CORPORATE FINANCE AND INVESTMENT

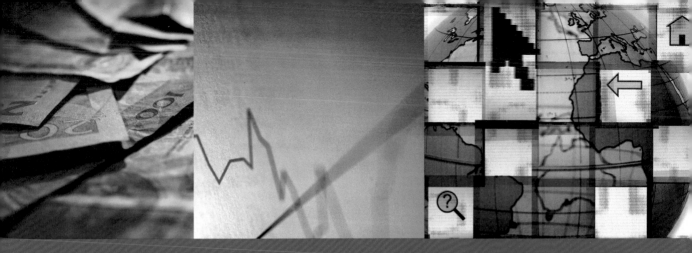

CORPORATE FINANCE AND INVESTMENT

DECISIONS AND STRATEGIES

Eighth Edition

Richard Pike, Bill Neale and Philip Linsley

PEARSON

Harlow, England • London • New York • Boston • San Francisco • Toronto • Sydney • Auckland • Singapore • Hong Kong
Tokyo • Seoul • Taipei • New Delhi • Cape Town • São Paulo • Mexico City • Madrid • Amsterdam • Munich • Paris • Milan

Pearson Education Limited

Edinburgh Gate
Harlow CM20 2JE
United Kingdom
England

Tel: +44 (0)1279 623623

Web: www.pearson.com/uk

First published 1993 (print)
Eighth edition published 2015 (print and electronic)

© Prentice Hall Europe 1993, 1999 (print)
© Pearson Education Limited 2003
© Pearson Education Limited 2012, 2015 (print and electronic)

The Financial Times. With a worldwide network of highly respected journalists, *The Financial Times* provides global business news, insightful opinion and expert analysis of business, finance and politics. With over 500 journalists reporting from 50 countries worldwide, our in-depth coverage of international news is objectively reported and analysed from an independent, global perspective. To find out more, visit www.ft.com/pearsonoffer.

ISBN: 978-1-292-06406-2 (print)
        978-1-292-06408-6 (PDF)
        978-1-292-06410-9 (eText)

British Library Cataloguing-in-Publication Data
A catalogue record for the print edition is available from the British Library

Library of Congress Cataloging-in-Publication Data
A catalog record for the print edition is available from the Library of Congress

10 9 8 7 6 5 4 3 2 1
19 18 17 16 15
Cover image © LeeYiuTung, iStock]

Print edition typeset in 9.5/12 Palatino LT Pro by 73
Printed in Slovakia by Neografia

NOTE THAT ANY PAGE CROSS REFERENCES REFER TO THE PRINT EDITION

Brief contents

Contents

Part I

A FRAMEWORK FOR FINANCIAL DECISIONS

Chapter 1

An overview of financial management   3

Chapter 2

The financial environment   23

Chapter 3

Present values, and bond and share valuation   54

Part II

INVESTMENT DECISIONS AND STRATEGIES

Chapter 4

Investment appraisal methods   83

Part III

VALUE, RISK AND THE REQUIRED RETURN

Part VI

INTERNATIONAL FINANCIAL MANAGEMENT

Chapter 21

Managing currency risk   657

Chapter 22

Foreign investment decisions   697

Chapter 23

Key issues in modern finance: a review   736

Appendices

Lecturer Resources

For password-protected online resources tailored to support the use of this textbook in teaching, please visit **www.pearsoned.co.uk/pikeneale**

ON THE WEBSITE

List of figures and tables

List of figures

List of tables

Preface

We are very pleased that the textbook is now in its eighth edition. It is unusual for a textbook to have such longevity and there are a series of people who need thanking – our publishers, who continue to support us in our endeavours to produce a contemporary and informative text, academics who recommend the book, and students who purchase the book and use it in their studies.

Corporate finance and the financial world continue to develop and change at a rapid rate, and the dynamic nature of financial markets is evident in movements in share prices and stock indices across the world. The financial crisis that commenced in 2007–8 is still having fundamental repercussions and making headlines. The crisis fully illustrates that finance should be studied and the potential consequences of financial decisions need to be understood. Futher, the crisis demonstrates that what happens in finance can have important ramifications for governments and individuals as well as businesses. Risk has always been a key facet of finance and financial markets, but now seems to have even greater significance. As a consequence, risk management has risen in prominence.

These considerations reinforce our view that finance should be about developing, explaining and, above all, *applying* key concepts and techniques to a broad range of contemporary management and business policy concerns and challenges. It is becoming more appropriate, certainly at the undergraduate level, to demonstrate the role finance has to play in explaining and shaping business development rather than concentrating on rigorous, quantitative aspects.

The focus of the eighth edition, as in previous ones, is distinctly corporate, examining financial issues from a managerial standpoint. To simplify greatly, we have tried, wherever possible, to present the reader with the question 'OK, but how does this help the managerial decision-maker?' and also to provide a few answers, or at least pointers.

Some might say we should include chapters on other financial issues deemed to have a degree of importance equivalent to those covered here. Yet we believe, as ever, that there is a trade-off between comprehensiveness and manageability. This edition is directed at those issues, which in our experience are regarded as the central issues in finance.

■ Distinctive features

The eighth edition retains a set of distinctive features, including the following:

- *A strategic focus*. Students often regard financial management as a subject quite distinct from management and business policy. We attempt to relate the subject to these matters, emphasising the integration of the finance function within the context of managerial decision-making and corporate planning, and to the wider external environment.
- *A practical approach*. Financial theory increasingly dominates some texts. Theory has its place, and this text covers an appreciable amount; however, we seek to blend theory and practice: to ask why they sometimes differ, and to assess the role of less-sophisticated financial approaches. In other words, we do not elevate theory above common sense and intuition.

- *A clear and accessible style.* Personal experience and feedback suggest that much of our target readership prefers a more descriptive, rather than heavily mathematical, approach but appreciates worked examples and illustrations. There is a place for formulae, proofs and quantitative analysis; however, where possible, an alternative narrative explanation is provided.
- *An international perspective.* Although emanating from the UK, our text continues to use, where appropriate, examples drawn from other regions and countries, especially mainland Europe and the USA.

■ Teaching and learning features

A range of teaching and learning features is provided, including the following:

- *Mini case studies.* Topical cameos, applying financial management principles to well-known companies, are presented at the start of chapters and elsewhere within the text.
- *Learning objectives.* Specified at the outset of each chapter, these highlight what the reader should achieve in terms of concepts, terminology and skills.
- *Worked examples.* Integrated throughout the text to illustrate the key principles.
- *Extracts from the press.* Each chapter includes at least one article mainly from either the *Financial Times* or *The Economist*, focusing on one of the key issues addressed in the chapter.
- *Key revision points.* Provided at the end of each chapter to summarise the main concepts covered.
- *Annotated further reading.* At the end of each chapter, a number of key books and articles are suggested to offer additional perspectives and enable subjects to be studied in more depth. Full details of all books and articles are given in the References at the end of the book.
- A quick reference *glossary* of simple definitions.

■ Assessment features

Flexible study and assessment is facilitated by a variety of activities:

- *Self-assessment activities (SAAs).* These include both short questions and simple numerical exercises designed to reinforce a point made in the text or to encourage the reader to pursue a particular line of thought. Questions are inserted in the text at appropriate points and the answers are packaged together at the end of the book in Appendix A.
- *Questions.* These test a mix of numerical, analytical and descriptive skills, offering a spread of difficulty. A selection of solutions is also provided in Appendix B at the end of the text, making these suitable for self-assessment, tutorial or examination purposes.
- *Practical assignments.* These provide the opportunity to look beyond the confines of the text to consider the application of concepts to a company or organisation, or to published financial reports and data, and are suitable where group or individually assessed coursework is set.

■ Readership

The text has proved successful both for newcomers to finance and also for students with a prior knowledge of the subject. It is particularly relevant to undergraduate,

MBA and other postgraduate and post-experience courses in corporate finance or financial management. Students seeking a professionally accredited qualification will also find it especially relevant to the financial management papers of the Association of Chartered Certified Accountants, Institute of Chartered Secretaries and Administrators, Certified Diploma in Finance and Accounting, Chartered Institute of Management Accountants and the Institute of Chartered Accountants in England and Wales.

■ Changes to the eighth edition

As with previous editions, our revisions are based on extensive market research, including reviewers' questionnaires and direct feedback from adopters and users. Feedback, while always interesting and helpful, was sometimes contradictory. Hopefully, we have achieved a balance between academic rigour and practical application.

In preparing this edition, we have battled with two opposing forces. We wanted to avoid expanding the text to an unmanageable size, yet we have been aware of several gaps in our coverage in previous editions, and the need for 'infill'.

The main changes to this edition in structure and in content are summarised below.

■ Structural changes

In the seventh edition we introduced more discussion of topics related to risk. We have built on this in the eighth edition and further extended these discussions on risk management and real options. We have also tried to make the text more accessible by 'breaking up' the chapters through the incorporation of additional self-test questions.

■ Structure and outline

An outline of the text is given below; however, a further description of the purpose and content of each section is given in the introduction to each.

Part I considers the underlying framework for corporate financing and investment decisions; key aspects of this part are the financial objectives of business, the financial environment within which firms operate, the time-value of money and the concept of value.

Part II addresses investment decisions and strategies within firms. Emphasis is placed on evaluation procedures, including treatments of taxation, inflation and capital rationing. Because, in practice, investment decision-making often bears little relationship to the theoretical approaches outlined in some texts, we persist in our attempt to promote an understanding of the practical evaluation of investment decisions by firms.

The importance of value, risk and the expected rate of return are examined in Part III, with six chapters devoted to this theme. Here we consider the investment project in isolation, including the rapidly developing and exciting field of options analysis. Other chapters view risk and return more from a shareholder perspective. Fundamental to this section are the rate of return on investment required by shareholders and the valuation of the enterprise.

Part IV discusses the short-term financing decisions and policies for acquiring assets. It covers treasury and working capital management.

Part V addresses long-term strategic financing and policy issues. What are the main sources of finance? How much should a company pay in dividends? How much should it borrow? The culminating chapter focuses on corporate restructuring, with particular reference to acquisitions.

Part VI examines international financial management issues. It explains the operation of the foreign currency markets and how firms can hedge against adverse foreign exchange movements, and sets out the principles underpinning firms' evaluation of foreign investment decisions.

A concluding chapter reviews developments in corporate finance, with specific focus on market efficiency and behavioural finance.

Acknowledgements

All textbooks include 'acknowledgements' but, on reflection, this seems too weak a word to use when assistance has so often been so freely given. *Roget's Thesaurus* offers as a synonym, 'the act of admitting to something', suggesting rather grudging recognition!

Our recognition of the wide range of people and organisations is anything but grudging. We extend our warm appreciation of the helpful comments provided by you over the years, and also for consent to use your material.

To the ever-lengthening roll of honour, we wish to add the following names and organisations, whom we sincerely hope will be happy to be associated with our efforts:

John Ward – Dealogic
Andrew Carr – CIMA
Janine of the Barclays Capital Equity–Gilt Study Team
Patrick Barber – Bradford University
Kathy Grieve – Birmingham City University
Ahmed El-Masry – University of Plymouth
Christopher Brown – JPMorgan Cazenove
Patrick McColgan – Aberdeeen University
Himanshu Dubey
Andrew Barfield
Maxim Kakareka
Professor Colin Mason – University of Strathclyde
Professor Andrew Marshall – University of Strathclyde
Sue Lane
Peter Blankenhorn – E.On AG
Andrew Naughton-Doe – Corus UK plc
Pat Rowham – LBS
Peter Aubusson – D.S. Smith plc
Sue Cox – BAA plc
ASJR Ramsay – International Power plc
"Sarah" at British Airways plc
Jane Lanyon – Thorntons plc
Ian Lomas – DTI
Ian Patterson – HM Customs & Excise
As ever, we apologise for any omissions.

Finally, we are especially grateful to the ever-patient, ever-tolerant editorial staff at Pearson Education, and to the anonymous contributors to the market research conducted by the publisher. We hope that you will agree that your comments have led to an improvement in the quality of the final product. Naturally, as ever, we claim sole responsibility for any remaining errors.

Richard Pike, University of Bradford
Bill Neale, Bournemouth University
Philip Linsley, The University of York

Publisher's acknowledgements

We are grateful to the following for permission to reproduce copyright material:

Figures

Figure 3.3 after YieldCurve.com, Reproduced with permission of YieldCurve.com. (c) Moorad Choudhry 2015; Figure 9.1 from *D.S. Smith Annual Report 2013*, D.S. Smith p.6; Figure 9.4 adapted from The Increasing Importance of Industry Factors, *Financial Analysts Journal*, Sep/Oct, Figure 4c, p.51 (Cavaglia, S., Brightman, C., & Aked, M. 2000), Copyright 2000, CFA Institute. Reproduced and republished with permission from CFA Institute. All rights reserved; Figure 13.4 from *A structured approach to Enterprise Risk Management and the Requirements of ISO 31000*, Institute of Risk Management (Airmic/Alarm/IRM 2010) p.14; Figure 13.5 adapted from *A structured approach to Enterprise Risk Management and the Requirements of ISO 31000*, Institute of Risk Management (Airmic/Alarm/IRM 2010) p.9; Figure 13.5 adapted from *BS ISO 31000:2009, Risk management – Principles and guidelines*, British Standards Institution (2009), Permission to reproduce extracts from British Standards is granted by BSI Standards Limited (BSI). No other use of this material is permitted. British Standards can be obtained in PDF or hard copy formats from the BSI online shop: http://www.bsigroup.com/Shop; Figure 17.1 from *Equity Gilt Study 2013*, 58th ed., Barclays (2013) Figure 11, p.78; Figure 22.1 from *Contemporary Strategic Analysis*, Basil Blackwell (Grant, R.M. 2010) p.374, Reproduced with permission from John Wiley & Sons Ltd.; Figure 22.2 from The optimal timing of a foreign direct investment, *Economic Journal*, Vol.92(361), pp. 75–87 (Buckley, P.J. & Casson, M. 1981); Figure 23.1 from Prospect theory: An analysis of decisions under risk, *Econometrica*, Vol.47(March), pp. 263–291 (Kahnemand, D. & Tversky, A.1979), The copyright to this figure is held by the Econometric Society, http://www.econometricsociety.org/. It may be downloaded, printed and reproduced only for personal or classroom use. Absolutely no downloading or copying may be done for, or on behalf of, any for-profit commercial firm or for other commercial purpose without the explicit permission of the Econometric Society. For this purpose, contact the Editorial Office of the Econometric Society at econometrica@econometricsociety.org.

Tables

Table 2.1 from Share price information for the retail sector, *Financial Times*, 01/07/2014, © The Financial Times Limited. All Rights Reserved; Table 6.1 from Strategic capital investment decision-making: A role for emergent analysis tools?: A study of practice in large UK manufacturing companies, *British Accounting Review*, Vol. 38(2), pp. 149–173 (Alkaraan, F. & Northcott, D. 2006); Table 7.6 adapted from A longditudinal survey on capital budgeting practices, *Journal of Business Finance and Accounting*, Vol. 23(1), pp. 79–92 (Pike, R. 1996); Table 7.6 adapted from Strategic capital investment decision-making: A role for emergent analysis tools?: A study of practice in large UK manufacturing companies, *British Accounting Review*, Vol. 38(2), pp. 149–173 (Alkaraan, F. & Northcott, D. 1996); Table 9.3 from Elroy Dimson and Paul Marsh (Eds), Risk Measurement Service, London Business School, January-March 2014.; Table 9.4a from *Equity Gilt Study 2013*, 58th ed., Barclays (2013) Figure2, p.75; Table 9.4b from *Equity Gilt Study 2013*, 58th ed., Barclays (2013) Figure. 2., p.80; Table 11.3 from *Annual Report 2013*, D.S. Smith plc (2013) Table1, p.31; Table 13.4 from Top 10 global business risks for 2014, *Allianz Risk Barometer on Business Risks 2014*, January, p.1 (2014); Tables 20.1, 20.2 from Office for National Statistics, First Release, March 2014, Source: Office for National

Statistics licensed under the Open Government Licence v.2.0.; Table 20.4 adapted from Office for National Statistics, First Release, March 2014, Source: Office for National Statistics licensed under the Open Government Licence v.2.0.; Table 20.7 from Shareholder wealth effects of corporate takeovers: the UK experience 1955-85, *Journal of Financial Economics*, Vol.23 (2), pp. 225–249 (Franks, J.R. & Harris, R.S.); Table 21.2 from *The Times*, 29/08/2007, © Times Newspapers Limited; Table 22.6 from *Annual Report 2013*, International Airlines Group (2013) p.135; Table 23.2 from Investor psychology and asset pricing, *Journal of Finance*, Vol.56(4), pp. 1533–1597 (Hirshleifer, D. 2001), (c) The American Finance Association 2001

Text

Extract on page 5 adapted from The key to industrial capitalism: limited liability, *The Economist*; Extract on page 15 adapted from Better Boards: Focus on boardrooms 'poses a danger', *The Financial Times*, 11/12/2013 (Whitehead, P.), © The Financial Times Limited. All Rights Reserved; Extract on page 23 adapted from Serco finance director departs as company seeks emergency funding, *The Guardian*, 30/04/2014, Copyright Guardian News & Media Ltd 2014; Extract on page 30 adapted from Alternative finance a big hope for small groups: funding for SMEs, *The Financial Times*, 03/03/2014 (Bollen,B.); Extract on page 33 adapted from UK's Social Stock Exchange set to include international members, *The Financial Times*, 31/08/2013 (Kortekass, K. and Sullivan, R.), © The Financial Times Limited. All Rights Reserved; Extract on page 38 adapted from It's true! The FT – and social media – really do move markets, *The Financial Times*, 04/01/2014 (Authers, J.), © The Financial Times Limited. All Rights Reserved; Extract on page 54 adapted from The fatal attraction of profits and share prices, *The Financial Times*, 30/10/2010 (Authers, J.); Extract on page 67 adapted from Neck-and-neck rally for US stocks and bonds, *Financial Times*, 04/03/2014, 24 (Mackenzie, M.), © The Financial Times Limited. All Rights Reserved; Box on page 75 from Short View: US yield curve, *Financial Times*, 22/02/2010 (Authers, J.); Extract on page 83 from Portrait of a frontier investor, *Financial Times*, 13/10/2013, p.12 (Manson, K.); Box on page 93 adapted from Bullish Ronson defies property slump, *Financial Times*, 03/06/2009 (Thomas, D.), © The Financial Times Limited. All Rights Reserved.; Box on page 96 from Is investing in pizza stores a no-brainer?, *Financial Times*, 03/01/2007 (Lex Column); Extract on page 113 adapted from The new market space: billionaire investors look beyond Earth, *The Financial Times*, 01/03/2014, p.1 (Sunyer, J.), © The Financial Times Limited. All Rights Reserved; Box on page 117 from The sleight of hand over shale costs, *Financial Times*, 21/03/2010 (Dizard, J.); Extract on page 123 adapted from Anger as no-tax company wins state mobile contract, *Financial Times*, 13/05/2013, p.4 (Mance, H. & Stacey, K.), © The Financial Times Limited. All Rights Reserved; Extract on page 140 from Disneyland Paris celebrates 20th birthday €1.9bn in debt, *The Guardian*, 11/04/2012 (Neate, R., Sylt, C. & Ried, C.), Copyright Guardian News & Media Ltd 2012; Extract on page 143 adapted from Toyota recalls more than 6.5m cars over steering and seat problems, *The Guardian*, 09/04/2014 (Rankin, J.), Copyright Guardian News & Media Ltd 2014; Extract on page 161 from Football's 'cajillionaires' go on record summer spending spree, *Financial Times*, 31/08/2013, p.7 (Blitz, R.), © The Financial Times Limited. All Rights Reserved; Extract on page 165 adapted from We all lose if failure is punished too harshly, *Financial Times*, 13/11/2013, p.14 (Johnson, L.); Box on page 189 from Lex live; Metro and the weather, *Financial Times*, 29/10/2004, © The Financial Times Limited. All Rights Reserved; Extract on page 198 adapted from Keeping the family fortune relatively intact, *Financial Times*, 23/09/2013, p.19 (Grant, J.), © The Financial Times Limited. All Rights Reserved; Extract on page 203 adapted from Concentration: the case for putting all your eggs in one basket, *Financial Times*, 30/09/2013, 6 (Bang, N.P. and Sakaldeepi, K.); Extract on page 208 adapted from Eggs in the investment basket need to be of varied hues, *The Guardian*, 01/08/2005 (Warner, E.), Copyright Guardian News & Media Ltd 2005; Extract on page 214 adapted from Too many stocks spoil the portfolio, *Financial Times*, 13/04/2013, p.7 (Smith, T.); Extract on page 234 adapted from The problem for active managers, *Financial Times*, 30/04/2012, p.6 (Skypala, P.); Extract on page 241 adapted from Vivendi faces challenge to keep evolving, *Financial Times*, 15/11/2013, p.23 (Thomson, A.), © The Financial Times Limited. All Rights Reserved; Extract on page 241 adapted from Anglo should hire a new boss who can do splits, *Financial Times*, 30/10/2012, p.16 (Guthrie, J.); Extract on page 242 adapted from Cookson review floats potential demerger, *Financial Times*, 18/05/2012, p.20 (Shotter, J.); Box on page 258 from Whitbread smells self-service success, *Financial Times*, 03/03/2011 (Jacobs, R.); Extract on page 264 adapted from Water operators hit by Ofwat's demands, *Financial Times*, 28/01/2014, p.23 (Kavanagh, M.), © The Financial Times Limited. All Rights Reserved; Box on pages 253–254 from Counting the cost, *Financial Times*, 24/03/2003 (Lex Column); Extract on page 270 adapted from Candy Crush game developer seeks $7.6bn valuation in IPO, *Financial Times*, 13/03/2014, p.15 (Cookson, R. & Davies, S.); Extract on page 270 adapted from King falls from grace with poor stock exchange debut, *Financial Times*, 29/03/2014, p.9 (Cookson, R. & Davies, S.), © The Financial Times Limited. All Rights Reserved; Box on page 274 from Club Méditerranée: An empire built on sand, *The Economist*, 14/08/2010, © The Economist Newspaper Limited, London; Extract on page 275 adapted from Lonely Planet losses prompt BBC rethink, *Financial Times*, 20/03/2013, p.4 (Kuchler, H. & Edgecliffe-Robert, A.), © The Financial Times Limited. All Rights Reserved; Extract on page 276 from BlackBerry ad campaign aims to calm customers, *Financial Times*, 15/10/2013, p.17 (Taylor, P.), © The Financial Times Limited. All Rights Reserved; Box on page 279 adapted from Ups and downs of global brands: Consumers luxuriate in shopping on the web, *Financial Times*, 12/05/2013, p.2 (Lucas, L.); Box on page 281 adapted from Cashmere if you can, *Financial Times*, 10/07/2013, p.10 (Lex Column), © The Financial Times Limited. All Rights Reserved; Box on page 290 adapted from End short-term financial reporting fudges, *Financial Times*, 31/05/2012, p.9 (Mauboussin M. & Rappaport, A.); Box on page 296 from The Godrej Group: Good-quality products can be made for low earners, *Financial Times*, 11/06/2013, p.2 (Moules, J.), © The Financial Times Limited. All Rights Reserved; Box on pages 286–287 from Social guessworking, *Financial Times*, 14/02/2011 (Lex); Box on page 318 adapted from Is it better to play it safe or to place bets that risk bankruptcy?, *Financial Times*, 11/12/2013, p.11 (Kay, J.), © The Financial Times Limited. All Rights Reserved; Case Study on page 323 adapted from BP in Russia: options, *Financial Times*, 06/03/2014, p.12 (Lex), © The Financial Times Limited. All Rights Reserved; Box on pages 319–320 adapted from Brussels to probe UK nuclear power plant deal, *Financial Times*, 12/12/2013, p.3 (Chazan, G. & Barker, A.), © The Financial Times Limited. All Rights Reserved; Box on page 331 from *Annual Report 2013*, D.S. Smith plc (2013) pp. 32–33; Box on page 338 adapted from Crisis alters risk outlook of corporate treasurers, *Financial Times*, 03/09/2010, p.21 (Milne, R.); Box on page 341 adapted from Hedging helps foodmakers through uncertainty, *Financial Times*, 21/08/2010 (Blas, J. & Farrell, G.), © The Financial Times Limited. All Rights Reserved; Box on page 342 adapted from Oil groups and utliities grab bigger share of airline hedging, *Financial Times*, 29/08/2013, p.19 (Makan, A.), © The Financial Times Limited. All Rights Reserved; Box on pages 349–350 adapted from A centuries-old concept, futures trading has kept pace with the times, *Financial Times*, 17/08/2010 (Flood, C.); Box on page 359 adapted from Invoice payments, *Financial Times*, 13/08/2013, p.10 (Lex), © The Financial Times Limited. All Rights Reserved; Box on page 362 adapted from Study warns of threat to shipping container groups, *Financial Times*, 25/03/2014, p.14 (Hale, T.), © The Financial Times Limited. All Rights Reserved; Box on page 364 adapted from Groups losing ground on cash handling, *Financial Times*, 25/06/2012, p.18 (Smith, A.); Box on page 369 adapted from You can have too much of a good thing, *Financial Times*, 05/02/2011, p.30 (Moules, J.); Box on page 375 from http://www.promptpaymentcode.org.uk/; Box on page 382 from Amazon - law of the jungle, *Financial Times*, 11/12/2012, p.2 (Armstrong, R. & Kirk, S.), © The Financial Times Limited. All Rights Reserved; Box on page 409 adapted from Invoice finance helps visionary businesses see their future, *The Telegraph*, 07/02/2014 (White, A.), copyright © Telegraph Media Group Limited 2014; Box on page 416 from You gonna buy that?, *The Economist*, 21/08/2010, © The Economist Newspaper Limited, London; Extract on page 444 adapted from Cream of Devon, *The Economist*, 02/11/2013, © The Economist Newspaper Limited, London; Box on page 453 from Listings worth $8bn lined up in IPO flurry, *Financial Times*, 19/02/2014 (Chassany, A. & Wigglesworth, R.), © The Financial Times Limited. All Rights Reserved; Box on page 454 from HgCapital poised to float Manx Telecom in AIM, *Financial Times*, 16/01/2014 (Thomas, D. & Chassany, A.), © The Financial Times Limited. All Rights Reserved; Box on page 456 adapted from Why even discounted rights issues need underwriting, *Financial Times*, 28/04/2008 (Hill, A.); Box on page 457 adapted from OFT draws critics over rights fees, *Financial Times*, 28/11/2011 (Johnson, M. & Murphy, M.); Box on page 459 adapted from Porsche to defy investors' fears with €5bn rights issue, *Financial Times*, 28/03/2011 (Schafer, D.); Box on page 461 from Small-cap week, *Financial Times*, 07/03/2014 (Wilson, J.), © The Financial Times Limited. All Rights Reserved; Example on page 462 after Mastercard stock split evokes 1990s spirit, *Financial Times*, 12/12/2013 (Massoudi, A.); Box on page 474 from Unilever in 'dim sum' bond move, *Financial Times*, 28/03/2011 (Lucas, L.); Box on page 477 from Unilever blazes sustainable trail with £250m 'green bond', *Financial Times*, 20/03/2014 (Daneshkhu, S. & Bolger, A.), © The Financial Times Limited. All Rights Reserved; Box on page 479 from Sukuk – growing up, *Financial Times*, 10/02/2014, © The Financial Times Limited. All Rights Reserved; Extract on page 481 from Banking on the ummah, *The Economist*, 05/01/2013, p.52 (Bahru, J.), © The Economist Newspaper Limited, London; Box on pages 446–447 from *Business Central Europe*, February (1995), © The Economist Newspaper Limited, London; Extract on pages 451–452 from Poundland gives the go-ahead for £700m IPO, *Financial Times*, 19/02/2014 (Felsted, A.), © The Financial Times Limited. All Rights Reserved; Extract on pages 465–466 from A big number from Verizon, *The Economist*, 14/09/2013, © The Economist Newspaper Limited, London; Extract on pages 468–469 from Back from the dead, *The Economist*, 11/01/2014, © The Economist Newspaper Limited, London; Box on pages 475–476 from Money will find a way, *The Economist*, 06/07/2013, © The Economist Newspaper Limited, London; Box on page 487 adapted from Personal goods - L'Oreal chief promises dividend is high priority, *Financial Times*, 13/02/2014, p.16 (Thomson, A.), © The Financial Times Limited. All Rights Reserved; Box on page 488 adapted from wolsey shares jump on bumper cash payout, *Daily Telegraph*, 01/10/2013 (Ficenec, J.), copyright © Telegraph Media Group Limited 2013; Box on page 490 adapted from Nokia slides after passing on dividend, *Financial Times*, 25/01/2013 (Stevenson, A.); Box on page 494 after Wm Morrison slips to five-year low, *Financial Times*, 15/02/2014, p.19 (Elder, B.), © The Financial Times Limited. All Rights Reserved; Box on page 498 adapted from China acts to relieve IPO backlog, *Financial Times*, 09/01/2013, p.30 (Noble, J. & Rabinovitch, S.), © The Financial Times Limited. All Rights Reserved.; Box on page 504 adapted from Costco – question of balance, *Financial Times*, 19/11/2012, p.14 (Lex Column); Box on page 509 adapted from Dividend reinvestment: scrips and drips, *Financial Times*, 27/10/2012, p.9 (Eley, J.); Box on page 511 adapted from Apple and tech stocks lift US markets, *Financial Times*, 20/03/2012, p.34 (Massoudi, A.); Box on page 512 from Apple to return extra $55bn to investors, *Financial Times*, 24/04/2013, p.1 (Bradshaw, T.), © The Financial Times Limited. All Rights Reserved; Box on page 512 from Icahn defeated in effort to force $50bn Apple buy-back, *Financial Times*, 11/02/2014, p.15 (Bradshaw, T. & Foley, S.), © The Financial Times Limited. All Rights Reserved; Box on page 513 adapted from Kimberly-Clark: mopping up, *Financial Times*, 20/04/2013, p.16 (Lex), © The Financial Times Limited. All Rights Reserved; Box on pages 507–508 adapted from Vodafone payout to bolster UK dividend payments to record £100bn, *Financial Times*, 12/10/2013, p.20 (Smith, A.); Box on pages 510–511 adapted from Share buybacks could provide equity inspiration, *Financial Times*, 22/08/2013, p.29 (Shellock, D.), © The Financial Times Limited. All Rights Reserved; Box on pages 514–515 from Where dividends fit in the financial puzzle, *Financial Times*, 05/03/2011 (Authers, J.); Box on page 522 adapted from 2014 outlook: Sugar high, *Financial Times*, 02/01/2014, p.7 (Alloway, T. & Mackenzie, M.), © The Financial Times Limited. All Rights Reserved; Box on page 530 adapted from Textron: Cessna turbulence, *Financial Times*, 18/04/2013, p.14 (Lex), © The Financial Times Limited. All Rights Reserved; Box on page 534 adapted from Debt ratios: the beautiful game, *Financial Times*, 18/02/2014, p.14 (Lex), © The Financial Times Limited. All Rights Reserved; Box on page 547 adapted from High street horror as Blockbuster's UK arm collapses again, *Financial Times*, 30/10/2013, p.17 (Felsted, A.), © The Financial Times Limited. All Rights Reserved; Box on page 548 adapted from Spain's airport that never took off up for sale at €100m, *Financial Times*, 09/12/2013, p.6 (Buck, T.), © The Financial Times Limited. All Rights Reserved; Box on page 549 adapted from UK high street closures accelerating, *Financial Times*, 28/02/2013, p.23 (Felsted, A.), © The Financial Times Limited. All Rights Reserved; Box on page 550 adapted from Brintons rolls out the red carpet for Middle East's revival, *Financial Times*, 25/11/2013, p.26 (Robinson, D.), © The Financial Times Limited. All Rights Reserved; Box on pages 544–545 from Broadband price blow for BT, *Financial Times*, 21/01/2011 (Parker, A.); Box on page 559 adapted from A theorem fit to terrify bankers, *Financial Times*, 09/03/2014, p.52 (Harford, T.), © The Financial Times Limited. All Rights Reserved; Box on pages 574–575 adapted from 'Climate of fear' for small business borrowers, *Financial Times*, 25/11/2013, p.2 (Parker, G. & Moore, E.), © The Financial Times Limited. All Rights Reserved; Box on page 593 adapted from Glencore Xstrata lifts cost-cutting target to $2bn, *Financial Times*, 11/09/2013, p.20 (Wilson, J. & Hume, N.), © The Financial Times Limited. All Rights Reserved; Box on page 594 adapted from RBS 'gamble' on ABN Amro deal: FSA, *The Guardian*, 12/12/2011 (Bowers, S. & Treanor, J.), Copyright Guardian News & Media Ltd 2011; Box on page 597 adapted from UK MPs seek 'cast iron' pledge on Astra jobs, *Financial Times*, 12/05/2014 (Ward, A., Rigby, E. & Fleming, S.), © The Financial Times Limited. All Rights Reserved; Box on page 600 adapted from Energy industry probe to test competition regulator's powers, *Financial Times*, 28/03/2014, p.3 (Binham, C.); Box on page 601 adapted from Greene King picks Cloverleaf chain, *Financial Times*, 11/02/2011 (Jacobs, R. & Wembridge, M.); Box on page 602 adapted from Barrick Gold chief hails benefits of Newmont merger, *Financial Times*, 23/04/2014, p.18 (Wilson, J.), © The Financial Times Limited. All Rights Reserved; Box on page 603 adapted from Swatch fills gap in portfolio with purchase of Harry Winston, *Financial Times*, 22/01/2013, p.2 (Shotter, J.), © The Financial Times Limited. All Rights Reserved; Box on page 603 adapted from China's Bright Food eyes Europe acquisitions, *Financial Times*, 11/02/2014, p.16 (Daneshkhu, S.), © The Financial Times Limited. All Rights Reserved; Box on page 604 adapted from Bunzl lifted at halfway by overseas acquisitions, *Financial Times*, 28/08/2013, p.18 (Wembridge, M.), © The Financial Times Limited. All Rights Reserved; Box on page 604 adapted from M&A opens door to markets for Assa Abloy, *Financial Times*, 23/01/2013 (Milne, R.), © The Financial Times Limited. All Rights Reserved.; Box on page 605 adapted from Eddie Stobart drives on to LSE, *Financial Times*, 16/08/2007 (Bryant, C.); Box on page 610 adapted from Costain sweetens offer for Mouchel, *Financial Times*, 23/01/2011 (Wilkinson, D. & Gray, A.); Box on page 616 adapted from DS Smith shows SCA unit takeover benefits, *Financial Times*, 07/12/2012, p.23 (Wembridge, M.), © The Financial Times Limited. All Rights Reserved; Box on page 619 after Better ways to play the merger mania, *Financial Times*, 03/08/2013, p.6 (Eley, J.), © The Financial Times Limited. All Rights Reserved; Box on page 624 adapted from Consultants offer advice at a 'dangerous moment', *Financial Times*, 08/11/2012, p.4 (Devi, S.); Box on page 625 adapted from Apollo Tyres skids 24% on Cooper deal fears, *Financial Times*, 14/06/2013, p.18 (Chilkoti, A.), © The Financial Times Limited. All Rights Reserved; Box on page 636 adapted from Vodafone forced to write down Indian business, *Financial Times*, 19/05/2011 (Parker, A.); Box on page 638 adapted from Qinetiq agrees to offload US services division, *Financial Times*, 23/04/2014, p.20 (Sharman, A.); Box on page 639 adapted from The southwest: dairies show how to be seen but not in the herd, *Financial Times*, 15/07/2013, p.19 (Brown, J.M.), © The Financial Times Limited. All Rights Reserved; Box on page 640 adapted from From wheels to deals for software sales chief, *Financial Times*, 20/03/2014, p.3 (Smedley, T.), © The Financial Times Limited. All Rights Reserved; Box on page 646 adapted from Infinis float to value group at up to £930m, *Financial Times*, 05/11/2013, p.23 (Chassany, A-S.), © The Financial Times Limited. All Rights Reserved; Box on pages 599–600 adapted from Brief Summary, http://www.thetakeoverpanel.org.uk/the-code/download-code; Box on pages 616–617 adapted from Paying the dire price of inflated ambition, *Financial Times*, 14/04/2012, p.17 (Lucas, L. & Thomas, D.); Box on pages 620–621 from Men's Wearhouse brings Pac-Man dealmaking tactic back to arena, *Financial Times*, 03/12/2013, p.23 (Hammond, E.), © The Financial Times Limited. All Rights Reserved; Box on pages 634–365 adapted from Marrying in haste, *Financial Times*, 12/04/2000 (Skapinker, M.); Box on pages 643–644 adapted from Return of the buyout kings, *Financial Times*, 08/03/2014, p.5 (Chessany, A-S.), © The Financial Times Limited. All Rights Reserved; Box on page 657 adapted from Currencies: Hedging your bets, *Financial Times*, 31/05/2012, p.9 (Hunter, M.); Box on page 659 adapted from To hedge or not to hedge, *Financial Times*, 01/04/2013, p.15 (Bollen, B.); Box on page 670 adapted from Europe's leaders warn currency volatility could harm the recovery, *Financial Times*, 17/03/2014, p.2 (Strauss, D.), © The Financial Times Limited. All Rights Reserved; Box on page 675 adapted from The Big Mac index. Grease-proof taper: Our bun-loving guide to currencies, *The Economist*, 24/01/2014, © The Economist Newspaper Limited, London; Box on page 678 adapted from Volvo aims to mitigate strong krona *Financial Times*, 10/09/2012, op. (Milne, R.); Box on page 681 adapted from Businesses look beyond EU for growth, *Financial Times*, 30/07/2012, p.4 (Bounds, A.,Brown, J.M., Tighe, C.); Box on page 684 adapted from Farmers embrace hedging to minimise currency risks, *Financial Times*, 30/09/2013, p.4 (Strauss, D.), © The Financial Times Limited. All Rights Reserved; Box on pages 674–675 adapted from Yen and Toyota: ups and downs, *Financial Times*, 06/02/2013, p.12 (Lex Column), © The Financial Times Limited. All Rights Reserved; Box on page 697 adapted from EM leads DM in cross-border M&A for first time, *Financial Times*, 30/04/2014, p.22 (Ratcliffe, V.), © The Financial Times Limited. All Rights Reserved; Box on page 701 after Nissan gears up to build cars in Nigeria, *Financial Times*, 10/10/2013, p.14 (Foy, H. & Blas, J.), © The Financial Times Limited. All Rights Reserved; Box on page 703 adapted from US and Mexico boost manufacturing credentials, *Financial Times*, 25/04/2014, p.4 (Crooks, E.), © The Financial Times Limited. All Rights Reserved; Box on page 704 adapted from Walmart plans big wholesale store push into India, *Financial Times*, 10/04/2014, p.16 (Kazmin, A.), © The Financial Times Limited. All Rights Reserved; Box on page 706 adapted from US courts foreign investment for economic boost, *Financial Times*, 31/10/2013, p.2 (Politi, J.), © The Financial Times Limited. All Rights Reserved; Box on page 722 adapted from Is Transparency International's measure of corruption still valid?, *The Guardian*, 03/12/2013 (Provost, C.), Copyright Guardian News & Media Ltd 2013; Box on page 724 adapted from When a haven harbours unseen risk, *Financial Times*, 25/03/2014, p.14 (Hill, A.), © The Financial Times Limited. All Rights Reserved; Box on page 726 adapted from $4bn Cnooc debt issue breaks Chinese records, *Financial Times*, 04/05/2013, p.20 (Wagstly, S.), © The Financial Times Limited. All Rights Reserved; Box on pages 699–700 adapted from Britain, the former empire, strikes back, *Financial Times*, 20/11/2013, p.4 (Groom, B.), © The Financial Times Limited. All Rights Reserved; Box on pages 713–714 adapted from The case study: How BMW dealt with exchange rate risk, *Financial Times*, 30/10/2012, p.12 (Bin, X. & Ying, L.), This article was based on a case study by Xu Bin, CEIBS Professor of Economics and Finance & Associate Dean (Research), and Liu Ying a research associate at CEIBS.; Box on page 738 adapted from More respect for behavioural studies, *Financial Times*, 03/01/2010 (Grene, S.), © The Financial Times Limited. All Rights Reserved.; Box on page 742 adapted from BP's $25bn annual profit sees confidence and dividends soar, *The Guardian*, 07/02/2012 (Macalister, T.), Copyright Guardian News & Media Ltd 2012; Box on page 745 adapted from Prize-winning work on asset prices goes to heart of financial crisis debate, *Financial Times*, 15/10/2013, p.2 (Giugliano, F. & Aglionby, J.), © The Financial Times Limited. All Rights Reserved; Box on page 746 adapted from Inefficient markets: dangerous hopes, *Financial Times*, 24/09/2013, p.12 (Lex Column), © The Financial Times Limited. All Rights Reserved; Box on page 749 adapted from Wanted: new model for markets, *Financial Times*, 29/09/2009 (Authers, J.); Box on page 750 adapted from Decoding the psychology of trading, *Financial Times*, 16/07/2010 (Mackiintosh, J.); Box on page 758 from Managing risk is the main task ahead, *Financial Times*, 03/01/2010 (Grene, S.); Box on page 759 adapted from Orthodox economists have failed their own market test, *The Guardian*, 20/11/2013 (Milne, S.), Copyright Guardian News & Media Ltd 2013; Box on pages 747–478 adapted from No more rules: a physicist argues that time is the only constant, *Financial Times*, 25/05/2014, p.9 (Tett, G.); Box on pages 751–752 adapted from Beware of your inner self, *Financial Times*, 01/06/2013, p.8 (Cohen, N.), © The Financial Times Limited. All Rights Reserved; Box on pages 756–757 adapted from Watch the herd, but don't join it, *Financial Times*, 03/07/2004 (Bloch, B.)

In some instances we have been unable to trace the owners of copyright material, and we would appreciate any information that would enable us to do so.

Part I

A FRAMEWORK FOR FINANCIAL DECISIONS

Business financial decisions are not made in a vacuum. An 'obvious' decision may often have to be tempered by an appreciation of the restrictions imposed by the prevailing environment. Although it is beyond our scope to consider the full social, political and economic complexity of the financial decision-making context, we provide an overview of the key features of the UK financial and economic system. A sound grasp of the framework for financial decisions is essential if the reader is to appreciate fully the issues discussed in subsequent chapters of this book.

Part I provides an introduction to the scope and the fundamental concepts of financial management. Chapter 1 provides a broad picture of the subject and the important role it plays in business. It examines the nature of financing and investment decisions, the role of the financial manager and the fundamental objective for corporate financial management. This leads on, in Chapter 2, to consideration of the financial and tax environment in which businesses operate. Particular attention is devoted to the characteristics and operation of the London Stock Exchange, which provides a barometer of the success of financial decisions via the market's valuation of the company's shares. The extent to which any market can provide 'accurate' valuations is also considered.

Central concepts in financial management are the time-value of money and present value, which are discussed in Chapter 3. The chapter also provides an understanding of the valuation of bonds and shares. Concepts of value and its measurement play important roles in subsequent chapters, where investment, financing and other key decisions are discussed.

1

An overview of financial management

Working for shareholders

Tesco and Walmart are two of the world's largest and best known retailers. Tesco was founded in the UK and Walmart in the USA, and both companies now have a significant international presence. The overlap between the two companies is not restricted to their competing in the same market sector. The two companies also have the same primary focus on shareholder value:

Everything we are doing reflects my determination to deliver shareholder value, an appropriate balance between investing for future growth, and delivering sustainable returns for our shareholders.

(Tesco 2013 Annual report)

Delivering strong returns to shareholders remains a top priority for Walmart.

(Walmart 2013 Annual report)

Sources: http://www.tescoplc.com, http://stock.walmart.com

Learning objectives

By the end of this chapter, you should understand the following:

■ What corporate finance and investment decisions involve.

■ How financial management has evolved.

■ The finance function and how it relates to its wider environment and to strategic planning.

■ The central role of cash in business.

■ The goal of shareholder wealth creation and how investors can encourage managers to adopt this goal.

1.1 INTRODUCTION

The objectives of Tesco and Walmart, summarised at the start, suggest that management has a clear idea of its purpose and key objectives. The mission is to deliver economic value to shareholders in the form of dividend and capital growth. Organisations such as Tesco and Walmart understand the importance of meeting the requirements of the **shareholders** – the owners of the business who need to be rewarded for their investment risk. Their objectives, strategies and decisions are all directed towards creating value for them.

One of the challenges in any business is to make investments that consistently yield rates of return to shareholders in excess of the cost of financing those projects and better than the competition. This book centres on that very issue: *how can firms create value through sound investment decisions and financial strategies?*

This chapter provides a broad picture of financial management and the fundamental role it plays in achieving financial objectives and operating successful businesses. First, we consider where financial management fits into the strategic planning process. This leads to an outline of the finance function and the role of the financial manager, and what objectives he or she may follow. Central to the subject is the nature of these financial objectives and how they affect shareholders' interests. Finally, we introduce the underlying principles of finance, which are developed in later chapters.

■ Starting a business: Brownbake Ltd

Ken Brown, a recent business graduate, decides to set up his own small bakery business. He recognises that a clear business strategy is required, giving a broad thrust to be adopted in achieving his objectives. The main issues are market identification, competitor analysis and business formation. He identifies a suitable market with room for a new entrant and develops a range of bakery products that are expected to stand up well, in terms of price and quality, against the existing competition.

Brown and his wife become the directors of a newly-formed limited company, Brownbake Ltd. This form of organisation has a number of advantages not found in a sole proprietorship or partnership:

- *Limited liability*. The financial liability of the owners is limited to the amount they have paid in. Should the company become insolvent, those with outstanding claims on the company cannot compel the owners to pay in further capital.
- *Transferability of ownership*. It is generally easier to sell shares in a company, particularly if it is listed on a stock market, than to sell all or part of a partnership or sole proprietorship.
- *Permanence*. A company has a legal identity quite separate from its owners. Its existence is unaffected by the sale of shares or death of a shareholder.
- *Access to markets*. The above benefits, together with the fact that companies enable large numbers of shareholders to participate, mean that companies can enjoy financial economies of scale, giving rise to greater choice and lower costs of financing the business.

Brown should have a clear idea of why the business exists and its financial and other objectives. He must now concentrate on how the business strategy is to be implemented. This requires careful planning of the decisions to be taken and their effect on the business. Planning requires answers to some important questions. What resources are required? Does the business require premises, equipment, vehicles and material to produce and deliver the product?

The key to industrial capitalism: limited liability

Shares, or 'equities', were first issued in the 16th century, by Europe's new joint-stock companies, led by the Muscovy Company, set up in London in 1553, to trade with Russia. (Bonds, from the French government, made their debut in 1555.) Equity's popularity waxed and waned over the next 300 years or so, soaring with the South Sea and Mississippi bubbles, then slumping after both burst in 1720. Share-owning was mainly a gamble for the wealthy few, though by the early 19th century, in London, Amsterdam and New York, trading had moved from the coffee houses into specialised exchanges. Yet the key to the future was already there. In 1811, from America, came the first limited-liability law. In 1854, Britain, the world's leading economic power, introduced similar legislation.

The concept of limited liability, whereby the shareholders are not liable, in the last resort, for the debts of their company, can be traced back to the Romans. But it was rarely used, most often being granted only as a special favour to friends by those in power.

Before limited liability, shareholders risked going bust, even into a debtors' prison maybe, if their company did. Few would buy shares in a firm unless they knew its managers well and could monitor their activities, especially their borrowing, closely. Now, quite passive investors could afford to risk capital – but only what they chose – with entrepreneurs. This unlocked vast sums previously put in safe investments; it also freed new companies from the burden of fixed-interest debt. The way was open to finance the mounting capital needs of the new railways and factories that were to transform the world.

Source: Based on *The Economist*, 31 December 1999.

Once these issues have been addressed, an important further question is: how will such plans be funded? However sympathetic his bank manager, Brown will probably need to find other investors to carry a large part of the business risk. Eventually, these operating plans must be translated into financial plans, giving a clear indication of the investment required and the intended sources of finance. Brown will also need to establish an appropriate finance and accounting function, to keep himself informed of financial progress in achieving plans and ensure that there is always sufficient cash to pay the bills and to implement plans. Such issues are the principal concern of financial management, which applies equally to small businesses, like Brownbake Ltd, and large multinational corporations, like Tesco and Walmart.

1.2 THE FINANCE FUNCTION

In a well-organised business, each section should arrange its activities to maximise its contribution towards the attainment of corporate goals. The finance function is very sharply focused, its activities being specific to the financial aspects of management decisions. Figure 1.1 illustrates how the accounting and finance functions may be structured in a large company. This book focuses primarily on the roles of finance director and treasurer.

It is the task of those within the finance function to plan, raise and use funds in an efficient manner to achieve corporate financial objectives. Two central activities are as follows:

1 Providing the link between the business and the wider financial environment.
2 Investment and financial analysis and decision-making.

■ Link with financial environment

The finance function provides the link between the firm and the financial markets in which funds are raised and the company's shares and other financial instruments are traded. The financial manager, whether a corporate treasurer in a multinational

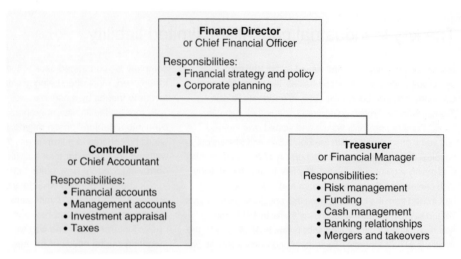

Figure 1.1 The finance function in a large organisation

company or the sole trader of a small business, acts as the vital link between financial markets and the firm. Corporate finance is therefore as much about understanding financial markets as it is about good financial management within the business. We examine financial markets in Chapter 2.

1.3 INVESTMENT AND FINANCIAL DECISIONS

Corporate finance is primarily concerned with investment and financing decisions and the interactions between them. These two broad areas lie at the heart of financial management theory and practice. Let us first be clear what we mean by these decisions.

The *investment decision*, sometimes referred to as the capital budgeting decision, is the decision to acquire assets. Most of these assets will be *real assets* employed within the business to produce goods or services to satisfy consumer demand. Real assets may be tangible (e.g. land and buildings, plant and equipment, and stocks) or intangible (e.g. patents, trademarks and 'know-how'). Sometimes a firm may invest in *financial assets*. Such investment does not form part of trading activity and may be in the form of short-term securities and deposits.

The basic problems relating to investments are as follows:

1 How much should the firm invest?
2 In which projects should the firm invest (fixed or current, tangible or intangible, real or financial)? Investment need not be purely internal. Acquisitions of other companies represent a form of external investment.

The *financing decision* addresses the problems of how much capital should be raised to fund the firm's operations (both existing and proposed), and what the best mix of financing is. In the same way that a firm can hold financial assets (e.g. investing in shares of other companies or lending to banks), it can also sell 'claims' on its own **real assets**, by issuing shares, raising loans, undertaking lease obligations, etc. A financial security, such as a share, gives the holder a claim on the future profits in the form of a dividend, while a bond (or loan) gives the holder a claim in the form of interest payable. Financing and investment decisions are therefore closely related.

real assets
Assets in the business (tangible or intangible)

Self-assessment activity 1.1

Take a look at the statement of financial position of Brownbake Ltd.

Assets employed	£
Machinery and equipment	15,000
Vehicles	8,000
Patents	12,000
Stocks	10,000
Debtors	3,000
Cash and bank deposit	4,000
	52,000

Liabilities and shareholders' funds	
	12,000
Trade creditors	8,000
Loans	32,000
Shareholders' equity	52,000

Identify the tangible real assets, intangible assets and financial assets. Who has financial claims on these assets?

(Answer in Appendix A at the back of the book)

1.4 CASH – THE LIFEBLOOD OF THE BUSINESS

Central to the whole of finance is the generation and management of cash. Figure 1.2 illustrates the flow of cash for a typical manufacturing business. Rather like the bloodstream in a living body, cash is viewed as the 'lifeblood' of the business, flowing to all essential parts of the corporate body. If, at any point, the cash fails to flow properly, a 'clot' occurs that can damage the business and, if not addressed in time, can prove fatal!

Good cash management therefore lies at the heart of a healthy business, and the major sources and uses of cash for a typical business are depicted in Figure 1.2.

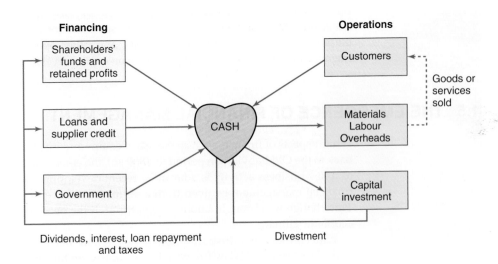

Figure 1.2 Cash – the lifeblood of the business

■ Sources and uses of cash

Shareholders' funds

shareholders' funds or equity capital
Money invested by shareholders and profits retained in the company

The largest proportion of long-term finance is usually provided by shareholders and is termed **shareholders' funds** or **equity capital**. By purchasing a portion of, or shares in, a company, almost anyone can become a shareholder with some degree of control over a company.

Ordinary share capital is the main source of new money from shareholders. They are entitled both to participate in the business through voting in general meetings and to receive dividends out of profits. As owners of the business, the ordinary shareholders bear the greatest risk, but enjoy the main fruits of success in the form of dividends and share price growth.

Retained profits

For an established business, the majority of equity funds will normally be internally generated from successful trading. Any profits remaining after deducting operating costs, interest payments, taxation and dividends are reinvested in the business (i.e. ploughed back) and regarded as part of the equity capital. As the business reinvests its cash surpluses, it grows and creates value for its owners. The purpose of the business is to do just that – create value for the owners.

Loan capital

debt finance/loan capital
Capital raised with an obligation to pay interest and repay principal

Corporate bonds
Medium- to long-term borrowing by a company

Money lent to a business by third parties is termed **debt finance** or **loan capital**. Most companies borrow money on a long-term basis by issuing loan stocks (or **corporate bonds**). The terms of the loan will specify the amount of the loan, rate of interest and date of payment, redemption date, and method of repayment. Loan stock carries a lower risk to the investor than equity capital and, hence, offers a lower return.

gearing
Proportion of the total capital that is borrowed

The finance manager will monitor the long-term financial structure by examining the relationship between loan capital, where interest and loan repayments are contractually obligatory, and ordinary share capital, where dividend payment is at the discretion of directors. This relationship is termed **gearing** (known in the USA as leverage).

Government

Governments and the European Union (EU) provide various financial incentives and grants to the business community. A major cash outflow for successful businesses will be taxation.

We now turn from longer-term sources of cash to the more regular cash flows from business operations as shown in Figure 1.2. *Cash flows from operations* comprise cash collected from customers less payments to suppliers for goods and services received, employees for wages and other benefits, and other operating expenses. The other major cash flow is long-term expenditure on capital investment.

1.5 THE EMERGENCE OF FINANCIAL MANAGEMENT

While aspects of finance, such as the use of compound interest in trading, can be traced back to the Old Babylonian period (*c.* 1800 BC), the emergence of financial management as a key business activity is a far more recent development. During the 20th century, financial management evolved from a peripheral to a central aspect of corporate life. This change was brought about largely through the need to respond to the changing economic climate.

With continuing industrialisation in the UK and much of Europe in the first quarter of the last century, the key financial issues centred on forming new businesses and raising capital for expansion and acquisitions.

As the focus of business activity moved from growth to survival during the depression of the 1930s, finance evolved by focusing more on business liquidity, reorganisation and insolvency.

Successive Companies Acts, Accounting Standards and corporate governance mechanisms have been designed to increase investors' confidence in published financial statements and financial markets. However, the US accounting scandals in 2002, involving such giants as Enron and Worldcom, have dented this confidence.

The 2007 credit crisis brought huge turmoil into the financial markets. This crisis resulted from banks expanding lending to sub-prime (i.e. riskier) borrowers and developed into a worldwide financial crisis that prompted comparisons with the Great Depression of the late 1920s and 1930s. The extent of the crisis resulted in significant financial support being provided to banks by governments, and, in 2009, the Bank of England reported that if 'all the facilities offered by central banks and governments were fully called upon, the scale of support to banking systems in the United Kingdom, the United States and euro area would exceed US$14 trillion' (Bank of England, 2009). This crisis has continued to have significant repercussions for governments, businesses and individuals. New banking regulations have been created, businesses have found it more difficult to access finance and individuals have found household budgets more difficult to manage.

Recent years have seen the emergence of financial management as a major contributor to the analysis of investment and financing decisions. The subject continues to respond to external economic and technical developments:

1 Successive waves of merger activity over the past 40 years have increased our understanding of valuation and takeover tactics. With governments committed to freedom of markets and financial liberalisation, acquisitions, mega-mergers and management buy-outs have become a regular part of business life.

2 Technological progress in communications and the liberalisation of markets have led to the globalisation of business. The single European market has created a major financial market with relatively unrestricted capital movement. Modern computer technology not only makes globalisation of finance possible, but also brings complex financial calculations and financial databases within easy reach of every manager.

derivative
A financial instrument whose value derives from an underlying asset

3 Complexities in taxation and the enormous growth in new financial instruments for raising money and managing risk have made some aspects of financial management highly specialised. The causes of the 2007 credit crisis stem, in part, from the risk management practices of the banks and the use of certain forms of **derivative** instruments.

4 Deregulation in the City is an attempt to make financial markets more efficient and competitive, although the lack of regulation in the banking sector was also judged a major factor in the 2007 banking crisis.

5 Greater awareness of the need to view all decision-making within a strategic framework is moving the focus away from purely technical to more strategic issues. For example, a good deal of corporate restructuring has taken place, breaking down large organisations into smaller, more strategically compatible businesses.

1.6 THE FINANCE DEPARTMENT IN THE FIRM

The organisational structure for the finance department will vary with company size and other factors. The board of directors is appointed by the shareholders of the company. Virtually all business organisations of any size are limited liability companies, thereby reducing the risk borne by shareholders and, for companies whose shares are listed on a stock exchange, giving investors a ready market for disposal of their holdings or for making further investment.

The financial manager can help in the attainment of corporate objectives in the following ways:

1 *Strategic investment and financing decisions.* The financial manager must raise the finance to fund growth and assist in the appraisal of key capital projects.
2 *Dealing with the capital markets.* The financial manager, as the intermediary between the markets and the company, must develop good links with the company's bankers and other major financiers, and be aware of the appropriate sources of finance for corporate requirements.
3 *Managing exposure to risk.* The finance manager should ensure that exposure to adverse movements in interest and exchange rates is effectively managed. Various techniques for hedging (a term for reducing exposure to risk) are available.
4 *Forecasting, coordination and control.* Virtually all important business decisions have financial implications. The financial manager should assist in and, where appropriate, coordinate and control activities that have a significant impact on cash flow.

Self-assessment activity 1.2

What are the financial manager's primary tasks?

(Answer in Appendix A at the back of the book)

1.7 THE FINANCIAL OBJECTIVE

For any company, there are likely to be a number of corporate goals, some of which may, on occasions, conflict. In finance, we assume that the objective of the firm is to *maximise shareholder value*. Put simply, this means that managers should create as much wealth as possible for the shareholders. Given this objective, any financing or investment decision expected to improve the value of the shareholders' stake in the firm is acceptable. You may be wondering why shareholder wealth maximisation is preferred to profit maximisation. Quite apart from the problems associated with profit measurement, it ignores the *timing* and *risks* of the profit flows. As will be seen later, value is heavily dependent on when costs and benefits arise and the uncertainty surrounding them.

The Quaker Oats Company (now part of Pepsico) was one of the first firms to adopt this goal:

> Our objective is to maximise value for shareholders over the long term . . . Ultimately, our goal is the goal of all professional investors – to maximise value by generating the highest cash flow possible.

However, many practising managers might take a different view of the goal of their firm. In recent years, a wide variety of goals have been suggested, from the traditional goal of profit maximisation to goals relating to sales, employee welfare, manager satisfaction, survival and the good of society. It has also been questioned whether management attempts to maximise, by seeking optimal solutions, or to seek merely satisfactory solutions.

Managers often seem to pursue a sales maximisation goal subject to a minimum profit constraint. As long as a company matches the average rate of return for the industry sector, the shareholders are likely to be content to stay with their investment. Thus, once this level is attained, managers will be tempted to pursue other goals. As sales levels are frequently employed as a basis for managerial salaries and status, managers may adopt goals that maximise sales subject to a minimum profit constraint.

earnings per share (EPS)
Profit available for distribution to shareholders divided by the number of shares issued

A popular performance target is **earnings per share (EPS)** and EPS growth. EPS focuses on the shareholder, rather than the company's performance, by calculating the earnings (i.e. profits after tax) attributable to each equity share.

Multiple objectives at GlaxoSmithKline (GSK)

GSK describes itself as a 'science-led global healthcare company that researches and develops a broad range of innovative products in three primary areas of Pharmaceuticals, Vaccines and Consumer Healthcare' and has a mission 'to help people do more, feel better, live longer'.

The company operates internationally and in 2013 achieved annual revenue of £26.5bn and core operating profit of £8.0bn.

The company does not solely seek to create shareholder value, but has multiple objectives:

Delivering innovation and maximising access to our products generates value for patients, shareholders and society more widely and enables us to reinvest back into the business.

Our primary contribution is to make products that provide benefits to patients and consumers.

Successful delivery of this generates profitable and sustainable performance. In turn this allows us to generate value and returns for our shareholders and enables us to reinvest in the business.

We also create value by making direct and indirect economic and social contributions in the countries where we operate. These wider benefits to society include contributions through tax, employment and enhancing the well-being of local communities through our global community initiatives.

Source: http://www.gsk.com

Other subsidiary targets may be employed, often more in the form of a constraint ensuring that management does not threaten corporate survival in its pursuit of shareholder goals. Examples of such secondary goals which are sometimes employed include targets for:

1 *Profit retention.* For example, 'distributable profits must always be, say, at least three times greater than dividends'.
2 *Borrowing levels.* For example, 'long-term borrowing should not exceed 50 per cent of total capital employed'.
3 *Profitability.* For example, 'return on capital employed should be at least 18 per cent'.
4 *Non-financial goals.* These take a variety of forms but basically recognise that shareholders are not the only group interested in the company's success. Other stakeholders include trade creditors, banks, employees, the government and management. Each stakeholder group will assess corporate performance in a slightly different way. It is therefore to be expected that the targets and constraints discussed above will, from time to time, conflict with the overriding goal of shareholder value, and management must seek to manage these conflicts.

The financial manager has the specific task of advising management on the financial implications of the firm's plans and activities. The shareholder wealth objective should underlie all such advice, although the chief executive may sometimes allow non-financial considerations to take precedence over financial ones. It is not possible to translate this objective directly to the public sector or not-for-profit organisations. However, in seeking to create wealth in such organisations, the 'value for money' goal perhaps comes close.

Alternative objectives: Divine Chocolate – a Fairtrade social enterprise

Divine Chocolate was set up in the 1990s as a Fairtrade chocolate company. The shares of the company are 45% owned by Kuapa Kokoo farmers' co-operative, and two people from the co-operative are on the board of directors. This structure is to ensure the cocoa farmers 'receive a better deal for their cocoa and additional income to invest in their community'.

The company is not focused on shareholders but has a social mission:

To grow a successful global farmer-owned chocolate company using the amazing power of chocolate to delight and engage, and bring people together to create dignified trading relations, thereby empowering producers and consumers.

Source: http://www.divinechocolate.com/uk/about-us/inside-divine

Self-assessment activity 1.3

It is common for companies to have multiple objectives and not to focus solely on shareholder value. What pressures are companies under that might cause them to have a range of objectives?

(Answer in Appendix A at the back of the book)

1.8 THE AGENCY PROBLEM

Potential conflict arises where ownership is separated from management. The ownership of most larger companies is widely spread, while the day-to-day control of the business rests in the hands of a few managers who usually own a relatively small proportion of the total shares issued. This can give rise to what is termed *managerialism* – self-serving behaviour by managers at the shareholders' expense. Examples of managerialism include pursuing more perquisites (splendid offices and company cars, etc.) and adopting low-risk survival strategies and 'satisficing' behaviour. This conflict has been explored by Jensen and Meckling (1976), who developed a theory of the firm under agency arrangements. Managers are, in effect, agents for the shareholders and are required to act in their best interests. However, they have operational control of the business and the shareholders receive little information on whether the managers are acting in their best interests.

principal–agent
The agent, such as board of directors, is expected to act in the best interests of the principal (e.g. the shareholder)

agency costs
Costs that owners (principals) have to incur in order to ensure that their agents (managers) make financial decisions consistent with their best interests

A company can be viewed as simply a set of contracts, the most important of which is the contract between the firm and its shareholders. This contract describes the **principal–agent** relationship, where the shareholders are the principals and the management team the agents. An efficient agency contract allows full delegation of decision-making authority over use of invested capital to management without the risk of that authority being abused. However, left to themselves, managers cannot be expected to act in the shareholders' best interests, but require appropriate incentives and controls to do so. **Agency costs** are the difference between the return expected from an efficient agency contract and the actual return, given that managers may be tempted to act more in their own interests than the interests of shareholders.

Self-assessment activity 1.4

Identify some potential agency problems that may arise between shareholders and managers.

(Answer in Appendix A at the back of the book)

1.9 MANAGING THE AGENCY PROBLEM

To attempt to deal with such agency problems, various incentives and controls have been recommended, all of which incur costs. Incentives frequently take the form of bonuses tied to profits (profit-related pay) and share options as part of a remuneration package scheme.

Share options only have value when the actual share price exceeds the option price; managers are thereby encouraged to pursue policies that enhance long-term wealth-creation. Most large UK companies now operate share option schemes, which are spreading to managers well below board level. The figure is far higher for companies recently coming to the stock market: virtually all of them have executive share option schemes, and many of these operate an all-employee scheme. However, a major

Incentivising executives at Marks and Spencer

To manage the principal–agent relationship at Marks and Spencer executives are remunerated as follows:

The Company has a staightforward and transparent approach to executive remuneration which comprises base salary, benefits, cash and shares awarded under an annual incentive scheme and shares awarded under a long-term incentive scheme. Three elements of our executive remuneration framework are performance-

related and two are subject to a three year deferral or performance period in order to encourage executive directors to remain with the Company and align their interests with those of shareholders. Executive directors are also required to hold a minimum number of shares in the Company within five years of their appointment.

Source: 2013 Annual Report http://corporate.marksandspencer .com/investors

problem with these approaches is that general stock market movements, due mainly to macroeconomic events, are sometimes so large as to dwarf the efforts of managers. No matter how hard a management team seeks to make wealth-creating decisions, the effects on share price in a given year may be undetectable if general market movements are downward. A good incentive scheme gives managers a large degree of control over achieving targets. Chief executives in a number of large companies have recently come under fire for their 'outrageously high' pay resulting from such schemes – especially the banks where 'huge' bonuses were paid in banks that had only recently been bailed out by the government.

Executive compensation schemes, such as those outlined above, are imperfect, but useful, mechanisms for retaining able managers and encouraging them to pursue goals that promote shareholder value.

Another way of attempting to minimise the agency problem is by setting up devices to monitor managers' behaviour. Examples include:

1 audited accounts of the company;
2 management audits and additional reporting requirements;
3 restrictive covenants imposed by lenders, such as ceilings on the dividend payable on the maximum borrowings.

To what extent does the agency problem invalidate the goal of maximising the value of the firm? In an efficient and highly competitive stock market, the share price is a 'fair' reflection of investors' perceptions of the company's expected future performance. So agency problems in a large publicly-quoted company will, before long, be reflected in a lower than expected share price. This could lead to an *internal* response – the share-holders replacing the board of directors with others more committed to their goals – or an *external* response – the company being acquired by a better-performing company where shareholder interests are pursued more vigorously.

1.10 SOCIAL RESPONSIBILITY AND SHAREHOLDER WEALTH

Is the shareholder wealth maximisation objective consistent with concern for social responsibility? In most cases, it is. As far back as 1776, Adam Smith recognised that, in a market-based economy, the wider needs of society are met by individuals pursuing their own interests: 'It is not from the benevolence of the butcher, the brewer, or the baker, that we expect our dinner, but from their regard to their own interest.' The needs of customers and the goals of businesses are matched by the 'invisible hand' of the free market mechanism.

Of course, the market mechanism cannot differentiate between 'right' and 'wrong'. Addictive drugs and other socially undesirable products will be made available as long as customers are willing to pay for them. Legislation may work, but often it simply creates illegal markets in which prices are much higher than before legislation. Other products have side-effects adversely affecting individuals other than the consumers, e.g. passive smoking and car exhaust emissions.

There will always be individuals in business seeking short-term gains from unethical activities. But, for the vast majority of firms, such activity is counterproductive in the longer term. Shareholder wealth rests on companies building long-term relationships with suppliers, customers and employees, and promoting a reputation for honesty, financial integrity and corporate social responsibility. After all, a major company's most important asset is its good name.

Not all large businesses are dominated by shareholder wealth goals. The John Lewis Partnership, which operates department stores and Waitrose supermarkets, is a partnership with its staff electing half the board. The Partnership's ultimate aim, as described in its constitution, 'shall be the happiness in every way of all its members'. The Partnership rule book makes it clear, however, that pursuit of happiness shall not be at the expense of business efficiency. Its constitution requires it to take account of its suppliers, customers and local community. In 2013, the firm reported an increase in profits of 16 per cent and an annual bonus for staff of 17 per cent of basic salary.

Stakeholder theory asserts that managers should make decisions that take into account the interests of all the firm's stakeholders. This will include shareholders, employees, suppliers, customers, local communities, the government and environment. It is undoubtedly true that management should consider all stakeholders in its decision-making, but where interests conflict it becomes a highly complex task to maximise multiple objectives, as we saw with GSK earlier in this chapter. This shareholder focus that also recognises the needs of other stakeholders is sometimes termed 'enlightened shareholder value'.

Environmental concerns have in recent years become an important consideration for the boards of large companies, including the source of supplies, such as timber and paper from 'managed forests'. Investors are also becoming more socially aware and many are channelling their funds into companies that employ environmentally and socially responsible practices. In 2010, Nestlé changed its sourcing of cocoa for its Kit Kat chocolate bar to Fair Trade. This benefits thousands of small farmers in Ivory Coast (which produces 40 per cent of the world's cocoa) by giving them a better price which helps them invest in long-term community and business development projects.

1.11 THE CORPORATE GOVERNANCE DEBATE

In recent years, there has been considerable concern in the UK about standards of corporate governance, the system by which companies are directed and controlled. While, in company law, directors are obliged to act in the best interests of shareholders, there have been many instances of boardroom behaviour difficult to reconcile with this ideal.

There have been numerous examples of spectacular collapses of companies, often the result of excessive debt financing in order to finance ill-advised takeovers, and sometimes laced with fraud. Many companies have been criticised for the generosity with which they reward their leading executives. The procedures for remunerating executives have been less than transparent, and many compensation schemes involve payment by results in one direction alone. Many chief executives have been criticised for receiving pay increases several times greater than the increases awarded to less exalted staff.

In the train of these corporate collapses and scandals, a number of committees have reported on the accountability of the board of directors to their stakeholders and risk management procedures, brought together as the 'Combined Code'.

The **Combined Code on Corporate Governance**, introduced in 2003, applies to all listed companies. The code is regularly updated by the Financial Reporting Council (FRC). Its main requirements for financial management are summarised below.

1 *Directors and the board*
   - There should be a clear division of responsibilities between the running of the board (chairman) and the executive responsibility for the running of the business (chief executive).
   - The board should include a balance of executive and independent non-executive directors.
   - The effectiveness of the board should be evaluated regularly.

2 *Directors' remuneration*
   - There should be transparent systems for establishing directors' remuneration.
   - The performance-related elements of remuneration should form a significant proportion of the total remuneration package of executive directors to ensure long-term success.

3 *Accountability and audit*
   - The board should present a balanced assessment of the company's position.
   - The directors should report that the business is a going concern, with supporting assumptions or qualifications as necessary.
   - The board should maintain a sound system of internal control and risk management to safeguard shareholders' investment and the company's assets.
   - The board should establish an audit committee to monitor the integrity of financial statements.

4 *Relations with shareholders*
   - The board should maintain regular contact with shareholders and keep in touch with shareholder opinion in whatever ways are practical and efficient.
   - The board should have separate resolutions on all major matters at general meetings.

Think-tank searches for good governance

Board Intelligence, a firm specialising in board information, is holding a series of debates called 'The Board is Dead, Long Live the Board'. Participants (who are not named) are asked: 'If you could rip up the rule book, what would good governance look like?' An alternative boardroom model was suggested, drawing on the way some executive committees operate, where the chief executive seeks consultation rather than consensus. Perhaps the chairman could have a similar function. This might also reflect the reality of the near-impossible task faced by non-executive directors. One participant said: 'A non-executive is on a hiding to nothing – and to do the job properly, they need smaller portfolios and better pay. When things go wrong, they can expect to be tried in the court of public opinion.' It was argued that this is becoming such a trend that many talented candidates are no longer willing to take on the role. 'I wouldn't take a non-executive role in a big and complex global bank. The mismatch between what you are accountable for and your ability to affect it is enormous,' one commented.

An interesting suggestion aimed at improving the principal–agent relationship, by which the independent directors are deemed primarily to represent the shareholders, was made: turn the agents (directors) into principals (investors). One participant said. 'The only way really to align their interests is to require that the board – and senior management – invest their own money in a "material" number of shares. "Material" meaning in relation to their personal wealth.

'In the Victorian era, it was extremely common for companies to have substantial directorial share ownership requirements included in their articles of association.' Views were expressed that this would also remove the need for long-term incentive plans and complex remuneration policies, which, it was argued, exist only to solve the agency problem in the first place.

Source: Based on Peter Whitehead, *Financial Times*, 11 December 2013.

Corporate governance is an important issue throughout the world and most countries have developed a code or recommendations. (A website for the relevant country codes is given at the end of this chapter.)

The main reservations centre on the issues of compliance and enforcement. These changes in the rules and responsibilities of directors and auditors are non-statutory. The Stock Exchange may not withdraw the listings of companies that fail to comply, although it hopes that any adverse publicity will whip offenders into line. This lack of 'teeth' has raised suspicions that determined wrongdoers can still exert their influence on weak boards of directors, to the detriment of the relatively ill-informed private investor in particular.

Debates surrounding corporate governance and the objectives that managers should pursue intensified in the wake of the 2007 financial crisis. For example, the current form of capitalism that ranks shareholders as the most important stakeholder group has been greatly debated, with questions being raised about fundamentally important issues such as trust, risk management, financial liberalisation, regulation of markets and the role of government in business. These debates will, inevitably, impact on future reforms of corporate governance codes. For example, in the UK, the corporate governance code was updated in 2012.

1.12 THE RISK DIMENSION

The objective of Tesco is to deliver shareholder value, as outlined at the start of the chapter. To create shareholder value requires a company to take risks. Some financial decisions incur very little risk (e.g. investing in government stocks, since the interest is known); others may carry far more risk (e.g. investing in shares). Risk and expected return tend to be related: the greater the perceived risk, the greater the return required by investors. This is seen in Figure 1.3.

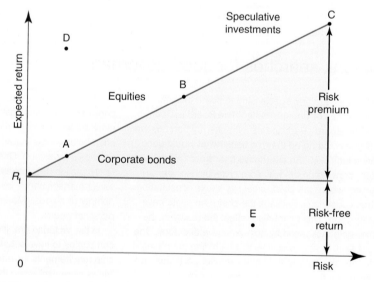

Figure 1.3 The risk–return trade-off

risk premium
The additional return demanded by investors above the risk-free rate to compensate for exposure to systematic risk

When the finance manager of a company seeks to raise funds, potential investors take a view on the risk related to the intended use of the funds. This can best be measured in terms of a **risk premium** above the risk-free rate (R_f) obtainable from, say, government stocks to compensate investors for taking risk. The capital market offers a host of investment opportunities for private and corporate investors, but in all cases there exists a clear relationship between the perceived degree of risk involved and the expected return. For example, R_f in Figure 1.3 represents the return on three-month UK Treasury Bills; point A represents a long-term fixed interest corporate bond; point B, a portfolio of ordinary shares in major listed companies; and point C, a more speculative investment, such as non-quoted shares. Studies indicate that the long-term average return on an investment portfolio consisting of the market index (e.g. the FTSE-100) is up to six percentage points higher than that from holding risk-free government securities.

One task of the financial manager is to raise funds in the capital markets at a cost consistent with the perceived risk, and to invest such funds in wealth-creating opportunities in the business. Here, it is quite possible – because of a firm's competitive advantage, or possession of superior brand names – to make highly profitable capital projects with relatively little risk (see D in diagram). It is also possible to find the reverse, such as project E. If the goal is to deliver cash flows to shareholders at rates above their cost of capital, managers should seek to invest in projects, such as D, that offer returns better than those obtainable on the capital market for the same degree of risk (A in the diagram).

1.13 THE STRATEGIC DIMENSION

To enhance shareholder value, managers could adopt a wide range of strategies. Strategic management may be defined as a systematic approach to positioning the business in relation to its environment to ensure continued success and offer security from surprises. No approach can guarantee continuous success and total security, but an integrated approach to strategy formulation, involving all levels of management, can go some way towards this.

Strategy can be developed at three levels:

1 *Corporate strategy* is concerned with the broad issues, such as the types of businesses the company should be in. Strategic finance has an important role to play here. For example, the decision to enter or exit from a business – whether through corporate acquisitions, organic growth, divestment or buy-outs – requires sound financial analysis. Similarly, the appropriate capital structure and dividend policy form part of strategic development at the corporate level.

2 *Business or competitive strategy* is concerned with how strategic business units compete in particular markets. Business strategies are formulated which influence the allocation of resources to these units. This allocation may be based on the attractiveness of the markets in which business units operate and the firm's competitive strengths.

3 *Operational strategy* is concerned with how functional levels contribute to corporate and business strategies. For example, the finance function may formulate strategies to achieve a new dividend policy identified at the corporate strategy level. Similarly, a foreign currency exposure strategy may be developed to reduce the risk of loss through currency movements. A typical strategic planning process is shown in Figure 1.4.

■ Strategic planning and value creation

The importance of competitive forces in determining shareholder wealth cannot be overestimated. They largely determine the price at which goods and services can be sold, the quantities sold, the cost of production, the level of required investment and the risks inherent in the business.

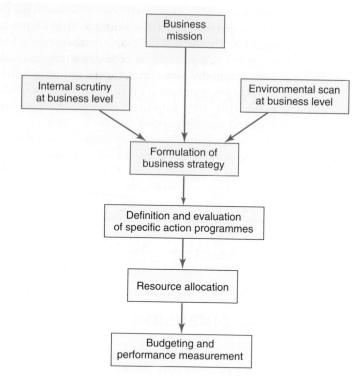

Figure 1.4 Main elements in strategic planning

However, individual companies can develop strategies leading to long-term financial performance well above the industry average. Figure 1.5 illustrates the main factors influencing the value of the firm. In any industry, all firms will be subject to much the same underlying economic conditions. Rates of inflation, interest and taxation and competitive forces in the industry will affect all businesses, although not necessarily to the same degree. The firm will develop corporate, business and operating strategies to exploit economic opportunities and to create sustainable competitive advantage. We are mainly concerned with those strategies affecting investment, financing and dividends. Operating and investment decisions create cash flows for the business, while financing decisions influence the cost of capital. The value of the

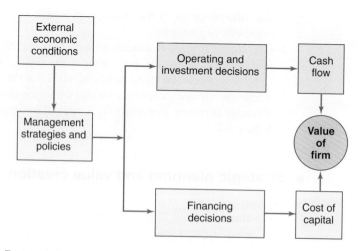

Figure 1.5 Factors influencing the value of the firm

firm depends upon the cash flows generated from business operations – their size, timing and riskiness – and the firm's cost of capital. Depending on the success of the firm's strategies and decisions, the value of the firm will increase or shrink.

While, in practice, some decisions appear to lack any rational process, most approaches to decisions of a financial nature have five common elements:

1 *Clearly defined goals.* It is particularly noticeable how, in recent years, corporate managements have realised the importance of defining and communicating their declared mission and goals, some more quantifiable than others, and some more relevant to financing decisions.

2 *Identifying courses of action to achieve these objectives.* This requires the development of business strategies from which individual decisions emanate. The search for new investment and financing opportunities for any organisation is far better focused and more cost-effective when viewed within well-defined financial objectives and strategies. Most decisions have more than one possible solution. For instance, the requirement for an additional source of finance to fund a new product launch can be satisfied by a multitude of possible financial options.

3 *Assembling information relevant to the decision.* The financial manager must be able to identify what information is relevant to the decision and what is not. Data gathering can be costly, but good, reliable information greatly facilitates decision analysis and confidence in the decision outcome.

4 *Evaluation.* Analysing and interpreting assembled information lies at the heart of financial analysis. A large part of this book is devoted to techniques of appraising financial decisions.

5 *Monitoring the effects of the decision taken.* However sophisticated a firm's financial planning system, there is no real substitute for experience. Feedback on the performance of past decisions provides vital information on the reliability of data gathered, the efficacy of the method employed in decision appraisal and the judgement of decision-makers.

Throughout this book, we shall attempt to allow for practical, real-world considerations when considering appropriate financial policy decisions. However, we hope that a clearer understanding of the concepts, together with an awareness of the degree of realism in their underlying assumptions, will enable the reader to make sound and successful investment and financial decisions in practice.

SUMMARY

This chapter has provided an overview of strategic financial management and the critical role it plays in corporate survival and success. We have examined how financial management has evolved over the years, its main functions and objectives.

Key points

■ It is the task of the financial manager to plan, raise and use funds in an efficient manner to achieve corporate financial objectives. This implies (1) involvement in investment and financing decisions, (2) dealing with the financial markets, and (3) forecasting, coordinating and controlling cash flows.

■ Cash is the lifeblood of any business. Financial management is concerned with cash generation and control.

■ Financial management evolved during the last century, largely in response to economic and other external events (e.g. inflation and technological developments), making globalisation of finance a reality and the need to concentrate on more strategic issues essential.

- The distinction should be drawn between accounting – the mere provision of relevant financial information for internal and external users – and financial management – the utilisation of financial and other data to assist financial decision-making.

- In finance, we assume that the primary corporate goal is to maximise value for the shareholders.

- The agency problem – managers pursuing actions not totally consistent with shareholders' interests – can be reduced both by managerial incentive schemes and also by closer monitoring of their actions.

- Investors require compensation for taking risks in the form of enhanced potential returns.

- Most of the assumptions underlying pure finance theory are not particularly realistic. In practice, market and other imperfections must also be considered in practical financial decision-making.

- Financial management has an essential role in strategic development and implementation at strategic, business and operational levels. Competitive forces, together with business strategy, influence the value drivers that impact on shareholder value.

Further reading

Students should get into the habit of reading the *Financial Times* and relevant pages of *The Economist* and *Investors Chronicle*.

Volume 22, Issue 1 (2010) of the *Journal of Applied Corporate Finance* contains a series of articles on executive compensation in the wake of the 2007 global financial crisis.

For more discussion on managerial compensation, see Goergen and Renneboog (2011). Jensen and Meckling (1976) and Fama (1980) are important articles on agency costs while Brickley *et al.* (2003) give a useful insight into organisational ethics and social responsibility. Koller *et al.* (2010) argue that shareholder wealth creation is good for all stakeholders, productivity and employment and Girerd-Potin *et al.* (2014) discuss how social responsibility can affect investors' risk perceptions of companies. Details on these and other references are provided at the end of the book. Discussions and critiques of shareholder value maximisation are provided by a range of authors including Adams, Licht and Sagiv (2011), Andreadakis (2012) and Stont (2012).

Useful websites

Financial Times: www.ft.com

Guardian: www.guardian.co.uk/money

The Economist: www.economist.com

Corporate governance codes in other countries: www.ecgi.org/codes/all_codes.php

Companies House: www.companieshouse.gov.uk

QUESTIONS

Questions with a **coloured number** have solutions in Appendix B on page 779.

1 Why is the goal of maximising owners' wealth helpful in analysing capital investment decisions? What other goals should also be considered?

2 Go4it plc is a young dynamic company which became listed on the stock market three years ago. Its management is very keen to do all it can to maximise shareholder value and, for this reason, has been advised to pursue the goal of maximising earnings per share. Do you agree?

(Solution on companion website www.booksites.net/pikeneale)

3 (a) 'Managers and owners of businesses may not have the same objectives.' Explain this statement, illustrating your answer with examples of possible conflicts of interest.

(b) In what respects can it be argued that companies need to exercise corporate social responsibility?

(c) Explain the meaning of the term 'Value for Money' in relation to the management of publicly owned services/ utilities.

(ACCA)

4 Discuss the importance and limitations of ESOPs (executive share option plans) to the achievement of goal congruence within an organisation.

(ACCA)

5 (a) A group of major shareholders of Zedo plc wishes to introduce a new remuneration scheme for the company's senior management. Explain why such schemes might be important to the shareholders. What factors should shareholders consider when devising such schemes?

(b) Eventually a short-list of three possible schemes is agreed. All pay the same basic salary plus:

(i) A bonus based upon at least a minimum pre-tax profit being achieved.

(ii) A bonus based upon turnover growth.

(iii) A share option scheme.

Briefly discuss the advantages and disadvantages of each of these three schemes.

(ACCA)

6 The primary financial objective of companies is usually said to be the maximisation of shareholders' wealth. Discuss whether this objective is realistic in a world where corporate ownership and control are often separate, and environmental and social factors are increasingly affecting business decisions.

7 The main principles of financial management may be applied to most organisations. However, the role of the financial manager may be affected by the type of organisation in which he or she works.

Required

Describe the key characteristics of the financial management function and the role of the financial manager in each of the following types of organisation.

(a) Quoted high-growth company

(b) Quoted low-growth company

(c) Unquoted company aiming for a stock exchange listing

(d) Small family-owned business

(e) Non-profit-making organisation, for example a charity

(f) Public sector, for example a government department

(CIMA)

8 (a) The Cleevemoor Water Authority was privatised in 2000, to become Northern Water plc (NW). Apart from political considerations, a major motive for the privatisation was to allow access for NW to private sector supplies of finance. During the 1980s, central government controls on capital expenditure had resulted in relatively low levels of investment, so that considerable investment was required to enable the company to meet more stringent water quality regulations. When privatised, it was valued by the merchant bankers advising on the issue at £100 million and was floated in the form of 100 million ordinary shares (par value 50p), sold fully paid for £1 each. The shares reached a premium of 60 per cent on the first day of stock market trading.

Required

In what ways might you expect the objectives of an organisation like Cleevemoor/NW to alter following transfer from public to private ownership?

(b) Selected biannual data from NW's accounts are provided below relating to its first six years of operation as a private sector concern. Also shown, for comparison, are the pro forma data as included in the privatisation documents. The pro forma accounts are notional accounts prepared to show the operating and financial performance of the company in its last year under public ownership as if it had applied private sector accounting conventions. They also incorporate a dividend payment based on the dividend policy declared in the prospectus.

The activities of privatised utilities are scrutinised by a regulatory body which restricts the extent to which prices can be increased. The demand for water in the area served by NW has risen over time at a steady 2 per cent per annum, largely reflecting demographic trends.

Key financial and operating data for year ending 31 December (£m)

	2000 (pro forma)	2002 (actual)	2004 (actual)	2006 (actual)
Turnover	450	480	540	620
Operating profit	26	35	55	75
Taxation	5	6	8	10
Profit after tax	21	29	47	65
Dividends	7	10	15	20
Total assets	100	119	151	191
Capital expenditure	20	30	60	75
Wage bill	100	98	90	86
Directors' emoluments	0.8	2.0	2.3	3.0
Employees (number)	12,000	11,800	10,500	10,000
P:E ratio (average)	–	7.0	8.0	7.5
Retail Price Index	100	102	105	109

Required

Using the data provided, assess the extent to which NW has met the interests of the following groups of stakeholders in its first six years as a privatised enterprise.

If relevant, suggest what other data would be helpful in forming a more balanced view.

(i) shareholders

(ii) consumers

(ii) the workforce

(iv) the government, through NW's contribution to the achievement of macroeconomic policies of price stability and economic growth.

(ACCA)

Practical assignment

Examine the annual report for a well-known company, particularly the chairman's statement. Are the corporate goals clearly specified? What specific references are made to financial management? What does it say about corporate governance and risk management? What does it say about corporate social responsbility and sustainability?

2

The financial environment

Serco finance director departs as company seeks emergency funding

Scandal-hit outsourcing company Serco – the business embroiled in controversy over billing the government for electronically tagging prisoners who had died – has parted company with its finance director after unveilling plans to raise an emergency £170m by selling new shares.

Serco, which runs services ranging from prisons to rail franchises and London's cycle hire scheme, said it would be 'uncomfortably close' to breaching its banking agreements and intended to sell nearly 50m new shares to raise cash.

The company commented: 'The proposed equity placing has a single purpose: to give us the opportunity to conduct a thorough review of the strategy of the business whilst remaining within the terms of our debt facilities.' The company, which has already warned it will take a big hit to profits as a result of the tagging scandal, said its performance this year had been 'more challenging than expected'.

Source: Based on *The Guardian*, 30 April 2014.

Learning objectives

By the end of this chapter, the reader should understand the nature of financial markets and the main players that operate within them. Particular focus is placed on the following topics:

- The functions of financial markets.
- The operation of the Stock Exchange.
- The extent to which capital markets are efficient.
- How taxation affects corporate finance.

Enhanced ability to read financial statements and the financial pages in a newspaper should also be achieved.

2.1 INTRODUCTION

The corporate financial manager, whether in Serco or any company, has the important task of ensuring that there are sufficient funds available to meet all the likely needs of the business. To do this properly, he or she requires a clear grasp both of the future financial requirements of the business and of the workings of the financial markets. This chapter provides an overview of these markets, and the major institutions within them, paying particular attention to the London Stock Exchange.

2.2 FINANCIAL MARKETS

financial market
Any market in which financial assets and liabilities are traded

A **financial market** is any mechanism for trading financial assets or securities. A **security** is a legal contract giving the right to receive future benefits under a stated set of conditions. Examples of financial securities range from the mortgage on a house or lease on a car to securities that are traded on financial markets, termed marketable securities.

Frequently, there is no physical marketplace, traders conducting transactions via computer. London is widely regarded as the leading European financial centre and is the largest by volume of dealing. Figure 2.1 shows the main financial markets, which are further explained below.

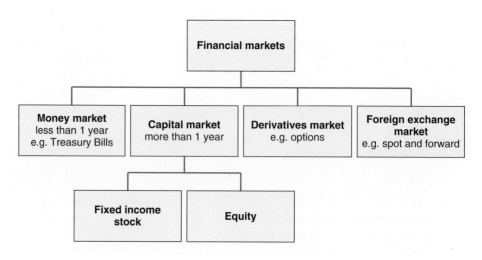

Figure 2.1 Financial markets

money market
The market for short-term money, broadly speaking for repayment within about a year

1 The **money market** channels wholesale funds, usually for less than one year, from lenders to borrowers. The market is largely dominated by the major banks and other financial institutions, but local government and large companies also use it for short-term lending and borrowing purposes. The official market is where approved institutions deal in financial instruments with the Central Bank. Other money markets include the inter-bank market, where banks lend short-term funds to each other, and the Euro-currency market where banks lend and borrow in foreign currencies.

securities/capital market
The market for long-term finance

2 The **securities** or **capital market** deals with long-dated securities such as shares and loan stock. The London Stock Exchange is the best-known institution in the UK capital market, but there are other important markets, such as the bond market (for long-dated government and corporate borrowing) and the Eurobond market.

spot
The spot, or cash market, is where transactions are settled immediately

3 The foreign exchange market is a market for buying and selling one currency against another. Deals are either on a **spot** basis (for immediate delivery) or on a **forward** basis (for future delivery).

forward
The forward market is where contracts are made for future settlement at a price specified now

4 Futures and options exchanges provide means of hedging (i.e. protecting) or speculating against movements in shares, currencies and interest rates. These are called **derivatives** because they are derived from the underlying security. A **future** is an agreement to buy or sell an asset (foreign currency, shares, etc.) at an agreed price at some future date. An **option** is the right, but not the obligation, to buy or sell such assets at an agreed price at, or within, an agreed time period. Examples of futures and options exchanges are Euronext NYSE Liffe, which operates exchanges in Europe (**www.euronext.com**) and the Chicago Mercantile Exchange in the USA (**www.cmegroup.com**).

The financial markets provide mechanisms through which the corporate financial manager has access to a wide range of sources of finance and instruments.

Capital markets function in two important ways:

1 *Primary market* – providing new capital for business and other activities, usually in the form of share issues to new or existing shareholders (equity), or loans.
2 *Secondary market* – trading existing securities, thus enabling share or bond holders to dispose of their holdings when they wish. An active secondary market is a necessary condition for an effective primary market, as no investor wants to feel 'locked in' to an investment that cannot be realised when desired.

Imagine what business life would be like if these capital markets were not available to companies. New businesses could start up only if the owners had sufficient personal wealth to fund the initial capital investment; existing businesses could develop only through re-investing profits generated; and investors could not easily dispose of their shareholdings. In many parts of the world where financial markets are embryonic or even non-existent, this is exactly what does happen. *The development of a strong and healthy economy rests very largely on efficient, well-developed financial markets.*

Financial markets promote savings and investment by providing mechanisms whereby the financial requirements of lenders (suppliers of funds) and borrowers (users of funds) can be met. Figure 2.2 shows in simple terms how businesses finance their operations.

derivatives
Securities that are traded separately from the assets from which they are derived

future
A tradable contract to buy or sell a specified amount of an asset at a specified price at a specified future date

option
The right but not the obligation to buy or sell a particular asset

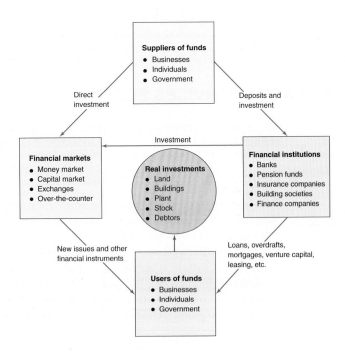

Figure 2.2 Financial markets, institutions, suppliers and users

financial intermediaries
Institutions that channel funds from savers and depositors with cash surpluses to people and organisations with cash shortages

Financial institutions (e.g. pension funds, insurance companies, banks, building societies, unit trusts and specialist investment institutions) act as **financial intermediaries**, collecting funds from savers to lend to their corporate and other customers through the money and capital markets, or directly through loans, leasing and other forms of financing.

Businesses are major users of these funds. The financial manager raises cash by selling claims to the company's existing or future assets in financial markets (e.g. by issuing shares, debentures or Bills of Exchange) or borrowing from financial institutions. The cash is then used to acquire fixed and current assets. If those investments are successful, they will generate positive cash flows from business operations. This cash surplus is used to service existing financial obligations in the form of dividends, interest, etc., and to make repayments. Any residue is re-invested in the business to replace existing assets or to expand operations.

We focus in this chapter on the financial institutions and financial markets shown in Figure 2.2.

■ Financial institutions provide essential services

The needs of lenders and borrowers rarely match. Hence, there is an important role for financial intermediaries, such as banks, if the financial markets are to operate efficiently. Financial intermediaries perform the following functions:

1 *Re-packaging, or pooling, finance*: gathering small amounts of savings from a large number of individuals and repackaging them into larger bundles for lending to businesses. The banks have an important role here.

2 *Risk reduction*: placing small sums from numerous individuals in large, well-diversified investment portfolios, such as unit trusts.

3 *Liquidity transformation*: bringing together short-term savers and long-term borrowers (e.g. building societies and banks). Borrowing 'short' and lending 'long' is acceptable only where relatively few savers will want to withdraw funds at any given time. The financial difficulties faced by Northern Rock in the UK in 2007 shows that this is not always the case.

4 *Cost reduction*: minimising transaction costs by providing convenient and relatively inexpensive services for linking small savers to larger borrowers.

5 *Financial advice*: providing advisory and other services for both lender and borrower.

2.3 THE FINANCIAL SERVICES SECTOR

The financial services sector can be divided into three groups of institutions: those engaged in (1) deposit-taking, (2) contractual savings and (3) other investment funds.

■ Deposit-taking institutions

retail banks
Retail banks accept deposits from the general public who can draw on these accounts by cheque (or ATM), and lend to other people and organisations seeking funds

Retail banks have three important roles: they manage nationwide networks of High Street branches and online facilities; they operate a national payments system by clearing cheques and by receiving and paying out notes and coins; and they accept deposits in varying amounts from a wide range of customers. The cheque clearing system in Great Britain is managed by the Cheque and Credit Clearing Company (**www.chequeandcredit.co.uk**). Because of the decline in cheque usage a target date of 2018 had been set to close central cheque clearing. However, in 2011 the Payments Council withdrew its plans. (Useful websites: **www.bba.org.uk**, **www.lendingstandardsboard.org.uk**)

The balance sheet of any clearing bank reveals that the main sterling assets are advances to the private sector, other banks, the public sector in the form of Treasury

Bills and government stock, local authorities and private households. Nowadays, the main instruments of lending by retail banks are overdrafts, term loans and mortgages.

In the European Union the Capital Requirements Directive (CRD) came into existence in 2007. The CRD enacted the Basel II Accord which aims to ensure banks hold sufficient capital to meet the market, credit and operational risks they face. Consequently, Basel II is endeavouring to ensure that banks and other credit institutions are financially sound and can withstand losses that may occur in the course of business. It also aims to improve risk management practices and market discipline. To strengthen the banking system in the wake of the 2007 financial crisis, the Basel Committee on Banking Supervision has agreed a Basel III Accord, although this will not come into being until 2018.

Wholesale banks

Wholesale banking (or investment banking) developed out of the need to finance the enormous growth in world trade in the 19th century. **Accepting houses** were formed whose main business was to accept Bills of Exchange (promising to pay a sum of money at some future date) from less well-known traders, and from **discount houses** which provided cash by discounting such bills. **Investment banks** nowadays concentrate on dealing with institutional investors, large corporations and governments. They have three major activities, frequently organised into separate divisions: corporate finance, mergers and acquisitions, and fund management.

Investment banks' activities include *giving financial advice to companies and arranging finance* through syndicated loans and new security issues. Investment banks are also members of the Issuing Houses Association, an organisation responsible for the *flotation of shares* on the Stock Exchange. This involves advising a company on the correct mix of financial instruments to be issued and on drawing up a prospectus and underwriting the issue. They also play a leading role in the *development of new financial products*, such as swaps, options and other derivative products, that have become very widely traded in recent years.

Another area of activity for wholesale banks is advising companies on corporate *mergers, acquisitions and restructuring*. This involves both assisting in the negotiation of a 'friendly' merger of two independent companies and developing strategies for 'unfriendly' takeovers, or acting as an adviser for a company defending against an unwanted bidder.

Finally, investment banks fulfil a major role as *managers of the investment portfolios* of some pension funds, insurance companies, investment and **unit trusts**, and various charities. Whether in arranging finance, advising on takeover bids or managing the funds of institutional investors, merchant banks exert considerable influence on both corporate finance and the capital market. Investment banks effectively grew out of merchant banks and, to all intents and purposes, provide similar services. The 1933 Glass–Steagall Act was implemented in the USA to enforce the separation of retail banks and investment banks. This Act was repealed approximately 50 years later. Following the 2007 financial crisis, the Independent Commission on Banking was set up and, in September 2011, recommended a clear boundary between retail and investment banking and to remove some risk from the banking sector.

The growth of *overseas banking* has been closely linked to the development of Eurocurrency markets and to the growth of multinational companies. Over 500 foreign banks operate in London. A substantial amount of their business consists of providing finance to branches or subsidiaries of foreign companies.

Following criticisms of the banks after the financial crisis, different governments have acted to reduce the possibility of a future crisis. A key action in the UK has been the development of the Banking Reform Bill, which is due to come into force in 2014. This will require UK banks to separate investment banking and retail banking activities by ring-fencing any deposits of individuals and SMEs.

accepting houses
Accepting houses are specialist institutions that discount or 'accept' Bills of Exchange, especially short-term government securities (see Chapter 15)

discount houses
Discount houses bid for issues of short-term government securities at a discount and either hold them to maturity or sell them on in the money market

investment banks
Investment banks are wholesale banks that arrange specialist financial services like mergers and acquisition funding, and finance of international trade fund management

unit trust
Investment business attracting funds from investors by issuing units of shares or bonds to invest in

building societies
Financial institutions whose main function is to accept deposits from customers and lend for house purchases

Building societies (www.bsa.org.uk) are a form of savings bank specialising in the provision of finance for house purchases in the private sector. As a result of deregulation of the financial services industry, building societies now offer an almost complete set of private banking services, and the distinction between them and the traditional banks is increasingly blurred. Indeed, many societies have given up their mutual status to become public limited companies with varying degrees of success.

Self-assessment activity 2.1

What are financial intermediaries and what economic services do they perform?

(Answer in Appendix A at the back of the book)

■ Institutions engaged in contractual savings

pension funds
Financial institutions that manage the pension schemes of large firms and other organisations

Pension funds accumulate funds to meet the future pension liabilities of a particular organisation to its employees. Funds are normally built up from contributions paid by the employer and employees. They can be divided into **self-administered schemes**, where the funds are invested directly in the financial markets, and **insured schemes**, where the funds are invested by, and the risk is covered by, a life assurance company. Pension schemes have enormous and rapidly growing funds available for investment in the securities markets. Pension funds enjoy major tax advantages. Subject to certain restrictions, individuals enjoy tax relief on their subscriptions to a fund. Together with insurance companies, pension funds make up the major purchasers of company securities.

self-administered schemes
A pension fund that invests clients' contributions directly into the stock market and other investments

insured schemes
A pension fund that uses an insurance company to invest contributions and to insure against actuarial risks (e.g. members living longer than expected)

Insurance companies' activities (www.abi.org.uk) can be divided into long-term and general insurance. Long-term insurance business consists mainly of *life assurance* and *pension provision*. Policyholders pay premiums to the companies and are guaranteed either a lump sum in the event of death, or a regular annual income for some defined period. With a guaranteed premium inflow and predictable aggregate future payments, there is no great need for liquidity, so life assurance funds are able to invest heavily in long-term assets, such as ordinary shares.

insurance companies
Financial institutions that guarantee to protect clients against specified risks, including death, and general risks in return for the payment of an annual premium

General insurance business (e.g. fire, accident, motor, marine and other insurance) consists of contracts to cover losses within a specified period, normally 12 months. As liquidity is important here, a greater proportion of funds is invested in short-term assets, although a considerable proportion of such funds is invested in securities and property.

portfolios
Combinations of securities of various kinds invested in a diversified fund

The investment strategy of both pension fund managers and insurance companies tends to be long-term. They invest in **portfolios** of company shares and government stocks, direct loans and mortgages.

■ Other investment funds

As we shall see in Section 2.4, private investors, independently managing their own investment portfolios, are a dying breed. Increasingly, they are being replaced by financial institutions that manage widely diversified portfolios of securities, such as unit trusts and investment trusts (www.investmentfunds.org.uk). These pool the funds of large numbers of investors, enabling them to achieve a degree of diversification not otherwise attainable owing to the prohibitive transactions costs and time required for active portfolio management. However, there are important differences between these institutions.

Investment trusts

Investment trusts are limited companies, whose shares are usually quoted on the London Stock Exchange, and set up specifically to invest in securities. The company's share price depends on the value of the securities held in the trust, but also on supply and demand. As a result, these shares often sell at values different from their net asset values, usually at a discount.

They are traditionally 'closed-ended' in the sense that the company's articles restrict the number of shares, and hence the amount of share capital, that can be issued. However, several open-ended investment companies (OEICs) have now been launched. To realise their holdings, shareholders can sell their shares on the stock market.

Unit trusts

Unit trusts are investment syndicates, established by trust deed and regulated by trust law. Investors' funds are pooled into a portfolio of investments, each investor being allocated tranches or 'units' according to the amount of the funds they subscribe. They are mainly operated by banks and insurance companies, which appoint managers whose conduct is supervised by a set of trustees.

Unit prices are fixed by the managers, but reflect the value of the underlying securities. Prices reflect the costs of buying and selling, via an initial charge. Managers also apply annual charges, usually about 1 per cent of the value of the fund. Unit-holders can realise their holdings only by selling units back to the trust managers.

They are 'open-ended' in the sense that the size of the fund is not restricted and the managers can advertise for funds.

Private equity funds

Private equity funds are typically limited partnerships where institutional investors make a commitment which is then drawn down over the term of the fund, as shown in Figure 2.3. The equity capital is invested either into companies that are already private or into public companies which are then taken private.

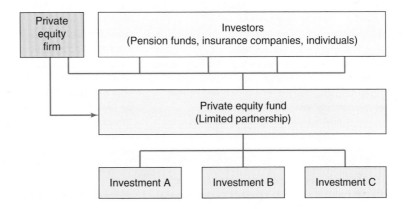

Figure 2.3 Private equity firm

Hedge funds

A hedge fund is a fund used by wealthy individuals and institutions. They are exempt from many of the rules and regulations governing other institutions, which allows them to accomplish aggressive investing strategies that are unavailable to others. These include:

- *Arbitrage* – simultaneous buying and selling of a financial instrument in different markets to profit from differences in prices.
- **Short-selling** – selling a security one does not own with the expectation of buying it in the future at a lower cost.
- *Leverage* – borrowing money for investment purposes.
- *Hedging* – using derivative instruments to offset potential losses on the underlying security.

Hedge fund managers receive their remuneration in the form of a management fee plus incentive fees tied to the fund's performance.

short selling
Selling securities not yet owned in the expectation of being able to buy them later at a lower price

Disintermediation and securitisation

disintermediation
Business-to-business lending that eliminates the banking intermediary

securitisation
The capitalisation of a future stream of income into a single capital value that is sold on the capital market for immediate cash

While financial intermediaries play a vital role in the financial markets, **disintermediation** is an important new development. This is the process whereby companies borrow and lend funds directly between themselves without recourse to banks and other institutions. Allied to this is the process of **securitisation**, the development of new financial instruments to meet ever-changing corporate needs (i.e. financial engineering). Some assets generate predictable cash returns and offer security. Debt can be issued to the market on the basis of the returns and suitable security. Securitisation usually also involves a credit-rating agency assessing the issue and giving it a credit rating. Securitisation can also be used to create value through 'unbundling' traditional financial processes. For example, a conventional loan has many elements, such as loan origination, credit status evaluation, financing and collection of interest and principal. Rather than arranging the whole process through a single intermediary, such as a bank, the process can be 'unbundled' and handled by separate institutions, which may lower the cost of the loan. Securitisation was a particular feature of the 2007 financial crisis.

Alternative finance a big hope for small groups: funding for SMEs

The need for small and medium-sized companies (SMEs) to access new sources of finance is well recognised globally. It seems that everywhere but in the US, such borrowers remain almost wholly dependent upon banks, whose ability to lend has become increasingly constrained since the global financial crisis. In this scenario, alternative finance has an increasingly important role to play in financing of the real economy in the UK and Europe.

The issue is likely to become even more pressing if Basel III regulations cause banks to lessen their commitment to longer-term lending because the new capital and liquidity rules make such activity less attractive for them.

The creation of new liquidity using securitised bonds is one of numerous proposals on the table, says Chris Redmond, global head of bond manager research at Towers Watson; he is one of many supporters of the notion.

Philippe Lespinard, chief investment officer, fixed income, at Schroders in London, says he, too, sees securitisation

as a viable option for SME financing. 'If driven by business needs rather than by arbitrage, it could be great news for the economy and for the investment community.'

Bill Blain, head of special situations, Mint Partners, the wholesale brokerage arm of BCG Partners, is almost evangelical about the potential for SMEs to take advantage of asset-backed securitisation (ABS). Mr Blain predicts that securitisation and ABS, including covered bonds (in the UK in the form of hybrid balance sheet securitisations, as opposed to legally-established European covered bonds) will become increasingly important funding for SME issuers – essentially a form of forward factoring. 'We expect to see an increasing number of asset classes from property, trade finance, leasing, publishing rights and other as yet unidentified asset cash flows securitised in coming years,' he adds.

Source: Based on Brian Bollen, *Financial Times*, 3 March 2014, p. 18.

Securitisation and disintermediation have permitted larger companies to create alternative, more flexible forms of finance. This, in turn, has forced banks to become more competitive in the services offered to larger companies. Recent, more exotic, forms of securitisation include pubs, gate receipts from a football club, future income from a pop star's recordings, and even the football World Cup competition for 2006.

2.4 THE LONDON STOCK EXCHANGE (LSE)

The capital market is the market where long-term securities are issued and traded. The London Stock Exchange is the principal trading market for long-dated securities in the UK (www.londonstockexchange.com).

A stock exchange has two principal economic functions: to enable companies to *raise new capital* (the primary market), and to *facilitate the trading of existing shares* (the secondary market) through the negotiation of a price at which title to ownership of a company is transferred between investors.

■ A brief history of the London Stock Exchange

The world's first joint-stock company – the Muscovy Company – was founded in London in 1553. With the growth in such companies, there arose the need for shareholders to be able to sell their holdings, leading to a growth in brokers acting as intermediaries for investors. In 1760, after being ejected from the Royal Exchange for rowdiness, a group of 150 brokers formed a club at Jonathan's Coffee House to buy and sell shares. By 1773, the club was renamed the Stock Exchange.

The Exchange developed rapidly, playing a major role in financing UK companies during the Industrial Revolution. New technology began to have a major impact in 1872, when the Exchange Telegraph tickertape service was introduced.

For over a century, the Exchange continued to expand and become more efficient, but fundamental changes did not occur until 27 October 1986 – the 'Big Bang' – the most important of which were:

1 All firms became brokers/dealers able to operate in a dual capacity – either buying securities from, or selling them to, clients without the need to deal through a third party. Firms could also register as market-makers committed to making firm bid (buying) and offer (selling) prices at all times.
2 Ownership of member firms by an outside corporation was permitted, enabling member firms to build a large capital base to compete with competition from overseas.
3 Minimum scales of commission were abolished to improve competitiveness.
4 Trading moved from being conducted face-to-face on a single market floor to being performed via computer and telephone from separate dealing rooms. Computer-based systems were introduced to display share price information, such as **SEAQ** (Stock Exchange Automated Quotations).

SEAQ
A computer-based quotation system on the London Stock Exchange where market-makers report bid and offer prices and trading volumes

In 2007, the Exchange launched a new trading system with greater capacity and speed of trading. Today, the London Stock Exchange is viewed as one of the leading and most competitive places to do business in the world, second only to New York in total market value terms.

The LSE has two tiers. The bigger market is the Official Main Market, providing a quotation for nearly 1,300 companies. To obtain a full listing, companies have to satisfy rigorous criteria relating to size of issued capital, financial record, trading history and acceptability of board members. These details are set out in a document called the company's 'listing particulars'. The **Financial Conduct Authority (FCA)** regulates admission of securities to the Official List. The UK Listing Authority (UKLA) is the division of the FCA responsible for approving applications to the Official List and companies seeking to have securities listed must comply with the FCA Listing Rules.

Financial Conduct Authority (FCA)
A regulatory body for maintaining confidence in the financial markets

Alternative Investment Market (AIM)
Where smaller, younger companies can acquire a stock market listing

The second tier is the **Alternative Investment Market (AIM)**. It attempts to minimise the cost of entry and membership by keeping the rules and application process as simple as possible. A nominated adviser (or NOMAD) firm (typically a stockbroker or bank) both introduces the new company to the market and acts as a mentor, ensuring that it complies with market rules. However, the requirement to observe existing obligations in relation to publication of price-sensitive information and annual and interim accounts remains. The AIM is unlikely to appeal to private investors unless they are prepared to invest in relatively high-risk businesses.

While the vast majority of share trading takes place through the Stock Exchange, it is not the only trading arena. For some years, there has been a small, but active over-the-counter (OTC) market, where organisations trade their shares, usually on a 'matched bargain' basis, via an intermediary.

Self-assessment activity 2.2

What type of company would be most likely to trade on:

(a) the main securities market?
(b) the Alternative Investment Market?
(c) the over-the-counter market?

(Answer in Appendix A at the back of the book)

■ Regulation of the market

Investor confidence in the workings of the stock market is paramount if it is to operate effectively. Even in deregulated markets, there is still a requirement to provide strong safeguards against unfair or incompetent trading and to ensure that the market operates as intended. The mechanism for regulating the whole UK financial system was established by the Financial Services Act 1986 (FSA86), which provided a structure based on 'self-regulation within a statutory framework' and established the Financial Services Authority (FSA), responsible to the Treasury. Its objectives were to sustain confidence in the UK's financial services industry and monitor, detect and prevent financial crime (**www.fsa.gov.uk**). This involved the regulation of the financial markets, investment managers and investment advisers.

The severe impact of the financial crisis resulted in the UK government identifying two primary policy issues: 'Improving regulation of the financial sector to protect customers and the economy' and 'Creating stronger and safer banks'. The idea underlying the first policy issue was that an appropriately regulated financial services sector was needed if the economy was to prosper. Consequently, the government undertook a major review of the regulation of the financial services sector to ensure the sector better managed its risks. This has led to the enactment of the Financial Services Act which came into force in April 2013. Formerly, under the tripartite system of regulation, responsibility was divided between the Financial Services Authority (FSA), the Bank of England and the Treasury. The new regulatory system comprises the Financial Policy Committee (FPC), the Prudential Regulation Authority (PRA) and the Financial Conduct Authority (FCA). The FPC is responsible for the macro-prudential regulation of risks that might impact the whole financial system. The PRA is responsible for micro-prudential regulation of financial firms, ensuring banks have appropriate amounts of capital and liquidity. The role of the FCA is to protect consumers by promoting competition and regulating financial services firms.

The strategic objective of the FCA is to ensure that the relevant markets function well and this is underpinned by three operational objectives:

■ to secure an appropriate degree of protection for consumers;
■ to protect and enhance the integrity of the UK financial system;
■ to promote effective competition in the interests of consumers.

The new regulatory system still has a connection to the Bank of England as the FPC is a committee of the Court of Directors of the Bank of England and the PRA is a subsidiary of the Bank of England. Other bodies overseeing aspects of the workings of the capital markets include the Competition and Markets Authority, and the Panel on Takeovers and Mergers.

Self-assessment activity 2.3

To what extent does an effective primary capital market depend on a healthy secondary market?

(Answer in Appendix A at the back of the book)

■ Share ownership in the UK

Back in 1963, over half (54 per cent) of all UK equities were held by private individuals. This proportion had dropped to 11 per cent by the end of 2012 (**www.ons.gov.uk**). Today, share ownership is dominated by financial institutions (the pension funds, insurance groups and investment and unit trusts) and 'rest of the world' investors. Financial institutions, acting for millions of pensioners and employees, policyholders and small investors, have vast power to influence the market and the companies they invest in. Institutional investors employ a variety of investment strategies, from passive index-tracking funds, which seek to reflect movements in the stock market, to actively managed funds.

Institutional investors have important responsibilities, and this can create a dilemma: on the one hand, they are expected to speak out against corporate management policies and decisions that are deemed unacceptable environmentally, ethically or financially. But public opposition to the management could well adversely affect share price. Institutions therefore have a conflict between their responsibilities as major shareholders and their investment role as managers seeking to outperform the markets.

Successive governments have promoted a 'share-owning democracy', particularly through privatisation programmes. However, individuals tend to hold small, undiversified portfolios, which exposes them to a greater degree of risk than from investing in a diversified investment portfolio. There are also a growing number of socially aware investors and the cameo below explains the UK's Social Stock Exchange.

■ Towards a European stock market?

The European Union is meant to be about removing barriers and providing easier access to capital markets. Until recently, this was still a pipe dream, with some 30 stock

UK's Social Stock Exchange set to expand internationally

A UK online portal that aims to connect investors with companies making a positive social impact is planning to expand internationally. The Social Stock Exchange, which admits only those London-listed companies that pass an independent assessment of their social and environmental contribution, said it was in talks with several overseas companies about joining its platform. 'We are looking at companies listed on Nasdaq OMX, NYSE Euronext and Deutsche Börse,' said Pradeep Jethi, chief executive of the SSE.

Launched in June, the exchange does not facilitate share trading but serves as a directory and research service for would-be social impact investors. Most of the SSE's 11 corporate members – including Good Energy Group, Straight and ITM Power – are listed on London's Alternative Investment Market, and Mr Jethi said he was aiming to increase the membership to 20 companies by the end of this year.

His move to include international companies follows support from the British prime minister at SSE's launch, just before this year's G8 Summit. Mr Cameron said the platform could help London 'cement its place as the home for social finance.'

Social finance, or social impact investment, is defined as buying into companies, organisations or funds that aim to achieve a measurable social or environmental impact as well as financial return. In 2012, $8bn was invested in this way and the figure is set to rise to $9bn this year, according to JPMorgan.

Mr Jethi said he identified two types of social impact investors. First, those that prioritise social returns. 'In their own mind, they say you cannot be delivering any less impact than this,' he explained. Second, those that need a financial return but also want a social upside.

However, there are also barriers to the market's growth, including the perceived riskiness of the companies, according to investment advisers. '[Social impact companies] are often small companies and sometimes don't meet all the financial criteria that we would be looking for,' said Elizabeth Haigh, of Rathbone Greenbank Investments, the ethical investment arm of Rathbones. She said social impact investments would only form part of a diversified portfolio for her clients.

Source: Based on Vanessa Kortekaas and Ruth Sullivan, *Financial Times*, 31 August 2013, p. 15.

exchanges within the EU, most of which had different regulations. With the introduction of a single currency, there is strong pressure towards a single capital market. But does this mean a single European stock exchange, with one set of rules for share listing and trading?

Euronext is a pan-European stock exchange based in Paris with subsidiaries in France, Belgium, the Netherlands, Portugal and the United Kingdom. Euronext merged with NYSE Group in 2007 to form NYSE Euronext, arguably the first global stock exchange.

2.5 ARE FINANCIAL MARKETS EFFICIENT?

If financial managers are to achieve corporate goals, they require well-developed financial markets where transfers of wealth from savers to borrowers are efficient in both pricing and operational cost.

allocative efficiency
The most efficient way that a society can allocate its overall stock of resources

operating/technical efficiency
The most cost-effective way of producing an item, or organising a process

social efficiency
The extent to which a socio-economic system accords with prevailing social and ethical standards

pricing/information efficiency
The extent to which available information is impounded into the current set of share prices

fair game
A competitive process in which all participants have equal access to information and therefore similar chances of success

Efficiency can mean many things. The *economist* talks about **allocative efficiency** – the extent to which resources are allocated to the most productive uses, thus satisfying society's needs to the maximum. The *engineer* talks about **operating** or **technical efficiency** – the extent to which a mechanism performs to maximum capability. The *sociologist* and the *political scientist* talk about **social efficiency** – the extent to which a mechanism conforms to accepted social and political values. The most important concept of efficiency for our purposes is **pricing** or **information efficiency**. This refers to the extent to which available information is built into the structure of share prices. If information relevant for assessing a company's future earnings prospects (including both past information and relevant information relating to future expected events) is widely and cheaply available, then this will be impounded into share prices by an efficient market. As a result, the market should allow all participants to compete on an equal basis in a so-called **fair game**.

We often hear of the shares of a particular company being 'under-valued' or 'over-valued', the implication being that the stock market pricing mechanism has got it wrong and that analysts know better. *In an efficient stock market, current market prices fully reflect available information* and it is impossible to outperform the market consistently, except by luck.

Consider any major European stock market. On any given trading day, there are hundreds of analysts – representing the powerful financial institutions which dominate the market – closely tracking the daily performance of the share price of, say, BSkyB, the broadcasting company. They each receive at the same time new information from the company – a major acquisition, a labour dispute or a revised profits forecast. This information is rapidly evaluated and reflected in the share price by their decisions to buy or sell BSkyB shares. *The measure of efficiency is seen in the extent and speed with which the market reflects new information in the share price.*

arbitrage
The process whereby astute entrepreneurs identify and exploit opportunities to make profits by trading on differentials in price of the same item as between two locations or markets

The Law of One Price suggests that equivalent securities must be traded at the same price (excluding differences in transaction costs). If this is not the case, **arbitrage** opportunities arise whereby a trader can buy a security at a lower price and simultaneously sell it at a higher price, thereby making a profit without incurring any risk. In an efficient market, arbitrage activity will continue until the price differential is eliminated.

■ The efficient markets hypothesis (EMH)

Information can be classified as historical, current or forecast. Only current or historical information is certain in its effect on price. The more information that is available, the better the situation. Informed decisions are more likely to be correct, although the use of inside information to benefit from investment decisions (insider dealing) is illegal in the UK.

Company information is available both within and without the organisation. Those within the organisation will obviously be better informed about the state of the business. They have access to sensitive information about future investment projects, contracts under negotiation, forthcoming managerial changes, etc. The additional knowledge will vary according to a person's level of responsibility and place in the organisational hierarchy.

Outsider investors fall into two categories: individual investors and the institutions. Of these two groups, the institutions are the better informed, as they have greater access to senior management, and may be represented on the board of directors.

Different amounts of financial information are available to different groups of people. There is unequal access to the information, called '**information asymmetry**', which may affect a company's share price. If you are one of the well-informed, this gives you the opportunity to keep one step ahead of the market. Otherwise, you may lose out. The share price reflects who knows what about the company. You should note, however, that in the UK, share dealings by company directors are tightly circumscribed; for example, they can only buy and sell at specific times, and details of all such trades must be publicly disclosed.

Market efficiency evolved from the notion of perfect competition, which assumes free and instantly available information, rational investors and no taxes or transaction costs. Of course, such conditions do not exist in capital markets, so just how do we assess their level of efficiency? Market efficiency, as reflected by the efficient markets hypothesis (EMH), may exist at three levels:

weak form
A weak-form efficient share market does not allow investors to look back at past share price movements and identify clear, repetitive patterns

1 The **weak form** of the EMH states that current share prices fully reflect *all information contained in past price movements*. If this level of efficiency holds, there is no value in trying to predict future price movements by analysing trends in past price movements. Efficient stock market prices will fluctuate more or less randomly, any departure from randomness being too expensive to determine. Share prices are said to follow a **random walk**.

random walk theory
Share price movements are independent of each other so that tomorrow's share price cannot be predicted by looking at today's

2 The **semi-strong form** of the EMH states that current market prices reflect not only all past price movements, but also *all publicly available information*. In other words, there is no benefit in analysing existing information, such as that given in published accounts, dividend and profits announcements, appointment of a new chief executive or product breakthroughs, after the information has been released. The stock market has already captured this information in the current share price.

semi-strong form
A semi-strong efficient share market incorporates newly released information accurately and quickly into the structure of share prices

3 The **strong form** of the EMH states that current market prices reflect *all relevant information* – even if privately held. The market price reflects the 'true' or intrinsic value of the share based on the underlying future cash flows. The implications of such a level of market efficiency are clear: no one can consistently beat the market and earn abnormal returns. Few would go so far as to argue that stock markets are efficient at this level, although some investors are often good at predicting what is happening inside companies before the information is officially released.

strong form
In a strong-form efficient share market, all information including inside information is built into share prices

You will have noticed that as the EMH strengthens, the opportunities for profitable speculation reduce. Competition between well-informed investors drives share prices to reflect their intrinsic values.

intrinsic worth
The inherent or fundamental value of a company and its shares

fundamental analysis
Analysis of the fundamental determinants of company financial health and future performance prospects, such as endowment of resources, quality of management, product innovation record, etc.

■ The EMH and fundamental and technical analysis

Investment analysts who seek to determine the **intrinsic worth** of a share based on underlying information undertake **fundamental analysis**. The EMH implies that fundamental analysis will not identify under-priced shares unless the analyst can respond more quickly to new information than other investors, or has inside information.

Another approach is **technical analysis**, its advocates being labelled **chartists** because of their reliance upon graphs and charts of price movements. Chartists are less interested in estimating the intrinsic value of shares, preferring to develop trading rules based on patterns in share price movement over time, or 'breakout' points of change. Charts are used to predict 'floors' and 'ceilings', marking the end of a share price trend. Figure 2.4 shows how charts are used to detect patterns of 'resistance' (for shares on the way up) and 'support' (for shares on the way down). This approach can often prove to be a 'self-fulfilling prophecy'. In the short term, if analysts predict that share prices will rise, investors will start to buy, thus creating a bull market and resulting in upward pressure on prices.

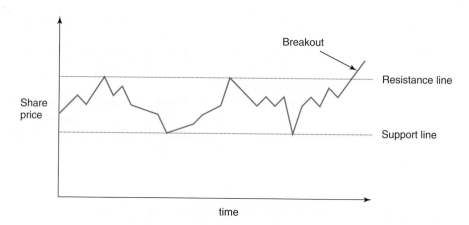

Figure 2.4 Chart showing possible breakout beyond resistance line

Even in its weak form, the EMH questions the value of technical analysis; future price changes cannot be predicted from past price changes. However, the fact that many analysts, using fundamental or technical analysis, make a comfortable living from their investment advice suggests that many investors find comfort in the advice given.

Considerable empirical tests on market efficiency have been conducted over many years. In the USA and the UK, at least until the 1987 stock market crash, the evidence broadly supported the semi-strong form of efficiency. More specifically, it suggests the following:

1 *There is little benefit in attempting to forecast future share price movements by analysing past price movements.* As the EMH seems to hold in its weak form, the value of charts must be questioned.

2 For quoted companies that are regularly traded on the stock market, analysts are *unlikely to find significantly over- or under-valued shares through studying publicly-held information.* Studies indicate (e.g. Ball and Brown, 1968) that most of the information content contained in annual reports and profit announcements is reflected in share prices anything up to a year before release of the information, as investors make judgements based on press releases and other information during the year. However, analysts with specialist knowledge, paying careful attention to smaller, less well-traded shares, may be more successful. Equally, analysts able to respond to new information slightly ahead of the market may make further gains. The semi-strong form of the EMH seems to hold fairly well for most quoted shares.

3 The strong form of the EMH does not hold, so superior returns can be achieved by those with 'inside knowledge'. However, it is the duty of directors to act in the shareholders' best interests, and it is a criminal offence to engage in insider trading for personal gain. The fact that cases of **insider trading** have led to the conviction of senior executives shows that market prices do not fully reflect unpublished information.

Recent governments have encouraged greater market efficiency in several ways:

- Stock market deregulation and computerised dealing have enabled speedier adjustment of share prices in response to global information.
- Mergers and takeovers have been encouraged as ways of improving managerial efficiency. Poorly performing companies experience depressed share prices and become candidates for acquisition.
- Governments have seen privatisation of public utilities as a means of subjecting previously publicly-owned organisations to market pressures.

How people trade in London

The Big Bang in 1986 gave the London Stock Exchange a huge advantage over most of its competitors. The result was strong growth in trading activity and international participation. But the Big Bang was only a partial revolution – automating the distribution of price information, but stopping short of automating the trading function itself.

Since 1986, global equity markets have become increasingly complex, with investors constantly looking for greater choice and lower costs. The London Stock Exchange made various attempts to retain its reputation as one of the most efficient stock markets. It took a major step by moving from a quote-based trading system, under which share dealing is conducted by telephone, to order-driven trading, termed SETS – the Stock Exchange Electronic Trading Service. The aim was to improve efficiency and reduce costs by automating trading and narrowing the spread between buying and selling prices. This it achieves by the automatic matching of orders placed electronically by prospective buyers and sellers.

The system works as follows. Instead of agreeing to trade at a price set by a market-maker, prospective buyers and sellers can:

(a) advertise through their broker the price at which they would like to deal, and wait for the market to move, or

(b) execute immediately at the best price available.

An investor wishing to buy or sell will contact his or her broker and agree a price at which the investor is willing to trade. The broker enters the order in the order book, which is then displayed to the entire market along with other orders. Once the order is executed, the trade is automatically reported to the Exchange. Time will tell whether it does lead to greater efficiency, but it is hoped that it will offer users more attractive, transparent and flexible trading opportunities.

■ Implications of market efficiency for corporate managers

In quoted companies, managers and investors are directly linked through stock market prices, corporate actions being rapidly reflected in share prices. This indicates the following:

1 Investors are not easily fooled by glossy financial reports or 'creative accounting' techniques, which boost corporate reported earnings but not underlying cash flows.
2 Corporate management should endeavour to make decisions that maximise shareholder wealth.
3 The timing of new issues of securities is not critical. Market prices are a 'fair' reflection of the information available and accurately reflect the degree of risk in shares.
4 Where corporate managers possess information not yet released to the market, there is an opportunity for influencing prices. For example, a company may retain information so that, in the event of an unwelcome takeover bid, it can offer positive signals such as an updated earnings forecast.

We return to the issue of market efficiency in discussing behavioural finance in Chapter 23.

Media – old and new – still move the markets

Newspapers report the news. They should never aim to be part of the story themselves. But in the stock market, that division is hard to sustain. A rigorous statistical study by academics at Warwick Business School has shown that we at the Financial Times regularly move the markets we write about. (A similar exercise for our best-known competitors would surely yield the same result; it happens that this study covered the FT.) The research is part of a growing effort to understand how to interpret people's use of data, and the trails they leave on the internet through search engines and social media, to predict how they, and markets, will behave.

The study looked at 1,821 FT issues published in the six years from 2007 to 2012 – years that included a historic stock collapse and a dramatic rebound. The researchers counted all mentions of the 31 stocks that were part of the Dow Jones Industrial Average during this period and linked their mentions in the paper to their share price performance the next day. It showed a strong correlation – a mention in the morning's FT meant a greater volume of trading.

Interestingly, their study involved the printed edition when much of the news on which the FT reported would already

have appeared online the previous day. So the news continued to have an impact on the next day. As there are now many sources that should move markets more swiftly than a printed newspaper, this also implies that it was the news itself, rather than any editorial choice about publishing stories, that moved prices.

How does the news about mentions in the FT, an externally driven event, affect these findings? It could go in one of two ways. As many stories are about share price moves that have just happened, the fact that the effect continues on the next day bears out that stock tend to have momentum once they have started moving.

But trading in reaction to news could also bear out the notion of market efficiency – that prices adjust to incorporate all known information and follow a 'random walk' in response to new news. The bubbles of the past two decades have shown that there is a lot wrong with the 'random walk' as a theory – but it is reassuring to confirm that traders do respond to news from the real world.

Source: Based on John Authers, *Financial Times*, 4 January 2014, p. 16.

Self-assessment activity 2.4

Consider why a dealing rule like 'Always buy in early December' should be doomed to failure. This rule is designed to exploit the so-called 'end-of-year effect' claiming that share prices 'always' rise at the end of the year.

(Answer in Appendix A at the back of the book)

Self-assessment activity 2.5

Share prices of takeover targets invariably rise before the formal announcement of a takeover bid. What does this suggest for the EMH?

(Answer in Appendix A at the back of the book)

2.6 READING THE FINANCIAL PAGES

Corporate finance is changing so quickly that it is essential for students of finance to read the financial pages in newspapers on a regular basis. In this section, we explain the main information contained in the Share Service pages of the *Financial Times*, and other newspapers.

■ The FT-SE Index

Every day, shares move up or down with the release of information from within the firm, such as a revised profits forecast, or from an external source, such as the latest government statistics on inflation or unemployment. To indicate how the whole share market has performed, a share index is used, the most common being the **FT-SE 100** – familiarly known as 'Footsie'. This index is based on the share prices of the 100 most valuable UK-quoted companies (sometimes termed 'blue chips'), mostly those with capitalisations above £3 billion, with each company weighted in proportion to its total market value. All the world's major stock markets have similar indices (for example, the Nikkei Index in Japan, the Dow Jones Index in the USA and the CAC 40 in France).

Every share index is constructed on a base date and base value. The FT-SE 100 started with a base value of 1,000 at the end of 1983 and reached a peak of 6,930 at the end of 1999. By February 2008, the index stood at around 6,029. Despite the collapse in world markets in 2000, and the subsequent slow recovery in confidence (punctuated by a fresh collapse at the time of the Iraq war), this still represented an annual compound growth rate of about 8 per cent, well above both the rate of inflation and the yield on low-risk investments over the same period. Moreover, it includes only capital appreciation – inclusion of dividend income would raise this percentage to about a 12 per cent return. However, the difficulties arising from the fallout of the 2007 financial crisis caused the index to fall to 3,530 in March 2009, although it had recovered to pass 6,800 in January 2014.

The FT-SE Actuaries Share Indices reveal share movements by sector. Their total gives the All-Share Index, representing the more frequently traded quoted companies.

Other FT indices

In recent years, the Stock Exchange has introduced several new indices including:

- FT-SE 350 provides the benchmark for investors who wish to focus on the more actively traded large and medium-sized UK companies, and covers 95 per cent of trading by value.
- FT-SE Small Cap offers investors a daily measure of the performance of smaller companies.
- FT-SE All-Share AIM covers companies on the Alternative Investment Market (AIM).

Using the published information

Financial managers and investors need to study the performance of the shares of their company, both against the appropriate sector as a whole and also against competitors within that sector. Two performance statistics that are most commonly reported are the **dividend yield** and **price:earnings ratio**.

Dividend yield

dividend yield
Gross dividend per ordinary share (including both interim and final payments) divided by current share price

Dividend yield is the gross, or pre-tax, dividends of companies and whole sectors in the last year as a percentage of their market value. Generally, sectors with low dividend yields are those with companies where the market expects high growth. Often we observe that the dividend yield for leading shares, and also on the overall index, is well below the return investors could currently earn on a safe investment in Treasury Bills. However, following the financial crisis, interest rates have been at extremely low levels and dividend yields have been above treasury rates in recent years.

Price:earnings (P:E) ratio

The P:E ratio is a much-used performance indicator. It is the share price divided by the most recently reported earnings, or profit, per share. So for the sector, it is the total market value of the companies represented in the sector divided by total sector earnings. The P:E ratio is a measure of the market's confidence in a particular company or industry. A high P:E usually indicates that investors have confidence that profits will grow strongly in future, perhaps after a short-term setback, although irregular events like a rumoured takeover bid will raise the P:E ratio if they lead to a higher share price.

Let us now turn to the performance of individual companies. Table 2.1 is an extract from the London Share Service pages in the *Financial Times*, giving the food and drug retailing sector. Transactions and prices of stocks are published continuously through SEAQ (the Stock Exchange Automatic Quotation).

Table 2.1 Share price information for the retail sector (selected companies)

	Price	Change	52 week high	52 week low	Yield	P/E	Average Vol.
Greggs	555.00	+19.00	565.00	388.40	3.64%	22.45	0.11m
Marks & Spencer	425.20	0.00	520.50	415.90	4.00%	13.20	3.86m
Morrisons	178.89	−4.51	312.30	178.70	7.09%	−	8.98m
Next	6,505.00	+40.00	6,907.90	4,514.96	1.99%	18.17	0.36m
Sainsbury	311.90	−3.30	428.00	301.50	5.48%	8.54	5.59m
Tesco	281.15	−3.15	386.40	278.50	5.19%	11.98	18.24m

Source: Financial Times, 1 July 2014. © Financial Times.

yield
Income from a security as a percentage of market price

price:earnings (P:E) ratio
The ratio of price per ordinary share to earnings (i.e. profit after tax) per share (EPS)

Tesco's closing share price of 281.15p is down 3.15p from the previous day's trading. The current price is 105p below its highest price over the past year. The **yield** of 5.19 per cent is the dividend yield, i.e. the dividend expressed as a proportion of the current share price. The **price:earnings (P:E) ratio** of 11.98 suggests that it would take 12 years for investors to get their money back in profit terms. Why should anyone be willing to wait that long? Remember that the calculation compares the last reported earnings per share with the current share price.

2.7 TAXATION AND FINANCIAL DECISIONS

Few financial decisions are immune from taxation considerations. *Corporate and personal taxation affects both the cash flows received by companies and the dividend income received by shareholders.* Consequently, financial managers need to understand the tax consequences of investment and financing decisions. Taxation may be important in three key areas of financial management:

1 *Raising finance*. There are clear tax benefits in raising finance by issuing debt rather than equity capital. Interest on borrowings attracts tax relief, thereby reducing the company's tax bill, while a dividend payment on equity capital does not attract tax relief. The tax system is thereby biased in favour of debt finance.

capital allowances
Tax allowances for capital expenditure

2 *Investment in fixed assets*. Spending on certain types of fixed asset attracts a form of tax relief termed **capital allowances**. This relief is intended to stimulate certain types of investment, such as in industrial plant and machinery. The taxation implications of an investment decision can be very important. We discuss capital allowances and tax implications for investment decisions in Chapter 5.

3 *Paying dividends*. Until 1973, in the UK, company profits were effectively taxed twice – first on the profits achieved and then again on those profits paid to shareholders in the form of dividends. Such a 'classical' tax system (which still exists in certain countries) is clearly biased in favour of retaining profits rather than paying out large dividends. The UK taxation system is more neutral, the same tax bill being paid (for companies making profits) regardless of the dividend policy.

Finally, the corporate financial manager should understand not only how taxation affects the company, but also how it affects the company's shareholders (**www.hmrc.gov.uk**). For example, some financial institutions (e.g. pension funds) pay no tax;

some shareholders pay tax at 20 per cent, while others pay higher-rate income tax at 40 per cent. Some may prefer capital gains to dividends.

Self-assessment activity 2.6

Explain why it is important to consider the tax implications of financial and investment decisions.

(Answer in Appendix A at the back of the book)

SUMMARY

This chapter has introduced readers to the financial and tax environment within which financial and investment decisions take place.

Key points

- Financial markets consist of numerous specialist markets where financial transactions occur (e.g. the money market, capital market, foreign exchange market, derivatives markets).
- Financial institutions (e.g. banks, building societies, pension funds) provide a vital service by acting as financial intermediaries between savers and borrowers.
- Securitisation and disintermediation have permitted larger companies to create alternative, more flexible forms of finance.
- The London Stock Exchange operates two tiers: the Main Market for larger established companies, and the Alternative Investment Market which mainly caters for very young companies.
- An efficient capital market is one where investors are rational and share prices reflect all available information. The efficient markets hypothesis has been examined in its various forms (weak, semi-strong and strong). In all but the strong form, it seems to hold up reasonably well, but it is increasingly unable to explain 'special' circumstances.
- Taxation can play a key role in financial management, particularly in raising finance, investing in fixed assets and paying dividends.

Further reading

Boakes (2010) provides a clear explanation of how to read the financial pages. More extensive discussions on financial markets are available in Stoakes (2013), Pilbeam (2010) and Valdez and Molyneux (2012).

Two classic review articles on market efficiency were written by Fama (1992), while Rappaport (1987) examines the implications for managers. Tests of capital market efficiency are found in Ross *et al.* (2010), Copeland *et al.* (2013) and Keane (1983). Ball (2009) discusses what the global financial crisis may tell us about market efficiency, as do Choudhry and Jayasekera (2013). Discussion on short-termism in the City is found in Marsh (1990) and Ball (1991). Lim and Brooks (2011) survey the empirical literature on stock market efficiency in a thorough review article.

Useful websites

www.moneyfactor.co.uk
www.moneysupermarket.com
www.moneyextra.com
www.find.co.uk
www.moneynet.co.uk
www.fool.com

Appendix
FINANCIAL STATEMENT ANALYSIS

Most readers will previously have undertaken a module in accounting and be familiar with financial statements. This appendix provides a summary of the key elements in analysing financial statements and the main ratios involved in interpreting accounts.

Investors, whether shareholders or bank managers, ask three basic questions when they examine the accounts of a business:

balance sheet/statement of financial position
A financial statement that lists the assets held by a business at a point in time and explains how they have been financed (i.e. by owners' capital and by third-party liabilities)

- *Position* – what is the current financial position, or state of affairs, of the business? This question is addressed by examining the **balance sheet**, also referred to as the **statement of financial position**.
- *Performance* – how well has the business performed over the period of time we are interested in, for example, the past year? This question is addressed by looking at the **profit and loss account**, otherwise termed the **income statement**.

profit and loss account/ income statement
A financial statement that details for a specific time period the amount of revenue earned by a firm, the costs it has incurred, the resulting profit and how it has been distributed ('appropriated')

- *Prospects* – what are the likely prospects of the business for which we are considering investment? A bank manager would probably request a cash flow forecast, showing the expected cash receipts and payments for the coming year. However, published accounts are historical documents and the shareholder will have to settle for the **cash flow statement** for the past year. Clues as to the expected future prospects may be found in the Chairman's Statement frequently published with the accounts.

cash flow statement
A financial statement that explains the reasons for cash inflows and outflows of a business, and highlights the resulting change in cash position

We will examine the three financial statements, drawing on the abridged accounts of a fictitious company called *Foto-U*, a business specialising in offering instant photographs through photo booths in public places throughout Europe.

■ The balance sheet or statement of financial position

non-current assets
Assets that remain in the balance sheet for more than one accounting period

Imagine it is possible to take a financial snapshot of *Foto-U* on 31 March 2015, the end of its trading year. What we would see are the very things we find in the balance sheet. Looking at *Foto-U*'s statement of financial position in Table 2.2, we see three main categories – assets, creditors (or liabilities), and shareholders' equity. This statement demonstrates the 'accounting equation': the money invested in the business by shareholders and creditors is represented by the assets in which they have been invested.

current assets
Assets that will leave the balance sheet in the next accounting period

$$\begin{array}{ccc} \textit{Where the cash came from} & = & \textit{Where the cash went} \\ \textit{(sources of funds)} & & \textit{(uses of funds)} \end{array}$$

intangible
Intangible assets cannot be seen or touched, e.g. the image and good reputation of a firm

Shareholders' funds of £78m + Liabilities (Creditors) £120m = Assets £198m

tangible
Tangible assets can quite literally be seen and touched, e.g. machinery and buildings

The more permanent assets (typically those with a life beyond a year) are termed **non-current assets** while the less permanent are termed **current assets**. For *Foto-U*, **intangible** non-current assets refer to patents and goodwill, the latter arising from acquiring another company and paying more for it than the balance sheet value of its underlying assets. **Tangible** non-current assets include land and buildings, photo booths, plant and machinery, vehicles, and fixtures and fittings. Their values are not stated at what they could be sold for, but at their **net book value** – what they originally cost less an estimate of the extent to which they have depreciated in value with use or age.

net book value
The original cost of buying an asset less accumulated depreciation charges to date

Table 2.2 *Foto-U* plc

Statement of Financial Position as at 31 March 2015

	2015	2014
	£m	£m
Non-current assets		
Intangible assets	15	10
Tangible assets	117	92
	132	**102**
Current assets		
Inventories	25	24
Receivables	29	25
Cash and cash equivalents	12	5
	66	**54**
Total assets	**198**	**156**
Current liabilities		
Payables*	60	62
Non-current liabilities		
Borrowings	60	23
Total liabilities	**120**	**85**
Net assets	**78**	**71**
Shareholders' equity		
Called-up share capital	2	2
Reserves	76	69
Total shareholders' equity	**78**	**71**
*The payables figures include trade creditors	40	42

Income Statement for the year ended 31 March 2015

	2015	2014
Turnover – continuing operations	**200**	**190**
Cost of sales (including depreciation of £27m)	(157)	(160)
Gross profit	**43**	**30**
Administration expenses	(21)	(20)
Operating profit (Earnings before interest and taxes)	**22**	**10**
Interest payable	(2)	(2)
Profit before taxation	**20**	**8**
Tax on profit	(6)	(4)
Profit after tax attributable to shareholders	**14**	**4**

Cash Flow Statement for the year ended 31 March 2015

	2015	2014
Net cash inflow from operations	**42**	**46**
Servicing of finance	(2)	(2)
Taxation	(6)	(4)
Capital expenditure	(57)	(33)
Dividends paid	(7)	(3)
Financing	37	2
Increase in cash in the year	**7**	**6**

Other data: Foto-*U* has 200 million shares in issue.
Share price at 31 March 2015 is 120p (50p for 2014).
Dividends declared and paid are £7 million (£3 million last year)

Current assets represent the less permanent items (typically less than a year) the business owns at the statement of financial position date. Our snapshot for *Foto-U* captures three items – inventories (also termed stocks), receivables (also termed debtors) and cash and cash equivalents. Unlike non-current assets, these items are continuously changing (or 'turning over') as trading takes place. Trade creditors and bank overdraft, where the amount has to be settled within one year, are deducted from the current assets to give the **net current assets** figure, commonly termed **working capital**. This is the amount of money likely to be turned into cash over the coming weeks. Creditors to be paid after more than a year (non-current liabilities) are typically in the form of medium/long-term loans. Finally, **shareholders' equity** represent the capital originally paid in by shareholders plus any reserves created since then. The most common reserve will be the profit retained in the business rather than paid to the shareholders as dividends.

net current assets
Current assets less current liabilities

shareholders' equity
The value of the owners' stake in the business – identically equal to net assets, or equity

Does the statement of financial position show the worth of the business?

Although the shareholders' equity for *Foto-U* of £78 million is the difference between what it *owns*, in the form of various assets, and what it *owes* to third parties, it would not be correct to say that this is what their investment is worth. The market value for the company is based on what investors are willing to pay for it. But the assets and liabilities are valued according to **Generally Accepted Accounting Principles (GAAP)**. We cannot explore them all here, but one principle is that assets are usually valued at their historical cost less a provision for such things as depreciation, in the case of non-current assets, and bad or doubtful debts, in the case of debtors. The key difference is that book values, based on GAAP, are backward-looking, while market values are forward-looking, based on expected future profits and cash flows.

Generally Accepted Accounting Principles (GAAP)
The set of legal regulations and accounting standards that dictate 'best practice' in constructing company accounts

To get some idea of the difference between the market and book values of the shareholders' funds we can look at the share price listed on the Stock Exchange on the balance sheet date. For *Foto-U* the share price at the balance sheet date was 120p. There are 200 million issued shares so the **market capitalisation** is:

market capitalisation
The market value of a firm's equity, i.e. number of ordinary shares issued times market price

(200 million shares × 120p a share) = £240 million

Comparing the market value with the book value for shareholders' equity, we find a ratio of approximately 3:1 (£240m/£78m). We should not be surprised to find that the market value is so much higher. Successful businesses are much more than a collection of assets less liabilities. They include creative people, successful trading strategies, profitable brands and much more. Generally, we can say that the greater the market-to-book value ratio, the more successful the business.

The income statement or profit and loss account

To gain an impression of how well *Foto-U* has performed over the past year we need to turn to the profit and loss account or income statement. This shows the sales income less the costs of trading. Shareholders are primarily interested in the **profit after tax (PAT)** available for distribution to them in the form of dividends. *Foto-U* has made a PAT of £14 million.

profit after tax (PAT)
Profit available to pay dividends to shareholders after tax has been paid

Investors also want to know how much profit (or earnings) has been made from its trading, before the cost of financing is deducted. **Earnings before interest and taxes (EBIT)** for *Foto-U* is:

earnings before interest and taxes (EBIT)
Earnings (i.e. profits) before interest and taxation

EBIT = total revenues − operating costs (including depreciation)

= £200m − £178m

= £22m

operating profit
Revenues less total operating costs, both variable and fixed – as distinct from financial costs such as interest payments

earnings before interest, tax, depreciation & amortisation (EBITDA)
A rough measure of operating cash flow, effectively, operating profit with depreciation added back. It differs from the 'Net Cash Inflow from Operating Activities' shown in cash flow statements due to working capital movements

This is also termed **operating profit**.

Profit is not the sole consideration for investors. They are perhaps more interested in how much cash has been created through successful trading. This can be estimated by adding back the depreciation (a non-cash cost) previously deducted in calculating EBIT. This is termed **earnings before interest, taxes, depreciation and amortisation (EBITDA)** (amortisation is just a fancy name for depreciating intangible assets). For our company, this is:

$$\begin{aligned} \text{EBITDA} &= \text{EBIT} + \text{Depreciation} \\ &= £22m + £27m \\ &= £49m \end{aligned}$$

■ The cash flow statement

The third and final financial statement in a published set of accounts is the cash flow statement. This statement is valuable because it reveals the main sources of cash and how it has been applied. For *Foto-U*, the main two sources of cash during the year are additional finance raised from new loans and net cash from operations (basically the EBITDA referred to above plus a few other adjustments for non-cash items). The main applications of this cash generated from trading are investment in capital expenditure, and dividends. The final line on this statement shows that, during the year, cash and cash equivalent has increased by £7 million.

■ A financial health check using ratios

Accountants and bank managers have formulated dozens of financial ratios to help diagnose the financial health of the business, its position, performance and prospects. We shall restrict our focus to those key financial ratios that every finance manager and investor should be acquainted with. These are summarised in Table 2.3 and discussed briefly below.

Profitability ratios
To assess the performance of *Foto-U*, we study a number of profitability ratios.

Profit margin
This ratio shows how much profit is generated from every £ of sales. It can be considered in the form of a percentage at both the gross and net profit levels.

Gross profit margin

$$\frac{\text{Gross profit}}{\text{Sales}} \times 100 = \frac{43}{200} \times 100$$
$$= 21.5\% \quad (15.8\% \text{ last year})$$

Net profit margin

$$\frac{\text{EBIT}}{\text{Sales}} \times 100 = \frac{22}{200} \times 100$$
$$= 11\% \quad (5.3\% \text{ last year})$$

(EBIT is earnings before interest and tax, i.e. operating profit.)

Table 2.3 *Foto-U* key ratios

Ratio	Form	2015	2014
Profitability			
Gross profit margin	%	21.5	15.8
Net profit margin	%	11.0	5.3
Return on total assets (ROTA)	%	11.1	6.4
Activity ratios			
Net asset turnover	times	1.01	1.22
Debtors	days	53	48
Stock	days	58	54
Supplier credit period	days	93	96
Liquidity and financing ratios			
Current ratio	times	1.1	0.9
Quick (acid test) ratio	times	0.7	0.5
Gearing	%	43.5	24.5
Interest cover	times	11	5
Investor ratios			
Return on shareholders' funds	%	17.9	5.6
Dividend per share	pence	3.5	1.5
Earnings per share	pence	7	2
Dividend cover	times	2	1.3
Price:earnings	times	17.1	25
Dividend yield	%	2.9	3

Return on total assets (ROTA)

This ratio, also termed the primary ratio, examines the rate of profit the business makes on the capital invested in it. *Foto-U* has total assets of £198 million.

$$\text{ROTA} = \frac{\text{EBIT}}{\text{Total assets}} \times 100 = \frac{22}{198} \times 100$$

$$= 11.1\% \quad (6.4\% \text{ last year})$$

Activity ratios

Here we examine how efficiently *Foto-U* manages its assets in terms of the level of sales obtained from the assets invested.

Asset turnover

$$\frac{\text{Sales}}{\text{Total assets}} = \frac{200}{198}$$

$$= 1.01 \text{ times} \quad (1.22 \text{ last year})$$

This can also be expressed in terms of each type of asset, but here, we usually express it in terms of days. For example, the average number of days it takes for debtors to pay is given by debtor days.

Debtor days

$$\frac{\text{Receivables}}{\text{Credit sales}} \times 365 = \frac{29}{200} \times 365$$

$$= 53 \text{ days} \quad (48 \text{ days last year})$$

Note also that we have used the asset figure at the year-end. A more accurate picture is given by finding the average asset value based on the values at the start and end of the year.

Similar calculations can be made for stock and creditors, but with one important difference. Stock and trade creditors are valued in the statement of financial position at original cost so instead of using sales, we use cost of sales, i.e. what it cost the firm to build these stocks.

Stockholding period

$$\frac{\text{Inventory}}{\text{Cost of sales}} \times 365 = \frac{25}{157} \times 365$$

$$= 58 \text{ days} \quad (54 \text{ days last year})$$

Supplier credit days

$$\frac{\text{Trade payables}}{\text{Cost of sales}} \times 365 = \frac{40}{157} \times 365$$

$$= 93 \text{ days} \quad (96 \text{ days last year})$$

It is preferable to use purchases rather than cost of sales, although this figure is not always available.

Liquidity and financing ratios

To assess whether the company is able to meet its financial obligations as they fall due, we need to compare short-term assets with short-term creditors. Two such ratios are commonly employed.

Current ratio

$$\frac{\text{Current assets}}{\text{Current liabilities}} = \frac{66}{60}$$

$$= 1.1 \text{ times} \quad (0.9 \text{ times last year})$$

Quick assets

For most firms, it is not easy to convert stock into cash with any great speed. The quick assets (or acid-test ratio) is a more prudent liquidity ratio which excludes stock entirely.

$$\frac{\text{Current assets} - \text{stock}}{\text{Current liabilities}} = \frac{66 - 25}{60}$$

$$= 0.7 \text{ times} \quad (0.5 \text{ times last year})$$

As a general rule of thumb, we would typically expect the current ratio to be 2 and the quick assets to match creditors (i.e. a quick ratio of 1). However, this guide may differ from industry to industry depending on the trade credit periods granted to customers and claimed from suppliers.

Gearing

A rather different question asks how the capital employed in the business is financed. The gearing ratio shows the proportion of capital employed funded by long-term borrowings.

$$\frac{\text{Long-term borrowings}}{\text{Debt} + \text{Equity capital}} \times 100 = \frac{60}{138} \times 100$$

$$= 43.5\% \quad (24.5\% \text{ last year})$$

An equally acceptable way of expressing the gearing ratio is by the Debt/Equity ratio.

$$\frac{\text{Long-term borrowings}}{\text{Shareholders' equity}} = \frac{60}{78} = 0.77{:}1$$

Interest cover

Another way of considering gearing is to look to the profit and loss account by assessing the degree of profits cover the firm has to meet its interest payments.

$$\frac{\text{Earnings before interest and taxes}}{\text{Interest payable}} = \frac{22}{2}$$

$$= 11 \text{ times} \quad (5 \text{ times last year})$$

An interest cover of 11 times is very safe. But were it to fall to, say, below three or four, concern may arise that taxation and dividends cannot be paid.

Investor ratios

Shareholders are more interested in the return they obtain on *their* investment rather than the return the company makes on the total business.

Return on shareholders' funds (return on equity)

This indicates how profitable the company has been for its shareholders.

$$\frac{\text{Earnings after tax and preference dividends}}{\text{Shareholders' equity}} \times 100 = \frac{14}{78} \times 100$$

$$= 17.9\% \quad (5.6\% \text{ last year})$$

Shareholders will also be interested in the earnings per share (what dividend could be paid) and dividend per share (what dividend is paid) for the year.

Earnings per share (EPS)

$$\frac{\text{Earnings after tax and preference dividends}}{\text{Number of ordinary shares in issue}} = \frac{14}{200}$$

$$= 7 \text{ pence per share}$$

$$(2 \text{ pence last year})$$

In practice, the EPS calculation is usually more complex than this, but the notes to the accounts will explain the calculation.

Dividend per share (DPS)

$$\frac{\text{Total ordinary dividend}}{\text{Number of ordinary shares in issue}} = \frac{7}{200}$$

$$= 3.5 \text{ pence per share} \quad (1.5 \text{ pence last year})$$

Dividend cover

This links the DPS and the EPS to indicate how many times the dividend *could* be paid, and, hence, how safe it is, in terms of exposure to a fall in EPS.

$$\frac{\text{Earnings per share}}{\text{Dividend per share}} = \frac{7}{3.5}$$

$$= 2 \text{ times} \quad (1.3 \text{ times last year})$$

The final two ratios relate earnings and dividends to stock market performance as reflected in the current share price. If the current share price for *Foto-U* is 120p, we can calculate the price:earnings ratio and dividend yield.

Price:earnings ratio (P:E)

$$\frac{\text{Current share price}}{\text{Earnings per share}} = \frac{120}{7}$$

$$= 17.1 \text{ times} \quad (25 \text{ times last year})$$

The share price, of course, is based on investors' expectations of *future* profits. A high P:E ratio indicates that investors expect future profits to grow – the higher the P:E, the greater the profit growth expectation.

Dividend yield

$$\frac{\text{Dividend per share (p)}}{\text{Share price (p)}} \times 100 = \frac{3.5}{120} \times 100$$

$$= 2.9\% \quad (3\% \text{ last year})$$

■ Interpretation of the accounts and ratios

The financial manager or investor needs to put together all the clues suggested by ratio analysis and reading the accounts to gain insights into the financial position, performance and prospects of the company. This will probably involve looking at the trend of financial indicators, not simply comparison with the previous year, together with comparison with industry and competitor data. It certainly requires a reasonable grasp of the business, its objectives and strategies. Table 2.4 offers a brief report to senior management of *Foto-U* by the finance manager on the company's published accounts.

Table 2.4 *Foto-U* annual corporate performance report

To: Senior Management of *Foto-U*
From: Finance Manager

Subject: **Annual corporate performance**
30 April 2015

I have reviewed the published accounts for the past year to establish how successful *Foto-U* was in financial terms.

Profitability. The Return on Total Assets has improved over the year from 6.4% to 11.1%. This is a significant improvement and well above the risk-free return we would expect from investing in say building society deposits, but we need also to compare the return against that achieved by our competitors. ROTA is a combination of two subsidiary ratios – net profit margin and asset turnover:

	ROTA	=	Net profit margin	×	Asset turnover
2014	6.4%	=	5.3%	×	1.22 times
2015	11.1%	=	11%	×	1.01 times

Continued

Both the gross and net profit margins have improved significantly as a result of the £10 million growth in sales over the year without any increase in costs. However, this growth has come at the expense of a poorer utilisation of our assets, as reflected in the significant decline in asset turnover. This is mainly attributable to a major capital expenditure programme during the year, the benefits of which will not be fully experienced for at least another year. A further factor is the increase in working capital. Last year, we actually managed to have negative working capital (i.e. our trade creditors and overdraft financed more than our current assets). This year, there has been a slight deterioration in all elements of working capital:

• We take five more days to collect cash from customers

• Stockholding period has increased by four days

• We pay suppliers a little quicker.

Liquidity. Our current and quick asset ratios are both well below the typical level for the industry of 1.8 and 1.0 respectively. However, this is largely due to the fact that our suppliers have been willing to grant us extended credit periods of about three months. Realistically, we cannot expect this to continue. Were they to demand payment within, say, 45 days, it is difficult to see where we would be able to find the cash. It is not good financial management for us to rely on the generous credit of suppliers over whom we have no control, and we need to address this issue urgently. Linked to this, we have just raised a large medium-term loan in order to fund our capital expenditure in the coming year. Our gearing ratio has now nearly doubled and we will have to find cash both for additional interest payments and, eventually, the loan repayments. Unless the new investment very rapidly produces higher profits and cashflow, I am concerned that we could be in serious financial difficulty, despite the strong level of profits. Perhaps it is time to consider asking shareholders to invest more capital in the business, or to reduce dividend payments.

Investment attractiveness. The company's share price has progressed from 50 pence to 120 pence over the year. No doubt this is due to the growth in sales, profits and dividends in the year. Many of the investment performance indicators have improved, particularly earnings per share and return on shareholders' funds, the latter looking much healthier at nearly 18%. However, the price:earnings ratio has slipped a little, suggesting that investors do not expect the company's profits and share price to continue to grow at quite the same rate as this year.

In summary, *Foto-U* has improved its performance over the past year, but there remain concerns regarding its liquidity. Management is urged to give urgent attention to this matter.

Questions with a **coloured number** have solutions in Appendix B on page 779.

1 When a company seeks a listing for its shares on a stock exchange, it usually recruits the assistance of an investment bank.

   (a) Explain the role of an investment bank in a listing operation with respect to the various matters on which its advice will be sought by a company.

   (b) Identify the conflicts which might arise if the investment bank were part of a group providing a wide range of financial services.

(CIMA)

2 (a) Briefly outline the major functions performed by the capital market and explain the importance of each function for corporate financial management. How does the existence of a well-functioning capital market assist the financial management function?

   (b) Describe the efficient markets hypothesis and explain the differences between the three forms of the hypothesis which have been distinguished.

   (c) Company A has 2 million shares in issue and company B 6 million. On day 1 the market value per share is £2 for A and £3 for B. On day 2, the management of B decides, at a private meeting, to make a cash takeover bid for A at a price of £3.00 per share. The takeover will produce large operating savings with a value of £3.2 million. On day 4, B publicly announces an unconditional offer to purchase all shares of A at a price of £3.00 per share with settlement on day 15. Details of the large savings are not announced and are not public knowledge. On day 10, B announces details of the savings which will be derived from the takeover.

   Required

   Ignoring tax and the time-value of money between days 1 and 15, and assuming the details given are the only factors having an impact on the share prices of A and B, determine the day 2, day 4 and day 10 share prices of A and B if the market is:

   1 semi-strong form efficient, and
   2 strong form efficient

   in each of the following separate circumstances:

   (i) the purchase consideration is cash as specified above, and

   (ii) the purchase consideration, decided upon on day 2 and publicly announced on day 4, is one newly issued share of B for each share of A.

(ACCA)

3 You are an accountant with a practice that includes a large proportion of individual clients, who often ask for information about traded investments. You have extracted the following data from a leading financial newspaper.

(i)

Stock	Price	P:E ratio	Dividend yield (% gross)
Buntam plc	160p	20	5
Zellus plc	270p	15	3.33

(ii) Earnings and dividend data for Crazy Games plc are given below:

	2011	2012	2013	2014	2015
EPS	5p	6p	7p	10p	12p
Div. per share (gross)	3p	3p	3.5p	5p	5.5p

The estimated before tax return on equity required by investors in Crazy Games plc is 20%.

Required

Draft a report for circulation to your private clients which explains:

(a) the factors to be taken into account (including risks and returns) when considering the purchase of different types of traded investments.

(b) the role of financial intermediaries, and their usefulness to the private investor.

(c) the meaning and the relevance to the investor of each of the following:

(i) Gross dividend (pence per share)

(ii) EPS

(iii) Dividend cover

Your answer should include calculation of, and comment upon, the gross dividends, EPS and dividend cover for Buntam plc and Zellus plc, based on the information given above.

(ACCA)

4 Beta plc has been trading for 12 years and during this period has achieved a good profit record. To date, the company has not been listed on a recognised stock exchange. However, Beta plc has recently appointed a new chairman and managing director who are considering whether or not the company should obtain a full stock exchange listing.

Required

(a) What are the advantages and disadvantages which may accrue to the company and its shareholders of obtaining a full stock exchange listing?

(b) What factors should be taken into account when attempting to set an issue price for new equity shares in the company, assuming it is to be floated on a stock exchange?

(Certified Diploma)

5 Collingham plc produces electronic measuring instruments for medical research. It has recorded strong and consistent growth during the past 10 years since its present team of managers bought it out from a large multinational corporation. They are now contemplating obtaining a stock market listing.

Collingham's accounting statements for the last financial year are summarised below. Fixed assets (i.e. non-current assets) including freehold land and premises, are shown at historic cost net of depreciation. The debenture is redeemable in two years although early redemption without penalty is permissible.

Profit and Loss Account (Income Statement) for the year ended 31 December 2014 (£m)

Turnover	80.0
Cost of sales	(70.0)
Operating profit	10.0
Interest charges	(3.0)
Pre-tax profit	7.0
Corporation tax (after capital allowances)	(1.0)
Profits attributable to ordinary shareholders	6.0
Dividends	(0.5)
Retained earnings	5.5

Statement of Financial Position as at 31 December 2014 (£m)

Assets employed		
Fixed: Land and premises	10.0	
Machinery	20.0	30.0
Current: Stocks	10.0	
Debtors	10.0	
Cash	3.0	23.0
Current liabilities: Trade creditors	(15.0)	

Bank overdraft	(5.0)	(20.0)
Net current assets		3.0
Total assets less current liabilities		33.0
14% Debentures		(5.0)
Net assets		28.0
Financed by:		
Issued share capital (par value 50p):		
Voting shares		2.0
Non-voting 'A' shares		2.0
Profit and Loss Account		24.0
Shareholders' funds		28.0

The following information is also available regarding key financial indicators for Collingham's industry.

Return on (long-term) capital employed	22% (pre-tax)
Return on equity	14% (post-tax)
Operating profit margin	10%
Current ratio	1.8:1
Acid test	1.1:1
Gearing (total debt/equity)	18%
Interest cover	5.2
Dividend cover	2.6
P:E ratio	13:1

Required
(a) Briefly explain why companies like Collingham seek stock market listings.
(b) Discuss the performance and financial health of Collingham in relation to that of the industry as a whole.
(c) In what ways would you advise Collingham:
  (i) to restructure its balance sheet prior to flotation?
  (ii) to change its financial policy following flotation?

Practical assignment

Select two companies from one sector in the Financial Times share information service. Analyse the share price and other data provided and compare this with the FT All-Share Index data for the sector. Suggest why the P:E ratios for the companies differ.

3

Present values, and bond and share valuation

The fatal attraction of profits and share prices

It is easy to put a value on a company. All you need to do is foresee the future. If not, it is impossible. And that is where the problems start. The value of a company is tied up in the future. It is worth the total cash flows that it produces in the future, discounted for the time value of money – the fact that a dollar today is worth much more than a dollar in 10 years.

The mathematics is not that difficult if you know the company's future cash flows, the cost of its equity and debt, and the relative proportions of debt and equity into the future. The problem is that all these four variables are unknown at the time you have to decide how much a company is worth.

This is why the art of valuing stocks is so imprecise, allowing investors to win and lose so much on the stock market. It is also why astute corporate financiers can get away with so much. With 'true' valuation unknowable, it is far easier to prompt buyers to pay ridiculous prices in acquisitions, or for managers to take damaging decisions that seem to enhance value in the short term.

Source: Based on John Authers, *Financial Times*, 30 October 2010, p. 16.

Learning objectives

Having completed this chapter, you should have a sound grasp of the time-value of money and discounted cash flow concepts. In particular, you should understand the following:

- The time-value of money.
- The financial arithmetic underlying compound interest and discounting.
- Present value formulae for single amounts, annuities and perpetuities.
- The valuation of bonds and shares.

Skills developed in discounted cash flow analysis, using both formulae and tables, will help enormously in subsequent chapters.

3.1 INTRODUCTION

Managers are expected to make sound long-term decisions and to manage resources in the best interests of the owners. To assess whether investment ideas are wealth-creating, we need to have a clear understanding of cash flow and the time-value of money. Capital investment decisions, security and bond value analyses, financial structure decisions, lease vs. buy decisions and the tricky question of the required rate of return can be addressed only when you understand exactly what the old expression 'time is money' really means.

In this chapter, we will consider the measurement of wealth and the fundamental role it plays in the decision-making process; the time-value of money, which underlies the discounted cash flow concept; and the net present value approach for analysing investment decisions.

3.2 MEASURING WEALTH

'Cash is King' seems to be the message for businesses today. Spectacular business collapses in recent years demonstrate that reliance on sales, profits or earnings per share as measures of performance can be dangerous.

Businesses go 'bust' because they run out of the cash required to fulfil their financial obligations. Of course, there are always reasons why this happens – recession, an over-ambitious investment programme, rapid growth without adequate long-term finance – but, basically, corporate survival and success come down to cash flow and value creation.

Boo.com, the internet fashion retailer, thought it had a promising future at the start of 2000. It had raised $135 million to set up the new business and invest in marketing to break into the competitive fashion retail sector. But less than six months later, it had virtually run out of cash and was forced into liquidation. The Chief Executive confessed: 'My mistake has been not to have an accountant who was a strong financial controller.'

Recall from Chapter 1 that the assumed objective of the firm is to create as much wealth as possible for its shareholders. A successful business is one that creates value for its owners. Wealth is created when the market value of the outputs exceeds the market value of the inputs, i.e. the benefits are greater than the costs. Expressed mathematically:

$$V_j = B_j - C_j$$

The value (V_j) created by decision j is the difference between the benefits (B_j) and the costs (C_j) attributable to the decision. This leads to an obvious decision rule: accept only those investment or financing proposals that enhance the wealth of shareholders, i.e. accept if $B_j - C_j > 0$.

time-value of money
Money received in the future is usually worth less than today because it could be invested to earn interest over this period

Nothing could be simpler in concept – the problems emerge only when we probe more deeply into how the benefits and costs are measured and evaluated. One obvious problem is that benefits and costs usually occur at different times and over a number of years. This leads us to consider the **time-value of money**.

3.3 TIME-VALUE OF MONEY

An important principle in financial management is that the value of money depends on *when* the cash flow occurs – £100 *now* is worth more than £100 at some *future* time. There are a number of reasons for this:

1 *Risk*. One hundred pounds now is certain, whereas £100 receivable next year is less certain. This 'bird-in-the-hand' principle affects many aspects of financial management that will be covered in later chapters.

2 *Inflation.* Under inflationary conditions, the value of money, in terms of its purchasing power over goods and services, declines.

3 *Personal consumption preference.* Most of us have a strong preference for immediate rather than delayed consumption.

More fundamental than any of the above, however, is the time-value of money. Money – like any other desirable commodity – has a price. If you own money, you can 'rent' it to someone else, say a banker, and earn interest. A business which carries unnecessarily high cash balances incurs an **opportunity cost** – the lost opportunity to earn money by investing it to earn a higher return. The investor's overall return, which reflects the time-value of money, therefore comprises:

opportunity cost
The value forgone by opting for a particular course of action

(a) the risk-free rate of return rewarding investors for forgoing immediate consumption, plus

(b) compensation for risk and loss of purchasing power.

Self-assessment activity 3.1

Imagine you went to your bank manager asking for a £50,000 loan, for five years, to start up a burger bar under a McDonald's franchise. Which of the considerations in the previous paragraph would the bank manager consider?

(Answer in Appendix A at the back of the book)

Before proceeding further, we need to understand the essential financial arithmetic for the time-value of money. Einstein once said 'compound interest is the 8th wonder of the world. He who understands it, earns it. He who doesn't, pays it.' The next section of the chapter considers compound interest and associated ideas.

3.4 FINANCIAL ARITHMETIC FOR CAPITAL GROWTH

■ Simple and compound interest

The future value (FV) of a sum of money invested at a given annual rate of interest will depend on whether the interest is paid only on the original investment (simple interest), or whether it is calculated on the original investment plus accrued interest (**compound interest**). Suppose you win £1,000 on the National Lottery and decide to invest it at 10 per cent for five years' simple interest. The future value will be the original £1,000 capital plus five years' interest of £100 a year, giving a total future value of £1,500.

compound interest
Interest paid on the sum which accumulates, i.e. the principal plus interest

With compound interest, the interest is paid on the original capital plus accrued interest, as shown in Table 3.1. The process of compounding provides a convenient way of adjusting for the time-value of money. An investment made now in the capital market of V_0 gives rise to a cash flow of $V_0(1 + i)^2$ after two years, and so on. In general,

Table 3.1 Compound interest on £1,000 over five years (at 10%)

Year	Starting balance £	+	Interest £	=	Closing balance £
1	1000		100		1100
2	1100		110		1210
3	1210		121		1331
4	1331		133		1464
5	1464		146		1610

the future value of V_0 invested today at a compound rate of interest of i per cent for n years will be:

$$FV_{(i,n)} = V_0(1 + i)^n$$

where $FV_{(i,n)}$ is the future value at time n, V_0 is the original sum invested, sometimes termed the principal (note that the 0 subscript refers to the time period, i.e. today), and i is the annual rate of interest.

Using this formula in the above example, we obtain the same future value as in Table 3.1.

$$FV_5 = £1,000(1 + 0.10)^5 = £1,610$$

Note that the effect of compound interest yields a higher value than simple interest, which yielded only £1,500.

■ More frequent compounding and annual percentage rates

Unless otherwise stated, it is assumed that compounding or discounting is an annual process; cash payments of benefits arise either at the start or the end of the year. Frequently, however, the contractual payment period is less than one year. Building societies and government bonds pay interest semi-annually or quarterly. Interest charged on credit cards is applied monthly. To compare the true costs or benefits of such financial contracts, it is necessary to determine the **annual percentage rate** (APR), or effective annual interest rate, taking into account any costs such as one-off fees. In the UK, lenders are required to disclose the APR before the loan is finalised. Taking compounding to its limits, we can adopt a continuous discounting approach.[*]

annual percentage rate
The true annual interest rate charged by the lender which takes account of the timing of interest and principal payments

Examples of more frequent compound interest

Returning to our earlier example of £1,000 invested for five years at 10 per cent compound interest, we now assume 5 per cent payable every six months.

After the first six months, the interest is £50, which is reinvested to give interest for the second half year of $(£1,050 \times 5\%) = £52$. The end-of-year value is therefore $(£1,050 + £52) = £1,102$. We can still use the compound interest formula, but with i as the six-monthly interest rate and n the six-monthly, rather than annual, interval:

$$\text{After 1 year, } FV_1 = £1,000(1 + 0.05)^2$$

$$= £1,102$$

$$\text{After 5 years, } FV_5 = £1,000(1 + 0.05)^{10}$$

$$= £1,629$$

Note that this value is higher than the £1,610 value based on the earlier annual interval calculation. In converting the annual compounding formula to another interest payment

Continued

---

[*]When the number of compounding periods each year approaches infinity, the future value is found by:

$$FV_n = V_0e^{in}$$

where i is the annual interest rate, n is the number of years and e is the value of the exponential function. Using a scientific calculator, this is shown as 2.71828 (to five decimal places).

Using the same example as before:

$$FV_4 = V_0e^{in} = £1,000\,e^{(0.1)5}$$

$$= £1,648.72 \text{ (slightly more than compounding on a weekly basis)}$$

frequency, the trick is simply to divide the annual rate of interest (i) and multiply the time (n) by the number of payments each year.

If, in the above example, interest is calculated at weekly intervals over five years, the future value will be:

$$\text{FV}_5 = \pounds1,000\left(1 + \frac{0.10}{52}\right)^{52(5)} = \pounds1,648$$

We calculate below the APRs based on a range of interest payment frequencies for a 22 per cent per annum loan. By charging compound interest on a daily basis, the effective annual rate is 24.6 per cent, some 2.6 per cent higher than on an annual basis.

Annually	$(1 + 0.22)$	$- 1 = 0.22$ or 22%
Semi-annually	$\left(1 + \dfrac{0.22}{2}\right)^2$	$- 1 = 0.232$ or 23.2%
Monthly	$\left(1 + \dfrac{0.22}{12}\right)^{12}$	$- 1 = 0.244$ or 24.4%
Daily	$\left(1 + \dfrac{0.22}{365}\right)^{365}$	$- 1 = 0.246$ or 24.6%

3.5 PRESENT VALUE

present value
The current worth of future cash flows

discounting
The process of reducing cash flows to present values

An alternative way of assessing the worth of an investment is to invert the compounding process to give the **present value** of the future cash flows. This process is called **discounting**.

The time-value of money principle argues that, given the choice of £100 now or the same amount in one year's time, it is always preferable to take the £100 now because it could be invested over the next year at, say, a 10 per cent interest rate to produce £110 at the end of one year. If 10 per cent is the best available annual rate of interest, then one would be indifferent to (i.e. attach equal value to) receiving £100 now or £110 in one year's time. Expressed another way, the *present value* of £110 received one year hence is £100.

We obtained the present value (PV) simply by dividing the future cash flow by 1 plus the rate of interest, i, i.e.

$$\text{PV} = \frac{\pounds110}{(1 + 0.10)} = \frac{\pounds110}{(1.1)} = \pounds100$$

Discounting is the process of adjusting future cash flows to their present values. It is, in effect, compounding in reverse.

Recall that earlier we specified the future value as:

$$\text{FV}_n = V_0(1 + i)^n$$

Dividing both sides by $(1 + i)^n$ we find the present value:

$$V_0 = \frac{\text{FV}_n}{(1 + i)^n}$$

which can be read as the present value of the future cash flow FV receivable in n years' time given a rate of interest i. This is the process of discounting future sums to their present values.

Let us apply the present value formula to compute the present value of £133 receivable three years hence, discounted at 10 per cent:

$$\text{PV}_{(10\%,\,3\,\text{yrs})} = \frac{\pounds133}{(1 + 0.10)^3} = \frac{\pounds133}{1.33} = \pounds100$$

The message is: do not pay more than £100 today for an investment offering a certain return of £133 after three years, assuming a 10 per cent market rate of interest.

Calculator tip

Your calculator should have a power function key, usually x^y. Try the following steps for the previous example.

Input	1.1
Press	x^y function key
Input	3
Press	=
Display	1.331
Press	1/x
Multiply	133
Press	=
Answer	99.9

Self-assessment activity 3.2

Calculate the present value of £623 receivable in eight years' time plus £1,092 receivable eight years after that, assuming an interest rate of 7 per cent.

(Answer in Appendix A at the back of the book)

■ Discount tables

Much of the tedium of using formulae and power functions can be eased by using discount tables or computer-based spreadsheet packages. In the previous example, the discount factor for £1 for a 10 per cent discount rate in three years' time is:

$$\frac{1}{(1.10)^3} = \frac{1}{1.33} = 0.751$$

This can be found in Appendix C by locating the 10 per cent column and the 3-year row. We call this the present value interest factor (PVIF) and express it as $\text{PVIF}_{(10\%,\, 3\text{yrs})}$ or $\text{PVIF}_{(10,3)}$.

Multiplying the cash flow of £133 by the discount factor yields the same result as before:

$$PV = £133 \times 0.751 = £100 \text{ (subject to rounding)}$$

annuity
A constant annual cash flow for a prescribed period of time

With a constant annual cash flow, termed an **annuity**, we can shorten the discounting operation. Appendix D provides the present value interest factor for an annuity (PVIFA). Thus, if £133 is to be received in each of the next three years, the present value is:

$$PV = £133 \times \text{PVIFA}_{(10\%,\, 3\text{yrs})}$$
$$= £133 \times 2.4868 = £331$$

It is standard practice to write interest factors as: Interest factor(rate, period).

Examples:

$\text{PVIF}_{(8,10)}$ is the present value interest factor at 8 per cent for 10 years.

$\text{PVIFA}_{(10,4)}$ is the present value interest factor for an annuity at 10 per cent for four years.

Example of present values: Soldem Pathetic FC Ltd

Soldem Pathetic Football Club has recently been bought up by a wealthy businessman who intends to return the club to its former glory days. He also wants to pay a good dividend to the shareholders of the newly formed quoted company by making sound investments in quality players. One such player the manager would dearly like in his squad is Shane Moony, currently on the market for around £9 million. The chairman reckons that, quite apart from the extra income at the turnstiles from buying him, he could be sold for £11 million by the end of the year, given the way transfer prices are moving. Should he bid for Moony?

Assuming a 10 per cent rate of interest as the reward that the other shareholders demand for accepting the delayed payoff, the present value (PV) of £11 million receivable one year hence is:

$$PV = \text{discount factor} \times \text{future cash flow} = \frac{1}{1.10} \times £11\,\text{million}$$
$$= £10\,\text{million}$$

How much better off will the club be if it buys Moony? The answer is, in present value terms:

$$£10\,\text{million} - £9\,\text{million} = £1\,\text{million}$$

net present value
The present value of the future net benefits less the initial cost

We call this the **net present value** (NPV). The decision to buy the player makes economic sense; it promises to create wealth for the club and its shareholders, even excluding the likely additional gate receipts. Of course, Moony could break a leg in the very first game for his new club and never play again. In such an unfortunate situation, the club would achieve a negative NPV of £9 million, the initial cost. Alternatively, he could be insured against such injury, in which case there would be premiums to pay, resulting in a lower net present value.

Another way of looking at this issue is to ask whether the investment offers a return greater than could have been achieved by investing in financial, rather than human, assets. The return over one year from acquiring Moony's services is:

$$\text{Return} = \frac{\text{Profit}}{\text{Investment}} = \frac{£11m - £9m}{£9m} \times 100 = 22.2\%.$$

If the available rate of interest is 10 per cent, the investment in Moony is a considerably more rewarding prospect.

In the highly simplified example above, we assumed that the future value was certain and the interest rate was known. Of course, a spectrum of interest rates is listed in the financial press. This variety of rates arises predominantly because of uncertainty surrounding the future and imperfections in the capital market. To simplify our understanding of the time-value of money concept, let us 'assume away' these realities. The lender knows with certainty the future returns arising from the proposal for which finance is sought, and can borrow or lend on a perfect capital market. The latter assumes the following:

1 Relevant information is freely available to all participants in the market.
2 No transaction costs or taxes are involved in using the capital market.
3 No participant (borrower or lender) can influence the market price for funds by the scale of its activities.
4 All participants can lend and borrow at the same rate of interest.

Under such conditions, the corporate treasurer of a major company like Shell can raise funds no more cheaply than the chairman of Soldem Pathetic. A single market rate of interest prevails. Borrowers and lenders will base time-related decisions on this unique market rate of interest. The impact of uncertainty will be discussed in later chapters; for now, these simplistic assumptions will help us to grasp the basics of financial arithmetic.

■ The effect of discounting

Figure 3.1 shows how the discounting process affects present values at different rates of interest between 0 and 20 per cent. The value of £1 decreases very significantly as the rate and period increase. Indeed, after 10 years, for an interest rate of 20 per cent, the present value of a cash flow is only a small fraction of its nominal value.

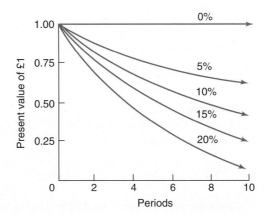

Figure 3.1 The relationship between present value of £1 and interest over time

Table 3.2 summarises the discount factors for three rates of interest. It is useful to develop a 'feel' for how money changes with time for these rates of interest. The 15 per cent discount rate is particularly useful, because this is a popular discount rate for evaluating capital projects. It also happens to be easy to remember: every five years the discounted value halves. Thus, with a 15 per cent discount rate, after five years the value of £1 is 50p, after 10 years 25p, etc.

Table 3.2 Present value of a single future sum

Year	10%	15%	20%
0	£1.00	£1.00	£1.00
5	0.60	0.50	0.40
10	0.40	0.25	0.16
15	0.24	0.12	0.06
20	0.15	0.06	0.03
25	0.09	0.03	0.01

Self-assessment activity 3.3

Your company is just about to sign a deal to purchase a fleet of lorries for £1 million. The payment terms are £500,000 down payment and £500,000 at the end of five years. No one present has a calculator or discount tables to hand. If the cost of capital for the company is 15 per cent, what is the present value cost of the purchase?

(Answer in Appendix A at the back of the book)

3.6 PRESENT VALUE ARITHMETIC

We have seen that the present value of a future cash flow is found by multiplying the cash flow by the present value interest factor. The present value concept is not difficult to apply in practice. This section explains the various present value formulae, and illustrates how they can be applied to investment and financing problems. Throughout, we shall use the symbol X to denote annual cash flow in pounds and i to denote the interest, or discount, rate (expressed as a percentage). Recall that PVIF is the present value interest factor and PVIFA is the PVIF for an annuity.

■ Present value

We know that the present value of X receivable in n years is calculated from the expression:

$$PV_{(i,n)} = \frac{X_n}{(1 + i)^n}$$
$$= X \text{ times } PVIF_{(i,n)}$$

Example

Calculate the present value of £1,000 receivable in 10 years' time, assuming a discount rate of 14 per cent:

$$PVIF_{(14\%,\,10\text{ yrs})} = \frac{1}{(1.14)^{10}} = 0.26974$$

Alternatively, the table in Appendix C provides a PVIF of 0.26974 for $n = 10$ and $i = 14$ per cent:

$$PV = £1,000 \times 0.26974 = £269.74$$

The present value of £1,000 receivable 10 years hence, discounted at 14 per cent, is thus £269.74.

Self-assessment activity 3.4

Calculate the present value of £1,000 receivable 12 years hence, assuming the discount rate is 12 per cent.

(Answer in Appendix A at the back of the book)

Example: Pay cash up front or by instalments?

Mary has agreed to purchase a new car for £18,500. She is considering whether to pay this amount in full now or by instalments involving £9,000 now and payments of £5,000 at the start of each of the next two years.

Her first thought is that by paying through instalments she pays £19,000 which is £500 more than the single payment option. She then recalls that the time-value of money principle argues that all future cash flows should be converted to present values to make a valid comparison. She estimates that the rate she could earn on her savings is 6 per cent. The calculations are:

		Present value
Down payment	£9,000	£9,000
Second payment	£5,000/1.06	£4,717
Third payment	£5,000/(1.06)^2	£4,450
Total present value		£18,167

Mary decides that it is better to go for the deferred payment package as it will cost her £18,167 in present value terms which is £333 cheaper than outright purchase. (The reader may wish to refer to Appendix C to check the present value calculations.)

In practice, most managers will use spreadsheets to do present value calculations, particularly when they involve multiple cash flows. We illustrate this using Microsoft Excel™ below.

1	A	B	C	D
2	**Year**	**Cash flow**	**Present value**	**Formula in column C**
3	0	−£9,000	−£9,000	=PV(B9,A3,0,B3)
4	1	−£5,000	−£4,717	=PV(B9,A4,0,B4)
5	2	−£5,000	−£4,450	=PV(B9,A5,0,B5)
6				
7	Total present value		−£18,167	=SUM(C3:C5)
8				
9	Discount rate	0.06		

■ Valuing perpetuities

Frequently, an investment pays a fixed sum each year for a specified number of years. A series of annual receipts or payments is termed an annuity. The simplest form of annuity is the infinite series or **perpetuity**. For example, certain government stocks offer a fixed annual income, but there is no obligation to repay the capital. The present value of such stocks (called irredeemables) is found by dividing the annual sum received by the annual rate of interest:

perpetuity
A constant annual cash flow for an infinite period of time

$$\text{PV perpetuity} = \frac{X}{i}$$

Example

Uncle George wishes to leave you in his will an annual sum of £10,000, starting next year. Assuming an interest rate of 10 per cent, how much of his estate must be set aside for this purpose? The answer is:

$$\text{PV perpetuity} = \frac{£10,000}{0.10} = £100,000$$

Suppose that your benevolent uncle now wishes to compensate for inflation, estimated to be at 5 per cent per annum. The formula can be adjusted to allow for growth at the rate of g per cent p.a. in the annual amount. (The derivation of the present value of a growing perpetuity is found in Appendix II at the end of the chapter.)

$$\text{PV} = \frac{X}{i - g}$$

As long as the growth rate is less than the interest rate, we can compute the present value required:

$$\text{PV} = \frac{£10,000}{0.10 - 0.05} = £200,000$$

This formula plays a key part in analysing financial decisions and will be developed further, below, when we consider the valuation of assets, shares and companies.

■ Valuing annuities

An annuity is an investment paying a fixed sum each year for a specified period of time. Examples of annuities are many credit agreements and house mortgages.

The life of an annuity is less than that of a perpetuity, so its value will also be somewhat less. In fact, the formula for calculating the present value of an annuity of £A is found by calculating the present value of a perpetuity and deducting the present value of that element falling beyond the end of the annuity period. This gives the somewhat complicated formula (see Appendix II at the end of the chapter for the derivation) for the present value of an annuity (PVA):

$$PVA_{(i,n)} = A\left(\frac{1}{i} - \frac{1}{i(1 + i)^n}\right)$$

$$= A \times PVIFA_{(i,n)}$$

In words, the present value of an annuity for n years at i per cent is the annual sum multiplied by the appropriate present value interest factor for an annuity.

Suppose an annuity of £1,000 is issued for 20 years at 10 per cent. Using the table in Appendix D, we find the present value as follows:

$$PVA_{(10\%,20 \text{ yrs})} = £1,000 \times PVIFA_{(10,20)}$$

$$= £1,000 \times 8.5136 = £8,513.60$$

Self-assessment activity 3.5

Calculate the present value of £250 receivable annually for 21 years plus £1,200 receivable after 22 years, assuming an interest rate of 11 per cent.

(Answer in Appendix A at the back of the book)

■ Calculating interest rates

Sometimes, the present values and future cash flows are known, but the rate of interest is not given. A credit company may offer to lend you £1,000 today on condition that you repay £1,643 at the end of three years. To find the compound rate of interest on the loan, we solve the present value formula for i:

$$PV_{(i,n)} = PVIF_{(i,n)} \times FV$$

Rearranging the formula:

$$PVIF_{(i,3)} = \frac{PV}{FV} = \frac{£1,000}{£1,643} = 0.60864$$

Turning to the tables in Appendix C and looking for 0.6086 under the Year 3 column, we find the rate of interest is 18 per cent. As we shall see in Chapter 4, this calculation is fundamental to investment and finance decisions and is termed the **internal rate of return**.

internal rate of return
The rate of return that equates the present value of future cash flows with initial investment outlay

Alternatively, it is also possible to solve the present value formula for i:

$$PV = \frac{FV}{(1 + i)^n}$$

$$(1 + i)^n = FV/PV$$

$$i = (FV/PV)^{1/n} - 1$$

In the above example:

$$i = (1,643/1,000)^{1/3} - 1 = 0.18 \text{ or } 18\%$$

Who wants to be a millionaire?

An advertisement in the financial press read: 'How to become a millionaire? Invest £9,138 in the M&G Recovery unit trust in 1969 and wait for 25 years.' So, for those of us who missed out on this investment, let us grudgingly calculate its annual return:

$$
\begin{aligned}
i &= (\text{FV}/\text{PV})^{1/n} - 1 \\
&= (\pounds 1 \text{ million}/\pounds 9{,}138)^{1/25} - 1 \\
&= 20.66\%
\end{aligned}
$$

By investing in a unit trust earning an annual rate of return of around 21 per cent, £9,138 turns you into a millionaire in 25 years' time. All you have to do is find an investment giving 21 per cent for 25 years!

3.7 VALUING BONDS

discounted cash flow (DCF) analysis
The process of analysing financial instruments and decisions by discounting cash flows to present values

bonds
A debt obligation with a maturity of more than a year

principal
The principal or face value or par value is the amount of the debt excluding interest

Now that we have explored the essential financial arithmetic of discounting, we can apply it to **discounted cash flow (DCF) analysis** in the analysis and valuation of financial instruments and investment projects. This chapter will cover the valuation of shares and **bonds**. When a company wants to make long-term investments, it may look to raising a long-term loan to finance it. One way of doing this is by issuing corporate bonds, promising investors that it will make a series of fixed interest payments and then repay the initial loan. A bond is a long-term (more than one year) loan which promises to pay interest and repay the loan in accordance with agreed terms. Governments, local authorities, companies and other organisations frequently seek to raise funds by issuing fixed interest bonds, offering a specific payment schedule for interest and repayment of **principal**. The return offered to the investor will depend on the creditworthiness of the issuer. For example, a UK government bond is seen as less risky than an unsecured corporate bond where the risk of default (the inability to meet its payment obligations) is higher. Accordingly, the return required for the corporate bond would typically be higher.

Once issued, bonds are traded in the bond markets. Although a bond has a par, or nominal, value – typically £100 – its actual value will vary according to the cash flows it pays (interest and repayments) and the prevailing rate of interest for this type of bond. This is the present value of the future interest and repayments.

$$
V_0 = \text{PV (interest payments)} + \text{PV (redemption value)}
$$

Example: Bondo Ltd

coupon rate
The nominal annual rate of interest expressed as a percentage of the principal value

Bondo Ltd issues a two-year bond with a 10 per cent **coupon rate** and interest payable annually. The bond is priced at its face value of £100:

$$
\pounds 100 = \frac{\pounds 10}{1.10} + \frac{\pounds 10 + \pounds 100}{(1.10)^2}
$$

The bond value above includes the present value of the first year's interest plus the present value of the two elements of the Year 2 cash flow (i.e. interest and redemption value).

Bond prices are subject to interest rate risk, increasing when interest rates fall and dropping when market interest rates rise. Typically, the longer the term of the bond, the greater the exposure to interest rate risk.

Continued

discount
The amount below the face value of a financial instrument at which it sells

Assume that the market interest rate unexpectedly rises to 12 per cent. The bond is now priced in the market at a **discount** at the lower value of £96.62, reflecting the fact that the 10 per cent interest rate is now less attractive to investors:

$$£96.62 = \frac{£10}{1.12} + \frac{£10 + £100}{(1.12)^2}$$

premium
The amount above the face value of a financial instrument at which it sells

Assume now that the market interest rate falls to 8 per cent. The bond would now be viewed as more attractive and lead it to be priced at a **premium**:

$$£103.57 = \frac{£10}{1.08} + \frac{£10 + £100}{(1.08)^2}$$

From the above example, we may conclude that bonds will sell:

- at a discount when the coupon rate is below the market interest rate, and
- at a premium when the coupon rate is above the market interest rate.

yield to maturity
The interest rate at which the present value of the future cash flows equals the current market price

In the above example, the market interest was known. It may be that we know the bond prices and wish to calculate the **yield to maturity**. This measures the average rate of return to an investor who holds the bond until maturity. Here, we use the same formula but the unknown is the interest rate:

$$£103.57 = \frac{£10}{1 + i} + \frac{£10 + £100}{(1 + i)^2}$$

Thus, where the market price is £103.57 we solve the equation (using a computer or trial and error) to find that 8 per cent is the yield to maturity. The bond has a 10 per cent coupon and is priced at £103.57 to yield 8 per cent.

Example: Valuing a bond in Millie Meter plc

Some time ago you purchased an 8 per cent bond in the fashion chain Millie Meter. Today, it has a par value of £100 and two years to maturity. Interest is payable half-yearly. What is it worth?

Assuming the current comparable rate of interest is 8 per cent, the value should equal the par value of £100.

$$V_0 = \frac{4}{(1.04)} + \frac{4}{(1.04)^2} + \frac{4}{(1.04)^3} + \frac{4}{(1.04)^4} + \frac{100}{(1.04)^4} = £100$$

Notice that because payments are made half-yearly, both the interest and discount rate are half the annual figures.

In reality, the required rate of return demanded by investors may be different from the original coupon rate. Let us say it is 10 per cent. As this is higher than the coupon rate, the bond value for Millie Meter will fall *below* its par value:

$$V_0 = \frac{4}{(1.05)} + \frac{4}{(1.05)^2} + \frac{4}{(1.05)^3} + \frac{4}{(1.05)^4} + \frac{100}{(1.05)^4} = £96.45$$

This example shows that an investor would have to pay £96.45 for a bond offering a 4 per cent coupon rate (i.e. based on the par value of £100) plus the redemption value in two years' time, assuming that the market rate of interest for this type of security is 10 per cent.

For actively-traded bonds there is little need to value them in this way because, if the bond market is efficient, it is already done for you. All you need do is to look at the latest quoted price. However, the required rate of return is less easy to obtain. Who says, in the above example, that 10 per cent is the return expected by the market for this type of bond? The answer is simple. If we know the current bond price, we put this in the above equation to find that discount rate which equates price with the discounted future cash flows – 10 per cent in the previous example.

US stocks and bonds enjoy rally in tandem

What does it portend when stock and bond prices both move higher? The two markets usually move in opposite directions, but US bonds and equities have rallied in tandem this year. One or other could tumble should the economy either accelerate or show more signs of softness that are not due to the current harsh winter.

Long-term bonds have returned nearly 7 per cent so far this year. The 10-year Treasury yield, which moves inversely to price, was heading above 3 per cent at the start of the year and is now at 2.6 per cent. Equities are a touch lower for the year after starting March on the defensive.

The broad view across Wall Street is that once the cold weather lifts, the economy will accelerate. Bond yields will be pushed higher, and the bullish tone in equities – led by surging biotech stocks and expectations of robust M&A (merger and acquisition) activity – will be vindicated.

Modest economic growth, moribund inflation and a delayed monetary tightening cycle may well keep stocks and bonds moving in the same direction longer than many currently believe.

Source: Based on Michael Mackenzie, *Financial Times*, 4 March 2014, p. 24.

■ Factors affecting interest rates

term structure of interest rates
Pattern of interest rates on bonds of the same risk with different lengths of time to maturity

It is common in financial management to talk about 'the interest rate ruling in the money market'. However, it is important to realise that there is never a single prevailing rate. At any time, there is a spectrum of interest rates on offer – along this spectrum the rates depend on the identity of the borrower, e.g. firm or government, and hence the degree of risk faced by the lender, the amount lent or borrowed and the period over which the loan is made available. The last of these aspects is referred to as the **term structure of interest rates**. This shows how the yields offered for loans of different maturities vary as the term of the loan increases. We discuss this, together with the **yield curve**, in Appendix I to this chapter.

3.8 VALUING SHARES: THE DIVIDEND VALUATION MODEL

Bond valuation is relatively straightforward because the cash flows and life of the bond are known in advance. When we consider valuing shares we realise that the share may exist for as long as the company exists, and the cash flows to the shareholder are far from certain. The main cash flow arising to a shareholder will be the dividend payment, but this can only be paid if the company has built up sufficient profits, and the dividend policy pursued by companies may vary. Shareholders attach value to shares because they expect to receive a stream of dividends and hope to make an eventual capital gain. Although shareholders are legally entitled to the earnings of a company, in the case of a company with a dispersed ownership body, their influence on the dividend payout is limited by their ability to exert their voting power on the directors. Other things being equal, shareholders prefer higher to lower dividends, but issues such as capital investment strategy and taxation may cloud the relationship between dividend policy and share value. With this reservation in mind, we now develop the **dividend valuation model (DVM)**. *This is appropriate for valuing shares of companies rather than whole enterprises.* This is because minority shareholders have little or no control over dividend policy and thus it is reasonable to project past dividend policy, especially as companies and their owners are known to prefer a steadily rising dividend pattern rather than more erratic payouts. Conversely, if control changes hands, the new owner can appropriate the earnings as it chooses.

■ Valuing the dividend stream

The DVM states that the value of a share now, P_0, is the sum of the stream of future discounted dividends plus the value of the share as and when sold, in some future year, n:

$$P_0 = \frac{D_1}{(1 + k_e)} + \frac{D_2}{(1 + k_e)^2} + \frac{D_3}{(1 + k_e)^3} + \cdots + \frac{D_n}{(1 + k_e)^n} + \frac{P_n}{(1 + k_e)^n}$$

However, since the new purchaser will, in turn, value the stream of dividends after year n, we can infer that the value of the share at any time may be found by valuing all future expected dividend payments over the lifetime of the firm.

Zero growth

If the lifespan is assumed to be infinite and the annual dividend is constant, we have:

$$P_0 = \sum_{t=1}^{\infty} \frac{D_t}{(1 + k_e)^t} = \frac{D_1}{k_e} \quad \text{where } D_1 = D_2 = D_3, \text{ etc.}$$

This is another application of valuing a perpetuity.

For example, the shares of Nogrow Ltd, whose owners require a return of 15 per cent, and which is expected to pay a constant annual dividend of 30p per share through time, would be valued thus:

$$P_0 = \frac{30p}{0.15} = £2.00 \text{ per share}$$

In reality, the assumptions underlying this basic model are suspect. The annual dividend is unlikely to remain unchanged indefinitely, and it is difficult to forecast a varying stream of future dividend flows. To a degree, the forecasting problem is moderated by the effect of applying a risk-adjusted discount rate because more distant dividends are more heavily discounted. For example, discounting at 20 per cent, the present value of a dividend of £1 in 15 years' time is only 6p, while £1 received in 20 years adds only 3p to the value of a share. In other words, for a plausible cost of equity, we lose little by assuming a time-horizon of, say, 15 years. Even so, reliable valuations still require estimates of dividends over the intervening years, and, by the same token, any errors will have a magnified effect during this period.

■ Allowing for future dividend growth

Dividends fluctuate over time, largely because of variations in the company's fortunes, although most firms attempt to grow dividends more or less in line with the company's longer-term earnings growth rate. For reasons explained in Chapter 17, financial managers attempt to 'smooth' the stream of dividends. For companies operating in mature industries, the growth rate will roughly correspond to the underlying growth rate of the whole economy. For companies operating in activities with attractive growth opportunities, dividends are likely to grow at a faster rate, at least over the medium term.

■ Allowing for dividend growth: the DGM

The constant dividend valuation model can be extended to cover constant growth, thus becoming the dividend growth model (DGM). This states that the value of a share is the sum of all discounted dividends, growing at the annual rate g:

$$P_0 = \frac{D_0(1 + g)}{(1 + k_e)} + \frac{D_0(1 + g)^2}{(1 + k_e)^2} + \frac{D_0(1 + g)^3}{(1 + k_e)^3} + \cdots + \frac{D_0(1 + g)^n}{(1 + k_e)^n}$$

If D_0 is this year's recently paid dividend,[*] $D_0(1 + g)$ is the dividend to be paid in one year's time, (D_1), and so on.

Such a series growing to infinity has a present value of:

$$P_0 = \frac{D_0(1 + g)}{(k_e - g)} = \frac{D_1}{(k_e - g)}$$

The growth version of the model is often used in practice by security analysts (it is popularly known as 'the dividend discount model'), at least as a reference point, but it makes some key assumptions. Dividend growth is assumed to result from earnings growth, generated solely by new investment that is financed by retained earnings. Such investment is, of course, worthwhile only if the anticipated rate of return, R, is in excess of the cost of equity, k_e. Furthermore, it is assumed that the company will retain a constant fraction of earnings and invest these in a continuous stream of projects all offering a return of R. It also breaks down if g exceeds k_e.

Example: Growmore Ltd

Growmore Ltd has just paid a dividend of 6p per share. The dividend grows at a steady rate of 5 per cent per year and the cost of equity is 12 per cent. Using the dividend growth model, the price per share is:

$$\begin{aligned} P_0 &= D_1/(k_e - g) \\ &= 6p \times 1.05/(0.12 - 0.05) \\ &= 6.3p/0.07 \\ &= 90p \end{aligned}$$

Where did Growmore's dividend growth rate, g, come from? It is a compound of the proportion of profits retained in the company and the return it expects to make on those reinvested profits. If we term the retention ratio b, and return on invested capital R, we can say:

$$g = (b \times R)$$

If Growmore regularly reinvested 40 per cent of its earnings and expected to get a 15 per cent return on the reinvested earning, the dividend growth rate would be 6 per cent:

$$\begin{aligned} g &= (b \times R) \\ &= 0.40 \times 0.15 \\ &= 0.06 \text{ or 6 per cent} \end{aligned}$$

An alternative approach to estimating the dividend growth rate is to determine the historical rate of growth in dividend over a number of years.

---

[*]If the dividend has recently been paid, i.e. the next dividend will be paid in, say, a year's time, the shares are said to be 'ex-dividend'. They trade without entitlement to a dividend for some considerable time.

In Chapter 17, we examine more fully the issues of whether and how a change in dividend policy can be expected to alter share value. For the moment, we are mainly concerned with the mechanics of the DGM and rely simply on the assumption that any retained earnings are used for worthwhile investment. If this applies, the value of the equity will be higher with retentions-plus-reinvestment than if the investment opportunities were neglected, i.e. the decision to retain earnings benefits shareholders because of company access to projects that offer returns higher than the owners could otherwise obtain.

Self-assessment activity 3.6

XYZ plc currently earns 16p per share. It retains 75 per cent of its profits to reinvest at an average return of 18 per cent. Its shareholders require a return of 15 per cent. What is the ex-dividend value of XYZ's shares? What happens to this value if investors suddenly become more risk-averse by seeking a return of 20 per cent?

(Answer in Appendix A at the back of the book)

3.9 PROBLEMS WITH THE DIVIDEND GROWTH MODEL

The Dividend Growth Model, while possessing some convenient properties, has some major limitations.

■ What if the company pays no dividend?

The company may be faced with highly attractive investment opportunities that cannot be financed in other ways. According to the model, such a company would have no value at all! Total retention is fairly common, either because the company has suffered an actual or expected earnings collapse, or because, as in some European economies (e.g. Switzerland), the expressed policy of some firms is to pay no dividends at all. The cash-rich American computer software firm Microsoft paid its first dividend only in 2003, while two other computer firms, Dell and Apple, only began paying dividends in 2012. Yet we observe that shares in such companies do not have zero values. Indeed, nothing could be further from the truth.

For inveterate non-dividend payers, the market is implicitly valuing the liquidating dividend when the company is ultimately wound up. Until this happens, the company is adding to its reserves as it reinvests, and continually enhancing its assets, its earning power and its value. In effect, the market is valuing the stream of future earnings that are legally the property of the shareholders.

■ Will there always be enough worthwhile projects in the future?

The DGM implies an ongoing supply of attractive projects to match the earnings available for retention. It is most unlikely that there will always be sufficient attractive projects available, each offering a constant rate of return, R, sufficient to absorb a given fraction, b, of earnings in each future year. While a handful of firms do have very lengthy lifespans, corporate history typically parallels the marketing concept of the product life cycle – introduction, (rapid) growth, maturity, decline and death – with paucity of investment opportunities a very common reason for corporate demise. It is thus rather hopeful to value a firm over a perpetual lifespan. However, remember that the discounting process compresses most of the value into a relatively short lifespan.

■ What if the growth rate exceeds the discount rate?

The arithmetic of the model shows that if $g > k_e$, the denominator becomes negative and value is infinite. Again, this appears nonsensical, but, in reality, many companies do experience periods of very rapid growth. Usually, however, company growth settles down to a less dramatic pace after the most attractive projects are exploited, once the firm's markets mature and competition emerges. There are two ways of redeeming the model in these cases. First, we may regard g as a long-term average or 'normal' growth rate. This is not totally satisfactory, as rapid growth often occurs early in the life cycle and the value computed would thus understate the worth of near-in-time dividends. Alternatively, we could segment the company's lifespan into periods of varying growth and value these separately. For example, if we expect fast growth in the first five years and slower growth thereafter, the expression for value is:

$$P_0 = \text{[Present value of dividends during Years 1–5]}$$
$$+ \text{[Present value of all further dividends]}$$

Note that the second term is a perpetuity beginning in Year 6, but we have to find its present value. Hence it is discounted down to Year 0 as in the following expression:

$$P_0 = \frac{D_0(1 + g_f)}{(1 + k_e)} + \frac{D_0(1 + g_f)^2}{(1 + k_e)^2} + \cdots + \frac{D_0(1 + g_f)^5}{(1 + k_e)^5} + \left(\frac{D_5(1 + g_s)}{(k_e - g_s)} \times \frac{1}{(1 + k_e)^5} \right)$$

$$= \sum_{t=1}^{5} \frac{D_0(1 + g_f)}{(1 + k_e)^t} + \sum_{t=6}^{\infty} \frac{D_5(1 + g_s)}{(1 + k_e)^t}$$

where g_f is the rate of fast growth during Years 1–5 and g_s is the rate of slower growth beginning in Year 6 (i.e. from the end of Year 5).

The DGM may be used to examine the impact of changes in dividend policy, i.e. changes in b. Detailed analysis of this issue is deferred to Chapter 17.

Example: The case of unequal growth rates

Consider the case of dividend growth of 25 per cent for Years 1–5 and 7 per cent thereafter. Assuming shareholders require a return of 10 per cent, and that the dividend in Year 0 is 10p, the value of the share is calculated as follows:

| Year | For Years 1–5 | | |
	Dividend (p)	Discount factor at 10%	PV (p)
1	$10(1.25) = 12.5$	0.909	11.4
2	$10(1.25)^2 = 15.6$	0.826	12.9
3	etc.　　$= 19.5$	0.751	14.6
4	$= 24.4$	0.683	16.7
5	$= 30.5$	0.621	18.9
			Total 74.5

For later years, we anticipate a perpetual stream growing from the Year 5 value at 7 per cent p.a. The present value of this stream as at the end of Year 5 is:

$$\frac{D_6}{k_e - g_s} = \frac{D_5(1 + 7\%)}{(10\% - 7\%)} = \frac{30.5p(1.07)}{0.03} = \frac{32.64p}{0.03} = £10.88$$

Continued

This figure, representing the PV of all dividends following Year 5, is now converted into a Year 0 present value:

$$PV_0 = £10.88 \, (PVIF_{10,5}) = (£10.88 \times 0.621) = £6.76$$

Adding in the PV of the dividends for the first five years, the PV of the share right now is:

$$PV_0 = (£0.745 + £6.76) = £7.51$$

However, we may note here that valuation of the dividend stream implies a known dividend policy. Because dividends are not controlled by shareholders, but by the firm's directors, the DGM is more applicable to the valuation of small investment stakes in companies than to the valuation of whole companies, as in takeover situations. When company control changes hands, control of dividend policy is also transferred. It seems particularly unrealistic, therefore, to assume an unchanged dividend policy when valuing a company for takeover. However, the growth formula can be used to value the earnings stream, i.e. by assuming all earnings are paid as dividend as, in effect, they would be if the enterprise became a 100 per cent-owned subsidiary of an acquiring firm.

SUMMARY

We have examined the meaning of wealth and its fundamental importance in financial management. For most investments, there is a time-lag between the initial investment outlay and the receipt of benefits. Consideration therefore must be given to both the timing and size of the costs and benefits. Whenever there is an alternative opportunity to use funds committed to a project (e.g. to invest in the capital market), cash today is worth more than cash received tomorrow. These concepts were then applied to valuing bonds and shares.

Key points

- Money, like any other scarce resource, has a cost. We allow for the time-value of money by discounting. The higher the interest cost for a future cash flow, the lower its present value.

- Discount tables take away much of the tedium of discounting – but computer spreadsheets eliminate it altogether.

- Standard discount factors are:

    PVIF = the present value interest factor,

    PVIFA = the present value interest factor for an annuity.

    Conventional shorthand is:

    Interest factor (rate of interest, number of years)

    e.g. $PVIFA_{(10,3)}$ reads 'the present value interest factor for an annuity at 10 per cent for three years'.

- Bonds are valued by discounting the interest payments and final repayment by the market interest rate for comparable bonds. The yield to maturity is the interest rate that equates the present value of bond payments to the bond price.

- Shares are more difficult to value because the future dividends are difficult to forecast. The dividend growth model offers a valuation approach where the dividend growth rate is constant.

- The value of a share can be found by discounting all future expected dividend payments.
- The retention of earnings for worthwhile investment enhances future earnings, dividends and, therefore, the current share price.
- The Dividend Valuation Model must be treated with caution. It embodies many critical assumptions.
- The term structure of interest rates shows how yields on bonds vary as the durations of loans increase.

Further reading

Early writers on discounted cash flow include Fisher (1930) and Dean (1951). Ross, Westerfield and Jordan (2010) have good chapters on bond and share valuation.

Useful websites

Discounted cash flow: **www.investopedia.com**
Annual percentage rate: **www.moneyextra.com**
www.investinginbonds.com
www.yieldcurve.com

Appendix I
THE TERM STRUCTURE OF INTEREST RATES AND THE YIELD CURVE

We saw in Section 3.7 that the interest rate depends on a number of factors, one of which is duration of the investment or loan. This relationship is called the **term structure of interest rates**. It shows how the yields offered for loans of different maturities vary as the term of the loan increases.

Relating this to bonds issued by the state, or government stock, the term structure shows the rate of return expected, or yield, by today's purchaser of stock who plans to hold to **maturity**, or redemption, i.e. when the stock will be repaid, or redeemed, by the government. It also shows how the yield varies for different lengths of time to maturity. In graphical terms, it is shown by a relationship called the **yield curve**.

yield curve
A graph depicting the relationship between interest rates and length of time to maturity

Normally, we find that yields to maturity increase as the term increases. In other words, rates of interest on 'longs' are higher than on 'shorts', as the blue curve in Figure 3.2 shows. Notice that the relevant yield is the gross redemption yield, which includes both interest payments and any capital gain or loss at redemption.

By tradition, short-dated stocks, with up to five years to maturity are called *shorts, mediums* have between five and 15 years before repayment and *longs* will be paid beyond 15 years. Notice that *longs* include a number of irredeemables or perpetuities which quite literally will never be repaid but will attract interest forever. These are also called undated stocks. Figure 3.3 presents the actual yield curves for UK Gilts and US Treasuries at 31 March 2014. Here we see that both stocks follow the normal shape of the yield curve. For example, the six-month yield for UK Gilts is 0.39 per cent, while the 30-year yield is 3.52 per cent.

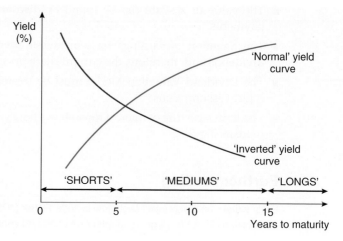

Figure 3.2 The term structure of interest rates

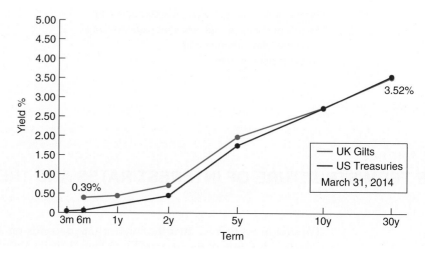

Figure 3.3 Yield curves

Source: From *www.yieldcurve.com* © Moorad Choudhry 2015. Reproduced with permission. Visit *www.yieldcurve.com*.

March 31, 2014

	6m	1y	2y	5y	10y	30y
UK Gilt	0.39	0.44	0.71	1.97	2.73	3.52

	3m	6m	2y	5y	10y	30y
US Treasuries	0.04	0.06	0.45	1.75	2.72	3.55

■ Explaining the shape of the yield curve

Three theories have been proposed to explain the shape of the yield curve – the expectations theory, the liquidity preference theory and the market segmentation theory. These are not mutually exclusive explanations – the influences incorporated in each theory all tend to operate at any one time but with different degrees of pressure. Sometimes, investors' expectations (e.g. about future inflation) are predominant, while, at other times, investors' desire for liquidity may govern the shape of the curve.

Expectations theory

This theory asserts that investors' expectations about future interest rates exert the dominant influence. When the curve rises with years to maturity, this suggests that people expect interest rates to rise in the future. This is reflected in the relative demand for short-dated and long-dated securities – investors expect to be able to earn higher rates in the future so they defer buying long-dated stocks, preferring to invest in shorts. This pushes up the price on shorts, and thus lowers the yields on them, and conversely, for longer-dated stock.

Short view: US yield curve

We ignore the yield curve at our peril. That is one of the lessons from the financial implosion that started in 2007, but how do we apply it now?

The yield curve is the popular name for the spread between the yields on ten-year and two-year Treasury bonds. Usually, investors require a bigger yield to compensate them for the greater risks that come with lending money over a longer term. When short-term yields rise above long-term ones, then market jargon holds that the yield curve is 'inverted'. This has been a great recession indicator, as it implies the market thinks short-term interest rates must imminently be cut. Each of the past seven recessions was preceded by a brief period when the yield curve was inverted and there has only been one false signal.

But what happens when the yield curve gets very steep? That is happening now and there are few, if any, precedents. Last week, ten-year yields exceeded two-year ones by 2.94 percentage points, the highest figure since the Federal Reserve's records for this indicator began in 1976. Its previous peaks were at about 2.5 percentage points in October 2003, when a brief bull market in equities was gathering pace, and October 1992, when years of expansion for both markets and the economy lay ahead.

Should this, then, be regarded as a big reason for optimism? Perhaps not. An implicit bet that rates will rise over the next 10 years is not daring when rates are virtually at zero. Neither is a call for an intermediate economic recovery after a savage recession. In any case, the extremes that financial markets have touched in the past few years make it dangerous to read any indicator with too much confidence. But it does seem to suggest that the market is more convinced than economists both that central banks will be raising rates sooner rather than later and that the US economy is enjoying a true recovery.

 *Source: Financial Times, 22 February 2010. © Financial Times*

Liquidity preference theory

Most investors, being risk-averse, prefer to hold cash rather than securities – cash is effectively free of risk (although banks do go bust!), while even the shortest-dated government stocks carry a degree of risk. Here, by risk, we mean not the risk of default, but the risk of not being able to find a willing buyer of the stock at an acceptable price, i.e. liquidity risk. Consequently, investors need to be compensated for having to wait for the return of their money. Preference for liquidity now, and risk avoidance, thus explains the shape of the yield curve. The longer the time to maturity, the greater the risk of illiquidity and the higher the compensation required.

Market segmentation theory

In developed markets, there is a wide range of investors with different needs and time-horizons who, therefore, focus on different segments of the yield curve. For example, some financial institutions, such as banks, are anxious to protect their ability to allow investors to withdraw their deposits freely – for them, shorts are very attractive as they need liquidity. Conversely, pension funds have far longer-term liabilities and wish to match the maturity stream of their assets to these quite predictable liabilities. For them, longs are more suitable.

According to this view, the 'short' market is quite distinct from the 'long' market and the two ends could behave quite differently under similar conditions. For example, if the government is expected to be a net repayer of its debt in the future, this suggests a shortage of longs. This is likely to increase the demand for those stocks presently available and thus reduce their yields. This would explain the case of the 'inverted', i.e. downward-sloping, yield curve, shown by the red curve in Figure 3.2.

In Chapter 16, we will examine how firms can use the information contained in the yield curve for their financial planning.

Appendix II
PRESENT VALUE FORMULAE

■ Formula for the present value of a perpetuity

This formula derives from the present value formula:

$$PV = \frac{X}{1+i} + \frac{X}{(1+i)^2} + \frac{X}{(1+i)^3} + \cdots$$

Let $X/(1+i) = a$ and $1/(1+i) = b$. We now have:

(i) $PV = a(1 + b + b^2 + \cdots)$

Multiplying both sides by b gives us:

(ii) $PVb = a(b + b^2 + b^3 + \cdots)$

Subtracting (ii) from (i) we have:

$PV(1 - b) = a$

Substituting for a and b,

$$PV\left(1 - \frac{1}{1+i}\right) = \frac{X}{1+i}$$

Multiplying both sides by $(1 + i)$ and rearranging, we have:

$$PV = \frac{X}{i}$$

■ Formula for the present value of a growing perpetuity

In the formula above, we obtained:

$PV(1 - b) = a$

Redefining $b = (1 + g)/(1 + i)$ and keeping $a = X/(1 + i)$:

$$PV\left(1 - \frac{1+g}{1+i}\right) = \frac{X}{1+i}$$

Multiplying both sides by $(1 + i)$ and rearranging, we have:

$$PV = \frac{X}{i - g}$$

■ The present value of annuities

The above perpetuities were special cases of the annuity formula. To find the present value of an annuity, we can first use the perpetuity formula and deduct from it the years outside the annuity period. For example, if an annuity of £100 is issued for 20 years at 10 per cent, we would find the present value of a perpetuity of £100 using the formula:

$$PV = \frac{X}{i} = \frac{100}{0.10} = £1,000$$

Next, find the present value of a perpetuity for the same amount, starting at Year 20, using the formula:

$$PV = \frac{X}{i(1 + i)^t} = \frac{£100}{0.10(1 + 0.10)^{20}} = £148.64$$

The difference will be:

$$PV \text{ of annuity} = \frac{X}{i} - \frac{X}{i(1 + i)^t}$$

$$= £1,000 - £148.64 = £851.36$$

The present value of an annuity of £100 for 20 years discounted at 10 per cent is £851.36.

The formula may be simplified to:

$$PV \text{ of annuity} = X\left(\frac{1}{i} - \frac{1}{i(1 + i)^t}\right)$$

Appendix III
THE P:E RATIO AND THE CONSTANT DIVIDEND VALUATION MODEL

If we examine the P:E ratio more closely, we find it has a close affinity with the growth version of the DVM. The P:E ratio is defined as price per share (PPS) divided by earnings per share (EPS). In its reciprocal form, it measures the **earnings yield** of the firm's shares:

earnings yield
The earnings per share (EPS) divided by market share price

$$\frac{1}{P:E} = \frac{EPS}{PPS} = \frac{Earnings}{Company\,value} = \frac{E}{V}$$

This equals the dividend yield plus retained earnings (bE) per share. As in the DGM, the growth version of the DVM, we define the fraction of earnings retained as b. We can then write:

$$\frac{E}{V} = \frac{D}{V} + \frac{bE}{V}$$

The ratio E/V is the overall rate of return *currently* achieved. If this equals R, the rate of return on reinvested funds, then bE/V is equivalent to the growth rate g in the DGM. In other words, the earnings yield, E/V, comprises the dividend yield plus the growth rate or 'capital gains yield' for a company retaining a constant fraction of earnings and investing at the rate R. The two approaches thus look very similar. However, this apparent similarity should not be overemphasised for three important reasons:

1 The earnings yield is expressed in terms of the current earnings, whereas the DGM deals with the *prospective* dividend yield and growth rate, i.e. the former is historic in its focus, while the latter is forward-looking.
2 The DGM relies on discounting cash returns, while the earnings figure is based on accounting principles. It does not follow that cash flows will coincide with accounting profit, not least due to depreciation adjustments.
3 For the equivalence to hold, the current rate of return, E/V, would have to equal the rate of return expected on future investments.

Despite these qualifications, it is still common to find the earnings yield presented as the rate of return required by shareholders, and hence the cut-off rate for new investment projects. Unfortunately, this confuses a historical accounting measure with a forward-looking cash flow concept.

QUESTIONS

Questions with a coloured number have solutions in Appendix B on page 780.

1 Explain the difference between accounting profit and cash flow.

2 Calculate the present value of a 10-year annuity of £100, assuming an interest rate of 20 per cent.

3 A firm is considering the purchase of a machine which will cost £20,000. It is estimated that annual savings of £5,000 will result from the machine's installation, that the life of the machine will be five years, and that its residual value will be £1,000. Assuming the required rate of return to be 10 per cent, what action would you recommend?

4 Brymo Ltd issued bonds two years ago that pay interest on an annual basis at 8 per cent. The bonds are due for repayment in two years' time. They will be redeemed at £110 per £100 nominal value. A yield of 10 per cent is required by investors for such bonds. What is the expected market value?

5 The gross yield to redemption on government stocks (gilts) are as follows:

Treasury 8.5% 2000	7.00%
Exchequer 10.5% 2005	6.70%
Treasury 8% 2015	6.53%

(a) Examine the shape of the yield curve for gilts, based upon the information above, which you should use to construct the curve.
(b) Explain the meaning of the term 'gilts' and the relevance of yield curves to the private investor.

6 Calculate the net present value of projects A and B, assuming discount rates of 0 per cent, 10 per cent and 20 per cent.

	A (£)	B (£)
Initial outlay	1,200	1,200
Cash receipts:		
Year 1	1,000	100
Year 2	500	600
Year 3	100	1,100

Which is the superior project at each discount rate? Why do they not all produce the same answer?

7 Brosnan plc generates cash flows of £5 million p.a. after allowing for tax and depreciation, which is used for reinvestment. It has issued 10 million shares. Shareholders require a 12 per cent return.

Required
Value each share:
(i) assuming all cash flows are distributed as dividend.
(ii) assuming 50 per cent of cash flows are retained, with a return on retained earnings of 15 per cent.
(iii) as for (ii), but assuming 10 per cent return on reinvestment.
(iv) assuming that cash flows grow at 7.5 per cent for each of the first three future years, then at 5 per cent thereafter.
Note: assume all cash flows are perpetuities.

8 Insert the missing values in the following table:

	P_0	D_0	D_1	g	b	R	k_e
(i)	£8.44	£0.35	?	8.5%	0.5	17%	13.0%
(ii)	£4.98	£0.20	£0.219	?	0.6	16%	14.0%
(iii)	?	£0.10	£0.108	8.0%	0.4	20%	15.0%
(iv)	£2.75	?	£0.220	10.0%	0.5	20%	18.0%
(v)	£10.20	£0.60	£0.610	2.0%	?	10%	8.0%
(vi)	£0.60	£0.05	£0.054	8.0%	0.8	20%	?
(vii)	£1.47	£0.12	£0.133	10.5%	0.7	?	19.5%

Note: answers may have some minor rounding errors.

9 Leyburn plc currently generates profits before tax of £10 million, and proposes to pay a dividend of £4 million out of cash holdings to its shareholders. The rate of corporation tax is 30 per cent. Recent dividend growth has averaged 8 per cent p.a. It is considering retaining an extra £1 million in order to finance new strategic investment. This switch in dividend policy will be permanent, as management believe that there will be a stream of highly attractive investments available over the next few years, all offering returns of around 20 per cent after tax. Leyburn's shares are currently valued 'cum-dividend'. Shareholders require a return of 14 per cent. Leyburn is wholly equity-financed.

Required
(a) Value the equity of Leyburn assuming no change in retention policy.
(b) What is the impact on the value of equity of adopting the higher level of retentions? (Assume the new payout ratio will persist into the future.)

Practical assignment

List three decisions in a business with which you are familiar where cash flows arise over a lengthy time period and where discounted cash flow (DCF) may be beneficial. To what extent is DCF applied (formally or intuitively)? What are the dangers of ignoring the time-value of money in these particular cases?

Part II

INVESTMENT DECISIONS AND STRATEGIES

Chapters 4 to 6 examine in depth the investment decision and how it is evaluated. The concepts of time-value of money and present value are extensively applied. The available methods for assisting the financial manager to evaluate investment proposals are examined in Chapter 4, both when capital is freely available and when it is in short supply. Methods of appraisal that do not utilise discounting procedures are also examined.

In Chapter 5, investment appraisal procedures are applied to practical situations, incorporating the impact of both taxation and inflation. Consideration is given to identifying the relevant information for project evaluation, particularly for replacement decisions.

Chapter 6 sets the whole project appraisal system in a strategic perspective and explores the wider aspects of the investment appraisal system within companies. It dispels the notion that investment analysis hinges solely on methods of appraisal, and it reveals how companies approach their project evaluations in practice.

4

Investment appraisal methods

Portrait of a frontier investor

No sooner had US investor Gabriel Schulze moved to China to gain a foothold in the world's most promising untapped markets eight years ago than he realised he was already behind. 'I moved to China thinking I'm on the frontier, I'm ahead of the curve, and of course as I lunched in China where are all the Chinese going? They're going to Africa.'

Mr Schulze, fifth generation of a billionaire mining family, quickly followed them to Ethiopia. 'People told me I'm nuts ... [but] if you were looking for a place that wasn't fully appreciated yet Ethiopia won hands down,' he says.

Mr Schulze is at the cutting edge of frontier investment, whose promise of reward for risk-taking is attracting increasing interest and delivering returns against the grain. He diverges from the prevailing trend of big funds that spread emerging market risk through regional diversification and controlling stakes. Instead he favours single-country funds and minority stakes. So far he says he has exited more than a dozen deals with internal rates of return in excess of 30 per cent.

But even North Korea may not be the final frontier. At a recent board meeting, Mr Schulze and his father discussed the potential for opportunities in outer space. 'The boundaries of frontier investment will keep moving,' he smiles. 'Some day in the decades to come we'll be looking for first-mover advantage on Mars.'

Source: Based on Katrina Manson, *Financial Times*, 31 October 2013, p.12.

Learning objectives

Having read this chapter, you should have a good grasp of the investment appraisal techniques commonly employed in business, and have developed skills in applying them. Particular attention will be devoted to the following:

- The net present value approach and why it is consistent with shareholder goals.
- The three discounted cash flow approaches – net present value, internal rate of return and profitability index.
- The underlying strengths and limitations of the above methods.
- How net present value and internal rate of return methods can be reconciled when they conflict.
- Non-discounting methods.
- Analysing investments when capital availability is an important constraint.

4.1 INTRODUCTION

Every day managers and investors, like Gabriel Schulze in the introductory cameo, make long-term investment decisions. How do they go about this? A major US company explains how it employs the net present value (NPV) approach in assessing capital projects:

> We measure all potential projects by their cash flow merit. We then discount projected cash flows back to present value in order to compare the initial investment cost with a project's future returns to determine if it will add incremental value after compensating for a given level of risk.

There are, however, a number of alternative techniques to the NPV method. The aim of this chapter is to present the main methods of investment appraisal and to consider their strengths and limitations. In Chapter 5, we consider their practical application in business, large and small.

4.2 CASH FLOW ANALYSIS

The investment decision is the decision to commit the firm's financial and other resources to a particular course of action. Confusingly, the same term is often applied to both real investment, such as buildings and equipment, and financial investment, such as investment in shares and other securities. While the principles underlying investment analysis are basically the same for both types of investment, it is helpful for us to concentrate here on the former category, usually referred to as capital investment. Our particular emphasis on strategic capital projects concentrates on the allocation of a firm's long-term capital resources.

Self-assessment activity 4.1

Investment projects do not only include investment in plant and equipment or buildings. Think of some other types of capital projects.

(Answer in Appendix A at the back of the book)

■ Cash flow matters more than profit

Managers in business usually pursue profit-related goals. It might, therefore, be assumed that capital project appraisal should seek to assess whether the investment is expected to be 'profitable'. Indeed, many firms do use such an approach.

There are, however, many problems with the profit measure for assessing future investment performance. Profit is based on accounting concepts of income and expenses relating to a particular accounting period, based on the *matching principle*. This means that income receivable and expenses payable, but not yet received or paid, along with depreciation charges, form part of the profit calculation.

Consider the case of the Oval Furniture Company with expected annual sales from its new factory of £400,000 and profits of £60,000. In order to stimulate demand, customers are offered two years' credit. While this decision has no impact on the reported profit, it certainly affects the cash position – no cash flow being received for two years. Cash flow analysis considers all the cash inflows and outflows resulting from the investment decision. Non-cash flows, such as depreciation charges and other accounting policy adjustments, are not relevant to the decision. We seek to estimate the stream of cash flows arising from a particular course of action and their timing.

■ Timing of cash flows

Project cash flows will usually arrive throughout the year. For example, if we acquire a machine with a four-year life on 1 January 2016, the subsequent cash flows related to it may involve the monthly payment purchases and expenses and daily receipt of cash from customers throughout each year. Strictly speaking, these cash flows should be identified on a monthly, even daily, basis and discounted using appropriate discount factors.

In practice, to facilitate the use of annual discount tables, cash flows arising during the year are treated as occurring at the year end. Thus, while the initial outlay is assumed to occur at the start of the project (frequently termed Year 0), subsequent cash flows are deemed to arrive later than they actually arise. This has the effect of producing an NPV slightly lower than the true NPV, assuming that subsequent cash flows are positive.

Decision-making can be viewed as an *incremental* activity. Businesses generally operate as going concerns with fairly clear strategies and well-established management processes. Decisions are part of a sequence of actions seeking to move the organisation from its current to its intended position. The same idea is apparent in analysing projects – the decision-maker must assess how the business changes as a direct result of selecting the project. Every project can be either accepted or rejected, and it is the difference between these two alternatives in any time period, t, expressed in cash flow terms (CF_t), that is taken into the appraisal.

Incremental analysis

Project CF_t = CF_t for firm *with* project − CF_t for firm *without* project.

4.3 NET PRESENT VALUE

We have assumed that the paramount objective of the firm is to create as much wealth as possible for its owners through the efficient use of existing and future resources. To create wealth, the present value of all future cash inflows must exceed the present value of all anticipated cash outflows. Quite simply, *an investment with a positive net present value increases the owners' wealth*. The elements of investment appraisal are shown in Figure 4.1.

Most decisions involve both costs and benefits. Usually, the initial expenditure incurred on an investment undertaken is clear-cut: it is what we pay for it. This includes the cash paid to the supplier of the asset plus any other costs involved in making the project operational. The problems start in measuring the worth of the investment project. What an asset is worth may have little to do with what it cost or what value is placed on it in the firm's statement of financial position or balance sheet. A machine standing in the firm's books at £20,000 may be worth far more if it is essential to the manufacture of a highly profitable product, or far less than this if rendered obsolete through the advent of new technology. To measure its worth, we need to consider the *value of the current and future benefits less costs* arising from the investment. Wherever possible, these benefits should be expressed in terms of *cash flows*. Sometimes (as will be discussed later) it is impossible to quantify benefits so conveniently. Typically, investment decisions involve an initial capital expenditure followed by a stream of cash receipts and disbursements in subsequent periods. The net present value (NPV) method is applied to evaluate the desirability of investment opportunities. NPV is defined as:

$$\text{NPV} = \frac{X_1}{(1 + k)} + \frac{X_2}{(1 + k)^2} + \frac{X_3}{(1 + k)^3} + \cdots + \frac{X_n}{(1 + k)^n} - I$$

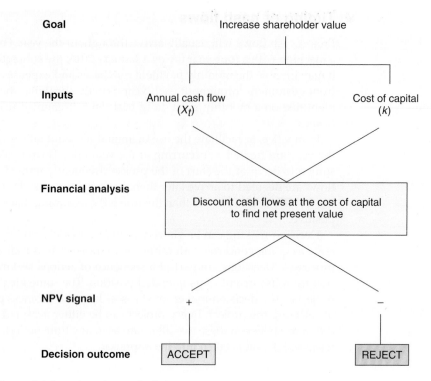

Figure 4.1 Investment appraisal elements

which may be summarised as:

$$\text{NPV} = \sum_{t=1}^{n} \frac{X_t}{(1 + k)^t} - I$$

where X_t is the net cash flow arising at the end of Year t, I is the initial cost of the investment, n is the project's life, and k the minimum required rate of return on the investment (or discount rate). (The Greek letter Σ, or sigma, denotes the sum of all values in a particular series.)

A project's net present value (NPV) is determined by summing the net annual cash flows, discounted at a rate that reflects the cost of an investment of equivalent risk on the capital market, and deducting the initial outlay.

Self-assessment activity 4.2

Define the main elements in the capital investment decision.

(Answer in Appendix A at the back of the book)

The net present value rule

Wealth is maximised by accepting all projects that offer positive net present values when discounted at the required rate of return for each investment.

Most of the main elements in the NPV formula are largely externally determined. For example, in the case of investment in a new piece of manufacturing equipment, management has relatively little influence over the price paid, the life expectancy or the discount rate. These elements are determined, respectively, by the price of capital goods, the rate of new technological development and the returns required by the capital market. Management's main opportunity for wealth creation lies in its ability to implement and manage the project so as to generate positive net cash flows over the project's economic life.

An NPV example: Sleek Ltd

The management of Sleek Ltd is currently evaluating an investment in hair dye products costing £10,000. Anticipated net cash inflows are £6,000 received at the end of Year 1 and a further £6,000 at the end of Year 2. Assuming a discount rate of 10 per cent, calculate the project's net present value.

We can compute the NPV for Sleek using three different approaches, all of which will be employed in later chapters.

1 *Formula approach*

$$\text{NPV} = \frac{£6,000}{1.1} + \frac{£6,000}{(1.1)^2} - £10,000$$
$$= £5,454 + £4,959 - £10,000$$
$$= £413$$

2 *Present value tables* (using Appendix C)

Year	Cash flow £		Discount factor at 10%		Present value £
1	6,000	×	0.90909	=	5,454
2	6,000	×	0.82645	=	4,959
			1.73554		10,413
	Less initial cost				(10,000)
			NPV		413

3 *Present value annuity tables* (using Appendix D)

$$\text{NPV} = (£6,000 \times \text{PVIFA}_{(10,2)}) - £10,000$$
$$= (£6,000 \times 1.7355) - £10,000$$
$$= £413$$

This approach is appropriate only when annual cash flows are constant. Notice that the present value interest factor for an annuity at 10 per cent for two years (taken from Appendix D) is simply the cumulative total of the individual factors in the previous approach.

How would the net present value differ if the perceived project risk were greater? The risk-averse management of Sleek would probably require a higher return from the project, reflected in a higher discount rate. Let us repeat the exercise using 13 per cent (average risk) and 16 per cent (high risk).

Using 13 per cent:

$$\text{NPV} = (£6,000 \times \text{PVIFA}_{(13,2)}) - £10,000$$
$$= (£6,000 \times 1.6681) - £10,000$$
$$= £8 \text{ (i.e. approximately zero)}$$

Using 16 per cent:

$$\text{NPV} = (£6,000 \times 1.6052) - £10,000$$
$$= (369)$$

Looking at the net present values, what interpretation can be made? With a 10 per cent discount rate, the project offers a *positive* NPV of £413. If the projected cash flows are generally expected to be achieved, the market value of the firm should rise by £413. Hence, the project should be accepted. On the other hand, if the project is classified as high risk, the cash inflows are discounted at a rate of 16 per cent and the NPV is estimated at −£369. Its acceptance would reduce the firm's value by £369. Hence, the project should not be accepted. Clearly, it would not be wise to exchange £10,000 today for future cash flows having a present value of less than this amount.

Continued

If the project is classified as having average risk, the discount rate used is 13 per cent, yielding an NPV of £8. The project is just acceptable; it yields 13 per cent, which is the required rate of return. We can draw two important conclusions:

1 Project acceptability depends upon cash flows and risk.
2 The higher the risk of a given set of expected cash flows (and the higher the discount rate), the lower will be its present value. In other words, the value of a given expected cash flow *decreases* as its risk *increases*.

■ Why NPV makes sense

The main rationale for the net present value approach may be summarised as follows:

1 Managers are assumed to act in the best interests of the owners or shareholders, even if agency costs – in the form of incentives or controls – have to be incurred. They seek to increase shareholders' wealth by maximising cash flows through time. The market rate of exchange between current and future wealth is reflected in the current rate of interest.
2 Managers should undertake all projects up to the point at which the marginal return on the investment is equal to the rate of interest on equivalent financial investments in the capital market. This is exactly the same as the net present value rule: accept all investments offering positive net present values when discounted at the equivalent market rate of interest. The result is an increase in the value of the firm and thus in the market value of the shareholders' stake in the firm.
3 Management need not concern itself with shareholders' particular time patterns of consumption or risk preferences. In well-functioning capital markets, shareholders can borrow or lend funds to achieve their personal requirements. Furthermore, by carefully combining risky and safe investments, they can achieve the desired risk characteristics for those consumption requirements.

Mini case

How NPV is used in debt relief to the poorest nations

The International Monetary Fund (IMF) and World Bank have designed a framework to provide special assistance for heavily indebted poor countries. It entails coordinated action by the international financial community, including banks and multinational companies, to reduce and reschedule the debt burden to levels that countries can service through exports and aid.

Net present value is central to the calculation of the sustainable debt level. The face value of debt stock is not a good measure of a country's debt burden if a significant part of it is contracted on concessional terms, for example with an interest rate below the prevailing market rate. The net present value of debt is used to find the sum of all future debt-service obligations (interest and principal) on existing debt, discounted at the market interest rate. Whenever the interest rate on the loan is lower than the market rate, the resulting NPV of debt is smaller than its face value, with the difference reflecting the grant element.

Question

Explain to a government official from one of the world's poorest countries why the NPV approach is an appropriate method for calculating the sustainable debt level.

Self-assessment activity 4.3

Why should managers seek to maximise net present value? Is business not about maximising profit?

(Answer in Appendix A at the back of the book)

4.4 INVESTMENT TECHNIQUES – NET PRESENT VALUE

Discounted cash flow (DCF) analysis is a family of techniques, of which the NPV method is just one variant. Two other DCF methods are the internal rate of return (IRR) and the profitability index (PI) approaches. Many managers prefer to use non-discounting approaches such as the payback and return on capital methods; others use both approaches. The following example illustrates the various approaches to investment appraisal.

Example: Appraising the Lampard and Gerrard projects

Sportsman plc is a manufacturer of sports equipment. The firm is considering whether to invest in one of two automated processes, the Lampard or the Gerrard, both of which give rise to staffing and other cost savings over the existing process. The relevant data relating to each are given below:

	Lampard (£)	Gerrard (£)
Investment outlay (payable immediately)	(40,000)	(50,000)
Year 1 Annual cost savings	16,000	17,000
2 Annual cost savings	16,000	17,000
3 Annual cost savings	16,000	17,000
4 Annual cost savings	12,000	17,000
The required return is 14 per cent p.a.		

The investment outlays are obviously additional cash outflows, while the annual cost savings are cash flow benefits because total annual expenditures are reduced as a result of the investment.

Should the company invest in either of the two proposals and, if so, which is preferable?

The NPV solution

The net present value for the Lampard machine is found by multiplying the annual cash flows by the present value interest factor (PVIF) at 14 per cent (using the tables) and finding the total, as shown in Table 4.1. An immediate cash outlay (treated as Year 0) is not discounted as it is already expressed in present value terms. The same factors could be applied to evaluate

Table 4.1 Net present value calculations

Year		Cash flow (£)	PVIF at factor 14%	Present value (£)
Lampard proposal				
0	Outlay	(40,000)	1	(40,000)
1	Cost savings	16,000	0.87719	14,035
2	Cost savings	16,000	0.76947	12,312
3	Cost savings	16,000	0.67497	10,800
4	Cost savings	12,000	0.59208	7,105
	Net present value at 14%			4,252
Gerrard proposal				
Cost savings	£17,000 × PVIFA $_{(14\%,4\text{ yrs})}$		2.9137	49,533
Outlay				(50,000)
	Net present value at 14%			(467)

Continued

the Gerrard proposal. However, as the annual savings are constant, it is far simpler to use the present value interest factor for an annuity (PVIFA) at 14 per cent for four years.

Comparison of the two proposals reveals the following:

1 The Lampard machine offers a positive NPV of £4,252, and would increase shareholder wealth.
2 The Gerrard machine offers a negative NPV of £467 and would reduce value.
3 Given that the proposals are mutually exclusive (i.e. only one is required), the Lampard proposal should be accepted.

What does an expected NPV of £4,252 from the Lampard proposal really mean? The project's future cash flows are sufficient for the firm to pay all costs associated with financing the project and to provide an adequate return to shareholders. From the shareholders' viewpoint, it means that the firm could borrow £44,252 (the cost plus the NPV) to purchase the machine and pay out a dividend today of £4,252, and still have sufficient funds from the project to pay off the interest at 14 per cent p.a. and annual repayments (see Table 4.2).

In practice, it is unlikely that the lender will agree to a repayment schedule that exactly matches the expected annual cash flows of the project. It is also somewhat imprudent to pay as a dividend the whole of the expected NPV before the project commences! However, in theory at least, the proposal creates wealth of £4,252 and the shareholders are that much better off than they were prior to the decision. Note that we assume that borrowing and lending rates of interest are the same. We discuss in later chapters how the discount rate is estimated; suffice it to say that it is the required rate of return that investors can expect on comparable alternative investment in the financial markets.

Table 4.2 Why NPV makes sense for shareholders

Year 0	Borrow: machine	£40,000	£
	Pay NPV as dividend	£4,252	44,252
1	Interest: £44,252 at 14%		6,195
			50,447
	Less: repayment		(16,000)
	(through annual savings)		34,447
2	Interest: £34,447 at 14%		4,822
			39,269
	Less: repayment		(16,000)
			23,269
3	Interest: £23,269 at 14%		3,257
			26,526
	Less: repayment		(16,000)
			10,526
4	Interest: £10,526 at 14%		1,474
			(12,000)
	Less: repayment		(12,000)
			—

4.5 INTERNAL RATE OF RETURN

IRR or DCF yield
The rate of return that equates the present value of future cash flows with the initial investment outlay

Managers frequently ask: 'What rate of return am I getting on my investment?' To calculate the correct return, or yield, requires us to find the rate that equates the present value of future benefits to the initial cash outlay. We call this the **internal rate of return (IRR)** or **DCF yield**.

The IRR is that discount rate, r, which, when applied to project cash flows (X_t), produces a net present value of zero. It is found by solving the equation for r:

$$\sum_{t=0}^{n} \frac{X_t}{(1 + r)^t} = 0$$

Where the IRR exceeds the required rate of return ($r > k$) the project should be accepted.

Suppose a savings scheme offers a plan whereby, for an initial investment of £100, you would receive £112 at the year end. The IRR is thus 12 per cent:

$$£100(1 + r) = £112$$
$$r = 12\%$$

If another scheme offered a single payment of £148 in three years' time, from an initial investment of £100, the IRR is found by solving:

$$£100(1 + r)^3 = £148$$

or

$$\frac{1}{(1 + r)^3} = \frac{£100}{£148} = 0.6757$$

Turning to the present value interest factor (PVIF) table (Appendix C) for three years, and looking for the rate that comes closest to 0.6757, we find that the IRR for the investment is approximately 14 per cent. The same approach is used to find the IRR for capital investment, but here the annual cash flows may differ. We find the IRR by solving for the rate of return at which the present value of the cash inflows equals the present value of the cash outflows. That is, we have to solve for

$$I_0 = \frac{X_1}{1 + r} + \frac{X_2}{(1 + r)^2} + \cdots + \frac{X_n}{(1 + r)^n}$$

This is the same as finding the rate of return that produces an NPV of zero.

The IRR solution

In our earlier example, the Lampard produced an NPV of £4,252 at 14 per cent. Given a 'normal' pattern of cash flows, i.e. an outlay followed by cash inflows, we can see that as the discount rate increases, the NPV falls. Trial and error will give us the discount rate that yields a zero NPV.

Trying 18 per cent, as shown in Table 4.3, gives a positive NPV of £976. Trying 20 per cent gives a *negative* NPV of £510. Clearly the IRR giving a zero NPV falls between 18 and 20 per cent, probably closer to 20 per cent. Using linear interpolation, we estimate the IRR by applying the formula:

$$IRR = r_1 + \left(\frac{N_1}{N_1 + N_2} \times (r_2 - r_1) \right)$$

where r_1 is the rate of interest and N_1 the NPV for the first guess, and r_2 and N_2, the NPV for the second guess. Applying the formula:

$$IRR = 18\% + \left(\frac{£976}{£976 + £510} \times 2\% \right) = 19.31\%$$

Note that the calculation includes the class interval, in this case $(20\% - 18\%) = 2\%$.

Continued

Table 4.3 IRR calculations for Lampard proposal

Year	Cash flow (£)	PVIF at 18%	PV (£)	PVIF at 20%	PV (£)
0	(40,000)	1.0	(40,000)	1.0	(40,000)
1	16,000	0.84746	13,559	0.83333	13,333
2	16,000	0.71818	11,490	0.69444	11,111
3	16,000	0.60863	9,738	0.57870	9,259
4	12,000	0.51579	6,189	0.48225	5,787
NPV			976		(510)

$$\text{IRR} = 18\% + \left(\frac{976}{976 + 510} \times 2\% \right) = 19.31\%$$

In the Lampard example, the NPV at various rates of interest is shown in Figure 4.2. The graph shows a clearer relationship between IRR and NPV. We also have an idea of the break-even rate of interest – or IRR – at around 19–20 per cent, as calculated earlier. The IRR of 19.31 per cent is well above the required rate of 14 per cent and the project is, therefore, wealth-creating.

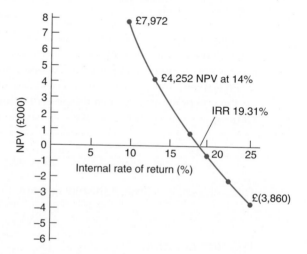

Figure 4.2 Lampard proposal NPV–IRR graph

Most managers have access to computer spreadsheets that solve the equation in a fraction of a second and avoid tedious manual effort. However, our analysis explains the logic behind the computer calculation.

For the Gerrard proposal, the IRR calculation is much more straightforward as the annual cash flows are constant.

$$£17,000 \times \text{PVIFA}_{(r,4\text{yrs})} = £50,000$$

$$\text{PVIFA}_{(r,4\text{yrs})} = \frac{£50,000}{£17,000} = 2.9411$$

Referring to annuity tables (Appendix D), we find that for four years at 13 per cent, the factor is 2.9745, and at 14 per cent it is 2.9137. The IRR is therefore between 13 and 14 per cent. This return falls just below the 14 per cent requirement, making it an uneconomic proposal.

Bullish Ronson defies property slump

Gerald Ronson strolls out of his Mercedes – the 'workhorse' he uses to cover 40,000 miles a year visiting his various projects in the UK – in front of his office building in Marylebone, London, looking every inch the fighter that his reputation makes out.

He's in characteristically bullish mood. Heron, the property company he started with his father in 1965, is in robust health considering the extent of the property slump, which has wiped out the value of some properties by half over the past two years.

Heron, partly because it sold its UK investments, and partly because European markets have performed relatively well, has held its net asset value almost static, and is looking for opportunities.

Mr Ronson says that most deals cross his large mahogany desk early on, but so far there have been few of interest. He has almost £140m to spend when the time is right. 'There will be interesting opportunities over the next 18–24 months but I have yet to see a deal that I consider we want

to do. This is not the time to overpay, and you need to see a respectable return. We [want] to see a return over 20 per cent on an IRR basis with low gearing,' he adds.

He would be interested in buying good investment properties as well as prime developments in London's West End, but predicts that the market still has further to fall, with a gap opening between qualities of property.

Mr Ronson says this downturn is worse than the 1990s recession, but that Heron is in better shape than last time, when massive losses and mounting debts forced a restructuring involving a consortium of US investors. The lesson, he says, was that problems had to be handled quickly, adding that there would be further casualties in the private property sector this time. 'The moral is to deal with things ahead of time, have the courage to face up to issues and take them head on, and not bury your head in the sand.'

Source: Based on Financial Times, 3 June 2009.

4.6 PROFITABILITY INDEX

profitability index (PI)
Ratio of the present value of benefits to costs

Another method for evaluating capital projects is the **profitability index (PI)**, sometimes called the benefit–cost ratio.

The profitability index

The profitability index is the ratio of the present value of project benefits to the present value of initial costs. The decision rule is that projects with a PI greater than 1.0 are acceptable.

Example: The PI decision rule

Referring back to the present values calculated in Table 4.1, we can find for the Lampard proposal:

$$PI = \frac{PV\ benefits}{PV\ outlay} = \frac{£44,252}{£40,000} = 1.1063$$

while for the Gerrard proposal:

$$PI = \frac{£49,533}{£50,000} = 0.9906$$

From this we see that the Lampard is acceptable on financial grounds as the PI exceeds 1. The higher the PI, the more attractive the project.

For *independent* projects, the PI gives the same advice as NPV and IRR methods, although there are important reservations when projects are 'mutually exclusive' (see Section 4.9).

The PI can also be expressed as the net present value per £1 invested, i.e.

$$PI = \frac{NPV}{PV \text{ of outlays}}$$

If NPV per £1 invested exceeds zero, then the project should be accepted.

Self-assessment activity 4.4

What are the three main DCF methods and how do you know when to accept a capital project with each?

(Answer in Appendix A at the back of the book)

4.7 PAYBACK PERIOD

Over the years, managers have come to rely upon a number of rule-of-thumb approaches to analyse investments. Two of the most popular methods are the payback period and the accounting rate of return.

payback period
Period of time a project's annual net cash flows take to match the initial cost outlay

The **payback period** (PB) is the period of time taken for the future net cash inflows to match the initial cash outlay.

Table 4.4 gives the cumulative cash flows for the two projects in our earlier example. After two years, the cumulative cash flow for the Lampard has reduced to −£8,000; but by the end of the third year it has improved to +£8,000. The project therefore breaks even, or pays back, in two and a half years. Similarly, the Gerrard pays back in 2.9 years. Many companies set payback requirements for capital projects. For example, if all projects are required to pay back within three years, both the Lampard and Gerrard are acceptable.

Table 4.4 Payback period calculation

Year		Lampard cash flow		Gerrard cash flow	
		Annual	Cumulative	Annual	Cumulative
0	Cost	(40,000)	(40,000)	(50,000)	(50,000)
1	Cost savings	16,000	(24,000)	17,000	(33,000)
2	Cost savings	16,000	(8,000)	17,000	(16,000)
3	Cost savings	16,000	8,000	17,000	1,000
4	Cost savings	12,000	20,000	17,000	18,000

$$\text{Payback: Lampard} \quad 2 + \frac{8,000}{16,000} \text{ years} = 2.5 \text{ years}$$

$$\text{Gerrard} \quad 2 + \frac{16,000}{17,000} \text{ years} = 2.9 \text{ years}$$

discounted payback
Period of time the present value of a project's annual net cash flows take to match the initial cost outlay

A number of modifications to simple payback are possible. **Discounted payback** addresses the problem of comparing cash flows in different time periods. It calculates how quickly discounted cash flows recoup the initial investment. Referring back to the NPV calculation for the Lampard, the discounted payback period at 14 per cent

Year	Present value at 14%	Cumulative PV
0	(40,000)	(40,000)
1	14,035	(25,965)
2	12,312	(13,653)
3	10,800	(2,853)
		Payback period 3.5 years
4	7,105	4,252
NPV	4,252	

interest is approximately three and a half years (see below). The cumulative present values recoup the initial outlay only in the final year.

A fuller discussion of the popularity of the payback period will be given in Chapter 5. However, we should note that this approach has some serious problems as a measure of investment worth:

1 The time-value of money is ignored (except in the case of discounted payback).
2 Cash flows arising after the payback period are ignored.
3 The payback period criterion that firms stipulate for assessing projects often has little theoretical basis. How do firms justify setting, say, a two-year payback requirement?

4.8 ACCOUNTING RATE OF RETURN

return on capital employed
Operating profit expressed as a percentage of capital employed

A key ratio in analysing accounts is the **return on capital employed**, or ROCE. This is calculated as:

$$\frac{\text{Profit before interest and tax}}{\text{Capital employed}} \times 100$$

This indicates a company's efficiency in generating profits from its asset base. All new investment should at least match existing assets in terms of its earning power. However, the annual ROCE on a project will change each year. Typically, it is less profitable in the early years but improves over time as the project's sales build up and as the book value of the asset (i.e. initial cost less depreciation) declines.

accounting rate of return
Return on investment over the whole life of a project

The **accounting rate of return** (ARR) seeks to provide a measure of project profitability over the entire asset life. It compares the average profit of the project with the book value of the asset acquired. The ARR can be calculated on the *original* capital invested or on the *average* amount invested over the life of the asset.

Accounting rate of return

$$\text{ARR (total investment)} = \frac{\text{Average annual profit}}{\text{Initial capital invested}} \times 100$$

$$\text{ARR (average investment)} = \frac{\text{Average annual profit}}{\text{Initial capital invested}} \times 100$$

Returning to our example, suppose the depreciation policy is to depreciate assets over their useful lives on a straight-line basis. The annual depreciation for the Lampard will be £10,000 (i.e. £40,000 over four years) and for the Gerrard, £12,500. The annual profit from the proposals will be the annual cash saving less the annual depreciation. The ARRs based on initial capital invested for the two proposals are shown in Table 4.5.

Table 4.5 Calculatation of the ARR on initial capital invested

	Year					
	1	**2**	**3**	**4**	**Average**	**ARR**
Project						
Lampard						
Cash flow (£)	16,000	16,000	16,000	12,000	–	
Depreciation[*] (£)	(10,000)	(10,000)	(10,000)	(10,000)	–	
Accounting profit (£)	6,000	6,000	6,000	2,000	5,000	5,000/40,000 = 12½%
Gerrard						
Cash flow (£)	17,000	17,000	17,000	17,000	–	
Depreciation[*] (£)	(12,500)	(12,500)	(12,500)	(12,500)	–	
Accounting profit (£)	4,500	4,500	4,500	4,500	4,500	4,500/50,000 = 9%

[*]Straight-line depreciation is used in each case.

Alternatively, we could base the calculation of ARR on the average investment, found by summing the opening and closing asset values and dividing by 2. This would yield answers for the Lampard and Gerrard of 25 per cent and 18 per cent, respectively, double the returns based on the initial capital. (In our case, the residual values are zero.)

A benefit of this profitability measure is that managers feel they understand it. It makes sense to use an investment evaluation measure that is broadly consistent with return on capital employed, which is the 'primary business' ratio. However, the ARR has some definite drawbacks. Suppose the Lampard proposal is expected to continue into Year 5, yielding a profit of £1,000 in that year. Common sense suggests that this would make the proposal more attractive. However, the new ARR actually declines from 25 to 21 per cent as a result of averaging over five rather than four years.

$$\text{ARR} = \frac{(£6,000 + £6,000 + £6,000 + £2,000 + £1,000)/5}{(£40,000 + 0)/2} \times 100 = 21\%$$

It also takes no account of the size and life of the investment, or the timing of cash flows. Moreover, this approach is based on profits rather than cash flows, the significance of

Is investing in pizza stores a no-brainer?

Lex Column

As Homer Simpson would no doubt agree, eating pizza is literally a no-brainer. Describing why people tuck into its products, Domino's Pizza, the US's largest pizza delivery company, cites the statistic that by 4.30pm on the average afternoon, almost three-quarters of Americans still have no idea what their families will eat for dinner that evening.

If buying pizzas is an easy way for parents to fill the bellies of their progeny, selling pizza can be very lucrative. The US alone generates $33bn in sales. CIBC estimates that a new Domino's store costs just $150,000–250,000 to build but yields an annual pre-tax cash return of 30–65 per cent. In addition, more than half the company's operating profit comes from franchised stores. These provide a stable royalties stream and a capital-light way to expand.

The big issue is growth. Toppings may get more adventurous but pizza has been around for years. Domino's focuses on home delivery, which is faster growing than eat-in meals – at some point, one has had so many slices it gets tricky to leave the sofa.

FT *Source: Financial Times, 3 January 2007.*

which we discuss in the next chapter. Such important weaknesses make ARR inappropriate as a main investment appraisal method, particularly when comparing projects. Now use this story to tackle Self-assessment activity 4.5.

Self-assessment activity 4.5

List four capital budgeting methods for evaluating project proposals. Identify the main strengths and drawbacks of each.

(Answer in Appendix A at the back of the book)

4.9 RANKING MUTUALLY EXCLUSIVE PROJECTS

For many investment projects, there will be a number of mutually exclusive proposals, only one of which can be accepted. For example, a firm may be considering a new IT system and needs to identify the best system from a number of possibilities.

Example: Ranking project performance

The manufacturers of the Lampard also make the Flintoff – a larger, more powerful, but more erratic model – offering a further 50 per cent in cost savings each year, but costing a further 50 per cent to purchase. The NPV will be 50 per cent greater than for the Lampard, but the other measures of performance – based on ratios or percentages – will be the same, as shown in Table 4.6.

Table 4.6 Comparison of various appraisal methods

	Lampard	Flintoff	Gerrard
Net present value (£)	4,252	6,378	(467)
Internal rate of return (%)	19.3	19.3	13.5
Profitability index	1.1	1.1	0.99
Payback period (years)	2.5	2.5	2.9
Accounting rate of return (%)	25.0	25.0	18.0

In ranking mutually exclusive capital projects, we can reject the Gerrard for having a negative NPV and performance indicators that are consistently inferior to the alternatives. While the Flintoff and Lampard are, pound-for-pound, identical, the Flintoff creates £2,126 additional wealth and is preferred.

Under the conditions typically found in business, no single method is ideal, which is why three or four different measures are often calculated. The ready availability of spreadsheet packages with graphics facilities makes this a straightforward and inexpensive procedure. Investment appraisal techniques are tools to assist managers in assessing the worth of a given project.

■ NPV or IRR?

In many cases, the choice of DCF method has no effect on the investment advice, and it is simply a matter of personal preference. In certain circumstances, however, the choice does matter. We shall consider three such situations:

1 Mutually exclusive projects.
2 Variable discount rates.
3 Unconventional cash flows.

■ Mutually exclusive projects

The decision to accept or reject a project cannot always be separated from other investment projects. For example, a company may have a spare plot of land that could be used to build a warehouse or a sports centre. In such cases, the problem is to evaluate mutually exclusive alternatives.

The earlier worked examples comparing the Lampard, Gerrard and Flintoff proposals are mutually exclusive. Recall that, while the Lampard and Flintoff offered the same IRR, the latter offered a much higher NPV because it was on a larger scale. The weakness of IRR is that it ignores the scale of the project. It implies that firms would prefer to make, say, a 60 per cent IRR on an investment of £1,000 than a 30 per cent return on a £1 million project. Clearly, project scale should be taken into consideration, which is why we recommend the NPV method when assessing mutually exclusive projects of different size or duration.

■ Variable discount rates

It is common to discount cash flows at a constant rate of return throughout a project's life. But this may not always be appropriate. The required rate of return is linked to underlying interest rates and cash flow uncertainties, both of which can change over time.

This presents little difficulty in the case of NPV: different discount rates can be set for each period. The IRR method, however, is compared against a single required rate of return and cannot handle variable rates.

■ Unconventional cash flows

There are three basic cash flow profiles:

Type	Cash flow pattern	Example
Conventional	Outlay followed by inflows (−+++)	Capital project
Reverse	Inflows followed by outflows (+−−−)	Loan
Unconventional	More than one change of sign (−+−+)	Two-stage development project

For a reverse cash flow pattern, such as a loan where cash is received and interest paid in subsequent periods, the IRR can be usefully applied. But in interpreting the result, remember that the lower the rate of return the better, so the decision rule is to accept the loan proposal if the IRR is below the required rate of return.

Unconventional cash flow patterns create particular difficulty for the IRR approach. Consider the following project cash flows and NPV calculation at 10 per cent required rate of return.

		£	PVIF at 10%	PV (£000)
Initial outlay	0	−100,000	1.00	−100
Year	1	+360,000	0.909	327
	2	−432,000	0.826	−357
	3	+173,000	0.751	130
		NPV		0

With an NPV of zero, the IRR is, by definition, 10 per cent. But at certain other rates, such as 20 per cent and 30 per cent, the NPV is still zero!

Multiple solutions may occur where there are multiple changes of sign. In our example there are three changes in sign – from negative cash flow at the start to positive in Year 1, negative in Year 2 and positive in Year 3. While a conventional project has only one IRR, unconventional projects may have as many IRRs as there are changes in the cash flow sign.

Self-assessment activity 4.6

Why do problems arise in evaluating mutually exclusive projects? What approach would you recommend in such circumstances?

(Answer in Appendix A at the back of the book)

To summarise, the use of NPV and IRR is a matter of personal preference in most instances. But where the evaluation is for mutually exclusive projects, where the discount rate is not constant throughout the project's life, or where an unconventional cash flow pattern is suspected, we recommend use of the net present value approach. To underline the superiority of NPV, we need to examine the respective reinvestment assumptions of the two methods.

The NPV method assumes that all cash flows can be reinvested at the firm's cost of capital. This is reasonable, since the discount rate is an opportunity cost of capital that should reflect the alternative use of funds. The IRR method assumes that a project's annual cash flows can be reinvested at the project's internal rate of return. Thus, a project offering a 30 per cent IRR, given a 12 per cent cost of capital, assumes that interim cash flows are compounded forward at the project's rate of return (30 per cent) rather than at the cost of capital (12 per cent). In effect, therefore, the IRR method includes a bonus of the assumed benefits accruing from the reinvestment of interim cash flows at rates of interest in excess of the cost of capital. This is a serious error for projects with IRRs well above the cost of capital.

Consider the mutually exclusive investment proposals given in Table 4.7: X and Y each cost £18,896. Project rankings reveal that X has the higher internal rate of return but the lower net present value. Figure 4.3 shows how this apparent anomaly occurs. (Strictly speaking, the graphs should be curvilinear.)

Table 4.7 Comparison of mutually exclusive projects

Proposal	Cash flows (£)					Undiscounted cash flow	IRR	NPV at 10%
	Year 0	Year 1	Year 2	Year 3	Year 4			
X	−18,896	8,000	8,000	8,000	8,000	13,104	25%	6,463
Y	−18,896	0	4,000	8,000	26,164	19,268	22%	8,290

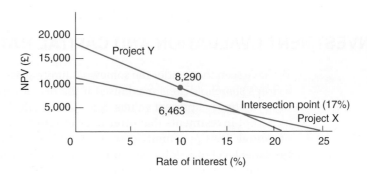

Figure 4.3 NPV and IRR compared

While Project Y has the higher NPV when discounted at 10 per cent, it has the lower IRR, the two projects intersecting on the graph at around 17 per cent. Wherever there is a sizeable difference between the project IRR and the discount rate, this problem becomes a distinct possibility.

Muggles away: new Harry Potter theme park opens in Florida

First came the books, then the blockbuster films. Now Harry Potter fans can visit the theme park. 'The Wizarding World of Harry Potter' – almost six years in the making and estimated to have cost around $200 million – opened to the public today in Universal's Islands of Adventure complex in Orlando, Florida.

I was there earlier this week to get a sneak preview, along with members of the cast of the first six films: Daniel Radcliffe (Harry Potter), Rupert Grint (Ron Weasley), Tom Felton (Draco Malfoy), Michael Gambon (Dumbledore) and author J.K. Rowling.

At the entrance to The Wizarding World – a 20-acre area within the Islands of Adventure theme park, rather than its own separate park – visitors are welcomed through a stone arch into Hogsmeade village by a steam-blowing Hogwarts Express train. Before them stretches a scene straight out of the movies: crooked-chimneyed Olde English shops crowd along a winding street, their snow-capped roofs glistening in the Florida sunshine.

But the real attraction at WWHP – the one that will appeal to wannabe wizards and blissfully unaware Muggles alike – is the much-hyped Forbidden Journey ride, hidden in the towering spires of Hogwarts Castle, which looks like it has been hacked from granite and left to moulder for 500 years in the Scottish damp.

Universal hasn't released predicted attendance figures, but the car park opened at 5.30 am today, so fans could be in for a long wait.

There are just two other rides in WWHP – the family-friendly Flight of the Hippogriff mini rollercoaster and Dragon Challenge, a high-speed double rollercoaster (with two trains running in opposite directions to create the impression they may crash), that is based on a Triwizard Tournament.

The limited number of rides may be disappointing for some, and at times it feels that half of Hogsmeade is up for sale in true 'exit through the gift shop' style. In Ollivanders' wand shop the walls are lined floor to ceiling with dusty wand boxes and visitors can have their wand 'choose' them, like Harry did in *The Philosopher's Stone*. It's a fun experience, if also a canny marketing tool for a $25 piece of plastic memorabilia. Next door you can send postcards back home via Owl Post with a Hogsmeade postmark and spend a small fortune in Dervish and Banges on Triwizard costumes, wizard robes, Hogswarts scarves and Golden Snitches. It's clear that Universal is banking on the money-making magic of Harry Potter to rub off on 'The Wizarding World of Harry Potter'.

Source: Based on Georgia Brown, *Guardian*, 18 June 2010.

Self-assessment activity 4.7

Take another look at the graphs in Figure 4.3. How would you explain to a manager that Project X, with the higher IRR, is actually less attractive than Project Y?

(Answer in Appendix A at the back of the book)

4.10 INVESTMENT EVALUATION AND CAPITAL RATIONING

We have seen that, under the somewhat limiting assumptions specified, the wealth of a firm's shareholders is maximised if the firm accepts all investment proposals that have positive net present values. Alternatively, the NPV decision rule may be restated as: **accept investments that offer rates of return in excess of their opportunity costs of capital**. The opportunity cost of capital is the return shareholders could obtain for the same level of risk by investing their capital elsewhere. Implicit in the NPV decision rule is the notion that capital is always available at some cost to finance investment opportunities.

In this section, we relax another assumption of perfect capital markets to include the situation where firms are restricted from undertaking all the investments offering positive net present values. Although individual projects cannot be accepted/rejected on the basis of the NPV rule, the essential problem remains: namely, to determine the package of investment projects that offers the highest total net present value to the shareholders.

■ The nature of constraints on investment

capital rationing
The process of allocating capital to projects where there is insufficient capital to fund all value-creating proposals

In imperfect markets, the capital budgeting problem may involve the allocation of scarce resources among competing, economically desirable projects, not all of which can be undertaken. This **capital rationing** applies equally to non-capital, as well as capital, constraints. For example, the resource constraint may be the availability of skilled labour, management time or working capital requirements. Investment constraints may even arise from the insistence that top management appraise and approve all capital projects, thus creating a backlog of investment proposals.

■ Hard and soft rationing

Capital rationing may arise either because a firm cannot obtain funds at market rates of return, or because of internally imposed financial constraints by management. Externally imposed constraints are referred to as hard rationing and internally imposed constraints as soft rationing.

The Wilson Committee (1980) found no evidence of any general shortage of finance for industry at prevailing rates of interest and levels of demand. A survey of managers (Pike, 1983) found that:

1 The problem of low investment essentially derives not from a shortage of finance but from an inadequate demand for funds.
2 Capital constraints, where they exist, tend to be internally imposed rather than externally imposed by the capital market.
3 Capital constraints are more acutely experienced by smaller, less profitable and higher-risk firms.

■ Soft rationing

Why should the internal management of a company wish to impose a capital expenditure constraint that may actually result in the sacrifice of wealth-creating projects? Soft rationing may arise because of the following:

1 Management sets maximum limits on borrowing and is unable or unwilling to raise additional equity capital in the short term. Investment is restricted to internally generated funds.
2 Management pursues a policy of stable growth rather than a fluctuating growth pattern with its attendant problems.
3 Management imposes divisional ceilings by way of annual capital budgets.
4 Management is highly risk-averse and operates a rationing process to select only highly profitable projects, hoping to reduce the number of project failures.
5 Management may feel they have limited capacity for taking on, and overseeing, additional projects.

The capital budget forms an essential element of the company's complex planning and control process. It may sometimes be expedient for capital expenditure to be restricted – in the short term – to permit the proper planning and control of the organisation. Divisional investment ceilings also provide a simple, if somewhat crude, method of dealing with biased cash flow forecasts. Where, for example, a division is in the habit of creating numbers to justify the projects it wishes to implement, the institution of capital budget ceilings forces divisional management to set its own priorities and to select those offering highest returns.

It is clear that capital rationing can be explained, in part, by imperfections in both the capital and labour markets, and agency costs arising from the separation of ownership from management. Of particular relevance are the problems of **information asymmetry** and **transaction costs**.

information asymmetry
The imbalance between managers and owners of information possessed about a firm's financial state and its prospects

Information asymmetry

Shareholders and other investors in a business do not possess all the information available to management. Nor do they always have the necessary expertise to appreciate fully the information they do receive. Capital rationing may arise because senior managers, convinced that their set of investment proposals is wealth-creating, cannot convince a more sceptical group of potential investors who have far less information on which to make an assessment and who may be influenced by the company's recent performance record.

Transaction costs

The issuing and other costs associated with raising long-term capital do not vary in direct proportion to the amount raised. Corporate treasurers in large organisations will not want to go to the capital market each year for relatively small sums of money if the costs can be significantly reduced by raising much larger sums at less frequent intervals. Capital rationing is therefore a distinct possibility in the intervening years, although this usually means delaying the start date for investments, and thus their benefits, rather than outright rejection.

■ One-period capital rationing

The simplest form of capital rationing arises when financial limits are imposed for a single period. For that period of time, the amount of funds available becomes the limiting factor.

Example: Mervtech plc

The manufacturing division of Mervtech plc has been set an upper limit on capital spending for the coming year of £20 million. It is not normal practice for the group to set investment ceilings, and it is anticipated that the capital constraint will not extend into future years. Assuming a cost of capital of 10 per cent, which of the investment opportunities set out in Table 4.8 should divisional management select?

Table 4.8 Investment opportunities for Mervtech plc

Project	Initial cost (£m)	Cash flows (£m) Year 1	Year 2	Present value at 10% (£m)	NPV at 10% (£m)
A	−15	+17	+17	30	15
B	−5	+5	+10	13	8
C	−12	+12	+12	21	9
D	−8	+12	+11	20	12
E	−20	+10	+10	17	−3

In the absence of any financial constraint, projects A–D, each with positive net present values, would be selected. Once this information has been communicated to investors, the total stock market value would, in theory at least, increase by £44 million – the sum of their net present values.

However, a financial constraint may prevent the selection of all profitable projects. If so, it becomes necessary to select the investment package that offers the highest net present value within the £20 million expenditure limit. A simple method of selecting projects under these circumstances is the profitability index. Recall that this measure is defined as:

Profitability index = Present value/Investment outlay

Project selection is made on the basis of the highest ratio of present value to investment outlay. This method is valuable under conditions of capital rationing because it focuses attention on the net present value of each project relative to the scarce resource required to undertake it. Appraising projects according to the NPV per £1 of investment outlay can give different rankings from those obtained from application of the NPV rule. For example, while in the absence of capital rationing, project A ranks highest (using the NPV rule), project B ranks highest when funds are limited, as shown in Table 4.9. Assuming project independence and infinite divisibility, divisional management will obtain the maximum net present value from its £20 million investment expenditure permitted by accepting projects B and D in total and £7 million or 7/15 of project A.

Table 4.9 NPV vs. PI for Mervtech plc

Project	Profitability index	Outlay (£m)	Outlay (£m)	NPV (£m)
B	2.6	5 accept	5	8
D	2.5	8 accept	8	12
A	2.0	15 accept 7/15	7	7
C	1.7	12 reject	—	—
E	0.8	20 reject	—	—
		60	20	27

However, the profitability index rarely offers optimal solutions in practice. First, few investment projects possess the attribute of divisibility. Where it is possible for projects to be scaled down to meet expenditure limits, this is frequently at the expense of profitability. Let us suppose that projects are not capable of division. How would this affect the selection problem? The best combination of projects now becomes A and B, giving a total net present value of £23 million. Project D, which ranked above A using the profitability index, is now excluded. Even more fundamental than this, however, is the limitation that the profitability index is appropriate only when capital rationing is restricted to a single period. This is not usually the case. Firms experiencing either hard or soft capital rationing tend to experience it over a number of periods.

In summary, the profitability index provides a convenient method of selecting projects under conditions of capital rationing when investment projects are divisible and independent, and when only one period is subject to a resource constraint. Where, as is more commonly the case, these assumptions do not hold, investment selections should be made after examining the total net present values of all the feasible alternative combinations of investment opportunities falling within the capital outlay constraints.

Self-assessment activity 4.8

What do you understand by 'soft' and 'hard' forms of capital rationing? Give two approaches available to resolve capital rationing problems.

(Answer in Appendix A at the back of the book)

■ Multi-period capital rationing

Many business problems have similar characteristics to those exhibited in the capital rationing problem, namely:

1 Scarce resources have to be allocated between competing alternatives.
2 An overriding objective that the decision-maker is seeking to attain.
3 Constraints, in one form or another, imposed on the decision-maker.

As the number of alternatives and constraints increases, so the decision-making process becomes more complex. In such cases, mathematical programming models are particularly valuable in the evaluation of decision alternatives, for two reasons:

1 They provide descriptive representations of real problems using mathematical equations. Because they capture the critical elements and relationships existing in the real system, they provide insights about a problem without having to experiment directly on the actual system.
2 They provide optimal solutions – that is, the best solution for a given problem representation.

A mathematical programming approach to solving more complex capital rationing problems is provided in Appendix II to this chapter.

SUMMARY

We have examined a number of commonly employed investment appraisal techniques and asked the question: to what extent do they assist managers in making wealth-creating decisions? The primary methods advocated involve discounting the incremental cash flows resulting from the investment decision, although non-discounting techniques are useful secondary methods for evaluating capital projects.

Key points

■ The net present value (NPV) method discounts project cash flows at the firm's required return and then sums the cash flows. The decision rule is: accept all projects whose NPV is positive.

■ The internal rate of return (IRR) is that discount rate which, when applied to project cash flows, produces a zero NPV. Projects with IRRs above the required return are acceptable.

■ The profitability index (PI) is the ratio of the present value of project benefits to the present value of investment costs. The decision rule is to accept projects with a PI greater than 1.

■ The NPV, IRR and PI methods give the same investment advice for independent projects. But where projects are mutually exclusive, differences can arise in rankings.

■ The NPV approach is viewed as more sound than the IRR method because it assumes reinvestment at the required return rather than the project's IRR.

■ The modified IRR (MIRR) is that rate of return which, when the initial outlay is compared with the terminal value of the project's cash flows reinvested at the cost of capital, gives an NPV of zero. This method provides a rate of return consistent with the NPV approach. This is discussed in Appendix I below.

■ Payback is a useful method, but ignores cash flows beyond the payback period. Simple payback also ignores the time-value of money.

- Accounting rate of return (ARR) compares the average profit of the project against the book value of the asset acquired. Its main merit is that, as a measure of profitability, it can be related to the accounts of the business. However, it takes no account of the timing of cash flows or of the size and life of the investment.

- Capital rationing, where it exists, tends to be of the 'softer' form where management voluntarily imposes investment ceilings in the short term.

- Single-period capital rationing is resolved by ranking projects according to their profitability index. More complex multi-period capital rationing problems demand a mathematical programming approach.

Further reading

Most good finance texts cover the topic of investment appraisal well, including Ross, Westerfield and Jordan (2010), and Brealey, Myers and Allen (2013). These texts also address the capital rationing problem.

Appendix I
MODIFIED IRR

Most managers prefer the IRR to the NPV method. The modified IRR seeks to adjust the IRR so that it has the same reinvestment assumption as the NPV approach.

■ The modified internal rate of return (MIRR)

modified internal rate of return (MIRR)
The internal rate of return modified for the reinvestment assumption

The **modified internal rate of return (MIRR)** is that rate of return which, when the initial outlay is compared with the terminal value of the project's net cash flows reinvested at the cost of capital, gives an NPV of zero.

This involves a two-stage process:

1 Calculate the terminal value of the project by compounding forward all interim cash flows at the cost of capital to the end of the project.
2 Find the rate of interest that equates the terminal value with the initial cost.

Example: Lampard revisited

We established earlier that the Lampard proposal offered an NPV of £4,252 (Table 4.1) and an IRR of approximately 19 per cent (Table 4.3). Table 4.10 shows that by compounding the interim cash flows at 14 per cent to the end of Year 4, the project offers a terminal value of £74,738. To find the Year 4 present value factor that comes closest to equating the terminal value with the initial outlay, we divide the initial outlay by the terminal value and look up the interest rate that gives this factor in Year 4 (see Appendix C). For the Lampard project, the MIRR is approximately 17 per cent, a good 2 per cent below the IRR figure. For more profitable projects, the deviation would be greater.

Find the rate of interest (denoted by x) which equates the terminal value with initial cost:

$$\text{PVIF}_{(x\%, 4 \text{ yrs})} = £40,000/£74,738 = 0.535$$

Using tables (Appendix C) for four years we find that 17 per cent gives a PVIF of 0.534.

Continued

Table 4.10 Modified IRR for Lampard

Year	Cash flow (£)	Future value factor at 14%	Terminal value (£)
Find the terminal value			
1	16,000	$(1.14)^3$	23,704
2	16,000	$(1.14)^2$	20,794
3	16,000	1.14	18,240
4	12,000	1.00	12,000
			74,738

	£
To check: £74,738 × 0.534 =	39,910
less initial investment	(40,000)
NPV	(90) i.e. close to zero

The modified IRR is approximately 17 per cent compared with the IRR of 19.3 per cent.
   You might like to check this out using an Excel spreadsheet. In cells A1 to A5 type in −40,000, 16,000, 16,000, 16,000, 12,000. In cell A6 click on the *fx* icon and select Financial/ MIRR. In the box enter for Values, A1:A5, and .14 for both Finance rate and Reinvestment rate.

Self-assessment activity 4.9

Describe how the modified IRR is calculated. What advantages does the MIRR have over the IRR in assessing capital investment decisions?

(Answer in Appendix A at the back of the book)

Appendix II
MULTI-PERIOD CAPITAL RATIONING AND MATHEMATICAL PROGRAMMING

Where an overriding financial objective exists (such as maximising shareholder wealth) and financial constraints are expected to operate over a number of years, the allocation of capital resources to investment projects is best solved by the mathematical programming approach.

   Many programming techniques have been developed. We shall concentrate on the most common technique: linear programming. The assumptions and limitations underlying the LP approach will be discussed later in the Appendix. Problem-solving using the LP approach involves four basic steps:

1 *Formulate the problem.* This requires specification of the objective function, input parameters, decision variables and all relevant constraints. Take a firm that produces two products, A and B, with contributions per unit of £5 and £10 respectively. The firm wishes to determine the product mix that will maximise its total contribution. The objective function may be expressed as follows:

   maximise contribution $= £5A + £10B$

A and B are the decision variables representing the number of units of products A and B that should be produced. The input values £5 and £10 specify the unit contribution values for products A and B respectively. Constraint equations may also be determined to describe any limitations on resources, whether imposed by managerial policies or the external environment.

2 *Solve the LP problem.* Simple problems can be solved using either a graphical approach or the simplex method. More complex problems require a computer-based solution algorithm.

3 *Interpret the optimal solution.* Examine the effect on the total value of the objective function if a binding constraint were marginally slackened or tightened.

4 *Conduct sensitivity analysis.* Assess, for each input parameter, the range of values for which the optimal solution remains valid.

These four stages in the LP process are illustrated in the following example.

Example: Multi-period capital rationing in Murray plc

Murray's five-year planning exercise shows that the cost of its six major projects, forming the basis of the firm's investment programme, exceeds the planned finance available. Murray is already highly geared and control is in the hands of a few shareholders who are reluctant to introduce more equity funds. Accordingly, the main source of funds is through cash generated from existing operations, estimated to be £300,000 p.a. over the next five years. The six projects are independent and cannot be delayed or brought forward. Each project has a similar risk complexion to that of the existing business. If necessary, projects are capable of division but no more than one of each is required. The planned investment schedule and associated cash flows are given in Table 4.11.

Table 4.11 Murray plc: planned investment schedule (£000)

| | Project outlays | | | | | | Total | Available |
Year	A	B	C	D	E	F	outlay	capital
0	−200	—	−220	−110	−24	—	−554	300
1	−220	−220	−100	−150	−48	—	−738	300
2		−66	−50			−500	−616	300
3					−200		−200	300
NPV	130	184	35	42	186	280		
Total NPV = £857,000								

The six projects, if implemented, are forecast to produce a total NPV of £857,000. However, the annual capital constraint of £300,000 means that for the next three years the required investment expenditure exceeds available investment finance, i.e. there is a capital rationing problem.

The solution sequence is as follows.

1 Specify the problem
The objective function seeks to maximise the NPV from the given set of projects available.

$$\text{Max NPV} = 130A + 184B + 35C + 42D + 186E + 280F$$

However, given the capital expenditure constraints over the coming years, we must express for each year the capital required for each project and the maximum capital available each year (i.e. £300,000):

Year 0 $200A + 200C + 110D + 24E \leq 300$
Year 1 $220A + 220B + 100C + 150D + 48E + \leq 300$
Year 2 $66B + 50C + 500F \leq 300$
Year 3 $200E \leq 300$

Continued

In addition to the capital constraints, we need to define the bounds for each variable. As no more than one of each project is required and projects are divisible, we can specify the bounds as:

$A, B, C, D, E, F \geq 0 \leq 1$

This linear programming formulation tells us to find the mix of projects producing the highest total net present value, given the constraint that only £300,000 can be spent in any year and that not more than one of each project is permitted.

2 Solve the problem

Using a linear program on the computer gives the solution in Table 4.12. Murray plc should accept investment proposals B and E in full plus 14.5 per cent of project A and 46.8 per cent of project F. This will produce the highest possible total net present value available, £520,000. This is significantly less than the £857,000 total NPV if no constraints are imposed.

Table 4.12 Projects accepted based on LP solution

Project	Proportion accepted	NPV (£000)	Capital outlay (£000)			
			Year 0	Year 1	Year 2	Year 3
A	0.145	19	−29	32	—	—
B	1	184		220	66	
C	0	—				
D	0	—				
E	1	186	−29	−48	—	−200
F	0.468	131	—	—	−234	—
		520	−58	−300	−300	−200

3 Interpret the optimal solution

Table 4.12 shows that only in Years 1 and 2 is the full £300,000 utilised. These years then impose binding constraints – their existence limits the company's freedom to pursue its objective of NPV maximisation because it restricts the investment finance available to the firm in those years. Conversely, Years 0 and 3 are non-binding: they do not constrain the firm in its efforts to achieve its objective. Hence while there is no additional opportunity cost (besides that already incorporated in the discount rate), for non-binding periods there is an additional opportunity cost attached to the use of investment finance in the two years where constraints are binding. These additional opportunity costs are termed shadow prices (or dual values). Shadow prices show how much the decision-maker would be willing to pay to acquire one additional unit of each constrained resource. In this case, computer analysis reveals that the shadow prices are:

Year	Shadow price (£)	Constraint
0	0	non-binding
1	0.59	binding
2	0.56	binding
3	0	non-binding

A £1 increase (reduction) in capital spending in Year 1 would produce an increase (reduction) in total NPV of £0.59. Similarly, for Year 2 a £1 change in investment expenditure would result in a £0.56 change in total NPV. Because the capital constraints in Years 0 and 3 are non-binding, their shadow prices are zero and a marginal change in capital spending in those years will have no impact on the NPV objective function. Shadow prices, while of value in indicating the additional opportunity cost, can be used only within a specific range. In addition, it is desirable to ascertain the effect of changes in input parameters on the optimal solution. These issues require some form of sensitivity analysis.

4 Perform sensitivity analysis

The computer output provides two additional pieces of information. First, it tells the decision-maker the maximum variation for each binding constraint. In our example, the shadow price for the Year 1 constraint has a range of −36 to +188. In other words, the shadow price of £0.59 would hold up to an increase in capital expenditure for that year of £188,000, or a reduction of £36,000.

The program also indicates the margin of error permitted for input parameters before the optimal solution differs. In our example, the actual NPV for the optimal investment mix could fall as indicated below and still not change the optimal solution:

Project	Maximum permitted fall in NPV (£000)
A	−68
B	−17
E	−158
F	−280

This facility is particularly appropriate as a means of assessing the margin of error permitted for risky projects under conditions of capital rationing.

■ LP assumptions

In order to assess the value of the basic linear programming approach, we must consider the assumptions underlying its application. These are as follows:

1. All input parameters to the LP model are certain.
2. There is a single objective to be optimised.
3. The objective function and all constraint equations are linear.
4. Decision variables are continuous (i.e. divisible).
5. There is independence among decision variables and resources available.

Most, if not all, of these limiting assumptions can be relaxed by using more complex mathematical programming. For example, uncertainty, multiple objectives and non-linearity can be better addressed by other approaches such as stochastic LP, goal programming and quadratic programming respectively.

For most businesses, the LP assumption that projects are divisible is unrealistic. Even if a project could be operated on a reduced scale, it is unlikely that the NPV would reduce *pro rata* because many of the fixed costs would remain while the benefits of sale would be reduced. *Integer programming* is more appropriate when projects are non-divisible. This is a special case of linear programming where variables can take only the values 0 (reject the project) or 1 (accept it *in toto*).

Applying integer programming to Murray plc requires only one change in the problem specification. The bounds become:

$$A, B, C, D, E, F = 0 \text{ or } 1$$

The solution, provided by an integer programming computer application, shows that only two projects should be accepted: projects B and E. These offer a combined NPV of £370,000, which is the best available given the capital constraints. This is well under half the £857,000 total NPV achievable in the absence of capital rationing (see Table 4.11). Were the shareholders of Murray plc aware of these lost wealth-creating opportunities, they might well be concerned and ask the chairman whether the capital constraints were really as fixed as they appeared to be!

QUESTIONS

Questions with a coloured number have solutions in Appendix B on page 781.

1 The directors of Yorkshire Autopoints are considering the acquisition of an automatic car-washing installation. The initial cost and setting-up expenses will amount to about £140,000. Its estimated life is about seven years, and estimated annual accounting profit is as follows:

Year	1	2	3	4	5	6	7
Operations cash flow (£)	30,000	50,000	60,000	60,000	30,000	20,000	20,000
Depreciation (£)	20,000	20,000	20,000	20,000	20,000	20,000	20,000
Accounting profit (£)	10,000	30,000	40,000	40,000	10,000	—	—

At the end of its seven-year life, the installation will yield only a few pounds in scrap value. The company classifies its projects as follows:

Required rate of return

Low risk	20 per cent
Average risk	30 per cent
High risk	40 per cent

Car-washing projects are estimated to be of average risk.

(a) Should the car-wash be installed?

(b) List some of the popular errors made in assessing capital projects.

2 Microtic Ltd, a manufacturer of watches, is considering the selection of one from two mutually exclusive investment projects, each with an estimated five-year life. Project A costs £1,616,000 and is forecast to generate annual cash flows of £500,000. Its estimated residual value after five years is £301,000. Project B, costing £556,000 and with a scrap value of £56,000, should generate annual cash flows of £200,000. The company operates a straight-line depreciation policy and discounts cash flows at 15 per cent p.a.

Microtic Ltd uses four investment appraisal techniques: payback period, net present value, internal rate of return and accounting rate of return (i.e. average accounting profit to initial book value of investment).

Make the appropriate calculations and give reasons for your investment advice.

3 Mace Ltd is planning its capital budget for 2015 and 2016. The company's directors have reduced their initial list of projects to five, the expected cash flows of which are set out below:

Project	2015	2016	2017	2018	NPV
1	−60,000	+30,000	+25,000	+25,000	+1,600
2	−30,000	−20,000	+25,000	+45,000	+1,300
3	−40,000	−50,000	+60,000	+70,000	+8,300
4	0	−80,000	+45,000	+55,000	+900
5	−50,000	+10,000	+30,000	+40,000	+7,900

None of the five projects can be delayed and all are divisible. Cash flows arise on the first day of the year. The minimum return required by shareholders of Mace Ltd is 10 per cent p.a. Which projects should Mace Ltd accept if the capital available for investment is limited to £100,000 on 1 January 2015, but readily available at 10 per cent p.a. on 1 January 2016 and subsequently?

4 The directors of Mylo Ltd are currently considering two mutually exclusive investment projects. Both projects are concerned with the purchase of new plant. The following data are available for each project:

	Project	
	1 (£)	2 (£)
Cost (immediate outlay)	100,000	60,000
Expected annual net profit (loss)		
Year 1	29,000	18,000
2	(1,000)	(2,000)
3	2,000	4,000
Estimated residual value	7,000	6,000

The company has an estimated cost of capital of 10 per cent and employs the straight-line method of depreciation for all fixed assets when calculating net profit. Neither project would increase the working capital of the company. The company has sufficient funds to meet all capital expenditure requirements.

Required
(a) Calculate for each project:
  (i) the net present value
  (ii) the approximate internal rate of return
  (iii) the profitability index
  (iv) the payback period
(b) State which, if any, of the two investment projects the directors of Mylo Ltd should accept, and why.
(c) State, in general terms, which method of investment appraisal you consider to be most appropriate for evaluating investment projects and why.

(Certified Diploma)

5 Mr Cowdrey runs a manufacturing business. He is considering whether to accept one of two mutually exclusive investment projects and, if so, which one to accept. Each project involves an immediate cash outlay of £100,000. Mr Cowdrey estimates that the net cash inflows from each project will be as follows:

Net cash inflow at end of:	Project A (£)	Project B (£)
Year 1	60,000	10,000
Year 2	40,000	20,000
Year 3	30,000	110,000

Mr Cowdrey does not expect capital or any other resource to be in short supply during the next three years.

Required
(a) Prepare a graph to show the functional relationship between net present value and the discount rate for the two projects (label the vertical axis 'net present value' and the horizontal axis 'discount rate').
(b) Use the graph to estimate the internal rate of return of each project.
(c) On the basis of the information given, advise Mr Cowdrey which project to accept if his cost of capital is (i) 6 per cent; (ii) 12 per cent.
(d) Describe briefly any additional information you think would be useful to Mr Cowdrey in choosing between the two projects.
(e) Discuss the relative merits of net present value and internal rate of return as methods of investment appraisal.

Ignore taxation.

(ICAEW)

6 The directors of XYZ plc wish to expand the company's operations. However, they are not prepared to borrow at the present time to finance capital investment. The directors have therefore decided to use the company's cash resources for the expansion programme.

Three possible investment opportunities have been identified. Only £400,000 is available in cash and the directors intend to limit the capital expenditure over the next 12 months to this amount. The projects are not divisible (i.e. cannot be scaled down) and none of them can be postponed. The following cash flows do not allow for inflation, which is expected to be 10 per cent per annum constant for the foreseeable future.

Expected net cash flows (including residual values)

Project	Initial investment £	Year 1 £	Year 2 £	Year 3 £
A	−350,000	95,000	110,000	200,000
B	−105,000	45,000	45,000	45,000
C	−35,000	−40,000	−25,000	125,000

The company's shareholders currently require a return of 15 per cent nominal on their investment. Ignore taxation.

Required

(a) (i) Calculate the expected net present value and profitability indexes of the three projects; and
 (ii) Comment on which project(s) should be chosen for the investment, assuming the company can invest surplus cash in the money market at 10 per cent. (Note: you should assume that the decision not to borrow, thereby limiting investment expenditure, is in the best interests of its shareholders.)

(b) Discuss whether the company's decision not to borrow, thereby limiting investment expenditure, is in the best interests of its shareholders.

(CIMA)

7 Raiders Ltd is a private limited company financed entirely by ordinary shares. Its effective cost of capital, net of tax, is 10 per cent p.a. The directors are considering the company's capital investment programme for the next two years, and have reduced their initial list of projects to four. Details of the projects' cash flows (net of tax) are as follows (in £000):

Project	Immediately	After 1 year	After 2 years	After 3 years	NPV (at 10%)	IRR (to nearest 1%)
A	−400	+50	+300	+350	+157.0	26%
B	−300	−200	+400	+400	+150.0	25%
C	−300	+150	+150	+150	+73.5	23%
D	0	−300	+250	+300	+159.5	50%

None of the projects can be delayed. All projects are divisible; outlays may be reduced by any proportion and net inflows will then be reduced in the same proportion. No project can be undertaken more than once. Raiders Ltd is able to invest surplus funds in a bank deposit account yielding a return of 7 per cent p.a., net of tax.

Required

(a) Prepare calculations showing which projects Raiders Ltd should undertake if capital for immediate investment is limited to £500,000, but is expected to be available without limit at a cost of 10 per cent p.a. thereafter.

(b) Provide a mathematical programming formulation to assist the directors of Raiders Ltd in choosing investment projects if capital available immediately is limited to £500,000, capital available after one year is limited to £300,000, and capital is available thereafter without limit at a cost of 10 per cent p.a.

(c) Outline the limitations of the formulation you have provided in (b).

(d) Comment briefly on the view that in practice capital is rarely limited absolutely, provided that the borrower is willing to pay a sufficiently high price, and in consequence a technique for selecting investment projects that assumes that capital is limited absolutely is of no use.

(ICAEW)

Practical assignment

Either drawing on your own experience, or by asking someone you know in management, find out the primary investment appraisal techniques employed in an organisation. How well does the appraisal system appear to operate?

5

Project appraisal – applications

The new market space: private investors are looking beyond Earth

'Investment in commercial space flight has become one of the big trends among the super-rich,' says Liam Bailey, head of global research at Knight Frank. The property agency has identified more than 70 ultra high net worth individuals (UHNWIs – people with at least $30m in net assets) investing in commercial space travel, 13 of whom are billionaires with a combined wealth of $175bn.

There are about 10 private companies engaged in space transport at present, including SpaceX, created by billionaire PayPal co-founder Elon Musk, and Blue Origin, founded by Amazon's chief executive Jeff Bezos. Space tourism, driven by companies such as Sir Richard Branson's Virgin Galactic and Jeff Greason's XCOR Aerospace, aim to give the super-wealthy a taste of what it is like to be an astronaut by sending them into sub-orbital space.

Aboard Virgin Galactic's SpaceShip Two, passengers will see the view that eluded mankind until 50 years ago, and one that only about 500 people have seen in reality: the curvature of the Earth set against the blackness of space. The two-hour journey will blast six passengers and two pilots nearly 70 miles into the sky, experiencing about five minutes of weightlessness before turning back and landing at Spaceport America in New Mexico.

The privilege does not come cheap; tickets cost $250,000 each. To date, Virgin Galactic has amassed about $80m in deposits. In customary happy-go-lucky style, Branson says he and his children will be on board the maiden flight later this year (although he initially predicted that his first passengers would take off in 2007).

About 700 people from 57 countries have signed up (and paid) for a seat on SpaceShip Two, including Leonardo DiCaprio, Stephen Hawking, Justin Bieber and the Candy brothers. Lady Gaga has also reserved a ticket and, if everything goes according to plan, will next year become the first singer to perform in outer space.

Of course, whether many space ventures will get off the ground, let alone turn a profit, is impossible to predict. Space projects have undeveloped markets and prolonged periods of development. They also eat up cash.

Source: Based on John Sunyer, *Financial Times*, 1 March 2014, p. 1.

Learning objectives

Having read this chapter, you should be well-equipped to handle most capital investment decision problems found either on examination papers or in business. Skills should develop in the following areas:

- Identifying the relevant information in investment analysis.
- Evaluating replacement and other investment decisions.
- Handling inflation.
- Assessing the effects of taxation on investment decisions.
- Investment appraisal practices, strengths and limitations.
- Identifying the appropriate discount rate.

5.1 INTRODUCTION

In the previous chapter, we examined a variety of approaches to assessing investment projects. The focus was almost exclusively on the appropriate appraisal method. But even the best appraisal method is of little use unless we can first identify the relevant information.

Investment decisions, particularly larger ones with strategic implications, are not usually made on 'the spur of the moment'. The whole process, from the initial idea through to project authorisation, usually takes many months, or even years, as suggested in the introductory cameo. A vital part of this process is gathering information to identify the *incremental cash flows* pertaining to the investment decision. In this chapter, we consider the principles underlying economic feasibility analysis and apply them to particular situations. We pay particular attention to the treatment of inflation and taxation in project evaluation.

■ Need for relevant information

In financial management, as with all areas of management, an effective manager needs to identify the right information for decision-making. In the case of capital investment decisions, committing a substantial proportion of the firm's funds to non-routine, largely irreversible actions can be risky and demands a careful examination of all the relevant information available.

Information on the likely costs and benefits of an investment proposal, its expected economic life, appropriate inflation rates and discount rates should be gathered to provide a clearer picture of the project's economic feasibility. Frequently, we find that the reliability of the information source varies. For example, a demand forecast from a marketing executive with a track record of making wildly inaccurate forecasts will be viewed differently from an official quote for the cost of a machine. The accounting system and formal reports provide a part of the relevant information, the remainder coming through informal channels, frequently more qualitative than quantitative in nature.

In identifying and analysing information, managers should remember that effective information should, wherever possible, be relevant, reliable, timely, accurate and cost-efficient.

5.2 INCREMENTAL CASH FLOW ANALYSIS

We stressed in the previous chapter that the financial input into any investment decision analysis should be based on the incremental cash flows arising as a consequence of the decision. These can be found by calculating the differences between the forecast cash flows from going ahead with the project and the forecast cash flows from not accepting the project.

This is not always easy. To illustrate this point, we consider how investment analysis handles opportunity costs, sunk costs, associated cash flows, working capital changes, interest costs and fixed overheads.

Self-assessment activity 5.1

What do you understand by the term 'incremental cash flows'?

(Answer in Appendix A at the back of the book)

■ Remember opportunity costs

Capital projects frequently give rise to opportunity costs. For example, a company has developed a patent to produce a new type of lawnmower. If it makes the product, the expected NPV is £70,000. However, this ignores the alternative course of action: to sell the patent to another company for £90,000. This opportunity cost is a fundamental element in the investment decision to manufacture the product and should be deducted from the £70,000, giving a negative NPV of £20,000. Alternatively, the sale of the patent is viewed as a mutually exclusive proposal which ranks above the proposal to manufacture the product.

Opportunity cost example: Belfry plc

We often see opportunity costs in replacement decisions. In Belfry plc, an existing machine can be replaced by an improved model costing £50,000, which generates cash savings of £20,000 each year for five years, after which it will have a £5,000 scrap value. The equipment manufacturers are prepared to give an allowance on the existing machine of £15,000, making a net initial cash outlay of £35,000. But in pursuing this course of action, we terminate the existing machine's life, preventing it from yielding £3,000 scrap value in three years. The prospective scrap value denied is the opportunity cost of replacing the existing machine. The cash flows associated with the replacement decision are therefore:

Year 0	Net cost	(£35,000)
Years 1–5	Annual cash savings	(£20,000)
Year 3	Opportunity cost (scrap value forgone on old machine)	(£3,000)
Year 5	Scrap value on new matchine	£5,000

Ignore sunk costs

sunk cost
A cost already incurred, or committed to

By definition, any costs incurred or revenues received prior to a decision are not relevant cash flows; they are **sunk costs**. This does not necessarily imply that previously incurred costs did not produce relevant information. For example, externally conducted feasibility studies are often commissioned to provide important technical, marketing and cost data prior to a major new investment. However, the costs of the study are excluded from project analysis. We are concerned with future cash flows arising as a consequence of the particular course of action.

Look for associated cash flows

Investment in capital projects may have company-wide cash flow implications. Those involved in forecasting cash flows may not realise how the project affects other parts of the business – senior management should therefore carefully consider whether there are any additional cash flows associated with the investment decision. The decision to produce and launch a new product may influence the demand for other products within the product range. Similarly, the decision to invest in a new manufacturing plant in Eastern Europe, or to take over existing facilities, may have an adverse effect on the company's exports to such countries.

Self-assessment activity 5.2

Waxo plc has developed a new wonder earache drug. The management is currently putting together an investment proposal to produce and sell the drug, but is not sure whether to include the following:

1 The original cost of developing the drug.
2 Production of the new product will have an adverse effect on the sale of related products in another division of Waxo.
3 Instead of producing the drug internally, the patent could be sold for £10 million.

How would you advise Waxo on the relevant costs?

(Answer in Appendix A at the back of the book)

■ Include working capital changes

working capital
Or net working capital is
current assets less current
liabilities

It is easy to forget that the total investment for capital projects can be considerably more than the fixed asset outlay. Normally, a capital project gives rise to increased stocks and debtors to support the increase in sales. This increase in **working capital** forms part of the investment outlay and should be included in project appraisal. If the project takes a number of years to reach its full capacity, there will probably be additional working capital requirements in the early years, especially for new products where the seller may have to tempt purchasers by offering more than usually generous credit terms. The investment decision implies that the firm ties up fixed and working capital for the life of the project. At the end of the project, whatever is realised is returned to the firm. For fixed assets, this will be scrap or residual value – usually considerably less than the original cost, except in the case of land and some premises. For working capital, the whole figure – less the value of damaged stock and bad debts – is treated as a cash inflow in the final year, because the finance tied up in working capital can now be re-leased for other purposes.

Occasionally, the introduction of new equipment or technology reduces stock requirements. Here the stock reduction is a positive cash flow in the start year; but an equivalent negative outflow at the end of the project should be included only if it is assumed that the firm will revert to the previous stock levels. A more realistic assumption may be that any replacement would at least maintain existing stock levels, in which case no cash flow for stock in the final year is necessary.

■ Separate investment and financing decisions

Capital projects must be financed. Commonly, this involves borrowing, which requires a series of cash outflows in the form of interest payments. These interest charges should not be included in the cash flows because they relate to the financing rather than the investment decision. Were interest payments to be deducted from the cash flows, it would amount to double-counting, since the discounting process already considers the cost of capital in the form of the discount rate. To include interest charges as a cash outflow could therefore result in seriously understating the true NPV.

Some companies include interest on short-term loans (such as for financing seasonal fluctuations in working capital) in the project cash flows. If so, it is important that both the timing of the receipt and the repayment of the loan are also included. For example, the NPV on a 15 per cent one-year loan of £100,000, assuming a 15 per cent discount rate, must be zero: £100,000 cash received today less the present value of interest and loan repaid after a year (i.e. £115,000/1.15).

■ Fixed overheads can be tricky

Only additional fixed overheads incurred as a result of the capital project should be included in the analysis. In the short term, there will often be sufficient factory space to house new equipment without incurring additional overheads, but, ultimately, some additional fixed costs (for rent, heating and lighting, etc.) will be incurred. Most factories operate an accounting system whereby all costs, including fixed overheads, are charged on some agreed basis to cost centres. Investment in a new process or machine frequently attracts a share of these overheads. While this may be appropriate for accounting purposes, only *incremental* fixed overheads incurred by the decision should be included in the project analysis.

The sleight of hand over shale gas costs

There is a grim argument in the energy industry over how much it really costs to produce natural gas from shale rock. The advocates of favourable shale gas economics seem to be winning, for now. That means energy bankers are kept busy selling interests in shale assets.

You would think this is an easy question to answer. Industry or government accountants could add up commonly agreed numbers for the nation's additions of gas reserves from shale, total the bills of shale gas exploration and production companies, and divide the one figure with the other, discounted for net present value.

You would be wrong. The data and analytic methods are not commonly agreed. This is disturbing. If more shale gas can only be produced with much greater difficulty, at far higher prices than believed, the clean energy future will be far less sunny than we see in all those advertisements and conference programmes.

For example, as a Texan gas man described the Marcellus gas fields in Pennsylvania: 'One company was saying they can develop reserves there for a little over $1.15 per mcf (thousand cubic foot). If you ask them, they say it costs them $3 million to drill and complete wells that average 3 billion cubic feet of reserves, produced over 40 years. Those reserves are calculated on the basis of high initial production rates that decline rapidly. There is insufficient data to have an accurate estimate for the assumed life of the wells. You can't check any of this, because unlike elsewhere in the US, the state doesn't release official monthly production numbers for three years.'

'There is a ton of sleight of hand going on here,' he alleges. 'The "costs" don't include the cost of the land, the seismic survey, the operating costs, and other expenses.' Remember, though, that no one with a competent securities lawyer ever needs to tell a lie.

Source: Based on *Financial Times*, 21 March 2010.

Self-assessment activity 5.3

Clegg – the marketing manager of a manufacturer of golf equipment – has recently submitted a proposal for the production of a range of clubs for beginners. He has just received the following response from Cameron, the managing director:

To: Rick Clegg
From: D. Cameron

I have examined your proposal for the new 'Clubs for Beginners' range which you say promises a three-year payback and a 30 per cent DCF return. Some hope! You seem to have forgotten the following relevant points.

1 We have a policy that all investment is subject to a depreciation charge of 25 per cent on the reducing balance.
2 The accounting department will need to recover factory fixed overheads on the new machine.
3 We need to charge against the project the £8,000 marketing research conducted to assess the size of the market for the new range.
4 I'd have to pay 15 per cent to finance the project.

Projects like this I can do without!

How would you reply to this e-mail if you were Clegg?

(Answer in Appendix A at the back of the book)

5.3 REPLACEMENT DECISIONS

The decision to replace an existing machine which has yet to reach the end of its useful life is often necessary because of developments in technology and generous trade-in values offered by manufacturers. In analysing replacement decisions, we assess the additional costs and benefits arising from the replacement, rather than the attractiveness of the new machine in isolation.

Example of replacement analysis: Ali plc

Ali plc manufactures components for the car industry. It is considering automating its line for producing crankshaft bearings. The automated equipment will cost £750,000. It will replace equipment with a residual value of £80,000 and a written-down book value of £200,000. It is anticipated that the existing machine has a further five years to run, after which its scrap value would be £5,000.

At present, the line has a capacity of 1.25 million units per annum but, typically, it has only been run at 80 per cent of capacity because of the lack of demand for its output. The new line has a capacity of 1.4 million units per annum. Its life is expected to be five years and its scrap value at that time £105,000. The main benefits of the new proposal are a reduction in staffing levels and an improvement in price due to its superior quality.

The accountant has prepared the cost estimates shown in Table 5.1 based on an output of 1 million units p.a. Fixed overheads include depreciation on the old machine of £40,000 p.a. and £130,000 for the new machine. It is considered that for the company overall, other fixed overheads are unlikely to change.

The introduction of the new machine will enable the average level of stocks held to be reduced by £160,000. After five years, the machine will probably be replaced by a similar one.

Table 5.1 Profitability of Ali's project

	Old line (per unit) (p)	New line (per unit) (p)
Selling price	150	155
Materials	(40)	(36)
Labour	(22)	(15)
Variable overheads	(14)	(14)
Fixed overheads	(34)	(40)
Profit per unit	40	50

The company uses a 10 per cent discount rate. We shall ignore taxation.

The solution is given in Table 5.2. Several comments are worthy of note:

1 It has been assumed that no benefits can be obtained from the additional capacity due to the sales constraints. In reality, it would be useful to explore whether – for example, by investing in advertising – demand could be increased.

2 Fixed costs are not relevant. Depreciation is not a cash flow, and we are told that other fixed costs will not alter with the decision. The incremental cash flow per unit is therefore 16p, giving £160,000 (i.e. 1 million units at 16p) additional cash each year on the expected sales.

3 In addition to the scrap values of £80,000 in Year 0 and £105,000 in Year 5 on the old and new machines respectively, there is a £5,000 opportunity cost in Year 5. This is the scrap value no longer available as a consequence of the replacement decision.

4 Working capital will be reduced by £160,000 for the period of the project and it therefore appears as a benefit in Year 0.

5 The book value of the existing machine represents the undepreciated element of the original cost, a sunk cost which is not relevant to the decision. The book value of assets, however, may be important in practice, as it can sometimes mean a heavy accounting loss in the year of acquisition. In this case, the loss would be £120,000 (i.e. book value of £200,000 less £80,000 residual value). This is not a cash flow, but, in practice, it may still be regarded as undesirable to depress reported profit figures in this way. This, of course, raises issues of market efficiency – will the market see through the accounting adjustment?

The replacement decision is a wealth-creating opportunity offering an NPV of £157,000, although the cumulative present value calculation in Table 5.2 shows that the project does not come into surplus, in net present value terms, until the final year.

Table 5.2 Ali plc solution

	Old line (pence per unit)				New line (pence per unit)	
Selling price		150			155	
Less:						
Materials		(40)			(36)	
Labour		(22)			(15)	
Variable overheads		(14)			(14)	
Variable costs		(76)			(65)	
Cash contribution		74			90	
Incremental cash flow per unit (90–74)					16p	
Total incremental cash flow on 1 million unit sales					£160,000	

Year (£000)	0	1	2	3	4	5
Cost savings		160	160	160	160	160
New machine	(750)					105
Scrap old machine	80					(5)
Working capital reduction	160					
Net cash flow	(510)	160	160	160	160	260
Net present value:						
10% discount factor	1.000	0.909	0.826	0.751	0.683	0.621
Present value	(510)	145	132	120	109	161
Cumulative present value	(510)	(365)	(233)	(113)	(4)	157
NPV	157					

5.4 INFLATION CANNOT BE IGNORED

Inflation can have a major impact on the ultimate success or failure of capital projects. In considering how it should be treated in discounted cash flow analysis, two problems arise: first, how does inflation affect the estimated cash flows from the project; and second, how does it affect the discount rate?

For example, a machine costs £18,000 and is projected to produce, in today's prices, cash flows of £6,000, £10,000 and £7,000 respectively over the next three years. The expected rate of inflation is 6 per cent and the firm's cost of capital is 16.6 per cent.

We can adopt one of two approaches:

1 Forecast cash flows in *money* terms and discount at the nominal or *money* cost of capital including inflation (i.e. 16.6 per cent).
2 Forecast cash flows in *constant* (i.e. current) money terms and discount at the *real* cost of capital.

'Money terms' here means the actual price levels that are forecast to obtain at the date of each cash flow; 'constant terms' means the price level prevailing today; and 'real cost of capital' means the net of inflation cost.

In Table 5.3 cash flows expressed at constant prices are converted to actual money cash flows by compounding at $(1 + I)$, where I is the inflation rate. These cash flows are then discounted in the normal manner at the money discount factor (the reason for such an awkward rate will become apparent later) to give a positive NPV of £977. Had we not adjusted cash flows for inflation, the NPV would have been incorrectly expressed as a negative value.

Table 5.3 The money terms approach

Year	Cash flow current prices (£)	Actual money prices (£)	Discount factor at 16.6%	Present value (£)
0	(18,000) × 1.0	(18,000)	1	(18,000)
1	6,000 × 1.06	6,360	$\dfrac{1}{1.166}$	5,454
2	10,000 × (1.06)²	11,236	$\dfrac{1}{(1.166)^2}$	8,264
3	7,000 × (1.06)³	8,337	$\dfrac{1}{(1.166)^3}$	5,259
			NPV	977

In this example, we undertook both compounding and discounting. The process could be simplified by multiplying the two elements. For example, in Year 2 we could multiply $(1.06)^2$ by $1/(1.166)^2$ to obtain a net of inflation discount factor of 0.8264 which, when multiplied by the cash flow in current prices, gives a present value of £8,264, as stated above. This gives rise to the formula for the real cost of capital, denoted by P.

Calculating the real cost of capital

$$(1 + P) = \frac{1 + M}{1 + I}$$

or

$$P = \frac{1 + M}{1 + I} - 1$$

where M is the money cost of capital, I is the inflation rate and P is the real cost of capital.

In our example, this gives us a real cost of capital of:

$$P = \frac{1.166}{1.06} - 1 = 0.10, \text{ i.e. a rate of 10 per cent}$$

Applying the real cost of capital gives the same NPV as before, as shown in Table 5.4.

Table 5.4 The real terms approach

Year	Cash flow current prices (£)	Real discount rate at 10%	PV (£)
0	(18,000)	1	(18,000)
1	6,000	$\dfrac{1}{1.1}$	5,454
2	10,000	$\dfrac{1}{(1.1)^2}$	8,264
3	7,000	$\dfrac{1}{(1.1)^3}$	5,259
		NPV	977

While the latter approach may be simpler, it is not without difficulties. In business, the use of a single indicator of the rate of inflation, such as the Retail Price Index, may be inappropriate. Selling prices, wage rates, material costs and overheads rarely change at exactly the same rate each year. Rent may be fixed for a five-year period; selling prices may be held for more than a year. Furthermore, when taxation is introduced into the analysis, we find that tax relief on capital investment is not subject to inflation. Such complexities lead us to recommend that both cash flows and discount rates should include inflation, i.e. the 'money terms' approach is preferred.

Self-assessment activity 5.4

What is the impact of firms not adjusting their investment 'hurdle' rates for changing levels of inflation? How would you advise a company which employs a 20 per cent discount rate which was based on a calculation made when inflation was twice the current level?

(Answer in Appendix A at the back of the book)

5.5 TAXATION IS A CASH FLOW

In Chapter 2, we introduced the subject of taxation and its broad implications for financial management. In this section, we examine in greater depth the taxation considerations for capital investment projects.

Recall that in the UK, Corporation Tax is assessed by HMRC on the profits of the company after certain adjustments. While it is not calculated on a project basis by HMRC, the actual tax bill will increase with every new project offering additional profits and reduce with every project offering losses. Corporation Tax is charged on the profits, gains and income of an accounting period, usually the period for which accounts are made up annually. In arriving at taxable profits, a deduction is made for capital allowances on certain types of capital investment. Following the principle outlined earlier of identifying the incremental cash flow, we need to ask: by how much will the Corporation Tax bill for the company change each year as a result of the decision? To answer this, we must consider the tax charged on project operating profits and the tax relief obtained on the capital investment outlay.

Example: Taxation implications of Tiger 3000 for Casey plc

Casey plc invests in a new piece of equipment, the Tiger 3000, costing £40,000 on 1 January 2014. It intends to operate the equipment for four years when the scrap value will be zero. Expected net cash flows from the project are £10,000 in the first year and £20,000 for each of the next three years. The discount rate is 15 per cent and the rate of Corporation Tax is 20 per cent.

No tax position

If we ignore taxation (perhaps Casey is making losses and is unlikely to pay tax for some time), the net present value of the project's pre-tax cash flows is £8,390, as shown in Table 5.5. The positive NPV suggests that, on economic grounds, it should be accepted.

With Corporation Tax but no capital allowances

Most companies have to pay Corporation Tax on taxable profits. A recent change in the UK is that for larger companies (profits over £1.5m) this tax is now paid in the same year as the

Continued

Table 5.5 Project Tiger 3000 (assuming no capital allowances)

Year	(1) Pre-tax cash flows £	(2) Tax at 20%	(3) After-tax cash flows £	(4) Discount factor at 15%	(1 × 4) PV pre-tax £	(3 × 4) PV post-taxt £
0	(40,000)	–	(40,000)	1.000	(40,000)	(40,000)
1	10,000	(2,000)	8,000	0.869	8,690	6,952
2	20,000	(4,000)	16,000	0.756	15,120	12,096
3	20,000	(4,000)	16,000	0.657	13,140	10,512
4	20,000	(4,000)	16,000	0.572	11,440	9,152
				NPV	8,390	(1,288)

related profits, usually by quarterly instalments. Hitherto, companies enjoyed a tax delay of at least a year, which meant that the tax payment would typically lag a full year behind the investment cash flows to which they relate. Most investments attract a capital allowance (equivalent to a depreciation charge) which reduces the tax bill. At this stage, we assume that the Tiger 3000 does not attract any capital allowances.

Table 5.5 shows that after deducting tax to be paid, the NPV for the project falls sharply to –£1,288. It is no longer economically viable.

With Corporation Tax and capital allowances

annual writing-down allowances (WDAs)
Allowances for depreciation on capital expenditure allowed for tax purposes

For many types of capital investment, tax relief is granted on capital expenditure incurred. In the United Kingdom, this can be in the form of **annual writing-down allowances (WDAs)**.

Assume the writing-down allowance is:

Plant and machinery   18 per cent on the reducing balance

So for expenditure on machinery of £1,000, the allowance would be as follows:

Year	Tax allowance (£)	Written-down value at year-end (£)
1	18% × 1,000 = 180	820
2	18% × 820 = 148	672
3	18% × 672 = 121 etc.	551 etc.

Clearly, the tax allowances diminish over time. Companies are allowed to write assets down for tax purposes to their disposal value. Any discrepancy between written-down value (WDV) and disposal value may trigger a tax liability (**balancing charge**) or qualify for tax relief (**balancing allowance**). In the above example, disposal of the asset for £600 after three years would mean that the capital allowances have been over-generous to the extent of £49 (i.e. disposal value of £600 – WDV of £551). This *balancing charge* of £49 would then be subject to Corporation Tax. Disposal for, say, £300 would qualify the company for a *balancing allowance* of £251 (i.e. £551 – £300), a loss that would be set against the taxable profits.

Let us return to the Casey plc example, this time assuming that the Tiger 3000 attracts an 18 per cent writing-down allowance. Table 5.6 calculates the WDAs. Tax is payable in the same year as the investment cash flows to which they relate.

The difference between what the investment finally sold for (in this case zero) and the balance at the start of the year is a balancing allowance, which is treated in the same way

Table 5.6 Casey plc – Tiger 3000 tax reliefs

End of accounting year	Tax written-down value £	Writing-down allowance £	20% tax saving £
1– Initial outlay	40,000	7,200	1,440
WDA at 18%	7,200		
	32,800		
2– WDA at 18%	5,904	5,904	1,181
	26,896		
3– WDA at 18%	4,841	4,841	968
	22,055		
4– Sale proceeds	–	22,055	4,411
Balancing allowance	22,055	40,000	8,000

as the writing-down allowance. (You should note that capital allowances are a potentially complex area of taxation and the above is a simple illustration of how they can interact with the investment appraisal decision.)

These cash flows can then be added to the earlier example, as in Table 5.7, showing that the investment offers a positive NPV of £4,015 after tax.

Table 5.7 Casey plc – Tiger 3000 with tax relief

Year	Pre-tax cash flows £	Tax at 20%	Tax saving £	Net cash flows £	Discount factor at 15%	PV £
0	(40,000)	–	–	(40,000)	1.000	(40,000)
1	10,000	(2,000)	1,440	9,440	0.869	8,203
2	20,000	(4,000)	1,181	17,181	0.756	12,989
3	20,000	(4,000)	968	16,968	0.657	11,148
4	20,000	(4,000)	4,411	20,411	0.572	11,675
						4,015

Taxation therefore affects cash flows from investments. It is payable on taxable profits arising from the investment decision after deduction of capital allowances. However, as the FT article below makes clear, many firms pay little or no tax because of the tax allowances on interest and investment.

Anger as no-tax company wins state mobile contract

A company that has paid no corporation tax for eight years has won a £150m government tender to improve mobile connectivity, despite calls for it to be excluded from public sector contracts. Arqiva said no additional pressure had been placed on its tax status, which is legal, during the year-long bidding process for the Mobile Infrastructure Project. George Osborne, the chancellor, announced plans in March to use public sector procurement as a weapon in fighting tax avoidance. Arqiva, which handled the UK's digital television switchover, had revenues of £843.8m in the year to last June, but reported pre-tax losses because of large debt repayments.

Its shareholders charged 13 per cent annual interest on unsecured loans to the company, contributing to total repayments of £365.6m last year.

Such loans, while agreed with HM Revenue & Customs, have been criticised by campaigners for allowing companies to return money to investors without declaring profits. Arqiva said its tax position stemmed from its debt and capital allowances relating to infrastructure investments.

Source: Based on Henry Mance and Kiran Stacey, *Financial Times,* 13 May 2013, p. 4.

Self-assessment activity 5.5

Your boss says: 'We only assess capital projects before tax. Every firm has to pay tax, so we can ignore it.' Do you agree?

(Answer in Appendix A at the back of the book)

5.6 USE OF DCF TECHNIQUES

It is a common misconception that the discounted cash flow approach is a relatively recent phenomenon. Historical records reveal an understanding of compound interest (upon which discounted cash flow techniques are based) as far back as the Old Babylonian period (*c.* 1800–1600 BC) in Mesopotamia. The earliest manuscripts setting out compound interest tables date back to the 14th century, while the first recorded reference to the net present value rule is found in a book by Stevin published in 1582.

In these early days, the application of discounted cash flow methods was restricted to financial investments such as loans and life assurance, where either the cash flows were known or their probabilities could be determined based on actuarial evidence. Only in the 19th century, with the Industrial Revolution well established, did the scale of capital investments lead some engineering economists to begin to apply discounted cash flow concepts to capital assets. However, in practice, these concepts were largely ignored until the early 1950s in the USA and the early 1960s in the UK.

Surveys between 1981 and 2003 provide a clearer picture of the changing trends in the practices of larger firms in the UK. Table 5.8 shows that, while all firms surveyed conduct financial appraisals on capital projects, the choice of method varies considerably, and most firms employ a combination of appraisal techniques.

Table 5.8 Capital investment evaluation methods in large UK firms

Firms using:	1981 (%)	1992 (%)	2003 (%)
Payback	81	94	96
Average accounting rate of return	49	50	60
Internal rate of return	57	81	89
Net present value	39	74	99

Sources: Pike (1988, 1996), Alkaraan and Northcott (2006).

The use of the NPV approach in large firms increased from 39 per cent in 1981 to 99 per cent by 2003. The IRR approach has also increased significantly over the same period. However, the use of the average accounting rate of return has not changed much over time.

The payback method has always been popular with smaller firms but Table 5.8 shows that virtually all larger UK firms use it within their evaluation process. It is clear that firms do not normally rely on any single appraisal measure, but prefer to employ a combination of simple and more sophisticated techniques. DCF methods therefore complement, rather than substitute for, traditional approaches.

Table 5.9 presents a wider picture on recent capital investment practices. It shows the main techniques employed for firms in the United States and major European countries.

We observe that the US has the highest use of DCF methods, while Germany and France employ these techniques far less, although France tends to favour the Profitability Index approach. However, Payback Period is still more commonly employed in European companies than IRR or NPV, particularly among smaller firms. The European study found that firms placing greater importance on maximising shareholder value preferred discounting techniques to payback approaches.

Table 5.9 Firms employing investment appraisal techniques 'always or almost always %'

	US	UK	Netherlands	Germany	France
Internal rate of return	76	53	56	42	44
Net present value	75	47	70	48	35
Payback period	57	69	65	50	51
Discounted payback period	29	25	25	31	11
Accounting rate of return	20	38	25	32	16
Profitability index	12	16	8	16	38

Sources: Graham and Harvey (2002), Brounen, de Jong and Koedijk (2004).

■ Dangers with DCF

While we have argued that DCF analysis offers a conceptually sound approach for appraising capital projects, a word of caution is appropriate.

From the emphasis devoted by most textbooks to advanced capital budgeting methods, one might be forgiven for assuming that successful investment is exclusively attributable to the correct evaluation method. However, DCF methods often create an illusion of exactness that the underlying assumptions do not warrant. As top management places more weight on the quantifiable element, there is a danger that the unquantifiable aspects of the decision, which frequently have a critical bearing on a project's success or failure, will be devalued. The human element is particularly important with regard to the project sponsor. The margin between a project's success or failure often hinges on the enthusiasm and commitment of the person sponsoring and implementing it.

Managers cannot afford to treat investment decisions in a vacuum, ignoring the complexities of the business environment. Any attempt to incorporate such complexities, however, will at best consist of abstractions from reality relying on generalised and simplified assumptions concerning business relationships and environments. A fundamental assumption underlying DCF methods is that decision-makers pursue the primary goal of maximising shareholders' wealth. For many firms, this may not be the case.

Common errors in applying DCF

- Discount rates are calculated on a pre-tax basis, while operating cash flows are calculated after tax.
- Discount rates are increased to compensate for non-economic statutory and welfare investments.
- Interest charges are included in cash flows.
- Cash flows are specified in today's money (excluding inflation), while hurdle rates are based on the money cost of capital (including inflation).
- Managerial aversion to uncertainty frequently results in conservative project life and terminal value assumptions.
- Use of a uniform cut-off rate instead of a rate reflecting individual project risk. This often leads to rejection of low-risk/low-return replacement projects.
- Failure to include scrap values.
- Neglect of working capital movements.
- Failure to consider what would have happened without the project.

Critical errors may often be seen in the way DCF theory is applied by managers. Usually, these errors are biased against investment. For example, many firms do not adjust their operating cash flows for inflation, but discount them at the money cost of capital, rather than the real rate of return before inflation. The effect is that cash flows in later years (typically the strong positive cash flows) are unduly deflated by the high discount factor, giving a lower net present value than should be the case.

Perhaps even more important, DCF methods ignore the value of investment options. This key topic is the subject of Chapter 12.

5.7 TRADITIONAL APPRAISAL METHODS

Managers have developed and come to rely upon simple rule-of-thumb approaches to analysing investment worth. Two of the most popular traditional methods are the *payback period* and the *accounting rate of return*, both of which were described in Chapter 4. Our present concern is to ask whether they have a valuable role to play in the modern capital budgeting process. Do they offer anything to the decision-maker that cannot be found in the DCF approaches?

■ Accounting rate of return (ARR)

We discussed the basic application of the ARR approach in Chapter 4. Table 5.8 reports that a little over half the companies surveyed employ the accounting rate of return approach in assessing investment decisions. This is not altogether surprising, given that the rate of return on capital is a very important financial goal in practice.

The ARR can be criticised on at least two counts: it uses accounting profits rather than cash flows, and it ignores the time-value of money. Nevertheless there has been a certain amount of support for the ARR in the literature. The absence of ARR leads to an inconsistency between the methods commonly used to *report* a firm's results and the techniques most frequently employed to *appraise* investment decisions. This is most acutely experienced where the divisional manager of an investment centre is expected to use a DCF approach in reaching investment decisions, while his or her short-term performance is being judged on a return on investment basis. Little wonder, then, that the divisional manager generally shows a marked reluctance to enter into any profitable long-term investment decisions that produce low returns in the early years.

A common assumption among managers is that the accounting rate of return and the internal rate of return produce much the same solutions. But while there is a relationship between a project's discounted return and the ARR, the relationship is not simple. Consider an investment costing £10,000 and generating an annual stream of net cash flows of £3,000. Assuming straight-line depreciation, the relationship between the internal rate of return and the accounting rate of return calculated on both the total investment and the average investment is as shown in Table 5.10.

Table 5.10 Relationship between ARR and IRR

Project duration (years)	5	10	20	25
IRR (%)	15.2	27.3	29.8	30
ARR on total investment (%)	10	20	25	27.5
Deviation from IRR	−5.2	−7.3	−4.8	−2.5
ARR on average investment (%)	20	40	50	55
Deviation from IRR	+4.8	+12.7	+20.2	+25

From this example, we can see that the accounting rate of return on *total* investment consistently *understates*, and the accounting rate of return on *average* investment *overstates*, the internal rate of return. The case for retaining the accounting rate of return is, therefore, valid only when applied as a secondary criterion to highlight the likely impact on the organisation's profitability upon which the divisional manager is judged.

Residual income approach: Pluto Electronics

residual income
Operating profit less the charge for capital

While the average accounting return can be a misleading decision indicator for capital projects, it is possible to employ a profit-based approach that is in line with net present value. This involves calculating the **residual income** (RI), the profit less a cost of capital charge based on the book value of the assets employed.

Pluto Electronics has acquired the rights to manufacture a product for three years and has set up a new division to do so. The investment outlay is £60 million and annual cash flows are forecast to be £30 million. The company operates a straight-line depreciation policy and has a cost of capital of 10 per cent.

We can calculate the NPV (£m) as:

$$NPV = -60 + (30 \times PVIFA_{10,3}) = -60 + (30 + 2.4868) = £14.6m$$

The same answer is given by calculating the residual income for each year and discounting at the cost of capital, as shown below. The annual profit is £10 million (i.e. £30 million cash flow less £20 million depreciation).

	£m	PV at 10% (£m)
Yr 1 profit	10	
Investment outlay: £60m		
10% capital charge on investment	(6)	
Residual income	4	× 0.909 = 3.636
Yr 2 profit	10	
Book value of assets: £40m		
10% capital charge	(4)	
	6	× 0.826 = 4.956
Yr 3 profit	10	
Book value of assets: £20m		
10% capital charge	(2)	
	8	× 0.751 = 6.008
Net present value		14.600

■ Payback period

Most finance texts have condemned the use of the payback period as potentially misleading in reaching investment decisions. However, Table 5.8 shows that it continues to flourish, being employed by most firms surveyed. Typically, the payback period required by firms is within 2–4 years (Arnold and Hatzopoulos, 2000). Why is payback so popular? Does it possess certain qualities not so apparent in more sophisticated approaches?

The two main objections to payback (PB)

1 It ignores all cash flows beyond the payback period.

2 It does not consider the profile of the project's cash flows within the payback period.

Although such theoretical shortcomings could fundamentally alter a project's ranking and selection, the payback criterion possesses a number of merits.

1 PB estimates DCF return

The payback period provides a crude measure of investment profitability. When the annual cash receipts from a project are uniform, the payback reciprocal is the internal rate of return for a project of infinite life, or a good approximation to this rate for long-lived projects.

$$\text{IRR} = \frac{1}{\text{payback period}}$$

In the case of *very* long-lived projects where the cash inflows are, on average, spread evenly over the life of the project, the payback reciprocal is a reasonable proxy for the internal rate of return. For example, a project offering permanent cash savings and giving a four-year payback period with relatively stable annual cash returns will have approximately a 25 per cent internal rate of return (i.e. the reciprocal of payback period). However, if the project life is only ten years, the IRR would fall to 21 per cent – some four percentage points below the payback reciprocal. In fact, the payback reciprocal consistently *overstates* the true rate of return for finite project lives.

2 PB considers uncertainty

Whereas more sophisticated techniques attempt to model the uncertainty surrounding project returns, payback assumes that risk is time-related; the longer the period, the greater the chance of failure. General economic uncertainty makes the task of forecasting cash flows extremely difficult; but for the most part, cash flows are correlated over time. If the operating returns are below the expected level in the early years, they will probably also be below plan in the later years.

Discounted cash flow, as practised in most firms, ignores this increase in uncertainty over time. Early cash flows, therefore, have an important information content on the degree of accuracy of subsequent cash flows. By concentrating on the early cash flows, the payback approach analyses the data where managers have greater confidence. If such evaluation provides a different signal from DCF methods, it highlights the need for a more careful consideration of the project's risk characteristics.

3 PB is a screening device

Payback provides a relatively efficient method for ranking projects when constraints prevail. The most obvious constraint is the time that managers can devote to initial product screening. Only a handful of the investment ideas may stand up to serious and thorough financial investigation. Payback period serves as a simple, first-level screening device which, in the case of marginal projects, tends to operate in their favour and permits them to go forward for more thorough investigation.

Many firms also resort to payback period when experiencing liquidity constraints. Such a policy may make sense when funds are constrained and better investment ideas are in the pipeline. The attractiveness of investment proposals considered during the interim period will be a function more of their ability to pay back rapidly than of their overall profitability. This does not necessarily lead to optimal solutions.

4 PB assists communication

Managers feel more comfortable with payback period than with DCF. In the first place, it is simple to calculate and understand. The non-quantitative manager is reluctant to rely on the recommendations of 'sophisticated' models when he or she lacks both the time and expertise to verify such outcomes. Confidence in, and commitment to, a proposal depend to some degree on how thoroughly the evaluation model is comprehended. The payback method offers a convenient shorthand for the desirability of each investment that is understandable at all levels of the organisation: namely, how quickly will the project recover its initial outlay? Some firms use a project classification system in which the payback period indicates how rapidly proposals should be processed and put into operation.

Ultimately, it is the manager – not the method – who makes investment decisions and is appraised on their outcome. Payback period is particularly attractive to managers not only because it is convenient to calculate and communicate, but also because it signals good investment decisions at the earliest opportunity.

While the payback concept may lack the refinements of its more sophisticated evaluation counterparts, it possesses many endearing qualities that make it irresistible to most managers; hence its resilience.

Self-assessment activity 5.6

The following reasons for using payback were given by finance executives from three different companies:

'We use payback in support of other methods. It is not a sufficiently reliable tool to be used in isolation.'

'When liquidity is under pressure, payback is particularly relevant.'

'Payback helps to give some idea of the riskiness of the project – a long time to get one's money back is obviously more risky than a short time.'

To what extent do you agree with these views?

■ The appropriate discount rate

So far, the examples used have simply stated the project discount rate based on the cost of capital, the rate of return required by investors. We discuss in some depth the appropriate discount rate in Chapters 9 and 10. Here, we outline one approach, the weighted average cost of capital (WACC).

This measures the rate of return that the firm must achieve in order to satisfy all of the people who invest in it. All of these investors incur an opportunity cost when placing their money in the hands of the firm's managers. This is the rate of return they could have achieved on the next best alternative investment.

Example: WACC

Wacky Ideas Ltd produces novelty toys. It currently finances its business one-third through loans and two-thirds through equity and reserves. Looking ahead, it does not expect to change this funding mix. The accountant estimates that the cost of equity is 12 per cent while the after-tax cost of borrowing is lower at 6 per cent. Given this information, we can calculate the average cost of capital for the company, duly weighted according to the proportion of capital represented by equity and borrowings respectively. For Wacky this is:

Source of capital	Proportion		Cost of capital		Weighted cost
Equity	67%	×	12%	=	8%
Loans	33%	×	6%	=	2%
WACC					10%

The weighted average cost of capital (WACC) approach multiplies the cost of each source of capital by the proportion of the total capital it represents. The results are summed to provide a WACC estimate of 10 per cent in Wacky's case. If we assume that each new investment project receives a slice of the total capital in the same 2:1 equity:borrowing proportion, and that the project has the same level of risk as the typical investments in the firm, we can apply a discount rate of 10 per cent in calculating the project's net present value. We leave the issue of determining the cost of capital for each source of finance to Chapter 11.

Self-assessment activity 5.7

Major plc has 20 million £0.50 ordinary shares and irredeemable loan capital with a nominal value of £40 million in issue. The ordinary shares have a current market value of £2.40 per share and the loan capital is quoted at £80 per £100 nominal value. The cost of ordinary shares is estimated at 11 per cent and the cost of loan capital is calculated to be 8 per cent. The rate of corporation tax is 25 per cent. What is the weighted average cost of capital for the company?

(Answer in Appendix A at the back of the book)

SUMMARY

One of the most difficult aspects of capital budgeting is identifying and gathering the relevant information for analysis. This chapter has examined the incremental cash flow approach to project analysis. Attention has been paid to the replacement decision and to the impact of inflation and taxation on investment decisions.

Key points

- Include only future, incremental cash flows relating to the investment decision and its consequences. This implies the following:

  1 Only additional fixed overheads are included.
  2 Depreciation (a non-cash item) is excluded.
  3 Sunk (or past) costs are not relevant.
  4 Interest charges are financing (not investment) cash flows and are therefore excluded from the cash flow profile.
  5 Opportunity costs (e.g. the opportunity to rent or sell premises if the proposal is not acceptable) are included.

- Replacement decision analysis examines the change in cash flows resulting from the decision to replace an existing asset with a new asset.

- Inflation can have important effects on project analysis. Two approaches are possible: (1) specify all cash flows at 'money-of-the-day' (i.e. including inflation) prices and discount at the money cost of capital, or (2) specify cash flows at today's prices and discount at the real (i.e. net of inflation) cost of capital. We recommend the former in most cases.

- Taxation is, for most organisations, a cash flow. Tax is calculated by deducting any cash benefits from tax relief on the initial capital expenditure from tax payable on additional cash flows. Care should be taken in estimating the timing of tax cash flows.

- In practice, most firms, particularly larger companies, employ a combination of DCF and traditional appraisal methods.

- One way of estimating the discount rate to be used is to calculate the firm's weighted average cost of capital.

Further reading

The Chartered Institute of Management Accountants (CIMA) has produced a report that discusses the use of investment appraisal within the context of strategic decision-making. This report has been prepared by Emmanuel *et al.* (2008). Most finance texts are not particularly strong on the applied aspects of capital budgeting. Pohlman *et al.* (1988) describe cash flow estimation practices in large firms. Levy and Sarnat (1994b) has useful chapters, but the US tax system is employed.

Studies on the investment practices of UK firms are well worth reading. See, for example, Pike (1982, 1988, 1996), McIntyre and Coulthurst (1985), Mills (1988), Pike and Wolfe (1988), Arnold and Hatzopoulos (2000), and Alkaraan and Northcott (2006). Useful references on the capital budgeting process are Cooper (1975), Pinches (1982) and Neale and Holmes (1991). Graham and Harrey (2002) examine US capital budgeting practices.

Appendix
THE PROBLEM OF UNEQUAL LIVES: POULTER PLC

Comparing mutually exclusive projects – such as retaining the old asset or replacing it with a new one – frequently involves the problem of assessing projects with different economic lives.

Poulter plc is seeking to modernise and speed up its production process. Two proposals have been suggested to achieve this: the purchase of a number of forklift trucks and the acquisition of a conveyor system. The accountant has produced cost savings figures for the two proposals using a 10 per cent discount rate, shown in Table 5.11.

Table 5.11 Poulter plc cash flows for two projects

Year	Forklift trucks	Conveyor system
0	(30,000)	(66,000)
1	10,000	12,000
2	15,000	20,000
3	18,000	20,000
4		18,000
5		15,000
6		15,000
NPV at 10%	5,010	6,538

At first sight, the more expensive conveyor system appears more wealth-creating. But it is not appropriate to compare projects with different lives without making some adjustment. Two approaches can be employed for this: the replacement chain approach and the equivalent annual annuity approach.

The **replacement chain approach** recognises that while, for convenience, we usually consider only the time-horizon of the proposal, most investments form part of a replacement chain over a much longer time period. We therefore need to compare mutually exclusive projects over a common period. In the example, this period is six years, two forklift truck proposals (one following the other) being equivalent to one conveyor system proposal. Assuming the cash flows for the original forklift trucks also apply to their replacements in Year 4 (a pretty big assumption, given inflation, improvements in technology, etc.), the replacement will produce a further NPV of £5,010 at the start of Year 4.

To convert this to the present value (i.e. Year 0) we must discount this figure to the present using the discount factor for 10 per cent for a cash flow three years hence:

$$\text{PV} = £5,010 \times \text{PVIF}_{(10,3)} = £5,010 \times 0.7513 \times £3,764$$

The NPV for the forklift truck proposal, assuming like-for-like replacement after three years, is therefore £5,010 + £3,764 = £8,774. This is well in excess of the NPV of the conveyor system proposal of £6,538 over the same time period.

replacement chain approach
The process of comparing like-for-like replacement decisions for mutually exclusive projects with different lives over a common time period

Poulter plc NPV comparison

Year		Forklift trucks £	Conveyor system £
1–3		5,010	
4–6	£5,010 × 0.7513	3,764	
1–6		8,774	6,538

equivalent annual annuity (EAA)
The constant annual cash flow offering the same present value as the project's net present value

A second approach, the **equivalent annual annuity (EAA)** approach, is easier than its name suggests. It seeks to determine the constant annual cash flow that offers the same present value as the project's NPV. This is found by dividing the project's NPV by the relevant annuity discount factor (i.e. 10 per cent over three years):

$$EAA = \frac{NPV}{PVIFA_{(10,3)}}$$

For the forklift proposal:

$$EAA = \frac{£5,010}{2.4868} = £2,015$$

For the conveyor system proposal:

$$EAA = \frac{NPV}{PVIFA_{(10,6)}} = \frac{£6,538}{4.3553} = £1,501$$

The forklift proposal offers the higher equivalent annual annuity and is to be preferred. Assuming continuous replacement at the end of their project lives, the NPVs for the projects over an infinite time-horizon are found by dividing the EAA by the discount rate:

NPV forklift truck = £2,015/0.10 = £20,150
NPV conveyor = £1,501/0.10 = £15,010

QUESTIONS

Questions with a coloured number have solutions in Appendix B on page 782.

1 Most capital budgeting textbooks strongly recommend NPV, but most firms prefer IRR. Explain.

2 A project costing £20,000 offers an annual cash flow of £5,000 over its life.

(a) Calculate the internal rate of return using the payback reciprocal assuming an infinite life.
(b) Use tables to test your answer assuming the project life is (i) 20 years, (ii) eight years.
(c) What conclusions can be drawn as to the suitability of the payback reciprocal in measuring investment profitability?

3 Your firm uses the IRR method and asks you to evaluate the following mutually exclusive projects:

Cash flows (£)	Year				
	0	1	2	3	4
Proposal L	−47,232	20,000	20,000	20,000	20,000
Proposal M	−47,232	0	10,000	20,000	65,350

Using the appropriate IRR method, evaluate these proposals assuming a required rate of return of 10 per cent. Compare your answer with the net present value method.

4 State two ways in which inflation can be handled in investment analysis. Which way would you recommend and why?

5 Bramhope Manufacturing Co. Ltd has found that, after only two years of using a machine for a semi-automatic process, a more advanced model has arrived on the market. This advanced model will not only produce the current volume of the company's product more efficiently, but allow increased output of the product. The existing machine had cost £32,000 and was being depreciated straight-line over a ten-year period, at the end of which it would be scrapped. The market value of this machine is currently £15,000 and there is a prospective purchaser interested in acquiring it.

The advanced model now available costs £123,500 fully installed. Because of its more complex mechanism, the advanced model is expected to have a useful life of only eight years. A scrap value of £20,500 is considered reasonable.

A comparison of the existing and advanced model now available shows the following:

	Existing machine	Advanced model
Capacity p.a.	200,000 units	230,000 units
	£	£
Selling price per unit	0.95	0.95
Production costs per unit		
Labour	0.12	0.08
Materials	0.48	0.46
Fixed overheads (allocation of portion of company's fixed overheads)	0.25	0.16

The sales director is of the opinion that additional output could be sold at 95p per unit.

If the advanced model were to be run at the old production level of 200,000 units per annum, the operators would be freed for a proportionate period of time for reassignment to the other operations of the company.

The sales director has suggested that the advanced model should be purchased by the company to replace the existing machine.

The required return is 15 per cent.

(i) You are required to calculate:

  (a) payback period
  (b) the net present value
  (c) the internal rate of return (to the nearest per cent).

(ii) What recommendation would you make to the sales director? What other considerations are relevant?

6 Argon Mining plc is investigating the possibility of purchasing an open-cast coal mine in South Wales at a cost of £2.5 million which the British government is selling as part of its privatisation programme. The company's surveyors have spent the last three months examining the potential of the mine and have incurred costs to date of £0.2 million. The surveyors have prepared a report which states that the company will require equipment and vehicles costing £12.5 million in order to operate the mine and that these assets can be sold for £2.5 million in four years' time when the coal reserves of the mine are exhausted.

The assistant to the Chief Financial Officer of the company has prepared the following projected profit and loss accounts (income statements) for each year of the life of the mine.

Projected Income Statements (Profit and Loss Accounts) (£m)

	Year			
	1	2	3	4
Sales	9.4	9.8	8.5	6.3
less Wages and salaries	(2.3)	(2.5)	(2.6)	(1.8)
Selling and distribution costs	(1.3)	(1.2)	(1.5)	(0.6)
Materials and consumables	(0.3)	(0.4)	(0.4)	(0.2)
Depreciation and equipment	(2.5)	(2.5)	(2.5)	(2.5)
Head office expenses	(0.6)	(0.6)	(0.6)	(0.6)
Survey costs	(0.4)			
Interest charges	(1.2)	(1.2)	(1.2)	(1.2)
Net profit (loss)	0.8	1.4	(0.3)	(0.6)

In his report to the Chief Financial Officer, the assistant recommends that the company should not proceed with the acquisition of the mine as the profitability of the proposal is poor.

The following additional information is available:

(i) The project will require an investment of £0.5 million of working capital from the beginning of the project until the end of the useful life of the mine.

(ii) The wages and salaries expenses include £0.5 million of working capital in Year 1 for staff who are already employed by the company but who would be without productive work until Year 2 if the project does not proceed. However, the company has no intention of dismissing these staff. After Year 1, these staff will be employed on another project with the company.

(iii) One-third of the head office expenses consists of amounts directly incurred in managing the new project and two-thirds represents an apportionment of other head office expenses to the project to ensure that it bears a fair share of these expenses.

(iv) The survey costs include those costs already incurred to date, and which are to be written off in the first year of the project, as well as costs to be incurred in the first year if the project is accepted.

(v) The interest charges relate to finance required to purchase the equipment and vehicles necessary to carry out the project.

(vi) After the mine has been exhausted, the company will be required to clean up the site and to make good the damage to the environment resulting from its mining operations. The company will incur costs of £0.4 million in Year 5 in order to do this.

The company has a cost of capital of 12 per cent.
Ignore taxation.

Required

(a) Using what you consider to be the most appropriate investment appraisal method, prepare calculations which will help the company to decide whether or not to proceed with the project.
(b) State, giving reasons, whether you think the project should go ahead.
(c) Explain why you consider the investment appraisal method selected in (a) above to be most appropriate for evaluating investment projects.

7 Consolidated Oilfields plc is interested in exploring for oil near the west coast of Australia. The Australian government is prepared to grant an exploration licence to the company for a five-year period for a fee of £300,000 p.a. The option to acquire the rights must be taken immediately, otherwise another oil company will be granted the rights. However, Consolidated Oilfields is not in a position to commence operations immediately, and exploration of the oilfield will not start until the beginning of the second year. In order to carry out the exploration work, the company will require equipment costing £10,400,000, which will be made by a specialist engineering company. Half of the equipment cost will be payable immediately and half will be paid when the equipment has been built and tested to the satisfaction of Consolidated Oilfields. It is estimated that the second instalment will be paid at the end of the first year. The company commissioned a geological survey of the area and the results suggest that the oilfield will produce relatively small amounts of high-quality crude oil. The survey cost £250,000 and is now due for payment.

The assistant to the project accountant has produced the following projected profit and loss accounts (income statements) for the project for Years 2–5 when the oilfield is operational.

		Year						
		2		**3**		**4**		**5**
	£000	£000	£000	£000	£000	£000	£000	£000
Sales		7,400		8,300		9,800		5,800
Less expenses								
Wages and salaries	550		580		620		520	
Materials and consumables	340		360		410		370	
Licence fee	600		300		300		300	
Overheads	220		220		220		220	
Depreciation	2,100		2,100		2,100		2,100	
Survey cost written off	250		–		–		–	
Interest charges	650		650		650		650	
		4,710		4,210		4,300		4,160
Profit		2,690		4,090		5,500		1,640

The following additional information is available:

1 The licence fee charge appearing in the accounts in Year 2 includes a write-off for all the annual fee payable in Year 1. The licence fee is paid to the Australian government at the end of each year.
2 The overheads contain an annual charge of £120,000, which represents an apportionment of head office costs. This is based on a standard calculation to ensure that all projects bear a fair share of the central administrative costs of the business. The remainder of the overheads relate directly to the project.
3 The survey costs written off relate to the geological survey already undertaken and due for payment immediately.
4 The new equipment costing £10,400,000 will be sold at the end of the licence period for £2,000,000.
5 The project will require a specialised cutting tool for a brief period at the end of Year 2, which is currently being used by the company on another project. The manager of the other project has estimated that he will have to hire machinery at a cost of £150,000 for the period the cutting tool is on loan.
6 The project will require an investment of £650,000 working capital from the end of the first year to the end of the licence period.

The company has a cost of capital of 10 per cent.
Ignore taxation.

Required

(a) Prepare calculations that will help the company to evaluate further the profitability of the proposed project.
(b) State, with reasons, whether you would recommend that the project be undertaken.
(c) Explain how inflation can pose problems when appraising capital expenditure proposals, and how these problems may be dealt with.

(Certified Diploma)

8 You are the chief accountant of Deighton plc, which manufactures a wide range of building and plumbing fittings. It has recently taken over a smaller unquoted competitor, Linton Ltd. Deighton is currently checking through various documents at Linton's head office, including a number of investment appraisals. One of these, a recently rejected application involving an outlay on equipment of £900,000, is reproduced below. It was rejected because it failed to offer Linton's target return on investment of 25 per cent (average profit-to-initial investment outlay). Closer inspection reveals several errors in the appraisal.

**Evaluation of profitability of proposed project NT17
(all values in current year prices)**

Item (£000)	0	1	2	3	4
Sales		1,400	1,600	1,800	1,000
Materials		(400)	(450)	(500)	(250)
Direct labour		(400)	(450)	(500)	(250)
Overheads		(100)	(100)	(100)	(100)
Interest		(120)	(120)	(120)	(120)
Depreciation		(225)	(225)	(225)	(225)
Profit pre-tax		155	255	355	55
Tax at 33%		(51)	(84)	(117)	(18)
Post-tax profit		104	171	238	37
Outlay					
Stock	(100)				
Equipment	(900)				
Market research	(200)				
	(1,200)				

$$\text{Rate of return} = \frac{\text{Average profit}}{\text{Investment}} = \frac{£138}{£1,200} = 11.5\%$$

You discover the following further details:

1 Linton's policy was to finance both working capital and fixed investment by a bank overdraft. A 12 per cent interest rate applied at the time of the evaluation.
2 A 25 per cent writing-down allowance (WDA) on a reducing balance basis is offered for new investment. Linton's profits are sufficient to utilise fully this allowance throughout the project.
3 Corporation tax is paid a year in arrears.
4 Of the overhead charge, about half reflects absorption of existing overhead costs.
5 The market research was actually undertaken to investigate two proposals, the other project also having been rejected. The total bill for all this research has already been paid.
6 Deighton itself requires a nominal return on new projects of 20 per cent after taxes, is currently ungeared and has no plans to use any debt finance in the future.

Required

Write a report to the finance director in which you:

(a) Identify the mistakes made in Linton's evaluation.
(b) Restate the investment appraisal in terms of the post-tax net present value to Deighton, recommending whether the project should be undertaken or not.

(ACCA)

9 (a) Explain how inflation affects the rate of return required on an investment project, and the distinction between a real and a nominal (or 'money terms') approach to the evaluation of an investment project under inflation.

(b) Howden plc is contemplating investment in an additional production line to produce its range of compact discs. A market research study, undertaken by a well-known firm of consultants, has revealed scope to sell an additional output of 400,000 units p.a. The study cost £0.1 million, but the account has not yet been settled.

The price and cost structure of a typical disc (net of royalties) is as follows:

	£	£
Price per unit		12.00
Costs per unit of output		
Material cost per unit	1.50	
Direct labour cost per unit	0.50	
Variable overhead cost per unit	0.50	
Fixed overhead cost per unit	1.50	
		(4.00)
Profit		8.00

The fixed overhead represents an apportionment of central administrative and marketing costs. These are expected to rise in total by £500,000 p.a. as a result of undertaking this project. The production line is expected to operate for five years and require a total cash outlay of £11 million, including £0.5 million of materials stocks. The equipment will have a residual value of £2 million. Because the company is moving towards a JIT stock management policy, it is expected that this project will involve steadily reducing working capital needs, expected to decline at about 3 per cent p.a. by volume. The production line will be accommodated in a presently empty building for which an offer of £2 million has recently been received from another company. If the building is retained, it is expected that property price inflation will increase its value to £3 million after five years.

While the precise rates of price and cost inflation are uncertain, economists in Howden's corporate planning department make the following forecasts for the average annual rates of inflation relevant to the project:

Retail Price Index	6% p.a.
Disc prices	5% p.a.
Material prices	3% p.a.
Direct labour wage rates	7% p.a.
Variable overhead costs	7% p.a.
Other overhead costs	5% p.a.

Note: You may ignore taxes and capital allowances in this question.

Required

(a) Given that Howden's shareholders require a real return of 8.5 per cent for projects of this degree of risk, assess the financial viability of this proposal.

(b) Briefly discuss how inflation may complicate the analysis of business financial decisions.

(ACCA)

Practical assignment: Engineering Products case study

The following case study brings together many of the issues raised in Part 2 of this book on the analysis of strategic investment decisions. In answering certain parts the student should also read Chapters 6 and 7.

Roger Davis, the newly appointed financial analyst of the Steel Tube division of Engineering Products plc, shut his office door and walked over to his desk. He had just 24 hours to re-examine the accountant's profit projections and come up with a recommendation on the proposed new computer numerically controlled (CNC) milling machine.

At the meeting he had just left, the managing director made it quite clear: 'If the project can't pay for itself in the first three years, it's not worth bothering with.' Davis was unhappy with the accountant's analysis, which showed that the project was a loss maker. But as the MD said, 'Unless you can convince me by this time tomorrow that spending £240,000 on this capital project makes economic sense, you can forget the whole idea.'

His first task was to re-examine the accountant's profitability forecast (Table 5.12) in the light of the following facts that emerged from the meeting:

1 Given the rapid developments in the market, it was unrealistic to assume that the product had more than a four-year life. The machinery would have no other use and could not raise more than £20,000 in scrap metal at the end of the project.
2 The opening stock in Year 1 would be acquired at the same time as the machine. All other stock movement would occur at the year ends.
3 This type of machine was depreciated over six years on a straight-line basis.
4 Within the 'other production expenses' were apportioned fixed overheads equal to 20 per cent of labour costs. As far as could be seen, none of these overheads were incurred as a result of the proposal.
5 The administration charge was an apportionment of central fixed overheads.

Table 5.12 Profit projection for CNC milling machine (£000)

| | Year | | | |
	1	2	3	4
Sales	400	600	800	600
Less costs				
Materials				
Opening stock	40	80	80	60
Purchases	260	300	360	240
Closing stock	(80)	(80)	(60)	–
Cost of sales	220	300	380	300
Labour	80	120	120	80
Other production expenses	80	90	92	100
Depreciation	40	40	40	40
Administrative overhead	54	76	74	74
Interest on loans to finance the project	22	22	22	22
Total cost	496	648	728	616
Profit (loss)	(96)	(48)	72	(16)

Later that day, Davis met the production manager, who explained that if the new machine was installed, it would have sufficient capacity to enable an existing machine to be sold immediately for £20,000 and to create annual cash benefits of £18,000. However, the accountant had told him that, with the machine currently standing in the books at £50,000, the company simply could not afford to write off the asset against this year's slender profits. 'We'd do better to keep it operating for another four years, when its scrap value will produce about £8,000,' he said.

Davis then raised the proposal with the marketing director. It was not long before two new pieces of information emerged:

(a) To stand a realistic chance of hitting the sales forecast for the proposal, marketing would require £40,000 for additional advertising and sales promotion at the start of the project and a further £8,000 a year for the remainder of the project's life. The sales forecast and advertising effort had been devised in consultation with marketing consultants whose bill for £18,000 had just arrived that morning.
(b) The marketing director was very concerned about the impact on other products within the product range. If the investment went ahead, it would lead to a reduction in sales value of a competing product of around £60,000 a year. 'With net profit margins of around 10 per cent and gross margins (after direct costs) of 25 per cent on these sales, this is probably the "kiss of death" for the CNC proposal,' Davis reflected.

The Steel Tube division was a profitable business operating within an attractive market. The investment, which employed new technology, had recently been identified as part of the group's core activities. The chief engineer felt that once they had got to grips with the new technology it should deliver improved product quality, and greater flexibility, enabling shorter production runs and other benefits.

The latest accounts for the division showed a 16 per cent return on assets, but the MD talked about a three-year payback requirement. His phone call to the finance director at head office, to whom this proposal would eventually be sent, was distinctly unhelpful: 'We have, in the past, found that whenever we lay down a hurdle rate for divisional capital projects, it merely encourages unduly optimistic estimates from divisional executives eager to promote their pet proposals. So now we give no guidelines on this matter.'

Davis decided to use 10 per cent as the required rate of return, made up of 6 per cent currently obtainable from risk-free government securities plus a small element to compensate for risk. Davis went home that evening with a very full briefcase and a number of unresolved questions.

1 How much of the information which he had gathered was really relevant to the decision?

2 What was the best approach to assessing the economic worth of the proposal? The company used payback and return on investment, but he felt that discounted cash flow techniques had some merit.

3 Cash was particularly limited this year and acceptance of this project could mean that other projects would have to be deferred. How should this be taken into consideration?

4 How should the strategic factors be assessed?

5 What about tax? Engineering Products plc pays corporation tax at 30 per cent, and annual writing-down allowances of 25 per cent on the reducing balance may be claimed. The existing machine has a nil value for tax purposes and tax is payable in the same year as the cash flows to which it relates.

Required

Prepare the case, with recommendations, to be presented by Davis at tomorrow's meeting. The report should address points 1–5 above.

6

Investment strategy and process

Disneyland Paris celebrates 20th birthday €1.9bn in debt

Twice as many people pass through its gates in search of Mickey Mouse as climb the Eiffel Tower, but Disneyland Paris celebrates its 20th anniversary burdened with vast debts.

Despite charging its 15.7 million annual adult visitors a minimum of £51 per visit, the theme park lost €55.6m (£45m) last year, and its debts are a towering €1.9bn. The debts are so huge that the company's chief executive has admitted it will still be paying them off for the next 12 years. The company's share price has crashed by 50% over the past year to just €4.43. One leading City analyst has even warned that the company's finances are in such a dire state that it will probably never make a profit.

The park is now the most popular tourist destination in Europe with more than double the number of visitors to the Louvre. But the increase in the number of visitors has come at a price. Twenty years ago Robert Fitzpatrick, Walt Disney's then chairman, boasted: 'My biggest fear is that we will be too successful.' But it didn't take long for the fairytale to turn into a financial disaster.

Visitor numbers began to increase and the company recorded its first quarterly profit in 1995. But rumours quickly circulated that the park was on the verge of bankruptcy and Walt Disney, which owns almost 40% of the company, and its banks were forced to bail out the park.

Philippe Gas, the park's sixth CEO, conceded this week that '[Disneyland] didn't work in the early years how we wanted. But now we are at the healthiest situation in our history ... It's been a long way, but now we have a calendar of payment that will see all the debt wiped out by 2024. We no longer need Mommy and Daddy to help us,' he told the AFP news agency.

But the analyst, who declined to be named, said Disneyland Paris 'should have a good outlook because of the anniversary ... [but] my guidance is that it will never make a profit.'

Source: Based on Rupert Neate, Christian Sylt and Caroline Reid, *The Guardian*, 11 April 2012.

Learning objectives

This chapter examines strategic issues in investment and the investment process:

- How strategy shapes investment decisions.
- Evaluating new technology and environmental projects.
- The investment decision and control process.
- Post-audit reviews.

6.1 INTRODUCTION

A company's ability to succeed in highly competitive markets depends to a great extent on its ability to regenerate itself through wealth-creating capital investment decisions compatible with business strategy. Applying capital to long-term capital projects in anticipation of an adequate return – as we saw in the introductory case of Disneyland Paris – is essential for the vitality and well-being of the organisation and the whole economy.

6.2 STRATEGIC CONSIDERATIONS

Where do positive NPV projects come from? By definition, a positive NPV means that a project offers returns superior to those obtainable in the capital market on investments of comparable risk. In the short run, it is quite feasible to find capital projects that do just this, but in a competitive market, it will not be long before other firms make similar investments, thereby ensuring that any superior returns are not perpetuated.

Selecting wealth-creating capital projects is no different from picking undervalued shares on the stock market. Earlier discussion on market efficiency argued that this is possible only if there are capital market imperfections that prevent asset prices reflecting their equilibrium values.

Companies that consistently create projects with high NPVs have developed a sustainable competitive advantage arising from imperfections in the product and factor markets. These imperfections generally take the form of entry barriers that discourage new entrants. Successful investments are therefore investments that help create, preserve or enhance competitive advantage.

Porter (1985) argues that there are really only three coherent strategies for strategic business units:

1 To be the lowest-cost producer.
2 To focus on a niche or segment within the market.
3 To differentiate the product range so that it does not compete directly with lower-cost products.

Investment expenditure that helps achieve the appropriate strategy is likely to generate superior returns. For example, Coca-Cola invests enormous sums into its product differentiation strategy through its brand support.

Capital projects should be viewed not simply in isolation, but within the context of the business, its goals and strategic direction. This approach is often termed **strategic portfolio analysis**.

strategic portfolio analysis
Assessing capital projects within the strategic business context and not simply in financial terms

The attractiveness of investment proposals coming from different sectors of the firm's business portfolio depends not only on the rate of return offered, but also on the strategic importance of the sector. Business strategies are formulated that involve the allocation of resources (capital, labour, plant, marketing support, etc.) to these business units. The allocation may be based on analysis of the market's attractiveness and the firm's competitive strengths, such as the **McKinsey–General Electric portfolio matrix** outlined in Figure 6.1.

McKinsey–General Electric portfolio matrix
An approach for assessing projects within the wider strategic context which focuses on the market attractiveness and business strength of the product and business unit relating to the capital proposal

The attractiveness of the market or industry is indicated by such factors as the size and growth of the market, ease of entry, degree of competition and industry profitability for each strategic business unit. Business strength is indicated by a firm's market share and its growth rate, brand loyalty, profitability, and technological and other comparative advantages. Such analysis leads to three basic strategies:

1 Invest in and strengthen businesses operating in relatively attractive markets. This may mean heavy expenditures on capital equipment, working capital, research and development, brand development and training.

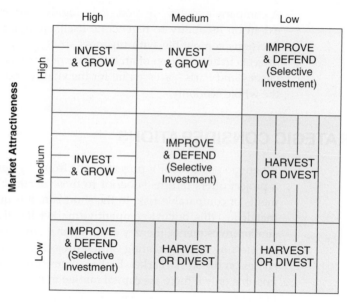

Figure 6.1 McKinsey–GE portfolio matrix

2 Where the market is somewhat less attractive and the business less competitive (the diagonal unshaded boxes), the optimal business strategy is to get the maximum out of existing resources. The financial strategy is therefore to maximise or maintain cash flows, while incurring capital expenditures mainly of a replacement nature. Tight control over costs and management of working capital leads to higher levels of profitability and cash flow.

3 The remaining businesses have little strategic quality and may, in the longer term, be run down or divested unless action can be taken to improve their attractiveness.

Boston Consulting Group approach

An approach for assessing capital proposals based on the market growth and market share of the products relating to the proposal

An alternative is the **Boston Consulting Group approach**, which describes the business portfolio in terms of relative market share and rate of growth (see Figure 6.2). This matrix identifies four product types within which a firm may offer: (1) 'stars' (high market share, high market growth), (2) 'cash cows' (high market share, low market growth), (3) 'question marks' (low market share, high market growth) and (4) 'dogs'

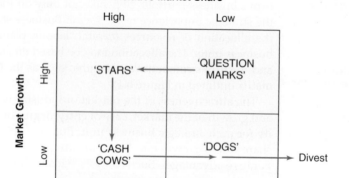

Figure 6.2 Typical progression of product over time

Toyota recalls more than 6.5m cars over steering and seat problems

Toyota is recalling more than 6.5m cars worldwide to fix a variety of problems, including faulty steering wheels and seats. The global recall tally is a huge blow to the world's biggest selling carmaker that has seen its reputation battered by a string of damaging recalls. Since early 2012, the company has recalled around 20m vehicles and sold 18.7m. The latest recall is not even the biggest in a single day: in October 2012 it was forced to call back 7.43m cars, mostly the Yaris and Corolla models to fix faulty window switches.

Toyota's reputation has not fully recovered since a faulty accelerator pedal led to it taking 10m cars off the road

in 2009–10. The company later admitted the faults were caused by over-hasty expansion, and last month was fined $1.2bn (£720m) by US regulators over an investigation into misleading statements the company had made about safety problems with its cars.

'Each announcement puts another dent in Toyota's efforts to recover its reputation and resurrects questions about the impact of its strategy of rapid expansion on previously enviable standards of design and production quality,' said Peter Shervington, an associate specialising in product liability and recall at Eversheds law firm.

Source: Based on *The Guardian,* 9 April 2014.

(low market share, low market growth). The normal progression starts with the potentially successful product ('question mark') and moves in an anticlockwise direction, eventually to be withdrawn (divested).

From this strategic analysis of the firm's business portfolio, we suggest the pattern of resource allocation outlined in Figure 6.3. Businesses offering high growth and the possibility of acquiring market dominance are the main areas of investment ('stars' and 'question marks'). Once such dominance is achieved, the growth rate declines and investment is necessary only to maintain market share. These 'cash cows' become generators of funds for other growth areas. Business areas that have failed to achieve a sizeable share of the market during their growth phase ('dogs') become candidates for divestment and should be evaluated accordingly. Any cash so generated should be applied to high-growth sectors.

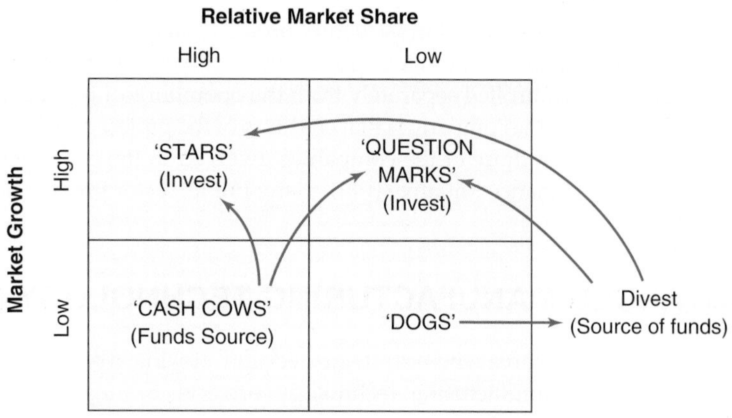

Figure 6.3 Investment strategy

Having developed its investment strategy, management can assess how individual projects fit into the firm's long-term strategic plan. Project appraisal – or, in the case of capital shortage, project ranking – is not only judged according to rates of return. Many companies will reject projects offering high returns because projects fall outside strategic thinking. Ultimately, the capital budget must tie up with corporate strategy so that each project contributes to an element of that strategy.

Shareholder value analysis (SVA) is a valuable planning tool and guide for strategic decision-making. It is basically an extension of the NPV approach where the focus is on business units, strategies and financial goals. A business is viewed as a portfolio of investment projects, but the emphasis is placed on maximising the value of strategic business units, not merely that of the capital projects within them.

Rather than dwell on short-term measures, such as annual earnings per share or return on capital, SVA manages cash flows over time. It is this long-term cash flow that determines the long-term value of the business. The value of adopting a new strategy is assessed in terms of the difference in the value of the business before and after implementation.

Self-assessment activity 6.1

Why is it important to view capital budgeting within a strategic framework?

(Answer in Appendix A at the back of the book)

Changes in strategy thinking

There has been a move away from the corporate planning view of strategy which held sway in the 1960s and 1970s towards a current emphasis on strategy as practice. The corporate planning approach saw strategic planning as a series of logical stages of analysing, planning, implementation and evaluation. The key criticism of this approach was that it failed to recognise that strategies may not always be deliberately conceived, but rather that strategies may emerge unexpectedly.

Hence, writers such as Mintzberg (1987) and Whittington and Cailluet (2008) now wish to emphasise that strategy should be seen as being crafted by managers as they find that it is necessary to respond to uncertain events as they unfold. Grant (2003) indicates that this results in less exhaustive strategic plans with shorter planning time-frames and gives divisional managers, who are under pressure to meet exacting financial targets, independence to self-determine strategies from the bottom up.

■ Project finance

Large-scale infrastructure projects, such as the construction of tunnels, roads and power stations, are often funded through project finance. Here the operation is financed and controlled separately from the operations of the constructor or user. The obvious benefit to the company is that creditors of the project only have claims on the project's cash flows, not those of the companies involved in the construction process. Following the Private Finance Initiative (PFI), many public sector projects have been funded in this manner.

6.3 ADVANCED MANUFACTURING TECHNOLOGY (AMT) INVESTMENT

An area where strategic decision-making is often required is the evaluation of advanced manufacturing technology projects. Strategic investment appraisal links corporate strategy to the costs and benefits associated with AMT and other strategic decisions. Frequently, it is insufficient to consider only financial issues; many of the benefits are less tangible and hard to quantify.

The past 30 years have seen growth in new technology capital projects, creating different challenges for the decision-maker. AMT projects offer a range of less tangible benefits: for example, greater flexibility with reduced 'downtime' on production changeover. Greater flexibility enables businesses to meet the challenges of increasing competition, shorter product life cycles and satisfying customers' specific requirements. AMT offers a flexible manufacturing system (FMS), in which a sequence of production operations are computer-controlled to respond to ever-changing production and design requirements.

AMT terminology

AMT investment helps companies achieve competitive advantage through a number of computer-controlled automated process technologies:

- **Computer-aided design (CAD)** helps the engineer test and modify a design from any viewpoint.

- **Computer-integrated manufacture (CIM)** brings together the manufacturing process and the computer.

- **Computer-numerically controlled (CNC)** machines can be easily reprogrammed to perform different tasks.

- **Flexible manufacturing systems (FMS)** enable the firm to produce a far greater variety of components quickly.

- **Direct numerical control (DNC)** systems connect a number of numerically-controlled machines by computer.

AMT example: Foster Engineering Ltd

Foster Engineering Ltd is considering introducing a flexible manufacturing system (FMS) to modernise production in a department currently using conventional metal-working machinery. The declining market and the awareness that its main competitors have recently introduced new technology have made the need to modernise plant facilities an urgent priority.

An AMT proposal has been put forward, offering an FMS capable of producing the present output. It involves two machining centres with CNC lathes, a conveyor system for transferring components and a computer for scheduling, tooling and overall control. The total investment would cost £2.4 million, half being incurred at the start and the other half after one year, at which point the existing machinery could be sold for £50,000. Any benefit would arise from Year 2 onwards for five years. The two quantified benefits are as follows:

1 A reduction in the number of skilled workers from 50 to 15. The annual cost of a skilled worker is £20,000 (savings of 35 × £20,000 = £700,000 p.a.).
2 Savings in scrap and re-work of £50,000 p.a.

The company requires all projects to offer a positive net present value discounted at 15 per cent.

The accountant produces the following evaluation showing that the FMS proposal has a negative NPV of £159,000 and fails to meet corporate investment criteria:

FMS proposal

Annual benefit		(£000)	
PV at Year 1	£700,000 × PVIFA$_{(15\%, 5 \text{ yrs})}$	2,346	
	£700,000 × 3.352		
PV at Year 0	£2,346 × PVIF$_{(15\%, 1 \text{ yr})}$		2,041
	£2,346 × 0.87		
Initial investment			
Year 0		(£1,200)	
Year 1 (£1,200 − 50) × 0.87		(£1,000)	(2,200)
NPV			(159)

Continued

An incensed production engineer in Foster Engineering, on hearing that the proposal is unacceptable, points to the 'intangible' benefits that the FMS will offer:

- Improved quality leading to a significant, but unknown, reduction in sales returns through faulty workmanship.
- Reduced stock and work-in-progress, enabling improved shopfloor layout, greater space and a lower working capital requirement.
- Lower total manufacturing time, enabling the company to respond more quickly to customer orders and to reduce work-in-progress further.
- Significantly improved machine utilisation rates, although the actual degree of improvement is difficult to quantify.
- Increased capacity with the option to operate unmanned night working.
- Greater flexibility, enabling shorter production runs and faster re-tooling and re-scheduling.

CIM involves the computerisation of functions and their integration into a system that regulates the manufacturing process. It brings together the individual manufacturing techniques referred to earlier under unified computer control.

Many of these benefits could be quantified, at least in part (e.g. the savings in working capital), although the degree of confidence in the underlying assumptions may not be high. But even so, there will still be a large intangible element that cannot be quantified. This has led to the charge that conventional methods of investment appraisal are biased against AMT investments.

Kaplan (1986) raises the question of whether AMT projects must be 'justified by faith alone'. Should managers in Foster Engineering replace the DCF approach with a belief that AMT is the key to the future and that strategic positioning must override economic analysis?

The answer is not to dismiss DCF analysis, but to see it within a wider strategic context. We advocate a three-stage approach to analysing AMT capital projects:

1 Does the project fit well within the company's overall corporate strategy?
2 Does the DCF analysis, based on the quantifiable elements of the decision, justify the investment outlay?
3 Where the net present value calculated in stage 2 is negative, examine the shortfall. Does management believe that the 'value' of the intangible benefits exceeds the shortfall? This last stage is essentially a subjective process whereby managers consider the strategic and operational benefits. No one can put an accurate value on flexibility, for example, but it would be wrong to exclude such a major benefit from consideration in the decision process.

Can firms afford not to invest?

Henry Ford once claimed: 'If you need a new machine and don't buy it, you pay for it without getting it.' The price paid is the loss in competitiveness from not taking advantage of new technology.

In evaluating proposed investments, managers have turned increasingly to sophisticated techniques. Their goal has been greater rationality in making investment decisions, yet their accomplishment has often been quite different – serious under-investment in the capital stock (the productive capacity, technology and worker skills) on which

their companies rest. As a result, they have unintentionally jeopardised their companies' futures.

Ingersoll Milling Machine Company took a strategic view that it needed to invest in the latest technology. Each production department manager annually had to write a justification to keep any machine that was over seven years old. The only generally accepted reason for not replacing equipment was that a new machine did not offer any significant improvements over older models.

6.4 ENVIRONMENTAL ASPECTS OF INVESTMENT

Much like AMT investment, many environmental capital projects have substantial costs or benefits which may not be wholly reflected in conventional net present value analysis. It should be recalled, from Chapter 1, that shareholders are not the only stakeholders in the company and the needs of other stakeholders, including the wider community, should also be incorporated into decisions. Environmental considerations have many dimensions, including economic, political, technological and social.

Pollution issues will be covered by legislation and regulation, but often the directors will want to go beyond the basic statutory requirements. While costs are not difficult to determine, the benefits are harder to quantify. These may take the form of fines and penalties avoided. For example, a greater sense of social responsibility may be costly but could have long-term benefits if the enhanced corporate image results in more business and improved shareholder value.

The steps involved in evaluating projects with environmental implications are:

1 Evaluate the projects using conventional capital appraisal methods.
2 Identify and incorporate statutory environmental costs as part of the evaluation.
3 Assess the costs and benefits of other environmental measures. For example, introducing anti-pollution measures should help reduce compensation claims.
4 Specify the internal controls to be introduced to ensure that pollution, etc. is minimised during construction and implementation.
5 Assess the impact of the decision on shareholder wealth, ethical and social responsibility goals.

Does Shell take the longer view?

The Royal Dutch Shell group operates in 140 countries and made total capital investments of $39bn in 2013. Most of its capital projects have sustainable environmental implications.

Take a look at Shell's annual report (**www.shell.com**) to examine the level of environmental capital investment and provisions for cost of decommissioning and site restoration. What is its policy on environmental investment and sustainable development? To what extent does Shell take a long-term view on investment and consider wider social and environmental aspects?

Table 6.1 presents the results of a survey on the importance of non-financial factors in assessing strategic investment projects. The leading factors are whether the project fits

Table 6.1 The importance of non-financial factors related to strategic investment projects

	Mean score (out of 5)*
Consistency with corporate strategy	4.4
Requirements of customers	4.0
Quality and reliability of outputs	3.7
Keeping up with competition	3.6
Ability to expand in future	3.5
Greater manufacturing flexibility	3.3
Reduced lead times	3.0
Reduced inventory levels	2.9
Experience with new technology	2.7

*5 = maximum importance, 1 = minimal importance
Source: Alkaraan and Northcott (2006).

with corporate strategy and customer requirements. Other important factors relate to quality, competitiveness, flexibility and the ability to expand in the future.

6.5 THE CAPITAL INVESTMENT PROCESS

So far we have focused on investment *appraisal*. Similar emphasis is found in much of the capital budgeting literature, the assumption being that application of theoretically correct methods leads to optimal investment selection and, hence, maximises shareholders' wealth. The decision-maker is viewed as having a passive role, acting more as a technician than as an entrepreneur. Somehow, investment ideas come to the surface; various assumptions and cash flow estimates are made; and risk is incorporated within the discounting formula to produce the project's net present value. If this is positive, the proposal becomes part of the admissible set of investment possibilities. This set is then further refined by the evaluation of mutually exclusive projects and the appraisal of projects under capital rationing, where appropriate.

Inherent in this approach to capital budgeting are the following assumptions, few of which bear much relevance to the world of business:

1 Investment ideas simply emerge and land on the manager's desk.
2 Projects can be viewed in isolation, i.e. projects are not interdependent.
3 Risk can be fully incorporated within the net present value framework.
4 Non-quantifiable or intangible investment considerations are unimportant.
5 Cash flow estimates are free from bias.

Increasingly, it has become apparent that the emphasis on investment appraisal rather than on the whole capital investment process is misplaced and will not necessarily produce the most desirable investment programme. Investment decision-making could be improved significantly if the emphasis were placed on asking the appropriate strategic question rather than on increasing the sophistication of measurement techniques. Managers need to re-evaluate the investment procedures within their organisations, not to determine whether they are aesthetically and theoretically correct, but to determine whether they allow managers to make better decisions.

Capital budgeting may best be understood as a process with a number of distinct stages. Decision-making is an incremental activity, involving many people throughout the organisational hierarchy, over an extended period of time. While senior management may retain final approval, actual decisions are effectively taken much earlier at a lower level, by a process that is still not entirely clear and that is not the same in all organisations.

Figure 6.4 shows the key stages in the capital budgeting process. The primary aim of such a process is to ensure that available capital resources are distributed to wealth-creating capital projects that make the best contribution to corporate goals. A second goal is to see that good investment ideas are not held back and that poor or ill-defined proposals are rejected or further refined. We shall explore the following four stages:

1 Determination of the budget.
2 Search for, and development of, projects.
3 Evaluation and authorisation.
4 Monitoring and control.

■ Determination of the budget

In theory at least, all capital projects could be put to the capital market for funding (individually or collectively as investment programmes), the availability of funds for projects and rate of return required being a function of the market's perception

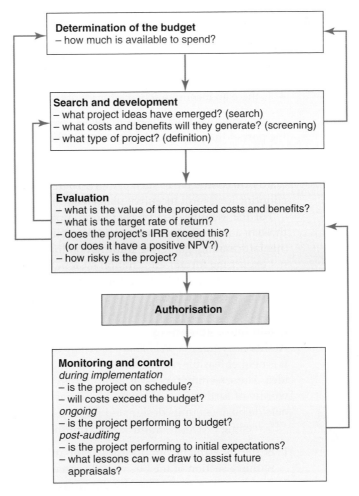

Figure 6.4 A simple capital budgeting system

of the prospective returns and associated risks. In practice, multi-divisional organisations operate an internal capital market in which senior management is better informed than the external capital market to assess capital proposals and allocate scarce resources.

If the investment decision-making body is a sub-unit of a larger group, the budget may be more or less rigidly imposed on it from above. However, for quasi-autonomous centres (divisions of larger groups with capital-raising powers) and/or independent units, the amount to be spent on capital projects is largely under their control, subject, of course, to considerations of corporate control and gearing.

■ Search for, and development of, projects

Economic theory views investment as the interaction of the supply of capital and the flow of investment opportunities. It would be wrong, however, to assume that there is a continuous flow of investment ideas. In general, the earlier an investment opportunity is identified, the greater is the scope for reward.

Possibly the most important role which top management can play in the capital investment process is to cultivate a corporate culture that encourages managers to search for, identify and sponsor investment ideas. Questions to be asked at the identification stage include the following:

1 How are project proposals initiated?
2 At what level are projects typically generated?
3 Is there a formal process for submitting ideas?
4 Is there an incentive scheme for identifying good project ideas?

Generating investment ideas involves considerable effort, time and personal risk on the part of the proposer. Any manager who has experienced the frustration of having an investment proposal dismissed, or an accepted proposal fail, is likely to develop an inbuilt resistance to creating further proposals unless the organisation culture and rewards are conducive to such activity. There is some evidence (Larcker, 1983) that firms adopting long-term incentive plans tend to increase their level of capital investment.

For the identification phase of non-routine capital budgeting decisions, especially those of a more strategic nature, to be productive, managers need to conduct environmental scanning, gathering information that is largely externally oriented. We should not expect the formal information system within most organisations, which is set up to help control short-term performance, to be particularly helpful in identifying non-routine investment ideas.

Preliminary screening

At this early stage, a *preliminary screening* of all investment ideas is usually conducted. It is neither feasible nor desirable to conduct a full-scale evaluation of each investment idea. The screening process is an important means of filtering out projects not thought worthy of further investigation. Ideas may not fit with strategic thinking, or may fall outside business units designated for investment.

Screening proposals address such questions as the following:

1 Is the investment opportunity compatible with corporate strategy? Does it fall within a section of the business designated for growth?
2 Are the resources required by the project available (expertise, finance, etc.)?
3 Is the idea technically feasible?
4 What evidence is there to suggest that it is likely to provide an acceptable return?
5 Are the risks involved acceptable?

As the quality of data used at the screening stage is generally poor, it makes little sense to apply sophisticated financial analysis. Accordingly, the simple payback method is frequently used at this stage because it offers a crude assessment of project profitability and risk.

Project definition

Any investment proposal is vague and shapeless until it has been properly defined. At the definition stage of the capital investment process, detailed specification of the investment proposal involves the collection of data describing its technical and economic characteristics. For each proposal, a number of alternative options should be generated, defined and, subsequently, appraised in order to create the project offering the most attractive financial characteristics.

Even at this early stage, proposals are gaining commitment. The very act of collecting information necessitates communicating with managers who may either lend support, or seek to undermine the proposal. The danger is that, in this process, commitments are accumulated such that investment becomes almost inevitable. The amount of information gathered for evaluation is largely determined by the following:

- The data perceived as desirable to gain a favourable decision.
- The ease and cost of its development.

- The extent to which the proposer will be held responsible for later performance related to the data.

Top management should seek to ensure that the most suitable projects are submitted by managers through establishing mechanisms that induce behaviour congruence. The accounting information system, reward system and capital budgeting procedures should all encourage managers to put forward the proposals that top management is looking for. For many firms, however, the accounting information system and reward mechanism encourage divisional managers to promote their own interests at the expense of those of the organisation, and to emphasise short-term profit performance at the expense of the longer term. Capital budgeting then becomes a 'game', with the accounting and reward systems as its rules. Cash flow estimates are biased to maximise the gains to individuals within such rules.

Self-assessment activity 6.2

Outline the key stages in the capital budgeting process.

(Answer in Appendix A at the back of the book)

Project classification

The information required and method of analysis will vary according to the nature of the project. A suggested investment proposal classification is given below under the headings replacement, cost reduction, expansion or improvement, new product, strategic, and statutory and welfare.

Replacement proposals are justified primarily by the need to replace assets that are nearly exhausted or have excessively high maintenance costs. Little or no improvement may be expected from the replacement, but the expenditure is essential to maintain the existing level of capacity or service (e.g. replacement of vehicles). Engineering analysis plays an important role in these proposals.

Cost reduction proposals (which may also be replacement proposals) are intended to reduce costs through addition of new equipment or modification to existing equipment. Line managers and specialists (such as industrial engineers and work study groups) should conduct a continuous review of production operations for profit improvement opportunities.

Expansion or improvement proposals relate to existing products, and are intended to increase production, service and distribution capacity, to improve product quality, or to maintain and improve the firm's competitive position.

New product proposals refer to all capital expenditures pertaining to the development and implementation of new products.

Strategic proposals are generated at senior management level and involve expenditure in new areas, or where benefits extend beyond the investment itself. A project may appear to offer a negative net present value and yet still create further valuable strategic opportunities. Three examples demonstrate this point:

1 Diversification projects may have the effect of bringing the company into a lower risk category. This is further considered in Chapter 12.
2 A patent may be acquired not for use within the firm, but to prevent its use by competitors.
3 Where information is difficult to obtain, such as in overseas markets, it may make sense to set up a small plant at a loss because it places the firm in a good position to build up information and to be ready for major investment at the appropriate time.

Statutory and welfare proposals do not usually offer an obvious financial return, although they may contribute in other ways, such as enhancing the contentment, and hence productivity, of the labour force. The main consideration is whether standards are met at minimum cost.

Each proposal should be ranked within each category in terms of its effect on profits, its degree of urgency, and whether or not it can be postponed.

It is quite possible that many projects do not fit into any of the above categories and will bypass the standard capital expenditure process. Examples include marketing expenditure, such as investment in brand development and support, and research and development projects. For example, Ericsson, the Swedish company providing telecommunications systems, spends around 25 per cent of its revenues on R&D projects. In such instances, it is important that separate procedures are in place.

■ Evaluation and authorisation

Evaluation

The evaluation phase involves appraisal of the project and decision outcome (accept, reject, request further information, etc.). Project evaluation, in turn, involves the assembly of information (usually in terms of cash flows) and the application of specified investment criteria. Each firm must decide whether to apply rigorous, sophisticated evaluation models, or simpler models that are easier to grasp yet capture many of the important elements in the decision.

The capital appropriation request forms the basis for the final decision to commit financial and other resources to the project. Typical information included in an appropriation request is given below:

1 *Purpose of project* – why it is proposed, and the fit with corporate strategy and goals.
2 *Project classification* – e.g. expansion, replacement, improvement, cost saving, strategic, research and development, safety and health, legal requirements.
3 *Finance requested* – amount and timing, including net working capital, etc.
4 *Operating cash flows* – amount and timing, together with the main assumptions influencing the accuracy of the cash flow estimates.
5 *Attractiveness of the proposal* – expressed by standard appraisal indicators, such as net present value, DCF rate of return and payback period calculated from after-tax cash flows.
6 *Sensitivity of the assumptions* – effect of changes in the main investment inputs. Other approaches to assessing project risk should also be addressed (e.g. best/worst scenarios, estimated range of accuracy of DCF return, discussed in Chapter 7).
7 *Review of alternatives* – why they were rejected and their economic attractiveness.
8 *Implications of not accepting the proposal* – some projects with little economic merit according to the appraisal indicators may be 'essential' to the continuance of a profitable part of the business or to achieving agreed strategy.
9 *Non-financial considerations* – those costs and benefits that cannot be measured.

Following evaluation, larger projects may require consideration at a number of levels in the organisational hierarchy before they are finally approved or rejected. The decision outcome is rarely based wholly on the computed signal derived from financial analysis. Considerable judgement is applied in assessing the reliability of data underlying the appraisal, fit with corporate strategy, and track record of the project sponsor. Careful consideration is required regarding the influence on the investment of such key factors as product markets, the economy, production, finance and people.

Authorisation

Following evaluation, the proposal is transmitted through the various authorisation levels of the organisational hierarchy until it is finally approved or rejected. The driving motive in the decision process is the willingness of the senior manager to make a commitment to sponsor a proposal. This is based not so much on the grounds of the proposal itself as on whether or not it will enhance the manager's reputation and career prospects. Sometimes those involved in the preliminary investigation and appraisal of major projects are promoted into head office decision-making positions in time to support and assist the approval of the same projects!

In larger organisations, the authorisation of major projects is usually a formal endorsement of commitments already given. Complete rejection of proposals is rare, but proposals are, on occasions, referred back. The approval stage appears to have a twofold purpose:

1 *A quality control function.* As long as the proposals have satisfied the requirements of all previous stages, there is no reason for their rejection other than on political grounds. Only where the rest of the investment planning process is inadequate will the approval stage take on greater significance in determining the destiny of projects.
2 *A motivational function.* An investment project and its proposer are largely inseparable. The decision-maker, in effect, forms a judgement simultaneously on both the proposal and the person or team submitting it.

Sometimes the costs associated with rejection of capital projects, in terms of managerial motivation, far exceed the costs associated with accepting a marginally unprofitable project. The degree of commitment, enthusiasm and drive of the management team implementing the project is a major factor in determining the success or failure of marginal projects.

Vodafone: four strategic priorities

Vodafone have set out four key strategic priorities for 2015:

Our strategy adapts to fit to, and shape, a fast-moving environment. But at its heart is our consistent commitment to differentiation through investment in our network and services.

Consumer 2015

A new strategic approach to consumer pricing and bundling in Europe, in order to offer customers greater freedom of usage and at the same time stabilise ARPU (average revenue per user).

Enterprise 2015

We are strengthening our position in enterprise, enhancing our product offering to large and medium-sized business and creating a dedicated enterprise operational structure.

Network 2015

We are focused on supporting high speed data services and delivering a consistently excellent data experience.

Operations 2015

We aim to further simplify our business model both across and within countries.

Source: Vodafone
www.vodafone.com/content/annualreport/annual_report13/strategy/strategy.html

Self-assessment activity 6.3

Read the above article and then access the Vodaphone website to ascertain what major capital investment projects they have undertaken in respect of their strategic priorities.

■ Monitoring and control

The capital budgeting control process can be classified in terms of pre-decision and post-decision controls. Pre-decision controls are mechanisms designed to influence managerial behaviour at an early stage in the investment process. Examples are setting authorisation levels and procedures to be followed, and influencing the proposals submitted by setting goals, hurdle rates and cash limits and identifying strategic areas for growth. Post-decision controls include monitoring and post-audit procedures.

Major investment projects may justify determining the critical path (i.e. a set of linked activities) in the delivery and installation schedule. The critical path is defined as the longest path through a network. Control is established by accounting procedures for recording expenditures. Progress reports usually include actual expenditure; amounts authorised to date; amounts committed against authorisations; amounts authorised but not yet spent; and estimates of further cost to completion.

6.6 POST-AUDITING

post-audit
A re-examination of costs, benefits and forecasts of a project after implementation (usually after one year)

The final stage in the capital budgeting decision-making and control sequence is the post-completion audit. A **post-audit** aims to compare the actual performance of a project after, say, a year's operation with the forecast made at the time of approval, and ideally also with the revised assessment made at the date of commissioning. The aims of the exercise are twofold: first, post-audits may attempt to encourage more thorough and realistic appraisals of future investment projects; and second, they may aim to facilitate major overhauls of ongoing projects, perhaps to alter their strategic focus. These two aims differ in an important respect. The first concerns the overall capital budgeting system, seeking to improve its quality and cohesion. The second concerns the control of existing projects, but with a broader perspective than is normally possible during the regular monitoring procedure when project adjustments are usually of a 'fire-fighting' nature.

Self-assessment activity 6.4

What are the main benefits from post-audits?

(Answer in Appendix A at the back of the book)

■ Problems with post-auditing

There are many problems with post-audits:

1 *The disentanglement problem.* It may be difficult to separate out the relevant costs and benefits specific to a new project from other company activities, especially where facilities are shared and the new project requires an increase in shared overheads. Newly developed techniques of overhead cost allocation (such as Activity-Based Costing) may prove helpful in this respect.

2 *Projects may be unique.* If there is no prospect of repeating a project in the future, there may seem little point in post-auditing, since the lessons learned may not be applicable to any future activity. Nevertheless, useful insights into the capital budgeting system as a whole may be obtained.

3 *Prohibitive cost.* To introduce post-audits may involve interference with present management information systems in order to generate flows of suitable data. Since post-auditing every project may be very resource-intensive, firms tend to be selective in their post-audits.

4 *Biased selection.* By definition, only accepted projects can be post-audited, and often only the underperforming ones are singled out for detailed examination. Because of this biased selection mechanism, the forecasting and evaluation expertise of project analysts may be cast in an unduly bad light – they might have been spot on in evaluating rejected and acceptably performing projects.

5 *Lack of cooperation.* If the post-audit is conducted in too inquisitorial a fashion, project sponsors are likely to offer grudging cooperation to the review team and be reluctant to accept and act upon their findings. The impartiality of the review team is paramount – for example, it would be inviting resentment to draw post-auditors from other parts of the company that may be competitors for scarce capital. Similarly, there are obvious dangers if reviews are undertaken solely by project sponsors. A balanced team of investigators needs to be assembled.

6 *Encourages risk-aversion.* If analysts' predictive and analytical abilities are to be thoroughly scrutinised, they may be inclined to advance only 'safe' projects where little can go awry and where there is less chance of being 'caught out' by events.

7 *Environmental changes.* Some projects can be devastated by largely unpredictable swings in market conditions. This can make the post-audit a complex affair, as the review team is obliged to adjust analysts' forecasts to allow for 'moving of the goalposts'.

■ The conventional wisdom

Studies conducted in North America and the UK have generated a conventional wisdom about corporate post-auditing practices. Its main elements are as follows:

- Few firms post-audit every project, and the selection criterion is usually based on size of outlay.
- The commonest time for a first post-audit is about a year after project commissioning.
- The most effective allocation of post-audit responsibility is to share it between central audit departments and project initiators to minimise conflicts of interest, while using relevant expertise.
- The 'threat' of post-audit is likely to spur the forecaster to greater accuracy, but it can lead to excessive caution, possibly resulting in suppression of potentially worthwhile ventures.

■ When does post-auditing work best?

What guidelines can we offer to managers who wish to introduce post-audit from scratch or to overhaul an existing system? Here are some key points:

1 When introducing and operating a post-audit, emphasise the learning objectives and minimise the likelihood of its being viewed as a 'search for the guilty'.

2 Clearly specify the aims of a post-audit. Is it to be primarily a project control exercise, or does it aim to derive insights into the overall project appraisal system?

3 When introducing post-audits, start the process with a small project to reveal, as economically as possible, the difficulties that need to be overcome in a major post-audit.

4 Include a pre-audit in the project proposal. When the project is submitted for approval, the sponsors should be required to indicate what information would be required to undertake a subsequent post-audit.

SUMMARY

We have examined the strategic framework for investment decisions, paying particular attention to new technology and environmental projects.

The resource allocation process is the main vehicle by which business strategy can be implemented. Investment decisions are not simply the result of applying some evaluation criterion. Investment analysis is essentially a search process: a search for ideas, for information and for decision criteria. The prosperity of a firm depends more on its ability to create profitable investment opportunities than on its ability to appraise them.

Key points

- Investments form part of a wider strategic process and should be assessed both financially and strategically.

- New technology projects are often particularly difficult to evaluate because of the many non-financial values.

- The four main stages in the capital budgeting process are:
  1 Determine the budget.
  2 Search for and develop projects.
  3 Evaluation and authorisation.
  4 Monitoring and control.

  Once a firm commits itself to a particular project, it should regularly and systematically monitor and control the project through its various stages of implementation.

- Post-audit reviews, if properly designed, fulfil a useful role in improving the quality of existing and future investment analysis and provide a means of initiating corrective action for existing projects.

Further reading

Because the business environment has become ever-more challenging, new approaches to thinking about managing projects successfully have been considered. Daniel, Ward and Franken (2011) explain how project portfolio management can help firms when conditions are volatile.

Further reading on AMT investment evaluation is found in Alkaraan and Northcott (2006), Pike *et al.* (1989) and Kaplan (1986). Neale and Buckley (1992) consider the practice of post-auditing, while Butler *et al.* (1993) examine strategic investment decisions. Grant (2003) and Whittington and Cailluet (2008) consider strategic planning and investment.

QUESTIONS

Questions with a coloured number have solutions in Appendix B on page 783.

1 'Capital budgeting is simply a matter of selecting the right decision rule.' How true is this statement?

2 What are the aims of post-audits?

3 AMT plc is increasing the level of automation of a production line dedicated to a single product. The options available are total automation or partial automation. The company works on a planning horizon of five years and either option will produce the 10,000 units which can be sold annually.

Total automation will involve a total capital cost of £1 million. Material costs will be £12 per unit and labour and variable overheads will be £18 per unit with this method.

Partial automation will result in higher material wastage and an average cost of £14 per unit. Labour and variable overhead are expected to cost £41 per unit. The capital cost of this alternative is £250,000.

The products sell for £75 each, whichever method of production is adopted. The scrap value of the automated production line, in five years' time, will be £100,000, while the line which is partially automated will be worthless. The management uses straight-line depreciation and the required rate of return on capital investment is 16 per cent p.a. Depreciation is considered to be the only incremental fixed cost.

In analysing investment opportunities of this type the company calculates the average total cost per unit, annual net profit, the break-even volume per year and the discounted net present value.

Required
(a) Determine the figures which would be circulated to the management of AMT plc in order to assist their investment analysis.
(b) Comment on the figures produced and make a recommendation with any qualifications you think appropriate.

(Certified Diploma)

4 Bowers Holdings plc has recently acquired a controlling interest in Shaldon Engineering plc, which produces high-quality machine tools for the European market. Following this acquisition, the internal audit department of Bowers Holdings plc examined the financial management systems of the newly acquired company and produced a report that was critical of its investment appraisal procedures.

The report summary stated:

Overall, investment appraisal procedures in Shaldon Engineering plc are very weak. Evaluation of capital projects is not undertaken in a systematic manner and post-decision controls relating to capital projects are virtually non-existent.

Required
Prepare a report for the directors of Shaldon Engineering plc, stating what you consider to be the major characteristics of a system for evaluating, monitoring and controlling capital expenditure projects.

(Certified Diploma)

What procedures should a business adopt for approving and reviewing large capital expenditure projects?

Practical assignment

Back in 1989, a *Harvard Business Review* article (Sept.–Oct. 1989) asked 'Must finance and strategy clash?' (Barwise, Marsh and Wensley). To what extent are the two disciplines difficult to reconcile?

Part III

VALUE, RISK AND THE REQUIRED RETURN

The preceding analysis of investment decisions has implied that future returns from investment can be forecast with certainty. Clearly, this is unlikely in practice. In Part III we examine the impact of uncertainty on the investment decision, the various approaches available to decision-makers to cope with this problem, and the implications for valuation of assets and companies.

In Chapter 7, we discuss a number of methods that may assist the decision-maker when looking at the risky investment project in isolation. This includes an examination of the contribution to project appraisal under risk and uncertainty promised by the field of options theory. In Chapter 8, we look at how more desirable combinations of risk and return can be achieved by forming a portfolio of investment activities. In Chapter 9, we examine the contribution to risk analysis of the Capital Asset Pricing Model, which offers a guide to setting the premium required for risk. The earlier study of how capital markets behave is particularly important here. Chapter 9 is highly important because it links the behaviour of individual investors, buying and selling securities, to the behaviour of the capital investment decision-maker. This focus is further developed in Chapter 10, which discusses how to alter the discount rate when faced by projects of degrees of risk that differ from the company's existing activities. In Chapter 11, many of the concepts of risk and return are brought together in the examination of various approaches to company, or enterprise, value, and equity, or owners', value. Finally, in Chapter 12 a detailed discussion of options and option pricing is provided.

7

Analysing investment risk

Football megadeals – risky investments

Even by football's profligate standards, this has been a summer of frenzied transfer megadeals to defy economic reality and plain common sense. Real Madrid are poised to shatter the world transfer record with the purchase of Tottenham Hotspur's Gareth Bale for about €100m. Premier League clubs' spending is storming past the 2008 record of £500m. Players are being bought simply to stop them from joining rival clubs.

This was meant to be the start of a new era of good housekeeping in football. Financial controls introduced by Uefa and the Premier League are meant to cut debt by forcing clubs to spend only what they earn. Football and prudence are awkward teammates. Debt, bankruptcy and liquidation can and do befall clubs, portending dire warnings about the game's financial future.

Real Madrid's Florentino Perez believes that €100m represents good value for a player like the 24-year-old Bale, despite his comparatively limited experience.

According to Pedro Garcia of the Universitat Internacional de Catalunya, the signing is in keeping with Mr Perez's business model of expanding Real Madrid's global media value. 'Hiring the intangible talent of football players is, of course, a risky investment,' he said.

Last season, the 20 Premier League clubs shared £1.06bn in broadcast income, with champions Manchester United picking up £60.8m. This season, the first of the new three-year deal, clubs can expect to share £1.6bn, with the winner's slice hitting £100m. All this leads wealthy club owners to abandon the path of moderation they promised to pursue. Manchester City, owned by Sheikh Mansour bin Zayed bin Sultan al-Nahyan of the Abu Dhabi royal family, have spent almost £100m, while Roman Abramovich, Chelsea's Russian owner, has paid out £65m.

Source: Based on Roger Blitz, *Financial Times,* 31 August 2013, p. 7.

Learning objectives

The aim of this chapter is to enable the reader:

- To understand how uncertainty affects investment decisions.
- To explore managers' risk attitudes.
- To appreciate the levels at which risk can be viewed.
- To be able to measure the expected NPV and its variability.
- To appreciate the main risk-handling techniques and apply them to capital budgeting problems.
- To understand the various forms of real options that can further enhance a project's value.

7.1 INTRODUCTION

The football industry is one of many cases where investment decisions turn out to be far riskier than originally envisaged, as expensive summer 2013 aquisitions by clubs such as Liverpool and Tottenham have demonstrated. The finance director of a major UK manufacturer for the motor industry remarked, 'We know that, on average, one in five large capital projects flops. The problem is: we have no idea beforehand which one!'

Stepping into the unknown – which is what investment decision-making effectively is – means that mistakes will surely occur. Only about 50 per cent of small businesses are still trading three years after start-up. Sir Richard Branson, head of Virgin Atlantic, once said, 'the safest way to become a millionaire is to start as a billionaire and invest in the airline industry'!

This does not mean that managers can do nothing about project failures. In this and subsequent chapters, we examine how project risk is assessed and controlled. The various forms of risk are defined and the main statistical methods for measuring project risk within single-period and multi-period time-spans are described. A variety of risk analysis techniques will then be discussed. These fall conveniently into methods intended to describe risk and methods incorporating project riskiness within the net present value formula. The chapter concludes by examining the various forms of investment options and how they can add value to a project.

■ Defining terms

At the outset, we need to clarify our terms:

- *Certainty*. Perfect certainty arises when expectations are single-valued: that is, a particular outcome will arise rather than a range of outcomes. Is there such a thing as an investment with certain payoffs? Probably not, but some investments come fairly close. For example, an investment in three-month Treasury Bills will, subject to the Bank of England keeping its promise, provide a precise return on redemption.
- *Risk and uncertainty*. Although used interchangeably in everyday parlance, these terms are not quite the same. Risk refers to the set of unique consequences for a given decision that can be assigned probabilities, while uncertainty implies that it is not fully possible to identify outcomes or to assign probabilities. Perhaps the worst cases of uncertainty are the 'unknown unknowns' – outcomes from events that we did not even consider.

The purest example of risk is the 50 per cent chance of obtaining a 'head' from tossing a coin. For most investment decisions, however, empirical experience is hard to find. Managers are forced to estimate probabilities where objective statistical evidence is not available. Nevertheless, a manager with little prior experience of launching a particular product in a new market can still subjectively assess the risks involved based on the information he or she has. Because subjective probabilities may be applied to investment decisions in a manner similar to objective probabilities, the distinction between risk and uncertainty is not critical in practice, and the two terms are often used synonymously.

Investment decisions are only as good as the information upon which they rest. Relevant and useful information is central in projecting the degree of risk surrounding future economic events and in selecting the best investment option.

Self-assessment activity 7.1

Why is risk assessment important in making capital investment decisions?

(Answer in Appendix A at the back of the book)

7.2 EXPECTED NET PRESENT VALUE (ENPV): BETTERWAY PLC

To what extent is the net present value criterion relevant in the selection of risky investments? Consider the case of Betterway plc, contemplating three options with very different degrees of risk. The distribution of possible outcomes for these options is given in Table 7.1. Notice that A's cash flow is totally certain.

Table 7.1 Betterway plc: expected net present values

Investment	NPV outcomes (£)		Probability		Weighted outcomes (£)
A	9,000	×	1	=	9,000
B	−10,000	×	0.2	=	−2,000
	10,000	×	0.5	=	5,000
	20,000	×	0.3	=	6,000
			1.0	ENPV =	9,000
C	−55,000	×	0.2	=	−11,000
	10,000	×	0.5	=	5,000
	50,000	×	0.3	=	15,000
			1.0	ENPV =	9,000

Clearly, while the NPV criterion is appropriate for investment option A, where the cash flows are certain, it is no longer appropriate for the risky investment options B and C, each with three possible outcomes. The whole range of possible outcomes may be considered by obtaining the **expected net present value (ENPV)**, which is the mean of the NPV distribution when weighted by the probabilities of occurrence. The ENPV is given by the equation:

expected net present value (ENPV)
The average of the range of possible NPVs weighted by their probability of occurrence

$$\overline{X} = \sum_{i=1}^{N} p_i X_i$$

where $\overline{X}$ is the expected value of event X, X_i is the possible outcome i from event X, p_i is the probability of outcome i occurring and N is the number of possible outcomes.

The NPV rule may then be applied by selecting projects offering the highest expected net present value. In our example, all three options offer the same expected NPV of £9,000. Should the management of Betterway view all three as equally attractive? The answer to this question lies in their attitudes towards risk, for while the *expected* outcomes are the same, the *possible* outcomes vary considerably. Thus, although the expected NPV criterion provides a single measure of profitability, which may be applied to risky investments, it does not, by itself, provide an acceptable decision criterion.

7.3 ATTITUDES TO RISK

Business managers prefer less risk to more risk for a given return. In other words, they are *risk-averse*. In general, a business manager derives less utility, or satisfaction, from gaining an additional £1,000 than he or she forgoes in losing £1,000. This is based on the concept of diminishing marginal utility, which holds that, as wealth increases, marginal utility declines at an increasing rate. Thus the utility function for risk-averse managers is concave, as shown in Figure 7.1. As long as the utility function of the decision-maker can be specified, this approach may be applied in reaching investment decisions.

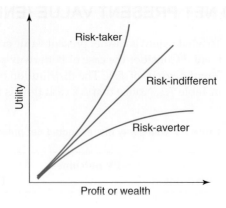

Figure 7.1 Risk profiles

Example: Carefree plc's utility function

Mike Cool, the managing director of Carefree plc, a business with a current market value of £30 million, has an opportunity to relocate its premises. It is estimated that there is a 50 per cent probability of increasing its value by £12 million and a similar probability that its value will fall by £10 million. The owner's utility function is outlined in Figure 7.2. The concave slope shows that the owner is risk-averse. The gain in utility (ΔU_F) as a result of the favourable outcome of £42 million is less than the fall in utility (ΔU_A) resulting from the adverse outcome of only £20 million.

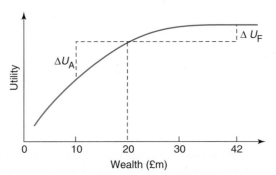

Figure 7.2 Risk-averse investor's utility function

The conclusion is that, although the investment proposal offers £1 million expected additional wealth (i.e. [0.5 × £12m] + [0.5 × −£10m]), the project should not be undertaken because total expected utility would fall if the factory were relocated.

While decision-making based upon the expected utility criterion is conceptually sound, it has serious practical drawbacks. Mike Cool may recognise that he is risk-averse, but is unable to define, with any degree of accuracy, the shape of his utility function. This becomes even more complicated in organisations where ownership and management are separated, as is the case for most large companies. Here, the agency problem discussed in Chapter 1 arises. Thus, while utility analysis provides a useful insight into the problem of risk, it does not provide us with operational decision rules.

We all lose if failure is punished too harshly

I suppose we are all fascinated by entrepreneurs going broke. Perhaps it is envy at work, possibly morbid curiosity, in some cases a desire to see justice served – or is it simply that such tales are full of human drama?

I would like to believe that educated citizens know such speculators are a vital element in the capitalist system. Without the risk-takers, innovation would be stunted, job-creation inhibited, tax proceeds reduced and society generally poorer. But often there is a fine line between winning and losing in business. And systems that punish failure too harshly discourage those who would seek opportunities – thereby making everyone a loser.

As a case study, Steve Oliver is the founder of MusicMagpie. His company is an online retailer of second-hand CDs, DVDs and computer games with almost £100m in revenue. That achievement was built using experience gained from a previous flop – Music Zone, that went into administration in 2007. If financiers, suppliers and other stakeholders had demonised him, his recent comeback would not have happened.

Whether in energy exploration or drug discovery, there will be more defeats than victories. But as Winston Churchill said: 'Success is not final, failure is not fatal. It is the courage to continue that counts.'

Source: Based on Luke Johnson, *Financial Times*, 13 November 2013, p. 14.

7.4 THE MANY TYPES OF RISK

Risk may be classified into a number of types. A clear understanding of the different forms of risk is useful in the evaluation and monitoring of capital projects:

operating gearing
The proportion of fixed costs in the firm's operating cost structure

1 *Business risk* – the variability in operating cash flows or profits before interest. A firm's business risk depends, in large measure, on the underlying economic environment within which it operates. But variability in operating cash flows can be heavily affected by the cost structure of the business, and hence its **operating gearing**. A company's break-even point is reached when sales revenues match total costs. These costs consist of fixed costs – that is, costs that do not vary much with the level of sales – and variable costs. The decision to become more capital-intensive generally leads to an increase in the proportion of fixed costs in the cost structure. This increase in operating gearing leads to greater variability in operating earnings.

financial gearing
Includes both capital gearing and income gearing

2 *Financial risk* – the risk, over and above business risk, that results from the use of debt capital. **Financial gearing** is increased by issuing more debt, thereby incurring more fixed-interest charges and increasing the variability in net earnings. Financial risk is considered more fully in later chapters.

relevant risk
The component of total risk taken into account by the stock market when assessing the appropriate risk premium for determining capital asset values

3 *Portfolio or market risk* – the variability in shareholders' returns. Investors can significantly reduce their variability in earnings by holding carefully selected investment portfolios. This is sometimes called **'relevant' risk**, because only this element of risk should be considered by a well-diversified shareholder. Chapters 8 and 9 examine such risk in greater depth.

Project risk can be viewed and defined in three different ways: (1) in isolation, (2) in terms of its impact on the business, and (3) in terms of its impact on shareholders' investment portfolios.

In this chapter, we assess project risk in isolation before moving on to estimate its impact on investors' portfolios (i.e. market risk) in Chapter 9.

Operating gearing example: Hifix and Lofix

Hifix and Lofix are two companies identical in every respect except cost structure. While Lofix pays its workforce on an output-related basis, Hifix operates a flat-rate wage system. The sales, costs and profits for the two companies are given under two

Continued

Table 7.2 Effects of cost structure on profits (£000)

	Hifix		Lofix	
	Normal	**Recession**	**Normal**	**Recession**
Sales	200	120	200	120
Variable costs	−100	−60	−160	−96
Fixed costs	−80	−80	−20	−20
Profit/loss	20	−20	20	4
Change in sales		−40%		−40%
Change in profits		−200%		−80%

economic states, normal and recession, in Table 7.2. While both companies perform equally well under normal trading conditions, Hifix, with its heavier fixed cost element, is more vulnerable to economic downturns. This can be measured by calculating the degree of operating gearing:

$$\text{Operating gearing} = \frac{\text{percentage change in profits}}{\text{percentage change in sales}}$$

$$\text{For Hifix} = \frac{-200\%}{-40\%} = 5$$

$$\text{For Lofix} = \frac{-80\%}{-40\%} = 2$$

The degree of operating gearing is far greater for the firm with high fixed costs than for the firm with low fixed costs.

Self-assessment activity 7.2

Which type of risk do the following describe?

1 Risks associated with increasing the firm's level of borrowing.
2 The variability in the firm's operating profits.
3 Variability in the cash flows of a proposed capital investment.
4 Variability in shareholders' returns.

(Answer in Appendix A at the back of the book)

7.5 MEASUREMENT OF RISK

A well-known politician (not named to protect the guilty) once proclaimed, 'Forecasting is very important – particularly when it involves the future!' Estimating the probabilities of uncertain forecast outcomes is difficult. But with the little knowledge the manager may have concerning the future, and by applying past experience backed by historical analysis of a project and its setting, he or she may be able to construct a probability distribution of a project's cash outcomes. This can be used to measure the risks surrounding project cash flows in a variety of ways. If we assume that the range of possible outcomes from a decision is distributed normally around the expected value, risk-averse investors can assess project risk using expected value and standard deviation. We shall consider three statistical

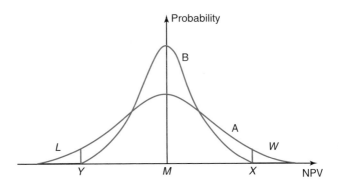

Figure 7.3 **Variability of project returns**

measures: the standard deviation, semi-variance and coefficient of variation for single-period cash flows.

Measuring risk for single-period cash flows: Snowglo plc

Standard deviation

We have seen that expected value overlooks important information on the dispersion (risk) of the outcomes. We also know that different people behave differently in risky situations. Figure 7.3 shows the NPV distributions for projects A and B. Both projects have the same expected NPV, indicated by M, but project A has greater dispersion. The risk-averse manager in Snowglo will choose B since he or she wants to minimise risk. The risk-taker will choose A because the NPV of project A has a chance (W) of being higher than X (which project B cannot offer), but also a chance (L) of being lower than Y. Hereafter, we make the reasonable assumption that most people are risk-averse, an assumption which is borne out by intuition, experience and empirical evidence.

The standard deviation is a measure of the dispersion of possible outcomes; the wider the dispersion, the higher the standard deviation.

The expected value, denoted by $\overline{X}$, is given by the equation:

$$\overline{X} = \sum_{i=1}^{N} p_i X_i$$

and the standard deviation of the cash flows by:

$$\sigma = \sqrt{\sum_{i=1}^{N} p_i (X_i - \overline{X})^2}$$

Table 7.3 shows the information on two projects for Snowglo plc.

Table 7.3 **Snowglo plc project data**

State of economy	Probability of outcome	Cash flow (£)	
		A	**B**
Strong	0.2	700	550
Normal	0.5	400	400
Weak	0.3	200	300

Table 7.4 Project risk for Snowglo plc

Economic state	Probability (a)	Outcome (b)	Expected value $(c = a \times b)$	Deviation $(d = b - \overline{X})$	Squared deviation $(e = d^2)$	Variance $(f = a \times e)$
Project A						
Strong	0.2	700	140	300	90,000	18,000
Normal	0.5	400	200	0	0	0
Weak	0.3	200	60	−200	40,000	12,000
			$\overline{X}_A = 400$		Variance $= \sigma_A^2$	$= 30,000$
					Standard deviation $= \sigma_A$	$= 173.2$
Project B						
Strong	0.2	550	110	150	22,500	4,500
Normal	0.5	400	200	0	0	0
Weak	0.3	300	90	−100	10,000	3,000
			$\overline{X}_B = 400$		Variance $= \sigma_B^2$	$= 7,500$
					Standard deviation $= \sigma_B$	$= 86.6$

Alternatively:

$$\overline{X}_A = 700(0.2) + 400(0.5) + 200(0.3) = 400$$

$$\sigma_A = \sqrt{[0.2(700 - 400)^2 + 0.5(400 - 400)^2 + 0.3(200 - 400)^2]}$$
$$= 173.2$$

$$\overline{X}_A = 550(0.2) + 400(0.5) + 300(0.3) = 400$$

$$\sigma_B = \sqrt{[0.2(550 - 400)^2 + 0.5(400 - 400)^2 + 0.3(300 - 400)^2]}$$
$$= 86.6$$

Table 7.4 provides the workings for projects A and B.

Applying the formulae, we obtain an expected cash flow of £400 for both project A and project B. If the decision-maker had a neutral risk attitude, he or she would view the two projects equally favourably. But as the decision-maker is likely to be risk-averse, it is appropriate to examine the standard deviations of the two probability distributions. Here we see that project A, with a standard deviation twice that of project B, is more risky and hence less attractive. This could have been deduced simply by observing the distribution of outcomes and noting that the same probabilities apply to both projects. But observation cannot always tell us by how much one project is riskier than another.

Semi-variance

While deviation above the mean may be viewed favourably by managers, it is 'downside risk' (i.e. deviations below expected outcomes) that is mainly considered in the decision process. Downside risk is best measured by the semi-variance, a special case of the variance, given by the formula:

$$SV_i = \sum_{j=1}^{K} p_j(X_j - \overline{X})^2$$

where SV_i is the semi-variance of decision i, j is each outcome value less than the expected value, and K is the number of outcomes that are less than the expected value.

Applying the semi-variance to the example in Table 7.4, the downside risk relates exclusively to the 'weak' state of the economy:

$$SV_A = 0.3 (200 - 400)^2 = £12,000$$
$$SV_B = 0.3 (300 - 400)^2 = £3,000$$

Once again, project B is seen to have a much lower degree of risk. In both cases, the semi-variance accounts for 40 per cent of the project variance.

Coefficient of variation (CV)

Where projects differ in scale, a more valid comparison is found by applying a relative risk measure such as the coefficient of variation. The lower the CV, the lower the relative degree of risk. This is calculated by dividing the standard deviation by the expected value of net cash flows, as in the expression:

$$CV = \sigma / \overline{X}$$

The Snowglo example (Table 7.4) gives the following coefficients:

	Standard deviation (1)	Expected value (2)	Coefficient of variation (1 ÷ 2)
Project A	£173.2	£400	0.43
Project B	£86.6	£400	0.22

Both projects have the same expected value, but project B has a significantly lower degree of risk. Next, we consider the situation where the two projects under review are different in scale:

	Standard deviation		Expected value		Coefficient of variation
Project F	£1,000	÷	£10,000	=	0.10
Project G	£2,000	÷	£40,000	=	0.05

Although the absolute measure of dispersion (the standard deviation) is greater for project G, few people in business would regard it as more risky than project F because of the significant difference in the expected values of the two investments. The coefficient of variation reveals that G actually offers a lower amount of risk per £1 of expected value.

Self-assessment activity 7.3

Project X has an expected return of £2,000 and a standard deviation of £400. Project Y has an expected return of £1,000 and a standard deviation of £400. Which project is more risky?

(Answer in Appendix A at the back of the book)

Mean–variance rule

Given the expected return and the measure of dispersion (variance or standard deviation), we can formulate the **mean–variance rule**. This states that one project will be preferred to another if either of the following holds:

1 Its expected return is *higher* and the variance is *equal* to or *less* than that of the other project.
2 Its expected return *exceeds* or is *equal* to the expected return of the other project and the variance is *lower*.

This is illustrated by the mean–variance analysis depicted in Figure 7.4. Projects A and D are preferable to projects C and B respectively because they offer a higher return for the same degree of risk. In addition, A is preferable to B because for the same expected return, it incurs lower risk. These choices are applicable to all risk-averse managers regardless of their particular utility functions. However, it is not possible to say whether Project D (high risk – high return) is superior to Project A (lower risk – lower return). This will depend on the preferences of the management team. This important issue will be discussed in Chapters 8 and 9.

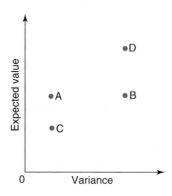

Figure 7.4 Mean–variance analysis

So far, our analysis of risk has assumed single-period investments. We have conveniently ignored the fact that, typically, investments are multi-period. The analysis of project risk where there are multi-period cash flows is discussed in the appendix to this chapter.

Self-assessment activity 7.4

What do you understand by the following?

(a) risk
(b) uncertainty
(c) risk-aversion
(d) expected value
(e) standard deviation
(f) semi-variance
(g) mean–variance rule

(Answer in Appendix A at the back of the book)

■ Risk-handling methods

There are two broad approaches to handling risk in the investment decision process. The first attempts to *describe* the riskiness of a given project, using various applications of probability analysis or some simple method. The second aims to *incorporate* the investor's perception of project riskiness within the NPV formula.

We turn first to the various techniques available to help describe investment risk.

Airline profits threatened by volcanic ash

The success of investment projects in the airline sector in 2010 was affected by a risk that few had ever considered – volcanic ash. This is a good example of those 'unknown unknowns' which, like a volcano, can erupt and seriously damage otherwise good projects. When the Eyjafjallajokull volcano in Iceland erupted, its plume of ash meant that all planes in Europe were grounded. When the volcano last erupted in 1821 it spewed ash into the atmosphere

for two years. How many tour operators and airlines today could survive large-scale flight cancellations over such a sustained period? The International Air Transport Association estimated the cost to the industry in April 2010 alone as $1.7 billion.

Undoubtedly, aerospace engine developers will be considering new capital projects which can help reduce the risk from volcanic ash to acceptable levels.

7.6 RISK DESCRIPTION TECHNIQUES

■ Sensitivity analysis

sensitivity analysis
Analysis of the impact of changes in assumptions on investment returns

In principle, **sensitivity analysis** is a very simple technique, used to isolate and assess the potential impact of risk on a project's value. It aims not to quantify risk, but to identify the impact on NPV of changes to key assumptions. Sensitivity analysis provides the decision-maker with answers to a whole range of 'what if' questions. For example, what is the NPV if selling price falls by 10 per cent? What is the IRR if the project's life is only three years, not five years as expected? What is the level of sales revenue required to break even in net present value terms?

Sensitivity graphs permit the plotting of net present values (or IRRs) against the percentage deviation from the expected value of the factor under investigation. The sensitivity graph in Figure 7.5 depicts the potential impact of deviations from the expected values of a project's variables on NPV. When everything is unchanged, the NPV is £2,000. However, NPV becomes zero when market size decreases by 20 per cent or price decreases by 5 per cent. This shows that NPV is very sensitive to price changes. Similarly, a 10 per cent increase in the capital cost will bring the NPV down to zero, while the discount rate must increase to 25 per cent in order to render the project uneconomic. Therefore, the project is more sensitive to capital investment changes than to variations in the discount rate. The sensitivity of NPV to each factor is reflected by the slope of the sensitivity line – the steeper the line, the greater the impact on NPV of changes in the specified variable.

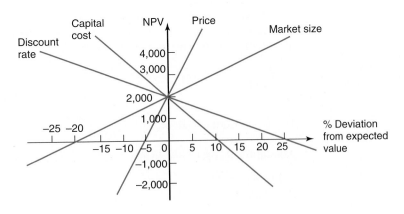

Figure 7.5 Sensitivity graph

Sensitivity analysis is widely used because of its simplicity and ability to focus on particular estimates. It can identify the critical factors that have greatest impact on a project's profitability. It does not, however, actually *evaluate* risk; the decision-maker must still assess the likelihood of occurrence for these deviations from expected values.

Break-even sensitivity analysis: UMK plc

The accountant of UMK plc has put together the cash flow forecasts for a new product with a four-year life, involving capital investment of £200,000. It produces a net present value, at a 10 per cent discount rate, of £40,920. His basic analysis is given in Table 7.5. Which factors are most critical to the decision?

Table 7.5 UMK cost structure

Unit data	£	£
Selling price		20
Less: Materials	(6)	
Labour	(5)	
Variable costs	(1)	
		(12)
Contribution		8
Annual sales (units)	12,000	
Total contribution		96,000
Less: Additional fixed costs		(20,000)
Annual net cash flow		76,000
Present value (4 years at 10%)		
76,000 × 3.17		240,920
Less: Capital outlay		(200,000)
Net present value		40,920

Investment outlay

This can rise by up to £40,920 (assuming all other estimates remain unchanged) before the decision advice alters. This is a percentage increase of:

$$\frac{£40,920}{£200,000} \times 100 = 20.5\%$$

Annual cash receipts

The break-even position is reached when annual cash receipts multiplied by the annuity factor equal the investment outlay. The break-even cash flow is therefore the investment outlay divided by the annuity factor:

$$\frac{£200,000}{3.17} = £63,091$$

This is a percentage fall of $\frac{£76,000 - £63,091}{£76,000} = 17.0\%$

Annual fixed costs could increase by the same absolute amount of £12,909, or

$$\frac{£12,909}{£20,000} \times 100 = 64.5\%$$

Annual sales volume: the break-even annual contribution is £63,091 + £20,000 = £83,091. Sales volume required to break even is £83,091/£8 = 10,386, which is a percentage decline of:

$$\frac{12,000 - 10,386}{12,000} \times 100 = 13.5\%$$

Selling price can fall by:

$$\frac{£96,000 - £83,091}{12,000} = £1.07 \text{ per unit}$$

a decline of $\frac{£1.07}{£20} \times 100 = 5.4\%$

Variable costs per unit can rise by a similar amount:

$$\frac{£1.07}{£12} \times 100 = 8.9\%$$

Discount rate

The break-even annuity factor is £200,000/£76,000 = 2.63. Reference to the present value annuity tables for four years shows that 2.63 corresponds to an IRR of 19 per cent. The error in cost of capital calculation could be as much as nine percentage points before it affects the decision advice.

Sensitivity analysis, as applied in the above example, discloses that selling price and variable costs are the two most critical variables in the investment decision. The decision-maker must then determine (subjectively or objectively) the probabilities of such changes occurring, and whether he or she is prepared to accept the risks.

■ Scenario analysis and stress testing

Sensitivity analysis considers the effects of changes in key variables only one at a time. It does not ask the question: 'How bad could the project look?' Enthusiastic managers can sometimes get carried away with the most likely outcomes and forget just what might happen if critical assumptions – such as the state of the economy or competitors' reactions – are unrealistic. Scenario analysis seeks to establish 'worst' and 'best' scenarios, so that the whole range of possible outcomes can be considered. It encourages 'contingent thinking', describing the future by a collection of possible eventualities.

Shell was an early adopter of scenario analysis in the 1970s and continues to use this approach as the company explains below (see box).

Stress testing is closely related to scenario analysis and, usually, involves assessing how resilient a company is to severe or crisis events. The term is now closely associated with the banking sector where regulators, governments and other stakeholders are very concerned to evaluate whether a bank has adequate capital should another financial crisis occur.

■ Simulation analysis

Monte Carlo simulation
Method for calculating the probability distribution of possible outcomes

An extension of scenario analysis is simulation analysis. **Monte Carlo simulation** is an operations research technique with a variety of business applications. The computer generates hundreds of possible combinations of variables according to a pre-specified probability distribution. Each scenario gives rise to an NPV outcome which, along with other NPVs, produces a probability distribution of outcomes.

Scenario analysis at Shell

Shell has been developing scenarios to explore the future since the early 1970s. Scenarios are stories that consider 'what if?' questions. Whereas forecasts focus on probabilities, scenarios consider a range of plausible futures and how these could emerge from the realities of today. They recognise that people hold beliefs and make choices that lead to outcomes. Our scenarios team considers changes such as in the global economic environment, geopolitics, resource stresses such as water, greenhouse gases, and energy supply and demand to help business leaders make better decisions.

Scenarios help decision makers reconcile apparent contradictions or uncertainties, such as how political change in one region impacts global society. They also have the potential to improve awareness around issues that could become increasingly important to society, such as increased urbanisation, greater connectivity or loss of trust in institutions.

By exploring plausible, as well as predictable outcomes, scenarios challenge conventional wisdom. Organisations using scenarios find it easier to recognise impending disruptions in their own operating environment, such as political changes, demographic shifts or recessions. They also increase their resilience to sudden changes caused by unexpected crises like natural disasters or armed conflicts.

In an industry often defined by uncertainty and volatility, Shell is stronger thanks to the forward planning capacity that scenarios bring.

Source: www.shell.com

One of the first writers to apply the simulation approach to risky investments was Hertz (1964), who described the approach adopted by his firm in evaluating a major expansion of the processing plant of an industrial chemical producer. This involved constructing a mathematical model that captured the essential characteristics of the investment proposal throughout its life as it encountered random events.

A simulation model might consider the following variables, which are subject to random variation.

Market factors	Investment factors	Cost factors
Market size	Investment outlay	Variable costs
Market growth rate	Project life	Fixed costs
Selling price of product	Residual value	
Market share captured by the firm		

Comparison is then possible between mutually exclusive projects whose NPV probability distributions have been calculated in this manner (Figure 7.6). It will be observed that project A, with a higher expected NPV and lower risk, is preferable to project B.

In practice, few companies use this risk analysis approach, for the following reasons:

1 The simple model described above assumes that the economic factors are unrelated. Clearly, many of them (e.g. market share and selling price) are statistically interdependent. To the extent that interdependency exists among variables, it must be specified. Such interrelationships are not always clear and are frequently complex to model.

2 Managers are required to specify probability distributions for the exogenous variables. Few managers are able or willing to accept the demands required by the simulation approach.

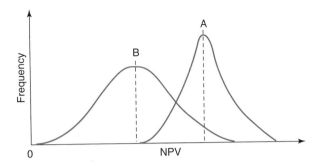

Figure 7.6 Simulated probability distributions

Self-assessment activity 7.5

What do you understand by Monte Carlo simulation? When might it be useful in capital budgeting?

(Answer in Appendix A at the back of the book)

7.7 ADJUSTING THE NPV FORMULA FOR RISK

Two approaches are commonly used to incorporate risk within the NPV formula.

■ Certainty equivalent method

This conceptually appealing approach permits adjustment for risk by incorporating the decision-maker's risk attitude into the capital investment decision. The certainty equivalent method adjusts the numerator in the net present value calculation by multiplying the expected annual cash flows by a certainty equivalent coefficient. The revised formula becomes:

$$\overline{NPV} = \sum_{t=1}^{N} \frac{\alpha \overline{X}_t}{(1 + i)^t} - I_0$$

where: $\overline{NPV}$ is the expected net present value; α is the certainty equivalent coefficient, which reflect's management's risk attitude; $\overline{X}_t$ is the expected cash flow in period t; i is the riskless rate of interest; n is the project's life; and I_0 is the initial cash outlay.

The numerator $(\alpha \overline{X}_t)$ represents the figure that management would be willing to receive as a certain sum each year in place of the uncertain annual cash flow offered by the project. The greater is management's aversion to risk, the nearer the certainty equivalent coefficient is to zero. Where projects are of normal risk for the business, and the cost of capital and risk-free rate of interest are known, it is possible to determine the certainty equivalent coefficient.

Example

Calculate the certainty equivalent coefficient for a project with a one-year life and an expected cash flow of £5,000 receivable at the end of the year. Shareholders require a return of 12 per cent for projects of this degree of risk and the risk-free rate of interest is 6 per cent.

Continued

The present value of the project, excluding the initial cost, and using the 12 per cent discount rate, is:

$$PV = \frac{£5,000}{1 + 0.12} = £4,464$$

Using the present value and substituting the risk-free interest rate for the cost of capital, we obtain the certainty equivalent coefficient:

$$\frac{\alpha \times £5,000}{1 + 0.06} = £4,464$$

$$\alpha = \frac{(£4,464)(1.06)}{£5,000}$$

$$= 0.9464$$

The management is, therefore, indifferent as to whether it receives an uncertain cash flow one year hence of £5,000 or a certain cash flow of £4,732 (i.e. £5,000 × 0.9464).

■ Risk-adjusted discount rate

Whereas the certainty equivalent approach adjusted the numerator in the NPV formula, the risk-adjusted discount rate adjusts the denominator:

$$\overline{NPV} = \sum_{t=1}^{N} \frac{\overline{X_t}}{(1 + k)^t} - I_0$$

where k is the risk-adjusted rate based on the perceived degree of project risk.

The higher the perceived riskiness of a project, the greater the risk premium to be added to the risk-free interest rate. This results in a higher discount rate and, hence, a lower net present value.

Although this approach has a certain intuitive appeal, its relevance depends very much on how risk is perceived to change over time. The risk-adjusted discount rate involves the impact of the risk premium growing over time at an exponential rate, implying that the riskiness of the project's cash flow also increases over time. Figure 7.7 demonstrates this point. Although the expected cash flow from a project

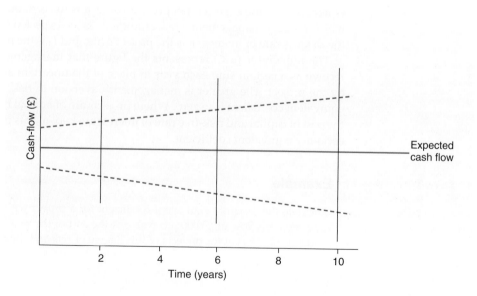

Figure 7.7 How risk is assumed to increase over time

may be constant over its 10-year life, the riskiness associated with the cash flows increases with time. However, if risk did not increase with time, the risk-adjusted discount rate would be inappropriate.

Adjusting the discount rate: Chox-Box Ltd

Chox-Box Ltd is a manufacturer of confectionery currently appraising a proposal to launch a new product that has had very little pre-launch testing. It is estimated that this proposal will produce annual cash flows in the region of £100,000 for the next five years, after which product profitability declines sharply. As the proposal is seen as a high-risk venture, a 12 per cent risk premium is incorporated in the discount rate. The risk-adjusted cash flow, before discounting at the risk-free discount rate, is therefore £89,286 in Year 1 (£100,000/1.12), falling to £56,742 in Year 5 (£100,000/1.12^5).

To what extent does this method reflect the actual riskiness of the annual cash flows for Years 1 and 5? Arguably, the greatest uncertainty surrounds the initial launch period. Once the initial market penetration and subsequent repeat orders are known, the subsequent sales are relatively easy to forecast. Thus, for Chox-Box, a single risk-adjusted discount rate is a poor proxy for the impact of risk on value over the project's life, because risk does not increase exponentially with the passage of time, and, in some cases, actually declines over time. The Eurotunnel project provides another illustration of this. By far the greatest risks were in the initial tunnelling and development phases.

A deeper understanding of the relationship between the certainty equivalent and risk-adjusted discount rate approaches may be gained by reading the appendix to this chapter.

7.8 RISK ANALYSIS IN PRACTICE

To what extent do companies employ the techniques discussed in this chapter? Table 7.6 shows changes since 1980.

Table 7.6 Risk analysis in large UK firms

	1980 (%)	1992 (%)	2003 (%)
Sensitivity analysis	42	86	89
Reduced payback period	30	59	75
Risk-adjusted rate	41	64	82
Probability analysis	10	47	77
Beta analysis	–	20	43

Source: Pike (1996), Alkaraan and Northcott (2006).

Use of sensitivity analysis has increased significantly over the period, and is now used in nearly all larger firms. Similar increases here occurred in the use of risk-adjusted discount rates and shortening the payback period. However, the greatest increase has taken place in the use of probability analysis and beta analysis (see Chapters 9 and 10 which cover the Capital Asset Pricing Model).

It is important to remember that investment appraisal and associated risk analysis is not simply a financial exercise. There is a human aspect to this that means that the processes may not be wholly rational. For example, managers in a firm have to compete with one another for funding of capital projects. Duchin and Sosyura (2013) have examined this aspect of capital projects in a US setting and find that divisional managers are more likely to receive funding for capital projects if they are socially connected to the CEO. Social connections may arise because the manager and CEO have worked together previously or are in the same alumni networks. This is potentially important as funds should ideally be allocated to those projects that will provide the best returns and taking into account the risk of the project, not based on whether a manager is connected to the CEO. Research by Greene *et al.* (2009) has found that multinational firms appear to be better at capital budgeting than purely domestic companies. The key reason proposed is that the managers' skills in multinational firms are stronger than in domestic firms.

7.9 CAPITAL INVESTMENT OPTIONS

real options
Options to invest in real assets such as capital projects

In financial markets 'options' are a type of financial instrument that gives the holder of the option the right to do something in the future but, very importantly, the holder has no obligation to do this thing. For example, the holder may have the right to sell a share in Marks & Spencer plc in three months' time at £5, but is not obliged to do so. Therefore, the holder of the option has flexibility. They can choose to do something or choose not to do something. Capital investment options (sometimes termed **real options**) are option-like features found in capital budgeting decisions. While discounted cash flow techniques are very useful tools of analysis, they are generally more suited to financial assets, because they assume that assets are held rather than managed. The main difference between evaluating financial assets and real assets is that investors in, say, shares, are generally *passive*. Unless they have a fair degree of control, they can only monitor performance and decide whether to hold or sell their shares.

Corporate managers, on the other hand, play a far more *active* role in achieving the planned net present value on a capital project. When a project is slipping behind forecast they can take action to try to achieve the original NPV target. In other words, they can create options – actions to mitigate losses or exploit new opportunities presented by capital investments. Managerial flexibility to adapt its future actions creates an asymmetry in the NPV probability distribution that increases the investment project's value by improving the upside potential while limiting downside losses.

We will consider three types of option: the abandonment option, the timing option and strategic investment options.

■ Abandonment option

option to abandon
Choice to allow an option to expire. With a capital investment, abandonment should take place where the value for which an asset can be sold exceeds the present value of its future benefits from continuing its operations

Major investment decisions involve heavy capital commitments and are largely irreversible: once the initial capital expenditure is incurred, management cannot turn the clock back and do it differently. The costs associated with divestment are usually very high. Most capital projects divested early will realise little more than scrap value. In the case of a nuclear power plant, the decommissioning cost could be phenomenal. Because management is committing large sums of money in pursuit of higher, but uncertain, payoffs, the **option to abandon**, without incurring enormous costs if things look grim, can be very valuable. To ignore this is to undervalue the project.

The development of new drugs in the pharmaceutical industry provides an example of an abandonment option. The research process for the development of a new drug takes considerable time, is very costly and there is no guarantee that it will be successful. Therefore, a pharmaceutical company may need to decide to abandon a research project at some point in its life. However, this might also create an opportunity to derive some value from the research carried out up to that point. For example, the company could potentially sell on the intellectual capital to another firm. Consequently, pharmaceutical companies can view drug development as having optionality, for at any time during the research process the company has the option to either continue development (and invest more in the research project) or to stop development and sell the intellectual capital.

Related to abandonment options are contraction options. For example, a company may find that the market it sells into starts to decline and because of this the company needs less space for warehousing its products. If it has leased the warehouse premises, then at the outset it may have been written into the lease that it can 'return' spare space to the landlord. Similarly, the company may have outsourced some of its production and as the market declines it is able to decrease production levels simply because it is a part of the contractual agreement with the other company that it can request less product when required. Another example of a contraction option is an oil company that decides to either slow down or close down oil production temporarily because the price of oil has dropped. It can then recommence production when the price of oil has risen sufficiently.

Example: Topvision plc

An established television manufacturer, Topvision plc, has decided to market a new product using technology new to the company, and is currently evaluating an £11 million capital project to enable its manufacture. The project has an infinite life and the discount rate is 10 per cent. Only two outcomes are possible, each with a 50 per cent probability:

At best outcome: annual cash benefits of £3 million, yielding an NPV of:

−£11 million (capital outlay) + £3 million/0.10 (PV of annual benefits)
= £19 million

At worst outcome: annual cash benefits of −£1 million giving an NPV of:

−£11 million − £1 million/0.10
= −£21 million

This yields an expected NPV of:

50% × £19 million + 50% × −£21 million = −£1 million.

On this basis the project would not be acceptable. However, on further consideration, management recognises that it would be able to identify which of the two outcomes would prevail by the end of the first year. This means that it has the option to abandon the project at that time.

The 'at worst' outcome now becomes a one-year project:

−£11 million −£1 million/1.10 = −£11.91 million

Exercising the abandonment option now suggests an expected NPV for the project of:

50% × £19 million + 50% × −£11.91 million
= £3.545 million.

The option to abandon the project after Year 1 turns the expected NPV from −£1 million to +£3.545 million and it now indicates that the project should be accepted. Arguably, project abandonment after one year would also realise a higher scrap value, further improving the 'at worst' outcome and strengthening the case for investment.

A further example: Cardiff Components Ltd

Cardiff Components Ltd is considering building a new plant to produce components for the nuclear defence industry. Proposal A is to build a custom-designed plant using the latest technology, but applicable only to nuclear defence contracts. A less profitable

Continued

scheme, Proposal B, is to build a plant using standard machine tools, giving greater flexibility in application and having a much higher salvage value than Proposal A.

The outcome of a general election to be held one year hence has a major impact on the decision. If the current government is returned to office, its commitment to nuclear defence is likely to give rise to new orders, making Proposal A the better choice. If the current opposition party is elected, its commitment to run down the nuclear defence industry would make Proposal B the better course of action. Proposal B has, in effect, an option attached to it, giving the flexibility to abandon the proposed operation in favour of some other activity. We underestimate NPV if we assume that the project must last for the prescribed project life, no matter what happens in the future.

A similar type of option is the option to redeploy. A utility company may have the option to switch between various fuels to produce electricity. This dual plant may cost more than one that is only capable of burning a single fuel, but the value of the redeployment option should be considered in reaching a decision.

■ Timing option

timing/delay option
The option to invest now or defer the decision until conditions are more favourable

The Cardiff Components example not only introduces an abandonment option, it also raises the **timing** or **delay option**. Management may have viewed the investment as a 'now or never' opportunity, arguing that in highly competitive markets there is no scope for delay. However, most project decisions have three possible outcomes – accept, reject or defer until economic and other conditions improve. In effect, this amounts to viewing the decision as an option that is about to expire on the new plant. If a positive NPV is expected, the option will be exercised; otherwise, the option lapses and no investment is made.

An immediate investment would yield either a negative NPV – in which case it would not be taken up – or a positive NPV. Delaying the decision by a year to gain valuable new information is a more valuable option. Managements sometimes delay taking up apparently wealth-creating opportunities because they believe that the option to wait and gather new information is sufficiently valuable.

A further example of a timing option could be a supermarket that buys land, but delays building the supermarket until it considers the time is appropriate. The reason for delaying the build may be because the supermarket believes there is currently insufficient market demand for its goods or because people living close by will react adversely to the development of a new supermarket at the present time. Of course, there also exists an abandonment option as the land has value in its own right and the supermarket can decide to sell the land if it judges it is strategically the better thing to do.

■ Strategic investment options

follow-on opportunities
Options that arise following a course of action

Certain investment decisions give rise to **follow-on opportunities** that are wealth-creating. New technology investment, involving large-scale research and development, is particularly difficult to evaluate. Managers refer to the high level of intangible benefits associated with such decisions. What they really mean is that these investments offer further investment opportunities (e.g. greater flexibility), but that, at this stage, the precise form of such opportunities cannot be quantified.

Valuation calculations applied to strategic investment options raise as many questions as they answer. For example, how much of the risk for the follow-on project is dependent upon the outcome of the initial project? But option pricing does offer insights into the problem of valuing 'intangibles' in capital budgeting, particularly where they create options not otherwise available to the firm. Real options will be further discussed in Chapter 12 where the main focus will be on their valuation. For example, a company may initially choose to establish only a small operation in an overseas country and, in effect, test the market. Subsequently, if there is strong demand for its products or services, then it can choose to expand the operation. This idea of follow-on options can apply not only to establishing an operation in a new market, but also to establishing a company's brand name in a new market. A company can undertake a marketing campaign in an overseas country and if a positive reaction occurs it can choose to commence selling into that market.

■ The use of real options in practice

The evidence suggests that, in practice, only a small number of companies are using a real options approach to appraise projects. For example, Baker *et al.*'s (2011) survey of Canadian firms found that only 16.8 per cent of respondents used real options approaches. When the managers of the sample firms ranked their use of capital budgeting techniques, net present value, internal rate of return and payback period were frequently used, but the barrier to using real options was a lack of knowledge and expertise. This was despite those firms that were using real options citing the primary reasons for doing so were that it enabled them to incorporate flexibility into managerial decision-making, and that it aided in the development of the strategic vision of the company.

SUMMARY

Risk is an important element in virtually all investment decisions. Because most people in business are risk-averse, the identification, measurement and, where possible, reduction of risk should be a central feature in the decision-making process. The evidence suggests that firms are increasingly conducting risk analysis. This does not mean that the risk dimension is totally ignored by other firms; rather, they choose to handle project risk by less objective methods such as experience, feel or intuition.

We have defined what is meant by risk and examined a variety of ways of measuring it. The probability distribution, giving the probability of occurrence of each possible outcome following an investment decision, is the concept underlying most of the methods discussed. Measures of risk, such as the standard deviation, indicate the extent to which actual outcomes are likely to vary from the expected value.

Key points

- The expected NPV, although useful, does not show the whole picture. We need to understand managers' attitudes to risk and to estimate the degree of project risk.

- Three types of risk are relevant in capital budgeting: project risk in isolation, the project's impact on corporate risk and its impact on market risk. The last two are addressed more fully in Chapters 9 and 10.

- The standard deviation, semi-variance and coefficient of variation each measure, in slightly different ways, project risk.

- Sensitivity analysis and scenario analysis are used to locate and assess the potential impact of risk on project performance. Simulation is a more sophisticated approach, which captures the essential characteristics of the investment that are subject to uncertainty.

- The NPV formula can be adjusted to consider risk. Adjustment of the cash flows is achieved by the certainty equivalent method. The risk-adjusted discount rate increases the risk premium for higher-risk projects.

- Capital investment decisions may have options attached such as the option to abandon, delay or expand. Conventional NPV analysis that ignores these options can seriously understate a project's value.

Further reading

Books on real options include Guthrie (2009). Useful research studies on the use of risk analysis are given in Pike (1988, 1996), Pike and Ho (1991), Mao and Helliwell (1969) and Bierman and Hass (1973). Risk analysis has become increasingly incorporated into risk management so that a very wide range of risk issues are considered across the company. There are significant numbers of risk management books now in publication. A recent book that covers many areas is Hopkin (2012).

Appendix
MULTI-PERIOD CASH FLOWS AND RISK

For simplicity, we have so far assumed single-period investments and conveniently ignored the fact that investments are typically multi-period. As risk is to be specifically evaluated, cash flows should be discounted at the risk-free rate of interest, reflecting only the time-value of money. To include a risk premium within the discount rate, when risk is already considered separately, amounts to double-counting and typically understates the true net present value. The expected NPV of an investment project is found by summing the present values of the expected net cash flows and deducting the initial investment outlay. Thus, for a two-year investment proposal:

$$\overline{NPV} = \frac{\overline{X}_1}{1 + i} + \frac{\overline{X}_2}{(1 + i)^2} - I_0$$

where $\overline{NPV}$ is the expected NPV, $\overline{X}_1$ is the expected value of net cash flow in Year 1, $\overline{X}_2$ is the expected value of net cash flow in Year 2, I_0 is the cash investment outlay and i is the risk-free rate of interest.

A major problem in calculating the standard deviation of a project's NPVs is that the cash flows in one period are typically dependent, to some degree, on the cash flows of earlier periods. Assuming for the present that cash flows for our two-period project are statistically independent, the total variance of the NPV is equal to the discounted sum of the annual variances.

For example, the Bronson project, with a two-year life, has an initial cost of £500 and the possible payoffs and probabilities outlined in Table 7.7. Applying the standard deviation and expected value formulae already discussed, we obtain an expected NPV of £268 and standard deviation of £206.

Table 7.7 Bronson project payoffs with independent cash flows

Probability	Year 1 cash flow (£)	Year 2 cash flow (£)
0.1	100	200
0.2	200	400
0.4	300	600
0.2	400	800
0.1	500	1,000
Expected value	£300	£600
Variance (σ^2)	£12,000	£48,000
Standard deviation	£110	£219

Assuming a risk-free discount rate of 10 per cent, the expected NPV is:

$$\overline{NPV} = \frac{300}{(1.10)} + \frac{600}{(1.10)^2} - 500 = £268$$

The standard deviation of the entire proposal is found by discounting the annual variances to their present values, applying the equation:

$$\sigma = \sqrt{\sum_{t=1}^{N} \frac{\sigma_t^2}{(1 + i)^2}}$$

In our simple case, this is:

$$\sigma = \sqrt{\frac{\sigma_1^2}{(1 + i)^2} + \frac{\sigma_2^2}{(1 + i)^4}} = \sqrt{\frac{12,000}{(1.1)^2} + \frac{48,000}{(1.1)^4}} = £206$$

The project therefore offers an expected NPV of £268 and a standard deviation of £206.

■ Perfectly correlated cash flows

At the other extreme from the independence assumption is the assumption that the cash flows in one year are entirely dependent upon the cash flows achieved in previous periods. When this is the case, successive cash flows are said to be perfectly correlated. Any deviation in one year from forecast directly affects the accuracy of subsequent forecasts. The effect is that, over time, the standard deviation of the probability distribution of net present values increases. The standard deviation of a stream of cash flows perfectly correlated over time is:

$$\sigma = \sum_{t=1}^{N} \frac{\sigma_t}{(1 + i)^t}$$

Returning to the example in Table 7.7, but assuming perfect correlation of cash flows over time, the standard deviation for the project is:

$$\sigma = \frac{£109}{1.1} + \frac{£219}{(1.1)^2}$$
$$= £280$$

Thus the risk associated with this project is £280, assuming perfect correlation, which is higher than that for independent cash flows. Obviously, this difference would be considerably greater for longer-lived projects.

In reality, few projects are either independent or perfectly correlated over time. The standard deviation lies somewhere between the two. It will be based on the formula for the independence case, but with an additional term for the covariance between annual cash flows.

■ Interpreting results

While decision-makers are interested to know the degree of risk associated with a given project, their fundamental concern is whether the project will produce a positive net present value. Risk analysis can go some way to answering this question. If a project's probability distribution of expected NPVs is approximately normal, we can estimate the probability of failing to achieve at least zero NPV. In the previous example, the expected NPV was £268. This is standardised by dividing it by the standard deviation using the formula:

$$Z = \frac{X - \overline{NPV}}{\sigma}$$

where X in this case is zero and Z is the number of standardised units. Thus, in the case of the independent cash flow assumption, we have:

$$Z = \frac{0 - £268}{£206}$$

$$= -1.30 \text{ standardised units}$$

Reference to normal distribution tables reveals that there is a 0.0968 probability that the NPV will be zero or less. Accordingly, there must be a $(1 - 0.0968)$ or 90.32 per cent probability of the project producing an NPV in excess of zero.

It is probably unnecessary to attempt to measure the standard deviation for every project. Even the larger European companies tend to use probability analysis sparingly in capital project analysis. Unless cash flow forecasting is wildly optimistic, or the future economic conditions underlying all investments are far worse than anticipated, the bad news from one project should be compensated by good news from another project.

Sometimes, however, a project is of such great importance that its failure could threaten the very survival of the business. In such a case, management should be fully aware of the scale of its exposure to loss and the probability of this occurring.

Probability of failure: Microloft Ltd

Microloft Ltd, a local family-controlled company specialising in attic conversions, is currently considering investing in a major expansion giving wider geographical coverage. The NPV from the project is expected to be £330,000 with a standard deviation of £300,000. Should the project fail (perhaps because of the reaction by major competitors), the company could afford to lose £210,000 before the bank manager 'pulled the plug' and put in the receiver. What is the probability that this new project could put Microloft out of business?

We need to find the value of Z where X is the worst NPV outcome that Microloft could tolerate:

$$Z = \frac{X - \overline{NPV}}{\sigma}$$

$$= \frac{-£210 - £330}{£300} = -1.8$$

Assuming the outcomes are normally distributed, probability tables will show a 3.6 per cent chance of failure from accepting the project. A family-controlled business, like Microloft, may decide that even this relatively small chance of sending the company on to the rocks is more important than the attractive returns expected from the project.

QUESTIONS

Questions with a coloured number have solutions in Appendix B on page 784.

1 Explain the importance of risk in capital budgeting.

2 Explain the distinction between project risk, business risk, financial risk and portfolio risk.

3 The 'woodpulp' project has an initial cost of £13,000 and the firm's risk-free interest rate is 10 per cent. If certainty equivalents and net cash flows (NCFs) for the project are as below, should the project be accepted?

Year	Certainty equivalents	Net cash flows (£)
1	0.90	8,000
2	0.85	7,000
3	0.80	7,000
4	0.75	5,000
5	0.70	5,000
6	0.65	5,000
7	0.60	5,000

4 Mystery Enterprises has a proposal costing £800. Using a 10 per cent cost of capital, compute the expected NPV, standard deviation and coefficient of variation, assuming independent interperiod cash flows.

Probability	Year 1 net cash flow (£)	Year 2 net cash flow (£)
0.2	400	300
0.3	500	400
0.3	600	500
0.2	700	600

5 Mikado plc is considering launching a new product involving capital investment of £180,000. The machine has a four-year life and no residual value. Sales volumes of 6,000 units are forecast for each of the four years. The product has a selling price of £60 and a variable cost of £36 per unit. Additional fixed overheads of £50,000 will be incurred. The cost of capital is 12.5 per cent p.a. Present a report to the directors of Mikado plc giving:

(a) the net present values
(b) the percentage amount each variable can deteriorate before the project becomes unacceptable
(c) a sensitivity graph

6 Devonia (Laboratories) Ltd has recently carried out successful clinical trials on a new type of skin cream, which has been developed to reduce the effects of ageing. Research and development costs in relation to the new product amount to £160,000. In order to gauge the market potential of the new product, an independent firm of market research consultants was hired at a cost of £15,000. The market research report submitted by the consultants indicates that the skin cream is likely to have a product life of four years and could be sold to retail chemists and large department stores at a price of £20 per 100 ml container. For each of the four years of the new product's life sales demand has been estimated as follows:

Number of 100 ml containers sold	Probability of occurrence
11,000	0.3
14,000	0.6
16,000	0.1

If the company decides to launch the new product, production can begin at once. The equipment necessary to make the product is already owned by the company and originally cost £150,000. At the end of the new product's life, it is estimated that the equipment could be sold for £35,000. If the company decides against launching the new product, the equipment will be sold immediately for £85,000 as it will be of no further use to the company.

The new skin cream will require two hours' labour for each 100 ml container produced. The cost of labour for the new product is £4.00 per hour. Additional workers will have to be recruited to produce the new product. At the end of the product's life the workers are unlikely to be offered further work with the company and redundancy costs of £10,000 are expected. The cost of the ingredients for each 100 ml container is £6.00. Additional overheads arising from the product are expected to be £15,000 p.a.

The new skin cream has attracted the interest of the company's competitors. If the company decides not to produce and sell the skin cream, it can sell the patent rights to a major competitor immediately for £125,000.

Devonia (Laboratories) Ltd has a cost of capital of 12 per cent.

Ignore taxation.

Required

(a) Calculate the expected net present value (ENPV) of the new product.

(b) State, with reasons, whether or not Devonia (Laboratories) Ltd should launch the new product.

(c) Discuss the strengths and weaknesses of the expected net present value approach for making investment decisions.

(Certified Diploma)

7 Plato Pharmaceuticals Ltd has invested £300,000 to date in developing a new type of insect repellent. The repellent is now ready for production and sale and the marketing director estimates that the product will sell 150,000 bottles per annum over the next five years. The selling price of the insect repellent will be £5 per bottle and the variable costs are estimated to be £3 per bottle. Fixed costs (excluding depreciation) are expected to be £200,000 per annum. This figure is made up of £160,000 additional fixed costs and £40,000 fixed costs relating to the existing business which will be apportioned to the new product.

In order to produce the repellent, machinery and equipment costing £520,000 will have to be purchased immediately. The estimated residual value of this machinery and equipment in five years' time is £100,000. The company calculates depreciation on a straight-line basis.

The company has a cost of capital of 12 per cent. Ignore taxation.

Required

(a) Calculate the net present value of the product.

(b) Undertake sensitivity analysis to show by how much the following factors would have to change before the product ceased to be worthwhile:

   (i) the discount rate

   (ii) the initial outlay on machinery and equipment

   (iii) the net operating cash flows

   (iv) the residual value of the machinery and equipment

(c) Discuss the strengths and weaknesses of sensitivity analysis in dealing with risk and uncertainty.

(d) State, with reasons, whether or not you feel the project should go ahead.

(Certified Diploma)

8 The managing director of Tigwood Ltd believes that a market exists for 'microbooks'. He has proposed that the company should market 100 best-selling books on microfiche, which can be read using a special microfiche reader that is connected to a television screen. A microfiche containing an entire book can be purchased from a photographic company at 40 per cent of the average production cost of best-selling paperback books.

The average cost of producing paperback books is estimated at £1.50, and the average selling price of paperbacks is £3.95 each. Copyright fees of 20 per cent of the average selling price of the paperback books would be payable to the publishers of the paperbacks plus an initial lump sum that is still being negotiated, but is expected to be £1.5 million. No tax allowances are available on this lump-sum payment. An agreement with the publishers would be signed for a period of six years. Additional variable costs of staffing, handling and marketing are 20p per microfiche, and fixed costs are negligible.

Tigwood Ltd has spent £100,000 on market research, and expects sales to be 1,500,000 units per year at an initial unit price of £2.

The microfiche reader would be produced and marketed by another company.

Tigwood would finance the venture with a bank loan at an interest rate of 16 per cent per year. The company's money (nominal) cost of equity and real cost of equity are estimated to be 23 per cent p.a. and 12.6 per cent p.a., respectively. Tigwood's money weighted average cost of capital and real weighted average cost of capital are 18 per cent p.a. and 8 per cent p.a., respectively. The risk-free rate of interest is 11 per cent p.a. and the market return is 17 per cent p.a.

Corporation tax is at the rate of 35 per cent, payable in the year the profit occurs. All cash flows may be assumed to be at the year end, unless otherwise stated.

Required

(a) Calculate the expected net present value of the microbooks project.

(b) Explain the reasons for your choice of discount rate in the answer to part (a). Discuss whether this rate is likely to be the most appropriate to use in the analysis of the proposed project.

(c) (i) Using sensitivity analysis, estimate by what percentage each of the following would have to change before the project was no longer expected to be viable:
  initial outlay
  annual contribution
  the life of the agreement
  the discount rate

  (ii) What are the limitations of this sensitivity analysis?

(d) What further information would be useful to help the company decide whether to undertake the microbook project?

(ACCA)

9 The general manager of the nationalised postal service of a small country, Zedland, wishes to introduce a new service. This service would offer same-day delivery of letters and parcels posted before 10 a.m. within a distance of 150 km. The service would require 100 new vans costing $8,000 each and 20 trucks costing $18,000 each. One hundred and eighty new workers would be employed at an average annual wage of $13,000, and five managers on average annual salaries of $20,000 would be moved from their existing duties, where they would not be replaced.

Two postal rates are proposed. In the first year of operation letters will cost $0.525 and parcels $5.25. Market research undertaken at a cost of $50,000 forecasts that demand will average 15,000 letters per working day and 500 parcels per working day during the first year, and 20,000 letters per day and 750 parcels per day thereafter. There is a five-day working week. Annual running and maintenance costs on similar new vans and trucks are estimated to be $2,000 per van and $4,000 per truck, respectively, in the first year of operation. These costs will increase by 20 per cent p.a. (excluding the effects of inflation). Vehicles are depreciated over a five-year period on a straight-line basis. Depreciation is tax-allowable and the vehicles will have negligible scrap value at the end of five years. Advertising in Year 1 will cost $500,000 and in Year 2 $250,000. There will be no advertising after Year 2. Existing premises will be used for the new service, but additional costs of $150,000 per year will be incurred.

All the above cost data are current estimates and exclude any inflation effects. Wage and salary costs and all other costs are expected to rise because of inflation by approximately 5 per cent p.a. during the five-year planning horizon of the postal service. The government of Zedland will not permit annual price increases within nationalised industries to exceed the level of inflation.

Nationalised industries are normally required by the government to earn at least an annual after-tax return of 5 per cent on average investment and to achieve, on average, at least zero net present value on their investments.

The new service would be financed half by internally generated funds and half by borrowing on the capital market at an interest rate of 12 per cent p.a. The opportunity cost of capital for the postal service is estimated to be 14 per cent p.a. Corporate taxes in Zedland, to which the postal service is subject, are at the rate of 30 per cent for annual profits of up to $500,000 and 40 per cent for the balance in excess of $500,000. Tax is payable one year in arrears. All transactions may be assumed to be on a cash basis and to occur at the end of the year, with the exception of the initial investment, which would be required almost immediately.

Required

(a) Acting as an independent consultant, prepare a report advising whether the new postal service should be introduced. Include a discussion of other factors that might need to be taken into account before a final decision was made. State clearly any assumptions that you make.

(b) Monte Carlo simulation has been suggested as a possible method of estimating the net present value of a project. Briefly assess the advantages and disadvantages of using this technique in investment appraisal.

(ACCA)

Practical assignment

Describe the types of risk associated with investment decisions in a firm known to you. (If necessary, read the Annual Report of a major company, like BP plc, to familiarise yourself with a company.) Suggest how these risks should be formally assessed within their investment appraisal process.

8

Relationships between investments: portfolio theory

Metro and the weather

Lex Live

Diversified investment strategies can be marvellous things. Suppose you face a choice of buying shares in a maker of sunscreen or in a maker of umbrellas. The textbook response is to invest in both. This guarantees a relatively high return at moderate risk levels, whatever the weather.

The same logic should apply to companies, too. Unfortunately, that has not been the recent experience of investors. On Friday, Metro, the German retail conglomerate, joined the growing list of companies blaming their lacklustre performance on a rainy European summer.

Wet weather may indeed have hit Metro's food sales. But the argument would carry more weight had the very same Metro a year ago not put weak department store sales down to last summer's heat. Groups such as Unilever and Cadbury Schweppes have also been keen to use the weather excuse in recent years, freely invoking the vagaries of the climate to explain away their performance.

This might sound like harmless spin, but it contains a real danger. This is that companies may actually believe their own PR and start to overlook structural challenges, such as the growth of own labels and discount retailers. These affect both Unilever and – arguably – Metro. The German retailer's weak like-for-like sales growth partly reflects lacklustre demand. But it also raises some doubts about the returns of its foreign expansion. When companies diversify, they take on a huge extra burden of management. If Metro cannot even cope with whatever is thrown at it by the weather gods, it should reconsider its foray abroad – and leave the task of diversifying to investors.

 Source: Financial Times, 29 October 2004. © Financial Times

Learning objectives

This chapter is designed to explore the financial equivalent of the maxim 'don't put all your eggs in one basket'. In particular, it aims:

- To give the reader an understanding of the rationale behind the diversification decisions of both shareholders and companies.

- To illustrate the mechanics of portfolio construction with a user-friendly approach to the key statistics, using numerical examples.

- To explain why optimal portfolio selection is a matter of personal choice.

- To examine the drawbacks of portfolio analysis as an approach to project appraisal.

A good grasp of the principles of portfolio analysis is an essential underpinning to understanding the Capital Asset Pricing Model, to be covered in Chapter 9.

8.1 INTRODUCTION

diversification
Extension of a firm's activities into new and unrelated fields. Although this may generate cost savings, e.g. via shared distribution systems, as a by-product, the fundamental motive for diversification is to reduce exposure to fluctuations in economic activity

portfolio
A combination of investments – securities or physical assets – into a single 'bundled' investment. A well-diversified portfolio has the potential capacity to lower the investor's exposure to the risk of fluctuations in the overall economy

contra-cyclical
A term applied to an investment whose returns fluctuate in opposite ways to general trends in business activity, i.e. contrary to the cycle

portfolio effect
The tendency for the risk on a well-diversified holding of investments to fall below the risk of most, and sometimes all, of its individual components

This chapter deals with the theory underlying **diversification** decisions. Diversification is a strategic device for dealing with risk. Whereas the previous chapter examined ways to analyse the risk of individual projects, here we study how the financial manager can exploit interrelationships between projects to adjust the risk–return characteristics of the whole enterprise. In the process, we will show why many firms develop a wide spread of activities or **portfolios**. The term 'portfolio' is usually applied to combinations of securities, but we will show that the principles underlying security portfolio formation can be applied to combinations of any type of asset, including investment projects.

Many firms diffuse their efforts across a range of products, market segments and customers in order to spread the risks of declining trade and profitability. If a firm can reduce its reliance on particular products or markets, it can more easily bear the impact of a major reverse in any single market. However, firms do not reduce their exposure to the threat of new products or new competitors for entirely negative reasons. Diversification can generate some major strategic advantages: for example, the wider the spread of activities, the greater the access to star-performing sectors of the economy. Imagine an economy divided into five sectors, with one star performer each year whose identity is always random. A company operating in a single sector is likely to miss out in four years out of five. In such a world, it is prudent to have a stake in every sector by building a portfolio of all five activities.

Diversification is designed to even out the bumps in the time profile of profits and cash flows. The ideal form of diversification is to engage in activities that behave in exactly opposite ways. When sales and earnings are relatively low in one area, the adverse consequences can be offset by participation in a sector where sales and profits are relatively high. With perfect synchronisation, the time profile of overall returns will describe the pattern shown in Figure 8.1. This shows the returns from two activities: A, which moves in parallel with the economy as a whole; and B, which moves in an *exactly* opposite way. The equal and opposite fluctuations in the returns from these two activities would result in a perfectly level profile for a diversified enterprise comprising both activities. In generally adverse economic conditions, the returns from activity A, closely following the economy as a whole, will be depressed, but involvement in activity B has an exactly compensating effect. The reverse applies when the economy is expanding. The returns from B are said to be **contra-cyclical**, and the dampening effect on the variability of returns is called a **portfolio effect**.

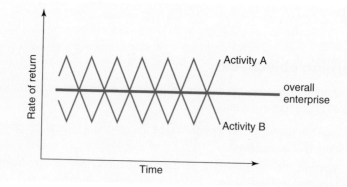

Figure 8.1 Equal and offsetting fluctuations in returns

For firms planning to diversify, there are two important messages. First, it is not enough simply to spread your activities. Different activities are subject to different types of risk, which are not always closely related. For an internationally diversified firm, the factors affecting domestic operations may be quite different from those affecting overseas operations. If changes in these influences are random and relatively uncorrelated, diversification may significantly reduce the variability of company earnings. Second, to generate an appreciable impact on overall returns, diversification must usually be substantial in relation to the whole enterprise. Hence, two key messages of portfolio diversification are: *look for unrelated activities* and *engage in significant diversification.*

8.2 PORTFOLIO ANALYSIS: THE BASIC PRINCIPLES

The theory of diversification was developed by Markowitz (1952). It can be reduced to the maxim 'don't put all your eggs in one basket'. This is a simple motto, but one that many investors persistently ignore. How often do we read heart-rending stories of small investors who have lost all their savings in some shady venture or other? Why do more than 50 per cent of private investors persist in holding a single security in their investment portfolios? Perhaps they are unaware of the advantages of spreading their risks, or have not understood the arguments. Perhaps they are not risk-averse or are simply irrational.* Rational, risk-averse investors appreciate that not all investments perform well at the same time, that some may never perform well, and that a few may perform spectacularly well. Since no one can predict which investments will fall into each category in any one period, it is rational to spread one's funds over a wide set of investments.

A simple example will illustrate the remarkable potential benefits of diversification.

■ Achieving a perfect portfolio effect

An investor can undertake one or both of the two investments, Apple and Pear. Apple has a 50 per cent chance of achieving an 8 per cent return and a 50 per cent chance of returning 12 per cent. Pear has a 50 per cent chance of generating a return of 6 per cent and a 50 per cent chance of yielding 14 per cent. The two investments are in sectors of the economy that move in direct opposition to each other. The investor expects the return on Apple to be relatively high when that on Pear is relatively low, and vice versa. What portfolio should the investor hold?

First of all, note that the expected value (EV) of each investment's return is identical:

Investment Apple: EV $= (0.5 \times 8\%) + (0.5 \times 12\%) = (4\% + 6\%) = 10\%$

Investment Pear: EV $= (0.5 \times 6\%) + (0.5 \times 14\%) = (3\% + 7\%) = 10\%$

At first glance, it may appear that the investor would be indifferent between Apple and Pear or, indeed, any combination of them. However, there is a wide variety of possible expected returns according to how the investor 'weights' the portfolio. Moreover, a badly weighted portfolio can offer wide variations in returns in different time periods.

For example, when Pear is the star performer, a portfolio comprising 20 per cent of Apple and 80 per cent of Pear will offer a return of:

$$\frac{Apple}{(0.2 \times 8\%)} + \frac{Pear}{(0.8 \times 14\%)} = \frac{Portfolio}{(1.6\% + 11.2\%)} = 12.8\%$$

When Apple is the star, the return is only:

$$(0.2 \times 12\%) + (0.8 \times 6\%) = (2.4 + 4.8\%) = 7.2\%$$

---

*A common reason is probably that they have applied for shares in a privatisation, or been given shares in a building society demutualisation! The biggest demutualisation was that by the Halifax Building Society (now part of the Lloyds Group). 'The Halifax' gave free shares to 7.5 million customers in June 1997.

Although there should be as many good years for Apple as for Pear, resulting over the long-term in an average return of 10 per cent, *in the shorter term*, the investor would be over-exposed to the risk of a series of bad years for Pear. Happily, there is a portfolio which removes this risk entirely.

Consider a portfolio invested two-thirds in Apple and one-third in Pear. When Apple is the star, the return on the portfolio (R_p) is a weighted average of the returns from the two components:

$$R_p = (2/3 \times 12\%) + (1/3 \times 6\%) = (8\% + 2\%) = 10\%$$

Conversely, when Pear is the star, the portfolio offers a return of:

$$R_p = (2/3 \times 8\%) + (1/3 \times 14\%) = (5.33\% + 4.67\%) = 10\%$$

With this combination, the risk-averse investor cannot go wrong! The portfolio completely removes variability in returns as there are only two possible states of the economy. Any rational risk-averse investor should select this combination of Apple and Pear to eliminate risk for a guaranteed 10 per cent return. Here, the portfolio effect is perfect, like that shown in Figure 8.1. However, not every investor would necessarily opt for this particular portfolio. Super-optimists might load their funds entirely on to Pear, hoping for 14 per cent returns every year. This may work for a year or two, but the chances of achieving a consistent return of 14 per cent year after year are very low. The chance of achieving 14 per cent in the first year is 50 per cent, but the chance of getting 14 per cent in *each* of the first two years is (50 per cent) $\times$ (50 per cent) = 25 per cent and so on. Diversification is usually the safest (and often the most profitable) policy. We will study later in the chapter how different portfolio weightings affect the overall risk and return.

In this example, the opportunity to eliminate all risk arises from the *perfect negative correlation** between the two investments, but this attractive property can only be exploited by weighting the portfolio in a particular way.

Regrettably, cases of perfect negative correlation between the returns from securities are rare. Most investment returns exhibit varying degrees of positive correlation, largely according to how they depend on overall economic trends. This does not rule out risk-reducing diversification benefits, but suggests they may be less pronounced than in our example. As we will see, *the extent to which portfolio combination can achieve a reduction in risk depends on the degree of correlation between returns*. Later in the chapter, we will examine rather more realistic cases, but first we need to explore more fully the nature and measurement of portfolio risk.

Self-assessment activity 8.1

What are the two required conditions for total elimination of portfolio risk?

(Answer in Appendix A at the back of the book)

8.3 HOW TO MEASURE PORTFOLIO RISK

We have just seen the importance of the degree of correlation between the returns from two investments. We saw also how the return from a portfolio could be expressed as a weighted average of the individual asset returns, the weights being the proportions of the portfolio accounted for by each of the various components. A

---

*Readers lacking a grounding in elementary statistics may want to consult an introductory text such as C. Morris, *Quantitative Approaches in Business Studies* (Pearson Education, 2008), in order to study the concept of correlation. Correlation is measured on a scale of −1 (perfect negative correlation) through zero to +1 (perfect positive correlation).

similar relationship applies before the event: that is, if we consider the *expected value* of the return from the portfolio. The expected return on a portfolio (ER_p) comprising two assets, A and B, whose individual expected returns are ER_A and ER_B respectively, is given by:

$$ER_p = \alpha ER_A + (1 - \alpha)ER_B \qquad (8.1)$$

where α and $(1 - \alpha)$ are the respective weightings of assets A and B, with $\alpha + (1 - \alpha) = 1$.

The riskiness of the portfolio expresses the extent to which the actual return may deviate from the expected return. This may be expressed by the variance of the return, σ_p^2, or by its standard deviation, σ_p.

Portfolio risk

The (rather fearsome!) expression for the standard deviation of a two-asset investment portfolio, σ_p, is:

$$\sigma_p = \sqrt{[\alpha^2 \sigma_A^2 + (1 - \alpha)^2 \sigma_B^2 + 2\alpha(1 - \alpha)\text{cov}_{AB}]} \qquad (8.2)$$

where

α = the proportion of the portfolio invested in asset A

$(1 - \alpha)$ = the proportion of the portfolio invested in asset B

σ_A^2 = the variance of the return on asset A

σ_B^2 = the variance of the return on asset B

cov_{AB} = the covariance of the returns on A and B.

covariance
A statistical measure of the extent to which the fluctuations exhibited by two (or more) variables are related

We need now to explain the meaning of the covariance. The **covariance**, like the **correlation coefficient**, is a measure of the interrelationship between random variables, in this case, the returns from the two investments A and B. In other words, it measures the extent to which their returns move together, i.e. their **co-movement** or **co-variability**. When the two returns move together, it has a positive value; when they move away from each other, it has a negative value; and when there is no co-variability at all, its value is zero. However, unlike the correlation coefficient, whose value is restricted to a scale ranging from -1 to $+1$, the covariance can assume any value. It measures co-movement in *absolute* terms, whereas the correlation coefficient is a *relative* measure.

correlation coefficient
A relative measure of co-movement that locates assets on a scale between -1 and $+1$. Where returns move exactly in unison, perfect positive correlation exists, and where exactly opposite movements occur, perfect negative correlation exists. Most investments fall in between, mainly with positive correlation

The correlation coefficient between the return on A and the return on B, r_{AB}, is simply the covariance, normalised or standardised, by the product of their standard deviations:

$$\text{Correlation coefficient between A's and B's returns} = r_{AB} = \frac{\text{cov}_{AB}}{\sigma_A \times \sigma_B}$$

co-movement/co-variability
The tendency for two variables, e.g. the returns from two investments, to move in parallel

The covariance, cov_{AB}, between the returns on the two investments, A and B, is given by:

$$\text{cov}_{AB} = \sum_{i=1}^{N} [p_i(R_A - ER_A)(R_B - ER_B)] \qquad (8.3)$$

where R_A is the realised return from investment A, ER_A is the expected value of the return from A, R_B is the realised return from investment B, ER_B is the expected value of the return from B, and p_i is the probability of any pair of values occurring.

Equation 8.3 tells us first to calculate, for each pair of simultaneously occurring outcomes, their deviations from their respective expected values; next, to multiply these deviations together and then to weight the resulting product by the relevant probability for each pair. Finally, the sum of all weighted products of paired divergences between expected and actual outcomes defines the covariance. This relationship is more easily understood with a numerical example. Table 8.1 shows possible returns from

Table 8.1 Returns under different states of the economy

State of the economy	Probability	Return from A	Return from B
E_1	0.25	-10%	$+60\%$
E_2	0.25	-10%	-20%
E_3	0.25	$+50\%$	-20%
E_4	0.25	$+50\%$	$+60\%$

Table 8.2 Calculating the covariance

R_A	ER_A	R_B	ER_B	$(R_A - ER_A)$	$(R_B - ER_B)$	Product	Probability	Weighted product
-10	20	$+60$	20	-30	$+40$	-1200	0.25	-300
-10	20	-20	20	-30	-40	$+1200$	0.25	$+300$
$+50$	20	-20	20	$+30$	-40	-1200	0.25	-300
$+50$	20	$+60$	20	$+30$	$+40$	$+1200$	0.25	$+300$
								covariance$_{AB} = 0$

Note: Although the rate of return figures are percentages, they have been treated as integers to clarify exposition.

two assets under four different economic conditions, with associated probabilities. First, do Self-assessment activity 8.2. Then, check through the calculation in Table 8.2.

Self-assessment activity 8.2

With the figures in Table 8.1, check that the expected values for both A and B are 20 per cent, and that their respective standard deviations are 30 per cent and 40 per cent, using the formulae presented in Chapter 7.

(Answer in Appendix A at the back of the book)

In this case, there is no co-variability at all between the returns from the two assets. If the return from A increases, it is just as likely to be associated with a fall in the return from B as a concurrent increase. If the covariance (which measures the degree of co-movement in absolute terms) is zero, we will find the correlation coefficient (the relative measure of co-movement) is also zero. We may now demonstrate this:

Correlation coefficient
between A's and B's returns $= r_{AB} = \dfrac{\text{cov}_{AB}}{(\sigma_A \times \sigma_B)} = \dfrac{0}{(30 \times 40)} = 0$

The case of zero covariance is a very convenient one, as we can see from looking at the expression for portfolio risk, σ_P (Equation 8.2 from page 193).

$$\sigma_P = \sqrt{[\alpha^2\sigma_A^2 + (1 - \alpha)^2\sigma_B^2 + 2\alpha(1 - \alpha)\text{cov}_{AB}]}$$

When the covariance is zero, the third term is zero, and portfolio risk reduces to:

$$\sigma_P = \sqrt{[\alpha^2\sigma_A^2 + (1 - \alpha)^2\sigma_B^2]}$$

With zero covariance, portfolio risk is thus smaller for any portfolio compared to cases where the covariance is positive. Even better, when the covariance is negative, the third term becomes negative and risk falls even further. In general, the lowest achievable portfolio risk declines as the covariance diminishes: if it is negative, all the better. There is, however, no limit on the covariance value. If we re-express portfolio risk in terms of the correlation coefficient, we can be more specific about the greatest achievable degree of risk reduction. The formula relating covariance and correlation coefficient (Equation 8.3) can be rewritten as:

$$cov_{AB} = (r_{AB} \times \sigma_A \times \sigma_B)$$

Substituting into the expression for portfolio risk (Equation 8.2), we derive:

$$\sigma_p = \sqrt{[\alpha^2\sigma_A^2 + (1 - \alpha)^2\sigma_B^2 + 2\alpha(1 - \alpha)r_{AB}\sigma_A\sigma_B]}$$

Inspection of this formula shows that when the correlation coefficient is negative, portfolio risk can be lowered by combining assets A and B. From a risk-minimising perspective, the most advantageous value of the coefficient is minus one, since when the portfolio is suitably weighted, the standard deviation of the portfolio return can be reduced to zero. We thus have a formulaic demonstration of the result intuitively obtained in the Apple and Pear example at the start of the chapter. Whether one works in terms of the covariance or the correlation coefficient is generally a matter of preference, but, sometimes, it is dictated by the information available.

■ The optimal portfolio

An obvious question to ask is: which is the best portfolio to hold? In this example, the two investments have the same expected values, so any portfolio we construct by combining them will also offer this expected value. The optimal portfolio is therefore the one that offers the lowest level of risk. Although very few decision-makers are outright risk minimisers, any rational risk-averse manager will adopt the risk-minimising action where every alternative offers an equal expected payoff.

The minimum risk portfolio with two assets

The expression for finding the weightings required to minimise the risk of a portfolio comprising two assets, A and B, where α_A^* = the proportion invested in asset A is:

$$\alpha_A^* = \frac{\sigma_B^2 - cov_{AB}}{\sigma_A^2 + \sigma_B^2 - 2cov_{AB}} \tag{8.4}$$

Substituting the figures for the AB example into Equation 8.4, we find:

$$\alpha_A^* = \frac{40^2}{30^2 + 40^2} = \frac{1{,}600}{2{,}500} = 0.64$$

This formula tells us that, to minimise risk, we should place 64 per cent of our funds in A and 36 per cent in B.

Self-assessment activity 8.3

Verify that the standard deviation of this risk-minimising portfolio is 24 per cent.

(Answer in Appendix A at the back of the book)

In the next section, we analyse the more likely, and more interesting, case where both the risks and expected returns of the two components differ.

8.4 PORTFOLIO ANALYSIS WHERE RISK AND RETURN DIFFER

Suppose we are offered the two investments, Z and Y, whose characteristics are shown in Table 8.3. Which should we undertake? Or should we undertake some combination? To answer these questions, we need to consider the possible available combinations of risk and return. Notice that correlation is negative.

Table 8.3 Differing returns and risks

Asset	Expected return (%)	Standard deviation (%)
Z	15	20
Y	35	40

Correlation coefficient$_{ZY}$ = −0.25; Covariance$_{ZY}$ = (−0.25) × (20) × (40) = −200

Table 8.4 Portfolio risk–return combinations

Z weighting (%)	Y weighting (%)	Expected return (%)	Standard deviation (%)
100	0	15	20
75	25	20	16
50	50	25	20
25	75	30	29
0	100	35	40

Let us assume that the two assets can be combined in any proportions, i.e. the two assets are perfectly divisible, as with security investments. There is an infinite number of possible combinations of risk and return. However, for simplicity, we confine our attention to the restricted range of portfolios whose risk and return characteristics are shown in Table 8.4.

If we wanted to minimise risk, we would invest solely in asset Z, since this has the lowest standard deviation. However, as we move from the all-Z portfolio to the combination 75 per cent of Z plus 25 per cent of Y, the risk of the whole portfolio diminishes and the expected return *increases*. Eventually, though, for portfolios more heavily weighted towards Y, the effect of Y's higher risk outweighs the beneficial effect of negative correlation, resulting in rising overall risk.

Figure 8.2 traces the full range of available opportunities (or **opportunity set**), shaped rather like the nose cone of an aircraft. The profile ranges from point A, representing total investment in Y, through to point C, representing total investment in Z, having described a U-turn at B.

opportunity set
The set of investment opportunities (i.e. risk–return combinations) available to the investor to select from

Self-assessment activity 8.4

Verify that the portfolio at B, involving 75 per cent of Z and 25 per cent of Y, is the minimum risk combination.

(Answer in Appendix A at the back of the book)

efficient frontier
Traces out all the available portfolio combinations that either minimise risk for a stated expected return or maximise expected return for a specified measure of risk

optimal portfolio
The risk–return combination that offers maximum satisfaction to the investor, i.e. his/her most-preferred risk–return combination

Not all combinations are of interest to the rational risk-averse investor. Comparing segment AB with the segment BC, we find that combinations lying along the latter are inefficient. For any combination along BC, we can achieve a higher return for the same risk by moving to the combination vertically above it on AB. Point S is clearly superior to T and, applying similar logic to the whole of BC, we are left with the segment AB summarising all efficient portfolios, i.e. those that maximise return for a given risk. AB is thus called the **efficient frontier**. Points along AB are said to dominate corresponding points along BC.

However, we cannot specify an **optimal portfolio**, except for the outright risk-minimiser, who would select the portfolio at B, and for the maximiser of expected return, who would settle at point A (all Y). A risk-averse person might select any portfolio along AB, depending on his or her degree of risk aversion: that is, what additional

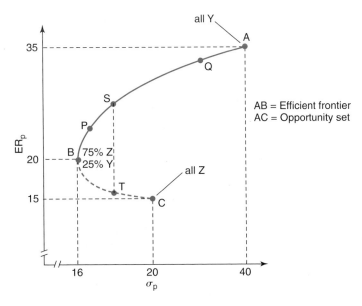

Figure 8.2 Available portfolio risk–return combinations when assets, risks and expected returns are different

return they would require to compensate for a specified increase in risk. For example, a highly risk-averse person might locate at point P, while the less cautious person might locate at point Q.

This is a crucial result. The most desirable combination of risky assets depends on the decision-maker's attitude towards risk. If we knew the extent of their risk-aversion – that is, how large a premium is required for a given increase in risk – we could specify the best portfolio.

Self-assessment activity 8.5

What is meant by an efficient frontier in portfolio analysis?

(Answer in Appendix A at the back of the book)

8.5 DIFFERENT DEGREES OF CORRELATION

Using arbitrary values for the correlation coefficient, we have found that negative correlation offers a handsome portfolio effect, and, to a lesser degree, also zero correlation. It is useful now to consider more carefully the general relationship between risk, correlation and return. To do this, we look at the full range of possible degrees of correlation, extending from perfect negative to perfect positive.

Say we are dealing with two investments, A and B, with asset A offering the higher expected return but also carrying greater risk. These are shown in Figure 8.3.

Consider the following degrees of correlation:

1 *Perfect positive.* In this case, it is not possible to achieve a portfolio effect at all. Combinations of A and B locate along the straight line AB. To achieve lower risk levels, we would simply invest more in asset B, while the risk-minimising 'portfolio' is simply asset B alone.

2 *Perfect negative.* In this case, combinations along AXB all become possible. With the returns from the two assets moving in perfect opposition to each other, it is possible to eliminate risk by adding B to A, but only by weighting the portfolio correctly is it possible fully to exploit the beneficial effect of correlation. Maximum risk-reduction

is achieved at point X where the portfolio risk is zero. Combinations along XB are clearly inefficient.

3 *Intermediate values.* For correlation coefficients between +1 and −1, it is still possible to generate a portfolio effect. The lower the correlation, i.e. the further away from +1, the greater the portfolio effect achievable. Two examples are shown in Figure 8.3 as dotted curves between A and B. The characteristic 'bow' shapes result from a progressively lower correlation bending the profile from its original position until we start observing 'nose cones' as identified earlier.

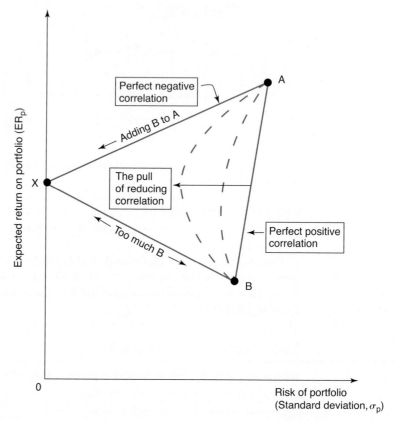

Figure 8.3 The effect on the efficiency frontier of changing correlation

Keeping the family fortune relatively intact

Family-controlled companies loom large in Asia, many tracing their origins to the 19th-century migration of mercantilist entrepreneurs from China. Many younger generation Asian family members have seen the need to diversify their family's businesses or risk oblivion.

One such family is Eu Yan Sang, a Singapore business founded in 1910 that has been transformed from a sleepy seller of traditional Chinese medicine into one with a global presence in the fast-growing 'health and wellness' sector. That turnaround was engineered by one of the city-state's best known entrepreneurs, Richard Eu, great-grandson of the founding patriarch. When he took over in the 1990s Eu Yan Sang was barely profitable from a few shops in

Singapore and Malaysia. Last year net profit was S$21m ($16.8m), from sales of modern, high-margin products.

'The family businesses that have survived did not just stick to their core business,' says Annie Koh, associate professor of finance at Singapore Management University. Others are seizing opportunities to expand regionally as they outgrow their home market. Some businesses are also moving further afield as they diversify, buying assets in the US and Europe. This year Eu Yan Sang bought a 22.5 per cent stake in Oriental & Western, a maker of food supplements and anti-ageing creams based in Oxfordshire, England.

Source: Based on Jeremy Grant, *Financial Times,* 23 September 2013, p. 19.

8.6 WORKED EXAMPLE: GERRYBILD PLC

Gerrybild plc is a firm of speculative housebuilders that builds in advance of firm orders from customers. It has a given amount of capital to purchase land and raw materials and to pay labour for development purposes. It is considering two design types – a small two-bedroomed terraced town house and a large four-bedroomed 'executive' residence. The project could last a number of years and its success depends largely on general economic conditions, which will influence the demand for new houses. Some information is available on past sales patterns of similar properties in roughly similar locations – the demand is relatively higher for larger properties in buoyant economic conditions, and higher for smaller properties in relatively depressed states of the economy. Since there appears to be a degree of inverse correlation between demand, and, therefore, net cash flows, from the two products, it seems sensible to consider diversified development. Table 8.5 shows annual net present value estimates for various economic conditions.

Table 8.5 Returns from Gerrybild

		Estimated NPV £ per:	
State of the economy	Probability	Large house	Small house
E_1	0.2	20,000	20,000
E_2	0.3	20,000	30,000
E_3	0.4	40,000	20,000
E_4	0.1	40,000	30,000

To analyse this decision problem, we need, first, to calculate the risk–return parameters of the investment, and, second, to assess the degree of correlation. This information may be obtained by performing a number of statistical operations:

1 *Calculation of expected values.* A shortcut is available, since some outcomes may occur under more than one state of the economy. Grouping data where possible:

$$EV_L = \text{Expected value of a large house} = (0.5 \times £20,000) + (0.5 \times £40,000)$$
$$= £30,000$$
$$EV_S = \text{Expected value of a small house} = (0.6 \times £20,000) + (0.4 \times £30,000)$$
$$= £24,000$$

2 *Calculation of project risks.* We now apply the usual expression for the standard deviation. The calculations for each activity are shown in Table 8.6. Clearly, the relative money-spinner, the large house project, is also the more risky activity.
3 *Calculation of co-variability.* Table 8.7 presents the calculation of the covariance in tabular form, following the steps itemised in Section 8.3.

The covariance of –£20 million suggests a strong element of inverse association. This is confirmed by the value of the correlation coefficient:

$$r_{LS} = \frac{\text{cov}_{LS}}{\sigma_L \times \sigma_S} = \frac{-£20,000,000}{(£10,000)(£4,899)} = -0.41$$

There are clearly significant portfolio benefits to exploit. To offer concrete advice to the builder, we would require information on his risk–return preferences, but we can still specify the available set of portfolio combinations. Rather than compute the full set of

Table 8.6 Calculation of standard deviations of returns from each investment

Outcome (£)	Probability	EV (£)	Deviation (£)	Squared deviation (£ million)	Weighted squared deviation (£ million)
Large houses					
20,000	0.5	30,000	−10,000	100	50.0
40,000	0.5	30,000	+10,000	100	50.0
				σ_L^2 = Variance =	100.0
				hence σ_L =	$\sqrt{100m}$
					= 10,000
					i.e. £10,000
Small houses					
20,000	0.6	24,000	−4,000	16	9.6
30,000	0.4	24,000	+6,000	36	14.4
				σ_S^2 = Variance =	24.0
				hence σ_S =	$\sqrt{24m}$
					= 4,899
					i.e. £4,899

Table 8.7 Calculation of the covariance

Outcomes (£)						
R_L	R_S	Probability	$(R_L - EV_L)$ (£)	$(R_S - EV_S)$ (£)	Product (£m)	Weighted product (£m)
20,000	20,000	0.2	−10,000	−4,000	40	+8
20,000	30,000	0.3	−10,000	+6,000	60	−18
40,000	20,000	0.4	+10,000	−4,000	40	−16
40,000	30,000	0.1	+10,000	+6,000	60	+6
					cov_{LS} =	−20
					i.e. −£20 million	

opportunities, we will identify the minimum risk portfolio, to enable construction of the overall risk–return profile.

■ The minimum risk portfolio

Using Equation 8.4, and defining α_L^* as the proportion of the portfolio (i.e. proportion of the available capital) devoted to large houses to minimise risk, we have:

$$\alpha_L^* = \frac{(\sigma_S^2 - cov_{LS})}{(\sigma_S^2 + \sigma_L^2 - 2\,cov_{LS})} = \frac{£24m + £20m}{£24m + £100m + £40m}$$

$$= \frac{£44m}{£164m} = 0.27$$

If Gerrybild wanted to minimise risk, it would have to invest 27 per cent of its capital in developing large houses and 73 per cent in developing small houses.

Self-assessment activity 8.6

Verify that the lowest achievable portfolio standard deviation is £3,496 and the expected NPV per house built from the minimum risk portfolio is £25,620.

(Answer in Appendix A at the back of the book)

■ The opportunity set

We now have assembled sufficient information to display the full range of opportunities available to Gerrybild. The opportunity set ABC is shown in Figure 8.4 as the familiar nose cone shape. If Gerrybild is risk-averse, only segment AB is of interest, but precisely where along this segment it will choose to locate depends on the attitude towards risk of its decision-makers.

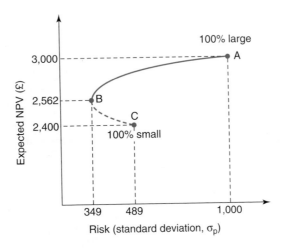

Figure 8.4 Gerrybild's opportunity set

Self-assessment activity 8.7

Using Figure 8.4, distinguish between risk minimisation and risk aversion.

(Answer in Appendix A at the back of the book)

8.7 PORTFOLIOS WITH MORE THAN TWO COMPONENTS*

Having so far looked only at simple two-asset portfolios, it is now useful to extend the analysis to more comprehensive combinations (see Figure 8.5). Imagine three assets are available, A, B and C, for each of which we have estimates of expected return and standard deviation, and also the covariance (and hence correlation) between each pair of assets. Imagine further that, whereas A and B are quite closely correlated, B and C are less so, and that correlation between A and C is even weaker.

Using a technique called Quadratic Programming, developed by Sharpe (1963), we can specify all available portfolios comprising one, two or three assets. Although there are only seven possible configurations of whole investments (A, B and C alone, A plus B, B plus C, A plus C and all three together), there are myriad combinations if we allow for divisibility of assets. The full range of available portfolios, i.e. risk–return combinations, is shown by the opportunity set in the form of an envelope, or 'bat-wing'.

The corners represent individual assets, while two-asset combinations are shown by the solid curves AB and BC and the dotted profile AC. Notice that by combining A

---

*As one might imagine, the mathematics of more complex portfolios becomes more awkward to handle as the number of components increases. The interested reader may wish to consult a more rigorous treatment, such as that given by Copeland, Weston and Shastri (2013). We will rely on an intuitive approach.

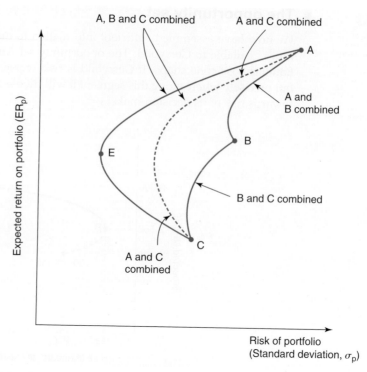

Figure 8.5 Portfolio combinations with three assets

and C, the investor can exploit their relative lack of correlation by accessing relatively more attractive portfolios in terms of their respective returns for particular levels of risk. The opportunity set thus moves inwards as assets with lower correlation are included. However, he can now access even more attractive combinations of A and C by combining all three assets. Points inside the envelope, or along the outer boundary, represent all possible combinations of A, B and C.

Notice that the investor now has access to a far wider range of investment combinations. If he is limited to combinations of only two assets, say A and B, as we saw in earlier analyses, he is restricted to risk–return combinations along AB or BC, depending on which two assets are combined. However, if access is opened up to include a third asset, the expanded range of combinations now available allows him to select far superior mixes of risk and return. For example, combinations within the envelope and on its upper bound, AEC, are superior to most of the two-asset portfolios available along AB and BC.

As before, we can differentiate between efficient and inefficient combinations. Clearly, all points lying beneath the upper edge AE and those along the segment EC are inefficient. The efficient set is therefore AE, identical in shape to our earlier profile, except that we are dealing with three-asset combinations (enabling investors to achieve lower levels of risk for specified returns by diversifying away yet more risk). Similar principles would apply if we were dealing with 30 or 300 assets, although the information requirements would become progressively more formidable.

Generally, we can conclude that the more assets that are available, the wider the range of choice open to the investor, and the greater the opportunities to achieve more desirable combinations of risk and return. The more assets under consideration, the nearer to the vertical axis lies the envelope of portfolios. Hence, the higher is the return achievable for a given risk, or conversely, the lower is the risk achievable for a specified expected return.

Notice also that the earlier conclusion about the optimal portfolio remains valid – it still depends on the particular investor's risk–return preferences.

Self-assessment activity 8.8

Draw an envelope of portfolios for the case where four assets are available to invest in, either individually or as portfolios.

(Answer in Appendix A at the back of the book)

The case for putting all your eggs in one basket

To date, portfolio diversification remains the most important lesson taught to students of investment and risk management. However, if we look at the portfolios of the rich and famous, they are, surprisingly, mostly concentrated.

Several great investors have very concentrated portfolios. Warren Buffett, George Soros, Rakesh Jhunjhunwala and many others are renowned proponents of portfolio concentration. To Mr Buffett, over-diversification presented a 'low-hazard, low-return' situation and thus he dismissed it. A concentrated portfolio pivots on the absolute conviction of the investor in his or her stocks and his or her risk appetite.

A diversified portfolio, on the other hand, works well if the investor is optimistic about the stock, but wary of the associated risk. Investors like the first billion-dollar Indian investor, Mr Jhunjhunwala, walk a fine line between the two.

Mr Buffett, echoing Benjamin Graham, the father of 'value' investing, says he does not just buy an insignificant thing that bounces by a small percentage every day on the stock market. He buys part of a real business and thinks like the owner of a business would.

Mr Buffett says: 'Wide diversification is only required when investors do not understand what they are doing.' Bruce Berkowitz, founder of Fairholme Capital and a leading 'value' proponent, adds that just a handful of significant positions are enough to do unbelievably well in a lifetime.

Source: Based on Nupur Pavan Bang and Khemchand Sakaldeepi, *Financial Times*, 30 September 2013, p. 6.

8.8 CAN WE USE THIS FOR PROJECT APPRAISAL? SOME RESERVATIONS

The Gerrybild example illustrates some drawbacks with the portfolio approach to handling project risk.

1 Most projects can be undertaken only in a very restricted range of sizes or even on an 'all-or-nothing' basis. This does not entirely undermine the portfolio approach – it simply means that the range of combinations available is much narrower. Besides, enterprises are often undertaken on a joint venture basis (e.g. in large, high-risk activities like Eurotunnel and Airbus and many cross-border automobile operations), where the various parties have some freedom to select the extent of their participation.

2 A more severe problem is the implication of constant returns to scale. Our analyses imply that if a smaller version of a project is undertaken, the percentage returns, or the absolute return per pound invested, will remain unchanged. For example, if the return on a whole project is 20 per cent, the return from doing 30 per cent of the same project is still 20 per cent. This may apply for investment in securities, but is unlikely for investment projects, where there is often a minimum size below which there are zero or negative returns, and, thereafter, increasing returns to scale.

3 We should be wary of any approach that relies on subjective assessments of probabilities, and wary of the probabilities themselves. In the case of repetitive activities, such as replacement of equipment, about which a substantial data bank of costs and benefits has been compiled, the probabilities may have some basis in reality. In other cases, such as major new product developments, probabilities

are largely based on inspired guesswork. Different decision analysts may well formulate different 'guesstimates' about the chances of particular events occurring. However, the subjective nature of probabilities used in practice need not be a deterrent if the estimates are well supported by reasoned argument, and therefore instil confidence.

4 Since attitudes to risk determine choice, we need to know the decision-maker's utility function, which summarises his or her preferences for different monetary amounts, if we wanted to pinpoint the optimal (as distinct from the risk-minimising) portfolio. The difficulties of obtaining information about an individual manager's utility function (let alone for a group) are formidable, as Swalm (1966) has shown. Besides, we should really be seeking to apply the risk–return preferences of shareholders rather than those of managers.

5 The portfolio approach to analysing project risk seems unduly management-oriented. Managers formulate the assessments of alternative payoffs, assess the relevant probabilities and determine what combinations of activities the enterprise should undertake. Managers are considerably less mobile and less well diversified than shareholders, who can buy and sell securities more or less at will. Managers can hardly shrug off a poor investment outcome if it jeopardises the future of the enterprise or, more pertinently, their job security. Most managers are more risk-averse than shareholders, resulting in the likelihood of sub-optimal investment decisions. Here, we see another manifestation of the agency problem – how do we get managers to accept the levels of risk that owners are prepared to tolerate?

Capital Asset Pricing Model (CAPM)
The CAPM is a model designed to explain how the stock market values capital assets, including ordinary shares, by assessing their relative risk–return properties

These may appear to be highly damaging criticisms of the portfolio approach, especially as it applies to investment decisions. However, although having limited operational usefulness for many investment projects, it provides the infrastructure of a more sophisticated approach to investment decision-making under risk, the **Capital Asset Pricing Model (CAPM)**. This is based on an examination of the risk–return characteristics and resulting portfolio opportunities of securities, rather than physical investment opportunities.

The CAPM explains how individual securities are valued, or priced, in efficient capital markets. Essentially, this involves discounting the future expected returns from holding a security at a rate that adequately reflects the degree of risk incurred in holding that security. A major contribution of the CAPM is the determination of the premium for risk demanded by the market from different securities. This provides a clue as to the appropriate discount rate to apply when evaluating risky projects. The CAPM is analysed in the next chapter.

SUMMARY

This chapter has examined some reasons why firms diversify their activities, and has considered the extent to which the theory of portfolio analysis can provide operational guidelines for diversification decisions.

Key points

- Both firms and individuals diversify investments – firms build portfolios of business activities and individuals build portfolios of securities.

- An important motive for business diversification is to reduce fluctuations in returns.

- Variations in returns can be totally eliminated only if the investments concerned have perfect negative correlation and if the portfolio is weighted so as to minimise risk.

- The expected return from a portfolio is a weighted average of the returns expected from its components, the weights being determined by the proportion of capital invested in each activity or security. For a portfolio comprising the two assets, A and B:

$$ER_P = \alpha ER_A + (1 - \alpha)ER_B$$

- Portfolio risk is given by a square-root formula that includes a measure of covariability:

$$\sigma_P = \sqrt{[\alpha^2 \sigma_A^2 + (1 - \alpha)^2 \sigma_B^2 + 2\alpha(1 - \alpha)\text{cov}_{AB}]}$$

- The degree of covariability between the returns expected from the components of the portfolios can be measured by the covariance, cov_{AB}, or by the correlation coefficient, r_{AB}. The lower the degree of covariability, the lower is the risk of the portfolio (for given weightings).

- The available risk–return combinations for mixing investments are shown by the opportunity set.

- Some combinations can be rejected as inefficient. Rational risk-averting investors focus only on the efficient set.

- The optimal portfolio for any investor depends on their attitude to risk, that is, how risk-averse they are.

- In practice, there are serious difficulties in applying the portfolio techniques to physical investment decisions.

Further reading

The classic works on portfolio theory are by Markowitz (1952), Sharpe (1964) and Tobin (1958) (all of whom have won Nobel Prizes for Economics). See also, Sharpe, Alexander and Bailey (1996), Levy and Sarnat (1994a) and Copeland, Weston and Shastri (2013) for more developed analyses, and also proofs and derivations of the formulae used in this chapter. Finally, Markowitz's Nobel address (1991) is well worth reading. Rubinstein (2002) gives a '50 years on' assessment of the impact of the CAPM. *ABACUS* journal has a special issue devoted to examining CAPM, Volume 49, January 2013. This special issue debates the importance, relevance and validity of CAPM.

QUESTIONS

Questions with a coloured number have solutions in Appendix B on page 785.

1 The returns on investment in two projects, X and Y, have standard deviations of 30 per cent and 45 per cent respectively. The correlation coefficient between the returns on the two investments is 0.2. What is the standard deviation of a portfolio containing *equal* proportions of the two investments?

2 Determine the risk-minimising portfolios for the following two-asset portfolios:

(i) $ER_A = 8\%$; $ER_B = 10\%$; $\sigma_A = 3\%$; $\sigma_B = 7\%$; $r_{AB} = -0.6$

(ii) $ER_A = 20\%$; $ER_B = 12\%$; $\sigma_A = 12\%$; $\sigma_B = 6\%$; $r_{AB} = -0.5$

(iii) $ER_A = 11\%$; $ER_B = 5\%$; $\sigma_A = 15\%$; $\sigma_B = 1\%$; $r_{AB} = 0$

3 Tomb-zapper plc manufactures computer video games. It is considering whether to expand production at its existing site in 'Silicon Glen' in Scotland, or to start production in a 'greenfield site' in China, where labour costs are considerably lower than in Europe. The IRRs for each project depend on average rates of growth in the world economy over the ten-year lifespan of the project. These are expected to be:

World growth	Probability	IRR China	IRR Scotland
Rapid	0.3	50%	10%
Stable	0.4	25%	15%
Slow	0.3	0%	16%

Tomb-zapper wants to exploit the less than perfect correlation between the returns from the two projects, without over-committing itself to the China investment.

Required

(a) What is the expected return and standard deviation of return for each separate project?

(b) Determine the expected return and standard deviation of an expansion programme that involves 25 per cent of available funds in China and 75 per cent in the Scottish location.

4 Nissota, a Japanese-based car manufacturer, is evaluating two overseas locations for a proposed expansion of production facilities at a site in Ireland and another on Humberside. The likely future return from investment in each site depends to a great extent on future economic conditions. Three scenarios are postulated, and the internal rate of return from each investment is computed under each scenario. The returns with their estimated probabilities are shown below:

	Internal rate of return (%)	
Probability	Ireland	Humberside
0.3	20	10
0.3	10	30
0.4	15	20

There is zero correlation between the returns from the two sites.

Required

(a) Calculate the expected value of the IRR and the standard deviation of the return from investment in each location.

(b) What would be the expected return and the standard deviation of the following split investment strategies:

 (i) committing 50 per cent of available funds to the site in Ireland and 50 per cent to Humberside?

 (ii) committing 75 per cent of funds to the site in Ireland and 25 per cent to the Humberside site?

5 The management of Gawain plc is evaluating two projects whose returns depend on the future state of the economy as shown below:

Probability	IRR_A(%)	IRR_B(%)
0.3	27	35
0.4	18	15
0.3	5	20

The project (or projects) accepted would double the size of Gawain.

Required

(a) Explain how a portfolio should be constructed to produce an expected return of 20 per cent.

(b) Calculate the correlation between projects A and B, and assess the degree of risk of the portfolio in (a).

(c) Gawain's existing activities have a standard deviation of 10 per cent. How does the addition of the portfolio analysed in (a) and (b) affect risk?

Practical assignment

Select a company with a reasonably wide portfolio of activities. Such companies do not always give segmental earnings figures, but they usually divulge sales figures for their component activities. By looking at the annual reports for three or four years, you can obtain a series of annual sales figures for each activity.

Assess the degree of past volatility of the sales of each sub-unit and their degree of inter-correlation. Also, see whether you can assess the extent of the correlation between each segment and the overall enterprise. How well diversified does your selected company appear to be? What qualifications should you make in your analysis?

9

Setting the risk premium: the Capital Asset Pricing Model

'Modern' portfolio theory

Overheard on the 6:41 from Bognor Regis to London Bridge:

Student 1: We did modern portfolio theory (MPT) yesterday. It was hard but I really enjoyed it.

Student 2: Yeah? What did it tell you?

Student 1: Well, for starters, you should own shares in both sun lotion manufacturers and umbrella manufacturers.

Student 2: Yeah, but what if the weather's just cloudy and dry?

Student 1: Dunno.

One answer offered by MPT is that the canny marketing men at All Weather Products plc will produce both products, just in case the weather takes a turn for either the better or the worse. So, it wins both ways. Another is that shares in AWP will fluctuate in value according to the financial rather than the meteorological weather, as they are protected from climatological vicissitudes. The rise of the large investment management houses was driven by MPT (no longer so modern now), which enjoyed its heyday in the 1980s. Investors were urged by its proponents to contemplate the benefits of diversification. Quantitative analysts drew up efficient frontier curves that purported to show how to achieve any given target rate of investment return at the lowest possible risk.

Investment was not just about picking stocks but about choosing the perfect combination of baskets among which to distribute one's nest eggs. Diversification takes two forms: owning a range of asset classes (bonds, shares, property, commodities and so on), and owning a range of investments within each class. To do justice to the portfolio theory requires a significant input from analysts and fund managers, which plays into the hands of the largest investment groups.

Unfortunately, having a big roster of investment professionals and having a critical mass of talented ones are very different things. As investment groups grew, their performance did not improve. In one respect it declined markedly, in that large size became a guarantee of ordinariness. With a small number of honourable exceptions, the leading fund managers delivered strikingly similar investment portfolios and, hence, returns for their customers. Portfolio theory is just that – a theory. It flounders on the constraints of time and resource that challenge all investors. Sometimes it is better to pick a small number of out-of-favour investments and wait for the weather to turn in their favour than condemn your performance to the depressing law of the average.

Source: Based on Edmond Warner, *Guardian*, 1 August 2005.

Learning objectives

This chapter deals with the rate of return required by shareholders of an all-equity financed company, building on the principles of portfolio theory covered in Chapter 8. Its specific aims are:

- To explain what type of risk is relevant for valuing capital assets.
- To explain what a 'Beta coefficient' is.
- To determine the appropriate risk premium to incorporate into a discount rate, whether for investment in securities or in capital projects.
- To examine the case for *corporate* diversification.
- To examine some criticisms of the CAPM.

An understanding of the significance of Beta coefficients is particularly important in appreciating how financial managers should view risk.

9.1 INTRODUCTION

In Chapters 7 and 8, we examined various methods of handling risk and uncertainty in project appraisal, ranging from sensitivity analysis to diversification that seeks to exploit the (normally) less than perfect correlation between the returns from risky investments. Most of these approaches aim to identify the sources and extent of project risk and to assess whether the expected returns sufficiently compensate investors for bearing the risk. Utility theory suggests that, as risk increases, rational risk-averse people require higher returns, justifying the common practice of adjusting discount rates for risk. However, none of these approaches offers an explicit guide to measuring the *precise* reward that investors should seek for incurring a particular level of risk.

The CAPM is a theory originally devised by Sharpe (1964) to explain how the capital market sets share prices. It now provides the infrastructure of much of modern financial theory and research and offers important insights into measuring risk and setting risk premiums. In particular, it shows how the study of security prices can help in assessing required rates of return on investment projects. However, as we shall see, the CAPM has not gone unchallenged.

9.2 SECURITY VALUATION AND DISCOUNT RATES

Asset value is governed by two factors – the stream of expected benefits from holding the asset and their 'quality', or likely variability. For example, the value of a single-project company is assessed by discounting future project cash flows at a discount rate reflecting their risk. The value, V_0, of a company newly formed by issuing 1 million shares to exploit a one-year project offering a single net cash flow of £10 million, at a 25 per cent discount rate, is:

$$V_0 = \frac{£10m}{(1.25)} = £8m$$

This suggests a market price per share of (£8m/1m shares) = £8. This would be the value established by an efficient capital market taking account of all known information about the company's future prospects.

Sometimes, the 'correct' discount rate is unclear to the firm. A major contribution of the CAPM is to explain how discount rates are established and, hence, how securities are valued. However, from the capital market value of a company, we can 'work backwards' to infer what discount rate underlies the market price. In the example, if we observe a market price of £8, this suggests a required return of 25 per cent.

By implication, if the market sets a value on a security that implies a particular discount rate, it is reasonable to conclude that any further activity *of similar risk* to current operations should offer about the same rate. This argument depends critically on market prices being unbiased indicators of the intrinsic worth of companies, i.e. that the efficient markets hypothesis applies.

Any discount rate is an amalgam of three components:

1 Allowance for the time value of money – the compensation required by investors for having to wait for their payments.
2 Allowance for price level changes – the additional return required to compensate for the impact of inflation on the real value of capital.
3 Allowance for risk – the promised reward that provides the incentive for investors to expose their capital to risk.

Ignoring expected inflation (or assuming that it is 'correctly' built into the structure of interest rates), discount rates have two components – the rate of return required on totally risk-free assets, such as government securities, and a risk premium.

9.3 CONCEPTS OF RISK AND RETURN

In this section, we examine risk and return concepts relevant for security valuation.

■ The returns from holding shares

Investors hold securities because they hope for positive returns. Purchasers of ordinary shares are attracted by two elements: first, the anticipated dividend(s) payable during the holding period; and second, the expected capital gain. Taken together, these elements make up the **Total Shareholder Return (TSR)**.

Total Shareholder Return (TSR)
The overall return enjoyed by investors, including dividend and capital appreciation, expressed as a percentage of their initial investment. Related to individual years, or to a lengthier time period, and then converted into an annualised, or equivalent annual return

Total Shareholder Return (TSR)

In general, for any holding period, t, and company, j, the TSR is the percentage return, R_{jt}, from holding its shares:

$$R_{jt} = \frac{D_{jt} + (P_{jt} - P_{jt-1})}{P_{jt-1}} \times 100$$

where D_{jt} is the dividend per share paid by company j in period t, P_{jt} is the share price for company j at the end of period t and P_{jt-1} is the share price for company j at the start of period t.

To illustrate this calculation, consider the following figures for a firm, for the calendar year 2014:

Share price at end of December 2013 = £11.61

Share price at end of December 2014 = £12.25

Net dividend paid during 2014 = 70p per share

The percentage return over this year was:

$$\frac{70p + (£12.25 - £11.61)}{£11.61} \times 100 = \frac{(70p + 64p)}{£11.61} \times 100 = 11.5\%$$

However, the TSR data relate to just one year, and may be influenced in either direction by random factors. A more meaningful measure of shareholder return would remove these short-term fluctuations, adverse or favourable. This is done by taking the overall return over a specific period, commonly five years, and converting this into an average annual or annualised equivalent rate of return. It is standard practice to make this calculation by assuming that dividends are re-invested in ordinary shares, i.e. the cash proceeds are used to buy shares at the prevailing market price at the date of dividend payment.

To illustrate this, figures from D.S. Smith, the UK packaging firm, are shown in Figure 9.1. For the period 2008–13, £100 invested in this firm would have grown at a rate above the growth in the FTSE 250 index of which D.S. Smith is a member.

Firms increasingly use TSR, usually in relation to other firms, as a performance benchmark as part of the executive reward scheme. For example, under its so-called Performance Share Plan, D.S. Smith bases a part of executive rewards on company TSR performance in relation to that of the constituents of the FTSE Industrial Goods and Services Supersector.

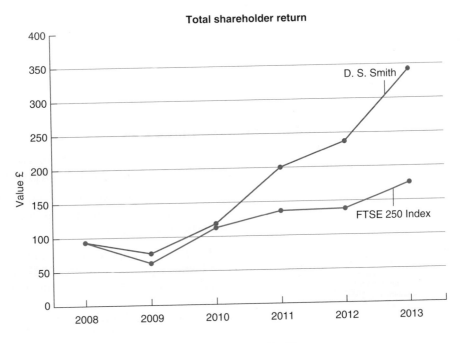

Figure 9.1 TSR of D.S. Smith vs. FTSE 250 Index 2008–13

Source: D.S. Smith *Annual Report* 2013.

Self-assessment activity 9.1

Determine the TSR for the year 201X in the following case:

- Share price 1 January: £2.20
- Share price 31 December: £2.37
- Interim dividend paid: £0.035 per share
- Final dividend paid: £0.065 per share

(Answer in Appendix A at the back of the book)

■ The risks of holding ordinary shares

In Chapter 8, we saw the power of portfolio combination in reducing the risk of a collection of investments. Risk was measured by the variance or standard deviation of the return on the combination. This measure can also be applied to portfolios of securities, with some remarkable results, as shown in Figure 9.2.

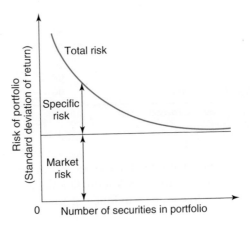

Figure 9.2 Specific vs. market risk of a portfolio

As the number of securities held in the portfolio increases, the overall variability of the portfolio's return, measured by its standard deviation, diminishes very sharply for small portfolios, but falls more gradually for larger combinations. This reduction is achieved because exposure to the risk of volatile securities can be offset by the inclusion of low-risk securities *or even ones of higher risk*, so long as their returns are not closely correlated.

■ Specific and systematic risk

Not all the risk of individual securities is relevant for assessing the risk of a portfolio of risky shares. The total risk of securities (and also of portfolios) has two components:

1 *Specific risk*: the variability in return due to factors unique to the individual firm.
2 *Systematic risk*: the variability in return due to dependence on factors that influence the return on all securities traded in the market.

specific risk
The variability in the return on a security due to exposure to risks relating to that security in isolation, e.g. risk of losing market share due to poor marketing decisions

Specific risk refers to the expected impact on sales and earnings of random events – industrial relations problems, equipment failure, R&D achievements, etc. In a portfolio of shares, such factors tend to cancel out as the number of securities included increases.

systematic risk
Variability in a security's return due to exposure to risks affecting all firms traded in the market (hence, **market risk**), e.g. the impact of exchange rate changes

Systematic risk refers to the impact of movements in the macroeconomy, such as fiscal changes, swings in exchange rates and interest rate movements, all of which cause reactions in security markets. These are captured in the movement of an index reflecting security prices in general, such as the FTSE in the UK or the DAX index in Germany. No firm is entirely insulated from these factors, and even portfolio diversification cannot provide total protection. Because these factors affect all firms in the market, such risk is often called 'market-related' (or just 'market') risk.

Returning to Figure 9.2, we see that the reduction in the total risk of a portfolio is achieved by gradual elimination of the risks unique to individual companies, leaving an irreducible, undiversifiable risk floor. The extent to which specific risk declines for a portfolio comprising N equally weighted and randomly selected securities is also shown in Table 9.1.

Table 9.1 How to remove portfolio risk

Number of securities (N)	Reduction in specific risk (%)
1	0
2	46
4	72
8	81
16	93
32	96
64	98
500	99

Source: Fosback (1985).

market portfolio
Includes all securities traded on the stock market weighted by their respective capitalisations. Usually, a more limited portfolio such as the FT All Share Index is used as a proxy

Substantial reductions in specific risk can be achieved with quite small portfolios, with the bulk of risk reduction being achieved with a portfolio of some 25–30 securities. To eliminate unique risk totally would involve holding a vast portfolio comprising all the securities traded in the market. This construct, called the '**market portfolio**', has a pivotal role in the CAPM, but for the individual investor, it is neither practicable nor cost-effective, in view of the dealing fees required to construct and manage it. However, since relatively small portfolios can capture the lion's share of diversification benefits, it is only a minor simplification to use a well-diversified portfolio as a proxy for the overall market, such as the FTSE-100, which covers approximately 81 per cent of the market capitalisation of all UK quoted companies (**www.ftse.com**).

Self-assessment activity 9.2

How many shares would an investor have to hold in order to *totally* eliminate specific risk?

(Answer in Appendix A at the back of the book)

■ Implications

Three major implications now follow:

1 *It is clear that risk-averse investors should diversify.* Yet in reality, over half of UK investors hold just one security (usually, shares in a privatised company). However, the major players in capital markets, holding well over two-thirds of all quoted UK ordinary shares (according to the Office of National Statistics, December 2012, **www .ons.gov.uk**[*]) are financial institutions such as pension funds and insurance companies, which do hold highly diversified portfolios.

2 *Investors should not expect rewards for bearing specific risk.* Since risk that is unique to particular companies can be diversified away, the only relevant consideration in assessing risk premiums is the risk that cannot be dispersed by portfolio formation. If bearing unique risk was rewarded, astute investors prepared to build portfolios would snap up securities with high levels of unique risk to diversify it away, while still hoping to enjoy disproportionate returns. The value of such securities would rise and the returns on them would fall until only systematic risks were rewarded.

3 *Securities have varying degrees of systematic risk.* Few securities exhibit patterns of returns rising or falling exactly in line with the overall market. This is partly because in the short term, unique random factors affect particular companies in different ways. Yet even in the long term, when such factors tend to even out, very few securities track the market. Some appear to outperform the market by offering superior returns and some appear to underperform it. However, performance relative to the market should not be too hastily judged, because the returns on different securities do not always depend on general economic factors in the same way.

For example, in an expanding economy, retail sales tend to increase sharply, but sales in less responsive sectors like water and defence are barely altered. Share prices of retailers usually increase quite sharply in an expanding economy, but the share prices of water companies and armaments suppliers respond far less dramatically. Retail sales are said to be 'more highly geared to the economy'. Systematic or market risk varies between companies, so we find different companies valued by the market at different discount rates. Already, we begin to see that the CAPM, based on the premise that rational investors can and do hold efficiently diversified portfolios, may show us how these discount rates might be assessed. Clearly, we need to measure systematic risk. This is covered in Section 9.5.

---

[*]At the end of December 2012, UK financial institutions held 27.1%, foreign investors 53.2% and private investors just 10.7%, with the balance of 9% held by the public sector and 'others'. The majority of foreign shareholdings (which have risen from 16% in 1994) is reckoned to represent institutional, rather than private, holdings.

Self-assessment activity 9.3

Give three examples of systematic and unique factors respectively that cause the returns on holding ordinary shares to vary over time.

(Answer in Appendix A at the back of the book)

Too many stocks spoil the portfolio

Diversification of a portfolio is a good thing. Right? Whether you reach that conclusion intuitively from the simple adage 'don't put all your eggs in one basket' or have heard of modern portfolio theory, you know it makes sense.

Unsurprisingly, the covariance of a portfolio of FTSE 100 stocks falls as the number of stocks in the portfolio increases, but the covariance – or risk – does not fall in a straight line. The risk falls sharply as the portfolio increases in number from just one stock, but by the time it has reached about 20 to 30 stocks most of the reduction in risk that can be attained has already been achieved. The problem is that increasing the number of stocks beyond this not only fails to achieve any significant further risk reduction, it also leads to other problems.

It is important to invest in good companies. But there is a severe limit to the number of good companies available and the more stocks you own the more you are likely to have to compromise on quality. It is also a fact that the more stocks you own the less you know about each of them and I have never found a theory of investment that suggests that the less you know about something, the more likely you are to generate superior returns.

There is even a term for this: 'diworsification', which was coined by the legendary fund manager Peter Lynch in his book *One Up On Wall Street*. He suggested that a business that diversifies too widely risks destroying itself, because management time, energy and resources are diverted from the original investment. Similarly, adding more investments to a portfolio can lead to diworsification.

Source: Based on Terry Smith, *Financial Times*, 13 April 2013, p. 7.

9.4 INTERNATIONAL PORTFOLIO DIVERSIFICATION

Most investors tend to adopt a local perspective when deciding which shares to buy. That is, they are inclined to invest in shares listed on their domestic stock market, thus demonstrating a 'home bias' when building portfolios. The prime reason cited for this home bias is that it is 'behavioural', being rooted in a preference for the familiar. Investors feel reassured when investing in the local stock market and perceive investing in other stock markets as high risk. This is despite financial markets having undergone a process of liberalisation since 1945, resulting in investors now facing increasingly greater possibilities to create portfolios that include international shares. Some argue that investors should grasp this opportunity and adopt a strategy of constructing international, rather than domestic, share portfolios. The implied rationale is that because correlations between different financial markets are quite low, investors can benefit from international diversification through reducing risk. For example, Odier and Solnik (1993) calculated the following correlation coefficients of the UK stock market with other markets over the 1980–90 period as: USA 0.6, Switzerland 0.5 and Germany 0.4. By contrast, correlation coefficients for 2013 of the UK stock market with these markets have been cited as : USA 0.55, Switzerland 0.78, Germany 0.81 (**www.bespokeinvest.com**). The overall effect of international diversification upon the risk of a portfolio is illustrated in Figure 9.3.

Whilst international diversification can have a beneficial effect upon the risk–return profile of an investor's portfolio, it introduces currency risk. However, it has generally been found that even if currency risk is left unhedged, it is preferable to invest internationally rather than just domestically.

Correlation coefficients between different stock markets do not remain static however. As financial globalisation has continued and stock markets have become more integrated, the question arises as to whether inter-market correlation

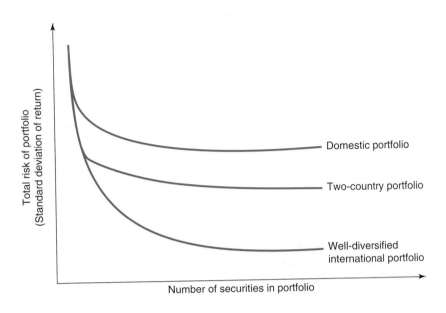

Figure 9.3 The effect of international diversification on portfolio risk

has increased. This is significant for investors as increased correlation coefficients erode the benefits of international diversification, and eventually a point is reached where it has no value. For example, Chiou (2008) analysed two time periods (1988 to 1996 and 1996 to 2004) and concluded that the advantages of global diversification have reduced overall. Chiou's findings also suggest these advantages are not evenly spread as investors based in emerging markets (particularly Latin America and East Asia) gain more from international diversification than investors based in developed countries. Driessen and Laeven's (2007) analysis of the effects of global diversification upon local investors in a diverse sample of 52 countries supports Chiou's findings. For the period 1985–2002, they concluded that correlations between markets have reduced as a result of greater market integration. However, they still find international diversification beneficial for all investors and particularly so for investors in developing countries. Within developing countries, the gains from global diversification are greatest for those countries with higher levels of country risk.

If home bias still deters investors from purchasing international stocks, an alternative strategy is for investors to maintain a sense of the familiar by diversifying regionally. Driessen and Laeven, in considering this strategy, suggest that regional diversification is beneficial, although not as advantageous as international diversification.

Another important issue concerns whether stock market correlations alter in periods of extreme volatility. For example, when a stock market crash occurs, it is plausible that with all markets falling simultaneously, the correlation coefficients between markets will increase substantially. If this does occur, the benefits of diversification diminish, and this at a time when these benefits are most needed. For this reason, studies examining correlations during bull and bear markets have been undertaken. For example, Longin and Solnik (2001) examined the period 1959–96 (which incorporates highly volatile episodes such as the 1987 Crash and the Gulf War crisis in the early 1990s), and Flavin and Panopoulou (2009) studied the period 1973–2005 which encompasses significant events such as the dotcom bubble. Longin and Solnik's principal conclusion from examining the five largest stock markets is that correlation increases in bear markets but not in bull markets. This has been supported by other research (for example, by Campbell, *et al.*, 2002; Meric *et al.*, 2002).

By contrast, Flavin and Panopoulou find that the benefits of international diversification are unaffected regardless of whether the market conditions are 'calm' or 'turbulent'. A particular difficulty in comparing the results of these types of study is that methods used to calculate correlations differ. In Flavin and Panopoulou's work, statistical correlations are not even considered – instead they investigate whether market linkages remain static over time. Their underlying argument is that if market linkages remain unchanged, this implies market contagion does not occur and international diversification will still deliver value for investors even when markets are highly unstable.

This discussion regarding international diversification neglects the issue of industry diversification. If, as already suggested, inter-market correlations have risen in recent years, country factors will have become less important for diversification. Concurrently, industry factors have risen in importance for investors' diversification strategies, and studies now suggest that industry diversification is of greater significance than country diversification. Therefore, investors should be considering purchasing shares in companies across a range of different industries to benefit their portfolios. The impact of industry and country diversification upon portfolio risk is shown in Figure 9.4.

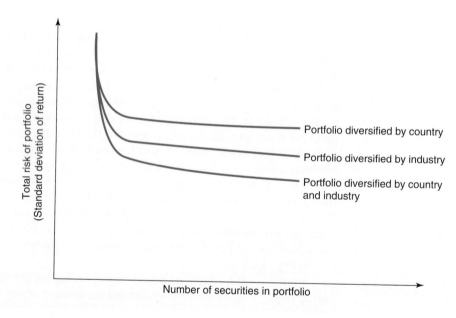

Figure 9.4 The effects of industry and country diversification on portfolio risk
Source: Adapted from Cavaglia, Brightman and Aked (2000).

When investors create portfolios, it is important to remember that shares are only one type of asset that they may decide to purchase. Property, commodities, bonds and other alternative assets can all form part of a portfolio. The risk–return profiles of these assets may differ substantially from the risk–return profiles of shares; more significantly, the correlation between returns on shares and alternative assets may be relatively low or even negative. This applies for bonds and shares where the correlation between their returns is normally found to be either very small or negative. Consequently, although bonds offer lower returns than shares, the relative lack of correlation can make them appealing to hold as a part of a diversified portfolio.

9.5 SYSTEMATIC RISK

As specific risk can be diversified away by portfolio formation, rational investors expect to be rewarded only for bearing systematic risk. Since systematic risk indicates the extent to which the expected return on individual shares varies with that expected on the overall market, we have to assess the extent of this co-movement. This is given by the slope of a line relating the expected return on a particular share, ER_j, to the return expected on the market, ER_m. It is important to appreciate that 'returns' in this context include both changes in market price and also dividends. For the overall market, dividend returns may be measured by the average dividend yield on the market index.

■ Example: Walkley Wagons

characteristics line (CL)
Relates the periodic returns on a security to the returns on the market portfolio. Its slope is the Beta of the security. The regression model used to estimate Betas is called the **market model**

The case of Walkley Wagons is shown in Table 9.2. Investors anticipate four possible future states of the economy. For every percentage point increase in the expected market return (ER_m), the expected return on Walkley shares (ER_j) rises by 1.2 percentage points. Walkley thus outperforms a rising market. The graphical relationship between ER_j and ER_m shown in Figure 9.5, is known as the **characteristics line (CL)**. Its slope of 1.2 is the **Beta coefficient**. Beta indicates how the return on Walkley is *expected* to vary alongside given variations in the return on the overall stock market.

Beta coefficients
Relate the responsiveness of the returns on individual securities to variations in the return on the overall market portfolio

Table 9.2 **Possible returns from Walkley Wagons**

State of economy	$ER_m(\%)$	$ER_j(\%)$
E_1	10	12
E_2	20	24
E_3	5	6
E_4	15	18

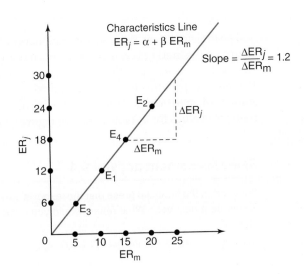

Figure 9.5 **The characteristics line: no specific risk**

■ The market model

In practice, because it is not easy to record people's expectations, the measurement of Beta cannot be done by looking forward. We have to measure Beta using *past* observations of the actual values of both the return on the individual company's shares, and also for the overall market, i.e. R_j and R_m respectively. So long as the past is accepted as a reliable indication of likely future events (i.e. people's expectations are moulded by examination of the frequency distribution of past recorded outcomes), observed Betas can be taken to indicate the extent to which R_j may vary for specified variations in R_m. A regression line[*] is fitted to a set of recorded relationships, as in Figure 9.6. The hypothesised relationship is:

$$R_j = \alpha_j + \beta_j R_m$$

and the fitted line is given by:

$$R_j = \hat{\alpha}_j + \hat{\beta}_j R_m + u$$

where $\hat{\alpha}_j$ and $\hat{\beta}_j$ are estimates of the 'true' values of α and β, and u is a term included to capture random influences, that are assumed to average zero. This regression model is called the **market model**.

market model
A device relating the expected (in practice, *actual*) return from individual securities to the expected/*actual* return from the overall stock market

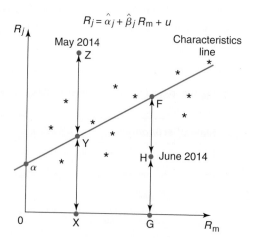

Figure 9.6 The characteristics line: with specific risk

The intercept term, α_j, deserves explanation. This is the return on security j when the return on the market is zero, i.e. the return with the impact of market or systematic risk stripped out. Consequently, it indicates what return the security offers for specific risk. We might expect this to average out at zero over time, given the random character of sources of specific risk. However, it is by no means uncommon empirically to record non-zero values for α. Notice that, in Figure 9.5, α is zero.

Self-assessment activity 9.4

You read in the financial press that the 'experts' are predicting overall stock market returns of 25 per cent next year. What return would you expect from holding Walkley Wagons ordinary shares?

(Answer in Appendix A at the back of the book)

---

[*]Readers unfamiliar with the technique of regression analysis might refer to C. Morris, *Quantitative Approaches in Business Studies* (Pearson, 2008).

■ Systematic and unsystematic returns

Figure 9.6 shows an imaginary set of monthly observations relating to a given year, say 2014, to which has been fitted a regression line. Clearly, unlike the *expected* values displayed in Figure 9.5, most values actually lie off the line of best fit. These divergences are due to the sort of random, unsystematic factors suggested in Section 9.3. For example, observation Z relates to the returns in May 2014. The overall return on security *j* in this month, XZ, can be broken down into the market-related return, XY, due to co-movement with the overall stock market, and the non-market return, or 'excess return', YZ, due to unsystematic factors, which, in this month, have operated favourably. The opposite appears to have applied in June 2014, indicated by point H. The market-related return 'should' have been FG, but the actual return of GH was dampened by unfavourable random factors represented by FH. *This analysis implies that variations in R_j **along** the characteristics line stem from market-related factors, which systematically affect all securities, and that variations **around** the line represent the impact of factors specific to company j. The systematic relationship is captured by β.*

Self-assessment activity 9.5

What is the significance of variations around the characteristics line? Relate this to a particular company, say, British Airways (now merged with Iberia to form International Airlines Group).

(Answer in Appendix A at the back of the book)

Beta values: the key relationships

Beta is the slope of a regression line. The slope coefficient relating R_j to R_m equals the covariance of the return on security *j* with the return on the market (cov_{jm}) divided by the variance of the market return (σ_m^2):

$$\text{Beta}_j = \frac{cov_{jm}}{\sigma_m^2}$$

Since the covariance is equal to the correlation coefficient times the product of the respective standard deviations ($r_{jm}\sigma_j\sigma_m$) (see Chapter 8), Beta is also equivalent to:

$$\text{Beta}_j = \frac{r_{jm}\sigma_j\sigma_m}{\sigma_m^2} = \frac{r_{jm}\sigma_j}{\sigma_m}$$

Beta is thus the correlation coefficient multiplied by the ratio of individual security risk to market risk. If the security concerned has the same total risk as the market, Beta equals the correlation coefficient. For a given correlation, the greater the security's systematic risk in relation to the market, the greater is Beta. Conversely, the lower the degree of correlation, for a given risk ratio, the lower the Beta. *Therefore, while Beta does not measure risk in absolute terms, it is a risk indicator, reflecting the extent to which the return on the single asset moves with the return on the market*, i.e. it is a measure of relative risk. To obtain a risk measure in absolute terms, we have to examine the total risk of the security in more detail, using a statistical technique called **analysis of variance**. This is explained in the appendix to this chapter.

analysis of variance
A statistical technique for isolating the separate determinants of the fluctuations recorded in a variable over time

■ Systematic risk: Beta measurement in practice

Betas are regularly calculated by several agencies. The Risk Measurement Service (RMS) operated by the London Business School (LBS) is one of the best known in the UK. The RMS is a quarterly updating service, based on monthly observations extending back over five years, which computes the Betas of all firms listed both on the main market and also on AIM. For each of the preceding 60 months, R_j is calculated for every security and regressed against R_m. An extract from the RMS showing selected companies is given in Table 9.3.

Table 9.3 Beta values of selected companies

Company name	FTSE-ICB classification	Market capit'n	Beta	Variability	Specific risk	Std err of Beta	R-sq'rd
British American Tobacco	Tobacco	61099	0.59	17	14	0.12	26
GKN	AutoPart	6122	1.55	35	27	0.19	41
Ladbrokes	Gambling	1644	1.02	32	29	0.20	21
National Grid	MultUtil	29395	0.46	17	16	0.13	15
Sainsbury	RetFood	6941	0.58	17	15	0.12	24
Smiths Group	Div Inds	5835	0.90	22	18	0.14	33
Tate & Lyle	FoodProd	3768	0.88	25	21	0.16	27
Tullow Oil	Exp&Prod	7780	0.80	28	26	0.18	17
Whitbread	RestBars	6781	0.95	22	18	0.14	38

Source: Risk Measurement Service, London Business School, January – March 2014.

The Beta values of securities can fall into three categories: 'defensive', 'neutral' and 'aggressive'. An aggressive security has a Beta greater than 1. Its returns move by a greater proportion than the market as a whole. In the case of GKN, with a Beta of 1.55, for every percentage point change in the market's return, the return on GKN's shares changes by 1.55 points. Such stocks are highly desirable in a rising market, although the excess return is not guaranteed due to the possible impact of company-specific factors. A defensive share is National Grid, with a Beta of 0.46, movements in whose returns tend to understate those of the whole market. The nearest stock to a neutral one, whose returns parallel those on the market portfolios, is Ladbrokes, with a Beta of 1.02. A truly neutral stock, of course, has a Beta of 1.0.

Notice that the total risk of each security is shown as 'variability', e.g. 35 for GKN. This is a standard deviation. Notice also that this invariably exceeds 'Specific risk', e.g. 27 for GKN. The difference indicates the market risk that cannot be diversified away. (See the appendix to this chapter for a fuller explanation.)

Self-assessment activity 9.6

Suggest why Beta values tend to cluster in a range of roughly 0.60 to 1.30.

(Answer in Appendix A at the back of the book)

9.6 COMPLETING THE MODEL

To recap, the CAPM suggests that only systematic risk is relevant in assessing the required risk premiums for individual securities, and we have established that Beta values reflect the sensitivity of the returns on securities to movements in the market return. However, the size of the risk premium on individual securities (or on efficient portfolios) will depend on the extent to which the return on the investment concerned is correlated with the return on the market. For a security that is perfectly correlated with the market, the market risk premium would be suitable; otherwise, the required return depends on the Beta.

security market line (SML)
An upward-sloping relationship tracing out all combinations of expected return and systematic risk, available in an efficient market. All traded securities locate on this schedule. In effect, the capital market line adjusted for systematic risk

The CAPM concludes that when an efficient capital market is in equilibrium, i.e. all securities are correctly priced, the relationship between risk and return is given by the **security market line (SML)**, as depicted in Figure 9.7.

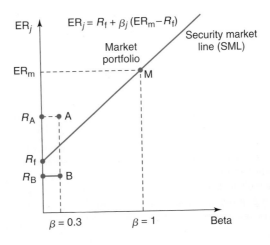

Figure 9.7 The security market line

Self-assessment activity 9.7

Why is the Beta of the overall market equal to 1.0?

(Answer in Appendix A at the back of the book)

■ The security market line

The equation of the SML states that the required return on a share is made up of the return on a risk-free asset, plus a premium for risk that is related to the market's own risk premium, but which varies according to the Beta of the share in question:

$$ER_j = R_f + \beta_j (ER_m - R_f)$$

If Beta is 1, the required return is simply the average return for all securities, i.e. the return on the benchmark market portfolio. Otherwise, the higher the Beta, the higher are both the risk premium and the total return required. *A relatively high Beta does not, however, guarantee a relatively high return.* The actual return depends partly on the behaviour of the market, which acts as a proxy for general economic factors. Similarly, expected returns for the individual security hinge on the expected return for the market. In a 'bull', or rising, market, it is worth holding high Beta (aggressive) securities. Conversely, defensive securities offer some protection against a 'bear', or falling, market. *However, holding a single high Beta security is foolhardy, even on a rising market. Undiversified investments, whatever their Beta values, are prey to specific risk factors. Portfolio formation is essential to diversify away the risks unique to individual companies.*

Self-assessment activity 9.8

As explained, the SML is an equilibrium relationship that traces out the set of required returns for securities of different levels of risk which an efficient capital market would demand.

How would you interpret securities such as A and B on Figure 9.7 that lie off the SML, yielding current returns of R_A and R_B respectively?

(Answer in Appendix A at the back of the book)

Risk-free status of government bonds comes under scrutiny

In recent weeks, some market commentators have asked a question that would once have seemed unthinkable. Should government bonds still be viewed as risk free? If a negative answer is anywhere near possible it has huge implications.

The question has become more urgent following the recent credit downgrade of Greece on concerns over its public debt burden. For institutional investors and other market participants, government debt is assumed to be the sole risk-free asset and has therefore been the cornerstone of capital allocation and diversified investment portfolios for many years.

This is because government debt is at the base of much of the applied theory of finance and portfolio management that institutional investment has been built on. For example, the risk-free asset is the foundation of the capital asset pricing model (CAPM), the capital market line (CML) and parts of modern portfolio theory. As government debt has always

been freely assumed to be risk free in practice, government debt is therefore key to diversified portfolio construction as well as capital and asset allocation. This is also the case with many of today's asset liability structures for pension funds.

The CAPM holds that an investor earns a premium for taking risk greater than that available from the risk-free rate. This premium comes from the beta of the investment (or its market return). The convention is to use the yield on local government debt as the risk-free rate, which has a beta of zero. If, however, the beta on government paper has a positive measure, then it is worth pondering the implications for investors who use these models. If the reference risk-free rate has risk, then the application of models such as the CAPM and the CML may need revisiting.

Source: Based on Michael Gordon, *Financial Times*, 7 January 2010, p. 22.

9.7 USING THE CAPM: ASSESSING THE REQUIRED RETURN

We may now apply the CAPM formula to derive the rate of return required by shareholders in a particular company. To do this, we require information on three components: the risk-free rate, the risk premium on the market portfolio and the Beta coefficient.

■ Specifying the risk-free rate

Treasury Bills
Short-dated (up to three months) securities issued by the Bank of England on behalf of the UK government to cover short-term financing needs

No asset is totally risk-free. Even governments default on loans and defer interest payments. However, in a stable political and economic environment, government stock is about the nearest we can get to a risk-free asset. Most governments issue an array of stock. These range from very short-dated securities, such as **Treasury Bills** in the UK, maturing in 1–3 months, to long-dated stock, maturing in 15 years or more and even, exceptionally, undated stock, such as the 3.5 per cent War Loan with no stated redemption date.

Alternatively, it is tempting to try to match up the life of the investment project with the corresponding government stock when assessing the risk-free rate. For example, when dealing with a ten-year project, we might look at the yield on ten-year government stock.

This may be unsatisfactory for several reasons. First, although the *nominal* yield to maturity is guaranteed, the *real* yield may well be undermined by inflation at an unknown rate. Second, there is an element of risk in holding even government stock. This is reflected in the 'yield curve', which normally rises over time to reflect the increasing liquidity risk of longer-dated stock. Third, although the yield to maturity is given, a forced seller of the stock might have to take a capital loss during the intervening period, since bond values fluctuate over time with variations in interest rates.

Usually, a better way to specify R_f is to take the shortest-dated government stock available, normally three-month Treasury Bills, for which these risks are minimised. The current yield appears in the financial press. This is about the same as the LIBOR, the London Interbank Offered Rate, the rate of interest at which banks lend to each other overnight. However, this rate is not always reliable as an indicator of long-term expectations; for example, following the global financial crisis in 2008, interest rates have been artificially kept down in Europe and the USA for political reasons. When the short-term money market is operating inefficiently, it seems sensible to take the long-term rate. Either way, it should be noted that inflation should be catered for via the risk-free rate because it ought to reflect the market's inflationary expectations.

■ Finding the risk premium on the market portfolio

The risk premium on the market portfolio, $(ER_m - R_f)$, is an expected premium. Therefore, having assessed R_f, we need to specify ER_m by finding a way of capturing the market's expectations about future returns. An approximation can be obtained by looking at past returns, which, taken over lengthy periods, are quite stable. The usual approach with ordinary shares is to analyse the actual total returns on equities as compared with total returns on fixed-interest government stocks over some previous time period. The results are likely to differ according to the period taken and the type of government stock used as the reference level (e.g. short-term securities such as Treasury Bills or long-term gilts). However, studies seem to come up with quite stable results. For example, Dimson and Brealey (1978), Day *et al.* (1987) and Dimson (1993) for the periods 1918–77, 1919–84 and 1919–92, respectively, showed average annual returns above the risk-free rate of 9.0, 9.1 and 8.7 per cent (before taxes) for the market index in the UK.

Similar estimates have been obtained in the USA. In 1985, Mehra and Prescott found that, after adjusting for inflation, equities delivered average *real* returns of 7 per cent p.a. over a quarter of a century, compared with 1 per cent for Treasury bonds – a real risk premium of 6 per cent. Mehra and Prescott found this premium 'puzzling' on the grounds that it seemed too large a premium for bearing non-diversifiable market risk, especially given international opportunities for diversification. Fama and French (2002) found the equity risk premium averaged 8.3 per cent p.a. over 1950–99, this being well in excess of the 4.1 per cent p.a average for 1872–1949.

Dimson (1993) reported similar premia in Japan (9.8 per cent, 1970–92), Sweden (7.7 per cent, 1919–90) and the Netherlands (8.5 per cent, 1947–89), although the last two estimates were in real terms, i.e. relative to domestic inflation.

A rather lower UK risk premium was recorded by Grubb (1993/4), at 6.2 per cent for 1960–92. Grubb suggests that returns to equities in the 1970s and 1980s were exceptional and that under a 'modern scenario of moderate growth and moderate inflation', a much lower premium on equities of only 2 per cent would be reasonable. This view was supported by Wilkie (1994), who, after exhaustive study of past trends in dividend yields and inflation, argued for a risk premium of 3 per cent for longer-term investment and 2 per cent for the short term. The evidence is inconclusive, but it is unlikely that many finance directors would contemplate recommending projects with such low premiums for risk.

However, for shorter periods, say five or ten years (more akin to project lifetimes), returns are highly volatile and sometimes negative. Clearly, people neither require nor expect negative returns for holding risky assets! It therefore seems more sensible to take the long-term average, and to accept that, in the short term, markets exhibit unpredictable variations.

The investment banking arm of Barclays Bank, Barclays Capital (**www.barcap.com**) publishes an annual analysis of equity and gilt-edged returns for various time periods called the 'Equity Gilt Study'. Their data show real investment returns on equities, and government stock, and also on cash deposits. For 2012 real investment returns on equities were 8.7 per cent in the UK and 14.1 per cent in the USA, and compare to gilt returns of 1.6 per cent and 2.1 per cent respectively. The Study notes that the risks associated with the aftermath of the financial crisis of 2008 have now abated and the likelihood is that equity prices will have low volatility in the medium term. The suggestion is that there will be something of a return to more normal market conditions. Looking ahead, two key events are judged as likely to have the most influence on investment returns in the next five years. First, China's economy will cease to grow at such a significant rate and, second, governments and their central banks will move away from following expansionary monetary policies that were put in place as a response to the crisis.

The Equity Gilt Study 2013 argues that the equity risk premium is likely to remain high when compared to historical equity risk premiums. This is because interest rates on risk-free (safe) assets – i.e. government bonds – have been low post-crisis. The low interest rates on government bonds have been caused by both a relative shortage of these bonds and a relatively high demand for these bonds. Demand for government bonds is forecast to stay high because of the introduction of more onerous banking regulations under the Basel III regime pushing banks into holding more of these 'safe' assets and an increasingly ageing population seeking out these bonds as investments to fund retirement.

Barclays Capital conclude that, although they estimate equity returns are likely to fall in the near future, 'the estimated equity risk premium remains in the 500–600bp (5%–6%) range, broadly consistent with historical experience . . . and if the low-volatility environment persists . . . the search for return will push investors more forcefully into equities'.

Table 9.4 shows Barclays data for real investment returns for different types of asset in the UK and the USA. The data are *real* geometric annualised returns, i.e. they exclude the effect of inflation.

Table 9.4 Real investment returns in the UK and USA

(a) Real investment returns (% pa): UK 1902–2012

	Equities	Gilts	Index-linked	Cash
1902–12	3.8	−0.4		1.6
1912–22	−1.9	−3.8		−1.6
1922–32	7.5	9.9		6.1
1932–42	4.3	0.8		−2.5
1942–52	1.7	−3.5		−2.6
1952–62	12.6	−0.7		1.1
1962–72	7.7	−1.7		0.8
1972–82	−1.2	−1.0		−1.9
1982–92	12.7	6.1		5.8
1992–2002	3.9	7.2	5.1	3.4
2002–12	5.0	3.4	3.5	−0.2

Source: Barclays (2013).

(b) Real investment returns (% pa): USA 1932–2012

	Equities	Government bond	Corporate bond	Cash
1932–42	7.6	1.7		−2.4
1942–52	11.9	−2.6		−3.7
1952–62	12.2	1.1		0.8
1962–72	6.7	−0.8		1.1
1972–82	−0.9	−2.8		−0.1
1982–92	11.2	8.4	9.3	3.0
1992–2002	6.1	6.8	5.7	1.8
2002–12	5.8	5.0	5.6	−0.8

Source: Barclays (2013).

In probably the most thorough analysis to date of the equity risk premium, Dimson, Marsh and Staunton (2002) updated and largely corroborated earlier results in a study of the equity risk premium for 16 countries, over a full century (1900–2000). They suggested that some earlier studies (including the earlier Dimson studies!) might have over-estimated the equity premium by excluding the First World War era, when equity returns were poor, and by confining the study to the performance of surviving firms, thus excluding the relatively poor performers that had expired.

They found:

- The average global real return on equity was 4.6 per cent.
- Germany had offered the highest risk premium at 6.7 per cent.
- Denmark offered the lowest risk premium at just 2 per cent.
- In the USA, for every 20-year period examined, equities outperformed bonds.
- Only four countries – Germany, the Netherlands, Sweden and Switzerland – exhibited any 20-year periods over which bonds outperformed equities.
- It is reasonable to expect a real equity premium of no more than 5 per cent or so in the UK in the future.

Credit Suisse updates on the real returns on equities and bonds allow us to infer the following risk premiums for equities over 1900–2012 for selected countries in Table 9.5. The figures are geometric means.

Table 9.5 **Real equity risk premium on equities 1900–2012**

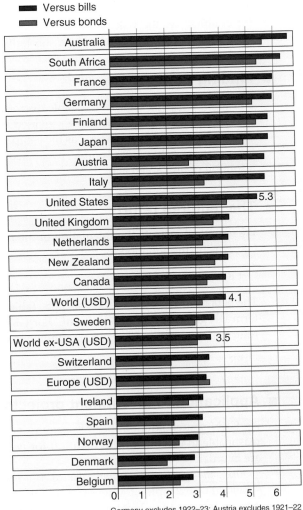

Germany excludes 1922–23; Austria excludes 1921–22

Dimson *et al.* have also discussed the 'puzzle' raised by Mehra and Prescott (1985), regarding the size of the equity premium. They suggest that, given the persistent worldwide out-performance by equities, the risk element in equity investment, at least in developed, efficient markets, is overplayed. McGrattan and Prescott (2003) have revisited this puzzle. They found that in the USA, after taking into account certain factors ignored by Mehra and Prescott, e.g. taxes, regulatory constraints, diversification costs, and focusing on long-term rather than short-term saving instruments, the puzzle is solved. Allowing for all these factors, they found that the difference between average equity and debt returns during peacetime is less than 1 per cent p.a., with the average real equity return just under 5 per cent, and the average real return on debt instruments a little under 4 per cent, a far lower premium than other writers have suggested.

In a later paper, Dimson *et al.* (2008), present data that suggest that past estimates of the equity premium have been overstated by some writers (thus resolving part of the 'puzzle'), partly due to 'survivorship bias' in the time series employed. After adjusting for non-repeatable factors that favoured equities in the past, they infer that investors expect an equity premium on the world index, relative to bills, of around 3–3.5 per cent, on the basis of geometric means, and on an arithmetic mean basis, a premium of around 4.5–5 per cent.

Whether the real equity premium is entering a period of long-term decline is still a matter of some debate. However, subsequent analysis will build in a risk premium for equities, i.e. the risk premium of the overall market portfolio, of 5 per cent, a 'guesstimate' that is supported by a substantial weight of recent evidence.

■ Finding Beta

Beta values appear to be fairly stable over time, so we can use Beta values based on past recorded data, such as those provided by the RMS, with a fair degree of confidence. This is acceptable so long as the company is not expected to alter its risk characteristics in the future: for example, by a takeover of a company in an unrelated field or a spin-off of unwanted activities.

■ The required return

We now demonstrate the calculation of the required return for the 'aggressive' share GKN, using the equation for the SML:

$$ER_j = R_f + \beta_j (ER_m - R_f)$$

The Beta recorded by the RMS was 1.55 (Table 9.3). At the same date, the yield on long-term UK gilts was about 3 per cent.[*] For GKN, this results in the following required return, assuming a market risk premium of 5 per cent:

$$ER = 3.0\% + 1.55\,(5\%) = 10.75\%$$

■ Application to investment projects

As GKN shareholders appear to require a return of 10.75 per cent, it may seem reasonable to use this rate as a cut-off for new investments. However, two warnings are in order.

First, the discount rate applicable to new projects often depends on the nature of the activity. For example, if a new project takes GKN away from its present spheres of activity into, say, food retailing, its systematic risk will alter, as suggested by the Beta

---

[*]The general level of interest rates at this time has been artificially depressed for political reasons since certain actions have been taken to manage the economic situation following the financial crisis.

for Sainsbury of 0.58. The relevant premium for risk hinges on the systematic risk of food retailing rather than that of engineering. This suggests that we 'tailor' risk premiums, and thus discount rates, to particular activities. This aspect is examined in the next chapter.

Self-assessment activity 9.9

What is the implied discount rate for investment by GKN into food retailing?

(Answer in Appendix A at the back of the book)

Second, the appropriate discount rate may depend upon the method of financing used. Until now, we have implicitly been dealing with an all-equity financed company whose premium for risk is a reward purely for the business risk inherent in the company's activity. In reality, most firms are partially debt-financed, exposing shareholders to financial risk. Using debt capital increases the risk to shareholders because of the legally preferred position of creditors. Defaulting on the conditions of the loan (e.g. failing to pay interest) can result in liquidation if creditors apply to have the company placed into receivership. The more volatile the earnings of the firm, the greater the risk of default.

Financial risk raises the Beta of the equity, as shareholders demand additional returns to compensate. The Beta of the equity becomes greater than the Beta of the underlying activity. In Chapter 19, we shall see that observed Betas have two components, one to reflect business risk and one to allow for financial risk. The Betas recorded by the RMS are actually equity Betas, so the required return computed for GKN is the shareholders' required return, part of which is to compensate for financial risk. However, when a company borrows, only the method of financing changes; nothing happens to alter the riskiness of the basic activity. The cut-off rate reflecting the basic risk of physical investment projects is often lower than the shareholders' own required return.

9.8 WORKED EXAMPLE

An investor holds the following portfolio of four risky assets and a deposit in a risk-free asset. The table shows their respective portfolio weightings and the current returns on the assets, together with their Beta coefficients.

Asset	Weighting (%)	Current return (%)	Beta
A	20	12.0	1.5
B	10	18.0	2.0
C	15	14.0	1.2
D	25	8.0	0.9
Risk-free asset	30	5.0	0

The *overall* return on the market portfolio of risky assets is 11 per cent, and this is expected to continue for the foreseeable future.

Required

(a) What is the current return on the whole portfolio, and its Beta value?
(b) Which of the four risky assets (if any) appear to be inefficient/efficient/super-efficient?
(c) In view of the answer to part (b), what predictions would you make regarding future asset values and, hence, their rates of return as the market moves to full equilibrium?

(d) What is the equilibrium return on this portfolio? (Assume the weightings remain unchanged.)

Answers

(a) The portfolio return is a weighted average of the individual asset returns, viz:

$$R_p = (0.2 \times 12\%) + (0.1 \times 18\%) + (0.15 \times 14\%) + (0.25 \times 8\%) + (0.3 \times 5\%)$$
$$= 2.4\% + 1.8\% + 2.1\% + 2.0\% + 1.5\%$$
$$= 9.8\%$$

The portfolio Beta is a weighted average of the individual asset Betas, viz:

$$\text{Beta}_p = (0.2 \times 1.5) + (0.1 \times 2.0) + (0.15 \times 1.2) + (0.25 \times 0.9) + (0.3 \times 0)$$
$$= 0.3 + 0.2 + 0.18 + 0.225 + 0$$
$$= 0.905$$

These results imply that the investor is relatively risk-averse, choosing to combine risky assets and the risk-free asset in such a way as to undershoot the overall market return of 11 per cent and the market Beta of 1.0.

(b) Efficient assets lie on the security market line, thus offering a return consistent with their Beta values. If we compare the actual with the required returns for each asset, we can judge the status of each one. The table shows this evaluation.

Asset	Risk-free rate (%)	Beta	Market premium (%)	Required return (%)	Actual return	Assessment
A	5	1.5	$(11\% - 5\%) = 6\%$	$5 + (1.5 \times 6) = 14\%$	12%	Inefficient
B	5	2.0	6%	$5 + (2.0 \times 6) = 17\%$	18%	Super-efficient
C	5	1.2	6%	$5 + (1.2 \times 6) = 12.2\%$	14%	Super-efficient
D	5	0.9	6%	$5 + (0.9 \times 6) = 10.4\%$	8%	Inefficient

Super-efficient assets offer in excess of what their Beta values warrant. The opposite is true for inefficient assets. Assets A and D are thus inefficient and B and C are super-efficient.

(c) Super-efficient assets are very attractive while they offer abnormal returns, and conversely, for inefficient assets. Investors will therefore scramble to buy the former and to sell the latter, triggering windfall gains for those lucky enough to be holding the former and losses for those holding the latter. Prices will adjust until every asset offers a return consistent with its Beta value. Hence, we would predict a rise in price for assets B and C, depressing their returns, i.e. the equilibrium return will be lower than the current return, and price falls for assets A and D until their expected returns increase accordingly.

(d) The equilibrium portfolio return is:

$$R_p = (0.2 \times 14.0\%) + (0.1 \times 17.0\%) + (0.15 \times 12.2\%) + (0.25 \times 10.4\%)$$
$$+ (0.3 \times 5\%)$$
$$= 2.8\% + 1.7\% + 1.83\% + 2.6\% + 1.5\%$$
$$= 10.43\%$$

Thus, the equilibrium portfolio return is a little above its initial level and closer to the market return.

9.9 THE UNDERPINNINGS OF THE CAPM

In the previous sections, we have concentrated on developing the operational aspects of the CAPM, without explaining the underlying theoretical relationships. The underlying theory is explained in Sections 9.9 and 9.10 and brought together in

Section 9.11, which you may omit at this stage. Section 9.12 discusses some general issues raised by the CAPM.

All theories rely on assumptions in order to simplify the analysis and expose the important relationships between key variables. In economics and related sciences, it is generally accepted that the validity of a theory depends on the empirical accuracy of its predictions rather than on the realism of its assumptions (Friedman, 1953). However, if we find that the predictions fail to correspond with reality, and we are satisfied that this is not due to measurement errors or random influences, then it is appropriate to reassess the assumptions. The ensuing analysis, based on an amended set of assumptions, may lead to the generation of alternative predictions that accord more closely with reality.

■ The assumptions of the CAPM

The most important assumptions are as follows:

1 All investors aim to maximise the utility they expect to enjoy from wealth-holding.
2 All investors operate on a common single-period planning horizon.
3 All investors select from alternative investment opportunities by looking at expected return and risk.
4 All investors are rational and risk-averse.
5 All investors arrive at similar assessments of the probability distributions of returns expected from traded securities.
6 All such distributions of expected returns are normal.
7 All investors can lend or borrow unlimited amounts at a similar common rate of interest.
8 There are no transaction costs entailed in trading securities.
9 Dividends and capital gains are taxed at the same rates.
10 All investors are price-takers: that is, no investor can influence the market price by the scale of his or her own transactions.
11 All securities are highly divisible, i.e. they can be traded in small parcels.

Several of these assumptions are patently untrue, but it has been shown that the CAPM stands up well to relaxation of many of them. Incorporation of apparently more realistic assumptions does not materially affect the implications of the analysis. A full discussion of these adjustments is beyond our scope, but van Horne (2001) offers an excellent analysis.

9.10 PORTFOLIOS WITH MANY COMPONENTS: THE CAPITAL MARKET LINE

capital market line (CML)
Traces out the efficient combinations of risk and return available to investors when combining a risk-free asset with the market portfolio

The theory behind the CAPM revolves around the concept of the 'risk–return trade-off'. This suggests that investors demand progressively higher returns as compensation for successive increases in risk. The derivation of this relationship, known as the **capital market line (CML)**, relies on the portfolio analysis techniques examined in Chapter 8.

The reader may find it useful to re-read Section 8.7, where we explained the derivation of the efficient set available to an investor who can invest in a large number of assets. One conclusion of this analysis was that the only way to differentiate between the many portfolios in the efficient set was to examine the investor's risk–return preferences, i.e. there was no definable optimal portfolio of equal attractiveness to all investors.

■ Introducing a risk-free asset

risk-free assets
Securities with zero variation in overall returns

The above conclusion applies only in the absence of a **risk-free asset**. A major contribution of the CAPM is to introduce the possibility of investing in such an asset. If we allow for risk-free investment, the range of opportunities widens much further. For example, in Figure 9.8, which is based on Figure 8.5 which showed an efficient frontier of AE, consider the line from R_f, the return available on the risk-free asset, passing through point T on the efficiency frontier. This represents all possible combinations of the risk-free asset and the portfolio of risky securities represented by T. To the left of T, both portfolio return and risk are less than those for T, and conversely for points to the right of T. This implies that between R_f and T the investor is tempering the risk and return on T with investment in the risk-free asset (i.e. lending at the rate R_f), while above T, the investor is seeking higher returns even at the expense of greater risk (i.e. borrowing in order to make further investment in T).

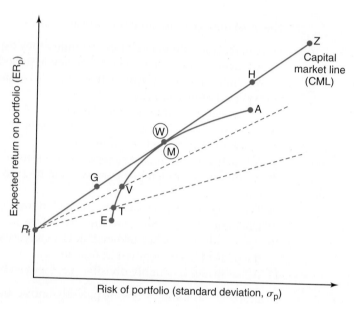

Figure 9.8 The capital market line

However, the investor can improve portfolio performance by investing along the line R_fV, representing combinations of the risk-free asset and portfolio V. He or she can do better still by investing along R_fWZ, the tangent to the efficient set. This schedule describes the best of all available risk–return combinations. No other portfolio of risky assets when combined with the risk-free assets allows the investor to achieve higher returns for a given risk. The line R_fWZ becomes the new efficient boundary.

Portfolio W is the most desirable portfolio of risky securities as it allows access to the line R_fWZ. If the capital market is not already in equilibrium, investors will compete to buy the components of W and tend to discard other investments. As a result, realignment of security prices will occur, the prices of assets in W will rise and hence their returns will fall; and conversely, for assets not contained in W. The readjustment of security prices will continue until all securities traded in the market appear in a portfolio like W, where the line drawn from R_f touches the efficient set. *This adjusted portfolio is the 'market portfolio' (re-labelled as M), which contains all traded securities, weighted according to their market capitalisations. For rational risk-averting investors, this is now the only portfolio of risky securities worth holding.*

There is now a definable optimal portfolio of risky securities, portfolio M, which all investors should seek, and which does not derive from their risk–return preferences. This proposition is known as the **separation theorem** – the most preferred portfolio is separate from individuals' attitudes to risk. The beauty of this result is that we need

separation theorem
A model that shows how individual perceptions of the optimal portfolio of risky securities is independent of (i.e. separate from) individuals' different risk–return preferences

not know all the expected returns, risks and covariances required to derive the efficient set in Figure 9.8. We need only define the market portfolio in terms of some widely used and comprehensive index.

However, having invested in M, if investors wish to vary their risk–return combination, they need only to move along R_fMZ, lending or borrowing according to their risk–return preferences. For example, a relatively risk-averse investor will locate at point G, combining lending at the risk-free rate with investment in M. A less cautious investor may locate at point H, borrowing at the risk-free rate in order to raise his or her returns by further investment in M, but incurring a higher level of risk. However, we would still need information on attitudes to risk to *predict* how individual investors behave.

The line R_fMZ is highly significant. It describes the way in which rational investors – those who wish to maximise returns for a given risk or minimise risk for a given return – seek compensation for any additional risk they incur. In this sense, R_fMZ describes an optimal risk–return trade-off that all investors and thus the whole market will pursue; hence, it is called the capital market line (CML).

The reader who refers back to Figure 1.3 in Chapter 1 will notice that the trade-off schedule R_fMZ is, in fact, a more fully developed version of the upward-sloping relationship in that earlier diagram.

The capital market line

The CML traces out all optimal risk–return combinations for those investors astute enough to recognise the advantages of constructing a well-diversified portfolio. Its equation is:

$$ER_p = R_f + \left[\frac{(ER_m - R_f)}{\sigma_m} \right] \sigma_p$$

Its slope signifies the rate at which investors travelling up the line will be compensated for each extra unit of risk, i.e. $(ER_m - R_f)/\sigma_m$ units of additional return.

For example, imagine investors expect the following:

$$R_f = 10\%$$
$$ER_m = 20\%$$
$$\sigma_m = 5\%$$

so that

$$\left[\frac{ER_m - R_f}{\sigma_m} \right] = \left[\frac{20\% - 10\%}{5\%} \right] = 2$$

Every additional unit of risk that investors are prepared to incur, as measured by the portfolio's standard deviation, requires compensation of two units of extra return. With a portfolio standard deviation of 2 per cent, the appropriate return is:

$$ER_p = 10\% + (2 \times 2\%) = 14\%$$

for $\sigma_p = 3\%$, $ER_p = 16\%$; for $\sigma_p = 4\%$, $ER_p = 18\%$; and so on.

Anyone requiring greater compensation for these levels of risk will be sorely disappointed.

To summarise, we can now assess the appropriate risk premiums for combinations of the risk-free asset and the market portfolio, and therefore the discount rate to be applied when valuing such portfolio holdings. The final link in the analysis of risk premiums is an explanation of how the discount rates for individual securities are established and hence how these securities are valued. This was already provided by the discussion of the SML in Section 9.6.

9.11 HOW IT ALL FITS TOGETHER: THE KEY RELATIONSHIPS

The CAPM sometimes looks complex. However, its essential simplicity can be analysed by reducing it to the three panels of Figure 9.9.

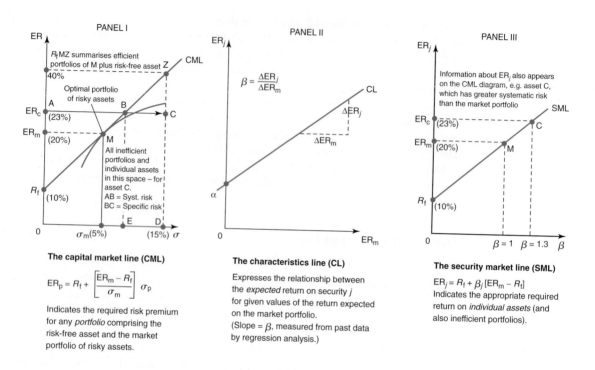

Figure 9.9 The CAPM: the three key relationships

Panel I shows the CML, derived using the principles of portfolio combination developed in Chapter 8. The CML is a tangent to the envelope of efficient portfolios of risky assets, the point of tangency occurring at the market portfolio, M. Any combination along the CML (except M itself) is superior to any combination of risky assets alone. In other words, investors can obtain more desirable risk–return combinations by mixing the risk-free asset and the market portfolio to suit their preferences, i.e. according to whether they wish to lend or borrow.

The slope of the CML, given by $[(ER_m - R_f)/\sigma_m]$ defines the best available terms for exchanging risk and return. It is desirable to hold a well-diversified portfolio of securities in order to eliminate the specific risk inherent in individual securities like C. When holding single securities, investors cannot expect to be rewarded for total risk (e.g. 15 per cent for C) because the market rewards investors only for bearing the undiversifiable or systematic risk. The extent to which risk can be eliminated depends on the covariance of the share's return with the return on the overall market. Hence, the degree of correlation with the return on the market influences the reward from holding a security and thus its price.

The characteristics line in Panel II shows how the return on an individual share, such as that represented by point C, is expected to vary with changes in the return on the overall market. Its slope, the Beta, indicates the degree of systematic risk of the security.

The security market line in Panel III shows the market equilibrium relationship between risk and return, which holds when all securities are 'correctly' priced. Clearly, the higher the Beta, the higher the required return. Although Beta is not a direct measure of systematic risk, it is an important indicator of relevant risk.

The decomposition of the overall variability, or variance, of the share's return into systematic and unsystematic components is explained in the appendix to this chapter. It can be demonstrated by focusing on security C in Panel III of Figure 9.9. Security C lies to the north-east of the market portfolio because its Beta of 1.3 exceeds that of the overall market. If the market as a whole is expected to generate a return of 20 per cent, and the risk-free rate is 10 per cent, C's expected return is:

$$ER_C = 10\% + 1.3(20\% - 10\%) = 10\% + 13\% = 23\%$$

This reward compensates only for systematic risk, rather than for the share's total risk. Looking at Panel I of the total risk of C, represented by distance OD, only OE is relevant.

The risk–return trade-off, given by the slope of the CML, is $(20\% - 10\%)/5\% = 2$, since the risk of the market itself is 5 per cent. For C, with overall risk of 15 per cent, we would not expect to obtain compensation at this rate (i.e. $2 \times 15\% = 30\%$ giving an overall return of 40 per cent), because much of the total risk can be diversified away.

Observe that a variety of required return figures could have emerged from our calculation – in fact, anything along the perpendicular ZD in Panel I of Figure 9.9, depending on the extent to which security C is correlated with the market portfolio. The nearer C lies to Z, the greater the correlation and the higher the required return, and conversely, should C be nearer to D. This reflects the changing balance between the two risk components along ZD.

If the market rewarded total risk, the return offered on security C would be the risk-free rate of 10 per cent supplemented by the risk–return trade-off ($2 \times$ the total security risk of 15 per cent), yielding a total of 40 per cent. However, because the total risk is partly diversifiable, the market offers a return of just 23 per cent for security C. This relationship is indicated on Panel I of Figure 9.9 by the distances AB and BC, representing respectively the systematic and specific risk components of security C's total risk (not to scale).

Self-assessment activity 9.10

You expect the stock market to rise in the next year or so. Could you beat the market portfolio by holding, say, the five securities with the highest Betas?

(Answer in Appendix A at the back of the book)

9.12 RESERVATIONS ABOUT THE CAPM

The CAPM analyses the sources of asset risk and offers key insights into what rewards investors should expect for bearing these risks. However, certain limitations detract from its applicability.

■ It relies on a battery of 'unrealistic' assumptions

It is often easy to criticise theories for the lack of realism of their assumptions, and certainly, many of those embodied in the CAPM, especially concerning investor behaviour, do not seem to reflect reality. However, if the aim is to provide predictions that can be tested against real-world observations, the realism of the underlying assumptions is secondary. Obviously, if the predictions themselves do not accord reasonably closely with reality, then the theory is undoubtedly suspect.

■ Single time period

A key assumption of the CAPM is that investors adopt a one-period time horizon for holding securities. Whatever the length of the period (not necessarily one year), the rates of return incorporated in investor expectations are rates of return over the whole holding period, assumed to be common for all investors. This provides obvious problems when we come to use a required return derived from a CAPM exercise in evaluating an investment project. Quite simply, we may not compare like with like. If an investor requires a return of, say, 25 per cent, over a five-year period, this is rather different from saying that the returns from an investment project should be discounted at 25 per cent p.a. Attempts have been made, notably by Mossin (1966), to produce a multi-period version of the CAPM, but its mathematical complexity takes it out of the reach of most practising managers, especially those inclined to scepticism about the CAPM itself.

The problem for active managers

Traditional active asset management has been under siege for some time, squeezed by the move to low-cost passive strategies on one hand and to expensive hedge funds and other alternative investments on the other.

According to a new paper from the 300 Club, a group of investment professionals, this trend is due to the far-reaching and unfortunate influence of the investment theories that underlie current practice, namely the efficient market hypothesis (EMH) and capital asset pricing model (CAPM).

These have persuaded people that active management does not work and 'spawned today's $4tn index fund industry', says the paper, written by Amin Rajan, chief executive of Create-Research and club member.

Mr Rajan maintains the theories have also contributed to the pervasive view among policy makers and others that the market knows best and interfering with its working through regulation is bound to cause distortions.

The paper does not go so far as to blame the financial crisis entirely on the ideas the theories promote (that investors are rational, market prices reflect all available information; price levels align with fundamental values over time and individual stock selection contributes little to portfolio returns), but it sees them as contributing factors.

It concludes that neither theory has much empirical support. They have been refined 'to the point where their principal inferences – that markets are efficient and active management does not work – are no longer tenable'.

Mr Rajan hopes that by questioning the tenets and implications of the EMH and CAPM, a new theory will emerge.

Source: Based on Pauline Skypala, *Financial Times*, 30 April 2012, p. 6.

9.13 TESTING THE CAPM

Many writers have observed that, in principle, the CAPM is untestable, since it is based on investors' expectations about future returns, and expectations are inherently awkward to measure. Hence, tests of the CAPM have to examine past returns and take these as proxies for future expected returns. This is based on the key premise that if a long enough period is examined, mistaken expectations are likely to be corrected, and people will come to rely on past average achieved returns when formulating expectations. Greatly simplified, the essence of the research methods is as follows.

Research usually proceeds in two stages. First, using time series analysis over a lengthy period applied to a large sample of securities (say 750), researchers estimate both the Beta for each security and its average return. Relying heavily on market efficiency, these estimates are taken to be estimates of the *ex ante* expected return, i.e. it is assumed that rational investors will be strongly influenced by past returns and their variability when formulating future expectations.

Second, the researcher tries to locate the SML to investigate whether it is upward sloping, as envisaged by the CAPM. The 750 pairs of estimates for Beta and the average return for each security are used as the input into a cross-section regression model of the form:

$$R_i = a_1 + a_2\beta_i + u_i$$

where R_i is the expected return from security i, a_1 is the intercept term (i.e. the risk-free rate), a_2 is the slope of the SML and u_i is an error term.

If the CAPM is valid, the measured SML would appear as in the steeper line on Figure 9.10, with an intercept approximating to recorded data for the risk-free rate: for example, the realised return on Treasury Bills.

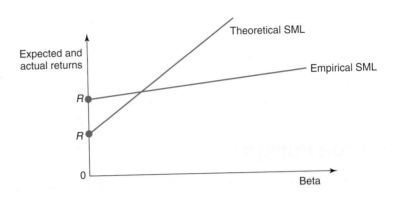

Figure 9.10 Theoretical and empirical SMLs

Several early studies (e.g. Black *et al.*, 1972; Fama and McBeth, 1973) did seem to support the positive association between Beta and average stock returns envisaged by the CAPM for long periods up to the late 1960s. However, evidence began to emerge that the empirical SML was much flatter than implied by the theory and that the intercept was considerably higher than achieved returns on 'risk-free' assets.

Some researchers have continued to test the validity of the CAPM, but others, following Ross (1976), have concluded that some of the 'rogue' results stem from intrinsic difficulties concerning the CAPM that make it inherently untestable. In the process, they have developed an alternative theory, based on the **Arbitrage Pricing Theory (APT)**, discussed in Section 9.15.

Other reasons why the CAPM is thought to be nigh impossible to test adequately are as follows:

1 It relies on specification of a risk-free asset – there is some doubt whether such an asset really exists.
2 It relies on analysing security returns against an efficient benchmark portfolio, the market portfolio, usually proxied by a widely used index. Because no index captures all stocks, the index portfolio itself could be inefficient, as compared with the full market portfolio, thus distorting empirical results.
3 The model is unduly restrictive in that it includes only *securities* as depositories of wealth. A full 'capital asset pricing model' would include all forms of asset, such as real estate, paintings or rare coins – in fact, any asset that offers a future return. Hence, the CAPM is only a *security* pricing model.

Fama and French (1992) made a thorough test of the CAPM, finding no US evidence for the 'correct' relationship between security returns and Beta over the period 1963–90. The cross-section approach supported neither a linear nor a positive relationship. It appeared that average stock returns were explained better by company size as measured by market capitalisation, large firms generally offering lower returns, and by the ratio of book value of equity to market value, returns being positively associated with this variable. They concluded that rather than being explained by a single variable, Beta, security risk was multi-dimensional.

Neither of the UK studies conducted by Beenstock and Chan (1986) and by Poon and Taylor (1991) found significant positive relationships between security returns and

Arbitrage Pricing Theory (APT)
An extension of the CAPM to include more than one factor (hence, an example of a **multi-factor model**) used to explain the returns on securities. Each factor has its own Beta coefficient

Beta. Acting on Levis' (1985) observation for the period 1958–82 that smaller firms tend to outperform larger firms (although erratically), Strong and Xu (1997) attempted to replicate the Fama and French analysis in a UK context. Specifically, they investigated whether Beta could explain security returns and whether it was outweighed by 'the size effect'.

For the period 1960–92, they found a positive risk premium associated with Beta in isolation, but this became insignificant when Beta was combined with other variables in a multiple regression. For the whole period, market value dominated Beta, but over 1973–92, it was itself insignificant compared with book-to-market value of equity, and gearing. However, the explanatory power of various combinations of variables used was poor, never exceeding an R^2 of 8 per cent. Overall, there appeared to be a size effect, but it did not operate in as clear or as stable a fashion as in the Fama and French study of US data.

9.14 FACTOR MODELS

It is not too surprising that some of the studies listed in the previous section do not support the notion that Beta is the most important determinant of the return on quoted securities. In the CAPM, the only independent variable driving individual security returns is the return on the market, i.e. there is a single factor at work. In reality, everyone knows there are many factors at work, but the researcher is hoping that their various impacts will all be rolled up into this single market factor.

However, the returns on a share react to general industry or sector changes in addition to general market changes. These aspects are all confused in Beta. This helps explain why the CAPM is such a poor explanatory model. The explanatory power of a regression model like the CAPM is measured by the R-squared, or Coefficient of Determination, which is measured on a scale of zero to +1. These are shown in Table 9.3 in the final column. While expert opinions vary on this, it is commonly accepted that an R-squared of above 50 per cent indicates a strong relationship, i.e. a high degree of explanatory power. The highest figure shown in the table is 41 per cent for GKN. The interpretation we have to put on this is that there are other, perhaps many other, factors at work impacting on security returns.

Whereas the CAPM is a single-factor model, many researchers like Fama and French (1992) have attempted to develop multi-factor models. A multi-factor model will include two elements:

- a list of factors that have been identified as having a significant influence on security returns;
- a measure of the sensitivity of the return on particular securities to changes in these factors.

In the CAPM, there is only the one factor, the return on the market portfolio, and the sensitivity is measured by each security's Beta. As in the CAPM, which distinguishes between specific and market-related risk, there are two types of risk – factor risk and non-factor risk. Thus, variations in the returns on stocks can be explained by variations in the identified factor(s) (analogous to market risk) and variations due to background 'noise', i.e. changes in factors not included in the model (analogous to specific risk).

■ A two-factor model

In the UK, 60 per cent of the economy is represented by consumer expenditure, which is largely driven by income growth and the 'feel-good factor' from rising house prices. Also bear in mind that the stock market is generally supposed to herald movements in the overall economy one to two years ahead. Therefore, a model devised to explain stock market returns in terms of income growth and house prices would be quite plausible.

This would be a two-factor model of the following form:

$$R_j = a + b_1 F_1 + b_2 F_2 + e_j$$

where R_j is the return on stock j in the usual sense, a is the intercept term, F_1 and F_2 are the two identified factors, income growth and house prices, b_1 and b_2 are the sensitivity coefficients and e_j is an error term.

The values of the parameters a, b_1 and b_2 would be found by multiple regression analysis, while the error term is assumed to average zero. Say the values established by empirical investigation are:

$$a = 0.01$$
$$b_1 = 2.0$$
$$b_2 = 0.2$$

This means that for every 1 per cent point change in income growth (F_1), individual security returns change by twice as much, i.e. by two percentage points. Similarly, for every 1 per cent point change in the house price index (F_2), security returns change by 0.2 of a percentage point.

It should be stressed that the explanatory factors in the equation would be common to all firms, but the sensitivity coefficients, the 'Betas', would vary according to how closely 'geared' the returns on each firm were to each factor. For example, if one identified factor was the sterling/dollar exchange rate, we would expect to see much higher sensitivity for a firm exporting to, or operating in, the USA, compared to one conducting most of its operations in the domestic arena.

9.15 THE ARBITRAGE PRICING THEORY

The most fully developed multi-factor model is the Arbitrage Pricing Theory (APT), developed by Ross (1976). Unlike the CAPM, APT does not assume that shareholders evaluate decisions within a mean–variance framework. Rather, it assumes the return on a share depends partly on macroeconomic factors and partly on events specific to the company. Instead of specifying a share's returns as a function of one factor (the return on the market portfolio), it specifies the returns as a function of multiple macroeconomic factors upon which the return on the market portfolio depends.

The expected risk premium of a particular share would be:

$$ER_j = R_f + \beta_1(ER_{factor\ 1} - R_f) + \beta_2(ER_{factor\ 2} - R_f) + \cdots + e_j$$

where ER_j is the expected rate of return on security j, $ER_{factor\ 1}$ is the expected return on macroeconomic factor 1, β_1 is the sensitivity of the return on security j to factor 1 and e_j is the random deviation based on unique events impacting on the security's returns. The bracketed terms are thus risk premiums, as found in the CAPM.

Diversification can eliminate the specific risk associated with a security, leaving only the macroeconomic risk as the determinant of required security returns. A rational investor will arbitrage (hence the name) between different securities if the current market prices do not give sufficient compensation for variations in one or more factors in the APT equation.

The APT model does not specify what the explanatory factors are; they could be the stock market index, Gross National Product, oil prices, interest rates and so on. Different companies will be more sensitive to certain factors than others.

In theory, a riskless portfolio could be constructed (i.e. a 'zero Beta' portfolio) which would offer the risk-free rate of interest. If the portfolio gave a higher return, investors could make a profit without incurring any risk by borrowing at the risk-free rate to buy the portfolio. This process of 'arbitrage' (i.e. taking profits for zero risk) would continue until the portfolio's expected risk premium was zero.

The Arbitrage Pricing Theory avoids the CAPM's problem of having to identify the market portfolio. But it replaces this problem with possibly more onerous tasks. First, there is the requirement to identify the macroeconomic variables. US research indicates that the most influential factors in explaining asset returns in the APT framework are changes in industrial production, inflation, personal consumption, money supply and interest rates (McGowan and Francis, 1991).

Tests of the APT, especially for the UK, are still in their relative infancy. However, in an early test, Beenstock and Chan (1986) found that, for the period 1977–83, the first few years of the UK's 'monetarist experiment', share returns were largely explained by a set of monetary factors – interest rates, the sterling M3 measure of money supply and two different measures of inflation, all highly interrelated variables. In 1994, Clare and Thomas reported results from analysing 56 portfolios, each containing 15 shares sorted by Beta and by size of company by value. For the Beta-ordered portfolios, the key factors were oil prices, two measures of corporate default risk, the Retail Price Index (RPI), private sector bank lending, current account bank balances and the yield to redemption on UK corporate loan stock. Using portfolios ordered by size, the key factors reduced to one measure of default risk and the RPI. Again, there was much intercorrelation among variables, but the return on the stock market index, although included in the initial tests, appeared in none of these final lists.

Once the main factors influencing share returns are established, there remain the problems of estimating risk premiums for each factor and measuring the sensitivity of individual share returns to these factors. For this reason, the APT is currently only in the prototype stage, and yet to be accepted by practitioners.

9.16 FAMA AND FRENCH'S THREE-FACTOR MODEL

An approach that marries the APT to the multi-factor approach is the three-factor model developed in a series of papers by Fama and French (1993, 1995, 1996). This has the distinctive merit of an empirical grounding, being based on their paper of 1992. In Section 9.13, we noted that they found that stock returns in the USA were explained better by company size and by the ratio of book value of equity to market value than merely by movements in the return on the whole market, magnified or moderated by Beta, as in the CAPM.

These two additional explanatory variables are utilised in the three-factor model. It states that stock returns above the risk-free rate (i.e. the equity premium) are determined by:

- The risk premium on the market portfolio.
- The difference between the return on a portfolio of small company shares and the return on a portfolio of large company shares (small less big, or SLB).
- The difference between the return on a portfolio of high book-to-market value stocks and the return on a portfolio of low book-to-market value stocks (high less low, or HLL).

The three-factor equation can be written thus:

Expected return on stock$_j$ =

$$ER_j = R_f + \text{Risk premium} = R_f + [Beta_1(ER_m - R_f) + Beta_2(SLB) + Beta_3(HLL)]$$

The logic behind the formulation of the model is that the average small company and its stock is assumed to be more risky than the average large firm and its stock and thus commands a higher risk premium. Larger firms are generally more stable as they are more diversified by products and markets, and have better credit ratings, partly because their stock of assets is larger. Similarly, a stock with a high book value relative to market value is assumed to be more risky than one with a low book value relative to market value. The former owes its higher valuation rating to a greater growth potential and/or greater endowment of intangible assets such as intellectual capital.

To make the model operational, information is required on the risk premiums related to each factor, and for the various Beta factors. For example, imagine that empirical evidence suggests that, in past years, the risk premium on the market portfolio has averaged 5 per cent, the risk premium for a small company stock compared to a larger firm has averaged 6 per cent, and the risk premium for the stock of a typical firm with a high book-to-market value compared to market price has averaged 4 per cent.

When the risk-free rate is 3 per cent, for a firm of average risk, i.e. average sensitivity to each of these three factors, and thus with Beta values of 1.0 across the board, the overall expected return will be:

$$ER_j = 3\% + [(1.0 \times 5\%) + (1.0 \times 6\%) + (1.0 \times 4\%)] = 3\% + 15\% = 18\%$$

In practice, firms exhibit varying sensitivities to these factors depending on their product and market profiles, for example, and thus carry Beta values different from one. Assume that Firm X has a low sensitivity to market movements (Beta = 0.4), a relatively high sensitivity in respect of relative size (Beta = 1.2) and a relatively low sensitivity to the book versus market value factor (Beta = 0.8), then its expected return is:

$$ER_j = 3\% + [(0.4 \times 5\%) + (1.2 \times 6\%) + (0.8 \times 4\%)] = 3\% + 12.4\% = 15.4\%$$

There has been extensive research in recent years based on Fama and French's highly influential approach. Most studies reinforce the view that Beta alone cannot adequately explain stock market returns, although they do not always agree on the most powerful determinants. In the process of analysis, a number of anomalies that the Fama and French model is unable to explain have emerged, for example, a negative relationship between returns and growth in assets, which appears counter-intuitive – why do firms invest in new projects if the returns are persistently negative? Among the most recent claimants to have developed a better 'three-factor model' is the model developed by Chen and Zhang (2010). This appears to account for many such anomalies and gives a good explanation of stock returns over a lengthy period as well as recording a non-significant alpha coefficient. Even so, their model does include the sensitivity of stock returns to the market excess returns (i.e. Beta as in the CAPM), as the first factor. The others are: the difference between the returns on a portfolio of low-investment stocks, and the returns on a portfolio of high-investment stocks, and the difference between the returns on a portfolio of stocks with high returns on assets, and the returns on a portfolio with low returns on assets. No doubt, such work will continue.

9.17 ISSUES RAISED BY THE CAPM: SOME FOOD FOR MANAGERIAL THOUGHT

The CAPM raises a number of important issues, which have fundamental implications for the applicability of the model itself and the role of diversification in the armoury of corporate strategic weapons.

■ Should we trust the market?

Legally, managers are charged with the duty of acting in the best interests of shareholders, i.e. maximising their wealth (although company law does not express it *quite* like this). This involves investing in all projects offering returns above the shareholders' opportunity cost of capital. The CAPM provides a way of assessing the rate of return required by shareholders from their investments, albeit based partly on past returns. If the Beta is known and a view is taken on the future returns on the market, then the apparently required return follows. This becomes the cut-off rate for new investment projects, at least for those of similar systematic risk to existing activities. This implies that managers' expectations coincide with those of shareholders or, more generally, with those of the market. If, however, the market as a whole expects a higher return from the market portfolio, some projects deemed acceptable to managers may not be worthwhile for shareholders.

The subsequent fall in share price would provide the mechanism whereby the market communicates to managers that the discount rate applied was too low. The CAPM relies on efficiently-set market prices to reveal to managers the 'correct' hurdle rate and any mistakes caused by misreading the market. The implication that one can trust the market to arrive at correct prices, and hence required rates of return, is problematic for many practising managers, who are prone to believe that the market incorrectly values the companies that they operate. Managers who doubt the validity of the EMH are unlikely to accept a CAPM-derived discount rate.

■ Should companies diversify?

The CAPM is based on the premise that rational shareholders form efficiently diversified portfolios, realising that the market will reward them only for bearing market-related risk. The benefits of diversification can easily be obtained by portfolio formation, i.e. buying securities at relatively low dealing fees. The implication of this is that *corporate diversification is perhaps pointless as a device to reduce risk because companies are seeking to achieve what shareholders can do themselves, probably more efficiently*. Securities are far more divisible than investment projects and can be traded much quicker when conditions alter. So why do managers diversify company activities?

An obvious explanation is that managers have not understood the message of the EMH/CAPM, or doubt its validity, believing instead that shareholders' best interests are enhanced by reduction of the total variability of the firm's earnings. For some shareholders, this may indeed be the case, as a large proportion of those investing directly on the stock market hold undiversified portfolios.

Many small shareholders were attracted to equity investment by privatisation issues or by Personal Equity Plans and their successor, ISAs (Individual Savings Accounts). Larger shareholders sometimes tie up major portions of their capital in a single company in order to take, or retain, an active part in its management. In such cases, market risk, based on the co-variability of the return on a company's shares with that on the market portfolio, is an inadequate measure of risk. The appropriate measure of risk for capital budgeting decisions probably lies somewhere between total risk, based on the variance, or standard deviation, of a project's returns, and market risk, depending on the degree of diversification of shareholders.

A more subtle explanation of why managers diversify is the divorce of ownership and control. Managers who are relatively free from the threat of shareholder interference in company operations may pursue their personal interests above those of shareholders. If an inadequate contract has been written between the manager – agents and the shareholder – principals, managers may be inclined to promote their own job security. This is understandable, since shareholders are highly mobile between alternative security holdings, but managerial mobility is often low. *To managers, the distinction between systematic risk and specific risk may be relatively insignificant, since they have a vested interest in minimising total risk in order to increase their job security.* If the company flounders, it is of little comfort for them to know that their personal catastrophe has only a minimal effect on well-diversified shareholders.

As we will see in Chapter 20, there are many motives for diversification beyond merely reducing risk. However, it is common to justify diversification to shareholders purely on these grounds, at least under certain types of market imperfection. When a company fails, there are liquidation costs to bear as well as the losses entailed in selling assets at 'knock-down' prices. These costs may result in both creditors and shareholders failing to receive full economic value in the asset disposal. Although this will not devastate a well-diversified shareholder, the resulting hole in his or her portfolio will require filling in order to restore balance. Company diversification may reduce these risks and also the costs of portfolio disruption and readjustment.

■ The conglomerate discount

Conglomerate companies are made up of businesses that operate in different industry or business sectors. Therefore, conglomerate companies are, by definition, diversified. The value of conglomerates is typically less than the value that would be assigned to the different parts of the business if they were operating separately from one another. Consequently, in stockmarkets there is often talk of a 'conglomerate discount' applying to the shares and this is illustrated in the examples below of Vivendi, Anglo American and Cookson.

Vivendi challenged to keep evolving

In March of last year, Jean-René Fourtou, Vivendi's chairman, wrote to shareholders and dared to ask something that investors had long wondered: 'Should the scope of the group be kept as it is? Should businesses be sold or should the group be split into two, or even into three?'

Over the past four months, Vivendi has embarked on sales almost as impressive as the dealmaking that transformed the company, under Jean-Marie Messier in the 1990s, from a boring water utility founded during the time of Napoleon III, into a glitzy media conglomerate intent on world domination.

The disposals are part of what Mr Fourtou has called a 'no taboos' examination of Vivendi's *raison d'être* as it grapples with the now apparent difficulties of realising synergies between media and telecoms businesses, and a share price long discounted for being a conglomerate.

In an interview with the *Financial Times*, Vincent Bolloré, the group's new vice-chairman and probable chairman if Mr Fourtou retires next year as expected, said the smaller but more coherent Vivendi had the right shape. 'Now we have a financial structure which is healthy so we don't need to sell anything and we don't intend to sell anything.'

Source: Based on Adam Thomson, *Financial Times*, 15 November 2013, p. 23.

Anglo should hire a new boss who can do the splits

The type of chief executive selected to replace Cynthia Carroll at Anglo American will signal whether the mining group plans to break itself up or not, according to one senior figure at a rival.

An operations specialist would probably keep the South African and international sides together, while tackling such problems as cost overruns on new projects. A recruit with a strategy bias would be more likely to split the two parts of the business, brought together through Anglo's merger with Minorco in 1999.

City investors would mostly prefer a splitter. Credit Suisse calculates that the conglomerate discount applying to shares in Anglo is about 17 per cent. The investment bank estimates that the South African and Botswanan parts of Anglo, consisting of a big thermal coal business and stakes in platinum, iron ore and diamond company De Beers, are worth some $37.2bn before debt of $1.8bn. The international side, including copper, coking coal and nickel, is valued at $16.5bn before debt of $8.6bn. The case for spinning it off is a good one. But a new chief executive would need diplomatic as well as strategy skills to present the move as a vote of confidence in South Africa, rather than the reverse.

Source: Based on Jonathan Guthrie, *Financial Times*, 30 October 2012, p. 16.

Cookson review raises possibility of demerger

Cookson has launched a strategic review that could lead to the industrial materials company splitting itself in two in a bid to boost shareholder value.

There has been speculation that Cookson might separate its performance materials business, which makes chemicals and pastes used in the production of circuit boards, from its ceramics business, which makes valve shutters and gates used in the steel industry.

Nick Salmon said that options such as a demerger had been considered regularly during his eight-year tenure as chief executive. Mr Salmon said a demerger would only be pursued if it was clear it would more than offset these costs, and that the company was also considering other options, including selling a division and maintaining the status quo.

Harry Philips, an analyst at Oriel Securities, said Cookson's shares would be fairly valued at 900p, but a demerger might lead to a higher valuation. 'It should unlock value that would otherwise be hindered by the conglomerate discount, and Cookson's history,' he said.

Source: Based on James Shotter, *Financial Times*, 18 May 2012, p. 20.

Self-assessment activity 9.11

What reasons may there be for a conglomerate discount existing?

(Answer in Appendix A at the back of the book)

SUMMARY

We have examined the nature of the risks affecting the holders of securities and have begun to discuss whether the return required by shareholders, as implied by market valuations, can be used as a cut-off rate for new investment projects.

Key points

- Security risk can be split into two components: risk specific to the company in question, and the variability in return due to general market movements.
- Rational investors form well-diversified portfolios to eliminate specific risk.
- The most efficient portfolio of risky securities is the market portfolio, although investors may mix this with investment in the risk-free asset in order to achieve more preferred risk–return combinations along the capital market line.
- The risk premium built into the required return on securities reflects a reward for systematic risk only.
- The risk premium on a particular share depends on the risk premium on the overall market and the extent to which the return on the security moves with that of the whole market, as indicated by its Beta coefficient.
- This premium for risk is the second term in the equation for the security market line:
  $$\text{ER}_j = R_f + \beta_j(\text{ER}_m - R_f).$$
- Practical problems in using the CAPM centre on measurement of Beta, specification of the risk-free asset and measurement of the market's risk premium.
- In an all-equity financed company, the return required by shareholders can be used as a cut-off rate for new investment if the new project has systematic risk similar to the company's other activities.
- There is some debate about whether managers should diversify company activities merely in order to lower risk.
- Empirical studies seem to throw increasing doubt on the CAPM.

■ The main proposed alternative, the Arbitrage Pricing Theory (APT), relies on fewer restrictive assumptions but is still in the prototype stage.

Further reading

Copeland *et al.* (2013) offer a rigorous treatment of the derivation of the formulae used in this chapter. Brealey *et al.* (2013) offer an alternative, less mathematical treatment. You should also read the famous critique of the CAPM by Roll (1977). Fama and French's paper (1992), although difficult, is essential reading, as is Strong and Xu (1997), for a UK perspective.

An excellent text on Modern Portfolio Theory is that by Elton *et al.* (2010) which covers the basic theory and includes an up-to-date survey of empirical work. There is a very good resumé of the Fama and French analysis in Ross *et al.* (2009). Meanwhile, they have not gone unchallenged – see, for example, the two articles by Black (1993a, 1993b) and that by Kothari *et al.* (1995).

Fama and French (1995, 2002) have updated the earlier study, reaching essentially similar conclusions, and Fama and French (2002) has also entered the debate on the equity premium.

Fama and French's latest contribution was in 2006, while Chen and Zhang (2010) have staked a claim on a 'better' three-factor model.

Dimson, Marsh and Staunton's latest estimates of risk premiums can be found in a book of essays edited by Mehra (2008).

The validity, and future, of CAPM is very much under debate. Finance researchers have different standpoints in these debates and a 2013 special issue of the journal *ABACUS* provides an excellent coverage of these (*ABACUS* special issue, 2013, vol. 49, issue supplement S1, January). The CAPM debates are also extensively covered in Levy (2012).

Appendix
ANALYSIS OF VARIANCE

The total risk of a security (σ_T), comprising both unsystematic risk (σ_{USR}), and systematic risk (σ_{SR}), is measured by the variance of returns, which can be separated into the two elements. Imagine an asset with total risk of $\sigma_T^2 = 500$, of which 80 per cent (400) is explained by systematic risk factors, the remainder resulting from factors specific to the firm:

$$\sigma_T^2 = 500 = \sigma_{SR}^2 + \sigma_{USR}^2 = 100 + 400$$

In terms of standard deviations, $\sigma_{SR} = \sqrt{400} = 20$ and $\sigma_{USR} = \sqrt{100} = 10$. Notice that we cannot express the overall standard deviation by summing the two component standard deviations – variances are additive, standard deviations are not – the square root of the total risk is $\sqrt{500} = 22.4$, rather than the sum of σ_{SR} and σ_{USR} (20 + 10 = 30).

In regression models, the extent to which the overall variability in the dependent variable is explained by the variability in the independent variable is given by the R-squared (R^2) statistic, the square of the correlation coefficient. The R^2 is thus a measure of 'goodness of fit' of the regression line to the recorded observations. If all observations lie on the regression line, R^2 equals 1, and the variations in the market return fully explain the variations in the return on security j. In this case, all risk is market risk. It follows that the lower is R^2 the greater the proportion of specific risk of the security. For investors wishing to diversify away specific risk, such securities are highly attractive. Notice that an R^2 of 1 does not entail a Beta of 1, as Figure 9.11 illustrates. All three

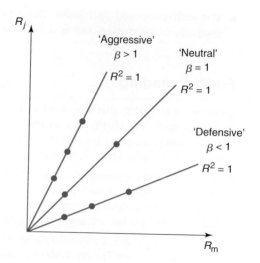

Figure 9.11 Alternative characteristics lines

securities have R^2 of 1, but they have different degrees of market risk, as indicated by their Betas.

In the example above, the R^2 of 80 per cent would correspond to a correlation coefficient, r_{jm}, of $\sqrt{0.8} = 0.89$. Looking at the standard deviations, we can infer that 0.89 of the standard deviation is market risk, i.e. $(0.89 \times 22.4) = 19.94$, while the specific risk = $(1 - r_{jm}) \times 22.4 = (0.11 \times 22.4) = 2.46$. Let us re-emphasise these relationships:

Market, or systematic, risk is:

$R^2 \times$ the overall variance, σ_T^2; or ($r_{jm} \times$ the overall standard deviation, σ_T)
$(0.8 \times 500) = 400$; or $(0.89 \times 22.4\%) = 19.94\%$

Specific risk is:

$(1 - R^2) \times$ overall variance, σ_T^2, or $(1 - r_{jm}) \times$ overall standard deviation σ_T
$(0.2 \times 500) = 100$; or $(0.11 \times 22.4\%) = 2.46\%$.

The reader may find it useful to test out these relationships using the data provided in Table 9.3 ('Variability' is total risk expressed as a standard deviation). However, not all cases work out neatly owing to rounding errors.

Questions with a **coloured number** have a solution in Appendix B on page 786.

1 The ordinary shares of Firm A have a Beta of 1.23. The risk-free rate of interest is 5 per cent, and the risk premium achieved on the market index over the past 20 years has averaged 11.5 per cent p.a. What is the future expected return on A's shares?

  If you believe that overall market returns will fall to 8 per cent in future years, how does your answer change?

2 Supply the missing links in the table:

	ER_j	R_f	β	ER_m
(i)	19%	?	1.10	18%
(ii)	17%	5%	?	12%
(iii)	?	4%	0.75	10%
(iv)	15%	7%	0.65	?

3 Locate the security market line (SML) given the following information: $R_f = 8\%$, $ER_m = 12\%$.

4 Which of the following shares are over-valued?

	Beta	Current rate of return
A	0.7	7%
B	1.3	13%
C	0.9	9%

The risk-free rate is 5 per cent, and the return on the market index is 10 per cent.

5 The market portfolio has yielded 12 per cent on average over past years. It is expected to offer a risk premium in future years of 7 per cent. The standard deviation of its return is 8 per cent. The risk-free rate is 5 per cent.

(i) What is the expected return from the market portfolio?
(ii) Draw a diagram to show the location of the capital market line.
(iii) What is the expected return on a portfolio comprising 50 per cent invested in the market portfolio and 50 per cent invested in the risk-free asset?
(iv) What is the risk of the portfolio in (iii)?
(v) What is the market trade-off between portfolio risk and return suggested by these figures?

6 The following figures relate to monthly observations of the percentage return on a widely used stock market index (R_m) and the return on a particular ordinary share (R_j) over a period of six months.

Month	R_m	R_j
1	5	4
2	-10	-8
3	12	9.6
4	3	2.4
5	-4	-3.2
6	7	5.6

(a) Plot these data on a graph and deduce the value of the Beta coefficient.
(b) To what extent are variations in R_m due to specific risk factors?
(c) Calculate the systematic risk of the security. (NB: systematic risk $= \beta^2 \sigma^2_m$)

7 Z plc is a long-established company with interests mainly in retailing and property development. Its current market capitalisation is £750 million. The company trades exclusively in the UK, but it is planning to expand overseas either by acquisition or joint venture within the next two years. The company has built up a portfolio of investments in UK equities and corporate and government debt. The aim of developing this investment portfolio is to provide a source of funds for its overseas expansion programme. Summary information on the portfolio is given below.

Type of security	Value £ million	Average % return over the last 12 months
UK equities	23.2	15.0
US equities	9.4	13.5
UK corporate debt	5.3	8.2
Long-term government debt	11.4	7.4
Three-month Treasury bonds	3.2	6.0

Approximately 25 per cent of the UK equities are in small companies' shares, some of them trading on the Alternative Investment Market. The average return on all UK equities, over the past 12 months, has been 12 per cent. On US equities, it has been 12.5 per cent.

Ignore taxation throughout this question.

Required

Discuss the advantages and disadvantages of holding such a portfolio of investments in the circumstances of Z plc.

(CIMA, November 1997)

10

The required rate of return on investment

Cost of equity

Calculating a cost of equity in practice can be difficult and there are different approaches that can be used. The following is taken from a 2012–13 cost of capital survey by KPMG.

■ 59 per cent of the surveyed companies derived the risk-free rate from the yield on government bonds with an average remaining life of 15 years; 39 per cent used the yield curve for the determination. The average risk-free rate used was 3.1 per cent and this had declined compared to the previous year.

■ The average market risk premium used was 5.2 per cent. The market risk premium is usually determined retrospectively based on a comparison between observable long-term stock yields and risk-free bond yields over a certain historical period.

■ As was the case in the previous year, the majority of companies derived their beta from a peer group, based on an average observation period of four years past.

■ The average cost of equity applied by the surveyed companies for the fiscal year 2011–12 was 9.3 per cent as an average.

Source: KPMG Cost of Capital Survey 2012–13.

Learning objectives

This chapter applies the models developed in earlier chapters to measuring the required rate of return on investment projects. After reading it, you should:

■ Understand how the Dividend Growth Model can be used to set the hurdle rate.

■ Understand how the Capital Asset Pricing Model also can be used for this purpose.

■ Be able to apply the required rate of return to firm valuation.

■ Appreciate that different rates of return may be required at different levels of an organisation.

■ Be aware of the practical difficulties in specifying discount rates for particular activities.

■ Appreciate how taxation may influence discount rates.

10.1 INTRODUCTION

No company can expect prolonged existence without achieving returns that at least compensate investors for their opportunity costs. Shareholders who receive a poor rate of return will vote with their wallets, depressing share price. If its share price under-performs the market (allowing for Beta), a company is ripe for reorganisation, takeover or both. A management team, motivated if only by job security, must earn acceptable returns for shareholders. This chapter deals with assessing such rates of return and showing how they can be used in valuing firms. Different returns may be required for different activities, according to their riskiness. Multi-division companies, which oper-ate in a range of often unrelated activities, may require tailor-made 'divisional cut-off rates' to reflect the risk of particular activities.

capital structure
The mixture of debt and equity resulting from decisions on financing operations

The return that a company should seek on its investment depends not only on its inherent business risk, but also on its **capital structure** – its particular mix of debt and equity financing. However, because determining this rate for a geared company is complex, we defer treatment of the impact of gearing until Chapters 18 and 19. *Here, we focus on the return required by the shareholders in an all-equity company*.

Shareholders seek a return to cover the cost of waiting for their returns, plus com-pensation for inflation, plus a premium to cover the exposure to risk of their capital, depending on the risk of the business activity.

Two widely adopted approaches are the Dividend Growth Model (DGM), encoun-tered in Chapter 3, and the Capital Asset Pricing Model (CAPM), developed in the last chapter. Under each approach, we determine the return that shareholders demand on their investment holdings. We then consider whether this return should dictate the hurdle rate on new investment projects.

10.2 THE REQUIRED RETURN IN ALL-EQUITY FIRMS: THE DGM

■ The DGM revisited

In Chapter 3, we discussed the value of shares in an all-equity firm which retained a constant fraction, b, of its earnings in order to finance investment. If retentions are ex-pected to achieve a rate of return, R, this results in a growth rate of $g = bR$. The share price is:

$$P_0 = \frac{D_0(1 + g)}{(k_e - g)} = \frac{D_1}{(k_e - g)}$$

where D_0 and D_1 represent this year's and next year's dividends per share respectively, and k_e is the rate of return required by shareholders.

cost of equity
The minimum rate of return a firm must offer owners to compensate for waiting for their returns, and also for bearing risk

■ The cost of equity

Rearranging the expression, we find the shareholders' required return is:

$$k_e = \frac{D_1}{P_0} + g$$

The shareholders' required return is thus a compound of two elements, the *prospective* dividend yield and the expected rate of growth in dividends.

It is important to appreciate that this formula for k_e is based on the *current* mar-ket value of the shares, and that it incorporates specific expectations about growth, dependent on current assumptions about both the retention ratio, b, and the expected rate of return on new investment, R. With b and R constant, the rate of growth, g, is also constant. These are highly restrictive assumptions. Often, the nearest we can get to assessing the likely growth rate is to project the past rate of growth, 'tweaking' it if we believe that a faster or slower rate may occur in future.

For example, assume Arthington plc is valued by the market at £3 per share, having recently paid a dividend of 20p per share, and has recorded dividend growth of 12 per cent p.a. Projecting this past growth rate into the future, we can infer that shareholders require a return of 19.5 per cent, viz:

$$k_e = \frac{20p\ (1.12)}{300p} + 0.12 = (0.075 + 0.12) = 0.195, \text{ i.e. } 19.5\%$$

If people felt this growth was unsustainable, then perhaps it might be 'nudged down' to a more achievable 10 per cent, say. In this case, the k_e becomes 17.3 per cent, a rather less demanding target.

Self-assessment activity 10.1

Determine the required return by shareholders in the following case:

Share price = £1.80 (ex div)
Past growth = 3%
EPS = £0.36
Dividend cover = 3 times

(Answer in Appendix A at the back of the book)

■ Whitbread plc (www.whitbread.co.uk.)

Let us relate this approach to a real company. Table 10.1 shows the dividend payment record and end-of-financial year share prices for Whitbread, the leisure conglomerate, for the years 2004–13.

Table 10.1 The dividend return on Whitbread plc shares 2004–13

Year	DPS (p)
2004–5	25.45
2005–6	27.30
2006–7	30.25
2007–8	36.00
2008–9	36.55
2009–10	38.00
2010–11	44.50
2011–12	51.25
2012–13	57.40

Source: Whitbread plc, *Annual Report.*

The dividend per share (DPS) grew from 25.45p in 2004–5 to 57.40p by 2012–13. Using discount tables, we find the average annual compound growth rate is about

10.7 per cent.* Applying this result to the share price of 4083p ruling at the date of analysis (29 April 2014) we find:

$$k_e = \frac{57.40(1 + 0.107)}{4083} + 0.107 = 0.016 + 0.107 = 0.123 \text{ (i.e. 12.3\%)}$$

■ Some problems

Apart from the restrictive assumptions of the Dividend Growth Model, some further warnings are in order.

1 The dividend growth depends on the time period used

The choice of time period can have a significant impact on the results. Too short a period and the estimate of growth is distorted by random factors, and too long a period exposes the result to the impact of structural changes in the business, e.g. divestment and acquisitions.

The calculation of g, and hence k_e, should certainly be based on a sufficiently long period to allow random distortions to even out. We may still feel that past growth is an unreliable guide to future performance, especially for a company in a mature industry, growing roughly in line with the economy as a whole. If past growth is considered unrepresentative, we may interpose our own forecast, but this would involve second-guessing the market's growth expectations, which is tantamount to challenging the EMH.

2 The calculated k_e depends on the choice of reference date for measuring share price

Our calculation used the price at the end of the accounting period, but this pre-dates the announcement of results and payment of dividend. Arguably, we should use the ex-dividend price, as this values all future dividends, beginning with those payable in one year's time. This would reduce the distortion to share price caused by the pattern of dividend payment (i.e. the share price drops abruptly when it goes 'ex-dividend', beyond which purchasers of the share will not qualify for the declared dividend). However, the eventual ex-dividend price may well reflect different expectations from those ruling at the company financial year end.

Conversely, in an efficient capital market, share prices gradually increase as the date of dividend payment approaches, so that, especially for companies that pay several dividends each year, some distorting effect is always likely to be present. Our practical advice is to take the ruling share price as the basis of calculation, but to moderate the calculation according to whether a dividend is in the offing. For example, if a 5p dividend is expected in two months' time, a prospective fall in share price of 5p should be allowed for. In our assessment, the error caused by using an out-of-date share price is likely to outweigh that from using a valuation incorporating a forthcoming dividend.

3 The calculation is at the mercy of short-term movements in share price

If, as many observers believe, capital markets are becoming more volatile, possibly undermining their efficiency in valuing companies, the financial manager may feel disinclined to rely on current market prices. Managers are generally reluctant to accept the EMH and commonly assert that the market undervalues 'their companies'. However,

---

*The growth rate, g, is found from the expression:

$$25.45/(1 + g)^8 = 57.40 \text{ or } (1 + g)^8 = 2.2554$$

The growth rate can be found directly from compound interest tables, or by inverting the expression from the present value tables, i.e. $1/(1 + g)^8 = 0.4434$, whence g approximates to 10.7 per cent.

there remains a need for a benchmark return to guide managers. One might examine, over a period of years, the actual returns received by shareholders in the form of both dividends and capital gains. One way of conducting such a calculation is to focus on average annual rates of return, based on the analysis adopted in Chapter 9, as applied to D.S. Smith plc. This evens out short-term fluctuations. However, it does not follow that the achieved return matches the required return.

4 Taxation

In Chapter 5, we argued the importance of allowing for taxation in project appraisal when estimating cash flows. Consistency seems to require discounting post-tax cash flows at a tax-adjusted cost of finance.

A project's NPV can be found on a post-tax or a pre-tax basis. If the NPV model is used on a pre-tax basis, both denominator and numerator must be on a pre-tax basis, and vice versa. If, for example, we wish to work in post-tax terms, the standard NPV expression for a one-off end-of-year cash flow, X, is:

$$NPV = \frac{X(1 - T)}{(1 + k_T)}$$

where T is the rate of corporation tax and k_T is the required return adjusted for tax. If shareholders seek a return of, say, 10 per cent after tax at 30 per cent, the company has to earn a pre-tax return of $10\%/(1 - 30\%) = 14.3$ per cent. In principle, computation on a pre-tax basis should generate the same NPV as that produced by a post-tax calculation, so long as the discount rate is suitably adjusted. However, this relationship is complicated by access to capital allowances. As a result, it is usual to compute NPVs on a post-tax basis.

The rate of tax applicable to corporate earnings might appear to be the rate of corporation tax. However, the picture is clouded by the prevailing type of tax regime (e.g. whether classical or an **imputation tax system**), and by the forms in which shareholders receive income (i.e. the balance between dividend income and capital gains, and the relevant rates of tax on these two forms of income). In other words, it is important to consider the interaction between the system of corporate taxation and the system of personal taxation.

Under an imputation tax, a shareholder receives a tax credit for the income tax component incorporated into the profits tax. Shareholders subject to tax at the standard rate face no further tax liability, while higher rate taxpayers face a supplementary tax demand. To add to the complexity, some imputation systems allow investors to reclaim all the tax paid on their behalf (full imputation), while others involve a discrepancy between the rate of corporation tax and the relevant rate of income tax (partial imputation). The UK system is a modified partial imputation system under which a tax credit is granted, but is not repayable to non-tax payers. The rate of tax imputed is 10 per cent.

When we calculated k_e using the DGM, the computation was based on the net-of-tax dividend payment, so it may appear that we have met the requirement to allow for taxation. However, the UK tax system imposes two possible tax distortions. First, the relative tax treatment of capital gains and dividend income has differed over time, and second, as we have just seen, different shareholders are subject to tax in different ways.

A major problem facing a company is divining the tax status of its shareholders. Inspection of the shareholder register may provide much information, but there is no easy solution to this problem. The share price is set by the market as a result of the interaction of the supply and demand for its shares as expressed by thousands of investors. Although each may well be in a different tax position, the resulting share price is the result of investors assessing whether the shares represent good value or not. In other words, the market automatically takes into account the average tax positions of its participants.

imputation tax systems
Taxation systems that offer shareholders tax credits (fully or partially) in respect of company tax already paid when assessing their income tax liability on dividends paid out

Under this view, it is not the function of the company to gauge the tax requirements of the investor and to adjust the discount rate accordingly. This is impossible in a capital market with large numbers of investors. The market imposes a required return for particular companies, and then it is up to individual investors to make their own arrangements regarding taxation. The market-determined rate of return can be regarded as the return that the company must make on its investments. This becomes the after-tax return that the company should use to discount the after-tax cash flows from capital projects. (The only adjustment that the company should make is to allow for the tax shield on debt, as explained in Chapter 18.)

To summarise: in principle, we could discount pre-tax cash flows, but the identification of the appropriate pre-tax required return is complicated by the existence and timing of capital allowances. Hence, a post-tax computation is preferable. Theoretically, we ought to allow for investors' personal tax positions as well as corporation tax (i.e. discount project cash flows net of both corporation tax and investors' personal tax liabilities). But this requires such detailed knowledge of the relevant tax rates applicable to shareholders as to render it impracticable. As a result, it is usual to discount post-corporation tax cash flows at the market-expressed required return, assuming that shareholders have made their own tax arrangements. This means that shareholders will gravitate to those companies whose dividend policies most suit their tax positions. This personal **clientèle effect** is discussed further in Chapter 17.

> **clientèle effect**
> The notion that a firm attracts investors by establishing a set dividend policy that suits a particular group of investors

---

Self-assessment activity 10.2

Specify the two situations under which the DGM breaks down completely. (You may have to revisit Chapter 3.)

(Answer in Appendix A at the back of the book)

10.3 THE REQUIRED RETURN IN ALL-EQUITY FIRMS: THE CAPM

In Chapter 9, we saw how the security market line (SML) traces out the systematic risk–return characteristics of all the securities traded in an efficient capital market. The SML equation is:

$$\text{ER}_j = R_f + \beta_j(\text{ER}_m - R_f)$$

ER_j is the return required on the shares of company j, and is therefore the same as k_e, R_f is the risk-free rate of return, and ER_m is the expected return on the market portfolio. We saw in Chapter 9 that, in order to utilise the CAPM, we needed either to measure, or to make direct assumptions about, these items. (Refer back to the discussion of measurement difficulties and the application to GKN.)

However, despite these problems, the CAPM has major advantages over the DGM. The DGM usually involves extrapolating past rates of growth and accepting the validity of the market's valuation of the equity at any time. If we suspect that past growth rates are unlikely to be replicated and/or that a company's share price is over- or under-valued, we might doubt the validity of an estimate of k_e derived from the DGM.

The CAPM does not require growth projections; nor does it totally depend on the instantaneous efficiency of the market. Recall that the Beta is derived from a regression model relating the returns from holding the shares of a particular company j to the returns on the market over a lengthy period. Taking, say, monthly observations over five years (60 in all) effectively irons out short-term influences. This requires semi-strong market efficiency for the period and a reasonably consistent relationship between security returns and the returns on the market portfolio.

■ Applying the CAPM to Whitbread plc

The Risk Measurement Service quoted a Beta of 0.95 for Whitbread shares as at January–March 2014. At that time, the yield on long-term UK gilts was about 3 per cent. Using a market risk premium of 5 per cent yields the following required return:

$$ER_j = R_f + \beta(ER_m - R_f) = 0.03 + 0.95(5\%)$$
$$= 0.03 + 0.0475 = 0.0775 = 7.75\%$$

This is somewhat below the DGM result of 12.3 per cent. As the two approaches, in principle, should yield about the same result, some reconciliation is required. At the time of this calculation, market interest rates were historically very low, at least in money terms, generating expectations of low interest rates for the future. It is doubtful whether Whitbread can sustain 10.7 per cent dividend growth in the future, so it might be more prudent to use a rate nearer to that of the industry as a whole.

It appears that estimates of k_e obtained by either method are susceptible to the date of the calculation and prevailing expectations for the future. More fundamentally, whereas the DGM looks at past performance over a number of years, the CAPM is essentially a forward-looking, one-period, model, although it is commonly used for long-term purposes.

Counting the cost

Lex Column

There are few more essential items in the corporate finance tool-kit than a company's cost of capital – the return its investors expect as compensation for putting their funds in one business rather than another. Estimating this cost of capital, however, involves as much art and guesswork as it does science, and the results can vary widely.

Three years ago, those companies that publish a figure for their cost of capital – usually those which have adopted a form of economic profit or economic value added performance framework – often came out with figures 1–2 percentage points higher than those implied by market values, or estimated by stock market analysts. Today, the gap has in many cases reversed. Lloyds TSB, for example, calculates its economic profit using a cost of equity of 9 per cent. Yet its share price appears to imply, even if you assume it will halve its dividend, a cost of equity in excess of 10 per cent.

Why does this matter? To create value for shareholders, companies need to make returns greater than their cost of capital. If companies are underestimating cost of capital, they will make acquisitions or invest in projects that destroy value. Conversely, if the market is setting the hurdle too high, investors will miss out on value-creating investments.

CAPM

Computing the cost of debt is fairly straightforward, at least for companies whose bonds are traded. The cost of equity is more complicated. The standard formula remains the capital asset pricing model, or CAPM, devised separately by William Sharpe, John Lintner and Jack Treynor. Though many academic studies have raised doubts about its empirical validity, three out of four chief financial officers use CAPM.

CAPM's starting point is the risk-free rate – typically a 10-year government bond yield. To this is added a premium, which equity investors require to compensate them for the extra risk they accept. This equity risk premium is multiplied by a factor, known as beta, to reflect a company's volatility and correlation with the market as a whole. Beta is designed to capture the risk that an investor cannot diversify away by holding a portfolio of other shares; a company whose share price tends to rise and fall more than the market will have a high beta. There are difficulties with all three of these elements. Government bond yields are currently very low, by historical standards. A company contemplating a long-term investment can lock in these low rates for its debt, but if interest rates then rise so will its cost of equity. It may generate the cash flows it anticipated from its investment, but these will no longer cover its cost of capital. It may be appropriate to use a somewhat higher normalised risk-free rate. Yet it looks as though many equity analysts have taken insufficient account of the fall of risk-free rates in their cost of capital estimates.

The equity risk premium is the element that has generated most controversy. In the early 1990s, most companies used numbers in excess of 6 per cent, drawing

Continued ➡

on data from Ibbotson Associates and others. Then market analysts started to use equity risk premiums of 3–4 per cent and these numbers began to filter into corporate use. Historical performance data compiled by Elroy Dimson, Paul Marsh and Mike Staunton give a world equity premium over bonds of 3.8 per cent over the last 103 years. Marakon Associates, the strategic consultancy, derives an equity risk premium of 5.3 per cent, rather higher than the recent average, from the implied internal rate of return of 1,190 stocks, but of 3.6 per cent on the basis of dividend yield and growth. Splitting the difference, that gives an estimate of about 4.5 per cent.

Beta

Beta can be even trickier to calculate. Ideally, companies would use a forward-looking beta but estimates depend on historical trading data. Yet as McKinsey analysts pointed out in a recent study, the TMT bubble of 1998–2001 has dramatically lowered the apparent betas of unaffected sectors. They calculate an improbably low current beta of 0.02 for the food, beverage and tobacco sector, against an average of 0.85 for 1990–97. Individual company betas can also deliver counter-intuitive results. An accident-prone company may have a very low beta, because its mishaps mean it shows less correlation with the overall market.

Take Allianz as an example: the German insurer bases its embedded value calculations on an 8.15 per cent risk discount rate for Europe and the US. This is based on a 5 per cent long-term view of risk-free rates, a 3.5 per cent equity risk premium and a beta of 0.9.

This beta, in particular, might raise an eyebrow, since the vulnerability of the company's capital base to equity market declines would prompt most investors to call it a high beta stock. Substituting a historical German equity risk premium of 5.7 per cent – according to Dimson, Marsh and Staunton – and a Bloomberg-calculated beta of 1.14 would yield a cost of equity of 11.5 per cent.

The finer points of CAPM mattered less when nominal interest rates were high. Take a company whose cash flows are growing at 3 per cent: using a 12 per cent cost of capital to discount these cash flows, only one third of its value lies more than 10 years out but, at 7 per cent, more than half is accounted for by these more distant years. Small adjustments to the cost of capital will also have a larger impact on the overall valuation at these lower rates. This effect weighs even more on non-financial companies with a significant amount of debt on their balance sheets, as their weighted average cost of capital will be lower than their cost of equity.

In most corporate investment decisions, the odd half point makes little difference, though in pricing acquisitions the precise cost of capital may be more significant. With equity markets still jittery, however, companies are better off setting a higher hurdle rate for investment than a straightforward CAPM calculation would imply. That might not be consistent with academic theory but it will, in practice, make them choose more carefully between their business units in allocating capital and lead to less wasteful investment than in the past.

 Source: Financial Times, 24 March 2003. © Financial Times

10.4 USING 'TAILORED' DISCOUNT RATES

Applying the discount rates derived using the CAPM to investment projects assumes that new projects fall into the same risk category as the company's other operations. This might be a reasonable assumption for minor projects in existing areas and perhaps for replacements, but hardly seems justifiable for major new product developments or acquisitions of companies in unrelated areas. If the expected return is positively related to risk, firms that rely on a single discount rate may tend to over-invest in risky projects to the detriment of less risky, though still attractive, projects. Many multi-divisional companies are effectively portfolios of diverse activities of different degrees of risk. The Beta of the firm as a whole is thus the weighted average of its component activity Betas. Each division contributes to the firm's overall business risk in a way similar to that in which individual shares contribute to the systematic risk of a portfolio of securities. The dangers of using a uniform discount rate are shown in Figure 10.1.

Figure 10.1 shows the relationship between the rate of return required on a particular project and that expected on the market portfolio, linked by the Beta. The overall portfolio of company activities may have a Beta of, say, 1.2, which is a weighted average of the Betas of component activities. For example, activity A has a greater than average degree of risk, with a Beta of 2.0, and thus a higher than average discount

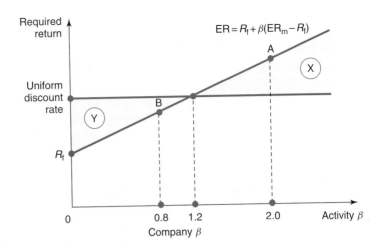

Figure 10.1 Risk premiums for activities of varying risk

rate would be applicable when appraising new projects in this area, while the reverse applies for activity B, which has a Beta of only 0.8. Clearly, to appraise all new projects using a discount rate based on the overall company Beta of 1.2 would invite serious errors. For example, in area X, application of the uniform discount rate would result in accepting some projects that should be rejected because they offer too low a return for their level of risk, while in area Y, some worthwhile, low-risk projects would be rejected. Firms should use 'tailor-made' cut-off rates for activities involving a degree of risk different from that of the overall company.

Self-assessment activity 10.3

What are the discount rates applicable to the firm as a whole and activities A and B in Figure 10.1, assuming a risk-free rate of 5 per cent, and a market risk premium of 6 per cent?

(Answer in Appendix A at the back of the book)

Figure 10.2 shows the three levels, or tiers, of risk found in the multi-activity enterprise, each requiring a different rate of return.

In Chapter 19, we will find that there is a fourth tier of risk that uniquely applies to ordinary shareholders. In a geared firm, that faces financial risk, the returns achieved by shareholders are more volatile than the firm's operating cash flows due to the interest payments that must be paid on debt. In response to this higher risk, shareholders demand a higher return. In other words, the Beta of the shares exceeds the Beta of the firm's business activities. To arrive at the activity Beta, we would need to 'ungear' the Beta of the shares.

If the company is entirely equity-financed, the risks that shareholders incur coincide with those incurred by the company as a whole, i.e. those related to trading and operational factors. In this case, the Beta of the ordinary shares coincides with that of the company itself.

Many companies are structured into separate strategic sub-units or divisions, organised along product or geographical lines. In such companies, it is unlikely that every activity faces identical systematic risk. So different discount rates should be applied to evaluate 'typical' projects within each division.

However, even within divisions, rarely do two projects have identical risk. Hence, different discount rates are required when new projects differ in risk from existing divisional activities.

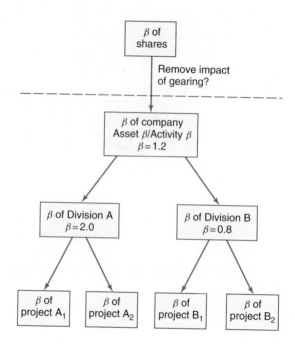

Figure 10.2 The Beta pyramid

Segmental Betas

The company Beta is a weighted average of component divisional Betas. For a company with two divisions, A and B, the overall Beta is a weighted average given by:

$$\text{Company } \beta = \left(\beta_A \times \frac{V_A}{V_A + V_B} \right) + \left(\beta_B \times \frac{V_B}{V_A + V_B} \right)$$

where the weights represent the proportion of company value accounted for by each segment. A similar expression would apply for each division, where the corresponding weights would represent the contribution to divisional value accounted for by each component activity. Figure 10.2 illustrates these concepts in the form of a 'Beta pyramid'.

Self-assessment activity 10.4

What is the company Beta for the firm shown in Figure 10.1 if activities A and B constitute 65 per cent and 35 per cent of its assets respectively?

(Answer in Appendix A at the back of the book)

Let us use Whitbread plc to illustrate the derivation of the appropriate discount rate at different levels of an organisation. It is organised into two broad product divisions, as shown in Table 10.2, which lists the operating divisions. These titles suggest quite different activities, although a firm's own description of its division is not always a reliable guide to the nature of those activities.

We performed a CAPM calculation earlier in relation to the equity of Whitbread, obtaining a result of 7.75 per cent. Should we apply this rate to all investments undertaken by Whitbread? The answer is 'no', if we believe there are risk differences between the divisions, in which case, we should calculate tailor-made discount rates.

Table 10.2 Divisional Betas for Whitbread plc

Activity	% share of sales	Surrogate company	Beta	Weighted beta
Hotels and Restaurants	67	Millennium and Copthorne	1.40	0.94
Costa	33	Snacktime*	0.87	0.29
	100			1.23

*There are no UK coffee shops quoted on the LSE. Snacktime manufactures coffee vending machines, so is probably subject to similar operating risks to a coffee retail operation.

Source: Whitbread plc Annual Report 2012–13; Risk Measurement Service January–March 2014.

■ The divisional cut-off rate

We need now to consider what are suitable Betas for the two Whitbread divisions. However, no Betas are recorded for company divisions, simply because no market trades securities representing title to a firm's divisional assets. Instead, we need to look for two surrogate companies and use their ungeared Betas as the 'stand-in' estimates for the Betas of the Whitbread divisions. This involves using what Fuller and Kerr (1981) called the **pure play technique**. It relies on the principle that: 'the risk of a division of a conglomerate company is the same as the risk of an undiversified firm in the same line of business (adjusted for financial risk)'.

pure play technique
Adoption of the Beta value of another firm for use in evaluating investment in an unquoted entity such as an unquoted firm, or a division of a larger firm

Consulting the RMS or Financial Times,* we look for suitable surrogate companies whose Betas we can use as proxies for those of the Whitbread divisions. The dangers of doing this should not be understated. Ideally, the surrogate should be a close match for the relevant Whitbread division, i.e. they should conduct the same activity or mix of activities in the same proportions, and should also be ungeared. (If they use debt finance, the gearing effect on their Betas should be stripped out, as explained in Chapter 19.) In principle, the weighted averages of these Beta values will coincide with the overall Beta of Whitbread plc if we have selected good surrogates. The weightings ought to be based on market values, but as these are unknown for company divisions, book values of net operating assets could be used. Not all companies reveal divisional asset values, so a proxy measure such as sales or operating profits may have to be used. For Whitbread, share of sales has been used. This is only a valid proxy for assets if the sales-to-assets ratio is similar from division to division, which is quite unlikely. (Actually, the respective shares of operating profit were 85 per cent for Hotels and Restaurants, and 15 per cent for Costa.)

Table 10.2 shows that the weighted average Beta for Whitbread is 1.23. This may differ from the Whitbread Beta we observe in any particular database and the discrepancy could be due to:

■ The chosen surrogates are not close enough matches for Whitbread's two activities.
■ Differences in gearing. As we will see in a later chapter, gearing has the effect of raising Beta values as shareholders seek an extra premium to compensate for the financial risk that gearing imposes. The RMS Beta values are all equity Betas – they include the effect of gearing, and, of course, different firms may have different gearing ratios. Hence, if we take a Beta from a low-geared firm and apply it to a high-geared one, our weighted average calculation will understate the true Beta of the

*Note: Betas can be obtained from different sources and databases. These different sources may calculate Betas in different ways. Hence, the Beta for a particular company may differ depending on the source or database.

focus firm, and vice versa. Ideally, we should compare like with like, either strip out the effect of gearing altogether, and work in terms of pure equity (or activity) Betas, or ungear the Betas of the surrogates, and then re-gear them to reflect the gearing of the focus firm. These issues we defer to Chapter 19.

■ Differences in how the Betas are calculated in the databases.

The following cameo shows an example of restructuring by Whitbread.

Self-assessment activity 10.5

Re-work the Whitbread weighted average Beta calculation, using share of operating profits as weightings (given above).

(Answer in Appendix A at the back of the book)

Whitbread smells self-service success

Andy Harrison is bringing the stripped-down service delivery he learnt at EasyJet to Whitbread, with a £59.5m deal that will launch the company's Costa Coffee division into the self-serve market.

The hotels and restaurants group said on Wednesday it would buy Coffee Nation, an operator of 900 self-service coffee machines across the UK, for 14 times the smaller group's earnings last year.

The machines will be relabelled 'Costa Express' – a new brand – and serve as a platform for growth in the UK's 'emerging self-serve coffee bar sector', according to the group.

It aims to expand to 3,000 stations over the next five years.

Mr Harrison, who joined as chief executive last autumn after five years at the low-cost carrier, said Coffee Nation's use of freshly ground beans and fresh milk in its machines would give Costa access to new types of locations and help it attract hurried customers without compromising on quality.

'There are 6bn cups of coffee sold through traditional vending machines. That tells us there's a huge customer demand for speed and convenience,' he said.

Research by Mintel showed steady growth over the past five years in the portion of coffee shop customers taking their purchases away. Mintel also said the portion of Britons visiting coffee shops – about 56 per cent – had held steady since 2007, suggesting this was a mature market.

The deal was announced alongside a fourth-quarter trading update showing like-for-like sales slowing at both Costa and Whitbread's hotel and restaurant division, which contributes 87 per cent of group profits.

Total sales rose 12.4 per cent in the quarter, on the back of 24 per cent growth at Costa and 12 per cent at Premier Inns. The company said full-year results would be in line with market expectations.

Mr Harrison warned that the economic environment was 'challenging'. Analysts raised concerns over higher value added tax and input costs, as well as Whitbread's vulnerability to UK consumer sentiment.

The shares fell 90p to £16.44.

Nigel Parson at Evolution Securities said the Coffee Nation purchase looked expensive on historic multiples but pointed to the expansion plans.

Geof Collyer at Deutsche Bank – one of Whitbread's brokers – estimated the multiple of earnings before interest, tax, depreciation and amortisation would fall to 4 times by year five of the takeover.

Investec Growth & Acquisition Finance, which alongside Milestone Capital and members of Coffee Nation's management team sold the self-serve operator, said the deal had returned double the amount it had invested in 2008 as part of a secondary management buy-out.

 Source: Rose Jacobs, *Financial Times*, 3 March 2011. © Financial Times

---

■ The project cut-off rate

If any division undertakes a new venture that takes it outside its existing risk parameters, clearly we must look for different rates of return – in effect, we need to obtain estimates for individual project Betas. Without access to internal records, our analysis can only be indicative, but the following principles offer broad guidance.

Essentially, we look for sources of risk that make the individual project more or less chancy relative to existing operations. There are two broad reasons why projects have different risks to the divisions where they are based – different revenue sensitivity and different operating gearing.

Revenue sensitivity

Imagine Whitbread is looking at developing a new coffee shop brand. The sales generated by the projected facility may vary with changes in economic activity to a greater or lesser degree than existing sales in the relevant division. For example, we may expect that, for a specified rise in the level of GDP, whereas overall retail sales of Whitbread existing outlets increase by 7 per cent, the sales of the new brand rise by 9 per cent.

The revenue sensitivity factor

revenue sensitivity factor (RSF)
The sensitivity to economic fluctuations of a project's sales in relation to that of the division to which it is attached

This magnifying effect is measured by the **revenue sensitivity factor (RSF)**. The RSF is calculated as follows:

$$RSF = \frac{\text{Sensitivity of project sales to economic changes}}{\text{Sensitivity of divisional sales to economic changes}} = \frac{9\%}{7\%} = 1.29$$

This relationship may stem from the nature of the product – if it is pitched at discretionary spenders (e.g. people who frequent more 'upmarket' outlets), it may be more closely geared to the economy as a whole.

Operating gearing

This concerns the extent to which the project cost structure comprises fixed charges. The higher the proportion of fixed costs in the cost structure, the greater the impact of a change in economic conditions on the operating cash flow of the project, thus magnifying the revenue sensitivity effect. Again, the project may exhibit a degree of operating gearing different from that of the division as a whole.

To illustrate the impact of operating gearing, consider the figures in Table 10.3, where the firm applies a 50 per cent mark-up on variable cost. An increase in sales revenue of 50 per cent will lead to an increase in net operating cash flow of 67 per cent because of the gearing effect. There is thus a magnifying factor of 1.34. This so-called **project gearing factor (PGF)** may well differ from the gearing factor(s) found elsewhere in the division.

project gearing factor (PGF)
The proportionate increase in a project's operating cash flow in relation to a proportionate increase in the project's sales

Table 10.3 The effect of operating gearing (£m)

Sales revenue	Variable costs	Fixed cash costs	Operating cash flow
90	60	5	25
60	40	5	15

operating gearing factor (OGF)
The operating gearing factor of an individual project in relation to that of the division to which it is attached

To measure the relative level of gearing, the **operating gearing factor (OGF)** is used. This is defined as:

$$OGF = \frac{\text{Project gearing factor}}{\text{Divisional gearing factor}}$$

If the divisional gearing factor is 1.80, for example, the project's OGF = 1.34/1.80 = 0.74.

The second step in assessing the project discount rate brings together these two sources of relative project risk into a project risk factor (PRF).

■ The project risk factor

This is the compound of the revenue sensitivity factor and the operating gearing factor:

Project risk factor $=$ RSF $\times$ OGF

In our example, this is equal to $(1.29 \times 0.74) = 0.95$. In this case, the project is less risky than the 'average' project within the division and merits the application of a lower Beta. Based on Whitbread's surrogate for Costa Beta, shown in Table 10.2, this is given by:

Project Beta $= (0.95 \times 0.87) = 0.83$

The final step calculates the required return using the basic CAPM equation, based on a 3.0 per cent risk-free rate and a market risk premium of 5 per cent:

Required return $= 0.03 + 0.83(0.05) = 0.03 + 0.041 = 0.071$ (i.e. 7.1%)

Self-assessment activity 10.6

Determine the required return on a project whose revenue sensitivity is 50 per cent and operating gearing 80 per cent compared to the division where it is located. The divisional Beta is 1.2, the risk-free rate is 5 per cent and the market risk premium 6 per cent.

(Answer in Appendix A at the back of the book)

■ Project discount rates in practice

Considering the informational requirements for obtaining reliable tailor-made discount rates for particular investment projects, few firms go to these lengths. A far more common practice is to seek an overall divisional rate of return, which becomes the average cut-off rate, but is then adjusted for risk on a largely intuitive basis, according to the perceived degree of risk of the project. For example, many firms group projects into 'risk categories' such as the classification in Table 10.4. For each category, a target or required return is established as the cut-off rate.

Table 10.4 Subjective risk categories

Project type	Required return (%)
Replacement	12
Cost saving/application of advanced manufacturing technology	15
'Scale' projects, i.e. expansion of existing activities	18
New project development:	
Imitative products	20
Conceptually new products, i.e. no existing competitors	25

Imagine the divisional required return is 18 per cent, the rate applicable to projects that replicate the firm's existing activities. Around this benchmark are clustered activities of varying degrees of risk, and as the perceived riskiness increases, the target return rises in tandem.

In all these cases, we are discussing a discount rate derived from the ungeared Beta. In other words, we are separating out the inherent profitability of the project from any financing costs and benefits. Analysis of financing complications is deferred to Chapters 18 and 19.

10.5 WORKED EXAMPLE: TIEKO PLC

Tieko plc is a diversified conglomerate that is currently financed entirely by equity. Its five activities and their respective share of corporate assets are shown in the table below. Also shown are the Beta coefficients of highly similar surrogate firms operating in the same markets as the Tieko divisions.

Division	% share of book value of Tieko assets	Beta of a close substitute
Electronics	30	1.40
Property	20	0.70
Defence equipment	30	0.20
Durables	20	1.05

The yield on short-term government stock is currently 6 per cent, and people expect the stock market portfolio to deliver an average annual return of 13 per cent in future years.

Required

In each of the following (separate) situations, determine Tieko's company Beta and the return required by shareholders:

(i) As it is currently structured. Also, calculate the hurdle rates for the four divisions.

(ii) If Tieko sells the defence division for book value and returns the cash proceeds to shareholders as a Special Dividend.

(iii) If Tieko sells the defence division for book value and places the cash proceeds on deposit.

(iv) If Tieko acquires a telecommunications firm that has a Beta of 1.60, and total assets equal in value to the defence division.

Solution

In each case, the Beta value is a weighted average of the Betas of the component activities, with each division's share of total assets providing the weights.

(i) At present, the Beta is:

$$(0.3 \times 1.4) + (0.20 \times 0.70) + (0.30 \times 0.20) + (0.20 \times 1.05)$$
$$= (0.42 + 0.14 + 0.06 + 0.21) = 0.83$$

Using the CAPM formula, the required return for the firm as a whole is thus:

$$6\% + 0.83 [13\% - 6\%] = (6\% + 5.8\%) = 11.8\%$$

The separate divisional hurdle rates are as shown in the following table.

Division	Risk-free rate	Beta	Market premium	Required return
Electronics	6%	1.40	7%	6% + 1.40(7%) = 15.80%
Property	6%	0.70	7%	6% + 0.70(7%) = 10.90%
Defence equipment	6%	0.20	7%	6% + 0.20(7%) = 7.40%
Durables	6%	1.05	7%	6% + 1.05(7%) = 13.35%

(ii) If Tieko 'downsizes' to 70 per cent of its previous size, the weightings for the three remaining divisions become:

Electronics $3/7 = 0.429$
Property $2/7 \;\; = 0.285$
Durables $2/7 \;\; = 0.285$

The overall Beta becomes:

$(0.429 \times 1.4) + (0.285 \times 0.70) + (0.285 \times 1.05)$
$= (0.60 + 0.20 + 0.30) = 1.10$

Clearly, Tieko has become more risky and the required return increases to

$6\% + 1.10\,[13\% - 6\%] = 6\% + 7.7\% = 13.7\%$

(iii) If it retains the cash, then the total assets remain unchanged but the Beta will alter as the Beta of cash is zero – it is uncorrelated with the risky securities quoted on the stock market.

The overall Beta becomes:

$(0.3 \times 1.4) + (0.20 \times 0.70) + (0.30 \times 0) + (0.20 \times 1.05)$
$= (0.42 + 0.14 + 0 + 0.21) = 0.77$

Having disposed of its least risky division and replaced it with risk-free cash, Tieko has become much less risky. As a result, its overall required return decreases to:

$6\% + 0.77\,[13\% - 6\%] = (6\% + 5.39\%) = 11.39\%$

(iv) If Tieko expands by adding another division of equal size to the electronics arm, i.e. a 30 per cent expansion, the new weightings are:

Electronics $3/13 = 0.230$
Property $\;\;\;\; 2/13 = 0.154$
Difence $\;\;\;\;\; 3/13 = 0.230$
Durables $\;\;\; 2/13 = 0.154$
Telecomms $3/13 = 0.230$

The overall Beta becomes:

$(0.230 \times 1.4) + (0.154 \times 0.70) + (0.230 \times 0.20) + (0.154 \times 1.05) + (0.230 \times 1.60)$
$= (0.322 + 0.108 + 0.046 + 0.162 + 0.368) = 1.006$

The required return increases to:

$6\% + 1.006\,[13\% - 6\%] = (6\% + 7.04\%) = 13.04\%$

After this expansion, Tieko has a Beta very similar to that of the market portfolio (1.0). It has thus managed to diversify itself into a portfolio of activities of virtually average risk.

10.6 ANOTHER PROBLEM: TAXATION AND THE CAPM

Empirical studies of the risk premium usually reveal gross-of-personal-tax results. To adjust for tax, one might consider the tax status of interest income from the risk-free asset, normally taken as government stock of some form, and the tax status of the return on the market portfolio.

Franks and Broyles (1979) recommended two adjustments. First, adjust the risk-free rate for the shareholders' rate of personal tax, then adjust the risk premium according to the relative proportions of excess return earned in dividend and in capital gain formed. There are practical difficulties in doing this. However, take for illustration 20 per cent as an average rate of capital gains tax (CGT) and 25 per cent as an average rate of tax on dividends, if we then assume half of the return on equities was from dividends and half from capital gain this yields a weighted average tax rate (WAT) of $(0.5 \times 0.20) + (0.5 \times 0.25) = 22.5\%$. Consequently the calculation of the post-tax required return on Whitbread's ordinary shares (ER_W) would be:

$$ER_W = R_f(1 - \text{present income tax rate}) + \beta[\text{market risk premium}][1 - \text{WAT}]$$
$$= 0.03(1 - 0.2) + (0.95)(0.05)(1 - 0.225)$$
$$= 0.024 + 0.037$$
$$= 0.061 \text{ (i.e. 6.1\%)}$$

There are obvious problems in taking average rates of tax over periods when tax regimes have altered. Wilkie (1994) argues that such a calculation is conceptually flawed, being based on the assumption that individuals would have invested in a tax-inefficient vehicle (government stock) – although many do! Most personal investors would have been subject to higher rates of income tax and thus would have taken steps anyway to shelter their income from tax. Finally, he points out that the securities market historically has been dominated by tax-exempt investors, in terms of both the percentages of market value held and, more crucially, the flow of new funds to the market, which dictates market prices. He concludes that little accuracy is lost by using the gross-of-tax risk premium, and ignoring any tax effect on the risk-free rate, especially as future tax rates on investment income are likely to be lower than past rates, following widespread tax cuts in the 1990s.

10.7 PROBLEMS WITH 'TAILORED' DISCOUNT RATES

The pure play technique is an appealing device for estimating discount rates for specific activities, but suffers from a number of practical difficulties.

1 *Selecting the proxy.* To select a proxy, the firm needs to examine the range of apparently similar candidates operating in the relevant sector. However, no two companies have the same business risk due to diversity of markets, management skills and other operating characteristics. How one chooses between a range of 'fairly similar' candidates is essentially an issue of judgement.

2 *Divisional interdependencies.* In practice, it is difficult to make a rigid demarcation of divisional costs and incomes, since most divisionalised companies share facilities, ranging from the highest decision-making level to joint research and development, joint distribution channels and joint marketing activities. Indeed, access to shared facilities often provides the initial motive for forming a diversified conglomerate, enabling the elimination of duplicated services and the exploitation of scale economies. If carefully evaluated and implemented, the merging of activities should create value and reduce business risk. Only when a merger has no operating impact across divisional lines can it be suggested that business risk itself is unaffected. Even so, there may well be synergies at the peak decision-making level.

3 *Differential growth opportunities.* Using a cut-off rate based on another firm suggests that the division in question has the same growth prospects as the surrogate. However, opportunities to grow are determined by dividend policy, the extent of capital rationing and the interaction between divisions, e.g. competition for scarce investment capital. In reality, because the firm's own decision processes help to determine the potential for growth, it is not accurate to assume that growth opportunities are externally derived.

4 *Joint ventures.* The use of differential discount rates may destroy the incentive to cooperate on projects that straddle divisional boundaries. For example, a joint venture whose expected return lies between the cut-off rates of the two divisions will be attractive to one and unacceptable to the other. Here, some form of mediation is required at peak level, which reassures the 'loser' of the decision that subsequent performance will be assessed after adjusting for having to operate with a project that it did *not* want, or without a project that it *did* wish to undertake.

Regulator turns screw on UK water operators

Ofwat (the UK water regulator) has turned the screw on water industry operators across England and Wales by demanding they accept lower rates of return on equity and capital in the next five-year regulatory period, which will run to 2020.

The regulator confirmed yesterday that companies should expect their weighted average cost of capital to be pegged to no more than 3.85 per cent.

WACC is a blended measure of the return on the mix of debt and equity needed to underpin investment and spending plans.

The regulator has concluded that an acceptable cost of debt to companies is in the range of 2.2 per cent to 2.8 per cent for the period.

It also set an acceptable average cost of equity at nearly 1 percentage point below companies' average claim of 6.6 per cent. The 'current total equity return expectations should be below historical evidence on returns', it said.

The guidelines suggested that an increase of half a percentage point in WACC – close to the spread between Ofwat's guidance of 3.85 per cent and average companies' assumption of 4.3 per cent – equated to an increase in annual bills of about £10.

Source: Based on Michael Kavanagh, *Financial Times*, 28 January 2014, p. 23.

10.8 A CRITIQUE OF DIVISIONAL HURDLE RATES*

Modern strategic planning has moved away from crude portfolio planning devices such as the Boston Consulting Group's market share/market growth matrix towards capital allocation methods that emphasise the creation of shareholder value. Central to value-based approaches is discounting projected cash flows to determine the value to shareholders of business units and their strategies. *A key feature of the DCF approach is the recognition that different business strategies involve different degrees of risk and should be discounted at tailored risk-adjusted rates.*

However, critics such as Reimann (1990) suggest that differential rates will increase the likelihood of internal dissension, whereby a manager of a 'penalised' division may resent the requirement to earn a rate of return significantly higher than some of his colleague-competitors. This resentment may be worsened by the observation that longer-term developments, especially in advanced manufacturing technology and other risky, but potentially high value-added activities, may be 'unfairly' discriminated against. As a result, managers may be reluctant to propose some potentially attractive projects.

As we saw in Chapter 7, risk-adjusted discount rates have the effect of compounding risk differences, making ostensibly riskier projects appear to increase in risk over time. One school of thought contends that in order to avoid this risk penalty, the attempt to tailor discount rates to divisions should be modified, if not abandoned. For example, instead of using differential discount rates, firms might use a more easily understood and acceptable, company-wide discount rate for projects of 'normal' risk, but appraise high-risk/high-return projects using different approaches.

---

*This section relies heavily on arguments used by Reimann (1990).

Underlying these arguments is the familiar assertion that diversification by firms differs crucially from shareholder diversification, so that applying the CAPM to the former could be misleading. If an investor adds a new share to an existing portfolio, the systematic risk of the portfolio will alter according to the Beta of the new security. If its Beta is higher than that of the existing portfolio, then the portfolio Beta increases, and vice versa. With corporate diversification, however, we are not dealing with a basket of shares of unrelated companies, which may be freely traded on the market. A firm that diversifies rarely adds totally unrelated activities to its core operations. It may add value if the new activity possesses synergy, or detract from value if the market views the combination as merely a bundle of disparate, unwieldy activities that are hard to manage.

Systematic risk can be altered by strategic diversification decisions at two levels. At the corporate level, decisions concerning business and product mixes, and operating and financial gearing can affect market risk. The effect of both types of gearing can be magnified by the business cycle, so that a firm which engages in contra-cyclical diversification may dampen oscillations in shareholder returns and thus reduce market risk. At the business level, market risk can be reduced by tying up outlets and supplier sources (i.e. by increasing market power), and by developing business activities that enjoy important interrelationships, such as common skills or technologies (i.e. by exploiting economies of scale).

Many managers feel that the emphasis on hurdle rates is probably misplaced insofar as accurate cash flow forecasts are more important to creating business value than the particular discount rate applied to them. This probably helps explain the continuing popularity of the payback method, and the relative reluctance in the UK, to adopt CAPM-based approaches. It may also explain why so many successful firms place great emphasis on post-auditing capital projects in order to sharpen up the cash flow forecasting and project appraisals of subordinate staff. Furthermore, there is (US) evidence (Pruitt and Gitman, 1987; Pohlman *et al.*, 1988) that senior managers manifest their suspicion of subordinates' cash flow predictions by deflating the figures presented to them when projects are submitted for approval.

In view of these arguments, there may be a case for reconsidering the merits of using certainty equivalents – adjusting the cash flow estimates and then discounting at the risk-free rate. However, this has not been widely adopted. Apart from the difficulty of specifying the risk-free asset, there is the problem of determining the certainty equivalent factors, which involves specifying the probabilities of different possible cash flows as a basis for assessing their utility values. While techniques are available for doing this (Swalm, 1966; Chesley, 1975), it has not been practicable in most firms.

Reimann (1990) suggests a 'management by exception' approach. The firm should establish and continuously update a corporate cost of capital, based on CAPM principles. This should be applied as a common hurdle rate for the majority of business activities, which, he argues, typically exhibit very similar degrees of risk. At the business level, major emphasis should be given to careful cash flow estimation, based on evaluation of long-term strategic opportunities and competitive advantage. A key element should be a multiple scenario approach, whereby the implications of 'best', 'worst' and 'most likely' states of the world are examined. For projects that, by their very nature, have a demonstrably greater level of risk, other procedures may be appropriate. Rather than adjust the corporate discount rate, Reimann suggests the risk adjustment be made to the cash flow estimates by the business unit executives themselves, i.e. those with closest knowledge both of the market and of competitors' behaviour patterns. Again, a multiple scenario approach should be adopted. This avoids the effect of compounding risk differences over time and thus penalising longer-term projects, which may have a demotivating effect on staff engaged in pursuing high-risk activities.

This discussion may seem to downgrade the importance of DCF and CAPM approaches in project appraisal. However, it is really intended to remind you that apparently neat mathematical models rarely hold the whole answer. If the rigid application of a numerical routine leads managers to question the basis of the routine itself (one which we believe offers powerful guidance in many situations) and to exhibit dysfunctional behaviour, it is far better to modify the routine itself to reflect real-world practicalities.

SUMMARY

We have considered the relative merits of using the DGM and the CAPM to derive the rate of return required by shareholders. The case for and against using tailor-made discount rates for particular business segments and projects was also discussed.

Key points

- The return required on new investment depends primarily on two factors: degree of risk and the method of financing the project.

- The return required by shareholders can be estimated using either the DGM or the CAPM.

- The DGM relies on several critical assumptions: in particular, sustained and constant growth, and the instantaneous reliability of the share price set by the market.

- The CAPM relies on a Beta estimate obtained after smoothing short-term distortions, but the estimated k_e may be affected by random influences on the risk-free rate.

- Application of a uniform company-wide discount rate to all company projects can lead to accepting projects that should be rejected and to rejecting projects that should be accepted.

- To resolve the problem of risk differences between divisions of a company, the Beta of a surrogate firm (adjusted for gearing) can be used to establish divisional cut-off rates.

- If individual projects within the division also differ in risk, the divisional Beta can be adjusted for differences in revenue sensitivity and/or differences in operating gearing.

- Not all academics and business people accept the need to define discount rates so carefully, preferring instead to concentrate on the problems of cash flow estimation.

- Reimann argues that a divisional cut-off rate should be used as a rough benchmark for projects, but alternative methods of risk analysis should be applied to explore more fully the risk characteristics and the acceptability of investment proposals.

Further reading

Analyses of the 'tailored' discount rate can be found in Dimson and Marsh (1982) and Andrews and Firer (1987). Weaver (1989), Gup and Norwood (1982) and Harrington (1983) all provide practical illustrations of how US corporations apply divisional discount rates, while Reimann (1990) gives a critique of the whole approach.

Recent articles reviewing required returns include those by King (2009) who surveys costs of equity for banks, van Binsbergen *et al.* (2010) who examine costs of debt, and DeLong and Magin (2009) who examine the US equity premium.

Questions with a coloured number have solutions in Appendix B on page 788.

1   The ordinary shares of Rasal plc have a market price of £10.50, following a recent dividend payment of £0.80 per share. Dividend growth has averaged 4.5 per cent p.a. over the past five years. What is the rate of return required by shareholders implied by the current share price?

2   Insert the missing values in the following table:

	k_e	P_0	g	D_0
(i)	11%	£8.00	3%	?
(ii)	14%	?	4%	£0.350
(iii)	?	£5.00	6%	£0.155
(iv)	12%	£4.60	?	£0.250

3   Lofthouse plc has paid out dividends per share over the past few years, as follows:

1996	11.0p
1997	12.5p
1998	14.0p
1999	17.0p
2000	20.0p

In March 2000, the market price per share of Lofthouse is £5.00 ex-dividend. What is the rate of return required by investors in Lofthouse's equity implied by the Dividend Growth Model?

4   The all-equity financed Lasar plc has a Beta of 0.8. What rate of return should it seek on new investment:

(i)   with similar risk to existing activities?
(ii) with 25 per cent greater systematic risk compared to existing activities?
(iii) with 25 per cent lower systematic risk compared to existing activities?

The risk-free rate of interest is 6 per cent, and the expected return on the market portfolio is 11 per cent.

5   Salas Ltd is an unquoted company that operates four divisions, all focused on single activities as shown in the table below. Salas identifies a proxy quoted company for each activity in order to calculate cut-off rates for new investment.

Division	Proxy Beta	Assets employed (£m)
Construction (C)	0.7	3.00
Engineering (E)	1.1	8.00
Road haulage (R)	0.8	4.00
Packaging (P)	0.6	5.00

The risk-free rate is 7 per cent, and the expected return on the market portfolio is 15 per cent.

Required
(i)   Calculate the required return at each division.
(ii) Calculate Salas' overall required rate of return.

6 Megacorp plc, an all-equity-financed multinational, is contemplating expansion into an overseas market. It is considering whether to invest directly in the country concerned by building a greenfield site factory. The expected payoff from the project would depend on the future state of the economy of Erewhon, the host country, as shown below:

State of Erewhon economy	Probability	IRR from project (%)
E_1	0.1	10
E_2	0.2	20
E_3	0.5	10
E_4	0.2	20

Megacorp's existing activities are expected to generate an overall return of 30 per cent with a standard deviation of 14 per cent. The correlation coefficient of Megacorp's returns with that of the new project is −0.36, Megacorp's returns have a correlation coefficient of 0.80 with the return on the market portfolio, and the new project has a correlation coefficient of −0.10 with the UK market portfolio.

■ The Beta coefficient for Megacorp is 1.20.
■ The risk-free rate is 12 per cent.
■ The risk premium on the UK market portfolio is 15 per cent.
■ Assume Megacorp's shares are correctly priced by the market.

Required
(a) Determine the expected rate of return and standard deviation of the return from the new project.
(b) If the new project requires capital funding equal to 25 per cent of the value of the existing assets of Megacorp, determine the risk–return characteristics of Megacorp after the investment.
(c) What effect will the adoption of the project have on the Beta of Megacorp?

Ignore all taxes.

7 PFK plc is an undiversified and ungeared company operating in the cardboard packaging industry. The Beta coefficient of its ordinary shares is 1.05. It now contemplates diversification into making plastic containers. After evaluation of the proposed investment, it considers that the expected cash flows can be described by the following probability distribution:

State of economy	Probability	Internal rate of return (%)
Recession	0.2	−5
No growth	0.3	8
Steady growth	0.3	12
Rapid growth	0.2	30

The overall risk (standard deviation) of parent company returns is 20 per cent and the risk of the market return is 12 per cent. The risk-free rate is 5 per cent and the FTSE-100 Index is expected to offer an *overall* return of 10 per cent per annum in the foreseeable future.

The new project will increase the value of PFK's assets by 33 per cent.

Required
(a) Calculate the risk–return characteristics of PFK's proposed diversification.
(b) It is believed that the plastic cartons activity has a covariance value of 40 with the company's existing activity.
 (i) Calculate the *total* risk of the company *after* undertaking the diversification.
 (ii) Calculate the new Beta value for PFK, given that the diversification lowers its overall covariance with the market portfolio to 120.
 (iii) Deduce the Beta value for the new activity.
 (iv) What appears to be the required return on this new activity?
(c) Discuss the desirability, from the shareholders' point of view, of the proposed diversification.

You may ignore taxes.

8   Lancelot plc is a diversified company with three operating divisions – North, South and West. The operating characteristics of North are 50 per cent more risky than South, while West is 25 per cent less risky than South. In terms of financial valuation, South is thought to have a market value twice that of North, which has the same market value as West. Lancelot is all-equity-financed with a Beta of 1.06. The overall return on the FT All-Share Index is 25 per cent, with a standard deviation of 16 per cent.

Recently, South has been under-performing and Lancelot's management plan to sell it and use the entire proceeds to purchase East Ltd, an unquoted company. East is all-equity-financed and Lancelot's financial strategists reckon that, while East is operating in broadly similar markets and industries to South, East has a revenue sensitivity of 1.4 times that of South, and an operating gearing ratio of 1.6 compared to the current operating gearing in South of 2.0.

Assume no synergistic benefits from the divestment and acquisition. You may ignore taxation.

Required
(a) Calculate the asset Betas for the North, South and West divisions of Lancelot. Specify any assumptions that you make.
(b) Calculate the asset Beta for East.
(c) Calculate the asset Beta for Lancelot after the divestment and acquisition.
(d) What discount rate should be applied to any new investment projects in East division?
(e) Indicate the problems in obtaining a 'tailor-made' project discount rate such as that calculated in section (d).

Note: More questions on required rates of return can be found in Chapter 19, where the additional complexities of gearing are discussed.

11

Enterprise value and equity value

How much is Candy Crush really worth?

Before . . . 13 March 2014

'Candy' studio eyes valuation of $7.6bn

King, the London-based games developer behind the app *Candy Crush Saga*, plans to float in New York with a market valuation of almost $7.6bn – four times the size of the company behind the hit game *Grand Theft Auto*. The pricing is at the top of the range and points to its confidence in being able to replicate *Candy Crush's* success.

King has had much growth in recent years and boasts about 324m monthly users. More than three-quarters of King's gross revenues are from a single game: *Candy Crush Saga*. It invites players to form rows of three jellied sweets. People can play free but have an option to pay to speed up progress and to pass difficult levels.

Ed Barton, gaming expert at Strategy Analytics, said that the sector was scattered with companies that experienced great success with a single game but were unable to repeat the success. There are already signs that growth is slowing.

And after . . . 29 March 2014

King falls from grace with poor stock exchange debut

Like King Louis XVI, King Digital has lost its top 15 per cent. Unlike the Frenchman, it might live to see another day. The games company had the worst stock exchange debut on record of any US listing. Having floated on the New York Stock Exchange as one of the UK's technology success stories, it closed the week with a reduced market capitalisation of about $5.8bn.

'It's one of those names you don't want to put your neck on the line for', a portfolio manager told the Financial Times. *Candy Crush's* popularity peaked in June 2013. Other titles including *Farm Heroes Saga* and *Pet Rescue Saga* accounted for only one-fifth of the company's $1.9bn in revenues last year. If they grow, King could avoid the fate of Zynga, the US games maker whose shares are down 70 per cent since a 2012 peak.

Sources: Based on Robert Cookson and Sally Davies, *Financial Times*, 13 March 2014, p. 15; and on Robert Cookson and Sally Davies, *Financial Times*, 29 March 2014, p. 9.

Learning objectives

The ultimate effectiveness of financial management is judged by its contribution to the value of the enterprise. This chapter aims:

- To provide an understanding of the main ways of valuing companies and shares, and of the limitations of these methods.

- To stress that valuation is an imprecise art, requiring a blend of theoretical analysis and practical skills.

A sound grasp of the principles of valuation is essential for many other areas of financial management.

11.1 INTRODUCTION

The concept of value is at the heart of financial management, yet the introductory case demonstrates that valuation of companies is by no means an exact science. Inability to make precisely accurate valuations complicates the task of financial managers.

The financial manager controls capital flows into, within and out of the enterprise, attempting to achieve maximum value for shareholders. The test of his/her effectiveness is the extent to which these operations enhance shareholder wealth. He/she needs a thorough understanding of the determinants of value to anticipate the consequences of alternative financial decisions. If there is an active and efficient market in the company's shares, it should provide a reliable indication of value. However, managers may feel that the market is unreliable, and may wish to undertake their own valuation exercises. Indeed, some managers behave as though they doubt the Efficient Markets Hypothesis (EMH), as outlined in Chapter 2.

In addition, there are specific situations where financial managers must undertake valuations, for example, when valuing a proposed acquisition, or assessing the value of their own company when faced with a takeover bid. Directors of unquoted companies may also need to apply valuation principles if they intend to invite a takeover approach from a larger firm or if they decide to obtain a market quotation.

Valuation skills thus have an important strategic dimension. In order to advise on the desirability of alternative financial strategies, the financial manager needs to assess the value to the firm of pursuing each option. This chapter examines the major difficulties in valuation and explains the main methods available.

11.2 THE VALUATION PROBLEM

Anyone who has ever attempted to buy or sell a second-hand car or house will appreciate that value, like beauty, is in the eye of the beholder. Value is whatever the highest bidder is prepared to pay. With a well-established market in the asset concerned, and if the asset is fairly homogeneous, valuation is relatively simple. *So long as the market is reasonably efficient, the market price can be trusted as a fair assessment of value.*

Problems arise in valuing unique assets, or assets that have no recognisable market, such as the shares of most unquoted companies. Even with a ready market, valuation may be complicated by a change of use or ownership. For example, the value of an incompetently managed company may be less than the same enterprise after a shake-up by replacement managers. But by how much would value increase? Valuing the firm under new management would require access to key financial data not readily available to outsiders. Similarly, a conglomerate that has grown haphazardly may be worth more when broken up and sold to the highest bidders. But who are the prospective bidders, and how much might they offer? Undoubtedly, valuation in practice involves considerable informed guesswork. (Inside information often helps as well!)

net asset value (NAV)
The value of owners' stake in a firm, found by deducting total liabilities (i.e. debts) from total assets

price–earnings multiples
The price–earnings multiple, or ratio (PER), is the ratio of earnings (i.e. *profit after tax*) per share (EPS) to market share price

discounted cash flow
Future cash flows adjusted for the time-value of money

Regarding the introductory case, we do not know how the valuation was arrived at, but we can see that even the 'experts' can get it wrong. This illustrates an important lesson – the only certain thing about a valuation is that it will be 'wrong'! However, this is no excuse for hand-wringing. A key question is whether the valuations were reasonable in the light of the information then available.

The three basic valuation methods are **net asset value**, **price–earnings multiples** and **discounted cash flow**. None of these is foolproof, and they often give different answers. Moreover, different approaches may be required when valuing whole companies from those appropriate to valuing part-shares of companies. In addition, the value of a whole company (i.e. the value of its entire stock of assets) may differ from the value of the shareholders' stake. This applies when the firm is partly financed by debt capital.

■ Enterprise value vs. equity value: Innogy plc

To persuade the present owners to sell, a bidder has to offer an acceptable price for their equity and expect to take on responsibility for the company's debt. Consider the purchase, by RWE Ag, the German multi-utility group of the British electricity supplier Innogy, itself a spin-off from the privatised company International Power. RWE's logic was to complement its previous acquisition of Thames Water in order to gain access to 10 million customer accounts to which it could offer gas, electricity and water. The overall deal was valued at around £5 billion, comprising some £3 billion of equity and £2 billion of debt.

Innogy's stock of assets was financed partly by equity and partly by debt. To obtain ownership of all the assets, i.e. the whole company, RWE was obliged to offer £3 billion to the shareholders to induce them to sell, *and* either pay off the debt or assume responsibility for it. Although RWE chose the latter route, either course of action made the total cost of the acquisition £5 billion.

Obviously, to make the acquisition worthwhile to RWE, its own (undisclosed) valuation would presumably have exceeded £5 billion. We thus encounter several different concepts of value:

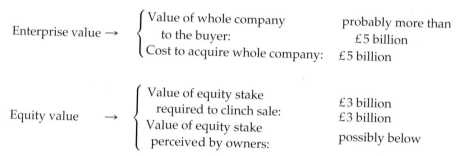

The distinction between company or enterprise value and the value of the owners' stake is clarified by considering the first method of valuation, the **net asset value approach**, which is based on scrutiny of company accounts.

> **net asset value approach**
> Calculation of the equity value in a firm by netting the liabilities against the assets

---

Self-assessment activity 11.1

Using the Innogy example, distinguish between the value of a whole company and the value of the equity stake. When would these two measures coincide?

(Answer in Appendix A at the back of the book)

11.3 VALUATION USING PUBLISHED ACCOUNTS

Using the asset value stated in the accounts has obvious appeal for those impressed by the apparent objectivity of published accounting data. The balance sheet shows the recorded value for the total of fixed assets* (sometimes, but not invariably, including intangible assets) and current assets, namely stocks and work-in-progress, debtors, and other holdings of liquid assets such as cash and marketable securities. After deducting the debts of the company, both long- and short-term, from the total asset value (i.e. the value of the whole company), the residual figure is the net asset value (NAV), i.e. the value of net assets, or the book value of the owners' stake in the company or, simply, 'owners' equity'.

The statement of financial position for D.S. Smith plc, the paper and packaging group, is shown in Table 11.1. The 'Consolidated Statement of Financial Position' pinpoints the NAV, the net assets figure, £1,084.9 million, which, by definition, must coincide with shareholders' funds, i.e. the value of the shareholders' stake net of all

---

*Also called 'non-current assets' following the adoption of IFRSs.

Table 11.1 Consolidated statement of financial position of D.S. Smith plc as at 30 April 2013

	£m	£m
Assets:		
Non-current assets (including intangibles of £1,044.3m)		2,536.2
Current assets		
Stocks	284.8	
Receivables	649.2	
Cash and cash equivalents	116.4	
Other	19.7	1,070.1
Total assets		3,606.3
Liabilities:		
Non-current liabilities (including borrowings of £903.9m)		(1,343.3)
Current liabilities (including trade payables of £955.8m)		(1,178.1)
Total liabilities		(2,521.4)
Net assets		1,084.9
Equity		
Issued capital		92.9
Share premium		710.0
Reserves		283.9
Non-controlling interests		(1.9)
Total equity (shareholders' funds)		1,084.9

Source: D.S. Smith plc Annual Report 2013.

liabilities (and, in this case, net of a small minority item, i.e. residual ownership in an acquired firm). The book value of the whole company, i.e. its total assets, is non-current assets plus current assets = (£2,536.2m + £1,071.1m = £3,606.3m). However, the NAV is a very unreliable indicator of value in most circumstances. Most crucially, it derives from a valuation of the separate assets of the enterprise, although the accountant will assert that the valuation has been made on a 'going concern basis', i.e. as if the bundle of assets will continue to operate in their current use. Such a valuation often, but not invariably, understates the earning power of the assets, particularly for profitable companies.

On 30 April 2013, the market value of D.S. Smith's equity was £2,164 million (share price of £2.33 times number of 10p shares, i.e. 929 million). Hence, the equity of the firm as a going concern with its existing and expected strategies, management and skills, all of which determine its ability to generate profits and cash flows, was worth less than its net assets. If the profit potential of a company is suspect, then asset value assumes great importance. The value of the assets in their best alternative use (e.g. selling them off) might then exceed the market value of the business, providing a signal to the owners to disband the enterprise and shift the resources into those alternative uses. Sometimes, we can adjust the NAV to take into account more up-to-date, or more relevant information, thus obtaining the **adjusted NAV**.

adjusted NAV
The NAV as per the accounts, adjusted for any known or suspected deviations between book values and market, or realisable values

Self-assessment activity 11.2

For D.S. Smith plc, identify:

(i) the value of the whole firm, i.e. enterprise value
(ii) the value of its total liabilities
(iii) the value of the owners' equity.

(Answer in Appendix A at the back of the book)

The cameo below gives an example of a well-known firm, whose assets appear to be valued at more than the market value of its shares.

An empire built on sand

Can the world's best-known holiday resort continue in its current form?

Club Med was celebrated in its early days as a socialist paradise where thanks to its villages' all-inclusive formula, money had no value. Holidaymakers are 'all multimillionaires', exclaimed *Paris Match* in 1965. Judging by its results, Club Med still has an anti-capitalist philosophy. It has lost about €250m ($310m) on revenues of €13 billion in the past eight years and its share price has fallen from over €120 in 2000 to €14 now. But there is no shortage of interest in the company.

Last year Club Med was the target of Bernard Tapie, a Marseilles businessman, who bought a chunk of shares and pushed for change before selling out last December. In June Fosun Group, a Chinese conglomerate, took a 7% stake. Most recently there have been reports that BMB Group, the Sultan of Brunei's investment company, wants to invest, though it has denied having direct talks with the firm.

For a long time, sun, sea and sex sold. A 1978 cult film, 'Les Bronzés', in which a group of holidaymakers attempt a record number of conquests, lampooned Club Med. But its mass-market formula did fairly well in the 1980s and 1990s. It peaked in 2000, with its village of Oyyo in Tunisia opening soon afterwards, at about €400 per person per week for unlimited food and music under the slogan '*Si tu dors t'es mort*' ('If you sleep you're dead').

Then the events of September 11th 2001 and the SARS virus hit tourism and Club Med's profits collapsed.

Desperate, a new chief executive, Henri Giscard d'Estaing (whose father was France's president) took the business upmarket. Club Med has shut its cheapest sites and spiffed up its properties. The culture has changed: its hosts and hostesses, known as *Gentils Organisateurs*, now have to address customers with the formal *vous* rather than *tu* in public. Its 'crazy signs' – choreographed communal dance moves – are scheduled far less frequently, according to 'Le Club Med: Réinventer la Machine à Rêves' ('Club Med: Reinventing the Dream Machine') by Jean-Jacques Manceau.

The strategy seems to be working. Thanks to richer customers spending more, Club Med announced a profit of €3m for the first half. It expects Chinese tourists to drive future growth. The partnership with Fosun Group, it says, will help it win 200,000 Chinese customers by 2015, up from 23,000 now. But observers are sceptical.

The company has several problems. It lacks distribution reach outside France, and powerful rivals such as Thomas Cook are copying its all-inclusive formula, says Matthias Desmarais of Exane BNP Paribas, a brokerage. At the same time, it owns some of the world's most valuable beach-front property. Much was purchased for a song in the 1960s and 1970s. There may be a large gap between the value of Club Med's assets and its shares. And that, not the crazy signs and fun-loving hostesses, may be what is tempting corporate suitors.

Source: The Economist, 14 August 2010.

■ Problems with the NAV

The NAV, even as a measure of break-up value, may be defective for several reasons.

1 Fixed asset values are based on historical cost

Book values of non-current assets, e.g. £2,536.2 million for D.S. Smith, are expressed net of depreciation, the result of writing down asset values over their assumed useful lives. Depreciating an asset, however, is not an attempt to arrive at a market-oriented assessment of value but an attempt to spread out the historical cost of an asset over its expected lifetime so as to reflect the annual cost of using it. It would be an amazing coincidence if the historical cost less accumulated depreciation were an accurate measure of the current value of an asset to the owners, especially at times of generally rising prices. Some companies try to overcome this problem by periodic valuations of assets, especially freehold property. Indeed, property companies are *required* to conduct an annual 'impairment' review. However, outside the property sector, few companies do this annually, and even when they do, the resulting estimate is valid only at the stated dates. Whichever way we look at it, fixed asset values are always out of date!

current cost accounting (CCA)
Attempts to capture the effect of inflation on asset values (and liabilities) by recording them at their current replacement cost, i.e. the cost of obtaining an identical replacement

replacement cost
The cost of replacing the existing assets of a firm with assets of similar vintage capable of performing similar functions

A more sophisticated approach (but thus far stoutly resisted by the accounting profession) is to adopt **current cost accounting (CCA)**. Under CCA, assets are valued at their **replacement cost**, i.e. what it would cost the firm now to obtain assets of similar vintage. For example, if a machine cost £1 million five years ago, and asset prices have inflated at 10 per cent p.a., the cost of a new asset would be about £1.6 million, i.e. $£1m \times (1.10)^5$. The historical cost less five years' depreciation on a straight-line basis, and assuming a ten-year life, would be £0.5 million. However, the cost of acquiring an asset of similar vintage would be around £0.8 million.

There are obvious problems in applying CCA. For example, estimating current cost requires knowledge of the rate of inflation of identical assets, and of the impact of changing technology on replacement values. Nevertheless, the replacement cost measure is often far closer to a market value than historical cost less depreciation. Ideally, companies should revalue assets annually, but the time and costs involved are generally considered prohibitive.

Asset values may also fall. Directors are legally required to state in the annual report if the market value of assets is materially different from book value. It is better to 'bite the bullet' and actually reduce the value of poorly performing assets in the accounts. In July 2007, Metronet, the five-firm consortium formed to upgrade London's underground system with capital of £350 million, collapsed owing over £2 billion, amidst allegations of management incompetence and poor cost control, with the job well short of completion. All five of its constituent shareholders made it clear that no extra funding would be forthcoming, but Bombardier, the Canadian conglomerate, went further by totally writing off its £70 million investment.

The highest write-off to date was the $50 billion write-down in 2003 by Worldcom (later renamed MCI) of assets acquired during an acquisition spree, following which several executives saw the inside of jails after convictions for false accounting. Write-offs are, in effect, an admission that profits have been overstated in the past, i.e. depreciation has been too low. Firms tend to increase write-offs during difficult trading times on the principle of unloading all the bad news in one go. The 2012 Duff and Phelps survey of goodwill write-downs recorded that US companies wrote off $29bn in 2011. This compares to write-offs totalling $188bn in 2008, the year of the financial crisis. In 2013 the BBC had to write down assets acquired, as explained in the cameo. During the 'credit crisis', many banks were laid low by the need to write down property assets.

Lonely Planet losses prompt BBC rethink

The BBC Trust has ordered an inquiry into the broadcaster's commercial arm after it offloaded Lonely Planet, the travel guide publisher, at a loss of £80m. The deal represented a 60 per cent loss on the £130.2m paid for Lonely Planet, the last tranche of which was bought in 2011. The broadcaster's governing body said it would not make this sort of acquisition again and demanded a review to examine whether BBC Worldwide overpaid for the business.

The original purchase of a majority stake in 2007 sparked complaints to the trust that the broadcaster's ambition to compete with the world's largest media companies would hurt private UK companies. BBC Worldwide had already committed itself to buying the second tranche when a review in 2009 decided that it should focus on profiting from BBC 'super brands' such as *Doctor Who, Top Gear* and *Dancing with the Stars*, the international version of *Strictly Come Dancing*.

Diane Coyle, the BBC Trust vice-chairman, said Lonely Planet had not been a 'good commercial investment' despite having a 'credible rationale' at the time. BBC Worldwide would now focus on selling BBC brands such as television series, merchandise and live events. BBC Worldwide's expansion has sparked debate on whether the publicly funded broadcaster was crowding out private competitors.

BBC Worldwide's revenue rose from £810m in 2007, when it bought the first chunk of Lonely Planet, to £1.1bn in 2012, pushing profit before goodwill impairments and other factors up from £111m to £155m over the period. The commercial arm contributed more than £200m to the BBC last year.

Source: Based on Hannah Kuchler and Andrew Edgecliffe-Robert, *Financial Times*, 20 March 2013, p. 4.

2 Stock values are often unreliable

Under **Generally Accepted Accounting Practice (GAAP)**, stocks are valued at the lower of cost or net realisable value. Such a conservative figure may hide appreciation in the value of stocks, e.g. when raw material and fuel prices are rising. Conversely, in some activities, fashions and tastes change rapidly, and although the recorded stock value might have been reasonably accurate at the balance sheet date, it may look inflated some time later. The cameo gives an example of a major stock (inventory) write-down.

BlackBerry aims to reassure

BlackBerry, the struggling Canadian smartphone maker which has put itself up for sale, is publishing an open letter intended to reassure its customers about its financial health. 'You can continue to count on BlackBerry,' the company says in the 660-word open letter due to be published in more than 30 daily newspapers, including some editions of the *Financial Times*, in nine countries today.

However, the decision to publish the letter is likely to fuel speculation that sales of the new BlackBerry 10 devices have taken a hit since the company said last month that it was undertaking a strategic review that might lead to the sale of all or part of the company. The letter reminds readers that the company 'has substantial cash on hand and a balance sheet that is debt-free', and notes that Black-Berry is in the midst of a restructuring, including job cuts, intended to reduce its expenses by 50 per cent.

'These are no doubt challenging times for us and we don't underestimate the situation or ignore the challenges,' it continues, 'we are making the difficult changes necessary to strengthen BlackBerry.'

BlackBerry's letter comes as the company struggles to reverse a sales decline following the launch of its BlackBerry 10 operating system this year and four new devices that use it. BB10 was supposed to help BlackBerry compete more effectively with its rivals, but the company has been forced to acknowledge that sales fell short of expectations.

Slow sales of new models such as the Z10 led to a 45 per cent revenue decline last quarter and prompted a near-$1bn inventory writedown together with the announcement of the strategic review.

Source: Based on Paul Taylor, *Financial Times*, 15 October 2013, p. 17.

3 The debtors' figure may be suspect

Similar comments may apply to the recorded figure for debtors. Not all debtors can be easily converted into cash, since debtors may include an element of dubious or bad debts, although some degree of provision is normally made for these.

The debtor collection period, supplemented by an ageing profile of outstanding debts, should provide clues to the reliability of the debtors' position.

4 A further problem: valuation of intangible assets

Even if these problems can be overcome, the resulting asset valuation is often less than the market value of the firm. 'People businesses' typically have few fixed assets and low stock levels. Based on the accounts, several leading quoted advertising agencies and consultancies have tiny or even negative NAVs.

However, they often have substantial market values because the people they employ are 'assets' whose interactions confer earning power – the quality that ultimately determines value. This may be seen most clearly in the case of professional football clubs, few of which place a value for players on their Balance Sheets. Manchester United led the way in this respect when it valued its players prior to flotation on the market in 1991.

Valuation of brands

However, some other companies have attempted to close the gap between economic value and NAV by valuing certain intangible assets under their control, such as brand names.

The brand valuation issue came to the fore in 1988 when the Swiss confectionery and food giant Nestlé offered to buy Rowntree, the UK chocolate manufacturer, for more than double its then market value. This generated considerable discussion about whether and why the market had undervalued Rowntree, and perhaps other companies that had invested heavily in brands, either via internal product development or by acquisition. Later that year, Grand Metropolitan Hotels (now Diageo) decided to capitalise acquired brands in their accounts, and were followed by several other owners of 'household name' brands, such as Rank Hovis McDougall, which capitalised 'home-grown' brands.

Decisions to enter the value of brands in balance sheets were partly a consequence of the prevailing official accounting guidelines, relating to the treatment of assets acquired at prices above book value, often termed 'goodwill'. These guidelines enabled firms to write off goodwill directly to reserves, thus reducing capital, rather than carrying it as an asset to be depreciated against income in the profit and loss account, as in the USA and most European economies. UK regulations allowed companies to report higher earnings per share, but with reduced shareholder funds, thus raising the reported return on capital, especially for merger-active companies. Such write-offs were stopped by a new accounting standard, FRS10, which also prevented capitalisation of 'home-grown' brands. FRS10 obliged UK firms to follow US practice by depreciating goodwill. Under IFRSs, adopted by all listed UK firms, acquired goodwill only needs to be depreciated if there is judged to be a 'substantial impairment' in the value of the asset.

Brand valuation raises the value of the intangible assets in the balance sheet and thus the NAV. Some chairpeople have presented the policy as an effort to make the market more aware of the 'true value' of the company. Under strong-form capital market efficiency, the effect on share price would be negligible, since the market would already be aware of the economic value of brands. However, under weaker forms of market efficiency, if placing a balance sheet value on brands provides genuinely new information, it may become an important vehicle for improving the stock market's ability to set 'fair' prices.

■ Methods of brand valuation

Many methods are available for establishing the value of a brand, all of which purport to assess the value to the firm of being able to exploit the profit potential of the brand.

1 Cost-based methods

At its simplest, the value of a brand is the historical cost incurred in creating the intangible asset. However, there is no obvious correlation between expenditure on the brand and its economic value, which derives from its future economic benefits. For example, do failed brands on which much money has been spent have any value? Replacement cost could be used, but it is difficult to estimate the costs of re-creating an asset without measuring its value initially. Alternatively, one may look at the cost of maintaining the value of the brand, including the cost of advertising and quality control. However, it is difficult to differentiate between expenditure incurred in merely maintaining the value of an asset and investment expenditure which enhances its value.

2 Methods based on market observation

Here, the value of the brand is determined by looking at the prices obtained in transactions involving comparable assets, for example, in mergers and acquisitions. This may be based on a direct price comparison, or by separating the market value of the company from its net tangible assets, or by looking at the P:E multiple at which the deal took place, compared to similar unbranded businesses. Although the logic is more acceptable, the approach suffers from the infrequency of transactions involving similar brands, given that individual brands are supposedly unique.

3 Methods based on economic valuation

In general, the value of any asset is its capitalised net cash flows. If these can be readily identified, this approach is viable, but it requires separation of the cash flows associated with the brand from other company cash inflows. The 'brand contribution method' looks at the earnings contributed by the brand over and above those generated by the underlying or 'basic' business. The identification, separation and quantification of these earnings can be done by looking at the financial ratios (e.g. profit margin, ROI), of comparable non-branded goods and attributing any differential enjoyed by the brand itself as stemming from the value of the brand, i.e. the incremental value over a standard or 'generic' product.

For example, if a brand of chocolates enjoys a price premium of £1 per box over a comparable generic product, and the producer sells 10 million boxes per year, the value of the brand is imputed as $(£1 \times 10m) = £10m$ p.a., which can then be discounted accordingly to derive its capital value. Alternatively, looking at comparative ROIs as between the branded manufacturer and the generic, we may find a 5 per cent differential. If capital employed by the former is £100 million, this implies a profit differential of £5 million, which is then capitalised accordingly.

Such approaches raise many questions about the comparability of the manufacturers of branded and non-branded goods, the lifespan assumed, and the appropriate discount rate. Adjustments should also be made for brand maintenance costs, such as advertising, that result in cash outflows.

4 Brand strength methods

Other, more intuitive, methods have been devised which purport to capture the 'strength' of the brand. This involves assessing factors like market leadership, longevity, consumer esteem, recall and recognition, and then applying a subjectively determined multiplier to brand earnings in order to derive a value. Although appealing, the subjectivity of these approaches divorces them from commercial reality.

No broad measure of agreement has yet been reached about the best method to use in brand valuation, or whether the whole exercise is meaningful. Indeed, a report commissioned by the ICAEW (1989), which rejected brand valuation for balance sheet purposes, was said to have been welcomed by its sponsors. The report claimed that brand valuation 'is potentially corrosive to the whole basis of financial reporting', arguing that balance sheets do not purport to be statements of value!

■ The role of the NAV

Generally speaking, the NAV, even when based on reliable accounting data, only really offers a guide to the lower limit of the value of owners' equity, but even so, some form of adjustment is often required. Assets are often revalued as a takeover defence tactic. The motive is to raise the market value of the firm and thus make the bid more expensive and difficult to finance. However, the impact on share price will be minimal unless the revaluation provides new information, which largely depends on the perceived quality and objectivity of the 'expert valuation'.

We conclude that while the NAV may provide a useful reference point, it is unlikely to be a reliable guide to valuation. This is largely because it neglects the capacity of the assets to generate earnings. We now consider the commonest of the earnings-based methods of valuation, the use of price-to-earnings multiples.

Prada leads the catwalk pack

Girls – and presumably boys too – just wanna have fun.

The companies whose brand values have risen the most in the 2013 BrandZ rankings are all about the fun things in life: designer outfits, cheap and cheerful fashion, beer, shops and movies. All washed down, of course, with lashings of Brazilian beer.

Leading the catwalk is Prada, the Italian luxury designer that listed on the Hong Kong stock exchange in June 2011 under the ticker 1913 – the year it was founded. Milan-based Prada raised $2.14bn when it became the first luxury brand to list in Hong Kong. Fast forward nearly two years and its brand value has pirouetted 63 per cent in the past year to $9.4bn, just ahead of the 61 per cent leap posted by Brazilian beer Brahma.

Peter Walshe, global director of BrandZ, dubs Prada 'exclusivity that travels': strong brand management that it has successfully transported to the likes of China and Latin America. Far from diluting the brand with lower price offerings, such as perfumes, it has opened entry points along the chain 'allowing different people access without having to dilute the brand too much'.

The same applies to Gucci, Prada's luxury fashion house stable mate, which saw its brand rise 48 per cent to $12.7bn. Gucci also holds the title of highest brand contribution in the category – as opposed to the financial component of the brand valuation. Alongside Burberry, it has the category's highest growing brand contribution.

'Gucci is exceptionally good at retaining the classic look but adding the modern touch, which is what Coca-Cola does so well,' says Robin Headlee, vice president for Europe at Millward Brown. 'They are keeping it modern but keeping the craftsmanship and doing a lot digitally: 13 per cent of online sales come from its mobile platform.'

Steve Wilkinson, head of consumer products at Ernst & Young in the UK, says social media has created a win–win for the luxury and apparel sectors. 'Brand owners, on the one hand, are able to get more feedback from consumers more quickly, while the most loyal consumers are able to get more engaged with the apparel and luxury lifestyle, on the other,' he says.

Source: Based on Louise Lucas, *Financial Times*, 21 May 2013, p. 2.

11.4 VALUING THE EARNINGS STREAM: P:E RATIOS

price-to-earnings multiple/P:E ratio
Another way of expressing the PER

It is well known that accounting-based measures of earnings are suspect for several reasons, including the arbitrariness of the depreciation provisions (usually based on the historic cost of the assets) and the propensity of firms to designate unusually high items of cost or revenue as 'exceptional' (i.e. unlikely to be repeated in magnitude in future years). Yet we find that one of the commonest methods of valuation in practice is based on accounting profit. This method uses the **price-to-earnings multiple** or **P:E ratio**.

■ The meaning of the P:E ratio

As we saw in Chapter 2, the P:E ratio is simply the market price of a share divided by the last reported earnings per share (EPS). P:E ratios are cited daily in the financial press and vary with market prices. A P:E ratio measures the price that the market attaches to each £1 of company earnings, and thus (superficially at least) is a sort of payback period. For example, for its financial year 2012–13, Severn Trent Water plc reported EPS of 98.9p. Its share price on 1 May 2014 was 1846p, producing a P:E ratio of 18.7. Allowing for daily variations, the market seemed to indicate that it was prepared to wait about 19 years to recover the share price, on the basis of the latest earnings. So would a higher P:E ratio signify a willingness to wait longer? Not necessarily, because companies that sell at relatively high P:E ratios do so because the market values their perceived ability to grow their earnings from the present level. Contrary to some popular beliefs, a high P:E ratio does not signify that a company has done well, but that it is *expected* to do better in the future. It is possible to identify companies with exceptionally high P:E ratios. For example, at the start of July 2014 Amazon had a P:E ratio of approximately 520.

The P:E ratio varies directly with share price, but it also *derives from* the share price, i.e. from market valuation, so how does this help with valuation? Investment analysts typically have in mind what an 'appropriate' P:E ratio should be for particular share categories and individual companies, and look for disparities between sectors and companies.

In May 2014, GlaxoSmithKline (GSK) plc, the UK pharmaceuticals firm, was selling at a P:E ratio above 14.5 with an EPS of 112.5p, while another comparable firm, Astra Zeneca (AZ) plc, was selling at a P:E ratio of 22.9, reporting an EPS of 204p. Did this imply that their respective share prices – 1631p for GSK and 4671p for AZ were out of line? Was there an arbitrage opportunity here by selling AZ and buying GSK?

Maybe so, but there is an element of circularity here. Acting in this way would have presumed that AZ is correctly valued and that GSK was under-valued, despite the apparent similarity to the outsider between these two 'Big Pharma' majors. There may have been sound reasons why they should have been valued differently. The reason for the significant difference at this point in time was that AZ was the subject of a bid by Pfizer.

Using P:E ratios to detect under- or over-valuation implies that markets are slow or inefficient processors of information, but there are reliable, rough benchmarks that can be utilised. The industry benchmark is established by one or more transactions, against which other deals in the same industry can be judged, and exceptions identified. In some industries, analysts use benchmarks other than the earnings figure implicit in the P:E ratio. Some examples are multiples of billings in advertising, sale price per room in hotels, price per subscriber in mail-order businesses, price per bed in nursing homes, and the more grisly 'stiff ratio' (value per funeral) in the undertaking business. At the height of the 'dotcom boom', some analysts attempted to explain the stratospheric valuations of internet companies in terms of number of 'hits' or visits to the site in question. More analysts are now utilising multiples based on cash flow. This development hints at the major problem with using P:E ratios – it relies on accounting profits rather than the expected cash flows which confer value on any item. We now consider cash-flow-oriented approaches to valuation.

Self-assessment activity 11.3

XYZ plc, which is unquoted, earns profit before tax of £80 million. It has issued 100 million shares. The rate of corporation tax is 30 per cent.

A similar listed firm sells at a P:E ratio of 15:1. What value would you place on XYZ's shares?

(Answer in Appendix A at the back of the book)

11.5 EBITDA – A HALFWAY HOUSE

Earnings Before Interest, Tax, Depreciation & Amortisation (EBITDA)
A rough measure of operating cash flow, effectively, operating profit with depreciation added back. It differs from the 'Net Cash Inflow from Operating Activities' shown in cash flow statements due to working capital movements

Cash flows and profits differ due to application of accruals accounting principles, but value depends upon cash generating ability rather than 'profitability'. An intermediate concept is that of **EBITDA**, an unattractive acronym standing for **Earnings Before Interest, Taxes, Depreciation and Amortisation**. EBITDA is equivalent to operating profit with depreciation and amortisation (the writing-down of intangible assets) added back. As such, it is a measure of the basic operating cash flow before deducting tax, but ignoring working capital movements.

Many companies use EBITDA as a measure of performance, especially when related to capital employed. However, being a *performance* measure, it can only be used in valuation if we look at the way in which the market values other companies' EBITDAs. As with P:E ratios, comparison with other companies is needed as a reference point.

The calculation 'EV/EBITDA' (where EV denotes Enterprise Value) is now commonly used to determine a market price for a company and to compare companies. Firms, such as Deloitte (see Table 11.2), provide analyses detailing this measure for companies. Enterprise value is calculated by adding to the market value of equity the market value of debt, minority interests and preferred equity and deducting cash and cash equivalents.

Table 11.2 EV/EBITDA for companies in cartonboard and corrugated sector

Company	EV/EBITDA as at 5 November 2013
D.S. Smith	8.2
Graphic Packaging	7.9
Mondi	7.0
Smurfit Kappa	6.5
Sonoco	8.7

Source: Deloitte M+A Roundup 2013.

The 'relative valuation' implicit in the use of EBITDA can be seen in the extract from the FT below.

Cashmere if you can

'My first bunny' is a soft toy made of real rabbit hair with a polyester interior. It will set you back a mere £2,045. This is just one of the products made by Loro Piana – The Italian cashmere brand in which LVMH has just invested €2bn for an 80 per cent stake. LVMH chairman and chief executive Bernard Arnault really is living up to his nickname 'the wolf in cashmere'.

With a market capitalisation of €67bn this is a bolt-on deal for the French luxury goods group that has been honing in on premium luxury (note LVMH's battle over Hermés). And the price looks fair. Including debt, the enterprise value of €2.7bn values the Italian brand on 19 times this year's earnings before interest, tax, depreciation and amortisation.

Granted, that is steep when considering LVMH trades on a multiple of 10 times, and its peer group on 11 times. But then Loro Piana's earnings are excepted to grow by at least 18 per cent each year on average over the next two years –

seven percentage points faster than the group, according to Morgan Stanley. Loro Piana's closest peer Brunello Cucinelli trades on an EV/ebitda multiple of 20 times.

All that makes Mr Arnault look quite the opportunist. LVMH bought Italy's family-owned jeweller Bulgari two years ago. Last week it bought a majority stake in Milanese coffee house Cova; a decade ago it took control of Fendi. After all, it costs dearly to finance a global distribution and marketing operation for luxury goods and as sales slow closer to home the need to expand intensifies. Analysts reckon that it now takes annual revenues of €1bn–€2bn to compete globally. The pride that exists within Italy's family-run luxury groups has prevented them from merging to form the country's own sizeable luxury conglomerate. Like the rabbit and the wolf, Italy's loss is definitely the French luxury conglomerates' gain.

Source: Based on Lex Column, *Financial Times*, 10 July 2013, p. 10.

Like a P:E multiple, an EBITDA multiple used in valuation stems from the value which the market attaches to other companies' EBITDAs, which invites the question of how it values those other companies, i.e. the EBITDA multiple is led by the valuation. Moreover, even when used crudely as a rough-and-ready comparison of value, one should appreciate that it is still based on accounting earnings. Although gross of depreciation and special items, it is still subject to different accounting practices between firms at the operating level, e.g. stock valuation.

Continuing to focus on income-generating methods, we now examine the genuine article, discounted cash flow.

11.6 VALUING CASH FLOWS

The value of any asset depends upon the stream of benefits that the owner expects to enjoy from his or her ownership. Sometimes these benefits are intangible, as in the case of Van Gogh's *Sunflowers*, which simply gives aesthetic pleasure to people looking at it. In the case of financial assets, the benefits are less subjective. Ownership of ordinary shares, for example, entitles the holder to receive a stream of future cash flows in the form of dividends plus a lump sum when the shares are sold on to the next purchaser, or if held until the demise of the company, a liquidating dividend when it is finally wound up. In the case of an all-equity financed company, the earnings over time should be compared on an equivalent basis by discounting them at the minimum rate of return required by shareholders or the **cost of equity capital** (henceforth denoted as k_e).

■ Valuing a newly created company: Navenby plc

Navenby plc is to be formed by public issue of 10 million £1 shares. It proposes to purchase and let out residential property in a prime location. It has been agreed that, after five years, the company will be liquidated and the proceeds returned to shareholders. The fully subscribed book value of the company is £10 million, the amount of cash offered for the shares. However, this takes no account of the investment returns likely to be generated by Navenby. In the prospectus inviting investors to subscribe, the company announced details of its £10 million investment programme. It has concluded a deal with a builder to purchase a block of properties on very attractive terms, as well as instructing a letting agency to rent out the properties at a guaranteed income of £1.3 million p.a. Based upon past property price movements, Navenby's management estimate 70 per cent capital appreciation over the five-year period. All net income flows (after management fees of £300,000 p.a.) will be paid out as dividends.

In the absence of risk and taxation, Navenby is easy to value. Its value is the sum of discounted future expected cash flows (including the residual asset value) from the project, i.e. (£1.3m – £300,000) p.a., plus the eventual sale proceeds:

	Year				
	1	**2**	**3**	**4**	**5**
Net rentals p.a. (£m)	+1.0	+1.0	+1.0	+1.0	+1.0
Sale proceeds (£m)					+17.0

If shareholders require, say, a 12 per cent return for an activity of this degree of risk, the present value (PV) of the project is found using the relevant annuity* (PVIFA) and single payment* (PVIF) discount factors, introduced in Chapter 3, as follows:

$$PV = (£1.0m \times PVIFA_{(12,5)}) + (£17.0m \times PVIF_{(12,5)})$$
$$= (£1.0m \times 3.6048) + (£17.0m \times 0.5674)$$
$$= (£3.61m + £9.64m) = £13.25m$$

The value of the company is £13.25 million and shareholders are better off by £3.25 million. In effect, the managers of Navenby are offering to convert subscriptions of £10 million into cash flows worth £13.25 million. If there is general consensus that these figures are reasonable estimates, and if the market efficiently processes new information, then Navenby's share price should be (£13.25m/10m) = £1.325 when information about the project is released. If so, Navenby will have created wealth of £3.25 million for its shareholders.

---

*Remember the notation convention – interest rate first, time period second. Hence, $PVIF_{(12,5)}$ refers to the PV factor at 12 per cent for five years.

Self-assessment activity 11.4

Navenby has a value of £13.25 million, but a major part of this reflects the eventual resale value of the assets. What final asset value would enable investors to just break even?

(Answer in Appendix A at the back of the book)

■ The general valuation model (GVM)

general valuation model
A family of valuation models that rely on discounting future cash flows to establish the value of the equity or the whole enterprise

In analysing Navenby, we applied the **general valuation model**, which states that the value of any asset is the sum of all future discounted net benefits expected to flow from the asset:

$$V_0 = \sum_{t=0}^{n} \frac{X_t}{(1 + k_e)^t}$$

where X_t is the net cash inflow or outflow in year t, k_e is the rate of return required by shareholders and n is the time period over which the asset is expected to generate benefits.

It should be noted that for a newly-formed company, such as Navenby, the valuation expression can be written in two ways:

value = cash subscription + NPV of proposed activities

or

value = present value of all future cash inflows less outflows

These are equivalent expressions. The value of Navenby is £13.25 million, and the net present value of the investment is £3.25 million, i.e. it would be rational to pay up to £3.25 million to be allowed to undertake the investment opportunity. Valuation of Navenby is relatively straightforward partly because the company has only one activity, but primarily because most key factors are known with a high degree of precision (although not the residual value). In practice, future company cash flows and dividends are far less certain.

■ The oxygen of publicity

Many corporate managers are somewhat parsimonious in their release of information to the market. Their motives are often understandable, such as reluctance to divulge commercially sensitive information. As a result, many valuations are largely based on inspired guesswork. The value of a company quoted on a semi-strong efficient share market can only be the product of what information has been released, supplemented by intuition.

Yet company chairpeople are often heard to complain that the market persistently undervalues 'their' companies. Some, for example Richard Branson (Virgin) and Andrew Lloyd-Webber (Really Useful Group), in exasperation, even mounted buy-back operations to repurchase publicly-held shares. The 'problem', however, is often of their own making. The market can only absorb and process that information which is offered to it. Indeed, information-hoarding may even be interpreted adversely. If information about company performance and future prospects is jealously guarded, we should not be surprised when the valuation appears somewhat enigmatic.

11.7 THE DCF APPROACH

The previous section implies that we should rely on a discounted cash flow approach. After all, it is rational to attach value to future cash proceeds rather than to accounting earnings, which are based on numerous accounting conventions, including the deduction of a non-cash charge for depreciation. Given that depreciation is not a cash item, surely all we need do is to take the reported profit after tax (PAT) figure and add back depreciation to arrive at cash flow and then discount accordingly?

As a first approximation, we could thus value a company by valuing the stream of annual cash flows as measured by:

$$\text{Cash flow} = (\text{operating profit} + \text{depreciation})$$
$$= (\text{cash revenues} - \text{cash operating costs})$$

The depreciation charge is added back because it is merely an accounting adjustment to reflect the fall in value of assets. If firms did replace capacity as it expired, in principle, this investment should equate to depreciation. In practice, however, only by coincidence does the annual depreciation charge accurately measure the annual capital expenditure required to maintain production, and thus earnings capacity. Moreover, most companies need investment funds for growth purposes as well as for replacement. The value of growing companies depends not simply on the earning power of their existing assets, but also on their growth potential: in other words, the NPV of the cash flows from all future non-replacement investment opportunities.

This suggests a revised concept of cash flow. To obtain an accurate assessment of value, we should assess total ongoing investment needs and set these against anticipated revenue and operating cost flows; otherwise, we might over-value the company.

■ Valuation and free cash flow (FCF)

The inflow remaining net of investment outlays is referred to as **free cash flow** (i.e. 'free' of 'must-do' outlays such as interest, tax and investment). The most common definition of this is:

$$\text{Free cash flow} = [\text{revenues} - \text{operating cost}] - [\text{interest payments}] - [\text{taxes}]$$
$$+ [\text{depreciation}] - [\text{investment expenditure}]$$

Using this measure, the value of the owners' stake in a company is the sum of future discounted free cash flows:

$$V_0 = \sum_{t=1}^{n} \frac{\text{FCF}}{(1 + k_e)^t}$$

Self-assessment activity 11.5

What is the free cash flow for the following firm?

Operating profit (after depreciation of £2m)	= £25m
Interest paid	= £1m
Tax rate	= 30%
Investment expenditure	= £3m

(Answer in Appendix A at the back of the book)

This approach removes the problem of confining investment financing to retentions, as in the **Dividend Growth Model**. However, we encounter significant forecasting problems in having to assess the growth opportunities and their financing needs in all future years.

Unfortunately, the accounting data for revenues and operating costs upon which this approach is based may fail to reflect cash flows due to movements in the various items of working capital. For example, a sales increase may raise reported profits, but if made on lengthy credit terms, the benefit to cash flow is delayed. Indeed, the net effect may be negative if suppliers of additional raw materials insist on payment before debtors settle.

It is important to mention another distortion. Stock-building, either in advance of an expected sales increase or simply through poor inventory control, can seriously impair cash flow, although the initial impact on profit reflects only the increased stockholding costs.

For these and similar reasons, accurate estimation of cash flow involves forecasting not merely all future years' sales, relevant costs and profits, but also all movements in working capital. Alternatively, one may assume that these factors will have a net cancelling effect, which may be reasonable for longer-term valuations but much less appropriate for short time-horizon valuations, as in the case of high-risk activities. Figure 11.1 provides a schema to show the calculation of FCF, and how it relates to other cash flow concepts.

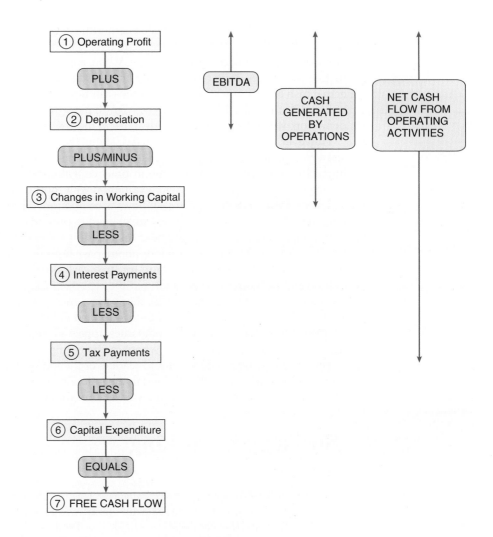

Notes : ① + ② is roughly equivalent to EBITDA.

① + ② + ③ corresponds to 'cash generated by operations' found on a UK firm's cash flow statement.

① + ② + ③ + ④ + ⑤ corresponds to 'net cash flow from operating activities' found on a UK firm's cash flow statement.

Item ⑥ is sometimes confined to Replacement Capital Expenditure.

Figure 11.1 Calculating free cash flow (FCF)

■ A warning!

The term 'free cash flow' is used in a wide variety of ways in practice. Here, we use it to signify cash left in the company after meeting all operating expenditures, all mandatory expenditures such as tax payments, and investment expenditure. It focuses on what remains for the directors to spend either as dividend payments, repayment of debts, acquisition of other companies or simply to build up cash balances. This broad definition is necessary because the cash inflow figure is defined to include revenues from both existing and future operations. Consequently, the investment expenditure required to generate enhancements in revenue must be allowed for. By the same token, a growth factor should be incorporated in the operating profit figures to reflect the returns on this investment.

A narrower definition could be used to confine cash inflows to those relating to existing operations and investment, and expenditures to those required simply to make good wear and tear, i.e. replacement outlays. This has the merit of expressing the cash flow before strategic investment, over which directors have full discretion. It also avoids financing complications, e.g. where a company wishes to invest more than its free cash flows, thus requiring additional external finance, which may distort the actual cash flow figure, as reflected in the cash flow statement.

The data in Table 11.3 relating to D.S. Smith plc are consistent with the first, broader definition, which is probably in widest use in the UK.

However, this yields a very restricted, static vision of the business, neglecting the strategic opportunities and their costs and benefits, which are truly responsible for imparting a major portion of value in practice. Failure to capture these longer-term strategic opportunities could yield a valuation well short of the market's assessment.

The problem of defining free cash flows is compounded by examination of UK company reports. Listed UK companies are obliged to present cash flow statements which report the net change in cash and near-cash holdings over the year. This is a backward-looking statement which says more about past liquidity changes than future cash flows. Some firms do report a figure for 'free cash flow', but often without defining it. Jupe and Rutherford (1997) analysed the reports of 222 of the 250 largest listed UK companies. They found that just 21 disclosed a free cash flow figure, although only 14 used the term itself, and few of these supplied either a definition or a breakdown. Analysis of the comments of 13 companies appeared to reveal the use of 13 different definitions. Clearly, this is an area where care is required in definition and usage.

Finally, it is appropriate to remind readers of the inherent difficulties in valuing an unquoted firm which are highlighted in the following extract from the *Financial Times*. This echoes the warning given at the very start of the chapter.

Social guessworking

Lex column

Have investors learnt anything from the dotcom bust? As the latest technology darlings – including Facebook, Twitter and LinkedIn – prepare to go public, almost everyone seems to believe the hype. That Facebook is worth $50bn or Twitter $10bn is recounted as fact. True, some social networks actually make a profit. But there are still precious few numbers to analyse and business models are no more proved than for dotcoms a decade ago.

To illustrate the ridiculousness of trying to value these things consider LinkedIn. Its S-1 registration statement (with US regulators) provides rudimentary financial statements from which to model the company. Revenues, operating costs, capital expenditure and depreciation and amortisation schedules are available for the past five years. It is then a hop to forecast earnings before interest, tax, depreciation and amortisation and, thus, future free cash flows. Discount these cash flows (made easier because there is no debt) and you've got a valuation.

But who on earth knows what forecasts to make? Private secondary markets supposedly value LinkedIn at $2.5bn–$3bn. To arrive at the bottom of that range requires sales to expand 60, 50 then 40 per cent over the next three years, before tailing off to a terminal growth rate of 3 per cent in 2019. Ebitda as a proportion of revenues has to double to 20 per cent and stay there. What is more, the elevated current high level of investment (23 per cent of sales) has to fall sharply and quickly.

That sounds like punchy stuff. If sales growth tapers off faster than expected or if systems spending becomes a bottomless pit, you can halve that valuation for starters. But what if LinkedIn's platform easily copes with millions of new members? Double Ebitda margins to 40 per cent and a $5bn company is easily within reach. Who knows? No wonder it's easier to simply quote the same price tag as everyone else.

 Source: Financial Times, 14 February 2011. © Financial Times

Table 11.3 D.S. Smith plc: cash flow

	2013 £m	2012 £m
Continuing operations		
Operating profit before amortisation and exceptional items	250.9	142.0
Depreciation	112.4	63.9
Adjusted EBITDA	363.3	205.9
Working capital movement	157.9	43.7
Provision and employee benefits	(18.3)	(28.8)
Other	0.4	4.7
Cash generated from operations before exceptional cash items	503.3	225.5
Capital expenditure	(161.0)	(94.2)
Proceeds from sale of property, plant and equipment and other investments	4.4	8.3
Tax paid	(41.7)	(25.3)
Net interest paid	(34.6)	(19.8)
Free cash flow	270.4	94.5
SCA Packaging acquisition costs	(31.6)	(7.0)
SCA Packaging integration costs	(52.9)	–
Other exceptional items	(27.8)	(19.5)
Dividends paid to Group shareholders	(36.8)	(31.5)
Acquisition of subsidiary businesses, net of cash and cash equivalents	(1,281.0)	(2.3)
Divestment of subsidiary and associate businesses, net of cash and cash equivalents	50.8	184.5
Net cash flow	(1,108.9)	218.7
(Transaction costs)/proceeds from issue of share capital	(0.4)	450.2
Purchase of own shares	(1.2)	(0.3)
Loans and borrowings acquired	(7.9)	(14.2)
Net movement on (debt)/cash	(1,118.4)	654.4
Foreign exchange and fair value movements	(27.5)	24.7
Net debt movement – continuing operations	(1,145.9)	679.1
Net debt movement – discontinued operations	7.2	(6.4)
Opening net debt	321.7	(351.0)
Closing net (debt) cash	(817.0)	321.7

Source: D.S. Smith *Annual Report* 2013.

11.8 VALUATION OF UNQUOTED COMPANIES

The inexact science of valuing a company or its shares is made considerably simpler if the firm's shares are traded on a stock market. If trading is regular and frequent, and if the market has a high degree of information efficiency, we may feel able to trust market values. If so, the models of valuation merely provide a check, or enable us to assess the likely impact of altering key parameters such as dividend policy or introducing more efficient management.

With unquoted companies, the various models have a leading rather than a supporting role, but give by no means definitive answers. Attempts to use the models inevitably suffer from information deficiencies, which may be only partially overcome. For example, in using a P:E multiple, a question arises concerning the appropriate P:E ratio to apply. Many experts advocate using the P:E ratio of a 'surrogate' quoted company, one that is similar in all or most respects to the unquoted subject. One possible approach is to take a sample of 'similar' quoted companies, and find a weighted average P:E ratio using market capitalisations as weights.

However, the shares of a quoted company are, by definition, more marketable than those of unquoted firms, and marketability usually attracts a premium, suggesting a lower P:E ratio for the unquoted company. Any adjustment for this factor is bound to be arbitrary, and different valuation experts might well apply quite different adjustment factors.

golden handcuffs
An exceptionally good remuneration package paid to executives to prevent them from leaving

Furthermore, a major problem in valuing and acquiring unquoted companies is the need to tie in the key managers for a sufficient number of years to ensure the recovery of the investment. The cost of such 'earn-outs', or **golden handcuffs**, could be a major component of the purchase consideration.

In principle, all the valuation approaches explained in this chapter are applicable to valuing unquoted companies, so long as suitable surrogates can be found, or if reliable industry averages are available. If surrogate data cannot be used, valuation becomes even more subjective. In these circumstances, it is not unusual to find valuers convincing themselves that company accounts are objective and reliable indicators of value. While accounts may offer a veneer of objectivity, we need hardly repeat the pitfalls in their interpretation.

11.9 SHAREHOLDER VALUE ANALYSIS

shareholder value analysis (SVA)
A way of assessing the inherent value of the equity in a company, taking into account the sources of value creation and the time horizon over which the firm enjoys competitive advantages over its rivals

During the 1980s, based on the work of Rappaport (1986), an allegedly new approach to valuation emerged, called **shareholder value analysis (SVA)**. In fact, it is not really novel, but a rather different way of looking at value, based on the NPV approach.

The key assumption of SVA is that a business is worth the net present value of its future cash flows, discounted at the appropriate cost of capital. Many leading US corporations (e.g. Westinghouse, Pepsi and Disney) and a growing number of European companies (e.g. Philips, Siemens) embraced SVA because it provides a framework for linking management decisions and strategies to value creation. The focus is on how a business can plan and manage its activities to increase value for shareholders and, at the same time, benefit other stakeholders.

value drivers
Factors that have a powerful influence on the value of a business, and the investors' equity stake

How is this achieved? Figure 11.2 shows the relationship between decision-making and shareholder value. Key decisions – whether strategic, operational, investment or financial – with important cash flow and risk implications are specified. Managers should focus on decisions influencing the **value drivers**, the factors that have greatest impact on shareholder value. Typically, these include the following:

1 *Sales growth and margin.* Sales growth and margins are influenced by competitive forces (e.g. threat of new entrants, power of buyers and suppliers, threat of substitutes and

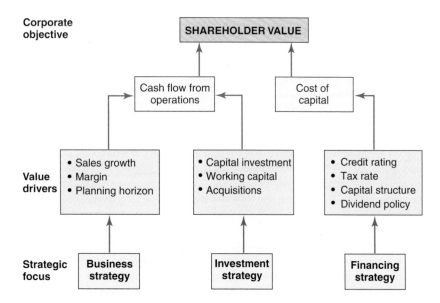

Figure 11.2 Shareholder value analysis framework

competition in the industry). The balance between sales, growth and profits should be based not only on profit impact, but also on value impact.

2 *Working capital and fixed capital investment.* Over-emphasis on profit, particularly at the operating level, may result in neglect of working capital and fixed asset management. In Section 11.7, the free cash flow approach advocated using cash flows after meeting fixed and working capital requirements.

3 *The cost of capital.* A firm should seek to make financial decisions that minimise the cost of capital, given the nature of the business and its strategies. As will be seen later, this does not simply mean taking the source of finance that is nominally the cheapest.

4 *Taxation* is a fact of business life, especially as it affects cash flows and the discount rate. Managers need to be aware of the main tax impacts on both investment and financial decisions. (This is not always negative.)

SVA requires specification of a planning horizon, say, five or ten years, and forecasting the cash flows and discount rates based on the underlying plans and strategies. Various strategies can then be considered to assess the implications for shareholder value.

A particular problem with SVA is specifying the terminal value at the end of the planning horizon. One approach is to try to predict the value of all cash flows beyond the planning horizon, based on that of the final year. Another is simply to take the value of the net assets predicted at the end of the horizon. Neither of these methods suggested is wholly satisfactory. It could be argued, however, that SVA does not have to be used to obtain the value of the business – rather, it can estimate the *additional* value created from implementing certain strategies. Assuming these strategies deliver competitive advantage, and therefore returns in excess of the cost of capital over the planning horizon, there may be no need to wrestle with the terminal value problem.

The real benefit of SVA is that it helps managers focus on value-creating activities. Acquisition and divestment strategies, capital structure and dividend policies, performance measures, transfer pricing and executive compensation are seen in a new light. Short-term profit-related activities may actually be counter-productive in value-creation terms.

End these short-term fudges in financial reporting

Over the past 20 years or so, executive compensation has been increasingly tied to stock prices as directors have pursued the laudable goal of aligning managers' and shareholders' interests. The unintended consequence has been executives attempting to boost their stock prices by maximising short-term results, irrespective of the long-term implications. Short-termism played a role in the corporate accounting scandals and the global financial crisis of the past decade and is setting up society for more pain.

Companies and investors fret over shortfalls of a few pennies in earnings per share even though the earnings number is incomprehensible – because it mixes realised cash flows with subjective estimates of highly uncertain future outlays

There is a better way. We need to adopt a corporate performance statement that is transparent and relevant for assessing value. This should include two separate sections: the cash flow the company realised during the reporting period and estimates of the company's future cash flow commitments. The statement begins with revenue and deducts cash outlays for operating expenses and capital investments to arrive at free cash flow.

The second section presents estimates of the cash flows that the company anticipates it will need to satisfy future financial commitments, such as pension liabilities. Reporting a single estimate to capture an uncertain amount leaves investors in the dark. This corporate performance statement presents a most likely, an optimistic and a pessimistic estimate for each account. Management's discussion of the factors driving the estimate, and the likelihood of each, enables investors to form their own expectations in an informed fashion.

The corporate performance statement would have been useful, for instance, in informing the debate over how to value mortgage-backed securities during the sub-prime lending crisis. Critics argued that forcing banks to write down their long-duration securities to fire-sale prices understated their value and exacerbated the financial meltdown. Other observers maintained that the low prices fairly reflected the poor decision companies had made, and that investors were entitled to know the unvarnished truth.

This type of controversy vanishes when there are three estimates. Fire-sale prices are appropriate for the pessimistic estimate if it is likely that creditors or regulators will force the bank to sell assets to stay afloat. The optimistic scenario reflects the present value of holding the securities until market prices recover. The most-likely estimate lies in between. This disclosure acknowledges that there is no right answer, only a range of possibilities.

Source: Based on Michael Mauboussin and Alfred Rappaport, *Financial Times*, 31 May 2012, p. 9.

11.10 USING VALUE DRIVERS

As we have observed, in recent years, there has been much greater appreciation of the need for managers to optimise the interests of shareholders. In general terms, this can be achieved by generating a rate of return on investment which, at the very least, matches their required return on investment, i.e. the cost of equity. Remember that shareholders incur an opportunity cost when subscribing capital for firms to use, and managers are legally obliged to safeguard those funds with all due diligence.

Sometimes, managers feel that 'their' companies are not 'correctly' valued by the stock market. Moreover, share prices can swing quite violently in the short term, which tends to undermine managers' faith in market efficiency. Often nonplussed by such gyrations, both managers and shareholders may require a more objective and reliable measure of value than simply the prevailing market price.

Such a measure can be provided by the shareholder value approach, propounded by Alfred Rappaport, drawing on Michael Porter's ideas. We now use the value driver concept to analyse inherent shareholder value (SV), which may be thought of as the fundamental, or inherent, value of the firm to its owners. The SV figure also provides a cross-check on the market's current valuation of the company. This may be regarded as a more stable, and possibly more reliable, indicator of the fundamental value of the firm that is unaffected by the short-term vagaries of the market.

The following example of Safa plc is the vehicle for investigating the SVA approach.

Rappaport developed a simple but powerful model to calculate the fundamental value of a business to its owners by focusing on the key factors that determine firm value. He identified seven value drivers, comprising three cash flow variables and four parameters:

- Sales, and its speed of growth
- Fixed capital investment
- Working capital investment
- Operating profit margin
- Tax rate on profits
- The planning horizon
- The required rate of return

In its simplest form, SVA takes the last four drivers as given, and assumes that the first three, the cash flow variables, change at a constant rate. The key to the analysis, as with any budgeting exercise, is the level of sales and the projected rate of increase. From the sales projections, we can programme the operating profits and cash flows over the planning horizon and discount at a suitable rate to find their present value.

In the full model, the value of the firm comprises three elements: the value of the equity, the value of the debt and the value of any non-operating assets, such as marketable securities. However, to keep the analysis simple, we focus on an all-equity-financed company with no holdings of marketable assets. In addition, we need to explain the treatment of investment expenditure. To generate value, firms have to invest, i.e. to generate future cash flows requires preliminary cash outflows. These appear to reduce value in the short term but should generate a more than compensating increase in value via future cash flows.

■ Categories of investment

Investment in working capital, especially inventories, is required to support a planned increase in sales. Often, companies attempt to apply a roughly constant ratio of working capital to sales so that an X per cent sales increase needs an equivalent increase in working capital investment. This is called *incremental working capital investment*.

Replacement investment is undertaken to make good the wear and tear due to using equipment, or 'depreciation'. However, there are phasing issues to consider. In reality, in relation to particular items, the act of replacement is infrequent, occurring in discrete chunks, whereas depreciation in the accounts is an annual provision, so that in all but the year of replacement, depreciation will likely exceed replacement expenditure. However, taken in aggregate, and especially for larger firms, replacement may be closely related to depreciation provisions.

New investment in fixed assets. This has two dimensions. First, if the firm wants to expand sales of existing products, then, unless it has spare capacity, it will need to invest in additional capital equipment to support the planned sales increase. Second, new investment may be undertaken to accompany a major strategic venture such as the development of a new product, which will also generate an increase in sales. Taken together, these may be related to the planned sales increase, although there is likely to be a time lag before strategic investment comes fully 'on stream' and is able to deliver higher sales quantities. Notwithstanding this qualification, we can link the amount of investment in new capacity, for whatever reason, and which adds to the firm's stock of assets, to a planned increase in sales. We call the resulting sum the *incremental fixed capital investment*.

In the following demonstration example of Safa plc, replacement investment is assumed to equal depreciation provisions (which are treated as part of operating expenses in accounting statements), and both working capital investment and incremental fixed capital investment are made a percentage of any planned sales increase.

11.11 WORKED EXAMPLE: SAFA PLC

The board of Safa plc is concerned about its current stock market value of £95 million, especially as board members hold 40 per cent of the existing 100 million ordinary shares (par value £1) already issued. They are vaguely aware of the SVA concept and have assembled the following data:

Current sales	£100 million
Operating profit margin[*]	20 per cent
Estimated rate of sales growth	5 per cent p.a.
Rate of corporation tax	30 per cent (with no delay in payment)
Long-term debt	zero
Net book value of assets	£120 million (net fixed assets plus net current assets)

To support the increase in sales, additional investment is required as follows:

(i) Increased investment in *working capital* will be 8 per cent of any concurrent sales increase.

(ii) Increased investment in *fixed assets* will be 10 per cent of any concurrent sales increase.

The risk-free rate of interest is 7.6 per cent, Safa's Beta coefficient is 0.8 and a consensus view of analysts' expectations regarding the overall return on the market portfolio is 15.6 per cent.

Safa presently pays out 20 per cent of profit after tax as dividend. The board estimates that Safa can continue to enjoy its traditional source of competitive advantage as a low-cost provider for a further six years, at the end of which it estimates the net book value of its assets will be £140 million.

What is the inherent underlying value of this company?

The following analysis is based on discounting all the cash inflows attributable to shareholders, and may thus be described as the 'Cash Flow-to-Equity' approach, or simply Flow-to-Equity (FTE). This is used in more complex cases where there is gearing present, as will be explained in Chapter 19.

Answer and comments: Evaluating the cash flows to equity

First of all, we need to find the return required by the shareholders of Safa, using the CAPM formula. This is:

$$
\begin{aligned}
k_e &= R_f + \beta \left[ER_m - R_f \right] \\
&= 7.6\% + 0.8 \left[15.6\% - 7.6\% \right] \\
&= (7.6\% + 6.4\%) = 14\%
\end{aligned}
$$

This becomes the appropriate rate at which to value Safa's future cash flows. There is no debt finance so all operating profits (less tax) are attributable to shareholders. There appears to be no long-term strategic investment programme, and wear-and-tear is made good at a rate roughly corresponding to tax-allowable depreciation provisions. This means that free cash flows are equal to operating profits less tax.

The firm enjoys a temporary cost advantage for six years, beyond which cash flows are uncertain. Post-Year 6 cash flows can be handled in a number of ways:

1 The Year 6 cash flow figure can be assumed to flow indefinitely. This seems quite an optimistic assumption to make both in relation to Safa plc and also more generally.

---

[*]After depreciation. On average, depreciation provisions are assumed to match ongoing investment requirements and are fully tax-deductible.

2 A view can be taken on the firm's efforts to restore competitive advantage and some growth assumption can then be incorporated. Again, this can only be speculative, as there is no information on this issue.

3 Perhaps the most prudent assumption to make is that the expected Year 6 book value of assets will approximate to the value of all future cash flows, i.e. the company has no further supernormal earnings capacity. This implies that any subsequent investment has an NPV of zero (i.e. there are no abnormal returns expected).

We adopt the third approach mainly for simplicity.

Table 11.4 shows the cash flows during the 'competitive advantage period', Years 1–6 inclusive. The base year (Year 0) figures are given to establish a reference line from which future cash flows will grow.

Table 11.4 Cash flow profile[1] for Safa plc

£m	0	1	2	3	4	5	6, etc.
1 Sales (5% growth)	100	105	110.25	115.76	121.55	127.63	134.00
2 Operating profit margin at 20%[2]	20	2	22.05	23.15	24.31	25.53	26.80
3 Taxation at 30%	(6)	(6.30)	(6.62)	(6.95)	(7.29)	(7.66)	(8.04)
4 Incremental working capital investment at 8% of sales increase		(0.40)	(0.42)	(0.44)	(0.46)	(0.49)	(0.51)
5 Incremental fixed capital investment at 10% of sales increase		(0.50)	(0.53)	(0.55)	(0.58)	(0.61)	(0.64)
6 Free cash flow	–	13.80	14.48	15.21	15.98	16.77	17.61
7 Present value at 14%		12.11	11.14	10.27	9.46	8.71	8.02

[1]Accuracy of figures influenced by rounding errors.

[2]These can be taken as operating cash flows given the assumption that depreciation = replacement investment.

■ Valuing Safa plc

Taking firstly the value created over the competitive advantage period (years 1–6):

PV of operating cash flows (line 7) = £59.7m

Second, we add in the estimated residual value, our proxy for all future operating cash flows:

$$\text{The PV of the residual value} = £140m \times \text{PVIF}_{14,6}$$
$$= £140m \times 0.4556 = £63.8$$

$$\text{Shareholder value} = £59.7m + £63.8m$$
$$= £123.5m$$

■ A note on taxation – two simplifications

You should appreciate how taxation is being handled in this example. All replacement investment is treated as being fully tax-deductible in the year of expenditure. This is a simplification adopted primarily for arithmetic convenience. In reality, the tax relief will be spread out over time as the firm claims the writing down allowance (WDA) each year. In addition, we have ignored the tax saving in relation to the WDA on the incremental fixed capital expenditure.

Correction for the first factor would reduce the valuation simply because delay in taking the tax relief would lower the PV of the stream of tax savings. On the other hand, inclusion of the second set of tax savings would raise the SV figure. If you calculate the 'true' valuation by allowing for these aspects, you will find a net increase in the valuation, although the calculation is a little messy.

We now turn to discuss the actual valuation obtained.

■ Commentary

Looking at the figures as calculated, we find, rather alarmingly, that a large proportion (52 per cent) of the SV is accounted for by the residual value. The SV of £125m more or less equals the current book value of £120m, both figures exceeding the market value of £95m. This seems to imply that the company might be worth more if it were broken up (although the resale value of the assets may not fetch book value).

This raises the obvious question of why the market should place such an apparently low value on Safa. We can consider some possible reasons for the market undervaluation of Safa.

- The market may currently apply a higher discount rate, for example, seeking a higher reward for risk.
- The growth estimate may be regarded as optimistic.
- The flow of information provided to the market may be inadequate – for example, if it does have plans for future investment, are these generally known and understood, at least in outline?
- Board control – presumably reflecting domination by members of the founding family – may look excessive. Such enterprises rarely enjoy a good stock market rating, because there is often a suspicion that the interests of family members may be allowed to dominate those of 'outside' shareholders.
- The dividend policy may be thought ungenerous – a 20 per cent payout ratio is low by UK standards, and there appears to be little scope for worthwhile strategic investment. Retentions may simply be going into cash balances.
- There may be doubts about whether Safa can recover some form of competitive advantage.
- The market may be unimpressed with its present cost advantage-based strategy.
- Its gearing – currently, zero – may be thought to be too low. There is no tax shield to exploit (see Chapter 19).

Whatever the reason(s), there is plenty for the board to consider!

11.12 ECONOMIC VALUE ADDED (EVA)

economic value added (EVA)
Post-tax accounting profit generated by a firm reduced by a charge for using the equity (usually, cost of equity times book value of equity)

Along with SVA comes another concept, **economic value added (EVA)**, trade-marked by the US consultancy house Stern Stewart (www.sternstewart.com). Whereas SVA is a forward-looking technique devised for assessing the inherent value of the equity invested in a firm, EVA is backward-looking, i.e. a measure of past performance. Like SVA, EVA relies heavily on the concept of the cost of capital. It is used as a device for assessing how much value or wealth a firm actually has created. Its roots lie in the accounting concept of Residual Income (e.g. see Horngren *et al.* 1998), which is simply the accounting profit adjusted for the cost of using the capital tied up in an activity.

However, the Stern Stewart version is rather more sophisticated as it attempts to adjust the recorded profit in various ways. The logic of these adjustments is, broadly, to avoid recording as a cost the items that are value-creating and that should perhaps be treated as capital rather than current expenditure. For example, spending on R & D and on product advertising and promotion contributes to wealth-creation in important ways. In addition, any goodwill that has been written off in relation to previous acquisitions is added back. The general impact of these adjustments – over 150 of these might be required in a full EVA calculation – is to raise the profit measure and also the capital employed.

Relating this, for simplicity, to an all-equity-financed firm, EVA is calculated after making a further adjustment for the opportunity cost incurred by shareholders when entrusting their capital to the firm's directors. The EVA formula can be written as:

$$\text{EVA} = \text{NOPAT} - (k_e \times \text{invested capital})$$

where:

NOPAT = the Net Operating Profit After Tax, and after adjustment for the items mentioned above

k_e = the rate of return required by shareholders

Invested capital = Net assets, or shareholders' funds.

To illustrate the concept, consider the data in Table 11.5.

Table 11.5 Calculation of EVA

	NOPAT	Equity	k_e	EVA
Firm A	£20m	£100m	15%	£20m − £15m = £5m
Firm B	£10m	£100m	15%	£10m − £15m = (£5m)

Both firms have the same equity capital employed of £100m, and both make positive accounting profits. However, after adjusting for the cost of the equity capital employed, Firm B has effectively made a loss for investors, i.e. the negative EVA indicates that it has destroyed value.

On the face of it, EVA is a simple and powerful tool for assessing performance, explaining why it has been adopted by many firms as an internal performance measurement device, e.g. for determining the performance of different operating units.

However, it is by no means problem-free:

1 Few firms have the resources required to compute EVA, division by division, with the same degree of rigour as the full Stern Stewart model with its myriad required adjustments.
2 It is based on book value, rather than market values (necessarily so for business segments).
3 It relies on a fair and reliable way of allocating shared overheads across business units, the Holy Grail of management accountants.
4 It is difficult to identify the cost of capital for individual operating units.
5 It may be dysfunctional if managers are paid according to EVA, especially short-term EVA. It is quite possible to encounter investment projects that flatter EVA in the short term by virtue of high initial cash flows but to have a negative NPV. Such projects might be favoured by managers who are paid by EVA. Similarly, some long-term projects that take time and money to develop may lower EVA in the early years but have a positive NPV. These, of course, could be rejected under an EVA regime.

The verdict is yet to be delivered on EVA, but like many other management tools, it is probably inadequate when used alone – it is one way of looking at the picture that should be supplemented by other perspectives.

Good-quality products can be made for low earners

The Godrej Group, the Indian conglomerate with interests ranging from high-tech engineering to consumer products, currently has a capitalisation of $3.8bn, employs a workforce of more than 28,000 people and has operations in more than 20 countries. It is estimated that 500m people in India alone currently use at least one Godrej product or service each day.

The current chairman, Mr Godrej, says that the key to the company's success has been in meeting the needs of the world's largest group of consumers, who also happen to be those with the lowest incomes on the planet.

By way of example, Mr Godrej talks about the hair dye market, where the Godrej group has the best-selling brands in 25 countries. 'L'Oréal is the world leader, but we have the largest-selling hair colourant,' he notes. 'Ours is a powder we sell in a sachet, and it sells for a tenth of the price of the L'Oréal cream hair product. It is not a question of competing on price. It is about innovation that meets the needs of low-income people.'

The group has around 100 manufacturing locations in India and abroad. Each generation of the Godrej family has spoken about its deep commitment to worker welfare, human development and environmental matters.

'We distinguish ourselves in a few areas,' Mr Godrej says, 'First, we use top-class business processes. We measure all our decisions, whether in marketing, advertising or acquisitions, based on economic value added. We also have a large number of our employees on variable remuneration, based on economic value added.'

Source: Based on Jonathan Moules, *Financial Times*, 11 June 2013, p. 2.

SUMMARY

We have discussed the reasons why financial managers may wish to value their own and other enterprises, the problems likely to be encountered and the main valuation techniques available.

Given the uncertainties involved in valuation, it seems sensible to compare the implications of a number of valuation models and to obtain valuations from a number of sources. A pooled valuation is unlikely to be correct, but armed with a range of valuations, managers should be able to develop a likely consensus valuation. This consensus is, after all, what a market value represents, based upon the views of many times more market participants. There should be no stigma attached to obtaining more than one opinion – doctors do not hesitate to call for second opinions when unsure about medical diagnoses.

Key points

- An understanding of valuation is required to appreciate the likely effect of investment and financial decisions, to value other firms for acquisition, and to organise defences against takeover.

- Valuation is easier if the company's shares are quoted. The market value is 'correct' if the EMH applies, but managers may have withheld important information.

- Using published accounts is fraught with dangers, e.g. under-valuation of fixed assets.

- Some companies attempt to value the brands they control. An efficient capital market will already have valued these, but not necessarily in a fully informed manner.

- The economic theory of value tells us that the value of any asset is the sum of the discounted benefits expected to accrue from owning it.

- A company's earnings stream can be valued by applying a P:E multiple, based upon a comparable, quoted surrogate company.

- Some observers like to compare the EBITDA (Earnings Before Interest, Tax, Depreciation and Amortisation) with share price for different companies as a cross-check on valuation. Market-based EBITDA multiples can be used as valuation tools.

- Valuing a company on a DCF basis requires us to forecast all future investment capital needs, tax payments and working capital movements.

- Valuation of unquoted companies is highly subjective. It requires examination of similar quoted companies and applying discounts for lack of marketability.

- Economic Value Added (EVA) is the residual profit after allowing for the charge for the firm's use of investors' capital.

- The two main lessons of valuation are: use a variety of methods (or consult a variety of experts), and don't expect to get it exactly right.

Further reading

The theory tells us that a company is worth the total amount of cash that it is expected to generate over its lifetime, discounted at the cost of capital to present value. But the theory is the easy part – the ongoing message in valuation is that it is a mix of theory and intuition. Wise birds will remember the words of Warren Buffett, the so-called Sage of Omaha:

> *It is far better to buy a wonderful company at a fair price than a fair company at a wonderful price.*

Therefore, the good books on valuation are those with a practical bent that look beyond the numbers. These include books by Koller *et al.* (2010) and by Damodaran (2012). Damodaran (2009) has also written about 'hard to value' companies.

Another useful and easy-to-read book is by Frykman and Tolleryd (2003). Antill and Lee (2005) offer an accounting-based approach that explains how to allow for the effect of International Financial Reporting Standards.

The brand valuation issue is addressed by Salinas (2009).

The text by Young and O'Byrne (2001) is a comprehensive primer on the application of EVA. Young (1997) provides a detailed practical example of the EVA concept related to a particular firm, and Klieman (1999) presents evidence on EVA generation in practice. Fernandez (2007) reviews a variety of discounted cash flow-based methods for valuing companies.

QUESTIONS

Questions with a coloured number have solutions in Appendix B on page 790.

1 Amos Ltd has operated as a private limited company for 80 years. The company is facing increased competition and it has been decided to sell the business as a going concern.

The financial situation is as shown on the balance sheet:

Statement of financial position as at 30 June 2014

	£	£	£
Fixed (non-current) assets			
Premises			500,000
Equipment			125,000
Investments			50,000
			675,000
Current assets			
Stock	85,000		
Debtors	120,000		
Bank	25,000		
		230,000	
Creditors: amounts due within one year			
Trade creditors	(65,000)		
Dividends	(85,000)		
		(150,000)	
Net current assets			80,000
Total assets less current liabilities			755,000
Creditors: amounts due after one year			
Secured loan stock			(85,000)
Net assets			670,000
Financed by			
Ordinary shares (50p par value)			500,000
Reserves			55,000
Profit and loss account			115,000
Shareholders' funds			670,000
The current market values of the fixed (non-current) assets are estimated as:			
Premises			780,000
Equipment			50,000
Investments			90,000

Only 90 per cent of the debtors are thought likely to pay.

Required

Prepare valuations per share of Amos Ltd using:

(i) Book value basis.

(ii) Adjusted book value.

2 The Board of Directors of Rundum plc are contemplating a takeover bid for Carbo Ltd, an unquoted company which operates in both the packaging and building materials industries. If the offer is successful, there are no plans for a radical restructuring or divestment of Carbo's assets.

Carbo's statement of financial position for the year ending 31 December 2014 shows the following:

	£m	£m
Assets employed (non-current and current)		
Freehold property		4.0
Plant and equipment		2.0
Current assets:		
stocks	1.5	
debtors	3.0	
cash	0.1	4.6
Total assets		10.6
Creditors payable within one year		(3.0)
Total assets less current liabilities		7.6
Creditors payable after one year		(1.0)
Net assets		6.6
Financed by		
Ordinary share capital (25p par value)		2.5
Revaluation reserve		0.5
Profit and loss account		3.6
Shareholders' funds		6.6

Further information:
(a) Carbo's pre-tax earnings for the year ended 31 December 2014 were £2.0 million.
(b) Corporation Tax is payable at 33 per cent.
(c) Depreciation provisions were £0.5 million. This was exactly equal to the funding required to replace worn-out equipment.
(d) Carbo has recently tried to grow sales by extending more generous trade credit terms. As a result, about a third of its debtors have only a 50 per cent likelihood of paying.
(e) About half of Carbo's stocks are probably obsolete with a resale value as scrap of only £50,000.
(f) Carbo's assets were last revalued in 2004.
(g) If the bid succeeds, Rundum will pay off the presently highly overpaid Managing Director of Carbo for £200,000 and replace him with one of its own 'high-flyers'. This will generate pre-tax annual savings of £60,000 p.a.
(h) Carbo's two divisions are roughly equal in size. The industry P:E ratio is 8:1 for packaging and 12:1 for building materials.

Required
(a) Value Carbo using a net asset valuation approach.
(b) Value Carbo using a price:earnings ratio approach.

3 Lazenby plc has been set up to exploit an opportunity to import a new product from overseas. It has issued two million ordinary shares of par value 25p, sold at a 25 per cent premium. Its projected accounts show the following annual operating figures:

Sales revenue	£500,000
Operating costs	(£300,000)
(after depreciation of £50,000)	
Operating profit	£200,000
Taxation at 30%	(£60,000)
Profit after tax	£140,000

Notes:
(i) Shareholders require a return of 10 per cent p.a.
(ii) Replacement investment is financed out of depreciation provisions and is fully tax-allowable.
(iii) 2 per cent of sales should be written off as bad debts.
(iv) Bad debt write-offs are 50 per cent tax-allowable.

Required

Value each share in Lazenby:

(a) assuming perpetual life.

(b) over a 10-year horizon.

4 The most recent statement of financial position for Vadeema plc is given below. Vadeema is a stock market-quoted company that specialises in researching and developing new pharmaceutical compounds. It either sells or licenses its discoveries to larger companies, although it operates a small manufacturing capability of its own, accounting for about half of its turnover:

Statement of financial position as at 30 June 2014

Assets employed	£m	£m	£m
Fixed (*non-current*) assets			
Tangible	50		
Intangible	120		170
Current assets			
Stock and work-in-progress	80		
Debtors	20		
Bank	5	105	
Current liabilities			
Trade creditors	(10)		
Bank overdraft	(20)	(30)	
Net current assets			75
10% loan stock			(40)
Net assets			205
Financed by			
Ordinary shares capital (25p par value)			100
Share premium account			50
Revenue reserves			55
Shareholders' funds			205

Further information:

1 In 2013–14, Vadeema made sales of £300 million, with a 25 per cent net operating margin (i.e. after depreciation but before tax and interest).

2 The rate of corporate tax is 33 per cent.

3 Vadeema's sales are quite volatile, having ranged between £150 million and £350 million over the previous five years.

4 The tangible fixed assets have recently been revalued (by the directors) at £65 million.

5 The intangible assets include a major patent (responsible for 20 per cent of its sales) which is due to expire in April 2015. Its book value is £20 million.

6 50 per cent of stocks and work-in-progress represents development work for which no firm contract has been signed (potential customers have paid for options to purchase the technology developed).

7 The average P:E ratio for quoted drug research companies at present is 22:1 and for pharmaceutical manufacturers is 14:1. However, Vadeema's own P:E ratio is 20:1.

8 Vadeema depreciates tangible fixed assets at the rate of £5 million p.a. and intangibles at the rate of £25 million p.a.

9 The interest charge on the overdraft was 12 per cent.

10 Annual fixed investment is £5 million, none of which qualifies for capital allowances.

Required

(a) Determine the value of Vadeema using each of the following methods:

    (i) net asset value

    (ii) price:earnings ratio

    (iii) discounted cash flow (using a discount rate of 20 per cent).

(b) How can you reconcile any discrepancies in your valuations?

(c) To what extent is it possible for the Stock Market to arrive at a 'correct' valuation of a company like Vadeema?

5 (a) The directors of Oscar plc are trying to estimate its value under its current strategy using a Shareholder Value Analysis framework. The last reported annual sales of Oscar plc were £30 million.

The key value drivers are estimated as follows:

Sales growth rate	7%
Operating profit margin (before tax)	10%
Corporation tax	30%
Fixed capital investment	15% of sales growth
Working capital investment	9% of sales growth
Planning period	6 years
Weighted average cost of capital	13%

Depreciation is currently charged on a reducing balance basis. The most recent charge was £0.5m. This is expected to remain constant over the next few years. All depreciation is tax-allowable.

The dividend payout ratio is 20 per cent.

Assume marketable securities held are £2.5m, and debt (in the form of a bank loan) is £6m (interest payable is at the rate of 8.33 per cent p.a.).

Required

Calculate the overall company (or enterprise) value, *and* the shareholder value.
(Clearly state any assumptions that you make.)

(b) The market value of Oscar's equity is £25m (lower than the directors' estimate of value), and also below the book value of net assets of £50m.

Several directors argue that Oscar is undervalued by the stock market, and are wondering how to improve the firm's stock market rating.

Required

Suggest possible reasons for this apparent undervaluation, and evaluate suitable *financial* policies that Oscar's directors might adopt to enhance its value.

6 AB is a telecommunications consultancy based in Europe that trades globally. It was established 15 years ago. The four founding shareholders own 25 per cent of the issued share capital each and are also executive directors of the entity. The shareholders are considering a flotation of AB on a European stock exchange and have started discussing the process and a value for the entity with financial advisers. The four founding shareholders, and many of the entity's employees, are technical experts in their field, but have little idea how entities such as theirs are valued.

Assume you are one of AB's financial advisers. You have been asked to estimate a value for the entity and explain your calculations and approach to the directors. You have obtained the following information.

Summary financial data for the past three years and forecast revenue and costs for the next two years is as follows.

Income Statement for the years ended 31 March

	Actual			Forecast	
	2012	**2013**	**2014**	**2015**	**2016**
	€ million	**€ million**	**€ million**	**€ million**	**€ million**
Revenue	125.0	137.5	149.9	172.0	198.0
Less:					
Cash operating costs	37.5	41.3	45.0	52	59
Depreciation	20.0	22.0	48.0	48	48
Pre-tax earnings	67.5	74.2	56.9	72	91
Taxation	20.3	22.3	17.1	22	27

Other information/assumptions:

■ Growth in after-tax cash flows for 2017 and beyond (assume indefinitely) is expected to be 3 per cent per annum. Cash operating costs can be assumed to remain at the same percentage of revenue as in previous years. Depreciation will fluctuate but, for purposes of evaluation, assume the 2016 charge will continue indefinitely. Tax has been payable at 30 per cent per annum for the last three years. This rate is expected to continue for the foreseeable future and tax will be payable in the year in which the liability arises.

Statement of financial position at 31 March

	2012 € million	2013 € million	2014 € million
Assets			
Non-current assets			
Property, plant and equipment	150	175	201
Current assets	48	54	62
	198	229	263
Equity and liabilities			
Equity			
Share capital (shares of €1)	30	30	30
Retained earnings	148	179	203
	178	209	233
Current liabilities	20	20	30
	198	229	263

Note: The book valuations of non-current assets are considered to reflect current realisable values.

- The average P:E ratio for telecommunication entities' shares quoted on European stock exchanges has been 12.5 over the past 12 months. However, there is a wide variation around this average and AB might be able to command a rating up to 30 per cent higher than this.
- An estimated cost of equity capital for the industry is 10 per cent after tax.
- The average pre-tax return on total assets for the industry over the past three years has been 15 per cent.

Required

(a) Calculate a range of values for AB, in total and per share, using methods of valuation that you consider appropriate. Where relevant, include an estimate of value for intellectual capital.

(b) Discuss the methods of valuation you have used, explaining the relevance of each method to an entity such as AB. Conclude with a recommendation of an approximate flotation value for AB, in total and per share.

(CIMA – Financial Strategy November 2006)

Practical assignment

Obtain the latest annual report and accounts of a company of your choice.* Consult the Statement of financial position and determine the company's net asset value.

- What is the composition of the assets, i.e. the relative size of fixed and current assets?
- What is the relative size of tangible fixed and intangible fixed assets?
- What proportion of current assets is accounted for by stocks and debtors?
- What is the company's policy towards asset revaluation?
- What is its depreciation policy?

Now consult the financial press to assess the market value of the equity. This is the current share price times the number of ordinary shares issued. (The notes to the accounts will indicate the latter.)

- What discrepancy do you find between the NAV and the market value?
- How can you explain this?
- What is the P:E ratio of your selected company?
- How does this compare with other companies in the same sector?
- How can you explain any discrepancies?
- Do you think your selected company's shares are under- or over-valued?

---

*Most large companies post their Annual Reports and Accounts on their websites. The most common address forms of UK companies are: companyname.co.uk or companyname.com.

12

Identifying and valuing options*

Learning objectives

By the end of this chapter, you should possess a clear understanding of the following:

- The basic types of option and how they are employed.
- The main factors determining option values.
- How options can be used to reduce risk.
- How option values can be estimated.
- The various applications of option theory in investment and corporate finance.
- Why conventional net present value analysis is not sufficient for appraising projects.

*The authors are grateful for the contribution to this chapter by Andrew Marshall.

12.1 INTRODUCTION

Business managers like to 'keep their options open'. Options convey the right, but not the obligation, to do something in the future. Managers should seek to create capital projects or financial instruments with valuable options embedded in them. For example, an investment proposal will be worth more if it contains the flexibility to exit relatively cheaply should things go wrong. This is because the 'downside' risk is minimised. Often it is not possible, or too costly, to build in such options. However, the financial manager can achieve much the same effect by creating options in financial markets.

Options are derivative assets. A 'derivative' is an asset which derives its value from another asset. The primary asset is referred to as the **'underlying' asset**. Option-like features occur in various areas of finance, and option theory provides a powerful tool for understanding the value of such options.

'underlying' asset
The asset from which option value is derived

This chapter examines the nature and types of options available and how they can reduce risk or add value. It also explains why the conventional net present value approach may not tell the whole story in appraising capital projects. But, to cover the basics of option theory, we will begin by considering the options as they relate to shares.

12.2 SHARE OPTIONS

In finance, *options are contractual arrangements giving the owner the right, but not the obligation, to buy or sell something, at a given price, at some time in the future*. Note the two key elements in options: (1) the right to *choose* whether or not to take up the option, and (2) at an *agreed* price. It is not a true option if I am free to buy in the future at the *prevailing* market price, or if I am *compelled* to buy at an agreed price. Many securities have option features: for example, convertible bonds and share warrants, where options to convert to, or acquire, equity are given to the owner.

■ Share options in Enigma Drugs plc

The simplest form of share option is when a company issues them as a way of rewarding employees. If the current share price of Enigma Drugs plc is £4, it might award share options to some of its employees at, say, the same price. If, over the period in which the shares can be exercised, the shares go up, employees could then purchase shares at a price below market price, either to sell at a profit or gain an equity interest.

Most options relate to assets which already exist. These are termed pure options. To begin with, we will consider pure share options, although much of our analysis could apply equally to interest rates, currency, oil and commodity markets. But first we need to go back to basics. Figure 12.1(a) depicts the payoff line for investing in ordinary shares in Enigma Drugs plc. If the shares are bought today at 400p, the payoff, or gain, from selling at the same price is zero. If, say, three months later, the share price has risen to 450p, the payoff is +50p; but if it has dropped to 350p, the payoff is −50p. The line is drawn at 45 degrees because a 50p increase in share price from its current level of 400p gives a 50p payoff.

We have all seen the warnings accompanying advertisements for financial products, reminding us that share prices can go up or down. But wouldn't it be nice if, whichever way prices moved, you ended up a winner? This can be done if you also acquire share options. With options you can create a 'no lose' option strategy providing protection from a drop in share price, as shown in Figure 12.1(b). The red arrowed line represents the payoff from the option to buy shares at a price of 400p. If share price increases above 400p, then we would exercise the option. That is, the holder of the option will exercise their right to buy the shares at 400p if the share price is above 400p. But if the

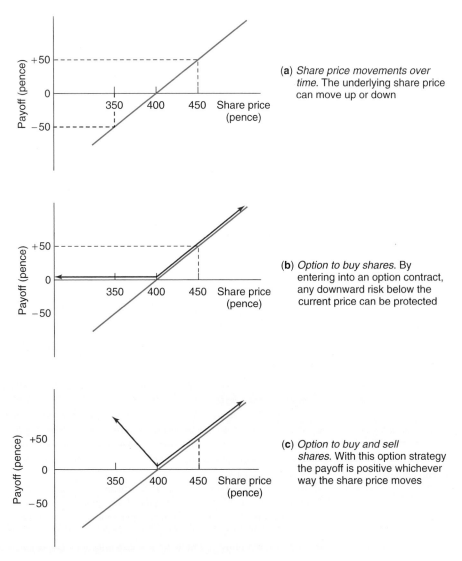

Figure 12.1 **Payoff lines for shares and share options in Enigma Drugs plc**
(underlying share price is blue, option contract is red)

share price falls below 400p, to say 350p, the option payoff remains at zero. In other words, the holder of the option will not exercise their right to buy the shares at 400p if the share price is below 400p.

By combining different types of option you can even create a 'win–win' situation. For example, Figure 12.1(c) shows the effects of combining options to buy and sell shares at a fixed price. Here, either a rise or a fall in share price gives you a positive payoff. At this stage, however, you do not need to know how this is achieved, simply that it can be done. Of course, few things in life are free and a share option is not one of them; there is a price for each option. Later in this chapter, we will show how to value such options.

■ Issuing options

Options on shares are not issued by the companies on whose shares they are written but by large financial institutions, such as insurance companies. The companies play no role in the issuing process. For the institutions issuing options the primary motivation is the fee income that their sale generates, but some also use options in their portfolio of management activities to limit their risk exposure.

Considerable interest has developed in recent years in share options, and there is a highly active market on the stock exchange for traditional and traded options. **Traditional options** are available on most leading shares and last for three months. A problem with these is that they are not particularly flexible or negotiable: investors must either exercise the option (i.e. buy or sell the underlying share) or allow it to lapse; they cannot trade the option.

traditional options
An option available on any security agreed between buyer and seller. It typically lasts for three months

traded options
An option traded on a market

To overcome these difficulties, **traded options** markets were established, first in Chicago, then in Amsterdam. In Europe, options markets are now run by NYSE Euronext in London, Paris, Amsterdam, Brussels and Lisbon (see **www.euronext.com**). NYSE Euronext was acquired by Intercontinental Exchange Group in 2013 (**www.theice.com**).

An exchange-traded contract is characterised by certain standardised features, particularly the exercise date and the exercise price. This makes it far easier to develop a continuous market in options than was the case for traditional options that were developed and traded on an ad hoc basis.

Options terminology

This topic has more than its fair share of esoteric jargon, some of the more essential of which are defined below.

- A **call option** gives its owner the right to *buy* specific shares at a fixed price – the **exercise price** or **strike price**.
- A **put option** gives its owner the right to *sell* (put up for sale) shares at a fixed price.
- A **European option** can be exercised only on a particular day (i.e. the end of its life), while an **American option** may be exercised at any time up to the date of expiry. These terms are a little confusing because most options traded in the UK and the rest of Europe are actually American options!
- The **premium** is the price paid for the option. Option prices are quoted for shares and traded in contracts (or units) each containing 1,000 shares.
- '**In the money**' is where the exercise price for a call option is *below* the current share price. In other words, it makes sense to take up the option.
- '**Out of the money**' is where the exercise price for a call option is *above* the current share price and it is not profitable to take up the option.
- **Long and short positions** – when an investor buys an option the investor is 'long', and when the investor sells an option the investor takes a 'short' position.

European options
Can only be exercised at the specified maturity date

American options
Can be exercised at any time up to the maturity date

option contract
A contract giving one party the right, but not the obligation, to buy or sell a financial instrument or commodity at an agreed price at or before a specified date

There are two parties to an **option contract**, the buyer (or option holder) and seller (or option writer). The buyer has the right, but not the obligation, to exercise the option. One feature of an option is that, if the share price does not move as expected, it can become completely worthless, regardless of the solvency of the company to which it relates. However, if it does move in line with expectations, very considerable gains can be achieved for very little outlay. Such volatility gives share options a reputation as a highly speculative investment. But, as will be seen later, options can also be used to reduce risk.

exercise price
Price at which an option can be taken up

In return for the option, the purchaser (option holder) pays a fee or **premium** (to the seller of the option). The premium is a small fraction of the share price, and offers holders the opportunity to gain significant benefits while limiting their risk to a known amount. The size of the premium depends on the **exercise price** and expected volatility of shares, which, in turn, is a function of the state of the market and the underlying risk of the share. The premium might range from as little as

3 per cent for a well-known share in a 'quiet' market to over 20 per cent for shares of smaller companies in a more volatile market. During past stock market collapses, or where there is substantial volatility, option premiums have shot up dramatically to reflect such uncertainty.

call option
The right to buy an asset at a specified price on or before expiry date

put option
The right to sell an asset at a specified price on or before expiry date

A **call option** gives the purchaser the right to buy a share at a given price within a set time period; a **put option** gives the right to sell. The seller of an option must meet his or her obligation to buy or sell shares if the right of the purchaser is so exercised. The reward to the seller of the option is, of course, the premium received. So a three-month call option with an exercise price of 220p on a share currently priced at 225p gives you the right to buy the share at 220p at any time before its expiry.

Table 12.1 shows the prices (or premiums) at which options on York plc are traded on a particular day on the traded options market. Two exercise prices are given: the first, at 230p, is below the current share price of 245p and the second, at 250p, is above the share price. Notice that option prices vary both with the exercise price and the exercise date. To buy a call option on York plc shares at an exercise price of 230p costs 24.0p for expiry in June, but costs 28.5p for expiry three months later in September.

Table 12.1 Option on York plc shares (current price 245p)

Exercise price	Call option prices (p)		Put option prices (p)	
	June	Sept	June	Sept
230	24.00	28.50	11.50	20.00
250	13.00	19.50	21.50	30.50

Self-assessment activity 12.1

By now your head may be spinning with all the terms and concepts introduced. It is therefore a good time to take stock of what you should know.

1 Define a call option and a put option.
2 What is the basic difference between European and American call options?
3 Options are available on what types of asset?
4 In relation to the information on traded options in Table 12.1 explain why the following features were observed:
  (a) the lower the exercise price, the higher the value of a call;
  (b) the greater the time to maturity, the higher the price of a call; and
  (c) the price paid for calls exceeds the gross profit that could be made by immediately exercising the call.

(Answer in Appendix A at the back of the book)

A call option has value if the price of the underlying share is *above* the option's exercise price ('in the money'). A put option has value if the price of the underlying share is *below* the option's exercise price. This would allow you to sell shares at a higher price (the exercise price) than they are currently trading at.

Options are only exercised if they have value (i.e. if they are 'in the money'). Conversely, options that are of no value (i.e. 'out of the money') are abandoned.

For a call option:

Profit = share price − exercise price − premium paid

For a put option:

Profit = exercise price − share price − premium paid

Self-assessment activity 12.2

1 Which of the following options has intrinsic value at the start of the contract?
   (a) A three-month call option with an exercise price of 230p on a share currently priced at 240p.
   (b) A three-month put option with an exercise price of 230p on a share currently priced at 240p.

2 Which of the following options is 'out of the money'?
   (a) A three-month call option with an exercise price of 240p on a share currently trading at 230p.
   (b) A three-month put option with an exercise price of 230p on a share currently priced at 215p.

(Answer in Appendix A at the back of the book)

■ Speculative use of options: Kate Casino

Kate Casino thinks that the York plc share price will move up sharply from its current level of 245p to a level in June sufficiently above the exercise price of 230p to justify the option price of 24p. Kate instructs her broker to purchase a contract for 1,000 June call options at a cost of (24p × 1,000) = £240. This is termed a *naked* option, held on its own rather than as a hedge against loss. It is a *long* call because Kate is *buying* the option.

The current share price of 245p is above the 230p exercise price, so the option is already 'in the money', since Kate could immediately exercise her option to buy shares at 230p to gain 15p, before transaction costs. Of course, she would not do this because the premium to be paid for the option is 24p.

Let us look at three possible share prices arising in June when the option expires:

Best – York plc share price will rise to 300p by June.
Likely – it will do no better than 255p.
Worst – it falls as low as 215p.

Her profit in each case would be:

Kate Casino's profit on the call option (pence)

	Best	**Likely**	**Worst**
Share price in June (pence)	300	255	215
Less exercise price (pence)	(230)	(230)	(230)
Profit on exercise (pence)	70	25	Not exercised
Less option premium paid (pence)	(24)	(24)	(24)
Profit (loss) before transaction costs	46	1	(24)
Profit on contract of 1,000 shares	£460	£10	(£240)

Kate would obviously not exercise her option if the price fell to 215p, so the loss in this case would be restricted to the 24p premium paid. The premium is the maximum loss on the contract. If York plc price on expiry is 255p, the contract profit is a modest £10. But if the share price shoots up to 300p, a large gain of £460 is made on the contract.

It is interesting to compare the option returns with those from investing directly in York plc shares. Table 12.2 shows that buying a call option has very different effects from buying the underlying share:

1 The capital outlay for the option contract for 1,000 shares is much smaller (£240 compared with £2,450 for the underlying shares).
2 The downside risk on the option contract is far greater in *relative* terms, but not in *absolute* terms. Consider if the expiry share price is 215p. Kate Casino loses all her initial investment on the option contract while the share value declines by only

Table 12.2 Returns on York plc shares and options

Expiry share price	300p	215p
	£	£
Buy 1,000 shares		
Cost 245p each	(2,450)	(2,450)
Proceeds from sale	3,000	2,150
Profit (loss)	550	(300)
Return over three months on original cost	+22.4%	−12.2%
	£	£
Call option on 1,000 shares		
Cost of option	(240)	(240)
Cost of exercise at 230p	(2,300)	−
	(2,540)	
Proceeds on sale	3,000	−
Profit (loss)	460	(240)
Return over three months	+192%	−100%

8 per cent. However, in money terms, the loss is £300 if the shares had been bought or £240 if the option premium had been paid.

3 The return achieved, if the shares reach 300p, is a phenomenal 192 per cent on the options contract compared with 22 per cent on the underlying shares (ignoring dividends).

The payoff chart in Figure 12.2 shows that, if the share price does not rise above the exercise price of 230p, the option is worthless. The option breaks even at 254p (230p + 24p premium) and the potential profit to be made thereafter is unlimited.

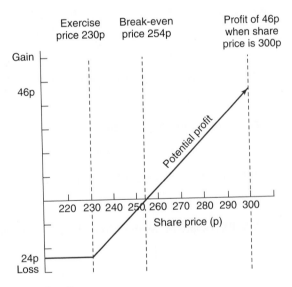

Figure 12.2 York plc call option

In general, the value of a call option at expiry (C_1) with a share price (S_1) and exercise price (E) is:

$$C_1 = S_1 - E, \text{ if } S_1 > E$$

At a share price of 300p, therefore, the option value is

$$C_1 = 300p - 230p$$

$$= 70p, \text{ giving a profit of 46p per share after paying the premium.}$$

■ Options as a hedge: Rick Aversion

hedging
Attempting to minimise the risk of loss stemming from exposure to adverse foreign exchange rate movements

While options offer an excellent opportunity to speculate, they are equally useful as a means of risk reduction, insurance or **hedging**. Rick Aversion is concerned that the current share price on his York plc shareholding will fall over the next two months. Because he wants to keep his shares as a long-term investment, he buys a put option (see Table 12.1), giving the right to sell shares in June at the strike price of 230p. This option costs him 11.5p.

By late June, the shares have fallen to 190p, and the option has increased in value to 40p (i.e. 230p − 190p). So Rick sells the option and retains the shares, using the profit on the option to offset the loss on the shares. This is administratively cheaper and more convenient than selling his shares and then buying them back. In this way, investors can capture any profits from a rise in share price and hedge against any price fall.

Figure 12.3 shows that when share prices are above the exercise price, the option value of the put is worthless. It should be exercised when prices fall below the 230p exercise price and breaks even at 218.5p (exercise price less premium).

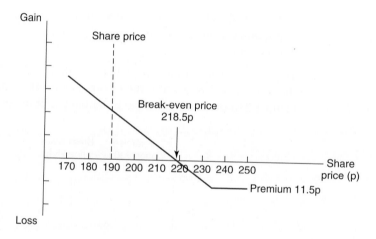

Figure 12.3 York plc put option

In general, the value of a put option (P_1) is:

$$P_1 = E - S_1, \text{if } S_1 < E$$

At a 190p share price, the value of the put option is therefore 40p:

$$P_1 = 230p - 190p$$
$$= 40p$$

This is because the holder could buy the shares in the market at 190p and exercise the option to sell at 230p. The profit on this transaction is (40p − 11.5p) = 28.5p.

■ Option strategies

Combinations of investments in options and the underlying shares are both of practical and analytical interest. From a practical standpoint a combination can provide a means of reducing exposure to the risks associated with substantial changes in the price of the underlying asset, or, from a speculative perspective, can provide some interesting payoff patterns. The analytical interest stems from the insights provided by such portfolios for the valuation of options.

Straddles or doubles

Combining investments in a put and a call, written on a share at the same exercise price and expiry date, produces what is referred to as a **straddle** (a long straddle is where you buy both the call and put option and the opposite is true: a short straddle is where you sell both the call and put option). Why should anyone wish to invest in calls and puts simultaneously (a short straddle)? This strategy will be employed by an investor who believes that the price of the underlying share is going to change quite significantly, but is unable to predict the direction of the change. Such an expectation will arise, for example, whenever an investor knows that a company is expected to make an important announcement, but has no knowledge of the content of the announcement.

This is a strategy to adopt whenever there is considerable short-term uncertainty about the price of a share, and it is anticipated that this uncertainty will be resolved before the expiry of the options. A straddle will lose an investor money if there is little change in the share price, but large price changes in either direction will produce gains.

Protective put

A protective put protects investment in the underlying asset by restricting the possible losses on the asset. Suppose an investor holds shares in Marks & Spencer. She may buy put options to help protect the value of her investment. The put options guarantee a minimum value for the shares up to the expiration date of the options. Whatever happens the shares can be sold at the option exercise price.

> For example: buy Marks & Spencer shares at 448p
>
> Protect the investment with *out of the money* puts
>
> Exercise price = 435p Premium cost = 15p

No matter how far the share price falls the investor can sell for 435p up to the expiration date. This is portfolio *insurance*, and the cost of the insurance is the put premium of 15p.

Alternatively, the investor might choose to protect the investment with *in the money* puts, e.g. exercise price of 465p. Obviously this guarantees a higher minimum selling price up to expiration, but the premium cost will be higher.

Covered call

The writing of calls is a risky business. One way of limiting the risk exposure is to buy the share on which the call is being written. When an investor simultaneously writes a call and purchases the underlying asset, the resulting combination is known as a covered call. The returns on the written call and the share are negatively correlated, as the liability implicit in the written call increases with rises in the value of the share. Covered calls may appeal to risk-averse investors who are mildly pessimistic about the future price performance of a share. The fee income from writing calls is attractive, and holding the share implies the risk from an unanticipated rise in the share price is neutralised. (Covered calls are of no interest to really pessimistic investors. They will not wish to purchase the share even if the writing of calls is attractive, and if they already hold the share they will consider its sale or the purchase of puts rather than the writing of calls.) Covered calls are the combination most frequently employed by financial institutions that regularly write calls.

12.3 OPTION PRICING

We now know that the value of a call and a put option at expiry date is as follows:

Option	Share price at expiry date	Option value at expiry
Call	above exercise price	share price – exercise price
	below exercise price	zero
Put	above exercise price	zero
	below exercise price	exercise price – share price

Option prices comprise two elements: intrinsic value and time-value. *Intrinsic value* is what the option would be worth were it about to expire; it reflects the degree to which an option is 'in the money' – in the case of a call option, the extent to which the exercise price is below the current share price. The *time-value* element depends on the length of time the option has to run – the longer the period, the better the chance of making a gain on the contract.

■ Put–call parity

We showed in the previous section how the combination of buying a call option and selling a put option gave the same payoff as the underlying share price. To find a combination that yields a riskless return, we reverse the options.

When a call and a put are written on the same asset with the same exercise price and expiry date, a relationship, referred to as the put–call parity, can be expected to hold between their market values. The price of one share (S) plus the price of one put option (P) must equal the value of investing the exercise price (E) until expiry at the risk-free rate of interest (R_f) plus the price of one call option.

Put–call parity

Value of share + Value of put = Present value of exercise price + Value of call

$$S \quad + \quad P \quad = \quad E/(1 + R_f) \quad + \quad C$$

It follows from the above that, given four of the five factors, the fifth can be estimated.

The net cash flow expected from investing in a put and a share is equivalent to that to be expected from investing in a call and placing the present value of the sum necessary to exercise the call in a risk-free investment. In both cases the investor will be left with a sum equivalent to the exercise price if the share price is less than the exercise price, and the value of the share if its price exceeds the exercise price.

Self-assessment activity 12.3

You take out contracts to sell a call option and buy a put option, both at the exercise price of 55p, exercisable one year hence. The cost of the put is 7p and the cost of the call is 1p. The current share price is 44p and the risk-free interest rate is 10 per cent. What is the present value of the exercise price?

(Answer in Appendix A at the back of the book)

Applying the put–call parity model

Melody plc has shares currently trading at 29p. Put and call options for the company are available with an exercise price of 30p expiring in one year. The price of a call option is 6p and the risk-free rate of interest is 6 per cent. What is the price of the put option?

Using the put–call parity model we know that:

$$S + P = E/(1 + R_f) + C \qquad \text{(Eqn 1)}$$

or

$$P = E/(1 + R_f) + C - S \qquad \text{(Eqn 2)}$$

$$= 30p/(1 + 0.06) + 6p - 29p$$

$$= 5.3p$$

The price of the put option is 5.3p. At any other price, investors would have an arbitrage opportunity to make a profit for zero risk by simultaneously buying and selling identical assets at different prices. Suppose that the actual market price of a put option for Melody plc was 6p. Looking at equation 2 above, we see that an arbitrage opportunity would arise from selling the put option at 6p and investing 30p in a riskless bond, for one year at 6 per cent, and at the same time acquiring a call option at 6p and selling a share priced at 29p.

■ Valuing a call

The following notation is employed with respect to valuing call options:

S_0 = Share price today
S_1 = Share price at expiry date
E = Exercise price on the option
C_0 = Value of call option today
C_1 = Value of call option on expiration date
R_f = Risk-free interest rate

A number of formal statements can be made about call options:

1 *Option prices cannot be negative.* If the share price ends up below the exercise price on the expiration date, the call option is worthless, but no further loss is created beyond that of the initial premium paid. In mathematical terms:

$$C_1 = 0 \text{ if } S_1 \leq E \qquad (12.1)$$

This is the case where an option is 'out of the money' on expiry.

2 *An option is worth on expiry the difference between the share price and the exercise price.*

$$C_1 = S_1 - E \text{ if } S_1 > E \qquad (12.2)$$

This is the case where an option is 'in the money' on expiry.

Thus far we have found the intrinsic values of the option – what it would be worth were it about to expire. We have previously noted that options with some time still to run will generally be worth more than the difference between current share price and exercise price because the share price may rise further.

3 *The maximum value of an option is the share price itself* – it could never sell for more than the underlying share price value.

$$C_0 \leq S_0 \qquad (12.3)$$

The minimum value of a call today is equal to or greater than the current share price less the exercise price:

$$C_0 \geq S_0 - E \text{ if } S_0 > E \qquad (12.4)$$

However, the exercise price is payable in the future. It was shown in the previous section that the payoffs from a share are identical to the payoffs from buying a call option, selling a put option and investing the remainder in a risk-free asset that yields the exercise price on the expiry date. In other words, we need to bring the exercise price to its present value by discounting at the risk-free rate of interest. This gives rise to the following revised statement.

4   *The minimum value of an option is the difference between the share price and the present value of the exercise price (or zero if greater).*

$$C_0 \geq S_0 - [E/(1 + R_f)^t] \tag{12.5}$$

The value of a call option can be observed in Figure 12.4. Bradford plc shares are currently priced at 700p. The diagram shows how the value of an option to buy Bradford shares at 1,100p moves with the share price. The upper limit to the option price is the share price itself, and the lower limit is zero for share prices up to 1,100p, and the share price minus exercise price when the share price moves above 1,100p. In fact, the actual option prices lie between these two extremes, on the upward-sloping curve. The curve rises slowly at first, but then accelerates rapidly.

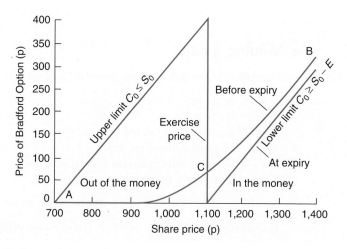

Figure 12.4 **Option and share price movements for Bradford plc**

At point A on the curve, at the very start, the option is worthless. If the share price for Bradford remained well below the exercise price, the option would remain worthless. At point B, when the share price has rocketed to 1,400p, the option value approximates the share price minus the present value of the exercise price. At point C, the share price exactly equals the exercise price. If exercised today, the option would be worthless. However, there may still be two months for the option to run, in which time the share price could move up or down. In an efficient market, where share prices follow a random walk, there is a 50 per cent chance that it will move higher and an equal probability that it will go lower. If the share price falls, the option will be worthless, but if it rises, the option will have some value. The value placed on the option at point C depends largely on the likelihood of substantial movements in share price. However, we can say that *the higher the share price relative to the exercise price, the safer the option* (i.e. more valuable).

5   *The value of a call option increases over time and as interest rates rise.* Equation 12.4 shows that the value of an option increases as the present value of the exercise price falls. This reduction in present value occurs over time and/or with rises in the interest rate.

6 *The more risky the underlying share, the more valuable the option.* This is because the greater the variance of the underlying share price, the greater is the possibility that prices will exceed the exercise price. But because option values cannot be negative (i.e. the holder would not exercise the option), the 'downside' risk can be ignored.

To summarise, the value of a call option is influenced by the following:

- The *share price*. The higher the price of the share, the greater will be the value of an option written on it.
- *The exercise price of the option.* The lower the exercise price, the greater the value of the call option.
- *The time to expiry of the option.* As long as investors believe that the share price has a chance of yielding a profit on the option, the option will have a positive value. So the longer the time to expiry, the higher the option price.
- *The risk-free interest rate.* As short-term interest rates rise, the value of a call option also increases.
- *The volatility in the underlying share returns.* The greater the volatility in share price, the more likely it is that the exercise price will be exceeded and, hence, the option value will rise.
- *Dividends.* The price of a call option will normally fall with the share price as a share goes ex-div (i.e. the next dividend is not received by the buyer).

contingent claim security
Claim on a security whose value depends on the value of another asset

A call option is therefore a **contingent claim security** that depends on the value and riskiness of the underlying share on which it is written.

Self-assessment activity 12.4

Explain why option value increases with the volatility of the underlying share price. List the factors that determine option value.

(Answer in Appendix A at the back of the book)

■ A simplified option-price model

Valuing options is a highly complex business, including a lot of mathematics or, for most traders, a user-friendly software package. But we can introduce the valuation of options by using a simple (if somewhat unrealistic) example. We argued earlier that it is possible to replicate the payoffs from buying a share by purchasing a call option, selling a put option and placing the balance on deposit to earn a risk-free return over the option period. This provides us with a method for valuing options.

Valuing a call option in Riskitt plc

In April, the share price of Riskitt plc is 100p. A three-month call option on the shares with a July expiry date has an exercise price of 125p. With the current price well below the exercise price it is clear that, for the option to have value, the share price must stand a chance of increasing by at least 25p over the next quarter.

Assume that by the expiry date there is an equal chance that the share price will have either soared to 200p or plummeted to 50p. There are no other possibilities. Assume also that you can borrow at 12 per cent a year, or about 3 per cent a quarter.

What would be the payoff for a call option on one share in Riskitt?

	Best	**Worst**
Share price	200p	50p
Less exercise price	(125p)	(125p)
Payoff	75p	–

You stand to make 75p if the share price does well, but nothing if it slips below the exercise price. To work out how much you would be willing to pay for such an option, you must replicate an investment in call options by a combination of investing in Riskitt shares and borrowing.

Suppose you buy 200 call options. The payoffs in July will be zero if the share price is only 50p and £150 (i.e. 200 × 75p) if the share price is 200p. This is shown in Table 12.3. Note that the cash flow you are trying to determine is the April premium, represented by the question mark.

To replicate the call option cash flows, you adopt the second strategy in Table 12.3: you need to buy 100 shares and borrow sufficient cash to give identical cash flows in July as the call option strategy. This means borrowing £50. The net cash flows for the two strategies are now the same in July whatever the share price. But the £50 loan repayment in July will include three months' interest at 3 per cent for the quarter. The initial sum borrowed in April would therefore be the present value of £50, i.e. £50/1.03 = £48.54. Deducting this from the share price paid gives a net figure of £51.46, which must also be the April cash payment for 200 call options. The price for one call option is therefore about 26p.

Table 12.3 Valuing a call option in Riskitt plc

Strategy	Cash flow in April	Payoff in July if share price is 200p	Payoff in July if share price is 50p
	£	£	£
1 Buy 200 call options	?	+150	–
2 Buy 100 shares	−100	+200	+50
Borrow	+48.54	−50	−50
	−51.46	+150	–

Value of call option = £51.46/200 call = 25.73p, say 26p

Risk-neutral method

In the previous Riskitt plc example we assumed that the two possible payoffs each had a 50 per cent probability. The same result is obtained even if we do not know the probabilities for the payoffs by assuming risk neutrality. Although most investors are risk averse, requiring a risk premium for taking on greater risk, both risk-averse and risk-neutral investors place the same value on a risk-free asset and, as was shown earlier in the put–call parity model, both place the same value on a hedged portfolio of options and shares.

Recall from the Riskitt plc example that the share price is 100 pence, a three-month call option has an exercise of 125 pence, and the risk-free rate of interest is 12 per cent a year (or approximately 3 per cent a quarter). The only two possible share price outcomes after three months are 200 pence and 50 pence, but in this example the probabilities of each are not known.

Assuming no dividends are paid in the period and that investors are risk-neutral, the expected share price in three months' time is 3 per cent more than the existing price, or 103 pence. From this we can infer probabilities for the two possible outcomes. Let the probability of the high outcome be p and the probability of the low outcome will therefore be $1 - p$. The expected payoff of 103 pence will be the sum of the two outcomes multiplied by their probabilities:

$$200 \text{ pence} \times p + 50 \text{ pence} \times (1 - p) = 103 \text{ pence}$$
$$150\,p = 53 \text{ pence}$$
$$p = 0.353$$
$$1 - p = 0.647$$

We can now use these probabilities to calculate the value of the call option valued at 125 pence. It is only of value if the high outcome of 200 pence is attained, the net gain being 75 pence. Therefore the expected cash flow is:

$$\text{Expected cash flow} = 75\,\text{pence} \times p = 75 \times 0.353$$
$$= 26.48\,\text{pence}$$

The present value of this is $26.48/(1.03) = 25.7$ pence or approximately 26 pence, as in the previous example.

■ Black–Scholes pricing model

The above example took a highly simplified view of uncertainty, using only two possible share price outcomes. Black and Scholes (1973) combined the main determinants of option values to develop a model of option pricing. Although its mathematics are daunting, the model does have practical application. Every day, dealers in options use it in specially programmed calculators to determine option prices.

For those who like a challenge, the complex mathematics of the Black–Scholes pricing model are given in the appendix to this chapter. However, the key message is that option pricing requires evaluation of five of the variables listed earlier: share price, exercise price, risk-free rate of interest, time and share price volatility.

Example

Acorn plc shares are currently worth 28p with a standard deviation of 30 per cent. The risk-free rate of interest is 6 per cent. What is the value of a call option on Acorn shares expiring in nine months and with an exercise price of 30p?

The fully worked solution to this problem is given in the appendix to this chapter, but we can identify here the five input variables:

Share price $(S) = 28$p

Exercise price $(E) = 30$p

Risk-free rate $(k) = 6$ per cent p.a.

Time to expiry $(t) = 9$ months

Share price volatility $(\sigma) = 30$ per cent

Application of the Black–Scholes formula to the above data (see Appendix) gives a value of the call option of 2.6p.

Black–Scholes option-pricing formula

Value of call option (C) is:

$$C = SN(d_1) - EN(d_2)e^{-tk}$$

where

$$d_1 = \frac{\ln(S/E) + tk}{\sigma t^{1/2}} + \frac{\sigma t^{1/2}}{2}$$
$$d_2 = d_1 - \sigma t^{1/2}$$

$N(d)$ is the value of the cumulative distribution function for a standardised normal random variable and e^{-tk} is the present value of the exercise price continuously discounted.

A simplified Black–Scholes formula can be used as an approximation for options of less than one year:

$$\frac{C}{S} \approx \frac{1}{\sqrt{2\pi}}\,\sigma\sqrt{t}$$

This formula emphasises the impact of volatility and time to expiry on the option price.

Applying the above to the previous example, we derive a slightly higher option price:

$$C \approx 0.398 \times 0.3\sqrt{0.75} \times 28 = 2.9\text{p}$$

Although the model is complex, the valuation equation derived from the model is quite straightforward to use, and is widely employed in practice. Four of the five variables on which it is based are observable: the only non-observable variable, the volatility or standard deviation of the return on the underlying asset, is generally estimated from historical data.

The Black–Scholes model is based on the following assumptions:

(a) there are no transactions costs or taxes;

(b) the expected risk-free rate of interest is constant for the period of the option life;

(c) the market operates continuously;

(d) share prices change smoothly over time – there are no jumps or discontinuities in the price series;

(e) the standard deviation of the distribution of returns on the share is known;

(f) the share pays no dividends during the life of the option; and

(g) the option may only be exercised at expiry of the call (i.e. a European-type option).

The assumptions on which the model is based are clearly quite restrictive. However, as these assumptions are consistent with mainstream theorising in finance, the model integrates well into the general body of finance theory. In practice the model appears to be quite robust and it is feasible to relax many assumptions and incorporate more 'real-world' features into the model without changing its overall character.

Is it better to play it safe or to place bets that risk bankruptcy?

Financial options are difficult to value. It isn't really the maths that is the problem. The Black–Scholes formula, which can be used to help value some of them, may look arcane to people who struggled with school algebra but is not – as they say – rocket science. (Rocket science is not very close to the frontier of mathematical knowledge either. Nor does Black–Scholes really solve the valuation question, though it is worth knowing that many people think it does.) The problem is that the valuation of options exposes difficulties humans encounter in assessing risks and uncertainties.

While options were invented recently, their pricing and evaluation is a question as old as time. When hunter-gatherers went out in search of prey, they were often in danger of becoming prey themselves. No doubt some prudent hunters took weapons to fend off predators, scoured the ground carefully for hostile animals or tribes and stayed at home when it was too dangerous. Others, less prudent, chose not to buy or exercise these options. They took more risks and caught more prey.

Back around the campfire, was it the meagre haul of the prudent, or the full bags of those of the imprudent who returned, that won the admiration of the tribe? Were the young women of the tribe more impressed when the cautious described their uneventful days, or when the bold recalled their heroic escape from danger?

Like all attempts to account for our behaviour by delving into our evolutionary past, this story should be taken with a large pinch of salt. But there does not have to be any historic truth in my narrative for its fundamental premise to be true. People who take foolish risks which mostly come off are likely to appear attractive mates and leaders. Our heroes are often drawn from precisely that population.

Financial regulators warn that dealing in options is for sophisticated players only and carries a risk of total loss. It is a lesson everyone should take to heart.

Source: Based on John Kay, *Financial Times*, 11 December 2013, p. 11.

12.4 APPLICATION OF OPTION THEORY TO CORPORATE FINANCE

Option theory has implications going far beyond the valuation of traded share options. It offers a powerful tool for understanding various other contractual arrangements in finance. Here are some examples:

1 *Share warrants*, giving the holder the option to buy shares directly from the company at a fixed exercise price for a given period of time.

2 **Convertible loan stock**, giving the holder a combination of a straight loan or bond and a call option. On exercising the option, the holder exchanges the loan for a fixed number of shares in the company.

3 *Loan stock* can have a call option attached, giving the company the right to repurchase the stock before maturity.

4 *Executive share option schemes* are share options issued to company executives as incentives to pursue shareholder goals.

5 *Insurance and loan guarantees* are a form of put option. An insurance claim is the exercise of an option. Government loan guarantees are a form of insurance. The government, in effect, provides a put option to the holders of risky bonds so that, if the borrowers default, the bond-holders can exercise their option by seeking reimbursement from the government. Underwriting a share issue is a similar type of option.

6 *Currency and interest rate options* are discussed in later chapters as ways of hedging or speculating on currency or interest rate movements.

7 *Underwriting* a new issue of shares when underwriters must take up any shares not subscribed for by investors.

Two further forms of option are equity options and capital investment (real) options.

convertible loan stock
A debenture that can be converted into ordinary shares, often on attractive terms, usually at the option of the holder. Some preference shares are convertible

■ Equity as a call option on a company's assets: Reckless Ltd

Option-like features are found in financially geared companies. *Equity is, in effect, a call option on the company's assets.*

Reckless Ltd has a single £1 million debenture in issue, which is due for repayment in one year. The directors, on behalf of the shareholders, can either pay off the loan at the year end, thereby having no prior claim on the firm's assets, or default on the debenture. If they default, the debenture-holders will take charge of the assets or recover the £1 million owing to them.

In such a situation, the shareholders of Reckless have a call option on the company's assets with an exercise price of £1 million. They can exercise the option by repaying the loan, or they can allow the option to lapse by defaulting on the loan. Their choice depends on the value of the company's assets. If they are worth more than £1 million, the option is 'in the money' and the loan should be repaid. If the option is 'out of the money', because the assets are worth less than £1 million, option theory argues that shareholders would prefer the company to default or enter liquidation. This option-like feature arises because companies have limited liability status, effectively protecting shareholders from having to make good any losses.

Brussels to probe Hinkley nuclear contract

Brussels is to launch a full investigation into whether the contract for Britain's first nuclear power plant in a generation offers illegal state support, casting the project into doubt until at least next summer.

The deal under scrutiny is the contract signed in October between the UK government and French utility EDF for Hinkley Point C nuclear power station in Somerset. It will provide 7 per cent of the country's

Continued

electricity. The agreement guarantees EDF a 'strike price' of £92.50 per megawatt hour – roughly double the current wholesale price – for electricity produced at the £16bn plant over 35 years.

However, it has always required approval from the European Commission, which can demand changes to any terms that distort competition through illegal state support. EDF says it cannot make a final decision on Hinkley or bring in co-investors before state aid clearance is received. A concern will be whether the government has 'overcompensated' EDF with too high a strike price.

Other elements to come under scrutiny are the rate of return on the project, the duration of the contract, arrangements for nuclear waste and decommissioning and insurance against a nuclear event, as well as the UK's infrastructure guarantee. The probe will be a crucial test case in a bitterly contested area of policy. There is huge uncertainty over

how state aid rules will be applied to plans for Europe's next generation of power plants, especially any new nuclear reactors.

Some have argued a formal investigation is likely because 'many people' are questioning the deal. 'Given the challenges from anti-nuclear groups, Brussels needs to show it has followed due process,' said one person close to the discussions.

The UK has argued that the contract does not qualify as state aid and, even if the commission decides it does, it would be compatible with EU treaties. People close to the discussions said the commission was unlikely to order a reduction in the strike price, or duration of the project, but may demand closer monitoring to ensure EDF did not make 'excessive' profits.

Source: Based on Guy Chazan and Alex Barker, *Financial Times*, 12 December 2013, p. 3.

12.5 CAPITAL INVESTMENT OPTIONS (REAL OPTIONS)

real options
Options to invest in real assets such as capital projects

In Chapter 7, the principal ideas underlying **real options** were explained. The key proposal was that managers can change future activities as a project progresses and events occur that require them to re-think the project strategy. Hence, different types of real option can be identified including, for example, options to postpone, expand, contract or abandon capital projects.

Real options are closely related to financial options, as they are concerned with building flexibility into capital investment projects. For example, a firm may buy a patent from an inventor. The acquisition of this patent permits the firm to manufacture a new and innovative product if it wants to, but it does not have to manufacture the product. This is equivalent to paying a premium on a call option. Buying the patent gives the firm the right to manufacture the product, but it has no obligation to do so.

We have seen that the value of a share option will be dependent upon five main variables and, similarly, the value of a real option is dependent upon five main variables:

Share call option	Real call option
Exercise price	Investment cost
Current value of share	Value of the project
Time to expiry	Time until investment opportunity disappears
Volatility of share price	Volatility of project flows
Risk-free interest rate	Risk-free interest rate

The first four of these variables can be further understood if we consider them within the context of the firm that has bought the patent.

Exercise price

In the case of the firm that buys the patent, if it decides to manufacture the product then capital expenditure will be needed at the outset. For example, it may need to invest in new machinery. This investment cost equates to the price incurred to exercise the option.

Current value

In making the decision whether to manufacture or not, the firm will estimate what the future cash inflows (generated from selling the product) and future cash outflows (arising from costs of manufacture and the like) will be for the capital project. The present value of the cash inflows and outflows associated with manufacturing, and then selling, the product represent the current value of the project.

Time to expiry

There will come a time after which the opportunity to manufacture the product has passed, for example, when the product is no longer considered innovative by the marketplace. Hence, the option to manufacture does not remain open indefinitely and the patent will have an expiry date after which the investment opportunity no longer exists.

Volatility

Additionally, just as share prices are uncertain then, so too, are the future expected cash flows from any project. Therefore, some assessment of the volatility of the future cash flows will be needed if a real option valuation is to be performed.

Example: Strategic options in Harlequin plc

Harlequin plc has developed a new form of mobile phone, using the latest technology. It is considering whether to enter this market by investing in equipment costing £400,000 to assemble and then market the product in the north of England during the first four years. (Most of the product parts will be bought in.) The expected net present value from this initial project, however, is −£25,000. The strategic case for such an investment is that by the end of the project's life sufficient expertise would have been developed to launch an improved product on a larger scale to be distributed throughout Europe. The cost of the second project in four years' time is estimated at £1.32 million. Although there is a reasonable chance of fairly high payoffs, the expected net present value suggests this project will do little more than break even.

'Obviously, with the two projects combining to produce a negative NPV, the whole idea should be scrapped,' remarked the finance director.

Gary Owen, a recent MBA graduate, was less sure that this was the right course of action. He reckoned that the second project was a kind of call option, the initial cost being the exercise price and the present value of its future stream of benefits being equivalent to the option's underlying share price. The risks for the two projects looked to be in line with the variability of the company's share price, which had a standard deviation of 30 per cent a year.

If, by the end of Year 4, the second project did not suggest a positive NPV, the company could walk away from the decision, the option would lapse and the cost to the company would be the £25,000 negative NPV on the first project (the option premium). But it could be a winner, and only 'upside' risk is considered with call options.

Gary knew that Harlequin's discount rate for such projects was 20 per cent and the risk-free interest rate was 10 per cent. Table 12.4 shows his estimation of the main elements to be considered.

Gary then entered the five variables (asset value, exercise price, risk-free discount rate, time period and asset volatility) into the Black–Scholes option pricing formula. The outcome was that the value of the option to invest in the follow-on project was approximately £80,000. This is because there is a chance that the project could be really profitable, but the company will not know whether this is likely until the outcome of the first project is known. The high degree of risk in the second project actually increases the

Continued

value of the call option. It seems, therefore, that the initial project launch, which creates an option value of £80,000 for a 'premium' of £25,000 (negative NPV) may make economic as well as strategic sense.

Table 12.4 Harlequin plc: call option valuation

Initial project	(£000)
Cost of investment	(400)
PV of cash inflows	375
Net present value	(25)
Follow-on-project in Year 4	
Cost of investment	(1320)
PV of cash inflows	1320
Net present value in Year 4	–
Main factors in valuing the call option:	
1 Asset value	PV of cash flows at Year 4 discounted to Year 0
	= £1.32m/$(1.2)^4$
	= £0.636m
2 Exercise price	= cost of follow-on project
	= £1.32m
3 Risk-free discount rate	= 10%
4 Time period	= 4 years
5 Asset volatility	= standard deviation of 30%

12.6 WHY CONVENTIONAL NPV MAY NOT TELL THE WHOLE STORY

Earlier chapters have rehearsed the theoretical argument that capital projects that offer positive net present values, when discounted at the risk-adjusted discount rate, should be accepted. In Chapter 6 we raised a number of practical shortcomings with discounted cash flow approaches; here we introduce an important theoretical point.

We have noted that orthodox capital projects analysis adopts a 'now or never' mentality. But the timing option reminds us that a 'wait and see' approach can add value. Whenever a company makes an investment decision it also surrenders a call option – the right to invest in the same asset at some later date. Such waiting may be passive, waiting for the right economic and market conditions, or active, where management seeks to gather project-related information to reduce uncertainty (further product trials, competitor reaction, etc.). Hence, the true NPV of a project being undertaken today should include the values of various options associated with the decision:

$$\text{True NPV} = \begin{matrix} \text{NPV of} \\ \text{basic} \\ \text{project} \end{matrix} + \begin{matrix} \text{NPV of} \\ \text{abandonment} \\ \text{option} \end{matrix} + \begin{matrix} \text{NPV of} \\ \text{follow-on} \\ \text{projects} \end{matrix} + \begin{matrix} \text{NPV of} \\ \text{option} \\ \text{to wait} \end{matrix}$$

If the total is positive, the project creates wealth. This is why firms frequently defer apparently wealth-creating projects or accept apparently uneconomic projects. Senior managers recognise that investment ideas often have wider strategic implications, are irreversible and improve with age.

Real options are particularly important in investment decisions when the conventional NPV analysis suggests that the project is 'marginal', uncertainty is high and there is value in retaining flexibility. In such cases, the conventional NPV will almost always understate the true value.

Although the ideas underlying real options are relatively new, they do appear to be of use to companies. In their survey of investment appraisal techniques, Graham and Harvey (2002) reported that more than a quarter of the companies studied used real options approaches in some form.

Icy options

Bob Dudley, BP's chief executive, likes to talk about 'optionality'. This makes the British oil major's decision to hive off onshore US operations sound like a subtle financial manoeuvre. Separate management might help the unit – still fully owned by BP – compete better with smaller shale operators. But all that's been said, really, is this: we might sell.

BP's real option play was made last year – in Russia. BP sold its stake in TNK-BP, returned some of that cash to shareholders, and put down a long-term bet on the Russian Arctic shelf (with 300bn barrels of oil equivalent recoverable resource) by accepting a fifth of Rosneft's equity as added payment.

BP will not, however, seek bids for its Rosneft stake any time soon – for good reason. Russia will contribute all of BP's production growth in the medium term. Looking out to 2017, Credit Suisse sees production volumes, on a barrel of oil equivalent basis, rising at 3 per cent annually. Remove Russian volumes and that growth almost evaporates. BP's proven reserves are about 18bn boe (barrels of oil equivalent): Rosneft's grand plans to develop its Arctic shelf could add as much as 48bn. Note also that Rosneft and its partners have agreed to pay the first $14bn of exploration outlays. BP's option will stay in the money so long as Rosneft can eventually deliver enough of these barrels.

Geopolitical tensions amid the Ukraine crisis may make BP's Russian option appear further out of the money. But compared with the risk of Russia expropriating western energy assets, currency moves and cost overruns still weigh more on BP's future income.

Source: Based on Lex Column, *Financial Times*, 6 March 2014, p. 12.

SUMMARY

The options literature has developed highly complex models for valuing options, but insufficient attention has been paid to value creation through options.

Options or option-like features permeate virtually every area of financial management. A better understanding of options and the development of option pricing have made the topic an increasingly important part of financial theory. We have sought to increase your awareness of what options are, where they are to be found, and how managers can begin to value them. The topic is still in its infancy, but its study will yield important insights into financial and investment decisions.

Key points

- Option features are to be found in most areas of finance (e.g. convertibles and warrants, insurance, currency and interest rate management, and capital budgeting).

- Pure options are financial instruments created by exchanges (e.g. stock markets) rather than companies.

- The two main types of option are (1) **call options**, giving the holder the right to buy a share (or other asset) at the exercise price at some future time, and (2) **put options**, giving the holder the right to sell shares at a given price at some future time.

- The minimum value of a call option is the difference between the share price and the present value of the exercise price.

- The value of call options increases as:

  – The underlying share price increases.

  – The exercise price falls.

  – The time to expiry lengthens.

– The risk-free interest rate rises.

– The volatility of the underlying share price increases.

- The Black–Scholes Option Pricing Model can be applied to estimate the value of call options.

- Capital investment decisions may have options attached covering the option to (1) abandon, (2) delay or (3) invest in follow-on opportunities.

- Where the value of a company's assets falls below the value of its borrowings, shareholders may not exercise their option to repay the loan, but prefer the company to default on the debt.

Further reading

There are a range of books that specifically focus on derivative instruments and within these options are treated in detail. For example, see Hull (2014) and McDonald (2013). Guthrie (2009) discusses the topic of real options and Dixit and Pindyck (1995) provide an easy-to-read article on the options approach to capital investment. Brennan and Trigeorgis (2000) offer a number of useful papers on real options. Those who like a mathematical challenge may want to try Black and Scholes' (1973) classic paper or Cox *et al.* (1979). Merton (1998) gives an excellent review of the application of option pricing, particularly to investment decisions.

Useful websites

Futures and Options World: **www.fow.com**
NYSE Liffe: **www.euronext.com**
International Swaps and Derivatives Association: **www2.isda.org**

Appendix
BLACK–SCHOLES OPTION PRICING FORMULA

The Black–Scholes formula, for valuing a call option (C), with no adjustment for dividends, is given by:

$$C = SN(d_1) - EN(d_2)e^{-tk}$$

where:

$$d_1 = \frac{\ln(S/E) + tk}{\sigma t^{1/2}} + \frac{\sigma t^{1/2}}{2}$$

$$d_2 = d_1 - \sigma t^{1/2}$$

We already have described S as the underlying share price and E as the exercise price. In addition, σ is the standard deviation of the underlying asset, t is the time, in years, until the option expires, k is the risk-free rate of interest continuously compounded, $N(d)$ is the value of the cumulative distribution function for a standardised normal random variable and e^{-tk} is the present value of the exercise price continuously discounted.

■ Example

Acorn plc shares are currently worth 28p each with a standard deviation of 30 per cent. The risk-free interest rate is 6 per cent, continuously compounded. Compute the value of a call option on Acorn shares expiring in nine months and with an exercise price of 30p.

We can list the values for each parameter: $S = 28$, $\sigma = 0.30$, $E = 30$, $K = 0.06$, $t = 0.75$.

$$\sigma t^{1/2} = (0.3)(0.75)^{1/2} = 0.2598$$

$$d_1 = \frac{\ln(S/E) + tk}{\sigma t^{1/2}} + \frac{\sigma t^{1/2}}{2}$$

$$= \frac{\ln(28/30) + 0.75(0.06)}{0.2598} + \frac{0.2598}{2}$$

$$= -0.2655 + 0.1732 + 0.1299$$

$$= 0.0376, \text{ say } 0.04$$

$$d_2 = d_1 - \sigma r^{1/2} = 0.0375 - 0.2598$$

$$= -0.2223, \text{ say } -0.22$$

Using cumulative distribution function tables:

$$N(d_1) = N(0.04) = 0.5160$$
$$N(d_2) = N(-0.22) = 0.4129$$

Inserting the above into the original equation:

$$C = SN(d_1) - EN(d_2)e^{-tk}$$

$$= 28(0.5160) - 30(0.4129)e^{-0.045}$$

$$= 2.6p$$

The value of the call is 2.6p.

Strictly speaking, adjustment for dividends on shares should be made by applying the Merton formula, not dealt with in this text.

QUESTIONS

Questions with a coloured number have solutions in Appendix B on page 791.

1 Give two examples where companies can issue call options (or something similar).

2 On 1 March the ordinary shares of Gaymore plc stood at 469p. The traded options market in the shares quotes April 500p puts at 47p. If the share price falls to 450p, how much, if any, profit would an investor make? What will the option be worth if the share price moves up to 510p?

3 What is the difference between traditional and exchange traded options?

4 Explain the factors influencing the price of a traded option and whether volatility of a company's share option price is necessarily a sign of financial weakness.

5 Frank purchased a call option on 100 shares in Marmaduke plc six months ago at 10p per share. The share price at the time was 110p and the exercise price was 120p. Just prior to expiry the share price has risen to 135p.

   Required
   (a) State whether the option should be exercised.
   (b) Calculate the profit or loss on the option.
   (c) Would Frank have done better by investing the same amount of cash six months ago in a bank offering 10 per cent p.a.?

6 Find the value of the call option given that the present value of the exercise price is 10p, the value of the put option is 15p and the current value of the share on which the option is based is 25p.

7 Find the present value of the exercise price given that the value of the call is 19p, the value of the put is 5p and the current market price of the underlying share is 30p.

8 The current price of a share is 38p and a call option written on this share with six months to run to maturity has an exercise price of 40p. If the risk-free rate of interest is 10 per cent per annum and the volatility of the returns on the share is 20 per cent, use the Black and Scholes model to estimate the value of the call.

9 The current price of a company's shares is 420.5p and the price of a call option with a strike price of 420p with six months to maturity is 50.5p. The value of a put option with the same strike price and time to maturity is 38.5p. Determine the annualised rate of interest if put–call parity holds.

10 The following are the closing prices of options on the shares of Gilling plc on 10 March 2014.

	Calls			Puts		
Exercise Price	**Apr**	**Jun**	**Sep**	**Apr**	**June**	**Sep**
Gilling 800	36.5	53.5	62.5	9.0	20.0	31.5
(*825) 850	11.0	25.5	35.0	33.0	42.0	55.5

*Current price

Refer to the table as required when answering this question.

(a) Explain the fundamental reasons for the large difference between the price of a September 800 call and an April 800 put.
(b) Outline a strategy that combines short calls and short puts. Why would an investor adopt such a strategy? Use data from the table to illustrate some possible payoffs.

11 *Spot the options in Enigma Drugs plc.* The mini-case presented below incorporates five options. Can you identify the type of option, its length and exercise price? Recall that American options offer the holder the right to exercise at any time up to a certain date, while a European option is exercised on one particular date.

> Enigma Drugs plc is an innovative pharmaceutical company. The management team is considering setting up a separate limited company to develop and produce a new drug.
>
> The project is forecast to incur development costs and new plant expenditure totalling £50 million and to break even over the next five years (by which time its competitors are likely to have found a way round the patent rights). Enigma's management is considering deferring the whole decision by two years, when the outcome of a major court case with important implications for the drug's success will be known.
>
> The risks on the venture are high, but should the project prove unsuccessful and have to be abandoned, the 'know-how' developed from the project can be used inside the group or sold to its competitors for a considerable sum. Enigma's management realises that there is little or no money to be made in the initial five years, but it should allow them to gain vital expertise for the development of a 'wonder drug' costing £120 million, which could be launched in four years' time.
>
> The newly formed company would be largely funded by borrowing £40 million in the first instance, repayable in total after eight years, unless the company prefers to be 'wound up' for defaulting on the loan. Some of the debt raised will be by 9 per cent Convertible Loan Stock, giving holders the right to convert to equity at any time over the next four years at 360p compared with the current price of 297p.

12 A European call option on shares has three months to expiry. The current share price is £3 and the exercise price of the option is £2.50. The standard deviation of the share is 20 per cent, and the risk-free rate is 5 per cent. Use the Black–Scholes model to value the call option of a share.

Practical assignment

1 Choose two forms of financial contracting arrangement with option features and show how option pricing theory can help in analysing them.

2 Consider a major capital investment recently undertaken or under review (e.g. the London Olympic Games project). Does it offer an option? Could an option feature be introduced? What would the rough value of the option be?

Part IV

SHORT-TERM FINANCING AND POLICIES

The acquisition of every asset has to be financed. Companies obtain two forms of finance, short and long term, although, in practice, it is difficult to make a rigid demarcation between them. Part IV is devoted to analysing short-term financing, while the analysis of long-term financing decisions appears in Part V.

Chapter 13 offers an overview of the financing operations of the modern corporation, focusing on balancing the inflows and outflows of funds in the process of treasury management. The chapter examines how the financial manager may use the derivatives market to manage interest rate risk, and explores treasury policy for a variety of issues including risk management.

Chapter 14 looks at managing short-term assets – cash, stocks, debtors – and the financing implications of different working capital policies. Chapter 15 describes the various forms of short- (and medium-) term sources of finance, especially trade credit and the banking system, and also discusses the analysis of leasing decisions and the finance of foreign trade.

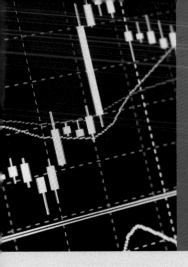

13

Risk and treasury management

Treasury management at D.S. Smith plc

The Group's overall treasury objectives are to ensure sufficient funds are available for the Group to carry out its strategy and to manage certain financial risks to which the Group is exposed. The Group's treasury strategy is controlled through the Treasury Committee, which meets regularly and includes the Group Chief Executive, the Group Finance Director, the Group Financial Controller, the Group Treasurer and the Group Tax Manager.

The Group Treasury function operates in accordance with policies and procedures approved by the Board and controlled by the Group Treasurer. The function arranges funding for the Group, provides a service to operations and implements strategies for financial risk management.

The Group regularly reviews the level of cash and debt facilities required to fund its activities. This involves preparing a business plan, determining the level of debt facilities required to fund the business, planning for repayments of debt at maturity and identifying an appropriate amount of headroom to provide a reserve against unexpected funding requirements.

At 30 April 2013, the Group's committed borrowing facilities totalled c. £1.4 billion of which £517 million were undrawn. Total gross borrowings at 30 April 2013 were £924.1 million. At 30 April 2013, the Group's committed borrowing facilities had a weighted-average maturity of 4.4 years.

In August 2012, the Group refinanced a €300 million bank term loan (due to mature in 2015) with the proceeds from a $400 million private placement of debt to US institutions with an average maturity of nine years. In addition, in November 2012, the Group repaid $105 million and £25 million of the private placement debt issued in 2002 at its maturity.

Source: D.S. Smith plc, *Annual Report*, 2013.

Learning objectives

Treasury management is central to the whole of corporate finance. After reading this chapter, you should appreciate the following:

- The purpose and structure of the treasury function.
- Treasury funding issues.
- How to manage banking relationships.
- Risk management, hedging and the use of derivatives.

13.1 INTRODUCTION

The introductory case study gives a flavour of the work of the Treasury in a large organisation (D.S. Smith is a leading packaging manufacturer). It also identifies some of the areas where things can potentially go wrong.

Treasury management, once viewed as a peripheral activity, today plays a vital role in corporate management. Most business decisions have implications for cash flow and risk, both of which are of direct relevance to treasury management. Many major firms have experienced problems through poor treasury management in recent years. This area has become a major concern in business, particularly the manner in which companies manage exposure to currency and other risks.

Most companies do not have a corporate treasurer; such a person is usually warranted only in larger companies. However, all firms are involved in treasury management to some degree. Treasury management can be defined in many ways. We will adopt the Association of Corporate Treasurers definition: 'the corporate handling of all financial matters, the generation of external and internal funds for business, the management of currencies and cash flows, and the complex strategies, policies and procedures of corporate finance.'

This chapter seeks to explain the main functions of treasury management and to provide an understanding of the risk management process.

13.2 THE TREASURY FUNCTION

The size, structure and responsibilities of the treasury function will vary greatly among organisations. Key factors will be corporate size, listing status, degree of international business and attitude to risk. For example, BP plc is a major multinational company with a strong emphasis on value creation, where currency and oil price movements can have a dramatic impact on corporate earnings. It is not surprising that it has a highly developed group treasury function, covering the following:

1 Ensuring liquidity sufficient to meet group requirements.
2 Optimising and managing cash flows.
3 Managing key financial risks including interest rate, foreign exchange, pension and financial institution credit risk.
4 Providing the interface between BP and the international financial markets.
5 Trading foreign exchange and interest rate products in the financial markets.

(*Source*: BP, *Annual Report*, 2013)

funding
Cash and liquidity management, short-term financing and cash forecasting

treasury operations
Financial risk management and portfolio management

In most companies, the treasury department is much simpler, typically with a distinction between **funding** (cash and liquidity management, short-term financing and cash forecasting) and **treasury operations** (financial risk management and portfolio management). The 2012 survey of global treasury management (*Treasury and Risk*, 2012) found that cash flow forecasting was regarded as the most important area of treasury operations, followed by risk management. Because of the slow economy, treasurers cited 'squeezing more cash from operations' as their priority for the next year as well as taking fewer risks.

It is the responsibility of the board of directors to set the treasury aims, policies, authorisation levels, risk position and structure. It should establish, for example, the following:

- The degree of treasury centralisation.
- Whether it should be a profit centre or cost centre.
- The extent to which the company should be exposed to financial risk.
- The level of liquidity desired.

Group Treasurer

- Working closely with Senior Management and international subsidiaries
- Group Borrowings
  - Ensure compliance with group covenants
  - Lead on structuring group finances
- Cash Management
  - Review/develop all cash processes and banking systems
  - Review surplus cash utilisation in the short, medium and long term
  - Ensure timely and tax effective remittance of surplus funds to the UK
  - Ensure tight control of all cash/cash transactions
  - Develop key banking relationships
- Working Capital Management
  - Improve Working Capital Management across the group
- Foreign Exchange
  - Manage the foreign exchange hedging process for all group companies
  - Manage foreign exchange exposure position
- Qualified Accountant and AMCT qualified

A typical job advertisement in the press

We pick up the last two points later, but deal with the structural issues in the following sections.

Degree of centralisation

Even in the most highly decentralised companies, it is common to find a centralised treasury function. The advantages of centralisation are self-evident:

1 The treasurer sees the total picture for cash, borrowings and currencies and is therefore able to influence and control financial movements on a global basis to achieve maximum after-tax benefit. The gains from centralised cash management can be considerable.
2 Centralisation helps the company develop greater expertise and more rapid knowledge transfer.
3 It permits the treasurer to capture any benefits of scale. Dealing with financial and currency markets on a group basis not only saves unnecessary duplication of effort, but should also reduce the cost of funds.
4 It enables the centre to cover a deficit in one area with surpluses from elsewhere, avoiding the costs of borrowing.

The major benefits from decentralising certain treasury activities are:

- By delegating financial activities to the same degree as other business activities, the business unit becomes responsible for all operations. Divisional managers in centralised treasury organisations are understandably annoyed at being assessed on profit after financing costs, over which they have little direct control.
- It encourages management to take advantage of local financing opportunities of which group treasury may not be aware and be more receptive to the needs of each division.

Profit centres and cost centres

In many large multinational firms, there is a substantial flow of cash each year in both domestic and foreign currencies. The volumes involved offer the opportunity to speculate, especially if the more favourable interest rates and exchange rates are available. Moreover, such firms probably employ staff skilled in cash and foreign exchange management techniques and may decide to use these resources pro-actively, i.e. to make a profit.

profit centre treasury (PCT)
A corporate treasury that aims to make a profit from its dealing – managers are judged on profit performance

In a **profit centre treasury (PCT)**, staff are authorised to take speculative positions, usually within clearly specified limits, by trading financial instruments in the same way as a bank. Such 'in-house banks' are judged on their return on capital achieved, although it is difficult to arrive at an accurate measure of capital employed. The main problem with operating a profit centre is that traders may exceed their permitted positions, either through negligence or in pursuit of personal gain.

cost centre treasury (CCT)
A treasury that aims to mini-mise the cost of its dealings

Conversely, a **cost centre treasury (CCT)** aims at operating as efficiently as possible, and eliminates risks as soon as they arise. D.S. Smith, the firm in the introductory case, clearly operates a CCT, i.e. it hedges rather than speculates, as a matter of policy.

Self-assessment activity 13.1

How would you define treasury management?

(Answer in Appendix A at the back of the book)

The four pillars of treasury management are: funding, banking relationships, risk management and working capital management. The first three of these are considered in this chapter and working capital management is covered in the next chapter.

13.3 FUNDING

Corporate finance managers must address the funding issues of: (1) how much should the firm raise this year, and (2) in what form? We devote Chapters 15 and 16 to these questions, examining long-, medium- and short-term funding. For the present, we sim-ply raise the questions that subsequent chapters will pursue in greater depth.

1 *Why do firms prefer internally generated funds?* Internally-generated funds, defined as profits after tax plus depreciation, represent easily the major part of corporate funds. In many ways, this is the most convenient source of finance. One could say it is equivalent to a compulsory share issue, because the alternative is to pay it all back to shareholders and then raise equity capital from them as the need arises. Raising equity capital, via the back door of profit retention, saves issuing and other costs. But, at the same time, it avoids the company having to be judged by the capital market as to whether it is willing to fund its future operations in the form of either equity or loans.

2 *How much should companies borrow?* There is no easy solution to this question. But it is a vital question for corporate treasurers. Borrow too much and the business could go bust; borrow too little and you could be losing out on cheap finance.

   The problem is made no easier by the observation that levels of borrowing dif-fer enormously among companies and, indeed, among countries. Levels of borrow-ing in Italy, Japan, Germany and Sweden are generally higher than in the UK and the USA. One reason is the difference in the strength of the relationship between lenders and borrowers. Bankers in Germany and Japan, for example, tend to take a longer-term funding view than UK banks. Japanese banks may even form part of the same group of companies. For example, the Bank of Tokyo–Mitsubishi UFJ, one of Japan's leading banks, is part of the Mitsibushi conglomerate (**www.mitsubishi.com**). We devote Chapters 18 and 19 to the key question of how much a firm should borrow.

3 *What form of debt is appropriate?* If the strategic issue is to decide upon the level of borrowing, the tactical issue is to decide on the appropriate form of debt, or how

to manage the debt portfolio. The two elements comprise the capital structure decisions. The debt mix question considers:

(a) *form* – loans, leasing or other forms?
(b) *maturity* – long-, medium- or short-term?
(c) *interest rate* – fixed or floating?
(d) *currency mix* – what currencies should the loans be in?

The first three issues are discussed in Chapters 15 and 16 and currency issues are dealt with in Chapters 21 and 22.

4 *How do you finance asset growth?* Each firm must assess how much of its planned investment is to be financed by short-term finance and how much by long-term finance. This involves a trade-off between risk and return.
Current assets can be classified into:

(a) *Permanent current assets* – those current assets held to meet the firm's long-term requirements. For example, a minimum level of cash and stock is required at any given time, and a minimum level of debtors will always be outstanding.
(b) *Fluctuating current assets* – those current assets that change with seasonal or cyclical variations. For example, most retail stores build up considerable stock levels prior to the Christmas period and run down to minimum levels following the January sales.

Figure 13.1 illustrates the nature of fixed assets and permanent and fluctuating current assets for a growing business. How should such investment be funded? There are several approaches to the funding mix problem.

First, there is the **matching approach** (Figure 13.1), where the maturity structure of the company's financing exactly matches the type of asset. Long-term finance is used to fund fixed assets and permanent current assets, while fluctuating current assets are funded by short-term borrowings.

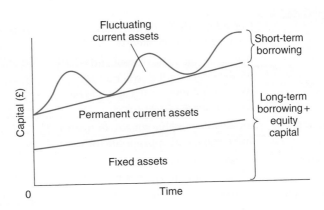

Figure 13.1 Financing working capital: the matching approach

A more aggressive and risky approach to financing working capital is seen in Figure 13.2, using a higher proportion of relatively cheaper short-term finance. Such an approach is more risky because the loan is reviewed by lenders more regularly. For example, a bank overdraft is repayable on demand. Finally, a relaxed approach would be a safer but more expensive strategy. Here most, if not all, the seasonal variation in current assets is financed by long-term funding, any surplus cash being invested in short-term marketable securities or placed in a bank deposit.

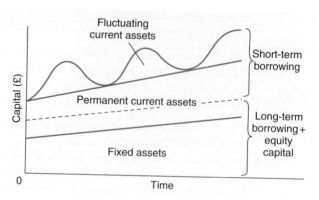

Figure 13.2 Financing working capital needs: an aggressive strategy

Self-assessment activity 13.2

What do you understand by the matching approach in financing fixed and current assets?
(Answer in Appendix A at the back of the book)

Example: Makepeace plc

Makepeace plc is a large UK multinational group. It is considering a major strategic capital project in Australia. What are the respective roles of the group's Treasury and Financial Control departments in appraising and implementing the new investment?

	Treasury	Financial Control
Project evaluation	Identify and quantify risks	Forecast operating costs and revenues
	Consider hedging or managing exchange rate and interest rate risks	Assess risk factors and conduct sensitivity or probability analysis
Discount rate	Advise on the costs of debt and equity for the target capital structure and recommend the cost of capital to be used for the specific project	Evaluate the project using the discount rate provided
Assess financing options	Investigate possible sources of finance and recommend appropriate form	
Arrange finance	Liaise with banks and other intermediaries to arrange finance	
Implementation and control	Prepare cash forecasts	Monitor implementation
	Provide the required finance and monitor cash flows	Prepare the operating budget and monitor project performance against budget
	Manage exchange rate and interest rate risk	Conduct post-completion audit
	Reinvest project cash inflows	

The issue of whether to borrow long term or short term is examined in more detail in the next section.

13.4 HOW FIRMS CAN USE THE YIELD CURVE

In Chapter 3, we examined the term structure of interest rates showing the yields on securities of varying times to maturity. The yield curve offers important information to treasury managers wanting to borrow funds. Although it is based on the structure of yields on government stock, similar principles apply to the market for corporate loans, or bonds. However, corporates have higher default risk than governments so that markets require higher yields on corporate bonds.

The market for government stock provides a benchmark that dictates the general shape of the yield curve with the curve for corporate bonds located above this. Figure 13.3 reproduces Figure 3.2 with an additional yield curve to describe yields in the market for corporate bonds. The distance between the two curves represents the premium required by the market to cover the risk of default by corporate borrowers. For top-grade corporate borrowers, with a very high credit rating, the premium will be relatively narrow, whereas firms considered to be more risky will be subject to higher risk premiums. The corporate versus government yield premium would usually widen with time to maturity, as corporate insolvency risk probably increases with time.

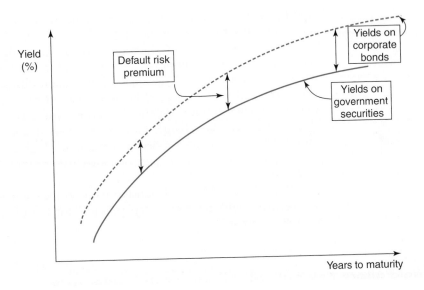

Figure 13.3 Yield curves

Today's yield curve incorporates how people expect interest rates to move in the future. An upward-sloping yield curve reflects investors' expectations of higher future interest rates and vice versa. The action points are clear:

■ A rising yield curve may be taken to imply that higher future interest rates are expected. This suggests firms might borrow long term now, and avoid variable interest rate borrowing.

■ A falling yield curve may be taken to imply that lower future interest rates are expected. This suggests firms might borrow short term now, and utilise variable interest rate borrowing.

■ Words of warning

In some circumstances, managers may be deceived by short-term rates. Say, they follow a policy of borrowing at short-term rates while the yield curve is upward-sloping, planning to switch to long-term borrowing when short-term rates exceed long-term rates.

For example, Jordan plc wants to borrow for six years, and the yield curve currently slopes upwards. The yields on five-year and six-year bonds are 5.5 per cent and 5.8 per cent respectively, while the yield on one-year bonds is 5.0 per cent. So, Jordan goes for one-year bonds, planning to issue a five-year bond a year later. But what if, a year later, the whole yield curve shifts upwards due to macroeconomic changes, e.g. a rise in the expected rate of inflation, so that Jordan has to pay say, 7.5 per cent on a five-year bond? Obviously, this is now more expensive than arranging to lock in the 5.8 per cent rate at the base year. Equally obviously, the reverse could apply – Jordan may benefit from a downward shift in the yield curve. However, the point is that firms should not be over-influenced by relatively small differentials along the yield curve.

We examine specific methods of short- and medium-term borrowing in Chapter 15 and methods of long-term borrowing in Chapter 16.

13.5 BANKING RELATIONSHIPS

Many large companies deal with several banks in order to maximise their access to credit. The 2011 Global Liquidity Investment Survey (J.P. Morgan, 2011) of treasurers found that the trend since the global financial crisis has been an increase in the number of banking relationships. The number of banks dealt with will depend on the company's size, complexity and geographical spread. While it makes sense to have more than one bank, too many can make it difficult to foster strong relationships. The real value of a good banking relationship is discovered when things get tough and when continued bank support is required.

We often hear the charge, particularly from smaller businesses, that banks are providing an inadequate service or charging too high interest rates. It seems that the banking relationship can be more of a love/hate relationship than a healthy financial partnership.

A flourishing banking relationship requires the company to deal openly, honestly and regularly with the bank, keeping it informed of progress and ensuring there are no nasty surprises.

Crisis alters risk outlook of corporate treasurers

Being a corporate treasurer has never been the most high-profile of jobs. Treasurers have long worked in the background. But the financial crisis gave companies a mantra of 'cash is king' and forced treasurers to take a more visible role. As Stuart Siddall, chief executive of the Association of Corporate Treasurers in the UK, says: 'Treasury as a profession has been catapulted into the spotlight by the crisis.' The crisis put a strain on companies as they scrambled to access liquidity and to secure funding as loans from banks dried up.

In interviews with the FT, treasurers at some of Europe's largest groups explain how their jobs have changed and how some of their innate conservatism has reaped rewards.

Many non-financial companies in Europe are sitting on record levels of cash. But rather than feeling it burning a hole in their pockets and splurging on an acquisition or share buy-back, companies are holding on to their cash.

Another change brought on by the crisis is that many groups have decided to diversify their funding. A treasurer at a UK group says: 'What should be my short-term and long-term mix? That has changed. Companies have become less reliant on short-term funding. But it is also important that you don't become too dependent on a single source of funding.'

The obvious manifestation was in the switch from bank finance to getting funds from the capital markets through bonds. Take MAN, the German truckmaker. Four years ago, it was entirely bank-financed. Now it does most of its financing through the capital markets.

Mr Siddall's advice to treasurers is to avoid complacency. 'You have to anticipate the unexpected. Make sure there has been an aggressive assessment of financial risks, and update it regularly.'

Source: Based on Richard Milne, *Financial Times*, 3 September 2010, p. 21.

13.6 TREASURY RISK MANAGEMENT

The financial manager should recognise the many types of risk to be managed:

- *Liquidity risk* – managing corporate liquidity to ensure that funds are in place to meet future debt obligations.
- *Credit risk* – managing the risks that customers will not pay.
- *Market risk* – managing the risk of loss arising from adverse movements in market prices in interest rates, foreign exchange, equity and commodity prices. It is this form of risk that we now consider.

Every business needs to expose itself to risks in order to seek out profit. But there are some risks that a company is in business to take, and others that it is not. A major company, like Ford, is in business to make profits from making cars. But is it also in business to make money from taking risks on the currency movements associated with its worldwide distribution of cars?

While the risks of business can never be completely eliminated, they can be *managed*. Risk management is the process of identifying and evaluating the trade-off between risk and expected return, and choosing the appropriate course of action.

With the benefit of hindsight, it is all too easy to see that some decisions were 'wrong'. In this sense, errors of commission are more visible than errors of omission; the decision to invest in a risky project which subsequently fails is more obvious than the rejected investment which competitors take up with great success. As with all aspects of decision-making, risk management decisions should be judged in the light of the available information when the decision is made. The treasurer plays a vital role in identifying, assessing and managing corporate risk exposure in such a way as to maximise the value of the firm and ensure its long-term survival.

Self-assessment activity 13.3

Take a look at the latest Annual Report of Wolseley plc (**www.wolseley.com**). What does the Directors' Report say about its financial risk management?

■ Stages in the risk management process

Identify risk exposure. Taking risks is all part of business life, but businesses need to assess exactly what risks they are taking. For example, while a firm will probably insure against the risk of fire, it may not consider the risk of loss of profits from the resulting disruption of the fire. The Brazilian coffee farmer could see his whole crop wiped out by a late frost. The UK fashion exporter could see her profit margins disappear because of the rising value of sterling against other currencies.

Before any attempt is made to cover risks, the treasurer should undertake a complete review of corporate risk exposure, including business and financial risks. Some of these risks will naturally offset each other. For example, exports and imports in the same currency can be netted off, thereby reducing currency exposure.

Evaluate risks. We saw, in Chapter 7, that there are various ways in which the risks of investments can be forecast and evaluated. The decision as to whether the risk exposure should be reduced will depend on the corporate attitude to risk (i.e. its degree of risk aversion) and the costs involved. **Hedgers** take positions to reduce exposure to risk. **Speculators** take positions to increase risk exposure.

Manage risks. The treasurer can manage risk exposure in four ways: risk retention, avoidance, reduction and transfer, each of which is considered below.

1 *Risk retention.* Many risks, once identified, can be carried – or absorbed – by the firm. The larger and more diversified the firm's activities, the more likely it is to be able

hedgers
Hedgers try to minimise or totally eliminate exposure to risk

speculators
Speculators deliberately take positions to increase their exposure to risk, hoping for higher returns

to sustain losses in some areas. There is no need to pay premiums to market institutions when the risk can easily be absorbed by the company. Firms may hold precautionary cash balances, or maintain lower than average borrowing levels, in order to be better able to absorb unanticipated losses. It should, of course, be borne in mind that there are costs associated with such actions, particularly the lower return to the firm from holding such large cash balances.

2 *Risk avoidance*. Some businesses prefer to keep well away from high-risk investments. For example, they may prefer to stick to conventional technology rather than promising new technology, and to avoid doing business with countries with volatile exchange rates. Such risk-avoiding behaviour may be acceptable in the short term, but, ultimately, it threatens the firm's competitiveness and survival.

3 *Risk reduction*. We all know that by having a good diet and taking the right amount of exercise, we can reduce our risk exposure to a variety of health problems. Similarly, firms can reduce exposure to failure by doing the right things. Risk of fire can be reduced by an effective sprinkler system; risk of project failure can be reduced by careful planning and management of the implementation process and clear plans for abandonment at minimum cost should the need arise.

4 *Risk transfer*. Where a risk cannot be avoided or reduced and is too big to be absorbed by the firm, it can be turned into someone else's problem or opportunity by 'selling', or transferring, it to a willing buyer. Bear in mind that most risks are two-sided. There may be a speculator willing to acquire the very risk that the hedger firm wishes to lose. It is this area of risk transfer which is of particular importance to corporate finance. Whole markets and industries have developed over the years to cater for the transfer of risk between parties.

Risk can be transferred in three main ways:

■ *Diversification*. We saw, in Chapter 8, that the risk exposure of the firm or shareholder can be considerably reduced by holding a diversified portfolio of investments. Diversification rarely eliminates all risk because most assets have returns positively correlated with the returns from other assets in the portfolio. It does, however, eliminate sufficient risk for the firm to consider absorbing the remaining risk exposure.

■ *Insurance*. This seeks to cover downside risk. A premium is paid to the insurer to transfer losses arising from insured events but to retain any gains. As we saw in Chapter 12, financial options are a form of insurance whereby losses are transferred to others while profits are retained.

■ *Hedging*. With hedging, the firm exchanges, for an agreed price, a risky asset for a certain one. It is a means by which the firm's exposure to specific kinds of risk can be reduced or 'covered'. Hence the fashion exporter can now enter into a contract guaranteeing an exchange rate for her exports to be paid in three months' time. Similar hedges can be created for risks in interest rates, commodity prices and many more transactions.

Hedging has a cost, often in the form of a fee to a financial institution, but this cost may well be worth paying if hedging reduces financial risks. The extent to which an exposure is covered is termed the *hedge efficiency*: eliminating all financial risk is a 'perfect hedge' (i.e. 100 per cent efficiency).

Bako Ltd is a medium-size bakery business. The financial manager has identified that its main risk exposures lie in the following areas:

Risk exposure	Market hedge
Raw material prices – specifically, flour and sugar	Commodity
Currency movements on imports and exports	Currency
Interest rate movements on its variable-rate borrowings	Financial
Loss of profits, e.g. lost production from a possible bakery fire or a bad debt	Insurance

The first three risks can be managed through hedging in the commodity, currency and financial markets, letting the market bear the risks. The last can be covered through various forms of insurance.

Hedging helps foodmakers through uncertainty

Imagine you supply the world's biggest supermarket chains with breakfast cereals, bottled beer and sliced bread. Or that you are one of the world's biggest meat producers, buying corn to feed cattle whose meat is your bottom line. Now imagine prices of wheat, corn, and other agricultural commodities, which comprise much of your input costs, jump 50 per cent in a matter of weeks because of a drought in Russia that has caused catastrophic crop failure. Worse, Moscow slaps a ban on exports. That is exactly what has happened to companies such as Kellogg and Kraft. Contrary to the fears of many investors, however, these big food companies are likely to weather the turmoil in commodities markets.

The reason? They learnt from bitter experience during the food crisis of 2007–08 and have protected themselves from the latest surge in prices by using derivatives. Companies have told investors that their commodity hedging strategies will largely insulate them from the effects of spiking wheat, corn and barley prices. Kellogg executives told investors that the cereal and snack company was 90 per cent hedged on a range of commodities. Anheuser-Busch InBev, the world's largest brewer, said it had hedged its barley purchases through 2011, avoiding a big cost problem.

The growing use of derivatives to lock in forward prices marks a big change from the situation multinational food producers found themselves in in 2007 and 2008, when they were caught off-guard by sudden jumps in prices. Bankers estimate that up to a third of the world's largest food companies launched fresh hedging programmes in the aftermath of the 2007–08 crisis.

For years, food companies did not worry too much about being caught out by unexpectedly steep price rises. Only the biggest groups hedged and, in most cases, they only bought protection for a few volatile commodities, such as coffee, sugar or cocoa. They sidelined other key agricultural commodities, from wheat and soyabeans to milk and corn, on the grounds that the prices in those markets were relatively stable. Moreover, the convention in the industry was to pass on to consumers any rise in costs. Companies learnt in 2007–08 there was a limit to shoppers' loyalty.

As a result, they overhauled their forward buying practices and locked in prices through buying futures and options traded on commodities exchanges in Chicago, New York, London and Paris. They dealt directly, too, with Wall Street banks on bespoke 'over-the-counter' derivatives deals that are not traded on exchanges.

Source: Based on Javier Blas and Greg Farrell, *Financial Times*, 12 August 2010.

▪ Derivatives

The financial instruments employed to facilitate hedging are termed **derivatives,** because the instrument derives its value from securities underlying a particular asset, such as a currency, share or commodity. One of the earliest derivatives was money itself, which for centuries derived its value from the gold into which it could be converted. 'Derivative' has today become a generic term that is used to include all types of relatively new financial instruments, such as options and futures.

The esoteric world of derivatives has hardly been out of the news in recent years. Barings Bank, Metallgesellschaft and Kodak are all examples of major businesses whose corporate fingers have been burned through derivative transactions. Société Générale revealed in 2008 that it had lost a staggering €4.9 billion from allegedly rogue derivatives trading. Although sometimes viewed as instruments of the devil, derivatives are really nothing more than an efficient means of transferring risk from those exposed to it, but who would rather not be (hedgers), to those who are not, but would like to be (speculators).

Derivatives are financial instruments, such as options or futures, which enable investors either to reduce risk or speculate. They offer the treasurer a sophisticated 'tool-box' to manage risk. A risk management programme should reduce a company's exposure to the risks it is *not* in business to take, while reshaping its exposure to those risks it does wish to take. Risk exposure comes mainly in unexpected movements in interest rates, commodity prices and foreign exchange, all of which should be managed.

There are, essentially, four main types of derivative: forwards, futures, options and swaps.

Oil groups and utilities grab bigger share of airline hedging

Oil companies and power and gas utilities are increasing their share of the airline hedging market according to participants, as physical operators extend their reach into a business long dominated by investment banks. The development reflects a shift in power in commodity markets, as expertise in derivatives spreads beyond banks to energy companies and trading houses. The growing prominence of non-banks in the hedging business also shows how physical operators are increasingly taking on financial market exposures, as well as physical contracts.

Airlines often enter derivative contracts with banks to manage their exposure to changes in the price of crude oil and jet fuel. During the financial crisis some airlines actively sought alternatives to banks and the trend has gathered pace in the past year, as some banks have scaled back their commitment to commodities and those that remain have tended to price credit risk more conservatively. It has been estimated that the energy companies' share of the European airline hedging market has grown from 5 per cent in 2008 to between a quarter and a third.

The trend is also present in the US, although less advanced as many US airlines opt for complex hedging deals, in which banks are still the preferred counterparty, according to market participants. BP, Royal Dutch Shell and Total, which trade crude oil and jet fuel as part of their business, have long offered hedges to airlines. But their market share has increased significantly, according to market participants. European power and gas utilities with trading arms, including RWE, EDF and GDF Suez, have also expanded into oil derivatives in recent years.

Bankers said they felt energy companies paid less attention to the credit risk involved in providing a long-term hedging contract, allowing them to price aggressively. 'We often hear on the floor that we've lost a trade with an airline by a few cents, and it will be exactly the same as our credit charge,' said the head of energy sales at one bank.

Source: Based on Ajay Makan, *Financial Times*, 29 August 2013, p. 19.

Forward contracts

forward contract
An agreement to sell or buy at a fixed price at some time in the future

A **forward contract** is an agreement to sell or buy a commodity (including foreign currency) at a fixed price at some time in the future. In business, buyers and sellers are often subject to exactly opposite risks. The manufacturer of confectionery is concerned that the price of sugar may rise next year, while the sugar cane producer is concerned that the price may fall. In a world where it is extremely difficult to predict future commodity prices, both parties may want to exchange uncertain prices for sugar delivered next year for a fixed price.

By agreeing a price for sugar delivery next year, the confectionery manufacturer hedges against prices escalating, while the sugar cane producer hedges against prices dropping. They do this by entering into a forward contract, enabling future transactions and their prices to be agreed today, but not to be paid for until delivery at a specified future date.

Forward markets exist for most of the major commodities (e.g. cocoa, metals and sugar), but even more important is the forward market in foreign exchange.

A forward currency contract is when a company agrees to buy or sell a specified amount of foreign currency at an agreed future date and at a rate that is agreed in advance.

For example, if you want to pay US$50,000 in six months' time, you can use a forward contract to hedge against adverse currency movements. You can agree a price today that will pay for the dollars by arranging with your bank to buy dollars forward. At the end of six months, you pay the agreed sum and take delivery of the US dollars (see Chapter 21 for a fuller explanation).

futures contract
A commitment to buy or sell an asset at an agreed date and price, and traded on an exchange

Futures contracts

Like a forward contract, a **futures contract** is a commitment to buy or sell an asset at an agreed date and at an agreed price. The difference is that futures are standardised in terms of period, size and quality and are traded on an exchange. In Europe, NYSE Euronext runs futures and options markets.

A chemical company plans to buy crude oil in three months' time. The spot price (i.e. current market price) for Brent crude is $108 a barrel and a three-month futures contract can be agreed at $110 a barrel. To guard against the possibility of an even higher price rise, the company enters a 'long' futures position (i.e. agrees to buy) at $110 a barrel, thereby reducing its exposure to oil price hikes. If, in three months' time, the spot oil price has risen beyond $110, the company will not suffer unforeseen losses.

If, however, just before delivery, the spot price has fallen to $98 a barrel, the company will want to benefit from the lower price. It will buy at the spot price and cancel the long contract by entering into a short contract (i.e. an agreement to sell) at around the $98 spot price. The loss of $12 a barrel on the two contracts is offset by the profit of $12 from buying at the spot rather than the original futures price.

Why might a company prefer a futures contract when a forward contract could be tailor-made to meet its specific requirements? The main reason lies in the obvious benefits from trading through an exchange, not least that the exchange carries the default risk of the other party failing to abide by the contract terms, so-called 'counterparty risk'. For this benefit, both the buyer and seller must pay a deposit to the exchange, termed the 'margin'.

Financial futures have become highly popular among both hedgers and traders, who buy or sell futures in order to profit from a view that the market will go up or down. The main forms of financial futures contracts cover short-term interest futures, bond futures and equity-linked futures using stock market indices.

Options

option
The right but not the obligation to buy or sell something at some time in the future at a given price

An **option** gives the right, but not the obligation, to buy or sell an asset at an agreed price at, or up to, an agreed time. It is this right not to exercise the option that distinguishes it from a future. We discussed options in Chapter 12.

A farmer has a ripening crop which he plans to sell in September. He would like to benefit from any price movements but also be 'insured' against any fall in price. A put option (i.e. the right to sell at an agreed price) is rather like insurance. If the price falls, the option to sell at an agreed price is exercised. If the price rises, the option is not exercised, and the spot price at the date of sale is taken.

Swaps

Swaps are arrangements between two firms to exchange a series of future payments. A swap is essentially a long-dated forward contract between two parties through the intermediation of a third party, such as a bank. For example, a company might agree to a currency swap, whereby it makes a series of regular payments in yen in return for receiving a series of payments in US dollars.

An interest rate swap effectively allows a firm to change between fixed and floating rate loans. At the end of June 2014, there was US$421 trillion of interest rate swaps outstanding (based on notional amounts outstanding: **www.bis.org**).

Example: Interest rate swap

X and Y are companies each looking to borrow £1 million for two years. X wants a floating rate loan while Y is looking for a fixed rate loan. X has a stronger credit rating than Y. The table below shows that X can borrow in the fixed rate market 1.5 per cent more cheaply than Y, but only 0.5 per cent more cheaply in the floating rate market. It therefore is considering a standard interest rate swap whereby X can swap interest payment on its floating rate loan for Y's fixed rate loan interest payments. This produces a total gain of 1 per cent

Continued

(i.e. $1.5\% - 0.5\%$). The table also shows the rates quoted by a swap dealer, the difference being the dealer's margin. We now must establish how the 1 per cent gain is to be shared between the two companies and the swap dealer.

	Floating	**Fixed**
X	LIBOR* + 0.5%	7%
Y	LIBOR + 1.0%	8.5%
Swap quote	LIBOR% − LIBOR + 0.1%	6.8% − 6.9%

X

Borrows fixed rate at 7% and swaps at 6.8%
This gives a loss of 0.2%
Swaps floating rate at LIBOR + 0.1% giving a gain on floating of 0.4 on the borrowing
   rate (LIBOR + 0.5%)
Net saving = 0.2%

Y

Borrows floating rate at LIBOR + 1% and swaps at LIBOR
This gives a gain of 1%
Swaps at 6.9% which is 1.6% less than the cost of a fixed rate loan
Net saving = 0.6%

The swap dealer makes 0.1% on the two swaps. The total gain of 1% on the swap is
   therefore 0.2% for X + 0.6% for Y + 0.2% for dealer = 1%

---

*LIBOR is the London interbank offered rate. This is a benchmark interest rate and indicates the rate at which key banks would pay if borrowing from one another. In 2012 a scandal erupted concerning the fixing of this rate, leading to regulatory reforms to aid in ensuring this manipulation would not happen again.

Self-assessment activity 13.4

(a) A futures contract can be customised to fit the particular needs of the customer. True or false?
(b) A currency swap can be used to hedge for a longer period than that offered by forward exchange contracts. True or false?
(c) Max International plc is due to receive €100,000 in three months' time for exports to a German customer and has decided to hedge the currency by taking a forward contract. The following rates have been quoted:

	Spot rate	Three-month forward
Euro per £	1.4925–1.4985	1.4892–1.4898

What is the sterling value that the company will receive from the forward contract?
(d) Consider the following example of a company which plans to buy aluminium. It enters into a call option contract, paying an appropriate premium for the right to buy aluminium at $1,500/tonne in three months' time. If, at the end of the period, the spot price is $1,400/tonne, should the company exercise its option or let it lapse?

(Answer in Appendix A at the back of the book)

■ To hedge or not to hedge

Does hedging enhance shareholder value? Some argue that it helps firms achieve competitive advantage over rivals by cost-effectively reducing risks over which it has little experience and exploiting those risks over which it has strong levels of competence. Pure theorists, on the other hand, argue that corporate hedging is a costly process doing no favours for shareholders. After all, portfolio diversification by investors is one form of hedging. Corporate hedging does nothing that shareholders could not do themselves, employing derivatives in exactly the same way as corporate treasurers to follow their own risk management strategy. So why do many large companies hedge and use derivatives? Consider the following case study.

Example

Yourfired plc is a global recruitment agency with exposure to macroeconomic risks concerning interest and exchange rates. The treasury function is considering who should manage such risks. Should it be the group treasury manager or left to the shareholders investing in the company?

The treasurer rehearsed the arguments for leaving risk management to portfolio managers rather than at the firm level. First, market, or systematic, risk is lower than total risk and therefore it will incur lower transaction costs. Second, companies are less experienced than portfolio managers in using potentially dangerous derivative instruments. There is therefore a good case for firms leaving risk management – particularly of the kind that employs derivatives – to the market, allowing large investors to decide whether and how to manage their portfolio risk.

However, the treasurer then recognised that this ignores some important issues.

1 These risks can bankrupt the company, and the realised value of a failed business is far lower than its value as a profitable going concern. All stakeholders, including investors, have a vested interest in the company's long-run prosperity.
2 Investors prefer steady earnings and cash flows to the more volatile ones likely when currency and interest rates are not managed.
3 The company's management may be reluctant to disclose to investors the full picture on risk exposure, making it difficult for them to make an accurate risk assessment on their portfolios.

The treasurer of Yourfired plc eventually decided that the company's hedging policy would be one of eliminating the worst 'down-side risk', but not attempt to hedge all risks. Whatever the risk management strategy, it is important that the treasurer explains to senior management what has been done and what risk exposure remains.

■ Interest rate management

Every company is exposed to a degree of interest rate risk. This occurs when changes in the interest rate affect a company's profits and/or the value of its assets and liabilities. The nature of the exposure depends on whether the company is a net borrower or net investor. Where a company with a high proportion of floating rate debt is exposed to the risk of rate increases, it will adversely affect the volatility of cash flows. Conversely, a company which has a high proportion of fixed interest rate debt would suffer from a loss of competitive advantage relative to floating rate borrowers if the prevailing interest rate falls.

The first form of interest rate risk is *basis risk* – the risk that the level of interest rates will change. A second form of risk relates to changes in the yield curve over time, as discussed earlier, and refers to differences in short- and long-term interest rates. The normal, upward-sloping yield curve arises where interest rates increase as the term lengthens. In practice, however, the curve can be flat or even inverted.

Steps to manage interest rate exposure

The treasurer needs to understand the company's interest rate risk exposure, how it is likely to change over time and, where any of these exposures are compensating, how they can be netted off against each other. The three-step process involves:

1 Identifying the expected future cash flows that are exposed to interest rate fluctuations.
2 Specifying those rates of interest beyond which steps must be taken to reduce exposure.
3 Reducing exposure by:

– *Natural (or internal) hedging.* This seeks to match liabilities against assets with similar interest rates. For example, an exposure to pay a rate of interest on a loan may be partially offset by an investment linked to the same or a similar rate.

– *Fixing the interest rate.* Loans can be taken out at a fixed rate rather than a floating rate.

– *Interest rate swaps.* This is an arrangement whereby two parties agree to exchange interest payments with each other over an agreed period. In other words, Company A agrees to pay the interest on Company B's loan, while Company B reciprocates by paying the interest on Company A's loan. Of course, what they are really swapping is the different characteristics of the two loans. The most common characteristic being exchanged is the fixed or variable interest rate, and this swap is termed a *plain vanilla* or *generic swap*.

– *Hedging contracts.* The corporate treasurer has a variety of techniques available to reduce interest rate risk, many of which have already been discussed. The main methods are forward rate agreements (FRAs), interest rate futures, interest rate options, interest rate swaps and more complex methods, such as options on interest rate swaps ('swaptions'). We are more concerned with the principles of interest rate management than the detailed application.

Table 13.1 summarises the findings of an international study of use of derivatives based on over 7,000 listed firms in 50 countries. The total picture indicates that forward contracts are most popular for foreign exchange hedging (37 per cent of firms), while swaps are most common for interest rate management (29 per cent). Japanese companies have by far the highest proportion of firms using derivatives, while German companies are far more reluctant to employ derivatives.

Table 13.1 International comparison of financial derivative usage

Country	Foreign exchange derivatives			Interest rate derivatives		
	Forward %	Swap %	Option %	Forward %	Swap %	Option %
Australia	48	9	18	4	39	15
Germany	27	11	13	2	18	10
Japan	71	33	18	1	60	14
UK	49	17	8	1	32	11
USA	31	6	7	1	36	7
Others	36	11	11	2	19	5
All firms	37	11	10	1	29	7

Source: Bartram *et al.* (2006).

Managing interest rate risk at MedExpress Ltd

It was Karen Bailey's first day as the financial controller of MedExpress Ltd, a fast-growing business in the medical support industry. A quick look at the statement of financial position revealed that the company, although highly profitable, was heavily geared, with large amounts of debt capital repayment due over the coming years. Interest rates had changed little over the past two years, but opinions were divided over whether the Bank of England would have to raise interest rates quite steeply in order to keep inflation within prescribed government limits, or whether rates would hold.

To Bailey's surprise, the company had taken no steps to manage its exposure to interest rate movements. Her first step was to identify the exposure to interest rate risk.

1 A £2 million overdraft, with a variable interest rate, would have a significant impact on profits and cash flow if the rate increased in the near future. If the interest rate rise was dramatic, it could seriously affect cash flows and increase the risk of liquidation.

2 The £5 million fixed-rate long-term loan would become much less attractive if interest rates fell. Paying unduly high interest rates adversely affects profitability.

3 Of the fixed rate loan, £1.8 million would mature shortly and need replacing. The company could choose to repay the loan at any time over the next two years. If rates were expected to rise over that period, early redemption would be preferable.

As Bailey sought to get a grip on the interest rate exposure, she considered the following ways of managing interest rate risk:

(a) *Interest rate mix.* A mix of fixed and variable rate debt to reduce the effects of unanticipated rate movements. She would need to give more thought to whether the existing ratio of £2 million variable/£5 million fixed rate debt was sufficiently well balanced.

(b) *Forward rate agreement (FRA).* Some risk exposure could be eliminated by entering into a forward rate agreement with the bank. This would lock the company into borrowing at a future date at an agreed interest rate. Only the difference between the agreed interest that would be paid at the forward rate and the actual loan interest is transferred.

(c) *Interest rate 'cap'.* It is possible to 'cap' the interest rate to remove the risk of a rate rise. If the cap is set at 8 per cent, an upper limit is placed on the rate the company pays for borrowing a specific sum. Unlike the FRA (see below), if the rate falls, the company does not have to compensate the bank.

(d) *Interest rate futures.* These contracts enable large interest rate exposures to be hedged using relatively small outlays. They are similar in effect to FRAs, except that the terms, the amounts and the periods are standardised.

(e) *Interest rate options.* Also termed interest rate guarantees, these contracts grant the buyer the right, but not the obligation, to deal at a specific interest rate at some future date. For example, if a company is borrowing money, then the interest rate option will protect the borrower from interest rate rises. However, if interest rates fall, then the borrower can benefit from the reduction in interest rates. The borrower will need to be willing to pay the premium for the interest option.

(f) *Interest rate 'swaps'.* These occur where a company (usually very large firms) with predominantly variable rate debt, worried about a rise in rates, 'swaps' or matches its debt with a company with predominantly fixed-rate debt concerned that rates may fall. A bank usually acts as intermediary in the process, but it can be through direct negotiations with another company. Each borrower will still remain responsible for the original loan obligations incurred. Typically, firms continue to pay the interest on their own loan and then, at the end of the agreed period, a cash adjustment will be made between the two parties to the swap agreement. Interest rate swaps can also involve exchanges in different currencies.

Example: Forward rate agreement (FRA)

A forward rate agreement (FRA) is a cash-settled forward contract on a short-term loan. No loan is actually given and contracts settle with a single cash payment on the first day of the underlying loan, termed the settlement date.

Frodo plc needs to raise a £1 million six-month fixed rate loan from 1 November. On 31 July, it enters into an FRA with a bank that fixes the rate of interest for borrowing for six months from 1 November, the relevant rate at that date being 6 per cent. This is termed a '3–9' FRA: it starts in three months' time and lasts for six months. What is the result of the FRA if the rate has moved to:

(a) 5 per cent?
(b) 8 per cent?

Answer

If the effective loan rate moves to 5 per cent, the company will pay the bank:

	£
FRA payment £1m $\times$ (6% $-$ 5%) $\times$ 6/12	(5,000)
Payment on underlying loan 5% $\times$ £1m $\times$ 6/12	(25,000)
Net payment on loan	30,000
Effective interest rate	6%

If the effective loan rate moves to 8 per cent, the bank will pay the company:

	£
FRA receipt £1m $\times$ (8% $-$ 6%) $\times$ 6/12	10,000
Payment on underlying loan at market rate 8% $\times$ £1m $\times$ 6/12	(40,000)
Net payment on loan	(30,000)
Effective interest rate	6%

Interest rate futures can be employed to hedge against changes in short-term interest rates for up to approximately two years. They are similar to FRAs, except that the terms, amounts and periods are standardised. This can make them less flexible as a hedging instrument because the corporate treasurer cannot always match them with specific interest rate exposures.

Lenders will want to hedge against the possibility of falling interest rates which would reduce the interest they receive. They can do this by purchasing futures now and selling futures on the date the lending commences. Conversely, borrowers can hedge against interest rate rises by selling futures now and buying futures on the date that the interest rate is fixed.

Example: Interest rate futures hedging strategy for X-factor plc

On 30 July, three-month sterling futures are quoted as follows:

September	94.45
December	94.30
March	94.22

The futures contracts have a notional value of £500,000.

X-factor plc is looking to raise a £1 million floating rate loan at the beginning of December for three months. The company is expecting to borrow at a rate of 6 per cent, but it is concerned that the interest rate may rise. Therefore, the company wishes to reduce this interest rate risk using interest rate futures.

Assume that at the beginning of December interest rates have risen and the company is borrowing at a rate of 6.5 per cent. Additionally, because of the rise in interest rates the price of three-month December contracts has moved to 93.85.

Answer

The increase in interest rates from 6 per cent to 6.5 per cent will cost X-factor plc an additional £1,250 (£1 million $\times$ 3/12 $\times$ 0.5%).

Using interest rate futures X-factor plc can offset this cost of £1,250 as follows:

As the contract size is £500,000, X-factor will need two futures contracts to hedge its loan of £1 million.

On 30 July, X-factor plc will enter into an agreement to sell two December contracts at 94.30 (note that the futures rate of 94.30 equates to an interest rate of 100 − 94.30 = 5.70%).

At the beginning of December, X-factor will then enter into an agreement to buy two December contracts at 93.85.

Consequently, X-factor plc will make a profit on its futures contracts. This is because it has agreed to buy two December contracts at 93.85 and agreed to sell two December contracts at 94.30.

The profit it makes is calculated as follows:

Contracts entered into on 30 July	94.30
Contracts entered into beginning of December	93.85
Difference	**0.45**

This difference is normally expressed as a number of *ticks*. A tick is the minimum price movement on a contract and in the case of short sterling futures this is 0.01.

Therefore, the futures difference in number of ticks = 0.45/0.01 = 45 ticks.

If **one** contract moves by **one** tick, then the change in the contract value = £500,000 $\times$ 0.01% $\times$ 3/12 = **£12.50** (this amount of £12.50 is referred to as the *tick value*).

X-factor plc had two contracts which both moved by 45 ticks and, therefore, the total futures profit for X-factor plc = 45 ticks $\times$ £12.50 $\times$ 2 contracts = £1,125.

Hence, although X-factor plc has an additional interest cost of £1,250, this is largely offset by the profit on the futures contracts of £1,125.

A centuries-old concept, futures trading has kept pace with the times

Since the dawn of commerce, merchants have used forward contracts to secure supplies and alleviate the risks inherent in trading. The terms of such contracts were usually individually negotiated to suit the needs of each trader, stipulating the delivery date of a fixed quantity of grain, rice or any other asset, for a fixed price.

Today, futures contracts have standard terms, which usually specify quantity [lot size], quality, contract expiration months, delivery dates and terms. These modern derivatives contracts allow market participants to trade at a fraction of the cost of the underlying asset, and have been essential for the massive growth of today's global commodity markets.

The exact origins of futures trading remain unclear, but the Dojima Rice Exchange in Osaka, Japan, which was formed in 1650, had by 1730 developed many of the key elements that a modern trader would recognise. The contracts traded were standardised rice bills, with contractual definitions for product quality as well as delivery time and location. They were traded on a central floor and the exchange provided the mechanism for determining official settlement prices.

More than a century later in the US, the Chicago Board of Trade [CBOT] was formed. It allowed its members to buy and sell grain for cash, but also facilitated the growing popularity

Continued

of forward contracts, known as 'to arrive' contracts. These allowed dealers to agree terms before the goods arrived, and led the CBOT to list a new type of standardised 'futures' contract in 1865, the first time the term had been used.

Traditionally, futures contracts were traded in a system called 'open outcry', in a designated 'pit', so that traders could use hand signals or shout orders to each other across a trading floor. However, since the late 1990s, futures markets have become increasingly dominated by electronic trading, and many pits have closed.

As well as shifting away from open outcry, the types of commodities traded have changed. Agricultural commodities dominated commodity futures trading for much of the 20th century, but energy commodity futures have become increasingly important since the West Texas Intermediate [WTI] crude-oil contract started trading on the New York Mercantile Exchange (Nymex) in the early 1970s.

Futures markets for gasoline [petrol], heating oil and distillates, such as diesel and jet fuel, have also developed since the 1970s.

In the market for base metals such as copper and aluminium, the global trading centre remains the London Metal Exchange [LME], which provides reference prices for producers and consumers around the world. From its beginnings in the Jerusalem Coffee House in the 19th century, it has expanded to become one of the great financial exchanges of the world, and last year it traded 111.9 million lots with a notional value of $7,410 billion.

Product innovations such as exchange traded funds have helped draw in new investors. Looking forward, steel futures trading is still in its infancy, and carbon credits are expected to make an increasingly substantial contribution to growth in energy futures trading as environmental regulations become stricter.

Source: Based on Chris Flood, *Financial Times*, 17 August 2010.

Self-assessment activity 13.5

Define in your own words the main forms of derivatives – forwards, futures, swaps and options.

(Answer in Appendix A at the back of the book)

13.7 RISK MANAGEMENT

The treasury function is predominantly concerned with the management of financial risks. However, it is important to recognise that companies have to manage all types of risk regardless of whether they are financial or non-financial risks. Alternative systems are available for classifying risks and Figure 13.4 provides one such example. This classification system suggests that, in addition to financial risks, there are three other fundamental drivers of risk: infrastructure risks, marketplace risks and reputational risks. In the wake of the problems stemming from the global credit crisis of 2008, even greater emphasis has been placed upon risk management, and this is reflected in the updated Corporate Governance Code published in the UK by the FRC (**www.frc.org .uk**). The Code now clearly specifies that 'the board (of directors) is responsible for determining the nature and extent of the significant risks it is willing to take in achieving its strategic objectives (and) should maintain sound risk management and internal control systems' (section C.2).

There are different ways that directors can approach risk management and each organisation must develop its own risk management systems, but, in essence, they all involve a similar process. For example, the international standard, ISO 31000 (Risk management – principles and guidelines, 2009), gives guidance on the implementation of risk management systems and how to ensure their effectiveness (**www.iso.org**). Typically, the risk management process is as summarised in Figure 13.5.

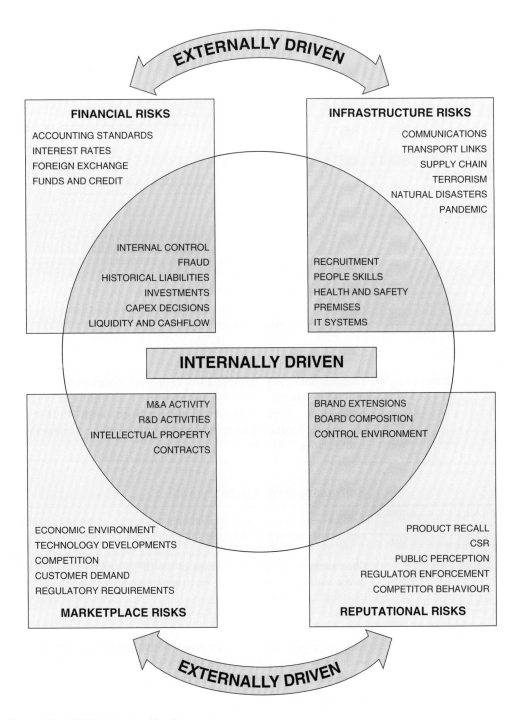

Figure 13.4 FIRM risk classification system

Source: From Airmic/Alarm/IRM (2010).

Potentially, a company can be exposed to a highly diverse range of risks and the first step in the risk management process is to *identify* all risks that a company may be subject to. To identify the risks to which they may be exposed, organisations must draw upon the knowledge of line managers. These line managers should

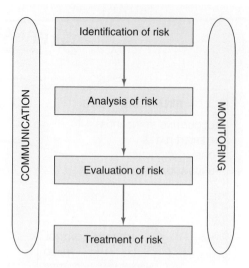

Figure 13.5 The risk management process

Source: Adapted from Airmic/Alarm/IRM/British Standards Institution (2010).

know what types of risks they face and, ultimately, they will be responsible for managing them. Risks can be identified in different ways, for example through workshops or questionnaires, and to begin with the list of risks may be rather imprecise. A process of refinement can take place during the next stages of the risk management process.

Self-assessment activity 13.6

Companies often state that reputational risk is one of the greatest threats that they face. Very high profile cases that illustrate the hugely harmful effect that reputational events can have upon a company's reputation include Perrier water, Ribena juice drink and Firestone Tyres. Read some of the press coverage of the BP oil spillage in the Gulf of Mexico in April 2010 (**www.guardian.co.uk**). How much reputational damage has BP suffered as a result of this incident?

(Answer in Appendix A at the back of the book)

The *analysis* and *evaluation* stages of the process initially require the company clearly to describe each risk that has been identified. An organisation may choose to create a register of risks which lists information on each individual risk such as:

- name of risk
- nature of risk
- likelihood of the risk occurring
- potential consequences if the risk occurs
- person responsible for managing the risk
- how the risk shall be monitored
- controls relevant to the risk.

reputation risk
Companies now cite reputation risk as one of the greatest threats

Because a company is subject to a potentially large number of risks, then it needs to focus its attention on the key (i.e. major) risks (for example, **reputation risk**). For example, Table 13.2 lists some of the key risks that The Coca-Cola Company has stated

Table 13.2 Examples of risk factors for The Coca-Cola Company

- Obesity concerns may reduce demand for some of our products.
- Water scarcity and poor quality could negatively impact the Coca-Cola system's production costs and capacity.
- If we do not anticipate and address evolving consumer preferences, our business could suffer.
- Increased competition and capabilities in the marketplace could hurt our business.
- Product safety and quality concerns, including concerns related to perceived artificiality of ingredients, could negatively affect our business.
- Increased demand for food products and decreased agricultural productivity may negatively affect our business.
- Changes in the retail landscape or the loss of key retail or foodservice customers could adversely affect our financial performance.
- If we are unable to expand our operations in emerging and developing markets, our growth rate could be negatively affected.
- We rely on our bottling partners for a significant portion of our business. If we are unable to maintain good relationships with our bottling partners, our business could suffer.
- Increase in the cost, disruption of supply or shortage of energy or fuels could affect our profitability.
- Significant additional labeling or warning requirements or limitations on the availability of our products may inhibit sales of affected products.

Source: The Coca-Cola Company Form 10-K (2013).

as being most significant for its business. To identify the key risks, two aspects of each risk must be estimated:

1 How likely is it that the risk will occur?
2 What is the possible consequence if the identified risk event did occur?

A common approach to the estimation of risks is to create a two-dimensional matrix (as below) and with each risk being allocated to one of the nine boxes:

		Possible consequence		
		High (3)	**Medium (2)**	**Low (1)**
Likelihood of occurrence	**High (3)**			
	Medium (2)			
	Low (1)			

To complete the matrix, the organisation needs to provide definitions that managers can use to evaluate each risk. For example, they may provide definitions as follows:

Likelihood of occurrence

High	Strong potential for the risk to occur in next period
Medium	Possible that the risk will occur in next period
Low	Unlikely the risk will occur in next period

Possible consequence	
High	Significant impact upon the organisation
Medium	Moderate impact upon the organisation
Low	Low impact upon the organisation

The risks of most concern are, of course, those where both the likelihood of occurring and the possible consequence is high. These risks will be placed in the top left-hand box of the matrix and an overall risk score of 9 can be assigned to these risks. This score is calculated by multiplying the possible consequence value of 3 (high) with the likelihood of occurrence value of 3 (high). If all risks are assigned an overall risk score following this method, then the company can rank its risks in order of overall risk score and, hence, it can determine the significance of each risk.

Once the most important risks are known, then the decision can be made as to whether existing controls are adequate to manage the risk, or if additional actions need to be taken to further mitigate or modify the risk. In making decisions about the *treatment* of a risk, organisations often refer to the '4Ts'. That is, there are four main options in respect of the treatment of a risk:

- Tolerate (i.e. accept) the risk.
- Transfer (i.e. remove) the risk through some appropriate measure such as insurance or using an appropriate hedging method.
- Treat (i.e. manage) the risk by introducing appropriate internal controls.
- Terminate (i.e. seek to eliminate) the risk.

Self-assessment activity 13.7

Companies are required to disclose their principal risks and uncertainties within the annual report. Download the annual report for BT (**www.btplc.com**). What are the major risks the company faces?

(Answer in Appendix A at the back of the book)

Risk management has evolved considerably in the past 15 to 20 years and is now considered an important aspect of the effective management of an organisation. One aspect of the evolution of risk management has been the recognition that risk management is not a static process. The company needs continually to *monitor* its risks. Risks change over time and new risks can arise very quickly. A further aspect is that it is now accepted that risk management cannot be viewed wholly as a negative, as it must also incorporate the management of opportunities alongside potential threats. Understanding that risk must be accepted as a normal part of business, and has a positive as well as a negative aspect, has led to the development of the interconnected ideas of risk appetite and enterprise risk management (ERM). ERM advocates suggest that firms need to understand that risk is best managed on a holistic basis across the entire organisation. This implies that any company needs to understand how risks in different business divisions may interact and correlate, as only then can risks be managed in a consistent and co-ordinated manner. To ensure that the management of risk across the enterprise is aligned with the company's strategy, the directors need to determine the risk appetite for the firm. Risk appetite refers to the overall maximum level of risk that the board of directors considers acceptable for the company. Determining the risk appetite for a company is not straightforward, as illustrated by HSBC's explanation of its risk appetite framework in Table 13.3.

Table 13.3 HSBC risk appetite

Risk appetite is a key component of our management of risk. The Board, advised by the GRC (Group Risk Committee), approves the Group's risk appetite, which describes the types and levels of risk that the Group is prepared to accept in executing our strategy and which is set out in the Group's Risk Appetite Statement. Embedding risk appetite statements and the related monitoring and reporting framework across the Group has continued to be an area of significant focus in 2013 with initiatives undertaken to:

- further enhance the Global risk appetite framework for consistent adoption by all regions and global businesses within the Group; and
- complete a formal triennial review and assessment that HSBC's risk appetite framework remains fit for purpose, is in line with best practice and adheres to the highest standards.

Our risk appetite framework is underpinned by the core characteristics listed below. These core characteristics are applied to define the risk appetite statements on Group-wide, global business and regional levels. The relevant strategic and operational objectives, within which we expect businesses and regions to operate, are expressed quantitatively across the following dimensions:

Risk appetite: core characteristics

- Risk must be commensurate with sustainable returns
- Strong balance sheet
- Healthy capital position
- Conservative liquidity management
- Strong brand
- Robust Group structure of separate legal entities
- The global businesses should produce sustainable long-term earnings growth
- Risk diversification

Source: HSBC Annual Report (2013).

The rise of the risk manager

It is now common for a range of organisations and consultants to compile lists of the most significant risks that companies face. The Allianz Risk Barometer is one such list and the top ten risks for 2014 are listed in Table 13.4. Inevitably the different league tables of risks differ from one another and there are continual debates as to which risks are most important. Additionally, there are discussions as to whether a risk such as loss of reputation (number 6 in the Allianz ranking) is an independent risk or whether it is a risk that occurs as a result of other risks. For example, banks that had to be bailed out by governments as a result of liquidity risks during the financial crisis then found that this adversely impacted on their reputations.

The World Economic Forum's 2014 Global Risk Report (**www.weforum.org**) notes that we have to understand that risks are now globally connected and it examines risks from this perspective. Therefore, it is understandable that key risks it cites are fiscal crises affecting economies, failure of a major financial mechanism or institution, extreme weather events and political instability. These reports that take a broader view of risk are useful to companies as they can assist the directors in seeing a 'bigger picture' and this helps the directors to see broader risks that might have some impact on the company's operations. The World Economic Forum risks are grouped into different categories: economic, geo-political, technological, societal and environmental risks. The financial crisis continues to be a theme in the risk discussions with the report emphasising that many governments still have high debt levels and fragile economies, and there remains a danger of financial crisis. Future crises could impact on the solvency of banks and, hence, have severe direct and indirect impacts on companies.

Because of the emphasis that is now being placed on understanding and managing risks in companies, there have been discussions regarding how risk management and corporate governance need to be connected. Hence, risk governance has become a key concept and is concerned with highlighting the responsibility that directors have for establishing robust and effective risk management systems, and for defining the risk appetite of the organisation. This

Continued

has resulted in other risk-related concerns arising. For example, many companies now look to understand their risk culture: namely, they are wanting to understand what attitudes to risk exist within the company and how these might affect its ability to manage risk effectively.

Table 13.4 Top ten business risks 2014: Allianz

	2014		2013 Rank	Trend
	1 Business interruption, supply chain risk	43%	46% (1)	—
	2 Natural catastrophes (for example, storm, flood, quake)	33%	44% (2)	—
	3 Fire, explosion	24%	31% (3)	—
	4 Changes in legislation and regulation	21%	17% (4)	—
	5 Market stagnation or decline	19%	12% (8)	↗
	6 Loss of reputation or brand value (for example, from social media)	15%	10% (10)	↗
	7 Intensified competition	14%	17% (5)	↘
	8 Cyber crime, IT failures, espionage	12%	(-) (-) ● NEW	
	9 Theft, fraud, corruption	10%	(-) (-) ● NEW	
	10 Quality deficiencies, serial defects	10%	13% (6)	↘

The third annual Allianz Risk Barometer survey was conducted among risk consultants, underwriters, senior managers and claims experts in the corporate insurance segment of both Allianz Global Corporate & Specialty (AGCS) and local Allianz entities. Figures represent the number of responses as a percentage of all survey responses (557)

Allianz ⑪

Source: Allianz (www.agcs.allianz.com)

SUMMARY

Treasury management is central to corporate finance in practice. Even in smaller businesses, where no formalised treasury function exists, the main treasury activities of managing corporate funding, risk, banking relationships, liquidity and working capital will still be conducted. This chapter has introduced the reader to those treasury activities, but most of them receive extensive treatment in subsequent chapters.

Key points

- Treasury management is the efficient management of liquidity and financial risk in the business.

- Each company should establish whether it requires a separate treasury function and whether it should be a cost or profit centre.

- Clear treasury policies are required for funding, banking relationships, risk management and working capital management.

- In general, long-term finance should be used to fund both fixed assets and permanent current assets, fluctuating current assets being funded by short-term borrowing.

- Hedging can take various forms, but derivative instruments, such as futures, forward contracts, options and swaps, are the most common.

- Risk management processes and systems seek to manage all risks in a company. The major difficulty is that risks continually change.

Further reading

Treasury management is a highly practical topic and books such as Bragg (2010) cover a wide range of treasury management issues, whilst texts such as Taylor (2010) give a sound explanation of the instruments available for hedging risk in the derivative markets.

Risk management books have proliferated in recent years. It should be borne in mind that risk management in non-financial companies differs from risk management in financial companies in many respects. Lam (2014) provides a guide to Enterprise Risk Management relevant to non-financial companies, whilst Saunders and Cornett (2013) cover risk management in the context of financial institutions. For an interesting, and alternative, discussion of the rise of risk management see Power (2007).

Useful websites

Websites that provide risk management information, as well as links to further risk-related topics, include the Association of Insurance and Risk Managers (**www.airmic.com**), the Institute of Risk Managers (**www.theirm.org**) and the Federation of European Risk Management Associations (**www.ferma.eu**). It is also important to note that, although risk management has developed significantly, there are differing views as to why it has become so prominent and whether it really is wholly beneficial.

QUESTIONS

1 Atlas Ltd is a newly formed digital media company with a number of locations in the UK, France and Germany. The board of directors is currently discussing whether the finance function should be centralised or decentralised. What advice would you offer?

2 What are the risks that a manufacturing company might encounter as a result of interest rate movements? Describe two financial instruments the company could use to reduce such risks.

3 ABC plc is a UK-based service company with a number of wholly owned subsidiaries and interests in associated companies throughout the world. In response to the rapid growth in the company, the Managing Director has ordered a review of the company's organisation structure, particularly the finance function. The Managing Director holds the opinion that a separate treasury department should be established. At present, treasury functions are the responsibility of the chief accountant.

Required
(a) Describe the main responsibilities of a treasury department in a company such as ABC plc and explain the benefits that might accrue from the establishment of a separate treasury function.
(b) Describe the advantages and disadvantages which might arise if the company established a separate treasury department as a profit centre rather than a cost centre.

(CIMA, November 1995)

Practical assignment

Look at the annual reports of two companies in the same industry. What do they say about the treasury function and treasury or risk management policies? How do the two companies differ and what might be the implications of such differences in treasury management?

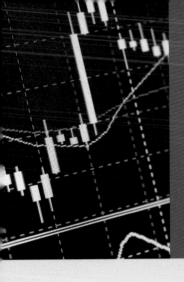

14

Working capital and short-term asset management

Invoice payments

Cheques, coins and cowrie shells have been in the post since time immemorial. Now the UK business secretary, Vince Cable, wants to fine companies that fail to pay suppliers quickly. What it does underline is how important and neglected working capital is to understanding the operation of companies.

Working capital is short-term assets tied up in running a business. It is current assets minus current liabilities. Lots of working capital sloshing around was once considered a good thing, representing a healthy balance sheet. Nowadays, however, treasurers try to keep as little working capital as possible. Why? Because more working capital equals less free cash flow. The three big components of working capital are accounts receivable (money owed to a company by customers), accounts payable (money a company owes suppliers) and inventories.

Thus in order to lower working capital and to raise cash flows, companies want as few inventories lying about as possible, and they want to pay their bills late while collecting their dues quickly. In large organisations, whole departments are devoted to this task. Investors, while sympathetic to the cause of small suppliers, should take note because the numbers can be significant. A third of the increase in Amazon's $4.1bn of operating cash flow last year, for example, was payables rising faster than receivables. But how often do changes in working capital make the business headlines?

Ultimately, though, the whole topic of working capital is a timing issue. Mostly, money is eventually paid and received. If a small business sends out invoices daily, in 30 or 60 days cheques will start arriving in the post every day.

Source: Based on Lex Column, *Financial Times*, 13 August 2013, p. 10.

Learning objectives

Having read this chapter, you should have a good appreciation of working capital policy and the importance of short-term asset management in corporate finance and of the basic control methods involved. Specific attention will be paid to the following:

- Working capital policies.
- The cash operating cycle and overtrading problems.
- Managing trade credit.
- Inventory management.
- Cash management.

14.1 INTRODUCTION

It is a common mistake to assume that financial management concerns only long-term financial decisions, such as capital investment, capital structure and dividend policy decisions. In reality, much of financial management addresses issues of shorter duration, such as short-term financing and working capital management. PwC claims in its 2013 Global Working Capital Review of 15,763 publicly-listed companies that 'if all companies achieved close to the best performance in their sector, a staggering €3.7 trillion of excess working capital could be released worldwide, averaging out at 10–12% of company turnover.' In this chapter, we provide an overview of working capital management and how short-term assets, such as debtors, inventory and cash, can be managed to maximise shareholder wealth.

14.2 WORKING CAPITAL MANAGEMENT

Let us first clarify the basic terms and ratios employed in working capital management.

net working capital
Current assets less current liabilities

Net working capital (or simply working capital) refers to current assets less current liabilities – hence its alternative name of net current assets. Current assets include cash, marketable securities, debtors and stock. Current liabilities are obligations that are expected to be repaid within the year.

Working capital management refers to the financing, investment and control of net current assets within policy guidelines. The finance manager acts as a steward of corporate resources and needs to devise and operate clear and effective working capital policies.

liquidity management
Planning the acquisition and utilisation of cash, i.e. cash flow management

Liquidity management is the planned acquisition and utilisation of cash – or near cash – resources to ensure that the company is in a position to meet its cash obligations as they fall due. It requires close attention to cash forecasting and planning. If the wheels of business are oiled by cash flow, the cash forecast, or cash budget, gauges how much 'oil' is left in the can at any time. Any predicted cash shortfall may require the raising of additional finance, disposal of fixed assets or tighter control over working capital requirements in order to avoid a liquidity crisis.

Various ratios are useful in assessing corporate liquidity, the following being the most commonly employed:

current ratio
Current assets divided by current liabilities

1 The **current ratio** is the ratio of current assets to current liabilities. A high ratio (relative to the industry) would suggest that the firm is in a relatively liquid position. However, if the current assets are largely in the form of raw materials and finished stocks, this may not be the case.

quick/'acid test' ratio
Current assets minus stocks, divided by current liabilities

2 The **quick** or **'acid test'** ratio recognises that stocks may take many weeks to realise in cash terms. Accordingly, it is computed by dividing current liabilities into current assets excluding stock.

Example: The Generally Eccentric Company (GEC)

The working capital of GEC is as follows:

	£m
Current assets	
Stocks and contracts in progress	1,195
Debtors	1,572
Investments	400
Cash at bank and in hand	1,009
	4,176
Less creditors due within one year	(2,037)
Net current assets	2,139

Notice that current assets are ranked in descending order of liquidity. The liquidity ratios for GEC and the industry are:

		GEC	Industry average
Current ratio	(4,176/2,037)	2.05	1.6
Acid test	(4,176 − 1,195)/2,037	1.46	1.2

GEC's current and acid test ratios are both higher than the industry averages, reflecting the company's healthy liquidity position. But what would the position look like if the £1 billion of cash were already committed, say, for major capital expenditure? If you recalculate the current and acid test ratios, you will find that the liquidity position then falls below the industry average.

days cash-on-hand ratio
Cash and marketable securities divided by daily cash operating expenses

3 **Days cash-on-hand ratio** is found by dividing the cash and marketable securities by projected daily cash operating expenses. As its name implies, it indicates the number of days for which the firm could meet its cash obligations, assuming that no further cash is received during the period. Daily cash operating expenses should be based on the projected cash flows from the cash budget, but a somewhat cruder approach is to divide the annual cost of sales, plus selling, administrative and financing costs, by 365.

14.3 PREDICTING CORPORATE FAILURE

Excessive levels of gearing are often responsible for corporate failure. However, very highly geared companies do survive and, conversely, some low-geared companies fail. This suggests that there are many other clues to the viability of a company, and it is not enough simply to examine a single balance sheet ratio when attempting to predict financial failure.

Z-score
A mathematically derived critical value below which firms are associated with failure

The **Z-score** method, developed by Altman (1968), attempts to balance out the relative importance of different financial indicators. This was based on examining the financial characteristics of two samples of failed and surviving US companies to detect which ratios were most important in discriminating between the two groups. For example, were past failures characterised by low liquidity ratios? What other ratios were important discriminators, and what was their relative importance?

Using a technique called discriminant analysis, the relative significance of each critical ratio can be expressed in an equation that generates a 'Z-score', a critical value below which failed firms typically fall, and above which survivors are located. In general terms, the equation is:

$$Z = a + bR_1 + cR_2$$

In this equation, a, b and c are constants derived from past observations and R_1 and R_2 are two identified key discriminatory ratios.

A Z-score model using data for UK firms was developed by Marais (1982), an extension of which is currently used by the Datastream database. For Datastream, Marais examined over 40 ratios before settling on four critical ones in his final model:

1 Profitability: $\dfrac{\text{Pre-tax profit } + \text{ depreciation}}{\text{Current liabilities}}$

2 Liquidity: $\dfrac{\text{Current assets less stocks}}{\text{Current liabilities}}$

3 Gearing:
$$\frac{\text{All borrowing}}{\text{Total capital employed less intangibles}}$$

4 Stock Turnover: $\dfrac{\text{Stock}}{\text{Sales}}$

Other analysts, using different samples of firms, employ different ratios and weightings in the equation for Z. In Marais' model, the critical Z-value is zero. This does not prove that an existing company displaying a Z-score of around zero is on the brink of insolvency, merely that the firm is displaying characteristics similar to previous failures. Given that there are accounting policy differences between companies, it may be more useful to look at changes in the Z-score over time. A declining Z-score suggests a worsening financial condition, while an improving Z-score indicates strong corporate financial management.

Corporate failure models, such as Z-scores, have their weaknesses (e.g. see Grice and Ingram, 2001):

(a) 'Failure' is difficult to define. Usually, its definition is wider than liquidation, but all sorts of restructuring and rescue operations arise for a variety of reasons.
(b) All models are based on the past, when macroeconomic conditions were different from the present.
(c) Companies employ different accounting policies, making comparison difficult.

Z-scoring is used primarily for credit risk assessment by banks and other financial institutions, industrial companies and credit insurers. While it does not tell the whole story behind the company's prospects, it is widely regarded as an important indicator of a company's financial health and hence its credit status.

Study warns of threat to shipping container groups

Listed shipping container companies face a greater risk of financial distress than at any time since 2010, a new report warns. The study draws on an index of 15 listed shipping companies within the container shipping industry. It suggests that average EBITDA interest cover – which divides EBITDA by interest payments to show how much of a company's earnings are needed to service its debt – fell to 4.9 in the 12 months to the end of September 2013, its lowest level since 2007.

The study, by consultant AlixPartners, also draws on the Altman Z-score, an academic measure used to forecast

bankruptcy. Over the 12 months to the end of September, this measure was on average 1.22 – lower than since the start of the financial crisis.

Esben Christensen, an author of the report, suggested a sluggish economic recovery had affected the rates paid by customers to container shipping groups. 'For the first time, we've seen sustained depression of rates. Larger carriers have accelerated the construction of bigger vessels to get economies of scale.'

Source: Based on Thomas Hale, *Financial Times*, 25 March 2014, p. 14.

14.4 CASH OPERATING CYCLE

For a typical manufacturing firm, there are three primary activities affecting working capital: purchasing materials, manufacturing the product and selling the product. Because these activities are subject to uncertainty (delivery of materials may come late, manufacturing problems may arise, sales may become sluggish, etc.), the cash flows associated with them are also uncertain. If a firm is to maintain liquidity, it needs to invest funds in working capital, and to ensure that the operating cycle is properly controlled.

cash operating cycle
Length of time between cash payment to suppliers and cash received from customers

The **cash operating cycle** is the length of time between the firm's cash payment for purchases of material and labour, and cash receipts from the sale of goods. In other words, it is the length of time the firm has funds tied up in working capital. This is calculated as follows:

Cash operating cycle = stock period + customer credit period − supplier credit period.

The cash operating cycle: Briggs plc

Briggs plc, a manufacturer of novelty toys, has the following working capital items in its balance sheet at the start and end of its financial year:

	1 January	31 December
Stock	£5,500	£6,500
Debtors	£3,200	£4,800
Creditors	£3,000	£4,500

Turnover for the year, all on credit, is £50,000 and cost of sales is £30,000. For how many days is working capital tied up in each item? What is the cash operating cycle period?

Our first task is to calculate the turnover ratios for each:

$$\text{Stock turnover} = \frac{\text{Cost of sales}}{\text{Average stock}} = \frac{£30,000}{£6,000} = 5 \text{ times p.a.}$$

$$\text{Debtors' turnover} = \frac{\text{Sales}}{\text{Average debtors}} = \frac{£50,000}{£4,000} = 12.5 \text{ times p.a.}$$

$$\text{Creditors' turnover} = \frac{\text{Cost of sales}}{\text{Average creditors}} = \frac{£30,000}{£3,750} = 8 \text{ times p.a.}$$

To find the number of days each item is held in working capital, we divide the turnover calculations into 365 days:

Stock period = 365/5 = 73 days

Debtors' (customer credit) period = 365/12.5 = 29.2 days

Creditors' (supplier credit) period = 365/8 = 45.6 days

The cash operating cycle is therefore:

$(73 + 29.2 − 45.6) = 56.6$ days

This is illustrated in Figure 14.1.

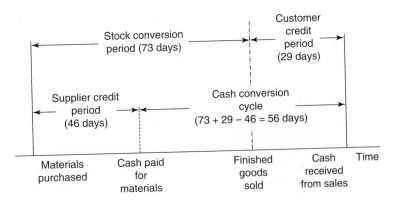

Figure 14.1 Cash conversion cycle

Self-assessment activity 14.1

Explain why two firms in the same industry could have very different cash operating cycles. What are the financial implications?

(Answer in Appendix A at the back of the book)

Groups losing ground on cash handling

Europe's largest companies wasted almost €800bn last year as a result of inefficient cash management, research suggests. A study of the 1,000 biggest listed European groups by sales suggests that they relaxed their efforts to improve their internal cash position as soon as they saw an uptick in sales.

REL, the working capital consultancy that carried out the research, says that the best-performing European companies have only about half as much working capital tied up in their operations as those with median performance. The gap between the upper quartile performance and the median was most marked when it came to stock levels: the best performers had only 12.7 days worth of inventory on-hand, compared with 38.6 days for the median.

Gavin Swindell, managing director of REL, says: 'Businesses are not set up to manage cash, but to manage profit. Because the focus is on revenues and costs, cash is not as well-managed – and can tend to get lost in the mix.'

He says that, at the beginning of the financial crisis, though companies were keen to chase customers and took longer to pay suppliers, their working capital position still suffered because they were caught with stock that was not selling as well as they had expected. During the following couple of years, the inventory position improved, and so companies benefited from more efficient working capital performance. But he says that better performance is now at risk of being lost, with only a small improvement in 2011 against 2010.

While the 1,000 companies collectively are managing their cash better than they were doing before the financial crunch, the gap between the strongest performers and the rest is widening. The study shows that only 99 companies – less than 10 per cent of those covered in the survey – were able to sustain an improvement in working capital over three years. During a five-year period, only one per cent of companies maintained or improved their cash management.

Even among those companies, none managed to improve all three elements of working capital performance – taking longer to pay suppliers; getting paid more quickly by customers; and not having too much cash tied up in stock – each year.

Source: Based on Alison Smith, *Financial Times*, 25 June 2012, p. 18.

14.5 WORKING CAPITAL POLICY

The finance manager should ensure that the firm operates sound working capital policies. These policies cover such areas as the levels of cash and stock held, and the credit terms granted to customers and agreed with suppliers. Successful implementation of these policies influences the company's expected future returns and associated risk, which, in turn, influence shareholder value.

Failure to adopt sound working capital policies may jeopardise long-term growth and even corporate survival. For example:

1 Failure to invest in working capital to expand production and sales may result in lost orders and profits.
2 Failure to maintain current assets that can quickly be turned into cash can affect corporate liquidity, damage the firm's credit rating and increase borrowing costs.
3 Poor control over working capital is a major reason for overtrading problems, discussed later in this chapter.

Typical questions arising in the working capital management field include the following:

■ What should be the firm's total level of investment in current assets?
■ What should be the level of investment for each type of current asset?
■ How should working capital be financed?

We now consider how firms establish and finance the levels of working capital appropriate for their businesses, and how they impact on profitability and risk. The level and nature of working capital within any organisation depend on a variety of factors, such as the following:

- The industry within which the firm operates.
- The type of products sold.
- Whether products are manufactured or bought in.
- Level of sales.
- Stock and credit policies.
- The efficiency with which working capital is managed.

We saw in Chapter 1 that the relationship between risk and the required financial return is central to financial management. Investment in working capital is no exception. In establishing the planned level of working capital investment, management should assess the level of liquidity risk it is prepared to accept, risk in the sense of the possibility that the firm will not be able to meet its financial obligations as they fall due. This is a further dimension of financial risk.

Working capital strategies: Helsinki plc

Helsinki plc, a dairy produce distributor, is considering which working capital policy it should adopt.

Figure 14.2 shows the two working capital strategies under consideration. Notice that both schedules are curvilinear, suggesting that economies of scale permit working capital to grow more slowly than sales. The firm operates with lower levels of stock, debtors and cash under a more *aggressive* approach than under a more relaxed strategy.

Figure 14.2 Helsinki plc working capital strategies

A *relaxed*, lower risk and more flexible policy for working capital means maintaining a larger cash balance and investment in marketable securities that can quickly be turned into cash, granting more generous customer credit terms and investing more heavily in stock. This may attract more custom, but will usually lead to a reduction in profitability for the business, given the high cost of tying up capital in relatively low profit-generating assets. Conversely, an aggressive policy should increase profitability, while increasing the risk of failing to meet the firm's financial obligations.

In Table 14.1, the relaxed working capital strategy involves a further £20 million investment in current assets. The additional stocks and more generous credit facilities enable Helsinki's management to attain an additional £5 million sales over the aggressive policy. This gives a 19.5 per cent return on capital employed and a secure current ratio of 2.7.

Table 14.1 Helsinki plc: profitability and risk of working capital strategies

	Relaxed (£m)	Aggressive (£m)
Current assets (CA)	40	20
Fixed assets	25	25
Total assets	65	45
Current liabilities (CL)	(15)	(15)
Capital employed (net assets)	50	30
Planned sales	65	60
Planned profit (15% of sales)	9.75	9.0
Return on capital employed	19.5%	30.0%
Net working capital (CA − CL)	£25m	£5m
Current ratio (CA/CL)	2.7	1.3

A more aggressive working capital strategy is likely to improve the return on capital. In Helsinki's case, the rate increases to 30 per cent. But this is achieved by increasing liquidity risk. Net working capital falls to only £5 million and the current ratio to 1.3.

■ Working capital costs

carrying costs
Stock costs that increase with the size of stock investment

shortage costs
Stock costs that reduce with size of stock investment

Managing working capital involves a trade-off not only between risk and required return, but also between those costs that increase and those costs that fall with the level of investment. Costs that increase with additional investment are termed **carrying costs**, while costs that fall with increases in investment are termed **shortage costs**. These two types of cost may be found in most forms of current assets, but particularly in stocks and cash.

The main form of carrying costs is opportunity costs associated with the cost of financing the investment.

■ Financing costs: Bedford Auto-Vending Machine Company

The Bedford Auto-Vending Machine Company is considering how much to invest in current assets. Two working capital policies are under investigation.

	Relaxed policy (£m)	Aggressive policy (£m)
Stock	32	25
Debtors	28	22
Cash and marketable securities	12	–
	72	47

It will be seen that the relaxed policy requires a further £25 million investment in working capital over and above that required for the aggressive policy. What is the cost of carrying this £25 million additional working capital? The main carrying cost is the return that could be earned by investing the additional £25 million in financial assets outside the business. If these could generate 10 per cent p.a., the additional earnings would be £2.5 million (less any interest earned on short-term cash and securities). Other carrying costs include the additional storage and handling costs for stock.

Aggressive or restrictive working capital policies are more susceptible to incurring shortage costs. These costs are usually of two types:

1 **Ordering costs** – costs incurred in placing orders for stock, cash, etc. (in the case of stocks, this may also include the production setup costs). Operating a restrictive policy means ordering stock more regularly and in smaller amounts than for more relaxed policies.
2 **Costs of running out of stock or cash** – the most obvious costs here are the loss of business and even the possible liquidation of the firm. Less tangible costs are the loss of customer goodwill, the disruption to the production schedule, and the time and cost of negotiating alternative sources of finance.

The trade-off between carrying costs and shortage costs is shown in Figures 14.3 and 14.4. In Figure 14.3, carrying costs are seen to increase steadily as current assets grow. Conversely, shortage costs fall with the level of investment in current assets. The cost of holding current assets is the combined cost of the two, *the minimum point being the optimal amount of current assets held*. For simplicity, we have shown current assets in total. Later, we consider each element, such as cash or stock, separately.

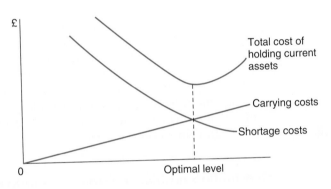

Figure 14.3 **Optimal level of working capital for a 'relaxed' strategy**

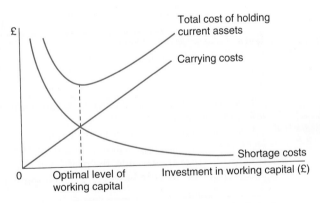

Figure 14.4 **Optimal level of working capital for an 'aggressive' strategy**

Different businesses will be more sensitive to certain types of cost. An aggressive policy is more appropriate when carrying costs are high relative to shortage costs, as in Figure 14.4. For example, a major car manufacturer like Ford will not want to hold excessive quantities of raw material stocks, but will buy in materials and parts just before they are to be used in car production, reflecting the Just-in-Time philosophy. Often there will be penalty clauses for non-delivery of such materials to the manufacturer by agreed dates. A flexible policy tends to be more suited to low carrying costs relative to shortage costs.

14.6 OVERTRADING PROBLEMS

overtrading
Operating a business with an inappropriate capital base, usually trying to grow too fast with insufficient long-term capital

Here, we address the problems arising from operating a business with an inappropriate capital structure, a phenomenon known as **overtrading**.

Overtrading arises from at least three serious managerial mistakes:

1 *Initial under-capitalisation.* Many businesses experience overtrading problems from the very start because they never invested sufficient equity at the time of formation to finance the anticipated level of trading. Experience suggests that the early years of trading are often difficult years.

2 *Over-expansion.* When a business expands to such a degree that its capital base is insufficient to support the new level of activity, the business is overtrading or, to put it another way, under-capitalised. In many senses, the business looks healthy, in that the level of activity is growing and the business is profitable. But unless sufficient cash is generated to finance the anticipated increase in working capital and fixed investment, the business may encounter serious overtrading problems.

3 *Poor utilisation of working capital resources.* Even when a business has been adequately capitalised and is not over-expanding its activity, overtrading can still occur in several ways:

(a) Failure to achieve planned profit and cash flow levels may mean that debt capacity, originally intended for working capital needs, is used to replace lost earnings.

(b) Cost overruns on fixed capital projects and other unanticipated capital investment can swallow up finance intended for working capital needs.

(c) Similarly, strategic decisions, such as a major acquisition, can have adverse effects on working capital finance unless the capital basis is adequately enlarged.

(d) Higher dividends mean reduced profit retentions, often the major source of finance for working capital.

Overtrading problems: Growfast Publishers Ltd

Growfast Publishers Ltd distributes books worldwide. Its most recent accounts reveal:

	£000
Sales	280
Cost of sales (all variable)	(240)
Profit	40

Stock is two months' cost of sales. Trade creditors pay within one month, while debtors take three months to pay.

Growfast Publishers has recently gained exclusive rights to publish *Corporate Finance and Investment* in Mongolia and is confident that this will lead to a doubling in total sales. Because all costs are variable, the profit will also double, giving a healthy £80,000 profit.

Cash flow for the year, however, is less impressive:

	£000
Trading profit	80
Increase in stocks (240/6)	(40)
Increase in debtors (280/4)	(70)
Increase in creditors (240/12)	20
Net cash flow from operating activities	(10)
Taxation on trading profit (30%)	(24)
Consequence	(34)

The consequence of a doubling in sales and profits is actually a reduction in cash by £34,000. If the increased working capital is thought to be permanent, it should be funded by longer-term finance.

■ Consequences of, and remedies for, overtrading

The consequences of overtrading can be extremely serious and possibly fatal. As the pace of activity increases, working capital needs will also increase. Without the necessary capital structure and cash flow, serious liquidity problems will arise. Business life then becomes a matter of crisis management: finding the cash to meet the wage bill, the creditors' claims and the tax charges. Such myopic behaviour takes attention away from the business of creating wealth and will, ultimately, lead to a decline in competitiveness and profitability.

What can management do to remedy the cash flow problems caused by overtrading?

1 The most drastic step is to *reduce the level of business activity*. Profitable orders may be rejected due to insufficient capital to finance additional working capital needs. If the alternative is to accept the order and, in so doing, jeopardise the business by exceeding the overdraft limit, a slower rate of growth is the preferred course of action.

2 The most obvious remedy is to *increase the capital base*. Figure 14.2 showed that an aggressive strategy for financing working capital operates on a lower long-term capital base, thus making overtrading more likely. Movement towards a matching approach is perhaps called for, where permanent increases in current assets are matched by the injection of permanent capital, preferably in the form of equity or long-term loans, perhaps with a moratorium on repayments in the early years.

3 Finally, steps should be taken to maintain tight control over working capital. Constant review of the working capital policy and its cash flow implications can allow the firm to minimise the extra capital resources required to fund expansion.

Self-assessment activity 14.2

Define overtrading. How does it arise and what are its consequences?

(Answer in Appendix A at the back of the book)

The remainder of the chapter considers short-term asset management, with particular focus on managing trade credit, inventory and cash.

You can have too much of a good thing

The team behind database business more2 has the kind of problem that most entrepreneurs would be happy to be stuck with right now: more clients than it can readily service. Last year, revenue climbed 30 per cent to £5m at more2, whose clever consumer databases have proved a hit with retailers such as Links of London and White Stuff, where they are used to better understand and sell to customers.

'I am not moaning,' says Sanjay Patel, more2's commercial director. 'It is really nice to be in a business where you can really plan some big growth.' Success, however, can be a problem if you cannot afford to service an increase in sales. It is an issue with a name – 'overtrading' – and it is something many insolvency practitioners believe will spark a new wave of bankruptcies as the economy emerges from recession.

Growing fast has proved challenging for more2 because the business needs to employ more skilled database builders as demand rises – and these technicians are in short supply. As a result, more2 has had to turn to India and Eastern Europe to fill its vacancies – but in doing this, the company has been hit by the UK government's tightening of immigration rules. Its aim is to avoid taking on too many clients and thus putting itself in danger of running out of cash.

Source: Based on Jonathan Moules, *Financial Times*, 5 February 2011, p. 30.

14.7 MANAGING TRADE CREDIT

trade credit
Temporary financing extended by suppliers of goods and services pending the customer's settlement

Trade credit is both a source and a use of finance because it can be received (via trade creditors or payables) and offered (via trade debtors or receivables). We will concentrate on the extension of trade credit and its management, although many of the issues raised apply also to the receipt of trade credit (discussed further in Chapter 15 because it is a form of finance).

Debtors represent the currently unpaid element of credit sales. While the extension of credit is accepted practice in most industries, credit is essentially an unproductive asset (unless it generates additional business) which both ties up scarce financial resources and is exposed to the risk of default, particularly when the credit period taken by customers is lengthy. Effective management of debtors is therefore an essential element of sound financial management practice.

■ Why offer trade credit?

Approximately one-third of the assets of UK businesses is in the form of trade debt – money to be paid at some future time for goods or services already received. The benefits to the customer are obvious, but why should the seller incur financing and other costs in extending credit to selected customers?

1 *Investment and marketing.* Trade credit should be viewed as an investment forming part of the sales package, the payoff being profitable repeat business. Most companies would lose a significant proportion of their customer base to their competitors were they to demand cash on delivery. As with all investment, there are risks involved. Credit risk exists when the company offering credit is exposed to the possibility that the debt will not be paid on time or at all.

The decision to grant credit involves a trade-off between the credit risk and the reward from the profit margin. A common mistake is to assume that a credit sale is a 'one-off', ignoring potential repeat business. If a firm loses business from refusing a customer £1,000 credit, what is the effect? It is more than simply the lost profit margin of, say, 40 per cent, or £400, on the sale. The business from many new customers will grow in time and offer significant repeat business. Assuming they would have entered into a very long-term relationship and ordered £10,000 p.a., growing at 3 per cent a year, the present value of the lost business (given an 8 per cent discount rate) could exceed £80,000:

$$PV = \frac{£10,000 \times (1.03)}{0.08 - 0.03} \times 0.4 = £82,400$$

2 *Industry and competitive pressures.* It is difficult for firms to offer credit terms that are less generous than their competitors' offerings.
3 *Finance.* Certain types of firm have better access to capital markets and can raise finance more cheaply than others. This competitive advantage can be reflected in offering generous credit to customers who experience greater difficulties in raising finance.
4 *Efficiency.* Information asymmetry exists between buyer and seller. The buyer does not know whether the product delivered is of the quality ordered until it has been thoroughly inspected. The credit period therefore provides a valuable inspection and verification period. Many companies deliver to customers on a daily basis. Trade credit is therefore a convenient means for separating the delivery of goods from the payment of deliveries.

Customer credit mission and goals for Makebelieve Ltd

Mission: To maintain and protect a portfolio of high-quality accounts receivable and to develop sound credit policies and administer credit operations in a manner that increases sales, contributes to profits, aids customer loyalty and improves shareholder value.

Goals:

1 To restrict monthly debtors to 45 days.

2 To achieve agreed monthly cash collection targets.

3 To limit overdue debts to 30 per cent of sales.

4 To limit bad debts to 1 per cent of sales.

5 To resolve credit-related customer queries within 3 days.

6 To improve the relationship between the credit function and major customers through regular contact and visits.

7 To convert 20 per cent of existing customers to direct debit in the year.

The aims of trade credit management are the following:

- To safeguard the firm's investment in debtors.
- To maximise operational cash flows by assessing customer credit risks, agreeing appropriate terms and collecting payments in accordance with these terms.

An example of the trade credit goals for Makebelieve Ltd is shown above.

The level of debtors in a company will depend on its terms of sale, credit-screening, cash discounts offered and cash collection procedures.

Effective debtor control policy requires careful consideration of the following:

- Credit period.
- Credit standards.
- Cost of cash discounts.
- Collection policy.

Each of these are discussed in this section.

While the main responsibility for setting credit policy lies within financial management, other functions should be involved, particularly marketing. However, all too often, this collaboration is lacking. The credit management process is shown in Figure 14.5.

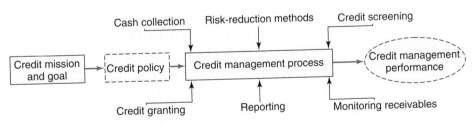

Figure 14.5 **The credit management process**

■ Credit period

The main factors influencing the period of credit granted to customers are:

1 *The normal terms of trade for the industry.* It is difficult to operate a trade credit policy where the period offered is considerably below the normal expectation for the

industry unless the company has another clear competitive advantage, such as a recognised better quality product.

2 *The importance of trade credit as a marketing tool.* Determining the optimum credit period requires the finance manager to identify the point where the costs of increased credit are matched by the profits made on the increased sales generated by the additional credit. The more vital the perception of credit as a marketing tool, the longer the likely period of credit offered.

3 *The individual credit ratings of customers.* Most firms operate regular credit terms for good-quality customers and specific credit terms for higher-risk customers.

credit limits

The maximum amount of credit that a firm is willing to extend to a customer

Credit limits should be set for each customer based on their creditworthiness. The firm should consider:

1 *Customer payment record*: is the customer a prompt payer?
2 *Financial signals*: is there evidence of the customer running up losses or having liquidity problems?

Very high-risk customers may be reviewed monthly and have to pay, in full or part, with order. Other customers may be granted credit on the basis of percentage of annual purchases.

Commonly-quoted trade credit terms

- **Cash before delivery (CBD)**
- **Cash on delivery (COD)**
- **Invoice terms** (e.g. 2/10, net 30). Payment terms offering a 2 per cent cash discount for payment within 10 days, otherwise the net amount is due after 30 days.
- **Consignment sales** – pay for goods when used or sold.
- **Periodic statement** – payment by a specific date for all invoices up to a cut-off date.
- **Seasonal dating** – payments due at specific dates to match the buyer's seasonal income.

■ Credit standards

We have noted that granting trade credit is partly a marketing exercise designed to increase sales. However, at the individual customer level, it is essentially a credit assessment and control exercise. In this sense, extending trade credit is no different from a bank granting a loan to a customer. The risk of granting trade credit can be seen when we consider the effect on profit of customer default. If a company sells a product for £1,000 with a 10 per cent net margin, which subsequently becomes a bad debt, the business must make ten similar sales to good customers simply to recover the £1,000 bad debt incurred.

Credit assessment should involve the following:

1 Prior experience with the particular customer. The credit extended and payment experiences in the past are useful guides, but it may relate to a time when the customer was not experiencing financial difficulty. Even so, it is wise to have more rigorous procedures for assessing new accounts.

2 Analysis of the customer's accounts and credit reports. Profit and loss accounts and balance sheets are available from the company's registered office, but can more easily be taken from computer databases. Credit reports include:

(a) Bank references

(b) Trade references expressing the views of other businesses trading with the customer

(c) Credit bureau reports. Credit-reporting agencies such as Dun & Bradstreet (www.dnb.co.uk) provide data and credit ratings that can be used in credit analysis. It is common practice for firms to offer credit agencies full disclosure of financial and trading information in order to gain a good rating. From an assessment of the customer's creditworthiness, it is possible to establish appropriate credit rules covering the terms of sale:

(i) the maximum period of credit granted;
(ii) the maximum amount of credit;
(iii) the payment terms, including any discounts for early payment and interest charges on overdue accounts.

The businesses most vulnerable to late payment are often those that do least to vet their customers. Many small firms fail to chase their late payers with any degree of urgency, partly because their credit management systems are not good enough to support such activity.

In evaluating customer creditworthiness, it is useful to remember the five Cs of credit: capacity, character, capital, collateral and conditions.

1 *Capacity* – does the customer have the capacity to repay the debt within the required period? This may require examination of the past payment record of the customer.
2 *Character* – will the customer make a serious effort to repay the debt in accordance with the terms agreed? Bank and trade references will be useful here.
3 *Capital* – what is the financial health of the customer? Is the firm profitable and liquid? Is it borrowing beyond its means? Financial accounts and credit agency reports will help here.
4 *Collateral* – should some form of security be required in return for extending credit facilities? Alternatively, should part payment in advance, or retention of title be specified?
5 *Conditions* – what are the normal terms for the industry? Are the firm's main competitors offering more generous terms?

■ Cash discounts

The longer a customer's account remains unpaid, the greater the risk that it will never be paid. But the cost of financing late payments is often greater than the cost of bad debts.

Cash discounts are financial inducements for customers to pay accounts promptly, but such discounts can be very costly.

Example: Yorko plc

Yorko plc offers terms of trade which are '2/10, net 30'. This means that a 2 per cent discount is offered for all accounts settled within 10 days, otherwise payment in full is to be made in 30 days. A 2 per cent discount may not seem much until one realises that it is given for a payment in advance of just 20 days (i.e. 30 – 10). The annualised cost is actually over 37 per cent, calculated by the formula below:

The cost of a discount

$$\text{Cost of cash discount} = \frac{\text{Discount \%}}{(100 - \text{discount \%})} \times \frac{365}{(\text{Final date} - \text{discount period})}$$

In the Yorko example, the annualised cost of forgoing the cash discount is:

$$\begin{aligned}
\text{Cost} &= \frac{2}{(100 - 2)} \times \frac{365}{(30 - 10)} \\
&= 0.0204 \times 18.25 \\
&= 37.23\%
\end{aligned}$$

Continued

A more precise calculation is to find the **effective annual rate of return**. We have already calculated for Yorko the two elements:

$$\text{Cost of discount} = 2/(100-2) = 0.0204\% \text{ per 20-day period}$$
$$\text{Number of 20-day periods a year} = 365/20 = 18.25 \text{ periods}$$
$$\text{Effective annual interest rate} = (1.0204)^{18.25} - 1 = 44\%$$

This expression of the cost is greater than in the first calculation because it correctly assumes compound rather than simple interest.

Where such generous terms are available, it probably makes sense for customers to opt for the discount even if it means borrowing, as long as the cost of finance is clearly below the annualised cost of discount. So why should firms offer such inducements? First, early payment can significantly improve cash flow and reduce bad debt risk. Second, cash discounts can encourage new customers who are attracted by the discounts. However, the financial manager should be aware of the true cost of such discounts and be able to justify why terms should be offered costing more than the cost of capital.

Self-assessment activity 14.3

A survey of large UK companies (Pike *et al.*, 1998) found that the normal credit period granted was 30 days, but the average credit period taken by customers was 46 days. Only 20 per cent of firms offered prompt payment cash discounts, with the most common terms being 2½ per cent/net 30 days. For a company offering those terms, what would be the effective interest rate for granting cash discounts assuming that firms would otherwise pay within 46 days?

(Answer in Appendix A at the back of the book)

■ Credit collection policy

A good credit collection policy is one in which procedures are clearly defined and customers know the rules. Debtors who are experiencing financial difficulties will always try to delay payment to companies with poor or relaxed collection procedures. The supplier who insists on payment in accordance with agreed terms, and who is prepared to cut off supplies or take action to recover overdue debts, is most likely to be paid in full and on time.

Figure 14.6 shows the debt collection cycle, starting with the customer order and ending with the cash received. Any speeding up of the order will reduce the required

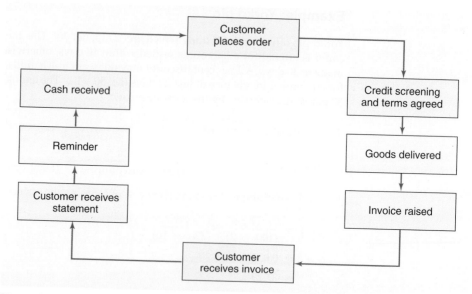

Figure 14.6 Ordering and debt collection cycle

working capital. Late payment by major customers often has a knock-on effect throughout the supply chain. For example, if a customer of company A pays its debts 60 days late, this may force Company A to pay its bills late to Company B, which might create sufficient cash flow pressures for B to go out of business.

It is a sad fact that firms usually only run out of cash once. Second chances are rare when it comes to cash failure. So getting on top of the credit-screening and control process is vital. Smaller businesses often complain that some larger companies take an unduly long time to settle their accounts. There is a real problem in British industry that far too much time and energy has to be devoted to chasing debts, for no apparent net gain to the business community. In 2008, the UK government initiated the Prompt Payment Code. The purpose of the code is explained in the following box:

The Prompt Payment Code

The Prompt Payment Code is about encouraging and promoting best practice between organisations and their suppliers. Signatories to the Code commit to paying their suppliers within clearly defined terms, and commit also to ensuring there is a proper process for dealing with any issues that may arise. This means that suppliers can build stronger relationships with their customers, safe in the knowledge that they will be paid, and confident that they are working with a business that values the service they deliver.

Code signatories undertake to:

1 Pay suppliers on time

- within the terms agreed at the outset of the contract
- without attempting to change payment terms retrospectively

- without changing practice on length of payment for smaller companies on unreasonable grounds

2 Give clear guidance to suppliers

- providing suppliers with clear and easily accessible guidance on payment procedures
- ensuring there is a system for dealing with complaints and disputes which is communicated to suppliers
- advising them promptly if there is any reason why an invoice will not be paid on the agreed terms

3 Encourage good practice

- requesting that lead suppliers encourage adoption of the code throughout their own supply chains

Source: www.promptpaymentcode.org.uk/

■ Using debtors as security

The financing of trade debtors may involve either the assignment of debts (invoice discounting) or the selling of debts (factoring). With invoice discounting, the risk of default on the trade debtors pledged remains with the borrower. Factoring, on the other hand, can be and usually is 'without recourse', i.e. the factor bears the loss in the event of a bad debt. Factors provide a wide range of services, the most common of which are as follows:

1 Advancing cash against invoices. Up to 80 per cent of the value of invoices can typically be obtained; repayments (together with interest on the advances) are paid from the subsequent cash collected from debtors.
2 Insurance against bad debts.
3 Administration of the credit control functions. This involves sending out invoices, maintaining the sales ledger and collecting payments.

We return to this topic in Chapter 15.

Self-assessment activity 14.4

What are the main elements in a firm's credit policy?

(Answer in Appendix A at the back of the book)

Federation of Small Businesses finds half of small firms have been paid late

New data from the Federation of Small Businesses (FSB) shows that more than 5 in 10 members were paid beyond the agreed payment date by large companies in 2013.
The FSB calls for Government to strengthen the Prompt Payment Code to make it easier for firms to complain about payment terms, and for a culture change amongst large companies who repeatedly pay late and who have been extending their payment terms sometimes to an unacceptable 120 days.

For those firms affected, being paid late or on extended terms hits them hard. It means reduced profitability (34%), paying their suppliers late (32%) and restricting their business growth (29%).

The FSB has urged the Government to consider re-launching the Prompt Payment Code (PPC) website and to promote more widely the existing 'challenge' function – where small firms can complain about a firm signed up to the code it feels isn't a prompt payer.

Additionally, to strengthen the PPC, the FSB wants to see all signatories clearly state what their maximum and average payment terms are as well as a named contact for small businesses who face difficulties. As included in the EU Directive enacted in the spring of last year, only in exceptional circumstances should payment terms be more than 60 days.

Fear of losing contracts is another issue, says the FSB. Even though they are legally entitled to do so, its research suggests just one in 10 (12%) had charged interest to clients for overdue payments because they fear losing business.

Source: Federation of Small Businesses, Press Release, 31 January 2014.

Worked example: Pickles Ltd

Pickles Ltd produces a single product sold throughout the UK. Its profit analysis is given below:

	Per unit	
	£	£
Selling price		40
Variable costs	(36)	
Fixed cost apportionment	(3)	(39)
Net profit per unit		1

Pickles has an annual turnover of £4.8 million and an average collection period for debtors of one month. It has conducted a study on entering new European markets and believes that this would produce an additional 25 per cent of sales, but the new business would require three months' credit. Stocks and creditors would rise by £400,000 and £200,000 respectively. The cost of financing any increase in working capital is 10 per cent.

Operating profit before finance costs increases as a result of the new business by £120,000:

Sales increase (25% × £4.8m) = £1.2m
Contribution/sales ratio (40 − 36)/40 = 10%
Increase in profit = £120,000

The question of whether profits increase as a result of the expansion into European markets very much rests on whether the existing UK customers also demand more favourable terms.

1 *Assuming only new customers take three months' credit*

	£000
New business (£4.8m × 25%)	1,200
New debtors (£1.2m × 3/12)	300
Additional stocks	400
Additional creditors	(200)
Required increase in working capital	500
Increase in operating profit (£1.2m × 10%)	120
Less financing cost (£500,000 × 10%)	(50)
Net profit increase	70

Thus net profits increase by £70,000. But what happens if *existing* customers demand the same credit terms?

2 *Assuming existing customers take three months' credit*

	£000
Sales (£4.8m + £1.2m)	6,000
New debtors level (3/12 × £6m)	1,500
Less existing debtors (1/12 × £4.8m)	(400)
	1,100
Additional stocks	400
Additional creditors	(200)
Additional working capital	1,300
Operating profit increase (as above)	120
Less financing cost (10% × £1.3m)	(130)
Net profit reduction after financing costs	(10)

After charging the cost of finance on additional debtors, stocks and creditors, the extra business does not increase profits.

14.8 INVENTORY MANAGEMENT

Inventory, or stock, may be classified into the following:

1 *Pre-production inventory* – stocks of raw materials and bought-in parts.
2 *In-process inventory* – work-in-progress at various stages of the production process.
3 *Finished goods inventory* – manufactured goods ready for sale.

In most cases, finished goods will convert most rapidly into cash; but where customer tastes change rapidly, such as in the fashion trade, this stock can also be the most risky.

Inventory is the least liquid of current assets. It is therefore vital to manage it in such a way that it can be converted from raw material to work-in-progress and finished goods as quickly as possible.

Stock is carried for two reasons:

1 *Business is uncertain.* Consumer demand and production requirements are difficult to forecast, and suppliers may not always be reliable in meeting delivery requirements. The cost of being out-of-stock, in terms of lost sales, profits and goodwill, is generally very high.
2 *Economies in ordering.* Every business needs to determine its economic order quantity for its main stock items.

Inventory control is an important topic for both production management and financial management, which should work closely to establish an inventory policy that meets customers' requirements while operating at optimum stock levels. It should avoid the twin evils of overstocking and understocking.

Overstocking results in the following:

- An unduly high level of working capital investment.
- Additional storage space requirements and greater handling and insurance costs.
- Possible deterioration and increased obsolescence risk.

Understocking reduces the working capital required, but can lead to out-of-stock situations ('stockouts') with orders unfulfilled, idle machines and underemployed workers.

In the past, carrying higher than necessary stocks has been a way of compensating for inefficient production and distribution or poor forecasting. But in today's highly competitive global markets, with Japanese and other overseas businesses operating efficient production schedules and minimal stock levels, European companies have been forced to examine their inventory management processes more closely.

■ Approaches to inventory management

There is now a whole variety of methods for improving stock control, some simple, others more sophisticated, using computer software. We will limit our discussion to three forms of stock control:

1 'Broad-brush' approaches.
2 Economic order quantity models.
3 Computer-based material requirements and Just-In-Time methods.

Broad-brush approaches

A simple, but useful, starting point is to consider the total stock position using the number of days' stock ratio:

$$\text{Number of days' stock} = \frac{\text{Average stock}}{\text{Cost of sales}} \times 365$$

Consider the stock levels of two companies, based on their latest accounts (see Table 14.2). U-Save, a discount supermarket chain, carries only finished stocks. Its generic strategy – to be the lowest-cost grocery retailer – requires tight control over its ordering, deliveries and stocks. Its stockholding period is 22 days, which means that stock will probably be turned into cash before the invoice for the goods is paid. By contrast, a major diversified producer like Unicom has very significant raw material stocks and a stockholding period which is double that of U-Save.

Table 14.2 Total inventory levels and stockholding periods

	U-Save (£m)	Unicom (£m)
Raw materials	—	1,380
Work-in-progress	—	175
Finished goods	148	1,894
Total stock	148	3,449
Cost of sales	2,403	25,926
Days' stock	22.5	48.5

While such cross-industry comparisons are interesting, U-Save will want to compare its stockholding period against Tesco and other competitors to see whether it is more efficient in its inventory control processes.

Major companies may well have thousands of items in stock. How should they determine the appropriate level of inventory control for each item? A simple stock classification, often called the **ABC system**, can help identify how closely stock items should be controlled. It divides a company's inventory into three groups according to importance to sales value, with high-value stocks requiring the highest stock control attention.

ABC system
A system of stock management that prioritises items accounting for greatest stock value

ABC stock classification in Boris plc

An analysis of stock items in Boris plc revealed the following:

Short-term financing and policies

Category	Stock items (%)	Stock value (%)
A	12	72
B	38	18
C	50	10
	100	100

Category A stock items have only 12 per cent of the total number of items in stock, but account for 72 per cent of stock value. It was decided that these items required a considerable degree of stock control attention, regular forecasting and monitoring, carefully assessed economic order quantities and an appropriate level of buffer stocks.

Category B stock items cover 38 per cent of total items, but only 18 per cent of stock value. The inventory policy for these items would be less sophisticated; forecasting would be simpler and less frequent.

Category C, which covers half the stock items but only 10 per cent of stock value, requires much simpler treatment, with few stock records and less regular monitoring. For example, stocks of nuts and bolts might simply require that an ample supply is always on hand.

Economic order quantity models

The costs of holding high levels of stocks include the interest lost in tying up capital in such assets, the costs of storing, insuring, managing and protecting stock from pilferage, deterioration, etc., and obsolescence costs. Against this, there are costs involved in holding low levels of stock or running out of stock:

1 Loss of goodwill from failure to deliver by the date specified by customers.
2 Lost production and disruption due to essential items being unavailable.
3 More frequent re-order costs (buyer's and storekeeper's time, telephone, postage, invoice-processing costs, etc.).

A variety of stock management models have been developed to help managers determine the optimal level of stock that balances holding costs against shortage costs. One way of addressing the issue is to determine the **economic order quantity (EOQ)** for the stock required.

economic order quantity (EOQ)
The most economic quantity to be ordered that minimises holding and ordering costs

Every firm should operate a clear stock control policy, which specifies for its main items the timing of stock replenishments, re-order quantities, safety stock levels and the implications of being out of stock. Figure 14.7 depicts the inventory cycle for a simple stock control model. It assumes a single product, immediate stock replenishment, constant usage and certainty.

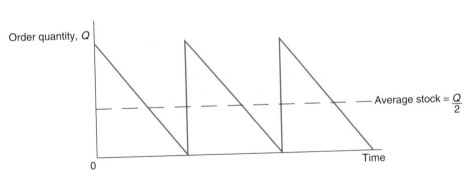

Figure 14.7 The inventory cycle

The total cost is:

Total cost = Ordering costs + Holding costs

Algebraically,

$$\text{Total cost} = \left(\frac{C}{Q} \times A \right) + \left(\frac{Q}{2} \times H \right)$$

where Q is the quantity ordered, C is the cost of placing an order, H is the cost of holding a unit of stock for one year and A is the annual usage of stock.

The economic order quantity is that quantity which minimises the total cost. We examined a similar cost function when we discussed total working capital investment earlier in this chapter.

At its simplest, the economic order quantity (EOQ) can be calculated as follows:*

$$\text{EOQ} = \sqrt{\frac{2AC}{H}}$$

Self-assessment activity 14.5

What do you understand by carrying costs and ordering costs? How do they fit into the economic order quantity formula?

(Answer in Appendix A at the back of the book)

EOQ example: Ivan plc

Ivan plc uses 2,000 units of stock item KPR each year. The cost of holding a single item for a year is £2 and the cost of placing each order is £45. The current order quantity is 200 units, but the company is considering changing to batches of 400. Is this the optimum re-order quantity?

Using the cost equation above:

$$\text{Total cost for 200} = \left(\frac{£45}{200} \times 2,000 \right) + \left(\frac{200}{2} \times £2 \right) = £650$$

$$\text{Total cost for 400} = \left(\frac{£45}{400} \times 2,000 \right) + \left(\frac{400}{2} \times £2 \right) = £625$$

$$\text{Total cost for 300} = \left(\frac{£45}{300} \times 2,000 \right) + \left(\frac{300}{2} \times £2 \right) = £600$$

The minimum total cost is achieved by ordering 300 units.

This is confirmed as the most economic order quantity by using the EOQ model:

$$\text{EOQ} = \sqrt{\frac{2 \times 2,000 \times £45}{£2}} = \sqrt{90,000}$$
$$= 300 \text{ units}$$

Each order will be placed for 300 units, which implies that orders will be placed every 55 days (i.e. $300/2,000 \times 365$).

---

*Mathematically, the EOQ is the value of Q that minimises the sum of ordering and holding costs. This is found by the technique of differentiation.

This simple model has two important limitations:

1 Demand, and therefore stock usage, may be seasonal. Hence the constant usage rate for stock assumed here may be unrealistic. Alternatively, demand may be difficult to predict, which necessitates holding **safety** or **buffer stocks**, and calls for a modification of the model.

2 Only the more easily quantifiable costs are included. Many of the other costs referred to earlier (lost goodwill, lost production, etc.) should also be considered.

safety or buffer stocks
Stocks held as insurance against stockouts (shortages)

We have so far assumed that stocks are used up at a constant rate and are replenished when the old level falls to zero. A **stockout** occurs when a firm is unable to deliver a product due to the lack of a specific inventory item. It is therefore tempting for firms to hold large levels of safety stocks to reduce this risk. In effect, this is a form of just-in-case management, as opposed to Just-In-Time management (see below).

stockout
Where a firm is unable to deliver due to shortage of stock

Holding costs will rise through carrying safety stocks, but costs associated with stockouts will fall. The level of safety stock will be affected by management's ability to forecast stock usage and lead time replenishment. Lead time is the delay between ordering and arrival of stock. Each stock item requires a re-order point to be set to cover safety stocks and lead time. The re-order point will be:

$$R = LW + S$$

In words, the re-order point (R) equals the lead time (L) times the weekly stock demand (W) plus the average safety stock (S).

Returning to the example of Ivan plc, if the stock item under consideration has a three-week re-order lead time and an average level of safety stocks is set at 40 units, we can determine the re-order point, assuming a 50-week working year.

$$
\begin{aligned}
R &= LW + S \\
&= 3 \times \frac{2,000}{50} + 40 \\
&= 160 \text{ units}
\end{aligned}
$$

In practice, rarely is demand uniform, and usage and lead times are uncertain. Determining the optimal stock levels and order quantities under conditions of uncertainty requires probabilistic inventory control models, which are beyond the scope of this book. However, the fundamental point remains that determining the optimal stock level involves balancing the expected costs of ordering and stockouts against the cost of holding additional stocks.

Materials requirement planning (MRP)

MRP is a computer-based planning system for scheduling stock replenishment, ensuring that adequate materials are always available for production purposes. Raw materials are determined from production schedules and lead times for replenishment. MRP can greatly reduce stockholding costs where the finished product requires a multi-stage production process with a large number of components and sub-assemblies, such as in motor car manufacture.

MRPII is a more comprehensive manufacturing resource planning system, which integrates all the resource requirements of the company. In addition to stocks, it also encompasses labour and machine requirements.

Just-In-Time

In recent times, managers in some manufacturing firms have been aiming for 'stockless production' and just-in-time (JIT) deliveries. JIT aims for an 'ideal' level of zero stocks, but with no hold-ups due to stock shortages. Materials and parts are delivered from suppliers just before they are needed, and products are manufactured just before they are needed for sale to customers. Where such an operation is successful, the consequent reduction in inventory and the cash operating cycle can be very considerable. Indeed, trade creditors can virtually match the current asset investment, thus enabling the business to operate with the minimum of working capital.

While it focuses on minimising stock levels, JIT forms part of a total quality production programme and rarely works well in isolation. A number of conditions are necessary for JIT to operate successfully:

- Strong links and shared information with suppliers and customers.
- Satisfied customers.
- A quality production process in a 'right-first-time' culture.
- Computerised ordering and inventory tracking systems.
- Smooth movement of materials from process to process.

Suppliers are typically located close to the manufacturer, making regular (often daily) deliveries in small quantities. They are tightly managed and deliver quality-assured components to meet agreed production schedules.

The main benefits of JIT, experienced by a growing number of companies, are:

1 Drastically reduced stock levels with commensurate savings in storage space, staff and financing costs.
2 A 'right-first-time' culture.
3 Reduced stock defects.
4 Increased productivity.

Amazon and law of the jungle

Proceed to checkout, review your order, click, done. Buying stuff on Amazon is easy. It is a wonder, however, that investors ever find the nerve to hit the place-your-order button for Amazon stock. That is because the online retailer's shares are expensive – basket-bustingly so. Yet 'buy investors' do. So what are the justifications for owning Amazon at these levels? Can its valuation possibly make sense?

Introducing Walmazon

To see the reason for owning Amazon in 2012, start by thinking about Walmart in 1991. The big-box retailer sold $44bn worth of merchandise that year, and had already changed the way Americans shop, using its sheer size to take costs out of its supply chain and pass the savings along to customers. Over the prior 10 years, Walmart's average annual sales growth had been 34 per cent.

Similarly, Amazon's sales reached $48bn last year, topping off a decade in which sales growth averaged 31 per cent. It too has changed the way many people in America (and to a somewhat lesser extent, Europe and Japan) shop for books (paper and digital), electronics, nappies, shoes – almost everything that can be delivered in a cardboard box or streamed over an internet connection.

The bottom line

In 1992, Walmart's growth, while still high, was decelerating. Amazon's growth was as high as ever last year. It takes an ever bigger slice of a pie – internet retail – that is itself expanding at a solidly double-digit pace in the US, and is expanding into other businesses. But whereas Walmart has delivered operating margins between 6 and 8 per cent for three decades, Amazon's margins peaked at 6 per cent in 2004, dropped several points for the following five years, and then, in 2011, dropped to around 2 per cent.

Part of the decline stems from Amazon's practice of subsidising delivery; shipping losses have been rising and now amount to more than 5 per cent of revenue. This company will cut profits to the bone to attract customers.

Amazon bulls will object that operating margin is not the right metric. Because Amazon pays its suppliers much more slowly than it is paid by its customers, in 2011 it averaged 90 days' worth of sales in payables (money due to be paid out) versus 16 days in receivables (money due to come in). Good inventory management also frees up cash. Over the past five years, these benefits (known as negative working capital) have accounted for almost a third of Amazon's free cash flow.

So operating profit does not reflect the company's cash profitability. Fair enough. Bear in mind two things, though. Free cash flow has declined alongside Amazon's operating profits in recent years. And this working capital benefit will decline when Amazon's growth slows. Working capital will not be a significant source of cash flow for ever.

Source: Based on Robert Armstrong and Stuart Kirk, *Financial Times*, 11 December 2012, p. 2.

14.9 CASH MANAGEMENT

Throughout this book, we have emphasised the importance of cash – rather than profit – in financial management. We now consider why cash has such a vital role to play, and how cash flow forecasts are prepared and used to help manage businesses operating in uncertain environments.

■ Why hold cash?

The word *cash* is something of a misnomer. While some 'cash' will be in the form of notes and coins, or bank accounts giving immediate access, much will be invested in short-term bank deposits.

Why should a company hold sums of money in cash or short-term deposits when the return is often quite low? There are a number of reasons why companies hold cash balances:

1 *Transactions motive.* Day-to-day cash inflows and outflows do not match perfectly; cash serves as a buffer to ensure that transactions occur at the appropriate time. Cash balances are particularly important where the patterns of cash inflows and outflows differ greatly, e.g. where business is highly seasonal.
2 *Precautionary motive.* Cash flows are often difficult to predict. Cash balances are required to cater for unanticipated cash disbursements.
3 *Speculative motive.* Cash allows the business to be highly flexible and to exploit wealth-creating opportunities more easily. Large cash balances are common among acquisitive companies where a cash alternative to a takeover bid is required.
4 *Compensation balances motive.* Banks provide a range of financial services, many of which are 'free' as long as the company keeps a positive bank balance.

Surplus cash is not always reinvested immediately in the business. The cash – or near cash – balance in some companies can be far greater than that required for normal trading purposes. The financial press publishes the main types of short-term financial investment opportunities available to companies, showing the relationship between maturity and interest rates.

Figure 14.8 illustrates the pivotal role played by cash in a typical firm. The cash balance is the result of the interactions of various activities with stakeholders.

■ *Operating activities* – cash from customers less payments to employees and suppliers.
■ *Servicing finance* – dividends and interest on loans.
■ *Taxation* – corporation tax and VAT.
■ *Investing activities* – purchase and sale of fixed assets.
■ *Financing activities* – new finance from shareholders and bondholders, and loan repayments.

The cash balance is restored to its appropriate level by short-term bank borrowing or repayment and the sale or purchase of marketable securities. The financial manager should therefore project the firm's ability to finance its operations and to manage corporate cash flow.

Self-assessment activity 14.6

What are the main motives for holding cash?

(Answer in Appendix A at the back of the book)

Even in well-diversified firms, it makes sense to centralise cash management:

1 It allows the treasurer to operate on a larger scale, which should lead to more competitive interest rates and lower staffing costs.

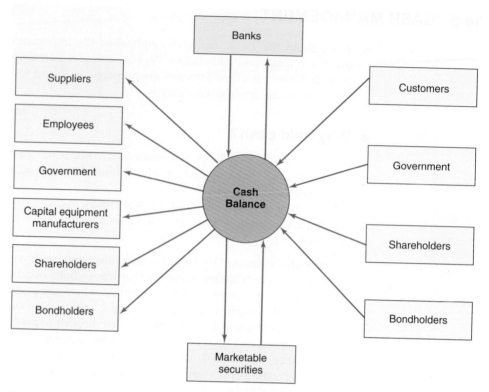

Figure 14.8 Cash flow activity for main stakeholders

2 Specialist staff can be employed to work in cash management.
3 Negative cash flows from one operating unit may be offset by positive cash flows from others, thus avoiding additional financing and loan-raising costs. This may well mean that the overall level of cash required to cover unanticipated cash shortfalls is reduced.
4 Banking operations become faster and more efficient, giving rise to advantageous banking arrangements.

■ Cash flow statements

International Accounting Standard (IAS) 7 requires companies to present a cash flow statement within their published accounts. The intention was to move away from over-reliance on profits.

A summarised cash flow statement for the chocolate manufacturer and retailer, Thorntons plc, is given in Table 14.3. The starting point in the statement is the company's ability to generate cash from its operations. A shareholder reading the cash flow statement can identify the reasons for the change in cash position over the year. For the year to 29 June 2013, Thorntons achieved £7.338 million positive cash flow from operating activities. However, the requirement to invest and repay loans resulted in a much smaller cash flow of £2.550 million.

■ Cash flow forecasting

The cash flow forecast, or cash budget, is the primary tool in short-term financial planning. It helps identify short-term financial requirements and surpluses based on the firm's budgeted activities. Cash budgeting is a continuous activity with budgets being rolled forward, usually in weeks or months, over time.

Table 14.3 Thorntons plc consolidated statement of cash flows

	52 weeks ended 29 June 2013 £'000	53 weeks ended 30 June 2012 £'000
Cash flows from operating activities		
Cash generated from operations	8,310	1,497
Corporate taxation (paid)/received	(972)	628
Net cash generated from operating activities	7,338	2,125
Cash flows from investing activities		
Proceeds from sale of property, plant and equipment	82	539
Purchase of property, plant and equipment	(4,275)	(4,875)
Net cash used in investing activities	(4,193)	(4,336)
Cash flows from financing activities		
Interest paid	(1,589)	(2,222)
Capital element of finance lease rental payments	(1,324)	(2,234)
Borrowings (repaid)/advanced	(600)	8,000
Dividends paid	—	(167)
Net cash (used in)/received from financing activities	(3,513)	3,377
Net (decrease)/increase in cash and cash equivalents and bank overdrafts	(368)	1,166
Cash and cash equivalents at beginning of period	2,918	1,752
Cash and cash equivalents at end of period	2,550	2,918

Source: Thorntons plc, *Annual Report* 2013 (**www.thorntons.co.uk**)

Preparation of the cash budget involves four distinct stages:

1 *Forecast the anticipated cash inflows.* The main source of cash is usually sales, and the sales forecast will therefore be the primary data source. Sales can be divided into cash sales and credit sales, the timing of the cash flow arising from the latter depending on the agreed credit terms. Thus, for example, the sales forecast for January would appear as a cash receipt in March if all sales were on credit terms of 60 days. Other cash inflows might be income from investments, cash from disposal of fixed assets, etc.
2 *Forecast the anticipated cash outflows.* The main payment is generally the payment of trade purchases. Once again, the credit period taken must be allowed for. Other cash outflows include wages and salaries, administrative costs, taxation, capital expenditure and dividends.
3 Compare the anticipated cash inflows and outflows to determine the *net cash flow* for each period.
4 Calculate the *cumulative cash flow* for each period by adding the opening cash balance to the net cash flow for the period.

■ **Float**

The 'cash at bank' position shown in a company's books will not usually be the same as that shown on the bank statement. Float is the money arising from the time lag between posting a cheque and it being cleared by the bank.

Float management in Marcus Ltd

On 1 July, the bank statement and cash account in the ledger of Marcus Ltd both show £40,000. The company pays suppliers £20,000 by cheque and receives cheques from suppliers for £15,000. The net cash balance in the accounts is therefore (£40,000 − £20,000 + £15,000) = £35,000. But the bank position is still £40,000. The cheques from customers will take 3 days to clear and the cheques paid will take more like 6–8 days to clear, including postal delay and time taken to pay in the cheque.

The cash controller must, therefore, regularly reconcile the two positions, but also manage the float by recognising that the actual cleared bank balance, upon which interest is calculated, is likely to be somewhat higher than the balance in the company's accounts. If Marcus can get its customers to pay by **direct debit**, this will speed up the banking process and further improve the bank position.

Another method of speeding up collections is **concentration banking**, where customers in a geographical area pay a local branch office rather than head office. The cheque is then deposited in the local bank branch. Where both the customer and the company have local banks, this can reduce both postal and clearing time.

Electronic funds transfer has certain benefits over cheque payment by post. Cost savings arise from the reduction in administration effort, time and postage. The transfer is instantaneous, which means that cash can stay in the company's bank account longer. The main disadvantage is that 'the cheque is in the post' excuse can no longer be employed. If payment is made on the same day as the cheque used to be posted, it impacts on the bank account quicker and results in more interest charges. BACS (Bankers' Automated Clearing Services) enables computerised funds transfers between banks. Corporate customers can use BACS, particularly for payment of salaries, by providing details of payments. Payment is made in two days. For large payments, same-day clearance can be made through CHAPS (Clearing House Automated Payment System).

direct debit
An automatic payment from a customer's bank account pre-arranged with the bank by both trading partners

concentration banking
Where customers in a geographical area pay bills to a local branch office rather than to the head office

electronic funds transfer
Instantaneous transfer of money from a debtor's bank account to a creditor

14.10 WORKED EXAMPLE: MANGLE LTD

Mangle Ltd produces a single product – a manually-operated spindryer. It plans to increase production and sales during the first half of next year; the plans for the next eight months are shown in Table 14.4.

Table 14.4 Mangle Ltd: production and sales (units)

Month	Production	Sales
November	70	70
December	80	80
January	100	80
February	120	100
March	120	120
April	140	130
May	150	140
June	150	160

The selling price is £100, with an anticipated price increase to £110 in June. Raw materials cost £20 per unit; wages and other variable costs are £30 per unit. Other fixed costs are £1,800 a month, rising to £2,200 from May onwards. Forty per cent of sales are for cash, the remainder being paid in full 60 days following delivery. Material purchases are paid one month after delivery and are held in stock one month before entering production. Wages and variable and fixed costs are paid in the month of production.

A new machine costing £10,000 is to be purchased in February to cope with the planned expansion of demand. An advertising campaign is also to be launched, involving payments of £2,000 in January and March. The directors plan to pay a dividend of £1,000 in May. On 1 January, the firm expects to have £2,000 in the bank. How will the cash position appear over the following six months?

Table 14.5 reveals that the first step is to determine the sales revenue each month. Forty per cent of sales are for cash and are therefore received in the selling month, while the remaining 60 per cent are received two months after the month of sale.

Table 14.5 Mangle Ltd: cash budget for six months to June (£)

		Jan.	Feb.	Mar.	Apr.	May	June
Inflows							
Receipts from cash sales		3,200	4,000	4,800	5,200	5,600	7,040
Receipts from debtors		4,200	4,800	4,800	6,000	7,200	7,800
	(A)	7,400	8,800	9,600	11,200	12,800	14,840
Outflows							
Payments to creditors		2,000	2,400	2,400	2,800	3,000	3,000
Variable costs		3,000	3,600	3,600	4,200	4,500	4,500
Fixed costs		1,800	1,800	1,800	1,800	2,200	2,200
Advertising		2,000		2,000			
Capital expenditure			10,000				
Dividend						1,000	
	(B)	8,800	17,800	9,800	8,800	10,700	9,700
Net cash surplus (deficit) in month (A – B)		(1,400)	(9,000)	(200)	2,400	2,100	5,140
Opening cash balance		2,000	600	(8,400)	(8,600)	(6,200)	(4,100)
Closing cash balance		600	(8,400)	(8,600)	(6,200)	(4,100)	1,040

Purchases are made in the month prior to entering production, but because a month's credit is taken, the payment to creditors is in the same month as production.

After including all cash flows, the net cash flow for each of the six months shows that, in the first three months, Mangle Ltd has a negative cash flow, and a negative cash balance for the February to May period. The company may decide that this is a seasonal business and that it is acceptable to operate with such monthly cash flow figures. In this case, the firm should seek to negotiate a loan to cover the shortfall. However, it would do well to consider ways of minimising the monthly deficits. For example, could cash receipts from debtors be collected more quickly? Could payment of creditors be deferred for a few weeks? Could the price increase be brought forward? Could payment terms on the capital equipment be extended over a longer period, possibly by leasing the equipment? The cash budget allows finance managers to consider such questions well ahead of events. Frequently, forward planning avoids the need to raise external finance through astute management of working capital.

14.11 CASH MANAGEMENT MODELS

We have already examined inventory control models. Cash is, in many ways, simply a form of inventory, the stock of cash required to enable a business to operate effectively. William Baumol (1952) recognised the similarity between cash and inventory for control purposes, particularly when the bank balance is simply a draw-down account.

This is when a firm has a cash balance upon which it draws steadily, and which it replenishes to the original balance at some point before running out (see the 'sawtooth' diagram for stock in Figure 14.7). Any surplus cash is invested in interest-bearing short-term securities.

In this case, the economic order quantity (EOQ) model can be employed, where EOQ represents the short-term securities to be sold to replenish the balance.

Recall that the equation is:

$$EOQ = \sqrt{\frac{2AC}{H}}$$

where C now represents the transaction cost for selling securities, H is the holding cost of cash (i.e. the interest rate) and A is the annual cash disbursements.

Example: Cash management model for Bizarre plc

The treasurer of Bizarre plc, a company specialising in unusual gifts for eccentric business managers (a rapidly growing market), has a sizeable sum invested in short-term investments, earning 6 per cent interest. Every time she sells investments to top up the bank balance the transaction cost is £25. Monthly cash payments are around £200,000. How often, and by how much, should she transfer money to the bank account?

The EOQ model gives an indication of the most economic amount of cash to be drawn each time:

$$EOQ = \sqrt{\left(\frac{2 \times \text{annual cash payments} \times \text{cost of selling securities}}{\text{annual interest rate}}\right)}$$

$$= \sqrt{\left(\frac{2 \times £2,400,000 \times £25}{0.06}\right)} = £44,721, \text{ say } £45,000$$

The frequency with which the treasurer will transfer cash is (£2.4 million/£45,000) = 53 times a year, or approximately weekly.

Self-assessment activity 14.7

As interest rates increase, it obviously becomes more attractive to transfer smaller quantities. Try reworking the Bizarre problem, assuming a doubling of the interest rate to 12 per cent p.a.
(Answer in Appendix A at the back of the book)

The above cash management model works quite well when daily cash drawings on the bank account are uniform. This is rarely the pattern of actual cash flows in business. Cash flows go up and down in what often appears a fairly random manner. Miller and Orr (1966) suggested that, instead of assuming a constant rate of cash payment, perhaps we should assume that daily balances cannot be predicted – they meander in a random fashion. This is further discussed in the Appendix to this chapter.

■ Short-term investment

When the cash budget indicates a cash surplus, the financial manager needs to consider opportunities for short-term investment. Any cash surplus beyond the immediate needs should be put to work, even if just invested overnight. The following considerations should be made in assessing how to invest short-term cash surpluses:

1 The length of time for which the funds are available.
2 The amount of funds available.

3 The return offered on the investment in relation to the investment involved.
4 The risks associated with calling in the investment early (e.g. the need to give three months' notice to avoid losing the interest).
5 The ease of realisation.

Examples of short-term investment opportunities are as follows:

- *Treasury Bills* – issued by the Bank of England and guaranteed by the UK government. No interest as such is paid, but they are issued at a discount and redeemed at par after 91 days. At any time, the bills can be sold on the money market.
- *Bank deposits* – a wide range of financial instruments is available from banks, but the more established investment opportunities are:
  (a) term deposits, where for a fixed period (usually from one month to six years) a fixed rate is given. For shorter periods (typically up to three months), the interest may be at a variable rate based on money market rates.
  (b) Certificates of Deposit, issued by the banks at a fixed interest rate for a fixed term (usually between three months and five years), but which can be sold on the money market at any time.
- *Money market accounts* – most major financial institutions offer schemes for investment in the money market at variable rates of interest (e.g. treasury accounts).

SUMMARY

The management of working capital is a key element in financial management, not least because, for most firms, current assets represent a major proportion of their total investment. Working capital policy is concerned with determining the total amount and the composition of a firm's current assets and current liabilities.

Key points

- Working capital policy trades off expected profitability and risk. An 'aggressive' working capital policy, which seeks to employ the minimum level of net current assets (including cash and marketable securities), will probably achieve a higher return on investment, but may jeopardise the financial health of the business.
- The cash operating cycle (the length of time between cash payment and cash receipt for goods) should be regularly reviewed and controlled.
- The consequences of overtrading (or under-capitalisation) can be extremely serious, if not fatal, for the firm.
- An effective debtor control policy should cover the credit period, credit standard, cost of cash discounts and collection policy.
- Credit terms should reflect the customer's credit rating, normal terms of the industry and the extent to which the firm wishes to use credit as a marketing tool.
- In evaluating customer creditworthiness, remember the five Cs: capacity, character, capital, collateral and conditions.
- Trade debtors can be used to raise finance through invoice discounting and factoring.
- Inventory management involves determining the level of stock to be held, when to place orders and how many units to order at a time.
- Inventory costs can be classified into carrying or holding costs, which increase as the level of stock rises, and shortage costs (or stockout costs and ordering costs), which fall as stock levels increase.

- A variety of economic order quantity models is available for determining the order quantity that will minimise total inventory cost. The basic model is:

$$EOQ = \sqrt{\frac{2AC}{H}}$$

where C is the cost of placing an order, A is the annual usage of stock and H is the cost of holding a unit of stock for one year.

- The cash flow forecast, or cash budget, is a vital tool in short-term financial planning.
- Cash management models (e.g. Baumol and Miller–Orr models) are useful in setting limits that trigger cash adjustment.

Further reading

Pike *et al.* (1998) report findings on trade credit management in large companies.

Brigham and Gapenski (1996) and Brealey, Myers and Allen (2013) provide fuller discussions on the issues addressed in this chapter. Sartoris and Hill (1981) provide a present value approach to credit evaluation. The pioneering work on cash management models is found in Baumol (1952) and Miller and Orr (1966).

Useful websites

Better Payments Practice Group: https://payontime.co.uk
Credit checks: www.checkit.co.uk
Companies House: www.companieshouse.gov.uk
Dun & Bradstreet: www.dnb.com

Appendix
MILLER–ORR CASH MANAGEMENT MODEL

When daily cash flows are very difficult to predict, it may be sensible to assume that the pattern of cash flows is random. This gives rise to the cash position shown in Figure 14.9. Rather than decide how often to transfer cash into the account, the treasurer sets upper

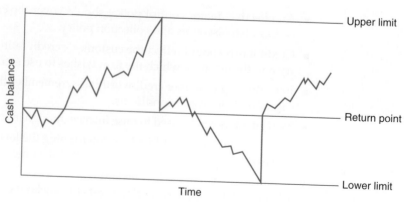

Figure 14.9 Miller–Orr cash management model

and lower limits that trigger cash adjustments, sending the balance back to the return point by selling short-term investments. The diagram prompts two questions:

1 How are the limits set?
2 Why isn't the return point midway between the two?

In general, the limits will be wider apart when daily cash flows are highly variable, transaction costs are high and interest on short-term investments is low. The Miller and Orr formula for setting the limits is:

$$\text{Range between upper and lower limits} = 3\left(\frac{3}{4} \times \frac{\text{transaction cost} \times \text{cash flow variance}}{\text{interest rate}}\right)^{1/3}$$

The cash balance does not return to a point mid-way between the upper and lower limits. The return point is:

$$\text{Return point} = \text{lower limit} + \frac{\text{range}}{3}$$

By having a return point below the mid-point between the two limits, the average cash balance on which interest is charged is reduced.

The Baumol and Miller–Orr models are really two extremes: the former assumes cash flows are constant, while the latter assumes they are unpredictable. In practice, an experienced cash controller, using a detailed cash budget, should perform better than a cash management model and should enable the company to operate on a lower cash balance. The primary value of simple cash management models may be to evaluate how much better the 'hands-on' expert can perform than the 'hands-off' control model.

Example

The financial manager at Millor Ltd believes that cash flows are almost impossible to predict on a daily basis. She knows that a minimum cash balance of £20,000 is required and transferring money to or from the bank costs £50 per transaction. Inspection of daily cash flows over the past year suggests that the standard deviation is £3,000 a day (i.e. £9 million variance). The interest rate is 0.03 per cent per day.

The Miller–Orr model specifies the range for the cash balance as below:

$$\text{Range} = 3\left(\frac{3}{4} \times \frac{50 \times 9,000,000}{0.0003}\right)^{0.3333} = £31,200 \text{ approx.}$$

The upper limit = lower limit + range = (£20,000 + £31,200) = £51,200

$$\text{The return point} = \text{lower limit} + \frac{\text{range}}{3} = £30,400$$

The decision rule is: if the cash balance reaches £51,200, buy (£51,200 − £30,400) = £20,800 of marketable securities. If the cash balance falls to £20,000, sell £10,400 of marketable securities for cash to return it to £30,400.

QUESTIONS

Questions with coloured numbers have solutions in Appendix B on page 793.

1 (a) (i) Discuss the theories, or arguments, which suggest that financial analysis can be used to forecast the probability of a given firm's failure; and

(ii) explain why such an analysis, even if properly applied, may not always predict failure.

(b) Discuss the following statement: 'It is always a sound rule to liquidate a company if its liquidation value is
above its value as a going concern.'

2 (a) Explain, with the use of a numerical example, the meaning of the term 'cash operating cycle' and its significance in relation to working capital management.

(b) Delcars plc own a total of ten franchises, in a variety of United Kingdom locations, for the sale and servicing
of new and used cars. Six of the franchises sell only second hand vehicles, with the remaining four operating
a car service centre in addition to retailing both new and used vehicles. Delcars operate different systems for
banking of sales receipts, depending on the type of sale. All monies from new car sales must be banked by the
garage on the day of the sale; receipts from second hand car sales are banked once a week on Mondays, and
receipts from car servicing work are banked twice a week on Wednesdays and Fridays. No banking facilities
are available at the weekend, i.e. Saturdays and Sundays. The sales mix of the three elements (as a percentage
of Delcars' total revenue) is as follows: 60 per cent new vehicles; 25 per cent second hand vehicles; 15 per cent
servicing. Total sales for all three business areas amounted to £25 million in 1999. Delcars pays interest at a
rate of 8.5 per cent per annum on an average overdraft of £65,000, and the company's finance director has
suggested that the company could significantly reduce the interest charge if all sales receipts were banked on
the day of sale. All the garages are open every day except Sunday. Assume that the daily sales value (for all
three areas of business) is spread evenly across the week.

Calculate the value of the annual interest which could be saved if all ten franchises adopted the finance
director's suggestion of daily banking.

(c) Using the example of a car dealership such as Delcars, as given in **(b)** above, outline the advantages and disadvantages of centralisation of the treasury function.

(ACCA)

3 Hercules Wholesalers Ltd has been particularly concerned with its liquidity position in recent months. The
most recent income statement and statement of financial position of the company are as follows:

Income statement for the year ended 31 May 20XX

	£	£
Sales		452,000
Less: Cost of sales		
Opening stock	125,000	
Add purchases	341,000	
	466,000	
Less: Closing stock	(143,000)	323,000
Gross profit		129,000
Expenses		(132,000)
Net loss for the period		(3,000)

Statement of financial position as at 31 May 20XX

	£	£	£
Fixed (non-current) assets			
Freehold premises at valuation			280,000
Fixtures and fittings at cost less depreciation			25,000
Motor vehicles at cost less depreciation			52,000
			357,000
Current assets		143,000	
Stock		163,000	
Debtors		306,000	
Less creditors due within one year			
Trade creditors	(145,000)		
Bank overdraft	(140,000)	(285,000)	
			21,000
			378,000
Less creditors due after more than one year			(120,000)
Loans			258,000
Capital and reserves			100,000
Ordinary share capital			158,000
Retained profit			258 ,000

The debtors and creditors were maintained at a constant level throughout the year.

Required

(a) Explain why Hercules Wholesalers Ltd is concerned with its liquidity position.
(b) Explain the term 'operating cash cycle' and state why this concept is important in the financial manage-ment of a business.
(c) Calculate the operating cash cycle for Hercules Wholesalers Ltd based on the information above. (Assume a 360-day year.)
(d) State what steps may be taken to improve the operating cash cycle of the company.

(Certified Diploma)

4 Micrex Computers Ltd was established in 1999 to sell a range of computer software to small businesses. Since its incorporation, the business has grown rapidly and demand for its products continues to rise. The most recent financial accounts for the company are set out below:

Statement of financial position as at 31 May 20XX

	£	£	£
Fixed (non-current) assets			
Freehold land and buildings at cost		55,000	
Less: Accumulated depreciation		(4,000)	51,000
Equipment and fittings at cost		20,000	
Less: Accumulated depreciation		(5,000)	15,000
Motor vehicles at cost		24,000	
Less: Accumulated depreciation		(6,000)	18,000
			84,000
Current assets			
Stocks		26,000	
Trade debtors		59,000	
		85,000	
Less creditors: amounts falling due within one year			
Trade creditors	(88,000)		
Proposed dividend	(1,000)		
Taxation	(6,000)		
Bank overdraft	(10,000)	(105,000)	(20,000)
			64,000
Less creditors: amounts falling due beyond one year			
14% bank loan (secured on freehold property)			(20,000)
			44,000
Capital and reserves			
Ordinary £1 shares			25,000
Retained profit			19,000
			44,000

Income statement for the year ended 31 May 20XX

	£	£
Sales		660,000
Less: Cost of sales		
Opening stock	22,000	
Purchases	426,000	
	448,000	
Less: Closing stock	(26,000)	422,000
Gross profit		238,000
Less: Selling and distribution expenses	(176,000)	
Administration expenses	(38,000)	
Finance expenses	(7,000)	(221,000)
Net profit before taxation		17,000
Corporation tax		(6,000)
Net profit after taxation		11,000
Proposed dividend		(1,000)
Retained profit for the year		10,000

The company is family-owned and controlled and, since incorporation, has operated without qualified finance staff. However, the managing director recently became concerned with the financial position of the company and therefore decided to appoint a qualified finance director to help manage the financial affairs of the business. Soon after joining the company, the finance director called a meeting of his fellow directors and at this meeting stated that, in his opinion, the company was overtrading.

Required

(a) What do you understand by the term 'overtrading' and what are the possible consequences of this type of activity?

(b) What are the main causes of overtrading and how might the management of a business overcome the problem of overtrading?

(c) Use financial ratios for Micrex Computers Ltd that you believe would be useful in detecting whether the company was overtrading. Explain the significance of each ratio you calculate.

(Certified Diploma)

5 Specify the basic formula for calculating the cost of cash discounts.

6 What are the main differences in the assumptions underlying the Baumol and Miller–Orr cash models?

7 Hunslett Express Company specifies payment from its customers at the end of the month following delivery. On average, customers take 70 days to pay. Sales total £8 million per year and bad debts total £40,000 per year.

The company plans to offer cash discounts for payment within 30 days. It is estimated that 50 per cent of customers will take up the discount, but that the remaining customers will take 80 days to pay. The company has an overdraft facility costing 13 per cent p.a. If the proposed scheme is introduced, bad debts will fall to £20,000 and savings in credit administration of £12,000 p.a. are expected.

Should the company offer the new credit terms?

8 Salford Engineers Limited, a medium-sized manufacturing company, has discovered that it is holding 180 days' stock while its main competitors are holding only 90 days' stock.

Required

(a) Discuss what you consider to be the most important factors determining the optimum level of stockholding for the company.

(b) What action would you take if you were asked to investigate the reasons for Salford's high level of stock?

(Certified Diploma)

9 Torrance Ltd was formed to produce a new type of golf putter. The company sells the putter to wholesalers and retailers and has an annual turnover of £600,000. The following data relate to each putter produced:

	£	£
Selling price		36
Variable costs	(18)	
Fixed cost apportionment	(6)	(24)
Net profit		12

The cost of capital (before tax) of Torrance Ltd is estimated at 15 per cent.

Torrance Ltd believes it can expand sales of this new putter by offering customers a longer period in which to pay. The average collection period of the company is currently 30 days. The company is considering three options in order to increase sales. These are as follows:

	Option		
	1	2	3
Increase in average collection period (days)	10	20	30
Increase in sales (£s)	30,000	45,000	50,000

Torrance Ltd is also reconsidering its policy towards trade creditors. In recent months, the company has suffered from liquidity problems, which it believes can be alleviated by delaying payment to trade creditors. Suppliers offer a 2.5 per cent discount if they are paid within 10 days of the invoice date. If they are not paid within 10 days, suppliers expect the amount to be paid in full within 30 days. Torrance Ltd currently pays suppliers at the end of the 10-day period in order to take advantage of the discounts. However, it is considering delaying payment until either 30 or 45 days after the invoice date.

Required

(a) Prepare calculations to show which credit policy the company should offer its customers.

(b) Discuss the advantages and disadvantages of using trade credit as a source of finance.

(c) Prepare calculations to show the implicit annual interest cost associated with each proposal to delay payment to creditors. Discuss your findings.

(Certified Diploma)

10 (a) Discuss:

(i) The significance of trade creditors in a firm's working capital cycle, and

(ii) the dangers of over-reliance on trade credit as a source of finance.

(b) Keswick plc traditionally follows a highly aggressive working capital policy, with no long-term borrowing. Key details from its recently compiled accounts appear below:

	£m
Sales (all on credit)	10.00
Earnings before interest and tax (EBIT)	2.00
Interest payments for the year	0.50
Shareholders' funds (comprising £1 million issued share capital, par value 25p, and £1 million revenue reserves)	2.00
Debtors	0.40
Stocks	0.70
Trade creditors	1.50
Bank overdraft	3.00

A major supplier which accounts for 50 per cent of Keswick's cost of sales is highly concerned about Keswick's policy of taking extended trade credit. The supplier offers Keswick the opportunity to pay for supplies within 15 days in return for a discount of 5 per cent on the invoiced value.

Keswick holds no cash balances but is able to borrow on overdraft from its bank at 12 per cent. Tax on corporate profit is paid at 33 per cent.

Required

Determine the costs and benefits to Keswick of making this arrangement with its supplier, and recommend whether Keswick should accept the offer. Your answer should include the effects on:

- The working capital cycle
- Interest cover
- Profits after tax
- Earnings per share
- Return on equity
- Capital gearing.

11 International Golf Ltd operates a large warehouse, selling golf equipment direct to the public by mail order and to small retail outlets. The cash position of the company has caused some concern in recent months. At the beginning of December, there was an overdraft at the bank of £56,000. The following data concerning income and expenses has been collected in respect of the forthcoming six months:

	December £000	January £000	February £000	March £000	April £000	May £000
Expected sales	120	150	170	220	250	280
Purchases	156	180	195	160	150	160
Advertising	15	18	20	25	30	30
Rent	40			40		
Rates		30				
Wages	16	16	18	18	20	20
Sundry expenses	20	24	24	26	26	26

The company also intends to purchase and pay for new motor vans in February at a cost of £24,000 and to pay taxation due on 1 March of £30,000.

Sales to the public are on a cash basis and sales to retailers are on two months' credit. Approximately 40 per cent of sales are made to the public. Debtors at the beginning of December are £110,000, 70 per cent of which are in respect of November sales.

Purchases are on one month's credit and, at the beginning of December, the trade creditors were £140,000. The purchases made in December, January and February are considered necessary to stock up for the sales demand from March onwards.

All other expenses are paid in the month in which they are incurred. Sundry expenses include £8,000 per month for depreciation.

Required
(a) Explain the benefits to a business of preparing a cash flow forecast.
(b) Identify and discuss the costs to a business associated with:
   (i) holding too much cash;
   (ii) holding too little cash.
(c) Prepare a cash flow forecast for International Golf Ltd for the six months to 31 May, which shows the cash balance at the end of each month.
(d) State what problems International Golf Ltd is likely to face during the next six months and how these might be dealt with.

(Certified Diploma)

12 (a) The Treasurer of Ripley plc is contemplating a change in financial policy. At present, Ripley's statement of financial position shows that fixed assets are of equal magnitude to the amount of long-term debt and equity financing. It is proposed to take advantage of a recent fall in interest rates by replacing the long-term debt capital with an overdraft. In addition, the Treasurer wants to speed up debtor collection by offering early payment discounts to customers and to slow down the rate of payment to creditors.

As his assistant, you are required to write a brief memorandum to other Board members explaining the rationales of the old and new policies and pinpointing the factors to be considered in making such a switch of policy.

(b) Bramham plc, which currently has negligible cash holdings, expects to have to make a series of cash payments (P) of £1.5 million over the forthcoming year. These will become due at a steady rate. It has two alternative ways of meeting this liability.

Firstly, it can make periodic sales from existing holdings of short-term securities. According to Bramham's financial advisers, the most likely average percentage rate of return (i) on these securities is 12 per cent over the forthcoming year, although this estimate is highly uncertain. Whenever Bramham sells securities, it incurs a transaction fee (T) of £25, and places the proceeds on short-term deposit at 5 per cent per annum interest until needed. The following formula specifies the optimal amount of cash raised (Q) for each sale of securities:

$$Q = \sqrt{\frac{2 \times P \times T}{i}}$$

The second policy involves taking a secured loan for the full £1.5 million over one year at an interest rate of 14 per cent based on the initial balance of the loan. The lender also imposes a flat arrangement fee of £5,000, which could be met out of existing balances. The sum borrowed would be placed in a notice deposit at 9 per cent and drawn down at no cost as and when required.

Bramham's Treasurer believes that cash balances will be run down at an even rate throughout the year.

Required

Advise Bramham as to the most beneficial cash management policy.

Note: ignore tax and the time-value of money in your answer.

(c) Discuss the limitations of the model of cash management used in part (b).

(ACCA)

Practical assignment

1 Sound credit management can play an important role in the financial success of a business.

Required

(a) Explain the role of the credit manager within a business.

(b) Discuss the major factors a credit manager would consider when assessing the creditworthiness of a particular customer.

(c) Identify and discuss the major sources of information that may be used to evaluate the creditworthiness of a commercial business.

(d) State the basis upon which any proposed changes in credit policy should be evaluated.

(Certified Diploma)

2 If you are based in a firm where credit management is important, apply the above question to your organisation.

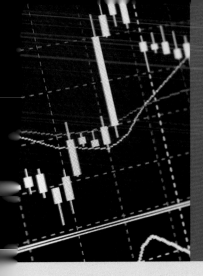

15

Short- and medium-term finance

Sharing, or shifting, the burden?

Small firms, especially via pressure groups such as the Federation of Small Businesses, have complained long and loud about how their larger brethren milk them for 'free' finance by delaying payments of invoices, forcing them to fall back on temporary and often expensive financing facilities such as overdrafts and invoice finance (see below). For example, Home Retail, owner of Argos and Homebase, takes 60 days to pay suppliers, reportedly one of the longest waits in the industry, and up from 51 days in 2012. (On the credit side, Mulberry, the ladies' handbag retailer, has an average payment time of 15 days, and Marks & Spencer, often criticised for pressing suppliers, pays up in 24 days).

However, in recent years, a more insidious development has surfaced under the seemingly innocuous label 'rebate schemes'. Retailers such as Laura Ashley, Debenhams, and John Lewis, as well as Home Retail, have sent letters to suppliers demanding discounts and rebates often retrospectively, i.e. after terms of payment have been agreed and the goods delivered.

Home Retail reportedly said in January 2014 that 'Our suppliers are very important to us. Payment is made in accordance with pre-agreed terms and reflects the markets in which we and our suppliers operate'. Yet a month later, it was reported as demanding a 2% turnover rebate on orders placed from the start of March. Also, in early 2014, Debenhams was reportedly seeking a fee of 2.5% from suppliers based on both outstanding payments and to orders that it had agreed with suppliers. Debenhams reportedly claimed that the discounts were a 'contribution' to the retailer's investment in new store openings and the £25m revamp of its flagship Oxford Street store. Earlier, in 2013, both Monsoon and Selfridges had provoked considerable opprobrium by demanding discounts on invoices (5% and 3–5%, respectively). In the latter case, the rebate demanded was presented as 'settlement discounts' in return for early payment for specific terms.

Sources: Based on various articles in *The Daily Telegraph*.

Learning objectives

This chapter aims to evaluate the advantages and disadvantages of the following means of short- and medium-term finance:

- Trade credit.
- Bank finance.
- Factoring and invoice discounting.
- Bills of exchange and acceptance credits.
- Hire purchase.
- Leasing.

Particular attention is given to leasing in view of its importance as a method of financing the acquisition of a wide range of assets. In addition, the commonest ways of financing foreign trade are also described in an appendix.

15.1 INTRODUCTION

For many years, the main UK banks have been heavily criticised for their allegedly miserly attitudes to small firms who rely heavily on short-term financing. While banks have taken a number of steps to address the criticisms raised by their detractors, many firms still find it difficult to arrange short-term finance, and many remain critical of the banking system. Such criticisms reached a crescendo during the 'credit crunch' when many small firms failed, allegedly due to lack of bank support, in part at least. (For news of developments in the field of finance for small firms, see the website of the British Bankers Association: **www.bba.org.uk**) Despite such problems, the banks remain the most important source of external finance for small and medium-sized firms, providing more than 50 per cent of their external finance. However, it is not only smaller firms that tend to rely on shorter-term finance; firms of all sizes use these sources to varying degrees. For example, many larger companies arrange access to overdraft finance to tide them over temporary liquidity shortages.

In this chapter, we examine the nature and characteristics of alternative sources of finance, ranging from very short-term facilities (e.g. trade credit) to rather longer-term ones (e.g. bank loans and finance leasing). Generally, we classify these under the heading of short and medium term, although the distinction is somewhat arbitrary. For example, lease finance can be used for varying time periods, ranging from a few weeks (operating leases) to as long as 15 years or more in the case of some finance leases. In addition, bank overdrafts are essentially short term in nature, but are often used continuously for lengthy periods, being 'rolled over' when the facility expires.

15.2 TRADE CREDIT

Trade credit is finance obtained from suppliers of goods and services over the period between delivery of goods (or provision of a service) and the subsequent settlement of the account by the recipient. During this time, the company can enjoy the goods or benefit from the service provided without having to pay up. Granting customers a credit period is part of normal trading relationships throughout most of UK industry. For this reason, it is sometimes called 'spontaneous finance'. Additional features of trade credit packages include the amount of credit that a company is allowed to obtain, whether interest is paid on overdue accounts, and whether discounts are offered for early payment.

A common way of expressing credit terms is as follows:

'2/10: net 30'

This means that the supplier will offer a 2 per cent discount for early settlement (in this case, within 10 days); otherwise, it expects payment of the invoice in full within 30 days. As shown below, *not* to take a discount is often an expensive option. Moreover, a very effective way of antagonising suppliers is to delay payment *and* attempt to claim the discount.

The length of the trade credit period offered depends partly on the following factors:

- *Industry custom and practice.* Terms of trade credit typically reflect traditional norms built up over years of trading. Although these terms often vary between industries, they are quite uniform within industries. Any supplier wanting to depart from the industry norm has to compensate with some other product offering, say, speed of delivery, to avoid losing sales.
- *Relative bargaining power.* If the supplier has a large range of customers, none of whom are crucial to it, and if the product is essential to buyers, the supplier has great power to impose its own terms. This power is enhanced by lack of strong

competitors. The lack of supplier bargaining power is seen very clearly in the introductory cameo.

■ *Type of product.* Products that turn over rapidly are often sold on short credit terms because they command small profit margins. Delay in settlement would severely erode the margin.

A firm's trade credit position is volatile, as it depends on which of its suppliers are awaiting payment and for how much, and these factors change continuously with the flow of business transactions. It is useful to express the average trade credit period in days, calculated as follows:

$$\text{Creditor days} = \frac{\text{Trade creditors}}{\text{Credit purchases}} \times 365$$

However, for the outside observer, this figure is only observed at the balance sheet date, and, even so, could have been 'window-dressed' by accelerated settlements immediately prior to drawing up the accounts. It is sometimes expressed in terms of total purchases and sometimes, when data for purchases is unavailable, in terms of overall cost of sales.

Self-assessment activity 15.1

Trade credit is often called 'spontaneous finance' or 'automatic finance'. Can you see why?

(Answer in Appendix A at the back of the book)

Because trade credit represents temporary borrowing from suppliers until invoices are paid, it becomes an important method of financing investment in current assets. Firms may be tempted to view trade creditors as a cheap source of finance, although statutory rights to claim interest on late payments now exist. Having a debtors' collection period shorter than the trade collection period may be taken as a sign of efficient working capital management. However, trade credit is by no means free – it carries both hidden and overt costs.

Excessive delay in settling invoices can undermine the stability of a business in a number of ways. Existing suppliers may be unwilling to extend more credit until existing accounts are settled. They may start to assign lower priority to future orders placed by the culprit, they may raise prices in the future or they may simply not supply at all. In addition, if the firm acquires a reputation as a bad payer among the business community, its relationships with other suppliers may be soured.

Finally, by delaying payment of accounts due, the company may be passing up valuable discounts, thus effectively increasing the cost of goods sold. This can be shown with a simple example.

Martock plc is offered a discount of 2.5 per cent on an invoice of £100,000 by a major supplier if it settles the account within 10 days, rather than taking the normal credit period of 30 days. Martock, which has at present a zero cash balance, can borrow from its bank at an interest rate of 15 per cent p.a. Should it borrow and exploit the discount, or take the full credit period of 30 days?

If it takes the discount and pays on (but not before!) day 10, it will have to borrow (97.5 per cent × £100,000) = £97,500 for an additional period of 20 days, since it would have to settle anyway after 30 days. If it waits until day 30, the cost of settling the bill is effectively the lost discount of £2,500. By advancing payment, Martock is borrowing £97,500 for 20 days in order to save £2,500, an interest rate over 20 days of 2.56 per cent. Expressed as an annual interest rate, this approximates to:

$$\frac{£2,500}{£97,500} \times \frac{365}{20} \times 100 = 46.8\%$$

A more accurate solution can be obtained by compounding over the number of 20-day periods in a year (18.25). The true rate is:

$$[(1.0256)^{18.25} - 1] = 58.6\%$$

As this compares very unfavourably with the 15 per cent cost of borrowing, Martock should borrow in order to advance this payment.

Typically, in times of recession, there emerges widespread concern over the tendency for more firms to delay payment of accounts. Larger firms allegedly exploited their industrial muscle by simultaneously spinning out their trade credit periods while insisting on prompter payment from small firm customers. This problem led the UK Government in 1998 to introduce legislation for a statutory right to demand interest on overdue accounts, initially for smaller companies only.

Until the passage of the Late Payments of Commercial Debts (Interest) Act in 1998, interest could only be claimed on late debts if it was included in the contract, or if awarded by a court. The Act enabled small businesses (50 or fewer employees) to claim interest from large businesses and the public sector. From November 2000, they were entitled to claim interest from other small businesses. From November 2002, all businesses obtained the statutory right to claim interest from any other firm or from the public sector.

In 2013, amended late payment legislation came into force with the implementation of the EU Directive 2011/7/EU on combating late payment in commercial transactions. Many of the measures contained in the EU Directive were already in place in UK legislation, but the main change was the provision that debtors should be forced to pay interest (at Bank of England base rate plus 8 per cent) and to reimburse the reasonable recovery costs of the creditor, if they fail to pay for goods and services on time, i.e. 60 days for private business and 39 days for public bodies. It should be noted that the statutory right to claim interest and recovery costs is not compulsory – it is up to the supplier to decide whether or not to use this right and fewer than 10% do so.

Firms that suffer from late payment face a difficult choice – delay settlement to their own suppliers or fall back on their banks for supplementary finance, via either overdraft or loan facilities. Moreover, if they push their customers too hard, or actually apply the interest sanction, they risk losing future business. Nevertheless, to quote a Department of Business, Innovation and Skills publication:[*]

> Evidence suggests that the best way of securing timely payment is to agree terms in advance of the transaction and to invoice timely and accurately – effort therefore needs to be focussed upon managing customer relationships and managing cash flow.

In the next section, we consider bank lending.

Self-assessment activity 15.2

What is the true annual interest rate paid when a firm delays payment under the following credit terms: '$1\frac{1}{2}$/15: net 40'?

(Answer in Appendix A at the back of the book)

15.3 BANK CREDIT FACILITIES

Major commercial banks extend a variety of credit facilities, ranging from short-term overdrafts to long-term loans of varying terms. The interest rate generally increases with the term of the advance, the actual rate being linked to the bank's base rate, which

---

[*]'A Users Guide to the recast Late Payment Directive', Department of Business, Innovation and Skills, March 2013, p. 5.

in turn depends on the base rate set by the national monetary authority (in the UK, the Monetary Policy Committee of the Bank of England).

■ Overdrafts

overdraft
Short-term finance extended by banks subject to instant recall. A maximum deficit balance is pre-agreed and interest is paid on the actual daily balance outstanding

The best-known form of bank finance is the **overdraft**, a facility available for specified short-term periods such as six months or a year. This facility specifies a maximum amount that the firm can draw upon either via direct cash withdrawals or in payments by cheque to third parties. Interest is paid on the negative balance outstanding rather than the maximum advance agreed. Compared with many other forms of finance, it is relatively inexpensive, with the interest cost set at some two or three percentage points above the Bank of England base rate. The interest rate is thus variable. Most banks also levy an arrangement fee (e.g. Lloyds Bank quoted up to 1.5% in March 2014) of the maximum facility.

In principle, overdrafts are repayable at very short notice, even on demand, although unless the company abuses the terms of the facility by exceeding the agreed overdraft limit, the overdraft is unlikely to be called in. Besides, it is not always in the best interests of a bank to do this suddenly, as it could exert such severe financial pressure on the client as to force it into liquidation.

Nevertheless, the bank retains the right to appoint a receiver if the client defaults on the debt. In practice, well-behaved clients can roll forward overdrafts from period to period. As a result, the overdraft effectively becomes a form of medium-term finance. Even in these cases, it is wise policy not to use an overdraft to invest in long-term assets that would be difficult to liquidate at short notice if the bank suddenly decided to call in the debt.

fixed charge
Applies when a lender can force the sale of pre-specified company assets in order to recover debts in the event of default on interest and/or capital payments

floating charge
Applies when a lender can force the sale of any (i.e. unspecified) of a company's assets in order to recover debts in the event of default on interest and/or capital payments. (Ranks behind a fixed charge)

To protect against risk of loss, the bank will usually demand that the overdraft be secured against company assets, i.e. in the event of default, the receiver will reimburse the bank out of the proceeds of selling these assets. Security can be in two forms: a **fixed charge**, where the overdraft is secured against a specific asset, or a **floating charge**, which offers security over all of the company's assets, i.e. those with a ready and stable second-hand market. A floating charge therefore ranks behind a fixed charge in the queue for payment. For trading companies, overdrafts are often secured against the inventory that the company purchases with the funds borrowed, or even against debtors. In this respect, the overdraft is '*self-liquidating*' – it can be reduced as the company sells goods and banks the proceeds.

Alternatively, and more to the liking of most bankers, overdrafts are secured against property. This often creates problems in times of recession, for example in the recent 'debit crunch' years. In a recession, property market prices typically fall quite sharply, thus reducing the value of assets upon which overdrafts are secured to below the balance outstanding. Many banks then make major provisions against the increasing likelihood of bad debts. In addition, they incur much ill-will by allegedly recalling overdrafts prematurely, thus exacerbating the liquidity difficulties of their clients, already seriously affected by falling sales. Many critics accuse the banks of forcing many essentially sound companies out of business.

Self-assessment activity 15.3

What do you think are the main considerations a banker makes in assessing an application for a loan or overdraft?

(Answer in Appendix A at the back of the book)

■ Term loans

term loans
Loans made by a bank for a specific period or term, usually longer than a year

Term loans are secured loans for a year or longer usually made at a fixed rate. UK banks have traditionally been reluctant to lend on a long-term basis, mainly because the bulk of their deposit liabilities are short-term. In the event of unexpectedly high demand by the public to withdraw cash, this could leave them vulnerable if they were unable to recall advances quickly from borrowers. This low exposure to default risk is generally regarded as the reason why banking collapses are relatively uncommon in the UK – notwithstanding the publicity given to a few high-profile cases such as Northern Rock.

However, because of criticism by a series of official reports on the financial system and the advent of intensive competition from London branches of overseas banks, the main UK banks are now far more willing to lend long-term. Term loans can be arranged at variable or fixed rates of interest, although the interest cost is usually higher in the latter case. For variable rate loans, the rate set may be two-to-five percentage points above the bank's base rate, depending on the credit rating of the client and the quality of the assets offered as security. In addition, an arrangement fee is usually charged. It is important to appreciate that interest is typically levied on the initial balance of the loan, regardless of ongoing repayments. This means that the effective rate of interest exceeds the quoted rate.

Self-assessment activity 15.4

Which are normally more expensive for firms – overdrafts or term loans? Why?

(Answer in Appendix A at the back of the book)

balloon loan
Where increasing amounts of capital are repaid towards the end of the loan period

bullet loan
Where no capital is repaid until the very end of the loan period

Tailor-made facilities are available to some firms, with repayment terms designed to suit their expected cash flow profiles. Sometimes, the bank may grant a 'grace period' at the outset of the loan when no capital is repayable and interest may be charged at a relatively low, but increasing, rate. This is particularly suitable for a small, developing company trying to establish itself. Similarly, a **balloon loan** is where increasing amounts of capital are repaid towards the end of the loan period, whereas a **bullet loan** is where no capital and, often, no interest, is repaid until the very end of the loan period.

The proportion of borrowing on overdraft by small businesses is in long-term decline. In its *Finance for Small Firms* report in 1995, the Bank of England estimated that fixed-term lending to small firms had overtaken overdraft finance, the proportion of total lending in the form of term loans then being 60 per cent, compared with 40 per cent only two years previously (see **www.bankofengland.co.uk** for small firm financing reports). This pattern has continued since then, so that by 2013, the British Bankers Association (**www.bba.org**) was reporting that overdraft lending accounted for only 11 per cent of its members' support for medium and smaller businesses, with term lending standing at 79 per cent (with 11 per cent represented by undrawn facilities).

Banks need to do more to win small business confidence says FSB

On the fifth anniversary of the Lehman Brothers crash, the FSB's survey of more than 2,000 small firms has uncovered that despite nearly half (49%) of businesses owners rating their business banking positively, the sector has much to do to improve small firms' confidence.

While banks score well on their customer satisfaction levels and reliability of payment services, more than half (56%) of respondents believe that banks do not care about small businesses. Concerns remain over disproportionate salaries and profits, with nearly half (49%) of respondents raising this as a concern. One third of businesses also highlighted an increase in the fees paid to their bank across the past year. The average charge paid by a small firm is £1,075, with some paying more than £4,000.

Continued

The FSB believes that for the recovery to take grip, and for small firms to turn to high street banks for their finance needs, this confidence gap needs to be closed. A crucial element in rebuilding that trust is for banks to repair communication with small business customers, having a relationship with them not only throughout the process of applying for finance but as they develop and grow their businesses over the long term.

For those unsuccessful in their applications for finance, signposting to other forms of lending when applications are denied is crucial. Only 37 per cent of small businesses knew about alternative lending such as peer-to-peer platforms, with only 18 per cent knowing about Funding Circle, a leading peer-to-peer lender, and a similar number for the challenger bank Handelsbanken. Equally disappointing is that while four in ten bank refusals are overturned on appeal, only 6 per cent knew about the appeal mechanism run by the banks.

It is clear more work needs to be done to publicise the diverse and growing range of non-bank finance providers. The Government needs to support and promote these new non-bank sources of finance either through regulatory means, direct funding through the business bank or by looking at the tax system.

John Allan, National Chairman, Federation of Small Businesses, said:

'Since the financial crash five year ago, small firms' confidence in the banking system has been hit. Not only have they been plagued by inability to access finance and overnight changes to their lines of credit, these latest figures show they have faced increasing fees for the banking service.

'Restoring this trust and getting banks to work in partnership with small firms is absolutely crucial for the recovery. We recognise the banks have done much and recognised their past mistakes, starting the culture change needed. However, our latest figures are a salutary reminder that process still has some way to go with more than half of our members believing the banks don't care about small firms.

'As much as a culture change in the banks, we must diversify the lending landscape as a whole. We fear that without real competition in the banking sector, small firms will only have the high street banks to turn to. We therefore urge the Government to maintain their efforts to promote non-bank sources of finance and thereby increase choice for small firms as well as competition in the market.'

Source: Federation of Small Businesses, Press release, 9 September 2013 (www.fsb.org.uk).

■ Revolving credit facilities (revolvers) (RCFs)

revolving credit facility
Enables a firm to borrow up to a pre-specified amount usually over 1–5 years. As repayments of outstanding balances are made, the loan facility is replenished

A term loan generally specifies an agreed payment profile and the amounts repaid cannot normally be re-borrowed. **Revolving credit facilities (RCF)**, or revolvers, allow the borrower to borrow, repay and re-borrow over the life of the loan facility, rather like a continuous overdraft. Like an overdraft, it is frequently secured on the borrower's working capital, e.g. using debtors and stocks as collateral, although very large firms (which tend to be the main users of RCFs) may not be asked for any security. The advantage of revolvers is the enhanced flexibility provided, i.e. funds can be re-used in a continuous credit line. The commitment by the bank thus 'revolves' – the borrower can continue to ask for loans, subject to giving suitable notice, so long as the committed total is not exceeded. The fees charged include:

- A front-end, or facility, fee for setting up the loan.
- A commitment fee to compensate the bank for having to commit some of its loan capacity by setting aside reserve assets to meet capital adequacy rules.
- The interest cost, usually expressed as so many basis points (one bp = 0.01%) above LIBOR, the rate at which London-based banks lend to each other.

Most large firms enter into RCF agreements. For example, GKN plc, the UK engineering firm (www.GKN.com) enjoys RCF facilities of £595m and £242m, operating until 2016 and 2017, respectively. In June 2013, Glencore plc (www.glencoreXstrata.com), the giant mining firm, reported a complex restructuring of the debt it had incurred in order to acquire Swiss-based miner, Xstrata. It signed syndicated RCF agreements totalling US$17.34bn, comprising a USD 12-month RCF for US$5.92bn, a US$7.07bn three-year revolver, and a US$4.35bn five-year revolver. In the USA, Facebook announced in August 2013 that it was to replace its existing $1.5bn unsecured revolver due in 2015 with a $6bn, five-year revolver. Both old and new RCFs carried an interest rate of LIBOR + 1 per cent with a 10 basis points commitment fee. Facebook also had a $5bn unsecured revolver due in 2017.

■ The Enterprise Finance Guarantee (EFG)

First known as the Loan Guarantee Scheme (and subsequently, the Small Firms Loan Guarantee Scheme), this was introduced in 1981 following the Report of the Committee to Review the Functioning of Financial Institutions, set up to investigate the provision of finance to business. The Committee pointed to the difficulty faced by smaller firms with little or no track record in obtaining suitable longer-term finance.

Such firms are reluctant to release control by issuing equity, while investors are reluctant to purchase equity owing to the risks involved, especially the difficulty of liquidating their investment on acceptable terms. Firms may also have difficulty persuading banks of the inherent viability of their businesses, and are frequently unable to offer sufficient and suitable security. Where banks do offer loans, they are often on less advantageous terms than those extended to larger firms and less likely to be augmented in times of difficult trading.

The EFG is financed by the Department of Business, Innovation and Skills (BIS). In its initial form, the scheme was supposed to be self-financing. The government originally guaranteed that, in the event of failure of a business, 80 per cent of the loan would be repaid to the financial institution making the loan. The cost of meeting guarantees would be met by borrowers paying the government a premium of three percentage points above the normal commercial rate applied by the bank. Loans were available for periods of two to seven years. Losses on the scheme turned out much higher than anticipated, largely, it was alleged, because banks contrived to shift existing shaky clients on to it. After many modifications over the years, it now (2014–15) embodies the following features:

- Small and medium-size firms of any age that operate in the UK may apply for loans directly to banks and other lenders.
- Applicants must demonstrate that they have applied for a conventional loan and have been rejected for lack of security or track reward.
- Want repayment terms from 3 months to 10 years.
- Only firms with annual turnovers no more than £41 million are eligible.
- 75 per cent of the loan is guaranteed but the borrower is responsible for the whole amount.
- Applicable for sums between 1,000 to £1 million. The loan is provided entirely by the lender.
- Borrowers pay a 'normal commercial' interest rate to the bank, plus a premium of 2.0 per cent p.a. on the outstanding amount of the loan, payable to the BIS Department.
- Term of loan available from 3 months to 10 years.

For updates on the EFG, see **www.bba.org.uk** and **www.bis.gov.uk**.

■ Alternative finance: Peer-to-Peer (P2P) lending

P2P is a way of removing the intermediary banker from lending/borrowing relationships. P2P 'platforms' bring together via online auctions (generally small) lenders with firms and individuals seeking funds on similar terms, often having been rejected by traditional banks. While pre-dating the financial crisis – Zopa (**www.zopa.com**), the oldest P2P firm in the world, and the largest in Europe, was set up in 2005 – the growth of P2P has undoubtedly been propelled by dissatisfaction with traditional banks among both lenders, dismayed by historically low deposit rates, and borrowers, often unable to obtain any finance in the post-crisis years, except on highly demanding terms. Other leading UK P2P platforms are Funding Circle (**www.fundingcircle.com**) and rebuildingsociety.com. (**www.rebuildingsociety.com**), while the market leader in the USA is Lending Club, which is part-funded by Google and is now a publicly-quoted company.

In 2013, in the UK, members of the Peer-to-Peer Finance Association, the industry trade body, provided finance of £608m, of which £193m (32 per cent) went to business borrowers. From April 2014, the P2P industry has been regulated by the Financial Conduct Authority which should enhance the confidence of lenders and provide a greater measure of security, an obvious concern to lenders (although P2P claims a lower failure rate than for traditional banks). At present, P2P is regarded as a means of funding SMEs, but it may well grow in size and reputation to provide a similar service to larger firms.

15.4 INVOICE FINANCE (OR 'ASSET-BASED FINANCE')

factors
Organisations that offer to purchase a firm's debtors for cash

Some companies, which need to offer trade credit to customers for competitive reasons, find that they need payment earlier than agreed in order to assist their own cash flow. Institutions called **factors**, mainly subsidiaries of the major banks and members of the Asset Based Finance Association (**www.abfa.org.uk**) (formerly known as the Factors and Discounters Association), exist to help such companies. Factors do not always provide new finance, but can accelerate the cash conversion cycle for client companies, allowing them to gain access to debtors more quickly than if they waited for the normal trade credit period to unwind. The essence of both factoring and invoice discounting is to use debtors (i.e. invoices) to provide security for financing, hence the term 'invoice finance'. Invoice finance thus includes both factoring proper and invoice discounting. The significance of this was seen in the introductory cameo.

Between 1993 and 2013, total domestic invoice financing, measured by ABFA clients' turnover, grew from £19 billion to £257 billion, over 90 per cent of which was invoice discounting. In 2013, invoice discounting itself grew by 11 per cent from £215 billion to £239 billion.

■ Factoring

factoring
A means of obtaining faster cash inflow, and thus increased funds. A firm appoints the factor to collect outstanding accounts payable and to administer debtors' accounts. It also lends money to the client based on the value of the firm's sales

Factoring involves raising immediate cash based on the security of the company's debtors, thus accelerating payment from customers. A factor provides three main services – sales administration, credit protection and provision of finance, commonly 80–85 per cent of the value of approved invoices.

Sales administration

A factor assumes the various functions of sales ledger administration, ranging from recording sales details to sending out invoices and reminders and collecting payment. The benefits for the client are the cost savings from reducing in-house administration and access to a more efficient, specialist debtor management team. This is particularly valuable to a young fast-growing company, which may outgrow its administration system and otherwise be exposed to the liquidity risks of overtrading. The fee for such an administration service would lie typically in the range of 0.75–2.5 per cent of the value of turnover handled, depending on whether credit protection against bad debt losses is included.

Credit protection

The factor may provide a credit evaluation service for clients, analysing customer characteristics before deciding on their creditworthiness. When all risks are borne by the factor, the service is termed 'without recourse', i.e. the factor has no 'comeback' on the client if customers default. Where this applies, the factor requires total control of credit approval, monitors customers' payments and attempts to collect payment. This suggests a possible problem with factoring – the intervention of the factor between the factor's client and the debtor company could endanger trading relationships and damage goodwill. For this reason, some clients prefer to retain responsibility for collection from problem debtors. This is known as 'undisclosed factoring'. In the case of '*with recourse*' factoring, the factor will call upon its client to reimburse the funds advanced on an invoice relating to a delinquent account.

Provision of finance

A factor will also advance funds to a client, based on a proportion, say 80 per cent, of approved (i.e. reliable) invoices. For example, a company with sales on 30-day credit terms from reliable customers of £500,000 per month would receive an advance of 80 per cent, i.e. £400,000 each month. The interest rate would be related to bank base rate, probably slightly above the cost of an overdraft. The client would receive the balance of the payment less interest and an administration charge, perhaps equal to 0.5 per cent of turnover.

Although factors provide valuable services, companies are sometimes wary of using them for reasons other than cost. Besides possible difficulties over collection of payment, widespread knowledge that a company is using a factor may arouse fears that the company is beset by cash flow problems. If so, its suppliers may impose more stringent payment terms, thus negating the benefits provided by the factor. Companies concerned by these risks may seek the more widely used, but less comprehensive, service of invoice discounting.

Self-assessment activity 15.5

Summarise the benefits of factoring for a small firm.

(Answer in Appendix A at the back of the book)

■ Invoice discounting

invoice discounting
Where a factor purchases selected invoices from a client firm, without providing debt collection or account administration services

Although factors provide a range of services, a company seeking merely to improve its cash flow is likely to use an **invoice discounting** facility. This involves the purchase of selected invoices, sometimes just one, by the discounter. The discounter will advance immediate cash up to 85 per cent of face value. It assumes no responsibility for the administration of the accounts receivable, or for the collection of the debts. The service is totally confidential, the client's debtors being unaware of the existence of the discounter. It is therefore equivalent to the financing service provided by a factor, although restricted to a narrower range of invoices.

Administration charges for this service are around 0.5 per cent of a client's turnover. It is more risky than factoring, since the client retains control of its credit policy. Consequently, such facilities are usually confined to established companies with turnovers above £1 million. Interest costs are usually 3–6 per cent above base rate, although larger companies and those that arrange credit insurance may receive keener terms.

How invoice discounting works

At the beginning of February, Menston plc sells goods for a total value of £300,000 to regular customers, but decides that it requires payment earlier than the agreed 30-day credit period for these invoices. A discounter agrees to finance 80 per cent of their face value, i.e. £240,000. Interest is set at 13 per cent p.a. The invoices were due for payment in early March, but were subsequently settled in mid-March, exactly 45 days after the initial transactions. The service charge is set at 1 per cent. As usually applies, a special account is set up with a bank, into which all payments are made. The sequence of cash flows is as follows:

February:
    Menston receives cash advance of £240,000
Mid-March:
    Customers pay up £300,000
    Invoice discounter receives the full £300,000
    Menston receives the balance less charges, i.e.

$$\text{Service fee} = 1\% \times £300,000 = £3,000$$
$$\text{Interest} = (13\% \times £240,000 \times 45/365) = \underline{£3,847}$$
$$\text{Total charges} = £6,847$$
$$\text{Net receipts} = (20\% \times £300,000) - £6,847$$
$$= (£60,000 - £6,847) = £53,153$$
$$\text{Total receipts by Menston} = (£240,000 + £53,153) = £293,153$$

In effect, Menston has settled for a discount of $(£6,847/£300,000) = 2.3$ per cent over 45 days for early receipt of 80 per cent of the accounts payable. As there are about eight 45-day periods in a year, this corresponds to an annual interest rate of:

$$(1.023^8 - 1) = 0.1995, \text{ i.e. } 19.95\%$$

To view the offerings of a typical factor, visit **www.rbsif.co.uk**, the website of the Royal Bank of Scotland's invoice financing operations.

Invoice discounting in action

Invoice discounting can often come into play when traditional lines of bank finance dry up, as Solo IT, a maker of thermal imaging helmets, based in Darlington, discovered. Solo's 'visionary headgear' assists fire-fighters in locating hotspots in areas such as dark corridors in buildings and cruise ships. It also produces a heat-seeking camera that is able to locate small ships at a distance, of particular use for merchant vessels concerned about pirates (Chelsea FC owner Roman Abramovitch's private yacht is equipped with one of these). It exports to the USA, Russia, China, Scandinavia and the Middle East.

Despite successfully operating over 18 years, it was unable to extend its bank overdraft to obtain required finance to invest in R&D and product development. It approached Platform Black (**www.Platformblack.com**), that operates on an auction basis, and one of several invoice discounters that arose out of the credit crunch to assist cash-strapped small–medium businesses. Solo IT's managing director, Victoria McLaren, said invoice discounting allowed the firm to 'release cash from 30-to-60 day invoices that helped us to fulfil our first order to Bulgaria'. Emphasising the short-term nature of this form of finance, Ms McLaren said 'the last thing we want is to become reliant on this form of debt. It's a means to an end, keeps liquidity and keeps us moving forward.'

Source: Based on an article by Anna White, *Daily Telegraph*, 7 February 2014.

15.5 USING THE MONEY MARKET: BILL FINANCE

A bill is often likened to a post-dated cheque or an IOU, as it represents a commitment to pay out a specific sum of money after a specified period of time. Bills are traded on the money market, which specialises in providing funds repayable over periods of less than a year. The major players in the money market are the commercial banks, which lend to each other, often overnight, to cover temporary cash shortages, at the London

Inter-Bank Offered Rate (LIBOR), and to the discount houses. The latter exist primarily to deal in short-term bills issued by the government (Treasury Bills), local governments and companies. They borrow on a very short-term basis from the commercial banks, usually at a very keen interest rate, and use the proceeds to purchase bills, which they may hold to maturity or sell at a profit in the money market.

A company can use two main types of bill to raise finance: a trade bill (Bill of Exchange) or a bank bill (acceptance credit).

■ Bills of Exchange

Bill of Exchange
A promise to pay at a specific time, issued to suppliers by purchasers in exchange for goods. Bills may be held to maturity or sold at a discount on the money market if cash is required sooner

Bills of Exchange are generally trade-related, connected to specific trading transactions. The trader purchasing goods draws up a bill stating a promise to repay at some future date, and then conveys the bill to the supplier of the goods.

The supplier may then hold the bill until maturity, or sell it in the market to a discount house, if cash is required earlier. The terms of the bill usually include an implicit interest charge, although no interest as such is paid, as the following example indicates.

Example: Bills of Exchange

A trader wishes to acquire goods to the value of £1 million. He draws up a Bill of Exchange, promising to pay £1 million in three months' time. The bill is immediately sold by the seller of the goods to a discount house, which pays out £975,000, i.e. a discount of £25,000. If the discount house holds the bill to its maturity, it earns a profit of £25,000. This is equivalent to an interest rate of (£25,000/£975,000) = 2.56% over three months, or in annual terms:

$$(1.0256)^4 - 1 = (1.1064 - 1) = 0.1064, \text{ i.e. } 10.64\%$$

If the discount house can borrow at less than this rate, it stands to make a profit. If interest rates fall, the discount house's profit margin widens. Alternatively, the discount house may sell the bill on the money market, its value rising as it nears maturity. The ultimate holder will present the bill to the trader, who assumes responsibility for payment and, by this time, hopes to have sold the goods at a profit.

Bills of Exchange are drawn up for periods of 60–180 days, for values of at least £75,000, reflecting interest rates based on LIBOR, but dependent on the riskiness of the companies concerned and their respective credit ratings.

■ Acceptance credits

acceptance credit
A facility to issue bank-guaranteed bills (bank bills) by a firm wanting to raise short-term finance. They can be sold on the money market, but are unrelated to specific trading transactions. The bank accepts the liability to exchange cash for bills when presented at the due date

Acceptance credits are often called 'bank bills' – whereas trade Bills of Exchange are drawn on the purchaser of goods by a supplier, an acceptance credit is drawn by a company on a bank. Acceptance credits were originally developed by merchant banks, but all large banks now offer this facility. The bank grants a credit facility whereby a client company can draw bills (up to an agreed limit) that the bank will 'accept', i.e. agree to honour, when presented for payment at a future specified date. The client company may not use the facility immediately, but may treat it as a stand-by to be used when required, usually in minimum tranches of £250,000, over a period of up to five years. Accepted bills are sold on the discount market by the bank on behalf of the client company at a relatively 'fine', or low, discount. The company thus effectively obtains finance from the purchaser of the discounted bills, using the name and reputation of the accepting bank as security. It is thus a somewhat roundabout way of one company lending to another, using the intermediary services of the bank. Bank bills have a period to maturity of 30, 60, 90 or 180 days. At the maturity date, the bank can either 'accept' a new bill (i.e. effectively roll over the old one) or receive the full value of the bill from the client's account, using the funds to pay the bearer of the bill. The cost to the client is the amount of discount on the bill plus a fee payable to the bank of around 0.6 per cent. It is not unusual for banks to require security for such facilities – the nature and type depending on the size and credit standing of the client.

Acceptance credits have become increasingly popular in recent years. Among their advantages are the following:

1 The 'interest' cost is relatively low, often below that of an overdraft, because the bills are backed by a bank.
2 The cost involved with the bill is known when it is discounted, and is not affected by subsequent interest rate changes, allowing greater accuracy in cash budgeting.
3 Acceptance credits can be negotiated for longer periods than overdrafts, thus offering more security to the borrower.
4 Unlike traditional Bills of Exchange, they are not tied to specific transactions.

However, they are available only to large companies with sound credit ratings, and they lack the flexibility of overdrafts, which a firm can reduce if it wishes to lower interest costs.

■ Commercial paper (CP)

commercial paper
A short-term promissory note or IOU, issued by a highly creditworthy corporate borrower to financial institutions and other cash-rich corporates

Another financial innovation imported from the USA that UK firms have been allowed to use since 1986, **commercial paper (CP)** is a means whereby the treasurer can circumvent the banking system by issuing promissory notes – effectively IOUs – directly to large financial institutions such as pension funds and insurance companies, or to corporates with temporary excess liquidity.

disintermediation
Business-to-business lending that eliminates the banking intermediary

CP is an example of **disintermediation** as it cuts out the banking intermediary as middleman and thus avoids paying the spread on the difference between the bank's lending rate and the rate it pays depositors, i.e. it is cheaper. In addition, CP avoids having to submit to the restrictive covenants that banks often impose on borrowers. However, because it is unsecured, the ability to issue CP is confined to the largest firms with the highest credit ratings, i.e. 'blue chips'.

Interest is not usually payable on CP – it has a maturity value greater than the amount lent, the difference being the cost to the issuer. There is virtually no secondary market in CP.

15.6 HIRE PURCHASE (HP)

hire purchase (HP)
A means of obtaining the use of an asset before payment is completed. An HP contract involves an initial, or 'down payment', followed by a series of hire charges at the end of which ownership passes to the user

With **hire purchase (HP)** (also known as asset purchase), the user of the asset will eventually own it. Small and medium-sized firms (SMEs) are particularly reliant on HP, which, although often an expensive option, is readily available because the loan is secured on the asset acquired. HP of equipment by firms is very similar to HP by consumers of durables such as washing machines. The equipment is purchased initially by specialist institutions called finance houses, most of which are subsidiaries of commercial banks and members of the Finance and Leasing Association (FLA, **www.fla.org.uk**). The hirer usually makes a down-payment and then signs a commitment to a series of (usually) monthly hire charges over a specified period, at the end of which the legal title to the article passes to the user. The hire charge contains two elements: an interest charge to reflect the borrowing of the capital involved; and a capital repayment element. The structure of an HP deal is shown in Figure 15.1.

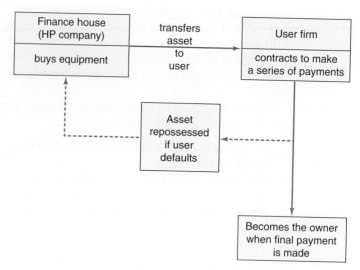

Figure 15.1 **How hire purchase works**

Two major advantages of HP are, first, the avoidance of a major cash outlay at the outset of the project and, second, the immediate availability of the asset for use, although the user assumes all the responsibilities of maintenance and insurance. However, if the user fails to fulfil the payment schedule, the owner can repossess the asset. The user then loses all title to the asset and obtains no credit for payments already made. HP tends to be used by smaller and riskier firms. Because of the default risk, the contract period is invariably less than the asset lifespan, so that in the event of repossession, the owner knows that it will hold a saleable asset with some working life remaining. Conversely, over longer-term HP contracts, the owner is exposed to the risk of technological progress outdating the asset and reducing its marketability. As a result of these considerations, HP is expensive.

How HP works

Boston Builders, wishing to obtain an earthmover using HP, contacts a manufacturer, which arranges an HP contract with a finance house. The finance house buys the asset, which has an expected useful life of four years, for £120,000 and arranges the following contract:

- The asset will be purchased over three years but operated for four years.
- A down-payment of £20,000 is required.
- Interest is charged at 15 per cent on the initial loan of (£120,000 – £20,000) = £100,000.
- Capital will be repaid in three equal annual instalments.

Note that, even though the balance outstanding declines over the three-year period, interest is applied to the initial loan of £100,000. The annual payments are thus:

Interest $= (15\% \times £100,000) = £15,000$ p.a.

Capital $= £100,000/3 = £33,333$ p.a.

Total $= £48,333$ p.a. (or £4,028 if paid monthly)

Because the interest is paid in this way, the true interest rate is roughly double the quoted rate. The annual interest charge of £15,000, applied to the average capital outstanding of £50,000, yields an effective interest rate of $(£15,000/£50,000) = 30$ per cent, although the precise rate depends on the actual timing of payments.

An advantage of HP is that the user qualifies for tax relief on the interest element in the repayment profile and also a writing-down allowance (WDA) on the capital expenditure component (18 per cent reducing balance), based on the total cash price of the asset. Table 15.1 shows the profile of tax reliefs for the Boston Builder's example, assuming tax is paid at 20 per cent, with no delay, and that the asset has a sale value of £20,000 after four years, i.e. tax-allowable depreciation totals £100,000 over the four-year lifespan of the asset.

Table 15.1 Tax relief on three-year HP contract with four-year asset lifetime (£)

Year	Interest at 15%	+	WDA at 18%*	=	Total tax reliefs	Tax saving at 20%
1	15,000		18,000		33,000	6,600
2	15,000		14,760		29,760	5,962
3	15,000		12,103		27,103	5,421
4	–		55,137**		55,137	11,027
Totals	45,000		100,000		145,000	29,010

* The outlay is assumed to occur on Day 1 of Year 1. Expenditure on the last day of Year 0 would bring forward the tax reliefs by a full year and raise the PV of the tax savings.

***Note:* Year 4 allowable depreciation = [Outlay less depreciation claimed for Years 1–3 less sale value]

= £120,000 − [£20,000 + £16,000 + £12,800] − £20,000
= £51,200

Tax relief is of value only to profitable companies with taxable capacity. Many of the smaller and higher-risk companies (often start-ups) that use HP are unable to exploit the tax breaks, often making HP a very expensive form of finance.

Self-assessment activity 15.6

What is the monthly payment on the following HP contract?

- Total cost of equipment = £40,000
- Down-payment = 30%
- Interest rate = 10%
- Hire period = 4 years

(Answer in Appendix A at the back of the book)

15.7 LEASING

Leasing resembles both HP and conventional borrowing, but deserves separate and extensive analysis for two reasons. First, it is highly significant as a means of financing fixed capital investment, having grown substantially since the 1970s. In 2013, members of the FLA provided £22.4 billion of new finance to the UK business and public sectors, 29 per cent of all fixed capital investment (excluding real estate). Of the total figure, HP accounts for roughly a third of this, while each of the two main forms of leasing discussed below, also account for a third.

Second, it provides an example of the interaction between investment and financing decisions, and an opportunity to show how DCF principles can be applied to financing as well as investment decisions.

■ What is leasing?

According to the International Accounting Standards Board:

> A leasing transaction is a commercial arrangement whereby an equipment owner conveys the right to use the equipment in return for payment by the equipment user of a specified rental over a pre-agreed period of time.

Thus, leasing is a way for companies to obtain the use of equipment when, for varying reasons, they may wish to avoid acquiring it outright using other financing methods. Leasing is a distinctive method of finance because it involves important interactions between the investment and financing decisions.

■ How a lease works

lessee
A firm that leases an asset from a lessor

lessor
A firm that acquires equipment and other assets for leasing out to firms wishing to use such items in their operations

Most leasing activity is undertaken by banking and similar institutions, such as HSBC Equipment Finance. In addition, some manufacturers, such as IBM and John Deere, operate leasing companies to market their own products. A company wishing to obtain the use of an asset (the **lessee**), such as an oil company wishing to lease a tanker, or a Development Corporation wishing to lease property, will approach the leasing specialist (the **lessor**) with its requirements. The deal will involve the lessor purchasing the tanker, or the site, and renting it to the lessee in return for a specified series of rental payments over an agreed time period.

■ Types of lease

capital lease/full payout lease
A lease that transfers most of the benefits and risks of ownership to the lessee

secondary lease
A second lease arranged to follow the termination of the initial lease period

rebate clause
An arrangement whereby the lessor pays a proportion of the resale value of an asset to the lessee

operating lease
A job-specific lease contract, usually arranged for a short period, during which the lessor retains most of the benefits and risks of ownership

part-payout lease
A lease contract which recovers a return lower than the capital outlay made by the lessor

Where the agreed term of the lease approximates to the expected lifetime of the asset, the lessee is clearly using the lease arrangement as an alternative form of finance to outright acquisition. As a result, it avoids having to incur the perhaps substantial cash outlay required at the outset of the project. Hence, this type of lease is called a **finance lease** (or a **capital lease**, or a **full payout lease**).

In the UK, it is important that the asset remains the legal property of the lessor, otherwise certain tax advantages may be lost. At the expiration of the lease contract, the two parties may negotiate a **secondary lease**, or the owner may otherwise dispose of the asset. For assets with long lives, the lessor may ignore the potential resale value of the asset when setting the rentals, since it is too distant in time to predict accurately. Instead, the lessor may agree to reimburse the lessee with a proportion, often over 90 per cent (but never 100 per cent) of the resale value, an agreement known as a **rebate clause**. Rebates are taxable in the hands of the lessee. Secondary leases are often undertaken at nominal or 'peppercorn' rentals to reflect their bonus nature – the owner will already have received back its outlay plus target profit once the contract has reached its full term.

However, not all forms of lease operate over long time periods. The user may not wish to incur the long-term contractual liability to pay rentals, especially if it wishes to obtain the use of the asset only to perform a specific job, e.g. drilling equipment to bore out a specific oil well. Lessors are willing to rent equipment to such firms on the basis of an **operating lease**. This is usually job-specific and can be cancelled easily, whereas cancellation of a finance lease usually involves financial penalties so severe that termination is rarely worthwhile. The lessor will hope to arrange a series of such contracts in order to recover its capital outlay and achieve a profit. For this reason, the operating lease is called a **part-payout lease**. Unlike the finance lease, where the user bears the full risks both of 'downtime' (inability to use the asset) and obsolescence, in an operating lease, the owner incurs the brunt of these risks. To compensate for the risk of having a yard full of idle and rusting equipment, the lessor will apply a rental that is higher per unit of time than that for a financial lease, thus effectively incorporating a risk premium.

Operating leases have another advantage for lessees. They are usually negotiated on a 'maintenance and insurance' basis, whereby the owner undertakes to insure and service the asset. This is normally the responsibility of the user in the case of the finance lease, although the owner may actually perform the servicing functions for a fee. The suitability of the operating lease for short-term projects explains its popularity in the construction industry under the guise of **plant hire**, and for assets with a rapid rate of technological advance such as photocopiers and computers, often called **contract hire**. To compensate for the risks of leasing out high-technology assets, lessors are sometimes able to protect themselves by using specialist computer leasing insurers, although premium rates are generally high.

plant hire
Hiring of construction
equipment

■ The characteristics of a finance lease

Until 1984, UK companies were able to disguise their true indebtedness by undertaking **financial leases**. Neither the asset acquired nor the contractual liability incurred had to appear on the balance sheet, although the rental payment obligation had to be stated in the notes to the accounts. To ensure that balance sheets would give a truer picture of a company's asset/liability position, the UK Accounting Standards Committee issued SSAP 21, 'Accounting for Leases and Hire Purchase'. This clarified the definition of a finance lease and issued instructions on how to account for leases. The subsequently released International Financial Reporting Standard, IAS 17, 'Leases', is consistent with SSAP 21.

finance lease
A method of acquiring an
asset that involves a series
of rental payments extending
over the whole expected lifetime of the asset

Since the period of a finance lease usually matches the expected lifetime of an asset, the old SSAP 21 defined a finance lease as one 'that transfers substantially all the risks and rewards of ownership to the lessee'. It assumes that such a transfer takes place if, at the start of the lease, the present value of the lease amounts to 90 per cent or more of the fair value of the asset (normally its cash price). Leases are still treated as financial leases if they meet one or more of the following criteria:

1 At the end of the lease period, the lessee is given the option to buy the asset at a price below its anticipated market value.
2 The lease period is no less than 75 per cent of the estimated working life of the asset.
3 Ownership of the asset can be transferred to the lessee at the end of the lease.

If, at the termination of a finance lease, the ownership of the asset does pass from lessor to lessee, all previously exploited tax benefits will be clawed back by the Inland Revenue.

The rules laid down for the accounting treatment of a finance lease are as follows:

1 The fair value is capitalised as a fixed asset in the Balance Sheet and is depreciated over its useful life (or lease term, if shorter).
2 Rental payments are treated as comprising two elements – a finance charge and a capital repayment. The finance charge is written off over the lease period at a constant periodic rate.
3 The obligation to pay the capital element of the future rentals is recorded as a long-term creditor in the balance sheet. At the outset of the lease period, the capital element should equal the cash value of the asset.
4 Every year, the appropriate finance charge is recorded in the profit and loss account.

The International Accounting Standards Board (IASB) and the Financial Accounting Standards Board (FASB) are jointly working on a project to investigate the feasibility of aligning the accounting treatment of finance and operating leases (i.e. to require that all leases are shown on the balance sheet) and published a set of revised proposals in May 2013 suggesting how this could be implemented (see **www.ifrs.org** and **www.fasb.org** for developments). The following cameo discusses the potential impact of these.

You gonna buy that?

NEW YORK

Businesses may have to start putting leases on their balance-sheets

When you lease something – a boat, a warehouse, a machine for making ball-bearings – you agree to pay for it bit by bit over time. So it is like incurring a debt, say the International Accounting Standards Board (IASB) and America's Financial Accounting Standards Board (FASB). Therefore, it should be on your balance-sheet. This new rule, proposed on August 17th by the two regulators, has shocked companies everywhere. It is up for public comment until December, but could be enacted as soon as June next year.

Today, companies can opt either for a 'capital lease', which goes on the balance-sheet, or an 'operating lease', which does not. This distinction makes a certain sense. But the IASB and FASB think it is open to abuse. By labelling leases as 'operating', firms can appear less indebted than they really are. The new rules would put the right to use the leased item in the assets column. The obligation to pay for it would go in the debit column.

That will make a lot of firms look wobblier: a survey by PricewaterhouseCoopers, an accounting firm, found that it would add about 58% to the average company's interest-bearing debt. Not only new leases but also existing ones would immediately be subject to the new rules. On the other hand, since rents will no longer be a running expense, operating earnings could see a bump upwards. But since the downturn, many companies are close to their maximum debt limits, and the new rules could push them over the edge. Small wonder they are howling.

The new rules' effects will vary widely. Retailers, who often lease prime property, will take a beating. Airlines, which seldom own their jets, will suffer too. Some businesses, such as utilities, will barely notice. But others will see their apparent return on capital plunge. Many firms will see their debt-to-equity ratios rise and their ability to borrow fall. Some will start leasing the tools of their trade on short-term contracts. Others will simply buy instead of lease, predicts Deloitte, an accounting firm.

Source: The Economist, 21 August 2010.

Self-assessment activity 15.7

What are the main differences between an operating lease (OL) and a finance lease (FL)?

(Answer in Appendix A at the back of the book)

15.8 LEASE EVALUATION: A SIMPLE CASE

We now formally evaluate the decision of whether to lease or purchase an asset. We begin by establishing the basic principles.

A lease requires a series of fixed rentals. This is a major appeal of a lease – the lessee can predict with certainty its future lease payments, and budget accordingly. Because leasing effectively offers fixed-rate finance, we examine the merits of a lease against the yardstick of the cheapest alternative form of borrowing that would otherwise be used to acquire the asset, normally a bank loan. In other words, *leasing is an alternative to borrowing at the risk-free rate (or, more realistically, the bank's lending rate) in order to buy the asset outright*. Because leasing involves incurring a fixed liability, astute lenders regard leases and debts as substitutes, so that an increase in the former should lead to an exactly compensating decrease in the other. While this 'one-for-one debt displacement hypothesis' is not universally accepted, we will assume that lenders recognise leasing for what it is. The leasing decision then amounts to evaluating the question: 'Is it preferable to lease or borrow-to-buy?'

It follows that the *appropriate rate of discount to use in lease evaluation is the lessee's cost of borrowing*. This is shown in the following example.

Example: Lease evaluation: Hardup plc

Hardup plc wishes to lease an executive jet aircraft from Flush Ltd, the leasing subsidiary of Moneybags Bank plc. The aircraft would otherwise cost £13.75 million to purchase via a bank loan at a 12 per cent interest rate. Flush quotes an annual rental of £5 million over three years, with the first instalment payable immediately, and the rest annually thereafter. Should Hardup lease or borrow-to-buy? With a lease, Hardup avoids the immediate cash outlay of £13.75 million, but loses out on any resale value (unless there is a rebate clause).

net advantage of a lease (NAL)
The NPV of the acquisition of an asset adjusted for financing benefits

We may assess the value of the lease on an incremental basis by finding the NPV of the decision to lease rather than borrow-to-buy, sometimes called the **net advantage of the lease (NAL)**. Table 15.2 sets out the relevant cash flows. For the purposes of this simple example, tax has been ignored (we will see later that the tax regulations have had an important bearing on the growth of leasing). We also ignore any resale value.

Table 15.2 Hardup plc's leasing analysis

Item of cash flow (£m)	Year		
	0	1	2
Lease (L)			
Rentals	−5.00	−5.00	−5.00
Buy (B)			
Outlay	−13.75		
Incremental cash flows (L − B)	+8.75	−5.00	−5.00
Present value at 12%	+8.75	−4.46	−3.99
Net present value = £0.30m			

The incremental cash flow profile shows that, by leasing, Hardup effectively obtains net financing of £8.75 million in exchange for debt service costs of £5 million in each of the following two years. (Notice that the timing of rental payments conflicts with our usual assumption of year-end payments. The lease rentals are actually paid at the start of Years 1, 2 and 3, respectively, which has negligible impact on the present value computations, but could have important tax implications.) After allowing for the 12 per cent cost of borrowing, the NPV of +£0.30 million indicates that the optimal form of financing arrangement is to obtain a lease from Flush. The same result could have been obtained by separately discounting the two cash flow streams and choosing the one with the lowest present value. This is simply a comparison between an outlay of £13.75 million and three payments of £5 million p.a. beginning now, with a present value of £13.45 million, discounted at 12 per cent. For many purposes, the incremental layout is easier and clearer: for example, it focuses attention directly on the relative merits of the two options.

■ An alternative method of evaluation: the equivalent loan

equivalent loan
The loan that would involve the same schedule of interest and loan repayments as the profile of rentals required by an equipment lessor

Another approach to lease evaluation is to compare the purchase price of the asset concerned with the **equivalent loan**, defined as the loan that would involve the same schedule of interest and repayments as the profile of rentals required by the lessor. The lease is adjudged worthwhile if the lease rental schedule provides more finance than the loan that would be required to purchase the asset outright. The appeal of this approach is that it emphasises the financing function of a lease. In the Hardup example, the equivalent loan is the maximum loan at 12 per cent that could be supported by a payment of £5 million now and two further payments of £5 million, after one and two years respectively. To find the equivalent loan, we simply calculate the present value of a two-year annuity of £5 million and add the undiscounted first payment of £5 million, yielding a total of:

$$PV = £5m + £5m \ (PVIFA_{(12,2)}) = (£5m + £8.45m) = £13.45m$$

Table 15.3 shows the behaviour of a loan of this amount, serviced by the same profile of payments as required by the lease itself.

Table 15.3 The behaviour of the equivalent loan (£m)

Year	0	1	2	3
1 Balance of loan at start of year	13.45	8.45	4.46	0
2 Payments, of which:	5.00	5.00	5.00	–
3 Interest at 12%	–	1.01	0.54	–
4 Capital	5.00	3.99	4.46	–
5 Balance of loan at end of year (1–4)	8.45	4.46	0	–

All we have done here is to express the calculation in a different way. We have found that the equivalent loan is £13.45 million, while the lease itself provides the ability to acquire an asset whose price is £13.75 million, i.e. for the same profile of payments, the lease allows the firm to 'borrow' an extra £0.30 million, which is precisely the NAL. We can now see that the lease evaluation effectively involves computing a loan equivalent. A lease is worthwhile if the required payment of cash flows could service a loan higher than the outlay required to undertake the project.

In other words, a lease is worthwhile if the effective financing obtained is higher than the equivalent loan. Some writers and analysts prefer to evaluate leases in terms of equivalent loans, but, in more realistic cases, the phasing of rental payments, intermingled with tax complications, can make the computation of an equivalent loan highly complex. Generally, we favour the incremental cash flow approach.

■ Leasing as a financing decision: the three-stage approach

In this section, we offer a note of warning. In the Hardup example, we found leasing was preferable to borrowing-to-buy. However, in many companies, the analysis might not have got this far. For example, had the underlying project (the acquisition of the jet) been revealed as unattractive, the financial manager might not have bothered to undertake a financing analysis. In other words, firms may evaluate decisions in two stages: first, to assess the basic desirability of the activity; and second, if the project is deemed acceptable, to assess the optimal form of financing. The danger in this sequence is that some projects that might be rendered worthwhile by especially favourable financing packages could be rejected. It may make more sense to *evaluate projects as linked investment and financing packages*. To explore further this interaction between investment and financing, we need to explain the *three-stage approach*.

In analysing Hardup's jet acquisition, it was assumed that the investment was inherently worthwhile, and that the remaining issue was how best to finance it. Let us now examine the underlying investment decision. Imagine that Hardup is all-equity financed and that its shareholders require a return of 15 per cent. Assume further that acquisition of the jet would result in annual benefits (such as savings in executive time and in travel expenses, and income from hiring) of £6 million p.a. for three years, treated as year-end lump-sum payments, and which, while uncertain, are no more risky than existing company operations. The NPV of the jet purchase is:

$$\text{NVP} = -£13.75\text{m} + £6\text{m} \, (\text{PVIFA}_{(15,3)}) = -£13.75\text{m} + £13.70\text{m} = -£0.05\text{m}$$

The project would be (just) rejected on the NPV criterion and the issue of how best to finance it might never arise (unless there were non-financial motives, such as corporate prestige, to justify it).

However, it could be acceptable using other methods of finance, such as borrowing or leasing. Of these, lease financing is the most attractive because we know the NAL is £0.30 million. In this example, the acquisition should be undertaken, since the NAL exceeds the negative NPV anticipated from all-equity financing. This suggests how and why a three-stage analysis should be applied. The three stages are as follows:

1 Determine whether the project is inherently attractive.
2 Even if the NPV is negative, evaluate the NAL to assess whether to lease or borrow-to-buy.
3 Assess the value of the project with the chosen financing method.

(N.B. Stage 2 could precede stage 1, of course, but all three should be undertaken.)

To examine stage 3, we compare the benefits anticipated from the project, discounted at the 'risky' rate of 15 per cent, with the costs associated with the cheapest financing method, in this case, the stream of rental payments.

As found earlier, the present value of project benefits is £13.70 million. Now applying the 12 per cent cost of debt finance to the rental stream, we have:

$$\text{PV of rentals} = £5\text{m} + £5\text{m} \, (\text{PVIFA}_{(12,2)}) = £13.75\text{m}$$

Since the project benefits exceed the costs associated with the cheapest financing method, the overall investment-cum-financing package is worthwhile. This is an important result. When judged on its intrinsic merits, and evaluated using 'normal' criteria, the project reduces shareholder wealth by £0.05 million. Yet when evaluated using alternative financing methods, it becomes worthwhile.

Thus we find:

PV of project cash flows = £13.70m

PV of lease rentals = (£13.45m)

NPV of project if leased = £0.25m

This equals the NPV of the basic project (−£0.05m) plus the NAL (+£0.30m).

Not all marginal investment decisions can be turned around by clever financing decisions, but a three-stage approach can help to avoid rejecting some projects that might be worth undertaking if financed in particular ways. Sometimes, the lease may yield net benefits due to the borrowing advantage of the lessor (e.g. a bank), which is passed on to the lessee. Alternatively, it is possible to exploit tax advantages for the mutual benefit of the two parties. Finally, in some cases, the lessor may have bulk-buying advantages not possessed by the lessee.

We will continue to assume that projects are worthwhile in their own right when their benefits are discounted at the appropriate risk-adjusted rate, although it is implicit that a full three-stage analysis is undertaken.

15.9 MOTIVES FOR LEASING

Some writers suggest that leasing is undertaken primarily to exploit tax advantages. Large numbers of firms in the 1970s and early 1980s found that their desired capital expenditures exceeded their taxable earnings and, as a result, they could not take advantage of the 100 per cent First Year Allowances then available, at least until their profitability had recovered. Under these circumstances, leasing was often a more cost-effective form of asset finance than borrowing-to-buy.

Many firms possessing taxable capacity set up leasing subsidiaries in order to shelter their own profits from tax by purchasing capital equipment on behalf of tax-exhausted firms. As a result, the list of active lessors included such odd-looking bedfellows as Tesco, Mothercare, Ladbrokes and Marks & Spencer, all highly profitable companies during this period. Such companies were able to obtain the tax benefits from equipment purchase considerably earlier than their tax-exhausted clients could expect to. In effect, lessors bought equipment on behalf of clients, took the tax benefits and passed these on to clients in the form of reduced rentals.

The extent to which tax benefits are actually passed on depends on the state of competition in the market for leasing and how near to the end of the lessor's tax year the negotiations take place. Sometimes, very attractive lease terms can be obtained from a lessor anxious to qualify for tax reliefs as soon as possible. In these cases, the lessor can profit from the contract, and the lessee may find leasing more attractive than outright purchase. Therefore, both parties can gain from the arrangement at the expense of the taxpayer.

While tax breaks have been important in explaining the rise of leasing, they do not account for the continuing popularity of leasing after the phased abolition of First Year Allowances between 1984 and 1986, and thereafter. Beyond the tax system, a variety of reasons have been proposed to explain the continuing popularity of leasing.

■ 'Leasing offers an attractive alternative source of funds'

For firms subject to capital rationing, leasing may offer an attractive means to access capital markets. This applies especially to small, growing businesses that lack a sufficiently impressive track record to satisfy lenders, or that possess inadequate assets upon which to secure a loan. With a lease, no security is required, since if the lessee defaults, the owner simply repossesses the asset and looks for another client. For this reason, it is unusual to find restrictive clauses in lease contracts, in contrast to debt covenants where the lender may stipulate, for example, that the borrower should not exceed a specified gearing ratio. In addition, few lenders will offer 100 per cent debt financing. They prefer instead to see the client inject a significant amount of equity. This is not the case with a lease contract, which may thus be seen as a 'back-door' method of obtaining total debt financing for the equipment needs of a project.

Some organisations, such as local authorities and government departments, persistently suffer from constraints on capital expenditure and may find leasing an appealing device. In such organisations, there is often a rigid distinction between 'revenue' budgets and 'capital' budgets, which can be exploited by managers aware of the leasing alternative. Equipment may be acquired not by using the tightly controlled capital budget, but by undertaking a lease contract where the rentals are paid out of the revenue budget. Indeed, in the short term, leasing may even be presented as a way of 'saving money'. In 1979, the ability of lessors to obtain tax relief on equipment purchase, regardless of the tax status of the lessee, was removed. Since then, tax relief has been available only in cases where the lessee is normally liable for corporation tax, even if, perhaps temporarily, tax-exhausted. However, the public sector remains an important source of leasing business.

■ 'Leasing has cash flow planning advantages'

Leasing removes the need for a substantial cash outlay at the outset of a project in return for a series of contractually agreed, predictable cash flows over the term of the lease contract. A lease thus has the effect of smoothing out cash flows, which facilitates budgetary planning. However, this is a rather spurious argument as the same effect could be achieved with a bank loan. So this argument only applies if a bank loan is not available. This would, of course, render the 'lease vs. borrow-to-buy' mode of evaluation redundant.

■ 'Leasing provides off-balance sheet financing'

Until SSAP 21 made capitalisation of leases mandatory, companies were not required to show lease obligations in published accounts. This had the effect of disguising their true indebtedness by lowering the recorded gearing ratio, and also raising the return on capital employed. However, lease obligations had to be mentioned in the notes to the accounts, but it may have been fanciful to imagine that lenders (perhaps with their own leasing subsidiaries) were unaware of this form of window-dressing when assessing corporate performance and borrowing levels. However, this argument does, for the moment at least, still apply for operating leases.

■ 'Leasing is cheaper than other forms of finance'

As well as its pragmatic attractions, leasing is often a more cost-effective way of acquiring an asset. We have seen how leasing can be a profitable alternative to bank borrowing under certain conditions. This is equivalent to saying that the effective rate of interest on a lease contract is lower than that on a bank loan. Indeed, many firms evaluate leases by comparing the bank's effective lending rate with the rate of interest implicit in the lease contract, i.e. the internal rate of return on the profile of lease payments, including the 'up-front' financing. Of particular interest is the case of an 'end-year lease', written on or just before the end of the lessor's tax year. At this juncture, the lessor is anxious to get the contract drawn up so as to claim the tax relief in the year just ending, rather than having to wait a further year before reaping the tax advantage. Many lessors have borrowing advantages owing to their size, which they may pass on to lessees in the form of lower rental charges.

15.10 ALLOWING FOR CORPORATION TAX IN LEASE EVALUATION

The Hardup example omitted the impact of taxation. Lease rentals qualify for tax relief, as do interest payments on loans, while expenditures to purchase capital equipment generally attract capital allowances against corporation tax. Including tax is particularly important, since the UK tax system was widely believed to be largely responsible for the original upsurge in leasing activity in the UK.

The current (2015–16) UK regime involves Corporation Tax paid at 20% and a Writing-Down Allowance of 18% p.a. A firm with sufficiently high taxable profits can set off a proportion of its outlay on capital equipment against profits in the year of expenditure, and in each subsequent year, based on a reducing balance. Consequently, by careful timing of expenditures, a company with sufficient taxable capacity can enjoy significant tax savings.

A firm that is not tax-exhausted can shelter its profits from tax by acquiring assets for leasing. In effect, the taxpayer subsidises the required outlay, making equipment purchase a more attractive proposition for the tax-paying enterprise. Conversely, tax relief on rental payments lowers their effective cost.

Self-assessment activity 15.8

What is the tax-adjusted interest rate when the nominal rate is 9 per cent for:

(i) a firm paying tax at 20 per cent?
(ii) a tax-exhausted firm?

(Answer in Appendix A at the back of the book)

■ The current tax treatment of lease rentals

However, lease rentals are not fully tax-deductible. In 1991, the UK tax authorities altered the rules, to bring the tax treatment of leases into line with SSAP 21. This dictates that finance leases be stated on the balance sheet and depreciated accordingly to reflect the 'substance' rather than the 'form' of a lease contract, thus treating it as quasi-ownership over the life of the asset. For leases taken out after April 1991, the Inland Revenue requires a separate treatment for the implicit finance charge and the implicit capital charge. The former depends on the interest rate implicit in the lease contract, and is tax-allowable in full in the relevant accounting period. The capital repayment element is derived by spreading the total capital charge – normally the asset's cash price – over its useful life. In other words, the depreciation charge in the accounts becomes the tax-allowable figure, dependent on the method of depreciation used and its acceptability to the Inland Revenue. An example should clarify this.

Example

Consider the case of a four-year lease contract to finance acquisition of an asset costing £10 million. The rental is £3.15 million p.a., paid at each year-end. The effective interest rate is the solution rate in the IRR expression formed by setting the finance raised equal to the sum of discounted payments:

$$£10m = \frac{£3.15m}{(1 + R)} + \frac{£3.15m}{(1 + R)^2} + \frac{£3.15m}{(1 + R)^3} + \frac{£3.15m}{(1 + R)^4}$$

R is exactly 10 per cent. The annual interest charge can now be found by analysing the implicit loan of £10 million as shown in Table 15.4.

Table 15.4 Interest charges on a lease contract (figures in £m)

Year	Opening balance	Interest at 10%	End of year debt	Repayment	Closing balance
1	10.00	1.00	11.00	3.15	7.85
2	7.85	0.78	8.63	3.15	5.48
3	5.48	0.55	6.03	3.15	2.88
4	2.88	0.29	3.17	3.15	0.02*

*Rounding errors prevent this reducing exactly to zero.

Applying straight-line depreciation to the asset cost, the annual charge is £10m/4 = £2.5m. This is fully allowable against tax in each of the four years. Table 15.5 compares the profiles of tax-allowable expenditures, and thus the impact of the 1991 changes. The present system accelerates the tax relief, and reduces the effective cost of the lease (for the tax-paying company). The interest charge is included under interest payments on the firm's profit and loss account, while the depreciation element is applied to lower the value of the asset in the usual way.

Table 15.5 Changes in tax-allowable lease costs (figures in £m)

Year	*Then* Rental	*Now* Interest	+	*Now* Capital charge	=	Total
1	3.15	1.00	+	2.50	=	3.50
2	3.15	0.78	+	2.50	=	3.28
3	3.15	0.55	+	2.50	=	3.05
4	3.15	0.29	+	2.50	=	2.79
Totals	12.60	2.62	+	10.00	=	12.62*

*Rounding error.

15.11 WORKED EXAMPLE OF LEASING TO INCLUDE TAXATION: PORLOCK plc

Porlock plc wishes to acquire an asset with a 4-year life. It can lease or buy.

■ The Buy alternative

To buy the asset requires an outlay of £10m, and will generate a residual value of £2m, payable at the end of year four. There is a Writing-Down Allowance (WDA) of 18 per cent p.a. available and the tax rate is 20 per cent, payable a year in arrears. Porlock plc can borrow at an annual rate of 7.5 per cent *before* tax.

■ The Lease alternative

Leasing requires an annual rental of £2.65m, paid in advance, i.e. at the end of each year, including Year 0. Tax relief can be claimed on the interest element of the rental payments and also on the implied depreciation of the asset on a straight-line basis.

■ Other information

The user will incur maintenance charges under either alternative. Whether purchaser or lessee, it can be assumed that the firm has sufficient taxable capacity to absorb all relevant tax allowances.

■ Cash flows and present value of the Buy alternative

First calculate the value of the annual tax allowances, offered at 18 per cent p.a. (see Table 15.6)

Table 15.6 Calculation of the tax savings

Year	£m Tax benefit @18% of WDA	£m Tax saving one year later	£m Written-down value
0	1.80	0.36	8.20
1	1.48	0.30	6.72
2	1.21	0.24	5.51
3	0.99	0.20	4.52
4	(4.52 − 2.00) = 2.52	0.50	0

Note that, in principle, total tax savings over time should equal (outlay, net of residual value, times tax rate) = £8m × 20% = £1.60m. This is the case here.

With tax relief on interest, the cost of borrowing after tax = 7.5% (1–20%) = 6%

The present value of the buy alternative is shown in Table 15.7.

Table 15.7 Present value of the Buy alternative

Year	0	1	2	3	4	5
Outlay (£m)	−10.00					
Tax savings (£m)		0.36	0.30	0.24	0.20	0.50
Residual value (£m)					2.00	
Net cash flows (£m)	−10.00	0.36	0.30	0.24	2.20	0.50
PV factors @ 6%	1.000	0.943	0.890	0.840	0.792	0.747
PV (£m)	−10.00	0.34	0.27	0.20	1.74	0.37

PV of costs of the Buy alternative = −£10.00m + £2.92 = **−£7.08m**.

Leasing is more worthwhile if the PV of costs, net of relevant tax reliefs, is less than £7.08m.

■ Cash flows and present value of the Lease alternative

First, calculate the implied interest rate on the finance involved.

The lease payments involve an up-front payment at the end of Year 0 plus three further instalments. The implied interest rate is thus the solution to the following IRR expression:

£10m = £2.65m + £2.65m (three-year annuity factor @ r%)
i.e. £10m = £2.65m (1 + PVIFA)

Whence 1 + PVIFA = £10m/£2.65m = 3.775. and PVIFA = 2.775.

Using the annuity tables, it can be seen that the interest rate = 4%

At 4% interest, the implied loan will thus behave as shown in Table 15.8:

Table 15.8 Behaviour of a loan at 4% interest

Year	0	1	2	3
Principal (£m)	10	7.35	4.99	2.54
Interest @ 4% (£m)	–	0.29	0.20	0.11
Balance (£m)	10.00	7.64	5.19	2.65
Rental (£m)	2.65	2.65	2.65	2.65
Closing balance (£m)	7.35	4.99	2.54	0

Porlock can claim tax relief on the stream of interest payments thus calculated, and also on the profile of depreciation payments. These latter are £10m/4 = £2.5m p.a.

Allowing for tax relief one year in arrears, the profile of cash flows for the lease alternative is as shown in Table 15.9:

Table 15.9 Profile of lease payments

Year	0	1	2	3	4
Rentals (£m)	−2.65	−2.65	−2.65	−2.65	
Interest (£m)		−0.29	−0.20	−0.11	
Tax savings (£m)			0.06	0.04	0.02
Depreciation	2.50	2.50	2.50	2.50	
Tax savings (£m)		0.50	0.50	0.50	0.50
Net cash flows (£m)	−2.65	−2.15	−2.09	−2.11	0.52
(Bold items)					
PV Factors @ 6%	1.000	0.943	0.890	0.840	0.792
PV (£m)	−2.65	−2.03	−1.86	−1.77	0.41

Thus, the PV of leasing costs = −£7.90m.

■ The decision

This compares with a figure of −£7.08m for the PV of the purchase costs. In this case, outright purchase is the cheaper option. This might alter if the lessor were to rebate some element of the resale value of the asset to the lessee (which is common for a finance lease) or if it chose to pay for maintenance costs (which would be unusual).

15.12 POLICY IMPLICATIONS: WHEN SHOULD FIRMS LEASE?

There are two lessons to be drawn from this analysis of leasing decisions:

1 Lease evaluation involves analysing a financing decision, as borne out by the three-stage analysis. Sometimes, especially favourable financing arrangements, available via a lease contract, may tip the balance between project rejection and acceptance. But these cases are rare, and the margin of acceptance offered by attractive financing will probably be fairly narrow. If the project is worthwhile only because of the financing package, this should be explicitly recognised and the concessionary finance regarded as a 'one-off', which may not be repeated in other cases. It seems unduly purist to argue that, if the financing deal is all that makes the project acceptable, then it should be rejected. Few financial managers would pass up an attractive financing opportunity. *However, policy is more profitably directed at finding genuinely worthwhile projects, rather than diverting resources to obtaining marginal financing advantages.*

2 The analysis enables us to pinpoint the factors that suggest the relative attractiveness of leasing as compared to other financing arrangements. We now list the factors that impact on the leasing decision, but note that these are mainly 'other things being equal' issues. 'Look before you lease' is a sensible motto.

Taxable capacity

Leasing is a means whereby lessors can exploit their own taxable capacity and pass on any tax savings to firms in less favourable tax positions. Hence, the greater the taxable capacity of would-be lessors and the lower that of users of capital equipment, the greater the attractions of leasing.

Competition among lessors

A major factor in the development of the UK leasing market was the entry of new players, eager to exploit their taxable capacity and thus shelter their profits from corporation tax. This had the effect of increasing competition for available leasing business and reducing the general level of lease rentals. Therefore, the greater the competition among lessors, the greater the attractiveness of leasing.

Investment incentives

Another major factor in the growth of the leasing industry was the availability of especially generous inducements to encourage firms to acquire plant, machinery and industrial buildings. Although UK incentives are now less attractive than those existing prior to 1984, there was no fall-off in leasing after the removal of First Year Allowances, probably owing to the other attractions of leasing. However, it seems reasonable to argue that, the greater the generosity of the tax authorities, the greater the attractiveness of leasing because tax-breaks lower the effective cost of equipment purchase for lessors, which may then pass on the benefits to lessees, whether or not they are tax-exhausted.

Corporation tax

Investment incentives are most valuable when high rates of corporation tax raise the value of the tax savings. Until 1984, with 100 per cent First Year Allowances (FYAs), the total (undiscounted) tax saving with corporation tax payable at 52 per cent for a £10 million investment would have been £5.2 million. This falls to £2.0 million with a tax rate of 20 per cent and, when discounted, even lower with annual WDAs rather than 100 per cent FYAs. The higher the rate of corporate profits tax, the more attractive leasing becomes, because lessors can shelter their profits to a greater extent.

Inflation

Rising price levels reduce the real value of future payments, such as a series of fixed rental payments. Therefore, the higher the expected rate of inflation, the greater the likely appeal of leasing. However, the inflation effect will benefit the lessee only if it correctly anticipates a higher rate of inflation than the lessor. As in all contractual arrangements, unanticipated inflation is what does the damage, and it is by no means certain that the lessee will be more successful than the lessor in forecasting inflation. If lessors feel confident in their ability to predict inflation, if the rentals they set incorporate their expectations, and if they are more or less correct, the benefits expected by lessees will evaporate. In addition, lease contracts may incorporate some form of inflation adjustment.

Interest rates

The relevant rate of discount in lease evaluation is the rate applicable to the best alternative bank loan. The higher the rate of interest, the greater the discounting effect on future contractual lease obligations. Generally, therefore, the higher the interest rate, the more attractive a lease appears, since the present value of a given set of rentals will become lower. However, this effect may be diluted by the impact of lessors applying higher rentals in order to cover their own increased borrowing costs. If there is any tendency for the spread of interest rates to widen at higher levels of interest rates, this effect may still operate, since lessors usually have access to borrowed capital at more advantageous rates than lessees.

SUMMARY

We have described a variety of short- and medium-term methods of financing company operations: trade credit, bank lending, factoring and invoice discounting, money market finance, HP and leasing. The key features of each source were examined, and particular emphasis was given to leasing and HP, where the tax implications were analysed.

Key points

- Companies have access to significant amounts of trade credit through normal trading relationships.

- Abuse of trade credit facilities can lead to severe liquidity problems.

- Companies are using term loans more extensively, even though these are generally more expensive than overdraft facilities.

- The money market can offer significant amounts of credit through bill finance.

- Hire purchase is often used by smaller, less creditworthy, companies to purchase equipment. The asset becomes the property of the user upon completion of the contract as scheduled. Users can exploit capital allowances in relation to assets acquired via HP.

- Leasing is a way of obtaining the use of an asset without incurring the initial 'lump' of capital outlay required for outright purchase.

- Leases may be 'job-specific' contracts applicable for periods less than the lifespan of assets (operating leases), or for periods coinciding with the asset's expected lifetime (financial leases).

- A lease contract normally involves a commitment to pay a series of fixed rental charges, which qualify the lessee for tax relief. A finance lease is an alternative to borrowing in order to purchase an asset, and the firm should expect its ability to borrow to fall by an equivalent amount.

- In the UK, if the ownership of a leased asset passes to the lessee, the tax breaks are clawed back by the Inland Revenue.

- SSAP 21 stipulates that leased assets acquired via finance leases must be included among fixed assets on the firm's balance sheet and that future rental obligations be recorded as liabilities.

- Evaluation of a lease, i.e. whether to lease or to borrow-to-buy, may be undertaken in three equivalent ways:

  1 by comparing the present values of the respective cash flow streams;

  2 by assessing what equivalent loan could be raised with the same stream of payments entailed by the lease;

  3 by comparing the effective rate of interest payable on the lease with the costs of raising an equivalent loan.

- Lease evaluation usually assumes that the asset is worth obtaining in its own right, regardless of financing method, but an unattractive investment could be rendered worthwhile by leasing. To investigate this, a three-stage analysis should be undertaken.

- Even though financial criteria may point to a definite preference, consideration of non-financial factors may reverse the lease or borrow-to-buy decision.

Further reading

The classic works on leasing are by Clark (1978) and Tomkins *et al.* (1979). Rutterford (1992) gives a more up-to-date treatment, while successive annual reports of the Finance and Leasing Association (**www.fla.org.uk**) will keep you abreast of developments. See Bowman (1980) and Narayanaswamy (1994) for empirical work that supports the leasing–debt equivalence view in the USA and the UK respectively, and Ang and Peterson (1984) for an exception. Myers *et al.* (1976) develop the standard lease evaluation model on which the analysis in the chapter is based. Jarvis *et al.* (2000) have conducted a historical appraisal of UK government policy in this area. See Koh (2006) for an overview of trends in the European leasing industry.

The availability of access to finance for small and medium-size (SME) firms differs greatly from large firms. Articles on the financing difficulties faced by SME firms include Beck et al. (2008) and Irwin and Scott (2010).

Appendix
FINANCING INTERNATIONAL TRADE

Obviously, it takes two parties to trade across country borders, the importer and the exporter, but here, we adopt the perspective of the exporter. Exporting carries particular risks, e.g. the risk of slow (or even non-) payment by customers and the risk of adverse currency movements. Hence, export finance is rather more complex than the finance of domestic trade. The banking system, both domestic and foreign, usually has a pivotal part to play both in arranging contract terms and making arrangements for the exporter to be paid.

open account
Where trading partners agree settlement terms with no formal contract

The simplest basis of trading is **open account**, where the parties simply make a 'gentleman's agreement' about the settlement date, prior to which the goods are shipped, received by the importer and used for production or sale. The exporter thus loses control over the goods and has recourse to the legal system if the importer fails to pay. Open account is thus confined to deals involving established, reliable and highly creditworthy customers located in countries that have rapid, fair and reliable payment and legal procedures. Much of the trade involving large UK firms with large EU-based firms is conducted on open account. The advent of the euro as the common currency of the EU has increased the proportion of intra-EU trade conducted on open account.

With less reliable, or new, customers based in other parts of the world, more formal procedures are required. As a first requisite, to overcome the fear of non-payment by a customer in a foreign country, the exporter enlists the help of a well-respected bank to act as intermediary. Using the reputation and good offices of the bank, the trade-cum-financing package typically works as follows:

- the importer secures the promise of the bank to pay on its behalf;
- the bank promises the exporter to pay on behalf of the importer;
- the exporter ships the goods, trusting to the bank's promise to pay;
- the bank pays the exporter at a pre-agreed juncture;
- the bank passes title to the goods to the importer;
- the importer pays the bank, often using the sale proceeds of the goods shipped.

■ Trade documents

letter of credit
A credit drawn up by an importer in favour of an exporter. It is endorsed by a bank that guarantees payment provided the beneficiary delivers the Bill of Lading proving that goods have been shipped

Most export deals involve three key documents:

- The bank's promise to pay is called a **Letter of credit**.
- When the exporter ships the goods to the importer's location, title to the goods is conveyed to the bank by a **Bill of lading**.
- When the exporter seeks payment from the bank, it presents a '**sight draft**'. When the bank has paid the exporter, title to ownership of the goods passes to the importer, who duly pays the bank.

bill of lading
A document that transfers title to exported goods to the bank that finances the deal when the goods are shipped

There is obvious potential for delay in these procedures, e.g. in trans-shipment of goods, in inspecting the goods, in acceptance of the documents, etc. Hence, the bank plays a key role in 'holding the ring' between importer and exporter and providing a source of short-term finance. The three documents help protect the two parties from the risk of non-completion of the contract.

sight draft
A document presented to a bank by an exporter seeking payment for an export deal

We now pay particular attention to the Letter of Credit, as this represents the bank's promise to pay.

■ Letters of credit (LOC)

An LOC, or documentary letter of credit (DLOC), is a document drawn up by an importer giving its bank detailed instructions as to the circumstances in which the credit can be honoured by the importer's bank (the 'opening bank') in favour of the exporter. It details the nature of the goods, their quality and price and the dates between which the LOC is valid. A DLOC enables the exporter to receive payment for goods in its country of location once shipment has taken place. The burden of financing is thus on the importer, who gains the comfort of knowing a definite date by which the exporter must ship the goods. The exporter's risk is reduced insofar as the creditworthiness of the involved banks is substituted for that of the buyer.

irrevocable DLOC
A written authority for a bank to make specified payments to an exporter, whose terms cannot be varied

There are two types of DLOC. An **irrevocable DLOC** is a written authority from the opening bank to its correspondent bank in the exporter's country (the 'advising bank') to make specified payments provided that the documents specified are presented between the specified dates. If requested, the advising bank will add its own undertaking to that of the opening bank by confirming the DLOC, which becomes a 'confirmed DLOC'. This type of DLOC is legally binding and thus cannot be modified or cancelled except with the consent of all parties involved.

revocable DLOC
A letter of credit whose terms can be varied without consulting the exporter

Conversely, a **revocable DLOC** can be altered or cancelled at any time without having to give prior notice to the beneficiary, i.e. the exporter. It cannot be confirmed and is not legally binding.

■ Drawbacks with letters of credit

DLOCs are not problem-free:

- They can be expensive. The importer is likely to demand a lower price if it uses a DLOC, as insurance against potential hitches in the transaction, removing the need for the exporter to build these into the price.
- The advising bank has to check that the documents presented exactly conform to the specifications stipulated. If they do not, payment will be refused.
- Banks do not accept responsibility for the goods shipped. A DLOC arrangement is simply about transferring documents at arm's length from the trading activity. If the documents are in order, the credit will be honoured.
- The opening bank bears a credit risk while the credit is open. It may thus demand a cash deposit or lower the importer's other borrowing facilities.

Other methods of financing international trade are: Bills of Exchange, documentary collections, forfaiting and export factoring.

Bills of Exchange in export trade

The use of Bills of Exchange in export trade is similar in essence to their domestic use. An exporter can send a Bill of Exchange for the value of goods shipped through the banking system for payment by a foreign buyer when presented. The exporter usually prepares the bill, drawn on the foreign-based importer, for the amount specified in the export contract.

Using the bill along with the other shipping documents via the banking system, the exporter retains greater control over the goods because, until the bill is paid or accepted by the foreign buyer, they cannot be released. The importer acknowledges its agreement to pay on the due date by writing an acceptance on the bill, but does not have to pay, or agree to pay, until delivery of the goods by the exporter.

The exporter may pass the bill to a domestic bank, which forwards it to a foreign branch of the same bank or to a correspondent bank in the importer's country. The so-called 'collecting bank' presents the bill to whoever it is drawn upon, either for immediate payment, if it is a 'sight draft', or for acceptance, if it is a 'term draft', payable after a specified credit term. Where no shipping documents are required, this is called a 'clean bill collection'.

Where the importer's financial standing is doubtful, the bill may be used in a 'documentary credit collection'. The exporter sends the bill to its bank which in turn sends it to its foreign-based correspondent, along with the shipping documents, including the title to the goods, represented by the Bill of Lading. The bank releases the documents to the importer only on payment or acceptance of the bill by the foreign buyer. In this way, greater control of the goods is achieved.

Bills of Exchange have several advantages:

- They are cheaper than letters of credit.
- Because the title documents can only be released on payment, the exporter has a stronger position than in open account trades.
- The bills can be discounted via the banking system to release finance for other uses. Effectively, the bank buys the customer's account payable, represented by the proceeds of the export deal at the time that the collection is remitted abroad.
- Banks may also give an advance based on an outward collection of Bills of Exchange, i.e. the anticipated payment.
- Bills of Exchange reduce the risk of non-payment, given that banks do not want to be associated with clients of poor credit standing.

Forfaiting

forfaiting
The practice whereby a bank purchases an exporter's sales invoices or promissory notes, that usually carry the guarantee of the importer's bank

Forfaiting is a form of medium-term export financing that involves the purchase by a bank (the 'forfaiter') of a series of promissory notes, usually due at six-month intervals over perhaps three to four years, signed by an importer in favour of an exporter. The notes are usually guaranteed ('avalised') by the importer's bank and then sold by the exporter to the forfaiting bank at a discount. The bank pays the exporter, allowing it to finance the production of the goods destined for export, and enabling the importer to settle later. The promissory notes are held by the forfaiter for collection as they mature, on a without-recourse basis, thus the exporter is not liable in case of default by the importer.

The rate of discount applied in forfaiting depends on the terms of the notes, the currencies of denomination, the credit ratings of the importer and of the bank that guarantees the notes, as well as the country risk of the importer's base. Because the forfaiting bank will quote a discount rate on demand, the exporter is able to quote a selling price to foreign customers that allows for financing costs.

■ Export factoring and invoice discounting

Export factoring is similar in essence to domestic factoring, with the added bonus that the factor usually assumes the foreign exchange risk. If an export receivable is to be settled on open account, rather than by DLOC or Bill of Exchange, the exporter can offer the receivable to a factor in exchange for domestic currency, thus offering protection against foreign exchange rate movements. The factor provides finance and also absorbs credit risk. Export factoring may therefore be expensive.

Factors may have their own offices abroad where they can investigate directly the credit status of firms' clients locally, or may be a member of a network of independent factoring organisations. The largest of these is Factors Chain International (FCI) (www.fci.nl), founded in 1968. FCI currently (March 2014) boasts 254 member firms, operating in 75 of the world's main commercial centres and accounting for over 80 per cent of world cross-border factoring activity.

As with domestic factoring, recourse and non-recourse versions are available, the latter being very convenient for export business, although more expensive. As well as a charge for providing finance, the factor applies a service fee of between 0.5 per cent and 2 per cent for running the sales ledger and collecting debts. In 2013, UK export invoice discounting grew 12 per cent, while export factoring rose by 18 per cent. However, at an activity level of £15.6bn compared to just £1.9bn, export invoice discounting is a far more popular facility.

QUESTIONS

Questions with a coloured number have solutions in Appendix B on page 795.

1 A supplier offers you the following trade credit terms: '3/15: net 45'.
  If you delay payment until day 45, what effective annual interest rate are you paying for additional trade credit?

2 A bank offers a client a choice between two financing options over a one-year period:

Option 1: a bullet loan for the full year of £500,000 to be repaid at end year with interest fixed at 12 per cent p.a.

Option 2: An overdraft, with a quoted rate of 14 per cent p.a., with interest charged quarterly on the average balance.
  The firm expects to need finance of £400,000 in the first quarter, £500,000 in quater 2, £500,000 in quarter 3 and only £200,000 in the final quarter due to the seasonal nature of its business. (These are all quarterly averages.)
  Unused funds can be invested at 2 per cent per quarter. The bank will not charge interest on accumulated quarterly interest charges.

(a) What advice would you give?
(b) What is the break-even rate on the overdraft, assuming the interest rate on the loan is fixed at 12 per cent?

3 A trader receives from a customer a Bill of Exchange set to mature in six months, and decides, after two months, to sell it to a bank. The face value is £200,000 and the bank discounts the Bill for £195,500.
  What effective annual interest rate is the trader paying to accelerate receipt of his money?

4 What is the monthly interest payment on the following HP contract?

- Total purchase cost of equipment = £100,000
- Down-payment = 15 per cent
- Interest rate = 7.5 per cent
- Equal monthly payments over four years.

5 Haverah plc is a manufacturer and distributor of denim garments. It employs a highly aggressive working capital policy, and uses no long-term borrowing. Highlights from its most recent accounts appear below:

	£m
Sales	45.00
Purchases	20.00
Earnings before interest and tax	5.00
Interest payments	2.00
Shareholder funds (comprising £1m issued shares, par value 50p, and £3m reserves)	4.00
Debtors	2.50
Stocks	1.00
Trade creditors	6.00
Bank overdraft	5.00

Killinghall is a supplier of cloth to Haverah and accounts for 40 per cent of its purchases. It is most anxious about Haverah's policy of taking extended trade credit, so it offers Haverah the opportunity to pay for supplies within 25 days in return for a discount on the invoiced value of 4 per cent.

Haverah is able to borrow on overdraft from its bank at 10 per cent. Tax on corporate profit is paid at 30 per cent.

Required

If Haverah made this arrangement with its supplier, what would be the effect on its working capital cycle and key accounting measures such as interest cover, profit after tax, earnings per share, return on equity and gearing? Should it accept the offer?

6 Raphael Ltd is a small engineering business which has annual credit sales of £2.4 million. In recent years, the company has experienced credit control problems. The average collection period for sales has risen to 50 days even though the stated policy of the business is for payment to be made within 30 days. In addition, 1.5 per cent of sales are written off as bad debts each year.

The company has recently been in talks with a factor who is prepared to make an advance to the company equivalent to 80 per cent of debtors, based on the assumption that customers will, in future, adhere to a 30-day payment period. The interest rate for the advance will be 11 per cent per annum. The trade debtors are currently financed through a bank overdraft which has an interest rate of 12 per cent per annum. The factor will take over credit control procedures of the business and this will result in a saving to the business of £18,000 per annum. However, the factor will make a charge of 2 per cent of sales for this service. The use of the factoring service is expected to eliminate the bad debts incurred by the business.

Raphael Ltd is also considering a change in policy towards payment of its suppliers. The company is given credit terms which allow a 2.5 per cent discount providing the amount due is paid within 15 days. However, Raphael Ltd has not taken advantage of the discount opportunity to date and has, instead, taken a 50-day payment period even though suppliers require payment within 40 days. The company is now considering the payment of suppliers on the fifteenth day of the credit period in order to take advantage of the discount opportunity.

Required

(a) Calculate the net cost of the factor agreement to the company and state whether or not the company should take advantage of the opportunity to factor its trade debts.

(b) Explain the ways in which factoring differs from invoice discounting.

(c) Calculate the approximate annual percentage cost of forgoing trade discounts to suppliers and state what additional financial information the company would need in order to decide whether or not it should change its policy in favour of taking the discounts offered.

(d) Discuss any other factors which may be important when deciding whether or not it should change its policy in favour of taking the discounts offered.

(Certified Diploma, June 1996)

7 Amalgamated Effluents plc, a chemical company currently in legal difficulties over its pollution record, is considering a proposal to acquire new equipment to improve waste generation. The equipment would cost £500,000 and have a working life of four years. At the end of Year 4, the disposal value of the equipment is expected to be £50,000. The machine is expected to generate incremental cash flows of £200,000 for each of the four years.

Amalgamated can acquire the equipment in two ways:

(a) Outright purchase via a four-year bank loan at a pre-tax interest cost of 7 per cent.

(b) A financial lease with rentals of £70,000 at the end of each of the four years.

Amalgamated is presently ungeared. Its shareholders seek a return of 10 per cent after allowing for all taxes. Corporation Tax is paid at 30 per cent with no tax delay. If the equipment is purchased, a 25 per cent writing-down allowance (reducing balance) is available.

Required

Should Amalgamated acquire the equipment and, if so, how should it be financed?

8 LEE is a manufacturing entity located in Newland, a country with the dollar ($) as its currency. LOR is a leasing entity that is also located in Newland.

LEE plans to replace a key piece of machinery and is initially considering the following two approaches:

- Alternative 1 – purchase the machinery, financed by borrowing for a five-year term.
- Alternative 2 – lease the machinery from LOR on a five-year operating lease.

The machinery and maintenance costs

The machinery has a useful life of approximately 10 years, but LEE is aware that the industry is facing a period of intense competition and the machinery may not be needed in five years' time. It would cost LEE $5,000 to buy the machinery, but LOR has greater purchasing power and could acquire the machinery for $4,000.

Maintenance costs are estimated to be $60 in each of Years 1 to 3 and $100 in each of Years 4 and 5, arising at the *end* of the year.

Alternative 1 – purchase financed by borrowing for a five-year term

$ interbank borrowing rates in Newland are currently 5.5 per cent per annum. LEE can borrow at interbank rates plus a margin of 1.7 per cent and expects $ interbank rates to remain constant over the five-year period. It has estimated that the machinery could be sold for $2,000 at the end of five years.

Alternative 2 – five-year operating lease

Under the operating lease, LOR would be responsible for maintenance costs and would charge LEE lease rentals of $850 annually *in advance* for five years.

LOR knows that LEE is keen to lease rather than buy the machine and wants to take advantage of this position by increasing the rentals on the operating lease. However, it does not want to lose LEE's custom and requires advice on how high a lease rental LEE would be likely to accept.

Tax regulations

Newland's tax rules for operating leases give the lessor tax depreciation allowances on the asset and give the lessee full tax relief on the lease payments. Tax depreciation allowances are available to the purchaser of a business asset at 25 per cent per annum on a reducing balance basis. The business tax rate is 30 per cent and tax should be assumed to arise at the end of each year and be paid one year later.

Alternative 3 – late proposal by production manager

During the evaluation process for Alternatives 1 and 2, the production manager suggested that another lease structure should also be considered, to be referred to as 'Alternative 3'. No figures are available at present to enable a numerical evaluation to be carried out for Alternative 3. The basic structure would be a five-year lease with the option to renew at the end of the five-year term for an additional five-year term at negligible rental. LEE would be responsible for maintenance costs.

Required:

(i) Use discounted cash flow analysis to evaluate and compare the cost to LEE of each of Alternatives 1 and 2.

(ii) Advise LOR on the highest lease rentals that LEE would be likely to accept under Alternative 2.

(Cima, May 2007)

Part V

STRATEGIC FINANCIAL DECISIONS

Financial managers face two key decisions: 'Which assets to invest in?' and, 'How to finance them?' Earlier in the book, we discussed strategic investment decisions, and we examined short-term financing in Part IV.

Also in Part IV, there was strong emphasis on the 'Golden Rule' of financing – that the term of financing should be matched to the term of the asset acquired finance (although we did encounter alternative stances). It is now appropriate to look at methods of financing long-term strategic investments, i.e. long-term sources of finance. This is done in Chapter 16.

Choices between alternative forms of finance essentially reduce to choices between different mixes of borrowing and equity capital in the firm's capital structure. We therefore examine, in Chapter 17, the factors that determine a firm's dividend policy – a decision to distribute higher dividends has implications for the debt/equity mix, but there are important constraints on dividend policy.

In Chapters 18 and 19, we examine how the use of borrowed funds can affect the value of the company and the return required on new investments. Chapter 18 presents the 'traditional' view on these issues, while Chapter 19 presents the 'modern' theory of capital structure, which emphasises the essential underlying relationships. We will also discover how borrowing affects the Beta coefficient, and how to tackle cases of investment evaluation where a firm alters its gearing and its (systematic) risk. We extend the analysis to cover interactions between investment and financing decisions and develop a decision rule – the adjusted present value – to handle complex interactions.

In Chapter 20, we examine mergers and takeovers – why they occur, how they are financed, and the effects they have on organisational structure and shareholder wealth. Other forms of restructuring are also considered.

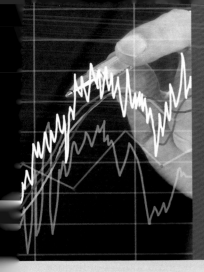

16

Long-term finance

Loss-making microblog firm sells for a macro-price (Chirpy-chirpy not so cheap)

One of the trickiest issues when making an initial public offering is setting the price – too low and the original owners feel short-changed, too high and investors are reluctant to buy, risking the embarrassment of unsold shares being left with the underwriters (see below). Valuation is reasonably straightforward when the firm has a track record of making profits, or owns sizeable assets. But when it has neither, the guessing games start. Eight-years old, but with revenues thought to be growing too slowly to warrant a floatation, Twitter had been tipped for an IPO for several years, but surprised the markets in September 2013, when it announced that it would go public on the New York Stock Exchange (rather than NASDAQ, the favoured outlet of many other hi-tech issues, such as Facebook) another two months later. Twitter's last reported quarterly sales were $169m and its net losses were $65m, compared to $22m a year earlier. Since 2010, it had lost over $440m.

Initial plans were to set the price at between $17 and $20 apiece, but expressions of enthusiasm for the company led its advisers to up the ante to $23–$25, which would have raised $1.75bn and valued the firm at $13.6bn.

In the event, the shares soared to an opening price of over $45, and briefly touched $50, valuing the company at $27bn, an opening gain of 74%.

But despite having over 230m users, Twitter has less broad appeal than Facebook, used by over half of Britons and Americans, and relies for its popularity on the deepest thoughts of celebrities and sportspeople as opposed to news stories from friends and family. Expected revenues were only a third of those already achieved by Facebook, and only a quarter of those achieved by LinkedIn, two much lower-valued firms.

So how does one explain the market's enthusiasm for Twitter? Wild expectations? Blind faith? Nostalgia for the 'dot.com boom' of a decade previously? Or just rose-tinted spectacles?

Whatever the reason, the risks are huge, e.g. a deluge of adverts that annoy users, breaches of privacy, people clogging up the 'Twittersphere' with too many pointless tweets or simply a change in tastes that spelt curtains for other short-lived social networking 'stars'.

One analyst said 'If you can get me to revenues of $6bn in 2018, I can get to $45 a share'. Forecast revenues for 2014 were just $1bn. His conclusion, shared by many others, was 'sell'.

By end-January 2014, it looked as if the naysayers had been routed, as the shares had climbed to $65, valuing Twitter at $36bn. Yet nemesis arrived a few days later when Twitter reported full year results for 2013. Although revenues had doubled to $655m, losses had soared to $645m, provoking a 22% fall in share price to $51. Equally seriously, there had been a dramatic slowdown in sales growth to a 'mere' 30%, well short of the 100% p.a. rate that analysts thought necessary to justify the share valuation. Short of this, as one analyst put it, the share price was in 'nosebleed territory'.

Maybe it is still early days for Twitter, but perhaps it attracts too many 'lurkers' – people who follow the tweets of others, but offering little data about themselves, making them virtually useless to advertisers.

Sources: Various articles in *The Telegraph, The Economist* and *The Financial Times.*

Learning objectives

After reading this chapter, you should understand the following:

- The key characteristics of the main forms of long-term finance.
- The benefits and drawbacks of each capital form.
- The factors that influence the choice between the various forms.

16.1 INTRODUCTION

hybrid
A security that combines features of both equity and debt

The next four chapters analyse the factors that determine a firm's long-term financing decisions. Before we can do this, it is important to present the main sources of finance and their essential characteristics. With an understanding of the pros and cons of different financial instruments, the reader will more fully appreciate the choices open to companies and the pressures that drive their choices.

The basic distinction in long-term financing is that between debt and equity, or, more accurately, between the various forms of debt and the various forms of equity. In recent years, the demarcation line between debt and equity has become increasingly blurred by the development of '**hybrid**' forms of finance, such as warrants and convertibles, as companies and their advisers have sought to exploit the advantages of each form of capital without incurring all the disadvantages.

In 1994, the UK accounting authorities issued a standard, FRS4 Capital Instruments, designed to clarify these differences and to offer guidance to companies in constructing and presenting their balance sheets. FRS4 divided capital instruments into debt and shareholder funds. Debt was defined as any instrument that creates a liability, including the obligation to deliver cash or shares at some specific future date and shareholder funds were defined as instruments that are not debt. These were split into equity and non-equity interests: broadly, ordinary shares and preference shares respectively.

The distinction between equity and non-equity was modified under International Accounting Standard 32 (Financial Instruments: Presentation). This classifies as equity non-redeemable preference shares and also those on which directors can exercise discretion in paying a dividend. However, in normal (i.e. 'everyday') financial parlance, when people talk of equity, it is almost invariably a reference to ordinary shareholders' capital.

Before examining specific sources and types of long-term finance, it is useful to consider some general principles that underpin the financing decision.

16.2 GUIDING LIGHTS: CORPORATE AIMS AND CORPORATE FINANCE

niche companies
Serve a limited segment of their markets, usually offering high-quality, differentiated products at a high margin

global companies
Serve a range of overseas markets both by exporting and direct investment

proprietorial companies
run by founders and their heirs to provide a livelihood for their families. They usually have limited growth aims

Strategists often divide companies into two categories: niche and global. A **niche company** sells high-quality products at a price that offers healthy profits. Such companies exist by exploiting a product differentiation advantage. A **global company** is able to compete in world markets with leading international firms by exploiting its own products at a competitive cost of production. Global companies thus combine product and cost advantages.

Not all companies aspire to global status; some are run by the proprietor to provide a livelihood for his or her family. Such **proprietorial companies** rarely offer sufficient potential to interest outside investors. Conversely, the **entrepreneurial company** has high growth potential and is driven by the desire of the owners to generate substantial wealth – in crude terms, to be 'seriously rich'.

Yet the predominant motive of many entrepreneurs is not money but the creative urge, the desire to build a thriving company, often for dynastic purposes. However, for the owners of such companies to realise their full potential, most of them eventually

entrepreneurial companies
Are driven by the growth ambitions and desire of the owners to create significant wealth

have to offer a share of the action to external participants, thus relinquishing a degree of control. Selling shares of equity involves releasing voting rights (it is possible to issue non-voting shares, but the Stock Exchange bans these for companies seeking a listing), and exposing the company's operations to outside scrutiny. Issuing debt usually involves some form of restrictive covenant over company financial policy, such as limits on subsequent borrowing and on dividend policy.

We now examine a short case to give a flavour of the strategic dimension of long-term financing.

■ Mitre Ltd: strategic financing issues

Mitre is a young, rapidly growing company, operating in the highly competitive computer software market. Its directors are the five founder members, all former employees of a giant US-owned computer manufacturer. All five found that 'working for a master' inhibited their creative energies. The company was set up on a shoestring, using the personal financial resources of the founders, supplemented by small inputs of capital from trusting close friends and relatives. After two years of struggle in rented premises, without paying its owners a salary, it managed to show an operating profit, on the basis of which it persuaded the local bank to extend overdraft facilities.

In subsequent years, Mitre has financed its operations through ploughing back the bulk of its profits, by further borrowing from the bank and by taking as much trade credit as possible from suppliers. It expects further rapid growth in the next few years, but is most concerned to avoid the problems of overtrading. It is, therefore, seeking to obtain long-term funding to support this growth.

Choosing the financing mix of short- and long-term debt and equity that best meets the investment requirements of any business is a key element of strategic financial management. Four issues need to be addressed.

Risk

How uncertain is the environment in which the business operates? How sensitive is it to turbulence in the economy? Mitre Ltd would probably be viewed by potential investors as having relatively high risk, particularly if the existing level of borrowing was high. Such a company will probably have a relatively inflexible cost structure, at least in the short term. As most of its costs will be fixed (unless it sub-contracts work), it exhibits a high level of **operating gearing**.

operating gearing
The proportion of fixed costs in the firm's operating cost structure

Ownership

A major injection of equity capital by financiers would dilute the control currently exercised by the founder members/directors. The desire to retain control of the company's activities may well make them prefer to borrow.

Duration

The finance should match the use to which it is put. If, for example, Mitre Ltd required finance for an investment in which no returns were anticipated in the early years, it might be desirable to raise capital that has little, if any, further drain on cash flow in these years. Conversely, it would be unwise for Mitre Ltd to raise long-term finance if the projects to be funded have a relatively short life. This could result in the business being over-capitalised, and unable to generate returns sufficient to service and repay the finance.

Debt capacity

debt capacity
Of an investment or a whole firm is the maximum amount of debt finance, and hence interest payments that it can support without incurring financial distress

If Mitre Ltd has a low level of borrowing at present, it has a greater capacity to raise debt than a similar firm with a higher borrowing level. However, **debt capacity** is not just a function of current borrowing levels, but also depends on factors such as the type of industry, and the security that the company can offer. An important benefit of borrowing is that the interest paid attracts tax relief and, hence, lowers effective financing charges, although this advantage can only be exploited when the company is profitable.

16.3 HOW COMPANIES RAISE LONG-TERM FINANCE IN PRACTICE

The financial manager can raise long-term funds internally, from the company's cash flow, or externally, via the capital market – the market for funds of more than a year to maturity. This exists to channel finance from persons and organisations with temporary cash surpluses to those with, or expecting to have, cash deficits. A critical intermediary function is provided by the major institutions such as pension funds, insurance companies and various types of bank. These collect relatively small savings and channel them to companies and other organisations seeking capital. As a result, the institutions are now the major holders of securities, both debt and equity, issued by companies.

The record of business financing patterns over the past 50 years or so shows several clear features:

- The majority of funds comes from internal sources – retained earnings and depreciation provisions (more strictly, cash flow), depending on company profitability and dividend policies.
- Bank borrowing plays a major role but is highly volatile, even negative in some years as firms repay debt. Firms tend to use bank finance as a buffer – borrowing heavily when interest rates are low and repaying when rates rise.
- Sales of shares on the New Issue Market are relatively unimportant, although many firms try to exploit high and rising stock markets by making rights issues.
- Historically, long-term debt issues have been relatively small contributors, along with preference share issues, but there was a huge upsurge in bond issues by highly creditworthy firms seeking to exploit the prevailing low interest rates of the post-financial crisis era.

We now consider the main forms of raising long-term finance to cast some light on these trends. In Chapters 18 and 19, we will examine several theories that attempt to explain firms' long-term financing decisions.

Self-assessment activity 16.1

What impact might the events of 11 September 2001 have had on corporate financing decisions?

(Answer in Appendix A at the back of the book)

16.4 SHAREHOLDERS' FUNDS

■ Ordinary shares

Articles of Association
A document drawn up at the formation of an enterprise, detailing the rights and obligations of shareholders and directors.

Share ownership lies at the heart of modern capitalism. By purchasing a portion or 'share' of the ownership of a firm, an investor becomes a shareholder with some degree of control over a company. A share is therefore a 'piece of the action' in a company. It used to be that when a company was formed, its **Articles of Association** specified how many ordinary shares it was authorised to issue. This maximum can be varied only with the agreement of ordinary shareholders. However, the requirement to have an authorised share capital was abolished from 1 October 2009 when the Companies Act 2006 came into effect. The issued share capital is the cornerstone of a company's capital structure. Ordinary shareholders carry full rights to participate in the business through voting in general meetings. They are entitled to payment of a dividend out of profits and, ultimately, repayment of capital in the event of liquidation, but only after all other claims have been met. As owners of the company, the ordinary shareholders bear the greatest risk, but also enjoy the fruits of corporate success in the form of higher dividends and/or capital gains.

Issued share capital

The accounts for Scottish and Southern Energy (SSE) plc (**www.sse.com**) as at 31 March 2014 showed:

Allotted, called up and fully paid	£m
974.9 million ordinary shares of 50p each	487.4

Notice that share capital is recorded in the accounts at par value, 50p in this case.

When ordinary shares are first issued, they are given nominal or par values. For example, a company could issue £5 million ordinary share capital in a variety of configurations, such as 10 million shares at a nominal value of £0.50 each, or 500,000 shares of £10 each. The main consideration is marketability. Investors tend to view shares with lower nominal values (e.g. 50p) as more easily marketable, particularly when, after a few years, shares often trade well above their nominal value. The most common unit nowadays is 25p. Issued share capital appears on the balance sheet at its par value, which explains why it often seems a minor item. For example, SSE's issued share capital (i.e. issued and paid for), denominated in 50p units, accounts for only 487.4 million (17 per cent) of ordinary shareholders' equity (£2,933 million). However, the market value of these shares on 31 March 2014 was many times higher than the par value, at 1468p each.

Once a company is established, its shares usually trade above the basic par value. A company wanting to sell new shares is therefore likely to issue them not at their nominal value, but at a **premium**. Share premium forms an integral part of the share capital, £861 million in the case of SSE. Most companies are limited liability companies incorporated under the Companies Acts. This implies that the owners (or shareholders) have obligations limited to the amount they have invested. If the company were ever wound up or liquidated, leaving outstanding debts, the shareholders would not be liable to meet such claims. Limited liability companies in the UK with a capitalisation over £50,000 and shares held by the public are termed public liability companies and denoted by the letters 'plc'. Public status does not necessarily mean that their shares are quoted on a stock exchange, simply that the shares can be traded among members of the public.

premium
The difference between the issue price of an ordinary share and its par (or nominal) value

■ Preference shares

preference shares
Hybrid securities that rank ahead of ordinary shares for dividend payment, usually at a fixed rate, and also in distributing the proceeds of a liquidation. Normally, they carry no voting rights

Preference shares are hybrids falling between pure equity and pure debt. Holders receive an annual dividend, usually a fixed percentage of the par value. Holders also have preferential rights over ordinary shareholders. Preferred dividends are paid before ordinary share dividends, and preference capital precedes ordinary share capital when assets are sold in a liquidation and the sale proceeds are distributed.

In the UK, they normally carry no voting rights except in the case of a proposed liquidation or a takeover, or when the company passes the preferred dividend. Preference share dividends do not qualify for tax relief. This lack of tax relief explains why preference shares are relatively unattractive to companies compared to other forms of fixed rate security. They may have some appeal to risk-averse investors looking for a relatively reliable income stream and a limited degree of participation in company affairs.

Types of preference share

Firms can issue many varieties of preference share. They can be:

- convertible
- cumulative
- redeemable
- participating

or some combination.

These terms have the following meanings:

- **Convertible** means that the preference shares can be converted into ordinary shares at some future date.
- **Cumulative** means that if a dividend is passed (i.e. not paid), it will be carried forward for payment at some future date.
- Some preference shares are **redeemable**, meaning that holders will eventually be repaid their capital, usually at par.
- Preference shares may also be **participating**. In an exceptionally good year, the directors may decide to declare an extra dividend for these preference shareholders above the regular fixed return, i.e. holders participate in the profits otherwise attributable to ordinary shareholders.

redeemable
Repayable (usually at nominal value)

participating
Preference shares that may qualify for payment of an additional dividend payment in a good year

Maybe one can now appreciate why these are called hybrids – they can exhibit characteristics of both equity and debt, but the question often arises as to which they *most* resemble, for example, when calculating gearing ratios. The answer really depends on what type of preference share we are dealing with, and the strength of the commitment made to investors:

- If they are cumulative, so that a passed dividend will eventually be paid, they resemble debt more than equity.
- If convertible, and the conversion date is near, they look more like equity than debt.
- If redeemable, they look more like debt.
- If participating, they look more like equity.

At one extreme, non-cumulative, convertible, irredeemable, participating preference shares look very much like equity, while the cumulative, convertible, redeemable, non-participating variety look very much like debt. However, there is plenty of room along the spectrum for preference shares with less clear-cut combinations of features.

■ Reserves

reserves
The funds that shareholders invest in a firm in addition to their initial subscription of capital

Reserves are also part of shareholders' funds. It is a common mistake to assume that reserves represent cash balances. There is a fundamental difference between cash, which is an asset, and reserves, which represent part of the firm's financing. Some reserves may once have had a cash counterpart, but this will almost certainly already have been re-invested in wealth-creating assets such as plant and machinery, stocks and debtors. In addition to share premium, reserves are created to account for profits retained from the recently ended, and preceding, years. These may be called revenue reserves, retained earnings or, simply, Profit and Loss Account, to indicate their origin. This reserve sets the limit on the amount of dividend that a company can pay (assuming it has the cash available!). A **revaluation reserve** is created when a revaluation of assets reveals a surplus – without such a reserve to represent enhanced value of the shareholders' stake, the balance sheet would not balance.

Internal finance, including retained profits, provides the main source of new capital for companies in general. This is partly because it is less costly than selling new shares, as it avoids expensive issuing costs. It may seem that retained earnings are a free source of finance and far more attractive to management than, say, raising interest-bearing loans. However, retention of earnings imposes an opportunity cost – if returned to shareholders as a dividend, the cash could be invested to yield a return. The cost of retained earnings is therefore the return that could be achieved by shareholders on investments of comparable risk to the company: in other words, the usual return required by shareholders, or cost of equity. However, the cost of using retained earnings can be adjusted as follows to reflect the issue costs saved:

$$\text{Cost of retained earnings} = k_{RE} = \frac{\text{normal cost of equity}}{(1 + f)}$$

where f is the percentage costs of issue, or flotation, costs that are avoided.

Self-assessment activity 16.2

Criticise the following statement made by your marketing director:

'Well, we can always finance the new product development from our reserves.'

(Answer in Appendix A at the back of the book)

16.5 HOW UNQUOTED FIRMS CAN RAISE EQUITY FINANCE

It is useful to make a distinction between companies not quoted on the Stock Exchange and those which are listed there. A listing opens up far greater access to capital of all kinds, and to a wider pool of shareholders. This is one reason why many private and other unquoted companies aspire to an eventual listing.

The supply of equity to an unquoted company depends partly on its size and partly on its stage of development. Most new companies find it virtually impossible to raise equity finance except of a 'personal' nature, i.e. from supportive friends and relatives. Some venture capitalists (see below) will provide start-up finance for highly promising activities, but most invariably look for a track record on the part of the entrepreneur(s). Until this is established, such companies need to rely on additional supplies of personal finance and retained earnings for further equity.

Having established some sort of record of operating success and potential, further avenues open up. Among these are the following.

Business angels

business angels
Wealthy private investors who take equity stakes in small, high-risk firms

A **business angel** is a private equity investor with spare funds to invest who wishes to gamble on the future prospects of young companies, often start-ups, managed by entrepreneurs lacking a track record but possessing a good idea plus enthusiasm. Angels are motivated partly by the prospect of riches and partly out of a desire to nurture the spirit of entrepreneurship. The umbrella organisation for introducing capital-hungry entrepreneurs to wealthy individuals is the UK Business Angels Association (BBAA, **www.bbaa.org.uk**). It estimates that there are some 18,000 active angels in the UK, investing around £850 million p.a. Unlike venture capitalists, which typically seek an exit in 3–5 years, angels tend to invest for much longer periods. However, despite attractive tax relief (see below) angel investment is not for the faint-hearted. Mason and Harrison

(2002) estimated that angels lose money in 40 per cent of their investments and make returns exceeding 50 per cent in less than a quarter of them.

Several networks or 'marriage bureaux' are designed to bring together prospective investors who seek high returns but are prepared to tolerate a high risk of total loss, and entrepreneurs needing capital and prepared to release an equity stake. Many are localised, and some are highly informal, operated by accountants and solicitors; others are more organised.

Increasingly, it is recognised that many businesses fail to raise equity, not merely because of 'finance gaps' on the supply side, but also because they are not 'investment ready' (Mason and Harrison, 2004). Accordingly, enterprise support agencies are now giving attention to provision of information on sources of finance and presentational skills, e.g. what to include in a business plan, and how to present it to potential investors in a convincing way. Many local networks provide 'investment readiness' training for entrepreneurs. Participants in these courses appear to have a relatively high success rate in converting presentations to investors into hard cash funding.

Equity crowdfunding

Whereas angels tend to invest relatively large tranches and funded firms tend to attract a limited number of angels, often a single one, crowdfunding appeals more to small investors. Relatively new in concept, it is a mechanism that uses the internet to enable wider groups of investors to combine in acquiring equity in start-ups and existing small firms. Typically, each investor will end up with only a small share of ownership. It allows potential investors to quiz entrepreneurs in some detail in online discussions to 'stress-test' their ideas. Larger investors tend to enter the fray at a relatively late stage, after smaller investors have acquired their stakes. In this sense, it harnesses the notion of 'the wisdom of crowds' to establish whether a proposal is attractive and viable. Although no statistics on success rates yet exist, the failure rate is thought to be high, although the amounts lost tend to be modest, and the gains potentially high.

Well-known equity crowdfunding sites are Seedrs, approved by the former Financial Services Authority in July 2012, Bank to the Future endorsed by Sir Richard Branson, and Crowdcube, formed in 2011, and officially approved in February 2013.

Cream of Devon

Has Tom Hanks just made life worse for real pirates as well as those on the big screen? David and Teresa Stevens run a small British company called Marine and Auto Security Solutions (MASS) that manufactures a device called Guardian. It fits to the guardrails of cargo ships and prevents pirates from attaching grappling-hooks and ladders. Despite a full order book, banks balked at lending MASS more money. The Stevenses experience with an early angel investor had been unhappy. But they needed more cash.

That is when they turned to Crowdcube, a website that helps entrepreneurs raise equity from the public. In five days in September MASS raised over £100,000 ($160,000) from tens of investors in return for a 12% stake. The offering came just before the release in Britain of 'Captain Phillips', a film in which Mr Hanks plays the captain of a vessel attacked by pirates. That helped the money roll in, says Mrs Stevens.

Darren Westlake, a technology entrepreneur, got the idea for Crowdcube when watching a TV series called 'Dragon's Den', in which founders of start-ups pitch their ideas to a panel of angel investors. Struck by the thought that he would have been prepared to put money into some of the schemes depicted, Mr Westlake began to ponder the power of an online platform to raise money from the masses. With his co-founder, Luke Lang, he launched Crowdcube in 2011. It has so far helped 76 early-stage firms to raise almost £15m in equity from investors who have either declared themselves sophisticated or passed a simple test about the risks of betting on start-ups. From its base in Exeter, a city known more for tourism and farming than finance, it has helped make Britain a leader in equity crowdfunding.

Source: The Economist, 2 November 2013.

Government-backed schemes

**enterprise investment
scheme (EIS)**
Introduced in January 1994
to give tax reliefs to investors

The **Enterprise Investment Scheme (EIS)** was introduced in January 1994. Under the EIS rules, 'unconnected' investors (those holding less than 30 per cent of the capital or voting rights in the firm) may invest up to £1 million (2014–15) in any tax year to receive relief from income tax at 30 per cent and freedom from capital gains tax if the investment is held for three years. Losses realised under the scheme are allowable against income tax. Companies cannot raise more than £5 million under the scheme in any one tax year. They must have gross assets of less than £15 million, have fewer than 250 employees and trade in the UK.

Using the EIS to raise equity

An example of equity funding under the EIS was the offer made by London Shipping Limited in early 2014. The entrepreneurs proposed to use a combination of debt and between £3.5m and £5m of equity to raise a total of £8m to acquire a mid-size bulk carrier to take advantage of a perceived weakness in both the resale values of vessels and the market for shipping rates, both of which they expected to improve in the medium-term. The operation would be managed by British Marine plc, a UK-owned and managed shipowner and operator, boasting a successful 14-year track record in the industry. The predicted IRR on the investment ranged between 17% and 26%, depending on the scenario specified, although the initial and ongoing management charges were not insignificant. Investors were invited to subscribe a minimum of £10,000 in the venture.

The exit route envisaged was a trade sale after three years, depending on conditions in the shipping market.

Source: Enterprise Investment Partners (**www.enterprise-ip.com**).

**Venture Capital Trusts
(VCTs)**
Stock-market listed financial
vehicles set up to invest in a
spread of highly risky new or
young firms

Venture Capital Trusts (VCTs) are a form of investment trust set up specifically to provide equity capital to small and growing companies. To attract investors concerned at the high risks of investing in small, unlisted companies, VCTs offer investors a wider spread of investments than is generally possible under the EIS, thus operating in a similar way to orthodox investment trusts. At present (2014–15), investors can obtain income tax relief at 30 per cent in the year of investment plus freedom from capital gains tax and from higher rate income tax on dividends if the funds remain invested for at least five years. As also applies to the EIS, the maximum investment in any tax year is £10 million, each company assisted can have no more than 250 employees, and have gross assets of no more than £15 million. The VCT itself must be quoted on the Stock Exchange.

More information on VCTs can be found on the website of the British Venture Capital Association (**www.bvca.co.uk**).

Corporate venturing

The Confederation of British Industry describes corporate venturing as: 'a formal, direct relationship usually between a larger firm, and an independent smaller company, in which both contribute financial management or technical resources, sharing risks and rewards equally for mutual growth'. The larger partner aims to foster the development of the small firm for a variety of reasons, partly altruistic. The arrangement can take a number of forms. The two parties could simply agree to cooperate in joint distribution or production, they could form a joint venture and/or the major company could take a minority equity stake in the small firm and inject cash into it. Aside from idealistic notions of nurturing the capitalist ethic, there are sound business reasons behind developing such links. For example:

- the large firm can tap into innovative R&D at low cost
- it may be able to use spare managerial capacity for training purposes
- it may develop a new source of supply
- it may gain access to a new market.

Venture capital (see also www.bvca.co.uk)

venture capital (VC)
Finance, usually equity, offered by specialist merchant banks wanting to take a stake in firms with high growth potential, but involving a high risk of loss

independent companies
Investment companies set up as 'stand-alone' entities by venture capitalists to invest money in risky but potentially attractive businesses

captive firms
Subsidiaries of banks and other institutions established to invest in risky but attractive businesses

management buy-out (MBO)
Acquisition of an existing firm by its existing management usually involving substantial amounts of straight debt and mezzanine finance

moral hazard
The temptation facing managers to engage in risky activities when they are protected from the consequences of failure, e.g. by guaranteed severance payments

information asymmetry
The imbalance between managers and owners of information possessed about a firm's financial state and its prospects

Venture capital (VC) is funding mainly for the development of existing companies with sound management and high growth potential, but sometimes for especially attractive start-ups. Funds are usually provided in large packages (typically over £250,000) of debt and equity, split this way partly to offer a degree of security, but mainly to allow the VC company to participate in any major success. VC companies will be hoping for an eventual flotation of the companies they assist, are usually prepared to see their investments 'locked in' for five to ten years, but will anticipate an annualised return of 30 per cent or more. VC companies often provide managerial assistance, and some (e.g. the biggest VC company, 3i, itself a listed company following its own Stock Exchange flotation in 1994) reserve the right to place their own appointee on the Board of Directors, although this is infrequently done.

VC companies fall into two groups: **independent companies** and **captive firms**. Independent funds are set up by private venture capitalists, raising funds from a variety of sources to invest in projects for a specified time and then to liquidate the investments. Captive funds are subsidiaries of major financial institutions, such as banks and insurance companies, set up to channel a portion of their capital into risky enterprises. Some VC firms operate with a strong social perspective. An example is Bridges Community Ventures which is partly government-funded. In 2002, it invested £345,000 in Simply Switch, the internet price comparison site set up by Karen Darby in a run-down area of Croydon. Its faith was rewarded in 2006 when Darby sold out to Daily Mail and General Trust for £22 million, of which £8 million went to the VC firm.

VC organisations devote much of their energies and funding to large **management buy-out (MBO)** investments, rather than concentrating on smaller and riskier start-up and development capital. In an MBO, the existing management of a company undertakes to purchase the firm from the present owners. Most MBOs involve managers buying out an unwanted, often underperforming, subsidiary from a larger parent, which feels that the business unit no longer fits its strategy. Exceptionally, the buy-out may involve taking an existing quoted company off the Stock Exchange, usually financed by large amounts of debt, but with equity provided by the managers, who themselves borrow heavily to provide these funds. There is an element of '**moral hazard**' here – managers wishing to buy out a company or division may be tempted to depress its performance so as to lower the price they need to pay to acquire it. Moreover, there is a problem of **information asymmetry** – managers are far better able to judge the value of a company or operating unit than an outside analyst or the head office of a larger company.

Piercing the jargon

Venture capitalists, suspended between the worlds of heady financiers and down-to-earth businessmen, have developed their own incomprehensible jargon. Here's an introduction to the terms that make their hearts beat faster:

Business plan: needed to apply for financing. A good plan should outline the business opportunity, the management's track record, the company's past and present performance, market demand, competition and trends, the structure of the company and the shareholders, long-term plans and goals, and the proposed role of venture capital (how much and what for). See *Due diligence*.

Control: one of the most hotly debated topics. Even where venture capitalists have a minority share, they want to be able to influence and/or have veto rights over decisions on strategy, like taking out credits, setting up subsidiaries or signing licensing agreements. This issue often creates conflict with entrepreneurs, but venture capitalists disagree among themselves as to whether control requires a majority share or just a good shareholders' agreement, and where the balance lies between supporting and stifling the entrepreneurial spirit. See *Hands on*.

Deal flow: the number and quality of applications for investment that come to the venture capitalist. Deal flow can come from referrals (banks, accountants, advisory services), walk-ins, or from hard work pounding the streets.

Development capital: also known as expansion capital. Venture capital financing used for expansion of an already established company.

Due diligence: several months of scrutiny designed to dig up all the necessary information for evaluating the business plan and establishing whether the entrepreneur is a solid investment.

Exit: the all-important sale of the shareholding in a company which enables the venture capitalist to (at least) recoup his investment and pacify his investors. Most exits in Central Europe will be by trade sale, but some might be by management buy-out or flotation on the stock market – or by write-off, if the investment is a disaster. The usual time-frame for exit is around five years, meaning there has been very little so far in the region.

Hands on: what most venture capitalists in Central Europe claim to be. It means that they're not interested in a passive shareholding but want to support the management with expertise, usually in marketing, finding export partners, or in financial planning.

Living dead: a company that is not a failure but which is making the sort of insignificant profits that make it almost impossible to sell, and even then would yield low returns.

Management buy-out: the purchase of a business by the existing management. The venture capitalist pays proportionately much more for his stake to recognise the value the management brings to the enterprise. Also used to describe a possible exit route, by which the management buys out the venture capitalist's share. The question is: at what price?

Second-round financing: most companies need more than the initial injection of capital, whether to enable them to expand into new markets, develop more production capacity, or to overcome temporary problems. There can be several rounds of financing.

Seed capital: capital used to turn a good idea into a commercially viable product or service; a very risky form of investment, although it generally involves small sums.

Start-up capital: capital used to establish a company from scratch or within the first few months of its existence. Also risky, but with huge returns for the few successes.

Trade sale: the sale of a company (or part of it) to a larger corporation. This is the main source of exits envisaged for Central Europe, but it means that the entrepreneur may have to become an employee or sell out his share.

Venture capital: equity finance in an unquoted, and usually quite young, company to enable it to start up, expand or restructure its operations entirely. It's cheaper than bank finance initially because paying dividends can be deferred; it also provides a strategic partner – but it implies handing over some control, a share of earnings and decisions over future sales.

Source: Business Central Europe, February 1995. Reprinted with permission.

Nevertheless, given the structure of the funding arrangements, the managers of MBOs are under considerable pressure to perform in order to service debts out of cash flow and to enhance the values of their own equity stake (and that of the venture capitalist). Many VC firms find the risk–return prospects of these deals more appealing than those of orthodox businesses. This is largely because the time taken before the venture capitalist can make an exit is usually much shorter.

management buy-in (MBI)
Acquisition of an equity stake in an existing firm by new management that injects expertise as well as capital into the enterprise

In a **management buy-in (MBI)**, an outside group of managers buys a stake in an existing company and assumes managerial responsibility for its operation. MBIs are largely financed in the same ways as MBOs, and occur for similar motives.

Private placing (or 'placement')

private placing
An issue of shares directly to a selected number of financial institutions

A **private placing** is a means whereby well-established companies can widen their shareholder base without going for a Stock Exchange listing. It is arranged through a stockbroker or issuing house, which buys the shares and then 'places' them with (i.e. sells them to) selected clients.

16.6 WORKED EXAMPLE: YZ AND VCI

This question appeared as Question 3 on CIMA Paper 9 Financial Strategy, November 2006.

VCI is a venture capital investor that specialises in providing finance to small but established businesses. At present, its expected average pre-tax return on equity investment is a nominal 30% per annum over a five-year investment period.

YZ is a typical client of VCI. It is a 100% family-owned transport and distribution business whose shares are unlisted. The company sustained a series of losses a few years ago, but the recruitment of some professional managers and an aggressive marketing policy returned the company to profitability. Its most recent accounts show revenue of $105 million and profit before interest and tax of $28.83 million. Other relevant information is as follows:

- For the last three years, dividends have been paid at 40% of earnings and the directors have no plans to change this payout ratio.
- Taxation has averaged 28% per annum over the past few years and this rate is likely to continue.
- The directors are forecasting growth in earnings and dividends for the foreseeable future of 6% per annum.
- YZ's accountants estimated the entity's cost of equity capital at 10% some years ago. The data they worked with was incomplete and now out of date. The current cost could be as high as 15%.

Extracts from its most recent statement of financial position are shown below.

	$ million
ASSETS	
Non-current assets	
Property, plant and equipment	35.50
Current assets	4.50
	40.00
EQUITY AND LIABILITIES	
Equity	
Share capital (Nominal value of 10 cents)	2.25
Retained earnings	18.00
	20.25
Non-current liabilities	
7% Secured bond repayable 2016	15.00
Current liabilities	4.75
	19.75
	40.00

Note: The entity's vehicles are mainly financed by operating leases.

YZ has now reached a stage in its development that requires additional capital of $25 million. The directors, and major shareholders, are considering a number of alternative forms of finance. One of the alternatives they are considering is venture capital funding and they have approached VCI. In preliminary discussions, VCI has suggested it might be able to finance the necessary $25 million by purchasing a percentage of YZ's equity. This will, of course, involve YZ issuing new equity.

Required:
(a) Assume you work for VCI and have been asked to evaluate the potential investment.
   (i) Using YZ's forecast of growth and its estimates of cost of capital, calculate the number of new shares that YZ will have to issue to VCI in return for its investment and the percentage of the entity VCI will then own. Comment briefly on your result.
   (ii) Evaluate exit strategies that might be available to VCI in five years' time and their likely acceptability to YZ.

(b) Discuss the advantages and disadvantages to an established business such as YZ of using a venture capital entity to provide finance for expansion as compared with long-term debt. Advise YZ about which type of finance it should choose, based on the information available so far.

Answer

(a) (i) First, it is necessary to calculate dividends and retained profit:

	$ m
Revenue	<u>105.00</u>
Profit before interest and tax (PBIT)	28.83
Interest ($15.0m $\times$ 7%)	(1.05)
Profit before tax (PBT)	27.78
Tax at 28%	(7.78)
Profit after tax (PAT)	20.00
Dividends at 40% pay-out	(8.00)
Retained profit	12.00

Using the dividend growth model, and assuming constant growth of 6%, the equity is valued as follows:

Cost of equity	10%	15%
Value $= \dfrac{D_1}{(k_e - g)}$	$\dfrac{(\$8.00m \times 1.06)}{(0.10 - 0.06)}$ = $212 million	$\dfrac{(\$8.00m \times 1.06)}{(0.15 - 0.06)}$ = $94 million
Implied P:E ratio	$212m/$20m = 10.6 times	$94m/$20m = 4.7 times
Value per share $ = Value/PAT Given 22,500,000 shares in issue	$212m/22.5m = $9.42	$94.2m/22.5m = $4.19
Shares to issue to VCI	2,653,928 ($25m/$9.42)	5,966,587 ($25m/$4.19)
Total shares in issue after new issue	25,153,928	28,466,587
Proportion owned by VCI	10.6% (2.654/25.154 $\times$ 100)	21.0% (5.967/28.467 $\times$ 100)

These figures suggest that YZ would need to issue between approximately 2.7 million and 6 million new shares depending on the valuation adopted, resulting in VCI owning between around 11% and 21% respectively of YZ. Even 21% is not a particularly high percentage, so long as VCI does not end up with the highest single shareholding. If this were the case, YZ managers would become vulnerable to pressure from VCI.

(ii) Possible exit strategies for VCI:

- *Sell back to YZ shareholders, perhaps via an MBO.* As founding shareholders, they might value the business more highly than a third-party investor. This would be an advantage for VCI, giving it a good base to negotiate a higher price. This might be a disadvantage to YZ shareholders, who might not be in a position to raise the necessary finance.
- *Encourage YZ to apply for a stock market listing.* YZ is too small for a main market listing, so it would have to be on the secondary market (AIM in the UK). This could be an administratively lengthy and expensive process. Also, YZ may not wish to make available the percentage of shares necessary (10% on AIM) to allow a market in its shares. However, there would be many advantages of listing at this stage in YZ's development.

■ *Sell to a ready buyer, for example via a trade sale*. If VCI is seeking a quick sale, it may be easier to do this, although it might require a lower price for speed and ease of disposal. YZ may be unhappy with the new shareholder unless it has some right of veto built into the initial deal with VCI.

VCI financing versus long-term debt:

Advantages

■ The money appears to be readily available.
■ VCI may bring much-needed management expertise and, possibly, take a seat on the board (although this could also be seen as a disadvantage, e.g. potential interference).
■ It lowers, rather than raises, gearing.

Disadvantages

■ VCI may want more control than management wish to cede, and may push for higher risk strategies than YZ is comfortable with in order to pursue its required rate of return.
■ VCI may demand a seat on the board (but this could be an advantage, as noted above).
■ VCI may eventually sell shares to an unwanted (to YZ) buyer, or push for an early flotation.
■ There are no tax advantages with dividend payments, as compared to debt.
■ It is difficult to value the shares. In these circumstances, we are valuing only part of the entity and estimates of value might need to be adjusted for a part-sale. Any adjustment will inevitably be subjective, but in some ways, it is no different from flotation where founding shareholders issue less than 50% of the share capital in order to retain control.
■ There may be higher set-up fees.

YZ has high gearing (based on book values) and appears dangerously illiquid, with a current ratio of less than 1. Borrowing from a bank could be difficult and expensive in these circumstances. However, although YZ is 'well established', thus meeting one of VCI's investment criteria, it has lower growth than would normally be expected by venture capitalists. Obtaining new finance from either route might therefore be problematic.

16.7 GOING PUBLIC

Seeking a quotation: from unquoted to quoted status

initial Public Offering (IPO)
The first issue of shares by an existing or a newly formed firm to the general public

Eventually, the unquoted company may require such a large amount of new capital that it may decide to 'go public' by issuing shares through a Stock Exchange. When a firm obtains a listing on a Stock Exchange by selling shares, this is called an **Initial Public Offering (IPO)**. Such issues are managed by sponsors, such as an investment bank or a member of the Stock Exchange, which advises on aspects such as the timing and the price of the shares to be issued.

To enhance the prospects of a successful IPO, the company ought to show a record of consistent and increasing profitability, and that it is managed by respected, experienced directors. There are numerous other criteria to qualify for a 'full listing' on the main London market that must also be satisfied, principally:

■ It must have a minimum market capitalisation of £700,000.
■ It must provide fully audited accounts covering at least three years.
■ It must be an independent business activity that has earned revenue for at least three years.
■ The senior management and key directors should not have changed significantly throughout the three-year period, and should possess appropriate expertise and experience.
■ If the company has a controlling shareholder, this must not prevent it from operating and making decisions independently.

- At least 25 per cent of the company's ordinary shares must be in public hands after listing. This is called 'free float'. However, this requirement was relaxed in February 2013. Firms joining the 'High Growth Segment' of the LSE will be able to launch their IPOs with only 10 per cent of their shares. This change was designed to attract firms that might otherwise have listed on NASDAQ in the USA, which requires free float of only 5 per cent.

The Stock Exchange* cites a seven-point list of benefits and possible drawbacks involved in obtaining a quotation:

- *Prestige.* Being seen to comply with the rules of the Stock Exchange may enhance the company's standing in the business community. This may lead to better relationships with suppliers, creditors and customers.
- *Growth.* The initial flotation can be used to raise cash, which can be used to lower gearing. Flotation may also lower the cost of using bank facilities. Access to the wider markets can be exploited if the company wishes to raise more finance in the future. Greater marketability of the shares increases the ability to conduct takeovers by offering equity in exchange for the target company's shares.
- *Access.* As well as giving companies greater access to fresh supplies of capital, flotation gives shareholders access to a wider market, enabling existing owners to convert shares into cash, and new ones to buy and sell more readily, i.e. it makes the company's shares more liquid.
- *Visibility.* The initial flotation gives the company publicity and more regular coverage by the media as it announces subsequent results. Greater awareness among the securities industry may enhance the ability to raise further capital on favourable terms.
- *Accountability.* Quotation imposes new responsibilities on directors and increases the need to consult shareholders before taking major decisions, such as a major acquisition.
- *Responsibility.* Directors must ensure that the company meets the listing rules of the Exchange, and that price-sensitive information is released in a timely and orderly way, so that every shareholder has equal access to it.
- *Regulation.* The Stock Exchange, as the only competent authority for listing, rigorously screens the applications of companies seeking a listing, monitors companies' ongoing compliance with its rules and deals with breaches of its rules.

Poundland banks on winning formula

Poundland has given the green light to its initial public offering of about £700m. Strong growth during the recession, and punchy valuation, have raised questions about whether it is cashing in ahead of a recovery, when Britons' appetite for £1 food, party goods, pet products and even gardening equipment might wane.

Poundland, which is 75 per cent owned by Warburg Pincus, the private equity group that bought it for about £200m in 2010, has increased sales from £641.5m in the year to March 2011 to £880.5m in March 2013. Underlying earnings before interest, tax, depreciation and amortisation has risen from £31.1m to £45.2m over the same period.

Poundland plans to double its UK store base to 1,000 stores over the next 10 years, and is preparing to add Spain to its operations in Ireland.

But Jim McCarthy, chief executive, who with about 150 colleagues shares management's 25 per cent stake in the company, says there is more to come.

'The notion that people will choose to waste their money having suffered for five years is a bit of a naive notion', he says, 'Will you buy a pair of shoes for £10 cheaper even when you have £10 in your pocket? ... You will still save money, and with the other £10 you will make choices.'

Continued

➡

Source: London Stock Exchange.

> Nick Bubb, the independent retail analyst, says it is not so much consumer sentiment, but competition in the discount sector, that could be a challenge for Poundland.
>
> Retailers such as 99p Stores and Pound World 'have been a bit of a thorn in their side', while Poundland could also be 'a bit overshadowed by B & M, the discount retailer chaired by Sir Terry Leahy, which is multi-price, rather than fixed price. 'I don't want to protest too much', says Mr McCarthy. 'But I'm absolutely convinced that Poundland will be in the winning camp.'
>
> Bryan Roberts, insights director at Kantar Retail, says Poundland will have to decide whether it can stick to its everything at a £1 formula, or adopt multiple price points, as some US dollar stores have done. He notes that some fixed-point US retailers have become more round price retailers, with products priced at $2, $5 or $10.

 Source: Financial Times, 19 February 2014.

■ Methods of obtaining a listing

There are four main methods of obtaining a quotation on the Stock Exchange:

offer for sale by prospectus
An issue of ordinary shares through an issuing house that promotes the shares in a detailed prospectus aimed at the public in general

1 **Offer for sale by prospectus**. Shares are sold to an issuing house, generally a merchant bank, and then are offered at a fixed price to the public at large, including both institutions and private individuals. Application forms and a prospectus, setting out all relevant details of the company's past performance and future prospects, as stipulated by Stock Exchange regulations laid down in 'The Yellow Book', must be published in the national press.

Usually such an issue is underwritten, i.e. the issuing house guarantees to buy up any shares not taken up by the public so as to ensure that the company receives the monies required. To spread the risk of being called upon to buy up possibly substantial blocks of shares, the lead underwriter usually makes sub-underwriting arrangements with other financial institutions.

Offers for sale are usually made at a fixed price, which is determined before the offer period based on the expertise and knowledge of the company's financial advisers. There is a tendency to price prospectus issues conservatively to ensure their success – companies whose shares have to be bought up by the underwriters often find it difficult to raise further capital through the Stock Exchange on attractive terms.

issue by tender
A share issue where prospective investors are invited to bid or 'tender' for shares at a price of their own choosing

2 A variant on this method is the **issue by tender**, where no prior issue price is announced, but prospective investors are invited to bid for shares at a price of their choosing. The eventual 'striking price' at which shares are sold is determined by the weight of applications at various prices. Essentially, the final price is set by supply and demand. A tender is often used when there is no comparable company already listed to use as a reference point in valuing the company. However, by underlining the uncertainty in valuation, it may deter investors. In a tender, the shares are underwritten at a certain minimum price. This is the most expensive form of issue, although it may be argued that there is less risk of underpricing.

placing
An issue of ordinary shares directly to selected institutional investors, who may re-sell them on the stock market when dealings officially commence

3 In a **placing**, shares are 'placed', or sold to, institutional investors, such as pension funds and insurance companies, selected by the investment bank advising the company, and the company's stockbroker. In this case, the general public has to wait until official dealing in the shares begins before it, too, can buy the shares. Placings are geared to smaller companies and involve relatively little publicity and, hence, limited expense. Conversely, although placings should aim at securing a wide distribution of shareholdings to promote liquidity on the secondary market, the resulting spread of holdings is inevitably far narrower than with offers for sale.

intermediaries offer
A placing made to stockbrokers other than the one advising the company making the issue

An **intermediaries offer** is a placing with financial intermediaries that allows brokers other than the one advising the issuing company to apply for shares. These brokers are allocated shares that they can subsequently distribute to their clients.

4 **Stock Exchange introduction**. This is applicable when the shares are already widely held, the proportion in public hands already exceeds 25 per cent, and existing shareholders do not intend to dispose of shares at the time of flotation. No money is actually raised from the public – the purpose of the exercise is merely to create a wider market in the company's shares. Because no underwriting is required, and advertising costs are minimal, this is the cheapest form of issue.

■ Continuing obligations

Once a company is listed, its directors have to obey a strict set of rules in order to safeguard its continued listing. In particular, it must observe the regulations relating to disclosure and directors' dealings.

1 **Disclosure**. A quotation places considerable demands on directors, especially in the release of price-sensitive information about the company's activities. The main occasions on which announcements are required through the Stock Exchange include:

- major developments in a company's activities, e.g. new products, contracts or customers
- decisions to pay (or not pay) a dividend
- preliminary announcements of profits for the year or half-year
- an acquisition or disposal of major assets
- a change in directors, or directors' responsibilities
- decisions to make major capital issues.

Listings worth $8bn lined up in IPO flurry

Europe's initial public offering market is on track for its busiest start to the year since the financial crisis as private equity companies seek to capitalise on demand from investors hungry for more exposure to the region's recovery.

The private equity backers of ISS, the Danish outsourcing group and Poundland, the UK discount retailer, yesterday announced their intention to float the companies in Copenhagen and London, just a day after GTT, the French engineering group, said it would seek a listing in Paris. Together they are seeking to sell more than $2.3bn worth of shares. Pets at Home, the UK pet shop chain owned by KKR, is expected to follow suit in the next few days.

The moves mean more than $8.3bn worth of European IPOs are currently being marketed, on top of the more than $3.2bn of flotations that have priced since the start of the year, according to data compiled by Dealogic. If all the IPOs go ahead as planned, the first quarter of 2014 will be the strongest start to the year since 2007.

Gareth McCartney, head of equity syndicate at UBS in Europe, said: 'Activity is picking up because markets are buoyant with attractive valuations and market conditions are expected to remain good.'

The flurry of offerings comes as market sentiment has sharply improved on hopes that Europe has shrugged off the debt crisis. IPOs have reflected the patchy international recovery since the financial crisis. Flotations quickly recovered in Europe, the US and Asia in 2010, after slumping to low points in 2009, but Europe's IPO market nosedived again in 2012 because of renewed market turmoil.

However, US fund managers including BlackRock and Fidelity are now hungry for a fresh crop of shares, following massive inflows into equity funds over the past year.

The performance of last year's IPOs has also whetted investor appetite. Shares in private equity-backed companies listed last year rose 25.3 per cent globally, according to EY. They were up 10 per cent in Europe.

'There's a lot of cash on the sideline and IPOs have made money for investors last year, so demand should continue to be there,' said Fotis Hasiotis, who advises private equity clients at Lazard.

Private equity groups, which struggled to return cash to investors in the wake of the financial crisis, have been quick to take advantage of the renewed demand for equities.

However, bankers predict that this year could see some more questionable companies come to market, as private equity groups exploit the buoyant environment to offload lower-grade assets.

 Source: Anne-Sylvaine Chassany and Robin Wrigglesworth. With additional reporting by David Oakely and Andrew Bolger in London. *Financial Times*, 19 February 2014.

directors' dealings
Share sales and purchases
by senior officers of the firm

2 **Directors' dealings**. Share dealings by the directors of a listed company are subject to the Criminal Justice Act 1993 and the Exchange's 'Model Code for Directors' Dealings', aimed to prevent insider dealing. Directors are precluded from dealing for a minimum period (normally two months) prior to an announcement of recurrent information such as trading results, or dealing in advance of the announcement of extraordinary events involving the publication of price-sensitive information. Companies whose directors infringe these rules are likely to jeopardise the continued listing of the company and also to sour relationships with investors, especially the financial institutions.

■ The Alternative Investment Market (AIM)

The AIM was set up by the Stock Exchange in 1995 to replace the declining Unlisted Securities Market. Its purpose is to provide a market for the shares of companies that are too young or too small to qualify for, or benefit from, a full listing. The Exchange organises a service called SEATS PLUS, which displays information about orders to buy and sell shares, to enable matching of buyers and sellers. To qualify for the AIM, companies have to satisfy certain criteria – in the main, less demanding than those of the full market – and to observe certain 'ongoing obligations' regarding the release of key information at appropriate times and the conduct of directors. In addition, the company must appoint and retain a nominated adviser (or 'Nomad') to assist with continuing compliance with the AIM's rules and a nominated broker to organise share transactions. At end-December 2013, there were 861 companies with an AIM listing with total market capitalisation of £76 billion. This compares with a peak of 1,694 firms in 2007. In recent years, many firms have left the AIM for various reasons, although after a six-year decline, AIM saw more new entrants than departures in the second half of 2013. In 2013 as a whole, the 69 IPOs raised a total of £1.2 billion, up from £700 million in 2012, a 65 per cent increase. The spectacular rise of the AIM to a position of international pre-eminence has been chronicled by Owen *et al.* (2007).

HgCapital poised to float Manx Telecom on Aim

Mobile & Telecoms

Manx Telecom, the Isle of Man group, is preparing for a float on the junior Aim market in a sign of private equity owners taking advantage of strong equity markets.

Manx Telecom, which provides more than two-thirds of mobile and fixed line services on the Isle of Man, is majority owned by HgCapital.

The private equity group bought the business from Telefónica for £159m in 2010.

Manx Telecom has appointed Liberum Capital and Oakley Capital to advise on the flotation, which could raise more than £150m depending on what stake is sold on the exchange.

The company is expected to be valued at about £250m in total.

No final decision has been made to list the group, although a flotation is seen as the most likely outcome by those with knowledge of the talks.

HgCapital declined to comment.

The group provides fixed line, mobile and data services to consumers and businesses on the island.

It employs 300 people with annual revenues of about £70m and a pre-tax profit of about £25m.

Manx Telecom was the first operator in Europe to launch a live 3G network, in part because it was used by Telefónica as a test case for developing new products and services before wider introduction elsewhere.

The group is now rolling out a 4G network for the island.

Telefónica acquired the business as part of the purchase of O_2, the former BT-owned mobile group.

Source: Daniel Thomas and Anne-Sylvaine Chassany, *Financial Times*, 16 January 2014.

16.8 EQUITY ISSUES BY QUOTED COMPANIES

rights issues
Sales of further ordinary shares at less than market price to existing shareholders who are usually able to sell the rights on the market should they not wish to purchase additional shares

pre-emption rights
The right for existing shareholders to be offered newly issued shares before making them available to outside investors

vendor placing/placing with clawback
A placing of new shares with financial institutions where existing investors have the right to purchase the shares from the institutions concerned to protect their rights

Once a company has achieved a quotation, it will find it easier to raise further equity, assuming a successful trading and profit record. The commonest method of raising new equity is by a **rights issue** (see below). The Companies Act of 1985 gives existing shareholders the right to subscribe to new share issues in proportion to their existing holdings. This generally rules out a public issue although these **pre-emption rights** can be waived with the agreement of shareholders at a properly convened meeting. With such agreement, a placing may be arranged whereby shares are sold to participating institutions provided that the price involves no more than a 10 per cent discount to the market price.

Shares can also be issued as full or partial consideration when acquiring another company. In some cases, this may be done via a **vendor placing**, or **placing with clawback**. In a vendor placing, the acquiring company places the new shares with a group of institutions, thus diluting the ownership and earnings of existing shareholders. For sufficiently large issues, existing shareholders have the right to reclaim the shares they would have been entitled to, had there been a rights issue. If they do not, they receive no compensation for the loss in value of their holdings as there are no detachable rights to sell (see below).

In view of their importance, we now give detailed consideration to rights issues.

■ Rights issues

It is much easier for a quoted firm to make a rights issue than for an unlisted firm. In a rights issue, shareholders are granted the right to subscribe for shares (or, less commonly, for other types of security) in proportion to their existing holdings, thus enabling them to retain their existing share of voting rights. Apart from the control factor, rights issues have certain other attractions:

prospectus
A document setting out the existing financial situation of a firm and its future prospects that is published to accompany a share issue

1 They are far cheaper than a public share issue. Provided the issue is for less than 10 per cent of the class of capital, there is no need for a **prospectus**, although a brochure must still be made available.

2 They may be made at the discretion of the directors without the consent of the shareholders or the Stock Exchange. At one time, a queuing system for all new issues was operated by the government broker, acting for the Bank of England, in order to ensure a measured flow of new securities on to the market.

3 When stock market prices are generally high, companies have been known to raise cash through rights issues and to place it on deposit while seeking suitable candidates for acquisition. This gives a high degree of flexibility in timing a bid, i.e. the cash is already to hand.

4 The finance is guaranteed, either from existing shareholders or from the underwriters. Existing shareholders are given an incentive either to take up their rights or to sell them. It is not a sensible option to do nothing: this effectively reduces their wealth, as shares are typically offered at a discount of about 20 per cent below the current market price. If, as is usual, they are underwritten, the company is guaranteed to receive the cash, although it is embarrassing to have to call upon the underwriters to fulfil their obligations.

However, underwriting is costly. It has been estimated that companies typically 'lose' around 2 per cent of the funds raised in an equity issue shared out as follows: lead underwriter, usually the lead investment bank that organises the issue, taking 0.5 per cent, the firm's stockbrokers taking 0.25 per cent, and the remaining 1.25 per cent split among the various institutional shareholders (who are in many cases already shareholders), who act as sub-underwriters. Conversely, putting out the underwriting business to tender can halve the underwriting fees. Nevertheless,

Why even discounted rights issues need underwriting

The ill wind blowing a flock of rights issues into UK markets brings with it the old debate about how much – if anything – underwriters and sub-underwriters should earn for insuring cash calls against failure.

Shareholders in Royal Bank of Scotland have just won themselves improved terms for insuring part of the bank's £12bn whopper share issue. They'll get 1 per cent of the sum insured for sub-underwriting it, while the principal underwriters receive 1.5 per cent plus an additional discretionary 0.25 per cent.

There's little high ground in the debate about how these fees are divvied up. Institutional investors complain that investment banks make a fat profit from underwriting, even after paying the institutions to take on much of the risk. But if the same institutions have already decided to subscribe for their rights – and are big enough to influence others to do the same – they have virtually guaranteed its success. At which point sub-underwriting is itself almost free of risk.

The bigger question is whether deeply discounted rights issues need underwriting at all. Asked to look into the system nine years ago, the old Monopolies and Mergers Commission expressed the wish for more frequent non-underwritten deeply discounted issues.

The problem is that the deep discount sends an emergency signal and is usually applied at times when equities are already in turmoil. This is an underwriters' market: capacity is low, demand high. Confidence is all. It would be reckless of RBS not to pay for its cash call to be underwritten. But could you not argue that the chance of RBS falling from 340p to below the 200p price of the new shares is negligible? Of course you could. But for anyone to have confidence in your argument, you would have to be the only person who successfully predicted both the run on Northern Rock and the bail-out of Bear Stearns.

 Source: Andrew Hill, *Financial Times*, 25 April 2008. © Financial Times

most issues are still not put out to tender, despite a report by the Monopolies and Mergers Commission in 1999, which stated that a 'complex monopoly' existed in the awarding of sub-underwriting contracts. Firms now have to justify the mode of underwriting to shareholders under revised Stock Exchange listing rules. It is likely that the persistence of traditional ways of handling the underwriting process is due to firms wishing to build a new, or protect an existing, relationship with key institutional shareholders whose support might be critical in a possible future crisis.

The issue of underwriting fees resurfaced in the aftermath of the credit crunch, when in June 2010, the Office of Fair Trading announced that it would conduct an enquiry into underwriting, following complaints from issuing firms. Fees are alleged to have rocketed in the recession period to 3–4 per cent of the sums raised as financial institutions sought more compensation for taking risks despite the tendency for discounts to deepen (see the cameo on discounted issues). For example, Xstrata, the mining conglomerate, paid 3 per cent in fees in 2009 when raising $4.1 billion.

The next cameo discusses the somewhat disappointing outcome of the OFT investigation.

■ Shareholders' choices in a rights issue: Grow-up plc

Grow-up plc decides to make a rights issue of one new share for every three held. The share price prior to the issue is 200p and the new shares are to be offered at 160p. In practice, rights issues are made at a discount, partly to make them *look* attractive and thus encourage shareholders to subscribe, and partly to safeguard against the risk of a fall in the market price during the offer period.

theoretical ex-rights price (TERP)
The share price that should in theory be established, other things being equal, after a rights issue is completed

The **theoretical ex-rights price (TERP)** is the price at which shares would trade with no account taken of the proposed use of the funds raised after the rights issue has

Watchdog criticised on rights fees

Leading investors have criticised a report into share underwriting services by the Office of Fair Trading, after it argued that shareholders should try harder to force down fees charged by investment banks.

After the third inquiry into UK underwriting since 1994, the OFT found that banks were operating in an uncompetitive market. But it declined to refer the issue to the Competition Commission. The OFT said that while it found that there was little effective competition on underwriting fees, it concluded that the issue 'can be tackled most effectively by companies and shareholders doing more to achieve more cost-effective outcomes'.

'This appears to be three–nil to the investment banking community,' said Richard Buxton, head of UK equities at Schroders.

'To acknowledge the market is not working effectively and that shareholders are being ripped off, but not to recommend any solid action is disappointing.'

The OFT found that average fees for underwriting had risen from about 2 per cent to 2.5 per cent between 2003 and 2005 to more than 3 per cent in 2009.

Last year the Institutional Investor Council, an umbrella body representing the UK's biggest long-term shareholders, said there was minimal evidence of competitive tendering for rights issues in the UK.

Since 2000, banks have generated £1.6bn from underwriting fees in the UK, with just three banks – UBS, JPMorgan and Royal Bank of Scotland – taking nearly 40 per cent of the total, according to data from Thomson Reuters.

'We do recognise there is a problem, but without transparency [on fees] it is very hard for us to be pragmatic and effective in tackling the problem,' said Ian Richards, head of regional corporate governance at Aviva Investors.

Mr Buxton said that companies often ignore investor protests. 'We have often raised the issue of fees with companies, but we rarely get a satisfactory response.'

Bankers argue that the UK underwriting market functions efficiently, with banks battling each other for market share.

They also argue that the OFT investigation faced two big problems.

First, the period it was examining saw a large number of companies shoring up their balance sheets. The OFT's analysis shows that while, between 2000 and 2007, there were fewer than 10 rights issues a year raising a total of less than £5bn, 2009 saw £40bn of issues from more than 30 companies.

The second problem is that even if the OFT concluded that there were significant failings, its remedial options are limited.

Barriers to entry in investment banking remain high. And with a government-appointed panel examining the future structure of the industry, if was never likely the OFT would push for new limits on a single business, bankers said. 'A complete and utter waste of time,' said one.

Source: Miles Johnson and Megan Murphy, *Financial Times*, 28 January 2011. © Financial Times

been completed. In effect, it is the price expected if the NPV of the proposed course of action is zero. It is calculated below at 190p.

Effect of a 1-for-3 rights issue		
Before	3 old shares prior to rights issue at 200p each:	600p
	1 new share at 160p:	160p
After	4 shares worth:	760p
	1 share is therefore worth (760p ÷ 4) = TERP =	190p

nil paid price of rights
The market value of the right to subscribe for new shares offered in a rights issue

The value of the rights is the difference between the pre-rights share price and the TERP. In the case of Grow-up plc, this is (200p − 190p) = 10p for every existing share held. This 10p is termed the '**nil paid price of rights**'. The first option for shareholders is to sell their rights, obtaining 10p per share, less any dealing costs. A shareholder with 3,000 shares in the company would have a holding with market value prior to the rights issue of (3,000 × £2) = £6,000. After the issue, the value will fall to (3,000 × £1,90) = £5,700, a decline of £300, which is the amount he or she would receive for the rights sold.

The formula for the TERP is thus:

$$\text{TERP} = \frac{(N \times \text{cum rights price}) + \text{issue price}}{N + 1}$$

where N = base number of shares held (i.e. number of rights required to buy one share). In this example, TERP is thus:

$$\frac{(3 \times 200p) + 160p}{(3 + 1)} = \frac{760p}{4} = 190p$$

Similarly, the value of a right = (TERP – issue price).
In the example, this is:

$$(190p - 160p) = 30p$$

The nil paid price can be expressed per existing share (10p), or more usually, per block of shares required to acquire one new share $(3 \times 10p) = 30p$, i.e. the difference between the TERP and the issue price.

The second option is to subscribe for the new shares by *taking up the rights.* This should happen only if the shareholder has the resources to acquire the additional shares and believes this is the best way to invest such money. Additional reasons for taking up the rights are the fact that no stamp duty or broker's commission is payable, and the desire to maintain one's existing share of voting power.

A third option is to *sell sufficient rights to provide the cash to take up the balance.* This option, known as 'tail-swallowing', makes sense for shareholders who want to maintain their existing investment in the company in value terms.

The formula for calculating the number of shares for a tail-swallower to buy is:

$$\frac{\text{Nil paid price}}{\text{Ex-rights price}} \times \text{Number of shares allotted}$$

As noted, the *nil paid price* is the difference between the TERP and the subscription price, i.e. $(190p - 160p) = 30p$. The number of new shares to which our investor with 3,000 existing shares retains acquisition rights is:

$$\frac{30p}{190p} \times 1,000 = 157 \text{ shares}$$

To buy 157 shares at 160p will cost £251.20, funded from (843/1,000) rights sold at 30p = £252.90. The total investment is now worth $(3,157 \times 190p) = £5,998$, which (when rounded) is equivalent to the original investment of £6,000

The final option is to *let the rights lapse* by doing nothing. In this case, the company may sell the new shares in the market and reimburse the shareholder net of dealing fees. Alternatively, the issuer may conduct an auction of rights not taken up to avoid the need to appoint underwriters.

The real message from rights issues is that shareholders cannot expect to receive something for nothing. The apparent gain from the invitation to purchase new shares at a discount on the existing price is more illusory than real.

To some, a rights issue may look damaging because the share price (in theory) has to fall due to the sale of shares at a discount, but again this apparent damage is illusory. Of course, the EPS, based on the last reported profits, will fall, as there are more shares in issue. But if people are bullish about the firm's prospects, then the post-issue price may exceed the TERP (and vice versa). In this case, the market would be pricing in the expected returns from new investment, i.e. adding in the NPV of the new project (and vice versa). In effect, investors are saying that the cash raised is worth more than its nominal value as it brings with it the promise of positive investment returns (and vice versa);

similarly, if the post-issue price is equal to the TERP, investors are assessing the NPV of the investment project at zero, and simply valuing the cash raised purely as cash.

However, if a rights issue is announced by a struggling firm, in adverse market conditions, this may not be seen as good news (see Porsche cameo below).

Porsche to defy investors' fears with €5bn rights issue

Porsche is to push ahead with plans to raise €5bn ($7bn) in much needed fresh captial, in spite of market turmoil triggered by the Japanese crisis.

The sports carmaker said it would launch 'in the coming weeks' what would be the first big capital issuance in Germany this year, defying investors' anxiety about a potential nuclear disaster in Japan.

Hans Dieter Pötsch, Porsche's chief financial officer, said: 'If one could have chosen, one would have selected a different environment to the current one. But there is no reason whatsoever to flinch.'

Rising market tensions have already spurred two Chinese internet companies and Canal Plus, of France, to postpone or scale back listing plans. Investment bankers agreed with Mr Pötsch that there was no need to reverse course. 'Market volatility is much lower than it was during the Greek sovereign debt crisis last year,' said the European head of equity capital markets at a large investment bank. 'If a large company comes to the market with a good story and at a fair price, there will not be any problems.'

The shaky market situation comes at a delicate time for Porsche, as it needs to raise capital to pay back €5bn in loans by the end of the year. Porsche's shareholder approval to raise fresh capital is only valid until the end of May and it has to repay a first €2.5bn of debt by the end of June.

'There is no plan B, C or D – we will proceed with the capital increase within the given time frame,' Mr Pötsch said.

The carmaker will use the money to reduce its €6.34bn net debt load to about €1.5bn, Mr Pötsch said.

Half of the planned rights issue is set to be backed by the Porsche and Piëch families and by Qatar Holding, a sovereign wealth fund, which holds a 10 per cent stake in the carmaker.

A debt reduction is a pre-requisite for the sports carmaker's merger with Volkswagen, in a move that would add Porsche to Europe's top-selling carmaker's stable of nine brands.

But tax and legal hurdles have threatened to derail the two companies' plan.

Legal battles with hedge funds in the US, a continuing investigation by German prosecutors against two former top managers and a potential tax burden have prompted Porsche to warn repeatedly that the merger could be delayed or even abandoned.

As an alternative to a merger, VW owns options that allow it from early 2013 to buy the remainder of Porsche's sports car business, which it already half-owns.

But Mr Pötsch said an exercise before mid-2014 would trigger a more than €1bn tax charge. Analysts see this as a prohibitively high hurdle.

 Source: Daniel Schäfer, *Financial Times*, 28 March 2011. © Financial Times

■ Open offers

An open offer, or 'entitlement offer', may also be made by a quoted company to its existing shareholders. Like a rights issue, it invites shareholders to buy new shares at a specified price, normally lower than the going market price. The investor's entitlement to buy is also based on his/her existing holdings. However, there is one important difference – an open offer cannot be traded on the market. If the offer is not taken up, it lapses. An additional difference is that the firm may invite investors to apply for more than their strict entitlement – a so-called 'excess application', although there is no guarantee that this excess will be satisfied, as demand for shares may exceed the amount the firm wishes to issue.

Open offers are not very common. One such was announced in February 2014 by the Exeter-based airline, Flybe. The open offer was part of a capital-raising exercise to generate some £155 million, partly to pay down and partly to finance expansion and also improve productivity. This would be raised by selling 141.5 million new shares at

110p per share, a 7 per cent discount to the prevailing share price. Shareholders were offered an exchange of existing ordinary shares for two new ones under a fully underwritten scheme.

Self-assessment activity 16.3

What is the TERP in the following case?

- pre-announcement share price = £5.
- rights issue of 1-for-6 at £3.50 issue price.

(Answer in Appendix A at the back of the book)

Analysis of a rights issue

On 3 March 2014, Royal Sun Alliance (RSA), a leading British insurance company, best known for its More Than brand, announced its intention to raise £7,773 million via a rights issue. After banking legal and underwriting fees of £25 million, the net proceeds would be £748 million. This news, not entirely unexpected by the market, arrived in the wake of revelations of 'accounting irregularities' in its Irish business. RSA's capital backing was at the time generally considered in the thin side at around 10% of liabilities, albeit above the level required by regulators, but well below the 15% level commanded by several peers in the industry.

Shareholders were invited to buy three new shares for every eight already held (i.e. '3-for-8'), at a price representing a 33% discount to the theoretical ex-rights price (the TERP), or compared to the day's opening share price of 93.50p, a more dramatic discount of 40%. Although such large discounts are generally regarded as bad news,

and analysts are not usually impressed by rights issues designed to bolster capital or cut debts, the share price did rise to 95.20p. Based on the day's opening price, the TERP can be calculated thus:

8 existing shares @ 93.50p	= £7.48
3 new shares @ 56p	= £1.68
Total 11 Shares representing value of:	£9.16
TERP	= £9.16/11 = 83.30p

Turning to the discount, the issue price of 56p divided by the TERP (56p/83.3p = 0.67) represented a discount of 33%, but more dramatically, as compared to the market price, it represented a discount of (93.50p − 56p)/93.50p = 40%. The issue being fully underwritten (at no little cost). RSA was assured of raising its cash. In the event the take-up was 96% of the issue, leaving the underwriters to pick up the balance.

Source: www.rsagroup.com

■ Placing (placement – USA)

Having already obtained a listing, firms can also make a secondary share issue via a placing. Just as in an IPO, such a placing involves selling shares directly to a small group of favoured and supportive investors. These need not be shareholders already. It is thus quick and relatively easy to issue shares this way, as it saves on administration and paperwork. However, as it involves bypassing existing shareholders' pre-emption rights, it needs their prior permission to do this. This is usually done at an AGM, where many companies simply roll forward their permission if no placing has been made in the year just ended. There are various restrictions on placing: pre-emption rights are normally disapplied for a maximum of 5 per cent of the issued capital in any year, and only 7.5 per cent on a rolling three-year basis. Also, any discount at which the new shares can be placed is limited to 5 per cent of the prevailing market price.

bonus or scrip issue
Issues of free shares to existing shareholders *in lieu* of, or in addition to, cash dividends. Reflected in lower reserves (hence the alternative label, **capitalisation issue**)

■ Scrip issues and bonus issues

Whereas the methods discussed above raise new finance, a **bonus or scrip issue** simply *gives* shareholders more shares in proportion to their existing holdings. As a result, the value of their total holdings is unchanged, but the share price will fall due to

Sirius secures £43m funding for Yorkshire potash plans

Sirius Minerals got more finance for its plans to build a potash mine in Yorkshire, raising £43m in a share placement shortly after it announced a big redesign of part of the project.

Sirius had to change tack last year on seeking planning approval for the mine in the North York Moors national park. Last month it scrapped plans for a pipeline to carry away polyhalite – a type of potash – saying it would build a conveyor system in a deep-level tunnel. It will add 15 per cent to building costs but should cut operating costs by a quarter. A share placing at 12p, a 7.7 per cent discount, raised funds to complete a definitive feasibility study. The share base will expand by almost 24 per cent. Investors also got warrants for further shares exercisable at 18p over 18 months.

Shares have traded in a narrow range this year, in contrast to the 43 per cent fall last year.

 Source: James Wilson, *Financial Times*, 8 March 2014.

earnings dilution. Scrip issues are often used by companies whose unit share price is 'high' – a high or '**heavy-weight**' share price (in the UK, £10 or above) is regarded as a deterrent to trading. This was the reason given by the German biotechnology company Geneart AG, the global market leader in gene synthesis technology in 2007, when it made a 'one-for-one' scrip issue. For every share held, owners were given a free share. According to the CFO of Geneart, the firm aimed 'to significantly increase the number of tradable shares . . . to support the liquidity and tradability of our shares'.

Companies like Geneart have built up substantial reserves by retention of earnings, making their issued share capital look relatively small. In the case of Geneart, the issued share capital was €2.243 million and the capital reserve was €16.900 million. The effect of the scrip issue was to double the issued share capital and to reduce the reserve by €2.243 million to €14.657 million. In other words, Geneart converted, or 'capitalised', its reserves into issued share capital, hence the common use of the synonym '**capitalisation issue**'.

Scrip issues do not always involve such a drastic reorganisation of shareholder funds. They are often given as '**bonus issues**' in addition to cash dividends, and are often taken by the market as a signal of higher future dividends. If a company makes, say, a one-for-ten scrip and maintains the dividend per share, this is tantamount to a future increase in dividends of 10 per cent (the new shares do not normally qualify for the dividend immediately). This signifies the company's expectation of greater capacity to pay dividends in the future, i.e. higher future earnings. In such cases, the share price may not fall quite so far as the simple arithmetic may suggest, i.e. by 1/11th, but may even increase as the market responds to the 'signals' emitted by the company.

■ Share splits ('stock splits' in the USA)

An alternative way of addressing the heavyweight status of a share is to **split** the ordinary shares into a larger number with lower par value. For example, one additional share may be given for every existing share in a '2-for-1' split (i.e. one share becomes two). In theory, this has no effect on the accounting numbers, i.e. the book value of the share capital will not change. Nor should it affect the share price since no additional funds are raised and each shareholder's interest in future profits is unchanged.

Microsoft Inc. has made nine stock splits between its IPO in March 1986 and February 2003 as shown in Table 16.1, when 5.4 billion shares were multiplied into a total of 10.8 billion in a 2-for-1 split. It is noteworthy that the share price did not always follow the terms of the splits (e.g.) a 2-for-1 split may not necesserily lead to a halving of the share price.

Table 16.1 History of Microsoft common stock splits

Split	Payable date	Type of split	Closing price before/after
First	Sept. 18, 1987	2 for 1	Sept. 18–$114.50/ Sept. 21–$53.50
Second	April 12, 1990	2 for 1	April 12–$120.75/ April 16–$60.75
Third	June 26, 1991	3 for 2	June 26–$100.75/ June 27–$68.00
Fourth	June 12, 1992	3 for 2	June 12–$112.50/ June 15–$75.75
Fifth	May 20, 1994	2 for 1	May 20–$97.75/ May 23–$50.63
Sixth	Dec. 6, 1996	2 for 1	Dec. 6–$152.875/ Dec. 9–$81.75
Seventh	Feb. 20, 1998	2 for 1	Feb. 20–$155.13/ Feb. 23–$81.63
Eighth	March 26, 1999	2 for 1	March 26–$178.13/ March 29–$92.38
Ninth	Feb. 14, 2003	2 for 1	Feb. 14–$48.30 Feb. 18–$24.96

Source: **www.microsoft.com**

Mastering the splits

In January 2014, Mastercard, the credit card issuing firm, announced a 10-for-1 split, along with an increase in the quarterly dividend of 83% and a $3.5 billion share buy-back. This was the latest set of goodies in a series of market-beating distributions since the firm's IPO in 2006. However, such splits are quite rare nowadays, having fallen in the US (where, historically, they have been most common) from around 100 each year in the dot.com boom years to just 12 in 2013. The reason ascribed to this is that with the fall in retail ownership of ordinary shares, a heavyweight share price is less of a barrier to trading as the increasingly important funds and other institutions buy in bulk. Nevertheless, the Mastercard share price did increase by 5% in the wake of the triple announcement. How much of this was due to the split *per se* was debateable.

 Source: article by Arash Massoudi, FT Dealing Room, **www.ft.com**, 12 December 2013.

Self-assessment activity 16.4

In a share split, e.g. '2-for-1', what is the effect on:

- the number of shares issued?
- the shareholders' capital in the balance sheet?
- the firm's assets?
- its market value – per share? in total?

(Answer in Appendix A at the back of the book)

Equity capital: checklist of key features

For:

- No fixed charges (e.g. interest payments). Dividends are paid if the company generates sufficient cash, the level being decided by the directors.

- No repayment is required. It is truly permanent capital.

- It carries a higher return than loan finance and acts as a better hedge against inflation for investors.

- Shares in most listed companies can be easily disposed of at a fairly predictable price.

Against:

- Issuing equity finance can be cost-effective (as in the case of retained profits or a rights issue), but it is expensive in the case of a public issue (often 5 per cent or more of the finance raised).

- Issuing ordinary shares to new shareholders dilutes the degree of control of existing members.

- Dividends are not tax-deductible, making equity relatively more expensive than borrowing.

- A higher proportion of equity can increase the overall cost of capital for the company (see Chapter 18).

- Shares in unlisted companies are difficult both to value and to dispose of.

■ Reversing the flow: going private again

The last decade or so has seen an upsurge in the number of firms being taken off the stock market by so-called private equity firms, generally specialist funds that are subsidiaries of banks or syndicates set up by a number of banks. Traditionally, they have specialised in funding management buy-outs or spin-offs of unwanted divisions of larger firms, but more recently, they have been active in taking quoted firms off the stock market.

Sometimes, they are set up specifically to acquire one particular firm. Some observers estimated that by the end of 2007, firms controlled by private equity firms accounted for around 20 per cent of private sector employment in the UK.

Not being quoted themselves, they do not face the same public scrutiny or continuous pressure to perform. Their aim is to restructure the acquired firm and sell it on, either in a trade sale or by a refloatation. Some spectacular successes have been achieved with substantial increases in the value of firms taken private and then refloated a few years later being recorded.

Among the reasons for relinquishing a listing are:

- *The weight of regulation and disclosure that listed firms have to bear,* for example, the move to International Reporting Standards in 2005, the ongoing requirements of the Combined Code, and the introduction of the Sarbanes–Oxley Act affecting firms with a US listing. Regarding the Combined Code, many firms do not see the need to separate the roles of Chairman and Chief Executive, arguing that it leads to lack of flexibility, which hampers swift and effective decision-making.

- *Greater liquidity among financial institutions.* Many institutions have curtailed their investment of new money into the stock market, and others have cut back their exposure, creating vacuums that they have filled by investing in private equity funds.

- *The ability to tolerate higher gearing.* With no public scrutiny, the amount of debt that they can carry is greater than for an equivalent listed firm. Private equity firms have tended to concentrate on asset-rich firms with solid cash flows, most notably firms in the retail store sector, which often need a re-vamp.

16.9 DEBT INSTRUMENTS: DEBENTURES, BONDS AND NOTES

The array of instruments for raising debt finance is even greater than for equity finance. Firms can raise long-term debt via the banking system, e.g. by a term-loan, or via the money and bond markets, by issuing a security that can be traded rather than held to maturity. The money markets supply short-term borrowing while the bond markets supply medium-to-long-term finance.

The word 'bond' is a general term used to describe a variety of longer-term loans to companies. In some markets, they are described as '**loan stock**', or, especially where the interest payable is variable, as '**notes**'. A bond is simply a receipt or promise to repay money on a loan, usually with interest, i.e. it binds the borrower to a commitment that can range between one and 30 years.

notes
Loan securities in general, but often referred to securities that carry a floating rate of interest

Characteristics of a bond are:

- the nominal or par value in the currency of denomination.
- the redemption value – usually the par value, but other possibilities include a stated premium, or index-linking.
- the rate of interest payable – known as the coupon – expressed as a percentage of the nominal value.
- the redemption date.

For example, Vodaphone Group plc, the telecommunications firm, is committed to the following bond:

Sterling 450 million 8.125% November 2018

The £450 million will be repaid in full in November 2018; and 8.125 per cent interest is payable per £100 of stock each year in two stages.

debenture
In law, any form of borrowing that commits a firm to pay interest and repay capital. In practice, usually applied to long-term loans that are secured on a firm's assets

■ Debentures

In strict legal terms, a **debenture** is a document acknowledging that the firm has borrowed money, whether or not any security has been given to back the loan. However, in normal business usage, this term is used to describe a loan which is secured on the assets of the company by mortgage deeds – a secured debenture is often called a **mortgage debenture**. If the issuer goes into liquidation, or defaults on interest or capital payments, the holders can apply for a court ruling to order the sale of either specified assets (called a **fixed charge**) or any of the firm's assets (a **floating charge**). The firm cannot dispose of assets subject to a fixed charge without the permission of the creditors.

mortgage debenture
A loan instrument under which the ownership of selected assets is mortgaged to the lender – in a default, the title passes to the lender

fixed charge
Applies when a lender can force the sale of pre-specified company's assets in order to recover debts in the event of default on interest and/or capital payments

As regards priority for payment, debts rank in order of issue – holders of the earliest issued debentures must be paid interest before the later comers. Where a firm has issued a series of bonds, a *pari passu* clause is inserted into the document acknowledging the priority of the debt. Debentures that rank lower down the priority list are called 'junior' or 'subordinated' stock.

An unsecured bond ranks behind a firm's secured borrowing, but ahead of any subsequently issued unsecured bonds. Unsecured stock is riskier than secured stock and investors thus require a higher coupon rate.

floating charge
Applies when a lender can force the sale of any (i.e. unspecified) of a company's assets in order to recover debts in the event of default on interest and/or capital payments. (Ranks behind a fixed charge)

The pejorative term '**junk bond**' is applied to the unsecured loan stock of a borrower that merits sub-investment grade by a bond-rating agency. The credit-rating agency Standard & Poor's investment grade is BBB or above – any security rated below this 'is regarded as having predominantly speculative characteristics with respect to capacity to pay interest and repay principal'. Obviously, junk carries much higher than average yields, hence the euphemism 'high yield bonds'.

junk bonds
Low-quality, risky bonds with no credit rating

restrictive covenants
Limitations on managerial freedom of action, stipulated as conditions of making a loan

Loan agreements usually specify **restrictive covenants**. Such conditions might include the following:

1 *Dividend restrictions* – limitations on the level of dividends a company is permitted to pay. This is designed to prevent excessive dividend payments, which may seriously weaken the company's future cash flows and thereby place the lender at greater risk.
2 *Financial ratios* – specified levels below which certain ratios may not fall, e.g. the current ratio, or exceed (e.g.) the gearing ratio.
3 *Financial reports* – regular accounts and financial reports to be provided to the lender to monitor progress.
4 *Issue of further debt* – the amount and type of debt that can be issued may be restricted. Subordinated loan stock (i.e. stock ranking below the existing unsecured loan stock) can usually still be issued.
5 *Asset backing* – a minimum level of tangible fixed assets may be specified.

Debentures and unsecured loan stock: checklist of key features

For:

- Most corporate loan stocks give ten or more years before repayment is due. A 'bullet' loan is where there is just one final repayment, and a 'balloon' loan is where increasing amounts of capital are repaid towards the end of the period of the loan.
- A successful company may eventually be able to redeem the loan stock through a new issue, without drawing upon operating cash flows (although the company is exposed to the risk of higher interest rates).
- Interest is tax-deductible.

Against:

- Restrictions are placed on the company in terms of either the charge over assets or the restrictive covenants imposed.
- Unsecured loan stock may impose demanding performance requirements.
- Greater monitoring and control takes place over a public issue such as a debenture than with, say, a term loan from a bank.

A big number from Verizon: Companies are still taking advantage of low yields to raise debt

Debt crisis? What debt crisis? The biggest corporate-bond issue ever was completed this week. Verizon Communications, an American telecoms group, issued a whopping $49 billion of bonds in order to finance the buy-out of Vodafone's stake in its wireless operations. That shattered the previous record, Apple's paltry $17 billion issue earlier this year.

The scale of Verizon's offering may be unprecedented, but its foray into the bond markets is anything but. In the first eight months of this year $1.4 trillion of corporate bonds were issued worldwide, according to Dealogic, a data provider, compared with $1.3 trillion in the same period of 2012. Firms have been keen to lock in long-term financing at low yields, particularly since borrowing costs started rising after the Federal Reserve hinted in May at slowing its asset purchases.

Oil and gas companies have been particularly enthusiastic issuers, according to Marcus Hiseman of Morgan Stanley, especially in the 'Yankee' market where foreign businesses sell bonds, priced in dollars, mainly to American investors. Previously many foreign firms would issue debt in euros and swap the proceeds into dollars, but regulatory restrictions on banks make that much more expensive these days. This year 72% of investment grade issuance has been in dollars, compared with 58% in 2009, according to Morgan Stanley.

If companies fear that bond yields are set to rise (meaning that bond prices will fall), why are investors so keen to

Continued

buy? There was plenty of demand to absorb the Verizon issue, for instance: orders reportedly reached $100 billion. One reason is that corporate bonds offer a spread (excess interest rate) over government bonds that is still attractive in historical terms. The average yield on ten-year investment-grade debt is 3.5%, compared with just 2.95% on Treasury bonds of the same maturity. The sheer size of the Verizon issue required it to be more generous towards investors, as did its BBB+ rating from Standard & Poor's, towards the bottom end of the investment grade category. The firm offered a yield of over 5% on its ten-year bonds, for example, more than two percentage points above the equivalent Treasury issue.

Many central banks, which hold a large part of their reserves in dollars, remain enthusiastic buyers of corporate debt. In addition, many investors in corporate debt are specialist fund managers who aim to beat the benchmark specific to their asset class, points out Paul Young of Citigroup; they care more about whether they pick the right bonds, as they are able to hedge the underlying interest-rate risk.

The influx of money nonetheless causes some to worry. The corporate-bond market is a lot less liquid than it used to be, thanks largely to the effect of regulations on the willingness of banks to hold large inventories of corporate debt. This could cause a problem should bond investors want to sell their holdings in a rush. For the moment, however, that does not seem likely. Corporate balance-sheets look strong and the default rate over the past 12 months, even on speculative debt, was just 2.9%, according to Moody's, another ratings agency.

Source: The Economist, 14 September 2013.

■ Deep-discount bonds

Some debt instruments are sold at a price well below the par value, with a so-called deep-discount. An extreme case of this is the zero-coupon bond, e.g. a bond issued at £70 with a five-year life to maturity when it will be repaid at par of £100. Such bonds carry no entitlement to interest as such, thus appealing to investors who would normally pay income or corporation tax on interest income, but who may not be liable to capital gains tax, or who wish to defer it. In this example, the annualised rate of return from the capital gain if held to maturity for the full five years is represented by the rate r in the following compound interest expression:

$$£70(1 + r)^5 = £100$$

This can be written as:

$$\frac{1}{(1 + r)^5} = \frac{£70}{£100} = 0.700$$

From the PVIF discount tables, it can be seen that the solution lies between 7 per cent and 8 per cent, more precisely, 7.3 per cent.

Self-assessment activity 16.5

What is the yield to maturity on a zero-coupon bond issued at £50, repayable at par of £100, in ten years' time?

(Answer in Appendix A at the back of the book)

asset-backed securities (ABS)
Bonds issued on the security of a stream of highly reliable income flows, e.g. mortgage payments to a bank, out of which interest payments are made

■ Asset-backed securities (ABSs)

In recent years, some companies – and even certain individuals – have issued a new breed of securities, backed not by physical assets but by a reliable long-term stream of future earnings. A category of assets commonly utilised has been intellectual property represented by patents and copyrights. Like most security issues, **asset-backed securities (ABS)** are sold essentially to raise cash for investing in other activities.

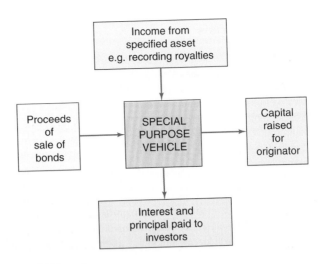

Figure 16.1 How an SPV works

Special Purpose Vehicle (SPV)
A financial vehicle set up to manage the issue of Asset-Backed Securities and arrange for payment of interest and eventual redemption

securitisation
The technique of packaging non-tradable claims into a traded security backed by an asset such as a flow of low-risk income payments

Organisations effectively *capitalise* their future income into a single lump sum and sell it on the financial markets to generate immediate cash. The firm's financial advisers set up a **Special Purpose Vehicle (SPV)**, as shown in Figure 16.1. This is effectively a 'bank' which handles the bond issue and into which the designated income stream is paid and from which is paid the stream of interest payments needed to service the borrowing.

This process of converting non-tradable claims into tradable ones is called **securitisation**. Like most financial innovations, securitisation originated in the USA. Banks parcelled up mortgage commitments made by house purchasers into bundles of mortgages to sell as interest-bearing securities, originally known as collateralised mortgage obligations (CMOs), now known as collateralised debt obligations (CDOs). Having both liquidity and a bank's guarantee, these could be offered at a lower interest rate than that charged on the underlying mortgages, the difference representing profit for the bank. This practice also became widespread in Europe, where it was increasingly seen as a cheaper alternative to unsecured bond issues.

The following examples of the ABS principle (not all of which involved SPVs) demonstrate its flexibility and versatility:

- In 1992, the Disney Corporation issued $400 million in seven-year notes with a variable rate of interest to be paid from royalties receivable from its portfolio of film copyrights, a path followed also by News Corporation in 1996.
- In 1997, David Bowie raised $55 million by selling bonds backed by his music copyright portfolio, with an average bond life of ten years. This tactic was also adopted by Rod Stewart and Michael Jackson, using a similar form of security.
- Holland's De Nationale Investeringsbank NV (DNIB) is a major player. Its ABS issue in March 1999, worth €290 million, was its fourth inside two years.
- Calvin Klein, GE Capital and Nestlé have all issued ABSs secured on trademarks.
- In 2004, British football club Leeds United issued bonds secured on future revenue from 'gate money', i.e. ticket sales, as part of a rescue package.
- Also in 2004, in the USA, Florida's Seminole Indian tribe sold $410 million of bonds to fund development of its gaming resorts in Tampa and Hollywood, Florida. The bonds were secured on future gambling takings, and income from a joint venture with Hard Rock Café.

CDOs and the credit crisis

In recent years, CDOs have received a bad reputation, especially those based on private mortgages. During the early 2000s, there was a surge in sales of such CDOs, especially in the USA, an estimated $600 million being sold in 2007. Mortgage CDOs were sold as packages of mortgages of varying quality (i.e. risk). They were said to be 'structured' according to riskiness, hence the term 'structured finance'. They were assigned risk ratings by the credit rating agencies depending on the risk of default of the underlying assets.

Banks were keen on CDOs because they offered a way to exchange relatively illiquid loan assets for cash, thus strengthening their balance sheets, and enabling them to take on more lending activities. The major banks also acquired CDOs from specialist mortgage banks and sold on CDO tranches to a wide range of investors across the financial system.

However, the quality of these CDOs was often overstated, with a larger proportion than investors had realised based on 'sub-prime mortgages' – loans made to high-risk borrowers with a high probability of default, and often, it was alleged, not adequately credit-screened by the original lender. As defaults occurred, the value of many CDOs plummeted, making it very difficult for holders to sell them on. As some CDOs use the same mortgage pool as collateral, any defaults in the pool cause a ripple effect through several investments. It was estimated that defaults of, say, $100 million could trigger losses throughout the financial system of $500 million. Investors who were attracted by relatively high rates of return for supposedly moderate risk investments were stunned to find that the market value of their CDOs had nose-dived, often to as low as 60 per cent of face value.

Many financial institutions that had acquired CDOs had to make substantial write-offs, the largest being $38 billion by Swiss bank UBS, $21 billion by Citigroup and $25 billion by Merrill Lynch. However, there was widespread suspicion that too few banks had 'come clean' about the scale of their losses with the result that the inter-bank lending market that provides temporary liquidity to banks with over-stretched balance sheets effectively dried up, which had a domino impact on other areas of the financial markets. In the UK, the most famous casualty was former building society Northern Rock, which was unable to refinance market borrowing that was due for repayment. Facing insolvency, it was offered for sale via the Bank of England, but with no acceptable offers forthcoming, the UK government was forced to nationalise it to prevent it collapsing.

By 2008, the CDO market had effectively seized up, no issues having been made since August 2007. Only time would tell whether the market would recover, but recover it did, as the next cameo reveals.

The return of securitisation: Back from the dead

A much-maligned financial innovation is in the early stages of a comeback

If you asked regulators in 2008 which financial instrument they most wished had never been invented, odds were that they angrily splurted a three-letter acronym linked to securitisation. The practice of bundling up income streams such as credit-card and car-loan repayments, repackaging them as securities and selling them on in 'tranches' with varying levels of risk once seemed like enlightened financial management. Not so after many a CDO, CLO, ABS, MBS and others (see table) turned out to be infested with worthless American subprime mortgages.

Find the same regulator today and he is probably devising a ploy to resuscitate the very financial vehicle he was bemoaning five years ago. Enthusiasm for the once-reviled practice of transforming a future income stream into a lump sum today – the essence of securitisation – is palpable. In Britain Andy Haldane, a cerebral official at the Bank of England, recently described it as 'a financing vehicle for all seasons' that should no longer be thought of as a 'bogeyman'. The European Central Bank (ECB) is a fan, as are global banking regulators who last month watered down rules that threatened to stifle securitisation.

Watchdogs will be pleased that, after once looking as if it was heading for extinction, securitisation is making a recovery. Issuance of ABSs (securities underpinned by car-loan receivables, credit-card debt and the like) are at double their 2010 nadir. Issuance of paper backed by non-residential mortgages is up from just $4 billion in 2009 to more than $100 billion last year. There have even been offerings of securities underpinned by more esoteric sources, such as cashflows from solar panels or home-rental income – the sort of gimmick once derided as a boomtime phenomenon. Excluding residential mortgages, where the American market is skewed by the participation of federal agencies, the amount of bundled-up securities globally is showing a steady rise (see chart).

Old alphabet soup, new taste

ABS (*asset-backed security*)	Most generic form of securitisation, includes credit-card debt, car loans, or any packaged income stream. Making steady comeback
MBS (*mortgage-backed security*)	Backed either by commercial (CMBS) or residential (RMBS) mortgages. The most problematic in the downturn, fuelled subprime crisis
CDO (*collateralised debt obligation*)	Pre-crisis these were often invested in 'tranches' of ABSs and MBSs or in other CDOs. Not popular with regulators
CLO (*collateralised loan obligation*)	Frequently filled with sliced and diced loans extended to poor-credit firms, such as those taken over by private equity. Making a comeback

Sources: Dealogic; *The Economist*.

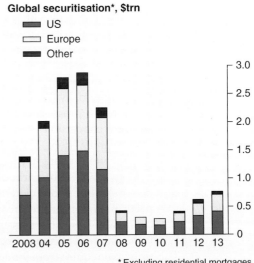

Global securitisation*, $trn

- US
- Europe
- Other

2003 04 05 06 07 08 09 10 11 12 13

* Excluding residential mortgages

The comeback of securitisation is related to the growth in economic activity: in order for car loans to be securitised, say, consumers have to be buying cars. Investors desperate for yield are also stimulating supply: securitised paper can offer decent returns, particularly at the riskier end of the spectrum, More important, though, is the regulators' enthusiasm.

Why are regulators so keen on the very product that nearly blew up the global economy just five years ago? In a nutshell, policymakers want to get more credit flowing to the economy, and are happy to rehabilitate once-suspect financial practices to get there. Some plausibly argue it was the stuff that was put into the vehicles (i.e., dodgy mortgages) that was toxic, not securitisation itself. This revisionist strand of financial history emphasises that packaged bundles of debt which steered clear of American housing performed well, particularly in Europe.

The need to revive slicing and dicing is felt most acutely in Europe. Whereas in America capital markets are on hand to finance companies (through bonds), the old continent remains far more dependent on bank lending to fuel economic growth. Its banks need more capital, and absent that are the weak link in the nascent recovery because they fail to meet demand for credit from consumers and small businesses.

This is in large part because regulators want banks to be less risky, by increasing the ratio of equity to loans. As banks are reluctant to raise capital, they need to shed assets. This is where securitisation helps: by bundling up the loans on their books (which form part of their assets) and selling them to outside investors, such as asset managers or insurance firms, banks can both slim their balance-sheet and improve capital ratios.

Securitisation 'airlifts assets off the balance-sheets of banks, freeing up capital, and drops them onto the balance-sheets of real-money investors,' in Mr Haldane's words.

That may not seem urgent now, as Europe's banks are flooded with cheap money from the ECB and have years before stricter capital ratios officially kick in. But at some point markets will have to take over financing banks. Such airlifts would nearly transform Europe's inflexible bank-led system into something more akin to America's.

Financial watchdogs are also keen on securitisation because they are confident that they can steer it along a different path from the one that ultimately wrought havoc in 2008. They believe that regulatory tweaks have made the practice safer.

One improvement is that those involved in creating securitised products will have to retain some of the risk linked to the original loan, thus keeping 'skin in the game'. The idea is to nip in the bud any temptation to adopt the slapdash underwriting practices that became a feature of America's mortgage market in the run-up to the financial crisis. Another tightening of the rules makes 're-securitisations', where income from securitised products was itself securitised, more difficult to pull off. If regulators have their way, financial Frankenstein monsters such as the 'CDO-squared' – a security underpinned by a security underpinned by a security underpinned by assets – are unlikely to make a comeback.

Perhaps the biggest change, however, is in investors' attitudes. Before 2008, many fell for the sales pitch of the whizzes who hatched CDOs, ABSs and the like. Reassured by somnolent credit-rating agencies, which backed the bankers' vision of handsome returns at virtually no risk, investors piled in with no due diligence to speak of. Aware of the reputational risks of messing up again, they now spend more time dissecting three-letter assets than just about anything else in their portfolio. Regulators will have to make sure that they retain this newfound discipline.

Source: The Economist, 11 January 2014.

■ Convertibles

A convertible begins life as a form of debt, but carries the right, at the holder's option, to convert into ordinary shares at some specified date in the future and on specified terms, e.g. how many new ordinary shares can be obtained on conversion per unit of convertible stock. They are, therefore, another form of hybrid securities.

Firms that issue convertibles increase their gearing ratios and may be viewed as being more risky. Yet the greater risk is not always reflected in a higher coupon rate. As there is a prospect of making a capital gain should the share price market perform strongly, convertibles can usually be issued at a lower rate of interest than straight or 'plain vanilla' debt. Until the date of conversion, the holder receives a fixed rate of interest and is a long-term creditor of the company.

Convertibles are particularly suitable for companies facing relatively high business risks, but strong potential growth, because they offer investors the possibility of participating in future prosperity. This explains the ease with which many 'dotcom' companies were able to issue so much convertible debt. The downside for companies is that interest, although tax-deductible, must be paid every year, good or bad, and the principal requires repayment if holders do not convert.

The downside for existing shareholders is the prospect of dilution of their equity, and hence a fall in EPS, as and when conversion occurs. Dilution is especially damaging if the conversion terms are misjudged, e.g. if growth is a lot stronger than expected, the conversion terms may be over-generous to convertible holders. It often makes sense for existing shareholders to hedge against this risk by acquiring the convertibles themselves. Indeed, convertibles may be issued initially to owners in a rights issue.

The language of convertibles

Convertible conversion terms can be complex.

- the **conversion date** (or range of dates) tells you when it can be converted.
- the **conversion rate** tells you the terms on which conversion can be made. This is stated either as a **conversion price** – the nominal value of loan stock that can be converted into one ordinary share – or as a **conversion ratio** – the number of ordinary shares that will be obtained from one unit of loan stock.
- the **conversion value** is the market value of ordinary shares into which a unit of convertible loan stock can be converted. This is equal to the conversion ratio times the current market price per ordinary share.
- the **conversion premium** is the difference between the market price of the convertible and its conversion value.
- the **rights premium** is the difference between the market value of the convertible and its value as straight debt. Each of the last two terms can be expressed as an absolute value or per share.

An example will help clarify this terminology.

Example: Cannon plc

Cannon plc's balance sheet shows 10 per cent convertible loan stock, par value of £100, redeemable at par in seven years. Each unit of stock can be converted at any time in the next three years into 20 ordinary shares. The debenture currently trades at £117, interest has just been paid and the current ordinary share price is £3.60. The ex-interest market price of the debentures of a company of similar risk is £109.

Current conversion value = (20 × £3.60) = £72
Current conversion premium = (£117 − £72) = £45 (or £2.25 per share)
Current rights premium = (£117 − £109) = £8 (or £0.40 per share)

At the initial issue date, the conversion value will be less than the issue price. Investors hope that as the conversion date nears, and as the market price of the underlying shares increases, the conversion value will rise accordingly, i.e. conversion becomes more attractive to investors. The conversion premium is proportional to the time remaining before conversion occurs. As conversion approaches, the market value and the conversion value converge until the conversion premium disappears. With no conversion premium, the value of the convertible is simply its value as straight debt with a similar coupon and maturity.

The market value of the convertible thus depends on:

- the current conversion value
- the time remaining to conversion
- the market's expectations regarding the expected returns
- the degree of risk of the underlying ordinary shares.

Nokia convertible bonds

In October 2012, Nokia, the Finnish cell-phone manufacturer, announced the decision to raise €750m from the sale of senior unsecured convertible bonds to improve its cash and liquidity position. These carry an interest rate of 5% and are due for repayment at par in October 2017. The initial conversion price was set at €2.6116, representing a 28% conversion premium to the recently prevailing average Nokia price. The maximum number of shares that may be converted (287m) represents almost 8% of Nokia's issued share capital. The right to convert bonds into shares operates from December 2012, at prices to be determined by Nokia.

Sources: Nokia Annual Report & Accounts, 2013, **www.nokia.com**; G. Kesarios, **www.seekingalpha.com**, 23 October 2012; *Reuters*, 23 October 2012.

Convertible loan stock: key features

- Convertible loan stock can be issued more cheaply than a 'straight' loan because it offers an equity incentive.
- Companies perceived as relatively high risk can attract loan finance by offering the possibility of participating in future growth.
- Interest on the loan (while it is a loan) is tax-deductible.
- The bonds can also be traded on the Stock Exchange.
- Where it is believed that the true worth of the company is not adequately reflected in the share price, convertibles provide a means of raising capital that may eventually become equity without diluting the value of existing equity.
- Convertibles offer the benefits of both equity and loan stock, thereby attracting additional investors.
- If all goes as planned, the conversion to equity will occur, reducing the gearing ratio (but also lowering Earnings per share).

■ Bond yields

interest yield
The annual interest on a bond or similar security divided by its market price

Investors who buy debentures and loan stock will want to know the rate of return, or yield, on their investments. Two ratios are of interest to investors. The **flat yield** or **interest yield** is the gross interest receivable, expressed as a percentage of the current market value of the stock. Thus a 7 per cent stock with a market value of £85 and a nominal value of £100 has a flat yield of:

$$\frac{£7}{£85} \times 100 = 8.2\%$$

This represents the gross yield. The net-of-tax yield to the investor depends on his or her tax position:

$$\text{Net interest yield} = \text{Gross yield} \times (1 - t_\text{p})$$

where t_p is the personal rate of tax incurred by the bond-holder.

redemption yield
The interest yield adjusted for any capital gain or loss if the security is held to maturity

The **redemption yield** combines the income accruing from interest payments with the capital gain or loss on maturity. It will be greater than the flat yield where the current value is below the redemption value because the investor will also receive a capital gain if the bond is held until maturity.

If the above stock has five years' life to maturity, someone who buys it for £85 will receive a capital gain on redemption of £15. Averaged over five years, this represents an additional gain of £3 p.a. Based on the purchase price of £85 this raises the yield to redemption thus:

$$\text{Flat yield} + £3/£85 = 8.2\% + 3.5\% = 11.7\%$$

However, this is only an approximation to the true redemption yield, which depends on the precise timing of the investor's returns. For example, assume he or she buys the stock now, having just missed out on the most recent interest payment, thus anticipating five future annual interest payments plus the redemption payment of £100 at the end of the fifth year. The yield to maturity is the solution R in the following internal rate of return expression:

$$£85 = \frac{£7}{(1 + R)} + \frac{£7}{(1 + R)^2} + \cdots + \frac{(£7 + £100)}{(1 + R)^5}$$

gross redemption yield
The redemption yield before allowing for income tax payable by investors

The precise solution is 10.9 per cent. As above, this would be offset by the investor's liability to tax. As this figure is gross-of-tax, it is also called the **gross redemption yield**. Similar principles apply in calculating yields on government securities.

Self-assessment activity 16.6

A bond with nominal value of £100 and coupon rate of 8.3 per cent has market value of £110. What is:

(a) its flat yield?

(b) its yield to maturity in three years?

(Answer in Appendix A at the back of the book)

■ Warrants

warrants
Options to buy ordinary shares at a pre-determined 'exercise price'. Usually attached to issues of loan stock

A **warrant** is an option to buy ordinary shares. We include warrants in the section on debt finance because they are more frequently linked to debt issues than to equity issues (although many companies distribute warrants to shareholders as a 'sweetener'). The warrant holder is entitled to buy a stated number of shares at a specific price up to a certain date. Each warrant will state the number of shares the owner may purchase and the time limit (unless it is a **perpetual warrant**) within which the option to purchase can be exercised.

perpetual warrant
A warrant with no time limit for exercising it

Companies issue warrants for a number of reasons. They can be attached to loan stock, thus providing loan stock holders with an opportunity to participate in the future growth and prosperity of the company, or, alternatively, used to attract investors by new and expanding companies. They may be also part of the purchase consideration in a takeover. In both cases, they act as a 'sweetener' to the investor. Frequently, such an inducement enables the company to obtain a lower rate of interest or less restrictive conditions in the debenture agreement. Whether or not warrants eventually give rise to additional finance by holders taking up their option to purchase depends, of course, on the future trading success of the company and the exercise price.

How warrants work

In 2008, when its ordinary shares carried a market price of £2.00, XYZ plc issued debenture stock with one warrant attached to each unit of stock giving the right to buy one ordinary share at a price of £2.50 in 2012. If, at the exercise date, the market share price is, say, £4.00 we would expect investors to exercise their rights, thus making a capital gain of £1.50 per share purchased. As a result of their purchases, the earnings of existing shareholders will be diluted – the company is, in effect, giving away £1.50 per share, which is not a problem if the same shareholders also hold the debentures, to which the warrants are attached, although this is rather unusual. The accounting mechanism would involve a reduction in the company's reserves. Warrants are often called 'time bombs' for this reason. This also explains why the issue of warrants may be used as a takeover defence tactic – warrants implant a 'poison pill' for the predator to swallow.

Warrants can be traded separately from the securities to which they were originally attached. In the XYZ example, if the ordinary shares are trading at £3.00, the warrants will be worth 50p each, because they embody the right to buy ordinary shares at a 50p discount. They also possess the attractive property of gearing. If the ordinary shares rise in value by 5 per cent from £3.00 to £3.15, the warrant would also rise by 15p in value, but by the considerably greater proportion of (15p/50p) = 30 per cent. For this reason, they are referred to as 'geared plays'.

Self-assessment activity 16.7

What is the market value of a warrant that gives the right to buy one new share for every four shares held, given the market price per share is £8, and the exercise price is £5?

(Answer in Appendix A at the back of the book)

■ Mezzanine finance

mezzanine finance
Covers hybrids such as convertibles that embody both debt and equity features

Mezzanine finance is frequently used in the financing of management buy-outs (MBOs). It is often described as a bridge between the secured debt that a business can raise and pay interest thereon with reasonable comfort plus the equity that the management team can raise, and the purchase price. Although it lies nearer the former, it ranks behind more formal borrowing contracts, which is why it is called 'subordinated' or 'intermediate' debt. Because of its low priority for payment, it attracts a relatively high interest rate, usually 3–5 per cent above LIBOR, and usually carries warrants and/or the right to convert into ordinary shares. The appeal of mezzanine finance to investors is that it offers investors exposure to the upside potential of the venture – if the MBO performs well, the warrants offer the prospect of capital gain. However, these are chancy investments – both the company and the instrument carry major risks.

■ Foreign bonds

foreign bonds
Loan stock issued on the domestic market by non-resident firms or organisations. In London, called 'bulldogs', in New York 'Yankees'

Foreign bonds are domestic issues by non-residents, e.g. an issue of stock by a US company in London (a 'bulldog'), or in Tokyo (a 'samurai') or in Australia (a 'kangaroo'). Such bonds are domestic bonds in the local currency – only the issuer is foreign. If a British firm makes a bond issue in New York, this is a 'Yankee' bond.

In recent years, 'dim sum' bonds have become popular, as the Unilever cameo illustrates.

Unilever tests 'dim sum' market

Unilever is set to become the first European multinational to launch an offshore renminbi-denominated 'dim sum' bond when it raises Rmb300m (£28m) from institutional investors in Hong Kong today, bankers say.

Dim sum bonds are gaining traction with multinationals, virtually all of which have China operations. McDonald's became the first US issuer last August when it raised Rmb200m. Caterpillar, the US-based maker of earthmoving equipment, followed with a Rmb1bn bond in November.

Unilever, which is also expected to be among the first clutch of foreigners to list renminbi-denominated A shares in Shanghai once the regulatory framework is in place, will hope the move demonstrates its commitment to China.

In addition to backing the nascent dim sum bond market, issuers are supporting Beijing's ultimate aim of internationalising the so-called red-back. The more foreign private sector issuers, as opposed to bodies like the Asian Development Bank, issue the bonds, the greater the credibility in the offshore market, bankers say.

The move comes an Unilever plays catch-up to US-based rival Procter & Gamble, which has stolen a march on it in China. Consultants in China attribute Procter & Gamble's stronger positioning to its early start and hefty investment in everything from advertising to distribution.

But Unilever, which has revenues in excess of €1bn (£880m) in China, is fighting back with beefed-up spending on research and development as well as consumer insights.

Dim sum bonds have raised $1.3bn so far this year, according to Dealogic, more than $1bn of which was tapped by Chinese issuers. But issuers from other countries are starting to dip in; Orix, the financial services company, became Japan's first issuer earlier this month.

Bankers say the coupon on Unilever's bond, which will be finalised on Monday, will be 'very competitive'. Caterpillar paid 2 per cent for its bond and McDonald's 3 per cent. Unilever, like fellow issuers, has sizeable renminbi outgoings, but these are more than covered by income. However, bankers say, the deal is seen as being less about securing reasonably priced funds than winning stripes in Beijing for good corporate citizenship. Backing by a multinational should help stimulate further interest in the dim sum bond market, one of the core components in Beijing's ambitious plan to internationalise the Chinese currency.

Foreign issuers have not been rushing to tap the market largely because the renminbi cannot be freely converted.

Strict regulations control the flow of the currency between Hong Kong and the mainland, making transfers for investment cumbersome. Most foreign issuance in the market since its creation in 2007 has come from banks and their China units.

 Source: Louise Lucas, *Financial Times*, 28 March 2011. © Financial Times

■ Eurobonds ('International bonds')

eurobonds or international bonds
Securities issued by borrowers in a market outside that of their domestic currency

The term **Eurobond** is a misnomer – they need not be issued in Europe or be denominated in a European currency! They are most easily understood as international loans denominated in a currency other than that of the issuer, but technically they are any long-term bonds issued outside the country of the currency in which the bonds are denominated. An example is a Eurodollar issue denominated (and thus repayable) in dollars by a US corporation, issued via the Frankfurt capital market. They are issued only by large, creditworthy companies, development banks and state-owned corporations, and are generally unsecured. The vast majority of Eurobond issues are denominated in euros and in US dollars, e.g. the issue by Ghana Telecommunications, in 2007, for $200 million.

Eurobond issues are mainly organised and underwritten by international syndicates of investment banks acting on behalf of borrowers. The market originally developed in response to the desire by US companies to avoid the now defunct withholding tax, which they were obliged to pay to the tax authorities on behalf of investors who purchased bonds sold locally.

Eurobonds are bearer bonds (i.e. they are transferable), with interest paid annually, and gross of tax, which may appeal to investors eager to delay (or evade) tax. Empirical evidence suggests that this feature may allow companies to borrow at rates lower than on their own domestic markets, although any such yield differential would be eliminated by arbitrageurs if the international bond market were efficient and unsegmented.

Lower overseas interest rates are not necessarily good news. Many corporate treasurers who try to take advantage of relatively low overseas interest rates often overlook the reasons why interest rates are lower overseas. Domestic interest rates are linked to future expected inflation rates and to expected exchange rate movements. If the inflation rate in Switzerland is lower than in the UK, the Swiss franc will appreciate against sterling, and current interest rates in London will exceed those in Zurich. This is to compensate both domestic investors for inflation and also overseas investors from, say, Switzerland for the prospective reduction in the Swiss franc value of investments in London. If a British corporate treasurer borrows 'cheap' in Zurich, he or she should not be surprised to find that, when it comes to repay the loan in Swiss francs, the sterling cost has increased, following depreciation of sterling. What is won from the interest rate savings will probably be lost from the capital value change. However, for treasurers who believe that exchange rate movements can be predicted in advance, Eurobonds may offer speculative opportunities. For those who simply want to create an overseas liability to offset an exposure in relation to an overseas income flow, Eurobonds may present an attractive way of hedging. (These aspects are examined in more detail in Chapter 21.)

In addition to interest cost advantages, Eurobonds usually involve fewer, if any, restrictive covenants, and usually require less disclosure of information than is required for similar issues on domestic markets. The unregulated nature of the market has probably contributed to its innovativeness in terms of the features attaching to many issues, whereby bonds can be tailored to specific corporate requirements. The following article from *The Economist* discusses current proposals to increase the reputation of financial markets, in the context of the success of the Eurobond market.

Money will find a way

The Eurobond's 50th birthday has lessons for governments about how not to regulate finance

Fifty years ago this week Autostrade, an Italian motorway operator, issued a $15m bond. The first Eurobond was less a piece of clever financial engineering than an elaborate tax dodge. The idea dreamed up by London bankers was to capture some of the dollars that were sloshing around Europe (hence the name Eurodollars) because of America's Regulation Q, which limited the interest rates paid on deposit accounts. Autostrade was chosen as the first issuer because it had the right to pay interest (in the form of coupons) without deducting Italian tax. The bond was issued in Schiphol airport in Amsterdam to avoid British stamp duty.

The coupons were payable in Luxembourg to avoid British income tax.

The new market's growth was boosted when President John Kennedy imposed a tax to discourage Americans from investing in foreign securities. International companies that wanted to borrow in dollars turned instead to the Eurobond market. Investors, such as the archetypal Belgian dentist, were looking for a safe home for their capital and a shelter from Europe's high taxes. Over the next four decades the market grew exponentially, hitting its first $1 billion year in 1966 and reaching a peak issue of $4.5 trillion in 2009.

Continued

With some encouragement from the Bank of England, London became the centre of this new market. The effect was to revive a financial centre that had been suffering from the country's economic troubles and the decline of the British empire, with its associated sterling area. The Eurobond market created lucrative work for the City's accountants, lawyers and merchant banks, and it attracted foreign banks to set up branches in London.

This was the dingy, decaying city's first step towards becoming the cosmopolitan capital of global finance that it is today. When exchange rates were allowed to float in the early 1970s London established itself as a currency-trading centre. More complex products like derivatives gravitated to it, too. Although Britain likes to lecture the world's tax havens on their need for transparency and reform, its own financial sector owes its modern success to the country's willingness to host an opaque, tax-evading capital market.

Capital punishment

The Eurobond market was the first big modern international capital market; in time it was followed by large cross-border markets in currencies and equities. Governments in continental Europe have always treated these with suspicion. To them, markets are made up of speculators who like to interfere in the smooth running of economies; when a government's policies are unconvincing, they drive currencies down and bond yields up. One reason why the European Union's leaders were so keen on the creation of the single currency was their frustration with the devaluations that dogged the old Exchange Rate Mechanism.

In recent years the wrath of European leaders has turned to the bond markets and the rise in the cost of government borrowing in some peripheral euro-zone countries. The politicians' response has been to put in place or propose a raft of regulations and taxes, from restrictions on short-selling (betting on falling prices) and limits on bankers' pay to taxes on financial transactions, in an attempt to curb the power of the dreaded markets.

Europe's governments should, instead, heed the lesson of the Eurobond's success: that elaborate rules will neither lower the borrowing costs of businesses nor persuade investors to forget their worries about the creditworthiness of governments, for money will always find a way round them. If trading becomes too expensive in Europe, volumes will shift elsewhere; and if regulations become too onerous the business will move to a more welcoming jurisdiction. Just as the American authorities handed a gift to London in the 1960s, the Europeans are now helping to ensure the eventual triumph of financial centres in Singapore and Hong Kong.

Source: The Economist, 6 July 2013.

■ Floating rate notes (FRNs)

Floating rate notes (FRN) are Eurobonds that pay a variable rather than a fixed interest rate. FRNs are especially favoured by financial institutions that conduct a great part of their business at a floating rate and therefore value the protection given by the ability to borrow at a floating rate. As rates of interest rise, banks' income rises, as do their costs – FRNs are thus a way of achieving a neat match between assets and liabilities.

HSBC bank is an active player in the Eurobond market, borrowing in several currencies, e.g. US dollars and euros, at both fixed and floating rates. The reason why it borrows in many currencies and at fixed rates is bound up with the swaps market. HSBC may not want the currency for itself (i.e. to finance operations) or even want a variable rate liability. It is borrowing in the currency in which, at prevailing market conditions, it is easiest and cheapest to borrow, say, euros. It can then use the swap market to exchange the euros for the currency it really requires.

A swap works in two stages. Take the case of HSBC's issue of €500 million FRNs repayable in 2020. This could have been swapped into sterling via another bank (the 'swap bank') at the time of issue, perhaps at a fixed rate. The parties would agree to swap back at maturity so that HSBC could repay the bond. The swap bank then passes to HSBC a stream of sterling until 2020 with which to pay the interest, in return for which it would receive from HSBC a fluctuating stream of euros with which to pay its own interest liability up to 2020.

In such a swap, there is an exchange not only of currencies but also a floating liability for a fixed one. This is called a Combined Interest Rate and Currency Swap (CIRCUS). The point of this is to enable the two parties to raise money where the terms are most attractive before swapping it into the currency they really want. At other times, HSBC itself might borrow at floating rates both in sterling and in other currencies.

■ Green bonds

Green bonds are issued to finance 'environmentally friendly' activities, thus tying in the proceeds of the issue to the 'green' activity. Until 2013, such bonds had mainly been issued by international organisations such as the World Bank. It operates an environmental department with the expertise to validate activities as sufficiently green to warrant a dedicated bond issue with the 'green' tag. The World Bank issued its first green bonds in 2008, but the market was slow to develop until the French energy firm EDF raised €1.4 billion, the first green bond issued by a large company. This appeared to mark a tipping point in the market, since which it has been exploited more by corporate issuers than by international organisations. For example, Toyota raised $1.75 billion to finance issues of loans for acquirors of hybrid and electric cars. However, the Unilever issue (see following cameo) appeared to be a game-changer. Whereas the EDF and Toyata bonds were for new, obviously green projects, renewable energy and electric vehicles, Unilever will use the cash to reduce the environmental impact of its ordinary activities. Similarly, the profile of acquirers of these bonds is changing – whereas 'traditional' green bond investors were public sector institutions such as US state pension funds, the 'new' bonds are being purchased by insurance companies and private fund managers. Whether the market will continue to flower, time will tell.

Unilever blazes sustainable trail with £250m 'green bond'

Unilever, the world's second largest food producer by sales, has issued a £250m 'green bond' – a development that could open a new chapter for this form of financing.

The market for green bonds that finance environmentally friendly projects increased more than five-fold last year, with Dealogic recording 29 deals worth a total of $11.2bn.

Most such bonds have so far been issued by supranational organisations such as the World Bank and the European Investment Bank. But in November EDF, the French power group, raised $1.9bn in the first euro-denominated green bond issued by a large corporate.

Marcus Hiseman, of Morgan Stanley, said Unilever's was a transformational deal that took sustainable bonds beyond those previously issued by development banks and utility groups – such as EDF for renewables – into the corporate mainstream.

'Our hope is that this deal will show other potential bond issuers that sustainability is not just an add-on, but can be an integral part of a company's strategy and finances,' he said.

Paul Polman, chief executive of Unilever, is one of the most vocal chief executives on environmental issues.

In 2010 – a year after becoming head – he set a target of doubling the Anglo-Dutch group's sales while halving its environmental impact by 2020. He told investors who disagreed with the strategy, dubbed the sustainable living plan: 'Don't put your money in our company.'

Mr Polman, whose company makes Lipton tea, Magnum ice creams and Dove soap, said sustainable consumption makes business sense because it 'saves us money'.

Jean-Marc Huët, Unilever's finance director, said the green bond was another step intended to demonstrate to the financial community the centrality of sustainability to the group's business model.

The five-year sterling bond, on which Morgan Stanley was the lead structuring adviser, pays a 2 per cent fixed coupon. The £250m raised will be used to fund a number of new factories, which will cut in half the amount of waste, water usage and greenhouse gas emissions of existing plants.

The planned new factories include a laundry liquid plant in South Africa, manufacturing Omo, Skip, Domestos and Comfort; and an ice cream factory, also in South Africa, producing brands such as Cornetto and Magnum.

Some of the money will be invested in expanding existing factories, such as a spread plant in Kansas, US. These will use 30 per cent less water, waste and greenhouse gas emissions.

FT *Source:* Scheherazade Daneshkhu and Andrew Bolger, *Financial Times*, 20 March 2014.

16.10 LEASING AND SALE-AND-LEASEBACK (SAL)

Lease contracts were discussed in Chapter 15 where long-term leases for certain assets, such as ships and aircraft, or for property, were discussed.

SAL involves selling assets (usually property) to a financial institution seeking good quality investments with potential for long-term growth in capital value. The seller, while giving up the ownership rights to the property, will then arrange to lease the premises from the new owner. SAL, therefore, is a transfer of ownership with retention of rights to use for a specified period. Its attraction to the vendor is the raising of capital, although its obvious disadvantage is usually the loss of any entitlement to capital appreciation. However, for a company eager to grow, the returns in the early years of strategic growth projects could outweigh the lost capital gains. This was the reasoning behind the SAL by Tesco, the supermarket chain, of many of its store sites in the 1980s when it was eager to claw back the market share advantage held by Sainsbury's (it subsequently grew to number one in the supermarket league by 1996). The finance generated by a series of SALs was used to purchase and develop new sites for stores.

After cementing its No. 1 position in the UK, Tesco pursued a policy of overseas expansion. To fund this, it announced a SAL in March 2007, selling over £500 million of property to British Land in a complex joint venture operation. The 21 stores involved accounted for 3 per cent of Tesco's UK floor space. Tesco is now selling part of its overseas estate to fund further development. In January 2014, it sold several of its South Korean stores (its largest international business with 550 stores) for some £355 million. Its wholly owned subsidiary, Homeplus Co. concluded the deal with Samsung SRA, a real-estate fund manager operating in Korea and other Asian countries.

Another firm that has recently raised money via SAL is HSBC, as the cameo below highlights.

SAL pays down the Dragon's debt

The Scottish entrepreneur, Duncan Bannatyne, Chair of Bannatyne Fitness Ltd, a chain of health clubs that operates at over 60 UK locations, is perhaps better known as a panellist on 'The Dragons' Den'. In February 2014, his firm negotiated a £92 million sale-and-leaseback deal for 39 of these clubs. The sale, to M&G Investments, was designed to pay down borrowings of £180 million from Anglo Irish Bank in 2006 incurred to finance the acquisition of 24 clubs from the Hilton Group. Since then, Anglo Irish had collapsed and was nationalised by the Irish government which appointed accountants KPMG to recover the bank's debts. The deal, involving ground-leases of 125 years, reportedly left Bannatyne 'virtually free of debt' which stood at £127 million at its last balance sheet date.

Source: articles in The Scotsman, The Northern Echo and The Daily Record, 25 February 2014.

■ Sale-and-manage-back

A variant of the SAL is the sale-and-manage-back (SAMB) tactic adopted by several hotel chains. Rather than lease back the sold property, the vendors undertake the management of it. One of the first exponents was Whitbread plc in October 2004, when it announced a wide-ranging disposal of properties, including its historic site in the City of London, for around £800 million. Half of the cash generated was to be returned to shareholders, and the remainder would be used to reduce its pension fund deficit and to pay down debt. Among the disposals were 12 Marriott-branded hotels (later increased to 46) that it would continue to manage.

Other hotel chains soon followed. In early 2005, the Hilton Group, Intercontinental and the French Accor group all announced SAMB programmes. The two British firms intended to return the sale proceeds to shareholders, while Accor planned to accelerate its expansion into budget hotels.

More recently, in March 2013, Intercontinental Group (IHG) sold its 447-room hotel in Park Lane, London for an estimated £600 million to Qatari investors. IHG is to continue to manage the hotel for 30 years, with three 10-year extensions leading to a potential 60-year contract length. IHG also stated that the sale (at a value 62 per cent above book value) was intended to reduce the amount of capital tied up in the business. Later in 2013, it announced a Special Dividend payment to shareholders of £228 million.

In all these cases, while the planned use of cash differed, the common thread was that the vendors felt they could earn higher returns on hotel management rather than owning upmarket hotels.

Sources: Whitbread plc press release, 28 October 2004, articles in the *Financial Times*, 29 October 2004, and in *The Economist*, 19 March 2005; *Asia One News*, 29 March 2013; *Daily Telegraph*, 7 August 2013.

Self-assessment activity 16.8

What is the effect of a sale-and-leaseback on a firm's balance sheet?

(Answer in Appendix A at the back of the book)

16.11 ISLAMIC FINANCE[*]

A relatively new phenomenon in the international financial markets has been the rise of Islamic banks offering *shariah*-compliant products that conform to the teaching and interpretation of the Koran by Islamic scholars. The key principles in Islamic finance are the strict, explicit prohibition of *riba*, or the earning of interest, which is, of course, at the core of traditional banking and finance, and the exclusion of transactions involving gambling, tobacco, alcohol, porcine products and pornography.

In recent years, Islamic finance is reckoned to have grown at 10–15 per cent p.a. while some estimates place the value of assets held under Islamic finance at around $1 trillion, with hundreds of financial institutions offering Islamic products. Its growth has been attributed to various factors, principally the heightened awareness and observance of Islamic principles among Muslims, the increase in liquidity in Middle Eastern nations following the increase in oil prices in the 1970s and more recently, in the 2000s, the presence of certain Western banks, such as HSBC, in the Middle East anxious to develop new products utilising their resources and expertise, including close knowledge and experience of local markets. London, where many international banks have located their Islamic banking and advisory services, is a leading centre for development of Islamic products, helped along by tax changes introduced in the 2007 Finance Act that clarify the treatment of costs of servicing loans. The UK was the first European country to authorise an exclusively Islamic bank, the Islamic Bank of Britain, which floated on the AIM in 2004.

Under *shariah,* interest is reckoned 'unfairly' to reward the provider of capital in a loan for little or no effort or risk undertaken. The Islamic economic model is based on a risk and profit/loss-sharing contract. Islamic financial products allow interest income to be replaced with sharing of the cash flows earned from profit-making activities, in effect, converting lending and borrowing into equity-based transactions. Because of this, most conventional equity products are judged to be acceptable under *shariah* (convertibles and warrants would be exceptions), although the distribution of profit is based more on reward for effort rather than for mere ownership of capital.

In terms of the provision of corporate finance, the main contribution of Islamic finance is in the bond market via the issue of *shariah*-compliant bonds, called *sukuks.*

---

[*]This section uses material from the paper published by the Financial Services Authority in November 2007, authored by Ainley *et al.*

Global issuance of sukuks peaked in 2007 at $35 billion, but dropped sharply to $15 billion in 2008, partly due to recessionary influences in the world economy, but also due to religious concerns about the *shariah* compliance of some forms of bond. The market remained flat in 2009 due to problems in the United Arab Emirates, but recovered in 2010. Malaysia is now the world leader in sukuk issuance, accounting for over 60 per cent of activity in 2010, followed by the UAE, Saudi Arabia, Bahrain and Indonesia.

There remains much controversy over Islamic financial products. What is or what is not *shariah*-compliant continues to be open to the varying interpretations among Islamic scholars of Islamic law, or *Fiqh*, as set out in the Koran. Similarly, there are many variants of the sukuk model. However, they all share the common feature that the returns to the investor are linked to the performance of a real asset, i.e. what is bought with the money raised. The word sukuk itself means certificates, namely, the documents issued when such a deal is set up. The design of the security resembles the more conventional securitisation process that sets up an SPV to acquire assets, issue financial claims on the asset and arrange for payment of returns. The certificates that encapsulate these financial claims represent a proportionate beneficial ownership for a stated period. The risk and the returns connected with the cash flows from the underlying asset are passed to the investors in the sukuk. The equivalent agency to the SPV is called a Special Purpose *Mudaraba* (SPM).

A *mudaraba sukuk* essentially records agreement between two parties whereby one party provides the capital required to finance the venture for the other party (the *Mudarib*) to work with, on the condition that the profit will be shared in accordance with a pre-agreed ratio, and that the capital will be returned when the sukuk are surrendered. They represent units of equal value in the equity of the business venture, and all investors receive returns in relation to their proportional ownership.

Mudaraba sukuks are used to enhance public participation in large investment projects, such as oil-field development. Sukuks that provide medium-term asset finance require a further device based on leasing principles (*ijara'*) now reckoned to be the commonest method of Islamic financing. The cash flows paid over to the SPM

Sukuk and see

The problem with being tagged a child prodigy is that you have to live up to expectations. Even Mozart had off days. The global market for sukuk – the Islamic equivalent of bonds, structured so that they provide a return but do not technically pay interest – is no different. This started to develop a decade ago; was knocked by global turmoil in 2008 and then spurted ahead for four years, leading to $140bn of issuance in 2012. But in 2013, it hit a sourer note as the value of instruments issued slipped 13 per cent, to about $120bn.

Explanations for the setback vary. General market uncertainty over US tapering did not help. Neither did hiccups in Malaysia, traditionally the dominant sovereign sukuk issuer due to its large public investment programme. As credit rating agencies hovered last year amid signs that national finances were deteriorating, the government took steps to cut the budget deficit. Investment growth slowed and Malaysian sukuk issuance fell by a quarter.

But there are good reasons to think business will be brisker this year. While corporates are smaller sukuk issuers than the sovereigns – in 2013, they supplied less than $30bn – their activity is rising fast. It was up a fifth last year and now both Standard & Poor's and Fitch expect further increases in 2014. Gulf banks, in particular, may want to tap the market as tougher regulatory capital standards kick in (sukuk hybrids can count towards capital). On top of that, it is likely that at least one non-Muslim country – perhaps the UK – will make an inaugural sukuk issue. This may be modest in dollar terms but it will open the bidding to host a lucrative hub for Islamic finance in the non-Muslim world.

Investors still face big issues in this market, such as lack of liquidity and standardised deal structures. But the buzz may be returning. And there's nothing child prodigies like better than a bit of attention.

FT *Source:* Lex Column, *Financial Times*, 10 February 2014.

Banking on the ummah: Malaysia leads the charge in Islamic finance

Of Malaysia's claims to fame, leadership in financial services is not an obvious one. Yet in some ways the country is the world's most important Islamic-finance centre. Just over a fifth of the country's banking system, by assets, is *sharia*-compliant; the average for Muslim countries is more like 12%, and often a lot less. Malaysia dominates the global market for *sukuk*, or Islamic bonds. The country issued the world's first sovereign *sukuk* in 2002; in the first three quarters of 2012 it was responsible for almost three-quarters of total global issuance. Malaysia is also home to the Islamic Financial Services Board, an international standard-setting body.

These are big achievements for a relatively small country of just 30m people, of whom only about 60% are Muslim. In neighbouring Indonesia, which is home to the largest Muslim population in the world, only about 4% of the financial sector is *sharia*-compliant. Although the much richer Gulf states and Saudi Arabia have bigger Islamic banks, it is Malaysia, argues Iqbal Khan of Dubai's Fajr Capital investment fund, that is the centre 'for thought leadership in Islamic Finance'.

How did the country carve out this niche? Malaysia's Muslim heritage, outward-looking nature and links with financial hubs like Britain and Singapore made the place a natural candidate to bridge the worlds of religion and capitalism. The central bank, the Bank Negara Malaysia, is also supportive.

Two institutions in particular, both set up by the central bank, have contributed to Malaysia's pre-eminence in the field. The first is the International Centre for Education in Islamic Finance (INCEIF). Established in 2005 and boasting about 2,000 students, INCEIF is the world's leading university for the study of Islamic finance, The International

Sharia Research Academy, housed within INCEIF, brings together scholars to produce an internationally acceptable rule-book for Islamic finance.

The second institution is the Islamic Banking and Finance Institute of Malaysia (IBFIM). It concentrates on vocational training, offering a variety of certificates in Islamic finance. IBFIM also acts as a consultancy to banks and firms that want to become *sharia*-compliant.

Zeti Akhtar Aziz, the head of the central bank, says that these bodies are the 'pipe-line to provide the banks with talent'. And not just in Malaysia. There are currently students from 80 countries at INCEIF; and IBFIM has taught people from Afghanistan, Nigeria, Palestine and elsewhere.

All of which gives Malaysia greater status within the *ummah*, the global Islamic community, important to a country that often feels on the periphery of the Muslim world. There are more tangible benefits, too. The Islamic subsidiary of Maybank, a big local lender, already accounts for about half of the group's customers and is expanding abroad: it set up a subsidiary in Singapore 18 months ago and has also moved into Indonesia.

Ms Zeti argues that *sharia*-compliant banks are inherently more stable than conventional peers. Speculation is forbidden, and because charging interest is prohibited under *sharia* law, returns are based on profit-sharing. Perhaps. Islamic finance is hardly foolproof: Dubai's debt crisis in 2009 showed that *sukuk* can help to inflate debt to unsustainable levels. But whatever its pros and cons, Malaysia will provide much of the evidence either way.

Source: The Economist, 5 January 2013.

that manages the lease contract are passed over to investors as payments that include elements of rental and principal. While this may be thought to come close to a conventional lease (or perhaps an HP) contract, it should be remembered that the sukuk gives the investor participation in the *'usufructs'* (earning or fruits) of the assets, *and also in any losses.* The risks inherent in purchasing sukuks were brought home to investors in Nakheel, a Dubai-based property developer which hit severe liquidity problems in 2010. The anatomy of an *ijara'*-based sukuk is explained more fully in Iqbal (1999).

SUMMARY

Chapter 16 has discussed the features of the principal forms of long-term finance available to companies, and their respective benefits and drawbacks.

Key points

- The main factors in considering the appropriate source of finance are risk, ownership, duration and debt capacity.

- Over half of the new finance raised for UK companies is usually through retained profits. This is not a free source of finance as it involves an opportunity cost in terms of the return that shareholders would have obtained had they received the profit as dividends and re-invested it elsewhere.

- New shares are issued through a private placing, stock exchange placing, public issue (prospectus issue, offer for sale or issue by tender) or by a rights issue.

- The enhanced ability to make a rights issue is a major attraction of a Stock Exchange listing.

- Equity capital is an attractive form of finance to companies because there are no interest charges or capital repayments; to investors, it offers a hedge against inflation, and a higher yield than loan stock. On the other hand, equity capital can be expensive to raise, and new issues to the public dilute the control of existing members.

- Debt finance (debentures, loan stock, etc.) is flexible, offering a wide range of financial products to the corporate treasurer. Interest payments are tax-deductible, but restrictions (e.g. charges over assets and monitoring of activities) are common practice.

- Convertible loan stock is a debt instrument that can, at the option of the holder, be converted into equity. It offers investors and firms the benefit of loan stock in the early years and, if all goes to plan, will enable the benefits of equity to be captured when the business is better established.

- The Eurobond market offers the opportunity for large firms to raise money in foreign markets.

- The rapidly growing sukuk market offers the opportunity for Islamic borrowers to raise money in *shariah*-compliant forms.

Further reading

Most UK finance textbooks carry a 'straight down the middle' description of methods of raising long-term finance in the UK. For a US perspective, see Emery and Finnerty (1997), Ross *et al.* (2009), or Block and Hirt (1994).

An excellent survey of the market for new issues of equity (IPOs), and an analysis of the tendency for new issues to be under-priced is given by Ritter (2006). Brown (2006) offers an up-to-date and highly practical guide to the bond markets. Colin Mason is the leading authority on business angels in the UK. See his 2006 paper for a comprehensive review of the angels' literature. A highly practical guide to raising venture capital is given by Pearce and Barnes (2006).

A useful source of information on Islamic finance is the *Handbook of Islamic Banking* (2005), edited by Hassan and Lewis (although it extends far beyond mere banking issues).

Both *The Economist* and the *Financial Times* provide a regular supply of examples of financing sources and methods covered in this chapter.

Jenkinson and Jones (2009) examine the role that investors play in IPOs in practice, and Aggarwal *et al.* (2009) look at IPO valuations. Kaplan and Lerner (2010) review the history of the venture capital industry in the USA and provide some thoughts on its future role.

QUESTIONS

Questions with a **coloured number** have solutions in Appendix B on page 797.

1 The ordinary shares of Anglia Paper Company are currently trading at £3.20. Existing shareholders are offered one new share at £2 for every three held.

(i) What is the theoretical ex-rights price?
(ii) What is the nil-paid rights price?

2 Cambridge Castings Ltd plans a major expansion to modernise its manufacturing plant, thereby improving productivity and reducing unit costs. The existing capital base is fairly evenly divided between equity and debt, and it is clear that the capital investment programme can only partly be funded through profit retention.

It is suggested that the additional finance could be raised through a preference share issue. You are required to evaluate this source of finance for the company, compared with equity or debt:

(a) from the company's point of view;
(b) from the viewpoint of investors.

3 Shaw Holdings plc has 20 million ordinary shares of 50p in issue. These shares are currently valued on the Stock Exchange at £1.60 per share. The directors of Shaw Holdings believe the company requires additional long-term capital and have decided to make a one-for-four rights issue at £1.30 per share.

An investor with 2,000 shares in Shaw Holdings has contacted you for investment advice. She is undecided whether to take up the rights issue, sell the rights, or allow the rights offer to lapse.

Required
(a) Calculate the theoretical ex-rights price of an ordinary share.
(b) Calculate the value at which the rights are likely to be traded.
(c) Evaluate each of the options being considered by the owner of 2,000 shares.
(d) Explain why rights issues are usually made at a discount.
(e) From the company's viewpoint, how critical is the pricing of a rights issue likely to be?
(ACCA Certified Diploma)

4 Burnsall plc is a listed company which manufactures and distributes leisurewear under the brand name Paraffin. It made sales of 10 million units worldwide at an average wholesale price of £10 per unit during its last financial year ending at 30 June 1995. In 1995–96, it is planning to introduce a new brand, Meths, which will be sold at a lower unit price to more price-sensitive market segments. Allowing for negative effects on existing sales of Paraffin, the introduction of the new brand is expected to raise total sales value by 20 per cent.

To support greater sales activity, it is expected that additional financing, both capital and working, will be required. Burnsall expects to make capital expenditures of £20 million in 1995–96, partly to replace worn-out equipment but largely to support sales expansion. You may assume that, except for taxation, all current assets and current liabilities will vary directly in line with sales.

Burnsall's summarised Balance Sheet (Statement of Financial Position) for the financial year ending 30 June 1995 shows the following:

Assets employed	£m	£m	£m
Fixed (non-current)			120
Current:			
stocks	16		
debtors	23		
cash	6		
	—	45	
Current liabilities:			
Corporation tax payable	(5)		
Trade creditors	(18)		
		(23)	
Net current assets			22
Long-term debt at 12%			(20)
Net assets			122
Financed by			
Ordinary shares (50p par value)			60
Reserves			62
Shareholders' funds			122

Burnsall's profit before interest and tax in 1994–95 was 16 per cent of sales, after deducting depreciation of £5 million. The depreciation charge for 1995–96 is expected to rise to £9 million. Corporation tax is levied at 33 per cent, paid with a one-year delay. Burnsall has an established distribution policy of raising dividends by 10 per cent p.a. In 1994–95, it paid dividends of £5 million net.

You have been approached to advise on the extra financing required to support the sales expansion. Company policy is to avoid cash balances falling below 6 per cent of sales.

Required

(a) By projecting its financial statements, calculate how much additional *external* finance Burnsall must raise.
    Note: You may assume that all depreciation provisions qualify for tax relief.

(b) Offer advice as to the appropriate method of financing for Burnsall's sales expansion.

(ACCA)

5 The managing director of Lavipilon plc wishes to provide an extra return to the company's shareholders and has suggested making either:

(i) a two-for-five bonus issue (capitalisation issue) in addition to the normal dividend.

(ii) a one-for-five scrip dividend instead of the normal cash dividend.

(iii) a one-for-one share (stock) split in addition to the normal dividend.

Summarised Balance Sheet (Statement of Financial Position) of Lavipilon plc (end of last year)

Fixed assets		65
Current assets	130	
Less: current liabilities	(55)	
Net current assets		75
Total assets less current liabilities		140
Less: Long-term liability		
11% debenture		(25)
Net assets		115
Capital and reserves:		
Ordinary shares (50 pence par value)	25	
Share premium account	50	
Revenue reserves	40	
Shareholders' funds		115

The company's shares are trading at 300 pence before the dividend is paid, and the company has £50 million of the (post-tax) profit from this year's activities available to ordinary shareholders, of which £30 million will be paid as a dividend if options (i) or (iii) are chosen. None of the £40 million revenue reserves would be distributed. This year's financial accounts have not yet been finalised.

(a) For each of the three proposals, show the likely effect on the company's Balance Sheet at the end of this year, and the likely effect on the company's share price.

(b) Comment on how well these suggestions fulfil the managing director's objective of providing an extra return to the company's shareholders.

(c) Discuss reasons why a company might wish to undertake:

(i) a scrip dividend,

(ii) a share (stock) split.

(ACCA)

6 Netherby plc manufactures a range of camping and leisure equipment, including tents. It is currently experiencing severe quality control problems at its existing fully depreciated factory in the south of England. These difficulties threaten to undermine its reputation for producing high-quality products. It has recently been approached by the European Bank for Reconstruction and Development, on behalf of a tent manufacturer in Hungary, which is seeking a UK-based trading partner which will import and distribute its tents. Such a switch would involve shutting down the existing tent manufacturing operation in the United Kingdom and converting it into a distribution depot. The estimated restructuring costs of £5 million would be tax-allowable, but would exert serious strains on cash flow.

Importing, rather than manufacturing, tents appears inherently profitable, as the buying-in price, when converted into sterling, is less than the present production cost. In addition, Netherby considers that the Hungarian product would result in increased sales, as the existing retail distributors seem impressed with the quality of the samples which they have been shown. It is estimated that for a five-year contract, the annual cash flow benefit would be around £2 million p.a. before tax.

However, the financing of the closure and restructuring costs would involve careful consideration of the financing options. Some directors argue that dividends could be reduced, as several competing companies have already done a similar thing, while other directors argue for a rights issue. Alternatively, the project could be financed by an issue of long-term loan stock at a fixed rate of 12 per cent.

The most recent Balance Sheet shows £5 million of issued share capital (par value 50p), while the market price per share is currently £3. A leading security analyst has recently described Netherby's gearing ratio as 'adventurous'. Profit after tax in the year just ended was £15 million and dividends of £10 million were paid.

The rate of Corporation Tax is 33 per cent, payable with a one-year delay. Netherby's reporting year coincides with the calendar year and the factory will be closed at the year end. Closure costs would be incurred shortly before deliveries of the imported product began, and sufficient stocks will be on hand to overcome any initial supply problems. Netherby considers that it should earn a return on new investment of 15 per cent p.a. net of all taxes.

Required

(a) Is the closure of the existing factory financially worthwhile for Netherby?

(b) Explain what is meant when the capital market is said to be information-efficient in a semi-strong form.

If the stock market is semi-strong efficient and without considering the method of finance, calculate the likely impact of acceptance and announcement of the details of this project to the market on Netherby's share price.

(c) Advise the Netherby board as to the relative merits of a rights issue rather than a cut in dividends to finance this project.

(d) Explain why a rights issue generally results in a fall in the market price of shares. If a rights issue is undertaken, calculate the resulting theoretical ex-rights share price of issue prices of £1 per share and £2 per share, respectively. (You may ignore issue costs.)

(e) Assuming the restructuring proposal meets expectations, assess the impact of the project on earnings per share if it is financed by a rights issue at an offer price of £2 per share, and loan stock, respectively. (Again, you may ignore issue costs.)

(f) Briefly consider the main operating risks connected with the investment project, and how Netherby might attempt to allow for these.

(ACCA)

Practical assignment

Consider the long-term financing of a company with which you are familiar. Evaluate each of the main sources of finance and suggest, with reasons, two methods of finance that are not currently used, but which may prove attractive to the company.

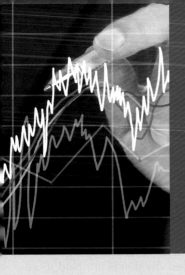

17

Returning value to shareholders: the dividend decision

L'Oréal chief promises dividend is high priority

L'Oréal intends to continue increasing dividend payments as the principal way of using its cash, chief executive Jean-Paul Agon has told the *Financial Times*. Mr Agon, head of the world's largest cosmetics group by sales, said that this was a higher priority than returning cash to shareholders through share buybacks.

'For investors today, a company that offers a very steady and increasing dividend year after year is important,' he said.

Mr Agon said: 'When you generate a lot of cash, the first thing to do is increase your dividends. It is the most logical and natural way to use your cash, and that is what we are doing.'

On Monday, as it reported 2013 full-year operating profit of €3.9bn on sales of €23bn, the company said that it would propose a dividend of €2.50 per share at its annual general meeting in April – an increase of 8.7 per cent compared with the dividend paid last year.

Source: Based on Adam Thomson, *Financial Times*, 13 February 2014, p. 16.

Learning objectives

After reading this chapter, you should:

- Understand the competing views about the role of dividend policy.
- Understand what factors a financial manager should consider when deciding to recommend a change in dividend payouts.
- Understand what is meant by the 'information content' of dividends.
- Know what alternatives to cash dividends may be used to deliver value to owners.
- Appreciate the impact of taxation on dividend decisions.
- Understand why changes in dividend payments usually lag behind changes in company earnings.

17.1 INTRODUCTION

The introductory cameo gives a flavour of the importance of dividends to investors. This chapter will help you to appreciate the factors that drive dividend decisions.

Most quoted companies pay two dividends to ordinary shareholders each year: an interim dividend based on half-year results, followed by the main, or final, dividend, based on the full-year reported profits. The amount of dividend is determined by the board of directors, advised by financial managers, and presented to the Annual General Meeting of shareholders for approval. The board and their advisers thus face a twice-yearly decision about what percentage of post-tax profits to distribute to shareholders (the 'payout ratio') and hence what percentage to retain (the 'retention ratio').

Until a specified **Record Day**, the shares are traded **cum-dividend**: that is, purchasers will be entitled to receive the dividend. The approved dividends are paid to all shareholders appearing on the share register on the Record Day, after which the shares are quoted **ex-dividend**, i.e. without entitlement to the dividend. In practice, there is a time lag between the shares going ex-dividend and the Record Day to allow the company's Registrar to update the shareholders' register to reflect recent dealings. The Financial Calendar of Scottish and Southern Energy plc, the electricity supply utility, is shown in Table 17.1. People purchasing Scottish and Southern Energy plc shares whose names did not appear on the register by 2 August 2013 would not have received the final dividend payable per share (56.1p).

Record Day
The cut-off date beyond which further entrants to the shareholder register do not qualify for the next dividend

ex-dividend
A share trades ex-dividend (xd) when people who buy are no longer entitled to receive the upcoming dividend payment

Table 17.1 Scottish and Southern Energy plc Financial Calendar 2013

Annual general meeting	25 July 2013
Ex-dividend date	31 July 2013
Record date	2 August 2013
Final dividend payment date	27 September 2013

Source: Scottish and Southern Energy plc, Annual Report and Accounts, 2013 (**www.sse.com**).

When the shares first trade ex-dividend, the share price will fall by the amount of the dividend. As dividends are usually quite a small proportion of the share price anyway, this is not a substantial fall. For example, in the case of SSE, the dividend of 56.1p compared to a share price of well over £11. However, sometimes, firms with a surplus of liquidity decide to pay a substantial special dividend (SD). This is good news at the time of announcement, and the shares usually rise, but it stores up the problem of a substantial fall in share price when the dividend is paid, which may alarm some investors. For example, Wolseley plc paid out a £350 million special dividend in 2013. The special dividend was based on a strong financial position and the disposal proceeds from selling off a number of businesses, as explained in the article below.

Wolseley shares jump on bumper cash payout

Wolseley, the largest plumbing supplies business in the world, is set to give investors a bumper payday by way of a special dividend. However, it is always useful to look more closely when capital is returned to shareholders as it is not always an unquestionable good. Sometimes special dividends can mask a company struggling to find growth in its core markets. The strongest sign of confidence in the future is a progressive full-year dividend policy. Annual dividend policies require much longer term planning and budgeting from management. The Wolseley capital return is encouraging as management has provided both a special dividend alongside a double-digit increase in the final dividend.

The group usually pursues a strategy of bolt-on acquisitions to drive growth. However, Wolseley did not find enough attractive targets during the year ended July so it is now hoping to spend about £210m on acquisitions, up from £140m previously. Wolseley's cash performance was also strong and this, when combined with the lack of acquisitions, led to the payout.

Source: Based on John Ficenec, *Daily Telegraph*, 1 October 2013.

How should top management approach the dividend decision? Should it be generous and follow a high payout policy, or retain the bulk of earnings? The pure theory of dividend policy shows that, under certain conditions, it makes no difference what they do! One authority argues: 'to the management of a company acting in the best interests of its shareholders, dividend policy is a mere detail' (Miller and Modigliani, 1961). However, the conditions required to support this conclusion are highly restrictive and unlikely to apply in real-world capital markets. Indeed, many financial managers and investment analysts take the opposite view, appearing to believe that the dividend payout decision is critical to company valuation and hence a central element of corporate financial strategy. These are the extreme views – an evaluation of the case for and against dividend generosity leads to more pragmatic 'middle-of-the-road' conclusions.

In this chapter, we consider the strategic, theoretical and practical issues surrounding dividend policy, and discuss some of the alternatives to dividend payment. *The basic message for management is: define the dividend policy, make a smooth transition towards it, and think very carefully before changing it, and avoid cutting dividends!*

Few people doubt that dividend levels influence share prices in some way or other. Indeed, a common method of valuation, the Dividend Valuation Model (introduced in Chapter 3) relies on discounting the future dividend stream. However, debate centres on what is the most attractive *pattern* of dividend payments, and the effects of *changes* in dividend policy.

Shareholders can receive returns in the form of dividends now and/or capital appreciation, which is the market's valuation of future expected dividend growth. But are shareholders more impressed by the higher near-in-time dividends than by the capital gain generated by a policy of low current payments, with retentions used to finance worthwhile investment? Graham *et al.* (1962) claimed that $1 of dividend was valued four times more highly by shareholders than $1 of retained earnings. Yet it is not uncommon to observe quite parsimonious (or even zero) payout ratios. Conventional wisdom warns companies subject to volatility of earnings to operate relatively high dividend covers to safeguard dividend payments in the event of depressed profitability. Similarly, smaller companies with less easy access to fresh supplies of capital are also advised to conserve cash and liquidity by operating a conservative dividend policy.

Dividend cuts are generally perceived as conveying bad news about the prospects of a company. However, it is difficult to generalise about optimal dividend policy and Figure 17.1 demonstrates that average dividend growth rates for FT All-Share companies have fluctuated over time. For example, following the financial crisis of 2008, companies cut dividends to conserve cash as many economies went into recession and because it was difficult to obtain external finance.

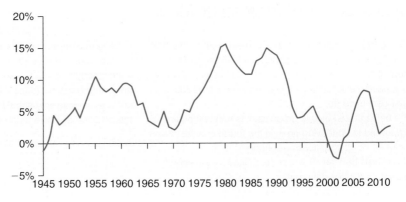

Figure 17.1 Five-year average dividend growth rates: FT All-Share companies
Source: Barclays Equity Gilt Study 2013.

In the following sections, we consider strategic and legal issues before examining the theory of dividend policy and, in particular, the 'irrelevance' hypothesis. We then consider the major qualifications to the theory, suggesting reasons why some shareholders may, in practice, prefer dividend income. You will see that dividend policy is an enigma with no obvious optimal strategy capable of general application. However, it will be possible to make some broad recommendations to guide the financial manager.

17.2 THE STRATEGIC DIMENSION

Formulating corporate strategy requires specification of clear objectives and delineation of the strategic options contributing to the achievement of these objectives. Although maximisation of shareholder wealth may be the paramount aim, there may be various routes to it. For example, diversifying into new industrial sectors involves a choice between internal growth and growth by acquisition. Whichever alternative is selected, the enterprise will need to consider both the level of required financing and the possible sources. The main alternatives for the listed company are short- and long-term debt capital, new share issues (normally rights issues) and internal financing (via retention of profits and depreciation provisions).

This is where we encounter the role of dividend policy. The amount of finance required to support the selected strategic option may exceed the borrowing capacity of the company, necessitating the use of additional equity funding. A capital-hungry firm therefore faces the choice between retention of earnings, i.e. restricting the dividend payout, or paying out high dividends but then clawing back capital via a subsequent rights issue. Neither policy is risk-free, as both may have undesirable repercussions on the ability to exploit strategic options. Retention may offend investors reliant on dividend income, resulting in share sales and lower share price, conflicting with the aim of wealth-maximisation, as well as exposing the company to the threat of takeover. Alternatively, the dividend payment-plus-rights issue policy incurs administrative expenses and the risk of having to sell shares on a flat or falling market. To this extent, the dividend decision is a strategic one, since an ill-judged financial decision could subvert the overall strategic aim. Consequently, financial managers must carefully consider the likely reaction of shareholders, and of the market as a whole, to dividend proposals.

Nokia slides as it forgoes dividend

Nokia's decision to withhold a dividend payment for the first time in its history triggered a strong reaction from shareholders. After a brief rally in response to what was a better than expected end to the financial year, the shares slid 5.5 per cent to €3.30.

The beleaguered mobile group said its handset business had returned to underlying profit in the fourth quarter, driven by sales of its new Lumia smartphone.

The shares had rallied 20 per cent since Nokia went public with the sales data earlier.

'[The market reaction] looks quite irrational to me as both net cash position as well as smartphone gross margins were clearly better than expected,' said Sami Sarkamies, analyst at Nordea. 'To me those were the two key unknowns. In what way should one be more concerned with the situation at Nokia today than yesterday?' he added.

Source: Based on Alexandra Stevenson, *Financial Times*, 25 January 2013, p. 22.

17.3 THE LEGAL DIMENSION

Legal factors impose further constraints on managers' freedom of action in deciding dividends. Although shareholders are the main risk-bearers in a company, other stake-holders, such as creditors and employees, carry a measure of risk. Accordingly, share-holders can be paid dividends only if the company has accumulated sufficient profits. They cannot be paid out of capital, except in a liquidation, as to do so would mean they would be paid ahead of prior claims on the business.

The Companies Act 1985 states that, in general, companies are restricted to accumulated realised profits. However, public companies are further restricted to realised profits less unrealised losses. Furthermore, bondholders may insist on restrictive covenants being written into loan agreements to prevent large dividends being declared.

Of course, paying the maximum legally permitted dividend is rarely likely to make strategic sense. Moreover, dividends are paid *out of profits* but *with* cash (or borrowings). It is quite common for companies to report low or negative profits, yet to maintain the previous year's dividend. This is both feasible and acceptable if the firm in question has built up sufficient reserves for previous years' retentions and has a reasonably healthy cash position. Indeed, the share prices of some struggling companies actually rise when they pay a maintained dividend out of reserves. This is because a maintained dividend is believed to be a signal to the market of expectations of better times ahead. Remember that managers have more information to hand than investors. So, in this case, many investors may believe that directors are conveying favourable information (the concept of information asymmetry again).

17.4 THE THEORY: DIVIDEND POLICY AND FIRM VALUE

The critical issue is how, if at all, does dividend policy affect the value of the firm? This section shows that the answer depends on whether or not a firm has access to external financing. In the absence of external financing, dividend payment may damage company value if the company has better investment opportunities than its shareholders. Payment of dividends may prevent access to worthwhile investment. With external financing, however, at least in a perfect market, dividends become totally irrelevant, since payment no longer precludes worthwhile investment, simply because the firm can recoup the required finance by selling shares.

In Chapter 3 we used the Dividend Valuation Model to show that the value of a company* ultimately depends on its dividend-paying capacity. For a company with constant and perpetual free cash flows[†] of E_t in any year t, paid wholly as dividend, D_t, the market will discount this stream at the rate of return required by shareholders, k_e so that:

$$\text{Value of equity} = V_0 = \sum_{t=1}^{N} \frac{E_t}{(1 + k_e)^t} = \frac{E_t}{k_e} \left(\text{or } V_0 = \frac{D_t}{k_e} \quad \text{since} \quad E_t = D_t \right)$$

If a proportion, b, of earnings is retained each year, beginning in period 1, for example, thus reducing the next dividend payable to $E_1 (1 - b)$, company value is given by the

---

*In this chapter, we assume no company borrowing, hence the value of the company is synonymous with the value of the equity. When referring to the present value of the whole equity, we use the symbol V_0, and when referring to the value of an individual share, P_0.

[†]In this and subsequent chapters, the letter E is used to denote a free cash flow concept of earnings, as explained in Chapter 11. Here, free cash flow is calculated *after* replacement investment but *before* strategic investment. Free cash flow is likely to deviate from accounting earnings, so when the latter accounting concept is intended, the phrases 'accounting profit' or 'reported earnings' are used.

forthcoming dividend divided by the cost of equity less the growth rate. The growth rate, g, is given by the retention ratio, b, times the return on reinvested funds, R (as explained in Chapter 3):

$$\text{Value of equity} = V_0 = \frac{E_1(1 - b)}{(k_e - g)} = \frac{D_1}{(k_e - g)} = \frac{D_1}{(k_e - bR)}$$

Self-assessment activity 17.1

Using the following figures, remind yourself why the growth rate of earnings $= (b \times R)$

Earnings in latest year $= £1,000$; $b = 60\%$; $R = 15\%$.

(Answer in Appendix A at the back of the book)

These expressions can cause confusion. In the first case, the market appears to value the stream of earnings, while in the second, the valuation is based upon the stream of dividends. Indeed, in the early stages of the debate about the importance and role of dividend policy, much attention was paid to the issue of whether the market values earnings or dividends. This apparent dichotomy can be easily resolved if we focus on the reasons for earnings retention. Retention may occur for two main reasons.

First, the company may wish to *bolster its holdings of liquid resources*. For example, dividend distribution may run down current assets or perhaps increase borrowings. Many profitable companies borrow to avoid having to reduce, or omit (or 'pass') a dividend, for reasons explained later.

However, the primary reason for retention is to *finance investment in fixed and other assets* to generate higher future earnings and, hence, enhance future dividend-paying capacity. By introducing retention and growth, the **Dividend Valuation Model** becomes the **Dividend Growth Model** (DGM).

Dividend Valuation Model
A way of assessing the value of shares by capitalising the future dividends. With growing dividend payments, it becomes the **Dividend Growth Model**

It is important to remember that the DGM assumes a constant retention ratio and a constant return on new investment projects. If these assumptions hold, both earnings and dividends grow at the same rate. Whether this rate is acceptable to shareholders depends on the return they require from their investments, k_e. The relationship between k_e and R, the return on reinvested earnings, provides the key to resolving the valuation dispute.

■ Dividend irrelevance in perfect capital markets

In 1961 Miller and Modigliani (MM) pointed out that earnings retention was simply one way of financing investment. If the company has access to better investment opportunities than its shareholders, under perfect capital market conditions, investors may benefit from retention.

dividend irrelevance
The theory that, when firms have access to external finance, it is irrelevant to firm value whether they pay a dividend or not

The original MM analysis proves **dividend irrelevance** in terms of a single dividend cut to finance worthwhile investment. MM envisaged an all-equity-financed company that has previously paid out its entire annual net cash flow as dividend. To illustrate their analysis, let us examine the case of Divicut plc.

One-off dividend cuts: Divicut plc

Divicut currently generates a perpetual free cash flow of £1,000 p.a. Shareholders require a return of 10 per cent. The market will value Divicut at $(£1,000/10\%) = £10,000$ on unchanged policies. If the management now decides to retain the whole of next year's earnings in order to invest in a project offering a single cash flow of £1,200 in the following year, the new market value of Divicut equals the present value of the revised dividend flow, assuming it reverts to 100 per cent payouts:

Year	1	2	3	4	etc.
Dividend (£)	0	2,200	1,000	1,000	⟶

This revised dividend flow is acceptable only if the resulting market value is at least equal to the pre-decision value, i.e. if the NPV of the project is at least zero. This is clearly the case, as the PV of the extra £1,200 in two years is greater than the PV of £1,000 less in one year, i.e.

$$\frac{£1,200}{(1.1)^2} > \frac{£1,000}{(1.1)}$$

or, £992 > £909

Divicut's shareholders are thus better off by £83.

Shareholder wealth is enhanced, since Divicut has used the funds released by the dividend cut to finance a worthwhile project. If these funds had been invested at only 10 per cent, the net effect would have been zero, while if investment had occurred at a rate of return of less than 10 per cent, shareholders would have been worse off. This simple example shows that the impact on company value is attributable to the investment, rather than the dividend, decision.

Self-assessment activity 17.2

Rework the Divicut example for the case where the returns on the new investment are £1,080 rather than £1,200 in year 2.

(Answer in Appendix A at the back of the book)

MM's dividend irrelevance conclusion was obtained in a world of certainty, and then extended to the case of risk/uncertainty, where the same conclusions emerge so long as investor behaviour and attitudes conform to conditions of 'symmetric market rationality'. This requires the following:

1 All investors are maximisers of expected wealth.
2 All investors have similar expectations.
3 All investors behave rationally.
4 All investors believe that other market participants will behave rationally and that other investors expect rational behaviour from them.

These assumptions were spelled out by Brennan (1971) and form part of the battery of conditions required for a perfect capital market. The additional assumptions required to support the 'irrelevance' hypothesis are as follows:

1 No transaction costs or brokerage fees.
2 All investors have equal and costless access to information.
3 All investors can lend or borrow at the same rate of interest.
4 No buyer or seller of securities can influence prices.
5 No personal or corporate income or capital gains taxes.
6 Dividend decisions are not used to convey information.

The full significance of some of these assumptions will be highlighted when we examine some of the reasons why shareholders may have a definite preference for either dividends or retentions.

Fears over dividend push Morrison to five-year low

Wm Morrison slipped to a five-year low yesterday as fears of a dividend cut eclipsed takeover hopes. The grocer had been bolstered earlier in the week by a report that its founding family had been sounding out private equity funds to take it private. But unless trading could be turned round, a takeover looked unlikely, said Exane BNP Paribas.

'Morrison is haemorrhaging market share and has a pricing problem requiring painful margin cuts to fix,' said the broker. 'The consumer's embrace of discounters has hurt all of the mainstream grocers, but Morrison's geographic and demographic positioning has left it exposed and its value credentials have been most tarnished.'

With online and convenience stores fragmenting the market share of supermarkets, property is not the value crutch it once was, said Exane. 'We would calculate property support based on a sustainable rent is perhaps only 50 per cent of the enterprise value of Sainsbury, Tesco (UK) and Morrison.'

'The cost of winning back custom will be painful. It means much lower profits and cash flows near term and requires a realistic view on the dividend.' The shares ended 1 per cent weaker at 233.8p.

Source: Based on Bryce Elder, *Financial Times*, 15 February 2014, p. 19.

■ Permanent dividend cuts: more Divicut

This argument can also be applied to the case of permanent retentions using the Dividend Growth Model, although the analysis is a little more complex. Retention may lower the dividend payment only temporarily, resulting in a rate of growth yielding higher future dividends. This is shown in Figure 17.2. At point-in-time t_1, the company, which currently pays out all its earnings, E_0, plans to cut dividends from D_0 to $(1-b)E_1$, where b is the retention ratio.

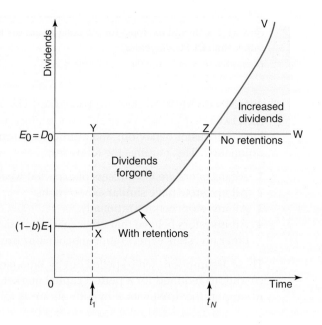

Figure 17.2 The impact of a permanent dividend cut

Dividends do not regain their former level until time t_N, involving a cumulative loss in dividend payments equal to the area XYZ. Beyond time t_N, dividends exceed their original level as a result of continued reinvestment. Clearly, shareholders will be better off if the area of higher future dividends, VZW, exceeds XYZ (allowing for the discounting process). This holds if R, the return on retained funds, exceeds k_e. This contention can be illustrated using the example of Divicut again.

Recall that, prior to alteration in dividend policy, the value of Divicut was £10,000, derived by discounting the perpetual earnings stream. Imagine the company announces its intention to retain 50 per cent of earnings in all future years (i.e. from and including Year 1) to finance a series of projects offering a perpetual yield of 15 per cent. Market value according to the dividend growth model is:

$$\text{Value of equity} = V_0 = \frac{E_1(1-b)}{(k_e - g)} = \frac{E_1(1-b)}{(k_e - bR)} = \frac{£1{,}000(1-0.5)}{0.1 - (0.5 \times 0.15)}$$

$$= \frac{£500}{0.025} = £20{,}000$$

This may seem a remarkable result. The decision to retain and reinvest doubles company value! Does this mean that dividend payments make shareholders worse off? The answer is simple.

Payment of dividends may make shareholders worse off than they otherwise might be if distribution results in failure to exploit worthwhile investment. In other words, the beneficial impact on Divicut's value is achieved because of the inherent attractions of the projected investments. Conversely, if the funds had been invested to yield only 5 per cent, market value would have fallen to £6,666.

The in-between case, where the return on reinvested funds, $R = k_e = 10$ per cent, leaves company value unchanged. This suggests that, if we strip out the effects of the investment decision, the dividend decision itself has a *neutral* effect. This can be done by assuming retentions are used to finance projects that yield an aggregate NPV of zero, i.e. yielding a return of k_e. With this assumption, dividend decisions are irrelevant to shareholder wealth. With a return on reinvested funds of 10 per cent, the company's value is:

$$\text{Value of equity} = V_0 = \frac{E_1(1-b)}{(k_e - g)} = \frac{£1{,}000(1-0.5)}{0.1 - (0.5 \times 0.1)} = \frac{£500}{0.05} = £10{,}000$$

Here we have valued the dividend stream, and the result is equivalent to valuing the steady stream of earnings with no retentions. This equivalence may perhaps be more readily seen by manipulating the expressions for value. If we neutralise the effect of the investment decision so that $k_e = R$, we may write:

$$\begin{array}{c}\text{Value} \\ \text{of} \\ \text{equity}\end{array} = V_0 = \frac{D_1}{(k_e - g)} = \frac{E_1(1-b)}{(k_e - g)} = \frac{E_1(1-b)}{(k_e - bR)} = \frac{E_1(1-b)}{(k_e - bk_e)} = \frac{E_1(1-b)}{k_e(1-b)} = \frac{E_1}{k_e}$$

There are clear conclusions from this analysis. In the absence of external financing:

1 *If the expected return on reinvested funds exceeds k_e,* it is beneficial to retain. A dividend cut will lead to higher value but only because funds are used to finance worthwhile projects.
2 *If the return on reinvested funds is less than k_e,* retention damages shareholder interests. A dividend cut would lower company value because shareholders have better uses for their funds.
3 *If the return on reinvested funds equals k_e,* the impact of a dividend cut to finance investment is neutral.

Self-assessment activity 17.3

How can dividend policy damage shareholder interests when no external financing is available?

(Answer in Appendix A at the back of the book)

■ Dividends as a residual

The dividend decision is simply the obverse of the investment decision. As observed earlier, we are examining the impact of one of the various ways in which proposed investment may be financed. Divicut is a case where the company is forced to retain funds through lack of alternative financing options. With the explicit assumption that the firm is capital-rationed with access only to internal sources of finance, we can illustrate the **residual theory of dividends**.

residual theory of dividends
Asserts that firms should only pay cash dividends when they have financed new investments. It assumes no access to external finance

This argues that dividends should be paid only when there are no further worthwhile investment opportunities. Having decided on the optimal set of investment projects, and determined the required amount of financing, the firm should distribute to shareholders only those funds not required for investment financing. This idea is shown graphically in Figure 17.3, using the **marginal efficiency of investment (MEI)** model, a construct borrowed from economic theory. The MEI traces out the rate of return on the last £1 invested, and thus shows investment opportunities ranked in declining order of attractiveness.

marginal efficiency of investment (MEI)
A schedule listing available investments, in declining order of attractiveness

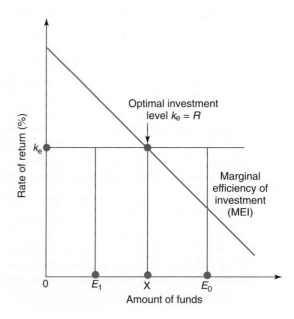

Figure 17.3 Dividends as a residual

With free cash flow of OE_0, there is scope for dividend payments. The limit of worthwhile new investment is at X, where the return on the last unit of investment is equal to the minimum required return k_e. The company can now make residual dividend payments of XE_0. However, if the free cash flow is only OE_1, distribution would impose an opportunity cost on shareholders. The whole cash flow should be reinvested, but it falls short of the finance required to support the optimal programme. The shortfall is E_1X, which could only be plugged by external financing if available.

Self-assessment activity 17.4

What dividend, if any, should the firm pay in the following situation? Earnings are £1 million, $k_e = 12$ per cent.

Project	Required outlay	IRR
A	£300,00	18%
B	£400,00	16%
C	£700,00	14%
D	£200,00	10%

(Answer in Appendix A at the back of the book)

■ External equity financing: yet more Divicut

We now consider the case where the firm has access to external financing. Rather than use earnings retention to finance investment, the firm may make a rights issue of shares, i.e. offer existing shareholders the right to buy new shares in proportion to their present holdings. If they all exercise their rights, the existing balance of control is unchanged, i.e. everyone ends up holding the same proportionate share of the firm. To sustain the irrelevance conclusion, we need to show that shareholder wealth is unaffected by choice of financing method, retention or new issues.

Consider the case where Divicut contemplates a one-off dividend cut to finance a project that requires a cash outlay of £1,000, and offers perpetual earnings of £200 p.a. The shares are not yet quoted ex-dividend. The options are to:

1 Retain the earnings.
2 Pay the dividend out of earnings and then recoup the cash via a rights issue.

The project itself is worthwhile, since its NPV is:

$$\text{NPV} = -£1,000 + \frac{£200}{0.1} = -£1,000 + £2,000 = +£1,000$$

The implications for shareholder wealth of each financing alternative are respectively:

1 If the dividend is passed, the value of shareholder wealth (W_0) is:

$$W_0 = (\text{dividend in year 0}) + (\text{PV of dividends from existing projects})$$
$$+ (\text{PV of dividends from new projects})$$

$$= 0 + \frac{£1,000}{0.1} + \frac{£2,00}{0.1} = (£10,000 + £2,000) = £12,000$$

Retention therefore benefits Divicut's shareholders, since £1,000 now is exchanged for a dividend stream with present value of £2,000.

2 If a rights issue is used to recoup the required capital, the wealth of shareholders is:

$$W_0 = (\text{dividend in year 0}) + (\text{PV of dividends from existing projects})$$
$$+ (\text{PV of dividends from new projects})$$
$$- (\text{amount subscribed for new shares})$$

$$= £1,000 + \frac{£1,000}{0.1} + \frac{£200}{0.1} - £1,000$$
$$= (£1,000 + £10,000 + £2,000) - £1,000 = £12,000$$

Shareholders' wealth is unaffected if they subscribe for the new shares, anticipating the higher future stream of dividends implied by the new venture. The attraction of the rights issue to some people is that it offers a choice between further investment in the company and an alternative use of capital (although this second option may be irrational if k_e accurately measures the opportunity cost of capital). Either way, in practice, companies often ensure they obtain the required funds by employing specialist financial institutions to underwrite such issues, as explained in Chapter 16.

■ Summary

This section has demonstrated that dividends are relevant to company valuation in the absence of external financing, but only in the sense that, if the company has better investment opportunities than its shareholders, payment of dividends prevents worthwhile investment. With external financing, however, in a perfect capital market, dividends become totally irrelevant since dividend payment no longer precludes worthwhile investment. The firm can simply recoup the required finance via a rights issue.

In the next section, we begin to unpick some of the assumptions underpinning the irrelevance theory and consider the implications of doing so.

Chinese groups get dividend guidance

Companies listed on the Shanghai Stock Exchange have been told by the bourse to return 30 per cent of profits to shareholders via dividends in the latest move by authorities to bolster confidence in China's equity markets.

Dividend payments by Chinese companies have been rising steadily in recent years, reaching about 30 per cent of aggregate profits for all listed companies in 2011, according to a statement from the exchange published on Monday. 'However, it must also be recognised that there is still a definite gap between cash dividend ratios for Shanghai-listed companies and those in mature markets, and high dividend ratios are largely concentrated in a minority of blue-chip stocks such as banks,' said the exchange.

Under the new exchange guidelines, those who regularly make dividend payments and 'satisfy' investors will be placed in a 'green light channel' for any financing and mergers and acquisition activity that relates to the exchange's supervision. Companies that do not meet the 30 per cent threshold for dividend payouts were told that they should provide a full explanation in their annual reports.

In the US for the third quarter, the percentage of earnings paid out in dividends for the S&P 500 companies was 29.1 per cent, according to Factset data. However, US companies also return large amounts of capital to shareholders through share buybacks. Based on 2011 earnings, the average dividend yield for members of the Shanghai Composite index was 2.2 per cent, compared with 3 per cent for companies in the MSCI Asia ex-Japan index, according to Bloomberg data.

Until last month, investors in Chinese shares had endured three years of poor performance. On 27 November, the benchmark Shanghai index dropped below 2,000 points for the first time since the depths of the financial crisis.

Source: Based on Josh Noble and Simon Rabinovitch, *Financial Times*, 9 January 2013, p. 30.

17.5 OBJECTIONS TO DIVIDEND IRRELEVANCE

This section examines some of the arguments advanced against the irrelevance theory. Financial managers should weigh up several important considerations before deciding upon the appropriate dividend payout policy:

- To what extent do shareholders rely on dividend income?
- Are nearer-in-time dividends less risky than future dividends?
- Do market imperfections lead companies to adopt policies that attract a particular clientèle of investors?
- Would investors accept a rights issue?
- How does taxation affect dividend policy?

Let us deal with these questions in turn.

■ Do shareholders rely on dividend income to support expenditure?

Shareholders who require a steady and reliable stream of income from dividends may be concerned by a sudden change in dividend policy, especially a dividend cut, albeit to finance worthwhile projects. Some groups of shareholders may well have a definite preference for current income: for example, the elderly, and institutions such as pension funds, that depend on a stable flow of income to meet their largely predictable liabilities. However, in an efficient capital market, such shareholders should be no worse off after a dividend cut, since the value of their holdings will rise on the news of the new

home-made dividend
Cash released when an investor realises part of his/her investment in a firm in order to supplement his/her income

investment. They can realise some or all of their gains, thus converting capital into income. The capital released is called a 'home-made dividend'. (This is similar to the 'equity release schemes' whereby UK home-owners extract some of the value locked up in their homes.) A worked example of this procedure is given in the appendix to this chapter.

There are several criticisms of the validity of the home-made dividends mechanism. Even in the absence of market imperfections, the investor is forced to incur the inconvenience of making the required portfolio adjustments. Allowing for brokerage and other transactions costs, the net benefits of the project for the income-seeking investor are reduced. Also, if capital gains are taxed, the enforced share sale may trigger a tax liability. In the case of only marginally attractive projects, these effects may be sufficient to more than offset the benefits of the project, at least for some investors. Conversely, it can be argued that payment of a dividend to investors who then incur brokerage fees in reinvesting their income is equally disadvantageous.

■ Are future dividends seen as more risky by shareholders?

The practical limitations on the unfettered ability to home-make dividends were spelt out by Myron Gordon (1963) in a ringing attack on MM's irrelevance conclusion. However, Gordon extended his critique of MM to argue that $1 of dividend now is necessarily valued more highly than $1 of retained earnings because investors regard the (albeit higher) future stream of dividends stemming from a new project as carrying a higher level of risk. In other words, investors prefer what Gordon called an 'early resolution of uncertainty'. Gordon was, in effect, arguing that shareholders evaluate future expected dividends using a set of rising discount rates. If present dividends are reduced to allow greater investment, thus shifting the dividend pattern into the future, company value will fall.

Keane (1974) refined Gordon's position by suggesting that it is secondary whether, in fact, future dividends are more risky than near ones. If investors *perceive* them to be riskier, a policy of higher retentions, while not actually increasing risk, may unfavourably alter investor attitudes. In capital markets where full information is not released about investment projects, investors' subjective risk assessments may result in low payout companies being valued at a discount compared to high payout companies: that is, investors' imperfect perceptions of risk may lead them to undervalue the future dividend stream generated by retentions.

The 'bird-in-the-hand fallacy'

bird-in-the-hand fallacy
The mistaken belief that dividends paid early in the future are worth more than dividends expected in later time periods, simply because they are nearer in time and viewed as less risky

If the firm's dividend policy does alter the perceived riskiness of the expected dividend flow, there may be an optimal dividend policy that trades off the beneficial effects of an enhanced growth rate against the adverse impact of increased perceived risk, so as to maximise the market value. However, advocates of dividend irrelevance argue that Gordon's analysis is inherently fallacious. More distant dividends are more risky only if they stem from inherently riskier investment projects. Risk should already have been catered for by discounting cash flows at a suitably risk-adjusted rate. To deflate future dividends for risk further would involve double-counting. There is no reason why risk necessarily increases with time – a model based on this supposition incorporates the **'bird-in-the-hand fallacy'**. According to MM (1961), dividend policy remains a 'mere detail' once a firm's investment policy, and its inherent business risks, is made known. This argument is examined more rigorously by Bhattacharya (1979).

Self-assessment activity 17.5

Why is Gordon's 'early resolution of uncertainty' argument in favour of paying early dividends logically flawed?

(Answer in Appendix A at the back of the book)

■ Market imperfections and the clientèle effect

The extent to which investors are willing and able to home-make dividends, and thus adjust the company's actual dividend pattern to suit their own personal desired consumption plans, depends on the degree of imperfection in the capital market. In practice, numerous impediments, especially when aggregated, may significantly offset the benefits of exploiting a profitable project. Some of these have already been mentioned, but the main ones are as follows:

- Brokerage costs incurred when shares are sold.
- Other transaction costs incurred, e.g. the costs of searching out the cheapest brokerage facilities.
- The loss in interest incurred in waiting for settlement.
- The problem of indivisibilities, whereby investors may be unable to sell the precise number of shares required, forcing them to deal in sub-optimal batch sizes.
- The sheer inconvenience of being forced to alter one's portfolio.
- Share sales may trigger a capital gains tax liability.
- If the company is relatively small, its shares may lack marketability, requiring a significant dealing spread and hence a leakage of shareholder capital.
- If the company is unquoted, it may be difficult or impossible to find a buyer for the shares.

Under such imperfections, maximising firm value may not be the unique desire of all shareholders; the pattern of receipt of wealth may become equally or more important. Some shareholders may prefer companies that offer dividend flows which correspond to their desired consumption, perhaps being prepared to pay a premium to hold these shares. In this way, they avoid having to make their own adjustments. The vehicle for aiding such investors is to provide a stable and known dividend stream. Shareholders can then perceive the nature of the likely future dividend pattern and decide whether or not the company's policy meets their requirements. In other words, the company attracts, and attempts to cater for, a **clientèle** of shareholders.

However, such a policy has costs, including the benefits forgone from projects that might have to be passed over, the costs of borrowing if debt finance is used, and/or the issue expenses of a rights issue if external financing is employed. The implications for control if rights are not fully exercised by the existing shareholders may be another problem.

The key difficulty facing the financial manager is lack of knowledge of shareholder preferences, without which it is difficult to balance the two sets of costs.

Self-assessment activity 17.6

What is meant by a shareholder clientèle? Which shareholders are most likely to prefer near-in-time dividends?

(Answer in Appendix A at the back of the book)

■ Problems with rights issues: Rawdon plc

Among the effects of a rights issue are the costs incurred. These can be substantial, and will affect the required return on new investment. Among the costs are the administrative expenses, the costs of printing brochures and circulation of these to shareholders, and also the underwriters' fees. The impact of these costs is examined using the case of Rawdon plc, whose details are shown in Table 17.2.

Although Rawdon's shareholders require a return of 20 per cent, the new project has to offer a return of *over* 20 per cent. This is because some of the finance raised by the share issue is required to meet the costs of the issue, but the holders of those shares

Table 17.2 Rawdon plc

- $k_e = 20\%$
- Rawdon's value = £5m
- 1m shares have been issued in the past
- Market price per share is £5
- Current company earnings = £1m (EPS = £1)
- Proposed investment outlay = £950,000
- The project has a perpetual life.
- Terms of rights issue:
  One share for every five held, i.e. 200,000 new shares.
  Purchase price £5: gross proceeds = £1m
  Issue costs: 5% of gross receipts = (0.05 × £1m) = £50,000
  Net proceeds = £950,000

will nevertheless demand a return. Total share capital is now £6 million, and earnings of £1.2 million are now required to generate a 20 per cent return overall. However, the required increase in earnings of £0.2 million must be generated by an investment of £950,000, necessitating a return of (£0.2m/£0.95m) = 21.1 per cent. Rawdon's required return on this project is given by:

$$\frac{\text{Normally required return}}{(1 - \%\ \text{issue costs})} = \frac{k_e}{(1 - c)} = \frac{0.2}{(1 - 0.05)} = 0.211, \text{ i.e. } 21.1\%$$

However, the problem of transactions costs may operate in another direction. Some shareholders, when paid a dividend, may incur some reinvestment costs. The higher the proportion of investors who wish to reinvest, either in the same or in another company, the greater the total saving of brokerage and other fees enjoyed by shareholders when the company retains earnings. Hence, the greater is the attraction of retained earnings to finance investment.

Bearing in mind the impact on share price, the announcement of a rights issue is not always greeted with delight. The shareholder is forced either to take up or sell the rights in order to avoid losing money (even sale of rights will result in brokerage fees), and thus incur the inconvenience involved. If the market takes a dim view of the proposed use of the capital raised (for example, if the funds are required to finance a takeover whose benefits look distinctly speculative), the share price may fall. *But it is important to realise that this would be a consequence of a faulty investment decision rather than of the financing decision itself.*

■ The impact of taxation

In many economies, the tax treatment of dividend income and realised capital gains differs, either via differential tax rates or via different levels of exemption allowed, or both. In such regimes, the theoretical equivalence between dividends and retention becomes further distorted. Typically, tax on capital gains is lower than tax on income from dividends. In some countries, there is *no* tax on capital gains. Some shareholders might prefer 'home-made dividends' (i.e. selling shares) now or in the future when the rate of **capital gains tax (CGT)** is lower than the marginal rate of income tax applied to dividends. Others may prefer dividend payments because their income tax liability (plus any reinvestment costs) is lower than CGT payments.

In addition to considerations of personal taxation, where the financial manager is often unaware of the particular tax positions of shareholders (a major exception to this is the case of institutional investors), complications may also be imposed by the corporate tax system. In an imputation tax system, shareholders receive dividend income net

capital gains tax (CGT)
Paid on realising an increase in share value. Capital gains are currently treated as income in the UK at the investor's marginal tax rate

of basic rate tax, while the rate of tax applied to corporate profits is designed to include an element of personal tax, thus making the distribution of dividends tax-neutral.

There are so many different tax regimes operated throughout the world, that it is difficult to generalise about the effect of taxation on dividend policy. However, the following simple example captures the flavour of some of the issues.

Barlow plc

Barlow plc is financed entirely by equity and its future cash flows have present value of £500 million at the start of 2014. During 2014, it earns £100 million – for simplicity, we assume that all transactions are in cash, so it now holds cash of £100 million. Profits are taxed at 30 per cent so Barlow must set aside £30 million for tax payments, leaving (70% × £100m) = £70m available for distribution. According to the EMH, the firm will be valued at (£500m + £70m) = £570m.

Should Barlow distribute or retain? The answer depends on three factors:

- shareholders' marginal rates of tax
- the relative rate of tax on dividends vs. tax on capital gains
- the type of tax regime.

classical tax system
A system where dividends are effectively taxed twice – the firm pays profits tax and then investors pay income tax on any dividend payment

Under a **classical tax system**, profits are taxed twice if distributed, firstly, as profits tax, and secondly, as income tax paid by investors. Imagine the firm makes a full distribution. Consider two rates of investor income tax:

(i) if investors pay tax at 10%, income tax is (10% × £70m) = £7m, and the total tax charge is (£30m + £7m) = £37m (or 37% of pre-tax earnings);

(ii) if investors pay tax at 50%, income tax is (50% × £70m) = £35m, and the total tax charge is (£30m + £35m) = £65m (or 65% of pre-tax earnings).

It looks better to retain in the second case, but the decision also depends on the rate of capital gains tax (CGT).

Assume the CGT rate is 20 per cent. If we also assume that the firm invests in zero-NPV projects (unlikely, but a necessary assumption to strip out the effect of the investment decision), the value of the firm will have risen from £500 million at start-year to £570 million at end-year. The CGT payable is thus (20% × £70m) = £14m. Along with the profits tax, the total tax payable is (£30m + £14m) = £44m.

Obviously, shareholders paying income tax at 50 per cent would prefer retention and vice versa.

Under an **imputation tax system**, the relative attractiveness of distribution and retention depends not only on the relative tax rates, but also on whether there is full or partial imputation.

With full imputation, investors get full credit for corporate profits tax already paid.

In case (i) above, the investor would face no further tax on income and may even get a tax rebate, depending on the tax regime, because the rate of corporate tax exceeds the rate of personal tax.

In case (ii), the investor obtains credit for the corporate tax already paid, and thus faces an additional income tax charge of (50% − 30%) × £70m = £14m. With these particular figures, investors would be indifferent between distribution and retention.

With partial imputation, it is less clear-cut – the relative desirability of distribution and retention depends on the degree of imputation, as well as the respective tax rates.

Current UK rates

Under the present UK system of partial imputation, income from dividends and capital gains are taxed at different rates, and different tax thresholds also apply. Following reforms implemented in 2008, there is now a discrimination in favour of capital gains. Individuals who pay income tax at 20 per cent, pay CGT at 18 per cent, and those who pay income tax at 40 per cent or more, pay CGT at 28 per cent.

Income tax on dividends

Dividends are paid net of tax, assumed payable at 10 per cent, thus generating a non-repayable tax credit. Currently (2013–14), dividends are treated as the top slice of income for tax purposes, and are thus taxed at the recipient's highest marginal rate of tax.

As the tax is applied to gross incomes, investors in the Starting Rate band of income pay no further tax, those in the Higher Rate band pay a further 22.5 per cent. These rates have the effect of equating dividend tax rates with tax rates on earned income, by adjusting for the tax credit.

Capital gains tax

Gains above the threshold £11,000 (2014–15) are taxed at 18 per cent for basic rate taxpayers and 28 per cent for higher rate taxpayers. The indexation and taper reliefs that mitigated tax were abolished in 2008, although husbands and wives continue to enjoy a double allowance for jointly owned assets.

■ The tax irrelevance thesis

Some argue that, under perfect capital markets, the question of relative tax rates is irrelevant because of arbitrage. Zero/low-rate taxpayers prefer to hold shares in firms with high payouts, and those with high marginal rates of tax prefer low payout firms. The process of tax-driven arbitrage would lead each group to bid up the share prices of the firms whose distribution policy suits their own particular tax positions, until in equilibrium, post-tax rates of return are equalised. This means there is no share price advantage to be obtained from following a particular dividend policy.

Elton and Gruber (1970) noted the importance of marginal tax brackets in determining the return required by shareholders. They defined the cost of using retained earnings as 'that rate which makes a firm's marginal shareholders indifferent between earnings being retained or paid out in the form of dividends'. Under differential tax treatments of dividend income and capital gains, the cost of using retained earnings is a function of the shareholder's marginal tax bracket. We might also expect companies whose shareholders incur high rates of income tax to exhibit low payout rates. Such a relationship between corporate dividend policy and shareholder tax brackets would support the notion of 'tax clientèles', whereby companies seek to tailor their payout policies to the tax situation of particular shareholders. Elton and Gruber's empirical work seemed to indicate that firms attract rational clientèles – *shareholders gravitate to companies whose distribution policy is compatible with their personal tax situations.*

17.6 THE INFORMATION CONTENT OF DIVIDENDS: DIVIDEND SMOOTHING

Possibly the most important consideration for corporate financial decision-makers when framing dividend policy is the information-processing capacity of the market. Any dividend declaration can be interpreted by the market in a variety of ways. In an uncertain world, information regarding a company's prospects is neither generally available nor costless to acquire. Managers possess more information about the company's trading position than is available to investors as a whole. This **information asymmetry** may mean that the announcement of a new or changed company policy may be interpreted by the market as a *signal* conveying particular information about a company's prospects, as in the Costco cameo below.

For example, the decision to pay an unexpectedly high dividend may be seized upon as evidence of greater expected dividend-paying capacity in the future. It may be taken as guaranteeing an ability to sustain at least the higher declared dividend and

information asymmetry
The imbalance between managers and owners of information possessed about a firm's financial state and its prospects

probably more. As a result, the financial manager should consider carefully how the market is likely to decode the signals contained in the dividend decision, and the likely consequences for share price.

Costco

The stock market is bad at maths, or accounting, or possibly both. Yesterday the discount warehouse club Costco announced a special dividend of $7 per share – a meaty payout for a stock that traded at about $97 before the announcement. Giddy buyers bid the shares up by as much as $6.

In theory, though, a dividend should not affect the value of a company. Costco's dividend will take $3bn in cash off the asset side of its balance sheet; retained earnings will drop by the same amount. Investors end up with $7 in their pockets and a share that is worth, on paper, $7 less.

There are forms of value not reflected by a balance sheet. The equity of a company is worth more if its management has a record of allocating capital wisely: deploying cash internally when high-returning opportunities are present, paying it out otherwise. A one-time dividend does not, however, demonstrate enough management skill to increase the value of a $42bn company by 6 per cent. One might argue that the special dividend signals insiders' confidence that profits are headed up. But Costco is not about to introduce an amazing new product or radical new strategy. It is a big-box retailer. The insiders can see Costco's future only slightly better than anyone who reads its reports.

The punters bidding up Costco might suggest, finally, that $7 is worth more to investors now than it will be next year, when US Federal taxes on dividends are expected to rise. Fair enough. How much should this boost the value of a Costco share before the dividend is paid? By, at most, the difference between the payout's current and future after-tax values. Assuming the current 15 per cent tax rate goes to a draconian 38 per cent, that is about $1.61. That leaves believers in the efficient market hypothesis with, say, $4.50 of share price change to explain away.

Source: Based on Lex Column, *Financial Times*, 29 November 2012, p. 14.

signalling
Using financial announcements to deliver more information than is actually spelt out in detail

Company finance directors (FDs) are well aware of the **signalling** power of dividends and their capacity to influence share price. This awareness is implied by the recent earnings and dividend record of the two firms, shown in Table 17.3.

Table 17.3 shows the EPS and DPS record of two firms in quite different operating environments. Scottish and Southern, which supplies electricity and water, faced a very stable marketplace, with demand highly predictable and operating costs relatively easy to manage. D.S. Smith plc, in contrast, faced a far more turbulent environment. Its main markets are subject to far more volatile influences as it supplies packaging products for final consumers, while its cost structure can rapidly be disrupted by rises in input costs, especially that of energy. Not surprisingly, we find that Scottish and Southern was able to pursue a far more progressive dividend policy than D.S. Smith, but it is clear that both firms endeavoured to smooth their DPS payment, i.e. both had far more stable DPS profiles than their corresponding EPS records.

This 'smoothing' of dividends can be found among many other firms and has been identified empirically. Lintner (1956) showed that companies appear to raise dividends only on the basis of reported earnings increases that they expect to be sustainable in the long term. In a survey of 179 Finance Directors of large quoted companies conducted by 3i (1993), 43 per cent said that the single most important factor influencing dividend policy was prospective long-term profit growth, while 93 per cent agreed with the statement that 'dividend policy should follow the long-term trend in earnings'.

So do companies ever cut dividends? Obviously, in adversity, dividend cuts are forced on firms in order to preserve cash. In the 3i survey, 55 per cent of FDs agreed with the statement that 'any cut in dividend payout sends adverse signals to the market and should be avoided'. Dividend-cutting is far more common in the USA than in the UK. Empirical work by Ghosh and Woolridge (1989) suggests that even when this

Table 17.3 Scottish and Southern plc and D.S. Smith plc: EPS and DPS

Year	EPS (p)	% change	DPS (p)	% change
Scottish and Southern				
2001	50.9	–	30.0	–
2002	54.7	7.5	32.4	8.0
2003	51.9	(5.1)	35.0	8.0
2004	52.2	0.6	37.7	7.7
2005	57.4	10.0	42.5	12.7
2006	74.7	30.1	46.5	9.4
2007	92.5	23.8	55.0	18.3
2008	105.6	14.2	60.5	10.0
2009	108.0	2.3	66.0	9.1
2010	110.2	2.0	70.0	6.1
2011	112.3	1.9	75.0	7.1
2012	112.7	0.4	80.1	6.8
2013	118.0	4.7	84.2	5.1
D.S. Smith				
2001	14.1	–	8.2	–
2002	13.1	(7.1)	8.2	0
2003	16.8	28.2	8.2	0
2004	13.6	(19.0)	8.2	0
2005	14.4	5.9	8.4	2.4
2006	10.0	(30.6)	8.4	0
2007	13.1	31.0	8.6	2.4
2008	19.9	(51.9)	8.8	2.3
2009	12.6	(36.7)	4.4	(50.0)
2010	12.9	2.4	4.6	4.5
2011	17.0	31.8	6.5	41.3
2012	*–	–	6.8	4.6
2013	*–	–	8.0	17.6

* Note: EPS restated after 2012 and not comparable to prior years.

Source: Respective company Annual Reports.

was motivated by the need to conserve funds for investment purposes, shareholders suffered significant capital losses, despite the merits claimed for the proposed investments. In the UK, it is almost unheard of for companies to cut dividends to finance investment – the dividend payment-plus-rights issue is invariably the preferred alternative. In the 3i survey, one FD said that 'a dividend cut is a sign of fundamental management failure – when management fails and the Board should change'. But, a dividend cut might be construed as a prudent move in sharply deteriorating market conditions as in the late 2000s. In adversity, *not* to cut a dividend may be seen as a sign of financial recklessness.

17.7 WORKED EXAMPLE

The data given below relates to three firms' dividend payouts over the last six years. None of the companies has issued, or cancelled, any shares over the period. All three firms are listed on the London Stock Exchange.

	2009	2010	2011	2012	2013	2014
Company A						
Shares issued	1,200m					
Profit after tax (£m)		600	630	580	600	640	660
Dividends declared (£m)		240	252	232	240	256	264
Company B						
Shares issued	2,000m					
Profit after tax (£m)		1,200	1,300	1,580	1,800	1,240	1,460
Dividends declared (£m)		120	132	145	160	176	194
Company C						
Shares issued	3,500m					
Profit after tax (£m)		2,200	1,400	2,100	1,950	2,200	2,560
Dividends declared (£m)		200	0	100	0	200	560

Required

Showing appropriate calculations, describe the dividend policy which each of the companies shown above appears to be following.

How would you justify each of these policies to the shareholders of each of the companies concerned?

Answer

General comments

Company A

This firm pays out a constant percentage (40 per cent) of profit after tax as dividend. It is thus prepared to tolerate fluctuations in the actual amount paid and, hence, DPS, as corporate profits, and thus EPS, oscillates. DPS fluctuates from a high of 20p in 2009 to a low of 19.3p in 2011, ending up at 22p in 2014. The range of fluctuation is thus quite narrow.

> *In brief*: constant payout (and cover)
> variable DPS

Company B

This firm increases the amount of dividend and thus the DPS by a constant 10 per cent p.a., come what may, in terms of PAT and EPS. The dividend cover thus takes the strain, although it is never less than 7 times (2013).

> *In brief*: rising DPS
> variable payout (and cover)

Company C

This firm pays out any excess of PAT above a base level of £2 billion, accepting a zero payout if PAT undershoots this figure.

> *In brief*: variable DPS
> variable payout (and cover)

Interpretation

The nature of the industry in which the firms operate could well be an important influence on dividend policy. Profits are relatively stable for Company A, but oscillate wildly in the case of Company C. Hence, A is able to pay out a relatively high proportion in dividends reasonably safe in the knowledge that profits will soon recover after a bad year as they did in 2012, exceeding the previous peak of 2010 shortly afterwards in 2013. The maintenance of a high payout (if not the actual DPS) might be taken as an expression of confidence in the future and thus perform an important signalling function. Indeed, the fall in DPS in 2011 might be taken as a sign of financial prudence – conserving cash at a time of faltering performance.

It is likely that Company A has a clientèle that relies on a high level of dividend income, although one that is prepared to accept some belt-tightening in lean years. A fluctuating DPS does impact on liquidity, e.g. in the leaner years, despite the cut in DPS, the amount of retained earnings and, by implication, free cash flow is reduced, perhaps impacting on investment expenditure. However, it is unlikely that firms would want to push ahead with substantial investments in the lean years (although there is a strong argument in favour of this, i.e. to be primed for the fat years when they arrive). Also, if the industry is stable, and the firm has a solid record of increasing profits over time, then it may have good access to capital markets. A high payout also has agency advantages – managers have less access to discretionary spending, that may not necessarily be in the best interests of the owners.

Looking at Company C, its base profits level of £2 billion before a dividend payment is made suggests that it has an ongoing investment programme to fund, and is thus concerned about liquidity, or that it is highly geared and faces debt covenants that stipulate this profits threshold before a dividend can be paid. The fluctuations in profits and the dividend policy imply that the shareholder clientèle is relatively unconcerned by dividend income, but is more interested in profits and value growth. The industry is probably a high-risk one, perhaps a New Economy one, with attractive long-term prospects. Clearly, this is a residual dividend policy where other demands on cash flow take precedence over distribution of profits. Eventually, however, like the cash-rich Microsoft ultimately did, the firm will exhaust its (organic) growth potential and will have to frame a coherent dividend policy.

Finally, Company B has a highly predictable dividend policy that allows shareholders to anticipate the next year's income with great accuracy and confidence. This will suit a variety of clientéles that rely on a predictable stream of income such as institutional investors and personal investors advanced in years. However, the payout ratio is not high, so the firm is taking no risks in terms of the sustainability of its policy, i.e. there is plenty of slack to enable an increase in DPS even in bad years such as 2013. This suggests that it is using retained earnings to a significant extent to finance growth, possibly because it faces difficult access to the capital markets – perhaps it is a relatively young firm or has high gearing. Either way, it is unlikely to have to endure the ignominy of cutting the dividend in the future – profits would have to fall over 80 per cent before the dividend was uncovered.

Vodafone's special payout poised to bolster dividend payments in UK to record £100bn

Gross dividend payments from UK companies are set to exceed £100bn next year for the first time, according to research from Capita Asset Services. The record payout will be boosted by the £16.6bn special dividend from Vodafone, the study points out. Altogether, the telecoms group is handing shareholders just over £54bn – almost three-quarters of the net proceeds from the sale of its 45 per cent stake in Verizon Wireless.

Without the Vodafone payment, the Capita research suggests that the outlook for dividend growth is far gloomier than the double-digit percentage increases seen in 2011 and 2012.

Capita says that, while dividend payments in the third quarter typically outstrip those paid in the second quarter, this year the headline payments to the end of October totalled £25.3bn – lower than the distribution in the three months to end of June. This is the first time since 2008 that the third quarter has not been the period of the largest dividend payout.

Year-on-year growth had also slowed with the 6.6 per cent increase in underlying dividends over the third quarter of 2012, lagging behind the 7.7 per cent rise in the first half of 2013 against last year.

Continued

17.8 ALTERNATIVES TO CASH DIVIDENDS

The motive for cutting a dividend is to save cash outflows. This suggests that liquidity considerations are another influence on the dividend decision. This section discusses how firms that wish to preserve liquidity can still offer 'dividends', and also how firms can cope with excessive liquidity. Alternatives to cash dividends are thus divided into those that preserve liquidity and those that reduce liquidity.

■ Liquidity-saving alternatives

(i) Scrip dividends

scrip dividends
Offered to investors in lieu of the equivalent cash payment. Also called a **scrip alternative**

Most major companies offer shareholders **scrip dividends**. This is an opportunity to receive new shares instead of a cash dividend payment. It has certain advantages for both the shareholder and the company.

From the firm's point of view, the scrip alternative preserves liquidity, which may be important at a time of cash shortage and/or high borrowing costs, although it could face a higher level of cash outflows if shareholders revert to preference for cash in the future. With more shares issued, the company's reported financial gearing may fall, possibly enhancing borrowing capacity. In this respect, the scrip dividend resembles a mini-rights issue.

For shareholders wishing to expand their holdings, the scrip is a cheap way into the company as it avoids dealing fees and Stamp Duty (currently, 0.5 per cent in the UK). A scrip dividend has no tax advantages for shareholders as it is treated as income for tax purposes.

In an efficient capital market, there is no dilution effect on the share price, because it would have fallen anyway with a cash dividend because of the 'ex-dividend effect'. However, if the additional capital retained is expected to be used wisely, the share price may be maintained or may even rise, giving shareholders who elect for the scrip dividend access to higher future dividends and capital gains. As a result, there may be a longer-term tax advantage for shareholders. However, most of these effects are marginal. Perhaps the main benefit of a scrip dividend is that, by giving shareholders a choice, it makes the shares more attractive to a wider clientèle.

(ii) Enhanced scrip dividends

To overcome the low take-up rate of scrip dividends, in 1993, several companies with chronic liquidity problems began to offer 'enhanced scrip dividends' (ESDs). The first to do so was BAT Industries (**www.bat.com**), which announced a scrip alternative 50 per cent above the equivalent cash dividend, designed to be so generous that shareholders could not refuse. BAT declared a 22.6p final dividend, and then, later that month, offered an ESD alternative of 33.9p. Had all of BAT's shareholders taken up the ESD, the cash saving would have been £423 million.

The ESD mechanism is a rights issue in disguise. To the extent that shareholders take the scrip alternative, the company is left with as much cash as if it had paid a cash dividend and then clawed it back from the same shareholders via a rights issue. As with a rights issue, the number of shares issued will rise. Finally, because the scrip is voluntary, the control of shareholders taking cash is diluted.

Self-assessment activity 17.7

How many shares would an investor receive in lieu of cash dividends of £1,000 if offered:

(i) a pro rata scrip alternative?

(ii) an ESD of 20%?

Share price is £20.

(Answer in Appendix A at the back of the book)

Scrips and Drips

The effect of dividend reinvestment is often illustrated by this startling statistic from the annual Barclays Equity-Gilt study: £100 invested in the UK stock market in 1899 would have been worth £12,655 (in nominal terms) by the end of 2010 without reinvestment, and £1.7m with all dividends reinvested.

Even over shorter time-frames, dividend reinvestment makes a difference. But how do you actually go about reinvesting dividends? It depends which companies' shares you own, and how you hold them.

A few big companies – including Shell, Aviva and SSE – operate scrip dividend schemes, where the company issues shares to the value of a cash dividend. Because these are new shares, there is no stamp duty or brokerage charge to pay, so it's the most cost-effective way of reinvesting dividends.

More common is the dividend reinvestment plan (Drip). These are operated by the company's registrar, and use the cash dividend to buy existing shares in the market. There is typically a charge of about 0.5 per cent of the transaction value. Any unused cash is carried forward. Many larger companies and investment trusts operate drips.

To participate in a scrip or a Drip, your name must appear on the company's share register, so you will need to hold share certificates or have personal membership of Crest, the UK's settlement system. If you hold your shares in a nominee account – as you must do if you have a self-select ISA – then your name will not appear on the register and you will be unable to use a Drip. However, many brokers offer a dividend reinvestment service, typically charging £1.50 per line of stock. For small shareholdings this may be uneconomic, but will make sense for larger ones.

Source: Based on Jonathan Elay, *Financial Times*, 27 October 2012, p. 9.

■ Liquidity-reducing alternatives

The dividend decision is contorted by the case of companies with too much cash.

As an alternative to paying cash dividends, the facility to repurchase shares, subject to shareholders' approval, was introduced in the UK by the 1981 Companies Act. It resulted from pressure from the small firms lobby, concerned that low marketability of unquoted firms' equity was hampering their development. Certain conditions were stipulated, designed principally to safeguard the position of creditors, and further restrictions were imposed by the Stock Exchange and the Takeover Panel, aimed at reducing the risk of market-rigging during takeover battles. The first major company to mount a **buy-back** was GEC in 1984, ostensibly to raise the EPS of the remaining shares. A component of British Airport Authority's (failed) defence package against a takeover bid in 2006 was share repurchase, designed to raise the cost of the bid.

buy-back
A method of obtaining payment for building a manufacturing unit overseas by taking the future physical product of the plant in return

The Bank of England (1988) cited five possible reasons for repurchases:

- To return surplus cash to shareholders.
- To increase underlying share value.
- To support share price during periods of temporary weakness.
- To achieve or maintain a target capital structure.
- To prevent or inhibit unwelcome takeover bids.

The hoped-for increase in share price works through the effect on EPS. A company may attempt a buy-back when it has a cash surplus beyond what it needs to finance normal business operations. This situation is assumed in Table 17.4, which shows the before-and-after situation of a company sitting on a cash pile of £100 million earning interest at 5 per cent. It buys in 20 million shares at 180p, above the market price of 172p, the discrepancy being due to the premium required to attract enough sellers. The total buy-back cost is therefore £36 million, on which the company will lose interest income.

Table 17.4 Analysis of a share repurchase

	Before	**After**
Trading profit (£m)	200.00	200.00
Interest income at 5% (£m)	5.00	3.20
Pre-tax profit (£m)	205.00	203.20
Tax at 30% (£m)	(61.50)	(60.96)
Profits available for shareholders (£m)	143.50	142.24
Number of shares in issue	500m	480m
EPS (p)	28.70	29.63
P:E Ratio	6:1	6:1
Share price (p)	172	178
Cash balances (£m)	100.00	64.00

US evidence suggests repurchasing shares may have a strong signalling effect, whereby executives can express confidence in their firms by investing in equity. Yet there remains a strong suspicion in the UK that such messages may be decoded adversely. To some observers, buy-backs are tantamount to an admission of managerial failure, signalling lack of confidence in their ability to identify and exploit wealth-creating projects.

Unclear outlook gives buy-backs a special appeal

Uncertainty about the outlook for global economic growth and corporate earnings has left equity market investors seeking fresh strategies. Could the current strength of companies' balance sheets provide inspiration? Brain Belski, chief investment strategist at BMO Capital Markets, says companies that repurchase shares consistently outperform the market.

'Repurchase strategies – often overlooked by investors – are particularly important during periods of anaemic earnings growth,' he says. 'We believe companies will struggle to deliver high rates of EPS growth in the upcoming reporting periods, given what is likely to be subdued economic growth. Unfortunately, most companies have been reluctant to part with their enormous cash piles in any significant way, 'despite vigorous pleas from investors to utilise cash in a more productive manner.'

'Therefore, until this scenario changes, overall market earnings growth is likely to struggle. In the meantime, companies that are in a position to repurchase shares are likely to benefit. For instance, we found that companies with the highest amount of share repurchases deliver the best average relative performance during periods of slow or negative overall EPS growth.'

'Robert Buckland, equity strategist at Citigroup, points out that, even though interest rates have increased during the last couple of months, debt financing is still cheap by historical standards, especially when compared with equity financing.'

'Given the large cash piles on company balance sheets, we think companies will continue to return capital to shareholders via buybacks,' he says. 'We find that companies doing buybacks have tended to be strong performers.'

'The percentage of S&P 500 earnings paid out as dividends – the payout ratio – has averaged 54 per cent since the early 1900s, yet stands at just 36 per cent today,' says Cheryl Rowan, portfolio strategist at Bofa ML. '[That] despite the fact that 82 per cent of securities in the index pay dividends – a level not seen since September 1999.'

Source: Based on Dave Shellock, *Financial Times*, 22 August 2013, p. 29.

However, investment expenditure is rarely a continuous process and small buy-backs may be a useful way of investing temporary cash surpluses, with the beneficial effects on EPS and share price providing a platform for a subsequent rights issue if development funds are needed. In addition, buy-backs may be a useful alternative to paying higher but unsustainable dividends, while preserving choice for investors.

Buy-backs: a word of warning

One of the unfortunate consequences of buy-backs is that (admittedly with the benefit of hindsight) they can make directors look rather foolish. If, after the buy-back, the share price falls, it means that more money has been expended on the buy-back than would have been required at the lower price.

An example of directors looking red-faced in retrospect was the case of Next plc, the fashion retail chain. In 2007, it announced a buy-back programme at a cash cost of £513 million, some 11 per cent of the shares then in issue, for an average of £19.74 per share. In accounting terms, this pressed the right buttons, as, assisted by a modest 4 per cent profits increase, EPS rose by 15 per cent in 2008. However, amid descending gloom for the retail sector, the share price had fallen to £11.08. The amount spent acquiring 26 million shares at the old price would have bought 46 million at the new, lower price. Obviously, those shareholders who did sell benefited significantly, but the remaining 89 per cent would have been far better off had the firm distributed its surplus cash as a dividend. In 2008, Next did raise its dividend by 15 per cent.

Further consolation for shareholders was that directors missed out on performance-related bonuses amounting to around £13 million.

The following FT articles set out how Apple decided it would commence paying dividends for the first time since 1995 and return cash to shareholders by way of a buy-back.

Apple gains as it prepares to make dividend payments

Technology stocks pushed the S&P 500 to another cyclical high yesterday as Apple once again dominated investor attention, saying it would begin making dividend payments for the first time since 1995.

Apple, the largest company in the world by market capitalisation, said it would return some of its estimated $100bn cash stockpile to shareholders by making quarterly dividend payments of $2.65 and spending up to $10bn on share repurchases.

The shares rose 2.7 per cent to close above the $600 mark at $601.10 for the first time in the company's history.

Source: Based on Arash Massoudi, *Financial Times*, 20 March 2012, p. 34.

Apple to return extra $55bn to investors and raise dividend 15%

Apple said it would return an additional $55bn to shareholders by the end of 2015, increasing its quarterly dividend by 15 per cent and boosting its share buy-back programme, after pressure from investors amid a falling share price.

The announcement of what Apple called the 'largest single share repurchase authorisation in history' came as it reported better than expected results for its second quarter.

Earlier this year, the company was targeted by activist shareholder David Einhorn, when his hedge fund Green-

light Capital sued Apple in his drive for greater returns of its cash pile to investors. Tim Cook, Apple chief executive, said in February he and the board were in 'very, very active discussions' about proposals for a new kind of high-yielding stock, increased dividend and other ideas for dispersing its cash hoard.

Source: Based on Tim Bradshaw, *Financial Times*, 24 April 2013, p. 1.

Icahn defeated in effort to force $50bn Apple buy-back

Carl Icahn has conceded defeat in his attempt to force Apple to return more of its $160bn cash pile to shareholders. The activist investor withdrew his proposal that Apple spend $50bn on share buy-backs before the end of September after the shareholder advisory firm ISS urged investors to vote against it, making a defeat likely at Apple's annual meeting this month.

The iPhone maker has already spent $14bn in buy-backs during the past two weeks, which has led some analysts to expect an expanded cash allocation scheme. Apple has said it will revisit its dividend and buy-back policy in March or April.

Tim Cook, Apple's chief executive, said last week that the company had launched the 'opportunistic' $14bn repurchase in light of an 8 per cent one-day share price decline after the Silicon Valley company released its earnings report. The buy-backs mean that Apple has now spent more than $60bn of a planned $100bn earmarked to return to shareholders through share repurchases and dividend payments.

Source: Based on Tim Bradshaw and Stephen Foley, *Financial Times*, 11 February 2014, p. 15.

Self-assessment activity 17.8

Suggest some arguments *against* share repurchases.

(Answer in Appendix A at the back of the book)

17.9 THE DIVIDEND PUZZLE

So where does all this leave us at a practical level? We encounter a dilemma known as the 'dividend puzzle'. Dividend cuts are generally viewed as undesirable, yet dividend payments may not always be in the best interests of shareholders. For example, under many tax regimes, dividends are immediately taxed, while the tax on capital gains can be deferred indefinitely. Dividend distribution may force a firm subsequently to issue equity or debt instruments which incur issue costs and interfere with gearing ratios (see Chapter 18). However, markets do react favourably to news of unexpectedly high dividend increases despite the acknowledged costs of dividends. The message conveyed by firms when raising dividends seems to be:

> Despite the cash flow costs of dividend payments, we are prepared to pay higher dividends because we are confident of our ability to withstand these costs and at least to maintain these higher disbursements.

■ The case for a stable dividend policy

Astute financial managers appreciate that different shareholders have different needs. A financial institution reliant on a stream of income to match its stream of liabilities will prefer stable dividends, while a 'gross fund' (i.e. one exempt from tax on its income) will prefer shares that offer a high level of dividends. The private individual in the 40 per cent tax bracket will prefer capital gains, at least up to the £11,000 exemption limit (2014–15), while the old-age pensioner with a relatively short time horizon is likely to seek income rather than capital appreciation.

Given the wide diffusion of shareholdings, it is almost impossible for most financial managers to begin to assess the needs of all their shareholders. This is a powerful argument for a stable dividend policy, e.g. the application of a fairly constant rate of dividend increase, implying that dividends rise at the same rate as corporate post-tax earnings, subject perhaps to the proviso that dividends should not be allowed to fall, unless earnings suffer a serious reverse. This will enable shareholders to gravitate towards companies whose payout policies suit their particular income needs and tax positions. In this way, companies can expect to build up a clientéle of shareholders attracted by a particular dividend pattern. Hardly surprising, then, that 75 per cent of FDs in the 3i survey said that 'Companies should aim for a consistent payout ratio.'

Kimberly-Clark: stability in an uncertain world

Cast your eyes over Kimberly-Clark's product portfolio and see your whole dreary life spooling out before you. Millions of dirty nappies. Uncounted messes mopped with paper towels. Decades of noses blown into tissues. Discreet, absorbent undergarments in which to shuffle about the old folks' home. Finally, the disposable masks and gowns worn by the hospital staff as they see you into the next world.

Companies that meet gritty human needs have been popular with investors recently and Kimberly-Clark has done particularly well. Its shares have returned nearly 75 per cent over two years, whipping the broader market and consumer stocks generally. The company's desirable characteristics include a large and stable dividend (capturing erstwhile fixed-income investors as they flee low bond yields) and staple products that appeal to stock investors still frightened about the economy. Kimberly-Clark reliably converts all of its earnings into cash, which it then spends on dividends and share buy-backs (and the odd acquisition). The company's first-quarter results, released yesterday, were characteristically solid: sales and profits ahead of expectations and a slight bump up for the earnings outlook. The stock gained 4 per cent.

Source: Based on Lex Column, *Financial Times*, 20 April 2013, p. 16.

Self-assessment activity 17.9

Rehearse the arguments in favour of a stable dividend policy.

(Answer in Appendix A at the back of the book)

However, the notion of consistency in dividend policy took a knock during the recession years of the late 2000s. Many firms cut dividends to conserve cash, and instituted a programme of cost-cutting to improve productivity, profitability and cash flow. As a result of their economy, 'blue chip' firms, in particular, found themselves sitting on substantial cash piles at the start of 2011. Given the great uncertainty in the economy following the financial crisis, it is not surprising that companies such as Kimberly-Clark (in the last cameo) have been attractive to investors. Kimberly-Clark makes products we all need and pays stable dividends based on this. For investors this provides some degree of certainty in an uncertain world.

17.10 CONCLUSIONS

What advice can be offered to practising financial managers? We suggest the following guidelines:

1 Remember the capacity of ill-advised dividend decisions to inflict damage. In view of the market's often savage reaction to dividend cuts, managers should operate a safe dividend cover, allowing sufficient payout flexibility should earnings decline. This suggests a commitment to a clientèle of shareholders who have come to expect a particular dividend policy from their company. This, in turn, suggests a long-term payout ratio sufficient to satisfy shareholder needs, but also generating sufficient internal funds to finance 'normal' investment requirements. Any 'abnormal' financing needs can be met by selling securities, rather than by dividend cuts. In the long term, it seems prudent to minimise reliance on external finance, but not to the extent of building up a 'cash mountain'. This may merely signal to the financial world that the company has run out of acceptable investment projects. If there is no worthwhile alternative use of capital, then dividends should be paid.

2 If an alteration in dividend policy is proposed, the firm should minimise the shock effect of an unanticipated dividend cut, e.g. by explaining in advance the firm's investment programme and its financing needs.

3 In an efficient capital market, the dividend announcement, 'good' or 'bad', will be immediately impounded into share price in an unbiased fashion. News of higher dividends will lead to a higher share price because it conveys the information that management believes there is a strong likelihood of higher future earnings and dividends. In view of this, many observers argue that the primary role of dividend policy should be to communicate information to a security market otherwise starved of hard financial data about future company prospects and intrinsic value, while pursuing a year-by-year distribution rate that does not conflict with the interests of the existing clientèle of shareholders.

4 While it is impossible to be definitive in this area, the following box lists the circumstances in which shareholders are likely to prefer dividends to retention and hence, when a dividend increase may raise share price.

5 Finally, the dividend decision is 'only' a financing decision, insofar as paying a dividend may necessitate alternative arrangements for financing investment projects. There can be few companies (at least, quoted ones) for which dividends have constrained really worthwhile investment. For most companies, it is often sensible to adopt a modest target payout ratio. It is not wise to pay large dividends and then have to incur the costs of raising equity from the very same shareholders.

The final cameo is an article that discusses the 'dividend puzzle', applying much of the theory discussed in this chapter.

Where dividends fit in the financial puzzle

Dividends should not matter, and yet they evidently do. This enduring puzzle of finance is very relevant now, as low yields on bonds combine with big cash piles on balance sheets to drive ever louder calls for higher dividends. New research might just provide a resolution.

That dividends really should not matter is not an over-elaborated financial theory, but rather something closer to a mathematical identity. If a company pays out cash, that cash is no longer on its balance sheet. The book value of the company (its assets minus its liabilities) reduces by the amount it has paid out. Cash belongs to shareholders whether it is on the balance sheet or paid out in a cheque.

If shareholders want to raise cash, they can withdraw as much cash as they need – when they need it – by selling shares.

It is not always quite as simple as this. Broking commissions make a difference. If capital gains and dividend income are taxed differently, investors may have a preference for dividends, or – more often – for share buy-backs.

Some successful stocks do not pay dividends. Microsoft was the success story of the 1980s and 1990s without ever paying a dividend. Now that it pays out lots of cash, its performance is mediocre. Neither Google nor Warren Buffett's Berkshire Hathaway pay dividends – and nobody complains.

But against this, dividends do to some extent reflect the vital issue of trust. They are a fixed data point. Mess with accounting conventions and you can change a company's earnings, but not the amount written on a dividend cheque. Once money has been paid out, the company's managers can no longer misuse it.

And then there is the evidence, which shows that higher yielding stocks (which pay out a higher proportionate dividend) deliver a much greater total return over time. Research for Credit Suisse by Elroy Dimson, Paul Marsh and Roy Staunton of the London Business School rams this home.

In the long term, stock investment is all about dividends. Invest $1 in the US in 1900, and its capital value alone would have reached $217 by the end of last year – an annualised gain of 5 per cent. Take dividends and reinvest them, however, and it would have been worth $21,766, or an annualised return of 9.4 per cent. The same point holds for all markets around the world – as the professors put it, 'for the seriously long-term investor, the value of a portfolio corresponds closely to the present value of dividends'.

Over time, dividend growth has barely kept pace with inflation, and yields have fallen – maybe reflecting a growing appreciation that dividends should not matter. Since 1900, the price/dividend ratio (the inverse of the dividend yield) has risen by 0.48 per cent per year. Thus less generous payouts have not, over time, meant worse returns for shareholders.

But in general, periods of growth for stocks correlate with periods of growth for dividends. Dividend growth is a symptom of other good things for equity investors.

What is fascinating, though, is that higher-yielding companies do outperform low-yielding stocks. In the UK, a strategy of buying the higher yielding 50 of the 100 biggest stocks each year crushes a strategy of buying the lower yielding 50. £1 invested in 1900 in low-yielders would now be £5,122; it would have turned into £100,160 in high-yielders.

Since 1975, high-yielders have outperformed low-yielders in 20 of 21 countries (New Zealand, a small market, is the only exception), by an average of 4.4 percentage points per year. Since 2000, just before the dot-com crash, this excess has been 9.1 percentage points. Among nations, high-yielding countries outperformed low-yielding ones.

If dividends do not matter, how can yield possibly make such a difference? High-yielders were no riskier than other stocks, and the differences are too big to explain by chance, or by tax effects. So the best explanation is the 'value effect'. Buy stocks when they are too cheap, and they will perform better. A high dividend yield, like a low price/earnings multiple, is a sign that the market is undervaluing a stock.

Dividends, 1900–2010
Per cent

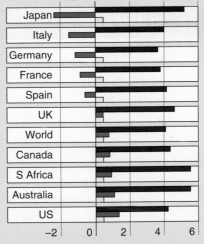

Source: Credit Suisse; London Business School.

In conclusion, a company's dividend-paying record, as it refers to the chances that it can disburse cash to shareholders in the future, is relevant. (Thus Google, which is a great bet to disgorge a lot of cash over the decades to come, is worth buying, even though it is yet to pay out anything.) It is a good way to find value, so there is money to be made by biasing your portfolio towards high-yielding stocks. Dividends do, in this sense, matter.

But the fact remains that if you need cash, you can equally easily get it by selling shares. And if you want a company to pay out a dividend because you don't trust management to treat cash responsibly – you should ask why you invested in the first place.

Credit Suisse Global Investment Returns Yearbook 2011. Contact London Business School at prowham@london.edu.

Dividends are likely to be higher:

- The greater the shareholders' reliance on current income.
- The more difficult it is to generate home-made dividends.
- The greater the impact of imperfections, e.g. brokerage fees.
- The lower are income taxes compared to capital gains taxes.
- The lower the costs of a rights issue.
- The greater the ease of reinvestment by shareholders.
- The more often that past dividend increases have heralded subsequent earnings and dividend increases.

SUMMARY

We have reviewed the competing arguments regarding the relative desirability of paying out dividends to shareholders and retaining funds to finance investment, resulting in capital gains.

Key points

- The market value of a company ultimately depends on its dividend-paying capacity.
- The irrelevance or residual theory of dividends argues that, under perfect capital market conditions, an alteration in the pattern of dividend payouts has no impact on company value, once the effect of the investment decision is removed.
- If retentions are used to finance worthwhile investment, company value increases, both for one-off retentions and for sustained retention to finance an ongoing investment programme.
- Failure to retain profits can damage shareholder interests if the company has better investment opportunities than shareholders, unless outside capital sources are available and utilised.
- Dividend irrelevance implies that shareholders are indifferent between dividends and capital gains, because the latter can be converted into income.
- In practice, various market imperfections, especially transactions costs and taxes, interfere with this conclusion, although it is difficult to be categoric about the net directional impact.
- Companies are generally unable to detect shareholder preferences, so they should follow a stable dividend policy, designed to suit a particular category, or 'clientèle', of shareholders.
- In practice, companies are reluctant to cut dividends for fear of adverse interpretation by the market of the information conveyed in the announcement.
- Similarly, companies are reluctant to increase dividends too sharply for fear of encouraging over-optimistic expectations about future performance.
- This 'information content' in dividend decisions provides a further argument for dividend stability.
- The advice regarding share re-purchases has to be 'use with care'.

Further reading

Firstly, a couple of health warnings. Fashions change in distribution policy, so important references that report the 'state-of-the-art' can quickly become out of date. Similarly, because of different tax regimes, the relevance of, for example, US studies in the UK context may be limited. However, some references are timeless. The best starting point is Gordon's first article (1959), followed by the original MM analysis, and Gordon's rejoinder (1963). Lintner (1956) was the first to reveal the smoothing strategy, and Brennan (1971) and Black (1976) present interesting discussions of the 'state of play' as the debate on dividend policy developed.

Bhattacharya (1979) gives a good analysis of the 'bird-in-the-hand fallacy'. Among the important studies that analyse signalling and the information content of corporate distribution announcements are Pettit (1972), Watts (1973), Vermaelen (1981), Healy and Palepu (1988), Asquith and Mullins (1986) and Bernatzi *et al.* (1997). Among more recent contributions that examine current trends are Fama and French (2001), an article and a case study respectively by Dobbs and Rehm (2006), and Wood (2006), published in Rutterford *et al.* (2006) give an up-to-date perspective on alterative distribution methods in the UK.

Benito and Young (2001) analyse reasons for dividend cuts and omissions. Pettit (2001) gives a highly readable assessment of the advantages and dangers of share buy-backs. Copeland *et al.* (2013) give a thorough analysis of the competing theories. Emery and Finnerty (1997) also contains two good chapters.

Becker *et al.* (2011) examine how older investors have a preference for investing in shares that pay higher dividends. Hence, they investigate the dividend clientèle effect and how demographics can affect the dividend policy. Shao *et al.* (2010) analyse the impact of national culture on dividend policy across a group of 21 countries and for the period 1995–2007.

Appendix
HOME-MADE DIVIDENDS

Kirkstall plc is financed solely by equity. Its cash flow from existing operations is expected to be £24 million p.a. in perpetuity, all of which has hitherto been paid as dividend. Shareholders require a return of 12 per cent. Kirkstall has previously issued 50 million shares. The value of the dividend stream is:

$$V_0 = \frac{£24m}{0.12} = £200m, \text{ yielding share price of } \frac{£200m}{50m} = £4 \text{ (ex-div)}$$

Imagine you hold 1 per cent of Kirkstall's equity, worth £2 million. This yields an annual dividend income of £240,000, all of which you require to support your lavish lifestyle. Kirkstall proposes to pass the dividend payable in one year's time in order to invest in a project offering a single net cash flow after a further year of £40 million, when the previous 100 per cent payout policy will be resumed. Your new expected dividend flow is:

Year 1	Year 2	Year 3
0	£240,000 + (1% × £40m) = £640,000	£240,000

The market value of Kirkstall rises to:

$$V_0 = 0 = \frac{£64m}{(1.12)^2} + \left[\frac{£24m}{(0.12)} \times \frac{1}{(1.12)^2} \right]$$
$$= (£51.02m + £159.44m) = £210.46m$$

The increase in value reflects the NPV of the project. Share price rises from £4 to £4.21, thus raising the value of your holding from £2 million to £2.104 million. To support your living standards, you could either borrow on the strength of the higher expected dividend in Year 2 or sell part of your share stake in Year 1, when no dividend is proposed.

In Year 1, the value of your holding will be £2.356 million, and each share will be priced at £4.71. To provide sufficient capital to finance expenditure of £240,000, you need to sell £240,000/£4.71 = 50,955 shares, reducing your holding to (500,000 − 50,955) = 449,045 shares. In Year 2, Kirkstall will distribute a dividend of £64 million (£1.28 per share), of which your share will be £574,778. Out of this, you will require £240,000 for immediate consumption, leaving you better off by £334,778. This may be used to restore your previous shareholding, and thus your previous flow of dividends. The ex-dividend share price in Year 2 will settle back to £4, at which price, the repurchase of 50,955 shares will require an outlay of £203,820, leaving you a surplus of (£334,778 − £203,820) = £130,958. The net effect of your transactions is to yield an income flow of:

Year	1	2	3, etc.
Dividend paid by company	0	£574,778	£240,000
Market transaction	£240,000	(£203,820)	
Net income	£240,000	£370,958	£240,000

Overall, your shareholding remains the same, and you earn extra income in Year 2 of £130,958. This has a present value of £104,000, the very amount of your wealth increase when Kirkstall first announced details of the project, i.e.

$$1\% \times \text{change in market value} = 1\% \times (£210.41\text{m} − £200\text{m}) = £104,000$$

(Note that rounding errors account for minor deviations.)

QUESTIONS

Questions with a **coloured number** have solutions in Appendix B on page 799.

1 Tom plc follows a residual dividend policy. It has just announced earnings of £10 million and is to pay a dividend of 20p per share. Its nominal issued share capital is £5 million with par value of 50p. What value of capital expenditure is it undertaking? (You may ignore taxes.)

2 Dick plc faces the following marginal efficiency of investment profile. All projects are indivisible.

Project	IRR (%)	Required outlay (£m)
A	15	3
B	24	5
C	40	2
D	12	4
E	21	7

Dick's shareholders require a return of 20 per cent. Dick has just reported earnings of £9 million. What amount of dividend would you recommend if Dick is unable to raise external finance?

3 Harry plc prides itself on its consistent dividend policy. Past data suggests that its target dividend payout ratio is 50 per cent of earnings. However, when earnings increase, Harry invariably raises its dividend only halfway towards the level that the target dividend payout ratio would indicate. The last dividend was £1 per share and Harry has just announced earnings for the recently ended financial year of £3 per share.

What dividend per share would you expect the Board to recommend?

4 Tamas plc, which is ungeared, earned pre-tax accounting profits of £30 million in the financial year just ended. Replacement investment will match last year's depreciation of £2 million. Both are fully tax-allowable.

Corporation tax is payable at 30 per cent. Tamas operates a 50 per cent dividend payout policy, and has previously issued 100 million shares, with par value of 25 pence each. Its shareholders require a return of 15 per cent p.a. Tamas holds £15 million cash balances.

Required
Determine the market price per ordinary share of Tamas, both cum-dividend and ex-dividend.
(N.B. Use the perpetuity formula to value Tamas' shares.)

5 Galahad plc, a quoted manufacturer of textiles, has followed a policy in recent years of paying out a steadily increasing dividend per share as shown below:

Year	EPS	Dividend (net)	Cover
2010	11.8p	5.0p	2.4
2011	12.5p	5.5p	2.3
2012	14.6p	6.0p	2.4
2013	13.5p	6.5p	2.1
2014	16.0p	7.3p	2.2

Galahad has only just made the 2014 dividend payment, so the shares are quoted ex-dividend. The main board, which is responsible for strategic planning decisions, is considering a major change in strategy whereby greater financing will be provided by internal funds, involving a cut in the 2015 dividend to 5p (net) per share. The investment projects thus funded will increase the growth rate of Galahad's earnings and dividends to 14 per cent. Some operating managers, however, feel that the new growth rate is unlikely to exceed 12 per cent. Galahad's shareholders seek an overall return of 16 per cent.

Required

(a) Calculate the market price per share for Galahad, prior to the change in policy, using the Dividend Growth Model.

(b) Assess the likely impact on Galahad's share price of the proposed policy change.

(c) Determine the break-even growth rate.

(d) Discuss the possible reaction of Galahad's shareholders and of the capital market in general to this proposed dividend cut in the light of Galahad's past dividend policy.

6 Laceby manufactures agricultural equipment and is currently all-equity financed. In previous years, it has paid out a steady 50 per cent of available earnings as dividend and used retentions to finance investment in new projects, which have returned 16 per cent on average.

Its Beta is 0.83, and the return on the market portfolio is expected to be 17 per cent in the future, offering a risk premium of 6 per cent.

Laceby has just made earnings of £8 million before tax and the dividend will be paid in a few weeks' time. Some managers argue in favour of retaining an extra £2 million this year in order to finance the development of a new Common Agricultural Policy (CAP) surplus crop disposal machine. This may offer the following returns under the listed possible scenarios:

	Probability	Cash flow (£m p.a.) (pre-tax)
WTO talks succeed	0.2	0.5
No reform of CAP	0.6	1.5
CAP extended to Eastern Europe	0.2	4.0

The project may be assumed to have an infinite life, and to attract an EU agricultural efficiency grant of £1 million. Corporation Tax is paid at 33 per cent (assume no tax delay).

Required

(a) What is the NPV of the proposed project?

(b) Value the equity of Laceby:

    (i) before undertaking the project,

    (ii) after announcing the acceptance of the project.

(c) Assuming you have found an increase in value in (b)(ii), explain what conditions would be required to support such a conclusion.

7 Pavlon plc has recently obtained a listing on the Stock Exchange. Ninety per cent of the company's shares were previously owned by members of one family, but, since the listing, approximately 60 per cent of the issued shares have been owned by other investors.

Pavlon's earnings and dividends for the five years prior to the listing are detailed below:

Years prior to listing	Profit after tax (£)	Dividend per share (pence)
5	1,800,000	3.60
4	2,400,000	4.80
3	3,850,000	6.16
2	4,100,000	6.56
1	4,450,000	7.12
Current year	5,500,000	(estimate)

The number of issued ordinary shares was increased by 25 per cent three years prior to the listing and by 50 per cent at the time of the listing. The company's authorised capital is currently £25,000,000 in 25p ordinary shares, of which 40,000,000 shares have been issued. The market value of the company's equity is £78,000,000.

The board of directors is discussing future dividend policy. An interim dividend of 3.16p per share was paid immediately prior to the listing and the finance director has suggested a final dividend of 2.34p per share.

The company's declared objective is to maximise shareholder wealth.

The company's profit after tax is generally expected to increase by 15 per cent p.a. for three years, and 8 per cent per year after that. Pavlon's cost of equity capital is estimated to be 12 per cent per year. Dividends may be assumed to grow at the same rate as profits.

Required

(a) Comment upon the nature of the company's dividend policy prior to the listing and discuss whether such a policy is likely to be suitable for a company listed on the Stock Exchange.

(b) Discuss whether the proposed final dividend of 2.34 pence is likely to be appropriate:
  (i) if the majority of shares are owned by wealthy private individuals;
  (ii) if the majority of shares are owned by institutional investors.

(c) Using the Dividend Valuation Model give calculations to indicate whether Pavlon's shares are currently undervalued or overvalued.

(d) Briefly outline the weaknesses of the Dividend Valuation Model.

(ACCA)

8 Mondrian plc is a newly formed company which aims to maximise the wealth of its shareholders. The board of directors of the company is currently trying to decide upon the most appropriate dividend policy to adopt for the company's shareholders. However, there is strong disagreement between three of the directors concerning the benefits of declaring cash dividends:

Director A argues that cash dividends would be welcomed by investors, and that as high a dividend payout ratio as possible would reflect positively on the market value of the company's shares.

Director B argues that whether a cash dividend is paid or not is irrelevant in the context of shareholder wealth maximisation.

Director C takes an opposite view to Director A and argues that dividend payments should be avoided as they would lead to a decrease in shareholder wealth.

Required

(a) Discuss the arguments for and against the position taken by each of the three directors.

(b) Assuming the board of directors decides to pay a dividend to shareholders, what factors should be taken into account when determining the level of dividend payment?

(ACCA Certified Diploma June 1996)

Practical assignment

Obtain the Annual Report and Accounts of any firm of your choice. Look at the five-year record provided, and work out the dividend cover each year and the annual rate of dividend per share increase as compared to the annual increase in EPS. Is there any obvious pattern to the dividend decisions over this period? Does the firm have a clear dividend policy?

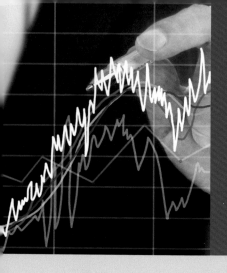

18

Capital structure and the required return

Sugar high – dangerous debt levels

As snow fell in New York City on a December afternoon, waiters bearing trays of cookies fanned out among the group of bankers and investors gathered at the New York Athletic Club. The sweet biscuits were courtesy of Leonard Tannenbaum, chief executive of Fifth Street Management, who had a message for those attending the financial conference. 'I believe there's another cycle coming,' said Mr Tannenbaum. 'So have the cookie. I want you to enjoy the sugar high – while it lasts.'

US credit markets rebounded in 2013 as a flood of central bank money and continued low interest rates pushed investors into riskier but higher-yielding assets. To the sceptics, the market is experiencing the kind of frothiness seen before the 2008 financial crisis. This, too, will end in tears, they warn.

Perhaps the foremost of these 'credit Cassandras' is Jeremy Stein, the US Federal Reserve governor who warned in February that markets may be overheating. 'A prolonged period of low interest rates, of the sort we are experiencing today, can create incentives for agents to take on greater duration or credit risks, or to employ additional financial leverage, in an effort to 'reach for yield', he said.

Issuance of syndicated leveraged loans – those made to companies that already carry high debt loads – reached $535.2bn in 2013. That is just shy of the $604.2bn sold in 2007, at the height of the last credit bubble. Meanwhile, loans that come with fewer protections for lenders, known as 'covenant-lite', accounted for almost 60 per cent of loans sold in 2013, compared with a 25 per cent share in 2007. Sales of 'payment-in-kind' notes, which give borrowers an option to repay lenders with more debt, reached $11.5bn in 2012 – a post-crisis high. Sales of 'junk', or high-yield, bonds surged to a record in 2013 as companies rushed to refinance and investors snapped up the resulting assets. Issuance of junk bonds rated 'triple C' – the lowest designation – jumped to $15.3bn, surpassing the pre-crisis peak.

Source: Based on Tracy Alloway and Michael Mackenzie, *Financial Times*, 2 January 2014, p. 7.

Learning objectives

This chapter has the following aims:

- To explain some of the ways of measuring gearing.
- To enable you to understand more fully the advantages of debt capital.
- To explain the meaning of, and how to calculate, the Weighted Average Cost of Capital (WACC).
- To enable you to understand the likely limits on the use of debt, and the nature of 'financial distress' costs.
- To help you understand the issues involved in financing foreign operations.
- To enable you to understand the factors that a finance manager should consider when framing capital structure policy.

18.1 INTRODUCTION

Most financing decisions in practice reduce to a choice between debt and equity. The finance manager wishing to fund a new project, but reluctant to cut dividends or to make a rights issue, has to consider the borrowing option. In this chapter, we further examine the arguments for and against using debt to finance company activities and, in particular, consider the impact of gearing on the overall rate of return that the company must achieve.

The main advantages of debt capital centre on its relative cost. Debt capital is usually cheaper than equity because:

1 The pre-tax rate of interest is invariably lower than the return required by shareholders. This is due to the legal position of lenders who have a prior claim on the distribution of the company's income and who, in a liquidation, precede ordinary shareholders in the queue for the settlement of claims. Debt is usually secured on the firm's assets, which can be sold to pay off lenders in the event of **default**, i.e. failure to pay interest and capital according to the pre-agreed schedule.

2 Debt interest can be set against profit for tax purposes, reducing the effective cost.

3 The administrative and issuing costs are normally lower, e.g. underwriters are not always required, although legal fees are usually involved.

default
The failure by a borrower to adhere to a pre-agreed schedule of interest and/or capital payments on a loan

The downside of debt is that high borrowing levels can lead to the risk of inability to meet debt interest payments during poor trading conditions. This often leads to managers having to pay more attention to managing the debt position than to managing actual business operations and strategy. Shareholders are thus exposed to a second tier of risk above the inherent business risk of the trading activity. As a result, rational shareholders seek additional compensation for this extra exposure. In brief, debt is desirable because it is relatively cheap, but there may be limits to the prudent use of debt financing because, although posing relatively low risk to the lender, it can be highly risky for the borrower, i.e. the risk is two-sided.

In general, larger, well-established companies are likely to have a greater ability to borrow because they generate more reliable streams of income, enhancing their ability to service (make interest payments on) debt capital. Ironically, in practice, we often find that small developing companies that should not over-rely on debt capital are forced to do so through sheer inability to raise equity, while larger enterprises often operate with what appear to be very conservative gearing ratios compared to their borrowing capacities. Against this, we often encounter cases of over-geared enterprises that thought their borrowing levels were safe until they were caught out by adverse trading conditions.

So is there a 'correct' level of debt? Quite how much companies should borrow is another puzzle in the theory of business finance. There are cogent arguments for and against the extensive use of debt capital, and academics have developed sophisticated models which attempt to expose and analyse the key theoretical relationships.

For many years, it was thought advantageous to borrow so long as the company's capacity to service the debt was unquestioned. The result would be higher earnings per share and higher share value, provided the finance raised was invested sensibly. The dangers of excessive levels of borrowing would be forcibly articulated by the stock market by a downrating of the shares of a highly geared company. The so-called 'traditional' view of gearing centres on the concept of an **optimal capital structure** which maximised company value. However, while the critical gearing ratio is thought to depend on factors such as the steadiness of the company's cash flow and the saleability of its assets, it has proved to be like the Holy Grail, highly desirable, but illusory and difficult to grasp. Some academics felt that a firmer theoretical underpinning was needed to facilitate the analysis of capital structure decisions and to offer more helpful guidelines to practising managers.

optimal capital structure
The financing mix that minimises the overall cost of finance and maximises market value

■ The Modigliani and Miller contribution

When Nobel laureates Modigliani and Miller (MM) published their seminal paper in 1958, finance academics began to examine in depth the relationship between borrowing and company value. MM's work on the pure theory of capital structure initially suggested that company value was unaffected by gearing. This conclusion prompted a furore of critical opposition, leading eventually to a coherent theory of capital structure, the current version of which looks remarkably like the traditional view.

traditional theory of capital structure
The theory that an optimal capital structure exists, where the WACC is minimised and market value is maximised

Because this is a complex topic, we have organised the treatment of the impact of gearing into two chapters. This chapter is mainly devoted to the **'traditional' theory of capital structure** and the issue of how much a company should borrow. In Chapter 19, we deepen the analysis by discussing the 'modern' theory. However, the present chapter gives a strong flavour of the main issues involved.

The two chapters together are designed to examine the following issues:

- How is gearing measured?
- Why do companies use debt capital?
- How is the cost of debt capital measured?
- What are the dangers of debt capital? How do shareholders react to 'high' levels of gearing?
- What do the competing theories of capital structure tell us about optimal financing decisions?
- How does taxation affect the analysis?
- What overall return should be achieved by a company using debt?
- What practical guidelines can we offer to financial managers?

18.2 MEASURES OF GEARING

capital gearing
The mixture of debt and equity in a firm's capital structure, which influences variations in shareholders' profits in response to sales and EBIT variations

There are two basic ways to express the indebtedness of a company. **Capital gearing** indicates the proportion of debt capital in the firm's overall capital structure. **Income gearing** indicates the extent to which the company's income is pre-empted by prior interest charges. Both are indicators of **financial gearing**.

income gearing
The proportion of profit before interest and tax (PBIT) absorbed by interest charges

■ Capital gearing: alternative measures

A widely used measure of capital gearing is the ratio of all long-term liabilities (LTL), i.e. 'amounts falling due after more than one year', to shareholders' funds, as shown in the balance sheet. This purports to indicate how easily the firm can repay debts from selling assets, since shareholder funds measure net assets:

financial gearing
Includes both capital gearing and income gearing

$$\text{Capital gearing} = \frac{\text{LTL}}{\text{Shareholders' funds}}$$

There are several drawbacks to this approach.

First, the market value of equity may be considerably higher than the book value, reflecting higher asset values, so this measure may seem unduly conservative. However, the notion of market value needs to be clarified. When a company is forced to sell assets hurriedly in order to repay debts, it is by no means certain that buyers can be found to pay 'acceptable' prices. The **break-up values (BUV)** of assets are often lower than those expressed in the accounts, which assume that the enterprise is a going concern. However, using book values does at least have an element of prudence. In addition, the oscillating nature of market values may emphasise the case for conservatism, even for companies with 'safe' gearing ratios.

break-up value (BUV)
The value that can be obtained by selling off the firm's assets piecemeal to the highest bidders

A second problem is the lack of an upper limit to the ratio, which hinders inter-company comparisons. This is easily remedied by expressing long-term liabilities as a fraction of all forms of long-term finance, thus setting the upper limit at 100 per cent. The gearing measure would become:

$$\frac{\text{LTL}}{\text{LTL} + \text{Shareholders' funds}}$$

A third problem is the treatment of provisions made out of previous years' income. Technically, provisions represent expected future liabilities. Companies provide for contingencies, such as claims under product guarantees, as a matter of prudence. Provisions thus result from a charge against profits and result in lower stated equity. However, some provisions turn out to be unduly pessimistic, and may be written back into profits, and hence equity, in later years. A good example is the provision made for deferred taxation. This is a highly prudent device to provide for possible tax liability if the firm were to sell its fixed assets before the end of their initially anticipated working lives.

Provisions could thus be treated as either equity or debt according to the degree of certainty of the anticipated contingency. If the liability is 'highly certain', it is reasonable to treat it as debt, but if the provision is the result of ultra-prudence, it may be treated as equity. For example, deferred taxation is a provision against the possibility of incurring a corporation tax charge if assets are sold above their written-down value for tax purposes. For most firms, this risk will diminish over time and the provision could safely be treated as equity. In practice, company accounts carry a mixture of provisions of varying degrees of certainty, and it is tempting to delete provisions from liabilities but not to include them in equity when expressing the gearing ratio. However, the nature of provisions should be questioned when the item appears substantial. Adjusted to exclude provisions, the capital gearing ratio becomes:

$$\frac{\text{Long-term borrowings (LTB)}}{\text{Shareholders' funds}} \quad \text{or} \quad \frac{\text{LTB}}{\text{LTB} + \text{Shareholders' funds}}$$

Arguably, any borrowing figure should take into account both long-term and short-term borrowing. Many companies depend heavily on short-term borrowing, especially bank overdrafts, and having to repay these debts quickly would place a significant burden on both the cash flow and liquidity of such companies. For this reason, some firms present their gearing ratios inclusive of such liabilities. For example, BP's (**www.bp.com**) measure of gearing focuses on 'finance debt', i.e. borrowing via the financial markets and from financial institutions:

$$\frac{\text{Finance debt}}{\text{Finance debt} + \text{Shareholders' funds}}$$

There are two objections to this approach. First, since short-term borrowing can be volatile, the year-end figure in the balance sheet is not always a reliable guide to short-term debts. However, many companies effectively use their bank overdraft as a long-term form of finance. In other words, the actual bank overdraft figure may include a hard core element of long-term debt and a fluctuating component, although it is not easy to separate these two items from external examination of the accounts.

Second, it may be argued that any holdings of cash and highly liquid, marketable securities ('near cash' assets) should be offset against short-term debt, to yield a measure of **net debt**. For example, BP expresses it thus:

net debt
A firm's net borrowing including both long-term and also short-term debt, offset by cash holdings. Expressed either in absolute terms, or in relation to owner's equity

$$\text{Net debt} = \frac{\text{Finance debt} - (\text{cash and liquid resources})}{\text{Equity}}$$

In fact, financial commentators increasingly use this measure of gearing, which is shown in the annual reports of many companies, expressed either in absolute terms or in relation to equity.

Self-assessment activity 18.1

Determine the following gearing ratios using the information supplied.

(i)   debt-to-equity ratio

(ii) debt-to-debt plus equity ratio

(iii) net debt

Equity = £100m

Long-term debt = £50m

Short-term debt = £20m

Cash = £10m

(Answer in Appendix A at the back of the book)

All the above measures are commonly used in the UK. In some other countries, a more direct measure of gearing (or leverage) is used. The UK ratios tend to focus on the relationship between debt and equity capital, which is reasonable since equity represents net assets. However, when necessary, debts are repaid by liquidating the assets to which the capital relates. Rather than this roundabout focus on capital, a direct focus on assets available to repay debts may give a clearer picture of ability to repay. For this purpose, many US commentators use an 'American gearing' ratio, such as:

$$\frac{\text{Total liabilities (including short-term liabilities)}}{\text{Total assets}}$$

■ Interest cover and income gearing

All the above measures purport to express the ability of the company to repay loans out of capital. However, they are only really helpful if book values and market values of the assets that would have to be sold to repay creditors approximate to each other. Yet, as we have noted, the market value of assets is volatile and difficult to assess. Moreover, capital gearing only indicates the security of creditors' funds in a crisis and may be an unduly cautious way of viewing debt exposure.

interest cover
The number of times the profit before interest exceeds loan interest

The trigger for a debt crisis is usually inability to make interest payments, and the 'front line' is therefore the size and reliability of the company's income in relation to its interest commitments. Although, in reality, cash flow is the more important consideration, the ability of a company to meet its interest obligations is usually measured by the ratio of *profit* before tax and interest, to interest charges, known as **interest cover**, or '**times interest earned**':

times interest earned
The ratio of profit before interest and tax (operating profit) to annual interest charges, i.e. how many times over the firm could meet its interest bill

$$\text{Interest cover} = \frac{\text{Profit before interest and tax}}{\text{Interest charges}}$$

Strictly, the numerator should include any interest received and the denominator should become interest outgoings. This adjustment is rarely made in practice; net interest charges are commonly used as the denominator (as we do for D.S. Smith plc below).

income gearing
The proportion of profit before interest and tax (PBIT) absorbed by interest charges

The inverse of interest cover is called **income gearing**, indicating the proportion of pre-tax earnings committed to prior interest charges. If a company earns profit before interest and tax of £20 million, and incurs interest charges of £2 million, then its interest cover is (£20m/£2m) = 10 times, and 10 per cent of profit before interest and tax is pre-empted by interest charges.

Arguably, cash flow-to-interest is a better guide to financial security, given that profits are expressed on the accruals basis, i.e., profit is recognised even though cash may not have been received yet for sales. Hence, the formula below is sometimes used:

$$\text{Cash flow cover} = \frac{\text{Operating cash flow}}{\text{Net interest payable}}$$

Self-assessment activity 18.2

Distinguish between capital gearing and income gearing. How is each measured?

(Answer in Appendix A at the back of the book)

■ Example: D.S. Smith plc's borrowings

The figures in Table 18.1 are taken from the Annual Report for D.S. Smith plc (www .dssmith.uk.com) for the year ended 30 April 2013. With these data, we can calculate various gearing indicators:

$$\frac{\text{LT borrowing}}{\text{Shareholder's funds}} = \frac{£904\text{m}}{£1,085\text{m}} = 83\%$$

$$\frac{\text{LT borrowing}}{\text{All LT funds}} = \frac{£904\text{m}}{£904\text{m} + £1,085\text{m}} = \frac{£904\text{m}}{£1,989\text{m}} = 45\%$$

$$\frac{\text{All borrowing}}{\text{Shareholder's funds}} = \frac{£904\text{m} + £58\text{m}}{£1,085\text{m}} = \frac{£962\text{m}}{£1,085\text{m}} = 89\%$$

$$\text{Net debt} = (£904\text{m} + £58\text{m} - £133\text{m}) = £829\text{m}$$
$$(76\% \text{ of equity})$$

$$\text{Interest cover} = \frac{£126\text{m}}{£36\text{m}} = 3.5 \text{ times}$$

$$\text{Income gearing} = \frac{1}{3.5} = 29\%$$

$$\frac{\text{Cash generated from operations}}{\text{Net interest payable}} = \frac{£374\text{m}}{£36\text{m}} = 10.4 \text{ times}$$

$$\frac{\text{Total liabilities}}{\text{Total assets}} = \frac{£2,521\text{m}}{£3,606\text{m}} = 70\%$$

Table 18.1 Financial data for D.S. Smith plc (2013)

	£m
Shareholders' funds (total equity)	1,085
Cash and short-term investments	133
Long-term borrowing (LTD)	904
Short-term borrowing	58
Group profit before interest and tax	126
Net financing costs	36
Total assets	3,606
Total liabilities	2,521
Cash generated from operations	374

Source: D.S. Smith plc, Annual Report, 2013

■ D.S. Smith net debt to EBITDA ratio

A further calculation that measures the gearing of a company is the ratio of net debt to EBITDA. For D.S. Smith this figure is reported in the 2013 annual report at 1.97 times. The company notes that this is below its target ratio for this calculation of 2.0 times, and significantly below a maximum of 3.25 times for its bank covenants. It is now common for bank covenants to stipulate a maximum net debt to EBITDA ratio.

Self-assessment activity 18.3

Obtain the accounts of a firm of your choice and conduct a similar exercise to the D.S. Smith plc calculations.

18.3 OPERATING AND FINANCIAL GEARING

A major reason for using debt is to enhance or 'gear up' shareholder earnings. When a company is financially geared, variations in the level of earnings due to changes in trading conditions generate a more than proportional variation in earnings attributable to shareholders if the interest charges are fixed. This effect is very similar to that exerted by **operating gearing** (see Chapter 10). We will now examine these two gearing phenomena and illustrate them numerically.

operating gearing
The proportion of fixed costs in the firm's operating cost structure

Most businesses operate with a combination of variable and fixed factors of production, giving rise to variable and fixed costs respectively. The particular combination is largely dictated by the nature of the activity and the technology involved. Operating gearing refers to the relative importance of fixed costs in the firm's cost structure, costs that have to be met regardless of output and revenue levels. In general, the higher the proportion of fixed to variable costs, the higher the firm's break-even volume of output. As sales rise above the break-even point, there will be a more than proportional upward effect on profits before interest and tax, and on shareholder earnings.

Firms with high operating gearing, mainly capital-intensive ones, are especially prone to fluctuations in the business cycle. In the downswing, as their sales volumes decrease, their earnings before interest and tax decline by a more than proportional amount, and conversely in the upswing. Hence, such companies are regarded as relatively risky. If such companies borrow, they add a second tier of fixed charges in the form of interest payments, thus increasing overall risk – the higher the interest charges, the greater the risk of inability to pay. Consequently, the risk premium required by investors in such companies is relatively high. It follows that companies that exhibit high operating gearing should use debt finance sparingly.

■ Operating and financial gearing: Burley plc

Burley plc produces and sells briefcases. It has issued 4 million 50p shares and has £2 million loan finance. Its gearing ratio, measured by the ratio of debt to equity at book values, is one-to-one (i.e. (4m × 50p)/£2m). Last year, Burley sold 60,000 units to large retailers at £30 per unit.

Its profit and loss account (income statement) is:

		£000	£000
Sales			1,800
Less:	Variable costs (VC)	(720)	
	Fixed operating costs (FC)	(480)	(1,200)
	Profit before interest and tax (PBIT)		600
Less:	Interest payable at 10%		(200)
	Profit before taxation (PBT)		400
Less:	Corporation tax at 30%		(120)
	Profit after tax (PAT)		280

The earnings per share (EPS) are:

$$\frac{\text{Profit after tax}}{\text{No of ordinary shares}} = \frac{£280,000}{4m} = 7.0p$$

contribution
Revenues (turnover) less variable costs, i.e. contribution to meeting fixed costs

Notice that the profit and loss account (income statement) hides the distinction between gross and net profit. The gross profit is the sales less variable costs, i.e. (£1,800,000 − £720,000) = £1,080,000, also called **contribution** because the fixed costs are paid from this amount. Any surplus over FC is the net or operating profit (PBIT). Operating profit is thus £600,000.

Now let us consider the break-even volume, initially ignoring the debt interest obligation. Recall that breaking even means just covering fixed operating costs and variable costs. In Burley's case, this requires an output sufficient to generate a gross margin high enough to cover the fixed operating costs of £480,000. The unit variable cost is:

(£720,000/60,000) = £12

Were it financed entirely by equity, Burley's break-even output would be found by dividing fixed cost by the gross profit margin of (£30 − £12) = £18:

(£480,000/£18) = 26,667 units

Allowing for the interest commitments of £200,000, Burley has to cover total fixed charges of (£480,000 + £200,000) = £680,000. This requires the higher output of (£680,000/£18) = 37,778 units to break even. Hence, using debt finance raises the break-even volume of production because fixed obligations are higher.

We can use this example to distinguish between operating and financial gearing. **Operating gearing** can be expressed in a variety of ways. Most simply, it is the proportion of total production cost accounted for by fixed costs: (£480,000/£1,200,000) = 40 per cent. Allowing for interest payments, Burley needs to generate a gross margin or contribution of (£480,000 + £200,000) = £680,000 to cover total fixed charges. At present, it is doing this fairly comfortably, since in percentage terms fixed charges account for (£480,000 + £200,000) ÷ £1,080,000 = 63 per cent of the contribution. Looking at the importance of financial gearing, out of its profit before interest and tax of £600,000, a third (£200,000) is required to cover interest payments, i.e. the interest cover is 3.3 times.

operating leverage
The ratio of contribution to profit before interest and tax

A more sophisticated way of viewing the impact of fixed charges is to calculate leverage ratios. **Operating leverage** is the number of times the contribution covers the profit before interest and tax (PBIT), i.e. a multiple of:

$$\frac{\text{Contribution}}{\text{PBIT}} = \frac{(\text{Sales} - \text{VC})}{\text{PBIT}} = \frac{£1,080,000}{£600,000} = 1.8 \text{ times}$$

This indicates the leeway between contribution and the PBIT, and hence the extent to which the fixed costs can increase without forcing the company into an operating loss. More significantly, the multiplier of 1.8 signifies the relationship between a given increase in sales and the resulting effect on PBIT. As we show below, a 10 per cent increase in sales will result in an increase in PBIT of 18 per cent.

financial leverage
The ratio of profit before interest and tax (PBIT) to profit before tax (PBT)

Similarly, **financial leverage** is the number of times the PBIT covers the profit before tax (PBT), i.e. a multiple of:

$$\frac{\text{PBIT}}{\text{PBT}} = \frac{£600,000}{£400,000} = 1.5 \text{ times}$$

The difference between PBIT and PBT is the interest charge, so this multiple indicates the extent to which interest charges can rise without forcing the company into pre-tax loss. More significantly, the multiplier of 1.5 magnifies the effect of operating leverage – the effect of a sales increase on PBT is greater in a financially geared firm than in one

Aircraft manufacturing operating leverage

First gold collapsed. Then premium cupcakes. Now corporate jets. Yesterday, Textron, maker of Cessna aircraft, reduced its 2013 outlook for business jet deliveries, foreseeing a decline from 2012, and brought down its earnings guidance by almost a tenth. The stock fell by 13 per cent. The depth of the guidance cut, and the reaction, might seem puzzling. Cessna accounted for a quarter of Textron's revenues last year, but only about 7 per cent of its segment profits (the company also makes helicopters and drones, among other things).

Part of the explanation is the high operating leverage in manufacturing aircraft: a little sales growth can mean a big jump in profit. Equally important, resurgence at Cessna has been long awaited, and is a key part of any bullish long-term view of Textron. The business jet market,

as JPMorgan has shown, was historically correlated with corporate profits, but jet sales have not come back as corporate earnings have boomed since the financial crisis. Cessna sold $5.6bn in aircraft in 2008; it sold $3.1bn worth in 2012.

The corporate jet is a symbol of excess some companies may be wary of, and the surge in corporate profits has less to do with growth than spending less on things like aircraft. Worse, the profit cycle appears to be turning over. Is there any reason for hope at Cessna? A key question is whether it can go where the growth is. Roughly 85 per cent of Cessna sales come from North America and Europe. If giddy corporate spending is going to blossom again soon, it is unlikely to happen there.

Source: Based on Lex Column, *Financial Times*, 18 April 2013, p. 14.

with no borrowing. Taking the two multipliers together, we obtain a combined leverage effect. In this case, a sales increase of 10 per cent will result in an increase in PBT of $(1.8 \times 1.5) = 2.7$ times as great, i.e. 27 per cent. For a given tax rate, here 30 per cent, the profit after tax and, hence, the EPS, will also rise by the same proportion.

To clarify these relationships, it is helpful to demonstrate the impact of Burley experiencing a sales increase of 10 per cent. Assuming no change in unit variable costs, the profit and loss account becomes:

		£000	£000	
Sales			1,980	(10% increase)
Less:	Variable costs (VC)	(792)		
	Fixed costs (FC)	(480)	(1,272)	
	Profit before interest and tax (PBIT)		708	(18% increase)
Less:	Interest payable at 10%		(200)	
	Profit before taxation (PBT)		508	(27% increase)
Less:	Corporation tax at 30%		(152)	
	Profit after tax (PAT)		356	(27% increase)

The new EPS is:

PAT/No. of shares = (£356,000/4m) = 8.9p (27% increase)

The increase in EPS of 27 per cent (rounded) is a far greater proportion than the sales increase, illustrating the operation of the combined gearing multiplier. It follows that the higher the proportion of fixed costs in overall costs, and the greater the commitment to interest charges, the greater will be the combined gearing effect. This may suggest that using fixed factors of production and using debt capital are both desirable things. However, as the following example demonstrates, financial gearing is double-edged. It is beneficial in favourable economic conditions, but because the gearing effect also works in reverse, it can spell trouble in adverse trading conditions.

Self-assessment activity 18.4

Show the effect on the combined gearing multiplier in the Burley example if fixed costs are £530,000 and interest charges are £240,000.

(Answer in Appendix A at the back of the book)

18.4 FINANCIAL GEARING AND RISK: LINDLEY PLC

Lindley plc retains no profit and its shareholders require a 20 per cent return. Issued share capital is £100 million, with par value of £1. Lindley's operating profit can vary as shown in Table 18.2, according to trading conditions characterised as bad, indifferent and good. These are denoted by scenarios A, B and C, which have probabilities of 0.25, 0.50 and 0.25, respectively.

Table 18.2 How gearing affects shareholder returns in Lindley plc

	Trading conditions		
	Scenario A ($p = 0.25$)	Scenario B ($p = 0.50$)	Scenario C ($p = 0.25$)
Profit before interest (PBIT)* (Net operating income)	£5m	£20m	£35m
Zero gearing (100m equity, £0m debt)			
Debt interest at 10%	—	—	—
Shareholder earnings	£5m	£20m	£35m
Return on equity (ROE)	5%	20%	35%
25% gearing (Debt/Equity $= \frac{1}{3}$) (£75m equity, £25m debt, interest 10%)			
Debt interest at 10%	£2.5m	£2.5m	£2.5m
Shareholder earnings	£2.5m	£17.5m	£32.5m
Return on equity (ROE)	3.3%	23.3%	43.3%
50% gearing (Debt/Equity $= \frac{1}{1}$) (£50m equity, £50m debt, interest 10%)			
Debt interest at 10%	£5m	£5m	£5m
Shareholder earnings	0	£15m	£30m
Return on equity (ROE)	0	30%	60%

*Taxes are ignored.

After all costs, but before deducting debt interest, earnings are £5 million, £20 million and £35 million under scenarios A, B and C, respectively. This measure of earnings is termed net operating income (NOI). (For simplicity, taxation is ignored.) Let us examine shareholder returns with gearing ratios of zero, 25 per cent and 50 per cent, measured by long-term debt (interest rate 10 per cent) to total long-term finance that is held constant at £100 million.

Notice that for a given increase in income, shareholder earnings rise by a greater proportion: for example, with gearing of 25 per cent, if NOI rises by 300 per cent from £5 million to £20 million, shareholder earnings increase by 600 per cent from £2.5 million to £17.5 million. It is easy to see why adding debt to the capital structure is called gearing – the change in earnings is magnified by a factor of 2.0 in shareholders' favour. Unfortunately, this effect also applies in a downward direction – a given proportionate fall in earnings generates a more pronounced *decrease* in shareholder earnings. Indeed, with 50 per cent gearing, under scenario A, shareholder earnings are entirely wiped out by prior interest charges. The return on equity would be negative at any higher gearing level under this scenario.

Negative returns are not necessarily fatal – companies often survive losses in especially poor trading years – but the likelihood of survival when continued trading losses combine with high fixed interest charges is lowered if the company cannot pay interest charges. In these cases, the enterprise is technically insolvent, although creditors may agree to restructure the company's capital, e.g. by converting debt into equity or preference shares. There is, however, an effective upper limit of gearing for Lindley. Beyond 50 per cent gearing, it may be unable to meet interest charges out of earnings. For practical purposes, the lower limit of earnings will dictate maximum borrowing capacity, although, in reality, this lower earnings limit is highly uncertain. This is why it is usually argued that the more reliable the company's expected cash flow stream, the greater its borrowing capacity.

Our Lindley example demonstrates that, under debt financing, although shareholders may achieve enhanced returns in good years, they stand to receive much lower returns in bad years. In other words, the residual stream of shareholder earnings exhibits greater variability. This can be examined by computing the expected value and the range, or dispersion, of the return on equity (ROE) with each of the three gearing levels.

Self-assessment activity 18.5

Calculate the expected value of Lindley's ROE under each scenario.

(Answer in Appendix A at the back of the book)

Table 18.3 shows that, although the expected value of the return on equity is greater at higher levels of gearing, the dispersion, or range, of possible returns is also wider, which might concern risk-averting shareholders. Notice also that we can decompose the overall risk incurred by shareholders into its underlying business and financial elements. Business risk refers to the likely variability in returns for an equivalent all-equity financed company, i.e. the dispersion of returns is due to underlying business-related factors. Financial risk is the additional dispersion in net returns to shareholders due to the need to meet interest charges whatever the trading conditions. At every gearing ratio, the range of returns due to business risk is unchanged – nothing has happened to its product range, its customer base or any other aspect of its trading activities. Lindley would simply share out the proceeds of its operations in different ways at different gearing ratios.

Table 18.3 How gearing affects the risk of ordinary shares

Gearing (%)	Expected ROE (%)	Total dispersion (%)	Due to: Business risk (%)	Financial risk (%)
0	20	30	30	0
25	23.3	40	30	10
50	30	60	30	30

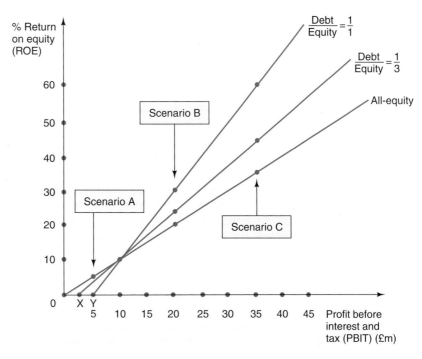

Figure 18.1 How gearing affects the ROE

It is also helpful to show the effect on ROE graphically. Figure 18.1 shows the data for Lindley's ROE for the three different capital structures. Clearly, the higher the debt-to-equity ratio, the greater the ROE for any level of profit before interest. Figure 18.1 also shows how the break-even value of profit before interest increases as gearing rises. As gearing increases from zero to 1:3 and to 1:1, the break-even earnings increase from 0 to 0X and to 0Y, corresponding to the three interest payment levels of zero, £2.5 million and £5 million respectively (Scenario A in Table 18.2 and Figure 18.1). Notice finally that earnings of £10 million would generate the same ROE under all three capital structures.

This discussion of the impact of gearing is incomplete in one important respect. The analysis has been based on book values, despite earlier remarks that gearing ratios may often be better measured in terms of market values. We have yet to consider the effect of gearing on the value of the firm – does gearing actually make shareholders better off?

To examine the effect on share price, we need to focus on the expected earnings figure and recall that the value of a share can be found by discounting its stream of earnings, in the simplest case, as a perpetuity. (No distinction is needed between earnings and dividends, as Lindley makes no retentions.) The expected values of shareholder earnings for each of the three gearing ratios are shown in Table 18.4. Recalling that Lindley's shares have a nominal value of £1, we can specify the number of shares corresponding to each gearing ratio and hence the expected value

Table 18.4 How gearing can affect share price

Gearing %	Number of shares	Expected value of shareholder earnings	EPS	Share price*
0	100m	£20m	20.0p	20.0p/0.2 = £1.00
25	75m	£17.5m	23.3p	23.3p/0.2 = £1.17
50	50m	£15m	30.0p	30.0p/0.2 = £1.50

*Share price is found by discounting the perpetual and constant EPS at 20 per cent.

of the EPS. Share prices are found by applying the valuation formula, discounting the perpetual EPS at the 20 per cent return required by Lindley's shareholders.

It appears that, by using debt capital, financial managers can achieve significant increases in shareholder wealth. However, we ought to be suspicious of this effect. Why should shareholders' wealth increase when there have been no changes in trading activity or in expected aggregate income?

The analysis assumes that shareholders are prepared to accept a return of 20 per cent at all permissible gearing levels – they seem to be unconcerned by financial risk. Even though there may be no risk of insolvency, gearing exposes shareholder earnings to greater variability. We might therefore expect shareholders to react to gearing by demanding higher returns on their capital. If they think gearing is too risky, they may sell their holdings, thus driving down the share price.

We need to examine in more detail the likely reaction of shareholders to increased gearing; we will find that this is a key element in the debate about optimal capital structure. In the next section, we examine the so-called 'traditional' view of gearing, probably still the most widely supported explanation.

Self-assessment activity 18.6

What is the effect on share price in the Lindley example if shareholders require returns of 25 per cent under 25 per cent gearing, and of 35 per cent under 50 per cent gearing?

(Answer in Appendix A at the back of the book)

Debt's all, folks

Are you too fat? Mass is an absolute measure, but the question is vexed all the same. Whatever the doctor may say, it is not as simple as taking, say, height or cholesterol into account. It is a matter of what one wants from life, and the risks one is prepared to run. Just so with corporate debt. Petrobras, for example, clearly has a debt problem. But how the problem is measured can make the Brazilian state oil company look a little chubby or morbidly obese. Start on the income statement. Can Petrobras cover its interest payments? No worries there. Operating profits covered interest payments eight times over in the nine months that ended in September.

Now compare profits to the stock of debt on the balance sheet. Net debt at Petrobras is three times its earning before interest, tax, depreciation and amortisation (EBITDA). The global average for this measure is 1.5 according to Datastream. So Petrobras's ratio seems high, but not wildly so. Private equity buyers are not spooked by ratios of four or more.

Or stick to the balance sheet, and compare the stock of debt to the stock of assets – judging what would be left to shareholders in case of liquidation. The average among the large US industrial companies is 60 per cent, according to S&P Dow Jones indices. Petrobras has 56 per cent of its equity covered by the debt. No red flag here.

But financial leverage must be seen in light of operational leverage. Oil exploration and production has high fixed costs, and revenue varies with the oil price. A price drop can change all debt ratios fast. Even other nationalised emerging oil majors have less net debt, on average, of 41 per cent of equity, and just 1.6 times ebitda.

The most important context for any measure is its trend through time. In just the first nine months of 2013, Petrobras's net debt rose from $72bn to $86bn as investment overshot earnings. All of its debt ratios are getting worse. Fat is a subjective matter, but objectively, Petrobras needs to go on a diet.

Source: Based on Lex Column, *Financial Times*, 18 February 2014, p. 14.

18.5 THE 'TRADITIONAL' VIEW OF GEARING AND THE REQUIRED RETURN

The traditional view emphasises the benefits of using relatively cheap debt capital as seen in the Lindley example: in particular, the effect on the rate of return required on investment. To analyse this approach in greater depth, we first need to make some definitions.

■ Value of an ungeared company

For an ungeared company, market value is found by discounting (or capitalising) its stream of annual earnings, E, all of which are attributable to shareholders, at the rate of return required by shareholders, k_e.

The value of an ungeared company, V_u, is simply the value of the ordinary shares, V_S. For a constant and perpetual stream of annual earnings, E:

$$V_u = V_S = \frac{E}{k_e} \quad \text{so that } k_e = \frac{E}{V_S}$$

capitalisation rate
A discount rate used to convert a series of future cash flows into a single capital sum

Much of the argument about capital structure centres on what happens to the discount rate (or **capitalisation rate**) as gearing increases and the share-out of earnings alters, due to the fixed interest charges imposed by debt. If the analysis is conducted in terms of *substituting* debt for equity, i.e. keeping size of firm constant as we did in the Lindley example, the effect of gearing can be examined while holding E constant. In this case, gearing simply rearranges the share-out of E among the company's stakeholders. We denote the book value of borrowings as B and the interest rate as i, thus involving a prior interest charge of $(i \times B)$. Gearing splits the earnings stream of the company into two components, the prior interest charge and the portion attributable to shareholders, the net income (NI) of $(E - iB)$. The overall value of the company is the value of the shares (V_S) plus the value of the debt, each capitalised at its respective rate of discount. For debt, where there is no discrepancy (as in this example) between book value (B) and market value (V_B), the capitalisation rate is simply the nominal interest rate. The overall value of the geared company, V_g, is the combined value of its shares and its debt:

$$V_g = V_S + V_B = \frac{(E - iB)}{k_e} + \frac{iB}{i} = \frac{(E - iB)}{k_e} + V_B$$

The *overall* capitalisation rate (denoted by k_0) for a company using a mixed capital structure is a weighted average, whose weights reflect the relative importance of each type of finance in the capital structure, i.e. V_S/V_g and V_B/V_g for equity and debt, respectively:

$$k_0 = \left(k_e \times \frac{V_S}{V_g} \right) + \left(i \times \frac{V_B}{V_g} \right)$$

Bearing in mind that $(k_e V_S)$ and iB (or iV_B, when $V_B = B$) represent the returns to shareholders and lenders respectively, i.e. their respective shares of corporate earnings, E, the weighted average expression simplifies to:

$$k_0 = \frac{k_e V_S + iB}{V_g} = \frac{E}{V_g}$$

weighted average cost of capital (WACC)
The overall return a firm must achieve in order to meet the requirements of all its investors

For both ungeared and geared firms alike, k_0 is found by dividing the total required earnings by the value of the whole firm. k_0 is also known as the **weighted average cost of capital (WACC)**, since it expresses the overall return required to satisfy the demands of both groups of stakeholders. The WACC may be interpreted as an average discount rate applied by the market to the company's future operating cash flows to derive the capitalised value of this stream, i.e. the value of the whole company.

It looks as if a company could lower the WACC by adding 'cheap' debt to an equity base. For instance, in the Lindley example, while the required return for the all-equity case is 20 per cent, i.e. the cost of equity, with gearing at 25 per cent, the WACC, using book value weights, becomes:

$$k_0 = (0.75 \times 20\%) + (0.25 \times 10\%) = 17.5\%$$

Apparently, gearing can lower the overall cost of capital if both k_e and i remain constant. The effect of this is highly significant. In the traditional view of gearing, shareholders are deemed unlikely to respond adversely (if at all) to minor increases in gearing so long as the prospect of default looks remote. If the cost of equity remains static, substitution of debt for equity will lower the overall cost of capital applied by the market in valuing the company's stream of earnings. This is shown in Figure 18.2 by the decline in the k_0 schedule between A and B. Corresponding to this fall in k_0 is an increase in the value of the whole geared company, V_g, in relation to that of an equivalent ungeared company, V_u.

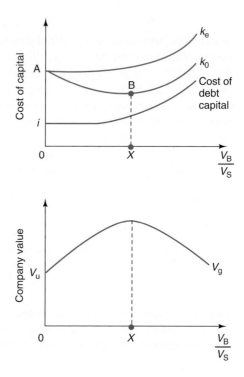

Figure 18.2 The 'traditional' view of capital structure

This benign impact of gearing has already been shown in the Lindley example. Looking back to Tables 18.3 and 18.4, consider the switch from 0 to 25 per cent gearing. Assuming shareholders continue to seek a return of 20 per cent, the EPS discounted to infinity yields a share price of £1.17. The market value of equity becomes (£1.17 × 75m) = £88m, and the overall company value is:

$$V_g = V_S + V_B = (£88m + £25m) = £113m$$

Gearing up to 25 per cent raises market value by £13 million above book value, thus demonstrating the benefits of gearing to shareholders. The market value of the whole company rises because the value per unit of the residual equity increases due to the increase in EPS. Without gearing, each share would sell at £1.

However, sooner or later, shareholders will become concerned by the greater financial risk to which their earnings are exposed and begin to seek higher returns. In addition, providers of additional debt are likely to raise their requirements as they perceive the probability of default increasing. The k_e schedule will probably turn upwards before any upturn in i, given the legally preferred position of debt-holders, although the phasing of these movements is not clear in this model. Whatever the sequence of the upward revisions in required returns, the WACC profile will eventually be forced to rise, and the value of the company will fall. The model involves a clear optimal debt/equity mix, where company value is maximised and the WACC is minimised. This is gearing ratio X in Figure 18.2.

To financial managers, a major disappointment of this approach is its failure to pinpoint a specific optimal gearing ratio for all firms in all circumstances. The optimal ratio is likely to depend on the nature of the industry (e.g. whether the activity generates strong cash flows), the general marketability of the company's assets, expectations about the prospects for the industry, and the general level of interest rates. Clearly, many of these factors vary over time as well as between industries. However, a few pointers are possible.

For example, a supermarket chain, characterised by strong cash flow, can sustain a higher level of gearing than a heavy engineering enterprise, where the operating cycle is lengthy. Similarly, an airline, for whose assets there is a ready and active second-hand market, might withstand a higher gearing level (especially as flights are often paid for well in advance) than a steel company with both a high level of operating gearing and assets that are highly specific and difficult to sell.

Self-assessment activity 18.7

What is this firm's WACC? (Ignore taxation.)

- debt-to-equity ratio = 40%
- cost of equity = 18%
- cost of debt = 8%

(Answer in Appendix A at the back of the book)

18.6 THE COST OF DEBT

Our analysis has so far assumed that market and book values of debt coincide. This is by no means always the case. Corporate bond values behave in a similar way to the market prices of government stock (gilt-edged securities). When general market interest rates increase, the returns on previously issued bonds may look unattractive compared with the returns available on newly issued ones. As a result, bond dealers mark down the value of existing stocks until they offer the same yield as investors can obtain by purchasing new issues. In other words, equilibrium in the bond market is achieved when all stocks that are subject to the same degree of risk and that have the same period to redemption offer the same yield.

The simplest case is perpetual (irredeemable) stock such as the UK government's 3.5 per cent War Loan. These were issued, never to be repaid, to support the British war effort between 1939 and 1945. They offer the holder a return of 3.5 per cent (the nominal rate of interest, or '**coupon rate**') on the par value of the stock, i.e. £3.50 per £100 of stock. With higher market rates, say 7 per cent, War Loan would look unattractive, and its value would fall, e.g. a £100 unit would have to sell at £50 to generate a yield of 7 per cent. An inverse relationship applies between fixed-interest bond prices and interest rates:

coupon rate of interest
The fixed rate of interest, as printed on the debt security, that a firm must pay to lenders

$$\text{The market value of an irredeemable bond} = \left(\text{nominal value} \times \frac{\text{coupon rate}}{\text{market rate}} \right)$$

Self-assessment activity 18.8

What is the market value of the 3.5 per cent War Loan when market rates are:

(i) 11%?

(ii) 3%?

(Answer in Appendix A at the back of the book)

Perpetually Tesco

Perpetual corporate bonds are very rare indeed. However, the longer the term of the bond, the more it resembles a perpetuity. For example, in February 2007 Tesco plc, the supermarket giant, issued a 50-year bond, maturing in 2057, to finance its overseas expansion plans. This is effectively a perpetuity (for proof, examine the size of the discount factors in the 30–50-year range for a plausible discount rate, say 10 per cent – they are very small indeed). The Tesco issue raised £500 million and was four times over-subscribed. It offered a yield of 5.23 per cent, compared to 4.06 per cent on an equivalent government bond, a quite modest risk premium of 1.17 percentage points.

Source: K. Allen, The Guardian, 27 February 2007.

In practice, the calculation is more complex when we consider the far more common case of bonds with limited lifetimes until maturity. In assessing the value of such bonds, the market value will also include the eventual capital repayment.

For example, if the market rate is 10 per cent, a 10-year bond with a coupon rate of 10 per cent, denominated in £100 units, would have the following (present) value:

$$
\begin{aligned}
PV &= \text{discounted interest} &+& \quad \text{discounted capital} \\
&\quad \text{payments over 10 years} && \quad \text{repayment in Year 10} \\
&= (10\% \times £100) \times (\text{PVIFA}_{(10,10)}) + &(£100)& \times (\text{PVIF}_{(10,10)}) \\
&= (£10 \times 6.1446) &+& \quad (£100 \times 0.3855) \\
&= £61.45 &+& \quad £38.55 = £100
\end{aligned}
$$

The market value coincides with the par value because the coupon rate equals the going market rate. If, however, the market rate were to rise to 12 per cent, all future payments to the bond-holder, both capital and interest, would be more heavily discounted, i.e. at 12 per cent, reducing the market value to £88.70.

Values of corporate bonds behave in essentially the same way, although, since companies are more risky than governments, they have to offer investors a rather higher rate of interest. This allows us to identify the cost of corporate debt capital. A company can infer the appropriate rate of interest at which it could raise debt by looking at the market value of its own existing debt or that of a similar company. For example, if the market value of each £100 unit of debenture stock is £95 and has to be repaid in full in two years' time, the cost of debt can be found by solving a simple IRR expression. Someone who decided to purchase the stock in the market would anticipate two interest payments of £10 and a capital repayment of £100. The return expected is denoted by k_d in the following IRR expression:

$$
£95 = \frac{£10}{(1 + k_d)} + \frac{(£10 + £100)}{(1 + k_d)^2}
$$

The solution for k_d is 13 per cent. The market signals this rate as the cost of raising further debt.

There is another adjustment to make for tax relief on debt interest payments. To allow for tax, we look at the cost of debt from the company's perspective, since it is the company that enjoys the tax break. With a corporation tax rate of 30 per cent, each £10 interest payment will generate a tax saving of £3 for the company, reducing the effective interest cost to £10(1 − 30%) = £7.0. The IRR equation becomes:

$$
£95 = \frac{£7.0}{(1 + k_d)} + \frac{(£7.0 + £100)}{(1 + k_d)^2}
$$

Self-assessment activity 18.9

Verify that the solution rate in the above IRR equation is 9.9 per cent.

The tax benefits from using debt can be substantial. Take the case of a 10-year bond, issued and redeemable at a price of £100, with a coupon rate of 10 per cent. The value of the tax savings on interest payments, or the '**tax shield**', is:

$$
\begin{aligned}
\text{Tax shield} &= \text{interest charge} \times (\text{tax rate}) \times \text{PVIFA}_{(10,10)} \\
&= (10\% \times £100) \times (30\%) \times 6.1446 \\
&= £18.43
\end{aligned}
$$

In practice, this value is reduced by any delay in tax payments, which in turn delays the receipt of tax benefits. It is also assumed that the company always has sufficient taxable profits to benefit from the tax relief on interest payments.

Self-assessment activity 18.10

What is the value of the tax shield for £10 million debt, coupon rate 6 per cent, tax rate 30 per cent:

(a) if the debt is perpetual?

(b) if it is to be repaid in 20 years?

(Answer in Appendix A at the back of the book)

Cost of capital in Europe: the importance of the tax shield

Lee *et al.* (2006) estimated the cost of equity capital and weighted average cost of capital (WACC) for a large sample of companies from 17 European countries between 1995 and 2005. They found that the equity premium (i.e. cost of equity minus risk-free rate of interest) was systematically lower in the UK (4.64 per cent) than in the rest of Europe (5.84 per cent). This is seen as the result of higher disclosure requirements and greater use of equity which leads to a lower cost of equity. However, firms in other European countries typically have much higher borrowings, offering a greater tax shield. This resulted in the WACC premium (WACC minus risk-free rate of return) for UK companies being no different to other European countries. The study also indicated that costs of capital in the IT, steel and materials, and mining sectors were consistently high while utilities and beverage sectors had lower equity and weighted average costs of capital.

Source: E. Lee, M. Walker and H. Christensen, 2006.

18.7 THE OVERALL COST OF CAPITAL

Section 18.5 discussed the weighted average cost of capital (WACC) concept, illustrated in Figure 18.2. This was interpreted as the overall rate of return required in order to satisfy all stakeholders in the company. It described a U-shaped profile as the firm's level of gearing increased. It fell initially, as cheap debt was added to the capital structure, reached a minimum at the optimal gearing ratio, then rose as gearing came to be regarded as 'excessive'. The behaviour of this schedule provides a clue to the appropriate rate of return required on the company's activities, and, by implication, on new investment projects. We will examine this issue using the Lindley example (covered in Section 18.4).

■ Lindley plc and the cut-off rate for new investment

Lindley's shareholders require a 20 per cent return and its pre-tax cost of debt is 10 per cent. Let us make the simplifying assumptions that Lindley's debt is perpetual and sells at par. Adjusting for tax at 30 per cent, as explained above, this corresponds to an after-tax cost of 7 per cent. What return on investment should Lindley achieve when issuing debt to finance a new project?

It is tempting to argue that the cut-off rate on this new project should be the cost of servicing the finance raised specifically to undertake the project. However, this is probably erroneous because using debt has an opportunity cost. The use of 'cheap' debt now may erode the company's ability to undertake worthwhile projects in the future by the depletion of credit lines. For example, assume that in 2015 Lindley uses debt costing 7.0 per cent after tax to finance a project offering a post-tax return of 12 per cent, but this exhausts its credit-raising capacity. As a result, it becomes unable to exploit a project available in 2016 that offers 14 per cent. This suggests that the 'true' cost of the finance used in 2015 exceeds 7.0 per cent. Hence, to assess the 'correct' cost of capital really requires forecasting all future investment opportunities and capital supplies.

In addition, our previous analysis leads us to expect, at some level of gearing, an adverse reaction by shareholders, who may demand higher returns to compensate for higher financial risk. Consider two possible cases, denoted by points A and B, respectively, on the WACC profile in Figure 18.2. Note that A corresponds to zero gearing and B to the critical ratio.

Case A

Lindley has no debt at present and shareholder capital is £100 million. A new project with perpetual life is to be financed by the issue of £10 million debt at an after-tax cost of 7 per cent. No impact on the cost of equity is expected. In this case, the company will have to generate additional post-tax annual returns of $(7\% \times £10m) = £0.70$ million in order to meet the extra financing costs associated with the new project, so that the hurdle rate for the new project is 7 per cent. Here, with the explicit assumption that shareholders will not react adversely, it may be reasonable to use the cost of debt as the cut-off rate. In this case, the required return would be simply the interest cost divided by the debt financing provided, i.e. the interest rate:

$$\text{Required return} = iB/B = i$$

However, this position is unlikely to be tenable, except for very small projects, and hence small borrowings, since significant changes in gearing (in either direction) are likely to provoke a market reaction.

Case B

We will assume that the optimal gearing ratio involves a capital structure with £50 million of each type of capital. Any further debt financing, even at a constant debt cost, will cause the cost of equity to increase. Assume that the extra £10 million debt financing will provoke shareholders to demand a return of 24 per cent. This would be expressed by downward pressure on share price until the return on holding Lindley's shares became 24 per cent. Now, the project has to meet not only the debt financing costs, but also the additional returns required by shareholders. The total additional required income is:

$$
\begin{aligned}
\text{Required} \atop \text{extra income} &= \text{debt financing} \atop \text{costs} + \text{extra return required} \atop \text{on equity} \\
&= (7\% \times £10m) + (4\% \times £50m) \\
&= £0.70m + £2m \\
&= £2.70m
\end{aligned}
$$

marginal cost of capital (MCC)
The extra returns required to satisfy all investors as a proportion of new capital raised

Instead of an apparent cost of just 7 per cent, the true cost of using debt to finance this project is actually $(£2.70m/£10m) = 27$ per cent. This figure of 27 per cent is the **marginal cost of capital (MCC)**.

In the next section, we pinpoint the conditions under which it is acceptable to use the WACC as the cut-off rate for evaluating new investment.

■ Required conditions for using the WACC

Some major requirements have to be satisfied before use of the WACC can be justified:

1 The project is a marginal, scalar addition to the company's existing activities, with no overspill or synergistic impact likely to disturb the current valuation relationships.
2 Project financing involves no deviation from the current capital structure (otherwise the MCC should be used).
3 Any new project has the same systematic risk as the company's existing operations. This may be a reasonable assumption for minor projects in existing areas and perhaps for replacements, but hardly for major new product developments.
4 All cash flow streams are level perpetuities (as in the theoretical models).

In the short term, at least, firms are almost certain to deviate from the target structure, especially as market values fluctuate and financial managers perceive and exploit ephemeral financing bargains, e.g. an arbitrage opportunity in an overseas capital market. It is thus unrealistic to expect the hurdle rate for new investment to be adjusted for every minor deviation from the target gearing ratio. To all intents and purposes, the capital structure is given – only for major divergences from the target gearing ratio should the discount rate be altered. Similarly, even where a project is wholly financed by debt or equity, so long as the project is a minor one with no appreciable impact on the overall gearing ratio, then it is appropriate to use the WACC as the cut-off rate.

The preceding discussions suggest that the marginal cost of capital (MCC), rather than the cost of debt or the WACC, should be used as the cut-off rate for new investment. However, the MCC does have operational limitations. In particular, we are required to anticipate *how* the capital market is likely to react to the issue of additional debt. Given that we seem unable to define the WACC profile or pinpoint the optimal gearing ratio at any one time, this presents a problem. We could assume that the present gearing ratio is optimal, but this prompts the question of why different firms in the same industry have different gearing ratios.

■ The target capital structure: a solution?

target capital structure
What the firm regards as its optimal long-term ratio of debt to equity (or debt to total capital)

A solution commonly adopted in practice is to specify a **target capital structure**. For example, RWE, one of Europe's largest electricity and gas companies, has set a target for gearing at 3.0 (gearing defined as the ratio of net debt to EBITDA). In 2012–13 the ratio achieved was higher than this at 3.5 and the company was working to move to the target ratio (**www.rwe.com**).

The firm defines what it regards as the optimal long-term gearing range or ratio, and then attempts to adhere to this ratio in financing future operations. If the optimal ratio is deemed to involve, say, 50 per cent debt and 50 per cent equity (i.e. a debt-to-equity ratio of 100 per cent), any future activities should be financed in these proportions. For example, a £10 million project would be financed by £5 million debt and £5 million equity, via retained earnings or a rights issue. The corollary is to use the WACC as the cut-off rate for new investment. When shareholders require 20 per cent and debt costs 7 per cent post-tax, the WACC is:

(cost of equity × equity weighting) + (post-tax cost of debt × debt weighting)
= (20% × 50%) + (7% × 50%) = (10% + 3.5%) = 13.5%

The WACC is recommended because it is difficult to anticipate with any precision how shareholders are likely to react to a change in gearing. The somewhat pragmatic solution proposed assumes that the new project will have no appreciable impact on gearing: in other words, that the company already operates at or close to the optimal gearing ratio and does not significantly deviate from it. Obviously, the WACC and the MCC will coincide in this case.

The panel explains how E.ON, the German utility group, calculates its WACC, based on a target debt/equity ratio of 50:50.

The WACC in practice

The cost of capital is determined by calculating the weighted-average cost of equity and debt. This average represents the market-rate returns expected by stockholders and creditors. The cost of equity is the return expected by an investor in E.ON stock. The cost of debt equals the long-term financing terms that apply in the E.ON Group. The parameters of the cost-of-capital determination are reviewed on an annual basis. The cost of capital is adjusted if there are significant changes.

Because a number of parameters changed significantly, we adjusted our cost of capital in 2013. Unlike in previous years, we used a current yield curve instead of a long-term average to calculate the risk-free interest rate. The yield curve along with a higher market-risk premium better reflects current developments on financial markets. The risk-free interest rate declined significantly owing to the low return on German treasury notes; however, this was offset by the increase in the market risk premium. The assumed debt-to-equity ratio for the E.ON Group was unchanged at 50:50.

On balance, the changes to the parameters had the effect of lowering the E.ON Group's after-tax cost of capital for 2013 from 5.6 to 5.5 per cent. Our pre-tax cost of capital declined from 7.7 to 7.5 per cent. There were also changes to some of our reporting segments' minimum ROACE requirements, which for 2013 ranged from 6.4 per cent to 20.7 per cent (before taxes, calculated in euros).

Source: E.ON Annual Report 2013, p. 49.

Cost of Capital

	2013	2012
Risk-free interest rate	2.5%	3.3%
Market premium[1]	5.5%	4.5%
Debt-free beta factor	0.59	0.59
Indebted beta factor[2]	1.02	1.02
Cost of equity after taxes	**8.1%**	**7.9%**
Average tax rate	27%	27%
Cost of equity before taxes	11.1%	10.8%
Cost of debt before taxes	3.9%	4.5%
Marginal tax rate	27%	27%
Cost of debt after taxes	**2.8%**	**3.3%**
Share of equity	50.0%	50.0%
Share of debt	50.0%	50.0%
Cost of capital after taxes	**5.5%**	**5.6%**
Cost of capital before taxes	**7.5%**	**7.7%**

[1]The market premium reflects the higher long-term returns of the stock market compared with German treasury notes.
[2]The beta factor is used as an indicator of a stock's relative risk. A beta of more than one signals a higher risk than the risk level of the overall market; a beta factor of less than one signals a lower risk.

18.8 WORKED EXAMPLE: DAMSTAR PLC

Damstar plc produces and sells computer modems. The company obtained a stock market quotation four years ago, since when it has achieved a steady annual return for its shareholders of 14 per cent after tax. It has an issued share capital of 2 million 50p ordinary shares. The ordinary shares sell at a P:E ratio of 11:1. In the year ended 31 March 2014, the company sold 20,000 units.

The profit and loss account (income statement) for the year to 31 March 2014 is as follows:

	£000	£000
Sales		1,600
Less: Variable expenses	(880)	
Fixed expenses	(350)	(1,230)
Profit before interest and taxation		370
Less: interest payable (10% loan stock)		(150)
Profit before taxation		220
Less: corporation tax (at 30%)		(66)
Profit after taxation		154
Dividend		(120)
Retained profit		34

In recent months, the company has been experiencing labour problems. As a result, it has decided to introduce a new highly automated production process in order to improve efficiency. The production process is expected to increase fixed costs by £140,000 (including depreciation), but will reduce variable costs by £19 per unit.

The new production process will be financed by additional debt in the form of a secured £1,000,000 debenture issue at an interest rate of 12 per cent. If the new production process is introduced immediately, the directors believe that sales for the forthcoming year will be unchanged.

Required

(a) Determine how the proposal affects Damstar's break-even volume.
(b) Assuming no change in P:E ratio, calculate the change in EPS and share price if Damstar introduces its new production process immediately.
(c) What is the effect of the new process on Damstar's weighted average cost of capital using market value weights?

Answer to Damstar example

(a) First, we establish the revenue and cost parameters. Currently, the price is $(£1.6m/20,000) = £80$ per unit. The average variable cost (AVC) $= (£0.88m/20,000) = £44$. Hence, the gross profit margin (GPM) $= (£80 - £44) = £36$.

The break-even volume (BEV) can be expressed in operating terms, i.e. before fixed financing charges, and also after allowing for interest. Ignoring interest, the BEV is:

(Fixed costs of £0.35m/£36) = 9,722 units

Allowing for interest of £0.15 million, the BEV is:

$(£0.35m + £0.15m/£36) = 13,889$ units.

With the new process, the AVC becomes $(£44 - £19) = £25$, and the GPM becomes $(£80 - £25) = £55$.

The new level of fixed operating costs is £0.49 million.

The BEV ignoring interest $= (£0.49m/£55) = 8,909$ units. Allowing for the interest, increased by $(12\% \times £0.12m)$ to $(£0.15 + £0.12m) = £0.27m$, the BEV is:

$(£0.49m + £0.27m)/£55 = 13,818$ units.

Notice that despite the increase in interest charges and the increase in fixed operating costs, the BEV has actually fallen due to the substantial fall in AVC. This warns that higher fixed costs does not always raise the BEV – it depends on what other changes are occurring at the same time.

(b) Currently, the EPS $= (£154,00/2m) = 7.7$p. With the 11:1 P:E ratio, the share price is $(7.7p \times 11) = 85$p.

Predicted profit and loss account for year ending 31 March 2015

	£(000)	£(000)
Sales		1,600
Variable Costs (20,000 × £25)	(500)	
Fixed Costs (£0.35m + £0.14m)	(490)	(990)
PBIT		610
Interest (£0.15m + £0.12m)		(270)
PBT		340
Taxation at 30%		(102)
PAT		238

EPS now becomes (£238,000/2m) = 11.9p, and with the same P:E ratio, the new share price would be (11.9p × 11) = £1.31.

(c) Based on market value weights, the WACC is:

	£	Weight
Value of equity = (£0.85 × 2m) =	1.7m	53
Value of debt = (£150,000/0.1) =	1.5m	47
(unknown market value, so book value used)		
Total	3.2m	100

$$\text{WACC} = (\text{cost of equity} \times \% \text{ of equity}) + (\text{post-tax debt cost} \times \% \text{ of debt})$$
$$= (14\% \times 53\%) + (10\% [1 - 30\%] \times 47\%)$$
$$= (7.4\% + 3.3\%) = 10.7\%$$

After the issue of £1 million debt at 12 per cent interest, there are now two categories of debt, senior and junior.

	£	Weight
Value of equity = (£1.31 × 2m) =	2.62m	54
Value of senior debt = (10/12 × £1.5m) =	1.25m	26
Value of junior debt =	1.00m	20
Total	4.87m	100

$$\text{WACC} = (14\% \times 54\%) + (10\%[1 - 30\%] \times 26\%) + (12\%[1 - 30\%] \times 20\%)$$
$$= (7.6\% + 1.8\% + 1.7\%) = 11.1\%$$

Comment: In this example, the increase in borrowing hardly affects the WACC, as the equity value increases to compensate. This result, of course, depends on the P:E ratio remaining at 11:1. Note also that the market value of the existing debt falls if interest rates rise. If the market rate of interest becomes 12 per cent, existing debt with a coupon of 10 per cent must sell at a discount.

Another practical application of the WACC

BT suffered a setback as the telecoms regulator Ofcom proposed cuts in the price of its wholesale products.

Ofcom wants BT to reduce the price of its wholesale broadband products in order to improve internet access in rural areas.

The regulator also outlined a lower-than-expected estimate of BT's cost of capital – the assumption of what it costs BT to fund its business. UBS analysts said that could cut BT's earnings by up to 8 per cent. Shares in the telecoms company fell 2.7p to close at 176.6p.

Ofcom is aiming to ensure that broadband prices fall for consumers in rural areas and, potentially, to increase download speeds available to them.

To achieve this, it is proposing that BT should cut the price of wholesale broadband products in parts of Scotland, Wales and Northern Ireland, together with certain English rural areas.

Those are all areas where BT is the sole provider of wholesale broadband services: mainly places not covered by infrastructure owned by Virgin Media, TalkTalk or British Sky Broadcasting. In those areas, Ofcom is proposing annual cuts in the price of BT's wholesale broadband products of between 11 per cent and 15 per cent over the next three years, after inflation.

Ofcom's calculations of its price controls for BT are partly based on its estimate of the company's cost of capital.

It proposed a lower cost of capital for BT Openreach, the subsidiary that provides the company's rivals with access to its fixed-line connections running to homes and offices.

The regulator reduced BT Openreach's weighted cost of capital from 10.1 per cent in May 2009 to 8.6 per cent in January 2011, partly to reflect lower interest rates. Analysts said this would in turn cut the price of the subsidiary's wholesale products across the country.

UBS analysts said the lower cost of capital could reduce BT's wholesale revenue by £50m in 2013–14 and cut group earnings by 3 per cent. TalkTalk, and other companies that use BT Openreach's products, could pass on any reduction in its wholesale charges to their customers. In these circumstances, BT Retail might feel obliged to make a similar move. If it did, group revenue could be cut by £150m in 2013–14. Earnings could decline by 8 per cent.

BT said Ofcom's proposed cost of capital for BT Openreach could reduce annual wholesale revenue by 'low tens of millions' of pounds. It added that the regulator's price controls for its wholesale broadband products should 'strike the right balance between control and incentives to invest in rural areas'.

 Source: Andrew Parker, *Financial Times*, 21 January 2011. © Financial Times

18.9 MORE ON ECONOMIC VALUE ADDED (EVA)

In Chapter 11, we explained the concept of EVA, a popular tool for assessing the amount of value created by a firm. In that chapter, we confined the analysis to all-equity-financed firms. In that form, the resulting EVA measured the wealth created for the owners of the business. EVA can also be calculated in a broader sense. Instead of focusing on wealth creation for the owners, one can focus on total economic value added for distribution to all the investors in the business. As such, for a geared firm, the EVA is arguably a better way of assessing managers' performance, i.e. the efficiency with which they utilise financial resources, because it is not distorted by the particular method of financing the business.

The adjustment is simple. Instead of applying the cost of equity to the net assets, we apply the WACC to the total capital employed to measure the capital cost, and deduct this from the NOPAT. For consistency, since the cost of debt appears in the WACC, the returns to debt should appear in the NOPAT, i.e. in this case the NOPAT is before charging interest, and thus includes returns to all types of investor.

The EVA formula thus becomes:

$$EVA = NOPAT - (WACC \times Capital\ employed).$$

It is usual to apply the WACC to long-term capital, given the relative volatility of short-term assets and liabilities.

Example

EVA plc's assets have a total book value of £900 million. It is financed by 60 per cent equity and 40 per cent debt. The costs of equity and debt are 12 per cent and 7 per cent (pre-tax) respectively. Operating profits are £100 million, and the tax rate is 30 per cent.

$$NOPAT = (Operating\ profit - tax) = £100m\ (1 - 30\%) = £70m$$
$$WACC = (60\% \times 12\%) + (40\% \times 7\%\ [1 - 30\%])$$
$$= 7.2\% + 1.96\% = 9.16\%$$
$$EVA = £70m - (9.16\% \times £900m) = (£70m - £82.44m) = -£12.44m$$

As this result is negative, EVA plc appears to have destroyed value.

Readers may notice that under the traditional view of gearing, as a firm raises the debt/equity ratio, the EVA is likely to increase, so long as the WACC declines.

18.10 FINANCIAL DISTRESS

This is an appropriate stage to clarify our terminology. Up to this point, we have implied that the reason for the upturn in the WACC profile is the threat of 'bankruptcy' resulting in 'liquidation', i.e. a company that fails to meet its debts will be forced by its creditors to liquidate. The term 'bankruptcy' in the UK strictly applies to personal insolvency. Individuals go bankrupt, and firms become insolvent. But what happens to a firm in severe financial distress? Broadly speaking, there are two main forms of treatment. The first is called 'receivership'.

Creditors – and it only takes one of many – may apply to a court to appoint a 'receiver' to recover the debt if the firm defaults on interest or capital repayments.

The order of priority for creditor payment

Creditors qualify for payment in the following order:

- *Secured creditors* These have a fixed legal charge over company assets such as land and buildings, plant and machinery, patents and other intellectual property such as trademarks. Factoring companies may also hold a fixed charge against specified debtors. Where there exist multiple fixed charge creditors, they rank in chronological order of registering the charge, hence the distinction between 'Senior' and 'Junior' debt.
- *Preferential creditors* These comprise employees' wages and other monetary entitlements, e.g. bonus payments.

- *Floating charge creditors* Floating charge assets are those that a firm uses in day-to-day operations including inventories, work-in-progress and non-factored debtors.
- *Unsecured creditors* These include trade creditors, VAT and PAYE debts payable to the tax authorities, loans that are not secured such as a bank overdraft, or a loan made by a director.

Shareholders are last in line, and rarely receive anything.

Source: Based on a listing provided by Wilson Field & Co. Ltd (**www.wilsonfield.co.uk**)

The receiver may sell the business, or parts of it, as a going concern, which continues to trade in a different guise, often involving a reduced scale of operation. However, the receiver's primary duty is to the appointing bank, and once sufficient funds have been realised to repay the loan, the receiver is under no obligation to maximise the proceeds of the sale of the remaining assets, or even to keep them operating. The receiver may choose to liquidate them *in toto* and disburse the net proceeds to remaining creditors and then any residue to shareholders.

administration
An attempt to reorganise an insolvent firm under an administrator, rather than liquidate it

The Insolvency Act 1986 introduced a new procedure, **administration**, as an attempt to rescue ailing companies and to protect employment, a procedure that became all too common during the recession years following the financial crisis, as the Blockbuster example (see next page) illustrates. The company is allowed to continue trading under the overall control of an administrator, who will attempt to reorganise the company's finances and its operating structure. The administrator is appointed by a court at the request of the directors and has an equal duty to all creditors. In effect, administration, rather like filing for Chapter 11 bankruptcy under the US Bankruptcy Code, is an attempt to protect the company from its creditors, thus giving the administrator a breathing space during which it can attempt to secure the company's survival as a reorganised going concern. The main difference compared with the US equivalent is that Chapter 11 bankruptcy allows the incumbent managers and owners to retain control. In addition, Chapter 11 enables the firm to impose a moratorium on interest payments on existing debts for a specified period and also to borrow more funds as money lent after the filing has a prior claim on assets.

Blockbuster on brink of collapse in UK for second time this year

The UK offshoot of the Blockbuster DVD rental chain is poised to enter administration for a second time this year, putting 2,000 jobs at risk after poor retail and rental sales. The expected administration comes only seven months after Blockbuster was saved by Gordon Brothers, the US private equity and investment company. It is a grim reminder of pressures on high street retailers, despite more confidence about their outlook. It comes almost exactly a year since Comet, the electricals retailer, plunged into administration.

In January, Deloitte was appointed administrator to the retailer, after Blockbuster failed to secure a sale of the UK business, after a plunge in profits. In March, the chain secured a lifeline from Gordon Brothers, which acquired 264 stores. At the start of the year, Blockbuster had 528 stores across the UK employing 4,190 staff. But yesterday Gordon

Brothers said it had tried to turn round the historically loss-making business. It had also tried to develop a new digital platform, but was unable to broker a licensing deal with Blockbuster's US parent company.

Frank Morton, chief executive of Gordon Brothers Europe, said: 'Since the acquisition we have worked extremely hard to reignite the Blockbuster brand, make our investment work and put the business on a viable footing. Despite our best efforts, we regret that we are now forced to make some redundancies'. Blockbuster has filed a notice of intention to appoint an administrator and is seeking a buyer for the business. Deloitte, which acted as administrator last time, is not thought to be being lined up this time.

Source: Based on Andrea Felsted, *Financial Times*, 30 October 2013, p. 17.

■ Distress costs

Any visitor to an auction of bankrupt stock will have no difficulty in appreciating the importance of postponing the break-up decision. Similarly, when repossessed assets, such as consumer durables and houses, are sold by creditors, they rarely fetch 'market values'. This is partly because the vendor often does not need to recover the market value, having deliberately set the loan itself at less than the market value of the asset upon which it is secured. The vendor is interested in a quick sale to minimise depreciation, interest and other carrying costs. Moreover, when it is generally known that the assets are offered under distressed conditions, asset values usually head south! In January 2002, Britain's BG Group plc announced it would pay distressed US energy firm Enron $350 million for its stake in oil and gas fields off the coast of India. The 30 per cent stake in the Tapti and Panna-Mukta fields plus 63 per cent of a further untapped field was valued by Dutch bank ABN AMRO at $450 million, 30 per cent above the agreed price.

The costs incurred at and during liquidation are called the 'direct' costs of financial distress. Empirical studies (e.g. van Horne, 1975; Sharpe, 1981) have suggested that liquidation costs, including legal and administrative charges, may lower the resale value of distressed companies by 50 per cent or more.

However, a more recent US study suggests that distress costs of this magnitude may be an overestimate. In a study of 31 Highly Leveraged Transactions (HLTs) occurring between 1980 and 1989, Andrade and Kaplan (1998) tried to differentiate between the costs of dealing with economic distress, e.g. reacting to loss of contracts, and direct costs of financial distress. Comparing enterprise values at the date of the HLT and at the date of resolution of the distress, they estimated an average loss in firm value of 38 per cent, of which 26 per cent was due to economic distress and 12 per cent due to financial distress.

A more insidious form of financial distress is the impact of increasing gearing on managerial decision-making and the performance of the firm – the so-called 'indirect' costs. As a firm's indebtedness begins to look excessive, it may develop an overriding concern for short-term liquidity. This may be manifested in reduced investment in training and R&D, thus damaging long-term growth capability, and reducing credit periods and stock levels, which may hamper marketing efforts. Supplier power triggered the collapse of US discount retailer K-Mart in January 2002. Its sole supplier of grocery products suspended payments after K-Mart failed to make a regular weekly payment.

More obviously, a distressed firm may sell established operations at bargain prices, sell or abandon promising new product developments, and, to the extent that it does continue to invest, may express a preference for short-payback projects, cash-generating projects, rather than strategic activities. Troubled companies often cut their dividends to preserve liquidity, but this often signals to the market the extent of their difficulties. Finally, there may be a pervasive 'corporate gloom effect', which saps morale internally and damages public image externally.

Such costs are likely to be encountered well before the trigger point of cash flow crisis, and, of course, many firms have successfully surmounted them, but not without an often prolonged dip in the value of the company. In other words, both actual and anticipated liquidation costs detract from company value, lowering the effective limit to debt capacity.

The practical importance of the facility to appoint an Administrator before creditors can appoint receivers may now be seen. Administration enhances the probability of survival of a company unable to meet its immediate liabilities and may thus lead to lower costs of financial distress. However, there may be an element of '**moral hazard**' to the extent that financial managers might undertake more dangerous levels of debt, knowing that there is a more relaxed legal procedure in the event of insolvency.

Two other procedures for managing distress situations are company voluntary arrangements, and so-called pre-pack insolvency. These are discussed in turn.

■ Company Voluntary Arrangements (CVAs)

A CVA is a device whereby an essentially profitable, but temporarily illiquid, firm can buy time to stave off its creditors in order to restructure its debts. The negotiations may involve repayment of a lesser sum than that owed, or payment over a longer period of time or both. As well as obtaining court protection from creditors, the main benefits are that deferral of payment will ease pressure on cash flow, and that the firm continues to trade under the control of the directors. A CVA may be accepted by creditors such as suppliers, who agree that the firm is inherently profitable, expecting to receive

---

Spain's airport that never took off goes up for sale

For sale: airport in provincial Spain, good as new, with 4km runway and passenger terminal built for 10m travellers a year; includes visitor centre, vast industrial park and 50m control tower. Good motorway access and ample parking. Asking price: €100m.

One of the ultimate symbols of Spain's real estate bubble will be put up for sale today in a process administrators hope, will secure a new future for Ciudad Real's infamous ghost airport. The project was completed in 2009, shortly after the bursting of the property bubble, reportedly at a cost of more than €1bn to private investors and the regional government.

Opened with high hopes, the airport never attracted more than a handful of flights per week, a fraction of its capacity. No aircraft has landed at Ciudad Real since April last year, when the airport was officially closed. CR Aeropuertos, the operator of the Ciudad Real terminal, went into bankruptcy three years ago, and the airport will now be sold to meet creditor demands.

The auction opens at 9am today and closes at 3pm on 29 December, according to a press statement issued by the administrators. Bidders will have to submit offers in excess of €100m and put up cash or a bank guarantee equivalent to 5 per cent of the bid.

A provincial capital of just 75,000 inhabitants, Ciudad Real is located in a thinly populated part of Castilla-La Mancha, halfway between Madrid and Cordoba, in southern Spain. There is no significant industry in the area and the city attracts relatively few visitors, especially from outside the country. The contrast between the ambition and scale of the airport and the apparent lack of demand for such a terminal in the region made it an obvious symbol of the folly and excess of Spain's boom years.

Source: Based on Tobias Buck, *Financial Times*, 9 December 2013, p. 6.

future orders. Moreover, they may feel that they will receive more money via a CVA than through more complex and therefore more expensive procedures such as outright liquidation. In recent years, several well-known retailers have signed a CVA, especially regarding rentals owed to landlords. Examples include Oddbins, the vintners, and JJB Sports (see the following cameo).

Gloom as store closures accelerate

Stores are disappearing from British high streets faster than ever before after a spate of retail casualties. Retailers with more than six stores across the UK are closing a net 28 stores a day – openings less closures – according to PwC, the professional services firm, and the Local Data Company, a retail information provider which warned that the situation could get worse. The figure for the past three months represents a significant acceleration from the net 20 a day on average that shut their doors in 2012.

Since the start of this year, Jessops, the photographic retailer, entertainment chains HMV and Blockbuster, and young fashion retailer Republic, have all gone into administration, with the loss of more than 10,000 jobs. This has come hard on the heels of the collapse of Comet, the electricals chain, in November, with the loss of more than 6,000 jobs.

Matthew Hopkinson, director of the Local Data Company, estimated that the casualties put about 1,400 stores at risk, while another 300 were being closed between December and February as solvent chains pruned their estates. He warned that the situation could get worse as retail conditions remained tough, independent retailers were also closing more stores than they were opening and there were questions over whether value retailers, which had filled much of the vacant space, would continue to take on empty sites.

'You can't see [the closures] getting any less, and therefore it's likely to get worse,' he said. 'The writing is on the wall.' PwC and the Local Data Company said the acceleration in store closures this year followed a grim 2012, when a net 1,779 closed. That is a 10-fold increase from the 174 in 2011, and reflected casualties including Game Group, JJB Sports, Black Leisure and Clinton Cards. Although many of the companies were salvaged in one form or another, hundreds of stores closed.

Mike Jervis, insolvency partner at PwC, said: '[The year] saw more retail chains go into insolvency than ever before. The failed chains generally shared two problems – too many stores and too little multi-channel activity. 'A number of them had failed to deal with their underlying issues by hiding behind light-touch restructuring processes, especially company voluntary arrangements; 2013 has seen the downward trend become even worse.'

Source: Based on Andrea Felsted, *Financial Times*, 28 February 2013, p. 23.

■ Pre-pack insolvency

A pre-pack insolvency deal is where an insolvent firm's business is sold before entering a formal insolvency process. The deal is usually agreed before the insolvency practitioner is appointed and then swiftly completed once the appointment is made. This procedure has been available for many years but has increased substantially since the Enterprise Act of 2002, and particularly during the recession of the late 2000s, when it attracted considerable adverse publicity. A pre-pack is often used for owner-managed firms or for those whose main value lies off balance sheet in the form of key staff who might leave, or in assets that may fall in value sharply once a formal insolvency is announced. Hence, the distressed firm is usually sold with a minimum of, or no, open marketing. Unsecured creditors are often only informed after the event, although secured creditors are normally made aware of the situation ahead of the finalised deal as they are required to release their security.

The main advantages of the pre-pack deal are that the debts of the business remain with the old company, and the new firm, often called a 'phoenix company', can start afresh unencumbered by debt. The old firm will move into administration and the new entity will start trading immediately. This speed of the process minimises the danger of 'drift' while an orthodox process of administration is conducted, and the consequent danger of loss of business and staff at a time of great uncertainty. The main problem with a pre-pack is the compromising of the interests of the unsecured creditors – it is always possible that a better deal might have been struck if the firm was put on the block for general sale, especially in cases where the outgoing directors were able to buy the business at a 'bargain price'. The UK government announced it would be undertaking a review of the pre-pack procedure to assess whether it provides value for creditors in 2014. The outcome of this review has been a set of recommendations designed primarily to improve the success rate of businesses that are sold to connected parties.

An explanation of modern insolvency procedures can be found in Bailey and Groves (2014).

Self-assessment activity 18.11

Identify examples of distressed behaviour by highly geared firms from your reading of the financial press.

Dubai recovery breathes life into Brintons

The economic recovery in Dubai is being felt in an unlikely location: Kidderminster. A resurgence of five-star hotels and fancy developments across the Middle East has helped Brintons, the 230-year-old Midlands-based carpet manufacturer, triple its earnings year-on-year. 'There are thousands of upscale five-star luxury projects, almost all of which got canned with the banking crisis,' said Don Coates, managing director. 'Those projects are coming back on stream again.'

The manufacturer of plush carpets saw its earnings before interest, tax, depreciation and amortisation triple from £3m to £9.1m for the year to September. This came despite revenues broadly staying flat at £81m. This marks a remarkable turnround for the group, which specialises in fitting out commercial buildings. It comes just two years after Carlyle, the private equity group, bought out Brintons in a pre-pack administration – a pre-negotiated sale of an insolvent business – to the chagrin of its owners at the time, the Brinton family. The family had controlled the group for more than two centuries.

'The insolvency came as a bit of a shock to Brintons employees,' said Mr Coates. 'They weren't aware of the precarious nature of the business.' Mr Coates said the group did attempt to do a deal that did not involve going into administration, but that effort failed. The company was eating up £1m of cash a month. 'When you have a near-death experience, you have a burning platform for change,' said Mr Coates. Although Brintons made about 250 staff redundant following its administration, it is looking to hire people once more as business picks up and it opens offices across the globe – including one in Dubai.

Source: Based on Duncan Robinson, *Financial Times*, 25 November 2013, p. 26.

The Sharks close in, and the Vultures circle

Not everyone loses in a distress situation. Clearly, the lawyers and insolvency practitioners who benefit from professional fees for services rendered, but also during the recession years of the late 2000s, a number of so-called 'activist' investors emerged, buying up the debt of struggling firms seeking to benefit from their distress. In many cases, the debt could be acquired at a substantial discount to face value, thus offering the prospect of handsome gains from their activities. These are some of the strategies they adopted:

Loan-to-influence lenders acquire the debt of distressed firms to obtain a voice in re-shaping the company's strategy and to secure management changes.

Loan-to-own lenders push for their holdings to be converted into an equity stake in the firm.

Loan-to asset sale investors exert their influence to force the company to sell assets and return the proceeds to shareholders (including themselves).

Loan-to-bust lenders push a firm into liquidation hoping that it will secure a pay-out that more than offsets the price paid for the debt. They can do this by calling in the debt that they own, by blocking a restructuring rescue deal, or by refusing to waive breaches of covenants.

Pay-to-shut lenders try to block restructuring proposals hoping that other lenders will buy them out.

Source: Based on an article by Elena Moyer and Aziz Durrani, *Guardian*, 4 May 2009.

18.11 TWO MORE ISSUES: SIGNALLING AND AGENCY COSTS

An unexpected reduction in indebtedness is usually greeted with pleasure by the market, whereas a debt increase can be regarded in a favourable or unfavourable light depending on the accompanying arguments. According to Ross (1977), managers naturally have a vested interest in not busting the company, so an increase in gearing might be construed by the market as signalling a greater degree of managerial confidence in the ability of the company to service a higher level of debt. This argument relies on asymmetric information between managers and shareholders, and reflects the pervasive principal/agent problem.

Financial managers, as appointees of the shareholders, are expected to maximise the value of the enterprise, but it is difficult for the owners to devise an effective, but not excessively costly, service contract to constrain managerial behaviour to this goal. In the context of capital structure theory, the financial manager acts as an agent for both shareholders and debt-holders. Although the latter do not offer remuneration, they do attempt to limit managers' freedom of action by including restrictive covenants in the debt contract, such as restrictions on dividend payouts, to protect the asset base of the company.

Such restraints on managerial decision-making may adversely affect the development of the firm and, together with the monitoring costs incurred by the shareholders themselves, may detract from company value. Conversely, it is possible that the close monitoring by a small group of creditors, aiming to protect their capital, may induce managers to pursue more responsible policies likely to enhance the wealth of a widely diffused group of shareholders.

18.12 CONCLUSIONS

What conclusions does this body of analysis lead to, and how does it help financial managers?

1 Gearing can lower the overall or weighted average cost of capital that the company is required to achieve on its operations, and can raise the market value of the enterprise. However, this benign effect can be relied upon only at relatively safe gearing levels. Companies can expect the market to react adversely to 'excessive' gearing ratios. The implications for project appraisal are reasonably clear. Strictly, the appropriate cut-off rate for new investment is the marginal cost of capital, but if no change in gearing is caused by the new activity, the WACC can be used.

2 Considerable care should be taken when prescribing the appropriate use of debt that will enhance shareholder wealth without ever threatening corporate collapse. Levels of gearing that look quite innocuous in calm trading conditions may suddenly appear ominous when conditions worsen. Corporate difficulties do not usually occur singly, and highly geared companies are relatively less well placed to surmount them.

3 The capital structure decision, like the dividend decision, is a secondary decision – secondary, that is, to the company's primary concern of finding and developing wealth-creating projects. Many people argue that the beneficial impact of debt is largely an illusion. Clever financing cannot create wealth (although it may enable exploitation of projects that would not otherwise have proceeded). It may, however, transfer wealth if some stakeholders are prepared, perhaps due to information asymmetry, to accept too low a return for the risks they incur, or if the government offers a tax subsidy on debt interest.

4 The decision to borrow should not be over-influenced by tax considerations. There are other ways of obtaining tax subsidies, such as investing in fixed assets, which

qualify for tax allowances. A highly geared company could find itself unable to exploit the other tax-breaks offered by governments when a favourable opportunity is uncovered.

5 Remember that interest rates fluctuate over time. If interest rates move from what seems a 'high' level, financial managers should take advantage of the reduction. For example, if 10 per cent seems like the 'normal' long-term level of interest rates, when rates next fall below 10 per cent, and bankers are offering variable rate loans at, say, 9 per cent, one should not be afraid to take a fixed rate loan at, say, 9.5 per cent. Readiness to work with a slightly higher than minimum rate in the short term could have significant payoffs in the longer term. Anyone who thinks that rates will continue to fall should reserve some borrowing capacity to retain flexibility.

6 Firms should avoid relying on too many bankers, as with syndicated loans, despite the benefits of access to a variety of banking facilities. If the company hits trading and liquidity problems, it is hard enough to convince one banker that the company should be saved. But if it has to persuade 10 or 20, and their decision has to be unanimous, it is virtually impossible to reach a satisfactory conclusion about capital restructuring. The ill-fated Eurotunnel had to deal with 225 banks at one stage of its troubled existence, later reduced to a mere 200. It was reported that Nissan had 170 banking relationships before implementing its recovery plan after the merger with Renault.

7 The finance manager should question whether debt is the most suitable form of funding in the circumstances. For example, there should be a clear rationale to support the case for debt rather than retentions (i.e. lower dividends) or a rights issue. He or she should recognise the value of retaining reserve borrowing capacity to draw upon under adverse circumstances or when favourable opportunities, like falling interest rates, arise.

8 These considerations are reflected in two popular theories that attempt to explain how firms address long-term financing decisions. These are:

- **The Trade-off Theory.** This recognises that firms seek to exploit the lower cost benefits of borrowing, especially the tax shield, but at the same time, they are reluctant to increase the financial risk entailed in entering contractual commitments to make ongoing interest and capital repayments. In other words, they trade off the returns (the cost benefits) against the risks. We might thus expect to find that firms enjoying higher and more stable profit levels, which offer greater scope to shelter profits from tax, should operate at higher borrowing levels.

- **The Pecking Order Theory.** This suggests that firms have an order of priorities in selecting among alternative forms of finance:

  - First, they prefer to use the internal finance generated by operating cash flow.
  - Second, they prefer to borrow when internal sources are drained.
  - Third, they regard selling new shares almost as a last resort.

information asymmetry
The imbalance between managers and owners of information possessed about a firm's financial state and its prospects

The reason for this order of preference lies yet again in **information asymmetry** – managers know far more about the firm's performance and prospects than outsiders. They are unlikely to issue shares when they believe shares are 'undervalued', but more inclined to issue shares when they believe they are 'overvalued'. Naturally, shareholders are aware of this likely managerial behaviour and thus regard equity issues with suspicion. For example, they may interpret a share issue as a signal that management thinks the shares are overvalued and mark them down accordingly – a very common occurrence – thereby increasing the cost of equity. Investors would expect managers to finance investment programmes, first, using internal resources, second, via borrowing up to an appropriate debt/equity combination, and finally through equity issues. Yet again, signalling considerations are crucial.

SUMMARY

We have explained the meaning of gearing, its likely benefits to shareholders, its dangers and its possible impact on the required return on investment projects.

Key points

- Borrowing often looks more attractive than equity due to its lower cost of servicing, tax-deductibility of interest and low issue costs.

- A company's indebtedness is revealed by its capital gearing and by its income gearing.

- The sum of discounted tax savings conferred by the tax-deductibility of debt interest is called the tax shield.

- In a geared company, variations in earnings before interest and tax generate a magnified impact on shareholder earnings.

- The downside of gearing is the creation of a prior charge against profits, which results in the risk of possible default as well as greater variability of shareholder earnings.

- Default risk is likely to impose further costs on the geared company's shareholders, referred to as the 'costs of financial distress'.

- An insolvent company, i.e. one unable to meet its immediate commitments, is unlikely to achieve full market value in a sale of assets.

- For companies using a mixture of debt and equity, there may be an optimal capital structure at which the overall cost of capital (WACC) is minimised.

- The WACC is found by weighting the cost of each type of finance by its proportionate contribution to overall financing, and may fall as gearing increases.

- The increased risks imposed by gearing are likely to cause lenders and shareholders eventually to demand a higher rate of return, raising the WACC.

- The WACC is the appropriate cut-off rate for new investment so long as the company adheres to the optimal capital proportions.

- When companies deviate from the optimal capital structure, the marginal cost of capital becomes the correct cut-off rate.

- Because the optimal gearing ratio is difficult to identify in practice, many firms aim for a target gearing ratio, which they regard as 'acceptable'.

- In view of the risks of gearing, an increase in borrowing may be a way of signalling to the market greater confidence in the future.

Further reading

Because Chapters 18 and 19 are 'paired', the reading guides have been amalgamated. A composite guide is given at the end of Chapter 19.

Appendix
CREDIT RATINGS

Standard & Poor's credit rating system is shown below, together with that of the other main credit rating agency, Moody's.

Credit risk	S & P	Moody's
Prime	AAA	Aaa
Excellent	AA	Aa
Upper Medium	A	A
Lower Medium	BBB	Baa
Speculative	BB	Ba
Very Speculative	B, CCC, CC	B, Caa
Default	C, D	Ca, C

Source: **www.moodys.com**, **www.standardandpoors.com**

Both agencies make further differentiation on the quality of bonds within each category. Moody's uses a numerical system (1,2,3) and S & P uses a plus or minus. For example, a rating of Aa1 from Moody's is a superior rating than Aa3, and an A+ from S & P is a better rating than A−.

Both rating systems are based on 'default risk and an assessment of the likelihood of recovery'. In each case, the cut-off between investment grade bonds and speculative ones is critical – anything of a speculative nature ('significant speculative characteristics' according to Moody's, and having 'speculative elements whose future cannot be considered as well-assured', according to Standard & Poor) is critical. Anything speculative attracts the unattractive label 'junk bonds', which, of course, incur higher rates of interest.

QUESTIONS

Questions with a **coloured number** have solutions in Appendix B on page 801.

1 Using the accounting information provided below, calculate the following measures of gearing:

- long-term debt (LTD) to equity
- LTD to LTD plus equity
- total debt to equity
- net debt in absolute terms
- net debt to equity
- total debt to total assets
- interest cover
- income gearing
- total liabilities to total assets

Shareholders' funds	£500m
Cash	£20m
Short-term deposits	£40m
Short-term bank borrowing	£50m
Debentures and other long-term debts	£200m
Total assets	£800m
Total liabilities	£300m
Profit before interest and tax	£120m
Net interest payable	£25m

2 Calculate the cost of debt facing a firm that issued £50 million in debentures in £100 units two years ago at a nominal interest rate of 8 per cent p.a., in each of the following cases:
   (i)   market value of debt is £45 million; perpetual life.
   (ii) as (i), but allowing for Corporation Tax at 30 per cent.
   (iii) as for (i), but lifespan of debt is 8 years.
   (iv) as for (iii), but with tax payable at 30 per cent.

3 Darnol plc is currently ungeared and is considering a buy-back of ordinary shares via an open market purchase, borrowing in order to do so. You have been commissioned to report on the likely impact of two alternative policies, depending on the level of sales and operating profit for its products. You are given the following information:

Level of sales	PBIT	Probability
Weak	£5m	0.3
Average	£50m	0.5
Strong	£150m	0.2

Equity is currently £200 million at book value. Tax is paid at 30 per cent. Two alternative share buy-back programmes are under consideration:
   (i)   Borrowing £40 million at 8 per cent.
   (ii) Borrowing £80 million at 8.5 per cent.

Required

(a) Calculate the current, and potential expected annual return on equity (ROE) under each programme.

(b) Calculate the standard deviation of the ROE in each case.

(c) Using the figures you have obtained, explain and illustrate the distinction between business and financial risk.

4 (a) Calculate the value of the tax shield in each of the following cases, all based on borrowing of £100 million at 10 per cent interest p.a., pre-tax.

   (i) Perpetual life debt, tax rate is 30 per cent.

   (ii) Debt repayable in full after five years.

   (iii) Debt repayable in equal tranches over five years, interest paid on the declining balance.

(b) Specify the factors that determine the value of the tax shield that a firm can exploit.

5 Calculate the weighted average cost of capital for the following company, using both book value and market value weightings.

	Statement of financial position (Balance sheet) values	Cost of finance
Ordinary shares: (par value 50p)	£10m	20%
Reserves:	£20m	20%
Long-term debt:	£15m	10%

The debt is permanent and its market value is equal to book value.
The rate of Corporate Tax is 30%.
The ordinary shares are currently trading at £4.50.

6 The directors of Zeus plc are considering opening a new manufacturing facility. The finance director has provided the following information:
Initial capital investment: £2,500,000.
Dividends for the last five years have been:

Year	2010	2011	2012	2013	2014
Net dividend per share (pence)	10.0	10.8	11.4	13.2	13.7

The following is an extract from the statement of financial position of Zeus plc for the year ended 31 December 2014.

Creditors due in more than one year

8% Debenture	£700,000
Long-term loan (variable rate)	£800,000
Capital and reserves	
2,000,000 shares of 25p each	£500,000

The authorised share capital is 4 million shares, the current market price per share at 31 December 2014 is 136p ex-dividend.

The current market price of debentures is £60 (ex-interest) and interest is payable each year on 31 December.

The interest rate on the long-term loan is 1 per cent above LIBOR, which at present stands at 16 per cent.

The debentures are irredeemable.

Ignore taxation.

Required

Calculate the weighted average cost of capital (WACC) for Zeus plc at 31 December 2014.

7 RH plc manufactures machine tools. It has issued two million ordinary shares, quoted at 168 pence each, and £1 million 10 per cent secured debentures quoted at par. To finance expansion, the directors of the company want to raise £1 million for additional working capital.

Cash flow from trading before interest and tax is currently £1 million per annum. It is expected to rise to £1.3 million per annum if the expansion programme goes ahead. To simplify placing a valuation on the company's equity, you should assume that:

- The forecast level of cash flow, and a tax rate of 33 per cent, will continue indefinitely.
- The required rate of return on the market value of equity, 18 per cent post-tax, will be unaffected by the new financing.
- There is no difference between taxable profits and cash flow.

The company's directors are considering two forms of finance – equity via a rights issue at 15 per cent discount to current share price, or 12 per cent unsecured loan stock at par.

Required
(a) Calculate for both financing options, the expected
    (i) increase in the market value of equity
    (ii) debt/(debt + equity) ratio
    (iii) weighted average cost of capital.
(b) Assume you are the financial manager for RH plc. Write a brief report to the board advising which of the two types of financing is to be preferred. Include in your report brief comments on non-financial factors which should be considered by the directors before deciding how to raise the £1 million finance.

(CIMA)

8 Celtor plc is a property development company operating in the London area. The company has the following capital structure as at 30 November 2014.

	£000
£1 ordinary shares	10,000
Retained profit	20,000
9% debentures	12,000
	42,000

The equity shares have a current market value of £3.90 per share and the current level of dividend is 20 pence per share. The dividend has been growing at a compound rate of 4 per cent per annum in recent years. The debentures of the company are irredeemable and have a current market value of £80 per £100 nominal. Interest due on the debentures at the year end has recently been paid.

The company has obtained planning permission to build a new office block in a redevelopment area. The company wishes to raise the whole of the finance necessary for the project by the issue of more irredeemable 9 per cent debentures at £80 per £100 nominal. This is in line with a target capital structure set by the company where the amount of debt capital will increase to 70 per cent of equity within the next two years.

The rate of corporation tax is 25 per cent.

Required
(a) Explain what is meant by the term 'cost of capital'. Why is it important for a company to calculate its cost of capital correctly?
(b) What are the main factors which determine the cost of capital of a company?
(c) Calculate the weighted average cost of capital of Celtor plc which should be used for future investment decisions.

9 Redley plc, which manufactures building products, experienced a sharp increase in operating profit (i.e. profits before interest and tax) from £27 million in 2012–13 to £42 million in 2013–14 as the company emerged from recession and demand for new houses increased. The increase in profits has been entirely due to volume expansion, with margins remaining static. It still has substantial excess capacity and therefore no pressing need to invest, apart from routine replacements.

In the past, Redley has followed a conservative financial policy, with restricted dividend payouts and relatively low borrowing levels. It now faces the issue of how to utilise an unexpectedly sizeable cash surplus. Directors have made two main suggestions. One is to redeem the £10 million of the secured loan stock issued to finance investment several years previously, the other is to increase the dividend payment by the same amount.

Redley's present capital structure is shown below:

	£m
Issued share capital (par value 50p)	90
Reserves	110
Creditors due after more than one year:	
9% secured loan stock 2004	30

Further information
(i) Redley has no overdraft.
(ii) Redley pays corporate tax at a rate of 33%.
(iii) The last dividend paid by Redley was 1.45 pence per share.
(iv) Sector averages currently stand as follows:

dividend cover	2.5 times
gearing (long-term debt/equity)	48%
interest cover	5.9 times

(v) Redley's P:E ratio is 17:1.

Required
(a) Calculate **(i)** the dividend cover and **(ii)** the dividend yield for both 2012–13 and for the reporting year 2013–14, if the dividend is raised as proposed.
(b) You have been hired to work as a financial strategist for Redley, reporting to the Finance Director. Using the information provided, write a report to your superior, which identifies and discusses the issues to be addressed when assessing the relative merits of the two proposals for reducing the cash surplus.

(ACCA)

Practical assignment

For a company of your choice, undertake an analysis of gearing similar to that conducted in the text for D.S. Smith plc. Pay particular attention to the treatment of provisions and other components of long-term liabilities. If you decide to include short-term indebtedness in your capital gearing measure, would you include trade and other creditors as well?

Try to form a view as to whether your company is operating with high or low gearing.

19

Does capital structure really matter?

A theorem fit to terrify bankers

Looking down the list of winners of the Nobel memorial prize in economics, two names are causing bankers across the world to break into a cold sweat. They are Franco Modigliani (laureate in 1985) and Merton H. Miller (laureate in 1990). Both men have been dead for years but their most important idea lives on with the undignified name of M&M.

M&M refers to an important-seeming decision for any company: how much should it be funded by borrowing, and how much through raising money by issuing shares or retaining profits? Some companies, famously Apple, have no debt to speak of. Others,

including any bank you can name, raise most of their resources by borrowing rather than issuing shares.

Regulators want banks to fund themselves more through equity and less through debt. Bankers are reluctant. Bankers have tended to argue that equity is scarce and expensive and too much equity means that banks will make fewer loans at higher rates. M&M shows us that this argument is wrong in theory. In practice, M&M roughly holds: as leverage falls, equity becomes substantially cheaper.

Source: Based on Tim Harford, *Financial Times*, 9 March 2013, p. 52.

Learning objectives

This chapter offers a more rigorous analysis of capital structure decisions. After reading it, you should:

- Understand the theoretical underpinnings of 'modern' capital structure theory.
- Appreciate the differences between the 'traditional' view of gearing and the Modigliani–Miller versions.
- Appreciate how the CAPM is integrated into capital structure analysis.
- Be able to identify the extent to which a Beta coefficient incorporates financial risk.

19.1 INTRODUCTION

The title of this chapter poses a question. In the last chapter, we warned that excessive debt could be lethal to the survival of firms. Yet such debt-burdened firms can, and often do, 'rise from the dead'.

Insolvency does not necessarily mean total loss of *enterprise value*. Insolvency is the formal acceptance that the business entity cannot meet its financial obligations, whether payment to creditors for supplies, or payments to lenders. Yet it is possible for insolvent firms to retain value as operating entities even though their owners' equity may have been wiped out. A few figures may help.

XYZ owes £10 million to lenders and its assets are only £8 million, so it is technically insolvent, unable to cover its debts with its assets, i.e. its net assets are negative – minus £2 million. However, if its operating activities generate more cash inflows than outflows, then as a debt-free entity, it would be viable and have value. Hence, it might look attractive as a restructured going concern to other investors prepared to take responsibility for the debts. Creditors might be prepared to exchange debt for equity or preference shares, or take a discount on their principal, accepting, say, 30p in the pound, just to salvage something from the mess. The equity value has disappeared but the enterprise still has value as a going concern if investors can be found to refinance it and reorganise it into a viable operation.

Even the heavily indebted Eurotunnel ('financial liabilities' of €3.9 billion in 2013) (**www .eurotunnel.com**) is able to deliver a positive EBITDA (€449 million in 2013). On this basis, it has an enterprise value even though the original equity has been all but wiped out.

One might then conclude that indebtedness does not really matter – a firm that cannot pay its way can be restructured and the jobs of the workers, if not the management, can be preserved.

In 2014 Readers Digest, the magazine publisher, was sold for £1. This might seem to be a small price to pay for a long-established company. However, the company had been struggling and filed for bankruptcy with liabilities of $1.2 billion and assets of $1.1 billion. Therefore, the price paid reflects the state of the company and the high level of indebtedness.

So long as assets can be sold at their full economic value, i.e. reflecting operating cash flows, then debt is of most consequence to the hapless owners whose equity is usually all but obliterated. Meanwhile, the business can proceed, often in a slimmed-down form and usually under different management, with a new set of backers hoping to do better next time round. This suggests that the sting of insolvency can be drawn.

The traditional theory of gearing says that debt should be handled with great caution but there is a body of analysis that proves that, under certain conditions, debt is truly irrelevant in determining company value and the cost of capital. This is the famous theory developed by Franco Modigliani and Merton Miller (MM), both Nobel prizewinners for Economics. Our next task is to explain this theory.

19.2 THE MODIGLIANI–MILLER MESSAGE

Modigliani and Miller's (MM)
Capital Structure Theories
(i) MM-no tax, which 'proves' that no optimal capital structure exists, and that the WACC is invariant to debt/equity ratios
(ii) MM-with tax which suggests that the tax shield should be exploited up to the point of almost 100 per cent debt financing

To **Modigliani and Miller (MM)**, the traditional perception of the impact and desirability of gearing seemed unsupported by a theoretical framework. In particular, there seemed little reason, apart from some form of market imperfection such as information deficiency, why merely altering the capital structure of a firm should be expected to alter its value. *After all, neither its earnings stream nor its inherent business risk would alter* – it would remain essentially the same enterprise, operating under the same managers and in the same industry.

MM contended that, in a perfect capital market, the value of a company depended simply on its income stream and the degree of business risk attaching to this, regardless of the way in which its income was split between owners and lenders, i.e. its capital structure. There-

fore, any imbalance between the value of a geared company and an otherwise identical ungeared company could only be a temporary aberration and would be quickly unwound by market forces. The mechanism for equalising the values of companies, identical except for their respective gearing, was the process of 'arbitrage', a feature of all developed financial markets which ensures that assets with the same risk–return characteristics sell at the same prices.

To support these contentions, some algebraic analysis is required, although readers will find that it is much less complex than may appear at first sight.

■ MM's analytical framework

No distinction is made between short- and long-term debt and we assume that all borrowing is perpetual. The company is expected to deliver constant and perpetual estimated annual earnings, described by a normally distributed range of possible outcomes. Investors are assumed to have homogeneous expectations, i.e. they all formulate similar estimates of company earnings, E, the net operating income (NOI) before interest and tax, or, more simply, revenues less variable costs less fixed operating costs. It is important to note that we are using a **free cash flow (FCF)** concept of earnings as explained in Chapter 11, i.e. income net of any investment required to rectify wear-and-tear on capital equipment and hence maintain annual earnings at E.

free cash flow (FCF)
A firm's cash flow free of obligatory payments. Strictly, it is cash flow after interest, tax and replacement investment, although it is measured in many other ways in practice, e.g. after all investment

The discount rate applied to the stream of expected earnings depends on the degree of business risk incurred by the enterprise. MM used the concept of 'equivalent risk classes', each one containing firms whose earnings depend on the same risk factors and from which the market expects the same return. In terms of the Capital Asset Pricing Model, this means that the earnings streams from firms in the same risk category are perfectly correlated and that member companies have identical activity Betas.

For consistency, we use the same definitions and notation as in Chapter 18. The key definitions are reproduced in Table 19.1.

The overall rate of return that the company must achieve to satisfy all its investors is the weighted average cost of capital (WACC), denoted by k_0. This can be expressed as:

$$k_0 = \left(k_e \times \frac{V_S}{V_0} \right) + \left(k_d \times \frac{V_B}{V_0} \right) = \frac{E}{V_0}$$

The WACC equals E / V_0, since net operating income is composed of earnings attributable to shareholders, $k_e V_S$, plus payments to lenders, iB.

Using this set of definitions, we now examine the impact of variations in capital structure on V_0 and k_0. Using debt-for-equity substitution rather than adding debt to equity has the major advantage of enabling us to hold constant both the book values of assets and capital employed and also the PBIT (a device used in the Lindley example in Chapter 18). Any gearing change alters only the company's capital structure, with no effect on company size or the level and riskiness of operating earnings. As a result, we can focus directly on the relationship between V_0 and k_0.

■ MM's assumptions

The MM thesis did not go unchallenged. Much criticism of MM's analysis stemmed from failure to understand positive scientific methodology. Their analysis attempted to isolate the critical variables affecting firm value under the restrictive conditions of a perfect capital market. This provided a systematic basis for examining how imperfections in real world markets could influence the links between value and risk. The key assumptions are:

■ All investors are price-takers, i.e. no individual can influence market prices by the scale of their transactions.

Table 19.1 Key definitions in capital structure analysis

$$V_0 = \text{the overall market value of the whole company}$$
$$V_S = \text{the value of the shareholders' stake in the company}$$
$$V_B = \text{the market value of the company's outstanding borrowings}$$
$$B = \text{the book value of borrowings (generally assumed equal to its market value)}$$
$$k_e = \text{the rate of return required by shareholders}$$
$$k_d = \text{the rate of return required by providers of debt capital}$$
$$k_0 = \text{the overall (weighted average) cost of capital}$$
$$i = \text{the coupon rate on debt}$$
$$iB = \text{annual interest charges (i.e. payments to lenders, based on book value)}$$
$$k_e V_S = \text{payments to shareholders} = (E - iB), \text{ so that}$$
$$E = \text{annual net operating income (NOI)} = (iB + k_e V_S)$$

It should be stressed that we are assuming no retention of earnings, i.e. D (dividends) = E, and hence no growth, and, for the moment, no taxes on corporate profits.

The value of equity in an all-equity firm is:

$$V_S = \frac{D}{k_e} = \frac{E}{k_e}$$

The value of a geared firm making interest payments of iB is:

$$V_S = \frac{(E - iB)}{k_e}$$

The value of the whole firm in either case is:
$$V_0 = V_S + V_B$$

- All market participants, firms and investors, can lend or borrow at the same risk-free rate.
- There are neither personal nor corporate income taxes.
- There are no brokerage or other transactions charges.
- Investors are all rational wealth-seekers.
- Firms can be grouped into 'homogeneous risk classes', such that the market seeks the same return from all member firms in each group.
- Investors formulate similar expectations about future company earnings. These are described by a normal probability distribution.
- The assets of an insolvent firm can be sold at full market values (i.e. no distress costs).

19.3 MM'S PROPOSITIONS

MM's analysis was presented as three propositions, the first being the crucial one.

■ Proposition I

The central proposition is that *a firm's WACC is independent of its debt/equity ratio, and equal to the cost of capital that the firm would have with no gearing in its capital structure.* In other words, the appropriate capitalisation rate for a firm is the rate applied by the market to an ungeared company in the relevant risk category, i.e. that company's cost of equity. The arbitrage mechanism will operate to equalise the values of any two companies whose values are temporarily out of line with each other. The example of Nogear plc and Higear plc will illustrate this.

Nogear plc and Higear plc

Nogear plc is ungeared, financed by 5 million £1 shares, while Higear plc's balance sheet shows £1 million debt, interest payable at 10 per cent, and 4 million £1 shares. Higear's debt/equity ratio is thus (£1m/£4m) = 25 per cent, at book values. The two firms are identical in every other respect, including their business risks and levels of annual expected earnings (E) of £1 million. The market requires a return of 20 per cent for ungeared streams of equity income of this risk.

Imagine that, temporarily, the market value of Nogear is £4 million and that of Higear is £6 million. Higear's equity is thus valued by the market at (£6m − £1m) = £5m. (Its debt/equity ratio expressed in terms of *market* values is thus £1m/£5m = 20 per cent.) These market values correspond to respective share prices of (£4m/5m shares) = 80p for Nogear and (£5m/4m shares) = £1.25 for Higear.

The different share values conform to the traditional relationship at relatively low gearing ratios. Higear has a greater value presumably due to its gearing. Also, it appears that Nogear is undervalued by the market since, at a required return of 20 per cent, its value should be (£1m/0.2) = £5m.

MM argue that such imbalances can only be temporary and the benefit obtained by Higear for its shareholders is largely illusory. It will pay investors to sell their holdings in the overvalued company and buy stakes in the undervalued one. Specifically, shareholders can achieve a higher return by selling holdings in Higear, and simultaneously replicate its gearing (MM call this '**home-made gearing**') and achieve a higher overall return. This process of arbitrage will force up the value of Nogear and lower Higear's value, until their values are equalised. There is thus little point in a firm borrowing to gear-up its capital structure when investors can achieve the same benefits by acting independently.

'home-made gearing'
Where an investor borrows to arbitrage between two identical but differently valued assets

Home-made gearing

Consider the case of an investor with a 1 per cent equity stake in Higear. At present, this stake is worth (1 per cent of £5m) = £50,000, attracting an income of 1 per cent of (£1 million less interest payments of 10% × £1m), i.e. (1% × £900,000) = £9,000. This investor could realise his or her holdings for £50,000 and duplicate Higear's debt/equity ratio of 20 per cent by borrowing £10,000 at 10 per cent and investing the total stake of £60,000 in Nogear shares. This would buy (£60,000/£4m) = 1.5% of Nogear's equity, to yield a dividend of (1.5% × £1m) = £15,000. Personal interest commitments amount to (10% × borrowings of £10,000) = £1,000 for a net return of (£15,000 − £1,000) = £14,000, well in excess of the income formerly obtained from their holding in Higear, i.e. £9,000. Clearly, it would pay all investors to undertake this arbitrage exercise, thus pushing down the value of Higear and pushing up the value of Nogear until there was no further scope to exploit such gains. This point would be reached when the market values of the two companies were equal and when each offered the appropriate 20 per cent return required by the market:

$$\text{Value of Nogear} = \text{Value of Higear} = \frac{E}{k_e} = \frac{£1m}{0.2} = £5m$$

At this equilibrium relationship, the price of each company's shares is £1. For Nogear, the calculation is (£5m/5m shares) = £1, while for Higear, the relevant figures are (£5m − £1m debt) divided by 4m shares = £1. *In an MM world, there are no prolonged benefits from gearing, and any short-term discrepancies between geared and otherwise identical ungeared companies quickly evaporate. As a result, MM concluded that both company value and the overall required return, k_0, are independent of capital structure.*

In reality, not all of the conditions required to support the arbitrage process may apply, suggesting that any *observed* benefits may derive from imperfections in the capital market. Moreover, if gearing does result in higher company value, there must have been a wealth transfer, since nothing has occurred to alter the fundamental wealth-creating properties of the company.

■ Proposition II: the behaviour of the cost of equity

Underpinning Proposition I is a statement about the behaviour of the relevant cost of capital concepts – in particular, the rate of return required by shareholders. This is expressed in MM's second proposition which states *'the expected yield of a share of equity is equal to the appropriate capitalisation rate, k_e, for a pure equity stream in the class, plus a premium related to the financial risk equal to the debt/equity ratio times the spread between k_e and k_d'*. This proposition can be expressed as:

$$k_{eg} = k_{eu} + (k_{eu} - k_d)\frac{V_B}{V_S}$$

where k_{eg} and k_{eu} denote the returns required by the shareholders of a geared company and an equivalent ungeared company, respectively. The expression is easily obtained from Proposition I. (See Appendix I to this chapter.) It simply tells us that *the rate of return required by shareholders increases linearly as the debt/equity ratio is increased,* i.e. the cost of equity rises exactly in line with any increase in gearing to offset precisely any benefits conferred by the use of apparently cheap debt. The relevant relationships are shown in Figure 19.1.

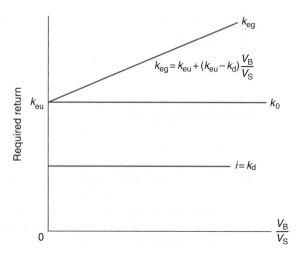

Figure 19.1 MM's Propositions I and II

If you check back to Chapter 18, which covered the traditional view of gearing, and to Figure 18.2 in particular, you will find that the behaviour of k_e is the critical difference between the MM version and the traditional theory. In the latter, there is little or no reaction by shareholders to an increase in debt-to-equity ratio over 'modest' levels of gearing. They presumably are not alarmed by the 'judicious' use of debt. By contrast, shareholders, in the MM view, respond immediately when any gearing is undertaken, i.e. to them, *any* use of debt introduces an element of financial risk.

It should now be appreciated that in the Nogear/Higear example, Higear shareholders were seeking too low a rate of return, i.e. Higear was overvalued, and the market was temporarily offering Nogear's shareholders too high a return, i.e. Nogear was undervalued. Via the process of arbitrage, their values were brought back into line, and appropriate rates of return on equity were established, reflecting their respective levels of gearing. The correct rate of return for Higear's equity, for its particular debt/equity ratio of 25 per cent (at equilibrium market values) is:

$$k_{eg} = k_{eu} + (k_{eu} - k_d)\frac{V_B}{V_S} = 20\% + (20\% - 10\%)\frac{£1m}{£4m} = 22.5\%$$

■ Proposition III: the cut-off rate for new investment

MM's third proposition asserts that *'the cut-off rate for new investment will in all cases be k_0 and will be unaffected by the type of security used to finance the investment'*.

A proof of this proposition is given in Appendix II to this chapter, but it is quite easy to justify intuitively. Proposition I states that the WACC, k_0, is constant and equal to the cost of equity in an equivalent ungeared company. Since k_0, is invariant to capital structure, it follows that however a project is financed, it must yield a return of at least k_0, the overall minimum return required to satisfy stakeholders as a whole.

It is worth illustrating this contention for the case where a company invests to yield a return *above* the cost of the debt used to finance the project, but *below* the cost of equity in an ungeared company.

Nogear: right and wrong investment cut-off rates

Nogear decides to raise £2 million via a debt issue at 10 per cent to finance a new project expected to yield an annual return of 15 per cent for many years into the future. Is this an acceptable project? Proposition I tells us that the initial value of the company, V_0, and hence the equity, V_{S0}, prior to the issue is:

$$V_0 = V_{S0} = \frac{E}{k_e} = \frac{£1m}{0.2} = £5m$$

Incorporating the new project's earnings, the post-issue value of the whole company, V_1, is:

$$V_1 = \frac{£1m + (15\% \times £2m)}{20\%} = \frac{£1.30m}{0.2} = £6.50m$$

Denoting R as the return on the new investment, I, and V_B as the value of the debt issued, the new value of the equity, V_{S1}, is:

$$V_{S1} = V_0 + \frac{RI}{k_0} - V_{B0} - I = £5m + \frac{£0.30m}{0.2} - 0 - £2m = (£6.50m - £2m)$$
$$= £4.50m$$

The value of the equity falls because the new project's return, although above the interest rate on the debt used to finance it, is less than the capitalisation rate applicable to companies in this risk category.

Self-assessment activity 19.1

Why does a geared company have the same value (allowing for size) as an ungeared company of equivalent risk in the 'basic' MM model?

(Answer in Appendix A at the back of the book)

19.4 DOES IT WORK? IMPEDIMENTS TO ARBITRAGE

The operation of the arbitrage process requires that corporate and personal gearing are perfect substitutes in a perfect capital market. The Nogear/Higear example showed how individual investors could replicate corporate gearing to unwind any transitory premium in the share price of a geared company. Much criticism of MM centres on the perfect capital market assumptions and hence the extent to which the arbitrage process can be expected to operate in practice.

In reality, brokerage fees discriminate against small investors, and other transaction costs limit the gains from arbitrage. Moreover, if companies can borrow at lower rates than individuals, investors may prefer the equity of geared companies as vehicles for obtaining benefits otherwise denied to them. It is well known that, for reasons of size, security and convenience, large firms can borrow at lower rates than small firms and individuals. In addition, some major UK investors (e.g. pension funds) face restrictions on their borrowing powers, limiting their scope for home-made gearing. Finally, whereas the shareholders in a geared firm have the protection of limited liability, personal borrowers enjoy no such protection in the event of bankruptcy.

Some authors suggest that such imperfections may foster investor demand for the equity of geared companies. However, to sustain this argument, we would need to produce evidence that relatively (but safely) geared companies are more attractively rated by the market. There is little evidence that such firms sell at relatively high P:E ratios. Indeed, UK investment trust companies, which invest in equities, often using substantial borrowed capital, typically sell at significant *discounts* to their net asset values – discounts far higher than can be plausibly explained by the transactions costs that would be incurred in liquidating their portfolios.

Self-assessment activity 19.2

What factors restrict the ability of investors to arbitrage in the way envisaged by MM?

(Answer in Appendix A at the back of the book)

19.5 MM WITH CORPORATE INCOME TAX

The analysis of MM's three propositions in Section 19.3 is a theoretical exercise, designed to isolate the key variables relating company value and gearing. This only becomes operational when 'real-world' complications are introduced. Perhaps the most important of these is corporate taxation. In most economies, corporate interest charges are tax-allowable, providing an incentive for companies to gear their capital structures. In a taxed world, the MM conclusions change significantly.

Because corporation tax is applied to earnings after deducting interest charges, the value of a geared company's shares is the capitalised value of the after-tax earnings stream (net income), i.e. $(E - iB)(1 - T)$:

$$V_S = \frac{(E - iB)(1 - T)}{k_{eg}}$$

where k_{eg} is the return required by shareholders, allowing for financial risk, and T is the rate of tax on corporate profits.

Assuming that the book and market values of debt capital coincide ($B = V_B$), so that the cost of debt, k_d, equates to the coupon rate, i, the value of debt is the discounted interest stream, i.e. $V_B = iB/i$. The value of the whole company is thus:

$$V_0 = V_S + V_B = \frac{(E - iB)(1 - T)}{k_{eg}} + \frac{iB}{i}$$

It can be shown that geared companies will sell at a premium over equivalent ungeared companies because of the benefits of tax-allowable debt interest. The post-tax annual expected earnings stream, E_T, comprises the earnings attributable to shareholders plus the debt interest:

$$E_T = (E - iB)(1 - T) + iB$$

This simplifies to:

$$E_T = E(1 - T) + TiB$$

This second expression is very useful: the first element is the net income that the shareholders in an equivalent ungeared company would receive, while the second element is the annual tax benefit afforded by debt interest relief. The total value of the geared company, V_g, is found by capitalising the first element at the cost of equity capital applicable to an ungeared company (k_{eu}), while the second is capitalised at the cost of debt, which we have assumed equals the nominal rate of interest, i:

$$V_g = \frac{E(1 - T)}{k_{eu}} + \frac{TiB}{i} = \frac{E(1 - T)}{k_{eu}} + TB = V_u + TB$$

This is a highly significant result. The expression for the value of the geared company comprises the value of an equivalent ungeared company, V_u, plus a premium derived by discounting to perpetuity the stream of tax savings that can be claimed so long as the company has sufficient taxable capacity, i.e. if $E > iB$ The introduction of this second term, TB, the discounted value of future tax savings, or the **tax shield**, is a major modification of MM's Proposition I, as shown in Figure 19.2.

tax shield
The tax savings achieved by setting tax-allowable expenses such as interest payments against profits

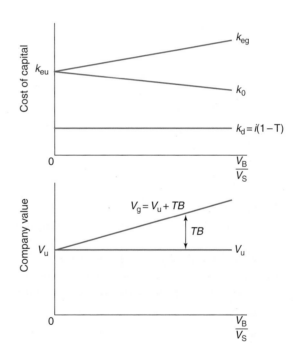

Figure 19.2 The MM thesis with corporate income tax

Self-assessment activity 19.3

Determine the respective values of geared and ungeared firms if:

- Earnings = £100m before tax
- Tax rate = 30%
- k_{eu} = 15%
- The geared firm borrows £200m.

(*Answer in Appendix A at the back of the book*)

■ Impact on the required return

The company value profile now rises continuously with gearing. Proposition II also needs modification. With no corporate tax, this stated that the shareholders in a geared company require a return, k_{eg}, of:

$$k_{eg} = k_{eu} + (k_{eu} - k_d)\frac{V_B}{V_S}$$

However, in a taxed world, the return required by shareholders becomes:

$$k_{eg} = k_{eu} + (k_{eu} - k_d)(1 - T)\frac{V_B}{V_S}$$

The return required by the geared company's shareholders is now the cost of equity in an identical ungeared company plus a financial risk premium related to the corporate tax rate and the debt/equity ratio.

The premium for financial risk required by shareholders is lower in this version owing to the tax deductibility of debt interest, making the debt interest burden less onerous. This relationship is also shown in Figure 19.2. It follows that if, at every level of gearing, the cost of equity is lower and also the cost of debt itself is reduced by interest deductibility, the WACC (k_0) is lower at all gearing ratios, and declines as gearing increases. Figure 19.2 shows the effect on the WACC.

The tax advantage of debt financing is incorporated in the revised equation for the WACC:

$$k_0 = \left[k_{eg} \times \frac{V_S}{V_S + V_B} \right] + \left[i(1 - T) \times \frac{V_S}{V_S + V_B} \right]$$

This can also be written as:

$$k_0 = k_{eu} \left[1 - \frac{T \times V_B}{V_S + V_B} \right]$$

Clearly, there are significant advantages from gearing, with the implication that companies should gear up until debt provides almost 100 per cent of its financing. However, this does not seem plausible. Surely there are practical, 'sensible' limits to company gearing, given the risks involved? More of this later!

Self-assessment activity 19.4

Compare the overall required return in geared and ungeared firms if:

■ $k_{eu} = 15\%$

■ Tax rate $= 30\%$

■ The geared firm has borrowed £200m at 7% interest, and has issued equity of £400m.

(Answer in Appendix A at the back of the book)

■ Example of the impact of corporate taxation

It is now helpful to demonstrate 'with-tax' relationships using the examples of Nogear and Higear. Recall that both companies had E of £1 million and their equilibrium market values were £5 million under the 'no-tax' version of the MM thesis. After taxation, shareholder earnings in Nogear fall to £1m$(1 - T)$. With 30 per cent corporate tax, this is £1m$(1 - 30\%) = £0.70$m. Capitalised at 20 per cent, the value of the ungeared company is:

$$V_u = \frac{£1m(1 - 30\%)}{k_{eu}} = \frac{£0.70m}{0.2} = £3.50m$$

In the case of Higear, net income for shareholders is given by taxable earnings of $(E - iB)$ less the tax charge of $T(E - iB)$ to yield net income of:

$$\text{NI} = (E - iB)(1 - T) = [\text{£1m} - (10\% \times \text{£1m})](1 - 30\%)$$

$$= (\text{£0.9m} \times 0.7) = \text{£0.63m}$$

This might be capitalised at the geared cost of equity and added to the value of debt to yield the overall company value. However, there is a circular problem here, since the calculation of the market value of the shares, V_S, derives from the calculation of k_{eg}, which itself depends on V_S. A remedy for this problem is to use the expression $V_g = V_u + TB$ encountered above. This yields:

$$V_g = V_u + TB = \text{£3.50m} + (30\% \times \text{£1m}) = (\text{£3.50m} + \text{£0.30m}) = \text{£3.80m}$$

It is useful also to cross-check on the components of V_g and the return required by Higear's shareholders. If $V_g = \text{£3.80m}$, and the value of debt is £1 million, the value of Higear's equity must be $(\text{£3.80m} - \text{£1m}) = \text{£2.80m}$. Using the revised expression for the return required by the shareholders of a geared company, we find:

$$k_{eg} = k_{eu} + (k_{eu} - i)(1 - T)\frac{V_B}{V_S}$$

$$= 20\% + (20\% - 10\%)(1 - 30\%)\frac{\text{£1m}}{\text{£2.8m}}$$

$$= (20\% + 2.5\%) = 22.5\%$$

The geared company clearly has a greater market value – it is worth more due to the value of the tax shield. The size of this tax shield depends on the gearing ratio, the rate of taxation and the taxable capacity of the enterprise. Since gearing has raised company value, the earlier conclusion, that the benefits of gearing are illusory, must be modified. The reason is that the stakeholders of Higear benefit at the expense of the taxpayer due to the tax deductibility of debt interest. (Whether this is desirable or not in a wider context depends on the value of the forgone tax revenues in their alternative use, which is an issue for welfare economists.)

In its tax-adjusted form, the MM thesis looks rather more like the traditional version, in so far as the WACC declines over some range of gearing. However, the benefits from gearing clearly derive from the tax system, rather than from the apparent failure of the shareholders to respond fully to financial risk by seeking higher returns. We will discover that the similarity becomes even closer when we allow for financial distress. Before doing this, we will show how the MM approach can be integrated with the CAPM.

19.6 CAPITAL STRUCTURE THEORY AND THE CAPM

A feature of MM's initial model was the classification of firms into 'homogeneous risk classes' as a way of controlling for inherent operating or business risk. The modern distinction between systematic and specific risk makes this device unnecessary, as relevant business risk is expressed by the Beta. The key point is that gearing introduces additional risk so that shareholders require additional compensation. Whereas in an ungeared firm the cost of equity is:

$$k_{eu} = R_f + \beta_u(ER_m - R_f)$$

where k_{eu} and β_u represent the required return and Beta values, respectively, that are applicable to an ungeared firm. In a geared firm, this becomes

$$k_{eg} = R_f + \beta_g(ER_m - R_f)$$

with

$$\beta_g > \beta_u$$

and

$$k_{eg} > k_{eu}$$

Clearly, gearing increases the equity Beta. It is a relatively simple task to integrate the MM analysis with the CAPM. This was first performed by Hamada (1969), who demonstrated that the required return on the equity of a geared firm in a CAPM framework is:

$$k_{eg} = R_f + (ER_m - R_f) \times \beta_u \times \left[1 + \frac{V_B(1 - T)}{V_S} \right]$$

where β_u is the Beta applicable to the earnings of an ungeared company, or the pure equity Beta. Multiplying out, we derive:

$$k_{eg} = R_f + \beta_u(ER_n - R_f) + (ER_m - R_f) \times \beta_u \times \left[\frac{V_B(1 - T)}{V_S} \right]$$

This looks unwieldy, but is a useful vehicle for making the distinction between business and financial risk. The Betas, recorded by the London Business School, are geared equity Betas, incorporating elements of both types of risk. Given that, and using Hamada's revised CAPM expression, the geared Beta, β_g, is:

$$k_{eg} = R_f + \beta_g(ER_m - R_f)$$

$$\beta_g = \beta_u \left[1 + \frac{V_B(1 - T)}{V_S} \right]$$

The ungeared equity Beta is therefore:

$$\beta_u = \frac{\beta_g}{\left[1 + \dfrac{V_B(1 - T)}{V_S} \right]}$$

This can also be written as:

$$\beta_u = \beta_g \times \left[\frac{V_S}{V_S + V_B(1 - T)} \right]$$

The shareholders of a geared company seek compensation for two separate types of risk – the underlying or basic risk of the business activity, and also for financial risk. The rewards for bearing these two forms of risk are the respective premiums for business risk and for gearing.

■ Higear and Nogear: separating the risk premiums

To explore this distinction, consider again the example of Nogear and Higear. Assume that the ungeared Beta applicable to this risk class is 1.11, the risk-free return is 10 per cent, the return expected on the market portfolio is 19 per cent and the corporate tax rate is 30 per cent. Recall that when we last encountered these companies (see Section 19.5) their respective values were:

Nogear: $V_u = V_S = £3.50m$

Higear: $V_g = V_u + TB = (£3.50m + £0.30m) = £3.80m$

$$V_B = £1m$$

$$V_S = (£3.80m - £1m) = £2.80m$$

First, we can verify the return required by Nogear's shareholders. This is:

$$k_{eu} = R_f + \beta_u[ER_m - R_f]$$
$$= 10\% + 1.11[19\% - 10\%] = (10\% + 10\%) = 20\%$$

Second, we can analyse the composition of the return required by Higear's shareholders. To find the overall return they seek, we need to know the geared Beta. This is given by:

$$\beta_g = \beta_u\left[1 + \frac{V_B(1-T)}{V_S}\right] = 1.11 \times \left[1 + \frac{£1m(1-30\%)}{£2.80m}\right] = 1.3875$$

For $\beta_g = 1.3875$, the return required by Higear's shareholders is:

$$k_{eg} = R_f + \beta_g[ER_m - R_f] = 10\% + 1.3875[19\% - 10\%]$$
$$= (10\% + 12.5\%) = 22.5\%$$

Analysing the cost of equity for Higear into its components, we find:

$$k_{eg} = \text{Risk-free rate} + \text{Business risk premium} + \text{Financial risk premium}$$

$$= R_f + \beta_u[ER_m - R_f] + [ER_m - R_f]\beta_u \times \frac{V_B(1-T)}{V_s}$$

$$= 10\% + 1.11[19\% - 10\%] + [19\% - 10\%]1.11 \times \frac{£1m(1-30\%)}{£2.80m}$$

$$= (10\% + 10\% + 2.5\%) = 22.5\%$$

This corresponds to the result obtained more directly with the CAPM formula. The two separate components of the geared Beta are shown in Figure 19.3. The increase in the geared Beta, as the debt/equity ratio increases, drives up the additional required premium *pro rata*.

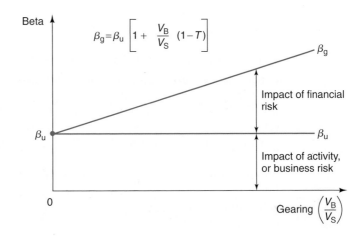

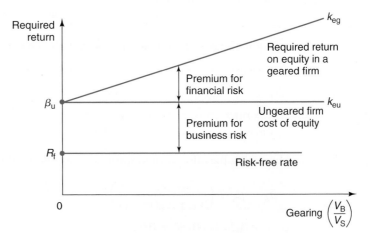

Figure 19.3 Business and financial risk premia and the required return

19.7 LINKING THE BETAS: UNGEARING AND RE-GEARING

There is a useful expression available to show how the various Betas are linked together. It is important to recall the MM message that the underlying business or activity risk is unaffected by the method of financing. If a firm chooses to borrow, thus introducing financial risk, the shareholders will respond by looking for a higher return as they perceive greater financial risk affecting their future income, but the risk attaching to the firm's actual operating activities is untouched – it is the same firm operating in the same business environment and operated by the same managers. All that has happened is a repackaging of the firm's flow of operating income resulting in lenders now having a prior claim. The size of the operating income itself is unaffected, only its distribution changes.

Given that the activity risk is unaffected by gearing, we can use the accounting equation to show the linkages. The accounting equation tells us that the assets are equal to the methods of financing them. Translating this into CAPM terms, the asset Beta (i.e. the activity Beta) equals the Beta of the methods of finance used to acquire those assets. In other words, the asset Beta equates to a weighted average of the Betas of the various methods of financing, according to the importance of each source of finance in the capital structure.

Algebraically, this is given by:

Beta of assets

= (Equity Beta × proportion of equity) + (Debt Beta × proportion of debt)

$$\text{Beta}_A = \left(\text{Beta}_S \times \frac{V_S}{V_S + V_B(1-T)} \right) + \left(\text{Beta}_B \times \frac{V_B(1-T)}{V_S + V_B(1-T)} \right)$$

Notice that the tax shield is reflected in applying the term $(1-T)$ to the debt component. Notice also that, as the debt proportion increases, the equity Beta must increase to preserve the constant asset Beta. It is usual to assume that the debt Beta is zero, although there is some evidence that corporate debt has a very low Beta, around 0.1 to 0.2.

However, if we do assume a debt Beta of zero, this becomes a very versatile expression, e.g. when moving into a new activity we can take a firm's equity Beta and ungear it to reveal the underlying activity Beta. This is particularly useful when diversifying into a new activity – we might borrow a Beta from another firm (a so-called 'surrogate'), whose gearing may differ from our own. In this case, we might ungear the borrowed Beta to strip out that firm's financial risk, and then re-gear to incorporate our own firm's gearing ratio.

To illustrate this, assume we have the following data:

Equity Beta of surrogate firm operating in new activity = 1.35

Gearing ratio (debt/equity) of this firm = 40:60

(i.e. debt proportion = 40:100)
Tax rate = 30%
Own gearing ratio = 10% (debt/equity)

Ungearing the other firm's equity Beta, assuming the debt Beta is zero, we have:

$$\beta_A = \beta_S \times \left(\frac{V_S}{V_S + V_B(1-T)} \right) = 1.35 \times \left(\frac{60}{60 + 40(1-T)} \right)$$

$$= 1.35 \times 60/88 = 0.92$$

Re-gearing to incorporate our own gearing, the equity β^* is given by:

$$0.92 = \beta_S \times \frac{100}{100 + 10(1 - T)} = \beta_S \times 100/107$$

Whence, equity Beta $= 0.92 \times 107/100 = 0.98$

Self-assessment activity 19.5

Ungear a β of 1.45 if:

- Tax rate $= 30\%$
- The debt–equity ratio $= 1:2$

(Answer in Appendix A at the back of the book)

19.8 MM WITH FINANCIAL DISTRESS

In Section 19.5, we saw how including corporate taxation in the MM model implied that companies should rely on debt for nearly 100 per cent of their financing. This implication is clearly at odds with observed practice – few companies gear up to extreme levels, through both their own and lenders' fear of insolvency, and its associated costs. MM's omission of liquidation costs from their analysis was a logical consequence of their perfect capital market assumptions. In such a market, where investors are numerous and rational, and have homogeneous expectations and plentiful access to information, the resale value of assets, even those being sold in a liquidation, will reflect their true economic values. Investors will recognise the worth of such assets as measured by the present values of their future income flows, and be prepared to bid up to this value, so that the price realised by a liquidator should not involve any discount.

costs of financial distress
The costs incurred as a firm approaches, and ultimately reaches, the point of insolvency

In effect, liquidation costs and the other **costs of financial distress** introduce a new imperfection into the analysis of capital structure decisions: namely the actual or expected inability to realise 'full value' for assets in a distress sale and the costs of actions taken to forestall this contingency.

Incorporating financial distress

Denoting the 'costs of financial distress' by *FD,* the value of a geared company becomes:

$$V_g = V_u + [TB - FD]$$

From this, we may conclude that the *financial manager should attempt to maximise the gap between tax benefits and financial distress costs, i.e. (TB – FD), and that there exists an optimal capital structure where company value is maximised.* This occurs where the marginal benefit of further tax savings equals the marginal cost of anticipated financial distress. This occurs with debt of X^* in Figure 19.4.

The costs of financial distress rise with gearing once the market starts to perceive a substantially increased risk of financial failure. The likelihood of *FD* being non-zero depends on the probability distribution of the firm's earnings profile. For example, in the Lindley example in Chapter 18, for gearing ratios up to 50 per cent the probability of inability to meet interest payments is zero, but it would be 0.25 for any higher gearing ratio. For most companies, the probability, *p,* of financial distress will increase

---

[*]A note on terminology and notation: the Beta of the shares, or the equity Beta, β_S, is the same here as β_g, since the latter denotes the Beta of the equity in a geared firm. Of course, β_S becomes equal to β_g in the case of the ungeared firm.

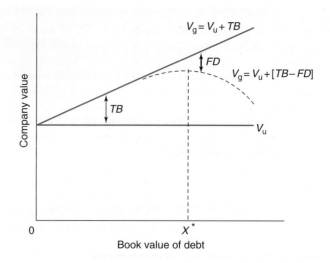

Figure 19.4 Optimal gearing with liquidation costs

with the book values of debt, B, so that the FD function increases with gearing. If d denotes the expected percentage discount on the pre-liquidation value in the event of a forced sale, the expected costs of financial distress are:

$$FD = (p \times d \times V_g)$$

and the value of the geared firm is:

$$V_g = V_u + (TB - p \times d \times V_g)$$

This suggests that market imperfections can be exploited to raise company value so long as TB exceeds $(p \times d \times V_g)$. Notice that the inverted U-shaped value profile now appears remarkably similar to the traditional version and, of course, is associated with a mirror-image WACC schedule.

You may recall our earlier comment that, after introducing market imperfections such as tax, the MM model begins to look more like the traditional version. With the inclusion of financial distress costs, this resemblance is closer still. However, the discussion of the impact of personal taxation in Appendix III at the end of this chapter shows that the debate is not yet dead.

'Climate of fear' for business borrowers

Royal Bank of Scotland is supposed to be at the heart of the British recovery; instead two reports out today accuse it of turning away good companies, exploiting its struggling customers and even presiding over a 'climate of fear'.

The first report, published this month, described the way RBS provided loans to customers as a failure. The final report will flesh out the claim that RBS is turning away three out of four small businesses that approach it for loans. But the report had a more worrying finding that a small number of borrowers had made serious allegations about the way they were treated by the bank when they showed signs of financial distress.

'Viable' companies across the country claimed RBS put them into the hands of what they called the bank's 'hit squad' – the Global Restructuring Group – and were hit with increased fees. The claim is the bank fostered a 'climate of fear' among its struggling customers: 'They are frightened of the bank. RBS acts very strongly against their customers when they complain.'

The report claimed that as well as paying more interest on loans, small businesses were often fined on entry into GRG. One business told the report that their time in GRG had cost them £256,000 in fees. The report notes there were multiple accounts of West Register, the bank's

19.9 CALCULATING THE WACC

Before progressing, you may find it useful to reread Chapter 10, where we discussed the hierarchy of discount rates and required rates of return, but deferred consideration of the problems posed by mixed capital structures until Chapter 18.

The WACC is the overall required return needed to satisfy all stakeholders. It is also the required return on the assumption that new projects are financed in exactly the same way as existing ones. If the company is all-equity financed, then the WACC is simply the return required by shareholders.

Gearing does not affect the underlying risk of the company's business activities. If a company uses debt capital, it is merely repackaging its operating income into different proportions of debt interest and equity income, but not influencing the size or the riskiness of this income before appropriation. What does change is the riskiness of the stream of residual equity income, which is why the equity Beta rises, pulling up with it the return required by shareholders.

We can explore this proposition with the case of Higear. The relevant figures for Higear were:

Value of debt $= V_B = £1m$

Value of equity $= V_S = £2.80m$

Shareholders' required return $= k_{eg} = 22.5\%$

Interest cost of debt $= i = 10\%$

Rate of corporate tax $= T = 30\%$

The expression for the WACC in the MM case with corporate tax is:

$$k_0 = \left(k_{eg} \times \frac{V_S}{V_S + V_B} \right) + \left[i(1 - T) \times \frac{V_B}{V_S + V_B} \right]$$

Using the data for Higear, this expression yields:

$$k_0 = \left(22.5\% \times \frac{£2.80m}{£2.80m + £1m} \right) + \left[10\%(1 - 30\%) \times \frac{£1m}{£2.80m + £1m} \right]$$

$$= (22.5\% \times 0.74) + (7\% \times 0.26)$$

$$= 16.6\% + 1.8\% = 18.4\%$$

Alternatively, we can obtain the same result by using the expression:

$$k_0 = k_{eu} \left[1 - T \times \frac{V_B}{V_S + V_B} \right]$$

$$= 20\% \left[1 - 30\% \frac{£1m}{£3.80m} \right]$$

$$= 20\% \times 0.92$$

$$= 18.4\%$$

■ Relaxing critical assumptions

Two important questions now arise. First, what happens to the discount rate if a company diversifies into an activity with a risk profile different from existing operations? Second, what happens if the gearing ratio is altered? The first issue is easier to handle.

Allowing for different risks

Imagine Higear proposes to diversify into a higher-risk business. Because the discount rate applicable to evaluating this project should reflect the systematic risk involved, the required return previously calculated is no longer appropriate. To cope with this problem, the following procedure is suggested:

1 Select a company already operating in the target activity, ideally, one with operating characteristics very similar to those exhibited by the project, and identify its Beta coefficient, e.g. by using the RMS.
2 If the surrogate company's gearing differs from that of Higear, the Beta must be adjusted by removing the effect of the surrogate's own gearing, and then superimposing Higear's gearing on the resulting ungeared Beta.
3 Calculate the WACC incorporating the surrogate activity Beta, adjusted for Higear's own gearing.

Assume Higear plans to enter an activity already served by Supergear, whose equity Beta is 1.8, and which has a debt/equity ratio of 1:2. Supergear's Beta is ungeared as follows:

$$\beta_u = \frac{\beta_g}{1 + \dfrac{V_B}{V_S}(1 - T)} = \frac{1.8}{1 + \dfrac{1}{2}(1 - 30\%)} = \frac{1.8}{1.35} = 1.33$$

The geared Beta applicable to Higear's capital structure (i.e. £1 million debt and £2.80 million equity) is:

$$\beta_g = \beta_u \left[1 + \frac{V_B}{V_S} \times (1 - T) \right]$$

$$= 1.33 \left[1 + \frac{£1m}{£2.80m} \times (1 - 30\%) \right]$$

$$= 1.33[1.25] = 1.663$$

For this risk, and with a 9 per cent market risk premium, Higear's shareholders require a return of:

$$ER_j = R_f + \beta_g [ER_m - R_f] = 10\% + 1.663[9\%] = 25\%$$

Finally, the WACC applicable to this activity risk and Higear's own gearing is:

$$(25.0\% \times 0.74) + (10\% [1 - 30\%] \times 0.26) = 18.5\% + 1.8\% = 20.3\%$$

The second issue, the effect of a change in gearing, poses more of a conundrum.

Allowing for a change of gearing

In the Higear example, no change in gearing was envisaged when financing new projects. However, as we have repeatedly warned, a significant change in gearing affects the market values of both debt and equity capital: for example, shareholders may respond adversely to higher gearing and the higher financial risk. Also, the value of debt may be marked down in the market. To compute the WACC, we would have to assess the new return required by shareholders, k_{eg}, given by:

$$k_{eg} = k_{eu} + (k_{eu} - i)(1 - T)\frac{V_B}{V_S} = R_f + \beta_g (ER_m - R_f)$$

where

$$k_{eu} = R_f + \beta_u (ER_m - R_f)$$

$$\beta_u = \text{the ungeared Beta coefficient}$$

To value the equity, i.e. to derive a measure for V_S, we would need to apply the (perpetuity) expression for valuing a stream of post-tax geared equity income:

$$V_S = \frac{(E - iB)(1 - T)}{k_{eg}}$$

We now encounter a circular problem, since the market value depends on k_{eg}, and to find k_{eg}, we need to know the market value!

A possible solution is to work in terms of a 'tailor-made' WACC based on the project's characteristics (i.e. its systematic risk, allowing for any divergence from existing operations) and on the project's own financing. For example, imagine the project in the previous example were to be financed 20 per cent by debt and 80 per cent by equity. You should verify that with $\beta_u = 1.33$, $\beta_g = 1.56$, that shareholders would seek a return of 24 per cent, and that the WACC is:

$$(24\% \times 4/5) + (10\% [1 - T] \times 1/5) = (19.2\% + 1.4\%) = 20.6\%$$

As it happens, use of the WACC in this situation may be inappropriate anyway, since unless the firm is at, and adheres to, the target ratio, the WACC and the marginal cost of capital (MCC) will diverge. If the firm is below the optimal capital structure, the MCC is less than WACC, and the MCC exceeds the WACC when it overshoots the optimal gearing ratio. We found, in Chapter 18, that when the firm departs from the optimal gearing ratio, the appropriate required return is the MCC:

$$MCC = \frac{\text{Change in total returns required by shareholders and lenders}}{\text{Amount available to invest}}$$

However, to calculate the MCC we again need to know the market values of both equity and debt at the higher level of gearing, i.e. we encounter the circular problem described earlier. It is clear that the WACC is suitable only for small-scale projects that do not materially disturb the gearing ratio, and that the theoretically more correct MCC is also problematic.

An 'off-the-cuff' solution is to work in terms of book values. This pragmatic approach has the merit of simplicity, as book values do not vary with gearing, and it might be appropriate for unlisted firms, which by definition have no market values. Nevertheless, it is desirable to work, whenever possible, in terms of market values, given that most investors are more concerned with the current values of their investments, and the returns thereon, than with historic balance sheet values.

Fortunately, as we shall see in the next section, help is at hand.

19.10 THE ADJUSTED PRESENT VALUE METHOD (APV)

adjusted present value APV
The inherent value of a project adjusted for any financial benefits and costs stemming from the particular method(s) of financing

The **adjusted present value (APV)** of a project is simply the 'essential' worth of the project, adjusted for any financing benefits (or costs) attributable to the particular method of financing it. The rationale for the APV method was provided by Myers (1974), using MM's gearing model with corporate tax, but is valid only so long as the WACC profile is declining due to the value of the tax shield. In Section 19.5, we saw that the value of a geared firm, V_g, is the value of an equivalent all-equity-financed company, V_g, plus a tax shield, TB, which is the discounted tax savings resulting from the tax-deductibility of debt interest:

$$V_g = V_u + TB$$

This can be translated from the value of a whole firm to the value of an individual project. However, different projects can probably support different levels of debt. For example, they may involve different inputs of easily resaleable fixed assets and may also have different levels of operational gearing. As a result, it may be more appropriate to evaluate the effects of the financing of each project separately.

The APV is calculated in three steps:

Step 1 Evaluate the 'base case' NPV, discounting at the rate of return that shareholders would require if the project were financed wholly by equity. This rate is derived by ungearing the company's equity Beta.

Step 2 Evaluate separately the cash flows attributable to the financing decision, discounting at the appropriate risk-adjusted rate.

Step 3 Add the present values derived from the two previous stages to obtain the APV. The project is acceptable if the APV is greater than zero.

A simple example will illustrate the use of the APV.

19.11 WORKED EXAMPLE: RIGTON PLC

Rigton plc has a debt/equity ratio of 20 per cent. The equity Beta is 1.30. The risk-free rate is 10 per cent and a return of 16 per cent is expected from the market portfolio. The rate of corporate tax is 30 per cent. Rigton proposes to undertake a project requiring an outlay of £10 million, financed partly by equity and partly by debt. The project, a perpetuity, is thought to be able to support borrowings of £3 million at an interest rate of 12 per cent, thus imposing interest charges of £0.36 million. It is expected to generate pre-tax cash flows of £2.3 million p.a.

Required

Using the APV method, determine whether this project is worthwhile.

Answer

Using the formula developed earlier for the ungeared Beta:

$$\beta_u = \frac{\beta_g}{\left[1 + \dfrac{V_B}{V_S} \times (1 - T)\right]} = \frac{1.30}{1 + 0.20(1 - 0.30)} = \frac{1.30}{1.14} = 1.14$$

This yields a required return on ungeared equity of:

$$ER_j = R_f + \beta_u (ER_m - R_f) = 0.10 + 1.14 (0.16 - 0.10) = (0.10 + 0.068)$$
$$= 0.168, \text{ i.e. } 16.8\%$$

The base case NPV is:

$$NPV = -£10m + \frac{£2.3m(1 - 0.30)}{0.168} = -£10m + \frac{£1.61m}{0.168}$$
$$= -£10m + £9.58m$$
$$= -£0.42m$$

The present value of the tax savings, i.e. the tax shield, *TB*, is given by:

$$\frac{TiB}{i} = \frac{(0.30)(0.12)(£3m)}{0.12} = \frac{(0.30)(£0.36m)}{0.12} = \frac{£0.108m}{0.12} = £0.9m$$

The adjusted present value is thus:

$$APV = -£0.42m + £0.90m = +£0.48m$$

and the project appears worthwhile. The significance of this result is that, although the base case NPV is negative, the project is rescued by the tax shield of £0.90 million. An essentially unattractive project is rendered worthwhile by the taxation system.

In the Rigton example, the project creates wealth only for Rigton's shareholders. From the perspective of the overall economy, it is wealth-reducing and, unless there are compelling 'social' reasons to justify it, should not be undertaken. This sort of reasoning led the UK government in 1984 to reduce the rate of corporation tax in order to lower the tax advantage of debt financing, and hence reduce the extent to which investment decisions were likely to be distorted by the system of tax breaks.

Self-assessment activity 19.6

What is the APV and how is it calculated?

(Answer in Appendix A at the back of the book)

19.12 FURTHER ISSUES WITH THE APV

Before leaving the APV, several related issues are worth examining.

1 The APV in practice is affected by the terms and conditions of a pre-arranged schedule for debt interest and capital repayment. Sometimes, the calculations can be exceptionally tedious. Rather than using the convenient assumption of perpetual debt financing, let us assume that the debt plus interest must be repaid over two years, with interest and two equal capital payments occurring at end-year. Table 19.2 shows the repayment schedule and the resulting tax savings.

Table 19.2 The tax shield with finite-life debt

Balance of loan at start of year	Interest at 12%	Tax saving (T = 30%)	Repayment	Balance of loan at end of year
£3.0m	£0.36m	$(30\% \times £0.36m) = £0.108m$	£1.5m	£1.5m
£1.5m	£0.18m	$(30\% \times £0.18m) = £0.054m$	£1.5m	0

With no tax delay assumed, the present value of the tax savings is:

$$\frac{£0.108m}{(1.12)} + \frac{£0.054m}{(1.12)^2} = (£0.096m + £0.043m) = £0.139m$$

Obviously, the value of the tax shield is much lower with the shorter payment profile.

2 Although our example focused on the side-effects of debt financing, the APV routine can be easily applied to any other financing costs and benefits, many of which are awkward to handle with the simple WACC. For example, if equity capital is externally raised, normally there are various issuing and underwriting costs to bear. Including these would alter the APV formula as follows:

$$\text{APV} = \text{Base case NPV} + \text{Tax shield} - \text{PV of issue costs}$$

A similar treatment would be applied to subsidised borrowing costs, investment grants and tax savings from exploiting investment allowances.

3 Tax savings are not certain because they depend on the inherent profitability of the company. As this is a random variable, the company's ability to set off interest payments (and other tax reliefs) against income is also random. Our examples assume continuous profitability, but if there are periods during which the company is expected to be tax-exhausted, this should be allowed for in the computation of the APV. If the future pattern of liability to tax is uncertain, then it is not appropriate to use a risk-free rate to discount the tax savings.

4 Finally, we have glossed over the issues that impact on the debt-supporting capacity of particular projects. In principle, the debt capacity of a project is given by the present value of future expected earnings from the firm as a whole, taking into account any existing borrowings. It might seem obvious that more profitable companies are able to borrow relatively more than unprofitable companies. However, this assumes that there are no costs of financial distress. Enhanced borrowing ability for more profitable companies is not universal, since a would-be lender would still look at the break-up value of the enterprise. In the final analysis, the crucial factor which governs debt capacity is how much can be raised by a distress sale of assets.

Self-assessment activity 19.7

How would you identify the point beyond which a firm would be unable to borrow?

(Answer in Appendix A at the back of the book)

19.13 WHICH DISCOUNT RATE SHOULD WE USE?

Specifying the correct discount rate to use when a new project involves financing and other differences from parent company activities is something of a puzzle. Now that we have examined the main variations on the discount rate theme, this checklist should help.

If the new project has:

Case 1 *Similar business risk and capital structure as the parent company.*
Use the parent's WACC.

Case 2 *Higher/lower business risk than the parent but similar financing mix.*
Adjust the Beta, using a surrogate firm's Beta as a basis but adjust for relative gearing, i.e. ungear the surrogate Beta and gear up the residual equity Beta. Then use the parent's capital structure weights to calculate the WACC.

Case 3 *Similar business risk, but capital structure different from that of the parent.*
Use the parent's equity Beta, gear it for the project financing mix and then use the project's financing mix to find the project WACC.

Case 4 *Higher/lower business risk, and a different capital structure.*
Use the project Beta, and, as in Case 2, gear it for the project financing, and calculate the WACC using the project financing mix.

Case 5 *Complex mixture of risk, financial structure and side-effects.*
Use the APV method.

19.14 VALUATION OF A GEARED FIRM

Having explained how to evaluate an investment project using the APV in Sections 19.11 and 19.12, it is a short step to reminding readers that this approach also provides a method for valuing a geared firm, and that is equivalent to two other approaches.

If the NPV of a geared project is found by following these steps:

- Forecast the future operating cash flows
- Adjust for expected taxation liabilities
- Discount future net-of-tax cash flows at the ungeared equity cost of capital
- Add in the PV of any financing benefits.

The result is the value of a geared enterprise, V_g, which is based on the expected income accruing to all investors before division into the respective equity and lenders' payments. The value of the equity, V_S, is then found by deducting the market value of the firm's debt, V_B:

$$V_S = V_g - V_B$$

The only difference from the APV of a new investment project is that when valuing a firm as a whole, the capital outlay term drops out of the equation, as it is a sunk cost, i.e. the firm is being valued as a set of existing investment projects that are already up-and-running. However, capital spending would come into play if the valuer were attempting to include in the calculation any **additional** cash flows stemming from new investment projects envisaged. Failing this, the APV thus values the firm as it stands.

In principle, this approach should yield exactly the same answer as the standard Weighted Average Cost of Capital approach to valuing a geared enterprise. This also discounts the stream of ungeared after-tax net income, i.e. before deducting interest, but after subtracting corporate taxation. As with the APV, this yields the enterprise value, as it is based on the expected stream of income accruing to all investors before dividing the spoils into the respective equity and lenders' payments. The value of the equity is found in the same way. Before making this split, the only adjustment for debt that is required is in calculating the geared cost of equity for insertion into the WACC formula.

Alternatively, it may be useful to focus directly on the value of the equity, V_S. This can be done by the 'Cash Flow-to-Equity', or 'Flow-to-Equity (FTE)' approach, noted in Chapter 10. The steps in the FTE approach are:

- Forecast the operating cash flows
- Deduct debt interest
- Apply the relevant rate of tax to obtain residual equity income (in cash flow terms)
- Discount at the geared cost of equity.

The value of the whole geared enterprise, V_g, is then found by adding the market value of the firm's debt, V_B:

$$V_g = V_S + V_B$$

All three approaches should yield the same answer, but whichever approach is adopted, it is essential to be consistent. The valuer should always compare like with like, either by discounting the ungeared stream of cash flows at the WACC to arrive at the enterprise value, or by discounting the geared flow of income to equity holders at the geared cost of equity.

The three methods are displayed schematically in Table 19.3.

Table 19.3 Valuing a geared firm: the three approaches

Approach	Focus	Method	Formulae*
APV (Adjusted Present Value)	Value of Geared firm, V_g whence $V_S = V_g - V_B$	■ Discount ungeared cash flows, using ungeared equity cost ■ Add in PV of financing benefits	$V_g = \dfrac{\overline{X}(1-T)}{k_{eu}} + TB$ whence $V_S = V_g - V_B$
WACC (Weighted Average Cost of Capital)	Value of Geared firm, V_g whence $V_S = V_g - V_B$	■ Discount ungeared cash flows, using the WACC	$V_g = \dfrac{(\overline{X} - iB)(1-T) + iB}{k_0}$ whence $V_S = V_g - V_B$
FTE (Flow-to-Equity)	Value of Equity, V_S whence $V_g = V_S + V_B$	■ Discount geared stream of equity income using geared equity cost	$V_S = \dfrac{(\overline{X} - iB)(1-T)}{k_{eg}}$ whence $V_g = V_S + V_B$

*Where: V_g = value of geared firm; V_S = value of equity; V_B = market value of debt; $\overline{X}$ = expected future operating cash flows; T = rate of corporate tax; k_{eu} = ungeared cost of equity; k_0 = Weighted Average of Capital; B = book value of debt; i = interest rate on debt; k_{eg} = geared cost of equity

19.15 PERFORMANCE EVALUATION IN A GEARED FIRM: THE EVA REVISITED

In Chapter 11, we briefly explained the notion of EVA and how it can be calculated in an ungeared firm. The EVA purports to measure the increase in wealth generated by a firm, after taking into account the cost of using scarce capital. In the ungeared firm, the relevant cost to consider is the cost of equity. The EVA can be expressed before or after tax, although from a shareholder perspective, the post-tax measure is probably more informative. However, the before-tax measure is the most relevant measure of basic wealth creation before the tax authorities carve out their share. As such, it offers an insight into managerial efficiency while the post-tax measure assesses contribution to the owners' disposable assets, or wealth.

In some firms, EVA is used as an internal performance measuring rod to assess the relative efficiencies of managers in the various operating divisions. As such, it can assist in the allocation of capital to new projects, or inform divestment decisions. For this purpose, the pre-tax measure of EVA is most suitable as it is an indicator of basic wealth or value creation. One firm that uses EVA to monitor the performance of individual business segments is the German utility group, E.ON. In the following extract from its Annual Report, one can see how the firm assesses the EVA (E.ON refers to this as its 'value added' approach) at the aggregate level, i.e. in terms of the whole enterprise, based on the pre-tax cost of capital of 7.5 per cent in 2013. This percentage is relevant for this purpose as the focus is on pre-tax EVA.

How E.ON calculates EVA

Analyzing value creation by means of ROACE and value added

Alongside EBITDA, our most important key figure for purposes of internal management control, we also use ROACE and value added to monitor the value performance of our operating business. ROACE is a pre-tax total return on capital. It measures the sustainable return on invested capital generated by operating a business. ROACE is defined as the ratio of EBIT to average capital employed.

Value added measures the return that exceeds the cost of capital employed. It is calculated as follows:

Value added = (ROACE) − cost of capital) × average capital employed

The table below shows the E.ON Group's ROACE, value added, and their derivation.

E.ON Group ROACE and value added

€ in millions	2013	2012
EBIT[1]	5,681	7,012
Goodwill, intangible assets, and property, plant, and equipment[2]	62,456	65,928
+ Shares in affiliated and associated companies and other share investments	7,590	5,678
+ Inventories	4,146	4,734
+ Other non-interest-bearing assets, including deferred income and deferred tax assets	−7,321	−3,653
− Non-interest-bearing provisions[3]	6,438	6,844
− Adjustments[4]	764	2,435
Capital employed in continuing operations (at year-end)	**59,669**	**63,408**
Capital employed in continuing operations (annual average)[5]	**61,539**	**63,286**
ROACE	**9.2%**	**11.1%**
Cost of capital before taxes	**7.5%**	**7.7%**
Value added	**1,066**	**2,139**

[1]Adjusted for extraordinary effects.

[2]Depreciable assets are included at half their acquisition or production costs. Goodwill represents final figures following the completion of the purchase-price allocation (see Note 4 to the Consolidated Financial Statements).

[3]Non-interest-bearing provisions mainly include current provisions, such as those relating to sales and procurement market obligations. They do not include provisions for pensions or for nuclear-waste management.

[4]Capital employed is adjusted to exclude the mark-to-market valuation of other share investment, receivables and liabilities from derivatives, and operating liabilities for certain purchase obligations to minority shareholdings pursuant to IAS 32.

[5]In order to better depict intra-period fluctuations in average capital employed, annual average capital employed is calculated as the arithmetic average of the amounts at the beginning of the year and the end of the year.

Source: E.ON *Annual Report* 2013.

SUMMARY

Chapters 18 and 19 have covered extensive ground, attempting to isolate the critical variables relating company value to capital structure. In this process, we have moved from the somewhat crude 'traditional' version to the pure and less pure MM analyses, before arriving at the model displayed in Figure 19.4. This closely resembles the traditional theory itself, with its U-shaped cost of capital schedule and optimal capital structure. We have established that *the benefits of debt stem mainly from market imperfections, especially the tax relief on debt interest, but that a different type of imperfection, distress costs, can offset these tax breaks at higher levels of gearing.* In addition, even the tax benefits of gearing may be overstated as they depend on the particular mix of personal and corporate tax rates faced by the company and its stakeholders (see Appendix III at the end of this chapter).

So in response to the question posed in the title of the chapter, 'Does capital structure really matter?' the answer seems to be 'yes', but in a number of complex ways. Debt, or rather, excessive debt, certainly matters to the owners but it may not destroy value. Distressed, but operationally viable, companies can still survive. For non-distressed companies, debt can offer significant tax advantages.

Key points

- MM argue that, as the method of financing a company does not affect its fundamental wealth-creating capacity, the use of debt capital, under perfect market conditions, has no effect on company value.

- Shareholders respond to an increase in the likely variability of earnings, i.e. financial risk, by seeking higher returns to offset exactly the apparent benefits of 'cheap' debt.

- The appropriate cut-off rate for new investment is the rate of return required by shareholders in an equivalent ungeared company.

- When corporate taxation is introduced, the tax-deductibility of debt interest creates value for shareholders via the tax shield, but this is a wealth transfer from taxpayers.

- The value of a geared company equals the value of an equivalent ungeared company plus the tax shield:

$$V_g = V_u + TB$$

- With corporate taxation, the rate of return required by the geared company's shareholders is less than that in the all-equity company, reflecting the tax benefits.

- A further effect of corporation taxation is to lower the overall cost of capital, which appears to fall continuously as gearing increases.

- However, this result relies on the absence of default risk and the consequent costs of financial distress incurred as a company reaches or approaches the point of insolvency.

- For geared companies, the required return can be derived by combining k_e with the after-tax debt cost to obtain the WACC.

- However, the WACC is acceptable only under restrictive conditions: in particular, when project financing replicates existing gearing, and when project risk is identical to that of existing activities.

- To resolve the problems of the WACC, the adjusted present value (APV) can be used. This is the 'basic' worth of the project, i.e. the NPV assuming all-equity financing, adjusted for any financing benefits such as tax savings on debt interest, or costs such as issue expenses.

- Eventually, the costs of financial distress may begin to outweigh the benefits of the tax shield. A major cost of financial distress is the inability to achieve 'full market value' in a 'distress sale'.

- There is, in theory, an optimal capital structure where the marginal benefit of tax savings equals the marginal cost of financial distress.

- In reality, while companies should balance the benefits of the tax shield against the likelihood of financial stress costs, most finance directors will restrain gearing levels, especially as tax savings are uncertain, depending on fluctuations in corporate earnings.

- There are three ways to value a geared enterprise, all of which generate the same answer if used consistently: the APV, the WACC approach and the Flow-to-Equity (FTE) approach.

- The Economic Value Added concept can be applied in the geared firm at either the pre-tax level to assess managerial operational effectiveness, or at the post-tax level to assess contribution to shareholder wealth.

Further reading

Similar health warnings apply here as with dividend policy, i.e. the fashion aspect, and the different taxation and institutional regimes that apply in different countries. But, as with dividend policy, the relevance of key papers is timeless and universal.

Look at the original articles by Modigliani and Miller (1958, 1963). Other important articles are those by Myers (1974, 1984), which analyse the interactions between financing and investment decisions, and Miller's attempt to resurrect the capital structure irrelevance thesis (1977) and his subsequent Nobel lecture (1991). As ever, Copeland *et al.* (2013) offer a more rigorous, mathematical development. Resumés of current thinking on capital structure theory can be found in Barclay *et al.* (1995) and Barclay and Smith (2006). Luehrman (1997a,b) offers two articles on the present state of valuation theory and analysis, with strong emphasis on APV, and also on strategic options.

A good textbook treatment can be found in Berk and Demarzo (2013).

Important articles include DeAngelo and Masulis (1980) on taxation and capital structure, Bradley *et al.* (1984) and Rajan and Zingales (1995) for empirical evidence, Ross (1977) on signalling, Warner (1977) on bankruptcy costs, Marsh (1982) on target debt ratios, Harris and Raviv (1990) on debt signalling, and (1991) for an overview of the debate, and Myers and Majluf (1984) on information asymmetry.

Appendix I
DERIVATION OF MM'S PROPOSITION II

Given that:

$$\frac{E}{V_S + V_B} = \frac{E}{V_0} = k_0$$

and

$$k_e = \frac{(E - iB)}{V_S}$$

we may write

$$E = k_0 V_0 = k_0 (V_S + V_B)$$

Substituting for E,

$$k_e = \frac{k_0(V_S + V_B) - iB}{V_S} = \frac{k_0 V_S + k_0 V_B - iB}{V_S} = k_0 + (k_0 - i) \times \frac{V_B}{V_S}$$

Since Proposition I argues that k_0 equals the return required by shareholders in an equivalent ungeared company, k_{eu}, and so long as the book and market values of debt capital coincide, thus ensuring that $i = k_d$, then this expression may be written as:

$$k_{eg} = k_{eu} + (k_{eu} - k_d)\frac{V_B}{V_S}$$

as in the text. In other words, the return required by shareholders is a linear function of the company's debt/equity ratio.

Appendix II
MM'S PROPOSITION III: THE CUT-OFF RATE FOR NEW INVESTMENT

MM's third proposition asserts that 'the cut-off rate for investment will in all cases be k_0 and will be unaffected by the type of security used to finance the investment'.

To show this, consider a firm whose initial value, V_0, is:

$$V_0 = V_{S0} + V_{B0} = \frac{E_0}{k_0} \qquad \text{(A)}$$

It contemplates an investment project, with outlay £I, involving a perpetual return of R per £ invested. After the investment is accepted, the new value of the firm, V_1, is:

$$V_1 = \frac{E_1}{k_0} = \frac{E_0 + RI}{k_0} = V_0 + \frac{RI}{k_0}$$

Assuming the project is debt financed, the post-project acceptance value of the shares is:

$$V_{S1} = (V_1 - V_{B1}) = V_1 - (V_{B0} + I) \qquad \text{(B)}$$

Substituting Equation A into Equation B yields:

$$V_{S1} = V_0 + \frac{RI}{k_0} - V_{B0} - I$$

and since

$$V_{S0} = (V_0 - V_{B0})$$

the change in V_S equals

$$(V_{S1} - V_{S0}) = \frac{RI}{k_0} - I$$

This exceeds zero only if $R > k_0$. Hence, *a firm acting in the best interests of its shareholders should only undertake investments whose returns at least equal k_0, the weighted average cost of capital, which itself is invariant to gearing according to Proposition I.*

Appendix III
ALLOWING FOR PERSONAL TAXATION: MILLER'S REVISION

The MM analysis including corporate earnings taxation still leaves something of a 'puzzle'. The expression for the value of a geared company indicates that the tax shield is equal to the corporate tax rate (T) times the book value of corporate debt (B), i.e. TB. With the present UK rate of corporation tax of 30 per cent, for every £1 of corporate debt the value of the company would be increased by £0.30. If such tax benefits can stem from corporate gearing, why do we find widely dispersed gearing ratios even in the same industry? And why are some of these so much lower than the MM theory (even allowing for the costs of financial distress) might suggest? According to Miller (1977), the answers to such questions lie in the interaction of the corporate taxation system with the personal taxation system, an issue omitted from the MM analysis.

Miller's agenda was to re-establish the irrelevance of gearing for company value, thus explaining why US firms did not appear to exploit apparently highly valuable tax shields. Miller argued that if individuals and corporations can borrow at the same rate, and if individuals invest in corporate debt as well as equity, there are no advantages to corporate borrowing because corporations that borrow are simply doing what personal investors can do for themselves. Any temporary premium in the market valuation of a geared company will be quickly unwound by the usual arbitrage process. However, this presupposes that individuals also can obtain tax relief on their personal borrowing (as applies in the USA, but not generally in the UK). Intuitively, we may expect to find some benefit to corporate borrowing in the UK because tax breaks on personal borrowing are not available.

Greatly simplifying, the Miller position can be expressed by the simple expression:

Post-tax cost of debt $= $ pre-tax cost $[1 - (T_c - T_p)]$

where T_c is the tax rate at which corporations enjoy relief on debt interest and T_p is the tax rate at which individuals enjoy relief on debt interest.

If $T_c = T_p$, then there is no tax advantage of corporate debt and hence no tax shield to exploit.

Only if T_c and T_p differ is there a tax shield. Note that for $T_c > T_p$ the tax shield is positive, and for $T_c > T_p$, the tax shield appears to be negative, as might apply for shareholders subject to very high rates of tax.

Miller introduced a further mechanism to support the irrelevance of gearing for company value. He argued that if there is a (temporary) tax advantage relating to debt financing, this will lead firms to increase their demand for debt (i.e. increase the supply of debt instruments), thus exerting upward pressure on interest rates until the advantage of issuing further debt disappears. If the effective tax rate on equity income were zero, and personal investors paid tax on debt interest income, companies would have to compensate investors for switching from untaxed equity to taxed debt investments by a higher interest rate. This would stop when the net-of-tax cost of debt to companies equalled the cost of equity. Miller concludes that movement to capital market equilibrium would eliminate any tax advantage of debt, so that $V_g = V_u$.

Ashton and Acker (2003) have undertaken an assessment of the average tax advantage of debt in a UK context, and conclude that it is 'likely to be no more than 13% of the value of debt'.

Questions with a coloured number **have solutions in Appendix B on page 803.**

1 With the following information about Rushden plc, determine its cost of equity according to the MM no-tax model.

$$k_{eu} = 20\%; \quad k_d = 8\%; \quad \frac{V_B}{V_B + V_S} = 20\%$$

2 Diamonds plc estimates its costs of debt and equity for different capital structures as follows:

% Debt	% Equity	k_d	k_e	WACC
–	100	–	20%	?
25	75	8%	24%	?
50	50	8%	32%	?
75	25	8%	56%	?

Required
(i)   What theory of capital structure is portrayed? (Complete the WACC column.)
(ii) Restate the table allowing for taxation of corporate profits (hence, tax relief on debt) at 30 per cent. Assume Diamonds plc always has sufficient taxable capacity to exploit the tax shield.
      Identify the relevant theory of capital structure.

3 Demonstrate how the process of home-made gearing-cum-arbitrage would operate in an MM world so as to equalise the values of the following two firms. The companies are identical in every respect except their capital structures.

	Geared	Ungeared
Expected earnings	£100	£100
Debt finance (nominal)	£200	–
Interest rate	5%	–
Market value of equity	£900	£950
Market value of company	£1,100	£950

Assume that the market value of geared debt is equal to the nominal value, and the investor holds 10 per cent of Geared's equity.

4 Kipling plc is a food manufacturer which has the following long-term capital structure:

	£
£1 ordinary shares (fully paid)	2,500,000
Share premium account	1,000,000
Retained profit	1,400,000
8% preference shares	1,200,000
10% debentures (secured)	2,600,000
	8,700,000

The directors of the company wish to raise further long-term finance by the issue of either preference shares or debentures. One director, who supports the issue of debentures, believes that, although a debenture issue will increase the company's gearing, it will reduce the overall cost of capital.

Required

(a) Discuss the arguments for and against the view that the company's overall cost of capital can be reduced in this way. The views of Modigliani and Miller should be discussed in answering this part of the question.

(b) Discuss the major factors which the directors should consider when deciding between preference shares and debentures as a means of raising further long-term finance.

(c) Identify and discuss the major factors which will influence the amount of additional debenture finance that Kipling plc will be able to raise.

(ACC Certified Diploma)

5 (a) Berlan plc has annual earnings before interest and tax of £15 million. These earnings are expected to remain constant. The market price of the company's ordinary shares is 86 pence per share cum div and of debentures £105.50 per debenture ex-interest. An interim dividend of six pence per share has been declared. Corporate tax is at the rate of 35 per cent and all available earnings are distributed as dividends. Berlan's long-term capital structure is shown below:

	£000
Ordinary shares (25 pence par value)	12,500
Reserves	24,300
	36,800
16% debenture 31 December 2017 (£100 par value)	23,697
	60,497

Required

Calculate the cost of capital of Berlan plc according to the traditional theory of capital structure. Assume that it is now 31 December 2014.

(b) Canalot plc is an all-equity company with an equilibrium market value of £32.5 million and a cost of capital of 18 per cent per year. The company proposes to repurchase £5 million of equity and to replace it with 13 per cent irredeemable loan stock.

Canalot's earnings before interest and tax are expected to be constant for the foreseeable future. Corporate tax is at the rate of 35 per cent. All profits are paid out as dividends.

Required

Using the assumptions of Modigliani and Miller, explain and demonstrate how this change in capital structure will affect Canalot's:

(i) market value

(ii) cost of equity

(iii) cost of capital

(c) Explain any weaknesses of both the traditional and Modigliani and Miller theories and discuss how useful they might be in the determination of the appropriate capital structure for a company.

(ACCA)

6 The ordinary shares of Stanley plc are quoted on the London Stock Exchange. The directors, who are also major shareholders, have been evaluating some new investment opportunities. If they go ahead with these, new capital of £38 million will be required. The directors expect the new projects to earn 15 per cent per annum before tax.

Financial information about the company for 2014 is as follows:

EBIT (existing operations)	£79.50 million
Number of shares in issue (par value £1)	50 million

The company is at present all-equity financed. It has the choice of raising the £38 million new capital by an issue of equity or debt. Equity would be issued by a new issue at a 15 per cent discount to current market price. Debt will be raised by an issue at par of 12 per cent unsecured loan stock.

If the finance is raised via equity, the company's P:E ratio is likely to rise from its current level of 9 to 9.5. However, if debt is introduced into the capital structure, the company's financial advisers have warned the two directors that the market is likely to lower the P:E ratio of the company to 8.5.

The company's marginal tax rate is 33 per cent.
Issue costs should be ignored.

(a) Determine the expected share price, total value of equity and value of the firm under the two financing options and comment briefly on which financing option appears the most advantageous.

(b) Assume the company's average cost of equity as an ungeared firm is 14 per cent and it expects to continue to pay tax at 33 per cent. The estimated cost of bankruptcy or financial distress is estimated at £5 million. According to Modigliani and Miller, what would be the value of equity and the firm if the company finances the expansion by (i) equity or (ii) debt?

(c) Explain the basic assumptions underlying MM's theories of capital structure and why, in an efficient market with no taxes, capital structure can have no effect on the value of the firm.

7 You are given the following information about Electronics plc. It has a payout ratio of 0.6, a return on equity of 20 per cent, an equity Beta of 1.33 and is expected to pay a dividend next year of £2.00. There are one million shares outstanding and it is fairly valued. It also has nominal debt of £20 million issued at 10 per cent and maturing in 5 years. Yields on similar debt have since dropped to 8 per cent. The risk free rate is 6 per cent and the expected market return is 13.5 per cent.

(a) Find Electronics' cost of capital and cost of equity.

(b) The company decides to retire half its debt at current prices. Find the company's cost of capital and equity and explain your results.

(c) The company decides to diversify into a completely different business area and decides to look at Betas of firms currently trading in the new business area. The information is given below.

Company	Beta	Debt/Equity	Market capitalisation
A	1.5	1:2	£20 million
B	1.8	1:1	£30 million
C	1.2	No debt	£50 million

What discount rate should the company use for the new business?

8 Claxby is an undiversified company operating in light engineering. It is all-equity financed with a Beta of 0.6. Total risk is 40 (standard deviation of annual return). Management want to diversify by acquiring Sloothby Ltd, which operates in an industrial sector where the average equity Beta is 1.2 and the average gearing (debt to total capital) ratio is 1:3. The standard deviation of the return on equity (on a book value basis) for Sloothby is 25 per cent. The acquisition would increase Claxby's asset base by 40 per cent. The overall return on the market portfolio is expected to be 18 per cent and the current return on risk-free assets is 11 per cent. The standard deviation of the return on the market portfolio is 10 per cent. The rate of corporation tax is 33 per cent.

(a) What is the asset Beta for Sloothby?

(b) Analyse both Sloothby's and Claxby's total risk into their respective specific and market risk components.

(c) What would be the Beta for the expanded company?

(d) Using the new Beta, calculate the required return on the expanded firm's equity.
    Under what conditions could this be taken as the cut-off rate for new investment projects?

(e) In the light of the figures in this example, discuss whether the acquisition of Sloothby may be expected to operate in the best interests of Claxby's shareholders.

9 The managing director of Wemere, a medium-sized private company, wishes to improve the company's investment decision-making process by using discounted cash flow techniques. He is disappointed to learn that estimates of a company's cost of equity usually require information on share prices which, for a private company, are not available. His deputy suggests that the cost of equity can be estimated by using data for Folten plc, a similar sized company in the same industry whose shares are listed on the AIM, and he has produced two suggested

discount rates for use in Wemere's future investment appraisal. Both of these estimates are in excess of 17 per cent p.a., which the managing director believes to be very high, especially as the company has just agreed a fixed rate bank loan at 13 per cent p.a. to finance a small expansion of existing operations. He has checked the calculations, which are numerically correct, but wonders if there are any errors of principle.

Estimate 1: Capital Asset Pricing Model
Data have been purchased from a leading business school
Equity Beta of Folten: 1.4
Market return: 18%
Treasury Bill yield: 12%

The cost of capital is 18% + (18% − 12%)1.4 = 26.4%. This rate must be adjusted to include inflation at the current level of 6 per cent. The recommended discount rate is 32.4 per cent.

Estimate 2: Dividend Growth Model

Folten plc

Year	Average share price (pence)	Dividend per share (pence)
2010	193	9.23
2011	109	10.06
2012	96	10.97
2013	116	11.95
2014	130	13.03

The cost of capital is: $D_1/(P - g)$, where D_1 is the expected dividend, P is the market price and g is the growth rate of dividends (= 14.20p/(138p − 9) = 11.01%).
When inflation is included, the discount rate is 17.01 per cent.
Other financial information on the two companies is presented below:

	Wemere £000	Folten £000
Fixed assets	7,200	7,600
Current assets	7,600	7,800
Less: Current liabilities	(3,900)	(3,700)
	10,900	11,700
Financed by:		
Ordinary shares (25 pence)	2,000	1,800
Reserves	6,500	5,500
Term loans	2,400	4,400
	10,900	11,700

Notes
1 The current ex div share price of Folten plc is 138 pence.
2 Wemere's board of directors has recently rejected a takeover bid of £10.6 million.
3 Corporate tax is paid at the rate of 35 per cent.

Required

(a) Explain any errors of principle that have been made in the two estimates of the cost of capital and produce revised estimates using both of the methods.
State clearly any assumptions that you make.

(b) Discuss which of your revised estimates Wemere should use as the discount rate for capital investment appraisal.

(ACCA)

Practical assignment

Reread the exposition in Chapter 10 of how we obtained tailored discount rates for the Whitbread plc divisions. How close do you think our surrogates were?

For another divisionalised company of your choice (try to find a two- or three-division company):

1 Consult the Risk Measurement Service for an up-to-date estimate of the equity Beta, and use the CAPM to assess the shareholders' required rate of return.

2 Estimate discount rates for each division. You will need to select surrogate companies, record their Betas, and obtain an indication of their own asset Betas by ungearing their equity Betas.

3 Determine whether the weighted average Beta for the company corresponds to its ungeared Beta. You will probably have to use weights based on earnings or sales as very few companies report book values (let alone market values!) of their segments.

20

Acquisitions and restructuring

Glencore chief sees synergies of $44bn deal

By outlining $2bn of synergies after taking over Xstrata and promising more to come, Ivan Glasenberg showed what he described as the 'Glencore way' of bearing down on costs – and repudiated many practices of the mining group with which he once intended to merge.

Glencore Xstrata's chief executive said that it expected synergies from the $44bn takeover to grow when it completes an operating review. 'There is still more to come,' said Mr Glasenberg. 'We have not really gone deep into the asset side.' Mr Glasenberg said that he had been surprised by how much 'fat' was to be cut at Xstrata.

Glencore said it found $1.4bn of extra savings from rationalising Xstrata's divisional offices, on top of marketing synergies identified when the commodities house planned to merge with the miner. Glencore has closed 33 offices since it took control of Xstrata.

Xstrata tended to 'gold-plate operations', had multiple offices in the same cities and was 'five plcs within a plc', said Steven Kalmin, Glencore Xstrata's chief financial officer. Mr Glasenberg said: 'We don't need a whole bunch of people analysing every asset purchase or whatever … we want mining engineers to run mines.'

Consistent with the hard-driving, trading mentality Glencore likes to portray, Mr Kalmin said that mine managers in coal – where the efficiency drive is most advanced – were now getting called 'every two days' in a vigilant approach to costs. 'There is pressure from us all at the top,' said Mr Kalmin.

Source: Based on James Wilson and Neil Hume, *Financial Times*, 11 September 2013, p. 20.

Learning objectives

A major aim of this chapter is to emphasise the interaction between the financial and strategic dimensions of takeovers. Having read it, you should understand the following:

■ Why firms select acquisitions rather than other strategic options.

■ How acquisitions can be financed.

■ How acquisitions should be integrated.

■ How the degree of success of a takeover can be evaluated.

■ How corporate restructuring can enhance shareholder value.

20.1 INTRODUCTION

Acquisitions of other companies are investment decisions and should be evaluated as (if not more) thoroughly and on essentially the same criteria as, say, the purchase of new items of machinery. However, there are two important differences between take-overs and many 'standard' investments.

First, because takeovers are frequently resisted by the target's managers, bidders often have little or no access to intelligence about their targets beyond published finan-cial and market data, and any inside information they may glean. (As and when take-over is accepted as inevitable, the defending board is obliged to provide key information to enable the bidder to conduct 'due diligence' examinations. This is essentially a search for 'skeletons in the cupboard'. See Sudarsanam (2010) for due diligence procedures.)

The takeover of ABN Amro by RBS for £49 billion was performed on the basis of inade-quate due diligence as explained in the box below. This deal is now cited as one of the most disastrous takeovers of all time after a write-off of approximately £15 billion was made.

Second, many takeovers are undertaken for longer-term strategic motives, and the benefits are often difficult to quantify. It is common to hear the chairmen of acquiring companies talk about an acquisition opening up a 'strategic window'; what they often do not add is that the window is usually not only shut, but also has thick curtains drawn across it! To a large extent, a takeover is a shot in the dark, partly explaining why so many firms that launch giant takeovers come to grief.

But there are other reasons. Targets are often too large in relation to bidders, so that excessive borrowings or unexpected integration problems throttle the parent.

There are important lessons to be learned from risk analysis and portfolio theory. When acquisitions have highly uncertain outcomes, the larger they are, the more cata-strophic the impact of any adverse outcomes. As a result, it may be rational and less risky to confine takeover activity to small, uncontested bids. Alternatively, a spread of large acquisitions might confer significant portfolio diversification benefits, so long as the components have low cash flow correlation. However, the greater the scale of takeover activity, the greater the resulting financing burden placed on the parent, and the greater the impact of diverting managerial capacity into solving integration problems.

RBS 'gamble' on ABN Amro deal

Financial Services Authority report finds 'extremely limited' due diligence by 'complacent' RBS board in £49bn ABN Amro bid

The board of Royal Bank of Scotland (RBS) was united in its collective enthusiasm for a £49bn record-breaking bid for the Dutch bank ABN Amro and was naively untroubled by the lack of due diligence that directors were able to conduct before agreeing the deal, according to a report by the Financial Services Authority. The City regulator said the size of the deal combined with the lack of visibility on the risks involved made it 'a gamble'. The 452-page report by the FSA into what went wrong at RBS found that the bank conducted inadequate due diligence into ABN, on the basis of just two lever arch files and a CD.

'The board was fully aware that it could undertake only extremely limited due diligence in respect of the ABN Amro acquisition. However, it appears to have treated the fact that such constraints on due diligence are normal in any contested bid as, at least to some degree, entitling it to disregard this impediment.' The report also noted that the board's investment banking advisers, led by Merrill Lynch's

Matthew Greenburgh, were 'largely remunerated on a suc-cess fee basis'. As a result, it is 'difficult' to argue that the advice they gave was independent.

In interviews with the then chairman, Sir Tom McKillop, and other board directors, the FSA was told that 'at no stage did any board member propose that we should not proceed'. One former director reflected, with hindsight, that there had been an element of 'group-think' in the board-room. To his knowledge, he added, no board member had ever expressed a worry about the deal.

'In the opinion of the [FSA] Review Team,' the report said, 'it is very difficult to reconcile this approach with the degree of rigorous testing, questioning and challenge that would be expected of an effective board process in dealing with such a large and strategic proposition.'

Source: Based on Simon Bowers and Jill Treanor, *The Guardian*, 12 December 2011.

asset stripping
Selling off the assets of a taken-over firm, often in order to recoup the initial outlay

The acquisition decision is thus a complex one. It involves significant uncertainties (except in purely **asset-stripping** takeovers), it often requires substantial funding and it may pose awkward problems of integration. Yet, as some takeover 'kings' have shown, spectacular payoffs can be achieved. These are some of the themes of this chapter – how to evaluate a takeover, how to finance it and how to integrate it. But first, we examine the phenomenon of takeover surges. Although it is too early to judge, there are indications that another surge could be imminent.

20.2 TAKEOVER ACTIVITY

takeover
Acquisition of the share capital of another firm, resulting in its identity being absorbed into that of the acquiror

mergers
Pooling by firms of their separate interests into newly constituted business, each party participating on roughly equal terms

Although the terms 'takeover' and 'merger' are used as synonyms, there is a technical difference. A **takeover** is the acquisition by one company of the share capital of another in exchange for cash, ordinary shares, loan stock or some mixture of these. This results in the identity of the acquired company being absorbed into that of the acquirer (although, of course, the expanded company may continue to use the acquired company's brand names and trademarks). A **merger** is a pooling of the interests of two companies into a new enterprise, requiring the agreement of both sets of shareholders. For example, in 2014 a US merger was announced between Safeway and Albertson. The merger of the two grocery store chains created a company with 2,400 stores and nearly 250,000 employees. By definition, mergers involve the friendly (initially, at least) restructuring of assets into a new organisation, whereas many takeovers are hotly resisted. In practice, the vast majority of business amalgamations are takeovers rather than mergers. However, mergers are quite common in some sectors, e.g. aviation. Air France merged with KLM in 2004, United Airlines and Continental merged in 2010, while British Airways and Iberia combined to form International Airlines Group in 2011 and in 2013 American Airlines merged with US Airways. This is undoubtedly due to the twin drivers of deregulation and chronic overcapacity.

Table 20.1 shows takeovers of UK firms over the past decade undertaken by other UK firms. It can be seen that the majority involve acquisitions of independent companies rather than trade sales, whether one looks at number, or value of, deals.

Table 20.1 Summary of mergers and acquisitions in the UK by UK companies

£ million

	Total all mergers and acquisitions		Mergers and acquisitions of independent companies		Sales of subsidiaries between company groups	
	Number	Value	Number	Value	Number	Value
2001	492	28 994	319	21 029	173	7 965
2002	430	25 236	323	16 998	107	8 238
2003	558	18 679	392	10 954	166	7 725
2004	741	31 408	577	22 882	164	8 526
2005	769	25 134	604	16 276	165	8 858
2006	779	28 511	628	20 180	151	8 331
2007	869	26 778	698	19 779	171	6 999
2008	558	36 469	445	33 469	113	3 000
2009	286	12 196	198	11 455	88	740
2010	325	12 605	243	7 775	82	4 830
2011	373	8 089	276	5 265	97	2 824
2012	266	3 413	216	2 536	50	877
2013	240	7 658	173	4 129	67	3 529

Source: Office for National Statistics, March 2014 (First Release, **www.statistics.gov.uk**). Crown copyright material is reproduced under the terms and conditions of the Open Government Licence (OGL).

If one examines the UK data for longer periods, there are clear examples of waves in motion, for example, in terms of number of firms, that of the early 1970s, the late 1980s and the mid-2000s. The significant rise in mergers and acquisitions in the mid-2000s was driven by factors such as globalisation. This wave ended abruptly in mid-2007 when the financial crisis began to emerge. When share prices are high and rising, it becomes easier to conduct a takeover bid by exchange of shares. Accordingly, the proportion of acquisitions completed in this way rose to historically high levels at this time. So, here we have one reason for takeover waves – takeover booms tend to reflect general stock market activity, so when the stock market booms, listed firms tend to become more acquisitive. Post-2008, following the financial crisis, there has been a noticeable drop in merger and acquisition activity but with some pickup in 2013.

There may be a 'chicken-and-egg' argument here. It has been argued that takeover activity often provides the trigger for a stock market recovery. When share prices fall, and the market value of firms looks low in relation to the replacement cost of their assets (i.e. the cost of setting up an equivalent operating facility), acquisition may seem the cheaper way for a firm wishing to expand compared to internal (or 'organic') growth.

According to the late Peter Doyle, the eminent marketing academic (1994), the motives for the mega-mergers of more recent years differ from those of the 1980s. In earlier waves, companies like Hanson and BTR were looking to exploit financial economies by restructuring badly-run companies and giving managers incentives to deliver strong cash flows to create value. By contrast, more recent mergers are more likely to be driven by strategic factors. Prominent among these are the increased globalisation of markets, with greater exposure to more aggressive international competition.

According to Doyle, this process was fuelled by deregulation and privatisation in many countries, which have freed companies in the telecommunications and airline industries, in particular, to seek out global strategic alliances. In addition, technological change raised the investment expenditures required to research and market new products, so that size of firm conferred a major advantage in industries like pharmaceuticals. Moreover, distance is no longer a barrier, given the improvements in transportation and information technology; hence, the wave of banking mergers in North America and Europe in the late 1990s, and the flurry of mergers in the US telecommunications industry in 2005.

The importance of cross-border acquisitions involving UK firms can be seen in Table 20.2, which shows data on both acquisitions and disposals abroad by UK companies, and also by foreign companies in the UK.

The international data clearly show the fall-back in activity following the 2007–8 financial crisis. Over the period, foreign companies have conducted a high level of net acquisitions of UK firms, which in value terms easily outweighs the acquisition of UK firms by other UK firms. In this sense, internal merger activity by UK firms has become a relative sideshow, although UK firms continue to spend large amounts on foreign firms as they increasingly globalise their activities.

The surge in foreign acquisitions has involved several high-profile, very large deals such as Tata Steel (India)/Corus, Telefonica (Spain)/O_2, Ferrovial (Spain)/British Airports Authority, and Dubai Ports World (United Arab Emirates)/P&O. In some of these cases, the acquirer was a 'sovereign wealth fund (SWF)' set up by the foreign government to invest income from oil or other sources. The increased ownership and involvement of such investors has raised issues of potential foreign influence in the economic affairs of the UK (and other countries), and appears to contradict the UK government's desire to reduce state ownership of industry. Following further foreign takeovers during 2010, e.g. Kraft's acquisition of Cadbury and train company Arriva's acquisition by Deutsche Bahn, a new set of concerns arose about dubious practices. Kraft was roundly reprimanded for promising to keep open a Cadbury plant at Summerdale, near Bristol, only to close it down seven

Table 20.2   Summary of cross-border mergers, acquisitions and disposals

£ million

	Transactions abroad by UK companies				Transactions in the UK by foreign companies			
	Acquisitions		Disposals		Acquisitions		Disposals	
	Number	Value	Number	Value	Number	Value	Number	Value
2001	371	41 473	139	28 494	162	24 382	62	4 464
2002	262	26 626	128	7 074	117	16 798	60	7 912
2003	243	20 756	136	8 643	129	9 309	55	3 620
2004	305	18 709	118	5 485	178	29 928	54	5 514
2005	365	32 732	110	12 668	242	50 280	61	8 387
2006	405	37 412	89	21 214	259	77 750	55	14 208
2007	441	57 814	104	10 221	269	82 121	66	7 524
2008	298	29 670	71	12 062	252	52 552	49	5 139
2009	118	10 148	37	5 101	112	31 984	38	7 820
2010	199	12 414	73	11 411	212	36 643	58	9 891
2011	286	50 234	80	14 111	237	32 967	69	11 748
2012	122	17 933	40	*	161	17 414	27	*
2013	50	*	*	*	135	31 144	25	1 586

* Data not disclosed

Source: Office for National Statistics, March 2014 (First Release, www.statistics.gov.uk). Crown copyright material is reproduced under the terms and conditions of the Open Government Licence (OGL).

days after the deal was closed, and then move production to Poland. Following this, the Takeover Panel introduced rules whereby it could act against companies that have not adhered to undertakings made as a part of a bid. This concern about post-bid practices was a feature of the Pfizer bid for AstraZeneca in 2014, as indicated in the box below.

UK MPs seek 'cast iron' pledge on Astra jobs

A group of influential MPs will on Tuesday demand that Pfizer offers 'cast iron' guarantees on British jobs and investment for up to 10 years if it buys AstraZeneca when they grill the company's boss over its £63bn takeover offer. Adrian Bailey, who chairs the business committee that will quiz Mr Read on Tuesday, said nothing less than 'cast-iron' guarantees would secure MPs' backing for what would be the biggest foreign takeover in UK history.

'We have been bitten once before on Kraft/Cadbury,' said Mr Bailey, referring to US-based Kraft's breaking of job pledges made before its takeover of Cadbury of the UK in 2010. 'Are the caveats they have given as legally binding as the commitments? If they are, they nullify each other.'

Pfizer has said it would be hard to make further promises without first talking to AstraZeneca about how a deal would work. In a statement on Monday, Pfizer said its commitments were 'tangible, legally binding and represent significant investment'. If Pfizer were to renege on the pledges it could fall foul of tougher but untested takeover rules introduced following the furore over the Kraft–Cadbury deal. The UK's Takeover Panel is now meant to monitor any undertakings Pfizer makes over issues such as the location of UK operations and employees and ensure the company sticks to them. If the Panel decided a pledge had been breached it could publicly criticise Pfizer, bring a court challenge, or 'cold-shoulder' the company.

The latter is the ultimate sanction at its fingertips and it would mean the Panel telling regulated firms in the City – investment banks, accountants, law firms – not to act for Pfizer on future deals. However, senior lawyers stressed that the strength of the revised rules had yet to be tested in a major deal and that Pfizer had left itself 'wriggle room' in its undertakings.

Source: Based on Andrew Ward, Elizabeth Rigby and Sam Fleming, *Financial Times*, 12 May 2014.

■ The regulation of takeovers

UK takeovers are regulated in three ways. The first mode of regulation is under the competition policy of the European Union, set out in the EC Merger Regulation 139/2004 (ECMR). The ECMR provides that a merger that creates a dominant position, as a result of which competition would be significantly impeded, shall be declared incompatible with the common market. The Regulation applies to all mergers with a 'Community Dimension', defined in terms of turnover levels. The ECMR was designed to provide 'one-stop' merger control to avoid the risk of mergers being investigated under two or more jurisdictions. National authorities may not normally apply their own competition laws to mergers falling within the ECMR, which are investigated by the Competition Commission. The 2009 bid by Kraft for Cadbury's was referred to the European Commission and was not dealt with by UK authorities.

Mergers falling outside the ambit of the ECMR are the responsibility of the Department for Business, Innovation and Skills. Mergers qualify for investigation if UK turnover of the target enterprise exceeds £70 million, or if the merger creates or increases a 25 per cent share in a market for goods or services in the UK, or in a substantial part of it (i.e. local monopolies can qualify).

Qualifying mergers are investigated by the Competition and Markets Authority (CMA) (**www.gov.uk/government/organisations/competition-and-markets-authority**). The CMA was established under regulations created by the Enterprise and Regulatory Reform Act 2013. This Act merged together the Competition Commission and the Office of Fair Trading, and the CMA began operating in April 2014. The overall mission of the CMA is to ensure 'markets work well in the interests of consumers, businesses and the economy'. Consequently, in respect of mergers, the CMA has a statutory duty to investigate any merger 'that could potentially give rise to a substantial lessening of competition, and require the merging parties to take steps to protect competition while the investigation takes place'. Mergers may come to the attention of the CMA either because a business notifies the CMA of the merger or through the CMA acting on its own initiative. Companies may opt to inform the CMA of an impending merger to reduce uncertainty.

The first phase of the CMA review must be completed within 40 working days and this review phase is to assess whether the merger will result in 'a realistic prospect of a substantial lessening of competition'. If there is a prospect of a substantial lessening of competition, a more detailed second review phase will take place and is normally completed with 24 weeks. The CMA will then set out any actions the two companies undertaking the merger would need to take to remedy any completion issues. For example, the CMA may stipulate that parts of the business must be sold prior to the merger. The two companies also have the option to suggest appropriate remedial actions at the end of the first review phase and, thereby, avoid the second review phase.

The CMA considers that substantial lessening of competition occurs 'when rivalry [between businesses] is substantially less intense after the merger than would otherwise have been the case, resulting in a worse outcome for customers [through, for example, higher prices, reduced quality or reduced choice]'. There ia a need for the use of judgement in determining whether this is the case, and a panel of independent members carries out the phase two review process.

The third control on takeovers is operated by **The Panel on Takeovers and Mergers** (**www.thetakeoverpanel.org.uk**), formed in 1968 to counter the perceived inadequacy of the statutory mechanisms for regulating the conduct of both parties in the takeover process. It states that 'its central objective is to ensure fair treatment for all shareholders in takeover bids'. The Panel consists of representatives from City and other leading business institutions, such as the CBI, the Stock Exchange and the ICAEW accounting body, thus representing the main associations whose members are involved in takeovers, whether as advisers, shareholders or regulators. The Panel promulgates and administers the **Takeover Code**, a set of rules originally with no

Takeover Code
The non-statutory rules laid down by the Takeover Panel to guide the conduct of participants in the takeover process

force of law, reflecting what those most closely involved with takeovers regard as best practice. It did, however, have some sanctions to enforce its authority, such as public reprimands, thereby damaging the reputation of violators of the Code, risking the collapse of the bid and, for financial advisers, jeopardising long-term business. Originally, the Panel's ultimate sanction was to request its members to withdraw the facilities of the City from offenders, although this was extremely rare.

In 2006, the EU Takeover Directive (2004/5/EC) came into force. This is very largely based on the UK Takeover Code, but with one important difference in that it is has statutory backing. The Panel can now order compensation to be paid in certain cases, and can pursue miscreants in the UK courts. It can also ask the Financial Services Authority to take enforcement action in cases of market abuse for which penalties include unlimited fines.

■ The chronology of a hostile bid

The following schedule details the necessary timing of bids and provision of information as required by the Takeover Code.

Day 1: Bid announced. Bidder has 28 days in which to post a formal offer to target's shareholders.

Day 14 after formal offer: Deadline for target company to publish its 'defence document'.

Day 21 after formal offer: First date at which the offer can be ended. Bidder must disclose how many of target's shares have been voted in its favour. If over 50 per cent, the bidder has won; if less, it may choose to walk away.

Day 39 after formal offer: Last day for defender to produce new arguments ('material new information') to encourage shareholder loyalty.

Day 46 after formal offer: Last day for offer or to revise its offer.

Day 60 after formal offer: Last day for offer to be declared unconditional as to acceptances.

Normally, the maximum time span allowed for the whole process is thus 89 days, although the Takeover Panel may 'stop the clock' pending clarification of key points. In the event of a reference to the CMA, the process is halted *sine die* to await its report. This can take upwards of six months, during which the initial 'urge to merge' has been known to evaporate.

The key requirements of the Takeover Code, now into its 11th edition (2013), are summarised by the Takeover Panel as:

- When a person or group acquires interests in shares carrying 30 per cent or more of the voting rights of a company, they must make a cash offer to all other shareholders at the highest price paid in the 12 months before the offer was announced.
- When interests in shares carrying 10 per cent or more of the voting rights of a class have been acquired by an offeror (i.e. a bidder) in the offer period and the previous 12 months, the offer must include a cash alternative for all shareholders of that class at the highest price paid by the offeror in that period.
- If the offeror acquires an interest in shares in an offeree company (i.e. a target) at a price higher than the value of the offer, the offer must be increased accordingly.
- The offeree company must appoint a competent independent adviser whose advice on the offer must be made known to all the shareholders, together with the opinion of the board.
- Favourable deals for selected shareholders are banned.
- All shareholders must be given the same information.
- Those issuing takeover circulars must include statements taking responsibility for the contents.
- Profit forecasts and asset valuations must be made to specified standards and must be reported on by professional advisers.

■ Misleading, inaccurate or unsubstantiated statements made in documents or to the media must be publicly corrected immediately.

■ Actions during the course of an offer by the offeree company which might frustrate the offer are generally prohibited unless shareholders approve these plans.

■ Stringent requirements are laid down for the disclosure of dealings in relevant securities during an offer.

■ Employees of both the offeror and the offeree company and the trustees of the offeree company's pension scheme must be informed about an offer. In addition, the offeree company's employee representatives and pension scheme trustees have the right to have a separate opinion on the effects of the offer on employment appended to the offeree board's circular, or published on a website.

New competition watchdog faces first significant test

The investigation of the UK energy market will be the first big test of the powers of the Competition & Markets Authority, legal experts have said. The CMA, which launches on 1 April, replaces the Office of Fair Trading and the Competition Commission in the biggest overhaul of UK competition regulators for decades.

One former regulator said the probe will put the CMA under 'massive pressure'. 'Everyone will think, "Great, the CMA will fix this market", but can they really? What possible remedies could it apply?' The CMA's powers to review entire markets and demand the break-up of companies even if they find no antitrust infringement – merely economic

evidence that a market is not working for consumers – are much the same as those of the old Competition Commission. But they remain almost unique among antitrust regulators in developed economies, lawyers say.

'It's not that the CMA has more power than the [Competition Commission], as that would have been pretty difficult to achieve,' said Mike Pullen, an antitrust partner at law firm DLA Piper. 'But this will be the first big test: you can bet that this will be a clash of the titans because it will be defended to the hilt by the companies.'

Source: Based on Caroline Binham, *Financial Times* 28 March 2014, p. 3.

20.3 MOTIVES FOR TAKEOVER

Managers seeking to maximise the wealth of shareholders should continually seek to exploit value-creating opportunities. There are two situations when managers feel able to enrich shareholders via takeovers:

1 *When managers believe that the target company can be acquired at less than its 'true value'.* This implies disbelief in the ability of the capital market consistently to value companies correctly. If a company is thought to be undervalued on the market, there may well be opportunities for 'asset-stripping', i.e. selling off the components of the taken-over company for a combined sum greater than the purchase price.

2 *When managers believe that two enterprises will be worth more if merged than if operated as two separate entities.* Thus for two companies, A and B:

$$V_{A+B} > V_A + V_B$$

value additivity
The notion that other things being equal, the combined present value of two entities is their separate present values added together

The principle of **value additivity** would refute this unless the amalgamation resulted in some form of synergy or more effective utilisation of the assets of the combined companies.

In practice, it is very difficult to differentiate between these two explanations for merger, especially as many mergers result in only partial disposals, when activities that appear to fit more neatly into existing operations are retained. Companies are valued by the market on the basis of information that their managements release regarding market prospects, value of assets, R&D activity, and so on. Market participants may suspect that an under-performing company could be operated more efficiently by an alternative management team, but until a credible bidder emerges, poor results may simply be reflected in a poor stock market rating.

■ How different types of acquisition create value

Acquisitions can be split into three types:

horizontal integration
The acquisition of a competitor in pursuit of market power and/or scale economies

1 **Horizontal integration** – where a company takes over another from the same industry and at the same stage of the production process: for example, a brewery acquiring a competitor, e.g. Greene King's acquisition of Cloverleaf, the pubs-and-eateries chain, in January 2011 (see the following cameo). The motivation is usually enhancement of market power and/or to obtain production economies.

Greene King picks Cloverleaf chain

Greene King has expanded its portfolio of food-led pubs with the purchase of Cloverleaf, a pub-restaurant chain.

The brewery and pub operator, whose 2,500 pubs include Old English Inns and Hungry Horse, has paid £55.8m for Cloverleaf's 12 sites and its 'strong growth story', according to Rooney Anand, Greene King chief executive. The price equates to 8.7 times annualised earnings before interest, tax, depreciation and amortisation.

Cloverleaf pubs, located in the Midlands and the north of England, beat Greene King's own south-east-focused managed estate in like-for-like sales growth, according to the bigger group.

Greene King plans to invest about £25m in the Cloverleaf division over the next two years – using up the remaining cash from a highly discounted rights issue in 2009.

'The total price therefore of £81m for 22 pub restaurants [£3.7m a site] appears on the high side,' said Simon French at Panmure Gordon.

'The deal is no steal, but overall looks like a sensible use of shareholders' money,' said analysts at Liberum Capital.

Mr Anand pointed out that 10 sites in the pipeline – which it expects to open within the next two years – as well as the brands' carvery offer add to the appeal. Carvery, he said, was 'an area where we've been under-represented'.

Cloverleaf's two founders, former Whitbread executives Gary Douglas and John Winder, will join Greene King.

Managed, food-led venues have proved more resilient following the recession than drink-led and tenanted pubs.

 Source: Rose Jacobs and Mark Wembridge, *Financial Times*, 1 February 2011. © Financial Times

---

vertical integration
Extension of a firm's activities further back, or forward, along the supply chain from existing activities

2 **Vertical integration** – where the target is in the same industry as the acquirer, but operating at a different stage of the production chain, either nearer the source of materials (backward integration) or nearer to the final consumer (forward integration), e.g. Ford's takeover of Kwikfit, the car spares firm.

conglomerate takeover
The acquisition of a target firm in a field apparently unrelated to the acquirer's existing activities

3 **Conglomerate takeover or unrelated diversification** – where the target is in an activity apparently dissimilar to the acquirer although some activities such as marketing may overlap (known as concentric diversification). These takeovers are often said to lack 'industrial logic', but can lead to economies in the provision of company-wide services such as Head Office administration and access to capital markets on improved terms, i.e. financial economies.

In reality, most mergers are difficult to classify into such neat categories, as they are motivated by a complex interplay of factors, which it is hoped will enhance the value of the bidder's equity. The more specific reasons cited for launching takeover bids usually reflect the anticipated benefits that a merger is expected to generate:

scale economies
Cost efficiencies, e.g. bulk-buying, due to increasing a firm's size of operation

1 *To exploit* **scale economies**. Larger size is usually expected to yield production economies if manufacturing operations can be amalgamated, marketing economies if

similar distribution channels can be utilised, and financial economies if size confers access to capital markets on more favourable terms. The 2014 Barrick Gold and Newmont Mining merger (see following cameo) is anticipated as leading to significant savings.

Barrick's chief burnishes benefits of gold merger

Peter Munk, the founder and chairman of Barrick Gold, has hailed the potential benefits of merging the world's largest gold miner with its US rival Newmont Mining, saying that investors should welcome the cost cuts and lower political risk that a combination could deliver. Attempts to broker a merger are made as the gold mining sector faces severe pressure to cut costs and to restructure, reversing a dash for growth that took place as the price of the metal soared for much of the past 12 years, before plummeting in 2013.

The companies – which have not commented on talks – have combined market capitalisation of more than $30bn and would produce about 12 per cent of annual gold mine output; three times more than the next-largest producer. Mr Munk said there were 'obviously synergies available' from combining Barrick and Newmont, pointing out that the two companies had many assets 'cheek by jowl' in Nevada,

US's foremost gold-producing state. People familiar with the talks said $1bn in synergies could result if a combined company concentrated on Nevada and spun off other assets – and suggested such a deal could still take place.

Mr Munk founded Barrick in 1982. He said he had long believed combination with Newmont would benefit shareholders. The fall in the gold price meant there was now more to be gained. 'Each dollar saved can make a difference – that is why savings are so essential and critical to shareholders,' Mr Munk said. 'At low gold price, they become much more important.'

Mr Munk, 86, turned the company into the world's largest and most valuable gold mining group, before embarking on a diversification by purchase of copper miner Equinox in 2011. He steps down as chairman at Barrick next week.

Source: Based on James Wilson, *Financial Times*, 23 April 2014, p. 18.

---

synergies

Gains in revenues or cost savings resulting from takeovers and mergers, not resulting from firm size, i.e. stemming from a 'natural match' between two sets of assets

2 *To obtain synergy.* **Synergies** is often used to include any gains from merger, but, strictly, it refers to benefits unrelated to scale. Gains may emerge from a particular way of combining resources. One company's managers may be especially suited to operating another company's distribution systems, or the sales staff of one company may be able to sell another company's, perhaps closely related, product as part of a package. Barrick Gold predicts there will be 'obvious' synergies that could amount to $1 billion.

3 *To enter new markets.* For firms that lack the expertise to develop different products, or do not possess the outlets required to access different market segments, takeover may be a simpler, and certainly a quicker, way of expanding, as with EADS' acquisition of Vector Aerospace, and Pepsico's acquisition of Wimm-Bill-Dann, Russia's biggest food company for about $5.5 billion in 2010.

4 *To fill in gaps in the product line.*

The Swatch Group acquisition of Harry Winston Diamond Corporation in 2013 was to fill a product gap. Swatch needed to add to its watch business a further business that would give it a position in the very 'high end' of the jewellery and watch market, and Harry Winston has filled this (see cameo).

5 *To provide 'critical mass'.* As many product markets have become more global and the lifespan of products has tended to diminish, greater emphasis has to be placed on R&D activities. In some industries, such as aerospace, telecommunications and pharmaceuticals, small enterprises are simply unable to generate the cash flows required to finance R&D and brand investment. This factor was largely responsible for the sale by Fisons and Boots of their drug-development activities in 1994 to much larger German companies. There is also a credibility effect. For example, companies may be unwilling to use small firms as a source of components when their future survival, and hence ability to supply, is suspect.

Swatch fills gap in portfolio with purchase of Harry Winston

For all its other successes, the ventures of Swatch Group into the world of high-end jewellery watches have not always ended in smiles. Its most recent foray collapsed in acrimony in 2011 when the Swiss watchmaker abruptly terminated a partnership with Tiffany, the US luxury jeweller, with accusations from both sides that the other had failed to honour the terms of their deal.

As well as sparking bitter legal tit-for-tat, the imbroglio left a gap in Swatch's portfolio in an area of the jewellery and watchmaking business that many observers think could see decent growth in coming years, and which is currently dominated by brands such as Cartier – owned by Swatch's Swiss rival, Richemont – and Chopard.

On 14 January, Swatch moved to fill the gap, disclosing that it had struck a deal to buy the watches and jewellery division of Harry Winston Diamond Corporation, a swanky brand immortalised by Marilyn Monroe in the song *Diamonds are a Girl's Best Friend*, and which remains a red carpet staple, counting the likes of Gwyneth Paltrow and Halle Berry among its Hollywood admirers.

Analysts were quick to approve the rationale of the deal, which accompanies a flurry of corporate activity in the luxury sector. 'Strategically it make sense,' says John Guy, an analyst at Berenberg Bank, pointing out that as well as filling a gap in Swatch's brand portfolio, the acquisition will also bulk up the watchmaker's hitherto slender presence in the Americas, which accounted for just 8 per cent of Swatch's sales in 2011, but which has been a traditional area of strength of Harry Winston.

The potential co-operation on diamond polishing also has significant strategic implications, Mr Guy says. 'Vertical integration is the holy grail in the luxury goods sector. This is particularly true where diamonds are concerned – if you can trace a diamond from the mine to the shelf in the boutique, then that is a big plus, given all the concerns around blood diamonds,' he says. 'It eliminates any ethical risk. But it is also important because the diamond market can be a volatile and capacity-constrained business. The greater your control over supply, the better,' he says.

Source: Based on James Shotter, *Financial Times*, 22 January 2013, p. 2.

6 *To impart or restore growth impetus.* Maturing firms whose growth rate is weakening may look to younger, more dynamic companies both to obtain a quick, short-term growth 'fix', and also for entrepreneurial ideas to achieve higher rates of growth in the longer term. For some years, British American Tobacco has been using its substantial cash flows to push into markets such as Serbia and Turkey where the health lobby is weaker than in Western Europe. The Chinese company Bright Food has undertaken a number of European acquisitions to secure growth (see the following cameo).

Bright Food hungry for buys

China's Bright Food is on the acquisition trail in Europe, visiting London, Dublin, Brussels and Barcelona as part of the state-controlled group's drive to double its international presence within the next three years. Ge Junjie, vice-president of the group that has majority stakes in the UK's Weetabix breakfast cereal and French wine merchant Diva Bordeaux, said Bright Food wanted to secure joint ventures, strategic partnerships and acquisitions.

Bright Food aims for international assets to account for 25 per cent of total assets in three years' time, from 12 per cent today, Mr Ge said. His comments come amid a jump in overseas acquisitions by Chinese companies to gain access to more advanced technologies and management and to secure a competitive advantage in an increasingly fierce domestic market.

Mr Ge said global expansion was a 'historic choice' for Chinese companies that would improve their competitiveness and give western companies access to China's 1.3bn

population. 'Chinese people eat three meals a day – that's a lot of food required, especially if you include snacks,' he said. Bright Food is one of China's biggest food groups and its third-largest dairy producer by revenues, according to China Confidential, a Financial Times research service. He said Bright Food's acquisition strategy included obtaining access to foreign management know-how – 'if we cannot keep the original management team, we won't acquire the company: stability is important.'

Asked about the cultural challenge of converting Chinese consumers to eating cold milk with cereal – regarded as unhealthy for the stomach – Mr Ge said the Weetabix acquisition had been premised on Chinese consumer demand for health and nutrition. 'Weetabix is not only a breakfast cereal, it is also about selling a lifestyle, and it has nutrition bars, biscuits and other formats,' he said.

Sorure: Based on Scheherazade Daneshkhu, *Financial Times*, 11 February 2014, p. 16.

Mergers are key to Assa Abloy's growth

When Johan Molin recently achieved his 100th acquisition as chief executive of lock maker Assa Abloy, it snuck up on him. 'I was surprised myself about it. When you are doing it you don't really think about it,' he says, a few weeks after the Swedish group purchased 4Front, a US maker of docking systems. The acquisitions have propelled Assa Abloy, the world's leading lock manufacturer by sales and owner of brands such as Yale, to impressive growth, with revenues almost doubling since Mr Molin took charge seven years ago to an estimated SKr47bn ($7.2bn) last year.

But, according to Morgan Stanley analysis, 91 per cent of the revenue increase in the past decade has been because of acquisitions, well above the 50–50 split with organic growth that the company itself targets. In a locks market that is

changing both technologically and geographically – electronic locks are becoming more popular, as are emerging markets – Mr Molin argues that the acquisitions were a necessity to allow the company to compete at a lower cost in developing markets.

The Stockholm company talks to acquisition targets frequently for several years to ensure that the often family-owned businesses are a good fit. 'The secret is to buy them at the right price. We have very skilled people centrally: the gatekeepers. The main gatekeeper is myself,' he says. The group normally works without hiring outside advisers, unless the target is listed, and Mr Molin has just two full-time merger and acquisition managers.

Source: Based on Richard Milne, *Financial Times*, 23 January 2013.

Similarly, the lock maker Assay Abloy has been undertaking acquisitions that have lead to revenue doubling over a seven-year period (see cameo).

7 *To acquire market power*. Obtaining higher earnings is easier if there are fewer competitors. Competition-reducing takeovers are likely to be investigated by the regulatory authorities, but are often justified by the need to enhance ability to compete internationally on the basis of a more secure home market. In addition, backward vertical integration, mergers undertaken to capture sources of raw materials (e.g. US oil firm Chevron's acquisition of Unocal in 2005 to increase its exploration and production capability), and forward vertical integration to secure new outlets for the company's products have the effect of increasing the firm's grasp over the whole supply chain, and are thus competition-reducing in a wider sense. Many past brewery takeovers were mounted not to obtain production capacity, but to secure access to the target's estate of tied public houses, and to acquire brands.

Deals deliver profits for Bunzl

A series of overseas acquisitions has helped Bunzl deliver stronger performance in the past six months, by offsetting a quieter performance from the distribution conglomerate's domestic market. The FTSE 100 company – which distributes everything from mops and buckets to coffee cups and carrier bags, for clients including supermarkets, hospitals and hotels – yesterday reported the pre-tax profit in the first half of 2013 had risen 9 per cent year-on-year, to £129.4m.

Bunzl said its aggressive acquisition strategy 'reached its highest level for eight years in 2012' – an approach that has continued into this year, with the purchase of companies including McNeil Surgical, an Australian distributor of healthcare products, and Vicsa Brasil, which sells eye and ear protection. Bunzl now operates in 27 countries and last year spent £272m on acquisitions.

However, Michael Roney, chief executive, said that the group had 'not reached the limit' of its acquisitive strategy, highlighting the recent purchases of Mexican safety products supplier Espomega, and TFS, a Rugby-based provider of promotional and marketing products. These two deals have taken Bunzl's spending on acquisitions to £203m so far this year.

'These acquisitions are more akin to capital expenditure for an industrial company,' Mr Roney argued. 'These are not arm-wrestling acquisitions, where one culture dominates. Essentially, we are trying to buy a stream of revenue and a good management team.'

Source: Based on Mark Wembridge, *Financial Times*, 28 August 2013, p. 18.

8 *To reduce dependence on existing, perhaps volatile, activities.* In Chapter 9, we concluded that risk reduction *per se* as a motive for diversification may be misguided. There is no reason why two enterprises owned by one company should have greater value unless the amalgamation produces scale economies or some other synergies. If shareholder portfolio formation is a substitute for corporate diversification, there is no point in acquiring other companies to reduce risk – rational shareholders will already have diversified away specific risk, and market risk is undiversifiable. There are two major qualifications to this argument. First, diversification into overseas securities may lower market risk, given that different economies, and hence stock markets, are not perfectly correlated (Madura and Fox, 2011). Second, it is possible that achieving greater size via conglomerate diversification may lower the costs of financial distress.

9 *To obtain a stock market listing.* This is achieved via a 'reverse takeover' in which an unlisted firm acquires a smaller listed firm. This 'back-door' method of achieving a listing is conducted by the listed firm issuing new shares in order to acquire the unlisted firm. Because of the difference in size, the bidder has to issue so many shares that the shareholders in the unlisted company emerge with a majority stake in the expanded firm, as in the case of the Eddie Stobart haulage firm 'backing into' Westbury Property Fund in 2007 (see cameo below).

Eddie Stobart drives on to LSE

Eddie Stobart, the haulage group renowned for its distinctive green lorries, is planning to list on the London Stock Exchange through a reverse takeover to create a £250m transport and logistics business.

The group has agreed to be acquired by Westbury Property Fund, the listed commercial property, port and rail operator for £137.7m in cash and shares, continuing a trend towards consolidation and scale in the logistics industry.

The merged entity, called Stobart Group, will combine Eddie Stobart's 900-vehicle haulage fleet with Westbury's port and rail assets, to create a transport and logistics business with net assets of more than £250m. It also plans to acquire O'Connor, a rail freight handling business.

The 25,000-strong Eddie Stobart fan club provides a loyal customer base and fans who compete to 'spot' its trucks. Each truck bears a different woman's name.

'Already we've had quite a few [fan club members] contact us this morning looking to buy some shares,' Mr Tinkler said. 'We're really excited about that.'

 Source: Chris Bryant, *Financial Times*, 16 August 2007. © Financial Times

■ The 'market for management control'

Several of the above motives for merger suggest that some companies can be more efficiently operated by alternative managers. A more general motive for merger is thus to weed out inefficient personnel. There are three ways in which the market mechanism can penalise managerial inefficiency:

1 Insolvency, which usually involves significant costs.

2 Shareholder revolt, which is difficult to organise given the diffusion of ownership and the general reluctance of institutional investors to interfere in operational management.

3 The takeover process, which may be regarded as a 'market for managerial control'. The threat of takeover provides a spur to inefficient managers; while removing inefficient managers lowers costs and removes barriers to more effective utilisation of assets. Theory suggests that incompetently managed firms will be acquired at prices

that ensure the owners of the acquirer suffer no loss in value. If a bid premium over the market price is payable, this should be recoverable from the higher cash flows generated from more efficient asset utilisation. To this extent, takeover activity is seen by authors such as Jensen (1984) as a perfectly healthy expression of the workings of the market system, potentially benefiting all parties.

■ Managerial motives for takeover

The motive of diversification to reduce risk suggests a second possible explanation for takeover activity. With the divorce of ownership and control, and the consequent high level of managerial autonomy, managers are relatively free to follow activities and policies, including acquisition of other firms, which enhance their own objectives, both in monetary and non-pecuniary forms.

Managerial salaries and perquisites are usually higher in large and growing firms, and since growth by acquisition is usually easier and swifter than organic growth, managers may view acquisition with some eagerness. If acquisitions are 'managerial' in this sense, then acquirers may be prepared to expend 'excessive' amounts to gain ownership of target companies simply to secure deals that promote managerial well-being, but at the expense of shareholder value. If this explanation is correct, acquisitions may result in a transfer of wealth from shareholders of acquiring firms to shareholders of acquired companies, even when presented as promoting the best interests of the former.

Takeovers may also be related to the way managers are remunerated. In the 1980s, UK managers increasingly came to be paid by results, with the commonest criterion of performance being growth in EPS. This is a notoriously unreliable measure of performance, as it is not only dependent on accounting conventions, but also relatively easy to manipulate and easy to increase by takeover. For example, shutting down a loss-making activity can raise reported EPS.

Self-assessment activity 20.1

Suggest some 'managerial' motives for growth by takeover.

(Answer in Appendix A at the back of the book)

■ How to increase EPS by takeover: Hawk takes over Vole

A common means of increasing EPS has been to acquire other companies with lower P:E ratios than one's own, these being companies out of favour with the market, either through poor performance or because too little was known about them. The acquisition of such companies, in certain conditions, can raise both EPS and share price. Consider the example in Table 20.3. Hawk, with a P:E ratio of 20, reflecting strong growth expectations, contemplates the takeover of Vole, whose P:E ratio is only 10. Hawk proposes to make an all-share offer. If it were able to obtain Vole at the current market price, it would have to issue 5 million shares to Vole's shareholders in exchange for their 20 million shares, i.e. (5 million × £4) = (20 million × £1) = £20 million.

Table 20.3 shows the impact of the exchange if the P:E ratio of the expanded company were to remain at 20. The new EPS is (£22m/105m) = 21p, resulting in a post-bid share price of £4.20 and an overall market value of £441 million. This apparently magical effect seems to have generated wealth of £21 million. If it works out this way, the beneficiaries are the two sets of shareholders: Hawk's existing shareholders find their 100 million shares valued at a price higher by 20p, i.e. £20 million in total, and Vole's

Table 20.3 Hawk and Vole

	Pre-bid		Post-bid	
	Hawk	**Vole**	**Hawk + Vole**	
Number of shares	100m	20m	100m + 5m	= 105m
Earnings after tax	£20m	£2m	£20m + £2m	= £22m
EPS	20p	10p	£22m ÷ 105m	= 21p
P:E ratio	20:1	10:1	20:1	
Share price	£4	£1	20 × 21p	= £4.20
Capitalisation (market value)	£400m	£20m	105m × £4.20	= £441m

former shareholders find they now hold shares valued at £21 million, rather than the value of £20 million placed on Vole prior to the bid, i.e.:

Gains to Hawk's shareholders $= £20m$

Gains to Vole's shareholders $\quad= \underline{£1m}$

Total gain $\qquad\qquad\qquad = £21m$

This so-called **'boot-strapping'** effect may simply be 'financial illusion' because it is unlikely to occur quite like this in reality. First, it assumes the absence of a bid premium. In practice, Hawk would have to offer above the market price to tempt Vole's shareholders into selling, thus altering the balance of gain. Second, it assumes that the market applies the same P:E ratio to the expanded group as the pre-bid ratio for Hawk. If no synergies were expected, then the likely post-bid P:E ratio is the total pre-bid value of the two firms relative to their total pre-bid earnings, i.e.:

$$\frac{(£400m + £20m)}{(£20m + £2m)} = \frac{£420m}{£22m} = 19.09$$

However, if Hawk is expected to reorganise Vole and impart the same growth impetus expected from Hawk itself, the P:E ratio post-bid could exceed this figure, and approach Hawk's pre-bid P:E value of 20. If this occurs, then both groups of shareholders can enjoy the value created by the expectation of more efficient operation of Vole's assets and higher cash flows thereafter. Conversely, expectations of integration difficulties might offset such gains.

It does not follow that a higher EPS will lead to a higher share price. If the acquisition moved Hawk into riskier areas of operation, its activity Beta should rise accordingly and the higher expected cash flows will be discounted at a higher required return. Similarly, if instead of financing the bid by a share exchange, Hawk had borrowed the required £20 million, then the share price might not rise if the greater gearing and accompanying financial risk resulted in a higher equity Beta. The suspicion remains that many acquisitions, ostensibly undertaken to raise the acquirer's share price, are really undertaken for 'managerial' reasons (see Gregory, 1997).

Certainly, the subsequent difficulties commonly experienced in post-merger integration and operation do not support the view that mergers are always in the best interests of the bidders' shareholders (see below).

Self-assessment activity 20.2

Suggest how managerial pay schemes might encourage takeovers against the interests of shareholders.

(Answer in Appendix A at the back of the book)

20.4 ALTERNATIVE BID TERMS

Table 20.4 shows UK data on the three main ways of financing takeovers: cash, issue of ordinary shares and fixed-interest securities (loan stock, convertibles and preference shares). Clearly, the first two methods predominate, although their relative importance varies over time. As a rule of thumb, share exchange is favoured when the stock market is high and rising, while cash offers are used more when interest rates are relatively low or falling, given that many cash offers are themselves financed by the acquirer's borrowing. This pattern is illustrated clearly by the figures for the early 2000s, when the stock market was depressed and interest rates low and falling. Increasingly, however, bidders offer their targets a choice of cash or shares, or even a three-way choice between straight cash, cash with shares, or shares alone.

Table 20.4 Mergers and acquisitions in the UK by UK companies: category of expenditure

£ million

| | | Expenditure | | | | Percentage of expenditure | | |
| | | Cash | | | | | | |
	Total	Independent companies	Subsidiaries	Issues of ordinary shares	Issues of fixed interest securities	Cash	Issues of ordinary shares	Issues of fixed interest securities
2001	28 994	8 489	6 704	12 356	1 445	52	43	5
2002	25 236	9 574	7 991	6 780	891	69	27	4
2003	18 679	8 956	7 183	1 667	873	86	9	5
2004	31 408	12 080	7 822	10 338	1 168	63	33	4
2005	25 134	13 425	8 510	2 768	431	87	11	2
2006	28 511	N/A	8 131	N/A	335	N/A	N/A	2
2007	26 778	13 671	6 507	4 909	1 691	76	18	6
2008	36 469	31 333	2 851	1 910	375	94	5	1
2009	12 195	2 937	709	8 435	114	30	69	1
2010	12 605	6 175	4 523	1 560	350	85	12	3
2011	8 089	4 432	2 667	719	271	87	10	4
2012	3 413	1 937	789	419	268	82	10	8
2013	7 658	3 683	3 475	353	147	92	6	2

Source: Office for National Statistics, March 2014 (First Release, **www.statistics.gov.uk**). Crown copyright material is reproduced under the terms and conditions of the Open Government Licence (OGL).

For example, when bidding for a smaller property company, City North plc, a former BES company, in 2005, the considerably larger Grainger Trust plc offered two alternatives. Shareholders of City North could either opt for a full cash consideration of 270 pence per share, or accept 180 pence in cash plus 0.2423 of a Grainger share, worth 95 pence on the last dealing day prior to the bid announcement. The cash plus paper offer was thus worth 275 pence, a little higher than the straight cash offer, which is typically the case, as the target shareholder bears the twin risks of exposure to share price falls and the danger of projected synergies not materialising.

Such complex offers are designed to appeal to the widest possible body of shareholders. The chosen package depends on the balance of relative advantages and disadvantages of the different methods, from both the bidder's and the target shareholders' viewpoints.

■ Cash

Everyone understands a cash offer. The amount is certain, there being no exposure to the risk of adverse movement in share price during the course of the bid. The targeted shareholders are more easily able to adjust their portfolios than if they received shares, which involve dealing costs when sold. Because no new shares are issued, there is no dilution of earnings or change in the balance of control of the bidder (unless, in the case of borrowed capital, creditors insist on restrictive covenants). Moreover, if the return expected on the assets of the target exceeds the cost of borrowing, the EPS of the bidder may increase, although perceptions of increased financial risk may mitigate this apparent benefit. A disadvantage from the recipient's viewpoint is possible liability to capital gains tax (CGT). However, in the case of cross-border takeovers there are major advantages in receiving cash rather than the shares of the bidder, traded only on a foreign stock exchange, one reason why Akzo Nobel offered cash to ICI shareholders. Nevertheless, the cash has to be found from somewhere.

■ Share exchanges

Any liability to CGT is delayed with a share offer, and the cash flow cost to the bidder is zero, apart from the administration costs involved. However, equity is more costly to service than debt, especially for a company with taxable capacity, and an issue of new shares may interfere with the firm's gearing ratio. There could be an adverse impact on the balance of control if a major slice of the equity of the bidder came to be held by institutions looking for an opportunity to sell their holdings. The overhanging threat of a substantial share sale may depress the share price of the bidder.

A disadvantage with a share offer is that it involves yielding a share of the ownership of the expanded firm, and thus a share of the benefits, to the owners of the target firm. Conversely, some part of the risk involved in exploiting synergies is also transferred. A further disadvantage of a share exchange is that the bid terms may be undermined by adverse stock market movements before the deal is agreed and completed, possibly necessitating a higher bid. For these reasons, a share offer is usually pitched higher in value than a corresponding cash offer when target shareholders are offered a choice.

■ Other methods

The use of other instruments is comparatively rare. When fixed-interest securities are used, they are usually offered as alternatives to cash and/or ordinary shares. Convertibles have some appeal because any diluting effect is delayed and the interest cost on the security, which qualifies for tax relief, can usually be pitched below the going market rate on loan stock, due to the expectation of capital gain on conversion. Preference share financing in general is comparatively rare, owing to the lack of tax-deductibility of preferred dividends and to limited voting rights.

Some takeover considerations are quite ingenious. In Sanofi's acquisition of Genzyme, the latter's shareholders were offered tradable 'Contingent Value Rights (CVRs)' to run until 2020, worth an extra $4 billion on paper, but only valid dependent on the success of new drugs in the Genzyme pipeline.

The Mouchel cameo shows how cash is often used in a takeover bid, i.e. to follow up an initial all-paper offer by adding a cash 'sweetener'.

Self-assessment activity 20.3

Why might the shareholders of a target company prefer to be paid in cash rather than shares?

(Answer in Appendix A at the back of the book)

Mouchel is offered cash sweetener by Costain

Costain, the engineering and construction group, has lifted its all-share bid for Mouchel with a 30p a share cash sweetener after two previous offers failed to win over the board of the struggling outsourcing specialist.

Unlike Costain's earlier proposals, Mouchel stopped short of rejecting outright the latest indicative take-over offer, which values the equity of the target company at £169m.

But Mouchel, which carries out maintenance work for local authorities, utilities and the Highways Agency, advised its shareholders 'to take no action' on what would be a transformational deal for both companies.

As part of its defence, Mouchel said that it was close to reaching an agreement with banks on a refinancing and also pointed out that it had received other approaches.

Shares in Mouchel, whose biggest equity investors include Schroders, Prudential and Invesco, rose 22¾p or 20 per cent, to close at 136½p on Friday – still a significant discount to the latest proposal.

Shares in Costain fell 3½p to 219¼p on Friday.

Costain's latest proposal comprises 0.5531 shares and 30p in cash for each Mouchel share.

Based on Costain's share price, the revised proposal values each Mouchel share at about 151.3p – a premium to the 135p a share indicative offer earlier this month.

That proposal was pitched about 25 per cent higher than the initial approach that Costain made in December.

The latest deal, including £83m of net debt, would result in an enterprise value for Mouchel of £253m.

'We think this is a good fit and believe that it is in the best interests of both sets of shareholders,' said Andrew Wyllie, Costain chief executive. 'It [Mouchel] is not challenging those points in its response.'

Geoff Allum, analyst at Arden Partners, said:? 'I can't see what justification Mouchel has for not opening the books to Costain.'

Mouchel has been hit by public sector cutbacks, and its banks – Barclays, Lloyds Banking Group and Royal Bank of Scotland – called in Deloitte, the accountancy firm, to conduct a review of its contracts ahead of debt renegotiations.

The company, which has previously warned it may need fresh funds if it fails to reach a refinancing deal with its banks, said it expected to finalise 'shortly' new medium-term facilities.

 Source: Damian Wilkinson and Alistair Gray, *Financial Times*, 23 January 2011. © Financial Times

20.5 EVALUATING A BID: THE EXPECTED GAINS FROM TAKEOVERS

Evaluating an acquisition is little different from other investments, assuming the motive of the bid is economic rather than managerial, i.e. designed to maximise the post-bid value of the expanded enterprise. It would be worthwhile Company A taking over Company B so long as the present value of the cash flows of the enlarged company exceeds the present value of the two companies as separate entities:

$$V_{A+B} > V_A + V_B$$

Thus, $[V_{A+B} - (V_A + V_B)]$ measures the increase in value. The net cost to the bidder is the value of the amount expended less the value of the target as it stands:

$$\text{Net cost} = [\text{Outlay} - V_B]$$

so that the net present value of the takeover decision is the gain less the cost, i.e.:

$$\text{NPV} = V_{A+B} - (V_A + V_B) - [\text{Outlay} - V_B]$$
$$= V_{A+B} - V_A - \text{Outlay}$$

The NPV will depend on the method of financing and, of course, the terms of the transaction. Essentially, the bidder is hoping to extract the maximum value of any expected cost savings and synergies from the takeover for its own shareholders. Conversely, the offer must be made attractive to the owners of the target to induce them to sell.

■ Fewston plc and Dacre plc

An example will illustrate the way in which the division of the spoils can depend on the method of financing. Fewston plc is launching a cash bid for Dacre plc, both are quoted companies and both are ungeared. The market value of Fewston is £200 million (100 million 50p shares, market price £2) and that of Dacre is £40 million (10 million 50p shares, market price £4). Fewston hopes to exploit synergies, etc., worth £20 million after the takeover. It offers the shareholders of Dacre £50 million in cash. The NPV of the bid to Fewston is thus:

$$\text{NPV} = V_{A+B} - V_A - \text{Outlay}$$
$$= (\pounds200m + \pounds40m + \pounds20m) - \pounds200m - \pounds50m = \pounds10m$$

The overall gain from the takeover (i.e. the synergies of £20 million) is split equally between the two sets of shareholders. The need to make a higher bid, or the appearance of another bidder, would probably tilt the balance of gain towards Dacre's shareholders.

If the bid is made in the form of a share-for-share offer to the same value, the arithmetic alters. In this case, Fewston is giving up part of the expanded firm and hence a further share of the gains to Dacre's shareholders. Assuming a bid of the same value, Fewston must offer them (£50/£2) = 25m shares. This would increase the shares in issue to 125 million shares, i.e. Fewston is handing over 20 per cent of the expanded company to Dacre's shareholders. In this case, the gain enjoyed by Fewston's shareholders will be lower. The NPV of the takeover is still the gain less the cost; but the cost is greater, i.e. the proportion of the expanded company handed over less the value of Dacre as it stands:

$$\text{Cost} = \left(\frac{25m}{100m + 25m} \times \pounds260m \right) - \pounds40m$$
$$= (\pounds52m - \pounds40m) = \pounds12m$$

Hence, the NPV of the takeover from Fewston's perspective is:

$$\text{NPV} = (\text{gain in value} - \text{cost}) = (\pounds20m - \pounds12m) = \pounds8m$$

Fewston's shareholders are thus left with only £8 million of the net gains from the takeover, 20 per cent lower than in the cash offer case, which is the same proportion as the share of the expanded company handed to Dacre's shareholders.

A share exchange of equivalent value to a cash bid generally leaves the bidder's shareholders worse off compared to a cash deal because their share of both the company and the gains from the takeover are diluted among the larger number of shares. The post-bid share prices in these two cases are as follows:

Cash bid: (£260m/100m) = £2.60

Share exchange: (£260/125m) = £2.08

Against this, given that takeovers carry risks, for example, the risk of inability to capture the anticipated synergies, a share-based deal has the merit of transferring a portion of these risks to the target's former owners.

However, if Fewston has to borrow in order to make the cash bid, the increase in gearing may result in shareholders seeking a higher return, thus lowering the market price. In addition, the analysis hinges on the existence of an efficient capital market whose assessment of the gains from takeover corresponds with that of the two parties.

Self-assessment activity 20.4

Predator is valued on the market at £1,000 million, and Prey at £200 million. Predator values the expected post-merger synergies at £50 million. If it bids £230 million for Prey what is the NPV of the bid? What is the share of the gains for each firm?

(Answer in Appendix A at the back of the book)

20.6 WORKED EXAMPLE: ML PLC AND CO PLC

The following part-question appeared on the CIMA Strategic Financial Management examination paper, May 1999. (It carried 15 of the total 20 marks available for the whole question.)

■ Question

ML plc is an expanding clothing retailer. It is all-equity financed by ordinary share capital of £10 million in shares of 50p nominal. The company's results to the end of March 1999 have just been announced. Pre-tax profits were £4.6 million. The Chairman's statement included a forecast that earnings might be expected to rise by 5 per cent per annum in the coming year and for the foreseeable future.

CO plc, a children's clothing group, has an issued share capital of £33 million in £1 shares. Pre-tax profits for the year to 31 March were £5.2 million. Because of a recent programme of reorganisation and rationalisation, no growth is forecast for the current year but, subsequently, constant growth in earnings of approximately 6 per cent per annum is predicted. CO plc has had an erratic growth and earnings record in the past and has not always achieved its often ambitious forecasts.

ML plc has approached the shareholders of CO plc with a bid of two new shares in ML plc for every three CO plc shares. There is a cash alternative of 135 pence per share.

Following the announcement of the bid, the market price of ML plc shares fell while the price of shares in CO plc rose. Statistics for ML plc and two other listed companies in the same industry immediately prior to the bid announcement are shown below. All share prices are in pence.

1998				
High	Low	Company	Dividend % Yield	PER
225	185	ML plc	3.4	15
145	115	CO plc	3.6	13
187	122	HR plc	6.0	12
230	159	SZ plc	2.4	17

Both ML plc and CO plc pay tax at 33 per cent.
ML plc's cost of capital is 12 per cent per annum and CO plc's is 11 per cent per annum.

Required

Assume you are a financial analyst with a major fund manager. You have funds invested in both ML plc and CO plc.

- Assess whether the proposed share-for-share offer is likely to be beneficial to the shareholders in ML plc and CO plc, and recommend an investment strategy based on your calculations.
- Comment on other information that would be useful in your assessment of the bid. Assume that the estimates of growth given above are achieved and that the new company plans no further issues of equity.

State any assumptions that you make.

Answer

First of all, some introductory calculations are needed before we can analyse the impact of the bid.

Basic information

	ML	CO	Combined
Profit after tax (PAT) for each firm is			
ML: (0.67 × £4.6m) CO: (0.67 × £5.2m)	£3.082m	£3.484m	£6.566m
Given respective P:Es, market values are:			
ML: (15 × £3.082m) CO: (13 × £3.484m)	£46.230m	£45.292m	£91.520m
Given the number of shares, share price is:			
ML: (£46.230m/20,000) CO: (£45.292m/33,000)	£2.31	£1.37	
EPS:			
ML: (£3.082m/20,000) CO: (£3.484m/33,000)	15.41p	10.56p	

Analysis

No. of shares post-bid: 20,000 + (2/3 × 33,000) = 42,000

Expected market prices post-bid = Total market value/No of shares

$\qquad\qquad$ = (£91.520m/42,000) = £2.18

Value of bid at post-issue price = (2 shares × £2.18) = £4.36

Cash value of bid per 3 shares offered: (£1.35 × 3) = £4.05

Assessment

Assuming no changes in the level of market prices, and no re-rating of the sector, ML's share price would fall post-acquisition to £2.18. At this price, the value of the 2-for-3 share offer should attract CO shareholders. They would get shares worth (2 × £2.18) = £4.36 in exchange for shares currently worth (3 × £1.37) = £4.11

The share-for-share offer is also worth more than the cash alternative: £4.36 vs £4.05.

This is a 'reverse takeover', where the shareholders of the target end up holding a majority stake in the expanded company – but who gains from this?

Former CO shareholders would hold (22,000/42,000) × £91.520m = £47.939m of the value of the expanded firm, a gain of (£47.939m – £45.292m pre-bid value of CO) = £2.649m.

ML shareholders would lose £2.649m, making the share-financed deal distinctly unattractive to them.

Conversely, the cash offer would create wealth for ML shareholders, i.e. they give £4.05 for something worth £4.11 post-bid.

The advice to the fund manager is: 'accept the bid in respect of CO shares and sell ML shares in the market if you can achieve a price above £2.18'.

Commentary on other information required

The advice given above hinges on the behaviour of ML's share price – it has already fallen on the announcement, but by how much? It may already be too late if the market is efficient, as it would already have digested the information contained in the announcement.

Also:

- What benefits are expected from the merger, i.e. cost savings and synergies? To make sense of the bid, ML must be setting the PV of these benefits above £2.649m to yield a positive NPV for the acquisition.
- How quickly are these benefits likely to show through? Any delay in exploiting these lowers the NPV.
- It is feasible that the market might apply a higher PER to the expanded company – maybe not as high as ML's but possibly at the market average, currently 14.25, compared to the weighted average PER for ML/CO of 14.
- Is ML likely to sell part of CO's operations? And to whom? If ML has already lined up a buyer, it must expect to turn a profit on the deal.
- Is the bid likely to be defended by the target's managers, fearful for their jobs? If so, a higher bid might be expected.
- Is a White Knight likely to appear with a higher bid on more favourable terms?
- Are there competition implications likely to attract the interest of the authorities?

20.7 THE IMPORTANCE OF STRATEGY

Considerable evidence has emerged that acquisitions have less than an even chance of success. Although definitions of 'success' may vary, any activity that fails to enhance shareholder interests is unlikely to be regarded favourably by the stock market. While it is often difficult to assess what would have happened had a company not embarked on the takeover trail, it is difficult to argue that the acquisition has not been a failure if post-acquisition performance is inferior to pre-acquisition performance, or if the acquisition actually leads to a fall in shareholder wealth.

The McKinsey firm of management consultants studied the 'value-creation performance' of the acquisition programmes of 116 large US and UK companies, using financial measures of performance. The criterion of success used was whether the company earned at least its cost of capital on funds invested in the acquisition process. On this basis, a remarkable 60 per cent of all acquisitions failed, with large unrelated takeovers achieving a failure rate of 86 per cent.

Acquisitions fail for numerous reasons:

1. Acquirers often pay too much for their targets, either as a result of a flawed evaluation process that overestimates the likely benefits or as a result of getting caught up in a competitive bidding situation, where to yield is regarded as a sign of corporate weakness.

2. 'Skeletons' appear in cupboards with alarming frequency. The infamous and disastrous takeover by defence contractor Ferranti of International Signal Corporation was a good example of a badly researched acquisition that ultimately destroyed the acquirer.

3. Acquirers often fail to plan and execute properly the integration of their targets, frequently neglecting the organisational and internal cultural factors. Inadequate knowledge about the target's business should be corrected in the process of due diligence. Lees (1992) explains how all too often this aspect is overlooked.

Yet many companies have sound acquisition records. Reckitt Benckizer, the Anglo-Dutch producer of household products is often held up as a prime example. Firms like Reckitt have several things in common. Their targets are carefully selected, they rarely get involved in competitive auctions, they often have the sense to walk away from deals when they realise the gravity of the likely integration problems, and they seem able quickly and successfully to integrate acquisitions once deals are completed. What these companies have in common is a coherent strategic approach to acquisitions.

20.8 THE STRATEGIC APPROACH

Most successful acquirers see their acquisitions as part of a long-term strategic process, designed to contribute towards overall corporate development. This requires acquirers to approach acquisitions only after a careful analysis of their own underlying strengths, and to identify candidates that satisfy chosen criteria and, most importantly, provide 'strategic fit' with the company's existing activities.

Figure 20.1 displays a simple strategic framework within which a thorough-going acquisition programme might be conducted. It begins with a full strategic review of the company as it stands, and its strategic options, followed by a detailed consideration of the role of acquisitions (i.e. the reasons why an acquisition target may be selected), leading to the process of selecting and bidding for the chosen prey, and culminating in the often neglected activities of post-merger integration and post-audit.

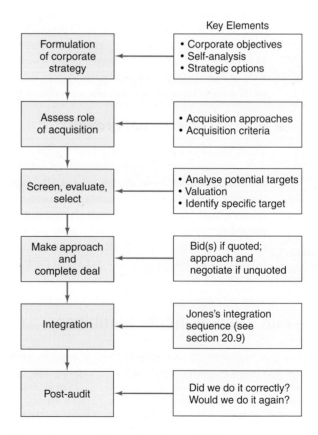

Figure 20.1 A strategic framework (based on Payne, 1987)

The takeover of SCA Group by DS Smith in 2012 was part of an overall strategy in respect of its European business as outlined below.

Purchase of Swedish rival packs punch for DS Smith

The takeover of a unit of a Swedish rival this year has buoyed interim revenues at packing specialist DS Smith, helping it offset weakness in the UK paper market. The FTSE 250 company in June completed the €1.6bn takeover of the packaging division of its Swedish rival SCA Group – a move that united the second and third biggest companies in Europe's €30bn cardboard packaging market. The reverse takeover also gave DS Smith a more solid foothold in the continental European recycling sector, where it provides recycled packaging materials for consumer goods customers such as Nestlé, Reckitt Benckiser and Unilever.

Miles Roberts, DS Smith chief executive, said that the deal 'more than doubled our size, and turned us from a UK company with a small continental Europe business to a huge continental business with a more modest UK side'. However, the takeover had further exposed DS Smith to recession-hit continental Europe, which has been struggling under the weight of the economic downturn and sovereign debt crises.

'We always planned for Europe being a zero-growth environment and prices still are relatively modest,' said Mr Roberts. 'But we can thrive due to the prevalence of such strong synergies [between SCA and DS Smith]. It is disappointing about Europe but it is in line with our expectations.'

Source: Based on Mark Wembridge, *Financial Times*, 7 December 2012, p. 23.

■ Objectives

Formulating strategy should begin with an expression of corporate objectives, concentrating on maximising shareholder wealth. Many firms now publish mission statements, but these are usually somewhat vague expressions of the image that the company would like to portray, often largely for internal consumption in order to motivate staff (Klemm *et al.*, 1991). If, in building the desired image, the company's managers fail to earn at least the cost of equity, they will themselves invite the risk of takeover. Strategy concerns the examination of alternative routes to achieving the ultimate aim, and then the optimal way of executing the chosen path. Achieving long-term goals usually involves expansion of the enterprise, a route often preferred by managers for personal motives.

■ Internal or external growth?

licensing
Involves the assignment of production and selling rights to producers located in foreign locations in return for royalty payments

joint venture
A strategic alliance involving the formal establishment of a new marketing and/or production operation involving two or more partners

There are two main ways of achieving growth: (1) by self-development of new products, markets and processes (internal growth) and (2) by acquisition (external growth). Although both of these routes are usually expensive in executive time and resources, external growth has the advantage of securing quick access to new markets or productive capacity. However, firms should not overlook intermediate strategies, such as **licensing**, whereby a royalty is paid to the developer of new technology in exchange for rights to exploit it, or **joint ventures**, where an existing company could be partially acquired, or a totally new one set up in partnership with another firm.

Paying the dire price of inflated ambition

Ambition has come with a big price for two once-proud British names. Cable & Wireless Worldwide, the demerged UK business of the 160-year-old telecoms group, was worth roughly the same as it was seven years ago until predators began circling last month. That has pushed up the share price but means the company now faces being swallowed up by either Vodafone, its once tiny rival, or Tata Group

of India, a country where C&W laid cables more than a century ago.

Premier Foods, which assembled Britain's biggest larder through a steady diet of acquisitions, last month promised lenders it would empty the shelves further to pay down more than £1bn of debt. Those borrowings had helped fund a shopping spree that has reduced its equity value from more than £2bn in 2007 to less than £400m today.

Their respective rises and falls took different routes but have in common over-ambitious (some say overbearing) chief executives, fee-hungry bankers and a predilection for overpaying.

Premier Foods' acquisitions of Campbell's UK and Irish businesses and RHM, owner of Hovis bread, were 'a flawed proposition' from the outset, says Clive Black, analyst at Shore Capital, who has downgraded the stock 11 times. He describes the acquisitions as 'the worst kind of deal' and blames gullible management and fee-hungry investment bankers – with the cleverer set being on the vendors' sides rather Premier Foods'.

Few executives from that era remain at Premier Foods, now run by Mike Clarke, but those close to the deals at the time deny they were flawed. Instead, they say, Premier Foods suffered from a confluence of external events unforeseen at the time the deals were hatched: input inflation, faltering consumer confidence, the end of ready money – in short, the end of favourable economic and debt cycles.

Premier Foods' maiden set of results showed hubris. Robert Schofield, then chief executive and architect of the acquisition strategy, lauded 'a year of unprecedented change for Premier'. Hindsight shows that the seeds of its demise were already evident: warnings about 'exceptional' cost inflation, implementation of a new bread strategy; and a revised set of banking covenants. Trading profit in the bread business virtually halved on a pro-forma basis in the first year under Premier Foods' ownership to £35m. The shredding of profits has continued: last year, trading profit was one-tenth the pro-forma 2007 level at £3.4m and less than one-twentieth of the 2006 number.

Source: Based on Louise Lucas and Dan Thomas, *Financial Times*, 14 April 2012, p. 17.

The decision to grow internally or externally will depend partly on an analysis of the strengths, weaknesses, opportunities and threats (SWOTs) of the firm. This self-analysis should make the potential acquirer aware of any competitive advantages it enjoys over rival companies. Competitive advantage stems from two sources: cost advantage, where products are virtually similar, and product differentiation. Exploitation of each of these creates value for shareholders. When areas of competitive advantage have been identified, the company can decide whether to build upon existing strengths or to attempt to develop distinctive competence in areas of perceived weakness. This evaluation may also result in a decision to divest certain activities where no obvious advantage is possessed, or where too many resources would be required to sustain an advantage.

Porter (1987) examined the acquisition record of 33 large diversified US companies. The criterion for judging 'success' was the subsequent divestment rate of earlier acquisitions. The main finding was that successful acquirers almost invariably diversify into related fields, and vice versa. In other words, diversifications into activities unrelated to the core business of the acquirer carry much greater risks of failure. Even companies with successful 'related diversification' records achieved poor results when they wandered into unrelated fields. Porter concluded that the corporate portfolio strategy of many diversifying companies had failed because most diversifiers fail 'to think in terms of how they really add value'.

External growth is often the result of a decision to move into a different sector. By acquiring other firms, the strategic aim of reconfiguring the firm's portfolio of activities can be more rapidly achieved. General Electric made several acquisitions in the oil services industry – for example, in 2011 the firm aquired the Aberdeen-based John Wood Group's well support division, famed for its electric submersible pumps, for $2.8 billion. This brought GE's spending on the drilling and production support business to about $10 billion since 2007.

■ Acquisition criteria

The bidder should next assess what specific role it hopes the acquisition will perform. Table 20.5, drawn from a publication (*Making an Acquisition*) by the investment bank 3i (Investors in Industry), which specialises in offering acquisition advice, lists possible strategic reasons for acquisition with suggested routes to achieving the stated aims.

Table 20.5 **Strategic opportunities**

Where you are	How to get to where you want to be
■ Growing steadily but in a mature market with limited growth prospects	■ Acquire a company in a younger market with a higher growth rate
■ Marketing an incomplete product range, or having the potential to sell other products or services to your existing customers	■ Acquire a company with a complementary product range
■ Operating at maximum productive capacity	■ Acquire a company making similar products operating substantially below capacity
■ Under-utilising management resources	■ Acquire a company into which your talents can extend
■ Needing more control of suppliers or customers	■ Acquire a company which is, or gives access to, a significant customer or supplier
■ Lacking key clients in a targeted sector	■ Acquire a company with the right customer profile
■ Preparing for flotation but needing to improve your Balance Sheet	■ Acquire a suitable company which will enhance earnings per share
■ Needing to increase market share	■ Acquire an important competitor
■ Needing to widen your capability	■ Acquire a company with the key talents and/or technology

Source: 3i (Investors in Industry).

At this stage, the company should reassess the alternatives to merger, in view of the many difficulties involved. Taking over another company is rather like moving to a larger, more expensive house. Mergers involve considerable disruptions during the planning and bidding phase; costs, such as legal advice and the printing and publishing of documents; possible exposure to increased financial risk; and the upheavals of integration. Just as some marriages do not survive the strains of house-moving, some companies often fail to recover after the stress of merger. Having identified the specific role of the acquisition, the company can now consider whether it can be achieved in other, perhaps more cost-effective ways.

Harrison (1987) suggests that, for every merger motive, there are several alternative ways of achieving the same end. For example, if the aim is sales growth, this can be achieved by internal expansion or by a joint venture. If the aim is to improve earnings per share, a loss-making subsidiary can be shut down or efficiency-enhancing measures can be implemented. If it is wished to use spare cash, this can be invested in marketable securities and trade investments, or even returned to shareholders as special dividends, or in the form of share repurchases. If an improvement in management skills is sought, appropriately skilled personnel can be bought in to replace existing managers, outside consultants can be used for advice, or incentive and bonus schemes can be introduced. In short, if the decision to grow by acquisition is made, the potential acquirer must be very sure that the stipulated aims are unattainable by alternative measures.

Most firms with corporate planning departments exercise a continuous review of the key members of the industry in which they operate and also of related and, often, unrelated areas. Some firms are known to 'track' potential takeover candidates, assessing their various strengths and weaknesses, and estimating the likely net value obtainable if they were acquired. Such target companies are continually cross-checked against a set of possible acquisition criteria.

When the decision to expand by acquisition is taken, the corporate planning staff should be able rapidly to provide a short-list of candidates, expressing the SWOTs of each, especially its vulnerability to takeover at that time. It is common for defending managements to dismiss takeover bids as 'opportunistic' in a pejorative way. For an acquisitive company that adopts the strategic approach, this means 'well-timed', as such companies are continually seeking opportune moments to launch a bid, especially when the stock market rating of the target appears low. The joint takeover by the former GEC and Siemens of Plessey in 1989 was opportunistic, in the sense that the target's return on capital was relatively low due to a recent substantial investment programme. Whether the market had correctly valued Plessey is arguable, but the bidders undoubtedly spotted a favourable opportunity to acquire Plessey at a time when its performance looked weak in relation to the market, thus eliminating a major competitor for lucrative British Telecom contracts. There has been a resurgence in M&A activity recently following a slowdown after the financial crisis of 2008. However, as the following cameo explains, this may not be all good news.

Better ways to play the merger mania

Mega mergers are back. This week, advertising groups Omnicom and Publicis announced a $35bn tie-up. Just a day or two earlier, Irish pharmaceuticals group Elan ended a long courtship by recommending a takeover by Perrigo. Closer to home, engineering group Invensys has recommended an offer from France's Schneider Electric.

The re-emergence of M&A has been long predicted, and there have been several false starts. Companies are sitting on big cash piles, having restructured and refinanced in the wake of the credit crunch, and that money is earning only trivial returns in cash and other short-term instruments. The global economic recovery might still be slow and uneven, but there are now at least some tangible signs that it is heading in the right direction, giving chief executives the confidence to deploy some of that cash.

Is this good news for investors? There's a mountain of academic evidence that takeovers destroy value for shareholders in the bidding company, and that the hubris of senior managers leads them to overestimate the benefits of combining one company with another. If you want a practical example, look no further than Rio Tinto's disastrous $38bn takeover of Alcan in 2007, which was followed by a dividend cut, a $15bn rights issue, a $10–11bn write-off – and a change of chief executive.

On the other hand, takeovers are a sign of growing confidence, and institutions generally have to reinvest whatever cash takeovers generate in other shares, which boosts the broader market. And for a private investor, a conventional cash takeover offer should be manna from heaven. You wake up one morning to find you've been offered a fat premium and no dealing costs to sell your shares. The only downside is that you might incur a capital gains tax liability on the profits, or face a conundrum when it comes to reinvesting them. Both are nice problems to have.

Source: Based on Jonathan Eley, *Financial Times*, 3 August 2013, p. 6.

■ Bidding (and defending)

Bidding is an exercise in applied psychology. Readiness to bid implies an assessment that the target is either undervalued as it stands or would be worth more under alternative management. In such cases, the bid itself provides new information about prospective value, and the bidder should expect to have to pay above the market price to secure control. However, it is often unclear before the event how much of a bid premium, if any, is already built into the market price as the market attempts to assess the probability of a bidder emerging and succeeding with its offer. The trick in mounting profitable takeover bids is to promise to use assets more effectively in order to entice existing shareholders to sell, without making such extravagant claims that the target's market price moves up too sharply before the acquisition is completed. Conversely, to accentuate the difficulties of reorganising the target could be regarded as disingenuous or even call into question the wisdom of the bid itself, leading to a fall in the bidder's own share price. The following box summarises some of the defence tactics which a bidder may encounter.

Choose your weapons! Takeover defence tactics

Takeover strategy is not a one-sided affair. Very few takeovers are recommended at once by the directors of target companies. Even if they expect to lose the fight, the incumbents usually reject the initial bid in the hope of attracting better terms. The first line of defence, therefore, is rejection because the bid is too low, or because the proposed union 'lacks industrial logic'.

Once defenders have had time to marshal their resources and get their public relations act together, more effective defences can be adopted. Some are more credible than others, and some are illegal in the UK but common in the USA. Typical defence ploys by UK firms are:

- Revalue assets – this is often a waste of time, as the market should already have assessed the market value.
- Denigrate the profit and share price record of the bidder, and hence the quality of its management. This invites retaliation in kind.
- Promise a dividend increase – this calls past dividend policy into question, and bidders usually offer this anyway.
- Publish improved profit forecasts – a dangerous ploy, since the forecast has to be plausible yet attractive, and once made, the company has to deliver. Companies that repel raiders but fail to meet profit forecasts are susceptible to further bids.
- Seek a **White Knight** – an alternative suitor that will acquire the target on more favourable terms (mainly for the management?).
- Lobby the competition authorities.

The following defences mostly originated in the USA and some are difficult to reconcile with the Takeover Code:

- The Crown Jewels defence – selling off the company's most attractive assets.
- Issuing new shares into friendly hands – this, of course, requires shareholder agreement.
- The Pacman defence – launching a counter-bid for the raider.
- Golden Parachutes – writing such attractive severance terms for managers that the bidder will recoil at the prospective expense.
- Tin Parachutes – offering excessively attractive severance terms for blue collar workers.
- Launching a bid for another company – if successful, this will increase the size of the firm, making it less digestible for the bidder.
- Leveraged buy-out – the purchase of the company by its own management using large amounts of borrowed funds.
- Poison pills – undertaking methods of finance that the bidder will find unattractive to unwind, e.g. large issues of convertibles that the bidder will have to honour.
- Repurchasing of shares to drive up the share price and increase the cost of the takeover (common now in the UK), although not allowed once an informal approach has been made (although it can be promised if the bid fails).

White Knight
A takeover bidder emerging after a hostile bid has been made, usually offering alternative bid terms that are more favourable to the defending management

Examples of poison pills are mechanisms to trigger deeply discounted rights issues if predator holdings rise above a certain level. Both Newscorp and Yahoo have implemented such arrangements. In the case of Yahoo's 'stockholder rights plan', a rights issue can be made if another firm builds a stake in Yahoo above 15 per cent. In Germany, the so-called 'VW law' of 1960 limits any investor's voting rights in the car-maker to 20 per cent, and confers a blocking vote on the minority stake held by the state of Lower Saxony (this has been declared illegal by the European Court of Justice).

Classic Pac-Man defence enters the retail arcade

Men's Wearhouse's counter-offer for Jos A Bank revives an old tactic

In the neon arcade world of Pac-Man, the game's greedy protagonist has only one sure-fire way of avoiding the ghosts that pursue him – turning the tables and eating them instead. The corporate defence tactic that draws its name from the eat-or-be-eaten video game returned to the dealmaking landscape last week as suit retailer Mens's

Wearhouse tried to block the overtures of a rival with a takeover offer of its own.

For two months, the Men's Wearhouse board had been unyielding in its refusal to entertain a takeover bid by Jos A Bank, dismissing as 'opportunistic' an offer that represented a 42 per cent premium to the retailer's then share price. But in what appears to be a tacit acceptance of the logic behind an enlarged company, Men's Wearhouse then made a $1.2bn offer that would see it gobble up its smaller rival.

The decision to deploy the Pac-Man defence is the latest twist in the battle to control America's multibillion-dollar discount menswear market. It also heralds the return of a dealmaking manoeuvre, out of fashion for a generation, that has yielded some unusual results.

In September 1982, aerospace company Martin Marietta took the unprecedented step of responding in kind to a takeover bid by its rival Bendix Corp. The ensuing dust-up dragged on for a month and ended without clear victory for either company. Instead, Allied Corp, which entered the fray to help Bendix vanquish Martin Marietta, swallowed Bendix for $2bn. Martin Marietta, while avoiding the ignominy of being taken over, was left nursing a debt burden four times larger than it started with, having borrowed $1bn to fund its own takeover effort.

Since then, the tactic has been used sparingly.

'Going with the Pac-Man basically means management are recognising that the deal makes sense, but are desperate to keep their jobs. It is good for the executives, but pretty rough for shareholders,' says a banker who has been involved in such a deal.

Since 1999, there have been just five examples of the Pac-Man defence being used, according to data from Dealogic. This reflects the flaw inherent to the tactic: more often than not, a target deploys the same industrial logic as its original bidder. In doing so it undermines its own rationale for a defence.

Source: Based on Ed Hammond, *Financial Times*, 3 December 2013, p. 23.

20.9 POST-MERGER ACTIVITIES

Probably the most difficult part of takeover strategy and execution is the integration of the newly acquired company into the parent. In the case of contested bids, the acquirer will normally have only a limited amount of information to guide its integration plans and should not be too shocked to encounter unforeseen problems regarding the quality of the target's assets and personnel. The difficulty of integration depends on the extent to which the acquirer wants to control the operations of the target. If only limited control is required, as in the case of unrelated acquisitions, integration will probably be restricted to meshing the financial reporting systems of the component companies. Conversely, if full integration of common manufacturing activities is required, integration assumes a different order of complexity.

Jones (1982, 1986) points out that the degree of complexity of integration depends on the type of acquisition: for example, whether it is a horizontal takeover of a very similar company, requiring a detailed plan for integrating supply, production and distribution; or, at the other extreme, a purely conglomerate acquisition where there is little or no overlap of functions. The relationship between type of acquisition, overlap of activity (split into financial, manufacturing and marketing) and the resulting degree of integrative complexity is shown in Figure 20.2. Because we believe that integration is perhaps the most important part of the acquisition process, we devote most of this section to further analysis of this issue.

Finally, the acquisition should be post-audited. The post-audit team should review the evaluation phase to assess whether, and to what extent, the appraisal was under- or over-optimistic, and whether appropriate plans were formulated and executed. The review should centre on what lessons can be learned to guide any subsequent acquisition exercise.

Poor planning and poorly executed integration are two of the commonest reasons for takeover failure. All too often, acquisitive companies focus senior management attention on the next adventure rather than devoting adequate resources to absorbing the newly acquired firm carefully. It is rash to lay down optimal integration procedures in advance, because the appropriate integration procedures are largely situation-specific. The 'right' way to approach integration depends on the nature of the company acquired, its internal culture and its strengths and weaknesses (Lees, 1992). However,

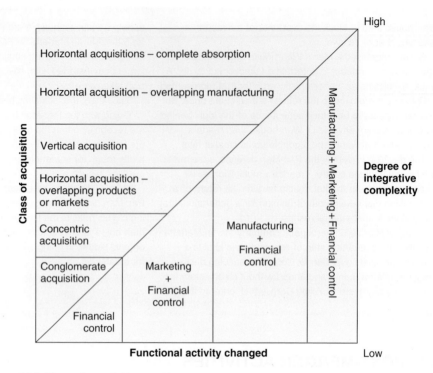

Figure 20.2 **Type of acquisition and integrative complexity** (Jones, 1986)

Drucker (1981) contends that there are Five Golden Rules to follow in the integration process:

1 Ensure that acquired companies have a 'common core of unity' with the parent. In his view, mere financial ties between companies are insufficient to obtain a bond. The companies should have significant overlapping characteristics like shared technology or markets in order to exploit synergies.

2 The acquirer should think through what potential skill contribution it can make to the acquired company. In other words, the takeover should be approached not solely with the attitude of 'what's in it for the parent?' but also with the view 'what can we offer them?'

3 The acquirer must respect the products, markets and customers of the acquired company. Disparaging the record and performance of less senior management is likely to sap morale.

4 Within a year, the acquirer should provide appropriately skilled top management for the acquired company.

5 Again, within a year, the acquirer should make several cross-company promotions.

These are largely common-sense guidelines, with a heavy emphasis on behavioural factors, but many studies have shown that acquirers fail to follow them. A study undertaken by Hunt and Lees of the London Business School with Egon Zehnder Associates (Hunt *et al.*, 1987) commented that 'unless the human element is managed carefully, there is a serious risk of losing the financial and business advantages that the acquisition could bring to the parent company'.

■ Jones's integration sequence

Jones (1986) explains that integration of a new company is a complex mix of corporate strategy, management accounting and applied psychology. Acquirers should follow an 'integration sequence', based on five key steps, the relative weight attaching to each step depending on the type of acquisition. The sequence is as follows:

1 Decide upon, and communicate, initial reporting relationships.
2 Achieve rapid control of key factors.
3 Review the resource base of the acquired company via a 'resource audit'.
4 Clarify and revise corporate objectives and develop strategic plans.
5 Revise the organisational structure.

Each of these is now examined.

Reporting relationships

Clear reporting relationships have to be established in order to avoid uncertainty. An important issue is whether to impose reporting lines at the outset or whether to await the new organisational structure. In resolving this issue, it is desirable to avoid managers establishing their own informal relationships, and to stress that some changes may only be temporary.

Control of key factors

Control requires access to plentiful and accurate information. To control key factors, acquirers should rapidly gain control of the information channels that export control messages and import key data about resource deployment. It may sometimes be desirable not to introduce controls identical to those of the parent, first, because group controls may not be appropriate for the acquired company, and second, because those group controls may no longer be appropriate for the revised organisation. If the acquired company's existing control systems are thought to be adequate, it may be worth retaining them. Two important financial controls are the setting of clear borrowing limits and an early review of capital expenditure limits and appraisal procedures.

Jones notes that poor financial controls are often found within newly acquired companies, and indeed, have often contributed to their acquisition. Examples are over-reliance on financial rather than management accounting systems (MAS), a MAS that provides inappropriate information in an inappropriate format, poor use of the MAS, and distortions in the overhead allocation mechanism, making it difficult to pinpoint unprofitable products and customers. The net result is often poor budgetary control, inadequate costing systems and inability to monitor and control cash movements.

Resource audit

The resource audit should examine both physical and human assets to obtain a clear picture of the quality of management at all levels. The extent of the audit required will depend on how much information is made available prior to the acquisition, but auditors should not be surprised if 'skeletons' are found in cupboards, requiring a reappraisal of the value of the acquired firm and possibly a different way of integrating it into the parent's future strategy and plans. For example, a business that was meant to be absorbed into the parent's operations may be divested if its capital equipment is unexpectedly dilapidated.

Corporate objectives and plans

These should be harmonised with those of the parent, but should also reflect any differences due to industrial sector, such as different 'normal' rates of return or profit margins in different industrial sectors. Managers of acquired firms should have some freedom to formulate their plans to meet the stated aims, but the degree of freedom should depend on the complexity of the merger. For example, in a conglomerate acquisition, where the primary aim is to secure financial control, it may be appropriate to allow executives to develop a system of management control suitable for their own

Consultants offer advice at a 'dangerous moment'

The skills needed to oversee a successful integration include having 'rhino skin'

Integration professionals are specialists who help companies make any kind of integration or change a success – from blue-chip mergers, to buy-outs by private equity firms, to the spinning off of company divisions.

A team of up 20 people might work on a blue-chip merger in an often highly charged and emotional atmosphere where people expect to – and do – lose their jobs. But the rewards can be great both financially – particularly for those working for PwC, Deloitte, Ernst & Young or KPMG, the 'big four' professional service firms – and in terms of career variety and challenge.

'You need listening skills but a rhinoceros skin. People share their innermost thoughts with you and blame you if things don't go well. But it's not personal and you have to say 'this is normal, they're not going crazy'. Mr Kelly likens an integration professional to a golf caddy who has walked the course, checked the wind conditions and the emotional status of the player, leaving them simply to take the shot.

'If you like daily interaction with clients and organisations, there is no question you've got a platform. You don't have to create the business case for a merger because that decision's already been taken and you've already got the attention of the client,' he says.

Richard Marsden at the Berkeley Partnership says integration professionals need to understand people and companies well in order to manage change effectively. 'You have to think about cultural change – all aspects of the customers, IT, the back office functions of HR, financial, talent management, and crucially, you have to have the right people in place quickly post-merger,' he says.

Source: Based on Sharmila Devi, *Financial Times*, 8 November 2012, p. 4.

operating patterns, so long as these are consistent with the aims of the takeover. In cases where cash generation is the main spur, all that may be needed is centralised cash management plus control over capital allocations.

Revising the organisational structure

A discussion of organisational design is beyond our scope, but obviously a demoralised labour force is unlikely to offer optimal performance.

Two important factors enhancing the success of a takeover are the thoroughness of the resource audit and the degree of senior management contact in the very early stages of the takeover. Employees of acquired companies seek a rapid resolution of uncertainty, especially regarding how they and their company fit into the future structure and strategy of the acquirer, and how soon the new management team will assume control. Particularly important for morale are the lifting of any previous embargo on capital expenditure and the provision of improved performance incentives, pension schemes and career prospects.

Some of these aspects are illustrated in the short case of GE capital.

■ Post-acquisition integration at GE Capital

According to Ashkenas, DeMonaco and Francis (1998) the process of melding one company into another is frequently badly done because few firms go through the process often enough to develop a pattern. They suggest that many firms see it as a one-off event rather than a replicable process – 'something to get finished, so everyone can get back to business'. Because 'the acquisition event is painful and anxiety-generating, involving change, disruption and job loss, most managers think how to get it over with, not how to do it better next time around'.

They reported on acquisition integration at GE Capital, a subsidiary of General Electric Corporation, founded in 1933 to provide consumers with credit to purchase GEC appliances. GE Capital has grown by acquisition, including over 100 in the five years prior to their report. From interviews with managers and key staff involved in acquisitions, both as former targets and subsequently as acquirers at GE Capital, they devised a framework for acquisition management based on four 'Lessons':

Lesson 1

Acquisition management is not a discrete phase of a deal and does not begin when the documents are signed. Rather, it is a process that begins with due diligence and runs through the ongoing management of the new enterprise.

Lesson 2

Integration management is a full-time job and needs to be recognised as a distinct business function, just like operations, marketing, or finance.

Lesson 3

Decisions about management structure, key roles, reporting relationships, lay-offs, restructuring, and other career-affecting aspects of the integration should be made, announced and implemented as soon as possible after the deal is signed – within days, if possible. Creeping changes, uncertainty, and anxiety that last for months are debilitating and immediately start to drain value from an acquisition.

Lesson 4

A successful integration melds not only the various technical aspects of the businesses but also the different cultures. The best way to do it is to get people working together quickly to solve business problems and accomplish results that could not have been achieved before.

Source: Ashkenas *et al.* (1998).

However, in the case of Apollo Tyres' acquisition of Cooper Tire and Rubber in 2014, a key concern has been that the post-merger strategy and integration will not work effectively (see the following cameo).

Apollo Tyres skids on fears over $2.5bn Cooper Tire deal

Shares in Apollo Tyres, India's largest tyre company by sales, plunged by a quarter yesterday amid investor concerns about higher debt related to the group's planned $2.5bn acquisition of US-based Cooper Tire and Rubber. The all-cash deal, which would be the largest-ever Indian acquisition of a US company, is also set to increase Apollo's consolidated net debt-to-equity ratio from 0.8 to around 3.8, according to Angel Broking, a Mumbai-based brokerage.

'The deal will leave the company with a huge debt and that is the biggest concern,' said Yaresh Kothari, an automotive analyst at the broker. The two companies say they expect a measure of profitability, of up to $120m a year for three years.

The duo have also said they expect to see benefits in operating scale, as well as greater efficiencies in sourcing, technology and manufacturing operations. Around two-thirds of Apollo's revenues come in India, but the company has long held global ambitions.

The acquisition of Ohio-based Cooper Tire, the world's 11th largest tyre company by revenue, will give the company a presence in the US and Chinese markets. Post-merger strategy has been cited as a potential concern of the deal, expected to be completed in the second half of the year.

'I'm not worried about the deal size; it's more about integration of the companies and how you use the opportunities in the marketplace,' said Abdul Majeed, head of automotive at consultants PwC in India. The two companies have said the incumbent management team will remain in place at Cooper and its manufacturing operations will continue at the company's existing facilities.

Source: Based on Avantika Chilkoti, *Financial Times*, 14 June 2014, p. 18.

Self-assessment activity 20.5

What are the key elements of an acquisition strategy?

(Answer in Appendix A at the back of the book)

20.10 ASSESSING THE IMPACT OF MERGERS

The impact of mergers can be assessed at various levels. At the macroeconomic level, if takeover activity is performing its function of weeding out inefficient managements, we might expect to find takeovers resulting in superior economic performance. However, over the long haul, the two economies where takeover activity is most prevalent – the USA and the UK – have underperformed economies where growth by takeover is less common (e.g. until the mould-breaking takeover of Mannesmann by Britain's Vodafone in 2000, there had been only four completed hostile takeovers in Germany since 1945 and not one completed by a foreign bidder). Measures of economic performance such as growth in gross domestic product (GDP) per head and capital formation as a percentage of GDP were, certainly until the 1990s, considerably lower in the UK than in Japan and Germany, as were figures for 'growth drivers' like R&D expenditure as a percentage of GDP.

Although such associations do not prove causation, the presumed link is via the impact of horizontal mergers reducing competition and through the pressures for short-term performance. It is often argued that managers in the 'Anglo-Saxon' economies are forced to pay out higher dividends to bolster share price in order to deter prospective raiders. Ever higher payouts represent cash that could have been used to finance investment and growth. However, it seems implausible to argue that the institutions would withhold funds from companies that showed a willingness to perform according to short-termist rules. Nevertheless, after reviewing the evidence, Peacock and Bannock (1991) concluded that mergers and takeovers did not create wealth, but merely transferred ownership of assets. The full explanation of why merger-active economies underperform is probably less simple, as Porter (1992) explains, involving a complex interplay of economic, social and political factors.

Another level of analysis is that of the performance of individual companies. If takeovers are beneficial, we should expect to see merger-active firms improving their performance post-merger.

Investigating the effects of merger activity is one of the busiest areas of contemporary applied finance research. There are two main ways of attempting to assess the impact of mergers.

The first, **the financial characteristics approach**, is based on examining the key financial characteristics of both acquiring and acquired firms before the takeover, to study whether they are more or less profitable (taking profitability as an indicator of efficiency) than firms not involved in acquisitions, and whether their profitability improves after the acquisition. The second, **'the capital markets approach'**, is based on examining the impact of the takeover on the share prices of both acquired and acquiring firms, to assess the extent to which expected benefits from merger are impounded in share prices and how these are shared between the two sets of shareholders.

The first method, the financial characteristics approach, suffers from severe limitations:

1 Different accounting conventions used by different firms (e.g. treatment of R&D) often make comparisons misleading.
2 Measures of profitability may have been distorted due to the application of acquisition accounting procedures. Prior to the issue of FRS 10 in 1997, firms in the UK were allowed to write off goodwill (the excess of purchase price over 'fair value') against reserves. This lowered their equity bases and raised their recorded return on investment. Goodwill now has to be shown on the balance sheet as an asset and amortised over its useful life up to 20 years. This abrupt change in the rules of accounting for goodwill means that pre- and post-takeover measurement of performance of firms active in takeovers before and after 1997 could be seriously distorted.
3 To assess properly the impact of the takeover requires an extended analysis ranging over, say, five to ten years. Many acquisitions are undertaken for 'strategic' purposes, the benefits of which may emerge only after several accounting periods, perhaps

following lengthy and costly reorganisation. Very frequently, when 'efficient' companies take over sizeable 'inefficient' companies, the group's return on net assets and fixed asset turnover ratios automatically fall.

4 Accounting studies are not capable of assessing what the performance of the expanded group would have been in the absence of the merger, and are thus unable to assess what improvement in performance (if any) was due to factors beyond the merger. This problem increases with the time period used for the post-merger investigation.

5 Any improvement in profitability may simply be due to a restriction of competition, rather than more efficient use of resources.

6 The approach does not allow for risk. If the aim of many mergers is to lower total risk (possibly for managerial reasons), or to shift the company into a lower Beta activity, a lower return post-merger is not especially surprising, since according to the EMH/CAPM, relatively low-risk investments offer relatively low returns.

The second method, **the capital markets approach**, caters for many of these difficulties, and is thus the most frequently used mode of analysis. By adopting a CAPM framework, it enables the returns on shares of acquiring firms to be examined prior to, and following, the merger. As noted in Chapter 9, the market model indicates that the expected return on any security, j, in any time period t, ER_{jt}, is a linear function of the expected return on the market portfolio:

$$ER_{jt} = \alpha_{jt} + \beta_j ER_{mt}$$

However, the actual return in any time period, R_{jt}, results from a compound of market-related and company-specific factors:

$$R_{jt} = \alpha_{jt} + \beta_j R_{mt} + u_{jt}$$

u_{jt} is an error term with zero expected value, indicating that random company-specific factors are expected to cancel out over several time periods.

If, over a suitable period, and allowing for overall movements in the market, we examine the differences between the expected returns and the actual returns, the 'residuals' or 'abnormal returns' should sum to zero, i.e. the expected value of the cumulated differences between ER_{jt} and R_{jt} is zero.

A takeover bid is a company-specific event likely to raise the share price, and hence, the return on holding the shares. When a bid occurs, the increase in returns can be attributed to the market's assessment of the impact of the bid, i.e. the evaluation of its likelihood of success, and if successful, its appraisal of the benefits likely to ensue. Therefore, both in the period leading up to the bid, as the potential bidder builds a stake, and also on the day of announcement of the bid, we might expect the residuals to be non-negative. For example, if the market thinks the takeover is a mistake, we may find negative residuals for the bidder but positive residuals for the target, if, as usually happens, the share price of the target rises sharply. Hence, the cumulated residual returns may be taken as the stock market's assessment of the value of the takeover to the shareholders of the acquirer and acquired companies, respectively.

To illustrate this use of the market model, consider the data in Table 20.6. This relates to the successful takeover bid for the Kennings Motor Group by the conglomerate Tozer Kemsley Milbourn (TKM) in 1986. There was a degree of industrial logic in this bid, as both TKM and Kennings retailed motor cars and Kennings operated a substantial car hire business. Kennings had attempted in previous years to diversify, but owing to the haphazard selection of targets and poorly executed integration, its core business was suffering, reflected in declining profitability and weakening cash flow. The data show the residual returns for both companies in the three months prior to, and also following, the bid; month 0 is the day of the bid, eventually completed at a price of £3.10 per share.

Table 20.6 Pre- and post-bid returns

Kennings Motor Group

Time period (months)	Share price (p)	Actual return (%)	Expected return (%)	Residual	Cumulated residuals
−3	140	−3.45	−0.29	−3.16	−3.16
−2	160	14.29	1.67	12.61	9.45
−1	158	1.25	−6.64	−7.89	1.56
0	212	34.18	7.63	26.54	28.10
1	268	26.42	−0.19	26.60	54.70
2	310	15.67	−3.04	18.71	73.41
3	310	0	3.08	−3.08	70.33

Tozer Kemsley Milbourn

−3	66	−2.94	−0.32	−2.62	−2.62
−2	81	22.73	1.87	20.86	18.24
−1	108	33.33	7.42	25.91	44.15
0	136	25.93	8.53	17.39	61.54
1	177	30.15	−0.21	30.36	91.90
2	172	−2.82	−3.40	0.58	92.48
3	180	4.65	3.44	1.21	93.69

Source: Data collected by Krista Bromley.

The data clearly show positive residuals for Kennings, before the bid, on the day of the bid itself, and also in the following periods as TKM raised its bid. In this case, both sets of shareholders enjoyed substantial returns. After allowing for the movement in the market as a whole, the returns on the shares of both companies were substantially positive, indicating market expectations that this merger would be wealth-creating. This proved to be the case, following very swift and effective reorganisation of Kennings by TKM.

Until quite recently, the bulk of the empirical evidence (e.g. see surveys by Jensen and Ruback (1983); Department of Trade and Industry (1988); Mathur and De (1989)) suggested that positive gains from takeovers accrue almost entirely to the shareholders of target firms. While the average abnormal returns (the cumulated residuals for all firms divided by the number of firms examined in the study) recorded in these studies are invariably positive and statistically significant, returns to the shareholders of bidding firms are negative for mergers and not significantly different from zero for takeovers. In other words, on average, takeovers and mergers are not wealth-creating, but the acquisition process transfers wealth from the shareholders of acquirers to those of the acquired. These are very important results as they seem to question the judgement or the motives, or both, of the instigators of takeover bids.

However, a very significant study by Franks and Harris (1989), based on both UK and US data, contradicted much earlier work in an important respect. The study is especially important for two reasons. First, the authors took mergers and takeovers over a much longer period (1955–85) than most other studies; and second, they examined a considerably larger sample than any previous study. For the UK, 1,900 acquisitions involving 1,058 bidders were studied and the US sample was 1,555 acquisitions involving 850 bidders. The targets were all publicly traded, facilitating a capital markets approach. Table 20.7 shows their results in terms of excess stock market returns as compared to the market portfolio, and allowing for systematic risk.

Table 20.7 The gains from mergers

	UK (months)		US (months)	
	0	−4 to +1	0	−4 to −1
Targets	+24%	+31%	+16%	+24%
Bidders	+1%	+8%	+1%	+4%

Source: Franks and Harris (1989).

As with earlier studies, these data record a substantial increase in wealth for the shareholders of target firms, but unlike earlier ones, they reveal a relatively smaller, but statistically significant, increase in wealth for the shareholders of acquirers over the whole period leading up to, and just after, the bid.

A subsequent study by Limmack (1991), using only UK data for the period 1977–86, suggested that 'the gains made by target company shareholders are at the expense of shareholders of bidder companies'. He also suggested that the average wealth decreases suffered by the shareholders of bidding companies were mainly confined to the period 1977–80, and that bids made in the years 1981–86 produced no significant wealth decrease for shareholders of bidding firms.

Limmack's study seemed to imply that bidding firms and the capital market in general might have learned from earlier mistakes, and that some of the gains from merger might be retained by the bidder.

However, Sudarsanam *et al.* (1996), in a study of returns around bid announcement dates over the period 1980–90, found significant negative CARs (Cumulative Abnormal Returns) of around 4 per cent for the announcement period minus 20 days to plus 40 days. In a subsequent study of 398 takeovers during 1984–92 involving bid values of over £10 million, Gregory (1997) found 'the post-takeover performance of UK companies undertaking large domestic acquisitions is unambiguously negative on average, in the longer term'. The results were clearly 'not compatible with shareholder wealth maximisation on the part of acquiring firms' management'. Gregory found that acquiring firms underperformed the stock market by 18 per cent on average for two years following a bid. The method of financing the takeover was also discovered to be significant, with share exchanges being especially poor for shareholders. Agreed bids were less successful for acquiring companies than hostile takeovers, and companies making their first takeovers were likely to be poorer performers than more experienced bidders. Finally, companies bidding to diversify their interests were less likely to succeed than takeovers in related business areas (which echoes many previous analyses).

US studies, by both academics and firms of consultants, have found parallel results. Research in 1995 by the Mercer consultancy and *Business Week* of 150 deals valued at $500 million or above during 1990–95 showed that about half destroyed shareholder wealth and only 17 per cent created results that were more than 'marginal'. These and similar studies appear to confirm the view that bidders overpay for their targets (Gregory found an average bid premium of around 30 per cent) and that managers underestimate the work required to make a takeover succeed. Moreover, many managers seem determined to ignore the warning signs.

Some researchers in both the USA and the UK have studied the post-merger behaviour of corporate cash flows. This has the merit of avoiding the problems of accounting measurement and policy when profitability data are used, and also avoids relying on the efficiency of the capital market if share price data is used. For example, Manson *et al.* (1994) studied 38 UK mergers over 1985–87, and found that, on average, takeovers produced significant improvements in operating performance, reflected in higher cash flow. This supports the view that the market for corporate control provides a discipline for managers, and is consistent with US studies using similar methods.

Franks and Mayer (1996a, 1996b) undertook an explicit test of the disciplinary role of hostile takeovers. They hypothesised that hostile takeovers would have a disciplinary impact, shown by association with, first, a high rate of managerial turnover, second, with substantial internal restructuring (asset sales exceeding 10 per cent of the value of post-acquisition fixed assets) and third, with weak firm performance post-acquisition.

Their study of hostile UK takeovers completed in 1985–86 found:

- 50 per cent of directors resign soon after a friendly bid as compared to 90 per cent after a hostile bid.
- Asset sales exceeded 10 per cent of the total fixed asset value in 26 per cent of friendly bids compared to 53 per cent of hostile bids.
- Bid premiums averaged 30 per cent of firm value for hostile bids compared to 18 per cent for friendly bids.
- Bid premiums on hostile bids were not correlated with rate of management turnover.
- Using four measures of performance – abnormal share price performance, dividend payments, pre-bid cash flow rates of return and Tobin's Q (the ratio of market value to replacement cost of assets) – they found little significant evidence that recipients of hostile bids were poor performers prior to the bid.

Overall, the evidence was not consistent with hostile takeovers exerting a form of natural selection in which underperforming managements are supplanted by alternative teams offering improved results.

Finally, what about international mergers? The accounting firm KPMG (1999) reported a study of 700 of the largest cross-border takeovers occurring between 1996 and 1998, in which it attempted to assess the value created. KPMG measured companies' share price performance before and after the deal, and compared the post-deal performance with trends in each of the firm's industries.

The results were:

- 17 per cent of takeovers added value to the combined company.
- 30 per cent produced no significant difference.
- 53 per cent actually destroyed value.

Commenting on why 83 per cent of mergers apparently fail to generate net benefits for shareholders, it was suggested that many firms concentrate too heavily on the business and financial mechanics and overlook the personnel-related issues, echoing the earlier study by Lees (1992).

KPMG identified six factors that merit close attention:

- evaluation of synergies
- integrated project planning
- due diligence
- selection of the right management team
- dealing with culture clashes
- communication with staff.

Not much new here, readers may think, but it is remarkable how often over-ambitious managers have to be reminded of the ingredients of a successful merger.

In a further survey released in 2002, KPMG claimed that over a third of giant international takeovers completed at the peak of the bull market were being unwound, that 32 per cent of chief executives or Finance Directors responsible for planning the original deals had moved on, and that two-thirds of firms acquired during 1996–98 still needed to be properly integrated. The lesson appears to be that, like Chris Gent of Vodafone, following the acquisition of Mannesmann, top managers should negotiate their bonuses after completion of the mega-deal, but before the problems begin to appear.

The KPMG study suggests the importance of internal cultural issues. One might be forgiven for thinking that acquisitions by British firms of US enterprises would have a greater chance of success given the similarity in language and corporate cultures. Yet research by Gregory and McCorriston (2004), based on a study of 197 major British takeovers in the USA (excluding banking – itself a disaster area), suggests exactly the opposite.

Failure to address cultural issues was also highlighted by a report by the Hay Group (Dion *et al.*, 2007). Its study of European mergers concluded that only 9 per cent of mergers achieve their pre-stated aims. The researchers found that only 29 per cent of acquirers had conducted a cultural audit of the target, suggesting that firms had over-prioritised the 'hard keys' like financial and IT due diligence.

However, although echoing many earlier findings, a slightly less gloomy picture was obtained in more recent KPMG surveys (2007, 2010). Using a telephone interview approach, this covered a sample of global companies that had conducted deals worth over US$100 million between 2002 and 2003. The KPMG team came to six broad conclusions.

1 More deals enhanced value (31 per cent), in terms of shareholder value relative to the relevant industry average, than in its earlier study, and more deals enhanced value than reduced value (26 per cent). Yet, still over two-thirds of deals failed to increase value. By contrast, executives from 93 per cent of firms claimed that their deals did enhance value. The 'perception gap' suggested that firms were not yet prepared to make an honest assessment of their deals.

2 There was strong correlation between firms that enhanced value and those that met or exceeded their synergy and performance improvement targets. This suggests that firms that set out to outperform their targets achieved the targets. KPMG surmised that synergies arrive from unexpected areas, and that narrow pursuit of cost savings may fail to capture the full benefit of revenue synergies.

3 Almost two-thirds of acquirers failed to meet their synergy targets, 43 per cent of which was included in the purchase price. This suggests that firms typically over-pay for synergies.

4 Firms found they did not start post-deal planning early enough. Although 59 per cent of firms had started planning for the integration process, the most commonly cited actions that firms said they would adopt on their next deal was earlier planning. Stated advantages of early planning were limiting the risk of losing customers, bringing forward synergy delivery, and avoiding a communication vacuum, in which rumour and speculation are rife.

5 Despite citing differences in organisational culture as the second greatest post-deal challenge, 80 per cent of firms said they had not been well prepared to handle this. The top three post-deal challenges were stated as: complex integration of two businesses, dealing with different organisational cultures and difficulty in integrating IT and reporting systems. About half said they had been well-prepared for challenges one and three, but over two-thirds had placed low emphasis on addressing people and cultural issues. Only 20 per cent said these issues were less important than expected. The top three actions that executives said they would adopt in their next deal were: to plan earlier, perform additional cultural due diligence, and to set up a dedicated team to handle the post-deal tasks.

6 It required on average nine months for companies to feel they had obtained control of the key issues facing the business post-deal. A third said it had taken longer than expected, and over 10 per cent took more than two years before being able to feel in control. More than two-thirds of firms stated that the two critical activities were gaining understanding of the target's finances and reporting systems, and understanding and overcoming the cultural difficulties between the two companies.

KPMG (2007, 2010) has undertaken a series of studies examining the association between M&A success and characteristics of deal transactions. In the first study, it analysed 510 worldwide deals by listed companies (thus excluding acquisitions by private equity houses) covering the period calendar 2000 to calendar 2004. In contrast to the earlier KPMG studies that focused on share price changes, the success of a deal was measured using the normalised share return (share price returns relative to share price returns in the same industry) at one and two years after the deal was announced. Only deals that involved a purchase price in excess of US$100 million were included (thus imparting a large-firm bias to the results). In addition to focusing on share returns, the impact on EBITDA margins was examined to assess whether acquisitions had delivered improved accounting results.

The research showed that:

- For the acquirers, there was an average gain in normalised share return of 3.7 per cent after one year and 10.8 per cent after two years, i.e. acquiring firms that performed better than their industry peers.
- Cash deals had significantly higher returns than deals financed with shares or a combination of cash and shares, being associated with a return of 15 per cent after one year, and 27 per cent after two years. All-share-financed deals delivered negative returns after one year (minus 2 per cent), but positive (4 per cent) after two years. Mixed-finance deals (shares plus cash) performed in between −4 per cent returns after one year and 10 per cent after two years. This is probably due to the fact that companies that use shares to finance a deal may perceive their shares to be a 'cheaper' currency than cash and may judge their stock prices to be around their peaks. Also, failures are 'easier' to write off when using shares (through impairment on the balance sheet) than when using cash, although this is not of benefit to the shareholders. In addition, cash deals are often (at least, partly) financed with debt, thus exerting more pressure to perform, as well as offering benefits to equity returns from gearing.
- Deals by acquirers with relatively low P:E ratios were most successful − 22 per cent returns after one year and 42 per cent after two years for acquirers in the lowest quartile P:E ratios. Acquirers that were able to purchase firms with below average P:E ratios also outperformed. These findings probably reflect the fact that it is difficult for companies with high P:E ratios, whose shares may be 'fully' valued, to further increase their value, and that acquirers already with low P:E ratios may be less tempted to engage in riskier deals.
- Deals by smaller firms were more successful, with returns of 6 per cent after one year and 16 per cent after two years, compared to larger firms (minus 4 per cent and minus 8 per cent respectively). The reasons for this discrepancy may be connected with other factors − large companies tended to conduct more deals and to have targets with higher P:E ratios. However, it could be that smaller companies are better prepared and are less willing to take risks. Also, such a deal will have a bigger impact on a smaller firm than it would have on a larger firm.
- Companies with above average deal activity were less successful than companies with below average deal activities. Negative returns were found for companies with more than ten deals a year, 7 per cent after one year and minus 8 per cent after two years, compared to positive returns for less active firms (one or two deals) − an 8 per cent increase after one year, and 18 per cent after two years Apparently, more deals, despite the experience obtained does not necessarily mean more success, presumably due to the increased complexity of controlling the integration of several targets.
- Different rationales for an acquisition lead to different results. When companies stated that their main reason for an acquisition was to increase financial strength or improve distribution channels, this resulted in an increase in normalised share price after one year. Vertical integration as a motivation, however, led to a significant decrease in share return. Deals driven by intellectual property and technology acquisition were significantly less successful than those driven by more mundane motives, possibly because the target firms had higher P:E ratios and key staff were more difficult to retain post-merger.

- Regarding the impact on EBITDA margins, it was found that these were 4 per cent higher for firms that made acquisitions. Results were broadly in line with those using share returns measures – firms that outperformed were those with lower deal activity, and deals motivated by financial strength tended to lead to an improved EBITDA margin.
- Geographical location was insignificant as a discriminating variable – it seemed not to matter if the acquirer and target were in the same or in different countries.

In 2010, KPMG updated the research when it examined 460 worldwide deals undertaken between 2002 and 2006 (KPMG, 2010), investigating the same variables as in 2007. The study showed largely the same results:

- Deals that were financed by cash, and acquirers with a relatively low P/E ratio were most successful.
- Too many deals lessen success: acquirers that made between six and ten deals were less successful than acquirers making between three and five deals.
- Again, this study showed that deals motivated by increasing financial strength were most successful, while deals motivated by a desire to purchase intellectual property or technology and to increase revenues were least successful.
- The main difference in findings was in the capitalisation area. Firms able to acquire targets with P:E ratios below the industry median suffered a negative return after one year (6 per cent) and also after two years (again, 6 per cent).
- In addition, size of acquiring firm was not a significant factor.
- Again, geographic location was insignificant.
- No results for the impact on EBITDA were reported.

In the next section, we return to a recurrent theme in this book: the meaning and reliability of the values placed on companies by the stock market.

Self-assessment activity 20.6

What are the main causes of 'failure' of takeovers?

(Answer in Appendix A at the back of the book)

20.11 VALUE GAPS[*]

Evidence from *some* studies indicates that there may be net gains from merger, while *most* surveys indicate that the shareholders of target companies experience a beneficial wealth effect. The near certainty that shareholders of targets will benefit suggests that market values typically fall short of the value that potential or actual bidders would place on them. These disparities in value are called value gaps, and there are four main explanations of how they arise.

■ Poor corporate parenting

Value gaps may arise because some business segments do not make their maximum possible cash or profit contributions to the parent. Ultimately, this is a reflection of poor central management, which is thus failing to add value to the group or actually reducing value. The following are some examples of management deficiencies:

1 Some assets, such as land and premises, may not be fully utilised by either the parent or its subsidiaries.

---

[*]This section relies on ideas presented in Young and Sutcliffe (1990).

2 The parent pursues too many ventures of dubious value, perhaps intending to gain entry into other areas of business, but in which it does not possess appropriate expertise.

3 HQ may fail to take sufficiently decisive action to prevent or correct poor profitability in business segments.

4 HQ may indulge in costly central activities or services that are a net burden rather than of benefit to business units.

5 Poor group structure may leave business units at a disadvantage compared with competitors. For example, a business unit may be too small to compete effectively in its main markets, or it may be denied sufficient capital resources to develop its activities. As a result, it may have a greater value under alternative, more perceptive, management.

■ Poor financial management

The HQ corporate finance department might have followed a gearing policy that fails fully to exploit its ability to borrow and gear up returns to equity; or alternatively, it may be severely over-borrowed. Similarly, its past dividend policy may have been over- or under-generous.

■ Over-enthusiastic bidding

It has been said that takeover bidders' greatest victims are themselves. Many bids are undoubtedly successful, such as the acquisition of Arcelor by Mittal. Lakshmi Mittal, CEO of the new entity, was able to report cost savings of US$973 million after just a year of operation, around two-thirds of the synergies of $1.6 billion promised at the time of the takeover. Reported earnings rose 42 per cent in 2006–7. However, many others are outright failures; and some, such as Morrisons' purchase of Safeway, are totally disastrous. Perhaps, at the time of the bid, the assessment of the bidding management was correct, but they were caught out by changed circumstances. A more likely explanation is that they were buoyed up with excessive enthusiasm about the bid. Although some bidders have the sense to walk away from a bid (e.g. Comcast's aborted bid for Disney in 2004), in too many cases, bidders delude themselves that the proposed takeover is vital to the development of the group.

Referring to such cases, cynics use the term 'winners' curse', for obvious reasons.

■ Stock market inefficiency

Does the stock market fail to assess the full value of a business, perhaps because it belongs to a sector that is 'out of favour', or because the market adopts too short-term a view of the prospects of the company?

Assessing the relative weights of these arguments is a major challenge for finance and business researchers.

Marrying in haste

Merger and acquisitions continue apace in spite of an alarming failure rate and evidence that they often fail to benefit shareholders. Last week's collapse of the planned Deutsche–Dresdner Bank merger tarnished the reputation of both parties. Deutsche Bank's management was exposed as divided and confused. Dresdner Bank lost its chairman, who resigned. Senior members of Dresdner Kleinwort Benson, its investment banking unit, walked out.

Deutsche–Dresdner was a fiasco that damaged both parties. But even if the takeover had gone ahead, it would probably still have claimed its victims. A long list of studies have all reached the same conclusion: the majority of takeovers damage the interests of the shareholders of the acquiring company. They do, however, often reward the shareholders of the acquired company, who receive more for their shares than they were worth before the takeover was announced. Mark Sirower, visiting professor at New York University, claims that 65 per cent of mergers fail to benefit acquiring companies, whose shares subsequently underperform their sector. Yet the evidence of failure has done nothing to dim senior managers' enthusiasm for takeovers.

Why do so many mergers and acquisitions fail to benefit shareholders? Colin Price, a partner at McKinsey, the management consultants, who specialises in mergers and acquisitions, says the majority of failed mergers suffer from poor implementation. And in about half of those, senior management failed to take account of the different cultures of the companies involved.

Melding corporate cultures takes time, which senior management does not have after a merger. 'Most mergers are based on the idea of "let's increase revenues", but you have to have a functioning management team to manage that process. The nature of the problem is not so much that there's open warfare between the two sides, it's that the cultures don't meld quickly enough to take advantage of the opportunities. In the meantime, the marketplace has moved on.'

Many consultants refer to how little time companies spend before a merger thinking about whether their organisations are compatible. The benefits of mergers are usually couched in financial or commercial terms: cost-savings can be made or the two sides have complementary businesses that will allow them to increase revenues.

Mergers are about compatibility, which means agreeing whose values will prevail and who will be the dominant partner. So it is no accident that managers as well as journalists reach for marriage metaphors in describing them. Merging companies are said to 'tie the knot'. When mergers are called off, as with Deutsche Bank and Dresdner Bank, the two companies fail to 'make it up the aisle' or their relationship remains 'unconsummated'. Yet the metaphors fail to convey the scale of risk companies run when they launch acquisitions or mergers. Even in countries with high divorce rates, marriages have a better success rate than mergers. And in an age of frequent pre-marital cohabitation, the bridal couple usually know one another better than the merging companies do.

Mr Sirower rejects the view that the principal problem is 'post-merger implementation'. 'Many large acquisitions are dead on arrival, no matter how well they are managed after the deal is done,' he says. He asks why managers should pay a premium to make an acquisition when their shareholders could invest in the target company themselves. How sure are managers that they can extract cost savings or revenue improvements from their acquisition that match the size of the takeover premium?

Perhaps it would help if senior managers abandoned the marriage metaphor in favour of the story of the princess and the toad. Warren Buffett, the US investor, said nearly 20 years ago that many acquisitive managers appeared to see themselves as princesses whose kisses could turn toads into handsome princes. Investors, he observed, could always buy toads at the going price for toads. 'If investors instead bankroll princesses who wish to pay double for the right to kiss the toad, those kisses better pack some real dynamite. We've observed many kisses, but very few miracles. Many managerial princesses remain serenely confident about the future potency of their kisses, even after their corporate backyards are knee-deep in unresponsive toads.'

Source: Based on Michael Skapinker, *Financial Times*, 12 April 2000.

20.12 CORPORATE RESTRUCTURING

Corporate *restructuring* is an important vehicle by which managements can enhance shareholder value by changing the ownership structure of the organisation. It involves three key elements:

1 Concentration of equity ownership in the hands of managers or 'inside' investors well-placed to monitor managers' efforts.
2 Substitution of debt for equity.
3 Redefinition of organisational boundaries through mergers, divestment, management buy-outs, etc.

In the dynamic environment within which companies operate, financial managers should be ever-alert to new and better ways of structuring and financing their businesses. The value-creation process will involve the following:

■ Review the corporate financial structure from the shareholders' viewpoint. Consider whether changes in capital structure, business mix or ownership would enhance value.

Vodafone forced to write down Indian business

Vodafone was forced to write down the value of its Indian business by more than 25 per cent yesterday, just three years after securing control of the country's second-largest mobile operator by revenue. The £2.3bn write-down on Vodafone's flagship emerging market business overshadowed the UK group's results where, for the first time, it set a three-year dividend growth target.

Vittorio Colao, chief executive, also tried to woo investors by holding out the possibility of a resumption of dividend payments from Verizon Wireless, the US mobile operator in which the UK group has a 45 per cent stake. But investors fretted over Vodafone's Indian challenges and the group's shares closed down 0.35p at 136p.

Vodafone's purchase of a controlling stake in Hutchison Essar, then India's fourth-largest mobile operator, was the signature acquisition of Arun Sarin, Mr Colao's predecessor.

Vodafone paid a hefty $10.9bn in 2007 for a 66 per cent stake in Hutchison Essar. But the operator, renamed Vodafone Essar, is slugging it out in a fierce price war involving an unusually large number of rivals. India has 15 network operators, whereas many developed countries have three or four.

Vodafone has written down the book value of its Vodafone Essar stake from £8bn to £5.7bn because of the price war, which has also dented the market capitalisations of domestic operators led by Bharti Airtel and Reliance Communications.

Mr Colao called on the Indian government to reform rules that prohibit consolidation between mobile operators. 'There is a need for political leadership in shaping the industry,' he said. Mr Colao also criticised proposals by the Indian telecoms regulator to impose retrospective radio spectrum charges on existing mobile operators.

 Source: Andrew Parker, *Financial Times*, 19 May 2011. © Financial Times

- Increase efficiency and reduce the after-tax cost of capital through the judicious use of borrowing.
- Improve operating cash flows through focusing on wealth-creating investment opportunities (i.e. those having positive net present values), profit improvement and overhead reduction programmes and divestiture.
- Pursue financially-driven value creation using various new financing instruments and arrangements (i.e. financial engineering).

■ Types of restructuring

Recent years have seen the development of new and elaborate methods of corporate restructuring. Restructuring can occur at three different levels:

1 *Corporate restructuring* refers to changing the ownership structure of the parent company to enhance shareholder value. Such changes can arise through diversification, forming strategic alliances, leveraged buy-outs and even liquidation.
2 *Business restructuring* considers changing the ownership structure at the strategic business unit level. Examples include acquisitions, joint ventures, divestments and management buy-outs.
3 *Asset restructuring* refers to changing the ownership of assets. This can be achieved through sale and leaseback arrangements, offering assets as security, factoring debts and asset disposals.

The levels of restructuring are summarised below:

Corporate	Business unit	Asset
Diversification/demerger	Acquisitions	Pledging assets as security
Share issues	Joint ventures	Factoring debts
Share repurchase	Management buy-outs	Leasing and HP
Strategic alliances	Sell-offs	Sale and leaseback
Leveraged buy-outs	Franchising	Divestment
Liquidation	Spin-offs	

Most of these devices have been covered elsewhere in this book. We devote the next two sections to a brief discussion of divestments and management buy-outs (MBOs), which have so far received only passing mention.

Divestment

A divestment is the opposite of an investment or acquisition; it is the sale of part of a company (e.g. assets, product lines, divisions, brands) to a third party. The heavy use of divestment as a means of restructuring reflects the continuing efforts of corporate management to adjust to changing economic and political environments.

One of the motives for acquisition, identified earlier, is the managerial belief that the two businesses are worth more when combined than separate. A form of reverse synergy is a major reason for divestment: the two elements of an existing business are worth more separated than combined. Whereas the arithmetic of synergy for acquisitions argues that $(2 + 2) = 5$, the arithmetic behind divestment, or reverse synergy, argues that $(5 - 1)$ can be worth more than 4. In other words, part of the business can be sold off at a greater value than its current worth to the company. The management team may not relish the prospect of divesting itself of certain business activities, but it is often necessary as the strategic focus changes.

Self-assessment activity 20.7

Suggest reasons why a firm may choose to divest part of its business.

(Answer in Appendix A at the back of the book)

Two particular forms of divestment are sell-offs and spin-offs. Sell-offs involve selling part of a business to a third party, usually for cash. The most common reason for sell-offs is to divest less profitable, non-core business units to ease cash flow problems. In spin-offs, there is no change in ownership. A new company is created with assets transferred to it, as in BT's spin-off of MMO$_2$ in 2002, but the shareholders now have holdings in two companies rather than one.

In theory, the value of the two companies should be no different from that of the single company prior to spin-off. But numerous US studies suggest that spin-offs usually result in strong positive abnormal returns to shareholders. Why should this be so?

1 It enables investors to value the two parts of the business more easily. Poor-performing business units are more exposed to the stock market, necessitating appropriate managerial action. For example, some high-street retailers have spun-off their properties into separate companies, so that investors can judge performance on retailing and property activities more easily.

2 The creation of a clearer management structure and strategic vision of the two companies should result in greater efficiency and effectiveness.

3 Spin-offs reduce the likelihood of a predatory takeover bid where the bidder recognises underperforming assets in a single company. They also make it easier for the group to sell a clearly defined part of its business at a price better reflecting its true worth.

Divestments enable companies to move their resources to higher-value investment opportunities. They should be evaluated along exactly the same lines as investment decisions, based on the net present value resulting from the divestment.

The motives for a demerger are broadly the same as for divestment discussed earlier. However, with the current vogue to focus on core businesses, it is easy to forget the drawbacks of demerger or divestment:

- Loss of economies of scale where the demerged business shared certain activities, including central overheads.
- A smaller firm may find it harder to raise finance or may incur a higher cost of capital.
- Greater vulnerability to takeover.

Qinetiq to offload struggling US arm

Qinetiq is to sell its US services division, closing a chapter on the defence technology company's aggressive expansion into the country. The London-listed group has agreed to offload its loss-making US business – one of the largest contractors to NASA – for as much as $215m in a deal with the SI Organization, the private US defence company. Qinetiq also announced that it would return £150m to shareholders – equivalent to a tenth of the company's market capitalisation – by way of a share buyback.

The US services operation was the product of what chief executive Leo Quinn called a 'flawed' strategy of buying up assets in US defence services, which pushed up debt levels at the former research arm of the Ministry of Defence. 'David [Mellors, finance director] and I have spent four years systematically unbundling what had been created, and this divestment is really the final piece in the jigsaw for creating a more focused strategy,' said Mr Quinn.

Deep defence cuts in Washington have plunged the US unit into the red. 'The fact that we're no longer exposed to that sector is very, very important,' said Mr Quinn, though the company retains interests – including robotics and sniper detection products – that serve the US.

The deal with SI Organization also excluded Cyveillance, the cyber intelligence operation that Qinetiq bought five years ago and which Mr Quinn sees as a key growth area. Qinetiq is refocusing that business away from defence towards what Mr Quinn calls its 'original, core base', namely banks, insurers and retailers.

JPMorgan Cazenove analysts said: 'Given ... that US services will no longer be a drain on management time, and that Qinetiq is now a "cleaner" company ... in our view makes it more likely Qinetiq could be acquired over time'.

Source: Based on Andy Sharman, *Financial Times*, 23 April 2014, p. 20.

Management buy-outs

management buy-out (MBO)
Acquisition of an existing firm by its existing management usually involving substantial amounts of straight debt and mezzanine finance

Management buy-outs (MBOs) occur when the management of a company 'buys out' a distinct part of the business that the company is seeking to divest. MBOs usually arise because a parent company decides to divest a subsidiary for strategic reasons. For example, it may decide to exit a certain activity; to sell off an unwanted subsidiary acquired by a takeover of the parent company; to improve the strategic fit of its various business units; or simply to concentrate on its core activities. MBOs can also be purchaser-driven, where the local management recognises that the business has greater potential than the parent company management realises, or where the alternative is closure, with high redundancy and closure costs.

Once a company decides to divest itself of part of its activities, it will usually seek to sell it as an ongoing business rather than selling assets separately. With an MBO, the firm sells the operation to its managers, who put in some of their own capital and obtain the remainder from venture capitalists.

The growth of MBO activity has been fuelled by venture capital firms enabling managers to raise large sums of capital through borrowings (leveraged buy-outs), particularly mezzanine finance, a cross between debt and equity, offering lenders a high coupon rate and, frequently, the right to convert to equity should the company achieve a quotation. The Finance Act 1981 gave considerable help by allowing finance raised to be secured on the acquired assets.

An MBO typically has three parties: the directors of the group looking to divest, the management team looking to make the buy-out and the financial backers for the buy-out team. A private company may agree to an MBO because the directors wish to retire or because it needs cash for the remaining operations.

It is quite common for the new management team to obtain a better return on the business than the old company. Reasons for this include:

- the greater personal motivation of management
- flexibility in decision-making
- lower overheads
- negotiating a favourable buy-out price.

Dairies demonstrate way to be seen but not be part of herd

In the sleepy mid-Devon town of Crediton, which only gets mentioned in the local news when there is barn fire or a seminar on horsebox safety, an Irish-born businessman has just bought the local dairy. Tim Smiddy had to remortgage his home to pull off the deal. But together with Neil Kennedy, a well-known west country dairyman, he paid an undisclosed sum to Arla Foods, the Danish co-operative and owner of the Lurpak brand, to acquire the Crediton UHT long-life milk processing plant.

A disposal of Crediton was a last-minute condition imposed by the European Commission competition authorities before approving the separate takeover by Arla of the Bristol-based Milk Link co-operative which, until then, owned Crediton. Mr Smiddy and Mr Kennedy had both worked for Milk Link – Mr Smiddy as finance director, Mr Kennedy as chief executive – so knew the Credition business well. Indeed, Mr Smiddy had been asked by Arla to run Crediton while it was being prepared for sale.

He only became interested in the possibility of a management buyout last March – but within six weeks, with the help of Lloyds Bank, had put together a bid and a business plan. 'We knew we were starting from behind. The others had done a few laps before we got going,' he recalls, as he takes a visitor round the processing plant.

With the deal set to be finally approved by Brussels in the next few weeks, Clive Hetherington of Lloyds Bank, who organised the financing package for the Crediton MBO, says one of the key features is that they enjoy close and long-term relations with their farmer suppliers, which ensures the quality and product reliability.

With the UK still a net importer of milk products, Mr Smiddy believes growth will continue to depend on the home market. But the company also has a small export presence – in markets such as Cyprus and Malta, where there is an expatriate British population. And this year, it is joining forces with one of its international packaging suppliers to exhibit at a food fair in China. Mr Smiddy believes that, with the end of quotas, many of the large European dairy companies will be looking at new markets to sell their products.

Source: Based on John Murray Brown, *Financial Times*, 15 July 2013, p. 19.

Checklist for a successful buy-out

The venture capitalist will ask a number of penetrating questions in evaluating whether the MBO is worth backing.

1 Has the management team got the right blend of skill, experience and commitment? The financial backers may require changes in personnel, frequently the introduction of a finance director.
2 What are the motives for the group selling and the management team buying? If the business is currently a loss-maker, how will the new company turn it round? A convincing business plan with detailed profit and cash flow projections will be required.
3 Is it the assets or the shares of the company that are to be purchased?

4 Will assets require replacement? What are the investment and financing needs?

5 What is an appropriate price?

6 Is there an exit strategy?

Buy-out failure is often the result of a wrongly priced bid, lack of expertise in key areas, loss of key staff or lack of finance.

Once the financial backers are satisfied that the MBO is worth backing, a financial package will be agreed. The management team will typically have a minority shareholding, with the financial backers (often more than one) taking the majority stake. While the venture capitalist company views the investment as long-term, it will look for a potential exit route, frequently through a stock market flotation.

The management team will usually be expected to demonstrate commitment by investing personal borrowings in the business. Redeemable convertible preference shares often form part of the financial arrangements. These shares give voting rights should the preference dividend fall into arrears and enable the holder to redeem shares should the investment fail, or to convert to equity if the business performs well.

Venture capitalists often make handsome returns from MBOs and similar deals – much higher than the returns on the stock market investments. The question must be asked as to whether large companies are acting in their shareholders' best interests in permitting buy-outs on such favourable terms. It is all very well to say that a particular division is a non-core activity; but firms are constantly changing their definitions as to what exactly is core. Restructuring, whether through MBOs or other forms, is wasteful and non-value-adding if the group selling the business could have achieved the same efficiency and other gains as the new company.

From wheels to deals for software sales chief

Not many people have beaten Sir Chris Hoy in a competitive cycling race. Very few have undertaken a management buyout – twice – before the age of 35. Jon Jorgensen has. Despite this, the co-owner and group sales director of software services company Access does not come across as a man in a hurry. Laid-back and affable, he is happy to recount his successes from the age of seven, when he was the national BMX champion, but you get the feeling he does not dine out on it.

Encouraged by a father who felt modern schooling lacked a competitive edge, BMXing saw him take titles, international tours and scalps including a young (though a couple of years older than Jorgensen) Hoy and Olympic champion Jamie Staff. When Essex-based Access ran a recruitment drive to find local talent, Mr Jorgensen, then a sixth-former in neighbouring Suffolk, felt he should go along. Much to his surprise, he successfully interviewed for a sales role: 'I didn't know anything about computers but they latched on to my BMX background – the competitive element seemed to help.'

Access today is a software developer that sells its own range of business applications (also known as ERP or enterprise resource planning) for finance, HR and payroll, supply chain and procurement, and provides associated consultancy to clients ranging from Marks and Spencer to the Bank of England.

Aged just 24, Mr Jorgensen was asked if he wanted to be part of a management buyout team. 'After I looked up "MBO" on the internet, I said: "So I get to own the

company? Yeah, I'm in." Forming a three-person debt-leveraged MBO team for a £2.8m turnover business was 'a massive learning curve', he says. 'The challenge comes with the way you leverage an MBO. Suddenly, you have a company that's doing very well trying to service a level of debt that needs to be paid before you stump up the salaries.' The MBO was ultimately successful and the debt paid off.

Then came his second MBO. 'When one person owns the majority of a company they are fearful of risk,' he says. 'We weren't able to do what we wanted to.' An MBO was mooted among the executive team as a way to 'unleash the shackles'. Unlike the First debt-financed MBO, this was better suited to private equity. 'This was a whole new ballgame ... The fees that were racked up were the size of a small company. You learn these terminologies of "below the line" "ebitda" ... We have more classes of shares now than there are Smarties in a tube.'

The eventual £50m deal with Lyceum Capital in 2011 gave Mr Jorgensen and his fellow MBO team the freedom they craved. 'Without private equity, we'd probably still be turning over about £25m–26m. As it is, we've gone from 230 people employed to 580 and a £50m turnover. 'More importantly, we got a lot skills from them. Two really good non-exec directors came on board. The equity house is also very involved ... They've never said "do this and do that" but they do help us look at the business in a slightly different way.' The company has had an impressive record for growth ever since.

Source: Based on Tim Smedley, *Financial Times*, 20 March 2014, p. 3.

management buy-in (MBI)
Acquisition of an equity stake in an existing firm by new management that injects expertise as well as capital into the enterprise

Management buy-ins (MBI) are the opposite of buy-outs. A group of business managers with the necessary expertise and skills to run a particular type of business search for a business to acquire. The ideal candidate is a business, or part of a business, with strong potential, but which has been underperforming or is in financial difficulty, perhaps because of poor management. The new team rarely has the necessary capital to buy in and often requires the backing of a venture capitalist.

Joint ventures and strategic alliances

Unlike mergers or acquisitions, **joint ventures** and other strategic alliances enable both sides to retain their separate identities. They have been employed to good effect to achieve a variety of objectives, but have become a particularly popular way of developing new products and entering new markets, especially overseas. One of the financial benefits is that the strength of two organisations coming together for some specific strategic purpose can often lower capital costs associated with the new investment.

There are two main types of joint venture. An *industrial cooperation* joint venture is for a fixed period of time, where the responsibilities of each of the parties are clearly defined. These are particularly popular in the emerging mixed economies of Central and Eastern Europe, and China. A *joint-equity* venture is where two companies make significant investments in a long-term joint activity. These are more common as a means of investing in countries where foreign ownership is discouraged, such as in Japan and parts of the Middle East.

Like any other investment, the potential partners need to assess the costs and benefits of the joint venture and identify and manage the activities critical to success. One problem can be the inability of the joint venture management team to make decisions without the approval of parent companies. This can be overcome by structuring the alliance with its own board of directors and financial reporting system.

How does restructuring enhance shareholder value? We suggest four ways in which value can be created.

1 Business fit and focus

As we saw with divestments, a business unit may 'fit' one company better than another. Management should review their strategic business units and ask whether they operate best under the present ownership or whether they would create more value under some other ownership through an external acquisition or management buy-out. When unrelated activities have been divested, management has a much better focus on its core businesses and can concentrate on pursuing wealth-creating investment opportunities and improving efficiencies.

2 Eliminate sub-standard investment

Managers commonly enter into investments that do not enhance shareholder value:

1 A decision to reduce reliance on a single business may lead to diversification. Quite apart from the additional overheads that may be created from diversification and the lack of managerial expertise, such diversification may have no real benefit for shareholders. As we saw in Chapters 8 and 9, shareholders can often achieve the same, or better, risk-reduction effects by creating diversified portfolios.

2 Pursuit of growth in sales and earnings brings power and, possibly, protection from takeover, but does little for shareholders. Rather than pay out larger dividends, management may be tempted to reinvest in projects or acquisitions that do not add value.

3 While a strategic business unit may be profitable, it is often an amalgamation of profitable and unprofitable projects, the former subsidising the latter. Restructuring the business creates a leaner operation with no room for cross-subsidisation.

3 Judicious use of debt

Cautious managers argue that borrowing should be minimised, as it increases financial risk and leaves little room for errors. Aggressive managers take a very different view.

Debt provides a powerful incentive to improve performance and minimise errors. The consequences of management's successes and mistakes are magnified through gearing, leaving little room for error. Managerial mediocrity is no longer acceptable. Cash flow – not profit – becomes the all-important yardstick, for it is cash flow that must be generated to service the debt and meet repayment schedules. In this respect, incurring debt obligations may provide an important signal to the market concerning the resolve of the management team.

Furthermore, debt is a cheaper source of finance because interest is tax-deductible, while dividends on equity are not. Restructuring the balance sheet by substituting debt for equity, within acceptable gearing limits, creates a tax shield and increases the company's market value.

4 Incentives

Raising debt to realise equity can be a powerful incentive to both shareholders and managers. Equity is concentrated in the hands of fewer shareholders, providing a greater incentive to monitor managerial actions. This often leads to the creation of managerial incentives to enhance shareholder value, through executive share options or profit-sharing schemes. Remuneration packages may increase profit-related pay at the expense of salaries and wages. This will also benefit loan stock holders, who have priority ahead of profit-sharing, but after employees' wages and salaries.

20.13 PRIVATE EQUITY

One of the most important mechanisms for industrial restructuring is the investment activity of private equity houses. Private equity investment is conducted by private equity fund management firms, usually in the form of a Limited Liability Partnership. The partners consist of syndicates of financial institutions, such as pension funds. They specialise in buying majority stakes in high growth businesses or firms where greater efficiencies can be achieved by restructuring activities. In principle, private equity covers all investment activities in unquoted firms including development and venture capital, management buy-outs and buy-ins. However, in recent years, the term has become associated, often in a pejorative context, with the practice of private equity firms buying out quoted companies, thus taking them off the Stock Exchange into private hands. These deals are usually associated with high levels of borrowing to gear up the capital structure while restructuring the firm, and paying the interest out of both existing cash flow and the proceeds of more efficient operations. In most cases, the ultimate aim is to refloat the firm on the Stock Exchange and make a capital gain. Until the enterprise is refloated, the private equity firm is the only shareholder in the business, and has total control over strategy and operations.

Despite achieving some notable successes, private equity has received considerable bad publicity for various reasons (see below). A flavour of the opprobrium can be gleaned from two cases.

In 2003, Debenhams, the stores group, was taken private, only to reappear on the Stock Exchange barely two years later with a market value greater than it was sold for, but loaded up with debt. The greater part of its property assets had been sold off, with the proceeds paid as dividends to the investors in the private equity firm, and in bonuses to the private equity fund managers. Since 2005, Debenhams has struggled to assert itself in the marketplace and its shares consistently traded below the (re)floatation price of 190p. By January, 2015, the share price was just 75p.

In July 2006, Boots, the chain of chemists, and Alliance, a firm of drug distributors, completed a £7 billion 'nil-premium' merger. Less than a year later, in March 2007, a private equity firm, Kohlberg Kravis Roberts (KKR), and Stefano Pessina, the former CEO of Alliance, made an indicative offer of £10 per share for Alliance Boots, as it was known. This was rejected, the offer was increased to £10.40, and accepted. Meanwhile, Terra Firma, another private equity firm, and the Wellcome Trust, a privately owned charitable organisation, made a counter-bid of £10.85 per share. KKR/Pessina responded with a bid of £10.90 that was accepted. Terra Firma then responded with a higher offer worth £11.15 per share, only to be trumped by KKR/Pessina with a winning bid of £11.39 per share, valuing the equity at £11 billion, making this Europe's biggest private equity deal, and the first time a FTSE 100 firm had been taken out by a private equity firm. The bid raised several ethical issues.

No details were given until after the battle was over as to how the bid would be financed, or what the winning consortium planned to do with its prize, and it was suggested that Pessina could well double his money in just five years if the venture paid off. As one observer put it: 'There remains a strong feeling among fund managers [other than private equity firms] that they may have been mugged by an inside job.' The books had been opened to KKR/Pessina at £10.40 per share, almost £1.00 below the final bid, suggesting the Board of Alliance Boots (many of whom were former colleagues of Pessina) had been far too ready to capitulate to Pessina and his partners. The following box gives a 'back-of-the-envelope' evaluation of the possible arithmetic underlying the bid.

Filling your Boots – did the numbers stack up?

- At the final bid price of 11.39 per share, making the equity worth £11 billion, and with net debt of £1.2 billion, the enterprise value was £12.2 billion.

- The projected restructuring thus appeared to involve £7.6 billion of debt plus £4.6 billion of direct equity investment (KKR £3.6 billion plus Pessina's £1.0 billion).

- At an interest rate of, say, 7.5 per cent (2 per cent above LIBOR), the interest bill would be about £500 million p.a.

- It could sell off property assets (100 freehold stores plus the Nottingham HO) to pay down debt. The property portfolio value was estimated at over £1 billion, but valued in the books at £400 million. This might lower debt to, say, £6.5 billion.

- After property disposals, the interest bill could fall by about (7 per cent × £1 billion =) £70 million to £430 million, compared to pre-tax profit estimated for 2007 of £600 million, a comfortable enough cushion, ignoring the rent that now became payable.

Return of the buyout kings

For many investors, 2013 was a very good year. For the founders of four of the top US private equity funds, it was a year of outrageous fortune. Leon Black, founder of Apollo Group, made $546.3m. His rival, Stephen Schwarzman of Blackstone, received $374.5m. Henry Kravis and George Roberts of KKR made more than $150m each, while Bill Conway, David Rubenstein and Daniel d'Aniello, the co-founders of Carlyle, shared $750m.

The enormous payouts, while exceptional, reflect a broader revival in the fortunes of private equity firms. As stock markets boomed, private equity firms were finally able to sell the companies in their portfolios – many of them bought before the crisis at high prices. And pension plans, sovereign wealth funds, insurers and wealthy families have started to entrust big buyout fund managers with their money again.

Continued

After four meagre years, private equity groups raised $485bn from investors last year, up 26 per cent from 2012. The 'mega funds' – criticised not so long ago as relics of the boom years – have had a dramatic revival. Apollo raised $18.4bn, 20 per cent more than what it amassed in 2008, on the eve of the crisis. Carlyle secured $13bn, while Warburg Pincus raised $11.2bn. In Europe, which has been attracting investors amid signs that it is emerging from the sovereign debt crisis, CVC Capital Partners attracted almost €11bn.

Buoyant credit and stock markets on both sides of the Atlantic helped private equity groups return $471bn to their investors last year from sales, initial public offerings or refinancings. This was 57 per cent more than the 2007 peak, according to Hamilton Lane, the pension fund adviser. 'It's an industry of cycles and private equity groups are good at playing the cycles, at being arbitrageurs of markets, equity or debt markets,' says Mr Albert.

Some deals that were left for dead ended up turning a handsome profit. Hilton went public in December, enabling Blackstone to post a gain of more than 100 per cent on an investment that had been written down by about 50 per cent. Permira has also marked up the value of its investment in Valentino and Hugo Boss to about twice the money.

Source: Based on Anne-Sylvaine Chassany, *Financial Times*, 8 March 2014, p. 5.

■ Criticisms of private equity

Against this background, it may be easier to appreciate some of the criticisms of private equity firms, or at least in the buy-out arena:

- They are only interested in 'quick flips', stripping out company assets, and cutting jobs before selling firms on, or closing them down.
- They increase unemployment.
- They may curtail the pension benefits of existing members.
- Returns paid out to investors and managers are 'excessive'.
- They pay little tax. Until 2008, UK private equity firms and their partners could pay capital gains tax on disposal at a concessionary rate applicable to business sales of 10 per cent, that often fell to as low as 5 per cent after allowances. CGT was raised to 18 per cent in 2008, but was still below the new threshold rate of income tax of 20 per cent.
- They lower government tax revenues – £130 million in corporation tax being at stake in the case of Alliance Boots. As equity is replaced by debt, so pre-tax profits reduce, thus reducing the firm's tax bill, given the tax shield.
- As they do not have to report to anyone other than their small number of shareholders, their activities are not transparent, allegedly unacceptable for a sector that accounts for such a high proportion of the economy.

■ Rejoinders

Such criticisms have not gone unchallenged. For example, using US data, Lerner (2008) has shown that the private equity investment period is much longer than popularly imagined – in the USA, this averages over five years and is increasing. There is a lower insolvency rate among private equity-owned firms than for orthodox firms, suggesting superior management. Against this, private equity-owned firms did cut more jobs in the two years after takeover – possibly because many taken-over firms were already distressed. However, private equity-owned firms tend to grow faster, and may create more employment as they recover in the longer term, as well as saving jobs in firms that might otherwise have failed.

In the UK, the trade association for the industry, the British Private Equity and Venture Capital Association (BVCA: **www.bvca.co.uk**) produces an annual report to chart the contribution of the industry, which boasted over 500 members as at 2015.

The BVCA reckons that firms with private equity involvement now account for about a fifth of the whole private sector force, and 8 per cent of the national workforce, having grown considerably faster than their listed peers, and the overall economy in terms of sales, employment and exports in the early-to-mid 2000s, although its growth has slackened sharply in the recession years. However, the BVCA does acknowledge that the industry has an 'image problem', and, partly at the urging of the Financial Services Authority, commissioned a report on the industry, published in November 2007. The committee, chaired by City 'grandee' Sir David Walker, was briefed to make recommendations about higher standards of transparency, and disclosure of operations and results, by private equity-backed firms, which it duly did, but was generally criticised for the anodyne nature of its conclusions.

This is doubtless an ongoing debate, although the recession of the late 2000s had taken the spotlight away from private equity. As the previous cameo illustrates there has been an upturn in the amounts raised by private equity groups in 2013. Time will tell whether private equity-inspired restructuring is on balance good or bad. For the moment, it may be useful to peruse Table 20.8 that shows the claimed advantages of private equity-backed firms over orthodox public companies.

Table 20.8 Public vs. private equity

Public companies	Private equity-backed firms
■ Large number of shareholders, many of them very small.	■ Small number of large shareholders.
■ Most shareholders have no say in strategy or operations, except at the AGM.	■ All private equity shareholders intimately involved in strategy and operations.
■ Shareholders may have conflicting personal investment aims and views on company strategy.	■ Shareholders usually have common interests.
■ Incentives of managers could lead to conflict with owners' interests.	■ Management highly incentivised; incentives closely aligned with investors' aims.
■ Public companies often over-focused on short-term earnings; may take decisions that damage long-term prospects to safeguard short-term earnings.	■ Freedom from stock-market pressures may encourage a more long-term focus.
■ Need shareholder approval for major decisions, e.g. mergers and divestments; may slow decision-making and execution.	■ Decision-making and implementation can be quicker; more likely to capture market opportunities.
■ Tend to be relatively low geared; WACC may be sub-optimal.	■ Able to employ much higher levels of gearing, so long as cash flow 'comfortably' exceeds interest commitments.
■ Difficult for shareholders to remove under-performing management.	■ Management changes can be quickly and easily made.
■ Possible that talented managers may seek higher rewards attainable in private equity.	■ Prospect of higher rewards can lure talented personnel.
■ Increasing burden of regulation and disclosure requirements, e.g. to meet corporate governance standards.	■ Less regulation and fewer disclosure requirements.
■ Pressure to increase, or at least to maintain, dividends.	■ No external pressure to pay dividends thus preserving cash flow for other uses.

Source: Based on JPMorgan/Cazenove Ltd (2008).

Private equity and renewable power

Infinis, the UK renewable power company owned by Guy Hands' private equity group Terra Firma, has given details of a planned flotation that will value the group at as much as £930m. The move is the latest example of a private equity-backed company seeking to tap markets that have been buoyed by signs of economic recovery in Europe and the deal on the US government's debt ceiling.

Last week, Merlin Entertainment, the owner of Madame Tussauds waxworks, said that it planned to raise up to £800m in an initial public offering that would value the Blackstone-backed theme park operator at up to £3.34bn.

Infinis, which announced its intention to float two weeks ago, said yesterday it would offer ordinary shares at between 260p and 310p each, implying a market capitalisation of between £780m and £930m. Terra Firma is expected to raise between £234m to £428m from the Infinis sale, having made an initial equity investment in the business of €61m in 2003.

The private equity group has been seeking to return cash to its investors as it attempts to raise a €3bn green energy infrastructure fund – its biggest fundraising effort since it lost a £1.75bn stake in EMI two years ago, which followed the seizure of the music company by its lender Citigroup.

Infinis owns a portfolio of 147 power generating plants that are situated across the UK, including gas generators and an onshore wind operation.

The list of private equity-backed businesses seeking a London initial public offering has been growing, largely as US institutional investors seek to increase their exposure to Europe after cutting it at the height of the eurozone debt crisis. Among the initial public offering hopefuls are Poundland, the discount retailer owned by Warburg Pincus.

Source: Based on Anne-Sylvaine Chassany, *Financial Times,* 5 November 2013, p. 23.

A 3-eyed venture capitalist (**www.3i.com**)

3i Group is way out in front as the UK's leading venture capital investment company, with assets under management of almost £13 billion in value in 2013. Its roots go back to 1929, when a report under the chairmanship of Lord Macmillan identified the 'Macmillan gap' – a shortage in the financing of small and medium-sized companies. Little was done, however, until 1945, when the Industrial and Commercial Finance Corporation, backed by the Bank of England, was created to bridge this gap with just £10 million of capital to invest. In 1973, it united with the Finance Corporation for Industry to form Investors in Industry, which later became simply 3i. It was floated on the stock market in 1994 in a £1.6 billion IPO making it a FTSE Top 100 company.

During its long history, spanning nearly 70 years, it has played a major role in helping to bridge the finance gap experienced by small companies and bringing many firms to their IPOs. Among its major successes were the sale in 2005 of foreign exchange specialist Travelex for a tenfold return on investment, and the sale of Go Fly, the low-cost airline in 2002 to easyJet for £374 million. But venture capital is a risky business, and 3i has had its share of failures, the largest of which was its investment in Isosceles, the company set up to mount a contested £2.4 billion management buy-in of the Gateway supermarket chain. The deal backfired, leaving 3i with £83 million debt and equity to write off. Many well-known businesses, like Waterstones, Geest and Laura Ashley, have benefited from its financial backing.

3i now has a major international presence, operating in 12 foreign countries including Germany, France, the USA, Norway, China and Singapore.

SUMMARY

We have explored various motives for merger and takeover activity, and have argued the importance of a coherently-structured strategic approach to acquisitions, including planned integration that emphasises human and organisational factors. Finally, we briefly discussed other forms of corporate restructuring.

Key points

- The decision to acquire another company is an investment decision and requires evaluation on similar criteria to the purchase of other assets.

- Added complications are the resistance of incumbent managers to hostile bids and the presence of long-term strategic factors.

- The takeovers most likely to succeed are those approached with a strategic focus, incorporating detailed analysis of the objectives of the takeover, the possible alternatives and how the acquired company can be integrated into the new parent.

- If the takeover mechanism works well, it is an effective and valuable way of clearing out managerial deadwood.

- Many takeovers appear to be launched for 'managerial' motives, such as personal and financial aggrandisement.

- The main reasons for failure of takeovers are poor motivation and evaluation, excessive outlays (often with borrowed capital) and poorly planned and executed integration.

- The complexity of takeover integration is related to the motive for the takeover itself, ranging from cash generation, requiring only a loose control over operations, to economies of scale, requiring highly detailed integration.

- The impact of mergers can be studied by comparing the financial characteristics of merger-active and merger-inactive firms to assess any performance differentials, but this approach suffers from many problems.

- The main alternative is a capital market-based approach to assess how the market judges a merger in terms of share price movements.

- The available evidence suggests that the bulk of the gains from merger accrue to shareholders of acquired companies, although some evidence suggests that shareholders of acquirers can also share in the benefits, presumably if the takeover is well-considered.

- Corporate restructuring enhances shareholder value through (i) improving the business fit and focus, (ii) judicious use of debt and (iii) providing incentives for management.

- Private equity houses are increasingly important agents for restructuring, but their activities have prompted mixed reactions.

Further reading

There has been an explosion in books on M&A in recent years, reflecting the ongoing high level of M&A activity, its increasingly cross-border nature and the amount of academic research resource devoted to understanding the whole process.

The most comprehensive UK text is Sudarsanam (2010), while a more international flavour can be gleaned from de Pamphilis (2013). Neither book is especially strong on valuation for takeover, but Arzac (2010), Damodaran (2012), and Koller *et al.* (2010) fill this gap. Rankine and Howson (2014) provide a clear guide to acquisitions.

As ever, Grant (2010) gives an excellent analysis of the strategic factors underpinning M&A. An important article that explains the market for corporate control is Jensen (1984).

As evidence accumulates about the disappointing results of M&A, more attention is being given to post-merger integration. Books that concentrate on this aspect are those by Gaughan (2010), Whitaker (2012) and Galpin and Herndon (2014).

A collection of leading papers in the M&A field is Gregoriu and Neuhauser (2007). Two useful papers that focus on post-merger integration are by Angwin (2004) and Quah and Young (2005).

KPMG is undertaking an ongoing survey of determinants of takeover success, the latest published in 2010. Zenner *et al.* (2008) provide a recent discussion of cross-border merger and acquisitions both from a European and US perspective.

QUESTIONS

Questions with a coloured number have solutions in Appendix B on page 805.

1 As treasurer of Holiday Ltd you are investigating the possible acquisition of Leisure Ltd. You have the following basic data:

	Holiday	Leisure
Earnings per share (expected next year)	£5	£1.50
Dividends per share (expected next year)	£3	£0.80
Number of shares	1 million	0.6 million
Share price	£90	£20

You estimate that investors currently expect a steady growth of about 6 per cent in Leisure's earnings and dividends. Under new management, this growth rate would be increased to 8 per cent per year, without any additional capital investment required.

Required
(a) What is the gain from the acquisition?
(b) What is the cost of the acquisition if Holiday pays £25 in cash for each Leisure share? Should it go ahead?
(c) What is the cost of the acquisition if Holiday offers one of its own shares for every three shares of Leisure? Should it go ahead?
(d) How would the cost of the cash offer and the share offer alter if the expected growth rate of Leisure were not changed by the takeover? Does it affect the decision?

2 The directors of Gross plc have made a 850p per share cash bid for Klinsmann plc, a company that is in a similar line of business. The summarised accounts of these two companies are as follows:

	Gross £m		Klinsmann £m	
Sales (all credit)		216		110
Operating costs		(111)		(69)
Operating profit		105		41
Interest		(8)		(10)
Earnings before tax		97		31
Tax		(25)		(10)
Earnings for shareholders		72		21
Fixed assets		76		50
Current assets				
Stock	20		25	
Debtors	40		24	
Cash	8		1	
	68		50	
Current liabilities				
Creditors	(28)		(12)	
Bank overdraft	–		(8)	
	(28)		(20)	
Net current assets		40		30
Total assets less current liabilities		116		80
Long-term liabilities		(60)		(50)
Net assets		56		30

Included in the operating costs for each company are the purchases made during this year – £100 million for Gross and £70 million for Klinsmann.

The number and market value of each company's shares are:

	Gross	Klinsmann
No. of shares issued	100m	20m
Share price	600p	700p

Required

Analyse this bid to include:

(a) Possible ways in which Gross may hope to recoup the bid premium when operating Klinsmann.

(b) The final and strategic effects on Gross if the bid is accepted by Klinsmann's shareholders.

3 Dangara plc is contemplating a takeover bid for another quoted company, Tefor plc. Both companies are in the leisure sector, operating a string of hotels, restaurants and motorway service stations. Tefor's most recent statement of financial position shows the following:

	£m	£m
Fixed assets (net)	800	
Current assets *less*		
Current liabilities	50	
Long-term debt		
(12% debenture 2002)	(200)	
		650
Issued share capital (25p units)	80	
Revenue reserves	420	
Revaluation reserve	150	
		650

Tefor has just reported full-year profits of £200 million after tax.
    You are provided with the following further information:

(a) Dangara's shareholders require a return of 14 per cent.

(b) Dangara would have to divest certain of Tefor's assets, mainly motorway service stations, to satisfy the competition authorities. These assets have a book value of £100 million, but Dangara thinks they could be sold on to Lucky Break plc for £200 million.

(c) Tefor's assets were last revalued in 1992, at the bottom of the property market slump.

(d) Dangara's P:E ratio is 14:1, Tefor's is 10:1.

(e) Tefor's earnings have risen by only 2 per cent p.a. on average over the previous five years, while Dangara's have risen by 7 per cent p.a. on average.

(f) Takeover premiums (i.e. amount paid in excess of pre-bid market values) have recently averaged 20 per cent across all market sectors.

(g) Many 'experts' believe that a stock market 'correction' is imminent, due to the likelihood of a new government, led by Bony Clair, being elected. The new government would possibly adopt a more stringent policy on competition issues.

(h) If a bid is made, there is a possibility that the Chairman of Tefor will make a counter-offer to its shareholders to attempt to take the company off the Stock Exchange.

(i) If the bid succeeds, Tefor's ex-chairman is expected to offer to repurchase a major part of the hotel portfolio.

(j) Much of Tefor's hotel asset portfolio is rather shabby and requires refurbishments, estimated to cost some £50 million p.a. for the next five years.

Required

As strategic planning analyst, you are instructed to prepare a briefing report for the main board, which:

(i) assesses the appropriate value to place on Tefor, using suitable valuation techniques. (State clearly any assumptions you make.)

(ii) examines the issues to be addressed in deciding whether to bid for Tefor at this juncture.

4 Larkin Conglomerates plc owns a subsidiary company, Hughes Ltd, which sells office equipment. Recently, Larkin Conglomerates plc has been reconsidering its future strategy and has decided that Hughes Ltd should be sold off. The proposed divestment of Hughes Ltd has attracted considerable interest from other companies wishing to acquire this type of business.

The most recent accounts of Hughes Ltd are as follows:

Statement of financial position as at 31 May 20XX

	£000	£000	£000
Fixed assets			
Freehold premises at cost		240	
Less Accumulated depreciation		(40)	200
Motor vans at cost		32	
Less Accumulated depreciation		(21)	11
Fixtures and fittings at cost		10	
Less Accumulated depreciation		(2)	8
			219
Current assets		34	
Stock at cost		22	
Debtors		20	
Cash at bank		76	
Creditors: amounts falling due within one year			
Trade creditors	(52)		
Accrued expenses	(14)	(66)	10
			229
Creditors: amounts falling due beyond one year			
12% Loan – Cirencester Bank			(100)
			129
Capital and reserves			
£1 ordinary shares			60
General reserve			14
Retained profit			55
			129

Income Statement for the year ended 31 May 20XX

	£000
Sales turnover	352.0
Profit before interest and taxation	34.8
Interest charges	(12.0)
Profit before taxation	22.8
Corporation tax	(6.4)
Profit after taxation	16.4
Dividend proposed and paid	(4.0)
	12.4
Transfer to general reserve	(3.0)
Retained profit for the year	9.4

The subsidiary has shown a stable level of sales and profits over the past three years. An independent valuer has estimated the current realisable values of the assets of the company as follows:

	£000
Freehold premises	235
Motor vans	8
Fixtures and fittings	5
Stock	36

For the remaining assets, the values on the the statement of financial position were considered to reflect their current realisable values.

Another company in the same line of business, which is listed on the Stock Exchange, has a gross dividend yield of 5 per cent and a price:earnings ratio of 12.

Assume a standard rate of income tax of 25 per cent.

Required

(a) Calculate the value of an ordinary share in Hughes Ltd using the following methods:
- **(i)** net assets (liquidation) basis
- **(ii)** dividend yield
- **(iii)** price:earnings ratio.

(b) Briefly evaluate each of the share valuation methods used above.

(c) Identify and discuss four reasons why a company may undertake divestment of part of its business.

(d) Briefly state what other information, besides that provided above, would be useful to prospective buyers in deciding on a suitable value to place on the shares of Hughes Ltd.

5 The directors of Fama Industries plc are currently considering the acquisition of Beaver plc as part of its expansion programme. Fama Industries plc has interests in machine tools and light engineering while Beaver plc is involved in magazine publishing. The following financial data concerning each company is available:

Income Statements for the year ended 30 November 20XX

	Fama Industries £m	Beaver £m
Sales turnover	465	289
Profit before interest and taxation	114	43
Interest payable	(5)	(9)
Profit before taxation	109	34
Taxation	(26)	9
Net profit after taxation	83	25
Dividends	(8)	(12)
Retained profit for the year	75	13

Statements of financial position as at 30 November 20XX

	Fama Industries £m	Beaver £m
Fixed assets	105	84
Net current assets	86	38
	191	122
Less creditors due beyond one year	(38)	(58)
	153	64
Capital and reserves		
Ordinary shares	50	30
Retained profit	103	34
	153	64
Price:earnings ratio prior to bid	16	12

The ordinary share capital of Fama Industries plc consists of 50p shares and the share capital of Beaver plc consists of £1 shares. The directors of Fama Industries plc have made an offer of four shares for every five shares held in Beaver plc.

The directors of Fama Industries plc believe that combining the two businesses will lead to after-tax savings in overheads of £4 million per year.

Required

(a) Calculate:
- **(i)** the total value of the proposed bid
- **(ii)** the earnings per share for Fama Industries plc following the successful takeover of Beaver plc

(iii) the share price of Fama Industries plc following the takeover, assuming that the price:earnings ratio is maintained and the savings are achieved.

(b) Comment on the value of the bid from the viewpoint of shareholders of both Fama Industries plc and Beaver plc.

(c) Identify, and briefly discuss, two reasons why the managers of a company may wish to take over another company. The reasons identified should not be related to the objective of maximising shareholder wealth.

6 Europium plc is a large conglomerate which is seeking to acquire other companies. The Business Development division of Europium plc has recently identified an engineering company – Promithium plc – as a possible acquisition target.

Financial information relating to each company is given below:

Income Statement for the year ended 30 November 20XX

	Europium plc	Promithium plc
Turnover	820	260
Profit on ordinary activities before tax	87	33
Taxation on profit on ordinary activities	(27)	(9)
Profit on ordinary activities after tax	60	24
Dividends	(15)	(5)
Retained profit for the year	45	19
Price:earnings ratio	16	10
Capital and reserves		
£1 ordinary shares	80	30
Retained profits	195	124
	275	154

The Business Development division of Europium plc believes that shares of Promithium plc can be acquired by offering its shareholders a premium of 25 per cent above the existing share price. The purchase consideration will be in the form of shares in Europium plc.

Required

(a) Calculate the rate of exchange for the shares and the number of shares of Europium plc which must be issued at the anticipated price in order to acquire all the shares of Promithium plc.

(b) Suggest reasons why Europium plc may be prepared to pay a premium above the current market value to acquire the shares of Promithium plc.

(c) Calculate the market value per share of Europium plc following the successful takeover and assuming the P:E ratio of Europium plc stays at the pre-takeover level. Would you expect the P:E ratio of Europium plc to stay the same?

(d) State what investigations Europium plc should undertake before considering a takeover of Promithium plc.

7 As a defence against a possible takeover bid the managing director proposes that Woppit make a bid for Grapper plc, in order to increase Woppit's size and, hence, make a bid for Woppit more difficult. The companies are in the same industry.

Woppit's equity Beta is 1.2 and Grapper's is 1.05. The risk-free rate and market return are estimated to be 10 and 16 per cent p.a. respectively. The growth rate of after-tax earnings of Woppit in recent years has been 15 per cent p.a. and of Grapper 12 per cent p.a. Both companies maintain an approximately constant dividend payout ratio.

Woppit's directors require information about how much premium above the current market price to offer for Grapper's shares. Two suggestions are:

(i) The price should be based upon the net worth on the statement of financial position of the company, adjusted for the current value of land and buildings, plus estimated after-tax profits for the next five years.

(ii) The price should be based upon a valuation using the Dividend Valuation Model, using existing growth rate estimates.

Summarised financial data for the two companies are shown below:

Most recent statements of financial position (£m)

	Woppit		Grapper	
Land and buildings (net)[a]		560		150
Plant and machinery (net)		720		280
Stock	340		240	
Debtors	300		210	
Bank	20	660	40	490
Less: Trade creditors	(200)		(110)	
Overdraft	(30)		(10)	
Tax payable	(120)		(40)	
Dividends payable	(50)	(400)	(40)	(200)
Total assets *less* current liabilities		1,540		720
Financed by:				
Ordinary shares[b]		200		100
Share premium		420		220
Other reserves		400		300
		1,020		620
Loans due after one year		520		100
		1,540		720

[a]Woppit's land and buildings have been recently revalued. Grapper's have not been revalued for four years, during which time the average value of industrial land and buildings has increased by 25 per cent p.a.

[b] Woppit 10p par value, Grapper 25p par value

Most recent income statements (£m)

	Woppit	Grapper
Turnover	3,500	1,540
Operating profit	700	255
Net interest	(120)	(22)
Taxable profit	580	233
Taxation	(203)	(82)
Profit attributable to shareholders	377	151
Dividends	(113)	(76)
Retained profit	264	75

The current share price of Woppit is 310 pence and of Grapper 470 pence.

Required

(a) Calculate the premium per share above Grapper's current share price that would result from the two suggested valuation methods. Discuss which, if either, of these values should be the bid price. State clearly any assumptions that you make.

(b) Assess the managing director's strategy of seeking growth by acquisition in order to make a bid for Woppit more difficult.

(c) Illustrate how Woppit might achieve benefits through improvements in operational efficiency if it acquires Grapper.

(ACCA)

Practical assignment

Select one of the merger/takeover situations that has been given prominence recently in the media. Analyse your selected case under the following headings (indicative guidelines are provided).

1 *Strategy* – How does the 'victim' appear to fit into the acquirer's long-term strategy?

2 *Valuation and bid tactics* – Has the acquirer bid or paid 'over the odds'? What were the pros and cons of the financing package?

3 *Defence tactics* – Were the tactics employed sensible ones? Were the managers of the target company genuinely resisting or simply seeking to squeeze out a higher offer?

4 *Impact* – Will the acquired company be difficult to integrate? Are any sell-offs likely?

INTERNATIONAL FINANCIAL MANAGEMENT

This section contains two chapters that deal with issues of international financial management (IFM). IFM adopts essentially the same perspective as domestic financial management, i.e. it looks at how decisions in the areas of investment appraisal, financing and dividend policy can be used to create wealth for the owners of the firm. However, there is a major difference – cash flows expected from foreign trading and investment activities are subject to exchange risk, the risk that the domestic currency value may be undermined by adverse exchange rate changes.

Chapter 21 explores the various types of exposure and explains how exporters and importers can, if they so choose, take precautionary measures against such exposures.

Chapter 22 examines how to evaluate foreign investment decisions (FIDs), using principles developed in earlier chapters, but focusing on the strategic motives for undertaking FIDs, and the particular problems, such as exchange exposure and multiple tax regimes, facing firms when evaluating FIDs. In particular, the issue of managing long-term operating exposure is examined in a strategic context.

JAPAN
MEXICO
NEW ZEALAND
S Korea
SINGAPORE
Sweden
Switzerland
TAHITI
TAIWAN
THAILAND

21

Managing currency risk

Hedging your bets

The perceived haven properties of sterling on international currency markets generate a clear problem for British business: a strong pound makes exports more expensive. At a time when domestic demand is also under pressure from faltering consumer confidence, the impact of adverse currency movements on competitiveness abroad adds a fresh layer of difficulty. For companies, this makes mitigating the impact of a strengthening pound all the more important.

Sarah French, finance manager at IT4Automation, started using currency hedging four years ago, after becoming aware that the business, which distributes networking products, was paying more than it needed to in euros for products bought from Taiwan. 'We brought in specialist help to reduce the frequency with which we had to revise prices, as well as to keep down our euro-costs. We were not getting a great exchange rate through the banks, and we also had to pay transaction costs. The services offered by our hedging provider have been more flexible and offer us greater clarity. For us, It definitely has worked, and has also been cost effective. If I was marking our strategy out of 10, I would give it a nine.'

Source: Based on Michael Hunter, *Financial Times*, 31 May 2012, p. 9.

Learning objectives

This chapter explains the nature of the special risks incurred by companies that engage in international operations:

- It explains the economic theory underlying the operation of international financial markets.
- It examines the three forms of currency risk: translation risk, transaction risk and economic risk.
- It explains how firms can manage these risks by adopting hedging techniques internal to the firm's operations.
- It explains how firms can use the financial markets to hedge these risks externally.

21.1 INTRODUCTION

With the huge growth in world trade over the last few decades, companies increasingly deal, as buyer, seller or investor, in foreign currency, making it a key factor in financial management. For competitive reasons, exporters are commonly obliged to invoice in the customer's currency – the greater the strength of competition from exporters based in other countries, the greater the likelihood of a UK exporter having to accept the foreign exchange risk and the associated exposure to the risk of loss.

Foreign currency can change in value relative to the home currency to significant degrees over a short time. Such changes can seriously undermine the often wafer-thin profit margin of a trader, say, a Japanese car exporter awaiting payment in foreign currency. If the yen appreciates, the yen value of the deal can evaporate before its eyes, while the likelihood of repeat business diminishes unless it lowers price, i.e. takes a smaller profit margin in yen terms. It is easy to understand the concern of a major exporter like Toyota, a great proportion of whose export trade is priced in dollars.

In this chapter, we explain both the theory of foreign exchange markets and also how they work in practice, and how exporters and importers can protect themselves against the risks of foreign exchange rate variations. There are two key issues for the treasurer of a company with significant foreign trading links to address:

1 *Whether* to seek protection against these variations, i.e. to '*hedge*', or to ride the risks, on the basis that in the long term they will even out. Most companies do seek hedges, being risk-averters. Yet some actively seek out foreign exchange risk, and use dealing opportunities as a source of profit by deliberately taking 'positions' in particular currencies. A multinational with a substantial two-way flow in several currencies can exploit its position (usually with quite strict dealing and exposure limits) to operate its currency dealing activity as a separate profit centre. Such companies are called '*speculators*'.

hedge
A hedge is an arrangement effected by a person or firm attempting to eliminate or reduce exposure to risk – hence to hedge and hedger

2 The second issue concerns the *extent* to which the firm wants to **hedge** – whether totally to avoid exposure to exchange rate risk or to control the degree of exposure to risk.

Some firms attempt to eliminate their exposures by matching their operating inflows in a foreign currency with operating outflows in that currency to achieve a perfect hedge. However, it is difficult to keep these two flows perfectly in unison due to timing differences in receipt and disbursement of cash.

A variation on this policy is to match operating cash flows with borrowings in the same currency. Such an approach is adopted by Compass Group plc. Its 2013 Annual Report stated that:

> The Group's policy is to match as far as possible its principal cash flows by currency to . . . borrowings in the same currency. As currency flows are generated, they are used to service and repay debt in the same currency.

Some firms actively court foreign exchange risks. In October 2003, Nintendo, the Japanese videogame producer, reported its first-ever loss of £16 million, largely as a result of the strength of the yen. Nintendo kept much of its foreign earnings in local currencies to take advantage of better interest rates outside Japan. This policy resulted in losses of some £215 million on foreign currency transactions as the yen rose strongly against the US dollar. Understandably, Nintendo now has policies in place to reduce currency risk, as the extract from its Annual Report (below) illustrates.

The task of this chapter is to explain the various types of exchange risk and the various ways they can be managed.

Nintendo distributes its products globally with overseas sales accounting for about 70% of its total sales. The majority of monetary transactions are made in local currencies. In order to reduce the influence of fluctuations in foreign exchange rates, we have implemented measures such as increasing purchases in U.S. dollars; however, it is difficult to eliminate the risks completely. In addition, the Company holds a substantial amount of assets in foreign currencies, including cash and deposits without exchange contracts. Thus, fluctuations in foreign exchange rates have a strong influence not only when accounts in foreign currencies are converted to Japanese yen but also when they are revalued for financial reporting purposes.

Source: Nintendo Annual Report, 2013.

To hedge or not to hedge – it all depends …

To hedge or not to hedge foreign currency investment exposure? That is a question posed repeatedly by investors, and answered by their advisers and investment managers. Some will advise to hedge fully. Some will advise to hedge partially. Some will advise that investors embrace the naked foreign exposure in full, enjoy it as much as possible and eventually profit from it. A central recurring phrase heard throughout the discussions that formed the research for this article was 'it all depends'.

Solutions should always be tailored to the needs and wants of the individual investor, however large or small. Ugo Lancioni, a currency portfolio manager at Neuberger Berman, sums it up neatly. Every investor has a different location, a different risk/return profile and different views. For John Normand, head of foreign exchange strategy at JP Morgan, the issue is a no-brainer. 'You should hedge if you think the currency in question is going down, any loss would be large relative to the value of the asset and the cost of hedging is low,' he recommends. He lists four principal reasons why investors might not hedge. One, they might not know the risk exists. Two, they know it exists but think it is trivial. Three, they perceive that it costs too much. Four, they think that any fall in the value of the currency will eventually be reversed.

In the end, it is clear, everything depends on the investors' understanding and tolerance of foreign currency risk. There is no single right answer to the question of whether to hedge or not to hedge. Consideration of the question does, however, prompt the posing of at least one other. If an investor has zero tolerance of foreign-currency risk, should that investor even be considering investing in a foreign-currency asset?

Source: Based on Brian Bollen, *Financial Times*, 1 April 2013, p. 15.

Self-assessment activity 21.1

What is the distinction between a foreign exchange 'speculator' and a 'hedger'? How would you describe Nintendo?

(Answer in Appendix A at the back of the book)

21.2 THE STRUCTURE OF EXCHANGE RATES: SPOT AND FORWARD RATES[*]

Most currency transactions are conducted between firms and individuals on one hand, and banks which make a market (i.e. quote an exchange rate in a variety of currencies) on the other. As in any other market, the two parties set a price – in this case, the

---

[*]Throughout the following sections, we use standard international abbreviations for currencies (based on SWIFT money transmission codes), e.g. pound sterling = GBP, US dollar = USD, etc. We also frequently use the abbreviation FX to denote foreign exchange (rates).

exchange rate is the price of one currency in terms of another. There are two ways of quoting the resulting price, which is often a source of confusion:

- **The direct quote** gives the exchange rate in terms of the number of units of the home currency required to purchase one unit of the foreign currency.
- **The indirect quote** gives the price in terms of how many units of the foreign currency can be bought with one unit of the home currency.

In London, dealers usually use the indirect quote (although this is changing). When we hear that the sterling/US dollar exchange rate (the so-called 'cable rate') is $2.00, this means that each pound can buy two units of the 'greenback', the US dollar. The corresponding direct quote would be £0.50 which indicates how many units of sterling that one US dollar can purchase. The direct quotation is simply the reciprocal of the indirect quotation.

In continental Europe, the direct quotation is used. In the USA, dealers generally use the indirect quotation when dealing with European banks, except for ones in London.

It is also misleading to talk of '*the* exchange rate' between currencies because there always exists a spectrum of rates according to when delivery of the currency traded is required.

The simplest rate to understand is the **spot market rate** that the bank quotes for 'immediate' (in practice, within two days) delivery. For example, assume on 13 June 2014 the closing quotation for the spot rate for Swiss francs (CHF) against sterling (GBP) was

1.5253–1.5255

spread
The difference between the exchange rates (interest rates) at which banks buy and sell foreign exchange (lend and borrow)

The first figure is the rate at which the currency can be purchased from the bank and the higher one is the rate at which the bank sells CHF. The difference (0.02 centimes), or **spread**, provides the bank's profit margin on transactions. At times of great volatility in currency markets, the spread usually widens to reflect the greater risk in currency trading.

It is also possible to buy and sell currency for delivery and settlement at specified future dates. This can be done via the **forward market**, which sets the rate applicable for advance transactions. On the above day, assume the following terms were quoted for CHF delivery in three months:

−24   −23

The numbers are referred to as 'points', with each point representing 1 per cent of a centime, or 0.0001 of a CHF. The negative sign in front of each number indicates that the CHF is selling at a *premium*, i.e. it is 'predicted' to appreciate versus sterling. Had the numbers been positive this would indicate CHF is selling at a *discount*. The terms forward premium and forward discount are typically abbreviated to 'pm' and 'ds' respectively.

The quotation given is not an exchange rate as such, but a 'prediction' of how the CHF spot exchange rate will change over the relevant period: in this case, depreciate against sterling. The rate itself (called an *outright*) is found by deducting the expected premium from the spot rate (or adding a discount to it). In this case, deduction is required because the market expects that one unit of sterling will purchase less CHF in the future, i.e.

Spot	1.5253	1.5255
F/w premium	(0.0024)	(0.0023)
F/w outright	1.5229	1.5232

Notice that the spread widens from 0.02 centimes (or 2 points) to 0.03 centimes (3 points). This is a reflection of the greater risk associated with more distant transactions. An important point to note is that, when a forward transaction is entered into, there exists a contractual obligation to deliver the currency that is legally binding on both parties. The rate of exchange incorporated in the deal is thus fixed. Hence, a forward contract is a way of locking in a specific exchange rate, and is appealing when there is great uncertainty about the future course of exchange rates.

From spot to forward

spot rate
The rate of exchange quoted for transactions involving immediate settlement. Hence, **spot market**

forward rate of exchange
The rate fixed for transactions that involve delivery and settlement at some specified future date

Spot and **forward rates** for other currencies against GBP are thus connected as follows:

$$\text{Forward rate} = \text{spot rate} \begin{cases} plus \text{ forward discount} \\ \text{OR} \\ minus \text{ forward premium} \end{cases}$$

Forward rates, therefore, appear to be an assessment of how the currency market expects two currencies to move in relation to each other over a specified time period, and are sometimes regarded as a prediction of the future spot rate at the end of that period. As we shall see, this is not entirely a correct interpretation.

The reader may wish to visit the website (**www.bis.org**) of the Bank of International Settlements (BIS) for statistics on the volume of trading on these markets. The BIS conducts a triennial survey of foreign currency trading activity on a specified trading day. In April 2013, 53 central banks and monetary authorities participated using data provided by some 1,300 dealers. The average *daily* turnover in April 2013 was US$2.0 trillion (2010, US$1.5 trillion) in spot transactions and US$680 billion (2010 US$475 billion) in outright forward transactions (BIS, 2013).

By currency, 87 per cent of all trades involved the US$, 33 per cent the euro, 23 per cent the Japanese yen, and 12 per cent sterling. The most frequent trading pair was US$/euro (24 per cent), while by location 41 per cent of activity was conducted via London, 19 per cent New York, 6 per cent Tokyo and 6 per cent Singapore.

Self-assessment activity 21.2

The spot rates and forward quotations for GBP versus two other currencies are as shown below. Calculate the forward outrights.

	Spot closing rates	Forward quotation (3 months)
Swedish krona	10.5895 − 10.6045	1 16 [i.e. a discount]
Singapore dollar	2.0499 − 2.0510	−18 − 3 [i.e. a premium]

Source: **www.forexpros.com**

(Answer in Appendix A at the back of the book)

21.3 FOREIGN EXCHANGE EXPOSURE

foreign exchange exposure
The risk of loss stemming from exposure to adverse foreign exchange rate movements

Foreign exchange exposures occur in three forms:

1 Transaction exposure
2 Translation exposure
3 Economic exposure

transaction exposure
The risk of loss due to adverse foreign exchange rate movements that affect the home currency value of import and export contracts denominated in a foreign currency

■ **Transaction exposure**

Transaction exposure is concerned with the exchange risk involved in sending money over a currency frontier. It occurs when cash, denominated in a foreign currency, is contracted to be paid or received at some future date.

For example, a UK company might contract to buy US$45 million worth of computer chips from a US company over a three-year period. When the contract is set up, the rate of exchange between the dollar and the pound is US$2.00 to £1, but what will happen in a year or two's time? What if the rate of exchange alters to US$1.75 to £1 in a year's time?

The US$45 million was equivalent to $45m/2.00 = £22.50m at the beginning of Year 1, but after the fall in the value of the pound against USD, the cost of the contract in GBP rises to $45m/1.75 = £25.71m. Such a substantial rise in costs could easily eliminate the UK company's profit margin.

Similar risks apply to expected cash inflows. If the UK company was due to receive 50 million Canadian dollars (CAD) and the CAD actually rose from C$2.2 to £1 to C$2.0 to £1, the UK company would gain £2.28 million on the contract (i.e. the difference between the expected income of £22.72m (C$50/2.2) and the actual income of £25m (C$50/2.0)).

Thus, unexpected changes in exchange rates can inflict substantial losses (and provide unexpected gains) unless action is taken to control the risk.

■ Translation exposure

translation exposure
Exposure to the risk of adverse currency movements affecting the domestic currency value of the firm's consolidated financial statements

Translation exposure is the exposure of a multinational's consolidated financial accounts to exchange rate fluctuations. If the assets and liabilities of, say, the Australian subsidiary of a UK parent firm are translated into sterling at year-end at a rate different from the start-year rate, exchange losses or gains will be reflected in the new balance sheet, and will also affect the profit and loss account. Similarly, the earnings of the subsidiary when translated into sterling are also affected by exchange rate changes.

Whereas transaction exposure is concerned with the effect on *cash flows* into the parent company's currency, translation exposure affects *balance sheet values*, and to a lesser extent (because assets typically exceed profits or cash flow in magnitude) the profit and loss account.

Examples of items that a treasurer might consider to be subject to translation exposure if denominated in foreign currency are debts, loans, inventory, shares in foreign companies, land and buildings, plant and equipment, as well as the subsidiary's retained profits.

Not everyone accepts that this risk is important. If the CAD falls in value by 3 per cent between the date an export contract is signed and the date the dollars are received in the UK, this represents a real loss to the UK company if no action is taken to hedge the exchange risk. But is a real loss sustained by a UK company with a Canadian subsidiary if C$30 million of its capital stock or C$10 million of its inventory are being held in Toronto at the time of a devaluation of the CAD against GBP? Or is this just a paper loss? This question has been much debated over the years.

It is often argued that translation risk is a purely accounting issue, i.e. it relates to past transactions, so it has no impact on the economic value of the firm and thus there is no need to hedge, i.e. people already know about it in an efficient market. However, it may become a problem if there are plans to realise assets held overseas and/or if earnings cannot be profitably reinvested in the location where they arise, and the parent wishes to repatriate them. (Arguably, these upcoming cash movements essentially reflect a transaction exposure rather than a translation exposure.) Moreover, a policy of 'benign neglect' tends to overlook possible effects on key performance measures and ratios, especially EPS, in relation to reporting overseas earnings, and gearing, via reported asset and liability values.

A multinational company may have significant borrowings in several currencies. If foreign currencies have been used to acquire assets located overseas, then, should the GBP decline in value, any adverse effect on the GBP value of borrowing will be offset by a beneficial effect on the sterling value of overseas assets. In this respect, the overseas borrowing is 'naturally' hedged, and no further action is required.

However, the UK company may face limits on its total borrowing which could be violated by adverse foreign exchange rate movements. For example, a weaker domestic currency, relative to currencies in which debt is denominated, could adversely affect borrowing capacity and the cost of capital.

Say a company has debt expressed in both GBP and USD, as in the following capital structure:

	£m
Equity	350
Loan stock: sterling	50
Loan stock: (US$80m)	40
Total	440

The valuation of the USD loan is translated at the exchange rate of $2.00:£1, the rate ruling at the end of the financial year. At this juncture, the gearing ratio (debt-to-equity) is (£90m/£350m) = 25.7%. Imagine there is a covenant attaching to the sterling loan which limits the gearing ratio to 30 per cent. If GBP falls to, say, $1.50:£1, the company has a problem. Its USD-denominated debt now represents a liability of $80m/1.50 = £53.33m, and the debt-to-equity ratio rises to:

$$(£50m + £53.33m) \div £350m = \frac{£103.33m}{£350m} = 29.5\%$$

The firm is now on the verge of violating the covenant. To avoid this situation occurring, the company could borrow in a range of currencies that might move in different directions relative to GBP, with adverse movements offset by favourable ones. For example, Bunzl plc (**www.bunzl.com**), the multinational distribution group, mixes a so-called currency cocktail that reflects its main operating currencies, as shown in Table 21.1.

Table 21.1 Net debt of Bunzl Group

Currency	Amount (£m)	%
GBP	292.7	34.5
USD	388.2	45.7
EUR	149.9	17.6
Other	18.7	2.2

Source: Bunzl plc, Annual Report 2013.

Bunzl, whose stated policy is not to hedge translation risk, reckons that a 10 per cent strenghening in sterling will result in a change in equity of around £72 million, a relatively small proportion of its balance sheet equity of nearly £940 million.

■ Economic exposure

Economic exposure is also known as long-term cash flow or operating exposure. Imagine a UK company which buys goods and services from abroad and sells its goods or services into foreign markets. If the exchange rate between sterling and foreign currencies shifts over time, then the value of the stream of foreign cash flows in sterling will alter through time, thus affecting the sterling value of the whole operation.

In general, a UK company should try to buy goods in currencies falling in value against GBP and sell in currencies rising in value against GBP.

Of course, the transaction exposure could be eliminated by denominating all its contracts in GBP, which shifts the risk to the trading partner. However, this tactic cannot remove economic exposure. The foreign company will convert the GBP cost of purchases and sales into its own currency for comparison with purchases or sales from companies in other countries using other currencies. Management of economic exposure involves looking at long-term movements in exchange rates and attempting to hedge long-term exchange risk by shifting out of currencies that are moving, to the detriment of the long-term profitability of the company. It is worth noting that many economic exposures are driven by political factors, e.g. changes in overseas governments resulting in different economic policies such as taxation.

Self-assessment activity 21.3

Distinguish between translation, transaction and economic exposure.

(Answer in Appendix A at the back of the book)

21.4 SHOULD FIRMS WORRY ABOUT EXCHANGE RATE CHANGES?

Purchasing Power Parity (PPP)
The theory that foreign exchange rates are in equilibrium when a currency can purchase the same amount of goods at the prevailing exchange rate anywhere in the world

Law of One Price
The proposition that any good or service will sell for the same price, adjusting for the relevant exchange rate, throughout the world

According to the theory of **Purchasing Power Parity (PPP)**, the answer to this question is a resounding 'No!'.

PPP says that the purchasing power of any currency should be equivalent in any location. It is based on the **Law of One Price**, which asserts that identical goods must sell at the same price in different markets, after adjusting for the exchange rate. For example, if the market rate of exchange between USD and GBP is $2.00:£1, a micro-computer could not sell for very long at simultaneous prices of, say, £1,500 in London and $2,000 (i.e. £1,000) in New York. People would buy in the 'cheap' market (New York) and ship the goods to London, thus tending to equalise the two prices at, say, a London price of £1,200 and a New York price of $2,400 (£1,200). (In reality, transport and other transaction costs may prevent the precise operation of PPP.)

The Law of One Price states that, for tradeable goods and services, the

$$(\text{£ price of a good} \times \text{\$/£ exchange rate}) = \text{USD price of a good}$$

However, part of the adjustment will occur via the effect on the exchange rate itself.

■ Absolute and relative PPP

In fact, the Law of One Price only applies under a rarified form of PPP called **absolute PPP (APPP)**. For the law to apply (i.e. for prices of similar products to be equal after adjusting for currency values), resources would have to be perfectly mobile so that the levels of supply and demand should equalise at just the appropriate level. In reality, the existence of transport costs, different local taxes such as VAT, barriers to trade such as tariffs, quotas and other government restrictions, not to mention sheer inertia, prevent APPP from operating, and price discrepancies will persist. One only has to think about land and property to appreciate that some resources are quite difficult to move (although titles to land can be traded).

In practice, market theorists put their faith in a more limited theory, the **relative PPP theory (RPPP)**, which allows for all the market imperfections listed above. RPPP theorists accept that the Law of One Price will probably not hold in its purest form, but it suggests that rates of change of prices will be similar when expressed in common currency terms, for a given set of trade restrictions. Take the previous example, with the computer selling at two different prices in New York and London ($2,000 and £1,500 respectively, or in terms of GBP, at the ruling exchange rate of $2.00 = £1, £1,000 and £1,500). It may be that this pair of prices reflects the market equilibria after all scope for price equalisation is exhausted. It should be noted that the prices infer a 'correct' exchange rate of:

US price/UK price = $2,000/£1,500 = US$1.33 per £1

This compares to the market rate of US$2.00 = £1. This implies the USD is undervalued or, to say the same thing, that the GBP is overvalued.

Obviously, the Law of One Price does not apply here, as the purchasing power of sterling is lower in London (where £1,000 buys only 2/3 of a computer) than in New York (where £1,000 buys a whole computer).

RPP focuses on the differential in inflation through time – if prices rise faster in one location, say London, the local currency would decline in relation to others such as the USD. If, say, prices rose by 10 per cent in London and only 5 per cent in the USA, the local prices for the computer would be £1,500(1.1) = £1,650 and $2,000(1.05) = $2,100 respectively. To preserve the purchasing power of both currencies, the exchange rate would have to alter to:

2.00 × US inflation/UK inflation = 2.00 × (1.05)/(1.10) = 1.91

This reflects a sterling depreciation of about 5 per cent, the inflation differential. Thus RPPP involves the assertion that a currency will fall (or is expected to fall) in relation to another according to the difference in actual (or expected) inflation rates between the two countries.

■ Exchange rate changes

If foreign exchange markets operate freely without government intervention, goods that can be easily traded on international markets, such as oil, are highly likely to obey the Law of One Price, although transport costs between markets may explain a continued price discrepancy. However, not all goods can be easily transported. Most notably, with land and property, which are physically impossible to shift, a sustained price discrepancy may apply between markets. In the longer term, however, even these differentials may close as investors and property speculators perceive that one market is cheap relative to the other.

PPP may be expected to operate broadly in the longer term for most goods and services, although it can be distorted by government intervention in the foreign exchange markets and the formation of currency blocs. The monetary authorities often attempt to smooth out currency fluctuations in order to minimise the dislocation to business activity that sudden sharp swings in currency values might cause. However, while exchange controls and official intervention can delay any adjustment necessary to reflect differential rates of inflation, the required change will eventually take place.

Accepting PPP and the Law of One Price, we arrive at a remarkable conclusion regarding the need to hedge FX risks – there is no need to worry! The Stonewall plc example explains the mechanics.

Example: Stonewall plc

A British-based firm, Stonewall plc has a factory in Baltimore, USA. It plans to produce and sell goods to generate a net cash inflow of $180 million at today's prices over the coming trading year. For simplicity, we assume all transactions are completed at year-end, and that any price adjustments resulting from inflation also occur at year-end.

Continued

At the current exchange rate of US$2.00 vs. £1, the sterling value of its planned sales = ($180m/2.00) = £90m. Stonewall is worried about the USD falling due to the annual rate of inflation in the US of 6 per cent compared to 3 per cent in the UK.

Concern about exposure to foreign exchange risk seems justified – with these inflation rates, PPP predicts the USD will decline to:

$2.00 × (1.06/1.03) = $2.058 after one year.

At this exchange rate, the sterling value of the USD cash flow is ($180m/2.058) = £87.46m, a fall of about 3 per cent on the start-year valuation. But should sleep be lost over this?

The answer is 'yes' if selling prices within the USA remained static. However, prices within the USA are *not* static – the reason why the FX rate will change is due to inflation at a higher rate in the USA relative to the UK.

With US prices rising at 6 per cent, the USD cash flow *ought* to rise to $180m (1.06) = $190.8m. Converted to sterling at the year-end rate, this is worth ($190.8/2.058) = £92.70m. This is precisely equal to its sterling-denominated value at the end of one year with UK price inflation at 3 per cent (£90m × 1.03 = £92.70).

So what has been lost from inflation affecting the relative value of sterling and USD? The answer is nothing if PPP operates! Should the firm take precautions against FX exposure? The answer is 'no' – why should it bother when it is automatically protected by market adjustments? Should the firm try to forecast future rates of exchange, e.g. by comparing the respective inflation rates? It could, but again, it is a waste of time, at least in theory, as the rate of $2.058 should already be quoted in the market for one-year forward deals.

However, it is not always this simple. In reality, prices rise in a continuous process rather than in a series of end-year adjustments. The policy of benign neglect only works if prices of the traded goods are adjusted *pari passu* as prices in general alter and the exchange rate 'crawls' in the appropriate direction, by the appropriate amount, and if the movement is synchronised.

In reality, FX rates adjust in response to relative inflation rates at the national level, as measured by a basket of goods. The basket may well inflate at a different rate from the goods traded. Indeed, competitive conditions (i.e. strategic considerations) may be so powerful that firms may be unable to raise prices even to compensate for inflation. For these reasons, most firms seek protection against FX movements.

21.5 ECONOMIC THEORY AND EXPOSURE MANAGEMENT

The first step in currency management is to identify the transaction, translation and economic exposure to which the company is subject. The second step is to decide how the exposure should be managed. Should the risk be totally hedged, or should some degree of risk be accepted by the company?

The international treasurer must devise a hedging strategy to control exposure to exchange rate changes. The precise strategy adopted is likely to be influenced by several economic theories that have evolved over the last century, and the extent to which they are considered valid. These theories are as follows:

1 The Purchasing Power Parity (PPP) Theory.
2 The Expectations Theory.
3 The Interest Rate Parity (IRP) Theory.
4 The Open, or International, Fisher Theory.
5 The international version of the efficient markets hypothesis (EMH).

We will provide brief sketches of these important contributions to the literature of international economics.

■ Purchasing Power Parity (PPP) Theory

In the last section, we encountered the Law of One Price and Purchasing Power Parity. PPP and the Law of One Price have important implications for the relationship between spot and forward rates of exchange. If people possessed perfect predictive ability, and the rates of inflation were certain, the market could specify with total precision the appropriate exchange rate between USD and GBP for delivery in the future (i.e. the *forward rate* of exchange).

More specifically, PPP states that foreign exchange rates will adjust in response to international differences in inflation rates and so maintain the Law of One Price. Thus the forward rate should be:

$$\text{Forward rate} = \text{Spot rate} \times \frac{(1 + \text{US inflation rate})}{(1 + \text{UK inflation rate})}$$

If the spot rate between sterling and the USD is $2.00 vs. £1, and people expect UK inflation at 10 per cent and only 3 per cent in the USA, this implies a one-year *forward rate* of:

$2.00:£1$ spot rate $\times (1.03)/(1.10) = \$1.87:£1$

Self-assessment activity 21.4

Use the Law of One Price and PPP to predict the relative local prices of a cup of coffee and the future sterling/dollar spot rate under the following conditions:

■ Price now in New York = $2.00
■ Price now in London = £1.00
■ Exchange rate for USD vs. GBP = $2.00:£1
■ UK inflation is 4 per cent; US inflation is 2 per cent

(Answer in Appendix A at the back of the book)

■ Expectations Theory

In the above example, the forward rate is predicting the spot rate that *should* apply in the future. If buyers and sellers of foreign exchange can rely on the currency markets to operate in this way, the risks presented by differential inflation rates could be removed by using the forward market. Forecasting future spot rates would then be a trivial exercise.

Expectations or unbiased forward predictor theory
The postulate that the expected change in the spot rate of exchange is equal to the difference between the current spot rate and the current forward rate for the relevant period

Unfortunately, the forward rate has been shown to be a poor predictor of the future spot rate. Yet it has also been shown to be an **unbiased predictor** in that, although the forward rate often underestimates and often overestimates the future spot rate, it does not consistently do either. In the long run, the differences between the forward rate's 'prediction' for a given date in the future and the actual spot rate on that date in the future should sum to zero. If the forward market operates in this way, firms can regard today's forward rate as a reasonable expectation of the future spot rate. This is the **Expectations Theory**.

■ Interest Rate Parity (IRP) Theory

Interest Rate Parity (IRP)
Asserts that the difference between the spot and forward exchanges is equal to the differential between interest rates prevailing in the money markets for lending/borrowing in the respective currencies

The **Interest Rate Parity (IRP)** Theory is concerned with the difference between the spot exchange rate (the rate applicable for transactions involving immediate delivery) and the forward exchange rate (the rate applicable for transactions involving delivery at some future specified time) between two currencies. Suppose the spot rate for USD to GBP is $2.00:£1, and the one-year forward rate is $1.85:£1. Here, the USD is selling at a

15 cent premium – it is more expensive in terms of GBP for forward deals. The currency market thus expects the USD to rise in value against GBP during the year by about 7.5 per cent.

IRP converts this expected rise in the value of the USD against GBP into a difference in the rate of interest in the two countries. The rate of interest on one-year bonds denominated in USD will be lower than bonds otherwise identical in risk, but denominated in GBP. The difference will be determined by the premium on the forward exchange rate. If depreciation of GBP against USD is expected, this should be reflected in a comparable interest rate disparity as borrowers in London seek to compensate lenders for exposure to the risk of currency losses. In other words, interest rates offered in different locations tend to become equal, to compensate for expected exchange rate movements.

The equilibrium relationship that operates under IRP is given by:

$$\text{Forward rate} = \text{Spot rate} \times \frac{(1 + \text{US interest rate})}{(1 + \text{UK interest rate})}$$

For example, if the interest rate available in London is 12 per cent p.a., the figures in our example will indicate a US interest rate as follows:

$$(1 + \text{US interest rate}) = 1.12 \times \frac{1.85}{2.00} = 1.036$$

So the US interest rate is $(1.036 - 1) = 0.036$, i.e. 3.6% p.a.

This is an interesting result. A New Yorker attracted by high UK interest, who is tempted to place money on deposit for a year in London, will find that what is gained on the interest rate differential will be lost on the adverse movement of GBP against USD over the year. To appreciate this 'swings and roundabouts' argument, consider the following figures, which relate to the two investment options faced by a US investor wanting to deposit $1,000:

1 *Invest in GBP:*

January   Convert $1,000 into GBP at 2.00 = £500.
           Invest for one year in London at 12%: £500(1.12) = £560.
December   Convert back to USD at 1.85 = $1,036.

vs.

2 *Invest in USD:*

January   Invest $1,000 in New York at 3.6% = $1,036 in December.

Clearly, the rational investor should be indifferent between these two alternatives, unless interest rates are expected to fall in New York relative to those in London, or the forward rate is not a good predictor of the spot rate in one year's time.

One reason why this predictive ability is weakened in practice is intervention in foreign exchange markets by governments. In the absence of such intervention, exchange rates seem to operate so as to smooth out interest rate disparities, but with the creation of artificial market inefficiencies, there often exist opportunities to arbitrage: for example, borrowing money at low interest rates in one market, hoping to repay it before IRP fully exerts itself. However, in the past, many corporate treasurers were wrong-footed by borrowing apparently cheap money overseas, but having to repay at exchange rates quite different from those envisaged when raising the loan, because market forces have eventually asserted themselves to remove the interest rate discrepancy.

arbitrageurs
Arbitrageurs attempt to exploit differences in the values of financial variables in different markets, e.g. borrowing in a low-cost location and investing where interest rates are relatively high (interest arbitrage)

This equalising process is effected by financial operators called **arbitrageurs**, who act upon any short-term disparities. For example, if in the previous example, the interest rate disparity were 3 per cent, it would pay to borrow in GBP and purchase US bonds in London.

Checking the agios: the scope for arbitrage

When currency and money markets are in equilibrium, any difference in interest rates available through investment in two separate locations should correspond to the differential between the spot and forward rates of exchange. The interest rate differential is called the **interest agio**, and the spot/forward differential is called the **exchange agio**. If these are not equal, arbitrageurs have scope to earn profits.

interest agio
The percentage difference between interest rates prevailing in the money markets for lending/ borrowing in two currencies

Consider this example. An investor has £1 million to invest for a year. The interest rate is 5 per cent in London and 8 per cent in New York. The current spot rate of exchange (ignoring the spread) is $2.00:£1 and the dollar sells at a one year forward discount of 5 cents, i.e. the forward outright is $2.05:£1. What is the best home for the investor's money?

exchange agio
The percentage difference between the spot and forward rates of exchange between two currencies

S/he could invest the £1 million on deposit in London to earn £50,000 interest over one year, thus increasing her/his cash holding to £1.05 million. Alternatively, s/he could engage in **covered interest arbitrage**. This works as follows:

covered interest arbitrage
Using the forward market to lock in the future domestic currency value of a transaction undertaken to exploit an interest arbitrage opportunity

1   Convert £1m at spot into USD, i.e.

   £1m × 2.00 = $2.00m

2   Invest $2.00m at 8 per cent for one year in the USA, i.e.

   $2.00m × 1.08 = $2.16m

3   Meanwhile, sell this forward over one year, i.e. for delivery in one year:

   $2.16m/2.05 = £1,053,658

The guaranteed proceeds from arbitrage are greater by £3,658. However, this so-called 'carry trade' cannot last for very long. As other investors spot the scope for risk-free profits and rush into the market, their actions will quickly eliminate the opportunity. This is why spot/forward relationships almost always reflect prevailing interest rate differentials.

For this reason, the forward rate is the product of a technical relationship linking the spot rate to relative interest rates, rather than a prediction in the true sense.

Equilibrium requires equality between the exchange agio and the interest agio, i.e. the spot/forward differential should equal the interest rate differential:

$$\frac{F_0 - S_0}{S_0} = \frac{i_\$ - i_\pounds}{1 + i_\pounds}$$

where F_0 is today's forward quotation, S_0 is today's spot quotation, $i_\$$ is the interest rate available by investment in USD, and $i_\pounds$ is the interest rate available by investment in GBP.

Note that the interest agio is found by discounting the interest differential over one year at the UK interest rate. If the period concerned were less than a year – say, three months – the equivalent three-monthly interest rate would be used.

In the above example, the two agios are:

$$\frac{2.05 - 2.00}{2.00} \quad \text{vs.} \quad \frac{0.08 - 0.05}{1.05}$$

i.e.:

   2.5% vs. 2.86%

uncovered arbitrage
Interest arbitrage without the use of the forward market to lock in future values of proceeds

This inequality signifies the scope for risk-free profit via covered interest arbitrage. **Uncovered arbitrage** is where the arbitrageur does not sell forward, but takes a gamble on how the spot rate changes over the year. This is the essence of **the carry trade**. In the example, he or she would earn bigger profits if the spot rate in one year turned out to be lower than $2.05:£1 (e.g. $2.02). This distinction highlights the difference between hedging and speculation. However, although differences in agios can persist for a while, transactions costs may preclude profitable arbitrage.

Self-assessment activity 21.5

If interest rates are higher in London than New York by 2.5 per cent p.a. and today's spot rate is $2.0250 vs. £1, what would you expect the three-month forward quotation to be if IRP applied?

(Answer in Appendix A at the back of the book)

Europe's leaders warn currency volatility could harm the recovery

Two years ago, European businesses were worrying about whether the euro would survive. Today, a bigger problem for many of them is its strength. With the single currency at its highest level since mid-2011 on a trade-weighted measure, politicians are warning that adverse exchange rates could stall the eurozone's fragile recovery. While the euro's rise against the dollar has been fairly moderate, turmoil in emerging currencies has stung many multinationals – which had bet heavily on growth in emerging economies in recent years to compensate for the lack of activity in their home markets, but now find themselves exposed to swings of as much as 20 per cent between the worst-hit local currencies and the resurgent euro.

'The most obvious [concern for 2014] is volatility in exchange rates,' says Carlos Ghosn, chief executive of Renault, which suffered a €600m loss from emerging market currency weakness last year. Adidas, whose euro-denominated revenues were hit last year by a slide in the Argentine peso and Brazilian real, warned this month that

it would suffer from weakness in the rouble, with political risk afflicting a region where it leads rivals. Siemens, the German conglomerate, Electrolux, Lafarge and Pernod Ricard have also reported a negative impact from exchange rate movements.

The reason this is proving so problematic is that multinationals – while accustomed to hedging against movements in major currencies – have tended not to hedge exchange rate risk in emerging markets that now account for a growing proportion of revenues. Treasurers find it expensive and at times impossible to protect against fluctuations in volatile and relatively illiquid currencies that may lack developed derivatives markets. 'If a company is going into an emerging market, it's a very big risk and the currency is a huge component of that,' says Martin O'Donovan, deputy policy and technical director at the Association of Corporate Treasurers.

Source: Based on Delphine Strauss, *Financial Times*, 17 March 2014, p. 2.

■ The Open Fisher Theory

The 'Open Fisher' Theory, sometimes called the 'International Fisher' Theory, claims that the difference between the interest rates offered on identical bonds in different currencies represents the market's estimate of the future changes in the exchange rates over the period of the bond. The theory is particularly important in the case of fixed-rate bonds having a long life to maturity, say, five to fifteen years' duration.

Suppose that a firm wishes to raise £50 million for a one-year period. It approaches a bond broker and is offered the following loan alternatives:

1 A loan in GBP at 12 per cent p.a.
2 A USD loan at 5 per cent p.a.

The Open Fisher Theory asserts that the interest rate difference represents the market's 'best estimate' of the likely future change in the exchange rates between the currencies over the next year. In other words, the market expects GBP to depreciate by around 7 per cent against USD over the next year.

To understand this, recall the relationship between 'real' and 'money' interest rates encountered in section 5.4 of Chapter 5. The Fisher Effect concerns the relationship between expectations regarding future rates of inflation and domestic interest rates – investors' expectations about future price level changes will be translated directly into nominal market interest rates. In other words, rational lenders will expect compensation not only for waiting for their money, but also for the likely erosion in real purchasing power. For example, if in the UK, the real rate of interest that balances the demand and supply for capital is 5 per cent, and people expect inflation of 10 per cent p.a., then the nominal rate of interest will be about 15 per cent (actually 15.5 per cent). Recall that real and nominal interest rates are connected by the Fisher formula:

$$(1 + P)(1 + I) = (1 + M)$$

where P is the real interest rate, I is the expected general inflation rate and M is the market interest rate.

The Open Fisher Theory asserts that all countries will have the same real interest rate, i.e. in real terms, all securities of a given risk will offer the same yield, although nominal or market interest rates may differ due to differences in expected inflation rates. It can be more precisely expressed by amalgamating the PPP and IRP theories:

$$\frac{(1 + \text{US interest rate})}{(1 + \text{UK interest rate})} \times \text{Spot rate} = \text{Forward rate}$$

$$= \frac{(1 + \text{US inflation rate})}{(1 + \text{UK inflation rate})} \times \text{Spot rate}$$

For example, suppose the London and New York interest rates are 12 per cent and 5 per cent, respectively, as quoted by our bond brokers, and the respective expected rates of inflation are 10 per cent and 3 per cent. If the spot rate is $2.00:£1, then the Open Fisher Theory predicts a depreciation in the pound as expressed by the forward rate thus:

$$\frac{1.05}{1.12} \times 2.00 = \mathbf{1.87} = \frac{1.03}{1.10} \times 2.00$$

In other words, when the spot rate is $2.00:£1, this combination of inflation rates and interest rates is consistent with a forward rate of $1.87:£1, as calculated earlier.

These economic theories are interlocking or mutually reinforcing, as shown by the 'equilibrium grid' in Figure 21.1. Several other factors, such as the timing of the change, tax and exchange controls can also affect the relative movement of currencies,

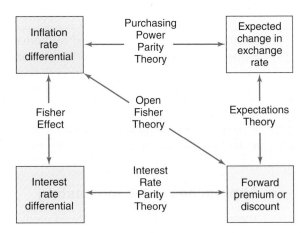

Figure 21.1 Interlocking theories in international economics

but the major factor influencing the movements in exchange rates is claimed to be the expected future movement in inflation rates, which is signalled by current differentials in interest rates.

■ The international efficient markets hypothesis (EMH)

The EMH claims that, in an efficient market, all publicly available information is very quickly incorporated into the value of any financial instrument. In other words, past information is of no use in valuation. Any change in value is due to future events, which are, by definition, unknowable at the present time. Past trends in exchange rates cannot provide any useful information to assist in predicting future rates.

This theory applies only to information-efficient markets. Currencies operating within a system of fixed average rates (or maximum permitted bands of fluctuation), such as the former European exchange rate mechanism (ERM), are operating within a controlled market, so the EMH will not apply fully. *Where markets are information-efficient, the EMH casts doubt on the ability of treasurers to make profits out of using exchange rate forecasts.*

This section of the chapter has provided a brief sketch of some economic theories relevant to devising a foreign exchange management strategy. We will shortly try to design such a strategy by applying these theories to the various types of foreign exchange exposure outlined earlier. But because these theories may not always apply (and some people think they rarely, if ever, apply), it is helpful to examine approaches to forecasting FX rates.

21.6 EXCHANGE RATE FORECASTING

First of all, consider why firms may want to forecast future exchange rates. There are both short-term and long-term reasons for this:

- To help decide whether to protect outstanding current assets and liabilities from potential foreign exchange losses.
- To assist in quoting prices in foreign currency when constructing an international price list.
- To aid working capital management, e.g. accurate exchange rate forecasts may assist the decision regarding the most efficient timing of transmitting currency in situations where the firm is able to lead and lag payments.
- To evaluate foreign investment projects requiring exchange rate forecasts over several years.

Because FX forecasts are required for both short- and long-term purposes, they may require continuous revision. In addition, long-term forecasts for investment appraisal purposes often require more intensive analysis of a range of different scenarios. In general, the firm's FX forecasting needs hinge on:

- The pattern of its trading and investment activities, i.e. its degree of globalisation.
- The required frequency of forecast revision.
- The internal resources and expertise available for forecasting analysis.

fundamental analysis
Estimation of the 'true' value of a share based on expected future returns

technical analysis
The intensive scrutiny of charts of foreign exchange rate movements attempting to identify persistent patterns

■ Approaches to FX forecasting

There are two broad approaches to FX prediction: **(a) fundamental analysis**, which bases forecasts on the financial and economic theories outlined earlier and **(b) technical analysis**, which is based on analysis and projection of time series trends.

(a) Fundamental analysis

This approach is sub-divided into two analytical perspectives:

(i) The balance of payments (BOP) perspective

This regards a country's BOP (more accurately, its balance of payments on current account) as an indicator of likely pressure on its exchange rate. When a country, say, the UK, spends more on foreign-produced goods and services than its export earnings, the resulting deficit on current account increases the probability of depreciation of its currency. Overseas residents accumulate monetary claims on sterling – when they convert into their own currencies, this will exert downward pressure on the GBP (and vice versa for a surplus of exports over imports).

Analysts who focus on the BOP try to evaluate not only the country's ongoing BOP performance but also the determinants of international competitiveness, such as prospects for inflation, e.g. a government budget deficit and how it is financed, and underlying productivity movements.

(ii) The asset market approach

This examines the willingness of foreign residents to hold claims on the domestic currency in monetary form. Their willingness depends on relative real interest rates and on a country's prospects for economic growth and the profitability of its industry and commerce. The asset market perspective could explain the continuing strength of the USD during the 'Greenspan Boom' of the 1990s, during which the USA received a massive inflow of overseas funds seeking a home in the stock markets, helping to offset the continuing gaping US current account deficit.

Any factor expected to increase real returns on investment, e.g. technological progress such as the rise of e-commerce, promising higher corporate profitability is thus likely to lead to relative exchange rate appreciation (and vice versa).

In practice, it is difficult to disentangle the various fundamental pressures on exchange rates to *identify* the true reasons for their movements. Some argue that short-term movements are largely determined by the relative attractiveness of international asset markets, interest rates and the expectations of market players plus a dose of speculation, while in the long term, equilibrium exchange rates depend on PPP.

(b) Technical analysis

chartist
Analyst who relies on charts of past share movements to predict future movements

Technical analysts conduct intensive scrutiny of charts to identify trends in foreign exchange rate movements. These **chartists** focus on both price and volume data to ascertain whether past trends are likely to persist into the future. The underlying premise behind chartism is that future FX rates are based on past rates. Chartists assert that FX movements can be split into three temporal categories:

(i) day-to-day movements, mainly random 'noise'
(ii) short-term movements, which extend from a few days to periods lasting several months
(iii) long-term movements, characterised by persistent upward and/or downward trends.

The longer the forecasting time horizon, the less accurate the prediction is likely to be. However, for most firms, a major part of their forecasting needs are short-to-medium term, so 'expert' forecasting may have some role to play. Forecasting for the long term, however, depends on the economic fundamentals of exchange rate determination, although some people believe in the existence of long-term waves in currency movements (at least, when they float!). A major flaw of technical analysis is that it is purely mechanical with no attempt to provide supporting theory regarding explanation of causation.

■ Forecasting in practice

Most leading banks offer FX forecasting services and many MNCs employ in-house forecasting staff. The value of these activities is open to question, but this really depends on the motivation for forecasting. A long-term forecast may be needed to underpin an investment decision in a foreign country. A forecast based on long-term fundamentals may not need to be perfectly accurate but may help in analysing more fully the risks surrounding the decision and its implementation.

Conversely, short-term forecasts may be needed to hedge debtors or creditors for settlement in a month or so. In such cases, long-term fundamentals may be less important than market-related technical factors, e.g. closing of positions, political factors or 'sentiment' in the market. The required degree of accuracy increases as the prospect of loss is more immediate and less remedial action is possible. In general, long-term forecasts are based on economic models reflecting fundamentals, while short-term forecasts tend to rely on technical analysis. Chartists often attempt to correlate exchange rate changes with various other factors regardless of the economic rationale for the co-movement.

■ FX forecasting and market efficiency

The likelihood of forecasts being consistently useful or profitable depends on whether the FX markets are efficient. The more efficient the market, the more likely that FX rates are random walks, with past behaviour having no bearing on future movements. The less efficient the market, the more likely that forecasters will 'get lucky' and stumble on a key relationship that happens to hold for a while. Yet, if such a relationship really exists, others will soon discover and exploit it, and the market will regain its efficiency regarding that item of information.

■ The role of central banks

A key requirement of market efficiency is that all market players are rational wealth seekers. This is often not the case with a major market participant, the central bank that tries to raise or lower its currency by buying or selling in the open market, often in defiance of market trends and sentiment. Evidence exists that at times when central banks intervene, markets become less efficient and it is possible to make money by betting against them. This happened most notably on 'Black Wednesday' in 1992 when sterling was evicted from the ERM despite the Bank of England spending billions of GBP worth of foreign exchange and raising bank base rate from 10 per cent to 15 per cent. However, these opportunities are likely to be only very short-term phenomena.

Forecasting in practice

The jury is still out on FX forecasting – it should not be possible to outguess the market, but sometimes it works: the question is 'when?' Meanwhile, some businesspeople derive comfort from having 'expert' forecasts available, possibly as a focus of blame! The implications for hedging are hazy – if one believes in PPP in the short term, then hedging is pointless, but PPP seems only to operate in the longer term and with unclear time lags. So, for peace of mind, most firms try to devise a hedging strategy.

Prius apart

During the yen's long rise, the bosses of Japan's export giants have been like executives forced into too-tight suits. Now a weaker currency and this earnings season provide an opportunity to see whether they adjusted their pants or simply breathed in until the pain passed. It is still early days to call the end of yen discomfort. Take Toyota. The world's

Continued

largest carmaker by sales has said that a US dollar rate between Y95 and Y100 is ideal. So the average for this financial year of Y81 is going to hurt.

Nomura estimates that Y1 of depreciation against the US dollar and the euro lifts Toyota's operating profits by Y35bn ($375m) and Y5bn respectively. But the impact over the longer term will not be as simple as that. Leaving to one side that forecasting currencies is a mug's game, the bigger issue for investors is gauging what a weaker yen will do to the whole supply chain. Toyota has used its considerable heft to wring bigger discounts from suppliers, according to Credit Suisse. Should margins expand, its supply chain will ask for its share, too. A lasting improvement should also lift Toyota's capital expenditure, which has hovered near 8 per cent of sales for the past two years, below its 11 per cent average.

Source: Based on Lex Column, *Financial Times*, 6 February 2013, p. 12.

The Economist magazine publishes an annual survey on PPP. This is based on the global price of a Big Mac (The Big Mac Index), and purports to identify – in a tongue-in-cheek fashion – cases where PPP does not apply between currencies. This has recently been extended to cover the worldwide price of Starbucks coffee, to widen the range of goods examined. Results are broadly similar although, of course, a more rigorous approach (as *The Economist* concedes) would scrutinise the prices of a standard 'basket' of goods, as in national price indices.

The Big Mac index: our bun-loving guide to currencies

Last summer mere talk from the Federal Reserve about 'tapering' (ie, phasing out) its monetary stimulus through asset purchases was enough to fry emerging-market currencies. The exchange rates of the 'fragile five' – Brazil, India, Indonesia, South Africa and Turkey – fell sharply. Now that tapering has, belatedly, commenced this month, which currencies look susceptible to further grilling?

The Big Mac index, *The Economist*'s gauge of exchange rates, offers some food for thought. The index is based on the theory of purchasing-power parity (PPP), which holds that currencies should in the long run adjust to rates that would make a basket of goods and services cost the same wherever they were bought. Our basket contains just one item, a Big Mac, since its ingredients are the same the world over, except in India, where the Maharaja Mac is made of chicken. Because buying a Big Mac in Norway, for instance, costs $7.80 at market exchange rates compared with $4.62 in America, our index suggests that the Norwegian krone is almost 70% overvalued.

Of the fragile five, Brazil looks the most vulnerable, because a Big Mac there costs $5.25, implying that the real is overheated by 13%. The other four all have undervalued currencies, to varying degrees. The Indonesian rupiah, the South African rand and the Indian rupee are undercooked by 50% or more.

The IMF is predicting growth for the euro area of just 1% this year. That forecast chimes with the message from the Big Mac index, which finds that the single currency is overvalued, by 7%. The strength of the euro is unwelcome for exporters and casts a shadow over the recovery in the 18-country zone that is already proving to be feeble and faltering. By contrast the British pound is at the right level, according to the index, which should help the much sturdier growth the IMF now expects in Britain this year, of 2.4%.

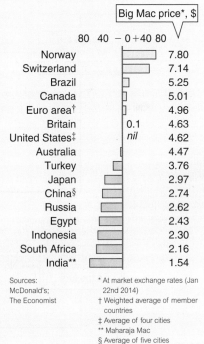

Local currency under (−)/over (+) valuation against the dollar, %

Big Mac price*, $

	Big Mac price*, $
Norway	7.80
Switzerland	7.14
Brazil	5.25
Canada	5.01
Euro area†	4.96
Britain	4.63
United States‡	4.62
Australia	4.47
Turkey	3.76
Japan	2.97
China§	2.74
Russia	2.62
Egypt	2.43
Indonesia	2.30
South Africa	2.16
India**	1.54

Sources: McDonald's; The Economist

* At market exchange rates (Jan 22nd 2014)
† Weighted average of member countries
‡ Average of four cities
** Maharaja Mac
§ Average of five cities

Our Big Mac index will soon be beefed up with the addition of the Vietnamese dong as McDonald's is soon to open its first branch in Vietnam, the first new country to welcome the golden arches in 15 years. Ketchup on this new entry to our index online next month.

Source: The Economist, 25 January 2014.

21.7 DEVISING A FOREIGN EXCHANGE MANAGEMENT (FEM) STRATEGY

■ Hedging translation exposure: balance sheet items

Total exchange exposure is made up of cash flowing across a national frontier plus the assets and liabilities of the company that are denominated in a foreign currency.

An international treasurer who does not believe the theories outlined above might decide to hedge all foreign currency transactions plus the total net worth of all foreign subsidiaries. This strategy is over-elaborate and very expensive, but is adopted by many companies, particularly those dealing in currencies that fluctuate widely in value over short periods.

Figure 21.2 illustrates a more systematic approach. The basic strategy is to remove from consideration all items that are self-hedging so far as exchange rate risk is concerned, and to concentrate attention on those cash flows, assets and liabilities that are subject to exchange rate risk in the short term.

We start with a position where all cash flows, assets and liabilities denominated in foreign currency values are assumed to be subject to exposure. Let us now try to eliminate some of these items from the exposure equation. First, we eliminate all non-monetary

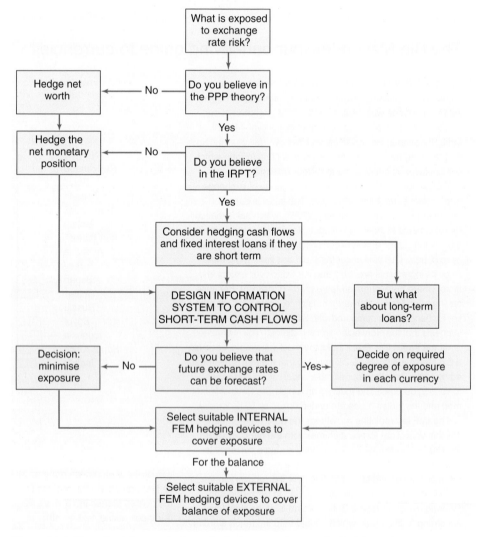

Figure 21.2 Flow chart demonstrating a logical approach towards devising a foreign exchange management strategy (based on McRae, 1996)

assets such as land, buildings and inventory. These should float in value with internal inflation. The rate of adjustment in value will vary, internationally traded goods will jump in local value faster than the value of land, but eventually the prices of all of these non-monetary assets should rise to compensate for the fall in value of the local currency. PPP relates inflation differences to changes in exchange rates. In time, the asset or liability denominated in the foreign currency will rise in value sufficiently to compensate for the fall in the foreign currency value. In other words, the owner of the asset could sell it for more foreign currency units, each commanding a lesser external value than before. The total in terms of home currency will remain unchanged.

Self-assessment activity 21.6

Langer plc, a UK firm, is worried about a fall in the Australian dollar by 5 per cent, compared to the present A$1.75 per £1, that might inflict translation losses regarding its A$100 million assets located in Adelaide. Why should it not worry?

(UK inflation is 2 per cent. Australian inflation is 7 per cent.)

(Answer in Appendix A at the back of the book)

Non-monetary assets are thus self-hedging at least in the long term. If the asset has to be sold in the short term and the foreign cash exchanged into local currency, the amount then becomes a part of transaction exposure because a real loss might be involved.

Short-term loans can, for the most part, also be considered self-hedged. The higher or lower interest rate on the foreign currency loan is a kind of insurance policy against the future fall or rise of the 'away' currency in terms of the 'home' currency. A forward contract could be taken out to cover the risk, but this would be a needless expense (given that spreads are wider on forward transactions), since the forward rate is an unbiased predictor of the future spot rate. On average, the forward contracts would make neither a profit nor a loss.

Long-term loans are more problematic. A fervent believer in the Open Fisher Theory would claim that the long-term loan, like the short, is also self-hedged. The interest rate difference is the market's best guess as to the future changes in the value of the currency. A lower-rate loan suggests a higher capital sum to repay in the home currency. A higher-rate loan suggests a smaller capital sum.

If in doubt about monetary assets or liabilities being self-hedging, one solution is to calculate the 'net monetary asset position' in each currency and make sure it is either in balance or in the 'right' direction. *In other words, if it is predicted that a currency will fall in value against GBP, the firm should owe money in that currency. If it is predicted that a currency will rise in value against GBP, then it should be owed money in that currency.* This might require some juggling with the financing mix of the firm via 'currency swaps', which we discuss later in the chapter.

The key problem in currency risk management is thus to identify the various types of exposure facing the company and then to hedge any unwanted exposure risks. Non-monetary assets and short-term loans in foreign currency are for the most part self-hedged. The exchange risk involved in financing with foreign loans and bonds is less clear. With regard to transaction exposure, a currency information system needs to be designed and installed to identify estimated short-term cash flow exposure in each currency.

■ Transaction exposure: hedging the cash flows

currency information system
An information system set up to identify values that are exposed to currency risk, e.g. cash in- and out-flows and asset and liability values

The first step in identifying and hedging cash flow exposure in foreign currency is thus to set up a **currency information system**. The control of currency risk is much simplified if this information system is centralised, but this is not a necessary condition of efficient currency management.

Once this system is in place, the company must decide whether it (1) believes that future exchange rates can be forecast, and (2) will permit speculation in currency. If the answer to either question is 'no', then the company must seek to minimise the exposure position in all currencies. If a profit-maximising strategy is adopted, the company will use currency forecasts to decide on an optimal position in each foreign currency. If the company believes that currency forecasting is impossible, or not profitable, then it has to adopt a **risk-minimising policy**. The aim will be to reduce exposure in all currencies to a minimum unless the cost of this policy is prohibitive.

risk-minimising policy
A foreign exchange policy designed to eliminate, as far as possible, the firm's exposure to currency risk

Once the estimated cash flows in each currency have been identified, the next step is to consolidate the data. The individual flows are netted to arrive at the estimated net balance in each currency for each future period. Monthly estimates for six months ahead are the most common requirement, but large companies holding, or trading in, many currencies may require weekly or even daily reports (especially if speculative positions are opened).

If the company believes that currency forecasting is both possible and profitable, it must decide, in the light of current currency forecasts, the degree of imbalance desirable in each currency in which it trades. Even if forecasting is thought to be possible and profitable, the company might decide to prohibit currency speculation as a matter of principle. Many UK multinationals take this position. In the past, US multinationals have been more willing than similar UK companies to speculate in currency.

The next step is to convert the 'natural' exposure position arising from normal trading into the 'desired' exposure position. This is done by using various currency hedging devices, some of which are internal to the firm and others external. Prindl (1978), who introduced the distinction between internal and external hedging, also pointed out that internal hedging is almost invariably cheaper than external hedging. The international treasurer should first adjust the 'natural' exposure position using

Volvo to build krona hedges

Volvo Cars is considering exporting vehicles from China to the US and even building an American factory as it seeks to counter the currency effects from a strong Swedish krona. Stefan Jacoby, chief executive, said the strength of the krona – the best-performing significant currency over the summer – was a 'disadvantage' in Volvo's fight with German premium carmakers such as BMW, Audi and Mercedes. 'We need natural hedging in US dollars. That could be production [a factory] or sourcing or exports out of China,' he told the *Financial Times*.

Volvo, based in Gothenburg but owned by Chinese carmaker Geely, is preparing to open two car plants and an engine factory in the coming years in China. The first is set to open next year in Chengdu, the capital of Sichuan province in central China, while a second is planned for Daqing in the north-west of the country. An engine plant in Zhangjiakou, near Beijing, will follow.

Any natural hedging in the US would have to cover about 10–15 per cent of Volvo's production, he added. Volvo produced 450,000 cars last year, generating SKr125bn ($19bn) in sales. However, Mr Jacoby hinted that importing cars from China and boosting local purchasing in the US might not be enough over time. 'It could be an interim solution

but maybe not a sustainable solution. Who knows what the Chinese renminbi is doing [in the next few years]? It would help to close that exposure that we have,' he added.

Mr Jacoby, a former senior executives at Volkswagen, is attempting to turn Volvo round and make it compete more directly with its much bigger German rivals. But its most recent results for the first half, released last week, show how difficult the task is for many midsize carmakers in an industry where economies of scale are important. The Swedish group suffered an 84 per cent decline in operating profit to Skr239m on revenues up 4 per cent to SKr65bn. Volvo has recently cut production, and laid off temporary workers, at its main Torslanda plant.

However, Mr Jacoby has scotched any suggestion that Volvo could cut back on investments in the next few years as it looks to almost double the number of cars it sells to 800,000 by 2020, including a fourfold increase in China to 200,000. Mr Jacoby acknowledged the risk he was taking: 'We have worsened our break-even point, obviously. This is a big risk that we are taking in a period of unpredictability. When the markets are going south it is an even bigger exposure.'

Source: Based on Richard Milne, *Financial Times*, 10 September 2012, p. 21.

internal techniques and use the more expensive external techniques only after the internal hedging possibilities have been exhausted.

21.8 INTERNAL HEDGING TECHNIQUES

Internal hedging techniques exploit characteristics of the company's trading relationships without recourse to the external currency or money markets. Most are simple in concept and operation.

netting
Offsetting a firm's internal currency inflows and outflows in the same currency to minimise the net flow in either direction

Netting applies where the head office and its foreign subsidiaries net off intra-organisational currency flows at the end of each period, leaving only the balance exposed to risk and hence in need of hedging. Netting is illustrated in the following simple example.

A UK-based multinational has a German operating subsidiary. In a particular month, it transfers components worth €20 million to Germany. In the same month, the subsidiary transfers finished goods worth €40 million to the UK. With netting, the company need only make a net currency transfer of €20 million rather than making two separate transactions totalling €60 million As well as reducing exposure, netting saves transfer and commission costs, but it requires a two-way flow in the same currency.

bilateral netting
Operated by pairs of firms in the same group netting off their respective positions regarding payables and receivables

Bilateral netting applies where pairs of companies in the same group net off their own positions regarding payables and receivables, often without the involvement of the central treasury. If the previous company also had a Swiss subsidiary, a bilateral netting arrangement could operate between the German and the Swiss subsidiaries. **Multilateral netting** is performed by the central treasury where several subsidiaries interact with the head office. Subsidiaries are required to notify the treasury of the intra-organisational flows of receivables and payments. Again, a common currency is required. To illustrate this, Oilex is a UK-based oil company with an exploration division based in Norway, major interests in the USA and chemical plants in the UK. The group treasury 'holds the ring' at the centre of this nexus, as shown in Figure 21.3. All intra-group transactions are conducted in USD, which is the operating currency of the oil industry.

multilateral netting
A central treasury department operation to minimise net flows of currency throughout an organisation

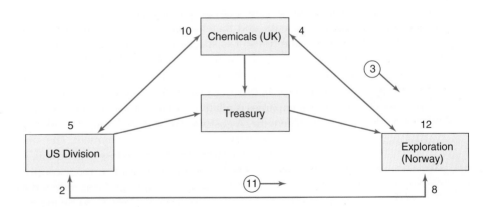

Figure 21.3 Illustration of multilateral netting

Table 21.2 shows transactions expected for one particular month. In total, currency flows of $41 million would be required with no treasury intervention. By multilateral netting, the treasury can reduce the exposed flows by $27 million. Such a system produces greatest benefits when the inter-subsidiary positions are most similar, and where payments are made directly to the relevant subsidiaries, thus avoiding cash transfers into and then out of the treasury. In this case, chemicals would transfer $3 million direct

Table 21.2 Oilex's internal currency flows

		Paying subsidiary ($m)				
		UK	US	Norway	Total	Net
Receiving	UK	–	10	4	+14	−3
subsidiary	US	5	–	2	+7	−11
($m)	Norway	12	8	–	+20	+14
	Total	−17	−18	−6	41	
	Net	−3	−11	+14		

Source: The Times, 29/08/2007, © The Times/NI Syndication.

to exploration and the US operation would transfer $11 million likewise, resulting in total flows of only $14 million.

Some experts dispute whether netting is a true hedging technique, rather than a cost-saving device, especially where the netted currency differs from the parent's reporting currency. However, if it does result in lower values of currency being shipped across the exchanges, then it is undeniable that it is capable of saving considerable banking and money transmission costs.

matching
Offsetting a currency inflow in one currency, e.g. a stream of revenues, by a corresponding stream of costs, thus leaving only the profit element unmatched. Firms may also match operating cash flows against financial flows, e.g. a stream of interest and capital payments resulting from overseas borrowing in the same currency

Matching is similar in concept to netting, but involves third parties as well as intra-group affiliates. A company tries to match its currency inflows by amount and timing with its expected outflows. For example, a company exporting to the USA and thus anticipating USD receipts could match this payable by arranging a USD outflow, perhaps by contracting to import from the same country. Clearly, as with netting, a two-way flow of currency is desirable – '**natural matching**'. 'Parallel matching' can be achieved by matching in terms of currencies that tend to move closely together over time, e.g. matching USD outflows to Canadian dollar inflows. Matching can also be achieved by offsetting balance sheet items against profit and loss account items. For example, a company with a long-term cash inflow stream in USD may also borrow in USD, to create an offsetting outflow of interest and capital payments. Earlier in the chapter, we observed Compass Group plc doing exactly this.

natural matching
A natural match is achieved where the firm has a two-way cash flow in the same currency due to the structure of its operations, e.g. selling in a currency in which it sources supplies

Leading and lagging currency payments is done to speed up or delay payments when a change in the value of a currency is expected. This involves forecasting future exchange rate movements, and therefore carries an element of speculation. Where payables are involved, the transfer is speeded up if the foreign currency is expected to appreciate against the domestic currency and slowed down if the overseas currency is expected to depreciate. A UK company importing from the USA at a time when the USD was falling against sterling may well have tried to lag payments. Leading and lagging within a group of companies is relatively easy to arrange, but when dealing with other firms, this can be problematic. A customer buying on credit will advance payment only if offered an inducement such as a discount for early payment. The same applies to delaying payment to an external supplier – the danger is loss of goodwill. Even for intra-firm transactions, there may still be local regulations and currency controls that limit flexibility.

leading
Advancing before the due date a payable denominated in a foreign currency that is expected to strengthen, or advancing a receivable in a currency expected to weaken

Currency transfers by companies into and out of less-developed countries, whose currencies tend to be weak, are closely scrutinised by the governments of those countries because of the destabilising effect they may have on their currency. In some cases, they are illegal, both for their ability to exacerbate currency weakness and also because of the effect on local minority shareholders of an overseas subsidiary. Leading a payment from the overseas subsidiary to the UK parent will raise the GBP profits of the parent, but lower the overseas currency profits of the subsidiary thus damaging local shareholders' interests, which risks alienating local opinion and antagonising the host government. This is one reason why repatriation of profits from overseas subsidiaries is often closely controlled by foreign governments.

Chocolate maker cuts euro exposure

Until recently Malachy McReynolds, managing director of Bristol-based chocolate maker Elizabeth Shaw, traded in euros, even outside the eurozone. But in the past six weeks the company, which exports about 10 per cent of its £10m sales, has insisted on being paid in sterling, or even the buyer's local currency rather than the euro. 'We took a policy decision to reduce our currency risk,' he said.

The company is reluctant to take out forward cover from the bank because it is too costly. Instead it uses a 'natural hedge'. The company not only sells into the EU but also sources part of its product range from euro area manufacturers on a contract basis. 'So we always look at our net euro exposure. If necessary we ask our euro area suppliers to invoice us in sterling,' said Mr McReynolds.

It is not just diversifying export markets that reduces euro exposure – companies can also switch suppliers. BSA Machine Tools in Birmingham used to buy parts from the Luxembourg branch of Fanuc, the Japanese manufacturer, paying in euros, but now buys from its UK branch.

Source: Based on National News Column, Financial Times, 30 July 2012, p. 4.

Self-assessment activity 21.7

Delete as appropriate.

Leading is advancing outflows in a *strong/weak* currency and advancing inflows in a *strong/weak* currency. Lagging is delaying inflows in a *strong/weak* currency and delaying outflows in a *strong/weak* currency.

(Answer in Appendix A at the back of the book)

price variation
Adjustment of a firm's pricing policy to take into account expected foreign exchange rate movements

The UK exporter might also consider a pre-emptive **price variation**. If it expects GBP to strengthen against the currency of an overseas customer, it may raise the contract price. However, this may have adverse consequences for sales, especially if competitors are prepared to shoulder currency risk by accepting payment in the overseas currency. Conversely, the acceptability of this ploy may be greater if the exporter quotes a price based on the forward rate rather than the spot rate when setting the value of the contract. Generally, however, such price variations require a strong competitive position in overseas markets. For this reason, another such device, switching the currency in which the contract is denominated to a third currency, say USD, also has to be used with caution. However, traders in basic commodities (most notably, oil) have no such flexibility, since most of these are priced in USD.

risk-sharing
An arrangement where the two parties to an import/export deal agree to share the risk, and thus the impact of unexpected exchange rate movements

Risk-sharing is a contractual arrangement whereby the buyer and seller agree in advance to share between them the impact of currency movements. This is recommended when the two parties want to build a long-term relationship. However, if exchange rate variations exceed tolerable limits, the arrangement may have to be renegotiated.

It might work like this. Firm X supplies Firm B in another country. They may agree that all transactions will be made at the ruling spot rate between the two parties' respective currencies. If, however, the rate at settlement varies by up to, say, 5 per cent either side of the original spot rate, X may accept the transaction exposure. If the rate varies by, say, 5–10 per cent of the original spot, they may share the difference equally, but for variations in excess of 10 per cent, the agreement may become void. Harley-Davidson is known to operate this policy with foreign importers.

re-invoicing centre
A corporate subsidiary set up usually in an off-shore location to manage transaction exposure arising from trade between separate divisions of the parent firm

Re-invoicing centres. A re-invoicing centre (RIC) is a separate corporate subsidiary that manages from one location, often off-shore, all the transaction exposure arising from intra-company trading.

For example, a manufacturing unit may sell goods to distribution subsidiaries of its parent firm indirectly by selling first to the re-invoicing centre, which then re-sells the goods to the distribution subsidiary. Title to the goods passes to the RIC but the goods are shipped directly from the manufacturing subsidiary to the distributor. The RIC thus manages the transactions on paper but keeps no physical stocks. All transactions exposure resides with the RIC.

A problem may arise due to allegations of profit-shifting via transfer pricing. To avoid such allegations, the RIC may sell at cost plus a commission for its services. The resale price is commonly the manufacturer's price times the forward exchange rate for the date when settlement by the distributor is expected.

RICs offer the major benefit of concentrating the management of all FX transactions in one location. As a result, the multinational corporation (MNC) can develop specialist expertise in judging which hedging technique is optimal at any one time. However, it should avoid conducting business with other firms in its country of location in order to establish non-resident status.

21.9 SIMPLE EXTERNAL HEDGING TECHNIQUES

forward contract
An agreement to sell or buy at a fixed price at some time in the future

The most widely used external hedging technique is the **forward contract**. It involves pre-selling/buying a specific amount of currency at a rate specified now for delivery at a specified time in the future. It is a way of totally removing risk of currency variation by locking in the rate quoted today by the forward market. However, there remain the risks of the trading partner (**credit risk**) defaulting and that of failure of the bank that arranges the deal (**counterparty risk**).

credit risk
The risk that a foreign customer might not pay up as agreed on time or at all

counterparty risk
The risk that the bank which is party to a hedging transaction such as a forward contract may not deliver the agreed amount of currency at the agreed time

Consider the case of a UK exporter entering an export contract in February for $10 million with a company in Denver. The companies agree on payment in three months' time, i.e. in May. The current spot rate is $2.00:£1, valuing the contract at $10m/2.00 = £5m. If the exporter is concerned by the possibility of a decline in the USD versus GBP, it will look carefully at the rate quoted for three-month delivery of USD. Assume the forward market quotes '2c discount'. The forward outright is thus:

Spot $2.00 plus 2.0c = $2.02:£1

If the exporter believes in the predictive accuracy of the forward market, it may decide to sell forward the anticipated $10 million receipt for $10m/2.02 = £4.95m. This involves taking a discount on the current spot value of the deal. Hedging costs the exporter £50,000, 1 per cent of the original value of the deal (although a higher proportion of his profits), but this may look trivial beside the losses that could materialise if GBP strengthens further than this. Conversely, the exporter is excluded from any gains if the USD appreciates in value.

forward option
A forward currency contract that incorporates a flexible settlement date between two fixed dates

If the exporter is unsure about the precise payment date by its customer, it may enter a **forward option**. In this case, the bank leaves the currency settlement date open, but books the deal at the worst forward rate ruling over the period concerned. Say the two companies had agreed on payment 'sometime over the next three months', but the exporter knows that the customer may delay payment for six months. The relevant forward quotations are:

1 month:	0.5c dis	Outright: 2.005
2 months:	1.0c dis	Outright: 2.010
3 months:	2.0c dis	Outright: 2.020
6 months:	3.0c dis	Outright: 2.030

The worst rate for the exporter is the six-month rate, so the deal will be booked for $10m/2.03 = £4.93m, again a minor increase in cost. If the customer pays up at any other time, the bank is committed to paying the exporter the amount agreed in the forward contract when the $10 million is handed over.

foreign currency swap
A way of using the forward markets to adjust the maturity date of an initially agreed contract with a bank

Another way of covering uncertainty over settlement dates is to undertake a **foreign currency swap**. The Bank of International Settlements (BIS, **www.bis.org**) defines a swap as follows:

> Foreign exchange swaps commit two counterparties to the exchange of two cash flows and involve the sale of one currency for another in the spot market with the simultaneous repurchase of the first currency in the forward market.

forward–forward swap
Where the original forward contract is supplemented by new contracts that have the effect of extending the maturity date of the original one

An exporter can take forward cover to a specified date, but if a later settlement date than this is agreed, it can extend the contract to the newly agreed date. For example, a **forward–forward swap** is needed if our exporter covers ahead from February until May, but if in March, a firm settlement date is agreed for June. Contractually, it has to meet the first contract maturing in May, and then take cover for a further month. This is done in March by buying $10 million two months forward, i.e. for delivery in May to meet the existing contract, and by selling $10 million three months forward for delivery in June. In this case, the exporter swaps the maturity date and ends up holding three separate contracts. Instead, it could adopt the riskier alternative of a **spot–forward swap**, fulfilling the May contract by buying the $10 million on the spot market, and also arranging to sell $10 million one month forward, i.e. in June. The BIS estimated average daily foreign exchange swap transactions at US$2,228 billion in its 2013 survey, 42 per cent of all foreign exchange-related transactions.

spot–forward swap
A less comprehensive forward swap that involves speculation on the future spot market

money market cover
Involves an exporter borrowing on the money market (i.e. creating a liability) in the same currency in which it expects to receive a payment

Money market cover involves the exporter creating a liability in the form of a short-term loan in the same currency that it expects to receive. The amount to borrow will be sufficient to make the amount receivable coincide with the principal of the loan plus interest. Assume the Eurodollar rate of interest, the annual rate payable on loans denominated in USD, is 8 per cent, i.e. 2.00 per cent over three months. The UK exporter would borrow ($10m/1.02 = $9.80m). This would be converted into GBP at the spot rate – in our example, $2.00:£1 – to realise ($9.80m/2.00) = £4.90m. This looks like a considerable discount on the spot value of the export deal (£5.00m), but the GBP proceeds of this operation can be invested for three months to defray the cost. Obviously, if the exporter could invest at a rate in excess of 8 per cent p.a., it would profit from this, but IRP should make this impossible, i.e. if USD sells at a forward discount, interest rates in New York should exceed those in London. If USD should unexpectedly fall in value against GBP, lower than expected receipts from the US contract are offset by the lower GBP payment required to repay the Eurodollar loan.

An alternative to a one-off loan to cover a specific contract is for the exporter to operate an overdraft denominated in one or a set of overseas currencies. The trader will aim to maintain the balance of the overdraft as sales are made, and use the sales proceeds as and when received to reduce the overdraft. This is a convenient technique where a company makes a series of small overseas sales, many with uncertain payment dates. A converse arrangement, i.e. a currency bank deposit account, may be arranged by a company with receivables in excess of payables.

Export invoice finance is a fast-expanding business among UK traders. Data published by the UK-based Asset Based Finance Association (ABFA) for the year-ended 30 June 2014 has estimated export factoring at £999m and export invoice discounting at £7,708m (www.abfa.org.uk). The international factor can provide many services to the small company, including absorbing the exchange rate risk. Once a foreign contract is signed, the factor pays, say, 80 per cent of the foreign value to the UK exporter in GBP. If the exchange rate moves against the UK company before receipt of the foreign currency, the factor absorbs the loss. In compensation, the factor also takes any gain arising from a change in rates. Factors make use of overseas 'correspondent' factors, enabling clients to benefit from expert local knowledge of overseas buyers' creditworthiness. Overseas factoring is usually expensive but offers the benefits of lower administration and credit collection costs.

Export receivables that involve settlement via **Bills of Exchange** can also be discounted with a bank in the customer's country and the foreign currency proceeds repatriated at the relevant spot rate. Alternatively, the bill can be discounted in the exporter's home country, enabling the exporter to receive settlement directly in home currency.

The most sophisticated external hedging facilities involve derivatives such as options, futures and swaps. These are treated in more detail below.

Farmers embrace hedging to minimise currency risk

The recent rally in sterling may reflect an upswing in the fortunes of the UK economy, but it comes at an unfortunate time for one sector: farming. The exchange rate at which EU subsidies totalling more than €3bn are paid to about 200,000 British farmers is fixed on the last day of September each year, adding currency risk to the vagaries of drought, floods and commodity prices they already contend with.

Almost all opt to receive the single farm payment [SFP], as the subsidy is termed, in sterling, which has gained about 2 per cent against the euro since farmers finalised their claims at the end of May, and 4 per cent since a low in early August. Most do nothing to mitigate the risk. 'We like to keep things simple,' said a spokesman for the Royal Society for the Protection of Birds, one of the biggest recipients, which receives a single payment of more than £1m.

But a sizeable minority now take out forward contracts to fix an acceptable exchange rate, with some following forex markets as closely as they do the weather. 'In the daytime if I come in for lunch, I'll watch [the exchange rate] and

when I'm happy with what I see and what I'm going to get, I hedge it,' said Llyr Hughes, who breeds Limousin cattle and early-lambing ewes on a 450-acre farm. Their single farm payment of about £30,000 represents roughly 40 per cent of profits.

For arable farmers in particular, who often rely on the single farm payment to break even and are still recovering from two of the wettest and coldest springs on record, the difference of a few thousand pounds can be critical to cash flow. Tony Keene, who owns two arable farms in Norfolk and Lincolnshire with a turnover of £1m each, said: 'The SFP is our net profit.' His daughters, who manage the farms, have hedged part of the exchange rate risk this year, judging the euro-sterling rate relatively stable. 'We watch it very carefully. We look at our budget and then we try to second guess how the eurozone and British economy are going to interplay. We really look and take a view,' Mr Keene said.

Source: Based on Delphine Strauss, *Financial Times*, 30 September 2013, p. 4.

21.10 MORE COMPLEX TECHNIQUES

■ Currency options

call option
A financial derivative that gives the buyer the right but not the obligation to buy a particular commodity or currency at a specific future date

A currency option confers the right, but (unlike the forward contract) not the obligation, to buy or sell a fixed amount of a particular currency at or between two specified future dates at an agreed exchange rate (the **strike price**).

A **call option** gives the purchaser of the option the right to buy, while a put option gives the right to sell. In each case, the buyer of the option pays the 'writer' of the option a premium. Options traded through exchanges are written in specified contract sizes: for example, on the Philadelphia Stock Exchange (PHLX – now owned by NASDAQ OMX), the contract size is 10,000 units of foreign currency except for Japanese yen (1,000,000 units). Most exchanges offer a limited number of alternative exercise prices and maturity dates. PHLX trades USD options against the British pound, the Australian dollar, Canadian dollar, Japanese yen and the Swiss franc, as well as euro contracts. Delivery dates are for the quarter months of March, June, September and December plus the two immediately upcoming months. For non-standard options, the would-be purchaser may have to shop around for a customised quotation on the **over-the-counter** (OTC) market. This may be necessary for unusual or 'exotic' currencies.

over-the-counter
An over-the-counter transaction, e.g. the purchase of an option, where the terms are tailor-made to suit the requirements of the purchaser

A '**European option**' can be exercised only at the specified maturity date, while an '**American option**' can be exercised at any time up to the specified expiry date. If an option is not exercised, it lapses and the premium is lost. However, the appeal of an option is that the maximum loss is limited to the cost of the premium, while the purchaser retains the upside potential. The size of the premium depends on the difference between the current exchange rate and the strike price (for an unlikely strike price, premiums will be very low), the volatility of the two currencies, the period to maturity and, for OTC contracts, the size of the contract.

Here is an example of how a trader could use a currency option for hedging purposes. A UK exporter sells goods for $5.95 million to a customer in Baltimore in June 2014 for settlement in September. The contract is worth £3.5 million when valued at spot of $1.70:£1, but the exporter is concerned that sterling might appreciate before settlement, thus eroding the profit margin. In this case, it might purchase a call option on GBP, i.e. an option to sell USD in exchange for GBP. The premiums in cents per option unit that were available at the Philadelphia Stock Exchange on 13 June 2014 are shown in Table 21.3.

Table 21.3 Sterling vs. US dollar options

Strike price 13 June 2014

	Calls		Puts	
$:£1	**September**	**December**	**September**	**December**
1.67	3.64	4.50	1.01	2.05
1.68	2.82	3.71	1.34	2.44
1.69	2.23	2.23	1.75	2.90
1.70	1.73	1.73	2.27	3.41

Source: Philadelphia Stock Exchange.

Note: the underlying contract size is generally 10,000 units of foreign currency for PHLX World Currency Options. Hence, contract size is £10,000.

Note: premium quotation – one point = $100. For example, a premium quote of 2.13 is $213.

Choosing the $1.70 strike price gives the exporter insurance against the value of sterling going higher than $1.70. The cost of purchasing September options is:

$$\text{Number of contracts} = \frac{\$5.95m}{\$1.70} \div £10,000 = 350$$

$$\text{Cost of option} = \$100 \times 1.73 \times 350 = \$60,550$$

i.e. £35,617 at spot.

If the spot rate in September is less than $1.70, the option is not worth exercising, and is said to be 'out of the money', while if the spot is over $1.70, say, $1.75, the option is 'in the money'. In the last case, export earnings of $5.95 million can be sold at $1.70 to realise £3.5m million, compared with a spot value of:

$$\frac{\$5.95m}{\$1.75} = £3.4m$$

Although the option has cost £35,617, it has prevented the exporter from losing (£3.5m − £3.4m) = £100,000. In this case, there is a net gain, allowing for the premium, of (£100,000 − £35,617) = £64,383.

It is important to appreciate that options are 'zero-sum games' – what the holder wins, the writer loses, and vice versa. It is relatively unusual to use currency options to hedge ongoing trading exposures – options are complex, they are often expensive compared to using the forward market and it is time-consuming to monitor an American option to judge whether it is worth closing out the position prematurely. Options tend to be used to cover major isolated expenditures, e.g. the cost of completing the acquisition of an overseas company or the phased payments in a major overseas construction project.

The Nasdaq trader website (**www.nasdaqtrader.com**) gives trading information on options.

■ Example: Hogan plc

Hogan plc exports computer components valued at 18 million Australian dollars (AUD) to Dundee Proprietary in Australia on three months' credit. The current spot exchange rate is A$1.80 vs. £1. Because of recent volatility in the foreign exchange markets, Hogan's directors are worried that a fall in the AUD could wipe out their profits on the deal. Three alternative hedging strategies have been suggested:

(i) using a forward market hedge
(ii) using a money market hedge
(iii) using an option hedge.

Hogan's treasurer discovers the following information:

- The three-month forward rate is A$1.805 vs. £1.
- Hogan could borrow in AUD at 9 per cent interest (annual rate), and could deposit in London at 4 per cent p.a.
- A three-month American put option to sell A$18 million at an exercise rate of A$1.81 vs. £1 could be purchased at a premium of £200,000 on the London OTC option market.

Required
Show how each hedge would work out, assuming the following spot rates apply in three months' time:

(a) A$1.78 vs. £1
(b) A$1.82 vs. £1.

In the course of your answer, consider whether interest rate parity applies as between these two currencies.

Answer
(i) The forward hedge
The bank contracts to buy A$18m for GBP in three months' time. The sterling value = (A$18m/1.805 = £9.97m).

(a) At future spot of A$1.78, Hogan could have received (A$18m/1.78 = £10.11m), involving an opportunity cost of:

(£10.11m − £9.97m) = £0.14m (1.4% of contract value)

(b) With future spot at A$1.82, Hogan would receive (A$18m/1.82 = £9.89m). The hedge offers a gain of:

(£9.97m − £9.89m) = £0.08m

(ii) The money market hedge
The three-month interest rate is (9%/4) = 2.25%. Hogan will borrow in AUD sufficient to accumulate at 2.25% to the AUD value of its receipts, i.e.:

(A$18m/1.0225) = A$17.60m

Exchanged for GBP at today's spot rate, this is worth:

(A$17.60m/1.80) = £9.78m

This can be invested at 4% p.a., i.e. (4%/4) = 1% over three months, accumulating to £9.78m(1.01) = £9.88m.

(a) At future spot of A$1.78 vs. £1, the unhedged income = £10.11m. The loss using the money market hedge is:

(£10.11m − £9.88m) = £0.23m (2.3% of the original contract value)

(b) At future spot of A$1.82 vs. £1, the unhedged income = £9.89m. Hence, the hedge still just loses, viz.:

(£9.89m − £9.88m) = −£0.01m

Apparently, IRP does not apply! With a difference in interest rates of 5% p.a. the forward rate should show the AUD trading at a greater discount than just half a cent, i.e. the AUD is overvalued on the forward market. If these interest rates prevail and IRP does reassert itself, we might conclude that the forward market is overstating the future spot rate (from an AUD perspective).

(iii) The OTC option hedge

(a) At future spot of A$1.78 vs. £1, the option is 'out of the money', i.e. it is better to sell AUD at spot rather than exercise the options at A$1.81 = £1. Hogan's unhedged income is £10.11m. Net of the option premium, the proceeds are:

(£10.11m − £0.20m) = £9.91m

Hogan's loss through the option hedge is simply the option premium.

(b) At future spot of A$1.82 vs. £1, the option is ' in the money', i.e. it is better to exercise it than sell GBP at spot to yield (A$18m/1.81 = £9.94m). This nets:

(£9.94m − £0.20m) = £9.74m

Self-assessment activity 21.8

What is the net cost/benefit of an option that is 'at the money'?

(Answer in Appendix A at the back of the book)

21.11 MORE COMPLEX TECHNIQUES: FUTURES AND SWAPS

■ Currency futures

In principle, a futures contract can be arranged for any product or commodity, including financial instruments and currencies. A currency futures contract is a commitment to deliver a specific amount of a specified currency at a specified future date for an agreed price incorporated in the contract. It performs a similar function to a forward contract, but has some major differences.

Currency futures contracts have the following characteristics:

1 They are marketable instruments traded on organised futures markets.
2 They can be completed (liquidated) before the contracted date, whereas a forward contract has to run to maturity.

3 They are relatively inflexible, being available for a limited range of currencies and for standard maturity dates. The world's largest market for currency futures is the Chicago Mercantile Exchange (CME). It trades futures in 11 different currencies for delivery four times each year: March, June, September and December.

4 They are dealt in standard lot sizes, or contracts.

5 The CME requires a down-payment called a 'performance bond' or 'margin' of about 1.5 per cent of the contract value, whereas forward contracts involve a single payment at maturity.

6 They also involve 'variation payments', essentially the ongoing losses on the contract to be paid to the exchange on which the contract is dealt.

7 They are usually cheaper than forward contracts, requiring a small commission payment rather than a buy/sell spread.

It is difficult to 'tailor make' a currency future to the precise needs of the parties involved, which explains why some exchanges have now stopped currency futures trading.

How a currency future works

This is best shown with an example. In June, a UK importer agrees to buy goods worth $10 million from a firm in Detroit. The sterling/dollar spot rate is $1.50:£1, valuing the deal at $10m/1.50 = £6,666,666. Settlement is agreed for 15 August, but the importer is concerned that appreciation of USD will undermine its profitability (it will have to find more GBP to meet the import cost). On the CME, the market price (i.e. the exchange rate) for September GBP futures is $1.48, suggesting that the market expects the USD to appreciate.

The importer needs eventually to acquire GBP to pay for its imports, so it should sell (i.e. go short of) GBP by selling GBP futures contracts at $1.48. With the standard contract size of £62,500 the number of whole contracts required is:

[$10m/(£62,500 × 1.48)] = 108 approx.

Note the indivisibility problem – 108 contracts covers exposure of only (108 × £62,500 × 1.48) = $9,990,000. This makes hedging by futures unattractive to small exporters. There is also a timing problem, as the importer has to supply USD before the expiry of the contract in August. When payment is due, the importer will close out the contract by arranging a reverse trade, i.e. one with exactly opposite features, which means buying 108 September GBP futures at the ruling market price. If USD has strengthened against GBP between June and August, the importer will make a profit on the futures contract.

Imagine this does happen and the spot rate on 15 August is $1.49 and the September futures price is $1.475. As payment for the goods is required, the importer converts GBP for USD on the spot market at a cost of ($10m/1.49) = $6,711,409. Compared with the cost of the deal at the June spot rate, it has made a loss of £44,743, owing to the feared USD appreciation. However, the importer holds 108 futures contracts, enabling it to sell GBP at $1.48. To close its position, the importer can buy the same number of contracts at an exchange rate of $1.475. It will thus make a profit on the futures market of:

Sells	108 × £62,500 × 1.480 =	$9,990,000
Buys	108 × £62,500 × 1.475 =	$9,956,250
Profit		$33,750

Valued at spot of $1.49, this is worth ($33,750/1.49) = £22,651, leaving a net loss of (£44,743 − £22,651) = £22,092. This demonstrates the difficulty of achieving a perfectly hedged position with currency futures. Moreover, the futures market may not always move to the same degree as the spot market, owing to expectations about future exchange rate movements.

The CME website (**www.cmegroup.com**) provides a beginner's guide to using the futures markets.

■ Currency swaps

The BIS defines currency swaps as follows:

> A currency swap (or cross-currency swap) commits two counterparties to several cash flows, which in most cases involve an initial exchange of principal and a final re-exchange of principal upon maturity of the contract, and, in all cases, several streams of interest payments.

currency swaps
Where two or more parties swap the capital value and associated interest streams of their borrowing in different currencies

Currency swaps originated from controls applied by the Bank of England over foreign exchange movements prior to 1979. Firms wishing to obtain foreign currency to invest overseas, say in the USA, found they could avoid these controls by entering an agreement with a US company that operated a subsidiary in the UK. In return for receiving a loan from the US company to finance its own activity in the USA, the UK company would lend to the UK-based subsidiary of the US company. The two firms would agree to repay the loans in the local currency after an agreed period, thereby locking in a particular exchange rate. The interest rate would be based on prevailing local rates. Such arrangements were called '**back-to-back loans**' – from the UK company's perspective, they involved agreeing to make a series of future USD payments in exchange for receiving a flow of GBP income.

back-to-back loans
A simple form of a swap where firms lend directly to each other to satisfy their mutual currency requirements

After exchange controls were removed in 1979, such loans were replaced by currency swaps. These need not involve two companies directly. In general terms, a currency swap is a contract between two parties (e.g. between a bank and an overseas investor) to exchange payments denominated in one currency for payments denominated in another. A simple example will illustrate this.

How currency swaps work

Currency swaps are complex. In particular, they require matching up two companies' mutual requirements in terms of type and amount of currency required and term of financing. The final agreement will reflect the bargaining power of the parties involved and is most viable when each party has a differential borrowing advantage in one currency which it can transfer to the other. This point is important – a currency swap almost invariably involves an interest rate swap.

To illustrate the process, consider the example of two companies, ABC and XYZ. ABC, which can borrow in Swiss francs (CHF) at 5.5 per cent, is seeking USD financing of $40 million for three years. The Dutch subsidiary of a US bank is prepared to act as intermediary, which involves finding a suitable matching company which has a borrowing advantage in USD and is seeking CHF finance. Until the match is found, the bank will be exposed to currency and interest rate risk, which it may cover by entering the spot market, or possibly using the options market. Company XYZ emerges as a suitable swap candidate. (More complex swaps might involve several participant companies if a directly corresponding currency requirement cannot be identified.)

XYZ has a borrowing advantage in USD, being able to borrow at 7 per cent, compared to ABC's borrowing rate of 7.75 per cent. Conversely, XYZ would have to borrow in CHF at 6 per cent. XYZ is seeking CHF finance of 52 million. At the ruling exchange rate of 1.3 CHF per USD, this is an exact match. With the bank's intermediation, the two companies now agree to swap currencies and assume each other's interest rate obligations over a three-year term, with transactions conducted via the bank. Figure 21.4 shows the structure of the swap and the sequence of transactions. In reality, the two companies would have to pay rather higher interest rates than those shown in order to yield a profit margin for the bank, sufficient to compensate it for assuming the risks of either company defaulting on interest payments or re-exchange of principal.

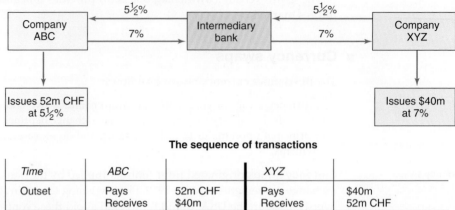

The sequence of transactions

Time	ABC		XYZ	
Outset	Pays Receives	52m CHF $40m	Pays Receives	$40m 52m CHF
Years 1–3	Pays Receives	7% on $40m 5½% on 52m CHF	Pays Receives	5½% on 52m CHF 7% on $40m
End Year 3	Pays Receives	$40m 52m CHF	Pays Receives	52m CHF $40m

Figure 21.4 Achieving the swap

There are three legs to such deals:

1 Exchange of principal at spot (either notional or a physical transfer) in order to provide a basis for computing interest.
2 Exchange of interest streams.
3 Re-exchange of principal on terms agreed at the outset.

The principal is fully hedged, unlike the interest rate payments, which may require hedging perhaps via the forward market.

fixed/fixed swap
A swap agreement where the parties agree to swap fixed interest rate commitments

cross-currency interest swap
A swap agreement where the parties agree to swap a fixed interest rate commitment for a floating interest rate

In the example, the company benefits from lower interest rates and effectively uses the superior credit rating of the swap specialist to access cheaper finance. Most currency swaps are undertaken to exploit such interest rate disparities, whereby one party can pass on to another the benefit of superior creditworthiness. There are two main forms of currency swap. In a **fixed/fixed swap**, one party swaps a stream of fixed interest payments for a corresponding stream of fixed interest payments in another currency (as in the above example). In a **fixed/floating swap**, or **cross-currency interest swap**, one or both payment streams are on a variable basis, e.g. linked to LIBOR.

21.12 CONCLUSIONS

The globalisation of world trade has forced financial managers to take a keener interest in managing foreign exchange exposure. There are three types of exposure: transaction exposure, affecting the flow of cash across a currency frontier; translation exposure, affecting the value of assets and liabilities denominated in a foreign currency; and economic exposure, which is the impact on long-term cash flows of possible changes in exchange rates.

Not all transactions, assets and liabilities denominated in foreign currencies are necessarily exposed to exchange rate risk. The essential skills in currency management are to identify the assets and cash flows which are at risk and to devise suitable means of hedging the risks. It is important to differentiate between hedging techniques internal and external to the firm. Several financial markets have been developed that allow the international treasurer to hedge foreign exchange risk, and financial instruments such as swaps, options, futures and forwards can be used for this purpose.

The international treasurer must decide whether or not exchange rates can be forecast with any degree of reliability. With exchange rates floating freely, research suggests that forecasting is not profitable. However, when governments begin to interfere with the free market, forecasting has proved to be a profitable activity. The dogged, but ultimately doomed, commitment by international monetary authorities to support artificially high or low exchange rates may make forecasting worthwhile.

SUMMARY

This chapter examined the nature and sources of a company's exposure to the risk of adverse foreign exchange rate movements. It explained a number of widely-used strategies to hedge or safeguard against these risks, applying techniques both internal to the firm and also available on external capital markets.

Key points

- Corporate profitability can be seriously affected by adverse movements in foreign exchange rates.

- Currency can be transacted for immediate payment on the spot market or for future delivery via the forward market.

- The international treasurer is faced with three kinds of foreign exchange exposure: transaction exposure, translation exposure and economic exposure.

- Transaction exposure relates to the likely variability in short-term operating cash flows: for example, the cost of specific imported raw materials and the income from specific exported goods.

- Translation exposure relates to the risk of exchange rate movements altering the sterling value of assets located overseas or the sterling value of liabilities due to be settled overseas.

- Economic exposure refers to the ongoing risks incurred by the company in its choice of long-term contractual arrangements, such as licensing deals or decisions to invest overseas. These risks are the long-term equivalent of transaction exposure.

- Companies that trade internationally should devise a foreign exchange strategy.

- The strategy might depend on the treasurer's belief in the validity of various international trade theories: Purchasing Power Parity (PPP), Interest Rate Parity (IRP), the Expectations Theory and the Open Fisher Theory.

- PPP states that, allowing for the prevailing exchange rate, identical goods must sell for a common price in different locations. If inflation rates differ between locations, exchange rates will adjust to preserve the Law of One Price.

- IRP asserts that any differences in international interest rates are a reflection of expected exchange rate movements, so that the interest rate offered in a location whose currency is expected to depreciate will exceed that in an appreciating currency location by the amount of the expected exchange rate movement.

- The forward premium or discount should equal the expected rate of appreciation or depreciation of a currency.

- The Open Fisher Theory asserts that investment in different countries will offer the same expected real interest rate, so that differences in nominal rates of interest can be explained by expected differences in rates of inflation.

- Once the exposure position of the company is identified and measured, the treasurer must devise a hedging strategy to control the foreign exchange risk faced by the firm.

- Many apparent exposures are often self-hedging: for example, holdings of plant and machinery that can be traded internationally.

- Generally, internal hedging techniques are cheaper to apply than using the external markets, which offer various financial instruments for hedging currency risks.

Further reading

There has been an upsurge in texts on international financial management, but a leading book in the field is generally reckoned to be that by Shapiro (2013), which also contains excellent bibliographies. The texts by Madura and Fox (2011) and Eiteman *et al.* (2012) are also highly regarded. The leading British text is Buckley (2012), while Pilbeam (2013) is also recommended.

Books on hedging include Chisholm (2010) and Taylor (2010).

Hedging is often considered to be useful as a means for reducing volatility and increasing shareholder value. Aretz and Bartram (2010) review the evidence for this claim and provide a sound analysis of the various theoretical arguments used to support it. For an article examining what factors affect financial derivative usage see Bartram *et al.* (2009).

To keep abreast of trends and emerging issues in the field, regular reading of *Euromoney* and *The Economist* magazines is recommended.

Questions with a **coloured number** have solutions in Appendix B on page 807.

1 The Local Bank plc quotes the following rates for the euro versus sterling:

1.6296–1.6320

(a) How many euros would a firm receive when selling £10 million?
(b) How much sterling would it receive when selling €12 million?

2 On 30 November, a UK exporter sells goods worth £10 million to a French importer on three months' credit. The customer is billed in euros, for which the spot rate versus sterling is €1.6 vs. £1. The three-month forward rate is €1.62 per £1.

(a) What is the amount invoiced?
(b) If the spot rate is €1.7 vs. £1 at the settlement date, what is the exporter's gain or loss, assuming it does not hedge
(c) If the spot rate is €1.5 vs. £1 at the settlement date, what is the exporter's gain or loss, assuming it does not hedge
(d) If the exporter takes forward cover, what is the cost of the hedge
   (i)   compared to the current spot rate?
   (ii) compared to case (**b**)?
   (iii) compared to case (**c**)?

3 Work out the forward outrights from the exchange rates versus sterling given in the table below.

Country/Currency	Closing market rates	One-month forward rates
Denmark/krona	10.960–10.967	−25–11 (pm)
Japan/yen	230.11–230.16	−110–97 (pm)
Norway/kronor	11.717–11.723	−21–4 (pm)

Source: The Times, 29 August 2007. © The Times/NI Syndication.

4 A selected bundle of goods costs £100 in the UK, and a similar bundle costs 1,200 krona (DKR) in Denmark. People generally expect the rate of inflation to be 5 per cent in the UK and 3 per cent in Denmark.

(a) Assuming that PPP applies, what is the current exchange between GBP and DKR?
(b) Assuming that PPP will continue to hold, what spot exchange rate would you predict for 12 months hence?
(c) Again assuming PPP, what exchange rate should be quoted for three-month forward transactions?

5 The respective interest rates in the USA and the UK are 9 per cent and 10 per cent respectively in annual terms. If the spot exchange rate is US$1.6000 to £1 what is the forward rate if IRP applies?

6 Assume you are the treasurer of a multinational company based in Switzerland. Your company trades extensively with the USA. You have just received US$1 million from a customer in the USA. As the company has no immediate need of capital you decide to invest the money in either US$ or Swiss francs for 12 months. The following information is relevant:

- The spot rate of exchange is CHF1.3125 to US$1.
- The 12-month forward rate is CHF1.275 to US$1.
- The interest rate on a 1-year Swiss franc bond is $4\frac{9}{16}$ per cent.
- The interest rate on a 1-year US$ bond is $7\frac{5}{8}$ per cent.

Assume investment in either currency is risk-free and ignore transaction costs.

Required

Calculate the returns under both options (investing in US$ or Swiss francs) and explain why there is so little difference between the two figures.

Your answer may be expressed either in US$ or in Swiss francs.

(CIMA May 1998)

7 The following situation is observed in the money markets.

Sterling: US dollar exchange rates:

	Spot	$1.6550–1.6600
	Forward (1 Year)	$1.6300–1.6450
Interest rates (fixed):	New York	5½%–5¼%
	London	5¾%–5⅝%

(a) Calculate *both* the interest and the exchange agios.

(b) Using the figures provided, investigate whether an arbitrageur operating in London could profit from covered interest arbitrage.

Notes:

(a) Assume he borrows £100,000.

(b) You may ignore commission and transaction costs other than the spreads.

8 Europa plc is a UK-based import–export company. It is now 15 May and the following transaction has been agreed:

The sale of pine furniture worth $1,250,000 to the USA receivable on 15 August.

$/£ FX rates

Spot	1.6480–1.6490
Two months' forward	−88–76 (premium)
Three months' forward	−130–124 (premium)
Three-month money market interest rates	
	£10%–8%
	$8%–6%

Required

(a) Hedge Europa's risk exposure on the forward market.

(b) Hedge Europa's risk exposure on the money market.

(c) Which is the more favourable hedge from Europa's point of view?

9 Slade plc is a medium-sized UK company with export and import trade links with US companies. The following transactions are due within the next six months. Transactions will be in the currency specified.

Purchase of components, cash payment due in 3 months:	$116,000
Sale of finished goods, cash receipt due in 3 months:	$197,000
Purchase of finished goods for resale, cash payment due in 6 months:	$447,000
Sale of finished goods, cash receipt due in 6 months:	$154,000
Exchange rates quoted on London market	$/£
Spot	1.4106–1.4140
3 months' forward	0.82–0.77
6 months' forward	1.39–1.34

Interest rates (annual)

3 months or 6 months	Borrowing	Lending
Sterling	7.5%	4.5%
Dollars	6.0%	3.0%

Required

Calculate the *net* sterling receipts which Slade might expect for both its three and six month transactions if it hedges foreign exchange risk on:

(a) the forward foreign exchange market;

(b) the money market.

10 Exchange-traded foreign currency option prices for dollar/sterling contracts are shown below:

	Sterling (£12,500) contracts			
	Calls		Puts	
Exercise price ($)	December	September	December	September
1.90	5.55	7.95	0.42	1.95
1.95	2.75	3.85	4.15	3.80
2.00	0.25	1.00	9.40	–
2.05	–	0.20	–	–

Option prices are in cents per £. The current spot exchange rate is $1.9405–$1.9425/£.

Required

Assume that you work for a US company that has exported goods to the United Kingdom and is due to receive a payment of £1,625,000 in three months' time. It is now the end of June.

Calculate and explain whether your company should hedge its sterling exposure on the foreign currency option market if the company's treasurer believes the spot rate in three months' time will be:

(a) $1.8950–1.8970/£

(b) $2.0240–2.0260/£

(ACCA)

11 Ashton plc, a UK-based firm, imports computer components from the Far East. The trading currency is Singapore dollars and the value of the deal is 28m Singapore dollars (S$). Three months' credit is given. The current spot exchange rate is S$2.80 vs. £1. Because of recent volatility in the foreign exchange markets, Ashton's directors are worried that a rise in the S$ could wipe out the profits on the deal. Three alternative hedging methods have been suggested:

■ a forward market hedge

■ a money market hedge

■ an option hedge.

Ashton's treasurer discovers the following information:

■ The three-month forward rate is S$2.79 vs. £1

■ Ashton can borrow in S$ at 2% interest (annual rate), and in London at 5% p.a.

■ Deposit rates are 1% p.a. in Singapore and 3% p.a. in London

■ A three-month American call option to buy S$28m at an exercise rate of S$2.785 vs. £1 could be purchased at a premium of £200,000 on the London OTC option market

Required

Show how *each* hedge would operate for *each* of the following spot rates in three months' time:

(a) S$2.78 vs. £1

(b) S$2.82 vs. £1

12 TLC Inc manufactures pharmaceutical products. The organisation exports through a worldwide network of affiliated organisations. Its headquarters are in the USA, but there is a large volume of inter-organisation sales, dividend flows and fee and royalty payments. These inter-organisational payments are made in US$. An example of payment flows among four affiliates for the past 6 months is shown in the diagram below:

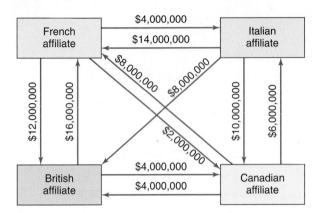

At present, each affiliate has control over its own cash management and foreign currency hedging decisions. The Corporate Treasurer is considering centralising cash and foreign currency management.

Required
(a) Explain, briefly, the characteristics of a bi- or multi-lateral netting system and, using the information in the diagram, advise the Corporate Treasurer of the pattern of cash flows that would have been evident if such a system had been in operation in TLC Inc.
(b) Discuss the advantages TLC Inc might obtain from centralising international cash management and foreign exchange management and advise on the potential disadvantages of such a change in policy.

(CIMA 2004)

Practical assignment

Many companies experience accounting problems in recording overseas transactions and in translating foreign currency values into their accounts. Select a company involved in international trade. Examine its report and accounts to determine its policy with regard to foreign exchange, and the extent of foreign currency losses or gains for the year concerned. Do you think these were 'real money' losses or gains, or merely accounting entries?

22

Foreign investment decisions

Emerging markets lead developed markets for first time in cross-border M&A

Transnational corporations (TNCs) from emerging market (EM) countries for the first time spent more on foreign acquisitions last year than companies from developed market (DM) countries. Led by some record-breaking acquisitions by Chinese and Russian companies, emerging markets transnational corporations (TNCs) accounted for as much as 56 per cent of total cross-border transactions in 2013. In total, the value of cross-border M&A deals – from EM and DM sources – rose 5 per cent in 2013 to $349bn.

More than two-thirds of cross-border purchases by EM companies involved the takeover of companies in other developing countries. Half of the companies bought by TNCs originating from developing countries were purchased from TNCs based in developed countries.

The $19bn acquisition of Canada's Nexen by Chinese state oil company CNOOC and $5bn buyout of US-based Smithfield Foods by Shuanghui were behind the increase. In developing markets, PetroChina's acquisition of a Mozambican subsidiary from italy's Eni for more than $4bn and Sinopec's $3bn purchase of Apache's Egyptian oil and gas business were also important.

While TNCs from developed countries stuck to investments in certain industries such as telecommunications, buyers from EMs invested in many sectors, particularly consumer goods and banking.

Source: Based on Verity Ratcliffe, *Financial Times*, 30 April 2014, p. 22.

Learning objectives

This chapter focuses on foreign investment decisions by multinational corporations (MNCs). It will:

- Study the advantages of MNCs.
- Discuss different ways of entering foreign markets.
- Consider the particular complexities of foreign direct investment (FDI).
- Analyse the appraisal of foreign FDI.
- Consider the impact of foreign exchange variations on foreign projects.
- Analyse ways of insulating projects against foreign exchange risk.
- Study political and country risk, and how to cope with it.

22.1 INTRODUCTION

portfolio investment
Investment in financial securities such as bonds and equities, with no stake in management

direct investment
Investment in tangible and intangible assets for business operating purposes

Foreign investment may be divided into **portfolio** (or financial) and **direct** (or strategic) **investment**. Portfolio investment involves the purchase of shares or loan stock in an overseas organisation, usually without control over the running of the business. **Foreign direct investment (FDI)** is a lasting interest in an enterprise in another economy where the investor's purpose is to have an effective voice in the management of the enterprise. Such direct investment may arise from the acquisition of a controlling interest in an overseas business or from setting up an overseas branch or subsidiary.

■ The strategic significance of FDI

Foreign direct investment (FDI)
Investment in fixed assets located abroad for operating distribution and/or production facilities

Firms that engage in FDI are called multinational corporations (MNCs). For such firms, FDI almost always has a strategic dimension for various reasons:

- **The outlay is often substantial**
  FDI thus places large amounts of capital at risk.
- **The investment is often not easily reversed.**
  One of the risks involved is the inability to exit quickly or cheaply. Because the firm is often lured to the country in question by tax breaks and other incentives, there is usually a lock-in time period before the firm can terminate the investment, or if it can exit, penalties may become payable. Finding a buyer for a failed overseas investment is difficult. Moreover, there is reputational damage in having to exit prematurely.
- **FDI is important for at least two parties:**
  (a) *The investing firm*
  FDI makes a difference in several financial areas. By accessing local cost advantages, such as lower labour costs, by exploiting scale economies such as bulk-buying or by tapping into more extensive overseas market, the FDI can provide major benefits to the parent firm's cash flows.
  (b) *The host country*
  The host country stands to benefit from greater employment (assuming no displacement of local firms), greater tax revenues and greater inflows of foreign currency, both initially, due to the up-front outlay, and also during the project's lifetime, if the facility is used as an exporting platform.
- **Risks are different to those in domestic investment**
  This aspect is explored in more detail below, but one should note the exposure to foreign exchange fluctuations, the operational risks involved in working in a different business and cultural context, and the danger of politically inspired interference by the host government (especially if it changes). Intuitively, one may conclude that FDI is more risky than domestic investment, which may be accurate regarding total risk, but due to the sort of favourable correlation effects discussed in earlier chapters, there may be useful portfolio effects. In other words, FDI may be a vehicle for diversifying risk across a wider range of global operating arenas.
- **FDI often opens up new opportunities.**
  The experience obtained in investing and operating abroad may reveal further opportunities to exploit the initial market, for example, by extending the product line or by taking over other firms, or by providing a springboard for expanding into other nearby territories, whereby the initial investment becomes a regional 'hub'. Thus, FDI may offer follow-on options, of which the firm may only be dimly aware at the outset.
- **FDI is a vehicle of competition**
  FDI is sometimes undertaken as an aggressive move to 'steal a march' over competing firms in a new market, or as a defensive move to exploit one particular market

after a rival has already secured an important presence elsewhere, and it would be too costly to challenge that established presence. Such moves are a reflection of the struggle among MNCs for market-leadership in a global context.

■ The multinational corporation

multinational company (MNC)
One that conducts a significant proportion of its operations abroad

A working definition of a **multinational company (MNC)** is: a firm that owns production, sales and other revenue-generating assets in a number of countries (although a wider definition would include firms that simply sell home-produced goods overseas). Foreign direct investment by MNCs includes establishment and acquisition of overseas raw material and component operations, production plants and sales subsidiaries. This occurs because of potentially greater cost-effectiveness and profitability in sourcing inputs and servicing markets through a direct presence in a number of locations, rather than relying solely on a single 'home' base and on imports and exports to support operations. A global firm is one that trades *and* invests abroad.

It is tempting to think of MNCs as 'Western' firms that invest in developing countries. The acquisition of firms in developed countries by firms in developing countries is increasingly common. For the year 2012, the United Nations Conference on Trade and Development (UNCTAD) reported that developed country FDI inflows and outflows totalled $561bn and $909bn respectively compared to developing country FDI inflows and outflows of $703bn and $426bn respectively (UNCTAD World Investment Report 2013). The UNCTAD Report notes that the so-called BRICS countries – Brazil, Russia, India, China, South Africa – accounted for approximately 10 per cent of world FDI. The USA is ranked as both the top host country ($168bn) and the top investor economy ($329bn) in the UNCTAD report; this compares to China, which is ranked second ($121bn) and third ($84bn) respectively. Following the financial crisis in 2007, global FDI fell as investors became cautious because of the economic uncertainty created by the crisis. Overall, global FDI totalled $1.35tn in 2012 and this compares to a pre-crisis average (based on 2005–7) of $1.49tn. The acquisition of the UK's Tetley tea operation by the Tata Corporation of India was an early example in 2000. The following cameo documents other examples of Tata group's acquisitions and also provides examples of FDI undertaken by Chinese companies.

Self-assessment activity 22.1

What is meant by a multinational corporation?

(Answer in Appendix A at the back of the book)

China and India seeking investments

Is it a great opportunity for mutual benefit or a case of the empire striking back? While Indians are investing in British steel, cars, tea and oil refining, the Chinese are piling into sensitive areas from telecoms to nuclear power. The UK's top sources of inward investment project in 2012–13 were the US followed by Japan, France and Italy, according to official data. India was the fifth largest source of projects and the third most important for creating new jobs, but it is communist China that is creating the most excitement.

Two state-owned Chinese companies, China General Nuclear Power Group and China National Nuclear Corp, are taking a 30–35 per cent stake in French utility EDF's project to build a £16bn nuclear power station in southwest England. China investment Corp (CIC), a sovereign wealth fund, owns 9 per cent of Thames Water and has discussed investing in the Thames super-sewer, a giant £4bn project under London. CIC, which has more than $400bn of assets, also owns about a third of Canary Wharf, the Docklands estate. Last November it took a 10 per cent

Continued

stake in Heathrow airport for £450m. Other potential areas for Chinese involvement include wind farms and the High Speed 2 rail project.

The biggest Indian investor is the Tata group, whose 50,000-strong UK workforce means it is vying with British Aerospace to be the country's largest manufacturer. It first opened an outpost in London in 1907 to buy supplies for its Indian operations, and Tata Consultancy Services, which pioneered the outsourcing of computing to India, opened in 1975. Tata bought Tetley tea in 2000, Brunner Mond chemical company in 2006, the Corus steel business in 2007 and Jaguar Land Rover (JLR) in 2008. Those purchases have

proved a mixed bag for Tata. JLR has boomed, driven by sales in emerging markets, but Tata Steel has been hit by weak European demand.

Britain is the favourite destination for Indian companies, with about $30bn invested, or about a quarter of India's outbound FDI stock. Essar, an Indian conglomerate, bought the Stanlow oil refinery in Cheshire this year. Meanwhile, Blackburn Rovers football club is owned by VH group an Indian poultry company.

Source: Based on Brian Groom, *Financial Times*, 20 November 2013, p. 4.

22.2 ADVANTAGES OF MNCS OVER NATIONAL FIRMS

The MNC may be in a position to enhance its competitive position and profitability in four main ways:

1 It can take advantage of differences in country-specific circumstances. In a world where countries are at different stages of economic evolution (some industrially advanced, others mainly primary producers), certain advantages in a country may have knock-on effects that the MNC can exploit on a global basis. For example, the MNC may locate its R&D establishments in a technologically advanced country in order to draw on local scientific and technological infrastructure and skills. Similarly, it may locate its production plants in a less-developed country in order to take advantage of lower input costs, especially cheap labour. JCB, the UK firm famous for its yellow diggers, operates plants in Brazil, India and China. Alternatively, the MNC may continue to produce its outputs in its 'home' country, but seek to remain competitive by sourcing key components from subsidiary plants based abroad.

2 MNCs can choose the appropriate mode of serving a particular market. For example, exporting may provide an entry route into a low-price, commodity-type market, with the MNC taking advantage of marginal pricing and the absence of set-up costs; licensing may be an appropriate mode if market size is limited or market niches are being targeted; direct investment in production and sales subsidiaries may be a more effective way of capturing a large market share where proximity to customers is important, or where market access via exporting is limited by tariffs. These various routes enable an MNC to pursue a complex global market-servicing strategy. For example, Ford operates assembly plants in 19 different countries (e.g. Argentina and China), and engine plants in 14 (e.g. Australia and Brazil). It ships engines from the latter to the former for final assembly according to the level of demand for the various models in different markets, including the export market. As a result, engine and car may be produced in two different locations and sold in a third one. The following box reproduces Ford's manufacturing policy with an emphasis on flexibility.

We are committed to maintaining an appropriate manufacturing footprint in markets around the world, both in the more mature markets in which we have an established presence, and in fast-growing newly-developed and emerging markets. We are making substantial investments in newly-developed and emerging markets, including in China, India, and Thailand, to increase our production capacity

with flexible new manufacturing plants. We and our unconsolidated affiliates in Asia Pacific Africa have launched four new plants in the past two years, and have announced that we expect to complete six more plants in the region by mid-decade.

Source: Ford Motor Company 2013 Form10-K.

3 'Internalisation' of the MNC's operations by foreign direct investment provides a unique opportunity for the firm to maximise its global profits by using transfer pricing policies. The transfer price is 'the price at which one affiliate in a group of companies sells goods and services to another affiliated unit' (Buckley, 2004). While a national, vertically-integrated firm needs to establish transfer prices for components and finished products that are transferred between component and assembly plants, and between assembly plants and sales subsidiaries, the greater scale of cross-frontier transactions by MNCs makes these transfer prices more significant because of the impact on relative profitability and tax charges in different locations.

4 An international network of production plants and sales subsidiaries enables an MNC to protect component supplies. The Swedish/Swiss engineering conglomerate Asea Brown Boveri (ABB) has built up a network of component-manufacturing subsidiaries in the Baltic region, including the former Soviet bloc, in order to diversify sources of supply. Networks also help in the simultaneous introduction of new products in several markets. This is important (where products have a relatively short life cycle and/or patent protection) in order to maximise sales potential. Equally importantly, it spreads the risk of consumer rejection across a diversified portfolio of overseas markets, so that failure in one market may be offset (or perhaps more than compensated by) rapid acceptance in another. Additionally, it enables the MNC to develop a 'global brand' identity (e.g. Coca-Cola, Levi's and Subway) or to 'customise' a product more effectively to suit local demand preferences.

Nissan gears up to build cars in Nigeria

Nissan will become the first global carmaker to build cars in Nigeria since west Africa's largest economy rolled out a policy to tempt investors to its nascent automotive industry. The Japanese carmaker, which has aggressively identified growth in emerging markets as the centrepiece of its global strategy, plans to build 45,000 cars a year in the country, probably starting with an SUV early next year.

Nissan, which last month announced it would be the first international carmaker to build vehicles in Myanmar, wants to double sales in Africa to 220,000 a year by 2016. Nigeria, which imports millions of dollars worth of new and used cars every year, has embarked on a drive to attract industrial and manufacturing investment into the country since former Goldman Sachs banker Olusegun Aganga was made minister of trade and investment this year.

While Nigeria is sub-Saharan Africa's biggest recipient of foreign investment with about $7bn last year, or 14 per cent of the region's total, investors complain that the country remains a challenging destination for industrial ventures due to power shortages, poor transport infrastructure and an unskilled labour force.

'Nissan is preparing to make Nigeria a significant manufacturing hub in Africa,' said chief executive Carlos Ghosn, the global car industry's most prominent believer in emerging market potential. 'As the first-mover in Nigeria, we are positioned for the long-term growth of this market and across the broader continent.'

Source: Based on Henry Foy and Javier Blas, *Financial Times*, 10 October 2013, p. 14.

22.3 FOREIGN MARKET ENTRY STRATEGIES

Firms enter foreign markets in pursuit of incremental profits and cash flows by exploiting advantages over local producers and other MNCs. The two basic vehicles for foreign market entry are, first, via transactions, and second, via direct investment. Each mode can be pursued in a number of ways. Figure 22.1 shows the spectrum of entry modes arranged by degree of commitment.

At one extreme, exporting (one-off or 'spot' transactions) involves least commitment, as it is relatively inexpensive and withdrawal is easy. At the other extreme, establishing a wholly-owned foreign operating subsidiary involves managing a range of complex functions including production, marketing and distribution. This is relatively expensive and requires substantial long-term commitment.

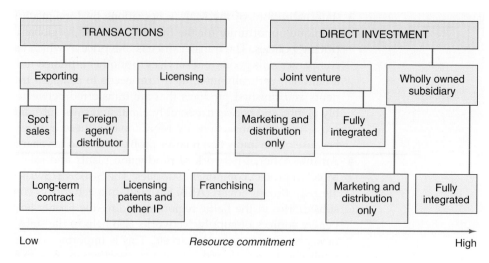

Figure 22.1 Alternative modes of overseas market entry
Source: Grant (2010), p. 374.

exporting
Sale of goods and services to a foreign customer

Exporting includes both indirect export of products from the home country via independent agents or distributors, and direct export of products through the firm's own export division to foreign markets. With exporting, most value-adding activity takes place in the home country, while FDI transfers many of these activities to the foreign location. Both exporting and FDI involve **internalisation**, i.e. retaining value-adding activities within the firm (although to different degrees).

internalisation
The retention by the MNC of key management functions and technology

externalisation
The transfer of key functions and expertise to an overseas strategic partner

Licensing is often a halfway house that results in **externalising** most of these activities. It involves transferring to a licensee the right to use corporate assets, such as a brand name, and often the sale of intermediate goods for the licensee to use in production. Licensing enables a firm to gain rapid overseas market penetration when it lacks the resources to set up overseas operations.

■ Choosing between entry modes: the determinants

The choice of entry mode hinges on several factors:

1 Whether the firm's source of competitive advantage is based on location-specific factors, e.g. low labour costs. If so, the firm is more likely to export. If managerial skills are transferable to other locations, FDI is more likely.

2 Whether the product is tradable, and whether barriers to trade exist. If import restrictions such as tariff barriers and government-imposed regulations make trade infeasible, licensing or FDI becomes more likely.

3 Whether the firm possesses the required skills and resources to build and exploit competitive advantage abroad. Marketing and distribution capabilities are essential for foreign operation, which argues in favour of appointing a distributor or agent when these skills are lacking. If a wider range of manufacturing and/or marketing skills is needed, the firm may license its product and/or technology to a local operator.

licensing
Involves the assignment of production and selling rights to producers located in foreign locations in return for royalty payments

In marketing-intensive industries, MNCs may offer their brands to local firms by trademark **licensing**. Licensing involves assigning production and selling rights to producers located in foreign locations in return for royalty payments. If tighter control over operations is required, a joint venture with a local firm may be set up.

patents
A legal device giving the holder the exclusive right to exploit the technology described therein

4 Whether the resources are 'appropriable' – can the technology be stolen? In some industries, technology can be closely guarded via **patents**, but in more service-oriented activities such as computer software, ownership rights are far more

difficult to enforce. In the former case, FDI involves less risk, while in the latter case, exporting may be preferred. When licensing a foreign partner, the firm must consider any potential damage to the reputation of its brand resulting from poor quality or service provided by a local operator.

Where a firm wants to exert close control over the use of its trademarks, technologies or trade secrets, **franchising** may be chosen as a way of licensing a fully packaged business system, as in the international fast food business.

franchising
Licensing out of a fully packaged business system, including technology and supply of materials, to an entrepreneur operating a separate legally constituted business

5 What transactions costs are involved? These are the costs of negotiating, monitoring and enforcing the terms of such agreements as compared with internationalisation via a fully owned subsidiary. With low or no transactions costs, exporting would usually be preferred.

US and Mexico boost reshoring credentials

The US and Mexico have become attractive as manufacturing locations relative to other large economies over the past 10 years, thanks to slow labour cost growth and falling natural gas prices. The analysis of the world's largest manufacturing economies from Boston Consulting Group shows that costs have been rising fastest in resource-rich countries such as Brazil, Australia and Russia, while China and some European countries such as France and Italy have also experienced significant increases.

The trends are expected to drive long-term movements in manufacturing activity towards the US and Mexico. The evidence of 'reshoring' in the US – the relocation of production away from previously low-cost centres such as China – is still only tentative. However, the international cost comparisons are an encouragement for expectations that American manufacturing will gather strength in the coming years.

The widening cost disadvantage of some western European countries is ominous for the outlook for their industries.

Hal Sirkin of BCG said: 'Unless things change, you're going to see significant falls in manufacturers opening factories in higher-cost countries, and more manufacturing plants shutting down.' Average cost indices calculated by the consultancy show the advantage enjoyed by China has been eroded rapidly over the past decade.

For the US, the most important factor behind the relative improvement in its costs has been the slow growth in manufacturing wages, which have risen much less than the average for large economies. Mexico has had wage rises in line with the global average, but has had much faster growth in labour productivity.

The impact of cost differences on location decisions will vary across industries. Sectors where transport costs are relatively high or being close to the customer is important offer the most attractive prospects for reshoring to the US.

Source: Based on Ed Crooks, *Financial Times*, 25 April 2014, p. 4.

■ Factors favouring foreign direct investment (FDI)

International expansion through FDI is an alternative to growth focused on the firm's domestic market. A firm may choose to expand horizontally on a global basis by replicating its existing business operations in a number of countries, or via international vertical integration, backwards by establishing raw material/components sources, or forwards into final production and distribution. Firms may also choose product diversification to develop their international business interests. Firms may expand internationally by greenfield (new 'start-up') investments in component and manufacturing plants, etc.; takeover of, and merger with, established suppliers; or forming joint ventures with overseas partners. In the case of foreign market servicing, the MNC may also choose to complement direct investment with some exporting and licensing.

FDI also provides opportunities for exploiting competitive advantages over rival suppliers. A firm may possess advantages in the form of patented process technology, know-how and skills, or a unique branded product that it can better exploit and protect by establishing overseas production or sales subsidiaries. A production facility in an overseas market may enable a firm to reduce its distribution costs and keep it in closer touch with local market conditions – customer tastes, competitors' actions, etc.

Moreover, direct investment enables a firm to avoid government restrictions on market access, such as tariffs and quotas, and the problems of currency variation. For example, the growth of protectionism by the European Union and the rising value of the yen were important factors behind increased Japanese investment in the EU, especially in the UK motor and electronics sectors.

Firms may benefit from grants and other subsidies by 'host' governments to encourage inward investment. Much Japanese investment (e.g. Nissan's plant near Sunderland) was attracted into the UK by regional selective assistance. In the case of sourcing, direct investment allows the MNC to take advantage of some countries' lower labour costs or provides them with access to superior technological know-how, thereby enhancing their international competitiveness.

Moreover, direct investment, by internalising input sourcing and market servicing within one organisation, enables the MNC to avoid various transaction costs: the costs of finding suppliers and distributors and negotiating contracts with them; and the costs associated with imperfect market situations, such as monopoly surcharges imposed by input suppliers, unreliable sources of supply and restrictions on access to distribution channels. It also allows the MNC to take advantage of the internal transfer of resources at prices that enable it to minimise its tax bill ('transfer pricing') or practise price discrimination between markets.

Finally, for some products (e.g. flat glass, metal cans, cement), decentralised local production rather than exporting is the only viable way an MNC can supply an overseas market because of the prohibitive costs of transporting a bulky product or one which, for competitive reasons, has to be marketed at a low price.

The following cameo illustrates an example of direct investment undertaken by the supermarket group, Walmart. Initially it had entered the Indian market via a joint venture and this had resulted in problems regarding regulation in India. Walmart dissolved the joint venture and adopted a new FDI strategy to overcome the regulatory problems.

Walmart renews Indian expansion with 50 new stores

Walmart plans to open another 50 wholesale stores in India, ending a self-imposed freeze on its expansion in a country where the US company has faced scrutiny for allegedly attempting to skirt a ban on foreign direct investment in retail businesses. The announcement by the world's largest retailer came in the same week that the Hindu nationalist Bharatiya Janata party – expected to win control of India's government in current elections – stated its opposition to FDI in retail businesses as part of its pre-election manifesto.

Walmart said its new stores, which it will open over the next four to five years, would be wholesale cash-and-carry outlets. These outlets provide bulk goods to small family-owned shops, hotels, restaurants, offices and other businesses. India permits 100 per cent foreign ownership of wholesale businesses, a policy not expected to be reversed under a new government.

Since 2009, Walmart has opened 20 cash-and-carry stores, called Best Price Modern Wholesale, in eight states. These stores were initially set up as a joint venture business with New Delhi-based Bharti Enterprises, which also operates a wholly-owned retail chain called Easy Day. In October, Walmart announced it was dissolving the partnership and buying out Bharti to take full control of the wholesale chain. Walmart has not opened a single new store since then.

'Walmart is committed to India and we are excited about our growth plans,' said Scott Price, president and chief executive officer of Walmart Asia. 'We will continue to focus on the cash-and-carry format as we are very happy with the way it has shaped up in the past few years.'

Walmart came under regulatory scrutiny in India in 2012 after it was accused of violating a ban on foreign direct investment in retail via the terms of its joint venture with Bharti. The announcement of expansion plans indicates Walmart is confident it has now put all regulatory issues behind it.

Source: Based on Amy Kazmin, *Financial Times*, 10 April 2014, p. 16.

22.4 THE INCREMENTAL HYPOTHESIS

incremental hypothesis
Suggests that firms tend gradually to build their degree of involvement in foreign markets, beginning with exporting and culminating in FDI

Johanson and Wiedersheim-Paul (1975) observed that firms tend to progress through several stages of foreign market servicing, typically beginning with exporting to obtain a 'bridgehead' and eventually graduating to FDI. A major factor in the progression is the relative cost of each servicing mode, which is a function of market size, or volume of sales.

The **incremental hypothesis** can be illustrated with a simple break-even diagram, using Buckley and Casson's (1981) model. Two possible entry modes, exporting and FDI, are displayed in Figure 22.2.

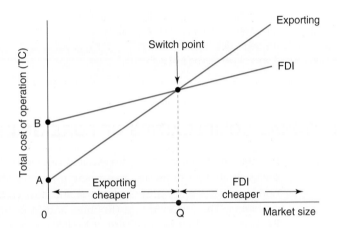

Figure 22.2 Exporting vs. FDI
Source: Buckley and Casson (1981).

These activities have quite different cost structures:

- Exporting involves relatively low fixed costs (0A) and relatively high unit variable costs, witness its steeper total cost profile.
- FDI involves relatively high investment fixed costs (0B) and relatively low variable costs due to lower production and distribution costs, reflected in a flatter TC profile.

For relatively low volumes, exporting may be more appropriate but the firm will eventually encounter a 'crossover' point where it becomes cheaper to switch to FDI. The switchover occurs at market size Q. Below this, exporting involves lower total operating costs, but beyond Q, a switch to FDI becomes preferable.

In practice, the switch decision is less clear-cut. Switchover costs would 'step' the FDI function, and most firms would wait a while before switching to ascertain whether the market expansion was permanent. Moreover, some firms 'jump' the intermediate stages if the foreign market size is already deemed sufficiently large.

Self-assessment activity 22.2

Consider how licensing would fit into Figure 22.2 – i.e. what is its likely cost structure relative to exporting and FDI?

(Answer in Appendix A at the back of the book)

US opens arms to foreign investors

Indian conglomerate Tata has placed a big bet on the US. It generates $8bn of annual revenues in the world's biggest economy and employs more than 18,000 people in IT centres, gourmet coffee production, and steel plants across the country. President Barack Obama would like many more global companies to follow suit, but the recent US record in attracting foreign investment has been worrying.

In 2000, the US gobbled up 37 per cent of the worldwide stock of inward foreign investment, but by 2012, that had shrivelled to 17 per cent. And annual inflows have almost halved from their 2008 peak. To boost those figures, the US president is donning his salesman cap for 'Brand USA' at an international conference starting today. 'This is the beginning of a sustained commitment to attracting FDI in the US,'

said Penny Pritzker, commerce secretary, who is hosting the two-day affair. 'We have so many great assets that should be celebrated and promoted at a time when the world is a very competitive place,' Ms Pritzker adds.

The US's need for inward investment is clear. 'The policy challenge isn't just that we need to create 20m jobs in the next 10 years, but we need to create 20m high-productivity, high-wage jobs,' said Matthew Slaughter, Associate Dean at the Tuck School of Business at Dartmouth University. 'Companies connected to the global economy tend to generate those types of jobs.'

Source: Based on James Politi, *Financial Times*, 31 October 2013, p. 2.

22.5 ADDITIONAL COMPLEXITIES OF FOREIGN INVESTMENT

Evaluation of foreign direct investment decisions is not fundamentally different from the evaluation of domestic investment projects, although the political structures, economic policies and value systems of the host country may cause certain analytical problems. There is evidence (Robbins and Stobaugh, 1973; Wilson, 1990; Neale and Buckley, 1992) that the majority of MNCs use essentially similar methods for evaluation and control of capital investment projects for overseas subsidiaries and for domestic operations, although they may well apply different discount rates.

Appraising foreign investment involves financial complexities not encountered in evaluating domestic projects. The main ones are:

1 Fluctuations in exchange rates over lengthy time periods are largely unpredictable. On the one hand, these may enhance the domestic currency value of project cash flows, but depreciation of the currency of the host country will reduce the domestic currency proceeds.

2 A foreign investment project may involve levels of operating risk quite different from those of the equivalent project undertaken in the domestic economy. This poses the problem of how to estimate a suitable required rate of return for discounting purposes.

3 Once up and running, the foreign investment is exposed to variations in economic policy by the host government (e.g. tax changes), which may reduce net cash flows.

4 Investment incentives provided by the host country government. Several countries in the 'New Europe' have been able to attract new investment from MNC firms, especially in the motor industry. Slovakia, with a tax rate of 22 per cent, can offer definite advantages over established EU members such as Germany (30–33 per cent) and France (33⅓ per cent), among the alleged losers in this process. Other EU countries with low tax rates (as at June 2014) include Bulgaria (10 per cent), Ireland and Cyprus (12.5 per cent) and Poland (19 per cent). Several developed countries have recently announced reductions in their rates of corporate tax in order to combat 'tax competition'. For example, in the UK, the corporate tax rate is falling, to 23 per cent in 2013, 21 per cent in 2014 and 20 per cent in 2015. (For updates, see **www.dits.deloitte.com** and **www.worldwidetax.com**).

5 Overspill effects on the firm's existing operations; e.g. goods produced overseas may displace some existing sales (referred to as 'cannibalisation').

6 The host government may block the repatriation of profits to the home country. A project that is inherently profitable may not be worth undertaking if the earnings cannot be remitted. This raises the issue of whether the evaluation should be conducted from the standpoint of the subsidiary (i.e. the project itself), or from that of the parent company. But for a company pursuing shareholder value, the relevant evaluation is from the parent's standpoint. Some companies have adopted ingenious ways of repatriating profits. PepsiCo, which invested in a bottling plant in Hungary, found it difficult to repatriate profits from this operation. To overcome this problem, it financed the local shooting of a motion picture (*The Ninth Configuration*), which was then exported to the West. It was not a box-office hit.

Usually, only remittable cash flows (whether or not they are actually repatriated) should be considered, and the project accepted only if the NPV of the cash flows available for investors exceeds zero. Thus, items like management fees, royalties, interest on parent company loans, dividend remittances, and loan and interest payments to the parent should all be included. In effect, a two-stage analysis is applied:

(i) specify the project's own cash flows
(ii) isolate the cash flows remittable to the parent.

Due allowance should be made for taxation in the foreign location.

■ Overcoming exchange controls

Possible ways of minimising the impact of controls over cash repatriation include:

(i) paying interest on loans or dividends on equity. Maximising dividend flows may involve 'creative accounting' to inflate the local profits, although this may be counter-productive if local tax rates exceed those in the home country. It may also antagonise local interests;
(ii) paying royalty fees where the foreign project utilises any process over which the parent claims proprietary rights, e.g. control of a patent or trade mark, such as Levi's;

transfer price
The cost applied to goods transferred between operating units owned by the same firm

(iii) **transfer pricing** policies that involve charging the overseas subsidiary high prices for components and other supplies;
(iv) applying a management charge if the senior managers are seconded from the parent. Similar charges can be used to make the foreign subsidiary pay for other services provided by the parent, e.g. IT and treasury costs. However, this may provoke close scrutiny by the host authorities.

Self-assessment activity 22.3

How does FDI differ from domestic investment?

(Answer in Appendix A at the back of the book)

22.6 THE DISCOUNT RATE FOR FOREIGN DIRECT INVESTMENT (FDI)

Opinions differ as to the appropriate discount rate to apply when discounting net cash flows from foreign investment. 'Gut feelings' may suggest that FDI should be evaluated at a higher discount rate than domestic investment 'simply because it involves more risk'. But is this valid?

Assuming all-equity finance, two commonly suggested possibilities are:

■ Use a required return based on the risk of similar activities in the home country. This would be the equity cost for projects in activities similar to existing ones, or a 'tailored' project-specific rate for ventures into new spheres.
■ Use a required return comparable to that of local firms.

Before deciding which approach is preferable, there are several issues to consider:

1 Foreign projects generally involve higher levels of risk than domestic ones. However, much of this risk can be dealt with in better ways than simply 'hiking' the discount rate. For example, currency risk can be handled by the sort of hedging techniques mentioned in Chapter 21 (if thought necessary), and political risk can be handled in the ways discussed later.

2 Although the total risk of FDI is often very high, the relevant risk is generally much lower, and sometimes lower than for comparable investment at home. FDI involves diversifying into overseas markets in the same way as an investor might diversify shareholdings across international markets. Solnik (1974) showed that the correlation between national stock markets is generally much less than one (although it may have increased in recent years). If investors can lower relevant risk by cross-border portfolio diversification, why should firms not do so? This is especially relevant for firms whose investors cannot diversify internationally, due to exchange controls or transactions costs, or into countries where no organised stock exchange operates' or, if one does exist, its efficiency may be in doubt.

The relevant Beta value for, say, a UK firm operating abroad may not be the Beta calculated by reference to the UK market portfolio, but the Beta in relation to the local market (if there is one). Consider the following example.

Example: Malaku Mining

Malaku Mining is the newly-formed Indonesian subsidiary of Mowmack plc, an all-equity-financed UK firm, whose shares have a Beta value of 0.9 relative to the UK market portfolio. The total risk (standard deviation) of the Malaku project is 30 per cent and the risk of the Jakarta Stock Exchange is 20 per cent. The UK stock market has a 50 per cent correlation with the Jakarta market.

Here, the parent Beta of 0.9 is inappropriate. Instead of using this value, it is more appropriate to consider the risk of the proposed activity in relation to the local market and allow for the low correlation between the London and Jakarta exchanges. We can do this by using a variation of the formula found in Section 9.5:

Project Beta = correlation coefficient × (risk of the activity/local market risk)

This yields a project-specific Beta of:

$(0.5 \times 30\%/20\%) = (0.5 \times 1.5) = 0.75$

The cost of equity would be calculated using the UK risk-free rate of, say, 5 per cent and the UK-equity market risk premium of, say, 5 per cent, as the firm has a UK investor base. Hence, the required rate of return for all-equity funding would be found from the usual CAPM formula:

$$k_e = R_f + \text{Beta}[ER_m - R_f] = 5\% + 0.75[5\%] = 8.75\%$$

Self-assessment activity 22.4

An ungeared UK firm, with a Beta of 1.4, plans to invest in an emerging country that has no stock exchange. Its economy has a weak correlation (0.4) with the UK. Due to operating gearing, the foreign project is 25 per cent more risky than the UK parent. The risk-free rate is 5 per cent and the expected overall return on the UK stock market is 11 per cent p.a. What return should the UK firm seek on this project?

(Answer in Appendix A at the back of the book)

22.7 EVALUATING FDI

Under certain conditions, analysing foreign project cash flows will yield the same result as analysing the cash flows to the parent. The key conditions are:

(i) Exchange rates adjust to reflect inflation differences between the parent country and the foreign location, i.e. PPP applies.
(ii) Project cash inflows and outflows move in line with prices in general in both locations.
(iii) No tax differentials exist between the two countries.
(iv) No exchange controls.

Because one or more of these conditions probably will not apply in practice, the following steps are generally recommended:

1 Predict local cash flows in money terms, i.e. including local inflation.
2 Allow for any 'overspill' effects like the 'cannibalisation' of existing exports. The opportunity cost is neither the sales revenue nor indeed the profit lost, but the gross margin or contribution.
3 Calculate the project's NPV using a discount rate reflecting the cost of finance in host country terms.
4 Allow for any management charges and royalties.
5 Estimate parent company cash flows by applying the expected future exchange rate to host country cash flows if there are no blocks on remittances, or to net remittable cash flows if exchange controls operate.
6 Allow for both local and parent country taxation.
7 Calculate the project's NPV.

■ Differences between host and parent country taxation

Quite apart from different tax rates, taxation issues can complicate FDI in several ways, most notably, if there are different systems of investment incentives in the two countries, and whether or not a **Double Taxation Agreement (DTA)** operates. Under a DTA, tax paid in the host country is credited in calculating tax in the parent country. The generally recommended procedure is to:

double tax agreements (DTAs)
Reciprocal arrangements between countries whereby tax paid in one location is credited in the second, thus avoiding doubling up the firm's tax bill. Hence, Double Tax Relief (DTR)

1 Allow for host country investment incentives before applying the local tax rate to local cash flows.
2 Apply the relevant UK rate of tax to remitted cash flows only.
3 Adjust stage 2 for any double tax rules. For example, with a DTA and host country tax payable at 15 per cent and where the rate of tax applicable in the UK is 30 per cent, the relevant rate of tax to apply to remittances is $(30\% - 15\%) = 15\%$.

Self-assessment activity 22.5

A UK MNC earns cash flow (all taxable) of $100 million in the USA. What is its overall tax bill if the rate of tax on profits in both the USA and the UK is 30 per cent and a DTA applies?

(Answer in Appendix A at the back of the book)

A full examination of the complexities of FDI is beyond our scope. However, several of these features are brought out in the example below.

22.8 WORKED EXAMPLE: SPARKES PLC AND ZOLTAN KFT

A UK company, Sparkes plc, is planning to invest £5 million in the Zoltan consumer electronics factory in Hungary. The project will generate a stream of cash flows in the local currency, Forints, which have to be converted into sterling as in Table 22.1. Should Sparkes invest?

Table 22.1 Sparkes and Zoltan: project details

■ Expected net cash flows from Zoltan in millions of Hungarian Forints (HUF) (at current prices):

Year	0	1	2	3	4
	−1,000	+400	+400	+400	+400

■ The project may operate for a further six years, but the local government has expressed its desire to purchase a 50 per cent stake at the end of Year 4. The purchase price will be based on the net book value of assets.

■ The spot exchange rate between sterling and Forints is 200 per £1. The present rates of inflation are 25 per cent in Hungary and 5 per cent for the UK. These rates are expected to persist for the next few years.

■ For this level of risk, Sparkes requires a return of 10 per cent in real terms.

First, we must consider the time dimension. The project is capable of operating for ten years, but the host government has expressed its desire to buy into the project after four years. This may signal to Sparkes the possibility of more overt intervention, possibly extending to outright nationalisation, perhaps by a successor government. It seems prudent to confine the analysis to a four-year period and to include a terminal value for the project based on net book values. If we assume a ten-year life, straight-line depreciation and ignore investment in working capital, the Net Book Value (NBV) after four years will be 60 per cent of Ft1,000m = Ft600m. Half of this can be treated as a cash inflow paid by the host government and half as a (perhaps conservative) assessment of the value of Sparkes' continuing stake in the enterprise.

In practice, we often encounter complications in assessing terminal values. For example, the assets may include land, which may appreciate in value at a rate faster than general price inflation. If so, there may be holding gains to consider, gains which may well be taxable by the host government. However, it is unwise to rely overmuch on terminal values – if project acceptance hinges on the terminal value, it is probably unwise to proceed with this sort of project.

Second, how should we specify the cash flows? Here, we have two problems: first, divergence between UK and Hungarian rates of inflation; and second, the need to convert locally denominated cash flows into sterling. To be consistent, we should discount nominal cash flows at the nominal cost of capital or real cash flows at the real cost. Each will give the same answer, but we conduct the analysis in nominal cash flows, thus incorporating the effect of inflation. Hence all cash flows are inflated at the anticipated Hungarian rate of inflation of 25 per cent.

As it is assumed that we are evaluating this project from the standpoint of Sparkes' owners, we need to obtain a sterling NPV figure. There are two ways of doing this.

The inflated cash flows in HUF are shown in Table 22.2. These are converted into sterling using forecast future spot rates. According to PPP, sterling will appreciate by the ratio of the respective inflation rates, i.e. $(1.25)/(1.05) = 19\%$ p.a. The predicted future spot rates are also shown in Table 22.2. The sterling cash flows are discounted at 15.5% ($[1.10] \times [1.05] - 1 = [1.155 - 1]$) to reflect the Fisher Formula.

Alternatively, we could proceed by discounting the inflated cash flows at a discount rate applicable to a comparable firm in Hungary, thus arriving at an NPV figure in local currency, and then convert to sterling. The local discount rate using the Fisher formula ((I_H) = Hungarian inflation) is:

$$(1 + P)(1 + I_H) - 1 = (1.10)(1.25) - 1 = (1.375 - 1) = 0.375, \text{ i.e. } 37.5\%.$$

Table 22.2 Evaluation of the Zoltan project

Year	Un-inflated cash flow in HUFm	Inflated at 25% (HUFm)	Forecast future spot rates: HUF vs. £1	Cash flows in sterling (£m)	PV in £m at 15.5%
0	(1,000)	(1,000)	200	(5.00)	−(5.00)
1	400	500	238	2.10	1.82
2	400	625	283	2.21	1.74
3	400	781	337	2.32	1.51
4	400	977	401	2.44	1.37
4	600*	600	401	1.50	0.73
				NPV =	+2.17
				i.e.	+£2.17m

*not inflated

To obtain a Sterling NPV, we adjust the NPV in HUF terms at *today's* spot rate of 200HUF vs. £1. Table 22.3 shows the result of this operation. Allowing for rounding, the NPVs are identical, i.e. the project is worth £2.18 m to Sparkes' shareholders.

Table 22.3 Alternative evaluation of the Zoltan project

Year	Inflated cash flows (HUFm)		PV in HUFm at 37.5%
0	(1,000)		(1,000)
1	500		364
2	625		331
3	781		300
4	977		273
4	600		168
		NPV =	436
	In sterling, at spot of 200HUF vs. £1	= 436/200	= £2.18m

■ The two equivalent approaches: which is best?

Consider the following example. Say a UK firm is investing in Canada. The two approaches are:

A The predicted C$ cash flows are converted to sterling cash flows, using expected future spot rates. These sterling cash flows are discounted at the sterling discount rate to yield a sterling NPV, numerically the same as in Approach B.

B The cash flows denominated in C$ are discounted at the local Canadian discount rate to generate a C$ NPV. This is then converted at the current spot rate for C$ against sterling to yield a sterling NPV.

Each approach has the same departure point, i.e. the C$ cash flows, and ends up at the same place, i.e. the sterling NPV. Which approach is 'better'? This depends on what information is available. Both approaches require forecasting cash flows in C$, so forecasts of Canadian inflation are required. Beyond this, it depends whether the financial manager is happier in forecasting future FX rates than in forecasting the required return in local currency terms. Approach B requires merely a one-year forecast of FX rates to derive the required return in C$ terms, whereas Approach A requires forecasts of FX rates over all future years of the project.

Remember that the equivalence of each approach depends on several factors, in particular, the operation of PPP and the existence of project inflation rates similar to those experienced at the national economy level. PPP ensures that if, say, the Canadian inflation rate exceeds the UK rate, the exchange rate of C$ vs. sterling will deteriorate, i.e. sterling will strengthen to ensure the parity of purchasing power of each currency in each country.

Either approach is acceptable, although the first is preferable as it has the advantage of allowing cash flows to be adjusted at inflation rates specific to the project where these may differ from the national rate, although this does require more detailed forecasting.

■ Using Interest Rate Parity as an alternative

In both of the previous examples, the calculation has relied on the validity of PPP. As an alternative, Interest Rate Parity might be used. Bear in mind that, in theory at least, the difference in interest rates at any one time should reflect expected differences in inflation rates. Taking the Zoltan example, where the difference in inflation rates is $(25\% - 5\%) = 20\%$, this would be consistent with a similar difference in interest rates.

Imagine that instead of being given information about expected inflation rates, we were told that the risk-free rate of interest in the UK was 7 per cent and that in Hungary it was 27 per cent: this would imply that the markets were expecting an inflation differential of 20 per cent, and thus, depreciation in the Forint versus Sterling. Future spot rates would be calculated as follows:

$$\text{Year 1 spot rate} = 200 \times (1.27)/(1.07) = 237.4$$
$$\text{Year 2 spot rate} = 200 \times (1.27)^2/(1.07)^2 = 281.8$$

Notice that the rates are slightly different to those above due to simplifying assumptions about converting from the real interest rate to the nominal interest rates, but the principle is identical. Obviously, one would only want to trust the first year's prediction as IRP is a technical relationship, but in later years, unless there is a forward market between these two currencies, predictions become far less reliable. A rate of exchange implied from interest rate differentials is called a **synthetic forward rate**.

22.9 EXPOSURE TO FOREIGN EXCHANGE RISK

You may appreciate now that FX variations are not always disastrous. The extent of FX exposure, and thus the urgency of dealing with it, depends on the structure of the firm's net cash flows in terms of its FX denomination. Firms with naturally hedged cash flows may be relatively unconcerned by FX variations. However, firms differ in the extent to which they are naturally hedged.

■ The four-way classification

Figure 22.3 shows a schema for classifying the extent of a firm's exposure to FX variations. Essentially, this depends on the sensitivity of their domestic currency cash flows to FX movements. Net cash inflows are broken down into their revenue and operating cost components, in order to focus on firms' net exposure. Classified by corresponding sensitivity, the four types of firm are:

- *Domestics* generate little or no income from abroad and source mainly from local suppliers. Their net exposure is indirect and usually low, stemming from the exposure suffered by their competitors on the UK markets, and by their local suppliers.

Sensitivity of cash outflows
to FX variations

	High	Low
High	GLOBALS – *LOW EXPOSURE*	EXPORTERS – *HIGH EXPOSURE*
Low	IMPORTERS – *HIGH EXPOSURE*	DOMESTIC TRADERS – *LOW EXPOSURE*

Sensitivity
of cash inflows
to FX variations

Figure 22.3 **Classification of firms by extent of operating exposure**

- *Exporters* source mainly from their own country, have high direct net exposures as their cash inflows and outflows are not naturally hedged, being in different currencies. They might consider adjusting their operating and/or financial strategies to achieve more insulated positions.
- *Importers* are in a similar position to exporters but in reverse – their net exposure is high because they source from abroad and sell on domestic markets.
- *Globals* have the lowest, and often minimal, net exposure. They have structured their operations so as to match as far as possible the currencies in which their inflows are denominated with those in which they incur costs. The match may not be perfect, given the indivisibility of some types of operation, e.g. production facilities, but regarding the overall profile of activities, their portfolios of cash inflow currencies should correlate highly with their portfolios of outflow currencies. At the group level, global firms should have little concern about FX exposures.

This is a powerful set of distinctions, but is counter-intuitive to many people. Firms heavily engaged in foreign operations may actually have low net exposures while many domestics, blissfully thinking they are insulated from overseas-generated exposures may, in reality, be more highly exposed. A high indirect exposure could conceivably outweigh a low direct exposure.

The BMW case below explains how moving production outside Germany reduced the company's exposure to foreign exchange risk. The case also illustrates that FDI strategies can have more than one benefit as BMW also gained from diversifying supply chains.

Managing foreign exchange risk – BMW moves production overseas

The story. BMW Group, owner of the BMW, Mini and Rolls-Royce brands, has been based in Munich since its founding in 1916. But by 2011, only 17 per cent of the cars it sold were bought in Germany. In recent years, China has become BMW's fastest-growing market, accounting for 14 per cent of BMW's global sales volume in 2011. India, Russia and Eastern Europe have also become key markets.

The challenge. Despite rising sales revenues, BMW was conscious that its profits were often severely eroded by changes in exchange rates. The company's own calculations in its annual reports suggest that the negative effect of exchange rates totalled €2.4bn between 2005 and 2009. BMW did not want to pass on its exchange rate costs to consumers through price increases. Its rival Porsche had done this at the end of the 1980s in the US and sales had plunged.

The strategy. BMW took a two-pronged approach to managing its foreign exchange exposure. One strategy was to use a 'natural hedge' – meaning it would develop ways

Continued

to spend money in the same currency as where sales were taking place, meaning revenues would also be in the local currency. However, not all exposure could be offset in this way, so BMW decided it would also use formal financial hedges. To achieve this, BMW set up regional treasury centres in the US, the UK and Singapore.

How the strategy was implemented. The natural hedge strategy was implemented in two ways. The first involved establishing factories in the markets where it sold its products; the second involved making more purchases denominated in the currencies of its main markets.

The overseas regional treasury centres were instructed to review the exchange rate exposure in their regions on a weekly basis and report it to a group treasurer, part of the group finance operation, in Munich. The group treasurer team then consolidates risk figures globally and recommends actions to mitigate foreign exchange risk.

The lessons. By moving production to foreign markets the company not only reduces its foreign exchange exposure but also benefits from being close to its customers. In addition, sourcing parts overseas, and therefore closer to its foreign markets, also helps to diversify supply chain risks.

Source: Based on Xu Bin and Liu Ying, *Financial Times*, 30 October 2012, p. 12.

■ Operating/economic/strategic exposure

If PPP always worked, forecasting FX rates would be very simple – in practice, prolonged uncertainty over future exchange rates and thus the effect on the firm's future cash flows in domestic currency terms greatly concerns many financial managers. The longer the time horizon that the firm works to, the greater is its concern. Continuing exposure over a period of years is called **economic exposure**. This refers to the effect of changing FX rates on the value of a firm's operations, generally the result of changing economic and political factors, hence the alternative label **operating exposure**. Because these variations will also affect the firm's competitive position, and because protecting or enhancing that position often provokes a change in strategy, it is also called **strategic exposure**.

These three terms are often used as synonyms. Whatever we call it, the impact is felt on the present value of the firm's operating cash flows over time, and thus the value of the whole enterprise. To prevent or mitigate damage, the firm can adopt various strategies to protect its inherent value. Measurement of exposure is the first step.

■ Measuring operating exposure

Operating exposure is both direct and indirect. Firms are concerned not only about how FX changes affect their own cash flows, but also how their competitors are affected by these changes. If the Chinese yuan declines against the US dollar, this may seem of no great consequence to a UK firm that sources in the US. However, it becomes important if, for example, competitors in the US that import from China see their import costs fall. These indirect effects are part of a firm's overall exposure.

Measurement of operating exposure thus involves identification and analysis of all future exposures both for the individual firm and also its main competitors, actual and even potential ones, bearing in mind that FX changes may even entice new entrants into existing markets.

It is worth repeating that operating exposure is concerned less with *expected* changes in FX rates, because, in efficient financial markets, both managers and investors will have already incorporated these into their anticipation of parent company currency cash flows. If the markets expect sterling to decline vs. the US dollar, the likely higher future sterling cash inflows of UK firms that export to the USA will have been factored into company valuations. In this situation, it is generally advisable to incorporate the forward rate of exchange into projections for future planning purposes. The damage is done when expectations are not fulfilled and/or when changes result from totally unexpected factors.

Example: Pitt plc

Pitt plc produces half its output in the USA, valued at today's exchange rate (US$1.50 vs. £1) at £100 million. The other half is sold in the UK. About 25 per cent of Pitt's supplies are sourced from the USA, valued at £15 million. Labour costs are £10 million per annum, and cash overheads are £5 million per annum. Shareholders require a return of 12 per cent per annum.

Required
(a) Determine the present value of Pitt's operating cash flows in sterling terms over a 10-year time horizon.
(b) Identify Pitt's direct and indirect operating exposures.
(c) What is the effect on Pitt's PV if the sterling/dollar exchange rate changes to US$1.40 vs. £1?

Solution
(a) At the present exchange rate, Pitt's cash flows are:
- Cash inflows: $2 \times$ £100m p.a. $\qquad$ = £200m
- Cash outflows:

Supplies ($4 \times$ £15m p.a.)	= (£60m)
Labour	= (£10m)
Overheads	= (£5m)
Net Cash Flow	= £125m

$$\text{Present value} = (£125m \times 10\text{-year annuity factor at } 12\%)$$
$$= (£125m \times 5.650) = £706\text{ m}$$

(b) Direct exposures:
- 50 per cent of cash inflows are exposed.
- 25 per cent of payments to suppliers are exposed.
- Any USD content of labour input and cash overheads would also be exposed.

Indirect exposures stem from the extent to which:
- US competitors are exposed to currency fluctuations.
- US suppliers are exposed.
- UK competitors are exposed.
- UK suppliers are exposed.

As discussed, it is important to realise that overall exposures transcend variations in the USD/£ rate. If, for example, suppliers in the UK import from India, they face exposure from the exchange rate of the rupee vs. sterling. Adverse variations are likely to spur them to recoup cost increases from their customers. Obviously, the extent to which they can achieve this depends on their own market power, e.g. the number and relative size of their own competitors and the importance of the components to customers like Pitt plc.

(c) Sterling depreciation to US$1.40 vs. £1 will increase the sterling value of the net cash inflows, because, at present, annual USD cash inflows exceed USD cash outflows. At the current exchange rate of US$1.50 vs. £1, the annual difference is (£100m − £15m) = £85m p.a.

Revised valuation:
- Inflows: [£100m + (£100m $\times$ 1.50/1.40)] $\qquad$ = £207m p.a.
- Outflows:

Supplies: ($3 \times$ £15m) + (£15m $\times$ 1.50/1.40)	= (£61m)
Labour	= (£10m)
Overheads	= (£5m)
Net Cash Inflow	= £131m

- PV at 12% = (£131m $\times$ 5.650) = £740m

Continued

In this example, depreciation of sterling by $(1 - 1.40/1.50) = 7\%$ has resulted in an increase in firm value of about 5 per cent. The sensitivity of a firm's value will depend on the structure of the firm's cash inflows and outflows – the greater the net foreign currency component, the greater the sensitivity of firm value.

Comment

The result is somewhat oversimplified for several reasons:

It assumes no change in the volumes of US-generated business in response to sterling depreciation. In reality, Pitt may lower the USD price to stimulate sales as it can now afford a price cut of up to 7 per cent and still achieve the same sterling cash inflow, after converting USD into sterling at the more favourable rate.

The effect will depend on:

(i) the extent of the price cut, i.e. whether Pitt matches the 7 per cent fall in sterling or takes some or all of this as windfall profit.

(ii) the elasticity of US demand for the product, i.e. the extent to which demand is stimulated by a price cut.

(iii) whether Pitt can produce enough to satisfy the demand increase.

(iv) the extent to which both US competitors and also other foreign firms supplying the US market follow a price cut.

Consequently, a full answer would depend on more rigorous strategic evaluation of the various consequences of the sterling depreciation. Similar comments apply to the increased sterling costs of supplies. Will Pitt try to absorb these costs? Will it try to pass them on wholly or partly? Will it seek alternative UK suppliers? In addition, there may be wider effects – will Pitt win sales from US competitors in the UK and elsewhere? How will fellow UK rivals respond to the sterling depreciation? How will non-exporting UK firms that import from the USA respond?

Having to grapple with these issues provides a powerful stimulus for seeking ways of trying to negate the effects of FX exposure.

Self-assessment activity 22.6

A UK-owned MNC produces in the USA and also exports to South American countries directly from the UK where it is paid in USD. Its US revenue is $50 million and its operating costs are $30 million. Export sales to South America are $100 million. What is its exposure to the USD/sterling exchange rate?

(Answer in Appendix A at the back of the book)

22.10 HOW MNCS MANAGE OPERATING EXPOSURE

Managing operating exposure involves taking steps to insulate the firm's operating cash flows as far as possible from the effect of unexpected FX changes, so as to minimise the effect on the value of the whole firm.

In Chapter 21, we explained a number of theories of the operation of FX markets. The upshot of these is that, if they are valid, firms need not worry about FX variations. However, because foreign exchange markets cannot always be relied upon to move quickly to new equilibria, it is often considered prudent to safeguard against the impact of future contingencies. Moreover, given the strongly competitive nature of many international markets, it is sensible to anticipate how competitors are likely to behave when operating conditions change.

There are two broad ways in which operating exposure can be minimised. The first involves structuring the firm's operations to insulate it from damage, and the second, structuring its financial policy to this end.

natural hedge
Where the adverse impact of FX rate variations on cash inflows are offset by the effect on cash outflows, or vice versa

The general aim is to construct a **natural hedge**. This occurs when there is little or no exposure because the adverse impact on cash inflows is exactly offset by the beneficial impact on cash outflows. A British firm producing and selling in the USA has a high degree of protection against sterling/dollar variations. If sterling appreciates, thus reducing the sterling value of dollar inflows, the adverse effect is largely counterbalanced by the corresponding fall in the sterling value of its USD-denominated inputs. Only the profit element is unhedged.

Firms that operate in the aerospace sector are particularly exposed to movements in the USD, the currency in which planes and engines are priced. Two firms that have tried to moderate their exposures are Rolls-Royce and Airbus. The former is constructing manufacturing and assembly plants in the USA and in Singapore, having already located the Head Office of its marine business on the island.

The following box shows details of how Airbus has attempted to moderate some of its operating exposure.

Airbus operations

The first Airbus final assembly line to operate outside of Europe, located in Tianjin, officially opened on 28 September 2008. This production site for A320 Family aircraft is a joint venture between Airbus and a Chinese consortium of Tianjin Free Trade Zone (TJFTZ) and China Aviation Industry Corporation (AVIC).

On 18 May 2009, the facili... the Chinese final ass... – complete... national Air... This same A...

Aviation Leasing for operation by Chengu-based carrier Sich... n Airlines, marking the first customer handover of an Air... etliner produced outside Europe.

... 1 January to 26 May 2010, Airbus delivered a ... n A320 Family jetliners assembled in Tianjin – ... ting that this facility's production ramp-up ... k at the rate of two aircraft per month. In ... t venture was extended to cover the period

...bsite: www.airbus.com

... e this 'self-hedging' effect in various

...ies where sales are made.
... or assemble the product.
...The stream of outflows (interest ...of inflows.
...currency received from sales.
...the Polish suppliers in USD

currency switching
Where an exporter pays for imported supplies in the currency of the export deal

The ...
tend ...
Canad...
stream. ...
Wher...
versified ...
exchange. 3

...ency. As some currencies ...sociated economies, e.g. ...e stream with a C$ cost

...n of operations. A diversified ...situations in foreign

parallel matching
Applies where a firm offsets inflows in one currency with outflows denominated in a closely correlated currency

■ If relativ... MNC can

■ If product ...
ing efforts t...

...ons, a diversified

...gthen its market- ...es are higher.

■ If raw material prices alter as between different locations, the MNC can alter its sourcing policy.

Admittedly, such adjustments are likely to trigger various conversion or switch-over costs, but the MNC may still benefit from favourable 'portfolio effects'. The variability of cash flows in domestic currency terms is likely to fall if the firm receives income in a variety of currencies – foreign exchange rate variations may increase competitiveness in some markets to offset lower competitiveness in others. This, of course, underpins the diversification motive for foreign investment, mentioned earlier in the chapter. Portfolio diversification was considered more fully in Chapter 8.

Self-assessment activity 22.7

Revisit self-assessment exercise 22.6.

Suggest three ways for the firm to lower its exposure.

(Answer in Appendix A at the back of the book)

22.11 HEDGING THE RISK OF FOREIGN PROJECTS

This issue has already been addressed. Operating a foreign investment involves both translation exposure and economic exposure. The translation risk stems from exposure to unexpected exchange rate movements: for example, a fall in the value of the Australian dollar (AUD) against GBP will reduce the GBP value of assets appearing in the Australian subsidiary's balance sheet. When consolidated into the parent's accounts, this will require a write-down of the value of assets in GBP terms. This problem can be avoided if the exposed assets are matched by a corresponding liability. For example, if the initial investment is financed by a loan denominated in AUD, the diminution in the sterling value of assets will be matched by the diminution in the GBP value of the loan.

Perfect matching of assets and liabilities is not always possible. Many overseas capital markets are not equipped to supply the required capital. Besides, it is probably politic to provide an input of parent company equity to signal commitment to the project, the government and the country. However, perfect matching is probably unnecessary, since some assets such as machinery can be traded internationally. The cause of the exchange rate depreciation (i.e. higher internal prices) will lead to a rise in prices, and if the Law of One Price holds, this appreciation in the value of locally-held assets will compensate for the reduced GBP value of the currency. As a result, the need to match probably applies only to property assets and items of working capital such as debtors, which cannot readily be traded on international markets. (Note the obvious attraction of operating with a sizeable volume of short-term creditors if sterling is strengthening, especially at the financial year-end.)

Economic exposure is the long-term counterpart of transaction exposure – it applies to a stream of cash inflows and outflows. In theory, the problem of variations in the prices of inputs and outputs should also be solved by the operation of the Law of One Price. For example, local price inflation at a rate above that prevailing in the parent company's country will be exactly offset by depreciation in the local currency, thus maintaining intact the GBP value of locally produced goods.

However, in practice, problems arise when PPP does not apply in the short term and when *project* prices alter at different rates from *prices in general*. The movement in the local price index is only an average price change, hiding a wide spread of higher and lower price variations. In principle, the firm could use the forward market to remove this element of unpredictability in the value of cash flows, but in practice, the forward market has a very limited time horizon, or is non-existent for many currencies.

Nevertheless, the parent company with widely spread overseas operations can adopt a number of devices. It can mix the project's expected cash flows and outflows with those of other transactions to take advantage of netting and matching opportunities. It can lead and lag payments when it expects adverse currency movements, although host governments usually object to this. It can also use third-party currencies. For example, if it invests in oil extraction, its output will be priced in USD and the otherwise exposed cost of inputs may be sourced or invoiced in USD or in a currency expected to move in line with USD. A more aggressive policy might involve invoicing sales in currencies expected to be strong and sourcing in currencies expected to be weak, perhaps including the local one.

Another tactic is to use the foreign project's net cash flows to purchase goods produced in the host country that are exportable, or can be used as inputs for the parent's own production requirements. This converts the foreign currency exposure of the project's cash flow into a world price exposure of the goods traded. This may be desirable if the degree of uncertainty surrounding the relevant exchange rate is greater than that attaching to the relevant product price.

Much world trade is conducted on the stipulation that the exporter accepts payment in goods supplied by the trading partner, or otherwise undertakes to purchase goods and services in the country concerned. This linking of export contracts with reciprocal agreements to import is known as **counter-trade**. It is usually found where the importer suffers from a severe shortage of foreign currency or limited access to bank credits.

counter-trade
A form of trade involving reciprocal obligations with a trading partner, or counterparty, e.g. a commitment to buy from a firm or country that the firm sells to

buy-back
A method of obtaining payment for building a manufacturing unit overseas by taking the future physical product of the plant in return

One form of counter-trade is **buy-back**, which is a way of financing and operating foreign investment projects. In a buy-back, suppliers of plant, equipment or technical know-how agree to accept payment in the form of the future output of the investment concerned. This long-term supply contract with the overseas partner raises some interesting principal/agent issues, concerning, in particular, the quality of the output and the management of the operation. Ideally, the output should be a product for which a ready market is available or that the exporter can use as an input to its own production process. In recent years, Iran has signed buy-back deals with European energy majors Shell, TotalFinaElf and ENI to finance the development of oil and gas projects.

The advantage of buy-backs for a Western company is that they secure long-term supplies and obviate any need to worry about exchange rate movements. The effective cost is the cost incurred in financing the original construction, and perhaps an opportunity cost if world prices of the goods received fall. Buy-backs thus offer a way of locking into the present world price for the goods transferred, which has some appeal in markets where prices fluctuate widely, for example, oil.

22.12 POLITICAL AND COUNTRY RISK

According to *Euromoney*, which conducts a regular analysis of political risk: 'Political Risk is the risk of non-payment or non-servicing of payment for goods and services, or trade-related finance and dividends, and the non-repatriation of capital.'

political risk
The risk of politically motivated interference by a foreign government in the affairs of a MNC, that adversely affects its net cash flows

country risk
The risk of adverse effects on the net cash flows of a MNC due to political and economic factors peculiar to the country of location of FDI

The definition and the above discussion imply a distinction between economic and **political risk**, the latter resulting from governmental interference and the former from general economic turbulence. But because these are usually intertwined, the two risks are often grouped under the heading of **country risk**.

It is not surprising that FDI by MNCs involves strong elements of political risk. Their very size and strength in relation to host countries creates the possibility of politically inspired action, whether favourable, e.g. granting generous incentives, or adverse, e.g. expropriation of oil company assets as in Venezuela in 2006. Where the goals of the host government and the MNC conflict, the political risk escalates. Political risk is heightened where political and social instability prevails, and host government objectives are unclear.

The task of the MNC's planners is to define, identify and predict these sources of instability. Instability results from internal pressures or civil strife that may be caused by factors such as inequities, actual or perceived, between internal factions (whether racial, religious, tribal, etc.), extremist political programmes, forthcoming independence or impending elections.

Any MNC that is considering FDI may observe the signals of political instability, but to measure its extent is a complex task. A major cause of political and social instability is due to economic influences. Factors such as oscillating oil prices, banking crises, foreign exchange crises and rampant inflation all promote instability.

As in Argentina, Turkey and Egypt in the early 2000s, economic instability often necessitates heavy overseas borrowing to finance reconstruction. Because reforms take time to implement, risk of default is ever-present. Default risk can be gauged by factors such as a country's debt service ratio (debt service payments relative to exports) and the debt age profile. The political risks of such pressures can provoke actions such as:

- exchange controls
- restrictions on registration of foreign companies
- restrictions on local borrowing
- expropriation or nationalisation
- tax discrimination
- import controls
- limitation on access to strategic sectors of the economy
- asset freezing.

Expropriation (confiscation of corporate assets with or without compensation), asset freezing (loss of control over asset management) and outright nationalisation represent the greatest political threat to foreign investors. The main risk is less that of expropriation *per se*, but the risk that compensation will be inadequate or delayed.

'Creeping' expropriation may also occur where mounting restrictions on prices, issue of work permits, transfer of shares, imports and dividends become likely when a nation feels threatened by the size and influence of MNCs. Hence, prior to deciding whether to operate in a new country, a pertinent question to consider is whether the MNC, either individually, or collectively with other MNCs, will dominate the industry, as occurs when oligopolistic rivals follow the strategic entry of a leader. If this is a strong probability, the political risk is greater than when penetration is low.

■ Assessing political and country risk (PCR)

There are several ways of assessing PCR:

1 Scoring systems

The magazines *Institutional Investor* and *Euromoney* produce country risk ratings on a regular basis. *Euromoney*'s ratings are based on a weighted average method, using the following scoring system, based on percentages:

- Political risk – 30 per cent
- Economic performance – 30 per cent
- Structural risk – 10 per cent
- Debt indicators – 10 per cent
- Credit ratings – 10 per cent
- Access to bank finance and capital markets – 10 per cent

The Euromoney 2012 Global Risk Trends guide explains how the world has become a riskier place. For example, the 2008 crisis has affected relative levels of risk in European countries. Table 22.4 shows the 'safest' countries based on the Euromoney Country Risk Survey for 2012 and Table 22.5 shows the most improved countries from 1993 to 2012.

Table 22.4 The world's 'safest' sovereigns

The leaders today...	Overall ECR score	Global rank	...and 20 years ago	Overall ECR score
Norway	90.4	1	Japan	99.4
Switzerland	88.8	2	United States	99.1
Singapore	88.0	3	Switzerland	99.0
Luxembourg	87.9	4	France	98.5
Sweden	86.8	5	Netherlands	98.2
Finland	84.3	6	Austria	97.9
Canada	84.3	7	Germany	97.9
Denmark	83.5	8	United Kingdom	97.8
Netherlands	83.1	9	Canada	97.8
Germany	82.2	10	Belgium	96.9
Hong Kong	82.2	11	Luxembourg	95.8
Australia	81.6	12	Denmark	95.2
New Zealand	80.7	13	Norway	94.7
Austria	79.8	14	Singapore	92.5
United States	75.7	15	Australia	92.5
Chile	74.9	16	Sweden	92.5
Taiwan	74.7	17	Spain	91.2
United Kingdom	74.2	18	Finland	91.2
France	73.9	19	New Zealand	91.1
Qatar	73.1	20	Ireland	90.5

Source: Euromoney Global Risk Trends (2012).

Table 22.5 The top-20 improvers in Euromoney's Country Risk Ratings

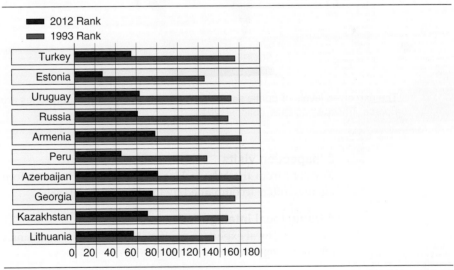

Source: Euromoney Global Risk Trends (2012).

2 Delphi technique

Also known as 'consulting the oracle', this involves canvassing a panel of experts for their opinions, via questionnaires or direct personal or telephone contact, and then aggregating the replies. The *Euromoney* analysis is essentially a combination of check-listing and the Delphi technique.

Measuring corruption

How can you measure the level of corruption in a country? If the abuse of public office for private gain is typically done in secret, under the table or behind closed doors, how can you systematically – and credibly – capture its scale and depth?

For nearly 20 years, campaigning NGO 'Transparency International' has scored and ranked countries according to how corrupt their public sectors are perceived to be. Drawing on 13 data sources, and based on the perceptions of businesspeople and country experts, the 2013 Corruption Perceptions Index (CPI) gives 177 countries a score from zero to 100, where zero is a perception that the country's public sector is 'highly corrupt' and 100 is 'very clean'.

Denmark and New Zealand top the list as the countries with the lowest perceived levels of public sector corruption; Afghanistan, North Korea and Somalia are the bottom three. More than two-thirds of the 177 countries examined scored below 50, a proportion similar to previous years.

Transparency International trumpets the CPI as 'the most widely used indicator of corruption worldwide'. The high-profile and widely reported index has, however, amassed its fair share of critics over the last two decades. Some have attacked the CPI's reliance on the opinions of a small group of experts and businesspeople.

Transparency International has defended its approach, arguing that capturing experts' perceptions is the most reliable method of comparing relative corruption levels across countries. 'Corruption generally comprises illegal activities, which are deliberately hidden and only come to light through scandals, investigations or prosecutions,' says the NGO. 'There is no meaningful way to assess absolute levels of corruption in countries or territories on the basis of hard empirical data. Possible attempts to do so, such as by comparing bribes reported, the number of prosecutions brought or studying court cases directly linked to corruption, cannot be taken as definitive indicators of corruption levels. Instead, they show how effective prosecutors, the courts or the media are in investigating and exposing corruption.'

Source: Based on Claire Provost, *The Guardian*, 3 December 2013.

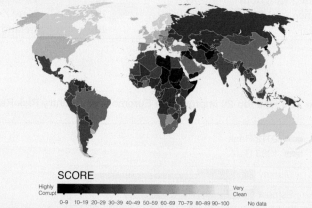

SCORE

Highly Corrupt — Very Clean

0–9 10–19 20–29 30–39 40–49 50–59 60–69 70–79 80–89 90–100   No data

The perceived levels of public sector corruption in 177 countries/territories around the world
Source: Transparancy International, 2013.

3 Inspection visits

Key staff from the MNC's Head Office make a 'Grand Tour' to the prospective host country, often accompanied by local embassy officials.

4 Using local intelligence

Consulting local experts, e.g. official insiders and credit analysts from banks, to advise on prevailing local trends.

▪ Corruption

A major issue in dealing with foreign officials is often corruption. Several agencies attempt to assess the extent to which local officials misuse their positions for personal gain when dealing with MNCs. For example, Transparency International (**www.transparency .org**) publishes a regular league table, based on a scale of 0–100 (100 = minimum perceived levels of public sector corruption). In its table published in 2013 covering 177 countries, Denmark, New Zealand and Finland were reckoned to be the least corrupt countries in the world. Other European countries ranked as follows: Germany (12), Britain (14), France (22), Italy (69), while North Korea and Somalia were reckoned to be the most corrupt.

22.13 MANAGING POLITICAL AND COUNTRY RISK (PCR)

Protection against the adverse consequences of changes in the political or economic complexion of a host country can be achieved in four ways:

- Pre-investment negotiation
- Laying down operating strategies
- Preparation of a contingency crisis plan
- Insurance

These aspects are now considered in turn.

■ Pre-investment negotiation

The best approach to PCR management is to anticipate problems and negotiate an understanding beforehand. Different countries apply different codes of ethics regarding the honouring of prior contracts, especially if concluded under a previous regime. Nevertheless, pre-negotiation does provide a better basis for subsequent wrangling.

An investment agreement sets out respective rights and obligations on both the MNC and the host government. It could cover aspects such as:

- The basis whereby financial flows, such as dividends, management fees, royalties, patent fees and loan repayments may be remitted back to the home country.
- The basis for setting transfer prices used for costing inputs delivered from the home country.
- Rights relating to third-country markets, i.e. who can serve them.
- Obligations to build or fund social infrastructure like schools and hospitals.
- Methods of taxation – rates and calculation procedures.
- Requirements for **offset**, i.e. local sourcing.
- Access to host country financial markets.
- Employment practices, especially regarding openings for nationals. This is very common in the Middle East, e.g. Oman has an 'Omanisation' policy, and the United Arab Emirates operates an 'Emiratisation' policy.

offset
The requirement for an MNC to undertake a proportion of local sourcing as condition of the award of an export deal (very common in the armaments industry)

■ Operating strategies

Flexible, risk-averting strategies that enhance the MNC's bargaining position can be devised in several areas.

Production and logistics

- Local sourcing increases local employment and may head off trouble if local interests would be damaged thereby.
- Siting production facilities to minimise risk, e.g. siting oil refineries in low-risk locations.
- Retaining control of transportation facilities like oil tankers and pipelines.
- Control of technology embodied in patents and the appointment of home country staff to manage complex technological processes. Coca-Cola has never divulged its magic formula, reputedly locked in a bank vault in Atlanta, Georgia.

Marketing

- Controlling markets by eliminating competition – locals are often happy to sell out.
- Controlling brand names and trademarks. McDonald's only franchises operations to local entrepreneurs.

Financial

- Issuing equity on the local stock market to extend ownership to locals. A Joint Venture is also an effective way to promote local participation.

- Restricting parental equity input – local debt financing is preferable to equity funding as it creates a hedge to offset local inflation and exchange rate depreciation, and also exerts leverage on local politicians if local banks stand to suffer from political intervention.
- Multi-source borrowing – raising loans from banks in several countries, and perhaps international development agencies, will build a wide nexus of vested interests in keeping the MNC healthy.

■ Preparation of a contingency crisis plan

Contingency planning helps in two ways, first, by providing an action plan to implement if things do go wrong, and second, it forces managers to think about the contingencies to which their foreign operation is most vulnerable.

■ Investment insurance

MNCs may be able to shift risk to a home country agency that specialises in accepting international risks. In the UK, the Export Credits Guarantee Department (ECGD) offers confiscation cover for new overseas investments, and Lloyds offers insurance facilities for existing and new investments in a comprehensive and non-selective form. In the USA, the government-owned Overseas Private Investment Corporation (OPIC) will cover risks relating to inability to convert overseas earnings into dollars, expropriation, war and revolution, and loss of business income arising from events of political violence that damage MNC assets.

■ A loaded dice?

In some countries, an apparently independent business partner may prove to have very strong links with the state, as BP has discovered with its joint ventures in Russia. In such countries, when difficulties arise, the local officials are more likely to side against the MNC as several firms have found in dealing with India, as well as Russia.

When a haven harbours unseen risk

If you had asked board directors at the beginning of last week which of two situations – the stand-off between Russia and Ukraine in Crimea, and the forthcoming British Budget – was politically riskier, they would have chosen the first. But for a few insurers involved in the lucrative business of offering annuities to pensioners, Britain turned out to be the more perilous place after George Osborne, the UK chancellor, astounded them by announcing reforms that could cut the size of that market by 90 per cent.

The Crimean crisis, for all its unpredictability, fits into the category of political risk that risk analysts love to analyse, risk managers to manage and insurers to insure against. If a capricious commander-in-chief orders men in fatigues in faraway places to do something that disrupts your supply chain or shuts down your factory, you may not like it, but the chances are you have braced yourselves for it. But if a minister in an industrialised country marches in and annexes your company's profit forecasts overnight, it may come as a shock. It should not. 'Safe' countries are riskier than they look.

Much recent economic growth has been concentrated in places where political and regulatory risk is high. Control

Risks estimated the share of global output generated in riskier countries, coloured amber or red on its 2014 political RiskMap, had more than doubled to 35 per cent in the preceding decade. Multinationals have of necessity focused their investment and attention there. As a result, Richard Fenning, the consultancy's chief executive, reckons boards now 'fixate on political risk as what can be covered by a Lloyd's of London insurance policy'.

Such an approach is understandable if you are Twitter, facing a ban in Turkey, Repsol, the Spanish company whose majority stake in Argentina's YPF was nationalised in 2012, or Glencore, which has mining operations in volatile areas overseen by trigger-happy local authorities. Before listing in 2011, Glencore outlined potential geopolitical threats that included 'terrorism, civil war, guerrilla activities, military repression, civil disorder, crime, workforce instability, change in government policy or the ruling party, economic or other sanctions imposed by other countries, extreme fluctuations in currency exchange rates or high inflation'.

Source: Based on Andrew Hill, *Financial Times*, 25 March 2014, p. 14.

The following cameo illustrates the difficulties faced by companies when governments make policy changes. Too much official interference can also be counterproductive, as Thailand discovered in 2007, when IKEA pulled out of a new store development, as it faced increasingly restrictive laws on foreign ownership.

22.14 FINANCING FDI

A multinational company (MNC) may have more opportunities to lower the overall cost of capital than a 'domestic'. This is often due to its larger size, and partly due to greater access to international financial markets, allowing it to exploit any temporary disequilibria, as well as receiving host government concessions.

The international financing decision has three elements:

1 *Whether* to borrow?
2 *How much* to borrow?
3 *Where* to borrow?

■ Key issues

The issues that determine these decisions are:

- **Gearing ratio.** The debt–equity mix selected for overseas activities is influenced by the gearing of the parent, or by the debt–equity ratios of comparable, competing firms in the location of the FDI. If the parent guarantees the subsidiary's borrowing, so long as the existing gearing of the parent is 'reasonable', the subsidiary's borrowing may be a separate issue, especially if a joint venture is formed and the borrowing of the overseas affiliate can be kept off-balance sheet. This enables fuller exploitation of subsidised loans and lower tax rates.
- **Taxation.** MNCs need to examine differences between the treatment of withholding taxes, losses, interest and dividend payments. Tax-deductibility of interest provides an incentive to borrow locally.
- **Currency risk.** Local borrowing can also reduce foreign exchange exposure by enabling a match of interest and capital repayments against locally generated cash inflows denominated in local currency.
- **Political risk.** Expropriation of assets or other interference is less likely if the MNC borrows from local banks or from the international markets. The host government is unlikely to want to offend the international financial community as it would damage its own credit standing. If the MNC borrows via the World Bank, it can include a **cross-default clause**, so that a default to any creditor automatically triggers default on a World Bank loan.

■ The case for borrowing

- Less risky than using equity which puts owners' capital at risk.
- Debt service is based on a strict schedule, helping cash flow planning and currency hedging. Dividends are more erratic.
- Debt service payments are less likely to antagonise host governments. Erratic dividend flows may interfere with a host government's attempts to manage the external value of its currency, especially if the MNC is a major contributor to local GDP.
- Tax relief on interest.
- Opportunity to hedge foreign exchange risk by matching.
- Protection against political risk.
- Access to concessionary local finance.
- Overseas equity markets (if they exist) can be highly inefficient.

■ The case against borrowing

- The parent's debt–equity ratio may already be high.
- There may be only limited local borrowing facilities.
- Local borrowing may entail more intensive credit risk investigation fees, and higher interest rates if the MNC has no local credit rating.
- The host government may place an upper limit on local borrowing to restrict tax avoidance.

$4bn CNOOC international debt issue breaks Chinese records

CNOOC, the Chinese state-run oil company, has joined the global rush to raise cheap corporate credit, with a $4bn bond, the biggest international issue in Asia in a decade. CNOOC said in a statement: 'The offering consists of $750m of 1.125 per cent guaranteed notes due 2016; $750m of 1.75 per cent guaranteed notes due 2018; $2,000m of 3.0 per cent guaranteed notes due 2023; and $500m of 4.250 per cent guaranteed notes due 2043.'

The net proceeds of $3.94tn will be used mainly to repay part of a $6bn short-term credit taken out to finance its $18bn acquisition of Nexen, the Canadian energy group, said CNOOC. A string of banks backed the deal, led by Bank of China, BOCI Asia, Bank of America Merrill Lynch, China International Capital Corporation, Citigroup, Credit Suisse, Goldman Sachs, JPMorgan, and UBS. The deal was five times subscribed, with investors offering about $24bn.

Chinese issuers led other Asian corporates by a long way in a year that is on course to beat 2012's totals, according to data from Dealogic. For 2012 as a whole, Chinese corporates raised $476bn, out of an Asian total of $881bn. Chinese companies also led the way in US dollar issues. Asia's annual total for 2012 was $131bn, with $29.2bn coming from Chinese companies. According to Dealogic, the largest Asian international bond issue was Hutchison Whampoa International's $5bn offering in 2003. CNOOC's is just bigger than Sinopec's $3.5bn offering last month.

Source: Based on Stafen Wagstyl, *Financial Times*, 4 May 2013, p. 20.

■ Assessment

The balance of argument usually points to borrowing to finance foreign subsidiaries; indeed, braver corporate treasurers may try to exploit perceived disequilibria in global financial markets to access 'cheap' finance. However, the international Fisher Effect (explained in Chapter 21) should caution against this. The benefit of borrowing at 'low' interest rates should always (eventually at least) be offset by the appreciation in currency in which debts are to be repaid.

Special Purpose Vehicles (SPV)
An entity set up specifically for managing a firm's financial requirements and obligations

Larger MNCs may set up their own financial subsidiaries as **Special Purpose Vehicles (SPV)**, established largely for the purpose of obtaining the funds required to finance the entire firm's ongoing growth needs. This avoids problems over costs and access to capital in the host country. The SPV simply borrows on world markets using the credit rating of the parent. Firms that use SPVs include General Electric Corporation (via GE Capital), BMW and Ford.

■ The currency cocktail

There is a strong argument for borrowing in a range or 'cocktail' of currencies to spread the risk over a diversified portfolio of borrowed currencies. By diversifying sources of finance, the MNC may take advantage of what it perceives as unusually low rates in certain financial centres. This requires the MNC to be well-known in international financial markets and to have established, sound banking relationships. Thus a firm needing to refinance a medium-term loan maturing in London where interest rates are 7 per cent may decide to borrow in Japan where interest rates for corporate borrowing are, say, 2–3 per cent.

To illustrate a currency cocktail, consider Table 22.6 which shows the long-term indebtedness of International Airlines Group by currency and by type of borrowing instrument.

Table 22.6 International Airlines Group borrowing at 31 December 2013

	(Millions)	(Millions)
	2013	**2012**
Loans		
Bank:		
US dollar	**$338**	$393
Euro	**€101**	€106
Japanese yen	**¥14,259**	¥32,268
Sterling	**£240**	£279
	€734	€1,037
Fixed rate bonds:		
Euro	**€321**	–
Sterling	**£249**	£561
	€618	€689
Finance leases		
US dollar	**$2,935**	$2,319
Euro	**€456**	€174
Japanese yen	**¥18,557**	¥9,332
Sterling	**£874**	£862
	€3,770	€3,072
	€5,122	€4,798

Source: International Airlines Group Annual Report, 2013.

22.15 THE WACC FOR FDI

In Section 22.6, we explained how a project-specific discount rate could be obtained for a foreign investment. At that point, we were assuming all-equity funding. But what if the project is partly debt-financed? This issue is often highly relevant where foreign governments offer concessionary interest rates, often prompting a level of local debt financing well above the parent's own gearing. The most appropriate solution is to use a tailor-made WACC calculated to reflect the particular financing mix of the project.

To illustrate this, let us revisit the case of Malaku Mining from page 708. Recall that it was decided that a local Beta value of 0.75 was appropriate to use, resulting in a project-specific equity cost of 8.75 per cent.

Now assume that Malaku can borrow in Indonesia at the concessionary rate of 3 per cent and that local regulations allow it to offset interest charges against local taxation, paid at 40 per cent. The WACC for the Indonesian mining project is found in the usual way by weighting the cost of each form of finance by its contribution to financial structure, in this case, project financing. Now assume that the project is financed 25 per cent by parental equity and 75 per cent by local borrowing. The WACC is thus:

$$(8.75\% \times \text{equity weight}) + (3\% [1 - 40\%] \times \text{debt weight})$$
$$= (8.75\% \times 25\%) + (1.8\% \times 75\%) = (2.2\% + 1.4\%) = 3.6\%$$

This is an interesting result indeed. The combination of low interest rate and high debt proportion results in a remarkably low required return. These sorts of calculation, although based on sound CAPM logic, can often generate much lower project cut-off rates than for comparable UK investment. To many executives, it is inconceivable that high-risk foreign projects should be evaluated at lower discount rates than UK projects.

Financial managers often have some difficulty in explaining and justifying lower WACCs to sceptical executives whose natural inclination is to use *higher* rates for foreign projects. The response is that, although foreign projects often have higher total risks, additional risks are usually project- and country-specific, and are thus very different from those affecting UK projects. These risks are best handled in more effective ways, e.g. by hedging foreign exchange risk, than by simply hiking the discount rate. Raising the hurdle rate, and possibly excluding an attractive, albeit risky, project is inferior to a considered policy of risk management.

22.16 APPLYING THE APV TO FDI

Discounting at the WACC implies that all the complex interactions involved in the investment can be factored into a single discount rate. In no case is this more difficult than for foreign investment projects that differ from domestic activities in aspects such as taxation, foreign exchange rate variability, concessionary financing and numerous additional dimensions of risk. This makes FDI a prime candidate for evaluation by the APV method.

For FDI, the evaluation procedure is:

1 Evaluate the core project assuming it is financed entirely by owners' equity to find the base case, as if the project were undertaken in the home country.
2 Separately evaluate the 'extras' such as the tax breaks and subsidies offered by the host government, and any spill-over effects on other activities, e.g. lost export trade.
3 Calculate APV = [base case NPV − PV of extras].
4 Accept the project if the APV is positive.

A simple APV model is shown in Figure 22.4. The APV is defined as the inherent value of the foreign-located project to the firm's owners, adjusted for all positive and negative side-effects. For foreign projects, the APV is particularly useful when project financing differs from the parent firm's capital structure, but suffers the limitation that calculation of these side-effects and their associated degrees of risk is difficult in practice. Inevitably, a high degree of judgement is required.

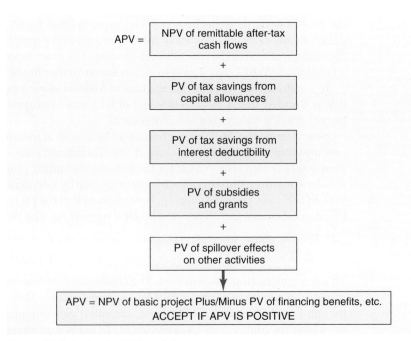

Figure 22.4 A simple APV model

22.17 WORKED EXAMPLE: APPLYING THE APV

(This question was part of a CIMA question in the May 2006 P9 Financial Strategy exam paper, in which it carried 15 of the available 25 marks.)

Question

GHI is a mobile phone manufacturer based in France with a wide customer base in France and Germany, with all costs and revenues based in the euro (€). GHI is considering expanding into the Benelux countries and has begun investigating how to break into this market.

After careful investigation, the following project cash flows have been identified:

Year	€million
0	(20)
1	5
2	5
3	4
4	3
5	3

The project is to be funded by a loan of €12 million at an annual interest rate of 5% and repayable at the end of five years. Loan issue costs amount to 2% and are tax-deductible.

GHI has a debt: equity ratio of 40:60 (at market values), a pre-tax cost of debt of 5.0% and a cost of equity of 10.7%.

Under the terms of a Double Tax Treaty, tax is payable at 25% wherever the earnings of a project are made, and not taxed again when cash is repatriated. The initial investment of €12 million will qualify for full tax relief.

Required

Advise GHI on whether or not to accept the project, based on a calculation of its Adjusted Present Value (APV), and comment on the limitations of an APV approach in this context.

Answer

The first step is to obtain an ungeared, equity discount rate. Substituting into the formula:

$$k_{eg} = k_{eu} + [k_{eu} - k_d]\frac{V_B(100 - t)\%}{V_S}$$

$$10.7\% = k_{eu} + [k_{eu} - 5\%] \times \frac{4 \times (100 - 35)\%}{6}$$

$$10.7\% = k_{eu} + 0.433k_{eu} - 2.167\%$$

Hence, the cost of equity is:

$$k_{eu} = 12.867\%/1.433 = 8.98\% \text{ or, approximately, } 9\%$$

Year	0	1	2	3	4	5
Project cash flows	−12	5	5	4	3	3
Local tax on cash flows at 25%		−1.25	−1.25	−1	−0.75	−0.75
Net cash flows	−12	3.75	3.75	3	2.25	2.25
Discount factor at 9%	1	0.917	0.842	0.772	0.708	0.650
Present Value	−12	3.43	3.15	2.32	1.59	1.46

NPV of basic project at 9% = −£12 million + £8.95 million = −£3.05 million

The next step is to find the PV of the 'extras'. Beginning with the tax shield on investment expenditure (assumed offsettable against earnings from other activities)

= 25% × £12 million = £3 million

The tax shield on debt is:

Tax relief on debt interest = €150,000 each year for five years (= €12 million × 5% × 25%)
PV of tax relief on debt interest = €0.67 million (= €150,000 × 4.452)

Finally, the issue costs:

Issue costs = €240,000 (= €12 million × 2%)
PV of tax relief on issue costs = €0.06 million (= €240,000 × 0.25 × 0.952)
The full APV calculation is thus:

Adjusted present value	€000
Base case NPV	(3.05)
Tax relief on initial outlay	3.00
PV of tax relief on debt interest	0.67
Issue costs	(0.24)
PV of tax relief on issue costs	0.06
Adjusted present value	0.44

Hence, although the basic project is not worthwhile, adding in the present value of the financing costs and benefits and the investment tax break, the APV is positive. The project should thus be accepted.

Limitations of the APV

- Determining the costs and benefits involved in the financing method to be used can be difficult (especially where they are based on an estimate of the enhanced debt capacity provided by the project, as in this case).
- Finding a suitable cost of equity for the base NPV calculation is subjective and may not truly reflect the risk associated with the new project, especially if the project is based abroad (as here – although there are no currency complications).
- Whether the tax rate will remain at this level, and the tax treaty will stay in force.
- Whether to discount the tax savings from the debt at the post-tax rate of interest or at the cost of equity.

Self-assessment activity 22.8

List eight ways in which MNCs can lower political risk.

(Answer in Appendix A at the back of the book)

SUMMARY

This chapter has examined the strategic motivations that drive firms to enter foreign markets, and methods of effecting entry, in particular, direct investment. Evaluating FDI is a complex process that differs in several important respects from evaluation of home country investment, not least the exposure to FX rate variations. As a result, FDI evaluation is more art than science, especially as it involves so many unquantifiable aspects such as the prevailing political mood of the host country, assessing political and other country risks and devising appropriate safeguards. Clearly, this topic transcends purely *financial* strategy.

Key points

- Foreign direct investment (FDI) may be undertaken for a variety of strategic reasons: for example, globalisation of component sources or meeting the threat of a competitor already based overseas.

- FDI is generally undertaken when exporting (with relatively high variable costs, but low fixed costs) becomes more expensive than overseas production (with relatively high fixed costs but low variable costs).

- In principle, the valuation of FDI is similar to appraisal of domestic investment, but there are important additional complications that may cloud the analysis.

- Among such complications are exchange rate complications, political risk, such as the risk of expropriation, exceptional inducements to invest in a particular location, and cannibalisation of existing export sales.

- Most of these complexities can be alleviated by (i) evaluating the project from the perspective of the parent company's shareholders, and (ii) as a first approximation at least, relying on the four-way parity relationships.

- If the parity relationships hold, then there are two equivalent ways of evaluating FDI: (i) predicting all future cash flows in the foreign currency, and discounting these at the local (i.e. overseas) cost of capital, and then converting to domestic currency at spot; and (ii) converting all the predicted foreign currency cash flows to the domestic currency using estimates of the future spot exchange rates, and discounting these at the domestic cost of capital.

- A tailor-made discount rate can be found by using the cost of capital of a comparable overseas firm, but allowing for the likely less than perfect correlation between the foreign economy and the domestic one.

- Foreign investment risk is mainly economic risk. This can be alleviated by strategic decisions, e.g. location of production facilities in a range of countries, and hence, operating in a variety of currencies.

- Similarly, diversification of markets can produce the same sort of currency cocktail.

- The extent to which a firm needs to hedge investment project risk depends on its international profile of activities, and thus the extent to which operating risks net off against each other in natural hedges, e.g. a firm producing in Italy and selling in France has no direct operating exposure as all transactions are conducted in euros.

- Counter-trade, i.e. making reciprocal dealing arrangements with firms and governments in other countries, can be used to mitigate foreign exchange risk. Available methods extend from crude barter to buy-back facilities.

- Political risk can be moderated in various ways, e.g. borrowing from local banks, but the guiding principle is to make the MNC indispensable to the local economy and society.

- Corruption is endemic in some foreign countries, so a sad fact of life is that failure to play the local game can lead to loss of business.

- If the complexities of evaluating FDI make the conventional DCF model too cumbersome, a short-cut approach is offered by the adjusted present value (APV) approach which separates out the cash flows from basic operations from those attributable to financing and other complexities.

Further reading and website

Books on international/multinational financial management (see Chapter 21) invariably carry chapters on evaluation of FDI – Shapiro (2013) has excellent coverage on this topic.

More general texts on international business such as those by Daniels *et al.* (2011) and Rugman and Collinson (2012) include extensive treatments of international strategy and operations, and usually cover appraisal of foreign projects also, but to a lesser depth. Buckley (2012) gives probably the most comprehensive coverage of overseas capital budgeting. Excellent analyses of operating exposure can be found in Lessard and Lightstone (2006) and in Grant and Soenen (2004).

Dunning and Lundan (2008) is perhaps the most authoritative text on the role of the MNC in the global economy.

The World Investment Report, published each autumn (usually September) by UNCTAD (**www.unctad.org**), is a mine of information on trends in FDI.

QUESTIONS

Questions with a coloured number have solutions in Appendix B on page 808.

1 The USD vs. GBP exchange rate is $1.50 vs. £1. A UK MNC operating in the US plans to sell goods worth $100 million at today's prices to US customers. Show that its GBP revenue *in real terms* will not be affected if PPP applies under each of the following conditions:

(i) UK and US inflation at 5% p.a.
(ii) UK inflation 5%, US inflation 2%.
(iii) UK inflation 2%, US inflation 5%.

2 OJ Limited is a supplier of leather goods to retailers in the UK and other Western European countries. The company is considering entering into a joint venture with a manufacturer in South America. The two companies will each own 50 per cent of the limited liability company JV (SA) and will share profits equally. £450,000 of the initial capital is being provided by OJ Limited, and the equivalent in South American dollars (SA$) is being provided by the foreign partner. The managers of the joint venture expect the following net operating cash flows which are in nominal terms:

	SA$ 000	Predicted future rates of exchange to £ sterling
Year 1	4,250	10
Year 2	6,500	15
Year 3	8,350	21

For tax reasons, JV (SA), the company to be formed specifically for the joint venture, will be registered in South America.

Ignore taxation in your calculations.

Assume you are a financial adviser retained by OJ Limited to advise on the proposed joint venture.

Required

(a) Calculate the NPV of the project under the two assumptions explained below. Use a discount rate of 16 per cent for both assumptions, and express your answer in sterling.

Assumption 1: The South American country has exchange controls which prohibit the payment of dividends above 50 per cent of the annual cash flows for the first three years of the project. The accumulated balance can be repatriated at the end of the third year.

Assumption 2: The government of the South American country is considering removing exchange controls and restrictions on repatriation of profits. If this happens, all cash flows will be distributed as dividends to the partner companies at the end of each year.

(b) Comment briefly on whether or not the joint venture should proceed based solely on these calculations.

(CIMA)

3 PG plc is considering investing in a new project in Canada that will have a life of four years. Initial investment is C$150,000, including working capital. The net cash flows that the project will generate are C$60,000 per annum for Years 1, 2 and 3 and C$45,000 in Year 4. The terminal value of the project is estimated at C$50,000, net of tax.

The current spot rate for C$ against the pound sterling is 1.70. Economic forecasters expect the pound to strengthen against the Canadian dollar by 5 per cent per annum over the next four years. The company evaluates UK projects of similar risk at 14 per cent per annum.

Required

Calculate the NPV of the Canadian project using the following two methods:

(i) Convert the foreign currency cash flows into sterling and discount at a sterling discount rate.
(ii) Discount the cash flows in C$ using an adjusted discount rate that incorporates the 12-month forecast spot rate.

(CIMA)

4 Kay plc, a UK-based chemical firm but with plants in Germany and the Netherlands, manufactures man-made fibres. It would like to expand its exports to Latin America and the country of Copacabana, in particular. However, Copacabana is unable to pay in Western currency and its own currency, the poncho, is subject to rapid depreciation, due to high local inflation. One solution to this problem is an arrangement whereby Kay manages and pays for the construction of a fibres plant and accepts payment in the form of the finished product of fibres (a so-called buy-back).

Construction will take two years and expenditures can be treated as four equal half-yearly payments of 10 million ponchos at today's prices, beginning in six months' time. The plant will have a 15-year life, but will attract no local investment incentives. The inflation rate in Copacabana is expected to average 20 per cent p.a. over the construction period. The current exchange rate of the poncho vs. sterling is 1:4 and inflation in the UK has recently averaged 5 per cent.

The fibres produced and taken as payment can be traded on world markets, probably in Europe, where the present price is €500 per tonne. Kay is not prepared to accept payment in this way for more than five years. The expected production rate of the plant is 20,000 tonnes per annum, and Kay would take 40 per cent of this in payment.

The current euro vs. sterling rate is €1.60 per £1, and sterling is expected to depreciate by 5 per cent per annum prior to joining the euro bloc.

Further information
- The project will be financed by equity only.
- Kay is at present debt-free. Its shareholders seek a return of 20 per cent p.a. for projects of this degree of risk.
- Profits from the operation will be taxed at 30 per cent when repatriated to the UK. Assume no delay in tax payment. All development costs will qualify for UK tax relief.
- Any losses will be carried forward to qualify for tax relief.
- There will be no tax liability in Copacabana.

Required

Determine whether Kay should undertake this project.

5 Brighteyes plc manufactures medical and optical equipment for both domestic and export sale. It is investigating the construction of a manufacturing plant in Lastonia, a country in the former Soviet bloc. Initial discussions with the Ministry of Economic Development in Lastonia have met with favourable response, providing the project can generate a 10 per cent pre-tax return. Shareholders look for a return of 15 per cent in real terms.

The investment will be partly import-substituting and partly export-based, selling to neighbouring countries. The project has been offered a local tax holiday, exempting it from all taxes for the first ten years, except for cash remittances, for which a 20 per cent withholding tax will apply. Modern factory premises on an industrial estate with convenient road and rail links have been offered at a reasonable rent.

The initial investment will be £10 million in plant, machinery and set-up costs, all payable in sterling by the parent company. Additional funds will come from a bank loan of 20 million latts, the local currency (4 latts = £1), negotiated with a local bank, at a concessionary rate of interest of 10 per cent p.a. This will be used to finance working capital. Operating cash flows, the basis for calculating tax, are estimated at L10 million in Year 1 and L22 million thereafter until Year 5.

The whole of the parent's earnings after payment of local interest and taxation will be repatriated to the UK. The Lastonia withholding tax is to be allowed as a deduction before calculating the UK corporation tax, currently at the rate of 30 per cent. All transfers can be treated as occurring on the final day of each accounting period, when all taxes become due.

The new venture is expected to 'cannibalise' exports that Brighteyes would otherwise have made to neighbouring countries, resulting in post-tax cash flow losses of £0.5 million in each of Years 2 to 5. For planning purposes, Year 5 is the cut-off year, when the realisable value of the plant and equipment is estimated at L24 million. The working capital will be realised, subject to losses of L2 million on stocks and L2 million on debtors. Funds realised will be used to repay the local borrowing, and the balance transferred to the UK without further tax penalty or restriction.

The exchange rate is forecast to remain at L4 vs. £1 until Year 2, when the Latt is expected to fall to L5 vs. £1.

Required

(i) Is the project acceptable from the Lastonian Ministry's point of view?
(ii) Is it worthwhile from the viewpoint of the foreign subsidiary?
(iii) Does it create wealth for Brighteyes' shareholders?

6 Palmerston plc operates in both the UK and Germany. In attempting to assess its economic exposure, it compiles the following data:

- UK sales are influenced by the euro's value as it faces competition from German suppliers. It forecasts annual UK sales based on three possible scenarios:

Euro: sterling exchange rate	Revenue from UK business
1.65:1	£200m
1.60:1	£215m
1.55:1	£220m

- Revenues from sales made in Germany are expected to be £120m p.a.
- Expected cost of goods sold is £120m p.a. from UK materials purchases, and €200m from purchases in Germany.
- Estimated cash fixed operating expenses are £50m p.a.
- Variable operating expenses are estimated at 20 per cent of total sales value (including German sales translated into sterling).
- Palmerston is financed entirely by equity and shareholders require a return of 15 per cent p.a.

Required
(i) Construct a forecast cash flow statement for Palmerston under each scenario.
(ii) Value Palmerston's equity under each scenario, assuming a ten-year operating time horizon. Ignore terminal values.
(iii) Suggest how Palmerston might restructure its operations to lower its sensitivity to exchange rate movements.

Ignore taxation.

7 A professional accountancy institute in the UK is evaluating an investment project overseas in Eastasia, a politically stable country. The project involves the establishment of a training school to offer courses on international accounting and management topics. It will cost an initial 2.5 million Eastasian dollars (EA$) and it is expected to earn post-tax cash flows as follows:

Year	1	2	3	4
Cashflow (EA$000)	750	950	1,250	1,350

The following information is available:

- The expected inflation rate in Eastasia is 3 per cent a year.
- Real interest rates in the two countries are the same. They are expected to remain the same for the period of the project.
- The current spot rate is EA$2 per £1 sterling.
- The risk-free rate of interest in Eastasia is 7 per cent and in the UK 9 per cent.
- The company requires a sterling return from this project of 16 per cent.

(CIMA)

Required
Calculate the sterling net present value of the project using *both* the following methods:

(i) by discounting annual cash flows in sterling,
(ii) by discounting annual cash flows in Eastasian $.

Practical assignment

Inspect the Annual Report for a company of your choice, to examine how its international profile of activities has changed over the years. You may find difficulty in obtaining a full set of accounts reaching very far back in time, but examination of a sample should give you a flavour of the company's policy regarding internationalisation.

Look also at the chairman's statements to glean an indication of the importance attached to overseas operations in the company's strategy.

Key issues in modern finance: a review

Voices of finance: fund manager at asset management firm

What I do: pension funds entrust us money to invest in the stock market, hoping that my team can achieve better returns than the market. We are so-called value investors, with a 'horizon' of about three to five years. After a lot of homework we buy shares in companies we hope to sell half a decade later for a good profit. We are like marathon runners, where traders are more like sprinters – they close their positions [sell all their stocks] at the end of each day.

Ultimately what you are after as a fund manager is what we call the underlying reality, the fundamentals of a particular company. What kind of returns can a company make? What kind of investment and growth opportunities are there? To what extent is management willing and able to take advantage of these opportunities? These key drivers determine the company's value. We then build a model that we can feed new developments into, to keep our assessment of the company's value and prospects up-to-date.

Finally we have to follow the psychology of the markets, because not everyone invests like we do, with a five-year perspective. There's a lot of herd behaviour. Successful investors are contrarians, they go where others are not.

Source: The Joris Luyendijk Banking Blog, *The Guardian*, 27 November 2011.

23.1 INTRODUCTION

This final chapter summarises the main principles of finance underpinning the book and it also provides the opportunity to extend the discussion to review key ideas relating to behavioural finance. This extension of the discussion is important as it reminds us that finance is not merely a technical subject. In finance it is commonly assumed that we are rational beings seeking to maximise wealth. However, this is not always the case and behavioural finance sets out to understand how our behaviour affects financial decision-making. Behavioural finance contends that individuals do not always act rationally. This is not to suggest that we act randomly, rather that there are observable patterns to individuals' behaviours arising from psychological biases. Behavioural finance has gained more followers in recent years and one reason for this is the 2007–8 financial crisis. The crisis caused many to observe that certain behaviours had played a role in the crisis. The topic of behavioural finance is considered later in this chapter.

A good finance theory is one that offers useful explanations of existing behaviour and provides a guide to future behaviour. We frequently find that rather restrictive assumptions are made in developing financial models. For example:

1 All markets – not just capital markets – are perfectly competitive.
2 Information is perfect and costless.
3 Transaction costs are zero.
4 No taxes exist.

These assumptions lead naturally to certain propositions that can be questioned. First, only shareholders really matter. A perfect labour market implies that managers and workers have sufficient mobility and can always find other equally attractive alternative employment. Second, shareholders are only interested in maximising the market value of their shareholdings. Given perfect, costless information, managers are tightly controlled by the shareholders to implement and pursue value-maximising strategies. Third, the pursuit of shareholder wealth is achieved by instructing managers to invest only in those projects that are worth more than they cost. Financing strategies, whether concerning dividends, capital structure or leasing, are largely irrelevant as they do little to increase shareholders' wealth.

The assumptions underlying the theory of finance appear to be at odds with reality. Information is imperfect; transaction costs and information costs may be sizeable. Markets are frequently highly imperfect; management will usually have a good deal of interest in the firm – an interest that may well conflict with that of shareholders. Managers have far from complete knowledge of the set of feasible financing strategies available, their cash flow patterns and impact on market values. Shareholders are even less well informed. Taxation policy, bankruptcy costs and other factors can have a major influence on financial strategies.

Whether we talk about markets, firms or managers, we are essentially looking at behaviour – the behaviour of individual managers, investors or groups.

Most readers will be familiar with the popular board game Monopoly. There is more than a passing resemblance between this game and corporate finance. Both are about maximising investors' wealth in risky environments, making investment decisions with uncertain payoffs, raising finance and managing cash flow. Players and managers must stick to the rules of governance and seek to devise appropriate investment, financing and trading strategies to gain competitive advantage. While rational analysis and sound judgement are essential, there remains room for sentiment, psychology, fun, and, to make the game interesting, a generous portion of luck!

Some aspects of finance, particularly routine finance decisions, can be operationalised through clear rules and procedures. But good finance managers look for something more than rules and procedures. They seek to understand the behaviour of markets and companies. Theories of finance seek to provide explanations for such behaviour – the better the theory, the better we understand how to make financing and investment decisions and set appropriate policies. Throughout this text we have sought to combine the 'why' with the 'how' in the theory and practice of corporate finance. This final chapter reminds the reader of the main pillars on which much of finance theory rests, many of which have been recognised as significant economic developments through the award of the Nobel Prize in Economic Sciences, and reflects on their practical relevance.

More respect for behavioural studies

The growing field of behavioural finance is attempting to explore the bounds of rationality in decision-making, working out whether our irrationality is systematic (it is) and whether a better understanding of it can improve investments (the jury's still out). Even more important for asset managers, it looks at how individuals value outcomes – not symmetrically. Losing something hurts more than gaining something of the notional equivalent value pleases us.

At the moment, behavioural finance as a discipline is still very largely based on the experiments done in controlled conditions, usually on college students. Critics like to point out that this is a far cry from financial markets, where billions of decisions are made, mostly by professionals, in distinctly uncontrolled conditions. But since the pure mathematical approach appears to have let down its proponents badly, whether because of a fundamental wrongness or because it was incorrectly applied, perhaps the behaviouralists should be allowed more respect (and possibly more funding for their research).

This is important, because in spite of the Nobel Memorial prize for Economics awarded in 2002 to Daniel Kahneman (a psychologist), behavioural finance is still not sufficiently developed for it to be properly integrated with market theory. It is true the turbulence of the past couple of years can be used to learn more about the risks of financial markets. It is even likely that complex mathematical models will have useful insights to offer chief risk officers, responsible for making sure asset management companies know what risks they are taking. But unless they somehow incorporate the discoveries of behavioural finance, they will be no better at understanding either how markets are likely to behave or how investors are likely to react to them.

 Source: Sophia Grene, *Financial Times*, 3 January 2010. © Financial Times

23.2 UNDERSTANDING INDIVIDUAL BEHAVIOUR

To understand how organisations function we must first understand individual behaviour. There are many models of human behaviour (e.g. sociological, psychological and political); we shall restrict our examination to two models of most relevance to finance.

The first is the traditional economic model of human behaviour. Here the manager is seen as a short-run wealth maximiser. The model is a useful starting point in studying finance because it offers a simple approach to model building, using only the pursuit of wealth as a goal. Much of the argument underlying the theories discussed in this book is based on this model. But we all know that this is a poor explanation of many aspects of human behaviour. For many people, and in many situations, money may not come before morality, honesty, love, altruism or having fun. As the song said, 'Money can't buy me love'.

This leads us to develop a more realistic model of human behaviour which Jensen and Meckling (1994) term the resourceful, evaluative, maximising model (or REMM). This model assumes that people are resourceful, self-interested maximisers, but rejects the notion that they are only interested in making money. They also care about respect, power, quality of life, love and the welfare of others. Individuals respond creatively to opportunities presented, seeking out opportunities, evaluating their likely outcomes, and working to loosen constraints on their actions.

Neither of the above models place much emphasis on psychological factors in human information-processing and decision-making. This growing area of finance, termed behavioural finance, is discussed in Section 23.5.

To sum up the foregoing discussion, money is not the only, or even the most important, thing in life. But when all else is equal, we act in a rational economic manner, choosing the course of action that **most** benefits us financially. Two fundamental concepts naturally follow.

Managers should only consider present and future costs and benefits in making decisions

This is the principle of incrementalism – only the additional costs or benefits resulting from a choice of action should be considered. For example, expenditures already incurred are not relevant to the decision in hand; they are **sunk costs**.

Choices often involve trade-offs, denying the possibility of other alternatives. The **opportunity cost** of making one decision is the difference between that choice and the next best alternative.

Managers are risk-averse

Most managers are risk-averse; given two investments offering the same return, they would choose the one with least risk. Unlike the risk-seeker or gambler, most managers try to avoid unnecessary risks. Risk aversion is a measure of a manager's willingness to pay to reduce exposure to risk. This could be in the form of insurance or other 'hedging' devices. Alternatively, it could be by preferring a lower-return investment because it also has a lower risk.

In business, risk and the expected return are usually related. Rational managers do not look for more risk unless the likely benefits are commensurately greater. This is the principle of **risk aversion**. One way in which investors can reduce risk is by spreading their capital across a range (portfolio) of investments. This is the principle of **diversification**, or not putting all your eggs in one basket. However, the key to risk management should not simply be to reduce it, but to take decisions in a risky business environment that also create value.

23.3 UNDERSTANDING CORPORATE BEHAVIOUR

■ Managers are agents for shareholders

A firm may be viewed as a collection of individuals and resources. More precisely, it is a set of contracts that bind individuals together, each with their own interests and goals. Agency theory explores the relationship between the shareholders (the principals) and the agents (e.g. board of directors) responsible for taking actions on their behalf.

Shareholders want managers to maximise firm value. It follows that to understand how firms behave, and whether managers pursue this goal, we must first understand the nature of the contracts, monitoring procedures and reward mechanisms employed.

Information is not available to all parties in equal measure. For example, the board of directors will know more about the future prospects of the business than the shareholders, who have to rely heavily on published information. This information asymmetry means that investors not only listen to the board's rhetoric and confident projections, but also examine the **information content** in its corporate actions. This **signalling effect** is most commonly seen in the reaction to dividend declarations and share dealings by the board. An increase in dividends signals that the company is expected to be able to sustain the level of cash distribution in the future, because it is usually regarded as the height of financial incompetence to be forced to cut a dividend.

information content
The extra, unstated intelligence that investors deduce from the formal announcement by a firm of any financial news, i.e. what people read 'between the lines', or 'financial body language'

■ Apply the NPV rule

A company will have perhaps thousands of shareholders, all with different levels of wealth and different risk attitudes. How can a firm make decisions that satisfy all of them? **The NPV rule states that decisions should be taken which maximise wealth and this can be achieved by accepting all positive net present value projects.** A firm's value is largely determined by two things: the cash generated over the life of the company and the risk of those cash flows. **Shareholder value analysis** advocates that firms should seek to maximise cash flows and manage risks. They should invest in those areas in which their firms have some competitive advantage, giving rise to superior return or positive net present value when discounted at the rate commensurate with the perceived level of risk. This rate reflects the return on risk-free investments plus a risk premium to compensate for the additional risk in the company's cash flow stream.

When properly applied, the NPV approach is the best method for evaluating forms of investment, where cash flows are fairly predictable and there are few investment options. However, two points are worth mentioning:

1 In long-run equilibrium all projects have a zero NPV. In other words, it may be possible for a firm to achieve positive NPVs because they are the first to spot a market opportunity, or have built entry barriers, but, ultimately, these will be overcome and competitors will continue to enter the market until the benefits no longer exist.

2 The DCF approach is most useful when evaluating bonds and financial leases, where cash flows are highly predictable. They become less relevant as risk and growth opportunities increase. Table 23.1 illustrates this.

Table 23.1 Usefulness of DCF methods

Usefulness of DCF methods	Financial investment	Capital investment projects
Very	Bonds and fixed-income securities	Financial leases
Moderate	Shares paying regular dividends	1 Replacement decisions 2 Businesses where there are no strategic options ('Cash Cows')
Limited	Shares where there are significant growth opportunities	Business with significant growth opportunities
Very low	Derivatives, e.g. share options	Pure research and development expenditure

■ Options have value

The DCF framework has come under increasing criticism in recent years for failing to consider the options embedded in investment opportunities. **An option allows an investor to buy or sell an asset at a fixed price during a given period.** A firm should only exercise its option if it adds value to the business. Unlike the conventional NPV approach, however, the more volatile the option, the more valuable it is, because the 'good news' is taken up. With capital projects, selecting projects offering the highest NPV at a specific point in time, conventional investment appraisal ignores the possibility that projects may have valuable options (called real options). Such options include greater flexibility for management in terms of growth, delay or abandonment options. The traditional approach of selecting the project with the highest NPV at a particular point in time disadvantages those projects offering greater flexibility to management and the benefits of possible add-on investments in the future. The price paid for an acquired company may look too high based on conventional NPV calculations. But this ignores any valuable strategic options embedded in the decision which may well justify the price paid. As a minimum, management should look to identify and evaluate subjectively any options linked to projects, particularly when projects with known options cannot be financially justified on conventional NPV grounds.

The increasing importance of options means that investors need to understand how they are valued. Black and Scholes (1973) first developed a formula for option pricing. In summary, it argues that **option value is based on the current market value of the underlying share, the strike price, the time to contract maturity, and the risk-free rate of interest**.

Options and other derivative instruments offer considerable scope for corporate treasurers in managing risk, such as foreign exchange and interest rate risk, by developing appropriate hedging strategies.

■ Look for an optimal capital structure and dividend policy

Managers need to know the cost of capital, or cut-off rate, for capital projects. Traditionally it was argued that the cost of capital depended, in part at least, on the mix of equity and debt in the company. The Modigliani–Miller propositions offer an elegant theory demonstrating that how the firm finances its investment schedule is irrelevant. The cost of capital for determining the cut-off rate for capital projects depended only on the risk class of the projects. In other words, financing decisions do not increase a firm's overall value. Value is therefore independent of capital structure.

For any company operating below the capital structure deemed 'appropriate', the private equity industry, with huge amounts of capital at its disposal, is ready to take over the business, introduce far higher gearing levels and return cash to shareholders. This is well illustrated by the car manufacturer Volvo. The company is known as a well-managed company maintaining prudent cash balances and relatively low gearing levels. In 2006, a venture capitalist, who had built up a 5 per cent stake in Volvo, began pressing the company to return to shareholders part of its sizeable cash balance of over £1 billion. The Volvo board responded by setting higher targets for profits, cash flow and gearing, the latter being an increase in the debt-to-equity ratio from 30 per cent to 40 per cent, and it stated that it would look favourably on opportunities to return cash to investors while also looking for suitable acquisitions.

Although the underlying assumptions are far removed from the world of everyday finance, even in practice, it is generally agreed that, in a no-tax world, issuing low-cost debt does not automatically reduce the overall cost of capital because the cost of equity will rise to compensate for the increased financial risk. However, in practice, we see that higher borrowing levels is a powerful incentive for managers to work harder and smarter, and offers tax advantages for firms through the tax relief on interest payments. On the other hand, excessive levels of debt threaten the firm's very existence and could lead to costly financial distress.

Related to the above is the need to identify the **optimal working capital** to be employed in the firm. This involves striking the right balance between minimising the cash conversion cycle and maintaining good supplier/customer relations. Many of the improvements in working capital management come through supply chain efficiencies and sound management of cash and accounts receivables/payables.

Much the same argument as for capital structure was made by Modigliani and Miller for the **irrelevance of dividends.** Under given assumptions, dividend policy does nothing to improve the value of the firm.

In a perfect capital market, rational investors are indifferent between a cash dividend and retention, once the impact of the investment decision is stripped out. If there is an increase in value when a firm retains, it is because investors expect the project to be wealth-creating. If a dividend increase raises value in such a market, it must be because investors have an extremely powerful desire for dividends rather than capital gains (i.e. an overwhelming preference for current dividends).

BP's $25bn annual profit sees confidence and dividends soar

BP has declared itself 'back on the right path' following the difficulties of the Gulf of Mexico oil spill with annual profits bouncing back from a $3.7bn (£2.3bn) loss to a $25.7bn profit. A 14% increase in the dividend to eight cents per share for the final three months of 2011 was a clear signal of management confidence although net debt still lies at almost $30bn.

'BP is on the right path,' said Bob Dudley, the chief executive who took over from Tony Hayward following the Deepwater Horizon accident. '2012 will be a year of increasing investment and milestones as we build on the foundations laid last year. As we move through 2013 and 2014, we expect financial momentum will build as we complete payments into the Gulf of Mexico Trust Fund, restore high-value production and bring new projects on stream,' he added.

The dividend hike was the first since the company resumed payouts last year and had been eagerly anticipated by the City.

Source: Based on Terry Macalister, *The Guardian*, 7 February 2012.

In imperfect markets, different conclusions apply. For example, dividends are said to be tax-disadvantaged compared to retention-plus-capital gains, as taxes on gains are delayed, and are often levied at a lower rate than the rate most investors face on their dividend income. Moreover, **dividends have a powerful signalling effect**. In a world where managers possess more information than investors, a dividend increase conveys the information that directors are confident about the future, while a dividend cut signals pessimism about the future. However, one should not exaggerate the signalling effect. When dividend changes are made, they are usually well-telegraphed – the market is usually aware that the firm is struggling and that a dividend cut is both sensible and likely. When the crunch comes, it is usually confirmation of what people generally expect. Indeed, failure to cut a dividend is often taken more seriously than a dividend cut in such circumstances. Converse arguments apply to the case of a dividend increase. This explains the positive reaction to BP's dividend increase and its signal of management confidence, as illustrated in the cameo. It is unexpected changes that have the most impact on price.

So, as dividend cuts are to be avoided, and most shareholders like dividends, for most firms, the sensible policy is to follow a 'progressive' dividend policy, steadily increasing payment, but only if supported by earnings increases that are regarded as sustainable. 'Declare a policy and stick to it' seems to be the message in order to attract and retain a clientèle of shareholders who find the policy in question suits their needs. However, as ever, there are exceptions. Firms with turbulent operating environments will be forgiven if dividend payouts fluctuate, while firms with highly stable environments, e.g. water and tobacco, had better tell a good story if they retain a high proportion of their earnings. Effective and clear communication, as in most walks of life, is essential.

■ Hedging adds value

Derivative instruments – like options, forward and futures contracts and swaps – can be used for speculation or for hedging. The main difference is that speculation is effectively a bet on a price move over time, whereas **hedging is used in combination with the underlying security; any gain or loss in the cash position is offset by an equivalent loss or gain in the derivatives position**.

At first sight it may seem questionable whether hedging is an appropriate tool for increasing the value of the firm. After all, if investors can eliminate all specific risk by holding a well-diversified investment portfolio, does incurring costs to hedge financial risks do anything for the shareholder? It seems that it does in the following ways:

1 Hedging reduces the probability of corporate failure. The greater security thereby extended to managers, suppliers and employees enables them to take a longer-term view in their decision-making. This is consistent with a net present value approach.
2 Hedging reduces the probability of financial distress which, in turn, reduces the firm's cost of capital.
3 Investors prefer a steady stream of corporate cash flows above the more volatile pattern likely without managing risk exposure.
4 Management may be reluctant to disclose to investors the full picture on risk exposure, making it difficult for investors to make an accurate assessment of the risk on their portfolios.

23.4 UNDERSTANDING HOW MARKETS BEHAVE

To make sound financial decisions consistently, managers need to have some understanding of how financial markets operate and behave. This involves understanding the time-value of money, how risk affects value, and the efficiency of markets.

■ Money has a time-value

To make sound financial decisions consistently, we need to understand how financial markets deal with the transfer of wealth between individuals or firms. This may take the form of investors lending money to borrowers in exchange for future interest and capital repayment, or purchasing a share of a company and participating in its future profits. This inevitably involves the transfer of wealth from one time period to another, based on the **time-value of money**. Put simply, we cannot add current and future money together in a meaningful way without first converting it into a common currency. This currency can be expressed in future value terms, but far more relevant to decisions being considered today is to express all future cash flows in **present value** terms. The value of money changes with time because it has an alternative use (opportunity cost): it can be invested in financial markets or elsewhere to earn a rate of return.

The present value of a cash flow is the amount of money today that is equivalent to the given future amount after considering the rate of return that can be earned. The higher the discount rate and the further the cash flow is from today, the lower its present value. In well-functioning financial markets, all assets of equivalent risk offer the same expected return. An asset's positive net present value implies that, after considering the time-value of money, its benefits outweigh the costs. This important concept allows investors and corporate managers alike – regardless of their attitudes to risk – to advocate a simple decision rule: accept investment opportunities that maximise net present value.

■ Non-diversifiable risk matters

In 1952, Harry Markowitz published a paper that provided a more accurate definition of risk and return for shares. The expected return on an investment is the weighted average of the returns of its possible outcomes, while the risk is the variance of those outcomes around the mean. These days we simply talk of the share's expected return and its variance (squared deviations around the expected mean). The significance of this is that risk is no longer seen as purely 'downside' risk, but also includes the likelihood of exceeding the expected value.

From this, Markowitz was able to calculate the risk and return for a portfolio which, in turn, could be used to select efficient portfolios which offered the best combinations of risk and return for investors. **Portfolio risk** is the weighted sum of the variance plus twice the weighted sum of the covariance. The implication of such a model is that investors should focus on portfolio risk rather than the risk of the individual shares within that portfolio. This diversification effect is not simply a matter of how many different shares are included in the portfolio, but the covariance between such shares.

While the mean–variance model offered insights into portfolio risk and return, it was less successful in practice in portfolio selection. However, it formed the basis for William Sharpe to develop his **Capital Asset Pricing Model (CAPM)**. Risk can be categorised into that which can diversify away and that which remains (non-diversifiable or market risk). The theory argues that investors should only really be concerned about the latter type of risk and the required return on an asset is commensurate to the amount of non-diversifiable risk. Sharpe's argument went as follows. Suppose every investor holds portfolios that are mean–variance efficient, and that they all have the same risk–return expectation. In such a world, all investors will hold the same portfolio of risky assets, termed the **market portfolio**. However, these investors may have very different risk attitudes – some may be more risk-averse than others.

Different risk profiles can be accommodated by holding different combinations of riskless investments (such as Treasury Bonds) and the market portfolio. It is even possible to further leverage risk and return by borrowing riskless assets and investing in the market portfolio. The investment strategy of investing in the market portfolio is followed by many institutions who invest in index (or tracker) funds employing passive investment strategies.

The attraction of the CAPM lies in its simplicity; the relationship between market (non-diversifiable) risk and the expected return on risky assets is reflected in the **security market line**, which is linear. The only risk that really matters is that which cannot be diversified away. The risk inherent in the market (the sensitivity of each share's returns to the market portfolio) is the only thing that changes with each investment. The expected return, ER_i, is a function of the risk-free rate of interest, R_f, and the risk premium on the market portfolio, $[ER_m - R_f]$, adjusted by the investment's Beta value, β_i.

$$ER_i = R_f + [ER_m - R_f] \times \beta_i$$

Everyone recognises that many of the assumptions behind the CAPM are far removed from the real world. But the issue is whether it is useful as a predictive model. Forty years of empirical observation suggests that while the model is fairly robust, it does not tell the whole story. Academics and practitioners may dispute just how deficient the model is, but most agree that it fails to capture the full effects of differences in:

■ *Size* – why do smaller firms seem to offer higher returns than large firms after adjusting for risk?
■ *Market-to-book ratio* – why do firms with high market-to-book ratios tend to exhibit higher returns than others?

Various models have been suggested that move away from a single factor pricing model (for example, Arbitrage Pricing Theory) but these too have their own problems.

From looking at financial markets over a lengthy period of time we observe that there is a reward for bearing risk and that the greater the potential reward, the greater is the risk.

■ Capital markets are efficient

Many of the theories in finance assume that capital markets are reasonably efficient in reflecting all available information. An efficient market is one where there are large numbers of rational profit-maximisers actively competing, with each trying to predict future market values of individual securities, and where important current information is almost freely available to all participants. The efficient markets hypothesis (EMH) argues that in such markets, new information on the intrinsic value of shares will be reflected instantaneously in actual prices.

The exact form of market efficiency in financial markets, in developed and developing countries, has been the subject of much debate and research. For major European stock markets, however, the consensus is that they exhibit efficiency in both the weak form (i.e. share prices contain all past data and superior returns cannot consistently be achieved from trading rules based on past stock market data) and the semi-strong form (i.e. share prices contain all publicly-available information, and superior returns cannot consistently be achieved from trading rules based on such information).

Prize-winning work on asset prices goes to heart of financial crisis debate

The Nobel Prize for Economics has been awarded to a trio of American academics for their work on what drives asset prices, a question that goes to the heart of the macroeconomic debate over the crisis. Eugene Fama, Lars Peter Hansen and Robert Shiller have all spent their careers analysing how the value of assets, such as stocks and bonds, vary over time. However, mirroring the broad disagreements that typically characterise the economics profession, the three scholars have come to radically different conclusions.

Prof Fama is one of the fathers of the so-called 'efficient market hypothesis'. This theory, which underlies his seminal 1965 paper 'Random Walks in Stock Market Prices', formulates that markets are 'informationally efficient', as investors immediately incorporate any new available information in the price of an asset.

In contrast Prof Shiller, from Yale University, believes that any explanation of investors' behaviour cannot be fully based on rationality and must acknowledge the role played by psychology. In the 1980s, he showed that stock prices tended to fluctuate more than corporate dividends. This should not happen if investors were fully rational, since stock prices forecast future dividends. In the 2000s, Prof Shiller applied his insights on investors' 'irrational exuberance' to the US housing market, which he believed was overvalued. Prof Hansen, a co-founder of the Becker Friedman Institute also at the University of Chicago, designed methods to explore the drivers of stock market volatility. His statistical brainchild, the 'Generalized Method of Moments', confirmed Prof Shiller's finding that swings in asset prices could not be explained via standard models based on rationality. Subsequent work has shown that at least some of this volatility can be explained by investors' different attitude towards risk.

At different stages over the past decade, the three academics have all individually been considered as possible favourites for the $1.23m prize. However, yesterday the economics community buzzed with astonishment at the joint award.

Source: Based on Ferdinando Giugliano and John Aglionby, *Financial Times*, 2 October 2013, p. 2.

Is it true that stock prices are essentially random walks? While the study of past stock prices may well produce interesting patterns, if they arise randomly they cannot, by definition, have predictive power when it comes to share prices or returns. This implies that, based on available information, there is no simple rule to generate above-average returns.

However, empirical studies suggest that share price movements are not truly random and the EMH moved its position to one where no gain can be made after allowance for transaction costs in buying/selling and changes in risk over time. The undeniable economic logic of the EMH is that if anyone finds a trading rule that consistently 'beats the market' by giving above-normal returns after all costs, it will quickly be imitated by others until the benefits from such a rule evaporate.

This does not mean that the market share price is perfectly 'correct' at any point in time. It does, however, imply that the market share price is an unbiased estimate of the true value of the share. While actual market prices may fluctuate in a random fashion around the 'true' value, investors cannot consistently outperform the market.

■ Criticisms of the EMH

Michael Jensen, a leading financial economist, argued in 1978 that 'the efficient markets hypothesis is the best-established fact in all of social science'. Why then is the EMH debate still hotly disputed? The main issue is whether investors react correctly to new information or whether they make systematic errors by over- or underreacting. The **overreaction hypothesis** argues that share prices tend to overshoot the true value due to excessive optimism or pessimism by investors in their initial reactions to new information. There is some evidence for this in UK financial markets (Dissanaike, 1997).

Much criticism of the EMH is misplaced because it is based on a misconception of what the hypothesis actually says. For example, it does not mean that financial expertise is of no value in stock markets and that a share portfolio might as well be selected by sticking a pin in the financial pages. This is clearly not the case. It does suggest, however, that in an efficient market, after adjusting for portfolio risk, fund managers will not, on average, achieve returns higher than that of a randomly-selected portfolio. Roll (see Ross *et al.*, 2002) makes the point that all publicly-available information need not be reflected in share prices. Instead, the link 'between unreflected information and prices is too subtle and tenuous to be easily or costlessly detected'.

Inefficient markets

It's a tricky one for the efficient market theory. Last Wednesday, the *Wall Street Journal* reported that BlackBerry was cutting 40 per cent of its staff. The company couldn't even manage a denial. This looked like final confirmation of the Canadian company's demise. Yet news of the layoffs did not move the shares. Perhaps, at $10.25, the stock was already trading on the assumption that BlackBerry would be sold for scrap. But then the group said on Friday it would report a terrible second quarter, with revenue falling by half from the first. The shares then tumbled by a fifth – stopped only by a conditional $9 buyout offer yesterday. Had Friday's sellers thought everybody was getting fired because things were going *well*?

How many hints did these misbegotten souls need?

The best explanation of the bizarre trading may be the same one that behavioural economists use to explain the allure of lottery tickets. Small probabilities of big gains do strange things to people's risk appetites. If the chance of a gain moves from, say, 51 per cent to 52 per cent, most people will pay just a bit more to invest. But if you move the probability from 0–1 per cent, some investors (or punters, if you prefer) will stump up big. This is the 'possibility effect' and it is ugly when it goes into reverse. Those who held on to BlackBerry until Friday were emotionally attached to the big gain they could make if BlackBerry fixed things. This sort of hope cannot be extinguished by strong evidence – only ironclad proof. The lesson is to be careful about buying a beat-up stock because 'the worst is priced in'. You may be co-investing with dangerous optimists.

Source: Based on Lex Column, *Financial Times*, 24 September 2013, p. 12.

Market efficiency also suggests that share prices are 'fair' in the sense that they reflect the value of that stock given the available information. So shareholders need not be unduly concerned with whether they are paying too much for a particular share.

The fact that many investors have done very well through investing on the stock market should not surprise us. For much of the last century, the market generated positive returns. Most investment advice, if followed over a long period of time, is likely to have done well; the point is that, in efficient markets, investors cannot consistently achieve above-average returns except by chance.

■ A few apparent anomalies in the EMH

There appear to be three main anomalies in the EMH: the effects of size and timing, and the periodic emergence of 'bubbles'.

Size effects

Market efficiency seems to be less in evidence among smaller firms. Shares of smaller companies tend to yield higher average returns than those of larger companies of comparable risk. Dimson and Marsh (1986) found that in the UK, on average, smaller firms outperformed larger firms by around 6 per cent per annum. Some of the difference can be accounted for by the higher risk and trading costs involved in dealing with smaller companies. Another explanation is institutional neglect. Financial institutions dominating the stock market often neglect small firms offering what appear to be high returns because the maximum investment is relatively small (if they are not to exceed their normal 5 per cent maximum stake). The costs of monitoring and trading may not warrant the sums involved.

Timing effects

In the longer term, disparities in share returns seem to correct themselves. A share performing poorly in one year is likely to do well the following year. Seasonal effects have also been observed. At the other extreme, it has been observed that share performance is related to the day of the week or time of the day. Prices tend to rise during the last 15 minutes of the day's trading, but the first hour of Monday trading is generally characterised by heavy selling. Investors may evaluate their portfolios over the weekend and decide what to sell first thing on Monday, but are more cautious in their buying decisions, preferring to take their broker's advice.

Stock market surges and bubbles

An investor holding a wide portfolio of shares (e.g. the FTA All-Share Index) for, say, 25 years, would have been rewarded handsomely. But the capital growth was not a steady monthly appreciation; the bulk of it came in just a fraction of the investment period through stock market surges. In an efficient market, few – if any – are clever enough to be able to predict short-term stock market surges.

The famous South Sea Bubble of 1722 was one of the early speculative stock market 'bubbles' where investors adopt the 'herd' instinct and drive up prices well above any rational valuation based on economic fundamentals. The economist J.M. Keynes described this in terms of a 'beauty contest' where investors are not following their own judgements but trying to guess how other investors are going to behave. The Internet Bubble of 1999 and the House Price Bubble of the 2000s show that speculative bubbles are still with us and the cost of following the trend can be considerable.

A physicist argues that time is the only constant

The world of money is a frustratingly unpredictable place. So when some economists decided in the middle of the last century that they could apply mathematics and physics to explain the movement of markets, it seemed like a thrilling development. Today, we need few reminders that their optimism was misplaced. But could it be that the effort to apply scientific laws to economics was itself wrong? Indeed, could it be foolhardy to think that universal, timeless laws of *any* type exist, be that in physics or elsewhere? These are some of the questions raised by Lee Smolin, an American theoretical physicist and writer, in his book *Time Reborn*.

Smolin argues that it is a mistake to view scientific laws as universal. The lay reader may find it difficult to work out exactly why Smolin feels so confident in making such claims. Nevertheless, the implication is clear: if he is correct, we need to drop our assumption that we will ever find a single formula that explains what makes the universe 'tick'.

And, as Smolin takes the opportunity to point out late in *Time Reborn*, this has serious implications for economics. For if there are no timeless truths, then the premise of orthodox economics – or, at least, the efficient market hypothesis – is also wrong. Economies do not have a 'natural balance'; nor do they operate according to timeless 'rules'. Rather, they too are 'path-dependent', in the sense that humans always react to each other and to what has happened before.

Continued

This assertion will come as no surprise to behavioural economists, who have been vociferous in their criticism of classical economics since the 2007 crisis; nor will it shock many Western policymakers, who often argue that it is wrong to presume that there is any single 'rule' to how economies should work. But to hear a physicist attacking the concept of timeless truth is nevertheless unnerving. For that reason alone, this book deserves to be debated widely; indeed, given the West's current predicament, the discussion it provokes is – dare I say it – timely.

Source: Based on Gillian Tett, *Financial Times*, 25 May 2013, p. 9.

Self-assessment activity 23.1

If the stock market is efficient, can no one beat the market average return?

(Answer in Appendix A at the back of the book)

■ A modern perspective – Chaos Theory

The EMH is based on the assertion that rational investors rapidly absorb new information about a company's prospects, which is then impounded into the share price. Any other price variations are attributable to random 'noise'. This implies that the market has no memory – it simply reacts to the advent of each new information snippet, registers it accordingly and settles back into equilibrium; in other words, all price-sensitive events occur randomly and independently of each other.

The crash of 1987, possibly attributed to the market's realisation that shares were overvalued and triggered by the collapse of a relatively minor management buy-out deal, has provoked more detailed scrutiny of the pattern of past share prices. This has uncovered evidence that share price movements do not always conform to a 'random walk'. For example, significant downturns happen more frequently than significant upturns.

A new branch of mathematics, chaos theory, has been harnessed to help explain such features. Observations of natural systems such as weather patterns and river systems often give a chaotic appearance – they seem to lurch wildly from one extreme to another. However, chaos theorists suggest that apparently random, unpredictable patterns are governed by sets of complex sub-systems that react interdependently. These systems can be modelled, and their behaviour forecast, but predictions of the behaviour of chaotic systems are very sensitive to the precise conditions specified at the start of the estimation period. An apparently small error in the specification of the model can lead to major errors in the forecast.

Edgar Peters (1991) has suggested that stock markets are chaotic in this sense. Markets have memories, are prone to major price swings and do not behave entirely randomly. For example, in the UK, he found that today's price movement is affected by price changes that occurred several years previously. The most recent changes, however, have the biggest impact. In addition, he found that price moves were persistent, i.e. if previous moves in price were upwards, the subsequent price move was more likely to be up than down. Yet chaos theory also suggests that persistent uptrends are also more likely ultimately to result in major reversals!

Peters' work suggests that world stock markets exhibit patterns that are overlaid with substantial random noise. The more noise, the less efficient the market. In this respect, the US markets appear to be more efficient than those in the UK and Japan. Other observers suggest that markets are essentially rational and efficient, but succumb to chaos on occasions, with bursts of chaotic frenzy being attributed to speculative activity. This suggests some scope for informed insiders to outperform the market during such periods.

Wanted: new model for markets

Modern portfolio theory, developed over the past 50 years in academia – particularly at the University of Chicago and Massachusetts Institute of Technology – has all been based on the common premise that market prices at all times attempt rationally to incorporate all known information.

From this emerged the ideas that drove countless investment decisions: that the pattern of returns in financial markets follows the normal 'bell curve' distribution often observed in natural sciences, that risk can be defined by the extent to which securities prices vary around their mean, and that observing how they have moved in relation to each other in the past allows a precise and measurable trade-off between risk and return.

In spite of the weight that was put on the theory, it has long been known to have problems. First, market returns do not follow a 'bell curve'. Instead, extreme events happen far more often than a 'normal' distribution would imply. Benoit Mandelbrot, the mathematician who invented fractal geometry, proved this more than 40 years ago, when efficient markets theory was in its infancy, and has continued to criticise the established theory ever since.

If stocks really followed a bell curve, he observed, then a swing of more than 7 per cent in a day for the Dow Jones industrial average should happen once every 300,000 years. In fact there were 48 such days during the 20th century. 'Truly, a calamitous era that insists on flaunting all predictions. Or, perhaps, our assumptions are wrong,' he concluded.

Another obvious weakness in efficient markets is the assumption that investors always make their decisions rationally. Virtually everyone knows this is not true. Indeed, over the past two decades, a new discipline of behavioural economics had started to substitute findings from psychology for the assumption of rationality. But last year's events inflicted fresh damage in the critical area of asset allocation – how to divide up an investment portfolio among broad asset classes such as stocks, bonds and commodities.

According to modern portfolio theory, there is an 'efficient frontier' in which different assets can be mixed to maximise return for a given level of risk. This rests on the correlation among the assets – the extent to which they tend to move in line with each other – and their risk, which is defined as the amount they tend to vary or move away from their long-term average. This is common sense – add an asset to a portfolio that will move up when the others move down and you have made the overall portfolio less risky.

But this relies on these correlations being static. Investing using this formula – and borrowing money to do so – can be a recipe for disaster if the correlations change. And that is what happened last year. According to Jeremy Siegel of the University of Pennsylvania's Wharton School, whose book *Stocks for the Long Run* was influential in persuading asset allocators to put a big weighting towards equities, says: 'The most serious attack on efficient markets is the change in correlation of asset classes under extreme conditions.'

He points out that oil and equities traditionally move in opposite directions – higher oil prices would damage the stock market. Thus buying oil would provide a hedge against lower stock prices. But for the past two years oil and stocks have been closely correlated, meaning that adding oil to a stock portfolio in effect makes the same bet twice.

By the time the stock market hit bottom in March, even the price of gold – normally a 'safe haven' that rises when equities fall – was declining. This calls into question the notion of gains from diversification. As Mr Siegel says, it might be possible to adapt the theory to account for changing correlations in times of high stress – but this would not only be complex but a 'very different framework than what we teach in finance classes today'.

 Source: Based on John Authers, *Financial Times,* 29 September 2009.

Which view is right? Are stock markets efficient, chaotic or somewhere in between? Pending the results of further research, it seems that corporate financial managers cannot necessarily regard today's market price as a fair assessment of company value, but that the market may well correctly value a company over a period of years. Examination of long-term trends gives more insight than consideration of short-term oscillations. For example, if a company's share price persistently underperforms the market, then perhaps its profitability really is low, or its management poor, or it has failed to release the right amount of information.

To conclude, it seems that the efficient markets hypothesis does not hold, except perhaps in its very weakest form, in today's capital markets. Evolving from both the EMH and chaos theory is a possible successor termed the coherent market hypothesis

(CMH) based on a combination of fundamental factors and market sentiment or technical factors (see Vaga, 1990). The CMH argues that capital markets are, at any point in time, in one of the following states, depending on a combination of economic fundamentals and 'crowd behaviour' in the market:

- Random walks – market efficiency with neutral fundamentals
- Unstable transition – market inefficiency with neutral fundamentals
- Coherence – crowd behaviour with bullish fundamentals
- Chaos – crowd behaviour with bearish fundamentals.

We will have to wait to see how well it helps explain stock market behaviour.

Decoding the psychology of trading

Before you even started reading this article, it had already been electronically scanned and its language examined by dozens of computers at hedge funds and investment banks. At MarketPsy Capital in Santa Monica, California, remote servers will have rated how positive or negative it is on the economy and checked for emotional content on thousands of companies. From the tens of thousands of newspaper articles, blogs, corporate presentations and Twitter messages being analysed every day, MarketPsy builds a picture of investor feelings about 6,000 companies. When emotions are running high, the hedge fund steps in and trades. MarketPsy is tiny by hedge fund standards, but it is at the cutting edge of behavioural finance, the intellectual offspring of psychology and economics.

Like others focused on behaviour, MarketPsy has long since discarded the idea that investors are rational, and tries instead to judge exactly how irrational they are. When people are deeply gloomy about a stock, it is time to buy; when they are raving about its brilliance, sell.

Measuring investor sentiment is not new; Dow Jones publishes an economic sentiment index based on textual analysis of 15 US newspapers, while investment banks measure everything from ratios of derivatives to the number of times the word 'crisis' is used in the media. MarketPsy itself publishes a 'fear index'. But advanced linguistic analysis is starting to allow a handful of companies and funds to go further.

One thing behavioural finance academics did not have to discover was that the finance industry jumps on any new trend. So it should be no surprise that many fund managers have been rebranding their business as based on the discipline. 'It has been co-opted as a marketing gimmick,' Dr Peterson laments. That behaviour, at least, was entirely predictable.

 Source: James Mackintosh, *Financial Times*, 16 July 2010. © Financial Times

23.5 BEHAVIOURAL FINANCE

Behavioural finance is the study of how psychological and sociological factors influence financial decision-making and financial markets. Financial economics traditionally assumes that people behave rationally. We have focused in this book on market efficiency and predictive models based on rational economic choices. This assumes that people have the same preferences, perfect knowledge of all alternatives, and understand the consequences of their decisions. The reality is frequently somewhat different. Behavioural finance relaxes the tight assumptions of financial economics to incorporate models based on observable, systematic and human departures from rationality. Its adherents claim that it helps understand stock market anomalies, including stock market overreaction, underreaction, bubbles and irrational pessimism. Some of the most successful investors have long held the view that to understand the stock market you must first understand the psychology of investors. There are common objections to the psychological approach to understanding market behaviour. However, as Hirshleifer has pointed out, there are equivalent objections to the rational approach (see Table 23.2).

Table 23.2 Common criticisms of the psychological and rational approaches

Objection to Psychological Approach	Objection to Fully Rational Approach
Alleged psychological biases are arbitrary.	Rationality in finance theory requires impossible powers of calculation.
Experiments that generate alleged psychological biases are not meaningful.	The evidence we possess does not support rational behaviour.
It is too easy to go theory fishing for psychological biases to match data ex post.	It is too easy to go theory fishing for factor structures and market imperfections to match data ex post.
Rational traders should arbitrage away mispricing.	Irrational traders should arbitrage away efficient pricing.
Rational investors will make better decisions and get richer.	Irrational investors will bear more risk and get richer.
Confused investors will learn their way to good decisions.	Accurate investors will learn their way to bad decisions

Source: Hirshleifer (2001).

Behavioural finance has attracted the attention of significant numbers of people who work in finance, including the financial regulator in the UK (see the following cameo), and draws on the work of psychologists such as Kahneman and Tversky. Their considerations of how we make decisions when there is uncertainty led to the development of prospect theory (Kahneman and Tversky, 1979) which has been hugely influential. Kahneman and Tversky have further developed their initial version of prospect theory (Figure 23.1) but fundamentally it encompasses a number of important propositions including:

- *We frame losses and gains relative to a subjective reference point*
  This means that we are not so much concerned about absolute wealth, but about our relative wealth. For example, if I have bought a house for £150,000 then this is likely

Beware the irrational side of your inner self

On a visit to the London School of Economics in 2008, the Queen asked the assembled professors why nobody had seen the financial crisis coming. Her Majesty's question was a pertinent one. Part of the answer is that there's a big problem with conventional economic and financial theory. Many of the big ideas that underpin it – from Eugene Fama's efficient market hypothesis to Harry Markowitz's modern portfolio theory – are based on the assumption that, when it comes to investing, the human mind is rational.

The financial crisis, and the fact that it came as a complete surprise to the vast majority of investors, has blown a hole in the whole notion of rationality. No longer is it assumed that froth and bubbles will be smoothed out by 'smart money' that knows enough to sell an overvalued asset.

But a new science of behavioural finance is emerging, led not by economists but by psychologists who argue – with masses of evidence – that we are far from rational when we invest. In fact, our brains are a kind of apothecary chest comprising all sorts of hidden drawers and cupboards, each containing biases and prejudices of which we are barely aware. We make mental short cuts, known as heuristics, that assume as fact what is really no more than belief.

Continued

Our fallibility hasn't gone unnoticed. The UK's own financial regulator has taken note. Earlier this spring, the Financial Conduct Authority said it would look at how investor psychology affected decision making and issued a paper on behavioural finance. 'One of the most significant challenges for modern financial regulators and financial services alike is to recognise that we operate within a very human environment,' FCA chief executive Martin Wheatley said at the time. 'A fallible world – not just of ratios and complex models but also responses, sometimes flawed, that behavioural economics helps us understand.'

It's not just retail investors that are fallible. Professionals fall into the same traps. Some have pointed out that investment bankers systematically underestimated the odds of catastrophic loss. 'Investors at all levels have similar biases,' says Paul Craven, co-head of distribution for Europe at Goldman Sachs Asset Management and an expert on behavioural finance. 'The smartest investors are aware of their biases and take them into account.'

Source: Based on Norma Cohen, *Financial Times*, 1 June 2013, p. 8.

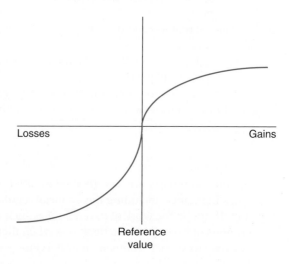

Figure 23.1 Prospect theory
Source: Kahneman and Tversky, 1979.

to become my reference point, and it is against this value that I measure any gains or losses. If I sell the house for more than £150,000 then I view this as a gain; if I sell the house for less than £150,000 then I view this as a loss. But note that my reference point may not remain static over time. If I hear that, on average, house prices have increased by 10 per cent in the period since I purchased the property, then I may shift my reference point and judge whether I have made a gain or loss relative to a reference value of £165,000. A parallel situation can occur in stock markets where I set the initial reference value according to the purchase price I paid for the shares; but I may shift the reference value in the future according to how the stock market has performed overall.

- *Twice the gain does not give twice the pleasure*
  Therefore, a gain of £200 does not give twice the pleasure of a gain of £100. This suggests that people become less willing to take risks as they make more gains.
- *Twice the loss does not give twice the pain*
  Therefore, a loss of £200 does not give twice the pain of a loss of £100. This suggests people become more willing to take risks as losses mount up.
- *But, we are loss-averse*
  Therefore, losing £100 hurts more than gaining £100. Losses and gains are felt asymmetrically.

Shefrin and Statman (1985) provide support for prospect theory in the context of stock markets by demonstrating that investors are inclined to sell 'winners' (i.e. shares that have gained value) too early, but hold on to 'losers' (i.e. shares that have lost value) for too long. Investors are unwilling to risk forfeiting gains and, hence, sell these shares early; but they hold on to losing shares in the hope the price may turn and rise. This is referred to as the 'disposition effect'.

Heuristics and biases

Researchers have found that when decisions have to be made that involve risk or uncertainty then we, unknowingly, use strategies to aid us in the decision-making process. These strategies help us to take mental short-cuts in processing information for decision-making and are termed 'heuristics'. The heuristic devices we use to assist us have patterns, and, therefore, they lead to systematic biases in our decision-making. Important heuristics identified include:

Anchoring

When asked to form a judgement about prices or values we are apt to do so by reference to prior information. For example, when Northcraft and Neale (1987) asked people to estimate the value of a house, they found that the estimates were significantly influenced by the asking price that was listed within the house details provided by the researchers to the study participants. The asking price became the anchor price for forming the estimate. A parallel situation in corporate finance might be if a board of directors is asked to place a valuation on an unlisted company prior to a takeover. In this situation the directors may be strongly influenced by the suggested price of the vendor, using this as the anchor for their estimate. Traditional budgeting is a further example of this phenomenon, where the current year's budget forms the basis for the next year's budget.

Hindsight bias

Once an event has occurred we find it difficult to recall what our initial prediction was prior to the event, and we often believe that we correctly predicted the eventual outcome. Therefore, our memories are not wholly reliable and we come to see the outcome that occurred as having been inevitable. In part, hindsight bias may be a process that helps us to 'impose' order upon the world. Hindsight bias can help explain why we come to view the stockmarket crash of 1987 or the global financial crisis of the late 2000s as events that were obviously going to occur. We believe that we really did see the signs of the crash or the crisis in advance of their happening. In an investment context, adjusting our view of the world in this way is potentially risky as it leads us to become overconfident about our abilities to spot good investment opportunities and we are less likely to learn from prior mistakes.

Sample size neglect

When we make decisions, we are disposed to draw conclusions based upon very limited evidence. This is the idea of a 'belief in the law of small numbers' (Tversky and Kahneman, 1971). This bias, which results in us arriving at unfounded conclusions, occurs in different parts of our lives. For example, Gilovich *et al.* (1985) have observed that we attribute 'hot hands' (when a player is on a real winning streak) to basketball players when, in fact, their prior performance in scoring baskets does not justify this. In the context of finance, this can be important as we may create stock market investment strategies based on an inadequate evidence base. For example, we act on the advice of an investment analyst we believe is on a 'winning streak', but if there is insufficient evidence to back this assumption then the advice may be flawed.

This idea is closely linked to the 'gambler's fallacy', whereby we are inclined to assume (incorrectly) that if the ball on the roulette wheel has just landed on red, then it is more likely it will land on black on the next spin of the wheel. But each spin of the wheel is an independent event and, therefore, it is as likely that the ball will land on red on the next spin.

Availability bias

Information which is more easy to recall causes us to be biased in our estimation of the likelihood of an event occurring. For example, we commonly overestimate the likelihood of a plane crash occurring and this is because when plane crashes do occur they are particularly dramatic and receive considerable publicity. Additionally, if the information is relatively recent, it has an even greater effect upon us. This can occur with investing, where it can be observed that investors overreact to bad news, causing the price of shares to fall to a greater extent than the bad news really justifies, and vice versa when the news is good (DeBondt and Thaler, 1985).

Overconfidence

We have a predisposition to overestimate our abilities. For example, it has been shown that the overwhelming majority of drivers are convinced that they are a better than average driver, and when individuals set up a new business they believe they have twice as much chance of making a success of the new venture as other individuals setting up a new business. This inclination to overconfidence is related to self-attribution bias whereby we attribute success to our own actions, whilst attributing failure to external factors beyond our control. Hence, if I am a trader, then when a trade goes well and I make substantial profits on the deal, it must be due to my great trading skills. However, when a trade makes a loss, it is due to the market turning in the wrong direction unexpectedly because of some unforeseen event such as a movement in interest rates or commodity prices. Heaton (2002) considers the problem of overconfidence in a corporate finance setting and discusses how overconfidence leads managers to believe that the marketplace undervalues the company's shares whilst the managers overvalue their own endeavours.

One reason that we are overconfident is that we attend more closely to evidence that will support our viewpoint, than evidence that challenges our viewpoint. This confirmation bias also implies that when we come across new information we misconstrue it so that our established viewpoint remains supported.

This propensity to be overconfident has also been noted in respect of illusions of control where we overestimate our ability to control and influence events. For example, traders have been observed to overestimate how much control they really have over events, and the relationship between illusion of control and performance has been found to be inverse (Fenton-O'Creevy *et al.*, 2003).

Behavioural finance raises some important issues.

1 Is it possible to exploit irrational behaviour when it arises? If any investor can identify that the market is acting irrationally, giving rise to a gap between market share price and underlying value, he or she has the potential to exploit this profitable opportunity.
2 How can investors avoid making irrational decisions, and so achieve returns superior to other investors?

We consider these as they relate to market efficiency and corporate managers.

▪ Mental accounting

In addition to using heuristics to make short-cuts in our decision-making, it has been suggested that our thinking is also influenced by what has been described as mental accounting. Ideas associated with mental accounting are particularly associated with the work of Richard Thaler. The basic idea is that the way we think is based upon having mental filing cabinets and this affects our decision-making. Consider an individual who is saving money to buy a second home and is earning interest at (say) 4 per cent, whilst, at the same time, this person is borrowing money to pay for a car purchase at an interest cost of (say) 11 per cent. Thaler, in his research, has observed that individuals in this position are unwilling to use their savings to pay off their borrowings even though they would be better off financially by doing so. The reason for this reluctance is that two mental accounts have been created. One account is for 'second home savings' and the other for 'car loan payments', and we will not merge the two accounts.

This idea of mental accounts has been developed in different ways. For example, Prelec and Loewenstein (1998) have found that a majority of people prefer to pay for a holiday in advance than in arrears, even though the concept of time-value of money tells us that it is better to pay later than earlier. The reasoning behind this seeming 'irrationality' is that we look to match costs to benefits within our mental accounts. If we pay for a holiday in arrears then the cost is incurred after we have received the benefit and we just don't like this. We are happy to incur the 'pain' of paying in advance for the holiday because we know we will then derive a *future* benefit. This kind of reasoning can also explain why, if we buy a pair of shoes that we subsequently find don't fit properly, we either continue to wear them even though they cause blisters, or refuse to throw them out. In the mental account for this shoe purchase, we have incurred the cost of buying the shoes and we also want to have a benefit to match the cost. Throwing the shoes out means we are closing the mental account with the cost unmatched by a benefit. It is only over time that we find it easier to close this mental account, and this is why it is less emotionally painful to get rid of the shoes after twelve months than after one month.

This idea of mental accounting can be applied to investing. If we place each of our investments into a different mental account then there is a danger that we do not look at our investments as a portfolio, in which case we may ignore the diversification benefits that arise from having a portfolio of shares. This can lead investors to make simplistic decisions about which shares to hold in a portfolio, as they do not take full account of the risk of the shares, or of how the share returns are correlated.

If we also add to mental accounting the ideas associated with prospect theory then we can begin to understand some other investment behaviours that appear to be irrational. It has been found investors are inclined to sell 'bundles' of loss-making shares at the same time. That is, they prefer to close a number of mental accounts (for each of the loss-making shares) all at once. Lim (2006) notes this is because investors prefer to take one overall hit of pain by closing these mental accounts simultaneously. On the other hand, investors prefer to separate out gains by selling such shares on different days. The irrationality in this is that investors should be selling shares at what they judge to be the right time, and they should not be timing sales to either minimise the pain of selling loss-making shares or maximise the happiness associated with selling shares that have made gains.

Richard Thaler, in conjunction with Cass Sunstein, has developed these initial ideas regarding mental accounting to suggest how we can 'nudge' people into making better decisions about, for example, investing in pension funds. These ideas have been influential with governments that want to find ways to persuade people to make better decisions. For example, the UK government now has a Behavioural Insights Team (often referred to as the 'Nudge Unit') which uses insights from behavioural finance to aid in making policy (**www.gov.uk**).

■ Behavioural finance and market efficiency

Behavioural finance has examined how investors react to new information. As explained earlier, share prices appear to underreact to financial news such as earnings announcements, but overreact to a series of good or bad news. Adherents of the efficient markets hypothesis argue that:

- Investors, in the main, value securities rationally.
- Even if some investors do not act rationally, their irrational behaviour is random and therefore cancels out.
- But even if most investors act irrationally, the market will be rectified by rational arbitrageurs who profit from the irrationality of others. Fama (1998) examined the impact of stock market anomalies on market efficiency. He concluded that 'market efficiency survives the challenge from the literature on long-run return anomalies. Consistent with the market efficiency hypothesis that the anomalies are chance results, apparent overreaction to information is about as common as underreaction, and post-event continuation of pre-event returns is about as frequent as post-event reversal.'

The psychology literature shows that people are irrational in a systematic manner.

Collective behaviour relates to the irrational behaviour of groups. Typically, this gives rise to excessive market swings. Two examples of such are 'herding' and 'price bubbles'. These arise when a large group of investors make the same choice based on the actions of others, which cannot be explained by fundamentals. The 'dotcom' price bubble of the 1990s is a clear example of this type of behaviour, as is the house price bubble of the 2000s. Most individuals find comfort in being part of a crowd, rather than acting independently. Of course, more often than not, the crowd can be right for a while, at least, until an overvalued market lurches downwards into its long-overdue correction phase.

Most financial practitioners are subject to bias. Bias, and emotion, cloud their judgement and misguide their actions. The question is whether they recognise this behaviour and take steps to minimise this bias. Practical steps that can be taken to reduce such bias include:

1 Recognise the circumstances leading to bias.
2 Have a written plan for each position, especially exit strategies.
3 Review actions.

Watch the herd, but don't join it

'Honey, it's only a paper loss,' is the classic financial self-delusion. Yet many investors cling desperately to bad investments rather than realising the losses and moving on.

This process of suppression is well known to psychologists and sociologists. Apart from the losses themselves, people are dominated by a fear of making mistakes and of losing prestige. These factors all play their part in distorting people's sense of perception.

The two disciplines of economics and psychology, separate for so many decades, are now united under the banner of behavioural finance. This combination is potentially extremely useful to investors. The objective of behavioural finance is to give investors insight into their own mistakes and those of others. The subject of behavioural finance has its origins in the research in the late 1970s of Americans Daniel Kanneman and Amos Tversky. Their work made waves at the time and the surf is still up.

Joachim Goldberg, a German behavioural finance guru, says many people are psychologically unable to follow rule Number One: 'Cut losses and let profits run.' This fundamental principle is broken time and time again because people are governed by the wrong psychology. Goldberg urges investors to forget what they paid because it is no longer relevant. It is a false reference point.

Likewise, the same misconceived psychology often encourages people to invest still more in a failed investment, thinking they can recoup their losses by buying at a bargain-basement price in a bear market. However, a bad investment does not get better when you pour more money into it.

Economists have always tended to underrate the importance of psychology and focus on so-called fundamentals. Yet, there are many unpredictable economic variables that affect stock markets. These range from political events, 'real' infections such as Sars and Chicken Flu, to interest rates, the gold price, the impact of the weather on commodity prices and a host of others. Psychology is simply another variable.

 Source: Brian Bloch, *Financial Times*, 3 July 2004.

■ Behavioural finance and corporate managers

While much of the behavioural finance literature considers the psychological aspects of stock market trading, it also applies to investment and financing decisions within firms, which is the main focus of this book. If finance managers are able to recognise the biases in their judgements, they will be better prepared to avoid or manage such bias in future.

Behavioural finance helps us understand:

- Why most boards believe the market undervalues 'their' firm's shares.
- Why, more often than not, acquisitions fail to deliver the hoped-for financial benefits.
- Why financial projections in capital investment proposals are usually over-optimistic.
- Why boards find it difficult to terminate (or even decide to escalate) unprofitable projects or strategies.

Share valuation

Good financial public relations and communication with shareholders is vital for any listed company, not least because the market should reflect all relevant information in the company's share price. Typically, we find that senior executives believe that the market tends to underprice 'their' shares and fails to recognise the true worth of the company. But in efficient markets the market price is an unbiased estimate of the true value of the investment. Corporate managers may be prone to biases of overconfidence, over-optimism and the illusion of control resulting in the self-deception that they are better judges of share price than the market, and that they can control outcomes.

In recent years, there has been a flurry of firms exiting the stock market, whereby managers use finance provided by private equity–capital specialists. Although the motivation for this is diverse, it is common to hear directors complaining that the market does not correctly value their firm, and/or analysts are insufficiently interested to generate much research about their prospects (Evans, 2005).

Acquisitions

The bias of over-optimism and overconfidence may also lead boards to believe that they can acquire a firm and produce greater returns than the previous management. As discussed in Chapter 20, there may be sound strategic and economic motives for mounting a takeover bid, but the evidence suggests that, on average, acquisitions are bad news for the shareholders of the acquiring firm.

When takeover bids are contested, the bidding company may end up paying far more for the target firm than was originally intended. In the language of behavioural finance, this may be seen as the loss aversion bias – the strong desire to have something because it looks like it is being taken away from you – and the associated desire to avoid regret from takeover failure.

Managing risk is the main task ahead

The main challenge for asset managers in the coming decade is understanding, managing and communicating risk. This was the overwhelming message of a survey of senior industry figures.

'The most important lesson [of the past decade] is about managing risk,' said Wolfgang Mansfeld, president of BVI, the German trade association. 'Managing risk is not mainly a question of tools and techniques. Far more, it is a matter of risk culture and risk governance. Risk management, in other words, has to be a boardroom issue.' Jan Straatman, chief

investment officer of ING IM, said: 'Risk has to go back to the heart of the investment approach of a solid investment manager.'

Many financial models failed in the past two years as markets demonstrated they did not behave according to conventional assumptions. John Belgrove, a principal consultant at Hewitt Global Investors, said: 'Markets are not efficient, investors do not have rational expectations, security prices do not reflect all known information and the market is not always right.' His proposed remedy is to include behavioural finance in risk management.

 Source: Sophia Grene, *Financial Times,* 3 January 2010. © Financial Times

Unprofitable projects and strategies

Many companies continue to operate projects or strategies long after they cease to be profitable or value-creating. Similarly, firms may continue to invest heavily in a corporate turnaround even though there is little likelihood of it ever recovering such investment. Overconfidence in management's ability to improve performance is one explanation. Another is termed **entrapment**; managers become entrapped in a strategy or project to which they have committed not just corporate capital, but also personal capital. Against all economic logic, they postpone decisions to terminate such projects or strategies in the hope that they will eventually come good. Sometimes, the only way to change direction is to remove the managers entrapped in this mindset.

There is considerable evidence (e.g. Staw, 1976, 1981) that managers are often reluctant to 'pull the plug' on failing projects, or may even decide, in the teeth of adversity, to escalate their commitment, hoping for an eventual turnaround, when the 'rational' thing to do is to abandon (Staw and Ross, 1987). However, for managers, blessed with information advantages, the rational course of action is to prolong their employment. Indeed, because they often have a reputation to protect or at least not to sully, prolongation is the lesser evil (Kanodia *et al.,* 1989).

Firms need to have in place clear guidelines preventing the above arising, through such mechanisms as regular post-audit reviews (Neale and Holmes, 1990). These mechanisms should specifically look for over-optimistic forecasts, irrational escalation of commitment, entrapment and other systematic biases in behavioural finance.

SUMMARY

In this final chapter of the book we have reviewed the main theories behind the corporate finance principles and practices outlined in previous chapters. The key material introduced was on the contribution that the emerging area of behavioural finance makes to our understanding of the subject.

This extension of the discussion is important as fundamental ideas in finance, such as the efficient markets hypothesis, have come under greater and greater scrutiny. It is always right to question the basic tenets of any discipline and this is as true in finance as in any other discipline. The re-evaluation of major aspects of financial theory has occurred as practitioners and academics have tried to reconcile these theories with the behaviour of markets in practice. The comparison of theory and practice takes place all the time, but there can also be periods when major episodes seem to demonstrate that the practice–theory divide needs to be examined even more closely than ever. The global credit crisis that commenced in the late 2000s has been just such an episode. The crisis has been persistent and has been well documented in newspapers, journals and on websites, and coming out of the crisis many government, industry and professional body reports have been researched and written. These crisis-related documents do different things; some aim to understand the origins of the crisis, some try to apportion blame and some offer solutions for future crisis-avoidance. The outcomes of the crisis include an increased interest in topics such as behavioural finance and risk management. It has also demonstrated that finance is a complex and dynamic subject, and that there is considerable scope for the refinement of existing theories and for the development of new theories. Recognising that much of finance theory is related to economics then it is understandable why students, as in the cameo below, are looking to their universities to give room in their teaching for ideas that help the students understand practice as well as theory.

Students demanding alternatives to a free-market dogma with a disastrous record

From any rational point of view, orthodox economics is in serious trouble. Its champions not only failed to foresee the greatest crash for 80 years, but also insisted such crises were a thing of the past. More than that, some of its leading lights played a key role in designing the disastrous financial derivatives that helped trigger the meltdown in the first place.

Any other profession that had proved so spectacularly wrong and caused such devastation would surely be in disgrace. You might even imagine the free-market economists who dominate our universities and advise governments and banks would be rethinking their theories and considering alternatives.

Alan Greenspan, the former chairman of the US Federal Reserve and high priest of deregulation, at least had the honesty to admit his view of the world had been proved 'not right'. The same cannot be said for others. Eugene Fama, architect of the 'efficeient markets hypothesis' underpinning financial deregulation, concedes he doesn't know what 'causes recessions' – but insists his theory has been vindicated anyway. Most mainstream economists have carried on as if nothing had happened.

Many of their students, though, have had enough. A revolt against the orthodoxy has been smouldering for years and now seems to have gone critical. Fed up with parallel universe theories that have little to say about the world they're interested in, students at Manchester University have set up a post-crash economics society with 800 members, demanding an end to monolithic neoclassical courses and the introduction of a pluralist curriculum. They want other schools of economic thought taught in parallel, from Keynesian to more radical theories – with a better record on predicting and connecting with the real world economy – along with green and feminist economics. The campaign is spreading fast: to Cambridge, Essex, the London School of Economics and a dozen other campuses, and linking up with university groups in France, Germany, Slovenia and Chile.

Source: Based on Seumas Milne, *The Guardian*, 20 November 2013.

Key points

- Financial management is more than applying rules and procedures. It explores the behaviour of markets, firms and individuals.

- Various theories explaining such behaviour include those of agency, risk aversion, present value, portfolio, information asymmetry, options, capital structure and market efficiency.

- Behavioural finance is the study of psychological traits that investors and managers display that prevent them acting in a purely rational manner.

- Examples of behavioural finance bias include regret, overconfidence, over-optimism, the illusion of control, herd behaviour, and anchoring and adjustment.

- Behavioural finance is particularly in evidence in stock market anomalies, share valuation, acquisitions, and loss-making projects.

Further reading

A number of texts have been written in the area of behavioural finance. These include texts by Forbes (2009), Baker and Nofsinger (2010), Redhead (2008) and Wilkinson and Klaes (2012). The work of Kahneman and Tversky has been of immense importance in establishing and developing ideas in behavioural finance and their 1979 prospect theory article is an important foundation. Kahneman's *Thinking Fast and Slow* (2012) is an excellent and accessible summary of how our judgement is biased when making decisions. The idea of mental accounting as developed by Thaler is also important and his 1999 paper provides a good summary of various key facets of this area. There are many other recent, interesting studies that also extend the ideas in behavioural finance: for example, Barber and Odean (2001) demonstrate how overconfidence affects the investment decisions of males. The textbooks listed above all refer to key studies.

The French academic Thomas Piketty (2014) has produced a bestselling book that examines whether the current economic system creates vast inequalities. Thaler and Sunstein's ideas on 'nudging' people into making better decision are discussed in their 2009 book *Nudge: Improving Decisions About Health, Wealth and Happiness*.

Appendix A

Solutions to self-assessment activities

CHAPTER 1

1.1 Tangible real assets: machinery and equipment, vehicles, stock
Intangible assets: patents
Financial assets: debtors, cash and building society deposits
Financial claims: trade creditors, loans, shareholders' equity

1.2 The financial manager has two broad responsibilities:

  (1) Providing financial information and advice for internal and external users. The financial accountant prepares the statutory financial accounts and deals with the auditors; the management accountant provides information for decision-making, planning and control. Other departments, such as taxation, may also report to the controller (or chief accountant).

  (2) Managing cash and raising finance at the best possible rate. This is the responsibility of the treasurer or financial manager. Typical functions within the treasury area are raising finance, the management of cash, credit and inventory, foreign currency management and financial risk management.

1.3 Companies are under pressure to be 'good corporate citizens' from a range of organisations. These can include activist groups, environmental groups, charities, religious organisations and government. These different groups and organisations have different agendas. This can mean that companies feel they should act responsibly in respect of the environment, deal fairly with suppliers, treat employees with respect, support initiatives in the local community, and provide customers with value for money.

1.4 **(1)** The goal of maximising owners' wealth is the normally accepted economic objective for resource allocation decisions. Rather than concentrate on the organisation, it evaluates investments from the viewpoint of the organisation's owners – usually shareholders. Any investment that increases their stock of wealth (the present value of future cash flows) is economically acceptable.

      In practice, many of the assumptions underlying this goal do not always hold (e.g. shareholders are only interested in maximising the market value of their shareholdings). In addition, owners are often far removed from managerial decision-making, where capital investment takes place. Accordingly, it is common to find that more easily measurable criteria are used, such as profitability and growth goals. There are also non-economic considerations, such as employee welfare and managerial satisfaction, which can be important for some decisions.

  (2) Separation of ownership from management can give rise to managerialism – self-serving behaviour by managers at the shareholders' expense, e.g. pursuing managerial 'perks' (company cars, etc.), adopting low-risk survival strategies, settling for less than the best.

CHAPTER 2

2.1 Financial intermediaries are the various financial institutions, such as pension funds, insurance companies, banks, building societies, unit trusts and specialist investment institutions. Their role is to accept deposits from personal and corporate savers to lend to customers (e.g. companies) via the capital and money markets.

    Financial intermediaries perform a vital economic service:

  (a) Re-packaging finance: collecting small amounts of finance and re-packaging into larger bundles for specific lending requirements (e.g. banks).

(b) Risk reduction: investing sums, on behalf of individuals and companies, into large, well-diversified investment portfolios (e.g. pension funds and unit trusts).

(c) Liquidity transformation: bringing together short-term lenders and long-term borrowers (e.g. building societies).

(d) Cost reduction and advice: minimising transaction costs and providing low-cost services to lenders and borrowers.

2.2 **(a)** Companies using the main market are generally those with a lengthy track record (i.e. a history of stable/growing sales and profits), seeking large amounts of capital, where the board is prepared to release a sizeable proportion of its controlling interest.

(b) The AIM is designed to appeal to smaller and growing companies which seek access to risk capital or where the board wishes to sell some of its holding, but cannot meet all the requirements for a full listing and prefers less regulation.

(c) The OTC market is for the remaining, smaller companies where shareholders occasionally wish to dispose of shares. This is performed on a 'matched bargain' basis, using facilities offered by authorised securities dealers.

2.3 A major function of an active capital market is to provide a mechanism whereby investors can realise their holdings by selling securities, and, obviously, for every seller, there has to be a buyer. Investors will be reluctant to commit their funds to the capital market by subscribing to new share issues if they doubt their ability to find a willing buyer as and when they decide to sell their holdings. The more liquid the market, the greater its ability to entice firms to make new share issues and investors to subscribe to them. Where market liquidity is poor, companies will have to offer much higher returns, making share issues uneconomic.

2.4 If these rules ever applied, investors would have soon realised the potential, and would have bought in November rather in advance of the expected price increase in December, thus creating a 'November effect', and so on.

Try the same argument on the old stock market advice 'Sell in May, and go away, and come back on St Leger Day' (the date of a horse race in the UK).

Many statistical tests have shown that all such dealing rules are usually inferior, and never superior, to a simple 'buy and hold' strategy.

2.5 **(a)** On the face of it, this represents insider dealing, by people in the know.

(b) It could represent speculation and rumour. If the company is known to be weak, then it is a candidate for takeover and people begin to speculate about how much the company may be worth in the hands of an alternative owner.

(c) Most bidders build up a 'strategic stake' in a takeover target prior to formal announcement. The present UK rules (*The City Code*) allow a holding of up to 3 per cent without declaration of beneficial ownership. The upward movement could simply be due to this buying pressure. In reality, 'abnormal' buying also promotes speculation.

2.6 The reader is referred to Section 2.7.

CHAPTER 3

3.1 Most likely, the banker would wish to reflect on the rate of interest required:

(a) the rate of interest available from a risk-free investment,
(b) the expected changes in purchasing power over the five years, and
(c) the risk that you may not be able to repay.

We consider other factors a banker will consider in a later chapter.

3.2 $PV = \dfrac{£623}{(1.07)^8} + \dfrac{£1,092}{(1.07)^{16}} = £732$

3.3 Discounting at 15 per cent, a pound halves in value every five years. The present value of the purchase cost is therefore £750,000 (£500,000 today and £250,000 in year 5).

3.4 $PV = \dfrac{£1,000}{(1.12)^{12}} = £257$

3.5 Using the tables:

$$PV = (\pounds 250 \times 8.0751) + (\pounds 1{,}200 \times 0.10067) = \pounds 2{,}140$$

3.6 Price per share $= \dfrac{D_1}{k_e - g} = \dfrac{D_0(1 + g)}{k_e - g}$

$D_0 = (25\% \times 16p) = 4p$

growth $= (0.75 \times 0.18) = 0.135$, i.e. 13.5% and $D_1 = 4p(1.135) = 4.54p$

Share price $= \dfrac{4.54}{(0.15 - 0.135)} = \pounds 3.03$

With shareholders seeking a 20% return, share price reduces to: $\dfrac{4.54p}{(0.20 - 0.1350)} = \pounds 0.70$

Because the return on reinvestment now is less than the cost of equity the firm should stop reinvesting, at least in the short term.

CHAPTER 4

4.1 Your answer could include the costs of developing a new product; a marketing campaign designed to increase long-term brand awareness; investment in training and management development; acquisition of other businesses; reorganisation and rationalisation costs (frequently in the form of redundancy payments), or research costs incurred in developing a strategic advantage.

4.2 The main elements in the capital budgeting decision are found in the formula

$$NPV = \frac{X_1}{1 + k} + \frac{X_2}{(1 + k)^2} + \cdots + \frac{X_n}{(1 + k)^n} - I$$

where X is the net cash flow arising at the end of year, k is the minimum required rate of return (or discount rate), I is the initial cost of the investment and n is the project's life.

4.3 The net present value rule states that a project is acceptable if the present value of anticipated cash flows exceeds the present value of anticipated cash flows. Wealth is maximised by accepting all projects offering positive net present values when discounted at the required rate of return.

4.4

	Accept when
Net Present Value	NPV > 0
Internal Rate of Return	IRR > k
Profitability Index	PI > 1(or PI >) 0 if based on NPV)

4.5

For	Against
Payback period	
Simple to calculate	Ignores time-value of money
Easily understood	Ignores cash flows beyond payback period
Crude measure of profitability	Problems in setting payback requirement
Emphasises liquidity	
Net present value	
Theoretically sound	Not well understood by non-financial managers
Based on cash flows	
Incorporates the time-value of money	Estimating the appropriate discount rate is difficult in practice
Internal rate of return	
Based on cash flows	Can incorrectly rank projects
Incorporates the time-value of money	Difficult to calculate without a computer
Accounting rate of return	
Can be related to accounts	Ignores time-value of money
Based on profits not cash flows	Problems in setting the required return

4.6 Evaluation of mutually exclusive projects using IRR and NPV approaches can produce different recommendations. This is particularly the case where projects are very different in scale or where the cash flow profiles of the various alternatives differ significantly. In such circumstances, the NPV approach is the better method.

4.7 Project Y offers the highest NPV for all discount rates up to 17 per cent. At the 12 per cent cost of capital, it offers a better cash return than Project X.

4.8 Soft capital rationing is internally imposed by the firm. This may be because management is unwilling to borrow or wishes to pursue a policy of stable growth. Hard rationing is externally imposed by the capital market. No additional external finance is available to the firm. Capital for a single period may be resolved by applying the profitability index to investment cash flows. Multi-period rationing requires a form of mathematical programming.

4.9 The modified IRR is that rate of return which, when the initial outlay is compared with the terminal value of the project's cash flows reinvested at the cost of capital, gives an NPV of zero. Whereas the IRR method implicitly assumes that cash flows generated by the project are reinvested at the project's internal rate of return, the modified IRR assumes reinvestment at the cost of capital. This means that it gives the same investment advice as the NPV approach.

CHAPTER 5

5.1 Incremental cash flows, applied to capital budgeting, are the additional cash flows created as a direct result of making an investment decision. Frequently, identifying these is not as straightforward as one might think, particularly where replacement decisions are involved or where decisions in one part of the business have ramifications for other parts.

5.2 The original cost of developing the drug is a sunk cost and should not form part of the analysis. Any adverse effects on other parts of the business resulting from the decision to manufacture the product are an associated cash flow and should be included in the analysis. The external sale value of the patent is an opportunity cost of proceeding with production. The £10 million cost should be deducted from the project's cash flows.

5.3 To: D. Cameron

From: Rick Clegg

Clubs for Beginners Proposal

I have re-examined the points raised in your e-mail and discussed them with our accountant.

In analysing capital projects, only future investment cash flows incremental to the business are relevant to the decision.

1 Depreciation is not a cash flow – it is a charge against profits. By comparing operating cash flows against initial outlay, the need for depreciation becomes unnecessary.
2 Only additional fixed costs resulting from the introduction of the new project should be charged. I have checked that no extra overheads are incurred.
3 The market research is a past cost. Its existence is not dependent upon the outcome of the decision, so it should not be included.
4 I agree that finance costs are important, but the cost of finance has already been accounted for within the discount rate.

My 'Clubs for Beginners' proposal is, I suggest, an attractive one, from which the business should benefit considerably.

5.4 Many companies have failed to take account of the relatively low inflation and interest rates when calculating the required return on investment projects. For example, a nominal rate of 20 per cent, which many firms use, may not be unreasonable during times of relatively high inflation, but is probably excessive during periods of low inflation. This makes it more difficult for economically attractive projects to be accepted.

5.5 Tax is a cash flow and shareholders want firms to maximise their after-tax cash flows. It affects companies in different ways, depending on their tax situations and the capital allowances available to them. Some types of business attract more generous allowances than others. However, for the majority of capital projects, the tax effect will have a relatively minor impact on the project outcome. Good projects are usually viable both before and after tax.

5.7 Weighted average cost of capital: Major plc

Capital	Market value £m	Weight	Cost %	Weighted cost
Ordinary shares	48	0.6	11	6.6
Loan	32	0.4	6	2.4
				9.0

Note that the 6% cost for the loan represents the after-tax cost = 8% (1 − 25%).

CHAPTER 6

6.1 The attractiveness of any project depends, in large measure, on how well it helps the business implement agreed strategies to achieve agreed goals. Investment is one of the main vehicles for implementing strategy.

It is quite possible for capital projects to be rejected because they are not compatible with long-term corporate intentions. An important element of the investment decision process is to ensure that there is a good 'fit' between projects proposed and corporate strategy.

6.2 Stages in the investment process:

Search for opportunities
Screening (is it worth evaluating further?)
Defining the project
Evaluation
Transmission through the organisation
Authorisation
Monitoring
Post-audit

6.4 Post-auditing may confer substantial benefits on the firm. Among these are the following:

1 The enhanced quality of decision-making and planning, which may stem from more carefully and rigorously researched project proposals.
2 Tightening of internal control systems.
3 The ability to modify or even abandon projects on the basis of fuller information.
4 The identification of key variables on whose outcome the viability of the current and similar future projects may depend.

CHAPTER 7

7.1 While a capital project may have a high expected return, the risks involved may mean that there is the possibility that it will be unsuccessful – even to the extent of putting the whole business in jeopardy.

7.2 **(1)** Financial risk; **(2)** Business risk; **(3)** Project risk; **(4)** Portfolio or market risk.

7.3 X has the lower degree of risk relative to the expected returns.

$$\text{Coefficient of variation:} \quad X = 400/2{,}000 = 0.2$$
$$Y = 400/1{,}000 = 0.4$$

7.4 **(a)** Risk – a set of outcomes for which probabilities can be assigned.
(b) Uncertainty – a set of outcomes for which accurate probabilities cannot be assigned.
(c) Risk-aversion – a preference for less risk rather than more.
(d) Expected value – the sum of the possible outcomes from a project each multiplied by their respective probability.
(e) Standard deviation – a statistical measure of the dispersion of possible outcomes around the expected value.
(f) Semi-variance – a special case of the variance which considers only outcomes less than the expected value.
(g) Mean–variance rule – Project A will be preferred to Project B if either the expected return of A exceeds that of B and the variance is equal to or less than that of B, or the expected return of A exceeds or is equal to the expected return of B and the variance is less than that of B.

7.5 Monte Carlo simulation involves constructing a mathematical model which captures the essential characteristics of the proposal throughout its life as it encounters random events. It is useful for major projects where probabilities can be assigned to key factors (e.g. selling price or project life) which are essentially independent.

CHAPTER 8

8.1 To eliminate the risk of, say, a two-asset portfolio, there would have to be perfect negative correlation between the returns from the two assets, and also the portfolio would have to be 'correctly' weighted.

8.2 Expected values:

A: EV $= (0.5 \times - 10\%) + (0.5 \times 50\%) = 20\%$
B: EV $= (0.5 \times - 20\%) + (0.5 \times 60\%) = 20\%$

Standard deviations

A: $\sigma_A = \sqrt{[(0.5)(-10\% - 20\%)^2 + (0.5)(50\% - 20\%)^2]}$
$\qquad = \sqrt{[(0.5 \times 900) + (0.5 \times 900)]}$
$\qquad = \sqrt{900} = 30, \text{i e. } 30\%$

B: $\sigma_B = \sqrt{[(0.5)(60\% - 20\%)^2 + (0.5)(-20\% - 20\%)^2]}$
$\qquad = \sqrt{[(0.5 \times 1600) + (0.5 \times 1600)]}$
$\qquad = \sqrt{1600} = 40, \text{i e. } 40\%$

8.3 The expected value $= 20\%$ as explained. The standard deviation is:

$\sqrt{[(0.64)^2(30)^2 + (0.36)^2(40)^2 + 0]}$
$\quad = \sqrt{(368.64) + (207.36)}$
$\quad = \sqrt{576}$
$\quad = 24, \text{ i.e. } 24\%$

8.4 To minimise portfolio risk, let α^* = the proportion invested in asset Z. Using the risk-minimising formula 8.4:

$$\alpha^* = \frac{\sigma_Y^2 - \text{cov}_{ZY}}{\sigma_Z^2 + \sigma_Y^2 - 2\,\text{cov}_{ZY}}$$

$$= \frac{40^2 - (-200)}{200^2 + 40^2 - (2 \times -200)}$$

$$= \frac{1600 + 200}{400 + 1600 + 400}$$

$$= 1800/2400 = 0.75, \text{ i.e. } 75\%$$

8.5 An efficient frontier is a schedule tracing out all the available portfolio combinations that either minimise risk for a given expected return or maximise expected return for a given risk.

8.6 Expected NVP $= (0.27 \times £30,000) + (0.73 \times £24,000)$
$$= £25,620$$

Standard deviation $= \sqrt{[(0.27)^2(10,000)^2 + (0.73)^2(4,899)^2 + 2(0.27)(0.73)(-20,000,000)]}$

$$= \sqrt{7.29m + 12.79m - 7.88m}$$

$$= \sqrt{12.22m}$$

$$= £3,496$$

8.7 The outright risk-minimiser locates at point B, the portfolio with minimum possible risk. However, risk-averters are willing to accept higher levels of risk if offered sufficient additional rewards, i.e. higher returns. Hence, any portfolio along AB is consistent with risk aversion. The lower the investor's concern with risk, the nearer to point A he/she will locate.

8.8 With four separate assets to choose from, the investor faces a wider array of available portfolios. The envelope that summarises his/her opportunities has the same basic shape as in the text, but with an extra 'corner' representing the fourth asset, denoted by point D in Figure A.1. Notice that all sorts of configurations of the envelope are possible, depending on the location of the four assets.

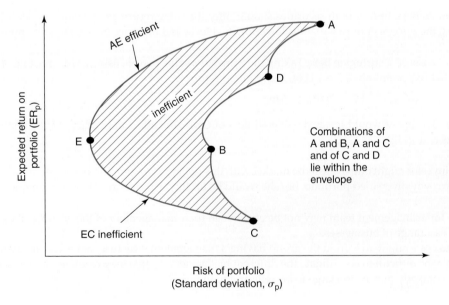

Figure A.1 Portfolio combinations with four assets

CHAPTER 9

9.1 TSR = [Dividend + Capital Gain]/Opening share price, expressed as a percentage.
= [£0.10 + £0.17]/£2.20 = £0.27/£2.20 = 0.123 i.e. 12.3%

9.2 To eliminate the specific risk, the investor would have to hold every share quoted on the markets, i.e. the market portfolio.

9.3 Systematic risk: political turmoil
exchange rate fluctuation
interest rate changes.
Unique risk: labour relations problems
announcement of a major new contract
discovery of a defect in a key product.

9.4 According to the CAPM, the Beta of Walkley Wagons is 1.2. Hence, the predicted return on its shares would be 1.2 × the predicted market return of 25%, i.e. 30%. (If you believe the experts!)

9.5 Variations around the characteristics line reflect the impact of factors unique to the firm. For BA, this could be due to a pilots' strike, pressure to relinquish landing slots at Heathrow, sale of its stake in Qantas, competition authorities blocking a proposed strategic alliance, etc.

9.6 The Beta values cluster in a relatively narrow range because these are large firms that are, themselves, mostly well diversified, and also because they constitute a major part of the overall market portfolio, which has a Beta of 1.0. Betas below 0.5 and above 1.50 are quite rare.

9.7 The market portfolio has a Beta of 1.0 simply because it varies in perfect unison with itself!

9.8 The SML traces out all combinations of risk and return that are efficient – anything currently located above or below the line represents an aberration from equilibrium that will be eliminated as market players realise the degree of mis-pricing. As they buy or sell, they help to move the market to equilibrium.
In the case of security A, the actual return is 'super-efficient', i.e. in excess of the return warranted by its Beta of 0.3. Conversely, security B is inefficient as it offers too low a return (actually below the risk-free rate) given its Beta. In fact, both securities should offer the same return as they share a Beta. To achieve equilibrium, the price of A must rise, thus lowering its return, and the price of B must fall to raise its return.

9.9 Here, we need a surrogate Beta. Taking the Sainsbury value of 0.58, using a risk-free rate of 3 per cent and the market risk premium of 5 per cent, the required return is:

3% + 0.58(5%) = 3% + 2.9% = 5.9%

This investment would lower the overall Beta of GKN, the effect depending on the relative size of the two areas of activity.

9.10 An investor might outperform the market with this policy, assuming it did actually rise. However, with such a narrowly diversified portfolio, he/she would be unduly exposed to risk factors unique to these five firms.

9.11 The top management team may not be effective in their management of the group as they cannot be experts across a range of businesses.
Extra costs might arise from the group having a management structure that is too hierarchical.
It may be difficult to co-ordinate the different businesses and this may result in inefficiencies.
The company may be too large to be agile and to innovate.

CHAPTER 10

10.1 With EPS = 36p, and the dividend covered three times, the dividend per share must be 12p (36p/12p = 3). Hence, the cost of equity is:

$$k_e = \frac{12p\,(1 + 3\%)}{£1.80} + 3\% = (6.9\% + 3\%) = 9.9\%$$

10.2 The DVM breaks down totally:

(i) when the firm pays no dividend

(ii) when the growth rate of dividends exceeds the cost of equity.

10.3 Overall, the required return = 5% + 1.2[6%] = 12.2%

For activity A, it is = 5% + 2.0[6%] = 17%

For activity B, it is = 5% + 0.8[6%] = 9.8%

10.4 Company Beta = (0.65 × Beta of A) + (0.35 × Beta of B)

= (0.65 × 2.0) + (0.35 × 0.8) = 1.58

10.5 The calculation is:

Activity	Weighting	Beta	Weighted Beta
Hotels and Restaurants	85%	1.40	1.19
Costa	15%	0.87	0.13
		Total	1.32

The change in weightings thus tends to raise the calculated Beta, reflecting the higher weighting of the more profitable Hotels and Restaurants division.

10.6 The project Beta = RSF × OGF × divisional Beta

= (0.5 × 0.8 × 1.2) = 0.48

Hence, the required return = 5% + 0.48[6%] = 5% + 2.9% = 7.9%

CHAPTER 11

11.1 The value of a whole company, or enterprise value, is the value of all its assets, whether measured at book value or market value (£5 billion in the case of Innogy plc). The value of the equity is the value of the owners' investment in the firm, or shareholders' funds (£3 billion in the case of Innogy). These are equal only when the firm is financed entirely by equity.

11.2 **(i)** D.S. Smith's enterprise value is the total value of its assets, i.e. £3,606.3m

(ii) Total liabilities are long-term and short-term creditors, valued at £1,343.3m and £1,178.1m respectively, total £2,521.4m. Minority interests represent remaining shares in firms previously taken over by Smith. These are neither Smith's liabilities nor Smith's owners' equity. They represent 'outsiders'' share of the total assets. Strictly, the figure given for total assets in (i) should be adjusted for this small item.

(iii) The value of owners' equity = shareholders' funds = net assets = NAV = £1,084.9m. These four terms are synonymous.

11.3 Profit after tax = [1 − 30%] × £80m = £56m

EPS = (£56m/100m) = 56p

Implied share value = EPS × surrogate P:E ratio = (56p × 15) = £8.40.

11.4 Break-even value is £1 million, of which £0.361 represents the PV of the rental income. To break even, the resale value must have a PV of (£1m – £0.361m) = £0.639m. Reversing the discounting process, this is a value of £0.639 × $(1.12)^5$ = £1.126m. Hence, the property must rise in value by about 13% to prevent investors from losing out.

11.5 Taxation = 30% × (£25m – £1m) = £7.2m

Free cash flow = Operating Profit + depreciation – interest – tax – investment expenditure

(£25m + £2m – £1m – £7.2m – £3m) = £15.8m.

CHAPTER 12

12.1 **(1)** A call option gives the owner the right to buy shares (or whatever) at a fixed price within a set period. A put option is the right to sell at a fixed price.

(2) A European option can only be exercised on the expiry date, while an American option can be exercised any time over the life of the option. Most traded options in Europe are actually the American variety.

(3) A wide range including shares, bonds, currency, interest rates, gold, silver, wool, soya beans, etc. Options are also available on interest rates.

(4) (a) The lower the exercise price, the more likely it is that it will be profitable to exercise the call, and therefore the more investors are prepared to pay for the call.

(b) The longer the time that a call has to run to maturity, the greater the scope for the price to drift above the exercise price. Of course there is also more time for prices to fall below the exercise price. However, the potential gains and losses are not symmetrically distributed. There are limits to the losses but not to the gains.

(c) The price exceeds the profit that can be made immediately by exercising the call, as over its remaining life there will be the opportunity to capitalise on further price movements. These may be upwards or downwards but we have already noted a bias in the consequence of price changes – this offers a higher expected value of potential gains than losses.

12.2 **(1) (a)** It has intrinsic value because you could buy the share (exercise the option) for less than the share price.

(2) (a)

12.3 Applying the equation below, we find that the put–call parity relationship holds:

$$Share\ price\ +\ value\ of\ put\ -\ value\ of\ call\ =\ E/(1\ +\ R_f)$$

$$44 \qquad\qquad 7 \qquad\qquad\quad 1 \qquad =\ 55/1.10$$

$$PV\ exercise\ price\ =\ 50p$$

12.4 Option value increases with the volatility of the underlying share price because the greater the variability in share price, the greater the probability that the share price will exceed the exercise price. Because option values cannot be negative, only the probability of exceeding the exercise price is considered.

Option values are determined by five main factors:

- share price
- exercise price of the option
- time to expiry of the option
- the risk-free rate of interest
- volatility of the underlying share price

In addition, the payment of dividends and underlying stock market trends have some influence on option values.

CHAPTER 13

13.1 Treasury management involves the efficient management of liquidity and risk in the business. The treasurer usually has primary responsibilities for funding, risk management, working capital management and liquidity, and managing banking relationships.

13.2 The matching approach to funding is where the maturity structure of the company's financing matches the cash flows generated by the assets employed. In simple terms, this means that long-term finance is used to fund both fixed assets and permanent current assets, while fluctuating current assets are funded by short-term borrowings.

13.3 Over to you!

13.4 **(a)** True
(b) False
(c) The company is selling euros so the higher three-month forward rate applies, i.e. 100,000/1.4898 = £67,123.
(d) It should let it lapse as the spot price is cheaper than the exercise price.

13.5 *Forward* – commits the user to buying or selling an asset at a specific price on a specific future date.
Future – a forward contract traded on an exchange.
Swap – a contract by which two parties exchange cash flows linked to an asset or liability.
Option – the right to buy or sell at an agreed price.

13.6 The reputational damage suffered by BP has been enormous. In its 2010 annual report BP acknowledged 'the Gulf of Mexico oil spill has damaged BP's reputation' and stated that this 'may have a long-term impact on the group's ability to access new opportunities, both in the US and elsewhere. Adverse public, political and industry sentiment towards BP, and towards oil and gas drilling activities generally, could damage or impair our existing commercial relationships with counterparties, partners and host governments and could impair our access to new investment opportunities, exploration properties, operatorships or other essential commercial arrangements with potential partners and host governments, particularly in the US.' The impact of spill on its financial position has also been huge and in 2010 BP recognised a charge of $40.9 billion in its accounts. The eventual cost to BP is highly uncertain.

13.7 The annual report contains a list of risk factors that BT has identified as significant. These include security and resilience, major contracts, pensions, competition, regulation, integrity and supply chain resilience. The risks are explained and the company also sets out how they go about mitigating the risks. The principal risks may change over time to reflect changes in the environment.

CHAPTER 14

14.1 A company with a simple production process, that makes to order, enjoys generous supplier credit terms and offers cash discounts for early payment could have a much shorter operating cycle than the industry average. A firm with a longer cycle demands more capital and is more exposed to bad debt and stock losses.

14.2 Overtrading arises when businesses operate with inadequate long-term capital. It occurs when firms:
(a) are set up with insufficient capital;
(b) expand too rapidly without a commensurate increase in long-term finance;
(c) utilise net current assets in an inefficient manner. The consequences can be extremely serious and possibly fatal unless the problem is addressed.

14.3 *Rough approximation*

$$\text{Cost of discount} = \frac{\text{Discount \%}}{100 - \text{discount \%}} \times \frac{365}{\text{Final date} - \text{discount date}}$$

$$= \frac{2.5}{100 - 2.5} \times \frac{365}{46 - 30} = 58.5\%$$

APR method

$$\text{Interest} = 2.5/(100 - 2.5) = 2.56\% \text{ per period}$$
$$\text{APR} = 1.0256^{365/16} - 1 = 78\%$$

In both cases, the cost of granting the cash discount terms looks prohibitive, unless it is thought likely that the customer would take much longer to pay than most other customers.

14.4 **(a)** Credit terms, including credit period.
  (b) Credit standards for offering credit to existing and new customers, including credit risk screening.
  (c) Credit collection policy, including use of cash discounts and collection agents.
  (d) Credit reporting.

14.5 Carrying costs include the cost of storing, insuring and maintaining stocks as well as the lost interest tied up in holding such assets.

  Ordering costs include not only the obvious administrative cost of making regular orders, but also the costs associated with running out of stock (lost orders, goodwill, etc.). These two types of cost are traded off to find the optimum order quantity, given by the formula:

$$EOQ = \sqrt{\frac{2AC}{H}}$$

  where C is the cost of placing an order, A is the annual stock usage and H is the cost of holding a unit of stock.

14.6 The main motives for holding cash are:
  (a) to act as a buffer to ensure that transactions can be paid for (transactions motive);
  (b) to cater for unanticipated cash outflows (precautionary motive);
  (c) to permit companies to take advantage of profitable opportunities (speculative motive);
  (d) to take advantage of 'free' banking services for firms with positive cash balances (compensation balances motive).

14.7 With interest at 12% p.a., the EOQ formula becomes:

$$EOQ = \sqrt{\frac{2 \times £2,400,00 \times £25}{0.12}} = £31,623 \approx £32,000$$

CHAPTER 15

15.1 Trade credit results from the time lag between receiving goods and having to pay for them. For as long as it takes the recipient of the goods to settle the account, the supplier is effectively financing the client. Hence, each order and delivery triggers a 'spontaneous' supply of finance.

15.2 Effective annual interest:
  Discount lost/Extra finance $= (1.5\%/98.5\%) = 1.523\%$
  Number of 25-day periods in a year $= (365/25) = 14.6$
  Effective interest rate $= (1 + 0.01523)^{14.6} - 1 = 0.247$, i.e. 24.7%.

15.3 The mnemonic PARTS is sometimes used to help remember this:
  Purpose: Is the purpose of the loan acceptable to the bank?
  Amount: Has the financial requirement been correctly specified (e.g. will additional working capital be required later)?
  Repayment: How will the loan be repaid? Will the funds generate sufficient income to enable repayment?
  Term: What is the duration of the loan?
  Security: What, if any, is the proposed security?

15.4 Overdrafts are normally cheaper than term loans because:
  - With an overdraft, interest is only paid on the credit used, not the credit available.
  - They can be recalled at short, or no, notice; term loans are for agreed durations.
  - Arrangement fees are higher for a term loan.
  - The interest rate is variable whereas it is usually fixed for a loan. Overdrafts are thus more risky for the borrower.

15.5 It receives cash to pay suppliers promptly and take advantage of any early payment discounts available.

- Growth can be financed through revenue from sales rather than through additional capital.
- Management need not devote so much time to chasing debtors and running the sales ledger.
- Finance is directly linked to sales. (Overdrafts are linked to the balance sheet and the security offered by assets.)
- If factoring is 'without recourse', any bad debts are no longer the firm's problem.

15.6 Loan $= (70\% \times £40{,}000) = £28{,}000$
Total interest $= (4 \times 10\% \times £28{,}000) = £11{,}200$
Total to be repaid $= (£28{,}000 + £11{,}200) = £39{,}200$
Monthly payment $= [£39{,}200/(4 \times 12)] = £816.67$

15.7
- *Purpose* – an OL is undertaken in order to perform a specific job over a short period of time, whereas an FL is usually contracted over a term which matches the expected working life of an asset.
- *Termination* – an OL can be easily terminated whereas cancellation penalties on an FL are prohibitive.
- *Obsolescence risk* – with an OL, this is borne by the lessor, while the lessee bears the risk with an FL.
- *Cost* – OLs are generally more expensive than FLs for the same period.

15.8 **(i)** $9\%[1 - 20\%] = 7.20\%$
(ii) The full 9%, as the firm cannot use the tax break.

CHAPTER 16

16.1 The events of 9/11 have made people more fearful for the future, and less inclined to invest. Equity would look safer for firms as it carries no interest obligations, although as the authorities used interest rate reductions to support their economies, this might encourage more borrowing, e.g. as firms re-finance existing loans at more favourable rates. So, on balance, probably a shift towards fixed interest financing to lock in historically low interest rates, certainly for as long as it takes fragile equity markets to recover.

16.2 The statement is nonsense. Reserves reflect financing of past investment, i.e. they represent funds already invested. The speaker is probably confused between reserves and 'cash reserves', common parlance for 'cash balances'.

16.3 Pre-issue, a shareholder holds $(6 \times £5) = £30$ in shares plus £3.50 in cash, totalling £33.50. Post-issue, this value is spread over 7 shares $(6 + 1)$ so the TERP $= £33.50/7 = £4.79$.

16.4 In a '2-for-1' split:

- the number of shares doubles, i.e. two new shares for each old one.
- both capital and assets are unchanged – no further cash is raised.
- the market value of the whole equity is unchanged but the value per share is halved.

16.5 £50 grows to £100 over 10 years, i.e. $£50(1 + g)^{10} = £100$.
Inverting, $1/(1 + g)^{10} = (£50/£100) = 0.5000$. From the present value tables, $g = 7.2\%$.

16.6 **(a)** Flat yield $=$ interest/market price $= (£8.30/£110) = 7.5\%$
(b) Yield to maturity is the interest rate that satisfies:
$£110 = (£8.3 \times 3\text{-year annuity factor}) + (£100 \times 3\text{-year discount factor})$.
The solution is 5.35%.

16.7 The warrant gives the right to buy something worth £8 for £5 – its value is thus £3. The one-for-four terms are irrelevant to the value per warrant. Someone holding 400 shares would have 100 warrants valued at $(100 \times £3) = £300$, etc.

16.8 Logic might suggest the following:

A SAL generates cash which raises assets, but as the lease is long-term it must be capitalised. It will thus appear (remain) as a fixed asset, but is offset by the corresponding PV of rental commitments, shown as long-term debt. Overall, it leaves net assets unchanged but, initially, it increases the calculated gearing ratio unless and until the cash generated is used to repay existing debt.

However, the reality is rather different, especially for property assets, which are usually classified as operating leases as the lessor retains the risks and rewards of ownership. Hence, most rented properties do not appear on the tenant's balance sheets. The balance sheet effect is largely cosmetic ('smoke and mirrors'), except that it does increase liquidity.

CHAPTER 17

17.1 Earnings in Year 0 = £1,000, of which 60%, i.e. £600, are retained. Returns on new investment = $(15\% \times £600) = £90$.

Next year's earnings $= (£1,000 + £90) = £1,090$.

Growth rate $= \dfrac{(£1,090)}{(£1,000)} - 1 = 9\% = (60\% \times 15\%)$

17.2 Divicut invests £1,000 in Year 1 to return £1,080 in Year 2.

The NPV of this is $£1,080/(1.1)^2$ vs. $£1,000/(1.1)$ or £893 vs. £909, thus a negative NPV of £16, because the return on reinvested earnings (8%) falls short of the required 10%.

17.3 Paying out dividends rather than investing in worthwhile projects otherwise inaccessible to shareholders reduces the PV of their future income below what it could have been, i.e. there is an opportunity cost imposed on them.

17.4 Projects A, B and C are all attractive, but C appears unavailable as it would lead to exceeding the budget. However, if C is divisible, the firm should undertake A, B and 3/7 of C; otherwise, it should pay a dividend of £300,000.

17.5 Gordon confuses the risk of the dividends with the risk of the underlying cash flows resulting from new investment. If risk (and any increase in it) is suitably allowed for in the discount rate used to deflate future cash flows, then to discount the more distant future dividend flow would entail double-counting for risk. (If the firm moves into a low risk area, the future dividends could even have lower risk than near-in-time dividends.)

17.6 A clientèle is a set of investors whose interests the firm tries to serve via its particular dividend policy. Investors with short time horizons are likely to include the relatively elderly or infirm, and those with pressing needs for rapid income payments, e.g. to repay debts or to fund a daughter's wedding.

17.7 **(i)** £1,000/£20 = 50 shares
(ii) 50 plus 20% = 60 shares.

17.8 Share repurchases may signal that the firm has exhausted investment opportunities or has become too risk-averse to devote funds to R&D. They may also trigger CGT liabilities for some investors. It may also cause embarrassment to directors if share prices subsequently fall.

17.9 A stable dividend policy gives reliability and security. Investors can plan their future income and expenditures more easily. Sharp cuts in dividends, as well as causing alarm, may force investors to sell shares on a weak market. Similarly, a sharp increase in dividends may force investors to reconfigure their portfolios, as well as triggering a CGT liability.

CHAPTER 18

18.1 **(i)** debt/equity = £50m/£100m = 50%.
(ii) debt-to-debt plus equity = £50m/(£50m + £100m) = 33.3%.
(iii) net debt = debt less cash = (£70m − £10m) = £60m, or as a percentage of equity = (£60m/£100m) = 60%

18.2 Both capital and income gearing are forms of financial gearing, i.e. they stem from the firm's financial structure. Capital gearing is obtained from the Balance Sheet and is measured by the amount of borrowing in relation to owners' equity. Income gearing can be gleaned from the P and L, and is measured by interest cover, or its inverse, the proportion of PBIT accounted for by interest charges.

18.4 Contribution is, of course, unaffected, but operating profit or PBIT would fall by £50,000 to £550,000, and PBT would fall a further £40,000 to £310,000. The two multipliers become:

Contribution/PBIT = (£1,080,000/£550,000) = 1.96

PBIT/PBT = (£550,000/£310,000) = 1.77

The combined multiplier = (1.96 × 1.77) = 3.47

18.5 **Scenario A:** EV = (0.25 × 5%) + (0.50 × 20%) + (0.25 × 35%) = 20%
Scenario B: EV = (0.25 × 3.3%) + (0.50 × 23.3%) + (0.25 × 43.3%) = 23.3%
Scenario C: EV = (0.25 × 0%) + (0.50 × 30%) + (0.25 × 60%) = 30%

18.6 With 25% gearing, share price = (23.3p/0.25) = £0.93
With 50% gearing, share price = (30p/0.35) = £0.86
It seems that shareholders' demand for a higher return outweighs the increase in EPS as gearing increases.

18.7 Debt-to-equity ratio of 40% means that debt is 2/7 of the total long-term funds and equity is 5/7. The WACC is thus:
(5/7 × 18%) + (2/7 × 8%) = (12.9% + 2.3%) = 15.2%

18.8 **(i)** With 11% interest, market value = (£100 × 3.5%/11%) = £31.82
(ii) With 3% interest, market value = (£100 × 3.5%/3%) = £116.67

18.10 **(a)** Perpetual debt: (30% × £10m debt) = £3m
(b) 20 years to maturity:
(20 year annuity of 6% × £10m × T) = (11.4699 × £600,000 × 30%)
= £2.06m

CHAPTER 19

19.1 Under MM assumptions, firms identical in all respects apart from capital structure (allowing for size) should have the same value. Value is determined by the stream of operating cash flows and the degree of business risk attaching to these, regardless of how the cash flows are 'packaged' or shared out between different classes of investor.

19.2 Arbitrage in pursuit of 'home-made gearing' is restricted by:
- Taxes on capital gains.
- Differences between the borrowing and lending rates available to all parties.
- Different borrowing rates available to firms and private investors.
- Restrictions on some institutions' ability to borrow.
- Transactions costs.

19.3 Value of ungeared firm $= \dfrac{£100m(1 - T)}{0.15} = \dfrac{£70m}{0.15} = £466.7m$

Value of geared firm $= V_u + TB = £466.7m + (30\% \times £200m)$
$= (£466.7m + £60m) = £526.7m$

19.4 In the ungeared firm, the overall cost of capital is simply the cost of equity, i.e. 15%. In the geared firm, the overall cost of finance is:

$k_{0u} = 15\%\left(1 - \dfrac{T \times V_B}{V_S + V_B}\right) = 15\%[1 - (30\% \times £200m/£600m)]$
$= 15\%(1 - 1.5\%) = 13.5\%$

19.5 Beta ungeared $= \dfrac{1.45}{\left[1 + (1 - 30\%) \times \frac{1}{2}\right]} = \dfrac{1.45}{1.35} = 1.074$

19.6 The APV is the value of an activity, based on its inherent worth as given by the PV of the stream of operating cash flows, adjusted for any 'special factors' such as tax concessions, financing costs, etc. It is thus the 'basic' NPV plus the PV of non-operating factors.

19.7 In theory, the limit to a firm's taxable capacity is where its interest charge equals the lowest possible level of future cash flows. In reality, it is much less than this. Based on asset-backing, the theoretical limit is where the book value of assets equals the book value of borrowings.

CHAPTER 20

20.1 Managerial motives reduce to the three Ps – power, pay and prestige, all of which are enhanced by size of firm.

20.2 If managers are paid according to growth in EPS, a takeover that exploits synergies may enhance their bonuses. However, if financed by debt, the value of the firm could actually fall. Takeovers that aim to reduce risk rarely benefit shareholders, for whom systematic risk is normally more relevant than total risk.

20.3 Cash is more certain, whereas the value of shares is volatile – by the time payment is made, the share value might have fallen. Investors wishing to liquidate the shares received will incur dealing fees.

20.4 The NPV of the bid for Predator's shareholders $=$ (£1,000m + £200m + £50m) − (£1,000m + £230m) = £20m. Prey's shareholders benefit by £30m (60 per cent of gains), and those of Predator by £20m (40 per cent), if the bid is completed at this price.

20.5 The strategic approach to takeover analysis and execution involves the following steps:

- Formulate corporate strategy.
- Assess the role of acquisition candidates in achieving that strategy.
- Screen, value and select from among possible candidates.
- Plan for future integration and/or disposals.
- Make informal approach.
- Announce hostile bid if necessary.
- Complete the deal.
- Integrate the acquisition following a detailed resource audit.
- Post-audit the acquisition and integration processes.

20.6 Takeovers fail to achieve the anticipated benefits due to:

- Managerial motivation rather than shareholder orientation.
- Inadequate evaluation of the target.
- Over-payment for the target.
- Failure to plan the integration process.
- Poor integration, e.g. neglect of the human factor.

20.7 There are many motives for divestment, including:

1 Dismantling conglomerates originally created by merger activity through defensive diversification strategies.

2 A change in strategic focus. This may involve a move away from the core business to new strategic opportunities. Alternatively, a business may decide that it is engaged in too wide a range of activities and seek to concentrate its efforts and resources on a narrower range of core activities. Non-core activities will then be divested.

3 Harvesting past successes, making cash flow available for new opportunities.

4 Selling off unwanted businesses following an acquisition. This is called 'asset-stripping'. Such sell-offs are often planned at the time of the bid.

5 Reversing (or learning from) mistakes.

CHAPTER 21

21.1 A speculator deliberately risks losing money by taking a long or short 'position' in a particular currency. A hedger tries to minimise exposure to risk. Nintendo is, at least to some extent, a hedger.

21.2

	Swedish krona (SEK)	Singapore dollar (SGD)	
Spot Forward points Forward outright	10.5895–10.60645 0.0001–0.0016	2.0499–2.0510 (0.0018–2.0003)	Remember to add the discount in the case of the currency quoted at a discount, and vice versa
	10.5896–10.6061	2.0481–2.0507	

21.3
- Transaction exposure is the risk of loss associated with short-term contractual obligations.
- Translation exposure is the risk of loss when constructing end-of-year financial statements.
- Economic, or operating, or strategic, exposure is the risk of the whole value of the firm falling due to adverse foreign exchange rate changes affecting the PV of future cash flows.

21.4 New York price in one year = $2.00(1.02) = $2.04
London price in one year = £1.00(1.04) = £1.04
Exchange rate under PPP = ($2.04/£1.04) = $1.96 per £1

21.5 Annual interest rate differential of 2.5% = 2.5%/4 over 3 months = 0.625% This is the interest *agio*. Forward rate should be spot less forward *agio* = (£2.0250 × 99.375%) = $2.0123. The US$ trades at a premium of 127 points.

21.6 Langer's assets are now worth (A$100m/1.75) = £57.14m. If all prices inflate at 7% in Australia, Langer's assets will appreciate to A$100m (1.07) = A$107m in one year. The AUD vs. GBP exchange rate should become (1.75 × 1.07/1.02) = A$1.836 per £1. At this rate, the sterling value of these assets = (A$1.07m/1.836) = £58.28m. This is the level to which they would have appreciated had they been located in Britain and experienced 2% UK inflation i.e. £57.14m (1.02) = £58.28m.

21.7 Leading is advancing outflows in a strong currency and advancing inflows in a weak currency. Lagging is delaying inflows in a strong currency and delaying outflows in a weak currency.

21.8 There is no point exercising an option 'at the money'. The purchaser simply loses the premium.

CHAPTER 22

22.1 Broadly, an MNC is a firm whose activities span national borders, but the term usually applies to firms that invest in foreign locations. A global firm both trades and invests abroad.

22.2 Licensing tends to have very low variable costs. Its fixed costs depend on the degree of supervision applied to the overseas operator (the agency costs). Fixed costs are probably higher than for exporting but lower than for FDI.

22.3 FDI differs from domestic investment for many reasons:

- Exposure to FX risk.
- Likelihood of inflation abroad occurring at rates different from home inflation.
- Risk of political intervention, leading to blocked funds, etc.
- Access to concessionary finance and grants.
- Overspill effects on existing operations.

22.4 Beta of project = $(1.4 \times 1.25) = 1.75$
Adjusted for correlation = $(1.75 \times 0.4) = 0.7$
Required return = $5\% + 0.7 [11\% - 5\%] = 5\% + 4.2\% = 9.2\%$

22.5 The firm will pay tax only in the USA, i.e. (US\$100m $\times$ 30%) = US\$30m, which is allowable in full against UK tax liability.

22.6 Exposure of US operations = US\$(50m − 30m) = US\$20m
Exposure in South America = US\$100m
Total exposure US\$120m

22.7 The net exposure could be reduced by:

- Producing more output in the USA and shipping direct to South America.
- Sourcing more USD-denominated inputs to support UK production.
- Borrowing in USD.

22.8
- Source materials and services from local suppliers.
- Employ locals in key management posts.
- Invest in training programmes for locals.
- Invest in sports and health facilities, open to the wider population.
- Sponsor local cultural events.
- Undertake joint ventures with local firms.
- Reinvestment rather than repatriation of profits.
- Use local sources of finance.

CHAPTER 23

23.1 **(1)** Some people are simply lucky.
(2) Some people stay lucky for several time periods, although shrewd ones remember to get out while ahead!
(3) In any time period, 50 per cent of investors ought to beat the market average.
(4) Some people deliberately assume high levels of risk for which a relatively high return is appropriate. We should therefore talk about 'risk-adjusted returns' rather than simple returns.
(5) Some people have access to inside information. This, of course, contravenes strong-form efficiency but it happens, although such information is unlikely to arrive in a steady stream over time.

Appendix B

Solutions to selected questions

CHAPTER 1

1 The goal of maximising owners' wealth is the normally accepted economic objective for resource allocation decisions. Rather than concentrate on the organisation, it evaluates investments from the viewpoint of the organisation's owners – usually shareholders. Any investment that increases their stock of wealth (the present value of future cash flows) is economically acceptable.

In practice, many of the assumptions underlying this goal do not always hold (e.g. shareholders are only interested in maximising the market value of their shareholdings). In addition, owners are often far removed from managerial decision-making, where capital investment takes place. Accordingly, it is common to find that more easily measurable criteria are used, such as profitability and growth goals. There are also non-economic considerations, such as employee welfare and managerial satisfaction, which can be important for some decisions.

CHAPTER 2

2 (c) (i) *For the cash offer*
On Day 1, the total value of each firm is:

A: £2 × 2m shares = £4m

B: £3 × 6m shares = £18m

Company B is making an offer of £6 million for Company A which is apparently worth only £4 million – this will reduce the market value of B by £2 million to £16 million or £16 million/6 = £2.67 per share. Against this, the anticipated savings would raise B's value to (£16m + £3.2m) = £19.2m or £3.20 per share (assuming the market accepts this assessment).

1 *Semi-strong form efficiency*
Under semi-strong form efficiency, the market prices will only react when the information about the bid enters the public domain. The advent of new information will produce the following share prices:

		Share price	
		A	**B**
Day 2	No new information	£2.00	£3.00
Day 4	Takeover bid announced. B appears to be paying £6m		
	for assets worth £4m	£3.00	£2.67
Day 10	Information available which revises the market		
	value of B	£3.00	£3.20

2 *Strong form efficiency*
If the market is strong form efficient, all information is reflected in the share price even if it is not publicly available information. This will mean that on Day 2, when the management of B decides to offer £3.00 for A,

the share prices will then react to reflect the full impact of the bid on both shares, perhaps via leakage of information by an informed insider. This will produce the following share prices:

		Share price A	Share price B
Day 2	Full impact of decision to bid and make savings reflected in share price	£3.00	£3.20
Day 4	Public announcement of bid, i.e. information of which the market is aware and therefore has no new information content	£3.00	£3.20
Day 10	Public announcement of savings to be derived from bid, i.e. further information of which the market is aware and therefore has no new information content	£3.00	£3.20

(ii) *For the share exchange*

Prior to the bid, the combined value of the two companies is (£4m + £18m) = £22m. If a share-for-share exchange were made on a one-for-one basis, the value per share of the expanded company would become £22m/8m = £2.75m, until further information about prospective savings emerged. Under semi-strong form efficiency, this will not happen until Day 10, but will leak out on to the market immediately under strong form efficiency. Spread over the whole 8m shares, the savings are worth £3.2m/8m = £0.4 per share.

The sequence of share price movements is thus:

	Level of efficiency			
	Semi-strong A	Semi-strong B	Strong A	Strong B
Day 2	£2	£3	£3.15	£3.15
Day 4	£2.75	£2.75	£3.15	£3.15
Day 10	£3.15	£3.15	£3.15	£3.15

Notice that the ultimate share price under the share exchange is lower than for the cash offer. This is because the benefits of the merger are spread out over a larger number of shares post-bid. In effect, the shareholders of B will have released part of the benefit they expect to receive from the bid to the former shareholders of A.

CHAPTER 3

1 Accounting profit is the excess of income over expenditure. Income and expenses relate to a specific period (e.g. the sales and costs for the month of January) based on accounting conventions such as depreciation. Cash flow is the cash receipts and payments from all operations including capital investment.

2 Using the table in Appendix D, the annuity factor for ten years and $i = 20\%$ is 4.1925:

$$PV = £100 \times 4.1925 = £419.25$$

3 Savings: £500,000 × 3.7908   £18,954
Residual value: £1,000 × 0.62092   £621
                                      £19,575
Less: initial cost: (£20,000)
NPV   £(425)

The NPV is negative. Recommend the project is rejected.

7 Free cash flow per share $= (£5m/10m) = £0.50$ or 50p

(i) $P_0 = (£0.5/0.12) = £4.17$

(ii) $P_0 = \dfrac{50\% \times 50p(1 + [15\% \times 50\%])}{12\% - [15\% \times 50\%]} = \dfrac{26.88p}{0.045} = £5.97$

(iii) $P_0 = \dfrac{50\% \times 50p(1 + [10\% + 50\%])}{12\% - [10\% \times 50\%]} = \dfrac{26.25p}{0.07} = £3.75$

(iv) Present value of dividends over Years 1–3:

Year 1 Dividend $= 26.88p$, as per part (ii) PV at 12% $= £0.239$
Year 2 Dividend $= 26.88p\,(1.075) = 28.89p$ PV at 12% $= £0.230$
Year 3 Dividend $= 28.89p\,(1.075) = 31.05p$ PV at 12% $= £0.221$
PV of dividends beyond year 3:

$$= \frac{31.05p\,(1.05)}{(12\% - 5\%)} \times \text{(3-year PV factor)}$$

$$= (£4.657 \times 0.7118) = \underline{£3.315}$$

Share price = Total PV $= £4.005$

8 (i) £0.37955

(ii) $(0.6 \times 16\%) = 9.6\%$

(iii) £0.65

(iv) £0.20

(v) $b = g/R = (2\%/10\%) = 0.2$

(vi) $k_e = ((D_1/P_0) + g) = (£0.054/£0.60) + 8\% = 17\%$

(vii) As $g = 10.5\%$, and
$b = 0.7$,
$$R = \frac{g}{b} = \frac{0.105}{0.7} = 15\%$$

CHAPTER 4

2 Microtic Ltd

		Project A (£)		Project B (£)	
1	*Payback period*	1,616,000/500,000		556,000/200,000	
	Outlay/annual flow	= 3.2 years		= 2.8 years	
2	*Net present value (15%)*				
	Annual cash flow five years £500 × 3.352	1,676,000	200 × 3.352	670,400	
	Scrap value £301 × 0.497	149,600	56 × 0.497	27,800	
	Outlay	(1,616,000)		(556,000)	
	NPV	209,600		142,200	
3	*Internal rate of return*				
	(use trial and error to obtain NPV of zero)	try 20%		try 25%	
	Annual cash flow £500 × 2,991	1,495,500	200 × 2,689	537,800	
	Scrap value £301 × 0.402	121,000	56 × 0.328	18,400	
	Outlay	(1,616,000)		(556,000)	
	NPV	500		200	
4	*Accounting rate of return*				
	Average profit before depreciation	500,000		200,000	
	Depreciation (£1616 − £301)/5	(263,000)	(556 − 56)/5	(100,000)	
		237,000		100,000	
	Average capital employed (£1616 + £301)/2	958,500	(556 + 56)/2	306,000	
	Rate	24.7%		32.7%	

Investment advice

All appraisal methods apart from the NPV approach recommend acceptance of Project B. This is because it generates a higher return for every £1 invested. The question is, however, which of the two projects creates most wealth for the owners. Clearly, the much larger Project A has the higher NPV. Unless the firm is experiencing severe capital rationing problems, Project A should be accepted.

3 Mace Ltd (£000)

Project	NPV per £ outlay	Ranking	Fraction accepted	Required capital (£)	NPV (£)
1	1.6/60 = 0.027	4	0	–	–
2	1.3/30 = 0.043	3	1/3	10	0.43
3	8.3/40 = 0.207	1	1	40	8.3
4				0	0.9
5	7.9/50 = 0.158	2	1	50	7.9
				100	17.53

CHAPTER 5

1 The preference for IRR in practice is because:

(a) It is easier to understand (this is debatable).
(b) It is useful in ranking projects (although not always accurate).
(c) Lower-level managers do not need to know the discount rate. Where a risk-adjusted hurdle rate is used, there may be considerable negotiation over the appropriate rate.
(d) Psychological. Managers prefer a percentage.

2 (a) Payback = four years. The reciprocal is 25 per cent, which is the IRR for a project of infinite life.
(b) For a 20-year life, IRR = 24%. For an eight-year life, IRR = 19%.
(c) The annual cash flows are approximately the same for a long-lived project, the payback reciprocal is a reasonable proxy for the IRR. The actual IRR is always something less than that given by the payback reciprocal.

4 The two basic approaches in handling inflation are:

(a) forecast cash flows in money terms (i.e. including inflation) and discount at the money cost of capital; or
(b) forecast cash flows in current terms and discount at the real cost of capital.
The relationship between the two is given by:

$$(1 + P) = \frac{(1 + M)}{(1 + I)}$$

where M is the money cost of capital, I is the inflation rate and P is the real cost of capital.

5 Bramhope Manufacturing

(i) **(a)** Additional investment: £123,500 –£15,000 = £108,500. Additional annual inflow = £24,300 (see below). Therefore payback period = £108,500/£24,300 = 4.5 years.

(b)

Time	Cash flow (£)	DF at 15%	PV (£)	DF at 17%	PV (£)
0	(108,500)	1	(108,500)	1	(108,500)
1–8	24,300	4.48732	109,042	4.20716	102,234
8	20,500	0.32690	6,701	0.28478	5,838
			7,243		(428)

(c) NPV AT 15% = £7,243; IRR = approx. 17%.
Workings: Existing project's annual cash inflow = £200,000 × (0.95 − 0.12 − 0.48) = £70,000.
Net project's annual cash inflow = £230,000 × (0.95 − 0.08 − 0.46) = £94,300.
Incremental cash flow = £94,300 − £70,000 = £24,300.

(ii) The project appears to offer a positive net present value and should be accepted. However, an NPV of £7,000 on a project costing £123,500 is relatively small, and questions should be asked as to how sensitive the key assumptions are to uncertainty. For example, is it realistic that the additional capacity can be sold at the current price? Will there really be no increase in fixed overheads? If an advanced machine has been developed after just two years, is an eight-year economic life optimistic?

CHAPTER 6

1 Capital budgeting involves the whole investment process from the original idea to the final post-audit.

The resource allocation process is the main vehicle by which business strategy can be implemented. Investment decisions are not simply the result of applying some evaluation criterion. The investment decision process is essentially one of search: search for ideas, search for information, search for alternatives and search for decision criteria. The prosperity of a firm depends more on its ability to create profitable investment opportunities than on its ability to appraise them.

Once a firm commits itself to a particular project, it must regularly and systematically monitor and control the project through its various stages of implementation. Post-audit reviews – if properly designed – fulfil a useful role in improving the quality of existing and future investment analysis and provide a means of initiating corrective action for existing projects.

2 Aims of post-audits:
   (a) improve the quality of existing decisions and underlying assumptions
   (b) improve the quality of future decisions
   (c) basis for corrective action

3 (a)

	Total automation £ per unit	Partial automation £ per unit
Sales price	75	75
Variable cost	(30)	(55)
Contribution	45	20
Fixed cost (see note 1)	(18)	(5)
Net profit	27	15
Total cost per unit	£48	£60
Annual net profit	£270,000	£150,000
Break-even units (p/a)	4,000	2,500
Net present value:		

	Cash flow £	Cash flow £
Outlay	−1,000,000	−250,000
Inflows Years 1–5	+450,000	+200,000
Scrap value Year 5	+100,000	–

	Present value £	Present value £
Outlay	−1,000,000	−250,000
Inflows at 3.27	+1,471,500	+654,000
Scrap value at 0.48	+48,000	–
Net present value	+519,500	+404,000

Note 1	$\dfrac{(1,000,000 - 100,000)}{5 \times 10,000}$	$\dfrac{(250,000)}{5 \times 10,000}$

(b) The total automation option produces a lower product cost. As the sales price and volume are identical for both alternatives, a higher annual profit is also reported by this alternative. Partial automation involves lower fixed costs (depreciation), but variable costs are substantially greater. With the cost pattern above, the total automation alternative results in a higher break-even point.

Remember that there is a higher initial capital cost with total automation. The accrual accounting assumptions applied above acknowledge this with an annual charge for depreciation. The net present value technique takes account of the capital cost in a different manner, charging the full cost immediately against discounted future cash flows. In this case, total automation generates a higher NPV but a higher initial outlay.

When the amount of the initial capital investment is considered, the option to undertake partial automation looks attractive. It achieves a net present value of 80 per cent of total automation with only one-quarter of the capital expenditure. Partial automation shows a profitability index of 2.62, compared with 1.52 for the total automation, which emphasises the attractiveness of the lower investment. The recommendation of the NPV technique must, however, be interpreted with care and considered in the light of the overall company situation. Investment in total automation is the course of action which will maximise the wealth of the owners (the extra benefit exceeds the extra capital cost at 16 per cent). If the company is not in a capital-constrained situation, then total automation should be pursued. If the company has a number of projects, all competing for limited capital, then we would need to know the returns from the other investment opportunities and compare them with the incremental investment being directed to total automation.

The data omit certain other factors which may be pertinent to the analysis, for example, quality differences, maximum machine capacities, maximum sales demand, the flexibility and interchangeability of parts and equipment which may be beneficial.

For a lower risk investment with an attractive return, the company should opt for partial automation. If they have extra capital available, electing for total automation of the product line will earn above their extra cost of capital but nothing is known about other projects competing for this extra capital.

CHAPTER 7

1 While a capital project may have a high expected return, the risks involved may mean that there is the possibility that the project will be unsuccessful – even to the extent of putting the whole business in jeopardy.

2 Project risk – variability in the projects' cash flows; business risk – variability in operating earnings of the firm; financial risk – risk resulting from the firm's financing decisions, e.g. the level of borrowing; portfolio risk – variability in the returns for an overall portfolio of investments.

3 Woodpulp project

Year	CE	NCF(£)	ENCF(£)	10% DF	PV(£)
1	0.90	8,000	7,200	0.90	6,480
2	0.85	7,000	5,950	0.83	4,938
3	0.80	7,000	5,600	0.75	4,200
4	0.75	5,000	3,750	0.68	2,550
5	0.70	5,000	3,500	0.62	2,170
6	0.65	5,000	3,250	0.56	1,820
7	0.60	5,000	3,000	0.51	1,530
				PV	23,688

NPV = £23,688 − £13,000 = £10,688. Accept the project. ENCF = Expected net cash flow.

4 Mystery Enterprises

Expected value Year 1 (£) $= 0.2(400) + 0.3(500) + 0.3(600) + 0.2(700) = £550$

Variance (£) $= 0.2(400 - 550)^2 + 0.3(500 - 550)^2$
$+ 0.3(600 - 550)^2 + 0.2(700 - 550)^2 = £10,500$

Standard deviation $= £102$

Expected value Year 2 (£) $= 0.2(300) + 0.3(400) + 0.3(500) + 0.2(600) = £450$

Variance (£) $= 0.2(300 - 450)^2 + 0.3(400 - 450)^2$
$+ 0.3(500 - 450)^2 + 0.2(600 - 450)^2 = £10,500$

Standard deviation $= £102$

Assuming a discount rate of 10 per cent and independent cash flows:

$$NPV = \frac{£550}{1.1} + \frac{£450}{(1.1)^2} - £800 = £71$$

$$SD = \sqrt{\frac{(£102)^2}{(1.1)^2} + \frac{(£102)^2}{(1.1)^4}} = £125$$

$$Coefficient\,of\,variation = \frac{£125}{£71} = 1.76$$

CHAPTER 8

1 Portfolio standard deviation $= \sqrt{\left[(0.5)^2\sigma_X^2 + (0.5)^2\sigma_Y^2 + 2(0.5)(0.5)(r_{XY}\,\sigma_X\,\sigma_Y)\right]}$

$$= \sqrt{\left[(0.5)^2 30^2 + (0.5)^2 45^2 + 2(0.5)(0.5)(0.2)(30)(45)\right]}$$

$$= \sqrt{\left[225 + 506.25 + 135\right]}$$

$$= \sqrt{866.25} = 29.4$$

This portfolio has a risk only slightly below that of investment X, even though the correlation coefficient is quite low. This suggests that the portfolio weighting involves too little of investment X if the intention is to lower portfolio risk.

2 The appropriate formula is:

$$Proportion\,invested\,in\,asset\,A = \frac{\sigma_B^2 - cov_{AB}}{\sigma_B^2 + \sigma_A^2 - 2cov_{AB}}$$

Also, remember that $cov_{AB} = r_{AB}\,\sigma_A\,\sigma_B$
(i) The covariance $= -12.6\%$ in $A = 74\%$, in $B = 26\%$
(ii) The covariance is -36% in $A = 29\%$, in $B = 71\%$
(iii) The covariance is 0% in $A = 0.44\%$, in $B = 99.56\%$

3 (a) China:

Expected value $= (0.3 \times 50\%) + (0.4 \times 25\%) + (0.3 \times 0) = 25\%$

Growth	Probability	IRR%	Deviation	Squared deviation	Times probability
Rapid	0.3	50	25	625	187.50
Stable	0.4	25	–	–	–
Slow	0.3	0	−25	625	187.50
					Sum = 375.00

Standard deviation $= \sqrt{375.0} = 19.4$, i.e. 19.4%

Scotland:
Expected value $= (0.3 \times 10\%) + (0.4 \times 15\%) + (0.3 \times 16\%) = 13.8\%$

Growth	Probability	IRR%	Deviation	Squared deviation	Times probability
Rapid	0.3	10	−3.8	14.44	4.33
Stable	0.4	15	1.2	1.44	0.58
Slow	0.3	16	2.2	4.84	1.45
					Sum = 6.36

Standard deviation $= \sqrt{6.36} = 2.5\%$

(b) Covariance calculation:

Covariance $= -45$

Expected portfolio return

$= (0.75 \times 13.8\%) + (0.25 \times 25\%) = 16.6\%$

Standard deviation

$$= \sqrt{[(0.25^2 \times 19.4^2) + (0.75^2 \times 2.5^2) + (2 \times 0.25 \times 0.75 \times -45)]}$$
$$= \sqrt{[(23.5) + (3.5) + (-16.9)]}$$
$$= \sqrt{10.1} = 3.2, \text{i.e. } 3.2\%$$

4 (a) *Ireland*: EV of IRR $= (0.3 \times 20\%) + (0.3 \times 10\%) + (0.4 \times 15\%)$

$= 6\% + 3\% + 6\% = 15\%$

Outcome (%)	Deviation	Sq'd Dev.	p	Sq'd Dev. $\times p$
20	+5	25	0.3	7.5
10	−5	25	0.3	7.5
15	0	0	0.4	0
			Variance = Total	15 $\sigma = 3.87$

Humberside: EV of IRR $= (0.3 \times 10\%) + (0.3 \times 30\%) + (0.4 \times 20\%)$

$= 3\% + 9\% + 8\% = 20\%$

Outcome (%)	Deviation	Sq'd Dev.	p	Sq'd Dev. $\times p$
10	−10	100	0.3	30
30	+10	100	0.3	30
20	0	0	0.4	0
			Variance = Total	60 $\sigma = 7.75$

(b) (i) For a 50/50 split investment:

EV of IRR $= (0.5 \times 15\%) + (0.5 \times 20\%) = 17.5\%$

$\sigma = \sqrt{(0.5)^2(15) + (0.5)^2(60) + 2(0.5)(0.5)(0)(3.87)(7.75)}$

$= \sqrt{[3.75 + 15]} = \sqrt{18.75} = 4.33$

(ii) 75/25 split:

EV $= (0.75 \times 15\%) + (0.25 \times 20\%) = 11.25\% + 5\% = 16.25\%$

$\sigma = \sqrt{(0.75)^2(15) + (0.25)^2(60)}$

$= \sqrt{[8.44 + 3.75]} = \sqrt{12.19} = 3.49$, i.e. lower risk than either project

CHAPTER 9

1 Expected return $= 5\% + 1.23[11.5\% - 5\%] = 13\%$. With more pessimistic expectations about market returns, this drops to:

$ER = 5\% + 1.23[8\% - 5\%] = 8.7\%$

2 (i) $R_f = 9\%$

(ii) Beta $= 1.71$

(iii) $ER_j = 8.5\%$

(iv) $ER_m = 19.3\%$

3 The intercept of the Security Market Line is the risk-free rate. It passes through the market portfolio which has a Beta of 1.0. In diagrammatic terms:

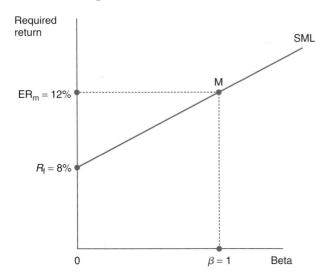

4 $\mathrm{ER}_A = 5\% + 0.7[10\% - 5\%] = 8.5\%$
$\mathrm{ER}_B = 5\% + 1.3[5\%] \qquad = 11.5\%$
$\mathrm{ER}_C = 5\% + 0.9[5\%] \qquad = 9.5\%$

Comparing the expected returns with those currently achieved, A and C generate returns lower than expected, which suggests they are overvalued. (B looks undervalued.)

5 (i) Projecting past returns into the future, the expected return on the whole market is $(5\% + 7\%) = 12\%$.

(ii)

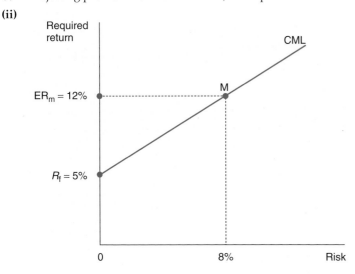

(iii) For a 50/50 portfolio:

$\mathrm{ER}_p = (0.5 \times 12\%) + (0.5 \times 5\%) = 8.5\%$

(iv) Bearing in mind there is no correlation between the risk-free rate and the market portfolio, the expression for portfolio risk is:

$\sigma_p = \sqrt{(0.5)^2 (8)^2}$
$\quad = \sqrt{16} = 4, \text{ i.e. } 4\%$

Alternatively, we could use the weighted average expression:

$(0.5 \times 8\%) + (0.5 \times 0) = 4\%$

(v) As risk increases from 4% (the 50/50 portfolio) to 8% (the market portfolio), the return required increases from 8.5% to 12%, suggesting a risk–return trade-off (assuming it is linear) of:

$(3.5\%/4\%) = 0.875$

Thus, for every one percentage point increase in the portfolio standard deviation, the investor must be compensated by an increase in portfolio return of 0.875%.

6 (a) Your graph should show every pair of observations lying along a straight line. This indicates perfect positive correlation between R_j and R_m. The slope of the line, and hence the Beta, is +0.8.

(b) Because all observations lie on the line of best fit, all variation in R_j appears to be explained by variation in R_m, i.e. there is no specific risk.

(c) $\sigma_m^2 =$ variance of the market return. The mean return on the market portfolio = 2.0. Hence

$$\sigma_m^2 = (5 - 2)^2 + (-10 - 2)^2 + \cdots + (6 - 2)^2 = 306$$

Thus, systematic risk $= (0.8)^2 (306) = 195.84$.

You should expect to find the total risk is also 195.84 because there is no unique risk.

CHAPTER 10

1 The shares are ex-dividend, so the future required return is:

$$k_e = \frac{£0.80(1.045)}{£10.50} + 0.045 = (0.08 + 0.045)$$
$$= 0.125, \text{ i.e. } 12.5\%$$

2 (i) $D_0 = £0.62$
(ii) $P_0 = £3.64$
(iii) $k_e = 9.3\%$
(iv) $g = 6.2\%$

3 Dividend growth is found by solving:

$$11p (1 + g)^4 = 20.0p$$
$$(1 + g)^4 = \frac{20.0p}{11.0p} = 1.8182$$

From tables, $g = 15.8\%$ approx.

$$\text{Implied } k_e = \frac{20p(1.158)}{£5.50} + 0.158$$
$$= 0.042 + 0.158 = 0.20, \text{ i.e. } 20\%$$

4 (i) $k_e = 6\% + 0.8[11\% - 6\%] = (6\% + 4\%) = 10\%$

(ii) Beta $= (0.8 \times 1.25) = 1.0$
$\quad k_e = 6\% + 1.0[11\% - 6\%] = (6\% + 5\%) = 11\%$

(iii) Beta $= (0.8 \times 0.75) = 0.6$
$\quad k_e = 6\% + 0.6[11\% - 6\%] = (6\% + 3\%) = 9\%$

5

Division	R_f	Beta	Market Premium	k_e	% of assets
C	7%	0.7	8.00	12.6%	15
E	7%	1.1	8.00	15.8%	40
R	7%	0.8	8.00	13.4%	20
P	7%	0.6	8.00	11.8%	5
Total	/	0.855	/	13.84%	100

Overall Beta $= (0.15 \times 0.7) + (0.04 \times 1.1) + (0.20 \times 0.8) + (0.25 \times 0.6)$
$$= (0.105 + 0.44 + 0.16 + 0.15) = 0.855$$

Overall required return $= 7\% + 0.855[8\%] = (7\% + 6.84\%) = 13.84\%$

6 (a) EV of return $= (0.6 \times 10\%) + (0.4 \times 20\%) = 14\%$.

Outcome	Deviation	Squared deviation	Prob.	Sq'd $\times$ dev. p
10%	−4%	16	0.6	9.6
20%	+6%	36	0.4	14.4
			Variance = Total	24.0 $\sigma = 4.9$

(b) Megacorp ER $= 30\%$ s.d. $= 14\%$ proportion $= 80\%$
Erewhon ER $= 14\%$ s.d. $= 4.9\%$ proportion $= 20\%$

ER $= (0.8 \times 30\%) + (0.2 \times 14\%) = 24\% + 2.8\% = 26.8\%$
S.d. $= \sqrt{[(0.8)^2 (14)^2 + (0.2)^2 (4.9)^2 + 2(0.8)(0.2)(-0.36)(14)(4.9)]}$

(c) The present Beta $= 1.20$.

$$\text{Beta of project} = \frac{\text{cov}_{jm}}{\sigma_m^2} = \frac{r_{jm}\sigma_j\sigma_m}{\sigma_m^2} = \frac{r_{jm}\sigma_j}{\sigma_m}$$

What is the risk of the market (σ_m)?
Rearranging:

$$\sigma_m = \frac{\sigma_j r_{jm}}{\text{Beta}_j}$$

For Megacorp:
$$\sigma_j = \frac{(14)(0.8)}{1.2} = 9.33$$

$$\text{Project Beta} = \frac{(-0.1)(4.9)}{9.33} = -\frac{0.49}{9.33} = -0.05$$

New Beta for Megacorp $= (0.8 \times 1.2) + (0.2 \times -0.05) = 0.95$. Therefore, the new project lowers Megacorp's Beta.

8 (a) Since the asset Beta is a weighted average of the component segment Betas:

$$\beta_A = \left(\frac{1}{4} \times \beta_N\right) + \left(\frac{1}{4} \times \beta_W\right) + \left(\frac{1}{2} \times \beta_S\right) = 1.06$$

where $\beta_N = \beta$ of North, $\beta_W = \beta$ of West, $\beta_S = \beta$ of South.

Since North is 50 per cent more risky than South, and West is 25 per cent less risky than South, it follows that:

$$\frac{(1.5\beta_S)}{4} + \frac{(0.75\beta_S)}{4} + \frac{\beta_S}{2} = 1.06$$

whence $\beta_S = 1.00$, $\beta_N = 1.50$, $\beta_W = 0.75$.

(b) The asset Beta for East β_E) is:

$\beta_E = \beta_S \times$ Relative risk factor

$\quad\ = \beta_S \times$ Revenue sensitivity factor $\times$ Operational gearing factor

$\quad\ = 1.0 \times 1.4 \times \dfrac{1.6}{2.0} = 1 \times 1.12 = 1.12$

(c) The asset Beta for Lancelot after the divestment and acquisition is again a weighted average of the component asset Betas:

$$\beta_A = \left(\frac{1}{2} \times \beta_E\right) + \left(\frac{1}{4} \times \beta_W\right) + \left(\frac{1}{4} \times \beta_N\right)$$

$$\ \ = \left(\frac{1}{2} \times 1.12\right) + \left(\frac{1}{4} \times 0.75\right) + \left(\frac{1}{4} \times 1.5\right)$$

$$\quad\quad\quad = 0.56 + 0.1875 + 0.375 = 1.12$$

(d) If we evaluate projects in East on the assumption of all-equity financing, the cut-off rate is:

$$R_f + \beta_E(ER_m - R_f) = 10\% + 1.12(15\%) = 26.8\%$$

(e) There are numerous problems involved in obtaining tailor-made project discount rates. First, given that we may have to take the Beta from a surrogate company, ungearing the Beta of its shares requires an accurate assessment of the values of the equity and debt. If the company is quoted, the market valuation of equity can be taken, but not all corporate debt is quoted. Thus the debt:equity ratio used will often be a mixture of market and book values, even for quoted companies. Second, decomposing the ungeared Beta into segmental asset Betas strictly requires weighted average calculations based on market values. Since corporate segments are not generally quoted on stock markets, book values invariably have to be used. Third, to measure project Betas requires consideration of whether the project is of a different order of risk from 'typical' projects in the division. If so, the revenue sensitivity factor requires estimation, mainly based on guesswork for unique projects. In addition, the project gearing factor must also be estimated. Fourth, the general problems relating to specification of the risk-free return and the risk premium on the market portfolio still have to be addressed.

CHAPTER 11

3 Free cash flow (£) = Revenue less bad debts less operating costs + depreciation less replacement investment less tax (allowing for relief on bad debts)

$\quad\ = (0.98 \times 500{,}000) - (300{,}000) + (50{,}000)$

$\quad\quad\quad - (50{,}000) - (60{,}000 + [0.3 \times 50\% \times 2\% \times 500{,}000])$

$\quad\ = (490{,}000 - 300{,}000 + 50{,}000 - 50{,}000 - 60{,}000 + 1{,}500)$

$\quad\ = £131{,}500$

(a) valued at 10% as a perpetuity:

$V = (£131{,}500/0.1) = £1.315$ million

i.e. $(£1.315m/2m) = £0.6575$ per share (65.75p)

(b) valued over 10 years:

$V = (£131{,}500 \times 10$ year annuity factor 10%)

$\quad = (£131{,}500 \times 6.1446) = £808{,}015m$, or £0.405 per share (40.5p).

CHAPTER 12

1 Companies issue a type of call option when issuing share warrants (giving the holder the right to buy shares at a fixed price) and convertible loan stock (giving the holder the right to exchange the loan for a fixed number of shares).

2 Gaymore plc
Traded options give the holder the right, but not the obligation, to buy (a call option) or sell (a put option) a quantity of shares at a fixed price on an exercise date in the future. They are usually in contracts of 1,000 shares and for three, six or nine months.

Holders of a put option in Gaymore plc have the right to sell shares in April at 500p. For this right they currently have to pay a premium of 47p, or £470 on a contract of 1,000 shares.

If the share price falls below 453p (i.e. 500p–47p), the shares become profitable and the holder is 'in the money'. So if they fall to 450p, the investor can buy shares at this price and exercise his or her put option to sell shares for 500p, a profit of 50p per share which, after the initial cost of the option, gives a net profit of 3p per share or £30 on the contract.

If the share price moves up to 510p by April, the option becomes worthless, and the investor loses his or her 47p premium.

Options such as this one can be used either to speculate or to hedge on share price changes for a relatively low premium.

3 The terms for an exchange traded option are standardised whereas the terms for traditional options can vary from contract to contract. It is the development of standardised options that has facilitated the trading of these instruments.

6 The put–call parity relationship is:

$S + P - C = E/(1 + R_f)$

From this:

$C = S - (E/(1 + R_f)) + P$

where $S = 25$, $P = 15$, $E/(1 + R_f) = 10$.

$C = 25 - 10 + 15 = 30$

The value of the call option is 30p.

7 The put–call parity relationship is:

$S + P - C = E/(1 + R_f)$

$E/(1 + R_f) = 30 + 5 - 19 = 16p$

8 Inputs:

$S_T = 38p \quad X = 40p$

$T = 0.5 \quad r_f = 0.10$

$SD(R) = 0.20$

Valuation equations:

$$C_t = S_t N(d_1) - Xe^{-rT} N(d_2)$$
$$d_1 = \frac{\ln(S_1/X) + (r + VAR(R)/2)t}{SD(r)\sqrt{t}}$$
$$d_2 = \frac{\ln(S_1/X) + (r + VAR(R)/2)t}{SD(r)\sqrt{t}} = d_1 - SD(r)\sqrt{t}$$
$$d_1 = [\ln 38/40 + (0.10 + 0.20^2/2)0.5]/0.2/\sqrt{0.5}$$

$$= [-0.05129 + 0.06]/[0.2 \times 0.7071]$$
$$= 0.06156$$
$$d_2 = [\ln 38/40 + (0.10 - 0.20^2/2)0.5]/0.2\sqrt{0.5}$$
$$= [-0.05129 + 0.04]/[0.2 \times 0.7071]$$
$$= -0.07986$$
$$N(d_1) = N(0.0615) = 0.5245$$
$$N(d_2) = N(-0.0798) = 0.4682$$
$$C_1 = 38.00 \times 0.5245 - 40.00e^{-0.10 \times 0.5} \times 0.4682$$
$$= 19.93 - 17.81$$
$$= 2.12$$

Calculations:
The estimated value of the call is 2.12p. This implies that if the call is bought at this price the share price would have to increase from 38.00p to 40.12p by the end of the six-month period for the investor to break even.

9 Put–call parity

$$S + P = C + ke^{-rt}$$
$$\Rightarrow 420.5 + 38.5 = 50.5 + 420e^{-0.5r}$$
$$\Rightarrow 0.9726 = e^{-0.5r}$$
$$\Rightarrow -0.5r = -0.02776$$
$$\Rightarrow r = 0.0555 = 5.55\%$$

10 (a) Intrinsic value: The intrinsic value of an option is the difference between the value of the underlying asset and the exercise price of the option. September 800 call is in the money while the April put is out of the money.

Time value: When options are more valuable the greater is the likelihood of a significant change in the value of the underlying asset. If an option expires tomorrow we can certainly say that there is a smaller likelihood of a significant change than if the option expires in six months. Quite simply, the longer the time to expiration, the more opportunity there is for the price to move and therefore at March the September option is more valuable than the April option.

(b) Short straddle (written straddle)

E.g. June 800 call + put: written premiums $= 53.5 + 20 = 73.5$p

The option writer receives 73.5p. If neither option is exercised, the writer gains all of this. However, this is the outcome only if $S_T = 800$.

If $S_T > 800$ the call is exercised, if $800 < S_T$ the put is exercised.

The writer will gain from the strategy if the intrinsic value of the exercised option is less than the 73.5 premiums received. Hence the writer will only profit if S_T is within the range 726.5 to 873.5.

If $S_T = 726.5$ the put is exercised, the writer must take delivery at 800, therefore losing 73.5, which exactly cancels the written premiums of 73.5, so net profit $= 0$.

If $S_T = 873.5$ the call is exercised, the writer must deliver the share at price 800, therefore losing 73.5, which exactly cancels out the written premiums, so net profit $= 0$.

Thus at any share price outside of that range the writer of the short straddle has an overall loss. If share price at expiration is within the range, the writer makes a net profit.

In general, the profit to short straddle $=$ written premiums $-$ intrinsic value of the option that is exercised.

Losses *could* be very high, e.g. if $S_T = 650$ loss $= 76.5$ (i.e. $73.5 - 150$), if $S_T = 1000$ loss $= 126.5$ ($73.5 - 200$). It is extremely risky.

12 Using the Black–Scholes formula

$$d_1 = \frac{\ln(P_s/X) + 0.5\sigma}{\sigma\sqrt{T}}\sqrt{T}$$

$$= \frac{\ln(3/2.50) + (0.5 \times 0.25)}{0.2 \times \sqrt{0.25}} + (0.5 \times 0.2 \times \sqrt{0.25})$$

$$= \frac{0.1823 + 0.0125}{0.1} + 0.5$$

$$= 1.9982$$

$$d_2 = d_1 - \sigma\sqrt{T}$$

$$= 1.9982 - 0.2\sqrt{0.25}$$

$$= 1.9982 - 0.1$$

$$= 1.8982$$

$$N(d_1) = 0.5 + 0.4767 + \frac{82}{100}(0.4772 - 0.4767)$$

$$= 0.9771$$

$$N(d_2) = 0.5 + 0.4706 + \frac{82}{100}(0.4713 - 0.4706)$$

$$= 0.9712$$

$$P_c = P_s N(d_1) - Xe^{-rT}N(d_2)$$

$$= (3 \times 0.9771) - (2.50e^{-0.05 \times 0.25} \times 0.9712)$$

$$= 2.9313 - (2.50 \times 0.9876 \times 0.9712)$$

$$= 53.35p$$

CHAPTER 14

3 Hercules Wholesalers Ltd

(a) The liquidity position may be examined by calculating the following ratios:

$$\text{Current ratio} = \frac{\text{Current assets}}{\text{Creditors due for repayment within one year}}$$

$$= \frac{£306,000}{£285,000}$$

$$= 1.1{:}1$$

$$\text{Acid-test ratio} = \frac{\text{Current assets (less stocks)}}{\text{Creditors due for repayment within one year}}$$

$$= \frac{£163,000}{£285,000}$$

$$= 0.6{:}1$$

The current ratio reveals that the current assets exceed the short-term liabilities of the company. However, the ratio of 1.1:1 seems rather low. If current assets were to be liquidated, they would only have to be sold off at a small discount on the cost to be insufficient to meet the short-term liabilities. The acid-test ratio excludes stocks from the calculation and represents a more stringent test of liquidity. The ratio of 0.6:1 is also low and suggests the company has insufficient liquid assets to meet its maturing obligations. When interpreting these ratios, it should be borne in mind that they are based on Balance Sheet figures and are therefore representative of only one particular moment in time. It would be useful to monitor the trends in these ratios over time. It would also be useful to prepare a cash flow forecast in order to gain a better understanding of the likely liquidity position of the business in the future. The bank overdraft is the major form of short-term finance and the continuing support of the bank is likely to be of critical importance to the company.

(b) The operating cash cycle of a business represents the time period between the outlay of cash on the purchase of stocks and the receipt of cash from trade debtors. In the case of a wholesale business it can be calculated as follows:

Average holding period for stocks + Average settlement period for debtors − Average settlement period for creditors

The operating cash cycle is important because the longer this period is, the greater the financing requirements of the business and the greater the risks involved.

(c) The operating cash cycle is:*ys*

		No. of days
Average period stocks are held $= \dfrac{\text{Average value of stocks held}}{\text{Average daily cost of sales}}$		
$= \dfrac{(£125,000 + £143,000)/2}{(£323,000/360)}$		149
Average settlement period for debtors $= \dfrac{\text{Average level of debtors}}{\text{Average daily sales}}$		
$= \dfrac{£163,000}{(£452,000/360)}$		130
		279
Less:		
Average settlement period for creditors $= \dfrac{\text{Average level of creditors}}{\text{Average daily purchases}}$		
$= \dfrac{£145,000}{(£341,000/360)}$		(153)
		126

(d) The operating cash cycle of the company seems to be quite long. It may be reduced by a reduction in the stocks, improving the collection period from debtors, extending further the average settlement period for creditors or some combination of these measures. The stockholding period and average settlement period for debtors seems high and might be reduced without difficulty. As the average settlement period of creditors appears to be high, it may be difficult to extend this further without incurring problems for the company.

5 Formula for the cost of cash discounts:

$$\frac{\text{Discount\%}}{(100 - \text{Discount\%})} \times \frac{365}{(\text{Final date} - \text{Discount period})}$$

6 The Baumol cash management model assumes cash is drawn down at an even rate and, at some point, is replenished to its original balance. The Miller–Orr model assumes that short-term cash movements cannot be predicted since they meander in a random fashion.

7 Hunslett Express Company

	(£000s)
Average level of debtors – current policy	
$70/365 \times £8m$	1,534
Average levels of debtors – proposed policy	
$50\% \times 30/365 \times £8m$	329
$50\% \times 80/365 \times £8m$	876
	1,205
Reduction in debtors under new policy	329
Financing cost savings ($13\% \times £329,000$)	43
Bad debt savings	20
Administration cost savings	12
	75
Cost of cash discounts	
$50\% \times £8m \times 2\%$	(80)
Estimated cost of scheme	(5)

The net cost of the proposed scheme is £5,000.

8 Salford Engineering Ltd

(a) The optimum stockholding level is a trade-off between the cost of holding stocks and the cost of not holding stock.

Stockholding costs include:

(i) Storage costs. Where stock is valuable these costs can be large.
(ii) Financing costs. Excessive stock requires unnecessary and expensive working capital.
(iii) Insurance costs against theft or damage.
(iv) Obsolescence costs. Stock held for long periods of time may become obsolete through new products coming to the market.

Costs of holding too little stock include:

(i) Loss of customer goodwill and business through not being able to supply goods on time.
(ii) Production stoppages. A 'stockout' can mean costly and harmful disruptions to the production process.
(iii) Lost flexibility. Shortage of stock makes it difficult for a firm to respond to unexpected demand or to extended production runs.

(b) In investigating the reasons for large stock levels for Salford Engineering, the following action should be taken:

(i) Examine the stock re-order levels for each stock line.
(ii) Examine how the optimum stock level is determined. Is any technique for assessing the optimum level employed?
(iii) Are stock requirements carefully budgeted?
(iv) Are ratios used (e.g. stock turnover) to monitor stock levels in total and by stock lines?
(v) Are stock records reliable and adequate?

CHAPTER 15

1 Cost of extra trade credit = lost discount of 3 per cent , i.e. £30 on an invoice of face value of £1,000. Over the extra 30 days during which you delay payment, you are paying a cost of roughly:

$$(£30/\text{extra finance}) \times 365/30 = (£30/£970) \times 12.167$$
$$= 3.09 \times 12.167 = 37.6\%$$

More accurately, the annual rate is

$$(1 + £30/£970)^{12.167} - 1 = (1.0309)^{12.167} - 1 = 1.448 - 1 = 0.448, \text{ i.e. } 44.8\%$$

2 (a) Option 1: The net cost of a full-year loan.

Interest £500,000 × 12%   = £60,000

Less interest received on surplus funds

Q1: (£500,000 − £400,000) × 2% = £2,000

     Compounded for Qs 2–4: = £2,000(1.02)^3 = (£2,122)

Q4: (£500,000 − £200,000) × 2%   = (£6,000)

                                              £51,878

Option 2: The cost of a fluctuating overdraft.

Quarterly interest rate = 14%/4 = 3.5%

Q1:£400,000 × 3.5% = £14,000

Q2:£500,000 × 3.5% = £17,500

Q3:£500,000 × 3.5% = £17,500

Q4:£200,000 × 3.5% =   £7,000

         Total = £56,000

Even without any interest charges on accumulated quarterly overdraft interest, the loan is the cheaper option. However, the overdraft offers possible access to lower interest rates. (Equally, they could rise!).

(Let I = average monthly overdraft rate

£51,878 = I × [£400,000 + £500,000 + £500,000 + £200,000]

I = [£51,878/£1,600,000]

I = 0.0324, rounded to 0.0325,   i.e. 3.25%, or 13% p.a.)

(b) An average annual interest rate of 13% on the overdraft (3.25% per month) is the break-even rate.

3 Cost of early discounting = (£200,000 − £195,500) = £4,500. This corresponds to an effective annual interest cost of roughly:

(£4,500/£195,500) × 12/4 = 6.9%

More accurately, the annual rate is:

$(1.023)^3 − 1 = 1.0706 − 1 = 0.0706$,   i.e. 7.06%

4 Net amount borrowed = (£100,000 − £15,000)   = £85,000

Total interest cost = (7.5% × £85,000 × 4)   =   £25,500

Total required payments   = £110,500

Required monthly payment = £110,500/(4 × 12)   =   £2,302.

7 Amalgamated Effluents plc

The evaluation should be conducted in three stages.

(i) Is the project inherently worthwhile? The basic project must first be evaluated assuming no change in financing, i.e. using the equity cost of capital. Assuming the outlay can be set against Year 0 profit, cash flows are:

	Cash flows (marked by *) (£m)				
	0	**1**	**2**	**3**	**4**
Operating cash inflow*		0.200	0.200	0.200	0.200
Equipment cost*	(0.500)				0.050
WDA	0.125	0.094	0.070	0.053	0.108
WDV	0.375	0.281	0.211	0.158	0.050
Taxable income	(0.125)	0.106	0.130	0.147	0.092
Tax impact at 30%	0.038	(0.032)	(0.039)	(0.044)	(0.028)
Net cash flows*	(0.462)	0.168	0.161	0.156	0.172
PV at 10%	(0.462)	0.153	0.133	0.117	0.117

The NPV = +0.58, i.e. + £58,000, hence the project is worthwhile.

(ii) Should the equipment be leased or purchased? The relevant discount rate is the post-tax cost of borrowing, i.e. $7\%(1-30\%)=5\%$

The respective cash flow implications of leasing and outright purchase are:

The PV of the rental stream $= 0.070(\text{PVIFA}_{5/4}) = 0.070(3.546) = 0.248$

The PV of the tax savings $= 0.248(0.30) = 0.074$, i.e. £74,000

Hence PV of leasing costs $= 0.248 - 0.074 = 0.174$, i.e. (£0.174m).

Purchase via bank loan:

The relevant cash flows are those connected with the purchase itself rather than the operation of the project, i.e. the outlay less tax savings and the residual value.

	Cash flows (marked by *) (£m)				
	0	**1**	**2**	**3**	**4**
Outlay*	(0.500)				0.050
WDA	0.125	0.094	0.070	0.053	0.108
Tax savings at 30%	0.041	0.031	0.023	0.017	0.036
Net cash flows*	(0.459)	0.031	0.023	0.017	0.036
PV at 5%	(0.459)	0.030	0.021	0.015	0.030

PV of cash flow $= (0.363)$, i.e. (£0.363m)

Hence, leasing is the preferable (least-cost) method of financing (£0.174m compared to £0.363m), i.e. the lease has a net advantage of £0.189m.

(iii) The third stage in the evaluation is now a formality – the optimal decision is to acquire the equipment using lease finance.

CHAPTER 16

1 (i)

	Pence
3 old shares prior to rights issue at 320p	960
1 new share at £2	200
4 shares worth	1,160
1 share therefore worth 1,160/4	290

(i) Value of the rights is the difference between the offer price and the ex-rights price: $(290p - 200p) = 90p$ for every new share issued.

2 Proposed preference share issue

(a) Benefits to the company:
- Dividends are only paid if funds are available.
- No asset security required as with some loans.
- Lower risk than for ordinary share capital, giving a cheaper source of finance.
- Suitable when a company does not want to increase the number of ordinary shares but is concerned that its gearing is already high.

Drawbacks to the company:
- Cost of preference shares is usually higher than for debentures because the risks are greater.
- No tax relief on the dividends (unlike loan interest).

(b) Benefits to the investor:
- Should produce a higher yield than fixed-interest securities.
- Lower risk than ordinary shares.
- Redeemable preference shares provide a means of liquidating the investment where markets are thin or non-existent.

Drawbacks to the investor:
– Unable to participate fully in the profits.
– Not usually secured.
– No guaranteed dividend.

Many of the drawbacks can be overcome where preference shares are cumulative, participating, redeemable and convertible into equity if desired.

4 (a) Burnsall needs additional finance to fund both working and fixed capital needs. As sales are expected to increase by 20 per cent, and since working capital needs are expected to rise in line with sales, the predicted working capital needs will be 20 per cent above the existing working capital level, i.e.

$1.2 \times$ [stock + debtors + cash − trade creditors]
$= 1.2 \times$ [£16m + £23m + £6m − £18m]
$=$ £32.4m, increase of £5.4m.

Together with the additional capital expenditures of £20m, the total funding requirement = (£5.4m + £20m) = £25.4m.

This funding requirement can be met partly by internal finance and partly by new external capital. The internal finance available will derive from depreciation provisions and retained earnings, after accounting for anticipated liabilities, such as taxation, that is, from cash flow.

Note that the profit margin on sales of £100m (£10 × 10m units) before interest and tax was 16 per cent in 1994–95. If depreciation of £5m for 1994–95 is added back, this yields a 'cash flow margin' of 21 per cent (ignoring movements in current assets/liabilities).

Using the same margin, and making a simple operating cash flow projection based on the accounts and other information provided:

Inflows	£m
Sales in 1995–96 = (£10 × 10m) + 20%	120.00
Cost of sales before depreciation at 79%	(94.80)
Operating cash flow	25.20
Outflows	
Tax liability for 1994–95	(5.00)
Interest payments: 12% × £20m	(2.40)
Dividends: 1.1 × £5m	(5.50)
	(12.90)
Net internal finance generated	12.30
Funding requirements	(25.40)
Net additional external finance required	(13.10)

(b) (i) Some new equipment could be leased, via a long-term capital lease. Tax relief is available on rental payments, lowering the effective cost of using the equipment. Lessors may 'tailor' a leasing package to suit Burnsall's specific needs regarding timing of payments and provision of ancillary services. Alternatively, good-quality property assets at present owned by Burnsall could be sold to a financial institution and their continued use secured via a leaseback arrangement, although this arrangement involves losing any capital appreciation of the assets.

(ii) If Burnsall's assets are of sufficient quality, i.e. easily saleable, it may be possible to raise a mortgage secured on them. This enables retention of ownership.

(iii) Burnsall could make a debenture issue, interest on which would be tax-allowable. The present level of gearing (long-term debt-to-equity) is relatively low at £20m/£120m = 16%, Burnsall has no short-term debt apart from trade creditors and the Inland Revenue, and its interest cover is healthy with profit before tax and interest divided by interest charges = [16% × £100m]/[12% × £20m] = 6.6 times. It is likely that Burnsall could make a sizeable debt issue without unnerving the market. Any new debenture would be subordinate to the existing long-term debt and probably carry a higher interest rate.

(iv) An alternative to a debt issue is a rights issue of ordinary shares. Because rights issues are made at a discount to the existing market price, they result in lower EPS and thus market price, although if existing shareholders take up their allocations, neither their wealth nor control is diluted. If the market approves of the intended use of funds, a capital gain may ensue, although the company and its advisers must carefully manage the issue regarding the declared reasons and its timing in order to avoid unsettling the market.

(v) Burnsall could approach a venture capitalist such as 3i, which specialises in extending development capital to small-to-medium-sized firms. However, 3i may require an equity stake, and possibly insist on placing an appointee on the Board to monitor its interests.

(vi) Burnsall could utilise official sources of aid, such as a regional development agency depending on its location, or perhaps the European Investment Bank.

CHAPTER 17

1 With a residual dividend policy:

Dividends = [Distributable Earnings − Capital Expenditure]

Tom has issued 10 million shares with par value 50p each, giving total book value of £5 million. Total dividends are (20p × 10m) = £2m. Hence, capex = (£10m − £2m) = £8m.

2 As all projects are indivisible, only whole projects with IRR > 20 per cent can be selected, i.e. B + C + E, with total expenditure of £14 million. As this infringes the capital availability constraint of £9 million, Dick is restricted to only B + C, with joint outlay of £7 million, leaving £2 million as a residual dividend.

3 According to Lintner's target adjustment theory, companies only partially adjust their dividends in line with earnings changes. The change in dividend will be half of the difference between current EPS and the last dividend, i.e.

$$\text{Dividend change} = 0.5 \times [0.5\,\text{EPS}_t - \text{Div}_{t-1}]$$
$$= 0.5 \times [0.5 \times (£3.0) - £1]$$
$$= 0.5 \times £0.5 = £0.25$$

so that the new dividend = (£1.0 + £0.25) = £1.25.

4
$$\text{Tamas' tax charge} = (30\% \times £30m) = £9m$$
$$\text{profit after tax} = (£30m - £9m) = £21m$$
$$\text{Dividend} = (50\% \times £21m) = £10.5m$$

$$\text{i.e. } (£10.5m/100m) = 10.5p \text{ per share}$$

Net (i.e. post-tax) cash flow = [Pre-tax profit + depreciation − replacement investment − tax]

$$= [£30m + £2m - £2m - £9m] = £21m$$

Value cum dividend = (£21m/15%) + £10.5m

$$= (£140m + £10.5m) = £150.5m$$

Per share, this is (£150.5m/100m) = £1.505 (cum dividend).

The ex-dividend share price is £1.505 reduced by the dividend per share of 10.5p, i.e. (£1.505 − £0.105) = £1.40.

5 (a) The price per share is given by:

$$P_0 = \frac{D_1}{(k_e - g)}$$

where D_1 is next year's dividend, k_e is the shareholder's required return and g is the expected rate of growth in dividends.

The growth rate can be found from the expression:

$$5.0p(1 + g)^4 = 7.3p$$

where g is the past (compound) growth rate.

$$(1 + g)^4 = \frac{7.3p}{5.0p} = 1.46$$

or

$$\frac{1}{(1 + g)^4} = 0.6849$$

From the present value tables, $g = 10\%$, whence:

$$P_0 = \frac{7.3p(1.1)}{(16\% - 10\%)} = \frac{8.03p}{0.06} = £1.34$$

(b) With D_1 at just 5.0p, using managerial expectations for the investment:

$$P_0 = \frac{5.0p}{(16\% - 14\%)} = \frac{5.0p}{0.02} = £2.50$$

(c) To break even, share price must not fall below £1.34, i.e.

$$£1.34 = \frac{5.0p}{(16\% - g)}$$

Solving for g, we find $g = 12.3\%$, marginally above the assessment of the more pessimistic managers.

(d) Until 2014, Galahad pursued a policy of distributing 40–50 per cent of profit after tax as dividend. Each year, it has offered a steady dividend increase, even in 2013, when its earnings actually fell. This was presumably out of reluctance to lower the dividend, fearing an adverse market reaction, and reflecting a belief that the earnings shortfall was a temporary phenomenon. In 2014 it offered a 12 per cent dividend increase, the highest percentage increase in the time series, possibly to compensate shareholders for the relatively small increase (only 8 per cent) in 2013. It would appear that Galahad has either already built up a clientéle of investors whose interests it is trying to safeguard, or that it is trying to do so.

The proposed dividend cut to 5.0p per share would represent a sharply increased dividend cover of 3.5, on the assumption that EPS also grows at 10 per cent p.a. Such a sharp rise in the dividend safety margin is likely to be construed by the market as implying that Galahad's managers expect earnings to be depressed in the future, especially as it follows a year of record dividend increase. Such an abrupt change in dividend policy is thus likely to offend its clientèle of shareholders at best, and at worst, to alarm the market as to the reliability of future earnings.

In an efficient capital market, with homogeneous investor expectations, the share price would increase by the amount calculated in (b), at least, if the market agreed with the managers' views about the attractions of the projected expenditure. However, in view of the information content of dividends, Galahad's board will have to be very confident of its ability to persuade the market of the inherent desirability of the proposed investment programme. This may well be a difficult task, especially given the stated doubts of some of its managers. The board will have to explain why they feel internal financing is preferable to raising capital externally, either by a rights issue, or by raising further debt finance. While the level of indebtedness of Galahad is not given, the implication is that it is unacceptably high, so as to obviate the issue of additional borrowing instruments. If this is the case, then it seems doubly risky to propose a dividend cut, as it may signal fears regarding Galahad's ability to service a high level of debt.

If the dividend cut is greeted adversely, then the ability of the shareholder clientèle to home-make dividends will be impaired, since, apart from the transactions costs involved, there will perhaps be no capital gain to realise. Any significant selling to convert capital into income will further depress share price.

If the investment programme is truly worthwhile, Galahad's managers perhaps should not shrink from offering a rights issue, since, despite the costs of such issues, shareholders will eventually reap the benefits in the form of higher future earnings and dividends. However, this might suggest a short-term reduction in share price, which may penalise short-term investors, but who still have the option of protecting their interests by selling their rights.

CHAPTER 18

1 LTD/Equity = (£200m/£500m) = 40%
LTD/(LTD + Equity) = £200m/(£200m + £500m) = 28%
Total Debt/Equity = (£200m + £50m)/£500m = 50%
Net Debt = (£200m + £50m) − (£20m + £40m) = £190m.
Net Debt/Equity = (£190m/£500m) = 38%
Total Debt/Total Assets = £250m/£800m = 31%
Interest Cover = (£120m/£25m) = 4.8 times.
Income Gearing = (1/4.8) × 100 = 21%
Total Liabilities/Total Assets = (£300m/£800m) = 37.5%

2 Market value of debt = £100 × (£45m/£50m) = £90

  (i) cost of debt = [8% × £100]/£90 = (£8/£90) = 8.9%
  (ii) cost of debt = £8(1 − 30%)/£90 = (£5.6/£90) = 6.2%
  (iii) cost of debt is the solution R to:

  $$£90 = \frac{£8}{(1 + R)} + \frac{£8}{(1 + R)^2} + \cdots + \frac{£8 + £100}{(1 + R)^6}$$

  Solution value for $R = 10.3\%$
  (iv) The cost of debt is the solution R to:

  $$£90 = \frac{£8(1 - 30\%)}{(1 + R)} + \frac{£5.6}{(1 + R)^2} + \cdots + \frac{(£5.6 + £100)}{(1 + R)^6}$$

  Solution value for $R = 8.25\%$

3 (a) £m

PBIT = (0.3 × £5m) + (0.5 × £50m) + (0.2 × £150m) = £56.5m

Current Structure – £200m equity.

Tax at 30%	(1.5)	(15)	(45)
PAT	3.5	35	105
ROE	1.8%	17.5%	52.5%

Programme (i) – £40m debt/£160m equity.

Interest at 8.5%	(3.2)	(3.2)	(3.2)
Taxable profit	1.8	46.8	146.8
Tax at 30%	(0.5)	(14.0)	(44.0)
PAT	1.26	32.8	102.8
ROE	0.8%	20.5%	64.3%

Programme (ii) – £80m debt/£120m equity.

Interest at 8.5%	(6.8)	(6.8)	(6.8)
Taxable profit	–	43.2	143.2
Tax at 30%	–	(14.0)	(44.0)
PAT	–	30.2	100.2
ROE	(1.5%)	25.2%	83.5%

(b) Risk is measured by the standard deviation of the returns on equity (ROE) around the respective expected values (EVs).

Current Capital Structure.
EV of ROE = $(0.3 \times 1.8) + (0.5 \times 17.5) + (0.2 \times 52.5) = 19.8\%$

Outcome	EV	Deviation	Squared	× probability
1.8	19.8	−18.0	324	97.2
17.5	19.8	−2.3	5.3	2.65
52.5	19.8	32.7	1069.3	213.86
				Total variance = 313.71

Standard deviation $= \sqrt{313.71} = 17.7$, i.e. 17.7%

Programme (i)
EV of ROE = $(0.3 \times 0.8) + (0.5 \times 20.5) + (0.2 \times 64.3) = 23.4\%$

Outcome	EV	Deviation	Squared	× probability
0.8	23.4	−22.6	510.76	153.228
20.5	23.4	−2.9	8.41	4.205
64.3	23.4	40.9	1672.81	334.56
				Total variance = 491.993

Standard deviation $= \sqrt{491.993} = 22.18$, i.e. 22.2%

Programme (ii)
EV of ROE = $(0.3 \times -1.5) + (0.5 \times 25.2) + (0.2 \times 83.5) = 28.9\%$

Outcome	EV	Deviation	Squared	× probability
−1.5	28.9	−30.4	924.16	277.248
25.2	28.9	−3.7	13.69	6.845
83.5	28.9	54.6	2981.16	596.230
				Total variance = 880.323

Standard deviation $= \sqrt{880.323} = 29.7$, i.e. 29.7%

(c) Business risk, exposure to the risk of fluctuations in business activity, can be measured in different ways, e.g. the variability in sales or in some measure of profitability. This example shows how ROE varies under three scenarios. By abstracting from financial risk, the ROE in the all-equity case shows inherent business risk – the ROE varies from 1.8 per cent to 52.5 per cent, with a standard deviation of 17.7 per cent.

Gearing adds a second layer of risk because it imposes an extra fixed cost, i.e. the prior interest charge – the higher the level of gearing, the higher the financial risk. Consequently, we see that the standard deviation of the ROE rises to 22.2 per cent under the relatively modest level of gearing, programme (i), while programme (ii) raises it to 29.7 per cent.

4 (a) (i) Perpetual debt:

$$\text{PV of Tax Savings} = \frac{(T \times i \times \text{Nominal Debt Value})}{i} = \frac{TiB}{i}$$
$$= (30\% \times 10\% \times \text{£100m})/10\%$$
$$= (\text{£3m}/0.1) = \text{£30m}$$

(ii) When debt is repaid in full after 5 years:
PV = £3m p.a. over 5 years at 10% discount rate = (£3m × 3.7908) = £11.37m

(iii) Debt repaid in equal tranches:

Year	Start-year debt	Interest	Tax saving	PV	Repayment
1	100	10	3	2.73	20
2	80	8	2.4	1.98	20
3	60	6	1.8	1.35	20
4	40	4	1.2	0.82	20
5	20	2	0.6	0.37	20

Total = £7.25m

(c) The value of the tax shield is higher:
- the higher the interest rate
- the higher the tax rate
- the higher the amount of debt
- the longer the term of the loan
- the slower that debt is repaid
- the greater the firm's taxable capacity

5 Book value weights:

			weight	cost
Equity [£10m + £20m] =	£30m	i.e.	66.7%	20%
Debt	£15m		33.3%	10% pre-tax
	£45m		100%	

WACC = (20% × 66.7%) + (10%[1 − 30%] × 33.3%)
       = (13.3% + 2.3%) = 15.6%

Market value of equity = (20m shares × £4.50) = £90m. The weights become:

Equity: £90m/£105m = 85.7%

Debt: £15m/£105m = 14.3%

WACC = (20% × 85.7%) + (10%[1 − 30%] × 14.3%)
       = (17.1% + 1.0%) = 18.1%

CHAPTER 19

1 (i) From MM's Proposition I, the cost of equity is:

$$k_{eg} = k_{eu} + (k_{eu} - k_d)\frac{V_B}{V_S}$$

If the proportion of debt to total finance is 20%, the ratio of debt to equity must be 1:4, i.e. 0.25. Hence,

$$k_{eg} = 20\% + (20\% - 8\%)(0.25) = 23\%$$

2 (i) Because the WACC is constant at 20% at all gearing levels, the figures correspond to the MM no-tax theory.
  (ii) This now illustrates the MM with-tax theory, wherein the WACC falls continuously as gearing increases. The cost of equity becomes:

$$k_{eg} = k_{eu} + (k_{eu} - k_d)(1 - T)\frac{V_B}{V_S}$$

The amended table is:

% Debt	% Equity	k_d	k_e	WACC
–	100	–	20%	20%
25	75	5.6%	22.8%	18.5%
50	50	5.6%	28.4%	17.2%
75	25	5.6%	45.2%	15.5%

3   Assume the investor holds 10 per cent of Geared's equity.
Value of stake $= 10\% \times £900 = £90$
Personal income initially $\quad = 10\% \times [£100 - (5\% \times £200)]$
$\qquad\qquad\qquad\qquad\qquad = 10\% \times £90 = £9$
Geared's gearing $= £200/£900 = 22.2\%$

Assume the investor sells the stake in Geared for £90, borrows £20 at 5 per cent to duplicate Geared's gearing and invests the whole stake in Ungeared's equity.

Now entitled to earnings of $(£110/£950) \times £100 = £11.58$
Personal interest liability $= (5\% \times £20) \qquad = \underline{(£1.00)}$
Net income $\qquad\qquad\qquad\qquad\qquad\qquad = £10.58$

The investor is better off by $(£10.58 - £9.00) = £1.58$

9 **(a)** CAPM
The stated Beta is an equity Beta so that the required return on equity is:

$\text{ER}_j = R_f + \beta_j(\text{ER}_m - R_f)$
$\qquad = 12\% + 1.4(18\% - 12\%) = 20.4\%$

This is unsuitable as a discount rate because:
(i) It is the required return on equity rather than the required return on the overall company.
(ii) The equity Beta of 1.4 reflects the financial risk of Folten's equity. Wemere's gearing differs from that of Folten, hence their equity Betas will differ.

The inflation adjustment is unnecessary since ER_m and R_f already incorporate the expected impact of inflation.

The equity Beta for Wemere can be estimated by ungearing Folten's equity Beta and regearing to reflect the financial risk of Wemere.

The market value-weighted gearing figures are:

Folten
Equity (138p $\times$ 7.2m shares) $= £9,936$m, i.e. 69.3% of total
Debt $= £4,400$m, i.e. 30.7% of total
Total $= £14.336$m

Wemere
Equity (using the takeover bid offer) $= £10.6$m, i.e. 81.5% of total
Debt $= £2.4$m, i.e. 18.5% of total
Total $= £13.0$m

Assuming corporate debt is risk-free, the ungeared equity Beta is

$$\beta_u = \beta_g \times \frac{1}{\left[1 + \dfrac{V_B}{V_S} \times (1 - T)\right]} = 1.4 \times \frac{1}{1 + (0.44)(1 - 35\%)}$$

$\qquad = 1.089$

Regearing Beta for Wemere,

$$\beta_g = \beta_u\left[1 + \frac{V_B}{V_S} \times (1 - T)\right]$$

$\qquad = 1.089 \, [1 + 0.23(1 - 35\%)] = 1.25$

The cost of equity for Wemere is thus:

$$12\% + 1.25[18\% - 12\%] = 19.5\%$$

Given the cost of debt is 13%:

$$\text{WACC} = [13\%(1 - 35\%) \times 18.5\%] + [19.5\% \times 81.5\%]$$
$$= 1.56\% + 15.89\% = 17.5\%$$

However, the WACC is only suitable as a discount rate if the systematic risk of the new investment is similar to that of the company as a whole.

Dividend Growth Model

The expression for this model relates to the cost of equity, not the overall cost of capital, i.e.

$$k_e = \frac{D_1}{P_0} + g = \frac{14.20p}{138p} + 9\% = 19.3\%$$

No inflation adjustment is required.

The WACC is: $[13\%(1 - 35\%) \times 18.5\%] + [19.3\% \times 81.5\%]$
$$= 1.56\% + 15.73\% = 17.3\%$$

(b) Neither method is problem-free. The surrogate company is unlikely to have identical characterisitics, either at an operating level or in terms of financial characteristics. For example, the cost of equity in the Dividend Growth Model is derived from a different set of data regarding dividend policy, growth and share prices.

Folten's managers may have different capabilities, and the company may face different growth opportunities. Before using the estimated WACC, Wemere must be confident that the two companies are a sufficiently close fit.

Even so, the calculated WACC is inappropriate if the systematic risk of any new project differs from that of the company as a whole, and/or if project financing involves moving to a new capital structure.

CHAPTER 20

1 (a) Value of target now:

$$P_0 = \frac{D_1}{k_e - g}$$

$$20 = \frac{80p}{k_e - 6\%}$$

whence $k_e = 10\%$.

Value of target would become

$$P = \frac{80p}{10\% - 8\%} = £40 \text{ per share}$$

Value of equity $= £40 \times 0.6m = £24m$, i.e. an increase of £12m.

(b) Cost of acquisition: $(£25 - £20) = £5$ per share. In total, $£5 \times 0.6m = £3m$. NPV of acquisition: $(£12m - £3m) = £9m$. Advise to proceed.

(c) Number of new shares required: $0.6m/3 = 0.2m$; new total $= 1.2m$.

$$\text{Value of new company} = \frac{£90m + £12m + £12m}{1.2m}$$

$$= £114/1.2m = £95 \text{ per share}$$

Cost of acquisition $= (0.2m \times £95m) - £12m = £7m$. NPV of acquisition $= (£12m - £7m) = £5m$. Again, advise to proceed.

(d) (i) Cost of cash bid unchanged. Pointless to proceed as there are no gains.
(ii) With the share exchange:

$$\text{Value of new company} = \frac{£90m + £12m}{1.2m} = £85 \text{ per share}$$

NPV of acquisition: $(0.2m \times £85) - £12m = (£5m)$. Advise not to proceed on this basis.

7 (a) The Balance Sheet net asset value is total assets minus total liabilities, i.e. £620m. Land and buildings have an estimated value of £150m $\times (1.25)^4 =$ £366m, i.e. £216m higher than the book value. Hence, the adjusted NAV is £836m.

Applying Grapper's 12 per cent growth rate, estimated PAT for the coming five years is:

£151(1.12) + £151(1.12)^2, etc.= £1,074m

This yields a total value of £836m + £1,074m = £1,910m. Grapper's market value is currently (400m shares $\times$ share price 470p) = £1,880m. The premium is thus £30m or 7.5p per share.

This is not a sound basis for valuation as it ignores the time-value of money. The premium of 1.6 per cent above the current market price is very small compared with those achieved in many 'real' bids.

Using the Dividend Valuation Model:

$$P_0 = \frac{D_1}{k_e - g} = \frac{D_0(1 + g)}{k_e - g}$$

Current dividend per share $= \frac{£76m}{400m} = 19p$

Hence $D_1 = 19p(1.12) = 21.3p$.

From the CAPM:

$k_e = ER_j = R_f + \beta_j (ER_m - R_f) = 10\% + 1.05(16\% - 10\%) = 16.3\%$

Thus:

$$P_0 = \frac{21.3p}{16.3\% - 12\%} = 495p$$

i.e. 5.3 per cent above the market price.

Restrictive assumptions underlying such a valuation include a constant growth rate, and an unchanged dividend policy. It is more rational to assess the value of Grapper incorporating post-merger rationalisation.

(b) The post-merger sales revenue of Woppit will be over £5,000 million, a size which could deter other takeover raiders, at least from the United Kingdom. However, bids from US and other European sources should not be ruled out. In addition, debt-financed bids from consortia like Hoylake (which bid for BAT) show that size alone is not an adequate protection against a takeover bid.

(c) An indication of the scope for improving Grapper's efficiency can be obtained by examination of key financial ratios.

	Woppit	Grapper
Operating profit margin (PBIT/sales)	20%	16.6%
Asset turnover (sales/total assets)	1.80	1.36
Debtors' collection period	31 days	50 days
Stock turnover	10.3	6.4
Current ratio	1.65:1	2.45:1

There are clear opportunities to improve Grapper's performance by rationalisation and restructuring of activities. For example:

- Grapper's operating profit margin could be brought into line with Woppit's by a price increase and/or cost reduction.
- Grapper's stock level looks high by comparison. There could well be stockholding economies in an expanded operation.
- Grapper's cash holdings look excessive – again, centralised cash management may generate economies.
- Grapper's asset turnover is relatively low. Some assets could well be sold and others worked more intensively.
- Grapper seems to have scope for reducing its investment in debtors.
- Introduction of such economies may well close the gap between Woppit's return on assets of 36 per cent and Grapper's present 22.5 per cent.

CHAPTER 21

1 Remember the bank always wins, so it sells euros at 1.6296, and buys at 1.6320.
  (a) Selling £10 million, its receipts are (10m × 1.6296) = €16.296 million.
  (b) Selling €12 million, its receipts are (12m/1.6320) = £7.353 million.

2 (a) Amount invoiced = (10m × €1.6) = €16m.
  (b) With spot at €1.7 vs. £1, proceeds = €16m/1.7) = £9.412m. Hence, the loss compared to the current spot rate = (£10m − £9.412m) = £0.588m.
  (c) With spot at €1.5 vs. £1, the sale proceeds are (€16m/1.5) = £10.667m. In this case, the exporter gains £0.667m from the exchange rate change.
  (d) If the exporter sells forward, the contracted proceeds are €16m/1.62 = £9.877m.
    (i) The cost of the hedge is thus £0.123m, i.e. 1.2% of the sterling value of the deal.
    (ii) If sterling falls to €1.5 vs. £1, the forward contract guarantees the exporter £9.877 million, but it could have received £10.667 million had it not hedged. There is thus an opportunity cost of (£10.667m − £9.877m) = £0.790m.
    (iii) If sterling rises to €1.7 vs. £1, the forward contract still guarantees the exporter £9.877m, but it would have received £9.412m had it not hedged. The exporter is thus better off by (£9.877m − £9.412m) = £0.465m.
  If the exporter thinks there is an equal chance of a 10 per cent variation in the €/£ exchange rate, it must balance an opportunity cost from hedging of £0.75 million if sterling falls, against being better off by £0.465 million if sterling rises.

3 The forward outrights are:

KRONA	10.960 − 10.967
Less forward premium	(0.025 − 0.011)
Forward outright	10.935 − 10.956
YEN	230.11 − 230.16
Less forward premium	(1.10 − 0.97)
Forward outright	229.01 − 229.19
KRONOR	11.717 − 11.723
Less forward premium	(0.021 − 0.004)
Forward outright	11.696 − 11.719

5 According to Interest Rate Parity,

$$\text{Forward rate} = \text{Spot rate} \times \frac{(1 + \text{US interest rate})}{(1 + \text{UK interset rate})}$$

$$= 1.6000 \times \frac{(1.09)}{(1.10)} = 1.5854, \quad \text{i.e. USD stronger on forward market}$$

The currency of the country in which interest rates are lower (presumably due to lower expected inflation) would be traded at a premium.

6 It is assumed it is desired to hold US$ at the year-end. By lending US$ at 7.625 per cent, the end-year balance will be £1m × 1.07625 = $1,076,250.
  If wishing to lend in Swiss francs, the treasurer would convert from dollars at spot of 1.3125 to obtain CHF of $1m × 1.3125 = CHF1,312,500. Over one year, invested at 4.5625 per cent, this would accumulate to CHF1,372,383.
  To cover the risk of adverse exchange rate movements, he will then sell CHF forward at the ruling rate of 1.275 to guarantee US$ delivery in one year's time of CHF1,372,383/1.275 = $1,076,379.
  The minimal difference of $129 can be attributed to the operation of IRP.
  Transactions costs would wipe out any gain from arbitrage.

11 With £1 = S$2.80:

Value of deal at today's spot = S$28m/2.80 = £10.00m

Hedged using a forward contract:

Value = S$28m/2.79 = £10.04m

Money market hedge:

Ashton borrows S$28m at 2%/4 = 0.5%
Borrowing = S$28m/1.005 = S$27.86m
Converts at spot (S$2.8 = £1) to yield S$27.86m/2.80 = £9.95m
Invested at 3%/4 (i.e. 0.0075%) this generates £9.95(1.0075) = £10.03m

The forward hedge is superior.

(a) If future spot is S$2.78 = £1

Value of deal at spot = S$28m/2.78 = £10.07m

Not hedging would have been preferable (with hindsight!)
The OTC option is out of the money and the premium is lost:

Net value = [£10.07m − premium of £0.2m] = £9.87m

(b) If future spot is £1 = S$2.82:

Value of deal at spot = S$28m/2.82 = £9.93m

Hedging would have been preferable (using the forward contract)
The OTC option is in the money.
Net of the premium, Ashton receives:

[S$28m/2.785] − £0.2m = £10.05m − £0.2m = £9.85m

But the forward contract would have been superior to this.

CHAPTER 22

1 In this question, we need to show that the receipts in sterling after adjusting for inflation at both locations remains unchanged.
Current exchange = US $1.50 against £1.
Sterling equivalent of US revenue = $150m/1.50 = 100m

Exchange rate	$ revenue	£ revenue	£ revenue (real terms)
(i) 1.05/1.05 × 1.50 = $1.50:£1	$157.5m	£105m	£105m/1.05 = £100m
(ii) 1.02/1.05 × 1.50 = $1.457:£1	$153m	£105m	£105m/1.05 = £100m
(iii) 1.05/1.02 × 1.50 = $1.544:£1	$157.5m	£102m	£102m/1.02 = £100m

2 (a) (i) With exchange controls:

Year	PAT (SA$000)	OJ share (SA$000)	50% div (SA$000)	Sterling (£000)	PV at 16% (£000)
0	—	—	—	(450)	(450)
1	4,250	2,125	1,062	106	91
2	6,500	3,250	1,625	108	80
3	8,350	4,175	2,088	100	64
			4,775	277	146
			(balance)		NPV = (69)

In this scenario, OJ should reject the project.

(ii) No exchange control:

Year	PAT (SA$000)	OJ share (SA$000)	Sterling (£000)	PV at 16% (£000)
0	–	–	(450)	(450)
1	4,250	2,125	212	183
2	6,500	3,250	217	161
3	8,350	4,175	199	127
				NPV = +21

In this scenario, the positive NPV indicates acceptance, but the project is marginal e.g. the Profitability Index (NPV/Outlay = 21/450) is only 0.047. Given the risk of exchange controls being imposed, this suggests that OJ should treat the project with great caution.

3 PG plc

Year	0	1	2	3	4
Method 1					
C$ Initial investment	(150,000)				50,000
Other cash flows		60,000	60,000	60,000	45,000
Net cash flows	(150,000)	60,000	60,000	60,000	95,000
C$ per £1	1.700	1.785	1.874	1.968	2.066
Sterling	(88,235)	33,613	32,017	30,488	45,983
DF at 14%	1.000	0.877	0.769	0.675	0.592
PV	(88,235)	29,479	24,621	20,579	27,222
NPV = £13,666					
Method 2					
C$ net cash flows	(150,000)	60,000	60,000	60,000	95,000
DF at 19.7%	1.000	0.835	0.698	0.583	0.487
C$	(150,000)	50,100	41,888	34,980	46,265
£ PV at 1.7	(88,235)	29,479	24,621	20,579	27,222
NPV = £13,666					

For the two approaches to generate the same answer, the discount rate applied to the C$ cash flows must be the combination of the sterling discount rate (14 per cent) and the expected strengthening of sterling, according to PPP. This yields:

$$(1.14 \times 1.05) - 1 = (1.197 - 1) = 0.197, \text{ i.e. } 19.7\%$$

A forecast 5 per cent appreciation of sterling against the C$ will be associated with UK inflation rates being 5 per cent less than the rate experienced in Canada. In practice, one might inflate the cash flows in C$ to reflect inflation internal to the Canadian economy.

6 Palmerston plc

Forecast Cash Flow Statement (£m)

Euros per £1	1.65	1.60	1.55
Sales			
UK	200	210	220
Germany	**182**	**188**	**194**
Total	382	398	414
Cost of Goods Sold:			
UK	(120)	(120)	(120)
Germany	(121)	(125)	(129)
Total	(241)	(245)	(249)
Gross Profit	141	153	165
Operating Expenses:			
UK – fixed	(50)	(50)	(50)
UK – variable (20% of total sales)	(76)	(80)	(83)
Total	(126)	(130)	(133)
Net Cash Flow	15	23	32
Firm value at 15%:	$(15 \times 5.019^*)$	(23×5.019)	(32×5.019)
*Annuity factor	= £75.3m	= £115.4m	= £160.61m

The analysis suggests that Palmerston benefits from a strong euro and vice versa. It could further reduce its exposure by shifting its cost base to Germany, or elsewhere in the euro area, preferably to a low-cost location, say, Greece or Portugal.

Present value interest factor (PVIF)

per £1.00 due at the end of *n* years for interest rate of:

n	1%	2%	3%	4%	5%	6%	7%	8%	9%	10%	n
1	0.99010	0.98039	0.97007	0.96154	0.95238	0.94340	0.93458	0.92593	0.91743	0.90909	1
2	0.98030	0.96117	0.94260	0.92456	0.90703	0.89000	0.87344	0.85734	0.84168	0.82645	2
3	0.97059	0.94232	0.91514	0.88900	0.86384	0.83962	0.81630	0.79383	0.77218	0.75131	3
4	0.96098	0.92385	0.88849	0.85480	0.82270	0.79209	0.76290	0.73503	0.70843	0.68301	4
5	0.95147	0.90573	0.86261	0.82193	0.78353	0.74726	0.71299	0.68058	0.64993	0.62092	5
6	0.94204	0.88797	0.83748	0.79031	0.74622	0.70496	0.66634	0.63017	0.59627	0.56447	6
7	0.93272	0.87056	0.81309	0.75992	0.71068	0.66506	0.62275	0.58349	0.54703	0.51316	7
8	0.92348	0.85349	0.78941	0.73069	0.67684	0.62741	0.58201	0.54027	0.50187	0.46651	8
9	0.91434	0.83675	0.76642	0.70259	0.64461	0.59190	0.54393	0.50025	0.46043	0.42410	9
10	0.90529	0.82035	0.74409	0.67556	0.61391	0.55839	0.50835	0.46319	0.42241	0.38554	10
11	0.89632	0.80426	0.72242	0.64958	0.58468	0.52679	0.47509	0.42888	0.38753	0.35049	11
12	0.88745	0.78849	0.70138	0.62460	0.55684	0.49697	0.44401	0.39711	0.35553	0.31863	12
13	0.87866	0.77303	0.68095	0.60057	0.53032	0.46884	0.41496	0.36770	0.32618	0.28966	13
14	0.86996	0.75787	0.66112	0.57747	0.50507	0.44230	0.38782	0.34046	0.29925	0.26333	14
15	0.86135	0.74301	0.64186	0.55526	0.48102	0.41726	0.36245	0.31524	0.27454	0.23939	15
16	0.85282	0.72845	0.62317	0.53391	0.45811	0.39365	0.33873	0.29189	0.25187	0.21763	16
17	0.84438	0.71416	0.60502	0.51337	0.43630	0.37136	0.31657	0.27027	0.23107	0.19784	17
18	0.83602	0.70016	0.58739	0.49363	0.41552	0.35034	0.29586	0.25025	0.21199	0.17986	18
19	0.82774	0.68643	0.57029	0.47464	0.39573	0.33051	0.27651	0.23171	0.19449	0.16351	19
20	0.81954	0.67297	0.55367	0.45639	0.37689	0.31180	0.25842	0.21455	0.17843	0.14864	20
21	0.81143	0.65978	0.53755	0.43883	0.35894	0.29415	0.24151	0.19866	0.16370	0.13513	21
22	0.80340	0.64684	0.52189	0.42195	0.34185	0.27750	0.22571	0.18394	0.15018	0.12285	22
23	0.79544	0.63414	0.50669	0.40573	0.32557	0.26180	0.21095	0.17031	0.13778	0.11168	23
24	0.78757	0.62172	0.49193	0.39012	0.31007	0.24698	0.19715	0.15770	0.12640	0.10153	24
25	0.77977	0.60953	0.47760	0.37512	0.29530	0.23300	0.18425	0.14602	0.11597	0.09230	25

n	11%	12%	13%	14%	15%	16%	17%	18%	19%	20%	n
1	0.90090	0.89286	0.88496	0.87719	0.86957	0.86207	0.85470	0.84746	0.84034	0.83333	1
2	0.81162	0.79719	0.78315	0.76947	0.75614	0.74316	0.73051	0.71818	0.70616	0.69444	2
3	0.73119	0.71178	0.69305	0.67497	0.65752	0.64066	0.62437	0.60863	0.59342	0.57870	3
4	0.65873	0.63552	0.61332	0.59208	0.57175	0.55229	0.53365	0.51579	0.49867	0.48225	4
5	0.59345	0.56743	0.54276	0.51937	0.49718	0.47611	0.45611	0.43711	0.41905	0.40188	5
6	0.53464	0.50663	0.48032	0.45559	0.43233	0.41044	0.38984	0.37043	0.35214	0.33490	6
7	0.48166	0.45235	0.42506	0.39964	0.37594	0.35383	0.33320	0.31392	0.29592	0.27908	7
8	0.43393	0.40388	0.37616	0.35056	0.32690	0.30503	0.28487	0.26604	0.24867	0.23257	8
9	0.39092	0.36061	0.33288	0.30751	0.28426	0.26295	0.24340	0.22546	0.20897	0.19381	9
10	0.35218	0.32197	0.29459	0.26974	0.24718	0.22668	0.20804	0.19106	0.17560	0.16151	10
11	0.31728	0.28748	0.26070	0.23662	0.21494	0.19542	0.17781	0.16192	0.14756	0.13459	11
12	0.28584	0.25667	0.23071	0.20756	0.18691	0.16846	0.15197	0.13722	0.12400	0.11216	12
13	0.25751	0.22917	0.20416	0.18207	0.16253	0.14523	0.12989	0.11629	0.10420	0.09346	13
14	0.23199	0.20462	0.18068	0.15971	0.14133	0.12520	0.11102	0.09855	0.08757	0.07789	14
15	0.20900	0.18270	0.15989	0.14010	0.12289	0.10793	0.09489	0.08352	0.07359	0.06491	15
16	0.18829	0.16312	0.14150	0.12289	0.10686	0.09304	0.08110	0.07078	0.06184	0.05409	16
17	0.16963	0.14564	0.12522	0.10780	0.09393	0.08021	0.06932	0.05998	0.05196	0.04507	17
18	0.15282	0.13004	0.11081	0.09456	0.08080	0.06914	0.05925	0.05083	0.04367	0.03756	18
19	0.13768	0.11611	0.09806	0.08295	0.07026	0.05961	0.05064	0.04308	0.03669	0.03130	19
20	0.12403	0.10367	0.08678	0.07276	0.06110	0.05139	0.04328	0.03651	0.03084	0.02608	20
21	0.11174	0.09256	0.07680	0.06383	0.05313	0.04430	0.03699	0.03094	0.02591	0.02174	21
22	0.10067	0.08264	0.06796	0.05599	0.04620	0.03819	0.03162	0.02622	0.02178	0.01811	22
23	0.09069	0.07379	0.06014	0.04911	0.04017	0.03292	0.02702	0.02222	0.01830	0.01509	23
24	0.08170	0.06588	0.05322	0.04308	0.03493	0.02838	0.02310	0.01883	0.01538	0.01258	24
25	0.07361	0.05882	0.04710	0.03779	0.03038	0.02447	0.01974	0.01596	0.01292	0.01048	25

continued

n	21%	22%	23%	24%	25%	26%	27%	28%	29%	30%	n
1	0.82645	0.81967	0.81301	0.80645	0.80000	0.79365	0.78740	0.78125	0.77519	0.76923	1
2	0.68301	0.67186	0.66098	0.65036	0.64000	0.62988	0.62000	0.61035	0.60093	0.59172	2
3	0.56447	0.55071	0.53738	0.52449	0.51200	0.49991	0.48819	0.47684	0.46583	0.45517	3
4	0.46651	0.45140	0.43690	0.42297	0.40960	0.39675	0.38440	0.37253	0.36111	0.35013	4
5	0.38554	0.37000	0.35520	0.34111	0.32768	0.31488	0.30268	0.29104	0.27993	0.26933	5
6	0.31863	0.30328	0.28878	0.27509	0.26214	0.24991	0.23833	0.22737	0.21700	0.20718	6
7	0.26333	0.24859	0.23478	0.22184	0.20972	0.19834	0.18766	0.17764	0.16822	0.15937	7
8	0.21763	0.20376	0.19088	0.17891	0.16777	0.15741	0.14776	0.13878	0.13040	0.12259	8
9	0.17986	0.16702	0.15519	0.14428	0.13422	0.12493	0.11635	0.10842	0.10109	0.09430	9
10	0.14864	0.13690	0.12617	0.11635	0.10737	0.09915	0.09161	0.08470	0.07836	0.07254	10
11	0.12285	0.11221	0.10258	0.09383	0.08590	0.07869	0.07214	0.06617	0.06075	0.05580	11
12	0.10153	0.09198	0.08339	0.07567	0.06872	0.06245	0.05680	0.05170	0.04709	0.04292	12
13	0.08391	0.07539	0.06780	0.06103	0.05498	0.04957	0.04472	0.04039	0.03650	0.03302	13
14	0.06934	0.06180	0.05512	0.04921	0.04398	0.03934	0.03522	0.03155	0.02830	0.02540	14
15	0.05731	0.05065	0.04481	0.03969	0.03518	0.03122	0.02773	0.02465	0.02194	0.01954	15
16	0.04736	0.04152	0.03643	0.03201	0.02815	0.02478	0.02183	0.01926	0.01700	0.01503	16
17	0.03914	0.03403	0.02962	0.02581	0.02252	0.01967	0.01719	0.01505	0.01318	0.01156	17
18	0.03235	0.02789	0.02408	0.02082	0.01801	0.01561	0.01354	0.01175	0.01022	0.00889	18
19	0.02673	0.02286	0.01958	0.01679	0.01441	0.01239	0.01066	0.00918	0.00792	0.00684	19
20	0.02209	0.01874	0.01592	0.01354	0.01153	0.00983	0.00839	0.00717	0.00614	0.00526	20
21	0.01826	0.01536	0.01294	0.01092	0.00922	0.00780	0.00661	0.00561	0.00476	0.00405	21
22	0.01509	0.01259	0.01052	0.00880	0.00738	0.00619	0.00520	0.00438	0.00369	0.00311	22
23	0.01247	0.01032	0.00855	0.00710	0.00590	0.00491	0.00410	0.00342	0.00286	0.00239	23
24	0.01031	0.00846	0.00695	0.00573	0.00472	0.00390	0.00323	0.00267	0.00222	0.00184	24
25	0.00852	0.00693	0.00565	0.00462	0.00378	0.00310	0.00254	0.00209	0.00172	0.00152	25

n	31%	32%	33%	34%	35%	36%	37%	38%	39%	40%	n
1	0.76336	0.75758	0.75188	0.74627	0.74074	0.73529	0.72993	0.72464	0.71942	0.71429	1
2	0.58272	0.57392	0.56532	0.55692	0.54870	0.54066	0.53279	0.52510	0.51757	0.51020	2
3	0.44482	0.43479	0.42505	0.41561	0.40644	0.39754	0.38890	0.38051	0.37235	0.36443	3
4	0.33956	0.32939	0.31959	0.31016	0.30107	0.29231	0.28387	0.27573	0.26788	0.26031	4
5	0.25920	0.24953	0.24029	0.23146	0.22301	0.21493	0.20720	0.19980	0.19272	0.18593	5
6	0.19787	0.18904	0.18067	0.17273	0.16520	0.15804	0.15124	0.14479	0.13865	0.13281	6
7	0.15104	0.14321	0.13584	0.12890	0.12237	0.11621	0.11040	0.10492	0.09975	0.09486	7
8	0.11530	0.10849	0.10214	0.09620	0.09064	0.08545	0.08058	0.07603	0.07176	0.06776	8
9	0.08802	0.08219	0.07680	0.07179	0.06714	0.06283	0.05882	0.05509	0.05163	0.04840	9
10	0.06719	0.06227	0.05774	0.05357	0.04973	0.04620	0.04293	0.03992	0.03714	0.03457	10
11	0.05129	0.04717	0.04341	0.03998	0.03684	0.03397	0.03134	0.02893	0.02672	0.02469	11
12	0.03915	0.03574	0.03264	0.02984	0.02729	0.02498	0.02287	0.02096	0.01922	0.01764	12
13	0.02989	0.02707	0.02454	0.02227	0.02021	0.01837	0.01670	0.01519	0.01383	0.01260	13
14	0.02281	0.02051	0.01845	0.01662	0.01497	0.01350	0.01219	0.01101	0.00995	0.00900	14
15	0.01742	0.01554	0.01387	0.01240	0.01109	0.00993	0.00890	0.00798	0.00716	0.00643	15
16	0.01329	0.01177	0.01043	0.00925	0.00822	0.00730	0.00649	0.00578	0.00515	0.00459	16
17	0.01015	0.00892	0.00784	0.00691	0.00609	0.00537	0.00474	0.00419	0.00370	0.00328	17
18	0.00775	0.00676	0.00590	0.00515	0.00451	0.00395	0.00346	0.00304	0.00267	0.00234	18
19	0.00591	0.00512	0.00443	0.00385	0.00334	0.00290	0.00253	0.00220	0.00192	0.00167	19
20	0.00451	0.00388	0.00333	0.00287	0.00247	0.00213	0.00184	0.00159	0.00138	0.00120	20
21	0.00345	0.00294	0.00251	0.00214	0.00183	0.00157	0.00135	0.00115	0.00099	0.00085	21
22	0.00263	0.00223	0.00188	0.00160	0.00136	0.00115	0.00098	0.00084	0.00071	0.00061	22
23	0.00201	0.00169	0.00142	0.00119	0.00101	0.00085	0.00072	0.00061	0.00051	0.00044	23
24	0.00153	0.00128	0.00107	0.00089	0.00074	0.00062	0.00052	0.00044	0.00037	0.00031	24
25	0.00117	0.00097	0.00080	0.00066	0.00055	0.00046	0.00038	0.00032	0.00027	0.00022	25

Appendix D

Present value interest factor for an annuity (PVIFA)
of £1.00 for a series of *n* years for interest rate of:

n	1%	2%	3%	4%	5%	6%	7%	8%	9%	10%	n
1	0.9901	0.9804	0.9709	0.9615	0.9524	0.9434	0.9346	0.9259	0.9174	0.9091	1
2	1.9704	1.9416	1.9135	1.8861	1.8594	1.8334	1.8080	1.7833	1.7591	1.7355	2
3	2.9410	2.8839	2.8286	2.7751	2.7232	2.6730	2.6243	2.5771	2.5313	2.4868	3
4	3.9020	3.8077	3.7171	3.6299	3.5459	3.4651	3.3872	3.3121	3.2397	3.1699	4
5	4.8535	4.7134	4.5797	4.4518	4.3295	4.2123	4.1002	3.9927	3.8896	3.7908	5
6	5.7955	5.6014	5.4172	5.2421	5.0757	4.9173	4.7665	4.6229	4.4859	4.3553	6
7	6.7282	6.4720	6.2302	6.0020	5.7863	5.5824	5.3893	5.2064	5.0329	4.8684	7
8	7.6517	7.3254	7.0196	6.7327	6.4632	6.2098	5.9713	5.7466	5.5348	5.3349	8
9	8.5661	8.1622	7.7861	7.4353	7.1078	6.8017	6.5152	6.2469	5.9852	5.7590	9
10	9.4714	8.9825	8.5302	8.1109	7.7217	7.3601	7.0236	6.7101	6.4176	6.1446	10
11	10.3677	9.7868	9.2526	8.7604	8.3064	7.8868	7.4987	7.1389	6.8052	6.4951	11
12	11.2552	10.5753	9.9539	9.3850	8.8632	8.3838	7.9427	7.5361	7.1607	6.8137	12
13	12.1338	11.3483	10.6349	9.9856	9.3925	8.8527	8.3576	7.9038	7.4869	7.1034	13
14	13.0038	12.1062	11.2960	10.5631	9.8986	9.2950	8.7454	8.2442	7.7861	7.3667	14
15	13.8651	12.8492	11.9379	11.1183	10.3796	9.7122	9.1079	8.5595	8.0607	7.6061	15
16	14.7180	13.5777	12.5610	11.6522	10.8377	10.1059	9.4466	8.8514	8.3125	7.8237	16
17	15.5624	14.2918	13.1660	12.1656	11.2740	10.4772	9.7632	9.1216	8.5436	8.0215	17
18	16.3984	14.9920	13.7534	12.6592	11.6895	10.8276	10.0591	9.3819	8.7556	8.2014	18
19	17.2261	15.6784	14.3237	13.1339	12.0853	11.1581	10.3356	9.6036	8.9501	8.3649	19
20	17.8571	16.3514	14.8774	13.5903	12.4622	11.4699	10.5940	9.8181	9.1285	8.5136	20
21	18.0457	17.0111	15.4149	14.0291	12.8211	11.7640	10.8355	10.0168	9.2922	8.6487	21
22	19.6605	17.6580	15.9368	14.4511	13.1630	12.0416	11.0612	10.2007	9.4424	8.7715	22
23	20.4559	18.2921	16.4435	14.8568	13.4885	12.3033	11.2722	10.3710	9.5802	8.8832	23
24	21.2435	18.9139	16.9355	15.2469	13.7986	12.5503	11.4693	10.5287	9.7066	8.9847	24
25	22.0233	19.5234	17.4131	15.6220	14.0939	12.7833	11.6536	10.6748	9.8226	9.0770	25

n	11%	12%	13%	14%	15%	16%	17%	18%	19%	20%	n
1	0.9009	0.8929	0.8850	0.8772	0.8696	0.8621	0.8547	0.8475	0.8403	0.8333	1
2	1.7125	1.6901	1.6681	1.6467	1.6257	1.6052	1.5852	1.5656	1.5465	1.5278	2
3	2.4437	2.4018	2.3612	2.3216	2.2832	2.2459	2.2096	2.1743	2.1399	2.1065	3
4	3.1024	3.0373	2.9745	2.9137	2.8550	2.7982	2.7432	2.6901	2.6486	2.5887	4
5	3.6959	3.6048	3.5172	3.4331	3.3522	3.2743	3.1993	3.1272	3.0576	2.9906	5
6	4.2305	4.1114	3.9976	3.8887	3.7845	3.6847	3.5892	3.4976	3.4098	3.3255	6
7	4.7122	4.5638	4.4226	4.2883	4.1604	4.0386	3.9224	3.8115	3.7057	3.6046	7
8	5.1461	4.9676	4.7988	4.6389	4.4873	4.3436	4.2072	4.0776	3.9544	3.8372	8
9	5.5370	5.3282	5.1317	4.9464	4.7716	4.6065	4.4506	4.3030	4.1633	4.0310	9
10	5.8892	5.6502	5.4262	5.2161	5.0188	4.8332	4.6586	4.4941	4.3389	4.1925	10
11	6.2065	5.9377	5.6869	5.4527	5.2337	5.0286	4.8364	4.6560	4.4865	4.3271	11
12	6.4924	6.1944	5.9176	5.6603	5.4206	5.1971	4.9884	4.7932	4.6105	4.4392	12
13	6.7499	6.4235	6.1218	5.8424	5.5931	5.3423	5.1183	4.9095	4.7147	4.5327	13
14	6.9819	6.6282	6.3025	6.0021	5.7245	5.4675	5.2293	5.0081	4.8023	4.6106	14
15	7.1909	6.8109	6.4624	6.1422	5.8474	5.5755	5.3242	5.0916	4.8759	4.6755	15
16	7.3792	6.9740	6.6039	6.2651	5.9542	5.6685	5.4053	5.1624	4.9377	4.7296	16
17	7.5488	7.1196	6.7291	6.3729	6.0472	5.7487	5.4746	5.2223	4.9897	4.7746	17
18	7.7016	7.2497	6.8399	6.4674	6.1280	5.8178	5.5339	5.2732	5.0333	4.8122	18
19	7.8393	7.3658	6.9380	6.5504	6.1982	5.8575	5.5845	5.3162	5.0700	4.8435	19
20	7.9633	7.4694	7.0248	6.6231	6.2593	5.9288	5.6278	5.3527	5.1009	4.8696	20
21	8.0751	7.5620	7.1016	6.6870	6.3125	5.9731	5.6648	5.3837	5.1268	4.8913	21
22	8.1757	7.6446	7.1695	6.7429	6.3587	6.0113	5.6964	5.4099	5.1486	4.9094	22
23	8.2664	7.7184	7.2297	6.7921	6.3988	6.0442	5.7234	5.4321	5.1668	4.9245	23
24	8.3481	7.7843	7.2829	6.8351	6.4338	6.0726	5.7465	5.4509	5.1822	4.9371	24
25	8.4217	7.8431	7.3300	6.8729	6.4641	6.0971	5.7662	5.4669	5.1951	4.9476	25

continued

n	21%	22%	23%	24%	25%	26%	27%	28%	29%	30%	n
1	0.8264	0.8197	0.8130	0.8065	0.8000	0.7937	0.7874	0.7813	0.7752	0.7692	1
2	1.5095	1.4915	1.4740	1.4568	1.4400	1.4235	1.4074	1.3916	1.3761	1.3609	2
3	2.0739	2.0422	2.0114	1.9813	1.9520	1.9234	1.8956	1.8684	1.8420	1.8161	3
4	2.5404	2.4936	2.4483	2.4043	2.3616	2.3202	2.2800	2.2410	2.2031	2.1662	4
5	2.9260	2.8636	2.8035	2.7454	2.6893	2.6351	2.5827	2.5320	2.4830	2.4356	5
6	3.2446	3.1669	3.0923	3.0205	2.9514	2.8850	2.8210	2.7594	2.7000	2.6427	6
7	3.5079	3.4155	3.3270	3.2423	3.1611	3.0833	3.0087	2.9370	2.8682	2.8021	7
8	3.7256	3.6193	3.5179	3.4212	3.3289	3.2407	3.1564	3.0758	2.9986	2.9247	8
9	3.9054	3.7863	3.6731	3.5655	3.4631	3.3657	3.2728	3.1842	3.0997	3.0915	9
10	4.0541	3.9232	3.7993	3.6819	3.5705	3.4648	3.3644	3.2689	3.1781	3.1090	10
11	4.1769	4.0354	3.9018	3.7757	3.6564	3.5435	3.4365	3.3351	3.2388	3.1473	11
12	4.2785	4.1274	3.9852	3.8514	3.7251	3.6060	3.4933	3.3868	3.2859	3.1903	12
13	4.3624	4.2028	4.0530	3.9124	3.7801	3.6555	3.5381	3.4272	3.3224	3.2233	13
14	4.4317	4.2646	4.1082	3.9616	3.8241	3.6949	3.5733	3.4587	3.3507	3.2487	14
15	4.4890	4.3152	4.1530	4.0013	3.8593	3.7261	3.6010	3.4834	3.3726	3.2682	15
16	4.5364	4.3567	4.1894	4.0333	3.8874	3.7509	3.6228	3.5026	3.3896	3.2832	16
17	4.5755	4.3908	4.2190	4.0591	3.9099	3.7705	3.6400	3.5177	3.4028	3.2948	17
18	4.6079	4.4187	4.2431	4.0799	3.9279	3.7861	3.6536	3.5294	3.4130	3.3037	18
19	4.6346	4.4415	4.2627	4.0967	3.9424	3.7985	3.6642	3.5386	3.4210	3.3105	19
20	4.6567	4.4603	4.2786	4.1103	3.9539	3.8083	3.6726	3.5458	3.4271	3.3158	20
21	4.6750	4.4756	4.2916	4.1212	3.9631	3.8161	3.6792	3.5514	3.4319	3.3198	21
22	4.6900	4.4882	4.3021	4.1300	3.9705	3.8223	3.6844	3.5558	3.4356	3.3230	22
23	4.7025	4.4985	4.3106	4.1371	3.9764	3.8273	3.6885	3.5592	3.4384	3.3254	23
24	4.7128	4.5070	4.3176	4.1428	3.9811	3.8312	3.6918	3.5619	3.4406	3.3272	24
25	4.7213	4.5139	4.3232	4.1474	3.9849	3.8342	3.6943	3.5640	3.4423	3.3286	25

n	31%	32%	33%	34%	35%	36%	37%	38%	39%	40%	n
1	0.7634	0.7576	0.7519	0.7463	0.7407	0.7353	0.7299	0.7246	0.7194	0.7143	1
2	1.3461	1.3315	1.3172	1.3032	1.2894	1.2760	1.2627	1.2497	1.2370	1.2245	2
3	1.7909	1.7663	1.7423	1.7188	1.6959	1.6735	1.6516	1.6302	1.6093	1.5889	3
4	2.1305	2.0957	2.0618	2.0290	1.9969	1.9658	1.9355	1.9060	1.8772	1.8492	4
5	2.3897	2.3452	2.3021	2.2604	2.2200	2.1807	2.1427	2.1058	2.0699	1.9352	5
6	2.5875	2.5342	2.4828	2.4331	2.3852	2.3388	2.2936	2.2506	2.2086	2.1680	6
7	2.7386	2.6775	2.6187	2.5620	2.5075	2.4550	2.4043	2.3555	2.3083	2.2628	7
8	2.8539	2.7860	2.7208	2.6582	2.5982	2.5404	2.4849	2.4315	2.3801	2.3306	8
9	2.9419	2.8681	2.7976	2.7300	2.6653	2.6033	2.5437	2.4866	2.4317	2.3790	9
10	3.0091	2.9304	2.8553	2.7836	2.7150	2.6495	2.5867	2.5265	2.4689	2.4136	10
11	3.0604	2.9776	2.8987	2.8236	2.7519	2.6834	2.6180	2.5555	2.4956	2.4383	11
12	3.0995	3.0133	2.9314	2.8534	2.7792	2.7084	2.6409	2.5764	2.5148	2.4559	12
13	3.1294	3.0404	2.9559	2.8757	2.7994	2.7268	2.6576	2.5916	2.5286	2.4685	13
14	3.1522	3.0609	2.9744	2.8923	2.8144	2.7403	2.6698	2.6026	2.5386	2.4775	14
15	3.1696	3.0764	2.9883	2.9047	2.8255	2.7502	2.6787	2.6106	2.5457	2.4839	15
16	3.1829	3.0882	2.9987	2.9140	2.8337	2.7575	2.6852	2.6164	2.5509	2.4885	16
17	3.1931	3.0971	3.0065	2.9209	2.8398	2.7629	2.6899	2.6202	2.5546	2.4918	17
18	3.2008	3.1039	3.0124	2.9260	2.8443	2.7668	2.6934	2.6236	2.5573	2.4941	18
19	3.2067	3.1090	3.0169	2.9299	2.8476	2.7697	2.6959	2.6258	2.5592	2.4958	19
20	3.2112	3.1129	3.0202	2.9327	2.8501	2.7718	2.6977	2.6274	2.5606	2.4970	20
21	3.2154	3.1158	3.0227	2.9349	2.8519	2.7734	2.6991	2.6285	2.5616	2.4979	21
22	3.2173	3.1180	3.0246	2.9365	2.8533	2.7746	2.7000	2.6294	2.5623	2.4985	22
23	3.2193	3.1197	3.0260	2.9377	2.8543	2.7754	2.7008	2.6300	2.5628	2.4989	23
24	3.2209	3.1210	3.0271	2.9386	2.8550	2.7760	2.7013	2.6304	2.5632	2.4992	24
25	3.2220	3.1220	3.0279	2.9392	2.8556	2.7765	2.7017	2.6307	2.5634	2.4994	25

Glossary

ABC system: a system of stock management that prioritises items accounting for greatest stock value.

Acceptance credit: a facility to issue bank-guaranteed bills (**bank bills**) by a firm wanting to raise short-term finance. They can be sold on the money market, but are unrelated to specific trading transactions. The bank accepts the liability to exchange cash for bills when presented at the due date.

Accepting houses: accepting houses are specialist institutions that discount or 'accept' Bills of Exchange, especially short-term government securities (see Chapter 15).

Accounting rate of return: return on investment over the whole life of a project.

Acquirees: taken-over firms. Also, 'targets' or 'victims'.

Acquirers: firms that make takeovers. Also, 'predators'.

Adjusted NAV: the NAV as per the accounts, adjusted for any known or suspected deviations between book values and market, or realisable values.

Adjusted present value (APV): the inherent value of a project adjusted for any financial benefits and costs stemming from the particular method(s) of financing.

Administration: an attempt to reorganise an insolvent firm under an administrator, rather than liquidate it.

Agency costs: costs that owners (principals) have to incur in order to ensure that their agents (managers) make financial decisions consistent with their best interests.

Aggressive stocks: generate returns that vary by a larger proportion than overall market returns. Their Betas exceed 1.0.

Allocative efficiency: the most efficient way that a society can allocate its overall stock of resources

Alternative Investment Market (AIM): where smaller, younger companies can acquire a stock market listing.

American options: can be exercised at any time up to the maturity date.

Amortisation: repayment of debt by a series of instalments. Also used as a term for depreciation of intangible assets.

Analysis of variance: a statistical technique for isolating the separate determinants of the fluctuations recorded in a variable over time.

Annual percentage rate (APR): the true annualised cost of finance.

Annual percentage rate: the true annual interest rate charged by the lender which takes account of the timing of interest and principal payments

Annual writing-down allowances (WDAs): allowances for depreciation on capital expenditure allowed for tax purposes.

Annuity: a finite series of cash flows.

Annuity: a constant annual cash flow for a prescribed period of time

Arbitrage: the profitable exploitation of divergences between the prices of goods (or between interest rates), that violate the Law of One Price. Also applied in MM's capital structure analysis to refer to the process of equalising the values of geared and ungeared firms. Hence, **arbitageur**.

Arbitrage: the process whereby astute entrepreneurs identify and exploit opportunities to make profits by trading on differentials in price of the same item as between two locations or markets.

Arbitrage Pricing Theory (APT): an extension of the CAPM to include more than one factor (hence, an example of a **multi-factor model**) used to explain the returns on securities. Each factor has its own Beta coefficient.

Arbitrageurs: arbitrageurs attempt to exploit differences in the values of financial variables in different markets, e.g. borrowing in a low-cost location and investing where interest rates are relatively high (interest arbitrage).

Articles of Association: a document drawn up at the formation of an enterprise, detailing the rights and obligations of shareholders and directors.

Asset or **activity Beta:** the inherent systematic riskiness of a firm's operations, before allowing for gearing. Also known as **firm Beta**, **company Beta**, or **ungeared Beta**.

Asset-backed securities (ABS): bonds issued on the security of a stream of highly reliable income flows, e.g. mortgage payments to a bank, out of which interest payments are made.

Asset stripping: selling off the assets of a taken-over firm, often in order to recoup the initial outlay.

Asymmetric information: one party to a contract is in possession of more information than the other.

Back-to-back loans: a simple form of a swap where firms lend directly to each other to satisfy their mutual currency requirements.

Balance sheet/statement of financial position: a financial statement that lists the assets held by a business at a point in time and explains how they have been financed (i.e. by owners' capital and by third-party liabilities).

Balloon loan: where increasing amounts of capital are repaid towards the end of the loan period.

Bancassurance: a term coined to denote the combination of banking and insurance business within the same organisation.

Bank loan: usually extended for a fixed term with a pre-agreed schedule of interest and capital repayments. Interest is usually payable on the initial amount borrowed, regardless of the falling balance as repayments are made.

Barter: the simplest form of counter-trade, involving direct exchange of goods with no money being exchanged.

Beta geared: the Beta attaching to the ordinary shares of a geared firm. These bear a risk higher than the firm's basic activity.

Beta ungeared: the geared Beta stripped of the effect of gearing. Corresponds to the activity Beta in an equivalent ungeared firm.

Betas or **Beta coefficients:** relate the responsiveness of the returns on individual securities to variations in the return on the overall market portfolio.

Bilateral netting: operated by pairs of firms in the same group netting off their respective positions regarding payables and receivables.

Bill of Exchange: a promise to pay at a specific time, issued to suppliers by purchasers in exchange for goods. Bills may be held to maturity or sold at a discount on the money market if cash is required sooner.

Bill of Lading: a document that transfers title to exported goods to the bank that finances the deal when the goods are shipped.

Bird-in-the-hand fallacy: the mistaken belief that dividends paid early in the future are worth more than dividends expected in later time periods, simply because they are nearer in time and viewed as less risky.

Bonds: any form of borrowing that firms can undertake in the form of a medium- or long-term security, that commits them to specific repayment dates, at fixed or variable interest.

Bonds: a debt obligation with a maturity of more than a year.

Bonus or **scrip issues:** issues of free shares to existing shareholders *in lieu* of, or in addition to, cash dividends. Reflected in lower reserves (hence the alternative label, **capitalisation issue**).

Book-to-market ratio: ratio of the book value of equity to the market value of the shares.

Boston Consulting Group approach: an approach for assessing capital proposals based on the market growth and market share of the products relating to the proposal.

Break-up value (BUV): the value that can be obtained by selling off the firm's assets piecemeal to the highest bidders.

Building societies: financial institutions whose main function is to accept deposits from customers and lend for house purchases.

Bullet loan: where no capital is repaid until the very end of the loan period.

Business angels: wealthy private investors who take equity stakes in small, high-risk firms.

Buy-back: a method of obtaining payment for building a manufacturing unit overseas by taking the future physical product of the plant in return.

Call option: the right to buy an asset at a specified price on or before expiry date.

Call option: a financial derivative that gives the buyer the right but not the obligation to buy a particular commodity or currency at a specific future date.

Capital: strictly, the funds invested in a firm by shareholders when they purchase ordinary shares, but often used to indicate all forms of equity, and often to refer to any form of finance, whether equity or debt.

Capital allowances: tax allowances for capital expenditure.

Capital asset: any investment that offers a prospective return, with or without risk. However, in finance, the term is usually applied to securities and ordinary shares in particular.

Capital Asset Pricing Model (CAPM): a theory used to explain how efficient capital markets value securities, i.e. capital assets, by discounting future expected returns at risk-adjusted discount rates.

Capital Asset Pricing Model (CAPM): the CAPM is a model designed to explain how the stock market values capital assets, including ordinary shares, by assessing their relative risk–return properties.

Capital gains tax (CGT): paid on realising an increase in share value. Capital gains are currently treated as income in the UK at the investor's marginal tax rate.

Capital gearing: the mixture of debt and equity in a firm's capital structure, which influences variations in shareholders' profits in response to sales and EBIT variations.

Capitalisation: the procedure of converting (by discounting) a series of future cash flows into a single capital sum.

Capitalisation rate: a discount rate used to convert a series of future cash flows into a single capital sum.

Capital lease/full payout lease: a lease that transfers most of the benefits and risks of ownership to the lessee.

Capital market line: a relationship tracing out the efficient combinations of risk and return available to investors prepared to combine the market portfolio with the risk-free asset.

Capital market line (CML): traces out the efficient combinations of risk and return available to investors when combining a risk-free asset with the market portfolio.

Capital rationing: the process of allocating capital to projects where there is insufficient capital to fund all value-creating proposals.

Capital structure: the mixture of debt and equity resulting from decisions on financing operations.

Captive firms: subsidiaries of banks and other institutions established to invest in risky but attractive businesses.

Carrying costs: stock costs that increase with the size of stock investment.

Cash flow statement: a financial statement that explains the reasons for cash inflows and outflow of a business, and highlights the resulting change in cash position.

Cash operating cycle: length of time between cash payment to suppliers and cash received from customers.

Characteristics line (CL): relates the periodic returns on a security to the returns on the market portfolio. Its slope is the Beta of the security. The regression model used to estimate Betas is called the **market model**.

Chartist: analyst who relies on charts of past share movements to predict future movements.

Chartists: analysts who use technical analysis.

Classical tax system: a system where dividends are effectively taxed twice – the firm pays profits tax and then investors pay income tax on any dividend payment.

Clientèle effect: the notion that a firm attracts investors by establishing a set dividend policy that suits a particular group of investors.

Commercial paper: a short-term promissory note or IOU, issued by a highly creditworthy corporate borrower to financial institutions and other cash-rich corporates.

Co-movement or **co-variability:** the tendency for two variables, e.g. the returns from two investments, to move in parallel. It can be measured using either:

(i) the **correlation coefficient:** a relative measure of co-movement that locates assets on a scale between −1 and +1. Where returns move exactly in unison, perfect positive correlation exists, and where exactly opposite movements occur, perfect negative correlation exists. Most investments fall in between, mainly, with positive correlation.

(ii) the **covariance:** an absolute measure of co-movement with no upper or lower limits.

Compound interest: interest paid on the sum which accumulates, i.e. the principal plus interest.

Concentration banking: where customers in a geographical area pay bills to a local branch office rather than to the head office.

Concentric acquisition: undertaken to exploit synergies in marketing of two firms' products, without production economies.

Conglomerate takeover: the acquisition of a target firm in a field apparently unrelated to the acquirer's existing activities.

Contingent claim security: claim on a security whose value depends on the value of another asset.

Contra-cyclical: a term applied to an investment whose returns fluctuate in opposite ways to general trends in business activity, i.e. contrary to the cycle.

Contribution: revenues (turnover) less variable costs, i.e. contribution to meeting fixed costs.

Convertible loan stock: a debenture that can be converted into ordinary shares, often on attractive terms, usually at the option of the holder. Some preference shares are convertible.

Corporate bonds: medium- to long-term borrowing by a company.

Cost centre treasury (CCT): a treasury that aims to minimise the cost of its dealings.

Cost of debt: the yield a firm would have to offer if undertaking further borrowing at current market rates.

Cost of equity: the minimum rate of return a firm must offer owners to compensate for waiting for their returns, and also for bearing risk.

Costs of financial distress: the costs incurred as a firm approaches, and ultimately reaches, the point of insolvency.

Counterparty risk: the risk that the opposite party to a contract defaults on its obligations.

Counterparty risk: the risk that the bank which is party to a hedging transaction such as a forward contract may not deliver the agreed amount of currency at the agreed time.

Counter-trade: a form of trade involving reciprocal obligations with a trading partner, or counterparty, e.g. a commitment to buy from a firm or country that the firm sells to.

Country risk: the risk of adverse effects on the net cash flows of a MNC due to political and economic factors peculiar to the country of location of FDI.

Coupon rate: the nominal annual rate of interest expressed as a percentage of the principal value.

Coupon rate of interest: the fixed rate of interest, as printed on the debt security, that a firm must pay to lenders.

Covariance: a statistical measure of the extent to which the fluctuations exhibited by two (or more) variables are related.

Covered interest arbitrage: using the forward market to lock in the future domestic currency value of a transaction undertaken to exploit an interest arbitrage opportunity.

Credit limits: the maximum amount of credit that a firm is willing to extend to a customer.

Credit risk: the risk that a foreign customer might not pay up as agreed on time or at all.

Crest: an electronic mechanism for settling and registering shares sold on the London Stock Exchange.

Critical mass: the minimum size of firm thought necessary to compete effectively, e.g. to finance R&D.

Cross-currency interest swap: a swap agreement where the parties agree to swap a fixed interest rate commitment for a floating interest rate.

Currency futures contract: a commitment to deliver a specific amount of foreign exchange at a specified future date at an agreed price incorporated in the contract. Contracts can be traded on an exchange in standard sizes.

Currency information system: an information system set up to identify values that are exposed to currency risk, e.g. cash in- and out-flows and asset and liability values.

Currency option: the right, but not the obligation, to buy or sell a fixed amount of currency at a pre-determined rate at a specified future date.

Currency swaps: where two or more parties swap the capital value and associated interest streams of their borrowing in different currencies.

Currency switching: where an exporter pays for imported supplies in the currency of the export deal.

Current assets: assets that will leave the balance sheet in the next accounting period.

Current cost accounting (CCA): attempts to capture the effect of inflation on asset values (and liabilities) by recording them at their current replacement cost, i.e. the cost of obtaining an identical replacement.

Current ratio: current assets divided by current liabilities.

Current ratio: ratio of current assets to current liabilities.

Days cash-on-hand ratio: cash and marketable securities divided by daily cash operating expenses.

Debentures: in law, any form of borrowing that commits a firm to pay interest and repay capital. In practice, usually applied to long-term loans that are secured on a firm's assets.

Debt capacity: of an investment or a whole firm is the maximum amount of debt finance, and hence interest payments that it can support without incurring financial distress.

Debt finance/loan capital: capital raised with an obligation to pay interest and repay principal.

Default: the failure by a borrower to adhere to a pre-agreed schedule of interest and/or capital payments on a loan.

Defensive stock: generates returns that vary by a smaller proportion than overall market returns. Its Beta is less than one.

Derivative: a financial instrument whose value derives from an underlying asset.

Derivatives: securities that are traded separately from the assets from which they are derived.

Direct debit: an automatic payment from a customer's bank account pre-arranged with the bank by both trading partners.

Direct investment: investment in tangible and intangible assets for business operating purposes.

Directors' dealings: share sales and purchases by senior officers of the firm.

Disclosure: release of financial and operating information about a firm into the public domain.

Discount: the amount below the face value of a financial instrument at which it sells.

Discounted cash flow: future cash flows adjusted for the time-value of money.

Discounted cash flow (DCF) analysis: the process of analysing financial instruments and decisions by discounting cash flows to present values.

Discounted payback: period of time the present value of a project's annual net cash flows take to match the initial cost outlay.

Discounting: the process of reducing cash flows to present values.

Discount houses: discount houses bid for issues of short-term government securities at a discount and either hold them to maturity or sell them on in the money market.

Discount rate: any percentage required return used to convert future expected cash flows into their equivalent present values.

Disintermediation: business-to-business lending that eliminates the banking intermediary.

Diversifiable risk: can be removed by efficient portfolio diversification.

Diversification: extension of a firm's activities into new and unrelated fields. Although this may generate cost savings, e.g. via shared distribution systems, as a by-product, the fundamental motive for diversification is to reduce exposure to fluctuations in economic activity.

Dividend irrelevance: the theory that, when firms have access to external finance, it is irrelevant to firm value whether they pay a dividend or not.

Dividend Valuation Model: a way of assessing the value of shares by capitalising the future dividends. With growing dividend payments, it becomes the **Dividend Growth Model**.

Dividend yield: gross dividend per ordinary share (including both interim and final payments) divided by current share price.

Double tax agreements (DTAs): reciprocal arrangements between countries whereby tax paid in one location is credited in the second, thus avoiding doubling up the firm's tax bill. Hence, Double Tax Relief (DTR).

Earnings before interest and taxes (EBIT): earnings (i.e. profits) before interest and taxation.

Earnings before interest, tax, depreciation & amortisation (EBITDA): a rough measure of operating cash flow, effectively, operating profit with depreciation added back. It differs from the 'Net Cash Inflow from Operating Activities' shown in cash flow statements due to working capital movements.

Earnings dilution: the dampening effect on EPS of issuing further shares at a discount as in a rights issue.

Earnings per share (EPS): profit available for distribution to shareholders divided by the number of shares issued.

Earnings yield: the earnings per share (EPS) divided by market share price.

Earnings yield: EPS divided by current share price. Sometimes, it refers to expected or 'prospective' EPS, becoming the '**prospective earnings yield**'. It is a simple way of expressing the investor's Return on Investment on the share.

Economic order quantity (EOQ): the most economic quantity to be ordered that minimises holding and ordering costs.

Economic value added (EVA): post-tax accounting profit generated by a firm reduced by a charge for using the equity (usually, cost of equity times book value of equity).

Efficient frontier: traces out all the available portfolio combinations that either minimise risk for a stated expected return or maximise expected return for a specified measure of risk.

Efficient markets: where current share prices fully reflect the information available.

Electronic funds transfer: instantaneous transfer of money from a debtor's bank account to a creditor.

Enhanced scrip dividends: scrip alternatives offered to investors that are worth more than the alternative cash payment.

Enterprise Investment Scheme (EIS): scheme offering tax relief to investors who are buying shares in smaller, more risky companies.

Enterprise value: the value of the whole firm.

Entrepreneurial companies: are driven by the growth ambitions and desire of the owners to create significant wealth.

Equity or **equity value:** the value of the owners' stake in a firm, however calculated.

Equity Beta: indicates the systematic riskiness attaching to the returns on ordinary shares. It equates to the asset Beta for an ungeared firm, or is adjusted upwards to reflect the extra riskiness of shares in a geared firm, to become '**Beta geared**'.

Equivalent annual annuity (EAA): the constant annual cash flow offering the same present value as the project's net present value.

Equivalent loan: the loan that would involve the same schedule of interest and loan repayments as the profile of rentals required by an equipment lessor.

Equivalent risk class: a concept used by MM to include all firms subject to the same business risks (i.e. all having the same Activity Betas).

Eurobonds or **international bonds:** securities issued by borrowers in a market outside that of their domestic currency.

European options: can only be exercised at the specified maturity date.

Exchange agio: the percentage difference between the spot and forward rates of exchange between two currencies.

Ex-dividend: a share trades ex-dividend (xd) when people who buy are no longer entitled to receive the upcoming dividend payment.

Ex-dividend (ex-div. or xd): when subsequent purchasers of a share no longer qualify for the forthcoming dividend payment. Until this point, the shares are quoted **cum-dividend**.

Exercise price: price at which an option can be taken up.

Exercise (strike) price: the price at which the option to buy or sell can be transacted.

Expectations or **unbiased forward predictor theory:** the postulate that the expected change in the spot rate of exchange is equal to the difference between the current spot rate and the current forward rate for the relevant period.

Expected net present value (ENPV): the average of the range of possible NPVs weighted by their probability of occurrence.

Exporting: sale of goods and services to a foreign customer.

Externalisation: the transfer of key functions and expertise to an overseas strategic partner.

Factoring: a means of obtaining faster cash inflow, and thus increased funds. A firm appoints the factor to collect outstanding accounts payable and to administer debtors' accounts. It also lends money to the client based on the value of the firm's sales.

Factors: organisations that offer to purchase a firm's debtors for cash.

Fair game: a competitive process in which all participants have equal access to information and therefore similar chances of success.

Finance lease: a method of acquiring an asset that involves a series of rental payments extending over the whole expected life-time of the asset.

Financial distress: in narrow terms, the difficulty that a firm encounters in meeting obligations to creditors. More broadly, it refers to the adverse consequences, e.g. restrictions on behaviour that result, usually from excessive borrowing by a firm.

Financial gearing: includes both capital gearing and income gearing.

Financial intermediaries: specialist financial institutions which collect funds from savers and lend to corporate and other borrowers.

Financial intermediaries: institutions that channel funds from savers and depositors with cash surpluses to people and organisations with cash shortages.

Financial leverage: the ratio of profit before interest and tax (PBIT) to profit before tax (PBT).

Financial market: any market in which financial assets and liabilities are traded

Financial Conduct Authority (FCA): a regulatory body for maintaining confidence in the financial markets.

Fixed charge: applies when a lender can force the sale of pre-specified company's assets in order to recover debts in the event of default on interest and/or capital payments.

Fixed/fixed swap: a swap agreement where the parties agree to swap fixed interest rate commitments.

Flat yield or **running yield:** on a bond is the ratio of the fixed interest payment to the current market price of the bond.

Floating charge: applies when a lender can force the sale of any (i.e. unspecified) of a company's assets in order to recover debts in the event of default on interest and/or capital payments. (Ranks behind a fixed charge.)

Floating rate note (FRN): a bond issue where interest is paid at a variable rate (often a Eurobond).

Follow-on opportunities: options that arise following a course of action.

Foreign bonds: loan stock issued on the domestic market by non-resident firms or organisations. In London, called 'bulldogs', in New York 'Yankees'.

Foreign currency swap: a way of extending the delivery date incorporated in a forward contract. A spot/forward swap involves completing the original contract by a spot transaction and entering a new forward contract for the additional of time.

Foreign currency swap: a way of using the forward markets to adjust the maturity date of an initially agreed contract with a bank.

Foreign direct investment (FDI): investment in fixed assets located abroad for operating distribution and/or production facilities.

Foreign exchange exposure: the risk of loss stemming from exposure to adverse foreign exchange rate movements.

Forfaiting: the practice whereby a bank purchases an exporter's sales invoices or promissory notes, that usually carry the guarantee of the importer's bank.

Forward: the forward market is where contracts are made for future settlement at a price specified now.

Forward contract: an agreement to sell or buy at a fixed price at some time in the future.

Forward–forward swap: where the original forward contract is supplemented by new contracts that have the effect of extending the maturity date of the original one.

Forward option: a forward currency contract that incorporates a flexible settlement date between two fixed dates.

Forward rate of exchange: the rate fixed for transactions that involve delivery and settlement at some specified future date.

Franchising: licensing out of a fully packaged business system, including technology and supply of materials, to an entrepreneur operating a separate legally constituted business.

Free cash flow (FCF): a firm's cash flow free of obligatory payments. Strictly, it is cash flow after interest, tax and replacement investment, although it is measured in many other ways in practice, e.g. after all investment.

Fundamental analysis: estimation of the 'true' value of a share based on expected future returns.

Fundamental analysis: analysis of the fundamental determinants of company financial health and future performance prospects, such as endowment of resources, quality of management, product innovation record, etc.

Funding: cash and liquidity management, short-term financing and cash forecasting.

Future: a tradable contract to buy or sell a specified amount of an asset at a specified price at a specified future date.

Futures contract: a commitment to buy or sell an asset at an agreed date and price, and traded on an exchange.

FX: abbreviation for foreign exchange.

Gearing: proportion of the total capital that is borrowed.

Generally Accepted Accounting Principles (GAAP): the set of legal regulations and accounting standards that dictate 'best practice' in constructing company accounts.

General valuation model: a family of valuation models that rely on discounting future cash flows to establish the value of the equity or the whole enterprise.

Global companies: serve a range of overseas markets both by exporting and direct investment.

Going concern value (GCV): the value of the assets as stated in the accounts that assume that the firm will continue as a viable entity as it stands, i.e. as an ongoing activity.

Golden handcuffs: an exceptionally good remuneration package paid to executives to prevent them from leaving.

Gross redemption yield: the redemption yield before allowing for income tax payable by investors.

Hedge: a hedge is an arrangement effected by a person or firm attempting to eliminate or reduce exposure to risk – hence to hedge and hedger.

Hedgers: hedgers try to minimise or totally eliminate exposure to risk.

Hedging: attempting to minimise the risk of loss stemming from exposure to adverse foreign exchange rate movements.

Hire purchase (HP): a means of obtaining the use of an asset before payment is completed. An HP contract involves an initial, or 'down payment', followed by a series of hire charges at the end of which ownership passes to the user.

Home-made dividends: cash released when an investor realises part of his/her investment in a firm in order to supplement his/her income.

Home-made gearing: where an investor borrows to arbitrage between two identical but differently valued assets.

Horizontal integration: the acquisition of a competitor in pursuit of market power and/or scale economies.

Hybrid: a security that combines features of both equity and debt.

Imputation tax systems: taxation systems that offer shareholders tax credits (fully or partially) in respect of company tax already paid when assessing their income tax liability on dividends paid out.

Income gearing: the proportion of profit before interest and tax (PBIT) absorbed by interest charges.

Incremental hypothesis: suggests that firms tend gradually to build their degree of involvement in foreign markets, beginning with exporting and culminating in FDI.

Independent companies: investment companies set up as stand-alone entities by venture capitalists to invest money in risky but potentially attractive businesses.

Information asymmetry: the imbalance between managers and owners of information possessed about a firm's financial state and its prospects.

Information content: the extra, unstated intelligence that investors deduce from the formal announcement by a firm of any financial news, i.e. what people read 'between the lines', or 'financial body language'.

Initial public offering (IPO): the first issue of shares by an existing or a newly formed firm to the general public.

Insider trading: dealing in shares using information not publicly available.

Insurance companies: financial institutions that guarantee to protect clients against specified risks, including death, and general risks in return for the payment of an annual premium.

Insured schemes: a pension fund that uses an insurance company to invest contributions and to insure against actuarial risks (e.g. members living longer than expected).

Intangible: intangible assets cannot be seen or touched, e.g. the image and good reputation of a firm.

Interest agio: the percentage difference between interest rates prevailing in the money markets for lending/ borrowing in two currencies.

Interest cover: the number of times the profit before interest exceeds loan interest.

Interest rate parity (IRP): asserts that the difference between the spot and forward exchanges is equal to the differential between interest rates prevailing in the money markets for lending/borrowing in the respective currencies.

Interest yield: the annual interest on a bond or similar security divided by its market price.

Intermediaries offer: a placing made to stockbrokers other than the one advising the company making the issue.

Internalisation: the retention by the MNC of key management functions and technology.

Internal rate of return: the discount rate that equates the present value of future cash flows with initial investment cost.

Internal rate of return: the rate of return that equates the present value of future cash flows with initial investment outlay.

International or **Open Fisher Theory:** the notion that, because real rates of interest are equalised throughout the world, given freedom of capital mobility, any observed differences in nominal rates between different locations must be due to different expectations of inflation between those locations.

Intrinsic worth: the inherent or fundamental value of a company and its shares.

Investment banks: investment banks are wholesale banks that arrange specialist financial services like mergers and acquisition funding, and finance of international trade fund management.

Invoice discounting: where a factor purchases selected invoices from a client firm, without providing debt collection or account administration services.

IRR or DCF yield: the rate of return that equates the present value of future cash flows with the initial investment outlay.

Irrevocable DLOC: a written authority for a bank to make specified payments to an exporter, whose terms cannot be varied.

Issue by tender: a share issue where prospective investors are invited to bid or 'tender' for shares at a price of their own choosing.

Joint venture: a strategic alliance involving the formal establishment of a new marketing and/or production operation involving two or more partners.

Junk bonds: low-quality, risky bonds with no credit rating.

Lagging: settling as late as possible a payable (receivable) denominated in a currency expected to weaken (strengthen).

Law of One Price: the proposition that any good or service will sell for the same price, adjusting for the relevant exchange rate, throughout the world.

Leading: advancing before the due date a payable denominated in a foreign currency that is expected to strengthen, or advancing a receivable in a currency expected to weaken.

lessee: a firm that leases an asset from a lessor.

lessor: a firm that acquires equipment and other assets for leasing out to firms wishing to use such items in their operations.

Letter of credit: a credit drawn up by an importer in favour of an exporter. It is endorsed by a bank that guarantees payment provided the beneficiary delivers the Bill of Lading proving that goods have been shipped.

Licensing: involves the assignment of production and selling rights to producers located in foreign locations in return for royalty payments.

Liquidity management: planning the acquisition and utilisation of cash, i.e. cash flow management.

Listed companies: firms whose shares are quoted on the Main List of the Stock Exchange.

Loan Guarantee Scheme: a facility whereby banks are able to lend to firms that would not otherwise qualify for bank finance due to lack of track record, the loan being guaranteed by the Department of Trade and Industry.

Main list: daily list of securities and prices traded on the London Stock Exchange.

Management buy-in (MBI): acquisition of an equity stake in an existing firm by new management that injects expertise as well as capital into the enterprise.

Management buy-out (MBO): acquisition of an existing firm by its existing management usually involving substantial amounts of straight debt and mezzanine finance.

Marginal cost of capital (MCC): the extra returns required to satisfy all investors as a proportion of new capital raised.

Marginal efficiency of investment (MEI): a schedule listing available investments, in declining order of attractiveness.

Market capitalisation: the market value of a firm's equity, i.e. number of ordinary shares issued times market price.

Market model: a device relating the expected (in practice, *actual*) return from individual securities to the expected/*actual* return from the overall stock market.

Market portfolio: includes all securities traded on the stock market weighted by their respective capitalisations. Usually, a more limited portfolio such as the FT All Share Index is used as a proxy.

Matching: offsetting a currency inflow in one currency, e.g. a stream of revenues, by a corresponding stream of costs, thus leaving only the profit element unmatched. Firms may also match operating cash flows against financial flows, e.g. a stream of interest and capital payments resulting from overseas borrowing in the same currency.

McKinsey–General Electric portfolio matrix: an approach for assessing projects within the wider strategic context which focuses on the market attractiveness and business strength of the product and business unit relating to the capital proposal.

Mergers: pooling by firms of their separate interests into newly constituted business, each party participating on roughly equal terms.

Mezzanine finance: covers hybrids such as convertibles that embody both debt and equity features.

Modified internal rate of return (MIRR): the internal rate of return modified for the reinvestment assumption.

Modigliani and Miller's (MM) Capital Structure Theories:

(i) MM-no tax, which 'proves' that no optimal capital structure exists, and that the WACC is invariant to debt/equity ratio.

(ii) MM-with tax which suggests that the tax shield should be exploited up to the point of almost 100 per cent debt financing.

Monetary Policy Committee: a body whose members are appointed by the Bank of England, responsible for setting UK interest rates at monthly meetings.

Money market: the market for short-term money, broadly speaking for repayment within about a year.

Money market cover: involves an exporter borrowing on the money market (i.e. creating a liability) in the same currency in which it expects to receive a payment.

Monte Carlo simulation: method for calculating the probability distribution of possible outcomes.

Moral hazard: the temptation facing managers to engage in risky activities when they are protected from the consequences of failure, e.g. by guaranteed severance payments.

Mortgage debenture: a loan instrument under which the ownership of selected assets is mortgaged to the lender – in a default, the title passes to the lender.

Multilateral netting: a central Treasury department operation to minimise net flows of currency throughout an organisation.

Multinational company (MNC): one that conducts a significant proportion of its operations abroad.

Natural hedge: where the adverse impact of FX rate variations on cash inflows are offset by the effect on cash outflows, or vice versa.

Natural matching: a natural match is achieved where the firm has a two-way cash flow in the same currency due to the structure of its operations, e.g. selling in a currency in which it sources supplies.

Net advantage of a lease (NAL): the NPV of the acquisition of an asset adjusted for financing benefits.

Net asset value (NAV): the value of owners' stake in a firm, found by deducting total liabilities (i.e. debts) from total assets.

Net asset value approach: calculation of the equity value in a firm by netting the liabilities against the assets.

Net book value: the original cost of buying an asset less accumulated depreciation charges to date.

Net current assets: current assets less current liabilities.

Net debt: a firm's net borrowing including both long-term and also short-term debt, offset by cash holdings. Expressed either in absolute terms, or in relation to owner's equity.

Net present value: the value of a stream of cash flows adjusted for the time-value of money. A positive NPV adds value.

Net present value: the present value of the future net benefits less the initial cost.

Netting: offsetting a firm's internal currency inflows and outflows in the same currency to minimise the net flow in either direction.

Net working capital: current assets less current liabilities.

Neutral stocks: generate returns that vary by the same proportion as overall market returns. Their Betas equal 1.0. Also called 'market-tracking' investments.

New Issue Market: the market for selling and buying newly issued securities. It has no physical existence.

Niche companies: serve a limited segment of their markets, usually offering high-quality, differentiated products at a high margin.

Nil paid price of rights: the market value of the right to subscribe for new shares offered in a rights issue.

Non-current assets: assets that remain in the balance sheet for more than one accounting period (i.e. they are fixed in the balance sheet).

Non-recourse (as distinct from recourse): factoring operates where factors are unable to reclaim bad debts from a client's accounts.

Notes: loan securities in general, but often referred to securities that carry a floating rate of interest.

Offer for sale by prospectus: an issue of ordinary shares through an issuing house that promotes the shares in a detailed prospectus aimed at the public in general.

Offset: the requirement for an MNC to undertake a proportion of local sourcing as condition of the award of an export deal (very common in the armaments industry).

Open account: where trading partners agree settlement terms with no formal contract.

Operating gearing: the proportion of fixed costs in the firm's operating cost structure.

Operating gearing factor: a ratio that compares the operating gearing of a particular activity, e.g. a product division within a larger firm to that of a larger entity such as the whole firm.

Operating gearing factor (OGF): the operating gearing factor of an individual project in relation to that of the division to which it is attached.

Operating/strategic exposure: the risk that adverse foreign exchange rate movements will affect the present value of the firm's future cash flows (effectively, long-term transactions exposure).

Operating/technical efficiency: the most cost-effective way of producing an item, or organising a process.

Operating lease: a method of hiring assets over periods less than the expected lifetime of those assets.

Operating lease: a job-specific lease contract, usually arranged for a short period, during which the lessor retains most of the benefits and risks of ownership.

Operating leverage: the ratio of contribution to profit before interest and tax.

Operating profit: revenues less total operating costs, both variable and fixed– as distinct from financial costs such as interest payments.

Opportunity cost: the value forgone by opting for a particular course of action.

Opportunity set: the set of investment opportunities (i.e. risk–return combinations) available to the investor to select from.

Optimal capital structure: the financing mix that minimises the overall cost of finance and maximises market value.

Optimal portfolio: the one chosen by an investor to achieve his/her most desired combination of risk and return. This choice depends on the investor's attitude to risk, or risk–return preference, i.e. how he/she rates different combinations of risk and return. If a risk-free asset is available, the optimal portfolio of risky assets is the market portfolio.

Optimal portfolio: the risk–return combination that offers maximum satisfaction to the investor, i.e. his/her most-preferred risk–return combination.

Option: the right but not the obligation to buy or sell a particular asset.

Option: the right but not the obligation to buy or sell something at some time in the future at a given price.

Option contract: a contract giving one party the right, but not the obligation, to buy or sell a financial instrument or commodity at an agreed price at or before a specified date.

Option to abandon: choice to allow an option to expire. With a capital investment, abandonment should take place where the value for which an asset can be sold exceeds the present value of its future benefits from continuing its operations.

Overdraft: short-term finance extended by banks subject to instant recall. A maximum deficit balance is pre-agreed and interest is paid on the actual daily balance outstanding.

Over-the-counter: an over-the-counter transaction, e.g. the purchase of an option, where the terms are tailor-made to suit the requirements of the purchaser.

Overtrading: where a firm has insufficient long-term capital to finance business growth.

Overtrading: operating a business with an inappropriate capital base, usually trying to grow too fast with insufficient long-term capital.

Owner's equity: in accounting terms, simply the NAV, but can also be expressed in market value terms, i.e. share price times number of ordinary shares issued, or 'capitalisation'.

Parallel matching: applies where a firm offsets inflows in one currency with outflows denominated in a closely correlated currency.

Participating: preference shares that may qualify for payment of an additional dividend payment in a good year.

Part-payout lease: a lease contract which recovers a return lower than the capital outlay made by the lessor.

Patents: a legal device giving the holder the exclusive right to exploit the technology described therein.

Payback period: period of time a project's annual net cash flows take to match the initial cost outlay.

Pension funds: financial institutions that manage the pension schemes of large firms and other organisations.

Perpetual warrant: a warrant with no time limit for exercising it.

Perpetuity: an infinite series of cash flows.

Perpetuity: a constant annual cash flow for an infinite period of time.

Placing: an issue of ordinary shares directly to selected institutional investors, who may re-sell them on the stock market when dealings officially commence.

Plant hire: hiring of construction equipment.

Poison pill: a provision designed to damage the interests of a takeover bidder, e.g. handsome severance terms for departing managers, activated on completion of the bid.

Political risk: the risk of politically motivated interference by a foreign government in the affairs of a MNC, that adversely affects its net cash flows.

Portfolio: a combination of investments – securities or physical assets – into a single 'bundled' investment. A well-diversified portfolio has the potential capacity to lower the investor's exposure to the risk of fluctuations in the overall economy.

Portfolio effect: the tendency for the risk on a well-diversified holding of investments to fall below the risk of most, and sometimes all, of its individual components.

Portfolio investment: investment in financial securities such as bonds and equities, with no stake in management.

Portfolios: combinations of securities of various kinds invested in a diversified fund.

Post-audit: a re-examination of costs, benefits and forecasts of a project after implementation (usually after one year).

Post-completion audit: audit of a capital project at an agreed time following implementation.

Pre-emption rights: the right for existing shareholders to be offered newly issued shares before making them available to outside investors.

Preference shares: hybrid securities that rank ahead of ordinary shares for dividend payment, usually at a fixed rate, and also in distributing the proceeds of a liquidation. Normally, they carry no voting rights.

Premium: the amount above the face value of a financial instrument at which it sells.

Premium: the difference between the issue price of an ordinary share and its par (or nominal) value.

Present value: the current worth of future cash flows.

Price–earnings multiples: the price–earnings multiple, or ratio (PER), is the ratio of earnings (i.e. *profit after tax*) per share (EPS) to market share price.

Price:earnings (P:E) ratio: the ratio of price per ordinary share to earnings (i.e. profit after tax) per share (EPS).

Price:Earnings ratio (PER): the current share price divided by the latest reported earnings (i.e. profits after tax) per share.

Price-to-earnings multiple/P:E ratio: another way of expressing the PER.

Price variation: adjustment of a firm's pricing policy to take into account expected foreign exchange rate movements.

Pricing/information efficiency: the extent to which available information is impounded into the current set of share prices.

Principal: the principal or face value or par value is the amount of the debt excluding interest.

Principal–agent: the agent, such as board of directors, is expected to act in the best interests of the principal (e.g. the shareholder).

Private placing: an issue of shares directly to a selected number of financial institutions.

Profitability index (PI): ratio of the present value of benefits to costs.

Profit after tax (PAT): profit available to pay dividends to shareholders after tax has been paid.

Profit and loss account/income statement: a financial statement that details for a specific time period the amount of revenue earned by a firm, the costs it has incurred, the resulting profit and how it has been distributed ('appropriated').

Profit centre treasury (PCT): a corporate treasury that aims to make a profit from its dealing – managers are judged on profit performance.

Project gearing factor (PGF): the proportionate increase in a project's operating cash flow in relation to a proportionate increase in the project's sales.

Project risk factor: the product of the Revenue Sensitivity Factor and the Operating Gearing Factor multiplied together.

Proprietorial companies: run by founders and their heirs to provide a livelihood for their families. They usually have limited growth aims.

Prospectus: a document setting out the existing financial situation of a firm and its future prospects that is published to accompany a share issue.

Provision: a notional deduction from profits to allow for some highly likely future financial contingency. In accounting terms, an appropriation of profit after taxation.

Proxy Beta: used when the firm has no market listing and thus no Beta of its own. It is taken from a comparable listed firm, and adjusted as necessary for relative financial gearing levels. Hence, **proxy discount rate**.

Purchasing power parity (PPP): the theory that foreign exchange rates are in equilibrium when a currency can purchase the same amount of goods at the prevailing exchange rate.

Pure play technique: adoption of the Beta value of another firm for use in evaluating investment in an unquoted entity such as an unquoted firm, or a division of a larger firm.

Put option: the right to sell an asset at a specified price on or before expiry date.

Quick/'acid test' ratio: current assets minus stocks, divided by current liabilities.

Random walk theory: share price movements are independent of each other so that tomorrow's share price cannot be predicted by looking at today's.

Real assets: assets in the business (tangible or intangible).

Real options: capital investment options rather than financial options.

Real options: options to invest in real assets such as capital projects.

Rebate clause: an arrangement whereby the lessor pays a proportion of the resale value of an asset to the lessee.

Record day: the cut-off date beyond which further entrants to the shareholder register do not qualify for the next dividend.

Redeemable: repayable (usually at nominal value).

Redemption yield: the interest yield adjusted for any capital gain or loss if the security is held to maturity.

Re-invoicing centre: a corporate subsidiary set up usually in an off-shore location to manage transaction exposure arising from trade between separate divisions of the parent firm.

Relevant risk: the component of total risk taken into account by the stock market when assessing the appropriate risk premium for determining capital asset values.

Replacement chain approach: the process of comparing like-for-like replacement decisions for mutually exclusive projects with different lives over a common time period.

Replacement cost: the cost of replacing the existing assets of a firm with assets of similar vintage capable of performing similar functions.

Reputation risk: companies now cite reputation risk as one of the greatest threats.

Reserves: the funds that shareholders invest in a firm in addition to their initial subscription of capital.

Residual income: operating profit less the charge for capital.

Residual theory of dividends: asserts that firms should only pay cash dividends when they have financed new investments. It assumes no access to external finance.

Restrictive covenants: limitations on managerial freedom of action, stipulated as conditions of making a loan.

Retail banks: retail banks accept deposits from the general public who can draw on these accounts by cheque (or ATM), and lend to other people and organisations seeking funds.

Retained earnings: reserves represented by retention of profits. Sometimes, labelled 'profit & loss account' on the balance sheet. Also called **revenue reserves**.

Revenue sensitivity: the extent to which revenue of an activity varies in response to general economic fluctuations.

Revenue sensitivity factor (RSF): the revenue sensitivity of a particular activity, e.g. a product division, relative to that of a larger entity, such as the whole firm.

Revenue sensitivity factor (RSF): the sensitivity to economic fluctuations of a project's sales in relation to that of the division to which it is attached.

Revocable DLOC: A letter of credit whose terms can be varied without consulting the exporter.

Revolving credit facility: enables a firm to borrow up to a pre-specified amount usually over 1–5 years. As repayments of outstanding balances are made, the loan facility is replenished.

Return on capital employed: operating profit expressed as a percentage of capital employed.

Rights issue: sales of further ordinary shares at less than market price to existing shareholders who are usually able to sell the rights on the market should they not wish to purchase additional shares.

Risk-free assets: securities with zero variation in overall returns.

Risk-minimising policy: a foreign exchange policy designed to eliminate, as far as possible, the firm's exposure to currency risk.

Risk premium: the additional return demanded by investors above the risk-free rate to compensate for exposure to systematic risk.

Risk-sharing: an arrangement where the two parties to an import/export deal agree to share the risk, and thus the impact of unexpected exchange rate movements.

Safety or **buffer stocks:** stocks held as insurance against stockouts (shortages).

Scale economies: cost efficiencies, e.g. bulk-buying, due to increasing a firm's size of operation.

Scrip dividend: offered to investors in lieu of the equivalent cash payment. Also called a **scrip alternative**.

SEAQ: a computer-based quotation system on the London Stock Exchange where market-makers report bid and offer prices and trading volumes.

Secondary lease: a second lease arranged to follow the termination of the initial lease period.

Securities/capital market: the market for long-term finance.

Securitisation: the technique of packaging non-tradable claims into a traded security backed by an asset such as a flow of low-risk income payments.

Securitisation: the capitalisation of a future stream of income into a single capital value that is sold on the capital market for immediate cash.

Security market line (SML): an upward-sloping relationship tracing out all combinations of expected return and systematic risk, available in an efficient market. All traded securities locate on this schedule. In effect, the capital market line adjusted for systematic risk.

Self-administered schemes: a pension fund that invests clients' contributions directly into the stock market and other investments.

Semi-strong form: a semi-strong efficient share market incorporates newly released information accurately and quickly into the structure of share prices.

Sensitivity analysis: analysis of the impact of changes in assumptions on investment returns.

Separation theorem: a model that shows how individual perceptions of the optimal portfolio of risky securities is independent of (i.e. separate from) individuals' different risk–return preferences.

Share buy-back: repurchase by a firm of its existing shares, either via the market or by a tender to all shareholders.

Shareholders' equity: the value of the owners' stake in the business – identically equal to net assets, or equity.

Shareholders' funds or **equity capital:** money invested by shareholders and profits retained in the company.

Shareholder value analysis (SVA): a way of assessing the inherent value of the equity in a company, taking into account the sources of value creation and the time horizon over which the firm enjoys competitive advantages over its rivals.

Share premium account: a reserve set up to account for the issue of new shares at a price above their par value.

Share splits (USA: stock splits): a way of reducing the share price of 'heavyweight' shares (prices above £10). Achieved by reducing the par value of issued shares, e.g. two shares of par value 50p to replace one share at £1 is a one-for-one split, halving the share price.

Shortage costs: stock costs that reduce with size of stock investment.

Short selling: selling securities not yet owned in the expectation of being able to buy them later at a lower price.

Sight draft: a document presented to a bank by an exporter seeking payment for an export deal.

Signalling: using financial announcements to deliver more information than is actually spelt out in detail.

Social efficiency: the extent to which a socio-economic system accords with prevailing social and ethical standards.

Special Purpose Vehicle (SPV): a financial vehicle set up to manage the issue of Asset-Backed Securities and arrange for payment of interest and eventual redemption.

Special Purpose Vehicles (SPV): an entity set up specifically for managing a firm's financial requirements and obligations.

Specific risk: the variability in the return on a security due to exposure to risks relating to that security in isolation, e.g. risk of losing market share due to poor marketing decisions.

Speculators: speculators deliberately take positions to increase their exposure to risk, hoping for higher returns.

Spot: the spot, or cash market, is where transactions are settled immediately.

Spot–forward swap: a less comprehensive forward swap that involves speculation on the future spot market.

Spot rate: the rate of exchange quoted for transactions involving immediate settlement. Hence, **spot market**.

Spread: the difference between the exchange rates (interest rates) at which banks buy and sell foreign exchange (lend and borrow).

Stockout: where a firm is unable to deliver due to shortage of stock.

Straight or **plain vanilla, debt:** fixed rate borrowing with no additional features such as convertibility rights or warrants.

Strategic portfolio analysis: assessing capital projects within the strategic business context and not simply in financial terms.

Stock Exchange introduction: where an established firm obtains a Stock Market listing without selling any shares.

Strong form: in a strong-form efficient share market, all information including inside information is built into share prices.

Sunk cost: a cost already incurred, or committed to.

Synergies: gains in revenues or cost savings resulting from takeovers and mergers, not resulting from firm size, i.e. stemming from a 'natural match' between two sets of assets.

Systematic risk: variability in a security's return due to exposure to risks affecting all firms traded in the market (hence, **market risk**), e.g. the impact of exchange rate changes.

Takeover: acquisition of the share capital of another firm, resulting in its identity being absorbed into that of the acquiror.

Takeover Code: the non-statutory rules laid down by the Takeover Panel to guide the conduct of participants in the takeover process.

Takeover Panel: a non-statutory body set up by, and with the participation of, leading financial organisations to oversee the conduct of takeover bids.

Tangible: tangible assets can quite literally be seen and touched, e.g. machinery and buildings.

Target capital structure: what the firm regards as its optimal long-term ratio of debt to equity (or debt to total capital).

Tax breaks: tax concessions, e.g. relief of interest payments against profits tax.

Tax credit: see **imputation systems**.

Tax shield: the tax savings achieved by setting tax-allowable expenses such as interest payments against profits.

Technical analysis: the detailed scrutiny of past time series of share price movements attempting to identify repetitive patterns.

Technical analysis: the intensive scrutiny of charts of foreign exchange rate movements attempting to identify persistent patterns.

Term loans: loans made by a bank for a specific period or term, usually longer than a year.

Term structure of interest rates: pattern of interest rates on bonds of the same risk with different lengths of time to maturity.

Theoretical ex-rights price (TERP): the market price to which the ordinary shares should gravitate following the completion of a rights issue.

Theoretical ex-rights price (TERP): the share price that should in theory be established, other things being equal, after a rights issue is completed.

Times interest earned: the ratio of profit before interest and tax (operating profit) to annual interest charges, i.e. how many times over the firm could meet its interest bill.

Timing/delay option: the option to invest now or defer the decision until conditions are more favourable.

Time-value of money: the notion that money received in the future is worth less than the same amount received today.

Time-value of money: money received in the future is usually worth less than today because it could be invested to earn interest over this period.

Total shareholder return (TSR): the overall return enjoyed by investors, including dividend and capital appreciation, expressed as a percentage of their initial investment. Related to individual years, or to a lengthier time period, and then converted into an annualised, or equivalent annual return.

Trade credit: temporary financing extended by suppliers of goods and services pending the customer's settlement.

Traded options: an option traded on a market.

Traditional options: an option available on any security agreed between buyer and seller. It typically lasts for three months.

Traditional theory of capital structure: the theory that an optimal capital structure exists, where the WACC is minimised and market value is maximised.

Transaction exposure: the risk of loss due to adverse foreign exchange rate movements that affect the home currency value of import and export contracts denominated in a foreign currency.

Transfer price: the cost applied to goods transferred between operating units owned by the same firm.

Translation exposure: exposure to the risk of adverse currency movements affecting the domestic currency value of the firm's consolidated financial statements.

Treasury Bills: short-dated (up to three months) securities issued by the Bank of England on behalf of the UK government to cover short-term financing needs.

Treasury operations: financial risk management and portfolio management.

Uncovered arbitrage: interest arbitrage without the use of the forward market to lock in future values of proceeds.

'Underlying' asset: the asset from which option value is derived.

Unit Trust: investment business attracting funds from investors by issuing units of shares or bonds to invest in.

Value additivity: the notion that other things being equal, the combined present value of two entities is their separate present values added together.

Value-based management: a managerial approach where the whole aim, strategies and actions are linked to shareholder value creation.

Value drivers: factors that have a powerful influence on the value of a business, and the investors' equity stake.

Vendor placing/placing with clawback: a placing of new shares with financial institutions where existing investors have the right to purchase the shares from the institutions concerned to protect their rights.

Venture capital (VC): finance, usually equity, offered by specialist merchant banks wanting to take a stake in firms with high growth potential, but involving a high risk of loss.

Venture Capital Trusts (VCTs): stock-market listed financial vehicles set up to invest in a spread of highly risky new or young firms.

Vertical integration: extension of a firm's activities further back, or forward, along the supply chain from existing activities.

Warrants: options to buy ordinary shares at a pre-determined 'exercise price'. Usually attached to issues of loan stock.

Weak form: a weak-form efficient share market does not allow investors to look back at past share price movements and identify clear, repetitive patterns.

Weighted average cost of capital (WACC): the overall return a firm must achieve in order to meet the requirements of all its investors.

White knight: a takeover bidder emerging after a hostile bid has been made, usually offering alternative bid terms that are more favourable to the defending management.

Working capital: or net working capital is current assets less current liabilities.

Yield: income from a security as a percentage of market price.

Yield curve: a graph of the relationship between the yield on bonds and their current length of time to maturity.

Yield curve: a graph depicting the relationship between interest rates and length of time to maturity.

Yield to maturity: the interest rate at which the present value of the future cash flows equals the current market price.

Z-score: a mathematically derived critical value below which firms are associated with failure.

Zero coupon bond: a bond that does not pay interest but is issued at a discount and redeemed at par (full) value.

References

3i *Making an Acquisition.*

3i (1993), *Dividend Policy*, April.

Adams, R.B., A.N. Licht and L. Sagiv (2011) 'Shareholders and stakeholders; how do directors decide?', *Strategic Management Journal*, Vol. 32, No. 12, pp. 1331–1355.

Aggarwal, R., S. Bhagal and S. Rangan (2009) 'The impact of fundamentals on IPO valuation', *Financial Management*, 38, pp. 253–284.

Ainley, M., A. Mashayekhi, R. Hicks, R. Rahman and A. Ravalia (2007) *Islamic Finance in the United Kingdom: Regulation and Challenges* (London: Financial Services Authority).

Airmic/Alarm/IRM (2010) *A structured approach to Enterprise Risk Management and the requirements of ISO 31000.*

Alkaraan, F. and D. Northcott (2006) 'Strategic capital investment decision-making: A role for emergent analysis tools? A study of practice in large UK manufacturing companies', *British Accounting Review*, Vol. 38, No. 12, [June], pp. 149–173.

Almazan, A., A. De Motta, S. Titman and V. Uysal (2010) 'Financial structure, acquisition opportunities, and firm locations', *Journal of Finance*, 65, pp. 529–563.

Altman, E.I. (1968) 'Financial ratios, discriminant analysis and the prediction of corporate bankruptcy', *Journal of Finance*, Vol. 23, No. 4, [September], pp. 589–609.

Andersen, J.A. (1987) *Currency and Interest Rate Hedging* (Prentice Hall).

Andrade, G. and S.N. Kaplan (1998) 'How costly is financial (not economic) distress? Evidence from highly-leveraged transactions that became distressed', *Journal of Finance*, Vol. 53, [October], pp. 1443–1493.

Andreadakis, S. (2012) 'Enlightened shareholder value: is it the new modus operandi for modern companies?' S. Boubaker, B.D. Nguyen, and D.K. Nguyen (eds) *Corporate Governance: Recent Developments and Trends*, pp. 415–432 (Springer).

Andrews, G.S. and C. Firer (1987) 'Why different divisions require different hurdle rates', *Long Range Planning*, Vol. 20, No. 5, [October], pp. 62–68.

Ang, A. and J. Chen (2007) 'CAPM over the long-run: 1926–2001', *Journal of Empirical Finance*, 14, pp. 1–40.

Ang, J., T. Arnold, C.M. Conover and C. Lancaster (2010) 'Maintaining a flexible payout policy in a mature industry: The Case of Crown Cork and Seal in the Connelly Era', *Journal of Applied Corporate Finance*, 22, pp. 30–44.

Ang, J. and P.P. Peterson (1984) 'The leasing puzzle', *Journal of Finance*, Vol. 39, No. 4, pp. 1055–1065.

Angwin, D. (2000) *Managing Successful Post-Acquisition Integration* (FT/Prentice Hall).

Angwin, D. (2004) 'Speed in M&A integration: The first 100 days', *European Management Journal*, Vol. 22, No. 4, pp. 418–430.

Antill, N. and K. Lee (2005) *Company Valuation under IFRSs* (Harrison House Publishing).

Aretz, K. and S.M. Bartram (2010) 'Corporate hedging and shareholder value', *The Journal of Financial Research*, 33, pp. 317–371.

Arnold, G. and P. Hatzopoulos (2000) 'The theory–practice gap in capital budgeting: evidence from the United Kingdom', *Journal of Business Finance & Accounting*, Vol. 27, Issue 5/6, [June], pp. 603–626.

Arzac, E. (2010) *Valuation for Mergers, Buyouts and Restructuring* (Wiley).

Ashkenas, R., L.J. De Monaco and S.C. Francis (1998) 'Making the deal real: How GE Capital integrates acquisitions', *Harvard Business Review*, Vol. 76, No. 1, [January–February], pp. 165–178.

Ashton, D. and D. Acker (2003) 'Establishing bounds on the tax advantage of debt', *British Accounting Review* Vol. 35, No. 4, [December], pp. 385–399.

Asquith, P. and D. Mullins (1986) 'Signalling with dividends, stock purchases and equity issues', *Financial Management*, Vol. 15, Issue 3, [Autumn], pp. 27–44.

Bailey, E. and Groves, H. (2014) *Corporate Insolvency: Law and Practice* (Butterworths).

Baker, H.K. and J.R. Nofsinger (2010) *Behavioural Finance: Investors, Corporations and Markets* (Wiley).

Baker, H.K., S. Dutta and S. Samir (2011) 'Management views on real options in capital budgeting', *Journal of Applied Finance*, Spring–Summer, 2011, Vol. 21, No. 1, pp. 18–29.

Ball, J. (1991) 'Short termism – myth or reality', *National Westminster Bank Quarterly Review*, August.

Ball, R. (2009) 'The global financial crisis and the efficient markets hypothesis: What have we learned?' *Journal of Applied Corporate Finance*, Vol. 21, No. 4, pp. 8–16.

Ball, R. and P. Brown (1968) 'An empirical evaluation of accounting income numbers', *Journal of Accounting Research*, Vol. 6, No. 2, [Autumn], pp. 159–178.

Bank for International Settlements (2007) 'Triennial Central Bank Survey of Foreign Exchange and Derivatives Market Activity in April 2007' (www.bis.org).

Bank of England (1988) 'Share repurchase by quoted companies', *Quarterly Bulletin,* Vol. 28, No. 3, [August], pp. 382–390.

Bank of England (2009) 'Financial Stability Report', June, Issue 25.

Bank of England (2011) 'Statistics on Capital Issuance', March 2011.

Barber, B. and T. Odean (2000) 'Trading is hazardous to your wealth: The common stock investment performance of individual investors', *Journal of Finance,* Vol. 55, No. 2, pp. 773–806.

Barber, B.M. and T. Odean (2001) 'Boys will be boys: Gender, overconfidence, and common stock investment', *The Quarterly Journal of Economics,* Vol. 116, pp. 261–292.

Barclay, M. and C. Smith, (2006) 'The capital structure puzzle: Another look at the evidence', in J. Rutterford, M. Upton and D. Kodwani (eds) *Financial Strategy,* 2nd edn (Wiley).

Barclay, M.J., C.W. Smith and R.L. Watts (1995) 'The determinants of corporate leverage and dividend policies', *Journal of Applied Corporate Finance,* Vol. 7, No. 4, [Winter], pp. 4–19.

Bartram, S., G. Brown and F. Fehle (2006) 'International evidence of financial derivative usage', *Social Science Research Network,* October.

Bartram, S.M., G. Brown and F.R. Fehle (2009) 'International evidence on financial derivatives usage', *Financial Management,* Vol. 38, pp. 185–206.

Barwise, P., P. Marsh, and R. Wensley (1989) 'Must finance and strategy clash?' *Harvard Business Review,* Vol. 67, No. 5, [September–October], pp. 85–90.

Baumol, W. (1952) 'The transactions demand for cash: An inventory theoretic approach', *Quarterly Journal of Economics,* Vol. 66, No. 4, [November], pp. 545–556.

Beck, T. and A. Demirguc-Kunt (2006) 'Small- and medium-size enterprises: Access to finance as a growth constraint', *Journal of Banking and Finance,* Vol. 30, pp. 2931–2943.

Beck, T., A. Demirguc-Kunt and V. Maksimovic (2008) 'Financing patterns around the world: Are small firms different?' *Journal of Financal Economics,* Vol. 89, pp. 467–487.

Becker, B., Z. Ivkovic and S. Weisbeener (2011) 'Local dividend clienteles', *Journal of Finance,* Vol. 66, pp. 655–683.

Beenstock, M. and K. Chan (1986) 'Testing the arbitrage pricing theory in the UK', *Oxford Bulletin of Economics and Statistics,* Vol. 48, No. 2, [May], pp. 121–141.

Bekaert, G., R.J. Hodrick and X. Zhang (2009) 'International stock return co-movements', *Journal of Finance,* Vol. 63, pp. 2591–2626.

Benartzi, S., R. Michaely and R. Thaler (1997) 'Do changes in dividends signal changes in the future or the past?', *Journal of Finance,* Vol. 52, No. 3, [July], pp. 1007–1034.

Benito, A. and G. Young (2001) *Hard Times or Great Expectations: Dividend Omissions and Dividend Cuts by UK Firms,* Bank of England Working Paper 147.

Bennet, N. (2001) 'One day we will go out of business', *Sunday Telegraph,* 9 December.

Berk, J. and P. Demarzo (2013) *Corporate Finance* (Pearson).

Bhattacharya, S. (1979) 'Imperfect information, dividend policy and the bird-in-the-hand fallacy', *Bell Journal of Economics and Management Science,* Vol. 10, No. 1, [Spring], pp. 259–270.

Bierman Jr, H. and J.E. Hass (1973) 'Capital budgeting under uncertainty: A reformulation', *Journal of Finance,* Vol. 28, No. 1, [March], pp. 1119–1129.

BIS (2013) *Triennial Central Bank Survey.* (BIS).

Black, F. (1976) 'The dividend puzzle', *Journal of Portfolio Management,* Vol. 2, No. 2, [Winter], pp. 5–8.

Black, F. (1993a) 'Estimating expected return', *Financial Analysts Journal,* Vol. 43, No. 2, pp. 507–528.

Black, F. (1993b) 'Return and Beta', *Journal of Portfolio Management,* Vol. 20, No. 1, pp. 8–18.

Black, F., M.C. Jensen and M. Scholes (1972) 'The capital asset pricing model: Some empirical tests', in M. Jensen (ed.) *Studies in the Theory of Capital Markets* (Praeger).

Black, F. and M. Scholes (1973) 'The pricing of options and corporate liabilities', *Journal of Political Economy,* Vol. 81, No. 3, [May–June], pp. 637–654.

Block, S. and G. Hirt (1994) *Foundations of Financial Management* (Irwin).

Boakes, K. (2010) *Reading and Understanding the Financial Times* (FT Prentice Hall).

Bodie, Z. and R. Merton (2000) *Finance* (Prentice-Hall).

Bowman, R.G. (1980) 'The debt equivalence of leases: An empirical investigation', *Accounting Review,* Vol. 55, No. 2, pp. 237–253.

Bradley, M., G. Jarrell and E. Kim (1984) 'The existence of an optimal capital structure: Theory and evidence', *Journal of Finance,* Vol. 39, No. 3, pp. 857–878.

Bragg, S.M. (2010) *Treasury Management: The Practitioner's Guide* (Wiley).

Branson, R. (1998) *Losing my Virginity* (Virgin Publishing).

Brav, O. (2009) 'Access to capital, capital structure, and the funding of the firm', *Journal of Finance,* Vol. 64, pp. 263–308.

Brealey, R.A., S.C. Myers and F. Allen (2013) *Principles of Corporate Finance* (McGraw-Hill).

Brennan, M. (1971) 'A note on dividend irrelevance and the gordon valuation model', *Journal of Finance,* Vol. 26, No. 5, [December], pp. 1115–1121.

Brennan, M. and L. Trigeorgis (eds) (2000) *Project Flexibility, Agency and Competition: New Developments in the Theory and Application of Real Options* (Oxford University Press).

Brett, M. (2003) *How to Read the Financial Papers*, 4th edn (Random House).

Brickley, J., C. Smith and J. Zimmerman (1994) 'Ethics, incentives, and organisational design', *Journal of Applied Corporate Finance*, Vol. 7, No. 2, [Summer], pp. 20–30.

Brickley, J., C. Smith and L. Zimmerman (2003) 'Corporate governance, ethics and organisational architecture', *Journal of Applied Corporate Finance*, Vol. 15, [Spring], pp. 34–45.

Brigham, E.F. and L.C. Gapenski (1996) *Financial Management Theory and Practice* (Dryden).

Bromwich, M. and A. Bhimani (1991) 'Strategic investment appraisal', *Management Accounting*, Vol. 69, [March], pp. 45–48.

Brooks, R. and L. Catao (2000) 'The new economy and global stock returns', *IMF Working Paper 216*, December.

Brounen, D., A. de Jong, and K. Koedijk (2004), 'Corporate finance in Europe: Confronting theory with practice', *Financial Management*, Vol. 33, No. 4, [Winter], pp. 71–101.

Brown, P. (2006) *An Introduction to the Bond Markets* (Wiley).

Bruner, R. and J. Perella (2004) *Applied Mergers and Acquisitions* (Wiley).

Buckley, A. (2004) *Multinational Finance*, (Financial Times/Prentice Hall).

Buckley, A. (2012) *International Finance: A Practical Perspective* (FT/Prentice Hall).

Buckley, P.J. and M. Casson (1981) 'The optimal timing of a foreign direct investment', *Economic Journal*, Vol. 92, No. 361, [March], pp. 75–87.

Butler, R., L. Davies, R. Pike and J. Sharp (1993) *Strategic Investment Decisions* (Routledge).

BVCA (2008) *The Economic Impact of Private Equity in the UK 2007* (The British Private Equity and Venture Capital Association).

Byoun, S. (2008) 'How and when do firms adjust their capital structures toward targets?' *Journal of Finance*, Vol. 63, pp. 3069–3096.

BZW (2008) *Equity–Gilt Study*, London.

Campbell, J. and T. Vuolteenako (2004) 'Bad Beta, good-Beta', *American Economic Review*, Vol. 94, No. 5, [December], pp. 1249–1275.

Campbell, R., K. Koedjik and P. Kofman (2002) 'Increased correlation in bear markets', *Financial Analysts Journal*, Vol. 58, No. 1, (Jan/Feb), pp. 87–94.

Cavaglia, S., C. Brightman and M. Aked (2002) 'The increasing importance of industry factors', *Financial Analysts Journal*, Vol. 56, No. 5, [Sept/Oct], pp. 41–54.

Chang, K. and C. Osler (1999) 'Methodical madness: Technical analysis and the irrationality of exchange rate forecasts', *Economic Journal,* Vol. 109, Issue 458, [October], pp. 636–661.

Chen, L. and L. Zhang, (2010) 'A better three-factor model that explains more anomalies,' *Journal of Finance*, Vol. 65, pp. 563–594.

Chesley, G.R. (1975) 'Elicitation of subjective probabilities: A review', *Accounting Review,* Vol. 50, No. 2, [April], pp. 325–337.

Chiou W.P. (2008) 'Who benefits from international portfolio diversification?', *Journal of International Financial Markets, Institutions and Money*, Vol. 18, No. 5, pp. 466–482.

Chisholm, A. (2010) *Derivatives Demystified* (Wiley).

Choudhry, T. and R. Jayasekera (2013) 'Level of efficiency in the UK equity market: Empirical study of the effects of the global financial crisis', *Review of Quantitative Finance and Accounting*, September.

Clare, A.D. and S.H. Thomas (1994) 'Macroeconomic factors, the arbitrage pricing theory and the UK stock-market', *Journal of Business Finance and Accounting*, Vol. 21, No. 3, [April], pp. 309–330.

Clark, T.M. (1978) *Leasing* (McGraw-Hill).

Collier, P., T. Cooke and J. Glynn (1988) *Financial and Treasury Management* (Heinemann).

Collier, P. and E.W. Davies (1985) 'The management of currency transaction risk by UK multinational companies', *Accounting and Business Research*, Vol. 15, No. 6, [Autumn], pp. 327–334.

Cooke, T.E. (1986) *Mergers and Acquisitions* (Blackwell).

Cooper, D.J. (1975) 'Rationality and investment appraisal', *Accounting and Business Research*, Vol. 5, No. 19, [Summer], pp. 198–202.

Copeland, T., T. Koller and J. Murrin (2000) *Valuation* (Wiley).

Copeland, T.E., J.F. Weston and K. Shastri (2013) *Financial Theory and Corporate Policy,* (Pearson).

Cox, J., S. Ross and M. Rubinstein (1979) 'Option pricing: A simplified approach', *Journal of Financial Economics*, Vol. 7, No. 3, [September], pp. 229–263.

Czinkota, M., T. Ronkainen and M. Moffet (1994) 'International business', in J. Dunning and S. Lundan *Multinational Enterprises and the Global Economy* (Edward Elgar).

Damodaran, A. (2009) *The Dark Side of Valuation* (Prentice Hall).

Damodaran, A. (2012) *Investment Valuation* (Wiley).

Daniel, E., J. Ward and A. Franken (2011) 'Project portfolio management in turbulent times', Vol. 7, No. 2. CIMA Executive Research Summary Series.

Daniels, J.D., L.H. Radebaugh and D.P. Sullivan (2011) *International Business: Environments and Operations*, 10th edn (Addison-Wesley).

Day, R., D. Allen, I. Hirst and J. Kwiatkowski (1987) 'Equity, gilts, treasury bills and inflation', *The Investment Analyst*, No. 83, [January], pp. 11–18.

DeAngelo, H. and R. Masulis (1980) 'Optimal capital structure under corporate and personal taxation', *Journal of Financial Economics*, Vol. 8, No. 1, pp. 3–30.

Dean, J. (1951) *Capital Budgeting* (New York, Columbia University Press).

DeBondt, W. F. M. and R. Thaler (1985) 'Does the stock-market overreact?', *Journal of Finance*, Vol. 40, No. 3, pp. 793–805.

DeLong, J.B. and K. Magin (2009) 'The US equity return premium: past, present and future', *Journal of Economic Perspectives*, Vol. 23, pp. 193–208.

De Pamphilis, D. (2013) *Mergers, Acquisitions and Other Restructuring Activities* (Academic Press).

Department of Trade and Industry (1988) *Mergers Policy* (HMSO).

Devine, M. (2002) *Successful Mergers: Getting the People Issues Right* (The Economist/Profile Books).

Dimson, E. (1993) 'Appraisal techniques', Proceedings of the Capital Projects Conference, May, Institute of Actuaries and Faculty of Actuaries.

Dimson, E. and R.A. Brealey (1978) 'The risk premium on UK equities', *The Investment Analyst*, No. 52, [December], pp. 14–18.

Dimson, E. and P. Marsh (1982) 'Calculating the cost of capital', *Long Range Planning*, Vol. 15, No. 2, [April], pp. 112–120.

Dimson, E. and P. Marsh (1986) 'Event study methodologies and the size effect: The case of UK press recommendations', *Journal of Financial Economics*, September.

Dimson, E., P. Marsh and M. Staunton (2002) *Triumph of the Optimists* (Princeton University Press).

Dimson, E., P. Marsh and M. Staunton (2008) 'The world-wide equity premium: A smaller puzzle', in R. Mehra, *Handbook of the Equity Premium* (Elsevier).

Dion, C., D. Allay, D. Derain and G. Lahiri (2007) *Dangerous Liaisons: The Integration Game* (The Hay Group).

Dissanaike, G. (1997) 'Do stock market investors overreact?' *Journal of Business Finance and Accounting*, Vol. 24, No. 1, pp. 27–49.

Dixit, A. and R. Pindyck (1995) 'The options approach to capital investment', *Harvard Business Review*, Vol. 73, No. 3, [May–June], pp. 105–115.

Dobbs, R. and W. Rehm (2006) 'The value of share buybacks', in J. Rutterford, M. Upton and D. Kodwani (eds) *Financial Strategy* (Wiley).

Doidge, C., G.A. Karoyli and R. Stulz (2010) 'Why do foreign firms leave U.S. equity markets?', *Journal of Finance*, Vol. 65, pp. 1507–1553.

Doyle, P. (1994) 'Setting business objectives and measuring performance', *Journal of General Management*, Vol. 20, No. 2, [Winter], pp. 1–19.

Driessen, J. and L. Laeven (2007) 'International portfolio diversification benefits: Cross-country evidence from a local perspective', *Journal of Banking and Finance*, Vol. 31, No. 6, pp. 1693–1712.

Drucker, P.F. (1981) 'Five rules for successful acquisition', *Wall Street Journal*, 15 October.

Duchin, R. and D. Sosyura (2013) 'Divisional managers and internal capital markets', *Journal of Finance*, Vol. 68, No. 2, pp. 387–429

Duckett, G. (2010) *Practical Enterprise Risk Management: A Business Process Approach* (Wiley).

Dunning, J.H. and S.M. Lundan (2008) *Multinational Enterprises and the Global Economy* (Edward Elgar).

Economist (2000) 'Making Mergers Work' (The Economist Newspaper Ltd, London).

Eiteman, D.K., A.I. Stonehill and M.H. Moffet (2012) *Multinational Business Finance*, 10th edn (Addison-Wesley).

Elton, E.J. (1970) 'Capital rationing and external discount rates', *Journal of Finance*, Vol. 25, No. 3, [June], pp. 573–584.

Elton, E.J. and M. Gruber (1970) 'Marginal stockholder tax rates and the clientele effect', *Review of Economics and Statistics*, Vol. 52, No. 1, [February], pp. 68–74.

Elton, E.J., M.J. Gruber, S.J. Brown and W.N. Goetzman (2010) *Modern Portfolio Theory and Investment Analysis* (Wiley).

Emery, D. and J. Finnerty (1997) *Corporate Financial Management* (Prentice Hall).

Emmanuel, C.R., E.P. Harris and S. Komakech (2008) 'Managerial judgement and strategic investment decision', Vol. 4, No. 1, CIMA research executive summaries services.

Evans, C. (2005) 'Private lessons', *Accountancy*, Vol. 135, No. 1337, [January], pp. 46–47.

Fama, E. (1980) 'Agency problems and the theory of the firm', *Journal of Political Economy*, Vol. 88, No. 2. [April], pp. 288–307.

Fama, E. (1998) 'Market efficiency, long-term returns, and behavioural finance', *Journal of Financial Economics*, Vol. 49, No. 3, [September], pp. 283–306.

Fama, E. and K. French (1993) 'Common risk factors in the returns on stocks and bonds', *Journal of Financial Economics*, Vol. 33, No. 1, pp. 3–56.

Fama, E. and K. French (1995) 'Size and book-to-market factors in earnings and returns', *Journal of Finance*, Vol. 50, No. 1, [March], pp. 131–155.

Fama, E. and K. French (1996) 'Multifactor explanations of asset pricing anomalies', *Journal of Finance*, Vol. 51, No. 1, [March], pp. 55–84.

Fama, E. and K. French (2001) 'Disappearing dividends: Changing firm characteristics or lower propensity to pay?' *Journal of Financial Economics*, Vol. 60, No. 1, [April], pp. 3–43.

Fama, E. and K. French (2002) 'The equity premium', *Journal of Finance*, Vol. 57, No. 2, pp. 637–659.

Fama, E. and K. French (2004) 'The CAPM – theory and evidence', *Journal of Economic Perspectives*, Vol. 18, No. 3, [Summer], pp. 25–46.

Fama, E.F. (1970) 'Efficient capital markets: A review of theory and empirical work', *Journal of Finance*, Vol. 25, No. 2, [May], pp. 383–417.

Fama, E.F. (1991) 'Efficient capital markets', *Journal of Finance*, Vol. 46, No. 5, [December], pp. 1575–1617.

Fama, E.F. and K.R. French (1992) 'The cross-section of expected stock returns', *Journal of Finance*, Vol. 47, No. 2, [June], pp. 427–465.

Fama, E.F. and K.R. French (2006) 'The value premium and the CAPM', *The Journal of Finance*, Vol. 61, pp. 2163–2185.

Fama, E.F. and J. McBeth (1973) 'Risk, return and equilibrium: Empirical tests', *Journal of Political Economy*, Vol. 81, No. 3, [May/June], pp. 607–636.

Fama, E.F. and M.H. Miller (1972) *The Theory of Finance* (Holt, Rinehart and Winston).

Feldman, S. (2005) *Principles of Private Firm Valuation* (Wiley).

Fenton-O'Creevy, M., N. Nicholson, E. Soane and P. Willman (2003) 'Trading on illusions: Unrealistic perceptions of control and trading performance', *Journal of Occcuptational and Organizational Psychology*, Vol. 76, No. 1, pp. 53–68.

Ferguson, A. (1989) 'Hostage to the short term', *Management Today*, March.

Fernandez, P. (2007) 'Valuing companies by cash flow discounting: Ten methods and nine theories', *Managerial Finance*, Vol. 33, pp. 853–876.

Finnie, J. (1988) 'The role of financial appraisal in decisions to acquire advanced manufacturing technology', *Accounting and Business Research*, Vol. 18, No. 70, [Spring], pp. 133–139.

Firth, M. and S. Keane (1986) *Issues in Finance* (Philip Allan).

Fisher, I. (1930) *The Theory of Interest,* reprinted in 1977 by Porcupine Press.

Flavin, T. J. and E. Panapoulou (2009) 'On the robustness of international portfolio diversification switching benefits to regime-switching volatility', *Journal of International Financial Markets, Institutions and Money*, Vol. 19, No. 1, pp. 140–156.

Foley, B.J. (1991) *Capital Markets* (Macmillan).

Forbes, W. (2009) *Behavioural Finance* (Wiley).

Fosback, N. (1985) *Stock Market Logic* (The Institute for Economic Research, Fort Lauderdale).

Franks, J. and J. Broyles (1979) *Modern Managerial Finance* (Wiley).

Franks, J. and C. Mayer (1996a) 'Do hostile take-overs improve performance?', *Business Strategy Review,* Vol. 7, No. 4, pp. 1–6.

Franks, J. and C. Mayer (1996b) 'Hostile take-overs and the correction of managerial failure', *Journal of Financial Economics,* Vol. 40, No. 1, pp. 163–181.

Franks, J.R. and R.S. Harris (1989) 'Shareholder wealth effects of corporate takeovers: The UK experience 1955–85', *Journal of Financial Economics,* Vol. 23, No. 2, pp. 225–249.

Friedman, M. (1953) 'The methodology of positive economics', in *Essays in Positive Economics* (University of Chicago Press).

Frykman, D. and J. Tolleryd (2003) *Corporate Valuation: An Easy Guide to Measuring Value* (Pearson Education).

Fuller, R.J. and H. S. Kerr (1981) 'Estimating the divisional cost of capital: An analysis of the Pure-Play Technique', *Journal of Finance*, Vol. 36, No. 5, pp. 997–1009.

Galati, G., A. Heath and P. McGuire (2007) 'Evidence of carry trade activity', *Bank of International Settlements Quarterly Review*, [September], pp. 27–42.

Galpin, T. J. and M. Herndon (2014) *The Complete Guide to Merger and Acquisitions*, (Wiley).

Gaughan, P. (2007) *Mergers, Acquisitions and Corporate Restructurings* (Wiley).

Graham J. and C. Harvey (2002) 'How do CFO's make capital budgeting and capital structive dicussion?' *Journal of Applied corporate Finance*, Vol 15 (1), pp. 8–23.

Girerd-Potin, I., S. Jimenez-Garess and P. Louvet (2014) 'Which dimensions of social responsibility concern financial investors?', *Journal of Business Ethics*, Vol. 121, No. 4, pp. 559–576.

Gentry, J. (1988) 'State of the art of short-run financial management', *Financial Management*, Vol. 17, No. 2, [Summer], pp. 41–57.

Ghosh, C. and J. Woolridge (1989) 'Stock market reaction to growth – induced dividend cuts: Are investors myopic?', *Managerial & Decision Economics,* Vol. 10, No.1, [March], pp. 25–35.

Giddy, I.H. (1994) *Global Financial Markets* (D.C. Heath).

Gilovich, T., R. Vallone and A. Tversky (1985) 'The hot hand in basketball: On the misperception of random sequences', *Cognitive Psychology,* 17, pp. 295–314.

Gluck, F.W. (1988) 'The real takeover defense', *The McKinsey Quarterly,* Issue 1, [Winter], pp. 2–16.

Goergen, M. and L. Renneboog (2011) 'Manageral compensation'. *Journal of Corporate Finance*, 17(4), pp.1068–1077.

Gordon, M. (1959) 'Dividends, earnings and stock prices', *Review of Economics and Statistics,*Vol. 41 [May], pp. 99–105.

Gordon, M. (1963) 'Optimal investment and financing policy', *Journal of Finance,* Vol. 18, No. 2, pp. 264–272.

Graham, B., D. Dodd and S. Cottle (1962) *Security Analysis: Principles and Techniques,* 4th edn (McGraw-Hill).

Graham, J. and C. Harvey (2002) 'How do CFOs make capital budgeting and capital structure decisions?', *Journal of Applied Corporate Finance,* Vol. 15, No. 1, [Spring], pp. 8–23.

Grant, R. and L. Soenen (2004) 'Strategic management of operating exposure', *European Management Journal,* Vol. 22, No. 1, [February], pp. 353–362.

Grant, R.M. (2003) 'Strategic planning in a turbulent environment: Evidence from the oil majors', *Strategic Management Journal,* Vol. 24, No. 6, pp. 491–517.

Grant, R.M. (2008) *Contemporary Strategic Analysis* (Basil Blackwell).

Graves, S.B. (1988) 'Institutional ownership and corporate R&D in the computer industry', *Academy of Management Journal,* Vol. 31, No. 2, [June], pp. 417–428.

Greene, W.H., A.S. Hornstein and L.J. White (2009) 'Multinationals do it better: evidence on the efficiency of corporations' capital budgeting', *Journal of Empirical Finance,* Vol. 16, No. 5, pp. 703–720.

Gregoriu, G. and K. Neuhauser (2007) *Mergers and Acquisitions* (Palgrave).

Gregory, A. (1997) 'An examination of the long-run performance of UK acquiring firms', *Journal of Business Finance and Accounting,* Vol. 24, No. 7–8, [September], pp. 971–1002.

Gregory, A. and S. McCorriston (2004) 'Foreign acquisitions by UK limited companies: Short and long-run performance', University of Exeter Centre for Finance and Investment Working Paper 04/01.

Grice, J.S. and R.W. Ingram (2001) 'Tests of the generalisability of Altman's bankruptcy prediction model',

Journal of Business Research, Vol. 54, No. 1, [October], pp. 53–61.

Grinyer, J.R. (1986) 'An alternative to maximisation of shareholders' wealth in capital budgeting decisions', *Accounting and Business Research,* Vol. 16, No. 64, [Autumn], pp. 319–326.

Grubb, M. (1993/4) 'A second generation of low inflation', *Professional Investor,* [December/January], pp. 53–57.

Gup, B.E. and S.W. Norwood (1982) 'Divisional cost of capital: A practical approach', *Financial Management,* Vol. 11, No. 1, [Spring], pp. 20–24.

Guthrie G. (2009) *Real Options in Theory and Practice* (OUP).

Habeck, M., F. Kroger and M.R. Traem (2000) *After the Merger* (Pearson Education).

Hamada, R.S. (1969) 'Portfolio analysis: Market equilibrium and corporate finance', *Journal of Finance,* Vol. 24, No. 1, [March], pp. 13–31.

Harar, S. (1998) 'Islamic banking: An overview', in J. Rutterford (ed.) *Financial Strategy: Adding Stakeholder Value* (Open Business School/Wiley).

Harrington, D. (1987) *Modern Portfolio Theory, The Capital Asset Pricing Model and Arbitrage Pricing Theory: A User's Guide* (Prentice Hall).

Harrington, D.R. (1983) 'Stock prices, Beta and strategic planning', *Harvard Business Review,* Vol. 6, No. 3, [May–June], pp. 157–164.

Harris, M. and A. Raviv (1990) 'Capital structure and the informational role of debt', *Journal of Finance,* Vol. 45, No. 2, pp. 321–350.

Harris, M. and A. Raviv (1991) 'The theory of capital structure', *Journal of Finance,* Vol. 46, No. 1, pp. 297–356.

Harrison, J.S. (1987) 'Alternatives to merger – joint ventures and other strategies', *Long Range Planning,* Vol. 20, No. 6, [December], pp. 78–83.

Haspeslagh, P. and D. Jemison (1991) *Managing Acquisitions: Creating Value Through Corporate Renewal* (The Free Press).

Hassan, M.K. and M.K. Lewis (eds) (2005) *Handbook of Islamic Financing* (Edward Elgar).

Hawkins, S.A. and R. Hastie (1990) 'Hindsight: Biased judgments of past events after the outcomes are known', *Cognitive Psychology,* Vol. 107, No. 3, pp. 311–327.

Healy, P. and G. Palepu (1988) 'Earnings information conveyed by dividend initiations and omissions', *Journal of Financial Economics*, Vol. 21, No. 2, [September], pp. 149–175.

Heaton, J. (2002) 'Managerial optimism and corporate finance', *Financial Management,* Vol. 31, pp. 33–45.

Hertz, D.B. (1964) 'Risk analysis in capital investment', *Harvard Business Review,* Vol. 42, No. 1, [January–February], pp. 95–106.

Hexter, O. (2007) 'Positive feeling', *Euromoney,* [September], pp. 200–206.

Hirshleifer, D. (2001) 'Investor psychology and asset pricing', *The Journal of Finance,* Vol. 56, No. 4, pp. 1533–1597.

Hirshleifer, J. (1958) 'On the theory of optimal investment decision', *Journal of Political Economy,* Vol. 66. No. 4, [August], pp. 329–352.

Hochberg, Y.V., A. Ljunqvist and Y. Lu (2010) 'Networking as a barrier to entry and the competitive supply of venture capital', *Journal of Finance,* Vol. 65, pp. 829–859.

Hodgkinson, L. (1989) *Taxation and Corporate Investment* (CIMA).

Hopkin, P. (2012) *Fundamentals of Risk Management* (Kogan Page).

Horngren, C.T., A. Bhimani, G. Foster and S.M. Datar (1998) *Management and Cost Accounting* (Prentice Hall Europe).

Howells, P. and K. Bain (2007) *Financial Markets and Institutions* (FT Prentice Hall).

Hull, J.C. (2014) *Options Future and Other Derivatives* (Prentice Hall).

Hunt, J., J. Grumber, S. Lees and P. Vivien (1987) *Acquisition – the Human Factors* (London Business School and Egon Zehnder Associates).

ICAEW (1989) *Accounting for Brands,* P. Barwise, C. Higson, A. Likierman and P. Marsh (Institute of Chartered Accountants in England and Wales, London Business School).

Iqbal, Z. (1999) 'Financial engineering in Islamic finance', *Thunderbird International Business Review,* Vol. 41, No. 4/5, [July–October], pp. 541–560.

Irwin, D. and J.M. Scott (2010) 'Barriers faced by SMEs in raising bank finance', *International Journal of Entrepreneurial Behaviour & Research*, Vol. 16, pp. 245–259.

Jarvis, R., J. Collis and P. Bainbridge (2000) 'The finance leasing market in the 1990s: A chronological review', Association of Certified and Corporate Accountants Occasional Paper No. 28.

Jenkinson, T. and H. Jones (2009) 'IPO pricing and allocation: a survey of the views of institutional investors', *The Review of Financial Studies,* Vol. 22, pp. 1477–1504.

Jensen, M. C. (1978). 'Some anomalous evidence regarding market efficiency', *Journal of Financial Economics,* Vol. 6, Nos. 2/3, pp. 95–101.

Jensen, M.C. (1984) 'Takeovers: Folklore and science', *Harvard Business Review,* Vol. 62, No. 6, [November–December], pp. 109–121.

Jensen, M.C. (2001) 'Value maximisation, stakeholder theory, and the corporate objective function', *Journal of Applied Corporate Finance,* Vol. 14, [Fall], p. 8.

Jensen, M.C. and W.H. Meckling (1976) 'Theory of the firm: Managerial behaviour, agency costs and ownership structure', *Journal of Financial Economics,* Vol. 3, No. 4, [October], pp. 305–360.

Jensen, M.C. and W.H. Meckling (1994) 'The nature of man', *Journal of Applied Corporate Finance,* Vol. 7, No. 2, [Summer], pp. 4–19.

Jensen, M.C. and R.S. Ruback (1983) 'The market for corporate control: The scientific evidence', *Journal of Financial Economics,* Vol. 11, No. 1/4, [April], pp. 5–50.

Johanson, J. and F. Wiedersheim-Paul (1975) 'The internationalisation of the firm – four Swedish cases', *Journal of Management Studies,* Vol. 12, No. 3, [October], pp. 305–323.

Jones, C.S. (1982) *Successful Management of Acquisitions* (Derek Beattie Publishing).

Jones, C.S. (1983) *The Control of Acquired Companies* (Chartered Institute of Cost and Management Accountants).

Jones, C.S. (1986) 'Integrating acquired companies', *Management Accounting,* April.

JPMorgan/Cazenove Ltd (2008) European Listed Private Equity Bulletin.

Junankar, S. (1994) 'Realistic returns: How do manufacturers assess new investment?', Confederation of British Industry, July.

Jupe, R.E. and B.A. Rutherford (1997) 'The disclosure of "free cash flow" in published financial statements: A research note', *British Accounting Review,* Vol. 29, No. 3, [September], pp. 231–243.

Kahneman, D. (2012) *Thinking Fast and Slow* (Penguin).

Kahneman, D. and A. Tversky (1979) 'Prospect theory: an analysis of decisions under risk', *Econometrica,* Vol. 47, [March], pp. 263–291.

Kahneman, D. and A. Tversky (1982) *Judgement Under Uncertainty: Heuristics and Biases* (Cambridge University Press).

Kanodia, C., R. Bushman and J. Dickart (1989) 'Escalation errors and the sunk cost effect: An explanation based on reputation and information asymmetries', *Journal of Accounting Research,* Vol. 27, No. 1, [Spring], pp. 59–77.

Kaplan, R.S. (1986) 'Must CIM be justified by faith alone?', *Harvard Business Review,* Vol. 64, No. 2, [March–April], pp. 87–97.

Kaplan, S.N. and J. Lerner (2010) 'It ain't broke: The past, present, and future of Venture Capital', *Journal of Applied Corporate Finance,* Vol. 22, pp. 36–47.

Kaplanis, E. (1997) 'Benefits and costs of international portfolio investments' in *Financial Times Mastering Finance* (FT/Pitman Publishing, London).

Keane, S. (1974) 'Dividends and the resolution of uncertainty', *Journal of Business Finance and Accountancy*, Vol. 1, No. 3, [September], pp. 389–393.

Keane, S.M. (1983) *Stock Market Efficiency: Theory, Evidence, Implications* (Philip Allan).

Kerr, H.S. and R.J. Fuller (1981) 'Estimating the divisional cost of capital: An analysis of the pure-play technique', *Journal of Finance*, Vol. 36, No. 5, [December], pp. 997–1009.

Kester, W.C. (1984) 'Today's options for tomorrow's growth', *Harvard Business Review*, Vol. 62, No. 2, [March–April], pp. 153–160.

Kindleberger, C.P. (1978) *International Economics* (Irwin).

King, M.R. (2009) 'The cost of equity for global banks: A CAPM perspective from 1990 to 2009', *BIS Quarterly Review*, September, pp. 59–73.

King, P. (1975) 'Is the emphasis of capital budgeting misplaced?', *Journal of Business Finance and Accounting*, Vol. 2, No. 1, [Spring], pp. 69–82.

Klemm, M., S. Sanderson and G. Luffman (1991) 'Mission statements: Selling corporate values to employees', *Long-Range Planning*, Vol. 24, No. 3, [June], pp. 73–78.

Klieman, R. (1999) 'Some new evidence on EVA companies', *Journal of Applied Corporate Finance*, Vol. 12, No. 2, [Summer], pp. 80–91.

Koh, P. (2006) 'Leasing gives loans a run for their money', *Euromoney*, October, pp. 90–92.

Koller, T., M. Goedhart and D. Wessels (2010) *Valuation: Measuring and Managing the Value of Companies* (Wiley).

Kotari, S.P., J. Shanken and R.G. Sloan (1995) 'Another look at the cross section of expected stock returns', *Journal of Finance*, Vol. 50, No. 1, pp. 185–224.

KPMG (1999) Global *M&A survey*. (KPMG Group, London).

KPMG (2007) *The Determinants of M&A Success; What Factors Contribute to Deal Success?* (KPMG Group, London).

KPMG (2010) *The Determinants of M&A Success: What Factors Contribute to Deal Success?* (KPMG Group, London).

Lam, J. (2014) *Enterprise Risk Management* (Wiley).

Lambert, R.A. and D.F. Larcker (1985) 'Executive compensation, corporate decision-making and shareholder wealth: A review of the evidence', *Midland Corporate Finance Journal*, Vol. 2, [Winter], pp. 6–22.

Larcker, D.F. (1983) 'Association between performance plan adoption and capital investment', *Journal of Accounting and Economics*, Vol. 5, No. 1, [April], pp. 3–30.

Lee, E., M. Walker and H. Christensen (2006) *The Cost of Capital in Europe*, Certified Accountants Educational Trust.

Lees, S. (1992) 'Auditing mergers and acquisitions – Caveat Emptor', *Managerial Auditing Journal*, Vol. 7, No. 4, pp. 6–11.

Lemon, M.L., M.R. Roberts and J.F. Zender (2008) 'Back to the beginning: Persistence and the cross-section of corporate capital structure', *Journal of Finance*, Vol. 63, pp. 1575–1608.

Lerner, J. (2008) *The Global Economic Impact of Private Equity Report 2008, Globalization of Alternative Investments*, Volume 1 (World Economic Forum).

Lessard, D. (1985) 'Evaluating foreign projects: An adjusted present value approach', in D. Lessard (ed.) *International Financial Management* (Wiley).

Lessard, D.R. and J.B. Lightstone (2006) 'Operating exposure', in J. Rutherford, M. Upton and D. Kodwani, *Financial Strategy* (John Wiley & Sons).

Levich, R.M. (1989) 'Is the foreign exchange market efficient?', *Oxford Review of Economic Policy*, Vol. 5, No. 3, pp. 40–60.

Levinson, M. (2002) *Guide to Financial Markets*, 3rd edn (London: Economist Books).

Levis, M. (1985) 'Are small firms big performers?', *The Investment Analyst*, No. 76, [April], pp. 21–27.

Levy, H. (2010) 'The CAPM is alive and well: A review and synthesis', *European Financial Management*, Vol. 16, pp. 43–71.

Levy, H. (2012) *The Capital Assets Pricing Model in the 21st Century: Analytical, Empirical, and Behavioral Perspectives* (Cambridge University Press).

Levy, H. and M. Sarnat (1994a) *Portfolio and Investment Selection: Theory and Practice* (Prentice Hall).

Levy, H. and M. Sarnat (1994b) *Capital Investment and Financial Decisions* (Prentice Hall).

Limmack, R.J. (1991) 'Corporate mergers and shareholder wealth effects: 1977–1986', *Accounting and Business Research*, Vol. 21, No. 83, [Summer], pp. 239–251.

Lintner, J. (1956) 'The distribution of incomes of corporations among dividends, retained earnings and taxes', *American Economic Review*, Vol. 46, [May], pp. 97–113.

Lim, S. (2006) 'Do investors integrate losses and segregate gains? Mental accounting and investor trading decisions', *The Journal of Business*, Vol. 79, No. 5, pp. 2539–2573.

Lim, K-P. and R. Brooks (2011) 'The evolution of stock market efficiency over time: a survey of the empirical literature', *Journal of Economic Surveys*, Vol. 25, No. 1, pp. 69–108.

Liu, Y., H. Szewczyk and Z. Zantout (2008) 'Underreaction to dividend reductions and omissions?', *Journal of Finance*, Vol. 63, pp. 987–1020.

Longin, F. and B. Solnik (2001) 'Extreme correlation of international equity markets', *Journal of Finance*, Vol. 56, No. 2, pp. 649–676.

Lorie, J.H. and L.J. Savage (1955) 'Three problems in capital rationing', *Journal of Business*, Vol. 28, No. 4, [October], pp. 229–239.

Luehrman, T.A. (1997a) 'What's it worth? A general manager's guide to valuation', *Harvard Business Review,* Vol. 75, No. 3, [May–June], pp. 132–142.

Luehrman, T.A. (1997b) 'Using APV: A better tool for valuing operations', *Harvard Business Review,* Vol. 75, No. 3, [May–June], pp. 145–154.

Madura, J. (2006) *International Financial Management* (West Publishing Co.).

Madura, J. and R. Fox (2011) *International Financial Management* (Thomson Publishers).

Madura, J. and A.M. Whyte (1990) 'Diversification benefits of direct foreign investment', *Management International Review,* Vol. 30, No. 1, pp. 73–85.

Maksimovic, V. and G. Philips (2008) 'The industry life cycle, acquisitions and investment: Does firm organization matter?', *Journal of Finance,* Vol. 63, pp. 673–708.

Manson, S., A. Stark and M. Thomas (1994) 'A cash flow analysis of the operational gains from takeovers', *ACCA Certified Research Report* 35.

Mao, J.C.T. and J.F. Helliwell (1969) 'Investment decisions under uncertainty: Theory and practice', *Journal of Finance,* Vol. 24, No. 2, [May], pp. 323–338.

Marais, D. (1982) 'Corporate financial strength', *Bank of England Quarterly Bulletin,* June.

Markowitz, H.M. (1952) 'Portfolio selection', *Journal of Finance,* Vol. 7, No. 1, [March], pp. 77–91.

Markowitz, H.M. (1991) 'Foundations of portfolio theory', *Journal of Finance,* Vol. 46, No. 2, [June], pp. 469–477.

Marosi, A. and N. Massoud (2008) 'You can enter but you cannot leave..: U.S. securities markets and foreign Firms', *Journal of Finance,* Vol. 63, pp. 2477–2506.

Marsh, P. (1982) 'The choice between debt and equity: An empirical study', *Journal of Finance,* Vol. 37, No. 1, [March], pp. 121–144.

Marsh, P. (1990) *Short-termism on Trial* (International Fund Managers Association).

Mason, C. (2006) 'Informal sources of venture finance', in S.C. Parker (ed.) *The Life Cycle of Entrepreneurial Ventures* (Springer), pp. 259–299.

Mason, C. and R. Harrison (2002) 'Is it worth it? The rates return from informal venture capital investments', *Journal of Business Venturing,* Vol. 17, No. 3, [May], pp. 211–236.

Mason, C. and R. Harrison (2004) 'Improving access to early stage venture capital in regional economies', *Local Economy,* Vol. 19, No. 2, pp. 159–173.

Mason, C. and R. Harrison (2010) 'Annual report on the business angel market in the United Kingdom: 2008/9', British Business Angels Association.

Mathur, I. and S. De (1989) 'A review of the theories of and evidence on returns related to mergers and takeovers', *Managerial Finance,* Vol. 15, No. 4, pp. 1–11.

McDaniel, W.R., D.E. McCarty and K.A. Jessell (1988) 'Discounted cash flow with explicit reinvestment rates: Tutorial and extension', *The Financial Review,* Vol. 23, No. 3, [August], pp. 369–385.

McDonald, R.L. (2013) *Derivatives Markets* (Pearson).

McGowan, C.B. and J.C. Francis (1991) 'Arbitrage pricing theory factors and their relationship to macroeconomic variables', in C.F. Lee, T.J. Frecka and L.O. Scott (eds), *Advances in Quantitative Analysis of Finance and Accounting* (JAI Press).

McGrattan, E.R. and E.C. Prescott (2003) 'Average debt and equity returns: Puzzling?', *The American Economic Review,* Vol. 93, No. 2, [May], pp. 392–397.

McIntyre, A.D. and N.J. Coulthurst (1985) 'Theory and practice in capital budgeting', *British Accounting Review,* Vol. 17, No. 2, [Autumn], pp. 24–70.

McRae, T.W. (1996) *International Business Finance* (John Wiley and Sons).

McSweeney, B. (2007) 'The pursuit of maximum shareholder value: vampire or Viagra?', *Accounting Forum,* Vol. 31, No. 4, pp. 325–331.

Meall, L. (2001) 'Dot.com dot.gone', *Accountancy,* Vol. 128, No. 1296, [August], p. 70.

Mehra, R. and E.C. Prescott (1985) 'The equity premium: A puzzle', *Journal of Monetary Economics,* Vol. 15, No. 2, [March], pp. 145–161.

Meric, I. L.W., Coopersmith, D. Wise and G. Meric (2002) 'Major stock market linkages in the 2000–2001 bear market', *Journal of Investing,* Vol. 11, No. 4 (Winter), pp. 55–62.

Merton, R. (1998) 'Applications of option pricing theory: Twenty five years later', *American Economic Review,* Vol. 88, No. 3, [June], pp. 323–349.

Miller, M. (1977) 'Debt and taxes', *American Economic Review,* Vol. 32, No. 2, [May], pp. 261–275.

Miller, M. (1986) 'Behavioural rationality in finance: The case of dividends', *Journal of Business,* Vol. 59, [October], pp. 451–468.

Miller, M. (1999) 'The history of finance: An eyewitness account', in J.M. Stern and D. Chew (2003) *The Revolution in Corporate Finance* (Blackwell Publishing).

Miller, M. (2000) 'The history of finance: An eyewitness account', *Journal of Applied Corporate Finance,* Vol. 13, [Summer], pp. 8–14.

Miller, M. and D. Orr (1966) 'A model of the demand for money by firms', *Quarterly Journal of Economics,* Vol. 80, No. 2, [August], pp. 413–435.

Miller, M.H. (1991) 'Leverage', *Journal of Finance,* Vol. 46, No. 2, [June], pp. 479–488.

Miller, M.H. and F. Modigliani (1961) 'Dividend policy, growth and the valuation of shares', *Journal of Business,* Vol. 34, No. 4, [October], pp. 411–433.

Mills, R.W. (1988) 'Capital budgeting techniques used in the UK and USA', *Management Accounting,* Vol. 61, [January], pp. 26–27.

Mintzberg, H. (1987) 'Crafting strategy', *Harvard Business Review,* Vol. 65, No. 4, pp. 66–75.

Modigliani, F. and M. Miller (1958) 'The cost of capital, corporation finance and the theory of investment', *American Economic Review,* Vol. 48, No. 3, [June], pp. 261–297.

Modigliani, F. and M.H. Miller (1963) 'Corporate income taxes and the cost of capital: A correction', *American Economic Review,* Vol. 53, No. 3, [June], pp. 433–443.

Morris, C. (2008) *Quantitative Approaches in Business Studies* (Pearson Education).

Mossin, J. (1966) 'Equilibrium in a capital assets market', *Econometrica,* Vol. 34, No. 4, [October], pp. 768–783.

Murphy, J. (1989) *Brand Valuation: A True and Fair View* (Hutchinson).

Myers, S. and N. Majluf (1984) 'Corporate financing and decisions when firms have information that investors do not have', *Journal of Financial Economics,* Vol. 13, No. 2, pp. 187–221.

Myers, S.C. (1974) 'Interactions of corporate financing and investment decisions – Implications for capital budgeting', *Journal of Finance,* Vol. 29, No. 1, [March], pp. 1–25.

Myers, S.C. (1984) 'The capital structure puzzle', *Journal of Finance,* Vol. 39, No. 3, [July], pp. 575–592.

Myers, S.C., D.A. Dill and A.J. Bautista (1976) 'Valuation of lease contracts', *Journal of Finance,* Vol. 31, No. 3, [June], pp. 799–820.

Narayanaswamy, V.J. (1994) 'The debt equivalence of leases in the UK: An empirical investigation', *British Accounting Review,* Vol. 26, No. 1, pp. 337–351.

Neale, B., A. Milsom, C. Hills and J. Sharples (1998) 'The hostile takeover process: A case study of Granada versus Forte', *European Management Journal,* Vol. 16, No. 2, [April], pp. 230–241.

Neale, C.W. and P.J. Buckley (1992) 'Differential British and US adoption rates of investment project post-completion auditing', *Journal of International Business Studies,* Third Quarter, Vol. 23, No. 3, pp. 419–442.

Neale, C.W. and D.E.A. Holmes (1988) 'Post-completion audits: The costs and benefits', *Management Accounting,* Vol. 66, No. 3, [March], pp. 27–30.

Neale, C.W. and D.E.A. Holmes (1990) 'Post-auditing capital investment projects', *Long Range Planning,* Vol. 23, No. 4, [August], pp. 88–96.

Neale, C.W. and D.E.A. Holmes (1991) *Post-Completion Auditing* (Pitman).

Nofsinger, J.R. (2008) *The Psychology of Investing* (Pearson Prentice Hall).

Northcraft, G. and M. Neale (1987) 'Experts, amateurs and real estate: An anchoring perspective on property pricing decisions', *Organizational Behavior and Human Decision Processes,* Vol. 39, pp. 84–97.

Odier, P. and B. Solnik (1993) 'Lessons for international asset allocation', *Financial Analysts Journal,* Vol. 49, No. 2, [Mar/Apr], pp. 63–77.

Office of National Statistics (2010) 'Share Ownership Survey'.

O'Shea, D. (1986) *Investing for Beginners,* Financial Times Business Information.

Otten, R. and D. Bams (2009) 'The performance of local versus foreign mutual fund managers', *European Financial Management,* Vol. 13, pp. 702–720.

Owen, G., J. Black and S. Arcot (2007) *From Local to Global – The Rise of the AIM* (London Stock Exchange Publications).

Payne, A.F. (1987) 'Approaching acquisitions strategically', *Journal of General Management,* Vol. 13, No. 2, [Winter], pp. 5–27.

Peacock, A. and G. Bannock (1991) *Corporate Takeovers and the Public Interest* (David Hume Institute).

Pearce, R. and S. Barnes (2006) *Raising Venture Capital* (Wiley).

Peel, M.J. (1995) 'The impact of corporate re-structuring: Mergers, divestments and MBOs', *Long Range Planning,* Vol. 28, No. 2, [April], pp. 92–101.

Peters, E.E. (1991) *Chaos and Order in the Capital Markets* (Wiley).

Peters, E.E. (1993) *Fractal Market Analysis* (Wiley).

Pettit, J. (2001) 'Is a share buyback right for your company?', *Harvard Business Review,* Vol. 79, No. 4, [October], pp. 141–147.

Pettit, R.R. (1972) 'Dividend announcements, security performance and capital market efficiency', *Journal of Finance,* Vol. XXVII, No. 5, pp. 993–1007.

Pike, R. (1996) 'A longitudinal survey on capital budgeting practices', *Journal of Business Finance and Accounting,* Vol. 23, No. 1, [January], pp. 79–92.

Pike, R., N. Cheng and L. Chadwick (1998) *Managing Trade Credit for Competitive Advantage* (CIMA).

Pike, R., J. Sharp and D. Price (1989) 'AMT investment in the larger UK firm', *International Journal of Operations and Production Management,* Vol. 9, No. 2, pp. 13–26.

Pike, R.H. (1982) *Capital Budgeting in the 1980s* (Chartered Institute of Management Accountants).

Pike, R.H. (1983) 'The capital budgeting behaviour and corporate characteristics of capital-constrained firms', *Journal of Business Finance and Accounting,* Vol. 10, No. 4, [Winter], pp. 663–671.

Pike, R.H. (1988) 'An empirical study of the adoption of sophisticated capital budgeting practices and decision-making effectiveness', *Accounting and Business Research,* Vol. 18, No. 2, [Autumn], pp. 341–351.

Pike, R.H. and S.M. Ho (1991) 'Risk analysis techniques in capital budgeting contexts', *Accounting and Business Research,* Vol. 21, No. 83, pp. 227–238.

Pike, R.H. and M. Wolfe (1988) *Capital Budgeting in the 1990s* (Chartered Institute of Management Accountants).

Piketty, T. (2014) *Capital in The Twenty-First Centuary* (Harvard University Press).

Pilbeam, K. (2010) *Finance and Financial Markets* (Palgrave MacMillan).

Pilbeam, K. (2013) *International Finance* (Palgrave Macmillan).

Pinches, G. (1982) 'Myopic capital budgeting and decision-making', *Financial Management,* Vol. 11, No. 3, [Autumn], pp. 6–19.

Pohlman, R.A., E.S. Santiago and F.L. Markel (1988) 'Cash flow estimation practices of larger firms', *Financial Management,* Vol. 17, No. 2, [Summer], pp. 71–79.

Pointon, J. (1980) 'Investment and risk: The effect of capital allowances', *Accounting and Business Research,* Vol. 10, No. 40, [Autumn].

Poon, S. and S.J. Taylor (1991) 'Macroeconomic factors and the UK stock market', *Journal of Business Finance and Accounting,* Vol. 18, No. 5, [September], pp. 619–636.

Porter, M.E. (1985) *Competitive Advantage* (Free Press).

Porter, M.E. (1987) 'From competitive advantage to corporate strategy', *Harvard Business Review,* Vol. 65, No. 3, [May–June], pp. 43–59.

Porter, M.E. (1992) 'Capital disadvantage – America's failing capital investment system', *Harvard Business Review,* Vol. 70, No. 4, [September–October], pp. 65–82.

Power, M. (2007) *Organized Uncertainty – Designing a World of Risk Management* (Oxford University Press).

Prasad, S.B. (1987) 'American and European investment motives in Ireland', *Management International Review* (Third quarter).

Prelec, D. and G. Loewenstein (1998) 'The red and the black: mental accounting of savings debt', *Marketing Science,* Vol. 17, No. 1, pp. 4–28.

Price, J. and S.K. Henderson (1988) *Currency and Interest Rate Swaps* (Butterworths).

Prindl, A. (1978) *Currency Management* (John Wiley).

Pritchett, P., D. Robinson and R. Clarkson (1997) *After the Merger* (McGraw-Hill).

Pruitt, S.W. and L.J. Gitman (1987) 'Capital budgeting forecast biases: Evidence from the Fortune 500', *Financial Management,* Vol. 16, No. 1, [Spring], pp. 46–51.

Quah, P. and S. Young (2005) 'Post-merger integration: A phases approach for cross-border M&As', *European Management Journal,* Vol. 23, No. 1, pp. 65–75.

Rajan, R. and L. Zingales (1995) 'What do we know about capital structure? Some evidence from international data', *Journal of Finance,* Vol. 11, No. 3, pp. 1421–1460.

Rankine, D. and P. Howson (2014) *Acquisition Essentials* (FT Publishing).

Rappaport, A. (1986) *Creating Shareholder Value: The New Standard for Business Performance* (Macmillan).

Rappaport, A. (1987) 'Stock market signals to managers', *Harvard Business Review,* Vol. 65, No. 6, [November–December], pp. 57–62.

Redhead, K. (1990) *Introduction to Financial Futures and Options* (Woodhead-Faulkner).

Redhead, K. (2008) *Personal Finance and Investments – A Behavioural Finance Perspective* (Routledge).

Reimann, B.C. (1990) 'Why bother with risk-adjusted hurdle rates?' *Long Range Planning,* Vol. 23, No. 3, [June], pp. 57–65.

Risk Measurement Service, London Business School.

Ritter, J. (2006) 'Initial public offerings', in J. Rutterford, M. Upton and D. Kodwani (eds) *Financial Strategy,* 2nd edn (Wiley).

Robbins, S. and R. Stobaugh (1973) 'The bent measuring stick for foreign subsidiaries', *Harvard Business Review,* Vol. 51, No. 5, [September–October], pp. 80–88.

Rodriguez, R.M. (1981) 'Corporate exchange risk management: Theme and aberrations', *Journal of Finance,* Vol. 36, No. 2, [May], pp. 427–444.

Roll, R. (1977) 'A critique of the asset pricing theory's tests; Part I: On past and potential testability of the theory', *Journal of Financial Economics,* Vol. 4, No. 2, [March], pp. 129–176.

Ross, S., R. Westerfield and J. Jaffe (2002) *Fundamentals of Corporate Finance* (McGraw-Hill).

Ross, S., R. Westerfield and J. Jaffe (2009) *Corporate Finance* (McGraw-Hill).

Ross, S., R. Westerfield and B. Jordan (2010) *Corporate Finance Fundamentals,* 9th edn (McGraw-Hill).

Ross, S.A. (1976) 'The arbitrage theory of capital asset-pricing', *Journal of Economic Theory,* Vol. 13, No. 3, pp. 341–360.

Ross, S.A. (1977) 'The determination of financial structure: The incentive signalling approach', *Bell Journal of Economics,* Vol. 8, No. 1, [Spring], pp. 23–40.

Ruback, R.S. (1988) 'An overview of takeover defenses', in A.J. Auerbach (ed.), *Mergers and Acquisitions* (University of Chicago Press).

Rubinstein, M. (2002) 'Markowitz's "portfolio selection": A fifty-year retrospective', *Journal of Finance*, Vol. 57, No. 3, pp. 1041–1045.

Rugman, A. and S. Collinson (2012) *International Business* (Pearson).

Rutterford, J. (1992) *Handbook of UK Corporate Finance* (Butterworths).

Rutterford, J.M., M. Upton and D. Kodwani (2006) *Financial Strategy: Adding Stakeholder Value* (John Wiley & Sons).

Salinas, G. (2009) *The International Brand Valuation Manual* (John Wiley).

Sartoris, W. and N. Hill (1981) 'Evaluating credit policy alternatives: A present value framework', *Journal of Financial Research*, Vol. 4, No. 1, [Spring], pp. 81–89.

Saunders, A. and M.M. Cornett (2013) *Financial Institutions Management: A Risk Management Approach* (McGraw Hill).

Savor, P.G. and Q. Lu (2009) 'Do stock mergers create value for acquirers?', *Journal of Finance*, Vol. 63, pp. 1061–1097.

Seasholes, M.S. and N. Zhu (2010) 'Individual investors and local bias', *Journal of Finance*, Vol. 65, pp. 1987–2010.

Shanken, J., R. Sloan and S. Kothari (1995) 'Another look at the cross-section of expected stock returns', *Journal of Finance*, Vol. 50, No. 1, [March], pp. 185–224.

Shao, L., C.C. Kwok and O. Guedhami (2010) 'National culture and dividend policy', *Journal of International Business Studies*, Vol. 41, pp. 1391–1414.

Shao, L.P. (1996) (ed.) 'Capital budgeting for the multinational enterprise', *Managerial Finance*, Vol. 22, No. 1.

Shapiro, A.C. (2013) *Multinational Financial Management* (Wiley).

Sharpe, P. and T. Keelin (1998) 'How SmithKline Beecham makes better resource-allocation decisions', *Harvard Business Review*, Vol. 76, No. 3, [March/April], pp. 45–57.

Sharpe, W. (1981) *Investments* (Prentice Hall).

Sharpe, W.F. (1963) 'A simplified model for portfolio analysis', *Management Science*, Vol. 9, No. 2, [January], pp. 277–293.

Sharpe, W.F. (1964) 'Capital asset prices – A theory of market equilibrium under conditions of risk', *Journal of Finance*, Vol. 19, No. 3, [September], pp. 425–442.

Sharpe, W.F., G.J. Alexander and J.W. Bailey (1999) *Investments* (Prentice Hall).

Shefrin, H. (1999) *Beyond Greed and Fear: Understanding Behavioural Finance and the Psychology of Investing* (Harvard Business School Press).

Shefrin, H. and M. Statman (1985) 'The disposition to sell winners too early and ride losers too long: theory and evidence', *The Journal of Finance*, Vol. 40, No. 3, pp. 777–790.

Short, T. (2000) 'Should foreign investors buy Polish shares?' in T. Kowalski and S. Letza (eds) *Financial Reform and Institutions* (Poznan University of Economics).

Smith, B.M. (2001) *Toward Rational Exuberance: The Evolution of the Modern Stock Market* (Farrar, Strauss & Giroux).

Smith, K.V. (1988) *Readings in Short-term Financial Management* (West Publishing).

Solnik, B.H. (1974) 'Why not diversify internationally rather than domestically?', *Financial Analysts Journal*, Vol. 30, No. 4, [July/August], pp. 48–54.

Staw, B.M. (1976) 'Knee-deep in the Big Muddy: A study of escalating commitment to a chosen course of action', *Organisational Behaviour and Human Performance*, Vol. 16, No. 1, [June], pp. 27–44.

Staw, B.M. (1981) 'The escalation of commitment to achosen course of action', *Academy of Management Review*, Vol. 6, No. 4, [October], pp. 577–587.

Staw, J. and S. Ross (1987) 'Knowing when to pull the plug', *Harvard Business Review*, Vol. 65, No. 2, [March/April], pp. 68–74.

Stoakes, C. (2013), *Know the City* (Christopher Stoakes Ltd).

Stonham, P. (1995) 'Reuter's share re-purchase', *European Management Journal*, Vol. 13, No. 1, pp. 99–109.

Stout, L. (2012) *The Shareholder Value Myth*. (Berrett-Koehler)

Strong, N. and X.G. Xu (1997) 'Explaining the cross-section of UK expected stock returns', *British Accounting Review*, Vol. 29, No. 1, [March], pp. 1–23.

Sudarsanam, P., P. Holl and A. Salami (1996) 'Shareholder wealth gains in mergers: Effect of synergy and ownership structure', *Journal of Business Finance and Accounting*, Vol. 23, No. 5/6, [July], pp. 673–698.

Sudarsanam, P.S. (1995) *The Essence of Mergers and Acquisitions* (Prentice Hall).

Sudarsanam, S. (2010) *Creating Value Through Mergers and Acquisitions: The Challenges* (FT/Prentice Hall).

Swalm, R.O. (1966) 'Utility theory – insights into risk-taking', *Harvard Business Review*, Vol. 44, No. 6, [November–December], pp. 123–136.

Taffler, R. (1991) 'Z-scores: An approach to the recession', *Accountancy*, July.

Takeover Panel (2009) Code for Takeovers and Mergers, London.

Taylor, F. (2010) *Mastering Derivatives Markets: A Step-by-Step Guide to the Products, Applications and Risks* (FT Prentice Hall).

Thaler, R., R. Michaely and S. Bernatzi (1997) 'Do changes in dividend policy signal the past or the future?' *Journal of Finance*, Vol. 52, No. 3, [July], pp. 1007–1034.

Thaler, R.H. (1999) 'Mental accounting matters', *Journal of Behavioral Decision Making*, Vol. 12, No. 3, 183–206.

Thaler, R. H. and C. R. Sunstein (2009) *Nudge: Improving Decisions About Health, Wealth and Happiness* (Penguin).

Tobin, J. (1958) 'Liquidity preference as behaviour towards risk', *Review of Economic Studies,* Vol. 25, [February], pp. 65–86.

Tomkins, C. (1991) *Corporate Resource Allocation* (Basil Blackwell).

Tomkins, C.R., J.F. Lowe and E.J. Morgan (1979) *An Economic Analysis of the Financial Leasing Industry* (Saxon House).

Tversky, A. and D. Kahneman (1971) 'Belief in the law of small numbers', *Psychological Bulletin*, Vol. 76, No. 2, pp. 105–110.

UNCTAD (2010) *World Investment Report,* United Nations Conference on Trade and Development (**www.unctad.org**).

Vaga, T. (1990) 'The coherent market hypothesis', *Financial Analysts Journal,* Vol. 46, No. 6, [November/ December], pp. 36–49.

Valdez, S. and P. Molyneux (2012) *An Introduction to Global Financial Markets* (Palgrave MacMillan).

Van Binsbergen, J.H., J.R. Graham and J. Yang (2010) 'The cost of debt', *Journal of Finance*, Vol. 65, pp. 2089–2136.

Van Horne, J. (1975) 'Corporate liquidity and bankruptcy costs', Research Paper 205, Stanford University.

Van Horne, J. (2001) *Financial Management and Policy* (Prentice Hall).

Vermaelen, T. (1981) 'Common stock repurchases and market signalling: An empirical study', *Journal of Financial Economics*, Vol. 9, No. 2, pp. 139–183.

Very, P. (2004) *Management of Mergers and Acquisitions* (Wiley).

Wallace, J.S. (2003) 'Value maximization and stakeholder theory: Compatible or not?' *Journal of Applied Corporate Finance*, Vol. 15, [Spring], pp. 120–127.

Walters, A. (1991) *Corporate Credit Analysis* (Euromoney Publications).

Wardlow, A. (1994) 'Investment appraisal criteria and the impact of low inflation', Bank of England *Quarterly Bulletin,* Vol. 34, No. 3, [August], pp. 250–254.

Warner, J. (1977) 'Bankruptcy costs: Some evidence', *Journal of Finance*, Vol. 32, No. 2, pp. 337–347.

Watts, R. (1973) 'The information content of dividends', *Journal of Business*, Vol. 46, No. 2, [April], pp. 191–211.

Wearing, R.T. (1989) 'Cash flow and the eurotunnel', *Accounting & Business Research*, Vol. 20, No. 77, [Winter], pp. 13–24.

Weaver, S. (1989) 'Divisional hurdle rates and the cost of capital', *Financial Management*, Vol. 18, [Spring], pp. 18–25.

Weaver, S.C., D. Peters, R. Cason and J. Daleiden (1989) 'Capital budgeting', *Financial Management,* Vol. 18, No. 1, [Spring], pp. 10–17.

Weingartner, H. (1977) 'Capital rationing: Authors in search of a plot', *Journal of Finance,* Vol. 32, No. 5, [December], pp. 1403–1431.

Weston, J.F. and T.E. Copeland (1992) *Managerial Finance* (Cassell).

Whitaker, S.C. (2012) *Merger and Acquisitions Integration Handbook* (Wiley).

Whittington, R. and L.L. Cailluet (2008) 'The crafts of strategy', *Long Range Planning*, Vol. 41, No. 3, pp. 241–247.

Wilkie, A.D. (1994) 'The risk premium on ordinary shares', Institute of Actuaries and Faculty of Actuaries, November.

Wilkinson, N. (2008) *An Introduction to Behavioral Economics* (Palgrave MacMillan).

Wilkinson, N. and M. Klaes (2012) *An Introduction to Behavioural Economics* (Palgrave Macmillion).

Wilson Committee (1980) 'Report of the committee to review the functioning of financial institutions', Cmnd. 7937, HMSO.

Wilson, M. (1990) (ed.) 'Capital budgeting for foreign direct investments', *Managerial Finance,* Vol. 16, No. 2.

Wood, A. (2006) 'Death of the dividend?', in J. Rutterford, M. Upton and D. Kodwani (eds) *Financial Strategy* (Wiley).

Wright, M. and K. Robbie (1991) 'Corporate restructuring, buy-outs and managerial equity: The European dimension', *Journal of Applied Corporate Finance*, Vol. 3, No. 4, [Winter], pp. 47–58.

Young, D. (1997) 'Economic value added: A primer for European managers', *European Management Journal,* Vol. 15, No. 4, [August].

Young, D. and B. Sutcliffe (1990) 'Value gaps – Who is right? The raiders, the market or the manager?', *Long Range Planning,* Vol. 23, No. 4, [August], pp. 20–34.

Young, S. and S. O'Byrne (2001) *EVA and Value-Based Management: A Practical Guide to Implementation* (McGraw-Hill).

Zenner, M., M. Matthews, J. Marks and N. Mago (2008) 'The era of cross-border M&A: How current market dynamics are changing the M&A landscape', *Journal of Applied Corporate Finance*, Vol. 20, pp. 84–96.

Index

Page references in **bold** refer to the Glossary